PRINCIPLES OF CONTRACT LAW

THIRD EDITION

PRINCIPLES OF CONTRACT LAW

THIRD EDITION

KEVIN S. MARSHALL
J.D., M.P.A., PH.D.
PROFESSOR OF LAW
UNIVERSITY OF LA VERNE COLLEGE OF LAW

JUANDA LOWDER DANIEL
J.D.
UNIVERSITY COUNSEL
CALIFORNIA STATE UNIVERSITY

Principles of Contract Law – Third Edition (2013)
Marshall, Kevin S. and Daniel, Juanda Lowder

Published by:

Vandeplas Publishing, LLC – July 2013

801 International Parkway, 5th Floor
Lake Mary, FL. 32746
USA

www.vandeplaspublishing.com

All Rights Reserved

ISBN: 978-1-60042-200-3

© 2013 Kevin S. Marshall and Juanda Lowder Daniel

PREFACE

The study of law is demanding, frustrating, and sometimes even exhausting. While it can be accomplished in the isolation of one's efforts, successful students realize early that there is value in collective discussion and inquiry. We often fill the voids of our ignorance by simply seeking the advice, counsel, and ideas of our colleagues. During any given semester, hardly a week goes by without one of your professors seeking guidance from his or her colleagues regarding any number of confounding issues; and they are generally better for it. With some discussion, one usually finds his or her bearings. We counsel you to welcome opportunities to discuss class topics with students not only in your assigned cohort or section, but also with students assigned to the other cohorts and sections. Keep in mind as you embark on your study of the law that you never, ever learn the law in any sort of absolute terms. Rather, you learn how to pursue the law, and the pursuit is typically a life-long endeavor. A little company along the way is sometimes of great value to each of us, especially as we confront those lonely and demoralizing moments of ignorance.

Collegial effort, however, cannot and will not, substitute for individual effort and preparation. You cannot succeed in law school riding on the coattails of others. Success in law school, as well as in the practice of law, requires great individual effort and continual preparation. While you are encouraged to pursue a collegial environment of inquiry, you are expected to engross yourselves in your studies. You are expected to read all of your assignments, attend all of your classes, and most importantly, come to each of your classes prepared to participate and contribute to the advancement of the class. Parasitic voyeurs should not be tolerated and certainly are not respected. While crying is sometimes allowed, remember that it likely will not advance your client's cause. Clients find comfort in their lawyers' strength, frequently exhibited by their steadfast commitment and resolve to master the legal issues beleaguering their cause, strength that is exhibited by their unwavering devotion to their own preparedness. Preparation is the great equalizer. This year you will yourself witness the greatest of intellects fail due to their lack of preparedness. The failure to show up prepared will doom even the most brilliant of attorneys to failure and possibly even to claims of malpractice. There is no excuse for such failure. As one of us will be happy to tell you, "excuses are the tools of incompetence used to build monuments of nothingness, and those who specialize in them seldom amount to anything."[*] To be prepared, you must be willing to do your own heavy lifting (with an occasional spot from one of your colleagues). This is why we frown upon your use of commercial outlines and case briefs. Have any of you ever gone to the gym and asked someone to work out for you? Lift weights for you? Run a mile for you? The answer is, of course, not. So roll up your sleeves and embrace your own preparedness where you will find strength, confidence, and, ultimately, success. As the other one of us likes to remind, the study and practice of law is one place where "action talks and bull*%$# walks!"[*]

As you study the law of contracts, you should think about the underlying public policies that drive its principles. In our supplemental reader we reference four relevant interests served by the law of contracts: 1) liberty, 2) morality, 3) economics, and 4) the Constitution. One of us approaches the study of contract law from a moral perspective (she often claiming

[*] Original author unknown.

[*] Original author unknown.

to be the moral one of the two of us). After all, a contract consists of a promise or a set of promises. And if one promises to do an act, should not that person be held accountable for failing to keep his or her promises? The other one of us approaches the study of contract law from an economic perspective (he often claiming to be the more efficient of the two of us). Since we all seek to thrive in an environment of scarcity, should not the law of contracts ultimately serve the policy goal of maximizing the efficient allocation of scarce resources? Surely, we are all familiar with the phrase "waste not, want not." But wait, that sounds more like a philosophical *mos*, or norm, or virtue? Or perhaps the minimization of waste is an economic principle? Throughout your study of law, we implore you to query as to the purpose of the law, and in your contracts class, particularly, the purpose of contract law.

Many law professors embrace the Socratic method of teaching in the classroom (which is yet another important reason for all of you to be prepared for your respective classes.) Being able to think on one's feet, to gracefully dance with the dynamics of the moment, all within a very stressful public environment, well . . . those are the skills of a good lawyer. To maximize your ability to dance with your professor and contribute to the advancement of knowledge in your class, you must be prepared. Accordingly, you are expected to brief each case sufficiently so you can participate on a moment's notice. We implore you to read Professor Christensen's article titled *The Psychology of Case Briefing*: *A Powerful Cognitive Schema,* 29 CAMPBELL L. REV. (Fall 2006) portions of which we have included in our supplement. Your case brief should be viewed as a tool to assist you in the Socratic dialogue in which we expect you to participate. You should view each class as your opportunity to volley with your professor and others, an opportunity to practice your trade, realizing that practice makes us better, and better, and better. So embrace the Socratic dialogue.

Finally, one of us emphasizes the use of the Restatement (Second) of Contracts as a supplemental source for understanding the principles of contract law. The other one of us emphasizes the use of problems as a supplemental mechanism for understanding the principles of contract law. Note our use of the term "supplemental." Regardless of the sources you might use to supplement your studies, remember they are supplemental resources to be used only after you have digested your assigned readings. The journey upon which you have now embarked is long and steep, and while a walking stick might be helpful to one's assent, a successful climb, nonetheless, requires each of us to power through each step. We wish you well as you pursue your path to the law. Happy trails.

Kevin Scott Marshall
Juanda Lowder Daniel

ACKNOWLEDGEMENTS

The authors wish to acknowledge the University of La Verne College of Law for its support through its faculty research and scholarship grant program. The authors also wish to acknowledge and thank our research assistants, Emeline Garcia, Sara Shirmohammadi, Sandy Perez, Merrill Hanson, Blake Harrison, Elizabeth Mouzakis, Crista Haynes, Taylor Bristol, Christina Rosier, Rebecca Onaitis, and Mark Sonefeldt for their tireless efforts in researching, compiling and formatting the material in this book.

Emeline Garcia graduated with a Bachelor of Arts degree in Political Science from the University of California, Riverside in 2009. Ms. Garcia will obtain a Juris Doctorate from the University of La Verne College of Law in 2015. While at the University of La Verne, Ms. Garcia served as a Staff Editor of the University of La Verne Society of Law, Business and Ethics Journal and as a research and teaching assistant for Professor Kevin Marshall. Ms. Garcia received CALI honors in Contracts and Legal Analysis and Writing I. Ms. Garcia was employed as a law clerk at Cho, Sheasby, Chung & Ignacio in Rancho Cucamonga, CA.

Sara Shirmohammadi received a Bachelor of Science degree in Chemistry and a Master of Business Administration degree with an option in management from California State University, Los Angeles. While at California State University, Los Angeles, Ms. Shirmohammadi worked in a bio-organic chemistry lab for a year and interned as both a graduate assistant and legal intern. Ms. Shirmohammadi will obtain a Juris Doctorate from the University of La Verne College of Law in 2015, with the hopes of pursing a career in patent law. Ms. Shirmohammadi also worked and managed her family's restaurant, doing their day to day operations.

Sandy Perez attended the University of California, Los Angeles and graduated in 2008 with a Bachelor of Arts degree in Political Science. Ms. Perez was a dual-degree student at the University of La Verne, obtaining her Juris Doctorate and Master of Business Administration in 2013. Ms. Perez was the Co-Technical Editor for the Journal of Law, Business and Ethics. Ms. Perez was the SBA American Bar Association Representative and one of the 9th Circuit Lt. Governors for the 2012-2013 academic year. Ms. Perez was also the Secretary for the Society of Legal Studies in Business.

Merrill Hanson received a Bachelor of Science degree from the University of La Verne in both Business Administration with a concentration on Business Management, and in Music with a concentration on Vocal Performance, and simultaneously graduated from the University's Honors Interdisciplinary Program. Mr. Hanson obtained a Juris Doctorate and a Master of Business Administration from the University of La Verne in 2013. While at the College of Law, Mr. Hanson served as a Staff Editor of the University of La Verne Law Review, as a research and graduate assistant for Professor Kevin Marshall, and was honored by being placed on the Dean's List of Academic Excellence. Mr. Hanson was employed as a clerk at Driskell & Gordon in Glendora, CA, and Crandall, Wade, & Lowe in Rancho Cucamonga, CA.

Blake Harrison received his baccalaureate degree *cum laude* from the University of La Verne with departmental honors in History in 2007. Mr. Harrison received his Juris Doctorate from the University of La Verne College of Law, where he graduated with honors and was the Spring 2010 graduating class recipient of the ALI-ABA award for scholarship and leadership. While at La Verne Law, Mr. Harrison served as the Juvenile Issue Editor of the University of La Verne Law Review, was a research assistant and graduate assistant for Professor Kevin Marshall, and was an intern for Judge Riemer of the Riverside Superior Court. Mr. Harrison received CALI honors in Contracts, Criminal Law, and Juvenile Law, and was several times honored by being placed on the Dean's List of Academic Excellence. Mr. Harrison also served as the President of the La Verne Law's Federalist Society, was recognized for his pro bono contributions, and served as a PASS scholar while in residency at La Verne Law.

Elizabeth Mouzakis graduated with a Bachelor of Arts degree in Global and International Studies from the University of California, Santa Barbara. Ms. Mouzakis received her Juris Doctorate from the University of La Verne College of Law in 2010. While at La Verne, Ms. Mouzakis served as a research assistant for Professor Kevin Marshall, was a member of the La Verne College of Law's travelling moot court team, which advanced to the quarter finals of the University of San Diego's National Criminal Procedure Moot Court Competition, and served the San Bernardino County District Attorney's Office as an intern. Ms. Mouzakis received CALI honors in Sales, Criminal Procedure: Investigations, and was several times honored by being placed on the Dean's List of Academic Excellence.

Crista Haynes graduated from the California State University at Long Beach with a Bachelor of Science degree in Criminal Justice, magna cum laude, in 2007. Ms. Haynes graduated from the University of La Verne College of Law in 2011. Ms. Haynes was appointed in 2010 to serve as Student Editor-in-Chief for the Journal of Law, Business and Ethics, an interdisciplinary, peer-reviewed journal published by the Pacific Southwest Academy for Legal Studies in Business. Ms. Haynes also worked as a research and teaching assistant for Professor Kevin S. Marshall and Professor Randall Rubin. Ms. Haynes received CALI honors in Property, Professional Responsibility, Business Organizations, and Sales.

Taylor Bristol earned a Bachelor of Arts in Political Science in 2007 from Point Loma Nazarene University in San Diego, California. Ms. Bristol graduated from the University of La Verne College of Law in 2011. Ms. Bristol was a Staff Editor from 2009-2010 and the Chief Managing Editor from 2010-2011 for the University of La Verne Law Review. In addition, Ms. Bristol was the President and Founder of the Public Interest Law Foundation at the University of La Verne.

Christy Rosier attended Knox College in Galesburg, Illinois, and graduated in 2005 with a Bachelor of Arts degree in Political Science. Ms. Rosier also earned a Master's Degree in Legal Studies from the University of Illinois at Springfield. Ms. Rosier graduated from the Chapman University School of Law in 2012 with a Juris Doctorate. While at the University of La Verne College of Law, Ms. Rosier earned a CALI award in Legal Writing and Analysis I and served as a Staff Editor for the University of La Verne Law Review. Additionally, Ms. Rosier was the SBA Historian at the University of La Verne College of Law for the 2010-2011 academic year.

Rebecca Onaitis is a 2006 graduate of Arcadia University in Glenside, Pennsylvania. Ms. Onaitis graduated with a Bachelor of Arts degree as a Psychology major and a Spanish minor. Ms. Onaitis earned her Juris Doctorate and Master of Business Administration at the University of La Verne in 2012. During the Summer of 2010, Ms. Onaitis worked as an intern at the Inland Valleys Justice Center. Ms. Onaitis was also a Staff Editor for the University of La Verne Law Review and an Articles Editor for the Journal of Law, Business and Ethics.

Mark Sonefeldt is a graduate of California State Polytechnic University, Pomona with a Bachelor of Arts degree in History. Before enrolling at the University of La Verne College of Law in 2009, Mr. Sonefeldt worked as a commercial real estate broker for five years in Orange County, California. Mr. Sonefeldt was an intern at the Riverside County Counsel's Office during the 2010 Summer and earned his Juris Doctorate in 2012.

TABLE OF CONTENTS

Chapter One

SOURCES OF CONTRACT LAW

The law is the witness and external deposit of our moral life. Its history is the history of the moral development of the race. The practice of it, in spite of popular jests, tends to make good citizens and good men.[*]

Justice O.W. Holmes

First, we would like to dispel any notion that "the law" is some abstract force that exists independent of human intervention. As you will come to realize through the course of your legal studies, the law is not constant nor is it abstract. Instead, the law is a living, breathing body that ideally reflects the social, political, and economic mores of society. Nevertheless, there are checks to prevent this organism from getting ahead of itself. Those checks are briefly discussed below.

The Constitution of the United States is the supreme law of the land. Thus, all federal and state laws must conform to the provisions of the Constitution. Beyond this, our system of federalism dictates that certain specifically enumerated powers are delegated to the federal government and are solely within its governing province; the rest are reserved to the states. Thus, the next "check" in the pecking order depends on whether it is a federal or state matter. Since most laws affecting contracts fall within the province of the state, state constitutions generally come next. Following this are enactments by state legislators in the form of codes and statutes.

One of the statutory schemes with which we will concern ourselves throughout this course is the Uniform Commercial Code (U.C.C.). This is a joint product of the National Conference of Commissioners on Uniform State Laws (NCCUSL) and the American Law Institute (ALI). The purpose is to provide a uniform set of laws governing commercial transactions in all states. Although it has no binding authority in and of itself, if and when any part of it is adopted by a state legislature, it then has the binding force of codes and statutes for that particular state. Of course, the intent to provide uniform laws is fulfilled only if all (or substantially all) of the states' legislatures adopt the provisions.

Article 2 of the U.C.C. governs transactions in goods. This article, along with Article 1 containing general provisions applicable to all nine of the U.C.C. articles, was promulgated by the NCCUSL and ALI in 1952 and has been adopted by 49 of the states (Louisiana, being the exception), as well as the District of Columbia. In 2003, Article 2 was substantially amended by the NCCUSL and ALI to address modern issues related to electronic commerce. However, none of the states have adopted the 2003 amendments. Thus, this course will focus on the pre-2003 version of Article 2, which continues to be the law in every state, except Louisiana.

By now, you should have noticed that we have yet to mention judicial rulings (or case law as it is commonly called) in this hierarchy of laws. This is because all case law is

---

[*] Justice O.W. Holmes, *The Path of the Law*, 10 HARV. L. REV. 457, 459 (1897).

subject to the above-referenced sources. In some cases, judicial rulings involve a question of whether a particular code or statute applies to the case before it. Often, this requires a judicial interpretation of the code or statute. In other cases, judicial rulings are not premised on codes or statutes. Instead, they are steeped in what we refer to as common law, a collective body of judicial decisions, or precedent, whereby courts use prior judicial rulings in order to resolve similar issues before it. The theory behind the use of precedent is that all cases involving the same or substantially similar facts and issues should be resolved in the same manner. This is the doctrine of *stare decisis*. When adhered to, it provides notice to society of acceptable versus unacceptable conduct, as well as the implications for running afoul of such expectations. As you will discover, both the study and practice of law focuses a great deal on whether the case at issue is substantially similar to previously decided cases, or whether the differences are of the magnitude that warrant different treatment.

Another source of contract law, albeit indirectly, is the Restatement of Contracts. This is a collection of propositions drafted by experts in the field of contracts and promulgated by the ALI. It was originally promulgated in 1932. In 1981, the ALI promulgated the updated version entitled the Restatement (Second) of Contracts. Unless otherwise indicated, all references in this book to the Restatement shall refer to the Restatement (Second) of Contracts.

Although it reads like a statute, please keep in mind that the Restatement is NOT the law. Thus, it should never be cited with the force of law. As you will see, in most cases (note the use of the word "MOST"), the relevant Restatement provisions track the actual state of the law in the majority of jurisdictions. Nevertheless, the only way any provision of the Restatement gets elevated to the status of binding authority is when a court with the force of binding authority specifically adopts the section and thereby incorporates it into common law. Otherwise, the Restatement should be treated as merely a persuasive statement of what the law should be. That being said, where the Restatement and the common law coincide, you will find that the Restatement succinctly states the rule of law in a usable and memorable form.

With this in mind, we turn to the study of contract law.

CHAPTER TWO

FORMATION

*The foundation of contracts is the reasonable expectation which the person who promises raises in the person to whom he binds himself; of which satisfaction may be extorted by force.**

Adam Smith

SECTION 1. WHAT IS A CONTRACT?

STEINBERG V. CHICAGO MEDICAL SCHOOL
Supreme Court of Illinois
371 N.E.2d 634 (1977).

DOOLEY, Justice:

Robert Steinberg received a catalog, applied for admission to defendant, Chicago Medical School, for the academic year 1974-75, and paid a $15 fee. He was rejected. Steinberg filed a class action against the school claiming it had failed to evaluate his application and those of other applicants according to the academic criteria in the school's bulletin. According to the complaint, defendant used nonacademic criteria, primarily the ability of the applicant or his family to pledge or make payment of large sums of money to the school.

The 1974-75 bulletin distributed to prospective students contained this statement of standards by which applicants were to be evaluated:

> Students are selected on the basis of scholarship, character, and motivation without regard to race, creed, or sex. The student's potential for the study and practice of medicine will be evaluated on the basis of academic achievement, Medical College Admission Test results, personal appraisals by a pre-professional advisory committee or individual instructors, and the personal interview, if requested by the Committee on Admissions.

Count I of the complaint alleged breach of contract . . . .

The real questions on this appeal are: Can the facts support a charge of breach of contract? Is an action predicated on fraud maintainable? Is this a proper class-action situation?

On motion to dismiss we accept as true all well-pleaded facts. (Acorn Auto Driving School, Inc. v. Board of Education (1963), 27 Ill.2d 93, 96, 187 N.E.2d 722.) Count I alleges Steinberg and members of the class to which he belongs applied to defendant and paid the $15 fee, and that defendant, through its brochure, described the criteria to be employed in

---

* Adam Smith, Professor of Moral Philosophy, Lectures on Jurisprudence 1766.

evaluating applications, but failed to appraise the applications on the stated criteria. On the contrary, defendant evaluated such applications according to monetary contributions made on behalf of those seeking admission.

A contract, by ancient definition, is "an agreement between competent parties, upon a consideration sufficient in law, to do or not to do a particular thing." People v. Dummer (1916), 274 Ill. 637, 640, 113 N.E. 934, 935.

An offer, an acceptance (Milanko v. Jensen (1949), 404 Ill. 261, 266, 88 N.E.2d 857; Geary v. Great Atlantic & Pacific Tea Co. (1937), 366 Ill. 625, 627, 10 N.E.2d 350; Dick v. Halun (1931), 344 Ill. 163, 165-66, 176 N.E. 440; Restatement (Second) of Contracts secs. 19, 22 (Tent. Draft No. 1, 1964)), and consideration (Moehling v. W. E. O'Neil Construction Co. (1960), 20 Ill.2d 255, 265, 170 N.E.2d 100; Green v. Ashland Sixty-Third State Bank (1931), 346 Ill. 174, 178, 178 N.E. 468) are basic ingredients of a contract. Steinberg alleges that he and others similarly situated received a brochure describing the criteria that defendant would employ in evaluating applications. He urges that such constituted an invitation for an offer to apply, that the filing of the applications constituted an offer to have their credentials appraised under the terms described by defendant, and that defendant's voluntary reception of the application and fee constituted an acceptance, the final act necessary for the creation of a binding contract.

This situation is similar to that wherein a merchant advertises goods for sale at a fixed price. While the advertisement itself is not an offer to contract, it constitutes an invitation to deal on the terms described in the advertisement. (1 A. Corbin, Contracts sec. 25 (1950); Restatement (Second) of Contracts sec. 25, comment b, illustration 1, and comment f (Tent. Draft No. 1, 1964); O'Keefe v. Lee Calan Imports, Inc. (1970), 128 Ill.App.2d 410, 262 N.E.2d 758; Montgomery Ward & Co. v. Johnson (1911), 209 Mass. 89, 95 N.E. 290; Lovett v. Frederick Loeser & Co. (1924), 124 Misc. 81, 207 N.Y.S. 753; Ehrlich v. Willis Music Co. (1952), 93 Ohio App. 246, 113 N.E.2d 252, 51 Ohio Op. 8.) Although in some cases the advertisement itself may be an offer (see Lefkowitz v. Great Minneapolis Surplus Store, Inc. (1957), 251 Minn. 188, 86 N.W.2d 689), usually it constitutes only an invitation to deal on the advertised terms. Only when the merchant takes the money is there an acceptance of the offer to purchase.

Here the description in the brochure containing the terms under which an application will be appraised constituted an invitation for an offer. The tender of the application, as well as the payment of the fee pursuant to the terms of the brochure, was an offer to apply. Acceptance of the application and fee constituted acceptance of an offer to apply under the criteria defendant had established.

Consideration is a basic element for the existence of a contract. (Moehling v. W. E. O'Neil Construction Co. (1960), 20 Ill.2d 255, 265, 170 N.E.2d 100; Green v. Ashland Sixty-Third State Bank (1931), 346 Ill. 174, 178, 178 N.E. 468.) Any act or promise which is of benefit to one party or disadvantage to the other is a sufficient consideration to support a contract. (Green v. Ashland Sixty-Third State Bank (1931), 346 Ill. 174, 178, 178 N.E. 468.) The application fee was sufficient consideration to support the agreement between the applicant and the school.

Defendant contends that a further requisite for contract formation is a meeting of the minds. But a subjective understanding is not requisite. It suffices that the conduct of the contracting parties indicates an agreement to the terms of the alleged contract. (Restatement (Second) of Contracts sec. 19, comment c, sec. 21 (Tent. Draft No. 1, 1964).) Williston, in his work on contracts, states:

> In the formation of contracts it was long ago settled that secret intent was immaterial, only overt acts being considered in the determination of such mutual assent as that branch of the law requires. During the first half of the nineteenth century there were many expressions which seemed to indicate the contrary. Chief of these was the familiar cliché, still reechoing in judicial dicta, that a contract requires the 'meeting of the minds' of the parties. (1 Williston, Contracts sec. 22, at 46-48 (3d ed. 1957)).

Here it would appear from the complaint that the conduct of the parties amounted to an agreement that the application would be evaluated according to the criteria described by defendant in its literature.

Defendant urges People ex rel. Tinkoff v. Northwestern University (1947), 333 Ill.App. 224, 77 N.E.2d 345, controls. There the plaintiff alleged that since he met the stated requirement for admission, it was the obligation of the university to accept him. Plaintiff was first rejected because he was 14 years of age. He then filed a mandamus action, and subsequently the university denied his admission, apparently because of the court action. That decision turned on the fact that Northwestern University, a private educational institution, had reserved in its charter the right to reject any applicant for any reason it saw fit. Here, of course, defendant had no such provision in its charter or in the brochure in question. But, more important, Steinberg does not seek to compel the school to admit him. The substance of his action is that under the circumstances it was defendant's duty to appraise his application and those of the others on the terms defendant represented.

A medical school is an institution so important to life in society that its conduct cannot be justified by merely stating that one who does not wish to deal with it on its own terms may simply refrain from dealing with it at all.

As the appellate court noted in a recent case in which this defendant was a party:

> A contract between a private institution and a student confers duties upon both parties which cannot be arbitrarily disregarded and may be judicially enforced. (People ex rel. Cecil v. Bellevue Hospital Medical College (N.Y.1891), 60 Hun. 107, 14 N.Y.S. 490; Baltimore University v. Colton (1904), 98 Md. 623, 57 A. 14; State ex rel. Nelson v. Lincoln Medical College (1908), 81 Neb. 533, 116 N.W. 294.) DeMarco v. University of Health Sciences (1976), 40 Ill.App.3d 474, 480, 352 N.E.2d 356, 361.

Here our scope of review is exceedingly narrow. Does the complaint set forth facts which could mean that defendant contracted, under the circumstances, to appraise applicants and their applications according to the criteria it described? This is the sole inquiry on this motion to dismiss. We believe the allegations suffice and affirm the appellate court in holding count I stated a cause of action. . . .

The judgment of the appellate court is affirmed in part and reversed in part, and the judgment of the circuit court of Cook County is affirmed in part and reversed in part. The cause is remanded to the circuit court with directions to proceed in a manner not inconsistent with this opinion.

Appellate court affirmed in part and reversed in part; circuit court affirmed in part and reversed in part; cause remanded.

NOTES AND QUESTIONS:

1. *See* Restatement (Second) of Contracts §§ 1 (Contract Defined), 2 (Promise; Promisor; Promisee; Beneficiary), 17 (Requirement of a Bargain), 18 (Manifestation of Mutual Assent), 19 (Conduct as Manifestation of Assent), and 71 (Requirement of Exchange; Types of Exchange) (1981).

SECTION 2. MANIFESTATION OF ASSENT AND THE OBJECTIVE THEORY OF CONTRACTS

Often, people are adjudged bound to promises under contractual theories even though they never intended for their statements or actions to have contractual ramifications. Justice Holmes observed in *The Path of the Law*, "[P]arties may be bound by a contract to things which neither of them intended, and when one does not know of the other's assent."[1] Before you delve into the following material, consider whether it is sound policy to bind a party to a deal that he never intended to make. Regardless of where you stand on this, consider how we are to determine whether such party, in fact, never intended to make the deal as opposed to later regretting his initial decision.

What is this "meeting of the minds" that is generally regarded as the foundation of a contract?

---

[1] Justice O. W. Holmes, *The Path of the Law*, 10 Harv. L. Rev. 457 (1897).

LUCY V. ZEHMER
Supreme Court of Appeals of Virginia
84 S.E.2d 516 (1954).

BUCHANAN, J., delivered the opinion of the court

This suit was instituted by W. O. Lucy and J. C. Lucy, complainants, against A. H. Zehmer and Ida S. Zehmer, his wife, defendants, to have specific performance of a contract by which it was alleged the Zehmers had sold to W. O. Lucy a tract of land owned by A. H. Zehmer in Dinwiddie county containing 471.6 acres, more or less, known as the Ferguson farm, for $50,000. J. C. Lucy, the other complainant, is a brother of W. O. Lucy, to whom W. O. Lucy transferred a half interest in his alleged purchase.

The instrument sought to be enforced was written by A. H. Zehmer on December 20, 1952, in these words: "We hereby agree to sell to W. O. Lucy the Ferguson Farm complete for $50,000.00, title satisfactory to buyer," and signed by the defendants, A. H. Zehmer and Ida S. Zehmer.

The answer of A. H. Zehmer admitted that at the time mentioned W. O. Lucy offered him $50,000 cash for the farm, but that he, Zehmer, considered that the offer was made in jest; that so thinking, and both he and Lucy having had several drinks, he wrote out "the memorandum" quoted above and induced his wife to sign it; that he did not deliver the memorandum to Lucy, but that Lucy picked it up, read it, put it in his pocket, attempted to offer Zehmer $5 to bind the bargain, which Zehmer refused to accept, and realizing for the first time that Lucy was serious, Zehmer assured him that he had no intention of selling the farm and that the whole matter was a joke. Lucy left the premises insisting that he had purchased the farm.

Depositions were taken and the decree appealed from was entered holding that the complainants had failed to establish their right to specific performance, and dismissing their bill. The assignment of error is to this action of the court.

W. O. Lucy, a lumberman and farmer, thus testified in substance: He had known Zehmer for fifteen or twenty years and had been familiar with the Ferguson farm for ten years. Seven or eight years ago he had offered Zehmer $20,000 for the farm which Zehmer had accepted, but the agreement was verbal and Zehmer backed out. On the night of December 20, 1952, around eight o'clock, he took an employee to McKenney, where Zehmer lived and operated a restaurant, filling station and motor court. While there he decided to see Zehmer and again try to buy the Ferguson farm. He entered the restaurant and talked to Mrs. Zehmer until Zehmer came in. He asked Zehmer if he had sold the Ferguson farm. Zehmer replied that he had not. Lucy said, "I bet you wouldn't take $50,000.00 for that place." Zehmer replied, "Yes, I would too; you wouldn't give fifty." Lucy said he would and told Zehmer to write up an agreement to that effect. Zehmer took a restaurant check and wrote on the back of it, "I do hereby agree to sell to W. O. Lucy the Ferguson Farm for $50,000 complete." Lucy told him he had better change it to "We" because Mrs. Zehmer would have to sign it too. Zehmer then tore up what he had written, wrote the agreement quoted above and asked Mrs. Zehmer, who was at the other end of the counter ten or twelve feet away, to sign it. Mrs. Zehmer said she would for $50,000 and signed it. Zehmer brought it back and gave it to Lucy, who offered him $5 which Zehmer refused, saying, "You don't need to give me any money, you got the agreement there signed by both of us."

The discussion leading to the signing of the agreement, said Lucy, lasted thirty or forty minutes, during which Zehmer seemed to doubt that Lucy could raise $50,000. Lucy suggested the provision for having the title examined and Zehmer made the suggestion that he would sell it "complete, everything there," and stated that all he had on the farm was three heifers.

Lucy took a partly filled bottle of whiskey into the restaurant with him for the purpose of giving Zehmer a drink if he wanted it. Zehmer did, and he and Lucy had one or two drinks together. Lucy said that while he felt the drinks he took he was not intoxicated, and from the way Zehmer handled the transaction he did not think he was either.

December 20 was on Saturday. Next day Lucy telephoned to J. C. Lucy and arranged with the latter to take a half interest in the purchase and pay half of the consideration. On Monday he engaged an attorney to examine the title. The attorney reported favorably on December 31 and on January 2 Lucy wrote Zehmer stating that the title was satisfactory, that he was ready to pay the purchase price in cash and asking when Zehmer would be ready to close the deal. Zehmer replied by letter, mailed on January 13, asserting that he had never agreed or intended to sell.

Mr. and Mrs. Zehmer were called by the complainants as adverse witnesses. Zehmer testified in substance as follows:

He bought this farm more than ten years ago for $11,000. He had had twenty-five offers, more or less, to buy it, including several from Lucy, who had never offered any specific sum of money. He had given them all the same answer, that he was not interested in selling it. On this Saturday night before Christmas it looked like everybody and his brother came by there to have a drink. He took a good many drinks during the afternoon and had a pint of his own. When he entered the restaurant around eight-thirty Lucy was there and he could see that he was "pretty high." He said to Lucy, "Boy, you got some good liquor, drinking, ain't you?" Lucy then offered him a drink. "I was already high as a Georgia pine, and didn't have any more better sense than to pour another great big slug out and gulp it down, and he took one too."

After they had talked a while Lucy asked whether he still had the Ferguson farm. He replied that he had not sold it and Lucy said, "I bet you wouldn't take $50,000.00 for it." Zehmer asked him if he would give $50,000 and Lucy said yes. Zehmer replied, "You haven't got $50,000 in cash." Lucy said he did and Zehmer replied that he did not believe it. They argued "pro and con for a long time," mainly about "whether he had $50,000 in cash that he could put up right then and buy that farm."

Finally, said Zehmer, Lucy told him if he didn't believe he had $50,000, "you sign that piece of paper here and say you will take $50,000.00 for the farm." He, Zehmer, "just grabbed the back off of a guest check there" and wrote on the back of it. At that point in his testimony Zehmer asked to see what he had written to "see if I recognize my own handwriting." He examined the paper and exclaimed, "Great balls of fire, I got 'Firgerson' for Ferguson. I have got satisfactory spelled wrong. I don't recognize that writing if I would see it, wouldn't know it was mine."

After Zehmer had, as he described it, "scribbled this thing off," Lucy said, "Get your wife to sign it." Zehmer walked over to where she was and she at first refused to sign but did so after he told her that he "was just needling him [Lucy], and didn't mean a thing in the world, that I was not selling the farm." Zehmer then "took it back over there . . . and I was still looking at the dern thing. I had the drink right there by my hand, and I reached over to get a drink, and he said, 'Let me see it.' He reached and picked it up, and when I looked back again he had it in his pocket and he dropped a five dollar bill over there, and he said, 'Here is five dollars payment on it.' . . . I said, 'Hell no, that is beer and liquor talking. I am not going to sell you the farm. I have told you that too many times before.'"

Mrs. Zehmer testified that when Lucy came into the restaurant he looked as if he had had a drink. When Zehmer came in he took a drink out of a bottle that Lucy handed him. She went back to help the waitress who was getting things ready for next day. Lucy and Zehmer were talking but she did not pay too much attention to what they were saying. She heard Lucy ask Zehmer if he had sold the Ferguson farm, and Zehmer replied that he had not and did not want to sell it. Lucy said, "I bet you wouldn't take $50,000 cash for that farm," and Zehmer replied, "You haven't got $50,000 cash." Lucy said, "I can get it." Zehmer said he might form a company and get it, "but you haven't got $50,000.00 cash to pay me tonight." Lucy asked him if he would put it in writing that he would sell him this farm. Zehmer then wrote on the back of a pad, "I agree to sell the Ferguson Place to W. O. Lucy for $50,000.00 cash." Lucy said, "All right, get your wife to sign it." Zehmer came back to where she was standing and said, "You want to put your name to this?" She said "No," but he said in an undertone, "It is nothing but a joke," and she signed it.

She said that only one paper was written and it said: "I hereby agree to sell," but the "I" had been changed to "We." However, she said she read what she signed and was then asked, "When you read 'We hereby agree to sell to W. O. Lucy,' what did you interpret that to mean, that particular phrase?" She said she thought that was a cash sale that night; but she also said that when she read that part about "title satisfactory to buyer" she understood that if the title was good Lucy would pay $50,000 but if the title was bad he would have a right to reject it, and that that was her understanding at the time she signed her name.

On examination by her own counsel she said that her husband laid this piece of paper down after it was signed; that Lucy said to let him see it, took it, folded it and put it in his wallet, then said to Zehmer, "Let me give you $5.00," but Zehmer said, "No, this is liquor talking. I don't want to sell the farm, I have told you that I want my son to have it. This is all a joke." Lucy then said at least twice, "Zehmer, you have sold your farm," wheeled around and started for the door. He paused at the door and said, "I will bring you $50,000.00 tomorrow. . . . No, tomorrow is Sunday. I will bring it to you Monday." She said you could tell definitely that he was drinking and she said to her husband, "You should have taken him home," but he said, "Well, I am just about as bad off as he is."

The waitress referred to by Mrs. Zehmer testified that when Lucy first came in "he was mouthy." When Zehmer came in they were laughing and joking and she thought they took a drink or two. She was sweeping and cleaning up for next day. She said she heard Lucy tell Zehmer, "I will give you so much for the farm," and Zehmer said, "You haven't got that much." Lucy answered, "Oh, yes, I will give you that much." Then "they jotted down something on paper . . . and Mr. Lucy reached over and took it, said let me see it." He looked at it, put it in his pocket and in about a minute he left. She was asked whether she saw Lucy offer Zehmer any money and replied, "He had five dollars laying up there, they didn't take it." She said Zehmer told Lucy he didn't want his money "because he didn't have enough money to pay for his property, and wasn't going to sell his farm." Both of them appeared to be drinking right much, she said.

She repeated on cross-examination that she was busy and paying no attention to what was going on. She was some distance away and did not see either of them sign the paper. She was asked whether she saw Zehmer put the agreement down on the table in front of Lucy, and her answer was this: "Time he got through writing whatever it was on the paper, Mr. Lucy reached over and said, 'Let's see it.' He took it and put it in his pocket," before showing it to Mrs. Zehmer. Her version was that Lucy kept raising his offer until it got to $50,000.

The defendants insist that the evidence was ample to support their contention that the writing sought to be enforced was prepared as a bluff or dare to force Lucy to admit that he did not have $50,000; that the whole matter was a joke; that the writing was not delivered to Lucy and no binding contract was ever made between the parties.

It is an unusual, if not bizarre, defense. When made to the writing admittedly prepared by one of the defendants and signed by both, clear evidence is required to sustain it.

In his testimony Zehmer claimed that he "was high as a Georgia pine," and that the transaction "was just a bunch of two doggoned drunks bluffing to see who could talk the biggest and say the most." That claim is inconsistent with his attempt to testify in great detail as to what was said and what was done. It is contradicted by other evidence as to the condition of both parties, and rendered of no weight by the testimony of his wife that when Lucy left the restaurant she suggested that Zehmer drive him home. The record is convincing that Zehmer was not intoxicated to the extent of being unable to comprehend the nature and consequences of the instrument he executed, and hence that instrument is not to be invalidated on that ground. It was in fact conceded by defendants' counsel in oral argument that under the evidence Zehmer was not too drunk to make a valid contract.

The evidence is convincing also that Zehmer wrote two agreements, the first one beginning "I hereby agree to sell." Zehmer first said he could not remember about that, then that "I don't think I wrote but one out." Mrs. Zehmer said that what he wrote was "I hereby agree," but that the "I" was changed to "We" after that night. The agreement that was written and signed is in the record and indicates no such change. Neither are the mistakes in spelling that Zehmer sought to point out readily apparent.

The appearance of the contract, the fact that it was under discussion for forty minutes or more before it was signed; Lucy's objection to the first draft because it was written in the singular, and he wanted Mrs. Zehmer to sign it also; the rewriting to meet that objection and the signing by Mrs. Zehmer; the discussion of what was to be included in the sale, the provision for the examination of the title, the completeness of the instrument that was executed, the taking possession of it by Lucy with no request or suggestion by either of the defendants that he give it back, are facts which furnish persuasive evidence that the execution of the contract was a serious business transaction rather than a casual, jesting matter as defendants now contend. . . .

If it be assumed, contrary to what we think the evidence shows, that Zehmer was jesting about selling his farm to Lucy and that the transaction was intended by him to be a joke, nevertheless the evidence shows that Lucy did not so understand it but considered it to be a serious business transaction and the contract to be binding on the Zehmers as well as on himself. The very next day he arranged with his brother to put up half the money and take a half interest in the land. The day after that he employed an attorney to examine the title. The next night, Tuesday, he was back at Zehmer's place and there Zehmer told him for the first time, Lucy said, that he wasn't going to sell and he told Zehmer, "You know you sold that place fair and square." After receiving the report from his attorney that the title was good he wrote to Zehmer that he was ready to close the deal.

Not only did Lucy actually believe, but the evidence shows he was warranted in believing, that the contract represented a serious business transaction and a good faith sale and purchase of the farm.

In the field of contracts, as generally elsewhere, "We must look to the outward expression of a person as manifesting his intention rather than to his secret and unexpressed intention. 'The law imputes to a person an intention corresponding to the reasonable meaning of his words and acts.' " *First Nat. Bank v. Roanoke Oil Co.,* 169 Va. 99, 114, 192 S.E. 764, 770. . . .

The mental assent of the parties is not requisite for the formation of a contract. If the words or other acts of one of the parties have but one reasonable meaning, his undisclosed intention is immaterial except when an unreasonable meaning which he attaches to his manifestations is known to the other party. Restatement of the Law of Contracts, Vol. I, § 71, p. 74.

". . . The law, therefore, judges of an agreement between two persons exclusively from those expressions of their intentions which are communicated between them . . . ." Clark on Contracts, 4 ed., § 3, p. 4.

An agreement or mutual assent is of course essential to a valid contract but the law imputes to a person an intention corresponding to the reasonable meaning of his words and acts. If his words and acts, judged by a reasonable standard, manifest an intention to agree, it is immaterial what may be the real but unexpressed state of his mind. 17 C.J.S., Contracts, § 32, p. 361; 12 Am. Jur., Contracts, § 19, p. 515.

So a person cannot set up that he was merely jesting when his conduct and words would warrant a reasonable person in believing that he intended a real agreement, 17 C.J.S., Contracts, § 47, p. 390; Clark on Contracts, 4 ed., § 27, at p. 54.

Whether the writing signed by the defendants and now sought to be enforced by the complainants was the result of a serious offer by Lucy and a serious acceptance by the defendants, or was a serious offer by Lucy and an acceptance in secret jest by the defendants, in either event it constituted a binding contract of sale between the parties. . . .

The complainants are entitled to have specific performance of the contracts sued on. The decree appealed from is therefore reversed and the cause is remanded for the entry of a proper decree requiring the defendants to perform the contract in accordance with the prayer of the bill.

Reversed and remanded.

LEONARD V. PEPSICO, INC.
United States District Court, S.D. New York
88 F. Supp. 2d 116 (1999).

KIMBA M. WOOD, District Judge.

. . . .

I. Background

This case arises out of a promotional campaign conducted by defendant, the producer and distributor of the soft drinks Pepsi and Diet Pepsi. (*See* PepsiCo Inc.'s Rule 56.1 Statement ("Def. Stat.") ¶ 2.) The promotion, entitled "Pepsi Stuff," encouraged consumers to collect "Pepsi Points" from specially marked packages of Pepsi or Diet Pepsi and redeem these points for merchandise featuring the Pepsi logo. (*See id.* ¶¶ 4, 8.) Before introducing the promotion nationally, defendant conducted a test of the promotion in the Pacific Northwest from October 1995 to March 1996. (*See id.* ¶¶ 5-6.) A Pepsi Stuff catalog was distributed to consumers in the test market, including Washington State. (*See id.* ¶ 7.) Plaintiff is a resident of Seattle, Washington. (*See id.* ¶ 3.) While living in Seattle, plaintiff saw the Pepsi Stuff commercial (*see id.* ¶ 22) that he contends constituted an offer of a Harrier Jet.

A. *The Alleged Offer*

. . . The commercial opens upon an idyllic, suburban morning, where the chirping of birds in sun-dappled trees welcomes a paperboy on his morning route. As the newspaper hits the stoop of a conventional two-story house, the tattoo of a military drum introduces the subtitle, "MONDAY 7:58 AM." The stirring strains of a martial air mark the appearance of a well-coiffed teenager preparing to leave for school, dressed in a shirt emblazoned with the Pepsi logo, a red-white-and-blue ball. While the teenager confidently preens, the military drumroll again sounds as the subtitle "T-SHIRT 75 PEPSI POINTS" scrolls across the screen. Bursting from his room, the teenager strides down the hallway wearing a leather jacket. The drumroll sounds again, as the subtitle "LEATHER JACKET 1450 PEPSI

POINTS" appears. The teenager opens the door of his house and, unfazed by the glare of the early morning sunshine, puts on a pair of sunglasses. The drumroll then accompanies the subtitle "SHADES 175 PEPSI POINTS." A voiceover then intones, "Introducing the new Pepsi Stuff catalog," as the camera focuses on the cover of the catalog. (*See* Defendant's Local Rule 56.1 Stat., Exh. A (the "Catalog").)[2]

The scene then shifts to three young boys sitting in front of a high school building. The boy in the middle is intent on his Pepsi Stuff Catalog, while the boys on either side are each drinking Pepsi. The three boys gaze in awe at an object rushing overhead, as the military march builds to a crescendo. The Harrier Jet is not yet visible, but the observer senses the presence of a mighty plane as the extreme winds generated by its flight create a paper maelstrom in a classroom devoted to an otherwise dull physics lesson. Finally, the Harrier Jet swings into view and lands by the side of the school building, next to a bicycle rack. Several students run for cover, and the velocity of the wind strips one hapless faculty member down to his underwear. While the faculty member is being deprived of his dignity, the voiceover announces: "Now the more Pepsi you drink, the more great stuff you're gonna get."

The teenager opens the cockpit of the fighter and can be seen, helmetless, holding a Pepsi. "[L]ooking very pleased with himself," (Pl. Mem. at 3,) the teenager exclaims, "Sure beats the bus," and chortles. The military drumroll sounds a final time, as the following words appear: "HARRIER FIGHTER 7,000,000 PEPSI POINTS." A few seconds later, the following appears in more stylized script: "Drink Pepsi-Get Stuff." With that message, the music and the commercial end with a triumphant flourish.

Inspired by this commercial, plaintiff set out to obtain a Harrier Jet. Plaintiff explains that he is "typical of the 'Pepsi Generation' . . . he is young, has an adventurous spirit, and the notion of obtaining a Harrier Jet appealed to him enormously." (Pl. Mem. at 3.) Plaintiff consulted the Pepsi Stuff Catalog. The Catalog features youths dressed in Pepsi Stuff regalia or enjoying Pepsi Stuff accessories, such as "Blue Shades" ("As if you need another reason to look forward to sunny days."), "Pepsi Tees" ("Live in 'em. Laugh in 'em. Get in 'em."), "Bag of Balls" ("Three balls. One bag. No rules."), and "Pepsi Phone Card" ("Call your mom!"). The Catalog specifies the number of Pepsi Points required to obtain promotional merchandise. (*See* Catalog, at rear foldout pages.) The Catalog includes an Order Form which lists, on one side, fifty-three items of Pepsi Stuff merchandise redeemable for Pepsi Points (*see id.* (the "Order Form")). Conspicuously absent from the Order Form is any entry or description of a Harrier Jet. (*See id.*) The amount of Pepsi Points required to obtain the listed merchandise ranges from 15 (for a "Jacket Tattoo" ("Sew 'em on your jacket, not your arm.")) to 3300 (for a "Fila Mountain Bike" ("Rugged. All-terrain. Exclusively for Pepsi.")). It should be noted that plaintiff objects to the implication that because an item was not shown in the Catalog, it was unavailable. (*See* Pl. Stat. ¶¶ 23-26, 29.)

---

[2] At this point, the following message appears at the bottom of the screen: "Offer not available in all areas. See details on specially marked packages."

The rear foldout pages of the Catalog contain directions for redeeming Pepsi Points for merchandise. (*See* Catalog, at rear foldout pages.) These directions note that merchandise may be ordered "only" with the original Order Form. (*See id.*) The Catalog notes that in the event that a consumer lacks enough Pepsi Points to obtain a desired item, additional Pepsi Points may be purchased for ten cents each; however, at least fifteen original Pepsi Points must accompany each order. (*See id.*)

Although plaintiff initially set out to collect 7,000,000 Pepsi Points by consuming Pepsi products, it soon became clear to him that he "would not be able to buy (let alone drink) enough Pepsi to collect the necessary Pepsi Points fast enough." (Affidavit of John D.R. Leonard, Mar. 30, 1999 ("Leonard Aff."), ¶ 5.) Reevaluating his strategy, plaintiff "focused for the first time on the packaging materials in the Pepsi Stuff promotion," (*id.,*) and realized that buying Pepsi Points would be a more promising option. (*See id.*) Through acquaintances, plaintiff ultimately raised about $700,000. (*See id.* ¶ 6.)

B. *Plaintiff's Efforts to Redeem the Alleged Offer*

On or about March 27, 1996, plaintiff submitted an Order Form, fifteen original Pepsi Points, and a check for $700,008.50. (*See* Def. Stat. ¶ 36.) Plaintiff appears to have been represented by counsel at the time he mailed his check; the check is drawn on an account of plaintiff's first set of attorneys. (*See* Defendant's Notice of Motion, Exh. B (first).) At the bottom of the Order Form, plaintiff wrote in "1 Harrier Jet" in the "Item" column and "7,000,000" in the "Total Points" column. (*See id.*) In a letter accompanying his submission, plaintiff stated that the check was to purchase additional Pepsi Points "expressly for obtaining a new Harrier jet as advertised in your Pepsi Stuff commercial." (*See* Declaration of David Wynn, Mar. 18, 1999 ("Wynn Dec."), Exh. A.)

On or about May 7, 1996, defendant's fulfillment house rejected plaintiff's submission and returned the check, explaining that:

> The item that you have requested is not part of the Pepsi Stuff collection. It is not included in the catalogue or on the order form, and only catalogue merchandise can be redeemed under this program.
>
> The Harrier jet in the Pepsi commercial is fanciful and is simply included to create a humorous and entertaining ad. We apologize for any misunderstanding or confusion that you may have experienced and are enclosing some free product coupons for your use (Wynn Aff. Exh. B (second)).

Plaintiff's previous counsel responded on or about May 14, 1996, as follows:

> Your letter of May 7, 1996 is totally unacceptable. We have reviewed the video tape of the Pepsi Stuff commercial ... and it clearly offers the new Harrier jet for 7,000,000 Pepsi Points. Our client followed your rules explicitly. . . .

> This is a formal demand that you honor your commitment and make immediate arrangements to transfer the new Harrier jet to our client. If we do not receive transfer instructions within ten (10) business days of the date of this letter you will leave us no choice but to file an appropriate action against Pepsi. . . . (Wynn Aff., Exh. C.)

This letter was apparently sent onward to the advertising company responsible for the actual commercial, BBDO New York ("BBDO"). In a letter dated May 30, 1996, BBDO Vice President Raymond E. McGovern, Jr., explained to plaintiff that:

> I find it hard to believe that you are of the opinion that the Pepsi Stuff commercial ("Commercial") really offers a new Harrier Jet. The use of the Jet was clearly a joke that was meant to make the Commercial more humorous and entertaining. In my opinion, no reasonable person would agree with your analysis of the Commercial. (Wynn Aff. Exh. A.)

On or about June 17, 1996, plaintiff mailed a similar demand letter to defendant. (*See* Wynn Aff., Exh. D.) . . . . PepsiCo moved for summary judgment pursuant to Federal Rule of Civil Procedure 56. The present motion thus follows three years of jurisdictional and procedural wrangling.

II. Discussion

A. *The Legal Framework*

1. *Standard for Summary Judgment*

On a motion for summary judgment, a court "cannot try issues of fact; it can only determine whether there are issues to be tried." *Donahue v. Windsor Locks Bd. of Fire Comm'rs,* 834 F.2d 54, 58 (2d Cir.1987) (citations and internal quotation marks omitted). To prevail on a motion for summary judgment, the moving party therefore must show that there are no such genuine issues of material fact to be tried, and that he or she is entitled to judgment as a matter of law. *See* Fed.R.Civ.P. 56(c); *Celotex Corp. v. Catrett,* 477 U.S. 317, 322, 106 S.Ct. 2548, 91 L.Ed.2d 265 (1986); *Citizens Bank v. Hunt,* 927 F.2d 707, 710 (2d Cir.1991). The party seeking summary judgment "bears the initial responsibility of informing the district court of the basis for its motion," which includes identifying the materials in the record that "it believes demonstrate the absence of a genuine issue of material fact." *Celotex Corp.,* 477 U.S. at 323, 106 S.Ct. 2548.

Once a motion for summary judgment is made and supported, the non-moving party must set forth specific facts that show that there is a genuine issue to be tried. *See Anderson v. Liberty Lobby, Inc.,* 477 U.S. 242, 251-52, 106 S.Ct. 2505, 91 L.Ed.2d 202 (1986). Although a court considering a motion for summary judgment must view all evidence in the light most favorable to the non-moving party, and must draw all reasonable inferences in that party's favor, *see Consarc Corp. v. Marine Midland Bank, N.A.,* 996 F.2d 568, 572 (2d Cir.1993), the nonmoving party "must do more than simply show that there is some metaphysical doubt as to the material facts." *Matsushita Elec. Indus. Co. v. Zenith Radio Corp.,* 475 U.S. 574, 586, 106 S.Ct. 1348, 89 L.Ed.2d 538 (1986). If, based on the submissions to the court, no rational fact-finder could find in the non-movant's favor, there is no genuine issue of material fact, and summary judgment is appropriate. *See Anderson,* 477 U.S. at 250, 106 S.Ct. 2505.

The question of whether or not a contract was formed is appropriate for resolution on summary judgment. As the Second Circuit has recently noted, "Summary judgment is proper when the 'words and actions that allegedly formed a contract [are] so clear themselves that reasonable people could not differ over their meaning.' " *Krumme v. Westpoint Stevens, Inc.,* 143 F.3d 71, 83 (2d Cir.1998) (quoting *Bourque v. FDIC,* 42 F.3d 704, 708 (1st Cir. 1994)) (further citations omitted); *see also Wards Co. v. Stamford Ridgeway Assocs.,* 761 F.2d 117, 120 (2d Cir. 1985) (summary judgment is appropriate in contract case where interpretation urged by non-moving party is not "fairly reasonable"). Summary judgment is appropriate in such cases because there is "sometimes no genuine issue as to whether the parties' conduct implied a 'contractual understanding.'.... In such cases, 'the judge must decide the issue himself, just as he decides any factual issue in respect to which reasonable people cannot differ.'" *Bourque,* 42 F.3d at 708 (quoting *Boston Five Cents Sav. Bank v. Secretary of Dep't of Housing & Urban Dev.,* 768 F.2d 5, 8 (1st Cir. 1985)). . . .

C. *An Objective, Reasonable Person Would Not Have Considered the Commercial an Offer*

Plaintiff's understanding of the commercial as an offer must also be rejected because the Court finds that no objective person could reasonably have concluded that the commercial actually offered consumers a Harrier Jet.

1. *Objective Reasonable Person Standard*

In evaluating the commercial, the Court must not consider defendant's subjective intent in making the commercial, or plaintiff's subjective view of what the commercial offered, but what an objective, reasonable person would have understood the commercial to convey. *See Kay-R Elec. Corp. v. Stone & Webster Constr. Co.,* 23 F.3d 55, 57 (2d Cir.1994) ("[W]e are not concerned with what was going through the heads of the parties at the time [of the alleged contract]. Rather, we are talking about the objective principles of contract law."); *Mesaros,* 845 F.2d at 1581 ("A basic rule of contracts holds that whether an offer has been made depends on the objective reasonableness of the alleged offeree's belief that the advertisement or solicitation was intended as an offer."); Farnsworth, *supra,* § 3.10, at 237; Williston, *supra,* § 4:7 at 296-97.

If it is clear that an offer was not serious, then no offer has been made:

> What kind of act creates a power of acceptance and is therefore an offer? It must be an expression of will or intention. It must be an act that leads the offeree reasonably to conclude that a power to create a contract is conferred. This applies to the content of the power as well as to the fact of its existence. *It is on this ground that we must exclude* invitations to deal or acts of mere preliminary negotiation, and *acts evidently done in jest* or without intent to create legal relations.

Corbin on Contracts, § 1.11 at 30 (emphasis added). An obvious joke, of course, would not give rise to a contract. *See, e.g., Graves v. Northern N.Y. Pub. Co.,* 260 A.D. 900, 22 N.Y.S.2d 537 (1940) (dismissing claim to offer of $1,000 which appeared in the "joke column" of the newspaper, to any person who could provide a commonly available phone number). On the other hand, if there is no indication that the offer is "evidently in jest," and that an objective, reasonable person would find that the offer was serious, then there may be a valid offer. *See Barnes,* 549 P.2d at 1155 ("[I]f the jest is not apparent and a reasonable hearer would believe that an offer was being made, then the speaker risks the formation of a contract which was not intended."); *see also Lucy v. Zehmer,* 196 Va. 493, 84 S.E.2d 516, 518, 520 (1954) (ordering specific performance of a contract to purchase a farm despite defendant's protestation that the transaction was done in jest as "'just a bunch of two doggoned drunks bluffing'").

2. *Necessity of a Jury Determination*

Plaintiff also contends that summary judgment is improper because the question of whether the commercial conveyed a sincere offer can be answered only by a jury. Relying on dictum from *Gallagher v. Delaney,* 139 F.3d 338 (2d Cir.1998), plaintiff argues that a federal judge comes from a "narrow segment of the enormously broad American socio-economic spectrum," *id.* at 342, and, thus, that the question whether the commercial constituted a serious offer must be decided by a jury composed of, *inter alia,* members of the "Pepsi Generation," who are, as plaintiff puts it, "young, open to adventure, willing to do the unconventional." (*See* Leonard Aff. ¶ 2.) Plaintiff essentially argues that a federal judge would view his claim differently than fellow members of the "Pepsi Generation."

Plaintiff's argument that his claim must be put to a jury is without merit. *Gallagher* involved a claim of sexual harassment in which the defendant allegedly invited plaintiff to sit on his lap, gave her inappropriate Valentine's Day gifts, told her that "she brought out feelings that he had not had since he was sixteen," and "invited her to help him feed the ducks in the pond, since he was 'a bachelor for the evening.' " *Gallagher,* 139 F.3d at 344. The court concluded that a jury determination was particularly appropriate because a federal judge lacked "the current real-life experience required in interpreting subtle sexual dynamics of the workplace based on nuances, subtle perceptions, and implicit communications." *Id.* at 342. This case, in contrast, presents a question of whether there was an offer to enter into a contract, requiring the Court to determine how a reasonable, objective person would have understood defendant's commercial. Such an inquiry is commonly performed by courts on a motion for summary judgment. *See Krumme,* 143 F.3d at 83; *Bourque,* 42 F.3d at 708; *Wards Co.,* 761 F.2d at 120.

3. *Whether the Commercial Was "Evidently Done In Jest"*

. . . Plaintiff argues that a reasonable, objective person would have understood the commercial to make a serious offer of a Harrier Jet because there was "absolutely no distinction in the manner" (Pl. Mem. at 13,) in which the items in the commercial were presented. Plaintiff also relies upon a press release highlighting the promotional campaign, issued by defendant, in which "[n]o mention is made by [defendant] of humor, or anything of the sort." (*Id.* at 5.) These arguments suggest merely that the humor of the promotional campaign was tongue in cheek. Humor is not limited to what Justice Cardozo called "[t]he rough and boisterous joke ... [that] evokes its own guffaws." *Murphy v. Steeplechase Amusement Co.,* 250 N.Y. 479, 483, 166 N.E. 173, 174 (1929). In light of the obvious absurdity of the commercial, the Court rejects plaintiff's argument that the commercial was not clearly in jest. . . .

III. Conclusion

. . . [T]he tongue-in-cheek attitude of the commercial would not cause a reasonable person to conclude that a soft drink company would be giving away fighter planes as part of a promotion. . . .

For the reasons stated above, the Court grants defendant's motion for summary judgment. The Clerk of Court is instructed to close these cases. Any pending motions are moot.

STEPP V. FREEMAN
Court of Appeals of Ohio
694 N.E.2d 510 (1997).

FREDERICK N. YOUNG, Presiding Judge.

Donald Freeman, defendant, appeals the trial court's holding in favor of Lionel Stepp, plaintiff, on the issues of equitable estoppel and implied contract.

I

This matter arose out of the events surrounding the purchase of a winning lottery ticket on March 1, 1993. Freeman and Stepp were members of a group of employees at the Chrysler Acustar Plant who jointly purchased lottery tickets. The group had been in existence in excess of five years. Freeman took over running the group approximately two years prior to the date the group purchased the winning ticket. The group had no written rules, but it had established certain unwritten rules of conduct.

The group was restricted to only twenty members. Freeman kept a list of the members. The members pooled their money to purchase lottery tickets whenever the jackpot reached $8 million or higher. Each member was expected to contribute $2.20 to the pool. Freeman would keep track of who had paid, whether payment was in advance, and who had not yet paid by noting it in the appropriate column on the list of the members. The group purchased forty tickets and four "kickers" with the pooled money.

To increase their chances of winning, the group would use half of the pooled money to purchase tickets in Cincinnati, Ohio, and the other half to purchase tickets in Beavercreek, Ohio. Freeman purchased the tickets in Beavercreek, Ohio, and Fred Krueger, another member of the group, purchased the tickets in Cincinnati, Ohio. The tickets were purchased either on Monday, for the Wednesday drawing, or on Thursday, for the Saturday drawing. In the weeks that the group played the lottery, Stepp was in charge of making photocopies of the tickets on Tuesday and/or Friday. Sometimes, however, another member of the group,

James Saul, would make the copies of the tickets if Stepp was unavailable. Stepp would leave the photocopies on Freeman's desk. Freeman would either leave the copies on his desk for the members to pick up or would sometimes distribute some of the copies to members.

Freeman was recognized as being in charge of receiving the money for the pool. Freeman testified that a few times he had to explicitly inform or remind some members that their money was due. Freeman further stated that he had to remind all of the members of the group at least once or twice during the two years that he ran the group that their shares were due. Freeman also often indirectly reminded members that their shares were due by walking around the plant with the list of members in his hand. When the members saw Freeman with the card in his hand, they knew it was time to contribute, and they would get out their money and pay their shares without Freeman having to expressly ask for their contributions.

Members would sometimes cover other members' shares when they ran into Freeman. Furthermore, Freeman or other members would cover another member's portion of the pool if the member was absent from work. When members knew that they would be on vacation or otherwise unavailable, they would pay their contribution in advance or would inform Freeman that they would pay when they returned. Since the time that Freeman began running the group, none of the members had ever failed to participate, and no fewer than forty tickets, two for each member, had ever been purchased.

Individuals who wanted to join the group had to put their names on a waiting list and could join the group only when one of the existing members decided to leave the group. The members that actually dropped out of the group while Freeman was running it were taken off the list only after Freeman had a conversation with them and the member had conveyed to Freeman that he or she was not going to contribute any longer and that he or she was leaving the group. No member had ever been unilaterally removed from the list by Freeman because the member had not timely paid his or her share. After a member left the group, Freeman would ask the first person on the waiting list if he or she wanted to join the group. If the individual decided to join the group, Freeman would add the individual's name to the list.

In the week prior to the group purchasing the winning lottery ticket, Freeman and Stepp had a serious work-related disagreement. As a result of their disagreement, Freeman called Stepp a derogatory name and, according to Stepp, threatened him. Following their disagreement, Freeman and Stepp did not speak to one another with the exception of a few brief work-related discussions. The lottery jackpot reached $8 million over the weekend following their conflict. On the ensuing Monday, Freeman collected money from the group for the drawing by, in part, walking around with the member list in his hand. Freeman, however, did not ask for Stepp's money, nor did he inform Stepp that the lottery had reached $8 million. Likewise, Stepp, who claims that he was unaware that the lottery had reached $8 million, did not offer his $2.20.

At the end of the day, Freeman gave Krueger the usual $20 to buy tickets in Cincinnati. Freeman put in the extra dollar himself. Freeman did not inform Krueger or Stepp that he did not consider Stepp to be included in the pool, but he did tell some other members that Stepp was out of the group because he had not paid his $2.20. Furthermore, Stepp never conveyed to Freeman that he was dropping out of the pool. Even though Freeman testified that he considered Stepp to be out of the pool, Freeman did not consult anyone on the waiting list to fill Stepp's spot. Freeman did, however, purchase nineteen, rather than twenty, tickets in Beavercreek, Ohio. Conversely, Krueger purchased the usual twenty tickets in Cincinnati. Therefore, the group had one more ticket than the group should have had if the group had purchased only enough tickets for nineteen members.

On Tuesday, Freeman asked James Saul, rather than Stepp, to make copies of the tickets, explaining that "Stepp hasn't come around." On Wednesday, March 3, 1993, the lottery group won the $8 million lottery jackpot. The winning ticket was one of the twenty tickets purchased in Cincinnati by Fred Krueger. When Stepp arrived at work on Thursday, he was informed by some of his coworkers that the group had won the lottery, and that the group considered that he was not entitled to a share of the money because he had failed to contribute his portion to the pool. The group, however, let one of the members, who was on vacation when the money for the lottery was collected, pay his $2.20 on the Friday after the group had won the lottery. The group let that member pay late because he had purportedly made arrangements with Freeman that he would pay when he returned from his vacation.

On September 1, 1993, Stepp commenced an action, claiming that he was denied his rightful share of the lottery winnings. In support of his claim, Stepp asserted three causes of action: breach of express contract, breach of implied contract, and equitable estoppel. The case was referred to a magistrate for a hearing pursuant to Civ.R. 53. The magistrate issued a finding in favor of Stepp on both the equitable estoppel and breach of contract claim, and recommended that the trial court enter judgment for Stepp in the amount of $60,000 for his portion of the accrued winnings in the years 1993-1996 and one-twentieth of each of the future jackpot payouts. Freeman put on objections to the magistrate's findings of fact and conclusions of law. The trial court considered Freeman's objections and independently reviewed the record as well as all of the evidence presented. After the court concluded its review, it rendered a thoughtful opinion in favor of Stepp on both the equitable estoppel and breach of implied contract claims. Freeman now brings this timely appeal of that decision.

II

Freeman presents the following . . . assignments of error: ". . . The trial court erred by holding that plaintiff could recover under an implied contract theory when plaintiff had not proven all of the essential contract elements."

We determine that we need not consider the assignments of error relating to the equitable estoppel claim because we believe that Stepp proved his cause of action for breach of an implied-in-fact contract, which is sufficient alone to support the court's monetary award. We find both that Stepp proved all of the elements of an implied-in-fact contract and that the court's finding that the contract was breached was not against the manifest weight of the evidence.

It is well established that there are three categories of contracts: express, implied in fact, and implied in law. Legros v. Tarr (1989), 44 Ohio St.3d 1, 6, 540 N.E.2d 257, 262-263. Express and implied-in-fact contracts differ from contracts implied in law in that contracts implied in law are not true contracts. Sabin v. Graves (1993), 86 Ohio App.3d 628, 633, 621 N.E.2d 748, 751-752. Implied-in-law contracts are a legal fiction used to effect an equitable result. Id. Because a contract implied in law is a tool of equity, the existence of an implied-in-law contract does not depend on whether the elements of a contract are proven. Id.

On the contrary, the existence of express or implied-in-fact contracts does hinge upon proof of all of the elements of a contract. Lucas v. Costantini (1983), 13 Ohio App.3d 367, 368, 13 OBR 449, 449-451, 469 N.E.2d 927, 928-929. Express contracts diverge from implied-in-fact contracts in the form of proof that is needed to establish each contractual element. Penwell v. Amherst Hosp. (1992), 84 Ohio App.3d 16, 21, 616 N.E.2d 254, 257-258. In express contracts, assent to the terms of the contract is actually expressed in the form of an offer and an acceptance. Lucas, supra. On the other hand, in implied-in-fact contracts the parties' meeting of the minds is shown by the surrounding circumstances, including the conduct and declarations of the parties, that make it inferable that the contract exists as a matter of tacit understanding. Point E. Condominium Owners' Assn. v. Cedar House Assn. (1995), 104 Ohio App.3d 704, 712, 663 N.E.2d 343, 348-349. To establish a contract implied in fact a plaintiff must demonstrate that the circumstances surrounding the parties' transaction make it reasonably certain that an agreement was intended. Lucas, supra.

Stepp proved all of the elements of an implied-in-fact contract. The circumstances surrounding this pool make it inferable that a contract existed as a matter of tacit understanding. The group membership was restricted to twenty. No new members could join until one of the twenty members dropped out of the group. There was a waiting list to join the group. Members joined the group by consulting Freeman and having Freeman place them on the group roster. Placing an individual's name on the roster created an implied agreement that the individual was a member of the group. Furthermore, there was an implied agreement that each member was to contribute $2.20 to the pool whenever the group played the lottery and that the members would share the winnings equally.

The members thought that the group was run very informally and left the details of running the group to Freeman. Many of the members knew very little about how the group was run. Some members did not even know that the group played the lottery only when the jackpot was $8 million or higher. Most members saw their duty as a member of the group as just contributing their share whenever they saw Freeman walking around the plant with the list in his hand or were otherwise informed that their shares were due.

There was an implied agreement among the members that once their names were on the list as members of the group, they would be informed when they owed their share of the pool and how much they owed. The implied agreement was that members would be informed when their money was due either verbally by Freeman, by other members, or by seeing Freeman walking about with the list in his hand. Freeman testified that he had to expressly remind some members that their money was due a few times and that he had to remind every member of the group that their money was due at least once or twice during the period that he ran the group. Freeman also admitted that he indirectly reminded people that there shares were due by frequently walking around the plant with the list in his hand when the group was going to be playing the lottery.

Because the members perceived the group as running informally and because Freeman had reminded the members that their money was due, a member could also count on not being dropped from the group after neglecting to make payment. No members had been unilaterally dropped from the group by Freeman because they had not paid their share in a timely manner. Those who had not paid their shares in a timely manner were dropped from the group only after Freeman had a conversation with them and they conveyed to him that they were not going to pay and that they were leaving the group.

Stepp had belonged to this group for over five years, and he had never failed to contribute to the lottery during those years. Stepp testified that he had always depended upon Freeman, who was in charge of the lottery, to inform him when the jackpot reached $8 million. Stepp testified that Freeman had always told him when his share was due and how much he owed. As consideration for being told that he owed his share, Stepp would contribute his $2.20 or Freeman would cover his $2.20.

Freeman admitted that he would sometimes cover Stepp's share even when Stepp was not absent from work. In particular, Freeman testified that sometimes the group would play the lottery twice a week and that in some instances he would only collect $2.20 from Stepp, and if they ended up playing a second time, he would put in the additional money for Stepp and collect it later. Freeman also admitted to putting in money for Stepp and collecting it later when Stepp was present but did not have enough money to contribute his share. Finally, Freeman sometimes put money in for Stepp and other members of the group when they were absent from work.

In addition to contributing his share to the group, Stepp performed a more formal role in the group than most of the other members in consideration for being informed when the group was playing the lottery. When Stepp was told that the group was playing the lottery, he would make copies of the lottery tickets. Stepp would pick up the tickets from Freeman on either Tuesday morning or Friday morning to make the copies and then return the tickets and copies to Freeman.

We believe from these facts and circumstances that there was an implied contract that Stepp, who had been a member of the group for over five years, who never had failed to contribute his share, who had a formal role in the group, whose share had been previously covered by Freeman under certain circumstances, and who had been reminded that his money was due in the past, would pay his share and perform his role in the group when he was informed that the group was playing the lottery. This contract was breached by Freeman when he failed to inform Stepp that the group was playing the lottery.

Moreover, we are of the opinion that there was an implied agreement that Stepp would not be dropped from the group unless he had expressed his wish to leave the group to Freeman or Freeman had informed him that he was being dropped from the group for the failure to pay his share. We determine that Freeman breached this implied agreement when he unilaterally dropped Stepp from the group. Accordingly, we find that Stepp proved all of the elements of breach of implied contract and that the trial court's decision was not against the manifest weight of the evidence. The assignments of error are overruled.

Based upon the foregoing the judgment of the trial court is affirmed.

Judgment affirmed.

WOLFF and FAIN, JJ., concur.

ANDERSEN INVESTMENTS, L.L.C. V. FACTORY CARD OUTLET OF AMERICA, LTD.
United States District Court, S.D. Iowa
630 F. Supp. 2d 1030 (2009).

JAMES E. GRITZNER, District Judge.

This matter comes before the Court on Defendant's Motion for Summary Judgment, which Plaintiffs resists. This matter came for hearing on March 27, 2009. Plaintiffs were represented by Robert Hatala. Defendant was represented by Rand Wonio and William Gantz. The matter is fully submitted and ready for disposition.

BACKGROUND

The following facts are either not in dispute or viewed in the light most favorable to the nonmoving party. See O'Brien v. Dep't of Agric., 532 F.3d 805, 808 (8th Cir.2008).

On November 1, 2007, Plaintiffs Andersen Investments, LLC, and Northridge Group I, LLC (collectively, Andersen), owner and lessor, respectively, of properties located near shopping malls, entered into a Letter of Intent (LOI) with Defendant Factory Card Outlet of America, Ltd. (FCOA) with respect to a commercial-property lease at a Coralville, Iowa, shopping center. The LOI stated that the lease "is subject to the approval of the [FCOA] Real Estate Committee, and the negotiation and the execution of a mutually acceptable lease between [FCOA] and [Andersen]." Def. App. 4. On November 15, 2007, the FCOA Real Estate Committee approved the Coralville shopping center as a site for a FCOA store and indicated that FCOA was "ready to move forward with the lease." Pl. App. 1.

After the parties entered into the LOI, lease negotiations began on December 3, 2007. Andersen was represented by attorney Tim Miedona (Miedona), and FCOA was represented by attorney Scott Weinberg (Weinberg). The parties negotiated various terms included in the LOI, such as the specifications for the Coralville lease site and the date Andersen would deliver the premises to FCOA. On January 8, 2008, Bob Kranz (Kranz), FCOA's real estate director, e-mailed David Wilson, Andersen's developer, "I know March 1 is right around the corner and constructing our build-out may be a push, but ... we will not want to miss the graduation selling season." Pl. App. 3. On January 9, 2008, Randy Parks (Parks), project manager for Build to Suit (Andersen's general contractor), prepared a construction schedule to begin on February 4, 2008, with a turnover date of April 11, 2008. Pl. App. 4, 91. On January 10, 2008, Kranz e-mailed Wilson stating, "So long as [Build to Suit] keeps pushing [its] contractor and architect forward I think we will be in good shape." Pl. App. 7.

On February 7, 2008, Kranz e-mailed Wilson that "if you cannot deliver by [the April 11] date, then we will not accept delivery until September 1." Def. App. 10. That same day, Gary Nekola (Nekola), FCOA's store-development director, e-mailed Kranz that Andersen's contractor was "planning to pour concrete slab on Monday and begin our build-out next week." Pl. App. 41. On February 19, 2008, Nekola made an inquiry about "our space" in Coralville and wanted an update on the project from Andersen's contractor. Pl. App. 42. On February 21, 2008, Wilson stated that he "just got a call from Kranz" and "he is ready to sign TODAY." Pl. App. 44. On February 25, 2008, Kranz reported the status of the Coralville lease to Timothy Gower (Gower), a vice president at FCOA, as follows:

> Coralville, IA-The lease has been completely negotiated and execution-ready copies are in [FCOA's real estate lawyers'] office pulling together exhibits. The developer has already commenced construction and is on schedule to deliver our space by April 11. Penalties are built into our lease against the developer if they do not deliver by April 11. We are planning on a soft opening the first week of May so we can capture the full graduation season, which is huge in this Iowa City-University of Iowa market. Pl. App. 59.

On March 10, 2008, Miedona e-mailed Weinberg stating, "[p]lease let me know what else you need to complete the lease." Def. App. 123. On March 11, 2008, Weinberg replied to Miedona as follows:

> I'll check with [Kranz] to see how he wants to handle circulating executing versions. Have you incorporated the change regarding square footage? If not, let me know and I can make the change. Also, we'd like to delete Section 9.6 in its entirety because we no longer utilize a satellite dish. If that's a problem, please let me know.

Def. App. 17. Miedona never responded to Weinberg's e-mail. The parties deleted the satellite dish provision from the final draft lease. For purposes of this motion, the Court assumes, without deciding, that the parties agreed on the appropriate square footage for the lease but that the parties did not include this change in the last draft of the lease agreement. All operative drafts of the lease that Andersen and FCOA discussed contained Section 20.18, which stated the lease will not bind either party until both sides have executed the agreement. Section 4.5 of the last draft lease agreement contemplated liquidated damages in the event that Andersen failed to deliver the Coralville premises to FCOA by April 11.

On March 12, 2008, Kranz advised Andersen that FCOA would not enter into the lease because FCOA had been recently acquired by Amscan Acquisitions Holding, and "they would not approve a new store in Coralville." Def. App. 19. By the time FCOA gave Andersen notice of their intent not to sign the lease, Andersen had completed approximately fifty percent of the work and spent approximately $232,000 on the project. On March 20, 2008, Mark Grossklag, FCOA's agent, told Wilson that FCOA withdrew because FCOA "was blindsided by the parent company when it went to get the lease approved to sign, as they told them they could not do so as Party [C]ity had exclusive rig[ht] to new Iowa deals." Pl. App. 64.

After FCOA withdrew from the lease negotiations with Andersen, Andersen filed the present lawsuit in the Iowa District Court for Johnson County, seeking (1) damages for breach of contract based on FCOA's terminating the lease negotiations, and (2) enforcement of FCOA's promise to enter into a lease under the promissory-estoppel doctrine. FCOA removed the case to this Court and then filed this Motion for Summary Judgment on all counts, arguing no genuine issues of material fact remain for trial and it is entitled to judgment as a matter of law. Andersen resists.

DISCUSSION

A. Summary Judgment Standard

"Summary judgment is appropriate when no genuine issue of material fact remains and the movant is entitled to judgment as a matter of law.... [I]f the record as a whole could not lead a rational trier of fact to find for the non-moving party, there is no genuine issue for trial." Walnut Grove Partners, L.P. v. Am. Family Mut. Ins. Co., 479 F.3d 949, 951-52 (8th Cir.2007) (citing Fed.R.Civ.P. 56(c) (internal quotation omitted)); see also Anderson v. Liberty Lobby, Inc., 477 U.S. 242, 247, 106 S.Ct. 2505, 91 L.Ed.2d 202 (1986). In order to defeat a motion for summary judgment, the nonmoving party "may not rely merely on allegations or denials in its own pleading," it must "set out specific facts showing a genuine issue for trial." Fed.R.Civ.P. 56(e). "Mere allegations, unsupported by specific facts or evidence beyond the nonmoving party's own conclusions, are insufficient to withstand a motion for summary judgment." Thomas v. Corwin, 483 F.3d 516, 527 (8th Cir.2007). "Only disputes over facts that might affect the outcome of the suit under the governing law will properly preclude the entry of summary judgment." Anderson, 477 U.S. at 248, 106 S.Ct. 2505; Wells Fargo Fin. Leasing, Inc. v. LMT Fette, Inc., 382 F.3d 852, 856 (8th Cir.2004).

B. Breach of Contract (Count Two)

In considering FCOA's motion, the Court must determine whether FCOA (1) breached a written contract when it entered into the LOI with Andersen and subsequently did not enter into a final lease agreement, and (2) breached an oral contract when it agreed to all material terms pertaining to the Coralville lease and subsequently did not enter into a final lease agreement.

1. Written Contract

FCOA argues there is no genuine issue of material fact remaining on Andersen's breach of contract claim because the parties never entered into a written lease agreement. Andersen asserts that FCOA and Andersen entered into a written contract to enter into a lease agreement when FCOA signed the LOI.

"A binding contract requires an acceptance of an offer." Heartland Express, Inc. v. Terry, 631 N.W.2d 260, 270 (Iowa 2001). "An '[a]cceptance of an offer is a manifestation of assent to the terms thereof by the offeree in a manner invited or required by the offer.'" Id. at 270 (quoting Restatement (Second) of Contracts § 30). "An agreement to agree to enter into a contract is of no effect unless all of the terms and conditions of the contract are agreed on and nothing is left to future negotiations." Scott v. Grinnell Mut. Reinsurance Co., 653 N.W.2d 556, 562 (Iowa 2002) (internal quotation omitted).

A LOI is defined as "[a] written statement detailing the preliminary understanding of parties who plan to enter into a contract or some other agreement; a noncommittal writing preliminary to a contract." Black's Law Dictionary 916 (7th ed. 1999). The Iowa Court of Appeals has held that a LOI does not constitute a contract as a matter of law. Crowe-Thomas Consulting Group, Inc. v. Fresh Pak Candy Co., 494 N.W.2d 442, 444-45 (Iowa Ct.App.1992) (holding that a LOI that is "subject to the negotiation and execution of a definitive agreement" was "nothing more than an invitation to attempt to reach an agreement of sale" and not an enforceable contract based on offer and acceptance).

The parties do not dispute that Andersen and FCOA entered into a LOI in November 2007. However, the LOI clearly indicated that the formation of a lease was "subject to ... the negotiation and the execution of a mutually acceptable lease between [FCOA] and [Andersen]." Def. App. 4. There is no dispute that the lease was not in executable form and that no contract would be binding until the parties executed a mutually acceptable lease. Because this condition precedent to form a binding contract did not occur, the "agreement to agree to enter into a contract is of no effect." Scott, 653 N.W.2d at 562; see Kopple v. Schick Farms, Ltd., 447 F.Supp.2d 965, 970-72 (N.D.Iowa 2006) (applying Iowa law and granting summary judgment to a prospective land purchaser who entered into a LOI, agreed on the contract terms, but later withdrew from the sale reasoning "it [was] undisputed ... that the parties contemplated the execution of a final written agreement after the signing of the letter of intent, [which] provide[d] a strong inference that the parties did not intend to be bound until the final terms were settled and a final contract was executed"). The Court finds as a matter of law the LOI did not create a written contract binding either side to enter into an executable lease agreement.

2. Oral Contract

FCOA also argues summary judgment is appropriate because no oral contract was formed. Andersen asserts that FCOA entered into an oral contract with Andersen to enter into a lease agreement when the parties orally agreed on all material terms and conditions but did not legally execute the agreement.

Iowa law recognizes the validity of oral contracts, even in those cases in which the parties intended to later reduce their agreement to writing. The Iowa Supreme Court has stated,

> It is generally held an oral agreement may be enforceable, even though the parties contemplate that it be reduced to writing and signed, if it is complete as to its terms and has been finally agreed to. Under such circumstances the writing is merely an expression of a contract already made. On the other hand, the parties may intend that obligation should arise only upon the signing of a written instrument embodying the terms they have tentatively agreed to.
>
> Faught v. Budlong, 540 N.W.2d 33, 35-36 (Iowa 1995) (quoting Elkader Coop. Co. v. Matt, 204 N.W.2d 873, 875 (Iowa 1973)); see also Bradley v. West Sioux Cmty. Sch. Bd. of Educ., 510 N.W.2d 881, 884 (Iowa 1994); Severson v. Elberon Elevator, Inc., 250 N.W.2d 417, 420 (Iowa 1977).

In order to prove the existence of an oral contract, the party asserting the oral contract must show that the terms of the alleged oral contract are "sufficiently definite for a court to determine with certainty the duty of each party and the conditions relative to performance." Seastrom v. Farm Bureau Life Ins. Co., 601 N.W.2d 339, 346 (Iowa 1999). "Generally, whether the parties intend an oral agreement to be binding or whether they did not intend to be bound until they executed a written agreement is a question of fact dependent upon all the circumstances present in the particular case." Schaller Tel. Co. v. Golden Sky Sys., 298 F.3d 736, 743 (8th Cir.2002) (citing Elkader, 204 N.W.2d at 875) (applying Iowa law). While the determination of whether an oral contract existed is ordinarily a question of fact, summary judgment is appropriate if "a party has not offered sufficient evidence to support the existence of a contract." Id. at 744.

The Iowa Supreme Court has set out legal principles to determine when the parties intended to be bound:

> a. Parties who plan to make a final written instrument as the expression of their contract necessarily discuss the proposed terms of the contract before they enter into it and often, before the final writing is made, agree upon all the terms which they plan to incorporate therein. This they may do orally or by exchange of several writings. It is possible thus to make a contract the terms of which include an obligation to execute subsequently a final writing which shall contain certain provisions. If parties have definitely agreed that they will do so, and that the final writing shall contain these provisions and no others, they have then concluded the contract.
>
> b. On the other hand, if either party knows or has reason to know that the other party regards the agreement as incomplete and intends that no obligation shall exist until other terms are assented to or until the whole has been reduced to another written form, the preliminary negotiations and agreements do not constitute a contract. Faught, 540 N.W.2d at 35-36 (quoting Restatement (Second) of Contracts § 27 cmts. a-b).

The analysis of any oral contract herein does not proceed in isolation, but in the shadow of the parties' written expressions. Thus, as a point of departure the Court recognizes there exists strong precedent that "a writing which clearly contemplates the subsequent execution of a formal agreement gives rise to an inference that the parties to the writing did not intend to be bound until the subsequent formal agreement is finalized." See, e.g., Kopple, 447 F.Supp.2d at 976. For example, the Iowa Court of Appeals concluded that a letter of intent that was "subject to the negotiation and execution of a definitive agreement" and inviting the recipients "to sign copies of the letter and turn this matter over to our respective attorneys for purposes of forming a definite contract" was "nothing more than an invitation to attempt to reach an agreement of sale," not an enforceable contract based on offer and acceptance. Crowe-Thomas, 494 N.W.2d at 444-45.

The parties' intent determines whether the parties entered into a binding oral contract. Referring to the Restatement (Second) of Contracts, Andersen argues this is a "comment a" case; that is, one where the parties have agreed on all material terms and have entered into an oral contract that includes a subsequent obligation to execute a final writing that contains the oral contract provisions. FCOA argues this is a "comment b" case; that is, one where the parties intended no obligation to exist until the entire agreement had been reduced to written form and executed by both parties.

There are two clauses from the parties' negotiations that inform the Court's analysis. First, all terms and conditions contained in the LOI were "subject to the approval of the [FCOA] Real Estate Committee, and the negotiation and the execution of a mutually acceptable lease between [FCOA] and [Andersen]." Def. App. 4. Second, all operative drafts of the lease that Andersen and FCOA discussed contained Section 20.18, which stated,

> Lease Execution. This lease shall not be binding until fully executed by both parties. [Andersen] agrees to provide [FCOA] with two (2) fully executed duplicate originals of this Lease within three (3) days after receipt of the partially executed Lease from [FCOA]. In the event [Andersen] fails to comply with such requirement, [FCOA] shall have the right to consider this Lease null and void. Def. SUF ¶ 4; Def. App. 67.

For purposes of this motion, the Court assumes that the parties agreed to all material terms but (1) did not incorporate in writing the revisions pertaining to the proper square footage for the lease and (2) the parties did not execute a mutually acceptable lease agreement.

This Court benefits from the analysis in Schaller Telephone Co. v. Golden Sky Systems, Inc., 139 F.Supp.2d 1071 (N.D.Iowa 2001), aff'd 298 F.3d 736 (8th Cir.2002), where two parties failed to close a deal involving the sale of exclusive rights to provide satellite dishes in a sales territory. Id. at 1075. The parties entered into a LOI and negotiations for an asset-purchase agreement, which conditioned the parties' obligations under the contract on the parties' ability to "negotiate and execute a mutually acceptable purchase agreement." Id. at 1085. The parties reached an oral agreement, and the seller sent the buyer a "draft letter memorializing what [the seller] believed had been agreed to in principle." Id. at 1076. Neither that draft nor any other agreement was ever signed by representatives of either party. Id. The Schaller court concluded that comment b controlled. While finding the parties had reached an oral agreement, there was no contract because the LOI's disclaimer "[made] it abundantly clear that [the buyer] had no intention to be bound in the absence of a written agreement." Id. at 1086. The court concluded,

> The language of the disclaimers expressly encompasses the entire negotiation process, creating an "umbrella" requirement of a signed writing to make a contract, thereby making clear that any agreement on individual terms or even all of the terms of the agreement would not result in a binding contract in the absence of an executed writing.
>
> The effect of such disclaimers is that summary judgment in favor of [the buyer] must be granted on [the seller's] claim of breach of an oral contract, because, as a matter of law, no oral contract could exist in the circumstances presented. Id. at 1093.

Schaller is particularly instructive in the present case because the LOI at issue in that case is almost identical to the LOI in this case. The only difference is that the LOI in this case contains the phrase "mutually acceptable lease," while the Schaller LOI contains the phrase "mutually acceptable purchase agreement." Id. at 1086. In this case, the repeated written statements in the LOI and Section 20.18 of the draft lease agreement demonstrate that the parties did not intend to be bound in the absence of an executed agreement.

Similarly, in Moore Development, Ltd. v. M.G. Midwest, Inc., No. C06-1014, 2007 WL 2331021, at *2-3 (N.D.Iowa Aug. 13, 2007), the two parties failed to close a deal for the building of a video-rental store. The parties entered into a LOI containing the following language:

> Tenant will send to Landlord a final Lease after all lease terms are fully negotiated. Landlord will execute the Lease, have it properly witnessed, and return the lease to the Tenant. Id. at *8.

After the landlord incurred substantial costs related to the tenant's request for "build-out construction" and was told by the tenant that the lease was a "'done deal' and to take the rental space off the market," the tenant decided not to enter into a final lease agreement with the landlord because the tenant was acquired by another competing video store. Id. at *3, *6. U.S. Magistrate Judge Jon S. Scoles concluded the case was a comment b case and granted the tenant's motion for summary judgment, holding,

> The [LOI] clearly requires [the landlord] and [the tenant] to reduce any lease agreement to writing. [The landlord] and [the tenant] did not reduce the lease agreement to writing. Because [the landlord] relies on the [LOI] to establish the definite terms of the lease and the [LOI] requires the lease to be reduced to writing and the parties did not comply with this requirement, the Court finds that [the Landlord] cannot establish an enforceable oral contract. Id. at *8.

Moore Development held that no oral contract can exist when (1) the party asserting an oral contract relies on a LOI that requires any final agreement be reduced to writing, and (2) the parties rely on the LOI to establish the definitive terms of the lease, meaning that any final agreement must be reduced to writing. Id., 2007 WL 2331021, at *8. Here, both the LOI and Section 20.18 contained in every draft lease agreement expressly contemplated that the parties would reduce their agreement to writing before either party was contractually bound. Unlike Moore Development, here both the LOI and the draft lease agreements expressly contemplated that any final agreement would be reduced to writing, clearly demonstrating the parties' intent that an executed lease agreement would be required before either party was bound by the agreement. Like Moore Development, Andersen incurred substantial building costs based on an anticipated lease deal, FCOA made representations about being ready to sign an executable version of the lease, and FCOA terminated negotiations "at the eleventh hour" after being acquired by another company. The Court finds that as a matter of law, however, these unfortunate facts do not alter the legal importance of the clear language contained in both the LOI and Section 20.18 of the draft lease agreements. See, e.g., Kopple, 447 F.Supp.2d at 976 ("Because it is undisputed here that the parties contemplated the execution of a final written agreement after the signing of the letter of intent, this circumstance provides a strong inference that the parties did not intend to be bound until the final terms were settled and a final contract was executed.").

Anderson has cited no authority, applying Iowa law or otherwise, supporting a breach of oral contract claim in the wake of a written LOI making any binding obligation contingent upon the parties' negotiation and execution of a lease. Although the Court recognizes the legal possibility that parties could enter into a subsequent oral contract negating a written LOI requirement for formal execution of a lease, that is an argument for another day on another record.

Assuming arguendo that the express writings in this case-the LOI and Section 20.18 of the lease agreement-did not control, then the Court would look to the Restatement (Second) of Contracts § 27 "comment c" factors to determine whether the case is governed by comment a or b. Comment c states,

> c. Among the circumstances which may be helpful in determining whether a contract has been concluded are the following: [1] the extent to which express agreement has been reached on all the terms to be included, [2] whether the contract is of a type usually put in writing, [3] whether it needs a formal writing for its full expression, [4] whether it has few or many details, [5] whether the amount involved is large or small, [6] whether it is a common or unusual contract, [7] whether a standard form of contract is widely used in similar transactions, and [8] whether either party takes any action in preparation for performance during the negotiations. Such circumstances may be shown by oral testimony or by correspondence or other preliminary or partially complete writings. Faught, 540 N.W.2d at 36 (quoting Restatement (Second) of Contracts § 27 cmt. c).

Four factors support treating the case as a "comment b" case, two factors support treating the case as a "comment a" case, and two factors are neutral. However, the two factors that support treating the case as a comment a case are easily distinguishable.

The Court accepts the allegation that the parties agreed on all terms, which favors the comment a approach. However, this factor cannot control since "[i]f either party intends not to be bound in the absence of a fully executed document, no amount of negotiation or oral agreement as to specific terms will result in the formation of a binding contract." Cont'l Labs., Inc. v. Scott Paper Co., 759 F.Supp. 538, 540 (S.D.Iowa 1990). The LOI and the draft lease agreement required the parties to reduce the lease into a final and executable form. Because the parties contemplated a condition precedent-execution of the lease-before being contractually bound, and that condition did not occur, the parties could not bind themselves to the oral agreement. See Desy v. Rhue, 462 N.W.2d 742, 746-47 (Iowa Ct.App.1990) ("The statement in the purported agreement that the parties would not be bound until acceptance clearly required the risks be assigned based on the status quo before contract negotiations until the agreement was, as it were, 'signed, sealed, and delivered.' Thus, because the purported agreement is clear as to the intent of the parties not to be bound, the jury should not have been asked to determine that issue."); see also Doll v. Grand Union Co., 925 F.2d 1363, 1370 (11th Cir.1991) (applying Georgia law, the court concluded no oral contract could exist as a matter of law because "when the parties make their intentions clear, there is no basis for a court to step in and contradict their explicit desires. A court surely would not infer consent to an unsigned agreement when the parties clearly predicated a binding agreement only on the actual execution of the contract. So here we are unwilling to allow a jury to infer an agreement to sign a lease when one of the parties specifically declared its intention not to be bound until a lease was drafted and signed by both parties....").

The factors inquiring whether the contract is one typically reduced to writing or whether it needs a formal writing for its full expression favors the comment b approach. The lease negotiations occurred over the five-month period between November 1, 2007, and March 11, 2008. On March 11, Miedona e-mailed Weinberg that he was "going to go ahead and prepare execution copies of the lease." Def. App. 17. Weinberg e-mailed Miedona that "[FCOA] typically prepare an execution version and send [it] to [the landlord's attorney] and the landlord.... I'll check with [Kranz] to see how he wants to handle circulating execution versions." Id. The parties proceeded in this typical manner, with Miedona preparing a copy of the lease that was Andersen's proposed draft of an execution-ready lease. These declarations by each party's representative anticipating an execution, read together with the LOI and the requirement that the parties reduce the lease into a final and executable form, support the conclusion that the parties did not intend an obligation to exist until the entire agreement was reduced to written form and executed by both parties. See Faught, 540 N.W.2d at 40 (concluding the second and third comment c factors support finding the existence of an oral contract when the parties were sophisticated business persons engaged in long, complex negotiations); see also Cont'l Labs., 759 F.Supp. at 541 (concluding the second and third comment c factors support a legal conclusion that no oral contract existed because "[t]he matter was a large and complex commercial undertaking, which is usually put into written form. The parties, who were both represented by legal counsel, negotiated for over seven months and exchanged numerous drafts of a written proposed agreement").

Whether the contract has few or many details and whether the contract involves small or large amounts of money favor the comment b approach. The proposed commercial-lease contract was forty-three pages long and contained an additional thirteen exhibits totaling another forty-nine pages. The ten-year term of the lease required FCOA to pay Andersen more than $1.3-million over the life of the lease. These factors support a conclusion that the parties contemplated final review of the lease, followed by a written execution of the lease, before either party would be bound. See Faught, 540 N.W.2d at 40 (concluding the fourth and fifth comment c factors support a legal conclusion that no contract existed because the deal involved a large sum of money ($130,000) and the contract involved many details); see also Kopple, 447 F.Supp.2d at 980 (concluding the fourth and fifth comment c factors support the legal conclusion no contract existed because "the matter was a complex undertaking" and "[t]he nearly $2,000,000 price tag for the stock transfer was a large sum of money [because] [o]ne would reasonably anticipate a written accord for such an undertaking"); Cont'l Labs., 759 F.Supp. at 541 (concluding the fourth and fifth comment c factors support a legal conclusion that no oral contract existed because "the 12 page contract contains many details and references numerous exhibits" and "the transaction at issue involves a commitment by Scott to purchase a minimum of $2.25-million worth of products from Continental during the term of the contract").

Whether the contract is common or whether it is a standard-form contract are inconclusive for lack of evidence and therefore supports neither comment a or comment b.

Whether either party took any action in preparation for performance during the negotiations supports the comment a approach. Andersen entered into a subcontract with Parks for a total contract amount of $472,544 and paid approximately $232,000 under the subcontract before FCOA informed Andersen it was terminating the lease negotiations. However, Andersen entered into a contract with Parks on February 4, which was three weeks before Andersen asserts that Kranz, acting as FCOA's agent, bound FCOA to an oral contract. This weakens Andersen's assertion that it acted in reliance on an oral contract purportedly formed on February 25. There is no evidence that (1) the parties entered into an exclusive negotiation, precluding Andersen from shopping the proposed lease site to a third party for a higher price, or (2) the parties contemplated a deposit fee or other type of indemnification for Andersen in the event FCOA withdrew from negotiations. See Venture Assoc. Corp. v. Zenith Data Sys. Corp., 96 F.3d 275, 278 (7th Cir.1996) (observing that sophisticated parties have ex ante remedies to apportion the risk of loss during preliminary negotiations such as deposit fees). Finally, Section 20.18 of the draft lease agreement, which states "[Andersen] agrees to provide [FCOA] with two (2) fully executed duplicate originals of this Lease within three (3) days after receipt of the partially executed Lease from [FCOA]," presupposes a requirement that the parties legally execute the agreement. Def. App. 68. If Andersen failed to provide FCOA with two copies of the fully executed lease agreement, then Andersen would lack any obligation to perform under the contract.

Whether the court considers the express terms of the LOI and Section 20.18 of the draft lease agreement writings or simply balances the comment c factors, the Court concludes that the evidence Andersen presents does not raise issues of material fact sufficient to preclude summary judgment. The Court concludes the oral contract is governed by comment b because no reasonable jury would conclude, taking the evidence in the light most favorable to Andersen, that the parties had concluded an oral agreement. . . .

CONCLUSION

Viewing the evidence in the light most favorable to Plaintiffs, and in the absence of any genuine issues of material fact, Plaintiffs' claims fail as a matter of law. Therefore, Defendant's Motion for Summary Judgment (Clerk's No. 11) must be granted as to all claims. Plaintiffs' case is hereby dismissed. The Clerk of Court is directed to enter judgment for Defendant and against Plaintiffs.

IT IS SO ORDERED.

NOTES AND QUESTIONS:

1. *See* Restatement (Second) of Contracts §§ 19 (Conduct as Manifestation of Assent) and 21 (Intention to Be Legally Bound) (1981).

2. *See* U.C.C. §§ 2-102 (Scope, Certain Security and Other Transactions Excluded From This Article); 1-103 (Construction of U.C.C. to Promote its Purposes and Policies: Applicability of Supplemental Principles of Law); 2-105 (Definitions: Transferability, "Goods", "Future" Goods,

"Lot"; "Commercial Unit"); 2-106 (Definitions: "Contract", "Agreement", "Contract for Sale", "Sale", "Present Sale", "Conforming" to Contract, "Termination", "Cancellation") (2002).

3. *See Dickerson v. Deno*, 770 So. 2d 63, 66-67 (Ala. 2000), wherein the Alabama Supreme Court distinguished *Stepp v. Freeman* as an agreement to jointly purchase and hold a lottery ticket. Unlike *Stepp*, *Dickerson* involved an agreement to share lottery winnings which the court ruled was unenforceable as a matter of law.

SECTION 3. OFFER

A. INVITATIONS TO ASSENT

In the previous section, we explored the standards by which it is determined whether parties have achieved the requisite mutual assent. That determination necessarily includes a determination that an offer and acceptance have occurred. Although these two aspects of mutual assent are interdependent, i.e. unless it can be determined that a valid offer exists, an acceptance cannot occur, each has its own set of complexities that require close examination.

LONERGAN V. SCOLNICK
District Court of Appeal, Fourth District, California
276 P.2d 8 (1955).

BARNARD, Presiding Justice.

. . . .

The complaint alleged that on April 15, 1952, the parties entered into a contract whereby the defendant agreed to sell, and plaintiff agreed to buy a 40-acre tract of land for $2,500; that this was a fair, just and reasonable value of the property; that on April 28, 1952, the defendant repudiated the contract and refused to deliver a deed; that on April 28, 1952, the property was worth $6,081; and that plaintiff has been damaged in the amount of $3,581. The answer denied that any contract had been entered into, or that anything was due to the plaintiff.

By stipulation, the issue of whether or not a contract was entered into between the parties was first tried, reserving the other issues for a further trial if that became necessary. The issue as to the existence of a contract was submitted upon an agreed statement, including certain letters between the parties, without the introduction of other evidence.

The stipulated facts are as follows: During March, 1952, the defendant placed an ad in a Los Angeles paper reading, so far as material here, "Joshua Tree vic. 40 acres, . . . need cash, will sacrifice." In response to an inquiry resulting from this ad the defendant, who lived in New York, wrote a letter to the plaintiff dated March 26, briefly describing the property, giving directions as to how to get there, stating that his rock-bottom price was $2,500 cash, and further stating that "This is a form letter." On April 7, the plaintiff wrote a letter to the defendant saying that he was not sure he had found the property, asking for its legal description, asking whether the land was all level or whether it included certain jutting rock hills, and suggesting a certain bank as escrow agent "should I desire to purchase the land." On April 8, the defendant wrote to the plaintiff saying "From your description you have found the property"; that this bank "is O.K. for escrow agent"; that the land was fairly level; giving the legal description; and then saying, "If you are really interested, you will have to decide fast, as I expect to have a buyer in the next week or so." On April 12, the defendant sold the property to a third party for $2,500. The plaintiff received defendant's letter of April 8 on April 14. On April 15 he wrote to the defendant thanking him for his letter "confirming that I was on the right land," stating that he would immediately proceed to have the escrow opened and would deposit $2,500 therein "in conformity with your offer," and asking the defendant to forward a deed with his instructions to the escrow agent. On April 17, 1952, the plaintiff started an escrow and placed in the hands of the escrow agent $100, agreeing to furnish an additional $2,400 at an unspecified time, with the provision that if the escrow was not closed by May 15, 1952, it should be completed as soon thereafter as possible unless a written demand for a return of the money or instruments was made by either party after that date. It was further stipulated that the plaintiff was ready and willing at all times to deposit the $2,400.

The matter was submitted on June 11, 1953. On July 10, 1953, the judge filed a memorandum opinion stating that it was his opinion that the letter of April 8, 1952, when considered with the previous correspondence, constituted an offer of sale which offer was, however, qualified and conditioned upon prompt acceptance by the plaintiff; that in spite of the condition thus imposed, the plaintiff delayed more than a week before notifying the defendant of his acceptance; and that since the plaintiff was aware of the necessity of promptly communicating his acceptance to the defendant his delay was not the prompt action required by the terms of the offer. Findings of fact were filed on October 2, 1953, finding that each and all of the statements in the agreed statement are true, and that all allegations to the contrary in the complaint are untrue. As conclusions of law, it was found that the plaintiff and defendant did not enter into a contract as alleged in the complaint or otherwise, and that the defendant is entitled to judgment against the plaintiff. Judgment was entered accordingly, from which the plaintiff has appealed.

The appellant contends that the judgment is contrary to the evidence and to the law since the facts, as found, do not support the conclusions of law upon which the judgment is based. It is argued that there is no conflict in the evidence, and this court is not bound by the trial court's construction of the written instruments involved; that the evidence conclusively shows that an offer was made to the plaintiff by the defendant, which offer was accepted by the mailing of plaintiff's letter of April 15; that upon receipt of defendant's letter of April 8 the plaintiff had a reasonable time within which to accept the offer that had been made; that by his letter of April 15 and his starting of an escrow the plaintiff accepted said offer; and that the agreed statement of facts establishes that a valid contract was entered into between the parties. In his briefs the appellant assumes that an offer was made by the defendant, and confined his argument to contending that the evidence shows that he accepted that offer within a reasonable time.

There can be no contract unless the minds of the parties have met and mutually agreed upon some specific thing. This is usually evidenced by one party making an offer which is accepted by the other party. Section 25 of the Restatement of the Law on Contracts reads:

> If from a promise, or manifestation of intention, or from the circumstances existing at the time, the person to whom the promise or manifestation is addressed knows or has reason to know that the person making it does not intend it as an expression of his fixed purpose until he has given a further expression of assent, he has not made an offer.

The language used in Niles v. Hancock, 140 Cal. 157, 73 P. 840, 842, "It is also clear from the correspondence that it was the intention of the defendant that the negotiations between him and the plaintiff were to be purely preliminary," is applicable here. The correspondence here indicates an intention on the part of the defendant to find out whether the plaintiff was interested, rather than an intention to make a definite offer to the plaintiff. The language used by the defendant in his letters of March 26 and April 8 rather clearly discloses that they were not intended as an expression of fixed purpose to make a definite offer, and was sufficient to advise the plaintiff that some further expression of assent on the part of the defendant was necessary.

The advertisement in the paper was a mere request for an offer. The letter of March 26 contains no definite offer, and clearly states that it is a form letter. It merely gives further particulars, in clarification of the advertisement, and tells the plaintiff how to locate the property if he was interested in looking into the matter. The letter of April 8 added nothing in the way of a definite offer. It merely answered some questions asked by the plaintiff, and stated that if the plaintiff was really interested he would have to act fast. The statement that he expected to have a buyer in the next week or so indicated that the defendant intended to sell to the first-comer, and was reserving the right to do so. From this statement, alone, the plaintiff knew or should have known that he was not being given time in which to accept an offer that was being made, but that some further assent on the part of the defendant was required. Under the language used the plaintiff was not being given a right to act within a reasonable time after receiving the letter; he was plainly told that the defendant intended to sell to another, if possible, and warned that he would have to act fast if he was interested in buying the land.

Regardless of any opinion previously expressed, the court found that no contract had been entered into between these parties, and we are in accord with the court's conclusion on that controlling issue. The court's construction of the letters involved was a reasonable one, and we think the most reasonable one, even if it be assumed that another construction was possible.

The judgment is affirmed.

CRAFT V. ELDER & JOHNSTON CO.
Court of Appeals of Ohio, Second District, Montgomery County
38 N.E.2d 416 (1941).

BARNES, Judge.

. . . .

On or about January 31, 1940, the defendant, the Elder & Johnston Company, carried an advertisement in the Dayton Shopping News, an offer for sale of a certain all electric sewing machine for the sum of $26 as a "Thursday Only Special." Plaintiff in her petition, after certain formal allegations, sets out the substance of the above advertisement carried by defendant in the Dayton Shopping News. She further alleges that the above publication is an advertising paper distributed in Montgomery County and throughout the city of Dayton; that on Thursday, February 1, 1940, she tendered to the defendant company $26 in payment for one of the machines offered in the advertisement, but that defendant refused to fulfill the offer and has continued to so refuse. The petition further alleges that the value of the machine offered was $175 and she asks damages in the sum of $149 plus interest from February 1, 1940.

Defendant interposed a general demurrer which was overruled. Thereupon defendant filed an answer and after certain admissions of purely formal allegations of the petition along with an admission that the Dayton Shopping News was an advertising paper distributed in Montgomery County and throughout the city of Dayton, then denies each and every allegation contained in the petition not previously admitted.

Following the joinder of issues, one branch of the case was submitted to the court by agreement of the parties. This agreement was carried into an entry approved by all counsel of record and reads as follows omitting the formal parts, "By agreement of the parties this case is submitted to the court for determination solely of the question as to whether the advertisement referred to in the petition of plaintiff constituted an offer. Further, by agreement of the parties, a copy of page 9 of the Dayton Shopping News for Thursday, February 1, 1940, is attached to this entry and made a part of the record in this case, and the advertisement appearing in the lower left hand corner of said page is stipulated and agreed to be the same advertisement as that referred to in plaintiff's petition."

The particular advertisement set forth on page 9 of the publication cannot be reproduced in this opinion, but may be described as containing a cut of the machine and other printed matter including the price of $26 and all conforming substantially to the allegations of the petition.

The trial court dismissed plaintiff's petition as evidenced by a journal entry, the pertinent portion of which reads as follows: "Upon consideration the court finds that said advertisement was not an offer which could be accepted by plaintiff to form a contract, and this case is therefore dismissed with prejudice to a new action, at costs of plaintiff."

Within statutory time plaintiff filed notice of appeal on questions of law and thus lodged the case in our court. Counsel for the respective parties have filed briefs presenting their respective theories with citation of authorities.

It seems to us that this case may easily be determined on well-recognized elementary principles. The first question to be determined is the proper characterization to be given to defendant's advertisement in the Shopping News. It was not an offer made to any specific person but was made to the public generally. Thereby it would be properly designated as a unilateral offer and not being supported by any consideration could be withdrawn at will and without notice. This would be true because no contractual relations of any character existed between the defendant company and any other person.

As supporting authority, we refer to Volume 9, Ohio Jurisprudence, page 257, Section 33, "In the absence of a consideration, an offer may be withdrawn at any time before acceptance." This part of the text is built from numberous Ohio cases cited under Note 7. In the cases cited under this Note 7, it will be found that none of the cases were predicated upon a unilateral offer made to the public generally under an advertisement. In all instances, the negotiations were between designated parties. The words "before acceptance" in the above quotation from Ohio Jurisprudence can have no significance in the instant case for the reason that no contractual relation of any kind existed between the plaintiff and defendant. Plaintiff's tendering of the money and demanding the article advertised would not create a contractual relation. Defendant's refusal to deliver the electric sewing machine would constitute in law a withdrawal of a unilateral offer.

It is argued that an offer can only be withdrawn where notice is given prior to the acceptance. This is true where the negotiations have advanced to the status of, at least, a unilateral contract. We distinguish between a unilateral offer and a unilateral contract.

There are instances where unilateral offers through advertisements may create contractual relations with members of the public, but these instances involve special circumstances.

> The most frequent case in which an advertisement has been construed as an offer in the technical sense, involves a published offer of a reward for the furnishing of certain information, the return of particular property, or the doing of a certain act. In such case all that is necessary to confer the benefit demanded by the offeror is performance of the required act. Such offers, of course, are unilateral contracts, and principles of unjust enrichment alone would prevent the offeror from refusing to perform his promise upon the doing of the act. 6 R.C.L. p. 607, paragraph 30.

Furthermore, conditions sometimes arise where an offer is made through an advertisement and a customer procures the articles without notice of the withdrawal of the offer and in such instances the advertiser will be held to his offer, but it must be noted that in these cases the relations of the parties have progressed to a consummated deal.

A case promulgating the above principle is that of Arnold v. Phillips, 1 Ohio Dec. Reprint 448. This case originated in Montgomery County and was decided by the Supreme Court, Wood C. J., delivering the opinion. The Arnolds advertised in the Western Empire, a paper published in the city of Dayton, as follows, "St. Clair Money-Notes of the above bank taken at par for goods at Arnold's, corner of Main and New Market streets." Phillips having seen the advertisement went to Arnold's store and there ordered merchandise. Nothing was said by either party how or in what funds the goods were to be paid for. The goods being selected and laid aside, Phillips left the store and Arnold sent the goods to Phillips' store with instructions not to take St. Clair bills. The clerk left the goods at the store of Phillips without communicating the instructions and returned to the store of Arnold, who sent him back in a few minutes to tell Phillips that he, Arnold, would not take St. Clair money for the goods-must have good money or return the goods-which Arnold's clerk communicated to clerk of Phillips, Phillips being absent as well as when the clerk first went there with the goods. Phillips had on hand $1,000 of the St. Clair bills, which were worth from twenty-five to forty per cent on their numerical value. In the afternoon of the same day, Phillips offered and tendered to Arnold in that kind of bills the price of the goods, which Arnold refused to receive. The tender was kept up, and the bills tendered were brought into court for the plaintiff. Wood, C. J., delivering the opinion, among other things, states the following: "That the proposition was general and indefinite in its terms as to time, and must be considered outstanding until publicly withdrawn, or unless notice that it had been withdrawn was given to each individual purchaser; that the proposition being to the public, any one had a right to accept it; that Phillips having seen the advertisement, and having purchased goods on the faith of it, the contract to receive payment in St. Clair money was complete, and could not be receded from, the moment the goods were delivered; that the delivery of the goods was complete when they were left at the store of Phillips by Arnold's clerk, and that the fact of the clerk's being instructed by his principal not to receive St. Clair money in payment, could not affect the rights of the parties unless those instructions were communicated to Phillips before, or at the time of the delivery."

The instant case is to be distinguished in that the electric sewing machine was not delivered and the fact that the defendant company refused to deliver the machine at the price of $26 was information that the unilateral offer was withdrawn.

We are referred to the case of Meyer v. Packard Co., 106 Ohio St. 328, 140 N.E. 118, 120, 28 A.L.R. 986. This case is interesting but readily distinguishable from the instant case. In the above Meyer case the motor company advertised rebuilt trucks as carrying the same guarantee as new trucks. Meyer purchased a truck and signed a written order therefor in which was contained the following, "All promises, verbal understandings or agreements of any kind pertaining to this purchase, not specified herein, are hereby expressly waived."

The entire controversy revolved around the question as to whether or not the Packard Company could be held liable under the newspaper guaranties in the face of the writing between the parties. The lower court held against the plaintiff, Meyer, but the Supreme Court reversed and remanded determining among other things that it was a question for the jury to determine whether or not the truck was defective within the terms of such general ad and the written order. Again in this reported case the deal concerning the subject matter advertised was completed and the sole question for determination was how far the advertisement might be considered. The question is entirely dissimilar to the one in the instant case.

From the cases cited in connection with our own independent investigation, we find that very generally courts hold against liability under offers made through advertisements. Very generally in these cases the courts base their findings upon theories quite different from our analysis. With all due respect to the pronouncements of able jurists, we are not impressed with these theories.

We will now briefly make reference to some of the authorities.

"It is clear that in the absence of special circumstances an ordinary newspaper advertisement is not an offer, but is an offer to negotiate-an offer to receive offers-or, as it is sometimes called, an offer to chaffer." Restatement of the Law of Contracts, Par. 25, Page 31.

"Under the above paragraph the following illustration is given, 'A, a clothing merchant, advertises overcoats of a certain kind for sale at $50. This is not an offer but an invitation to the public to come and purchase.' "

"Thus, if goods are advertised for sale at a certain price, it is not an offer and no contract is formed by the statement of an intending purchaser that he will take a specified quantity of the goods at that price. The construction is rather favored that such an advertisement is a mere invitation to enter into a bargain rather than an offer. So a published price list is not an offer to sell the goods listed at the published price." Williston on Contracts, Revised Edition, Vol. 1, Par. 27, Page 54.

"The commonest example of offers meant to open negotiations and to call forth offers in the technical sense are advertisements, circulars and trade letters sent out by business houses. While it is possible that the offers made by such means may be in such form as to become contracts, they are often merely expressions of a willingness to negotiate." Page on the Law Contracts, 2d Ed., Vol. 1, Page 112, Par. 84.

"Business advertisements published in newspapers and circulars sent out by mail or distributed by hand stating that the advertiser has a certain quantity or quality of goods which he wants to dispose of at certain prices, are not offers which become contracts as soon as any person to whose notice they may come signifies his acceptance by notifying the other that he will take a certain quantity of them. They are merely invitations to all persons who may read them that the advertiser is ready to receive offers for the goods at the price stated." 13 Corpus Juris 289, Par. 97.

"But generally a newspaper advertisement or circular couched in general language and proper to be sent to all persons interested in a particular trade or business, or a prospectus of a general and descriptive nature, will be construed as an invitation to make an offer." 17 Corpus Juris Secundum, Contracts, page 389, § 46, Column 2.

Syllabus 1: "A general advertisement in a newspaper for the sale of goods is a mere invitation to enter into a bargain, and is not an offer." Syllabus 3: "To consummate a contract of sale, there must be a meeting of minds." Georgian Co. v. Bloom, 27 Ga.App. 468, 108 S.E. 813.

We are also referred to the following: Salisbury v. Credit Service Inc., 9 W.W. Har., Del., 377, 199 A. 674. Schenectady Stove Co. v. Holbrook et al., 101 N.Y. 45, 4 N.E. 4. Montgomery Ward & Co. v. Johnson, 209 Mass. 89, 95 N.E. 290.

We are constrained to the view that the trial court committed no prejudicial error in dismissing plaintiff's petition.

The judgment of the trial court will be affirmed and costs adjudged against the plaintiff-appellant.

LEFKOWITZ V. GREAT MINNEAPOLIS SURPLUS STORE, INC.
Supreme Court of Minnesota
86 N.W.2d 689 (1957).

MURPHY, Justice.

. . . .

This case grows out of the alleged refusal of the defendant to sell to the plaintiff a certain fur piece which it had offered for sale in a newspaper advertisement. It appears from the record that on April 6, 1956, the defendant published the following advertisement in a Minneapolis newspaper:

> Saturday 9 A.M. Sharp 3 Brand New Fur Coats Worth to $100.00 First Come First Served $1 Each

On April 13, the defendant again published an advertisement in the same newspaper as follows:

> Saturday 9 A.M. 2 Brand New Pastel Mink 3-Skin Scarfs Selling for $89.50 Out they go Saturday. Each ... $1.00
>
> 1 Black Lapin Stole Beautiful, worth $139.50 ... $1.00 First Come First Served

The record supports the findings of the court that on each of the Saturdays following the publication of the above-described ads the plaintiff was the first to present himself at the appropriate counter in the defendant's store and on each occasion demanded the coat and the stole so advertised and indicated his readiness to pay the sale price of $1. On both occasions, the defendant refused to sell the merchandise to the plaintiff, stating on the first occasion that by a "house rule" the offer was intended for women only and sales would not be made to men, and on the second visit that plaintiff knew defendant's house rules.

The trial court properly disallowed plaintiff's claim for the value of the fur coats since the value of these articles was speculative and uncertain. The only evidence of value was the advertisement itself to the effect that the coats were "Worth to $100.00," how much less being speculative especially in view of the price for which they were offered for sale. With reference to the offer of the defendant on April 13, 1956, to sell the "1 Black Lapin Stole . . . worth $139.50 . . ." the trial court held that the value of this article was established and granted judgment in favor of the plaintiff for that amount less the $1 quoted purchase price.

The defendant contends that a newspaper advertisement offering items of merchandise for sale at a named price is a "unilateral offer" which may be withdrawn without notice. He relies upon authorities which hold that, where an advertiser publishes in a newspaper that he has a certain quantity or quality of goods which he wants to dispose of at certain prices and on certain terms, such advertisements are not offers which become contracts as soon as any person to whose notice they may come signifies his acceptance by notifying the other that he will take a certain quantity of them. Such advertisements have been construed as an invitation for an offer of sale on the terms stated, which offer, when received, may be accepted or rejected and which therefore does not become a contract of sale until accepted by the seller; and until a contract has been so made, the seller may modify or revoke such prices or terms. Montgomery Ward & Co. v. Johnson, 209 Mass. 89, 95 N.W. 290; Nickel v. Theresa Farmers Co-op. Ass'n, 247 Wis. 412, 20 N.W.2d 117; Lovett v. Frederick Loeser & Co. Inc., 124 Misc. 81, 207 N.Y.S. 753; Schenectady Stove Co. v. Holbrook, 101 N.Y. 45, 4 N.E. 4; Georgian Co. v. Bloom, 27 Ga.App. 468, 108 S.E. 813; Craft v. Elder & Johnson Co., 38 N.E.2d 416, 34 Ohio L.A. 603; Annotation, 157 A.L.R. 746.

The defendant relies principally on Craft v. Elder & Johnston Co. supra. In that case, the court discussed the legal effect of an advertisement offering for sale, as a one-day special, an electric sewing machine at a named price. The view was expressed that the advertisement was (38 N.E.2d 417, 34 Ohio L.A. 605) "not an offer made to any specific person but was made to the public generally. Thereby it would be properly designated as a unilateral offer and not being supported by any consideration could be withdrawn at will and without notice." It is true that such an offer may be withdrawn before acceptance. Since all offers are by their nature unilateral because they are necessarily made by one party or on one side in the negotiation of a contract, the distinction made in that decision between a unilateral offer and a unilateral contract is not clear. On the facts before us we are concerned with whether the advertisement constituted an offer, and, if so, whether the plaintiff's conduct constituted an acceptance.

There are numerous authorities which hold that a particular advertisement in a newspaper or circular letter relating to a sale of articles may be construed by the court as constituting an offer, acceptance of which would complete a contract. J. E. Pinkham Lumber Co. v. C. W. Griffin & Co., 212 Ala. 341, 102 So. 689; Seymour v. Armstrong & Kassebaum, 62 Kan. 720, 64 P. 612; Payne v. Lautz Bros. & Co., City Ct., 166 N.Y.S. 844, affirmed, 168 N.Y.S. 369, affirmed, 185 App.Div. 904, 171 N.Y.S. 1094; Arnold v. Phillips, 1 Ohio Dec. Reprint 195, 3 West.Law J. 448; Oliver v. Henley, Tex.Civ.App., 21 S.W.2d 576; Annotation, 157 A.L.R. 744, 746.

The test of whether a binding obligation may originate in advertisements addressed to the general public is "whether the facts show that some performance was promised in positive terms in return for something requested." 1 Williston, Contracts (Rev. ed.) § 27.

The authorities above cited emphasize that, where the offer is clear, definite, and explicit, and leaves nothing open for negotiation, it constitutes an offer, acceptance of which will complete the contract. The most recent case on the subject is Johnson v. Capital City Ford Co., La.App., 85 So.2d 75, in which the court pointed out that a newspaper advertisement relating to the purchase and sale of automobiles may constitute an offer, acceptance of which will consummate a contract and create an obligation in the offeror to perform according to the terms of the published offer.

Whether in any individual instance a newspaper advertisement is an offer rather than an invitation to make an offer depends on the legal intention of the parties and the surrounding circumstances. Annotation, 157 A.L.R. 744, 751; 77 C.J.S., Sales, § 25b; 17 C.J.S., Contracts, § 389. We are of the view on the facts before us that the offer by the defendant of the sale of the Lapin fur was clear, definite, and explicit, and left nothing open for negotiation. The plaintiff having successfully managed to be the first one to appear at the seller's place of business to be served, as requested by the advertisement, and having offered the stated purchase price of the article, he was entitled to performance on the part of the defendant. We think the trial court was correct in holding that there was in the conduct of the parties a sufficient mutuality of obligation to constitute a contract of sale.

The defendant contends that the offer was modified by a "house rule" to the effect that only women were qualified to receive the bargains advertised. The advertisement contained no such restriction. This objection may be disposed of briefly by stating that, while an advertiser has the right at any time before acceptance to modify his offer, he does not have the right, after acceptance, to impose new or arbitrary conditions not contained in the published offer. Payne v. Lautz Bros. & Co., City Ct., 166 N.Y.S. 844, 848; Mooney v. Daily News Co., 116 Minn. 212, 133 N.W. 573, 37 L.R.A.,N.S., 183.

Affirmed.

NOTES AND QUESTIONS:

1. *See* Restatement (Second) of Contracts §§ 3 (Agreements Defined; Bargain Defined), 4 (How a Promise May Be Made), 9 (Parties Required), 19 (Conduct as Manifestation of Assent), 21 (Intention to Be Legally Bound), 22 (Mode of Assent; Offer and Acceptance), 23 (Necessity That Manifestation Have Reference to Each Other), 24 (Offer Defined) and 26 (Preliminary Negotiations) (1981).

2. *See Nebraska Seed Co. v. Harsh*, 98 Neb. 89, 152 N.W. 310 (1915), in which Defendant Harsh directly passed to the Plaintiff Nebraska Seed Co. a price quote in a correspondence which read:

> Lowell, Nebraska, 4-24-1912
>
> Neb. Seed Co., Omaha, Neb.—Gentlemen: I have about 1800 bu. or thereabouts of millet seed of which I am mailing you a sample. This millet is recleaned and was grown on sod and is good seed. I want $2.25 cwt. for this seed f.o.b. Lowell.
>
> H.F. Harsh

Although Plaintiff Nebraska Seed forwarded a letter of acceptance on April 26, 1912, Defendant Harsh refused to deliver the seed. The court held that "the letter of defendant cannot be fairly construed to be an offer to sell to the plaintiff. . . . The language used is general, and such as may be used in an advertisement, or circular addressed generally to those engaged in the seed business, and is not an offer by which he may be bound, if accepted, by any or all of the persons addressed." *Id* at 310-311. Specifically, the court noted:

> If a proposal is nothing more than an invitation to the person to whom it is made to make an offer to the proposer, it is not such an offer as can be turned into an agreement by acceptance. Proposals of this kind, although made to definite persons and not to the public generally, are merely invitations to trade; they go no further than what occurs when one asks another what he will give or take for certain goods. Such inquiries may lead to bargains, but do not make them. They ask for offers which the proposer has a right to accept or reject as he pleases.
> The letter as whole shows that it was not intended as a final proposition, but as a request for bids. It did not fix a time for delivery, and this seems to have been regarded as one of the essentials by plaintiff, for in his telegram he requests defendant to 'wire how soon can load.'
>
> The mere statement of the price at which property is held cannot be understood as an offer to sell. *Id.* at 311.

3. Revisit *Leonard v. Pepsico,* 88 F. Supp. 2d 116, 122-128 (S.D.N.Y. 1999) for discussion of advertisements as offers.

4. *See Mesaros v. United States*, 845 F.2d 1576 (Fed. Cir. 1988) wherein the plaintiffs claimed that the promotional "materials sent to plaintiffs by the Mint, including the order form, constituted an offer that upon acceptance by the plaintiffs created a binding contract . . . whereby the government was bound and obligated to deliver the coins ordered by them." *Id.* at 1581. The Court explained that:

> [a] basic rule of contracts holds that whether an offer has been made depends on the objective reasonableness of the alleged offeree's belief that the advertisement or solicitation was intended as an offer. Generally, it is considered unreasonable for a person to believe that advertisements and solicitations are offers that bind the advertiser. Otherwise, the advertiser could be bound by an excessive number of contracts requiring delivery of goods far in excess of amounts available. That is particularly true in the instant case where the gold coins were limited to 500,000 by the Act of Congress. We conclude that a thorough reading, construction, and interpretation of the materials sent to the plaintiffs by the Mint makes clear that the contention of the plaintiffs that they reasonably believed the materials were intended as an offer is unreasonable as a matter of law. This is especially true in view of the words 'YES, Please accept my order . . .' that were printed on the credit card form, which showed that the credit card order was an offer *from the plaintiffs* to the Mint to buy the coins, which offer might or might not be accepted by the Mint. *Id.*

B. CLEAR AND DEFINITE TERMS

YODER V. ROCK ISLAND BANK
Appellate Court of Illinois, Third District
362 N.E.2d 68 (1977).

BARRY, Justice.

. . . .

In July of 1973, Yoder executed three separate construction mortgages to the Bank on Lots 1, 2 and 5 in Timothy Sirkl Second Addition to Coal Valley, Illinois. These three mortgages were placed of record. The Bank did advance money on the house being constructed on Lot 1, but no money was ever advanced on the mortgages on Lots 2 and 5.

In early November of 1974, Mr. Yoder discussed these particular mortgages and his financial obligations that were then due and owing to the Bank with Mr. Arvid Johnson, who was the vice president of the Bank and in charge of the Bank's real estate loan department. At that time, Mr. Johnson advised Yoder to have his attorney send him something in writing with respect to this problem. This was done, and in response to this letter, the Yoders' attorney, Sidney S. Deutsch, was referred to the Bank's attorney, Mr. H. Reed Doughty. He spoke to Mr. Doughty about this, but he wanted something in writing.

Thereafter, Mr. Deutsch received a letter from Mr. Doughty dated November 29, 1974. In this letter Mr. Doughty stated that he discussed Deutsch's letter with Mr. Arvid Johnson. The letter continued:

> . . . It would appear to me that we can make a resolution of Mr. Yoder's problems with the bank as follows:
>
> Previously, your client has offered to convey good title to the bank of Lot 1 in Timothy Sirkl, 2nd Addition, to the bank in exchange for a release on the mortgage thereon, together with a release by the bank of the judgment obtained against your client in cause 74 LM 7.
>
> In addition to this the bank will agree to release the mortgages on Lots 2 and 5 of the same addition. I must emphasize, however, that clear title must be provided to the bank for Lot 1 if this is to be accomplished. If your client is willing would you please advise at your earliest convenience and furnish me with abstract of title or commitment for title insurance "owners policy." If he is not willing we will proceed to foreclose the mortgage on Lot 1.

Since both Deutsch and Doughty were possible witnesses, the cause was tried by other counsel. Deutsch testified that after he received the letter of November 29, 1974, he called his client into the office and then called Doughty, explaining that the Yoders were going to go ahead and do what was necessary. Doughty testified that he has no recollection of Deutsch contacting him after his letter of November 29, 1974. He does, however, admit that he did receive a commitment for a title insurance policy, but he can't remember the date of receipt. The effective date on the schedule of commitment appears to be December 9, 1974.

Doughty further testified that, after writing the letter, he had a conversation with Mr. John Miller, who was then the president of The Rock Island Bank. Miller had discussed this matter with Johnson and learned of the terms of the letter which had been written to Yoder's attorney on November 29. Miller advised Doughty that he was unhappy with those terms and that he wanted to cancel or revoke the terms set forth in the letter of November 29. As a result of this conversation Doughty wrote a letter on December 20, which stated that Miller did not wish to proceed in accordance with the suggestions made in the letter of November 29, 1974.

Deutsch testified that after obtaining the commitment for title insurance and after the recording of the deed, which was done by the title company, he called Doughty and informed him that they had a commitment for title insurance, that there was a judgment to the Bank that could be taken care of since it was their property. He also testified that in this telephone conversation he commented that the taxes would be taken care of when they got together, that the judgment of the Bank could be withdrawn and that, although there may be another mortgage or lien for security for fees due him, that mortgage would also be taken care of, so the defendant would receive clear title. Deutsch further testified, in the same telephone conversation, that Doughty told him that the president had countermanded Johnson and that the offer would be withdrawn. Deutsch replied that Doughty should go back and talk to the president and that they should not run out on a commitment. Doughty stated he would go back and talk to them again. Subsequently Deutsch received the letter dated December 20. That was the last communication Deutsch had with Doughty.

A deed dated December 6, 1974, conveying Lot 1 of Timothy Sirkl Second Subdivision to the Village of Coal Valley, situated in Rock Island County and State of Illinois, from the Yoders to the Bank was recorded at 12:09 p.m. on December 9, 1974, in the Rock Island County Recorder's Office. This deed was delivered to the abstract company at the time the plaintiffs requested a title policy. A commitment for title insurance was issued, effective December 9, 1974, in the amount of $22,000, an owner's policy to be issued to the proposed insured, The Rock Island Bank, an Illinois corporation, with fee simple title vested in The Rock Island Bank, an Illinois corporation, to the land referred to as Lot No. 1 in Timothy Sirkl Second Subdivision, located in Rock Island County, Illinois, as of the effective date. Certain exceptions were listed. The taxes for the year 1974 were a lien but were not due and payable. Another exception was the taxes for 1973 in the amount of $58.59, which are unpaid. Likewise, a release of the mortgage recorded July 11, 1973, by The Rock Island Bank was required, as well as a release of the judgment of The Rock Island Bank versus John Yoder, Case No. 74 LM 7. The commitment is signed by The Rock Island County Abstract Title & Guaranty Company representatives for Chicago Title Insurance Company. This commitment was received by the Bank's attorney, Mr. Doughty, who had a copy of the commitment in his file. However, the title company apparently missed a mortgage from the Yoders to Deutsch. Doughty discovered Deutsch's mortgage after the lawsuit was filed. That mortgage, in the amount of $5,270.00 covering Lots 1, 2, 3, 4, and 5 of Timothy Sirkl 2nd Subdivision to the Village of Coal Valley, situated in the County of Rock Island and State of Illinois, except that portion of Lot 5 which has been deeded to Dwaine C. Halverson, dated October 26, 1973, filed October 30, 1973, in the Recorder's Office of Rock Island County, Illinois, in Record Book 580, page 220, Document No. 746721, has not yet been released, but Deutsch has acknowledged in open court that he would release it without receiving consideration from the Bank.

The evidence presented by the Bank indicated that the amount of the principal balance left on the Lot 1 mortgage was $17,973.90, the total amount of money paid out by the Bank. Adding interest, there is a total due on the mortgage of $21,003.45.

It was stipulated by the Bank that the only issue was the outcome of the specific performance action. If relief was denied in that case, then it is stipulated that the Bank was entitled to a decree of foreclosure. Therefore the only issue raised on review is whether the trial court erred in refusing to grant specific performance to the plaintiffs. The underlying, and controlling, question is whether there was a contract which could be specifically enforced.

It is the most elemental principle of law that, for a contract to come into existence, there must have been an offer and an acceptance. If the offer does not specify a particular mode of acceptance, the offer may be accepted by a performance of the desired acts. (Central National Bank v. Consumers Construction Company (2nd Dist., 1972), 5 Ill.App.3d 274, 282 N.E.2d 158). Nevertheless, the acceptance must conform exactly to the terms of the offer. (Brook v. Oberlander (1st Dist., 1964), 49 Ill.App.2d 312, 199 N.E.2d 613).

The purported offer in this case recited that the acceptance be made either by advising the Bank's attorney that the Yoders were willing to transfer the land in exchange for a release of the mortgage or by furnishing this same attorney with an abstract of title or a commitment for title insurance. There is a dispute in the facts as to whether Deutsch informed Doughty by telephone of the plaintiffs' acceptance of the purported offer. However, there is no dispute that Doughty's file contained a commitment for title insurance, or that the deed was recorded prior to the defendant Bank's December 20 withdrawal letter. Therefore, if the letter of November 29 conveyed an offer, there was clearly an acceptance which conformed exactly to the terms of the offer.

The defendant argues that the letter was not an offer. Rather, the argument continues, it was merely one step in a negotiation process. "It is not enough to show that an agreement of some kind existed between the parties, or even that it has in whole or in part been performed by the plaintiff, but the contract must be clear, certain and unambiguous in its terms, and give an absolute right without further negotiations." (Milani v. Proesel (1958), 15 Ill.2d 423, 430, 155 N.E.2d 38, 42).

The Bank points out in its brief that:

> The letter does not set forth the name of the Bank that the writer represents; does not set forth the amount of the title insurance that would be acceptable; does not state when the Plaintiffs-Appellants or the Defendant-Appellee are to perform; and does not give a complete description of the property concerned, other than to state the Lot number, and the name of the Addition, but the description is not located with reference to the City, County, Township, Section, or State in which it is located; and does not discuss possession, and transfer thereof.

None of these are sufficient reason to infer that the letter was not an offer. Although the letter does not set forth the name of the bank the author represents, it does state the name of the bank's agent. No question has been raised concerning Doughty's authority and, considering the ongoing relationship of the parties, the identity of the agent and other references (to the mortgage, to Arvid Johnson by name and to the case number) in the letter are sufficient to identify the bank referred to in the letter.

Generally, the terms of a contract are considered reasonably certain if there is a basis for determining breach of contract. (Restatement (Second) of Contracts § 32(2) (Tent. Draft, 1973)). Minor items may be left to the option of one of the parties or may be determined by what is customary or reasonable. (Restatement (Second) of Contracts § 32, comment F at 78 (Tent. Draft, 1973)). It is customary and reasonable that if transfer of possession is not determined, possession will be transferred when title is transferred. Likewise, although the amount of title insurance is not specified, it is reasonable and customary that the policy be issued in an amount at least equal to the amount due and owing on the mortgage. In the case at bar, the policy was issued in the next even thousand dollar amount greater than that due and owing on the mortgage. Since part performance of an agreement may remove uncertainty and establish an enforceable contract (Restatement (Second) of Contracts § 33(2) & comment C at 81 (Tent. Draft, 1973)), the action of the plaintiffs in providing a commitment for title insurance in the amount of $22,000.00 provided certainty to the contract. The plaintiffs' action is especially conclusive here because they were invited to provide such a commitment as a means of acceptance. Where a time for performance is not specified, the law implies that the parties intended the contract to be performed within a reasonable time. (Pel-Aire Builders, Inc. v. Jimenez (1st Dist., 1975), 30 Ill.App.3d 270, 332 N.E.2d 519).

It is also not fatal to this contract that the complete legal description of the land is not contained in the letter. The description contained in the letter, combined with the reference to the Yoders' mortgage and the judgment against the Yoders, is sufficient to inform any court in which enforcement is sought precisely to what land the contract pertains. For these reasons, this court finds that the letter is an offer, not merely a step in an ongoing process of negotiation; that the acceptance by the plaintiffs created a contract, and that this contract is sufficiently certain to be specifically enforced. . . .

Accordingly, the judgment of the Circuit Court of Rock Island County in Case Number 75 CH 1 is reversed, as is the judgment of the same court in the consolidated foreclosure action, Case Number 75 CH 49, and the cause is remanded to the Circuit Court of Rock Island County to proceed in accordance with the views expressed in this opinion.

Reversed and remanded with directions.

LUCEY V. HERO INTERNATIONAL CORP.
Supreme Judicial Court of Massachusetts, Berkshire
281 N.E.2d 266 (1972).

HENNESSEY, Justice.

This case involves a bill for specific performance of an option to purchase land. The defendant appeals from an interlocutory decree confirming the master's report and from a final decree ordering it to convey certain land to the plaintiff. The evidence is not reported.

We summarize the facts as found by the master. The defendant was the owner of a large tract of land in Richmond. On February 15, 1969, a clergyman, Father John P. Lucey (the plaintiff), offered to purchase five acres of the defendant's land and the buildings thereon for $65,000, and paid a broker $1,000 as a deposit. The broker told the plaintiff that his firm represented one Henry Rose, the defendant's president. At that time no mention was made of the corporation. The broker also prepared a real estate agreement describing the parcel and stating that "This agreement subject to an option to purchase additional land north of the house and along road at rate of $1,000.00 per acre." This agreement, however, was not executed.

On March 5, 1969, the defendant's board of directors voted that the corporation sell to the plaintiff "a piece of land on the easterly side of Lenox Road in Richmond, Massachusetts, for the sum of Sixty-Five Thousand ($65,000.00) Dollars and that the President be authorized to sign the deed and any other papers needed to effectuate this transfer." No other corporate vote on this matter was ever taken.

At a closing on March 13, 1969, the defendant conveyed to the plaintiff by warranty deed dated March 10, 1969, the five acre parcel. The transaction was consummated by the defendant's attorney, who, the master found, had authority to deliver the deed and accept the sale price on behalf of the defendant. At that same meeting, the plaintiff executed a real estate sales agreement which contained a paragraph granting the plaintiff "an option to purchase additional land belonging to . . . (the defendant), which said land shall be Northerly of the conveyed premises and along Lenox Road as mutually agreed upon by both parties." The option further provided that the land would be sold at a rate of $1,000 an acre. The master found that the words "as mutually agreed upon by both parties" were inserted at the suggestion of the defendant's attorney "in order to prevent the possibility that the option might be exercised by the purchase by the plaintiff of any portion of the seller's remaining land which would destroy the value of the residue of the land owned by the seller." The agreement also provided that the option provision "shall survive the closing."

The agreement was mailed to Rose who, without consulting the other officers of the corporation, deleted from the option paragraph the words "which said land shall be Northerly of the conveyed premises and along Lenox Road" and signed the agreement as so modified. The agreement was forwarded to the plaintiff's attorney whose attention was directed to the deletion made by Rose. The attorney was requested to have the plaintiff initial the modified agreement which was subsequently done. The master found that the plaintiff initialed the agreement "for the purpose of indicating his assent to all of the changes made thereon."

In late August, 1969, the plaintiff met Rose and told him that the defendant was obliged to sell to the plaintiff "whatever portion of the defendant's remaining land he wished to buy." Thereupon, the plaintiff hired a registered land surveyor who prepared a plan and a legal description of a five acre parcel selected by the plaintiff alone. The parcel selected was the one located immediately north of the parcel previously purchased. On September 2, 1969, the plaintiff's attorney notified the defendant that the plaintiff had elected to exercise the option with respect to the five acre parcel previously surveyed. Subsequently, Rose offered to sell and convey to the plaintiff a different parcel of land. No agreement was reached, whereupon the plaintiff commenced this litigation.

Since the evidence is not reported, the master's subsidiary facts must stand unless they are "mutually inconsistent, contradictory, or plainly wrong." Madigan v. McCann, 346 Mass. 62, 64, 190 N.E.2d 215, 216. Since his ultimate findings are conclusions of law, they are subject to review by this court on appeal. Ryan v. Stavros, 348 Mass. 251, 253, 203 N.E.2d 85.

The defendant advances as grounds for reversing the final decree that . . . the option agreement was too indefinite to be specifically enforceable . . . . Since we agree with . . . the defendant's arguments, the final decree must be reversed. . . .

We are also of the opinion that the option agreement is too indefinite to be specifically enforced. For that additional reason, the final decree is wrong. "An option to purchase real estate is a unilateral contract by which the owner of the property agrees with the holder of the option that he has the right to buy the property according to the terms and conditions of the contract." Morgan v. Forbes, 236 Mass. 480, 483, 128 N.E 792, 793. Since, therefore, an option is a contract, "(a)ll the essential terms . . . must be definite and certain so that the intention of the parties may be discovered, the nature and extent of their obligations ascertained, and their rights determined." Cygan v. Megathlin, 326 Mass. 732, 733-734, 96 N.E.2d 702, 703; Geo. W. Wilcox, Inc. v. Shell E. Petroleum Prod., Inc., 283 Mass. 383, 390, 186 N.E. 562. "The court cannot make for the parties a contract which they did not make for themselves." Read v. McKeague, 252 Mass. 162, 164, 147 N.E. 585, 586.

Applying these principles to the present case, we believe that the option provision as finally agreed upon by the parties did not contain a sufficient description of the land subject to the option. The provision stated, "(i)n addition, and for the same consideration . . . (the defendant) will give to . . . (the plaintiff) an option to purchase additional land belonging to . . . (the defendant), *as mutually agreed upon by both parties*" (emphasis added). As written, the words of the provision indicate that the parties contemplated a further agreement with respect to the location of the land subject to the option. To hold, as the plaintiff urges, that this option provision created a unilateral right on his part to designate the particular parcel to be purchased would ignore the very words of the provision. Furthermore, from the master's findings it appears that the words "as mutually agreed upon by both parties" were inserted by the defendant's attorney in order to prevent the exact situation which ultimately occurred, namely, the unilateral selection by the plaintiff of a parcel disagreeable to the defendant. In view of such a finding, we would also frustrate the intention of the parties in adopting the plaintiff's argument.

Given the manner in which the option was written, it is unenforceable. The location of the parcel subject to the option was left for future agreement. "(A)n agreement to enter into a contract which leaves the terms of that contract for future negotiation is too indefinite to be enforced." Caggiano v. Marchegiano, 327 Mass. 574, 580, 99 N.E.2d 861, 865; Rosenfield v. United States Trust Co., 290 Mass. 210, 217, 195 N.E. 323. Cf. Shayeb v. Holland, 321 Mass. 429, 73 N.E.2d 731. "Although a promise may be sufficiently definite when it contains an option given to the promisor or promisee, yet if an essential element is reserved for the future agreement of both parties, the promise can give rise to no legal obligation until such future agreement. Since either party by the very terms of the promise may refuse to agree to anything to which the other party will agree, it is impossible for the law to affix any obligation to such a promise." Williston, Contracts (3d ed.) § 45.

The plaintiff relies on a letter from the defendant's attorney to his attorney in which it was stated that because Rose deleted the description, "(i)t is my interpretation . . . that . . . (the defendant) is enlarging the option given to . . . (the plaintiff)." We first observe that the language requiring a future agreement also appeared in the original provision containing a description of the locus subject to the option. Secondly, the interpretation given, if entitled to any weight, is not necessarily inconsistent with our holding that the parties intended a future agreement since the only effect of deleting the description was to give the plaintiff a right to negotiate and agree with the defendant as to a greater area of land. The requirement of a future agreement, however, remained and is a fatal element of this contract.

The interlocutory decree is affirmed. The final decree is reversed and a new final decree is to enter dismissing the bill.

FAIRMOUNT GLASS WORKS V. CRUNDEN-MARTIN WOODEN WARE CO.
Court of Appeals of Kentucky
51 S.W. 196 (1899).

HOBSON, Justice.

On April 20, 1895, appellee wrote appellant the following letter:

St. Louis, Mo., April 20, 1895. Gentlemen: Please advise us the lowest price you can make us on our order for ten car loads of Mason green jars, complete, with caps, packed one dozen in a case, either delivered here, or f. o. b. cars your place, as you prefer. State terms and cash discount. Very truly, Crunden-Martin W. W. Co.

To this letter appellant answered as follows:

Fairmount, Ind., April 23, 1895. Crunden-Martin Wooden Ware Co., St. Louis, Mo.- Gentlemen: Replying to your favor of April 20, we quote you Mason fruit jars, complete, in one-dozen boxes, delivered in East St. Louis, Ill.: Pints $4.50, quarts $5.00, half gallons $6.50, per gross, for immediate acceptance, and shipment not later than May 15, 1895; sixty days' acceptance, or 2 off, cash in ten days. Yours, truly, Fairmount Glass Works.

Please note that we make all quotations and contracts subject to the contingencies of agencies or transportation, delays or accidents beyond our control.

For reply thereto, appellee sent the following telegram on April 24, 1895:

Fairmount Glass Works, Fairmount, Ind.: Your letter twenty-third received. Enter order ten car loads as per your quotation. Specifications mailed. Crunden-Martin W. W. Co.

In response to this telegram, appellant sent the following:

Fairmount, Ind., April 24, 1895. Crunden-Martin W. W. Co., St. Louis, Mo.: Impossible to book your order. Output all sold. See letter. Fairmount Glass Works.

Appellee insists that, by its telegram sent in answer to the letter of April 23d, the contract was closed for the purchase of 10 car loads of Mason fruit jars. Appellant insists that the contract was not closed by this telegram, and that it had the right to decline to fill the order at the time it sent its telegram of April 24. This is the chief question in the case. The court below gave judgment in favor of appellee, and appellant has appealed, earnestly insisting that the judgment is erroneous.

We are referred to a number of authorities holding that a quotation of prices is not an offer to sell, in the sense that a completed contract will arise out of the giving of an order for merchandise in accordance with the proposed terms. There are a number of cases holding that the transaction is not completed until the order so made is accepted. 7 Am. & Eng. Enc. Law (2d Ed.) p. 138; Smith v. Gowdy, 8 Allen, 566; Beaupre v. Telegraph Co., 21 Minn. 155. But each case must turn largely upon the language there used. In this case we think there was more than a quotation of prices, although appellant's letter uses the word "quote" in stating the prices given. The true meaning of the correspondence must be determined by reading it as a whole. Appellee's letter of April 20th, which began the transaction, did not ask for a quotation of prices. It reads: "Please advise us the lowest price you can make us on our order for ten car loads of Mason green jars.... State terms and cash discount." From this appellant could not fail to understand that appellee wanted to know at what price it would sell it ten car loads of these jars; so when, in answer, it wrote: "We quote you Mason fruit jars ... pints $4.50, quarts $5.00, half gallons $6.50, per gross, for immediate acceptance; ... 2 off, cash in ten days,"- it must be deemed as intending to give appellee the information it had asked for. We can hardly understand what was meant by the words "for immediate acceptance," unless the latter was intended as a proposition to sell at these prices if accepted immediately. In construing every contract, the aim of the court is to arrive at the intention of the parties. In none of the cases to which we have been referred on behalf of appellant was there on the face of the correspondence any such expression of intention to make an offer to sell on the terms indicated. In Fitzhugh v. Jones, 6 Munf. 83, the use of the expression that the buyer should reply as soon as possible, in case he was disposed to accede to the terms offered, was held sufficient to show that there was a definite proposition, which was closed by the buyer's acceptance. The expression in appellant's letter, "for immediate acceptance," taken in connection with appellee's letter, in effect, at what price it would sell it the goods, is, it seems to us, much stronger evidence of a present offer, which, when accepted immediately, closed the contract. Appellee's letter was plainly an inquiry for the price and terms on which appellant would sell it the goods, and appellant's answer to it was not a quotation of prices, but a definite offer to sell on the terms indicated, and could not be withdrawn after the terms had been accepted. It will be observed that the telegram of acceptance refers to the specifications mailed. These specifications were contained in the following letter: "St. Louis, Mo., April 24, 1895. Fairmount Glass-Works Co., Fairmount, Ind.-Gentlemen: We received your letter of 23rd this morning, and telegraphed you in reply as follows: 'Your letter 23rd received. Enter order ten car loads as per your quotation. Specifications mailed,'-which we now confirm. We have accordingly entered this contract on our books for the ten cars Mason green jars, complete, with caps and rubbers, one dozen in case, delivered to us in East St. Louis at $4.50 per gross for pint, $5.00 for quart, $6.50 for one-half gallon. Terms, 60 days' acceptance, or 2 per cent. for cash in ten days, to be shipped not later than May 15, 1895. The jars and caps to be strictly first-quality goods. You may ship the first car to us here assorted: Five gross pint, fifty-five gross quart, forty gross one-half gallon. Specifications for the remaining 9 cars we will send later. Crunden-Martin W. W. Co." It is insisted for appellant that this was not an acceptance of the offer as made; that the stipulation, "The jars and caps to be strictly first-quality goods," was not in their offer; and that, it not having been accepted as made, appellant is not bound. But it will be observed that appellant declined to furnish the goods before it got this letter, and in the correspondence with appellee it nowhere complained of these words as an addition to the contract. Quite a number of other letters passed, in which the refusal to deliver the goods was placed on other grounds, none of which have been sustained by the evidence. Appellee offers proof tending to show that these words, in the trade in which parties were engaged, conveyed the same meaning as the words used in appellant's letter, and were only a different form of expressing the same idea. Appellant's conduct would seem to confirm this evidence.

Appellant also insists that the contract was indefinite, because the quantity of each size of the jars was not fixed, that 10 car loads is too indefinite a specification of the quantity sold, and that appellee had no right to accept the goods to be delivered on different days. The proof shows that "10 car loads" is an expression used in the trade as equivalent to 1,000 gross, 1,000 gross being regarded a car load. The offer to sell the different sizes at different prices gave the purchaser the right to name the quantity of each size, and, the offer being to ship not later than May 15th, the buyer had the right to fix the time of delivery at any time before that. Sousely v. Burns' Adm'r, 10 Bush, 87; Williamson's Heirs v. Johnston's Heirs, 4 T. B. Mon. 253; Wheeler v. Railroad Co., 115 U. S. 34, 5 Sup. Ct. 1061, 1160. The petition, if defective, was cured by the judgment, which is fully sustained by the evidence. Judgment affirmed.

NOTES AND QUESTIONS:

1. *See* Restatement (Second) of Contracts §§ 17 (Requirement of a Bargain), 18 (Manifestation of Assent), 22 (Mode of Assent: Offer and Acceptance), 24 (Offer Defined), 26 (Preliminary Negotiations), 33 (Certainty), and 34 (Certainty and Choice of Terms; Effect of Performance or Reliance) (1981).

2. Recall that Article 2 of the U.C.C. "applies to transactions in goods." U.C.C. § 2-102 (2002). Also recall that the principles of law and equity apply to transactions in goods, unless displaced by the particular provisions of the U.C.C. U.C.C. § 1-103 (2001). Accordingly, it is important that the contract student commence reviewing the U.C.C. for the purpose of determining whether it may apply to the transaction in question. It is also important that the student understand when and how the U.C.C. differs from common law principles of law and equity. In assessing whether a particular provision of the U.C.C. applies to a transaction in question, the student should also seek to understand whether the U.C.C. provision displaces or supplements otherwise relevant common law principles. For example, New York Uniform Commercial Code § 2-204 (Formation in General) provides:

> (1) A contract for sale of goods may be made in any manner sufficient to show agreement, including conduct by both parties which recognizes the existence of such a contract.
>
> (2) An agreement sufficient to constitute a contract for sale may be found even though the moment of its making is undetermined.
>
> (3) Even though one or more terms are left open a contract for sale does not fail for indefiniteness if the parties have intended to make a contract and there is a reasonably certain basis for giving an appropriate remedy.

Query: Does U.C.C. § 2-204 displace or supplement the common law principles of law and equity regarding the formation of a contract?

3. The court in *Yoder v. Rock Island Bank*, *supra*, instructed that under the common law "[g]enerally, the terms of a contract are reasonably certain if there is a basis for determining breach of contract. Minor terms may be left to the option of one of the parties or may be determined by what is customary or reasonable." *Yoder*, 362 N.E.2d at 72. How does this common law principle compare with the provisions of U.C.C. § 2-204?

4. The court in *Lucey v. Hero International Corp.*, *supra*, instructed that "an agreement to enter into a contract which leaves the terms of the contract for future negotiation is too indefinite to be enforced." *Lucey*, 281 N.E.2d at 270. How does this common law principle compare with the provisions of U.C.C. § 2-204?

5. While we will continue to inquire whether the U.C.C. supplements or displaces the common law (as we continue to get acquainted with the U.C.C. and its provisions), it merits noting that Article 2 contains a number of gap-filling provisions that may likely displace common law principles and standards of certainty and definiteness. For example, a review of U.C.C. § 2-305 (Open Price Term) reveals that under Article 2 "parties if they so intend can conclude a contract for sale even though the price is not settled . . .[even if] the price is left to be agreed upon by the parties and they fail to agree. . . ." While the court in *Yoder v. Rock Island Bank*, *supra*, suggested that the common law will permit minor terms to be left open, price is not necessarily a minor term. And while the court in *Lucey v. Hero International Corp*, *supra*, suggested agreements to agree under the common law are too indefinite to be enforceable, U.C.C. § 2-305(1)(b) states that agreements under the U.C.C. are nonetheless enforceable even if "price is left to be agreed by the parties and they fail to agree." Thus, does U.C.C. §2-204 displace or supplement the common law with respect to the requirement of certainty and definiteness?

6. Compare Restatement (Second) of Contracts § 33 (Certainty) and its Comments with U.C.C. § 2-204 and its Comments.

7. There are instances in which statements of opinion may be regarded as "clear and definite offers." *See Cirafic v. Goffen, D.D.S.*, 407 N.E.2d 633, 634 (Ill. App. Ct. 1980) (During patient's consultation visit for dental implants, the dentist assured patient that "she would be able to eat 'corn on the cob' and other foods for which natural teeth are particularly suitable.").

SECTION 4. ACCEPTANCE

A. KNOWLEDGE OF THE OFFER

GLOVER V. JEWISH WAR VETERANS OF UNITED STATES, POST NO. 58
Municipal Court of Appeals for the District of Columbia
68 A.2d 233 (1949).

CLAGETT, ASSOCIATE JUDGE

. . . .

The controversy grows out of the murder on June 5, 1946, of Maurice L. Bernstein, a local pharmacist. The following day, June 6, Post No. 58, Jewish War Veterans of the United States, communicated to the newspapers an offer of a reward of $500 "to the person or persons furnishing information resulting in the apprehension and conviction of the persons guilty of the murder of Maurice L. Bernstein." Notice of the reward was published in the newspaper June 7. A day or so later Jesse James Patton, one of the men suspected of the crime, was arrested and the police received information that the other murderer was Reginald Wheeler and that Wheeler was the "boy friend" of a daughter of Mary Glover, plaintiff and claimant in the present case. On the evening of June 11 the police visited Mary Glover, who in answer to questions informed them that her daughter and Wheeler had left the city on June 5. She told the officers she didn't know exactly where the couple had gone, whereupon the officers asked for names of relatives whom the daughter might be visiting. In response to such questions she gave the names and addresses of several relatives, including one at Ridge Spring, South Carolina, which was the first place visited by the officers and where Wheeler was arrested in company with plaintiff's daughter on June 13. Wheeler and Patton were subsequently convicted of the crime.

Claimant's most significant testimony, in the view that we take of the case, was that she first learned that a reward had been offered on June 12, the day after she had given the police officers the information which enabled them to find Wheeler. Claimant's husband, who was present during the interview with the police officers, also testified that at the time of the interview he didn't know that any reward had been offered for Wheeler's arrest, that nothing was said by the police officers about a reward and that he didn't know about it "until we looked into the paper about two or three days after that."

We have concluded that the trial court correctly instructed the jury to return a verdict for defendant. While there is some conflict in the decided cases on the subject of rewards, most of such conflict has to do with rewards offered by governmental officers and agencies. So far as rewards offered by private individuals and organizations are concerned, there is little conflict on the rule that questions regarding such rewards are to be based upon the law of contracts.

Since it is clear that the question is one of contract law, it follows that, at least so far as private rewards are concerned, there can be no contract unless the claimant when giving the desired information knew of the offer of the reward and acted with the intention of accepting such offer; otherwise the claimant gives the information not in the expectation of receiving a reward but rather out of a sense of public duty or other motive unconnected with the reward. "In the nature of the case," according to Professor Williston, "it is impossible for an offeree actually to assent to an offer unless he knows of its existence."[2] After stating that courts in some jurisdictions have decided to the contrary, Williston adds, "It is impossible, however, to find in such a case [that is, in a case holding to the contrary] the elements generally held in England and America necessary for the formation of a contract. If it is clear the offeror intended to pay for the service, it is equally certain that the person rendering the service performed it voluntarily and not in return for a promise to pay. If one person expects to buy, and the other to give, there can hardly be found mutual assent. These views are supported by the great weight of authority, and in most jurisdictions a plaintiff in the sort of case under discussion is denied recovery."

The American Law Institute in its Restatement of the Law of Contracts follows the same rule, thus: "It is impossible that there should be an acceptance unless the offeree knows of the existence of the offer." The Restatement gives the following illustration of the rule just stated: "A offers a reward for information leading to the arrest and conviction of a criminal. B, in ignorance of the offer, gives information leading to his arrest and later, with knowledge of the offer and intent to accept it, gives other information necessary for conviction. There is no contract."[3] . . .

Affirmed.

NOTES AND QUESTIONS:

1. See Restatement (Second) of Contracts § 23 (1981).

2. See the following excerpt from *Choice v. City of Dallas*, 210 S.W. 753, 756 (Tex. Ct. App. 1919):

It is settled in this state that the recovery of rewards offered by individuals is governed by the principles of the law of contract, and that before recovery can be had it must appear that the party claiming the reward knew of and acted upon the offer when the services for the rendition of which the reward is claimed were rendered. *Broadnax v. Ledbetter*, 100 Tex. 375, 99 S.W. 1111, 9 L.R.A. (N.S.) 1057. The court in that case, however, suggests this distinction, which appellant Mrs. Firmin seeks to apply in this case:

---

[2] 1 Williston, Contracts, (rev. ed.) § 33.

[3] 1 Restatement, Contracts, § 53. See also: ibid., § 55; Reynolds v. Eagle Pencil Co., 285 N.Y. 448, 35 N.E.2d 35, rehearing denied 286 N.Y. 607, 35 N.E.2d 944; Rubenstein v. Frost, Sup., 116 N.Y.S. 681; Arkansas Bankers' Ass'n v. Ligon, 174 Ark. 234, 295 S.W. 4, 53 A.L.R. 534; Wilson v. Stump, 103 Cal. 255, 37 P. 151, 42 Am.St.Rep. 111; Williams v. West Chicago St. R. Co., 191 Ill. 610, 61 N.E. 456, 85 Am.St.Rep. 278; Kincaid Trust & Savings Bank v. Hawkins, 234 Ill.App. 64; Taft v. Hyatt, 105 Kan. 35, 180 P. 213, rehearing denied 105 Kan. 35, 181 P. 561; Fidelity & Deposit Co. of Maryland v. Messer, 112 Miss. 267, 72 So. 1,0004; Broadnax v. Ledbetter, 1,000 Tex. 375, 99 S.W. 1111, 9 L.R.A.,N.S., 1057; Tobin v. McComb, Tex.Civ.App., 156 S.W. 237.

> While we have seen no such distinction suggested, it may well be supposed that a person might become legally entitled to a reward for arresting a criminal, although he knew nothing of its having been offered, where it was offered in accordance with law by the government. A legal right might in such a case be given by law without the aid of contract.

A suggestion of such a distinction was also made in the cases of *Clinton County v. Davis*, 162 Ind. 60, 69 N.E. 680, 64 L.R.A. 780, 1 Ann. Cas. 282, and *Drummond v. United States (U.S.)* 35 Ct. Cl. 372. The only case we have found in which the distinction was actually applied is that of *Smith v. State*, 38 Nev. 477, 151 Pac. 512, L.R.A.1916A, 1276. In that case the Governor of the state of Nevada, acting under the provisions of an act of the Legislature, offered a reward for the arrest and conviction of the murderers of certain ranchmen, and the plaintiffs, who claimed the reward, were not aware of the fact that it had been offered when they did the acts on account of which the reward was claimed. The case of *Broadnax v. Ledbetter, supra*, was referred to in the opinion, and the above paragraph from the decision was quoted with approval, and it was concluded by the court that in cases of this kind it was not contemplated by the Legislature that any contractual relation was necessary; "that the right to the reward follows by operation of law if a compliance with the provisions of the statute has been shown." It seems that a general reward offered by the government is regarded by these authorities somewhat in the nature of a bounty. While an ordinance is not a law, in one sense of the word it is a local law, emanating from legislative authority and operative within its limited sphere as effectively as a general law of the sovereignty. Words and Phrases, vol. 6, p. 5024; Second Series, vol. 3, p. 77. Following these authorities, we hold that it was not necessary for the cross-petitioner to allege knowledge of the existence of the reward at the time she took action to secure the arrest and conviction of Mary Wright.

B. POWER OF ACCEPTANCE AND THE MIRROR IMAGE RULE

GREENBERG V. STEWART
Supreme Court of North Dakota
236 N.W.2d 862 (1975).

SAND, Judge.

This an appeal from a summary judgment of the District Court of Grand Forks County for the defendant, Alice Stewart, dismissing the action brought by plaintiff, Greenberg, for specific performance of a purported contract to sell land.

The respondents, Darrel Adams and Charles Bateman, were made parties to this action because they purchased the property in question from the defendant at a public sale conducted after the contract negotiations had been carried on between the plaintiff and the defendant.

Mrs. Stewart acquired the property involved in this case as the result of a transaction with a trust fund of which she was one of the principal beneficiaries. She expressed a desire to sell her interest in the land-which information was made known to Greenberg, who later contacted her regarding such a sale. On June 22, 1973, Greenberg submitted the following offer to Mrs. Stewart for the purchase of the property:

OFFER

I hereby offer to purchase from you those premises situated in the County of Grand Forks, State of North Dakota, described as the East 50% Of the acreage located in the West Half of Section 18 and the Northwest Quarter of Section 19, Township 151, Range 50, on the following terms and conditions:

1. The price to be paid shall be $400.00 an acre, it being understood and agreed that the total acreage in the above described premises is 232.135 acres more or less. The actual determination of the acreage involved shall be made by a registered engineer or surveyor at the expense of the seller.

2. This offer shall be subject to and dependent upon your acquiring good and marketable title to the property to be purchased.

3. The cash rent payable in the year 1973 shall be divided equally between the Seller and the undersigned.

4. The taxes for the year 1973 shall be prorated as of the date of possession based on the 1972 taxes.

5. This offer shall remain open and be binding upon the offeror for a period of 30 days from and after the date of acceptance by the seller, but this offer shall terminate and be null and void subsequent to that time.
6. The seller agrees that upon acceptance of this offer she will immediately cause to be commenced all Court proceedings necessary for an exchange of property as above described.

7. This offer must be accepted on or before the 10th day of July, 1973, to be binding on the undersigned.

8. The undersigned recognizes that seller may wish to negotiate other terms than cash payment and the undersigned is willing to arrange for an exchange of like properties of agreed upon equal value and is also agreeable to negotiate terms of an installment sale based on contract for deed.

9. Seller shall furnish to the buyer an Abstract of Title to said premises brought down to date showing good and marketable title in the name of the seller and the buyer shall have 15 days in which to examine such abstract to determine the marketability of the title. In the event the title cannot be made marketable, this agreement shall be void.

On August 6, 1973, Mrs. Stewart responded to Greenberg by letter, setting forth certain modifications to the offer:

> I received your offer dated June 22, 1973 and found it acceptable subject to the following modification:
>
> 1. Item 2 shall state my intention to provide good and marketable title to the property subject to any rights, covenants, conditions, restrictions, easements, and other encumbrances of record. I have no objections to your right to review that abstract of title within a reasonable period of time nor to your right to rescind your offer if such abstract reveals significant encumbrances.
>
> 2. Item 3 shall read "cash rents to be divided pro rata based upon the fiscal year for which they were collected."
>
> 3. Item 6 Due to the vagaries involved in securing judicial consents, I will use my best efforts to cause all court proceedings necessary for the exchange of property to be commenced but will not warrant all judicial consents will be given. If such consents are not obtained within 90 days either party may rescind this agreement.
>
> 4. Item 8 should be revised to provide for cash sale only. Upon acceptance of this contract by both parties the buyer will deposit 10% (ten percent) of the purchase price of the property into escrow. The balance of the purchase price shall be paid in cash upon close of escrow which is to be January 5, 1974. I am currently attempting to locate and acquire investment property in California and plan to use the proceeds from this sale for that purpose. In the unlikely event that such property is located this year and it is necessary to close escrow on that property prior to January 5, 1974, I retain the right to accelerate the close of this escrow to coincide with that purchase.
>
> 5. Item 9 should be deleted as it is covered adequately in Item 2.
>
> By copy of this letter to Mr. Peter Nielsen, I am directing him to prepare a contract of sale containing the points set forth in your offer as modified by my comments. If this is acceptable to you, please notify Mr. Nielsen.

On August 15, 1973, Greenberg, by letter, clarified a few points and transmitted to Mrs. Stewart a partially executed contract for the sale of the property between Mrs. Stewart and the plaintiff.

> Enclosed find purchase agreement executed in duplicate with an extra copy for your file.
>
> I had my lawyer look over the changes suggested in your letter of August 6, and he has incorporated these changes into the agreement.
>
> However, we have taken the liberty of clarifying a few other points which would be actually to your benefit. For instance, we have provided that you get all of the cash rents for 1973, and I get the cash rents thereafter. However, you would have to pay the taxes for 1973 and we would pay the

taxes thereafter. This is customary and would seem to be fair. As the closing date is set for January 5, 1974, this is most likely what would happen anyway.

We have made all of the remaining changes. Mr. Nielsen tells me that things are progressing as far as the estate proceedings are concerned and that this matter will undoubtedly go through.

You might send me the abstract of title, or let me know where it might be. All I want is your assurance you will pay the cost of continuation of the abstract to date and I will make the arrangements for having it continued.

Upon receipt from you of a signed copy of this agreement, I will deposit ten percent of the purchase price with the escrow agent. I am assuming you would want the First National Bank in Grand Forks to act as escrow agent.

AGREEMENT OF PURCHASE AND SALE

THIS AGREEMENT, made and entered into this _ _ day of August, 1973, by and between Alice E. Stewart of Lafayette, California, hereinafter called First Party, and Arthur Greenberg, Jr., of Grand Forks, North Dakota, hereinafter called Second Party, WITNESSETH:

WHEREAS, First Party desires to sell and Second Party desires to purchase the following described premises situated in the County of Grand Forks, State of North Dakota, to-wit:

The East fifty percent of the acreage located in the West Half (W 1/2) of Section Eighteen (18) and the Northwest Quarter (NW 1/4) of Section Nineteen (19), Township One Hundred Fifty-one (151), Range Fifty (50), Grand Forks County, North Dakota.

NOW THEREFORE, it is hereby agreed as follows:

1. The selling price shall be Four Hundred Dollars ($400.00) an acre, it being further agreed that the total acreage in the described premises is 232.135 acres, but that such acreage may be adjusted by a survey by a registered engineer or surveyor to be provided at the expense of the Seller for purposes of determining the actual acreage to be purchased at the above rate per acre.

2. It is the intention of the Seller to provide good and marketable title to the property subject to any rates, covenants, conditions, restriction and easements of record, and for that purpose the Seller shall furnish an abstract of title to the Buyer brought down to date; the Buyer shall have the right to rescind this proposal if such abstract reveals significant encumbrances.

3. The cash rent payable for the farming year 1973 shall be retained by the Seller and the cash rent for the farm year 1974 and thereafter shall be kept by the Purchaser.

4. The taxes for the year 1973 shall be paid by the Seller and the taxes for the years 1974 and thereafter shall be paid by the Purchaser.

5. The Seller shall use her best efforts to cause all necessary court proceedings for the exchange of properties to be commenced for purposes of establishing title in the name of the Seller. At the option of the Purchaser, if the Seller shall not be able to obtain approval of the court proceedings within ninety days from the date of this agreement, Purchaser may then rescind this agreement.

6. The selling price shall be paid in cash and upon acceptance of this contract by both parties, the Buyer will deposit ten percent of the estimated purchase price of the property into an escrow account with a mutually agreeable escrow agent. The balance of the purchase price shall be paid in cash upon close of the escrow on January 5, 1974. Seller may, at her option, accelerate the closing date of the escrow in the event she obtains investment property in California and is in need of funds for such purpose. If Seller accelerates the closing, she shall give the Purchaser a minimum of fifteen days notice of such Seller acceleration in order to enable the Purchaser to arrange for the cash payment.

IN WITNESS WHEREOF, the undersigned have set their hands on the day and year first above written.

PURCHASER:
S/ ARTHUR GREENBERG JR. __________

Arthur Greenberg, Jr.

SELLER:

____

Alice E. Stewart

(Jurats omitted.)

This contract was never signed or returned by Mrs. Stewart.

On October 11, 1973, Mr. Huff[1] informed Greenberg that, due to the inability of Mr. Greenberg and Mrs. Stewart to come to terms, the property would be sold at public auction. The property was sold to respondents Adams and Bateman at a public auction on November 11, 1973. The plaintiff attended the sale and submitted a written bid for an amount substantially more than what he had previously offered to pay for the property.

Greenberg then brought this action, claiming that a valid, enforceable contract existed between himself and Mrs. Stewart and demanding specific performance of that contract, and asking that all claims of Adams and Bateman to the property be declared null and void. . . .

The trial court found that there was no genuine issue as to any material fact and that the defendant was entitled to judgment as a matter of law. Greenberg contends that if a trial were held evidence would be brought out that would show that the parties intended to have a contract for the sale of the land. Greenberg readily admits that in the documents exchanged between the parties certain modifications were included, but contends and argues that a clarification of the modifications would support his contention that a contract existed. Any clarification of an ambiguous modification would not necessarily establish the existence of a contract. . . .

Thus the only issue remaining before the trial court was, and the only issue before this Court is, whether the documents exchanged do, as a matter of law, form a contract. This is a question amenable to resolution by summary judgment. We therefore affirm the trial court's conclusion that the matter was appropriate for summary judgment under Rule 56, N.D.R.Civ.P.

We now direct ourselves to the primary question of whether or not a valid contract existed between the parties.

Greenberg claims that the four documents exchanged between himself and Mrs. Stewart-the letter to Mrs Stewart of June 22, 1973, signed by Greenberg; the letter addressed to Greenberg signed by Mrs. Stewart dated August 6, 1973; the letter by Greenberg addressed to Mrs. Stewart dated August 15, 1973; and the partially executed agreement of purchase and sale transmitted with the letter of August 15-constitute a binding contract between the parties.

The trial court found that there was no meeting of the minds between the parties with respect to all of the terms and conditions of the sale and that there was no unqualified and absolute acceptance of an offer by either party. The trial court found as a matter of law that the letter of Mrs. Stewart of August 6, and the letter of Greenberg of August 22, did not constitute acceptances, but were counter offers.

The rule is fundamental that an acceptance must comply with the terms of the offer. In order to form a contract the offer and acceptance must express assent to the same thing. The acceptance must be unequivocal and unconditional and it may not introduce additional terms and conditions. 17 Am.Jur.2d Contracts § 62, p. 400.

[1] Mr. Huff was described by Mrs. Stewart as her financial adviser. He is not an attorney at law.

A conditional acceptance is itself a counter offer and rejects the original offer. 1 Williston on Contracts § 77, p. 251 (1967); Simpson, Contracts, § 33, p. 48 (1965).

The rule has been frequently stated by the North Dakota Supreme Court. In Beiseker v. Amberson, 17 N.D. 215, 116 N.W. 94 (1908), the Court stated:

> It is also equally well established that any counter proposition or any deviation from the terms of the offer contained in the acceptance is deemed to be in effect a rejection, and not binding as an acceptance on the person making the offer, and no contract is made by such qualified acceptance alone. In other words the minds of the parties must meet as to all the terms of the offer and of the acceptance before a valid contract is entered into. It is not enough that there is a concurrence of minds of the price of the real estate offered to be sold. If the purchaser adds anything in his acceptance not contained in the offer, then there is no contract. See also, Swanson v. Linder, 75 N.D. 751, 33 N.W.2d 62 (1948); First State Bank of Ray v. Hardgrove, 57 N.D. 396, 222 N.W. 265 (1928); Carns v. Puffett, 44 N.D. 438, 176 N.W. 93 (1920).

Section 9-03-21, NDCC, is pertinent to the question under consideration, which provides as follows:

> Except as provided by section 41-02-14, an acceptance must be absolute and unqualified, or must include in itself an acceptance of that character which the proposer can separate from the rest and which will conclude the person accepting. A qualified acceptance is a new proposal.

The reference to § 41-02-14, dealing with sales under the Uniform Commercial Code, has no significance in this case, because the UCC generally does not apply to real estate transactions.

Greenberg contends that any modifications made by the parties were insignificant and did not affect the motive of the transaction. He claimed that the proposed changes involved only mechanics relating to the closing of the sale and that there was a meeting of the minds on all necessary issues. He argues that not every modification of terms qualifies an acceptance and that there is a factual question of the degree of modification which must be resolved for each contract individually. Greenberg claims that the facts in this case show that the modifications are not of such significance as to qualify the acceptance of the offer and make it a counter offer.

Beiseker v. Amberson, supra, was an action for damages claimed under an alleged breach of a contract to sell and convey real estate. The alleged contract was evidenced solely by letters between the parties. The plaintiff, in purporting to accept the defendant's offer, added a new term asking the defendant to send the deed to the land to one of two banks named in the letter. The court held that this qualified the acceptance and that there was no binding contract. The court stated that if the plaintiff had accepted the offer unconditionally, his right to a deed could have been made effectual only by a tender of the price to the defendant personally; and, by requiring the defendant to send the deed elsewhere, a new condition was attached to the acceptance which the defendant was under no legal obligation to accept. The appellant contended that there was an unqualified acceptance contained in the letter and what followed was merely a suggestion for the most convenient way of completing the transaction. The court refused to accept this, holding that the place where the deed was to be sent was significant.

In Carns v. Puffett, supra, the alleged contract was based upon exchange of letters between the parties. The defendant wrote a return letter stating that she would sell the property for the offered price if the plaintiff would pay the taxes due on the property and send his note and mortgage to a New York bank. The plaintiff replied by stating that he would deliver his note and mortgage to a bank in North Dakota upon receipt of the deed and that he would pay the taxes due if the plaintiff would credit him for the cost of insuring the property. The court held that these modifications constituted terms of the proposed contract and were not matters merely relating to the execution and performance of it; that they therefore constituted counter offers, and that there was no contract between the parties. . . .

We find that there is substantial evidence to support the findings of fact of the trial court and that they are not clearly erroneous. We also find that the conclusions of law made by the trial court are in accordance with the law.

The summary judgment of the trial court dismissing the action is affirmed.

ERICKSTAD, C.J., and PAULSON, PEDERSON and VOGEL, JJ., concur.

RULE V. TOBIN
Supreme Court of Vermont
719 A.2d 869 (1998).

DOOLEY, Justice.

Plaintiffs, William and Beverly Rule and Danielle Swain, brought a civil rights action under 42 U.S.C. § 1983 against a Rutland police officer, Gary Tobin, and the City of Rutland alleging that Tobin unlawfully entered plaintiffs' apartment and unlawfully arrested Beverly Rule, using excessive force. A Rutland Superior Court jury returned a verdict for defendants, and plaintiffs appeal on a number of grounds, including that the trial court erred in failing to enforce a settlement agreement. We agree that the parties entered into a binding settlement agreement and reverse for entry of judgment consistent with that agreement.

This case was tried twice. On April 10, 1997, between the first and second trials, defendants' attorney sent plaintiffs an offer of judgment which read as follows:

> Now comes defendants ... and in accordance with the provisions of V.R.C.P. 68, and without prejudice to the rights of the defendant to proceed with the defense and its general denial of liability as envisioned by the rules, makes the following offer of judgment:

> The defendant offers to allow the plaintiff to take judgment against it in the amount and to the extent of Four Thousand and no/100 ($4,000.00), having thoroughly reviewed the liability and damages aspect of this case.

On April 15, 1997, plaintiffs' attorney answered, purporting to accept the offer of judgment, as follows:

> Assuming the defendants' 10 April Offer of Judgment does not include costs and attorney's fees pursuant to 42 U.S.C. § 1988 or any other entitlement, the plaintiffs accept the defendants' $4,000 offer.
>
> The plaintiffs understand that attorney's fees and costs will be determined in a later hearing pursuant to V.R.C.P. 54(d).

Asserting that they intended to include attorney's fees and costs in the offer, defendants objected to plaintiffs' answer and claimed that the offer had not been accepted.

The court apparently agreed with defendants' position. Over plaintiffs' objection, the court ordered the parties to start over with a new offer and acceptance, if appropriate. It directed that the new offer explicitly cover "everything, including all attorney's fees." Thereafter, defendants submitted an offer of judgment of $7,000, including "all claims for damages, costs, attorney's fees and every other potential claim." Plaintiffs rejected this offer.

On appeal, plaintiffs argue that (1) defendants' offer cannot be interpreted to include attorney's fees, (2) plaintiffs accepted defendants' offer, and (3) the court had no discretion to set aside the resulting agreement. Defendants respond that their offer must be interpreted to include costs and attorney's fees or, alternatively, it was ambiguous and the court had the discretion to rescind it because there was no meeting of the minds. We agree with plaintiffs' position. . . .

The leading case on construing offers of judgment in civil rights cases after *Marek* is *Erdman v. Cochise Cty.,* 926 F.2d 877 (9th Cir.1991). The court reinforced the direction of *Marek* for two main reasons: (1) "a settlement agreement is analyzed in the same manner as any contract, i.e., any ambiguities are construed against the drafter," *id.* at 880; and (2) "any waiver or limitation of attorney fees in settlements of § 1983 cases must be clear and unambiguous." *Id.* Other courts have also emphasized that offers of judgment put particular pressure on plaintiffs because they cannot be freely rejected without consequences; and, therefore, plaintiffs should not be put in the position where ambiguities in the offer might be construed against them. See *Chambers v. Manning,* 169 F.R.D. 5, 8 (D.Conn.1996); *Said v. Virginia Com. Univ./Med. College,* 130 F.R.D. 60, 63 (E.D.Va.1990).

Marek and its progeny hold that failure to explicitly deal with costs, and particularly attorney's fees, in an offer of judgment means that the plaintiff is free to accept the offer and seek attorney's fees and other costs in addition to the amount specified in the offer. Defendants' offer in this case was silent on costs and attorney's fees. Under *Marek,* we must interpret the offer as allowing plaintiffs to obtain costs and attorney's fees in addition to the judgment amount specified in the offer.

We must next determine whether plaintiffs accepted defendants' offer. In general, we turn to contract law to determine whether there has been a valid offer and acceptance. See *Radecki v. Amoco Oil Co.,* 858 F.2d 397, 399 (8th Cir.1988). Under contract law, an acceptance of an offer must be unconditional. See *Benya v. Stevens & Thompson Paper Co.,* 143 Vt. 521, 525, 468 A.2d 929, 931 (1983). It must "substantially comply with the terms of the offer" because "[a]n acceptance that modifies or includes new terms is not an acceptance of the original offer; it is a counteroffer...." *Id.*

Defendants argue that plaintiffs' purported acceptance of the offer of judgment was invalid because it was conditional and varied from the terms of the offer. Specifically, they rely on the language of the acceptance that conditioned acceptance on a construction of the offer that allowed plaintiffs to pursue attorney's fees and costs. Defendants argue that plaintiffs' assumption was at variance with their intent in making the offer.

Because we have held that the offer did not have to include attorney's fees and costs within the stated amount, it is clear that plaintiffs' acceptance did not vary the terms of the offer. At best, defendants' argument is that the acceptance is invalid because it was conditional, even if the condition is a correct statement of the legal effect of the offer. We do not believe that the applicable contract formation law is this formalistic.

As we have held, the condition imposed by plaintiffs was implied in the offer as a matter of law. In such a case, the acceptance is sufficient to form a contract. See *Chambers v. Manning,* 169 F.R.D. at 7; *Rohrer v. Slatile Roofing & Sheet Metal Co.,* 655 F.Supp. at 738. A leading contract treatise explains the rationale:

> Sometimes an acceptor from abundance of caution inserts a condition in his acceptance which merely expresses what would be implied in fact or in law from the offer. As such a condition involves no qualification of the acceptor's assent to the terms of the offer, a contract is not precluded. Thus an offer to sell land may be accepted subject to the condition that the title is good, for unless the offer expressly specifies that the offeree must take his chance as to the validity of the title, the meaning of the offer is that a good title will be conveyed.

1 W. Jaeger, Williston on Contracts § 78, at 257-58 (3d ed.1957); see also Restatement (Second) of Contracts § 59, Comment b, Illustration 3 (1981). Case law supports this interpretation. See *State Dept. of Transp. v. Providence & Worcester R.R.,* 674 A.2d 1239, 1243 (R.I.1996) (acceptance not equivocal if offeree merely puts into words that which was already reasonably implied in terms of offer); *In re Lamarre,* 34 B.R. 264, 266 (Bankr.D.Me.1983) ("[T]he offeree from an abundance of caution may condition his acceptance on a fact which would be implied in fact or in law from the offer."); *Panhandle Eastern Pipe Line Co. v. Smith,* 637 P.2d 1020, 1023 (Wyo.1981) (acceptance still effective if addition only asks for something implied from offer). Because plaintiffs' acceptance only clarified what they were already entitled to by law, it was unconditional. Accordingly, a valid agreement was entered into between plaintiffs and defendants for a judgment of $4,000, plus costs and attorney's fees.

Reversed and remanded for entry of judgment in accordance with defendants' offer of April 10, 1997 and further proceedings not inconsistent with this opinion.

NOTES AND QUESTIONS:

1. *See* Restatement (Second) of Contracts §§ 22 (Mode of Assent: Offer and Acceptance), 23 (Necessity That Manifestation Have Reference to Each Other), 29 (To Whom an Offer Is Addressed), 35 (The Offeree's Power of Acceptance), 39 (Counter-Offers), 40 (Time When Rejection or Counter-Offer Terminates the Power of Acceptance), 50 (Acceptance of Offer Defined; Acceptance by Performance; Acceptance by Promise), 52 (Who May Accept an Offer), 57 (Effect of Equivocal Acceptance), 58 (Necessity of Acceptance Complying with Terms of Offer), 59 (Purported Acceptance Which Adds Qualifications), 60 (Acceptance of Offer Which States Place, Time or Manner of Acceptance), and 61 (Acceptance Which Requests Change of Terms) (1981).

2. It is helpful to the formation analysis to understand that an "offer" instills in an "offeree" the power of acceptance. Such power is usually of a temporal nature, and once terminated, an offer can no longer be accepted. *See* Restatement (Second) of Contracts §§ 29 and 35 (1981). *See also Kurio v. United States*, 429 F. Supp. 42, 64 (S.D. Tex. 1970) ("By making an offer, a person creates in an offeree a power of acceptance. 1 Corbin §§ 11 and 35; 1 Williston § 50; Restatement § 34. As he is free not to make any offer at all, a person making an offer is free to restrict the power of acceptance in any way, reasonable or unreasonable, that he may wish. 1 Corbin § 88; 1 Williston § 76; Restatement § 61. Unless the offeree exercises his power of acceptance before it expires, there is no contract, for there is no power to accept. Therefore, where the offer has terminated by lapse of time, an attempt to accept is ineffectual to create a contract.").

3. Note Restatement (Second) of Contracts § 35 comment b (1981):

> [T]he offeree's power arises when the offeror's manifestation of assent is complete. Since the acceptance must have reference to the offer it is ordinarily necessary that the offeree have knowledge of the offer. *See* § 23. Once the power arises it continues until terminated . . . .
>
> There is no requirement that the offeror, or the mental assent which exists at the time of the offer, continue until the time of acceptance. *See* § 49.

C. TERMINATION OF POWER OF ACCEPTANCE

1. LAPSE OF TIME

AKERS V. SEDBERRY
Court of Appeals of Tennessee, Middle Section, at Nashville
286 S.W.2d 617 (1955).

FELTS, Judge.

These two consolidated causes are before us upon a writ of error sued out by J. B. Sedberry, Inc., and Mrs. M. B. Sedberry, defendants below, to review a decree of the Chancery Court, awarding a recovery against them in favor of each of the complainants,

Charles William Akers and William Gambill Whitsitt, for damages for breach of a contract of employment.

The principal question presented is whether complainants resigned their employment, or were wrongfully discharged by defendants; and if there was a breach of contract for which complainants are entitled to recover, there are some further questions as to the measure or extent of the recovery.

J. B. Sedberry, Inc., was a Tennessee corporation with its principal place of business at Franklin, Tennessee. Mrs. M. B. Sedberry owned practically all of its stock and was its president and in active charge of its affairs. It was engaged in the business of distributing "Jay Bee" hammer mills, which were manufactured for it under contract by Jay Bee Manufacturing Company, a Texas corporation, whose plant was in Tyler, Texas, and whose capital stock was owned principally by L. M. Glasgow and B. G. Byars.

On July 1, 1947, J. B. Sedberry, Inc., by written contract, employed complainant Akers as Chief Engineer for a term of five years at a salary of $12,000 per year, payable $1,000 per month, plus 1% of its net profits for the first year, 2% the second, 3% the third, 4% the fourth, and 5% the fifth year. His duties were to carry on research for his employer, and to see that the Jay Bee Manufacturing Company, Tyler, Texas, manufactured the mills and parts according to proper specifications. Mrs. M. B. Sedberry guaranteed the employer's performance of this contract.

On August 1, 1947, J. B. Sedberry, Inc., by written contract, employed complainant Whitsitt as Assistant Chief Engineer for a term of five years at a salary of $7,200 per year, payable $600 per month, plus 1% of the corporation's net profits for the first year, 2% for the second, 3% for the third, 4% for the fourth, and 5% for the fifth year. His duties were to assist in the work done by the Chief Engineer. Mrs. M. B. Sedberry guaranteed the employer's performance of this contract.

Under Mrs. Sedberry's instructions, Akers and Whitsitt moved to Tyler, Texas, began performing their contract duties in the plant of the Jay Bee Manufacturing Company, continued working there, and were paid under the contracts until October 1, 1950, when they ceased work, under circumstances hereafter stated.

In 1947, when these employment contracts were made, Mrs. Sedberry owned no stock in the Jay Bee Manufacturing Company. In 1948 she purchased the shares of stock in this company which were owned by the Glasgow interests, and in 1949 she purchased the 750 shares owned by her brother, B. G. Byars, and gave him her note therefore in the sum of $157,333.93, pledging the 750 shares with him as collateral to her note.

Glasgow had been general manager of the Jay Bee Manufacturing Company, but when he sold his stock, he was succeeded by A. M. Sorenson as manager. There soon developed considerable friction between Sorenson and complainants Akers and Whitsitt. The Jay Bee Manufacturing Company owed large sums to the Tyler State Bank & Trust Co.; and the bank's officers, fearing the company might fail under Sorenson's management, began talking to Akers and Whitsitt about the company's financial difficulties.

One of the bank's vice-presidents, J. Harold Stringer, made a trip to Franklin to see Mrs. Sedberry about the company's indebtedness to the bank. He told her that they could not get along with Sorenson and did not agree with the way he was managing the company's affairs. Mrs. Sedberry asked Stringer as soon as he got back to Tyler to see Akers and Whitsitt and discuss with them plans for the refinancing and the operation of the company; and thereafter the bank's officers had a number of conferences with Akers and Whitsitt about these matters.

While these matters were pending, Akers and Whitsitt flew to Nashville and went to Franklin to talk with Mrs. Sedberry about them. They had a conference with her at her office on Friday, September 29, 1950, lasting from 9:30 a.m. until 4:30 p.m. As they had come unannounced, and unknown to Sorenson, they felt Mrs. Sedberry might mistrust them; and at the outset, to show their good faith, they offered to resign, but she did not accept their offer. Instead, she proceeded with them in discussing the operation and refinancing of the business.

Testifying about this conference, Akers said that, at the very beginning, to show their good faith, he told Mrs. Sedberry that they would offer their resignations on a ninety-day notice, provided they were paid according to the contract for that period; that she pushed the offers aside-"would not accept them," but went into a full discussion of the business; that nothing was thereafter said about the offers to resign; and that they spent the whole day discussing the business, Akers making notes of things she instructed him to do when he got back to Texas.

Whitsitt testified that at the beginning of the meeting Akers stated the position for both of them, and told Mrs. Sedberry, as evidence of their good faith, "we would resign with ninety-days notice if she paid us the monies that she owed us to that date, and on the other hand, if she did not accept that resignation, we would carry forth the rest of our business." He said that she did not accept the offer, but proceeded with the business, and nothing further was said about resigning.

Mrs. Sedberry testified that Akers and Whitsitt came in and "offered their resignations"; that they said they could not work with Sorenson and did not believe the bank would go along with him; and that "they said if it would be of any help to the organization they would be glad to tender their resignation and pay them what was due them." She further said that she "did not accept the resignation," that she "felt it necessary to contact Mr. Sorenson and give consideration to the resignation offer." But she said nothing to complainants about taking the offer under consideration.

On cross-examination she said that in the offer to resign "no mention was made of any ninety-day notice." Asked what response she made to the offer she said, "I treated it rather casually because I had to give it some thought and had to contact Mr. Sorenson." She further said she excused herself from the conference with complainants, went to another room, tried to telephone Sorenson in Tyler, Texas, but was unable to locate him.

She then resumed the conference, nothing further was said about the offers to resign, nothing was said by her to indicate that she thought the offers were left open or held under consideration by her. But the discussion proceeded as if the offers had not been made. She discussed with complainants future plans for refinancing and operating the business, giving them instructions, and Akers making notes of them.

Following the conference, complainants, upon Mrs. Sedberry's request, flew back to Texas to proceed to carry out her instructions. On the way back, and while in Nashville, Friday evening, Akers telephoned her in Franklin to tell her that he had just learned that the bank had sued both the companies and process had been served that day. On the next morning, September 30, Akers had a conference with the bank officials about the refinancing of the company, the results of which he reported to Mrs. Sedberry by long-distance telephone conversation that day.

On Monday, October 2, 1950, Mrs. Sedberry sent to complainants similar telegrams, signed by "J. B. Sedberry, Inc., by M. B. Sedberry, President," stating that their resignations were accepted, effective immediately. We quote the telegram to Akers, omitting the formal parts:

> 'Account present unsettled conditions which you so fully are aware we accept your kind offer of resignation effective immediately. Please discontinue as of today with everyone employed in Sedberry, Inc., Engineering Department, discontinuing all expenses in this department writing.'

While this said she was "writing," she did not write. Akers wrote her, but held up sending his letter, at the request of her brother, Mr. Byars, who was one of the officers of the bank in Tyler, Texas. Akers later rewrote practically the same letter and mailed it to her on October 16, 1950. Whitsitt also sent her a similar letter on the same day.

In his letter, Akers said that he was amazed to get her telegram, and called her attention to the fact that no offer to resign by him was open or outstanding when she sent the telegram; that while he had made a conditional offer to resign at their conference on September 29, she had immediately rejected the offer, and had discussed plans for the business and had instructed him and Whitsitt as to things she wanted them to do in the business on their return to Tyler.

This letter further stated that Akers was expecting to be paid according to the terms of his contract until he could find other employment that would pay him as much income as that provided in his contract, and that if he had to accept a position with less income, he would expect to be paid the difference, or whatever losses he suffered by her breach of the contract. Whitsitt's letter contained a similar statement of his position.

On November 10, 1950, Mrs. Sedberry wrote a letter addressed to both Akers and Whitsitt in which she said that "no one deplored the action taken more than the writer," but she did not recede from her position as expressed in the telegram. She stated her contention that the offers to resign had been without condition; and though she also said she would like to make an amicable settlement, no settlement was made. . . .

An employee's tender of his resignation, being a mere offer is, of course, not binding until it has been accepted by the employer. Such offer must be accepted according to its terms and within the time fixed. The matter is governed by the same rules as govern the formation of contracts. Nesbit v. Giblin, 96 Neb. 369, 148 N.W. 138, L.R.A.1915D, 477, Ann.Cas.1916A, 1008; 1 Labatt's Master & Servant (2d ed.) section 181; Note, Ann.Cas.1916A, 1011, 1012.

An offer may be terminated in a number of ways, as, for example, where it is rejected by the offeree, or where it is not accepted by him within the time fixed, or, if no time is fixed, within a reasonable time. An offer terminated in either of these ways ceases to exist and cannot thereafter be accepted. 1 Williston on Contracts (1936), §§ 50A, 51, 53, 54; 1 Corbin on Contracts (1950), §§ 35, 36; 1 Rest., Contracts, §§ 35, 40.

The question what is a reasonable time, where no time is fixed, is a question of fact, depending on the nature of the contract proposed, the usages of business and other circumstances of the case. Ordinarily, an offer made by one to another in a face to face conversation is deemed to continue only to the close of their conversation, and cannot be accepted thereafter.

The rule is illustrated by Restatement of Contracts, § 40, Illustration 2, as follows:

> 2. While A and B are engaged in conversation, A makes B an offer to which B then makes no reply, but a few hours later meeting A again, B states that he accepts the offer. There is no contract unless the offer or the surrounding circumstances indicate that the offer is intended to continue beyond the immediate conversation.

In Mactier's Adm'rs v. Frith, 1830, 6 Wend.N.Y., 103, 114, 21 Am.Dec. 262, 268, the rule was stated as follows:

> 'Although the will of the party making the offer may precede that of the party accepting, yet it must continue down to the time of the acceptance. Where parties are together chaffering about an article of merchandise and one expresses a present willingness to accept of certain terms, that willingness is supposed to continue, unless it is revoked, to the close of their interview and negotiation on the same subject, and if during this time the other party says he will take the article on the terms proposed, the bargain is thereby closed. Pothier Traite du Contract de Vente, p. 1, sec. 2, art. 3, no. 31.'

Professor Williston says:

> 'A reasonable time for the acceptance of most offers made in conversation will not extend beyond the time of the conversation unless special words or circumstances indicate an intention on the part of the offeror that it shall do so.' Williston on Contracts (1938), § 54.

Professor Corbin says:

> 'When two negotiating parties are in each other's presence, and one makes an offer to the other without indicating any time for acceptance, the inference that will ordinarily be drawn by the other party is that an answer is expected at once. . . . If, when the first reply is not an acceptance, the offeror turns away in silence, the proper inference is that the offer is no longer open to acceptance.' 1 Corbin on Contracts (1950), § 36, p. 111.

The only offer by Akers and Whitsitt to resign was the offer made by them in their conversation with Mrs. Sedberry. They made that offer at the outset, and on the evidence it seems clear that they expected an answer at once. Certainly, there is nothing in the evidence to show that they intended the offer to continue beyond that conversation; and on the above authorities, we think the offer did not continue beyond that meeting.

Indeed, it did not last that long, in our opinion, but was terminated by Mrs. Sedberry's rejection of it very early in that meeting. While she did not expressly reject it, and while she may have intended, as she says, to take the offer under consideration, she did not disclose such an intent to complainants; but, by her conduct, led them to believe she rejected the offer, brushed it aside, and proceeded with the discussion as if it had not been made.

> 'An offer is rejected when the offeror is justified in inferring from the words or conduct of the offeree that the offeree intends not to accept the offer or to take it under further advisement (Rest. Contracts § 36).' 1 Williston on Contracts, § 51.

So, we agree with the Trial Judge that when defendants sent the telegrams, undertaking to accept offers of complainants to resign, there was no such offer in existence; and that this attempt of defendants to terminate their contract was unlawful and constituted a breach for which they are liable to complainants. Nesbit v. Giblin, supra; Brady v. Oliver, 125 Tenn. 595, 147 S.W. 1135, 41 L.R.A.,N.S., 60, Ann.Cas.1913C, 376; Church of Christ Home For Aged, Inc. v. Nashville Trust Co., 184 Tenn. 629, 642, 202 S.W.2d 178, 183; Lazarov v. Nunnally, 188 Tenn. 145, 149, 217 S.W.2d 11. . . .

All of the assignments of error are overruled and the decree of the Chancellor is affirmed. Decrees will be entered here for complainants for the amount of the decrees below with interest. The costs are adjudged against defendants and the sureties on their cost bond. The causes are remanded to the Chancery Court for further proceedings not inconsistent with this opinion.

HICKERSON and SHRIVER, JJ., concur.

MINNESOTA LINSEED OIL CO. v. COLLIER WHITE LEAD CO.
Circuit Court, D. Minnesota
4 Dill. 431, 17 F. Cas. 447 (1876).

Reported by Hon. John F. Dillon, Circuit Judge:

This action was removed from the state court and a trial by jury waived. The plaintiff seeks to recover the sum of $2,151.50, with interest from September 20, 1875—a balance claimed to be due for oil sold to the defendant. The defendant, in its answer, alleges that on August 3d, 1875, a contract was entered into between the parties, whereby the plaintiff agreed to sell and deliver to the defendant, at the city of St. Louis, during the said month of August, twelve thousand four hundred and fifty (12,450) gallons of linseed oil for the price of fifty-eight (58) cents per gallon, and that the plaintiff has neglected and refused to deliver the oil according to the contract; that the market value of oil after August 3d and during the month was not less than seventy (70) cents per gallon, and therefore claims a set-off or counter-claim to plaintiff's cause of action. The reply of the plaintiff denies that any contract was entered into between it and defendant.

The plaintiff resided at Minneapolis, Minnesota, and the defendant was the resident agent of the plaintiff, at St. Louis, Missouri. The contract is alleged to have been made by telegraph.

The plaintiff sent the following dispatch to the defendant:

> 'Minneapolis, July 29, 1875. To Alex. Easton, Secretary Collier White Lead Company, St. Louis, Missouri: Account of sales not enclosed in yours of 27th. Please wire us best offer for round lot named by you-one hundred barrels shipped. Minnesota Linseed Oil Company.'

The following answer was received:

> 'St. Louis, Mo., July 30, 1875. To the Minnesota Linseed Oil Company: Three hundred barrels fifty-five cents here, thirty days, no commission, August delivery. Answer. Collier Company.'

The following reply was returned:

> 'Minneapolis, July 31, 1875. Will accept fifty-eight cents (58c), on terms named in your telegram. Minnesota Linseed Oil Company.'

This dispatch was transmitted Saturday, July 31, 1875, at 9:15 p.m., and was not delivered to the defendant in St. Louis, until Monday morning, August 2, between eight and nine o'clock.

On Tuesday, August 3, at 8:53 a.m., the following dispatch was deposited for transmission in the telegraph office:

'St. Louis, Mo., August 3, 1875. To Minnesota Linseed Oil Company, Minneapolis: Offer accepted-ship three hundred barrels as soon as possible. Collier Company.'

The following telegrams passed between the parties after the last one was deposited in the office at St. Louis:

'Minneapolis, August 3, 1875. To Collier Company, St. Louis: We must withdraw our offer wired July 31st. Minnesota Linseed Oil Company.'

Answered:

'St. Louis, August 3, 1875. Minnesota Linseed Oil Company: Sale effected before your request to withdraw was received. When will you ship? Collier Company.'

It appeared that the market was very much unsettled, and that the price of oil was subject to sudden fluctuations during the month previous and at the time of this negotiation, varying from day to day, and ranging between fifty-five and seventy-five cents per gallon. It is urged by the defendant that the dispatch of Tuesday, August 3d, 1875, accepting the offer of the plaintiff transmitted July 31st, and delivered Monday morning, August 2d, concluded a contract for the sale of the twelve thousand four hundred and fifty gallons of oil. The plaintiff, on the contrary, claims, 1st, that the dispatch accepting the proposition made July 31st, was not received until after the offer had been withdrawn; 2d, that the acceptance of the offer was not in due time; that the delay was unreasonable, and therefore no contract was completed.

NELSON, District Judge:

It is well settled by the authorities in this country, and sustained by the later English decisions, that there is no difference in the rules governing the negotiation of contracts by corespondence [*sic*] through the post-office and by telegraph, and a contract is concluded when an acceptance of a proposition is deposited in the telegraph office for transmission. See 14 Am. Law Reg. 401, "Contracts by Telegraph," article by Judge Redfield, and authorities cited; also, Trevor v. Wood, 36 N. Y. 307.

The reason for this rule is well stated in Adams v. Lindsell, 1 Barn. & Ald. 681. The negotiation in that case was by post. The court said: "That if a bargain could not be closed by letter before the answer was received, no contract could be completed through the medium of the post-office; that if the one party was not bound by his offer when it was accepted (that is, at the time the letter of acceptance is deposited in the mail), then the other party ought not to be bound until after they had received a notification that the answer had been received and assented to, and that so it might go on ad infinitum." See, also, 5, Pa. St. 339; 11 N. Y. 441; Mactier v. Frith, 6 Wend. 103; 48 N. H. 14; 8 C. B. 225. In the case at bar the delivery of the message at the telegraph office signified the acceptance of the offer. If any contract was entered into, the meeting of minds was at 8:53 of the clock, on Tuesday morning, August 3d, and the subsequent dispatches are out of the case. 1 Pars. Cont. 482, 483.

This rule is not strenuously dissented from on the argument, and it is substantially admitted that the acceptance of an offer by letter or by telegraph completes the contract, when such acceptance is put in the proper and usual way of being communicated by the agency employed to carry it; and that when an offer is made by telegraph, an acceptance by telegraph takes effect when the dispatch containing the acceptance is deposited for transmission in the telegraph office, and not when it is received by the other party. Conceding this, there remains only one question to decide, which will determine the issues: Was the acceptance of defendant deposited in the telegraph office Tuesday, August 3d, within a reasonable time, so as to consummate a contract binding upon the plaintiff?

It is undoubtedly the rule that when a proposition is made under the circumstances in this case, an acceptance concludes the contract if the offer is still open, and the mutual consent necessary to convert the offer of one party into a binding contract by the acceptance of the other is established, if such acceptance is within a reasonable time after the offer was received.

The better opinion is, that what is, or is not, a reasonable time, must depend upon the circumstances attending the negotiation, and the character of the subject matter of the contract, and in no better way can the intention of the parties be determined. If the negotiation is in respect to an article stable in price, there is not so much reason for an immediate acceptance of the offer, and the same rule would not apply as in a case where the negotiation related to an article subject to sudden and great fluctuations in the market.

The rule in regard to the length of the time an offer shall continue, and when an acceptance completes the contract, is laid down in Parsons on Contracts (volume 1, p. 482). He says:

> 'It may be said that whether the offer be made for a time certain or not, the intention or understanding of the parties is to govern. . . . If no definite time is stated, then the inquiry as to a reasonable time resolves itself into an inquiry as to what time it is rational to suppose the parties contemplated; and the law will decide this to be that time which as rational men they ought to have understood each other to have had in mind.'

Applying this rule, it seems clear that the intention of the plaintiff, in making the offer by telegraph, to sell an article which fluctuates so much in price, must have been upon the understanding that the acceptance, if at all, should be immediate, and as soon after the receipt of the offer as would give a fair opportunity for consideration. The delay here was too long, and manifestly unjust to the plaintiff, for it afforded the defendant an opportunity to take advantage of a change in the market, and accept or refuse the offer as would best subserve its interests.

Judgment will be entered in favor of the plaintiff for the amount claimed. The counter-claim is denied. Judgment accordingly.

NOTES AND QUESTIONS:

1. *But see Caldwell v. E.F. Spears & Sons*, 216 S.W. 83 (Ky. Ct. App. 1919), where the court determined that circumstances surrounding a face-to-face offer were sufficient to allow a timely acceptance the following day.

---

2. DEATH OR INCAPACITY OF A PARTY

Generally speaking, an offer is terminated upon the death or supervening incapacity of either party. This is true regardless of whether the offeree has actual knowledge of the offeror's death or incapacity before attempting to accept. The justification for this rule stems from the fact that there can be no meeting of the minds where one of the two "minds" ceases to exist. However, some question the fairness of this rule to an offeree who materially changes his position in response to an offer where no notice of termination has been received, thus preferring a construction that would put the burden of notification upon the executor of the estate or the guardian of the ward. Restatement (Second) of Contracts § 48 reflects the prevailing view of treating the offer as terminated immediately upon the death or incapacity. For a discussion of the general rule, *see Jordan v. Dobbins*, 122 Mass. 168 (1877). *But see Swift & Co. v. Smigel*, 279 A.2d 895, *aff'd*, 289 A.2d 793 (N.J. App. 1972).

---

3. DIRECT AND INDIRECT REVOCATION

DICKINSON V. DODDS
Chancery Division
2 Ch.D. 463 (1876).

On Wednesday, the 10th of June, 1874, the Defendant John Dodds signed and delivered to the Plaintiff, George Dickinson, a memorandum, of which the material part was as follows:

> I hereby agree to sell to Mr. George Dickinson the whole of the dwelling-houses, garden ground, stabling, and outbuildings thereto belonging, situate at Croft, belonging to me, for the sum of £800. As witness my hand this tenth day of June, 1874.
>
> £800 /signed/ John Dodds
>
> P.S.—This offer to be left open until Friday, 9 o'clock, A.M. J.D. (the twelfth), 12th June 1874.
>
> /signed/ J. Dodds

The bill alleged that Dodds understood and intended that the Plaintiff should have until Friday 9 a.m. within which to determine whether he would or would not purchase, and that he should absolutely have until that time the refusal of the property at the price of £800, and that the Plaintiff in fact determined to accept the offer on the morning of Thursday, the

11th of June, but did not at once signify his acceptance to Dodds, believing that he had the power to accept it until 9 a.m. on the Friday.

In the afternoon of the Thursday the Plaintiff was informed by a Mr. Berry that Dodds had been offering or agreeing to sell the property to Thomas Allan, the other Defendant. Thereupon the Plaintiff, at about half-past seven in the evening, went to the house of Mrs. Burgess, the mother-in-law of Dodds, where he was then staying, and left with her a formal acceptance in writing of the offer to sell the property. According to the evidence of Mrs. Burgess this document never in fact reached Dodds, she having forgotten to give it to him.

On the following (Friday) morning, at about seven o'clock, Berry, who was acting as agent for Dickinson, found Dodds at the Darlington railway station, and handed to him a duplicate of the acceptance by Dickinson, and explained to Dodds its purport. He replied that it was too late, as he had sold the property. A few minutes later Dickinson himself found Dodds entering a railway carriage, and handed him another duplicate of the acceptance, but Dodds declined to receive it, saying, "You are too late. I have sold the property."

It appeared that on the day before, Thursday, the 11th of June, Dodds had signed a formal contract for the sale of the property to the Defendant Allan for £800, and had received from him a deposit of £40.

The bill in this suit prayed that the Defendant Dodds might be decreed specifically to perform the contract of the 10th of June, 1874; that he might be restrained from conveying the property to Allan; that Allan might be restrained from taking any such conveyance; that, if any such conveyance had been or should be made, Allan might be declared a trustee of the property for, and might be directed to convey the property to, the Plaintiff; and for damages.

The cause came on for hearing before Vice-Chancellor Bacon on the 25th of January, 1876. . . .

JAMES, LJ:

After referring to the document of the 10th of June, 1874, continued:

The document, though beginning "I hereby agree to sell," was nothing but an offer, and was only intended to be an offer, for the Plaintiff himself tells us that he required time to consider whether he would enter into an agreement or not. Unless both parties had then agreed there was no concluded agreement then made; it was in effect and substance only an offer to sell. The Plaintiff, being minded not to complete the bargain at that time, added this memorandum—"This offer to be left over until Friday, 9 o'clock A.M., 12th June, 1874." That shows it was only an offer. There was no consideration given for the undertaking or promise, to whatever extent it may be considered binding, to keep the property unsold until 9 o'clock on Friday morning; but apparently Dickinson was of opinion, and probably Dodds was of the same opinion, that he (Dodds) was bound by that promise, and could not in any way withdraw from it, or retract it, until 9 o'clock on Friday morning, and this probably explains a good deal of what afterwards took place. But it is clear settled law, on one of the clearest principles of law, that this promise, being a mere nudum pactum, was not binding, and that at any moment before a complete acceptance by Dickinson of the offer, Dodds was as free as Dickinson himself.

Well, that being the state of things, it is said that the only mode in which Dodds could assert that freedom was by actually and distinctly saying to Dickinson, "Now I withdraw my offer." It appears to me that there is neither principle nor authority for the proposition that there must be an express and actual withdrawal of the offer, or what is called a retraction. It must, to constitute a contract, appear that the two minds were at one, at the same moment of time, that is, that there was an offer continuing up to the time of the acceptance. If there was not such a continuing offer, then the acceptance comes to nothing. Of course it may well be that the one man is bound in some way or other to let the other man know that his mind with regard to the offer has been changed; but in this case, beyond all question, the Plaintiff knew that Dodds was no longer minded to sell the property to him as plainly and clearly as if Dodds had told him in so many words, "I withdraw the offer." This is evident from the Plaintiff's own statements in the bill.

The Plaintiff says in effect that, having heard and knowing that Dodds was no longer minded to sell to him, and that he was selling or had sold to some one else, thinking that he could not in point of law withdraw his offer, meaning to fix him to it, and endeavouring to bind him, "I went to the house where he was lodging, and saw his mother-in-law, and left with her an acceptance of the offer, knowing all the while that he had entirely changed his mind. I got an agent to watch for him at 7 o'clock the next morning, and I went to the train just before 9 o'clock, in order that I might catch him and give him my notice of acceptance just before 9 o'clock, and when that occurred he told my agent, and he told me, you are too late, and he then threw back the paper."

It is to my mind quite clear that before there was any attempt at acceptance by the Plaintiff, he was perfectly well aware that Dodds had changed his mind, and that he had in fact agreed to sell the property to Allan. It is impossible, therefore, to say there was ever that existence of the same mind between the two parties which is essential in point of law to the making of an agreement. I am of opinion, therefore, that the Plaintiff has failed to prove that there was any binding contract between Dodds and himself.

MELLISH, LJ:

I am of the same opinion. The first question is, whether this document of the 10th of June, 1874, which was signed by Dodds, was an agreement to sell, or only an offer to sell, the property therein mentioned to Dickinson; and I am clearly of opinion that it was only an offer, although it is in the first part of it, independently of the postscript, worded as an agreement. I apprehend that, until acceptance, so that both parties are bound, even though an instrument is so worded as to express that both parties agree, it is in point of law only an offer, and, until both parties are bound, neither party is bound. . . . Well, then, this being only an offer, the law says--and it is a perfectly clear rule of law--that, although it is said that the offer is to be left open until Friday morning at 9 o'clock, that did not bind Dodds.

He was not in point of law bound to hold the offer over until 9 o'clock on Friday morning. He was not so bound either in law or in equity. Well, that being so, when on the next day he made an agreement with Allan to sell the property to him, I am not aware of any ground on which it can be said that that contract with Allan was not as good and binding a contract as ever was made. Assuming Allan to have known (there is some dispute about it, and Allan does not admit that he knew of it, but I will assume that he did) that Dodds had made the offer to Dickinson, and had given him till Friday morning at 9 o'clock to accept it, still in point of law that could not prevent Allan from making a more favourable offer than Dickinson, and entering at once into a binding agreement with Dodds.

Then Dickinson is informed by Berry that the property has been sold by Dodds to Allan. Berry does not tell us from whom he heard it, but he says that he did hear it, that he knew it, and that he informed Dickinson of it. Now, stopping there, the question which arises is this--If an offer has been made for the sale of property, and before that offer is accepted, the person who has made the offer enters into a binding agreement to sell the property to somebody else, and the person to whom the offer was first made receives notice in some way that the property has been sold to another person, can he after that make a binding contract by the acceptance of the offer? I am of opinion that he cannot. The law may be right or wrong in saying that a person who has given to another a certain time within which to accept an offer is not bound by his promise to give that time; but, if he is not bound by that promise, and may still sell the property to some one else, and if it be the law that, in order to make a contract, the two minds must be in agreement at some one time, that is, at the time of the acceptance, how is it possible that when the person to whom the offer has been made knows that the person who has made the offer has sold the property to someone else, and that, in fact, he has not remained in the same mind to sell it to him, he can be at liberty to accept the offer and thereby make a binding contract?

It seems to me that would be simply absurd. If a man makes an offer to sell a particular horse in his stable, and says, "I will give you until the day after to-morrow to accept the offer," and the next day goes and sells the horse to somebody else, and receives the purchase-money from him, can the person to whom the offer was originally made then come and say, "I accept," so as to make a binding contract, and so as to be entitled to recover damages for the non-delivery of the horse? If the rule of law is that a mere offer to sell property, which can be withdrawn at any time, and which is made dependent on the acceptance of the person to whom it is made, is a mere nudum pactum, how is it possible that the person to whom the offer has been made can by acceptance make a binding contract after he knows that the person who has made the offer has sold the property to some one else? It is admitted law that, if a man who makes an offer dies, the offer cannot be accepted after he is dead, and parting with the property has very much the same effect as the death of the owner, for it makes the performance of the offer impossible. I am clearly of opinion that, just as when a man who has made an offer dies before it is accepted it is impossible that it can then be accepted, so when once the person to whom the offer was made knows that the property has been sold to some one else, it is too late for him to accept the offer, and on that ground I am clearly of opinion that there was no binding contract for the sale of this property by Dodds to Dickinson, and even if there had been, it seems to me that the sale of the property to Allan was first in point of time. However, it is not necessary to consider, if there had been two binding contracts, which of them would be entitled to priority in equity, because there is no binding contract between Dodds and Dickinson.

BAGGALLAY, LJ:

I entirely concur in the judgments which have been pronounced.

PETTERSON V. PATTBERG
Court of Appeals of New York
161 N.E. 428 (1928).

KELLOGG, Justice.

The evidence given upon the trial sanctions the following statement of facts: John Petterson, of whose last will and testament the plaintiff is the executrix, was the owner of a parcel of real estate in Brooklyn, known as 5301 Sixth avenue. The defendant was the owner of a bond executed by Petterson, which was secured by a third mortgage upon the parcel. On April 4th, 1924, there remained unpaid upon the principal the sum of $5,450. This amount was payable in installments of $250 on April 25th, 1924, and upon a like monthly date every three months thereafter Thus the bond and mortgage had more than five years to run before the entire sum became due. Under date of the 4th of April, 1924, the defendant wrote Petterson as follows:

> 'I hereby agree to accept cash for the mortgage which I hold against premises 5301 6th Ave., Brooklyn, N. Y. It is understood and agreed as a consideration I will allow you $780 providing said mortgage is paid on or before May 31, 1924, and the regular quarterly payment due April 25, 1924, is paid when due.'

On April 25, 1924, Petterson paid the defendant the installment of principal due on that date. Subsequently, on a day in the latter part of May, 1924, Petterson presented himself at the defendant's home, and knocked at the door. The defendant demanded the name of his caller. Petterson replied: 'It is Mr. Petterson. I have come to pay off the mortgage.' The defendant answered that he had sold the mortgage. Petterson stated that he would like to talk with the defendant, so the defendant partly opened the door. Thereupon Petterson exhibited the cash and said he was ready to pay off the mortgage according to the agreement. The defendant refused to take the money. Prior to this conversation Petterson had made a contract to sell the land to a third person free and clear of the mortgage to the defendant. Meanwhile, also, the defendant had sold the bond and mortgage to a third party. It, therefore, became necessary for Petterson to pay to such person the full amount of the bond and mortgage. It is claimed that he thereby sustained a loss of $780, the sum which the defendant agreed to allow upon the bond and mortgage if payment in full of principal, less that sum, was made on or before May 31st, 1924. The plaintiff has had a recovery for the sum thus claimed, with interest.

Clearly the defendant's letter proposed to Petterson the making of a unilateral contract, the gift of a promise in exchange for the performance of an act. The thing conditionally promised by the defendant was the reduction of the mortgage debt. The act requested to be done, in consideration of the offered promise, was payment in full of the reduced principal of the debt prior to the due date thereof. 'If an act is requested, that very act and no other must be given.' (Williston on Contracts, § 73.) 'In case of offers for a consideration, the performance of the consideration is always deemed a condition.' (Langdell's Summary of the Law of Contracts, § 4.) It is elementary that any offer to enter into a unilateral contract may be withdrawn before the act requested to be done has been performed. (Williston on Contracts, § 60; Langdell's Summary, § 4; *Offord v. Davies*, 12 C. B. [N. S.] 748.) A bidder at a sheriff's sale may revoke his bid at any time before the property is struck down to him. (*Fisher v. Seltzer*, 23 Penn. St. 308.) The offer of a reward in consideration of an act to be performed is revocable before the very act requested has been done. (*Shuey v. United States*, 92 U. S. 73; *Biggers v. Owen*, 79 Ga. 658; *Fitch v. Snedaker*, 38 N. Y. 248.) So, also, an offer to pay a broker commissions, upon a sale of land for the offeror, is revocable at any time before the land is sold, although prior to revocation the broker performs services in an effort to effectuate a sale. (*Stensgaard v. Smith*, 43 Minn. 11; *Smith v. Cauthen*, 98 Miss. 746.)

An interesting question arises when, as here, the offeree approaches the offeror with the intention of proffering performance and, before actual tender is made, the offer is withdrawn. Of such a case Williston says:

> 'The offeror may see the approach of the offeree and know that an acceptance is contemplated. If the offeror can say "I revoke" before the offeree accepts, however brief the interval of time between the two acts, there is no escape from the conclusion that the offer is terminated.' (Williston on Contracts, § 60-b.)

In this instance Petterson, standing at the door of the defendant's house, stated to the defendant that he had come to pay off the mortgage. Before a tender of the necessary moneys had been made the defendant informed Petterson that he had sold the mortgage. That was a definite notice to Petterson that the defendant could not perform his offered promise and that a tender to the defendant, who was no longer the creditor, would be ineffective to satisfy the debt. 'An offer to sell property may be withdrawn before acceptance without any formal notice to the person to whom the offer is made. It is sufficient if that person has actual knowledge that the person who made the offer has done some act inconsistent with the continuance of the offer, such as selling the property to a third person.' (*Dickinson v. Dodds*, 2 Ch. Div. 463, headnote.) To the same effect is *Coleman v. Applegarth* (68 Md. 21). Thus, it clearly appears that the defendant's offer was withdrawn before its acceptance had been tendered. It is unnecessary to determine, therefore, what the legal situation might have been had tender been made before withdrawal. It is the individual view of the writer that the same result would follow. This would be so, for the act requested to be performed was the completed act of payment, a thing incapable of performance unless assented to by the person to be paid. (Williston on Contracts, § 60-b.) Clearly an offering party has the right to name the precise act performance of which would convert his offer into a binding promise. Whatever the act may be until it is performed the offer must be revocable. However, the supposed case is not before us for decision. We think that in this particular instance the offer of the defendant was withdrawn before it became a binding promise, and, therefore, that no contract was ever made for the breach of which the plaintiff may claim damages.

The judgment of the Appellate Division and that of the Trial Term should be reversed and the complaint dismissed, with costs in all courts.

LEHMAN, J. (dissenting).

The defendant's letter to Petterson constituted a promise on his part to accept payment at a discount of the mortgage he held, provided the mortgage is paid on or before May 31st, 1924. Doubtless by the terms of the promise itself, the defendant made payment of the mortgage by the plaintiff, before the stipulated time, a condition precedent to performance by the defendant of his promise to accept payment at a discount. If the condition precedent has not been performed, it is because the defendant made performance impossible by refusing to accept payment, when the plaintiff came with an offer of immediate performance. 'It is a principle of fundamental justice that if a promisor is himself the cause of the failure of performance either of an obligation due him or of a condition upon which his own liability depends, he cannot take advantage of the failure.' (Williston on Contracts, § 677.) The question in this case is not whether payment of the mortgage is a condition precedent to the performance of a promise made by the defendant, but, rather, whether at the time the defendant refused the offer of payment, he had assumed any binding obligation, even though subject to condition.

The promise made by the defendant lacked consideration at the time it was made. Nevertheless the promise was not made as a gift or mere gratuity to the plaintiff. It was made for the purpose of obtaining from the defendant something which the plaintiff desired. It constituted an offer which was to become binding whenever the plaintiff should give, in return for the defendant's promise, exactly the consideration which the defendant requested.

Here the defendant requested no counter promise from the plaintiff. The consideration requested by the defendant for his promise to accept payment was, I agree, some act to be performed by the plaintiff. Until the act requested was performed, the defendant might undoubtedly revoke his offer. Our problem is to determine from the words of the letter read in the light of surrounding circumstances what act the defendant requested as consideration for his promise.

The defendant undoubtedly made his offer as an inducement to the plaintiff to "pay" the mortgage before it was due. Therefore, it is said, that 'the act requested to be performed was the completed act of payment, a thing incapable of performance unless assented to by the person to be paid.' In unmistakable terms the defendant agreed to accept payment, yet we are told that the defendant intended, and the plaintiff should have understood, that the act requested by the defendant, as consideration for his promise to accept payment, included performance by the defendant himself of the very promise for which the act was to be consideration. The defendant's promise was to become binding only when fully performed; and part of the consideration to be furnished by the plaintiff for the defendant's promise was to be the performance of that promise by the defendant. So construed, the defendant's promise or offer, though intended to induce action by the plaintiff, is but a snare and delusion. The plaintiff could not reasonably suppose that the defendant was asking him to procure the performance by the defendant of the very act which the defendant promised to do, yet we are told that even after the plaintiff had done all else which the defendant requested, the defendant's promise was still not binding because the defendant chose not to perform.

I cannot believe that a result so extraordinary could have been intended when the defendant wrote the letter. "The thought behind the phrase proclaims itself misread when the outcome of the reading is injustice or absurdity." (See opinion of CARDOZO, Ch. J., in *Surace v. Danna*, 248 N. Y. 18.) If the defendant intended to induce payment by the plaintiff and yet reserve the right to refuse payment when offered he should have used a phrase better calculated to express his meaning than the words: "I agree to accept." A promise to accept payment, by its very terms, must necessarily become binding, if at all, not later than when a present offer to pay is made.

I recognize that in this case only an offer of payment, and not a formal tender of payment, was made before the defendant withdrew his offer to accept payment. Even the plaintiff's part in the act of payment was then not technically complete. Even so, under a fair construction of the words of the letter I think the plaintiff had done the act which the defendant requested as consideration for his promise. The plaintiff offered to pay with present intention and ability to make that payment. A formal tender is seldom made in business transactions, except to lay the foundation for subsequent assertion in a court of justice of rights which spring from refusal of the tender. If the defendant acted in good faith in making his offer to accept payment, he could not well have intended to draw a distinction in the act requested of the plaintiff in return, between an offer which unless refused would ripen into completed payment, and a formal tender. Certainly the defendant could not have expected or intended that the plaintiff would make a formal tender of payment without first stating that he had come to make payment. We should not read into the language of the defendant's offer a meaning which would prevent enforcement of the defendant's promise after it had been accepted by the plaintiff in the very way which the defendant must have intended it should be accepted, if he acted in good faith.

The judgment should be affirmed.

---

4. COUNTER-OFFER AND REJECTION

LIVINGSTONE V. EVANS
Alberta Supreme Court
3 W.W.R. 453, 4 D.L.R. 769 (1925).

Walsh, Justice.

The defendant, Thomas J. Evans, through his agent, wrote to the plaintiff offering to sell him the land in question for $1,800 on terms. On the day that he received this offer the plaintiff wired this agent as follows:

'Send lowest cash price. Will give $1,600 cash. Wire.'

The agent replied to this by telegram as follows:

'Cannot reduce price.'

Immediately upon the receipt of this telegram the plaintiff wrote accepting the offer. It is admitted by the defendants that this offer and the plaintiff's acceptance of it constitute a contract for the sale of this land to the plaintiff by which he is bound unless the intervening telegrams above set out put an end to his offer so that the plaintiff could not thereafter bind him to it by his acceptance of it.

It is quite clear that when an offer has been rejected it is thereby ended and it cannot be afterwards accepted without the consent of him who made it. The simple question and the only one argued before me is whether the plaintiff's counter offer was in law a rejection of the defendant's offer which freed him from it.

Hyde v. Wrench, 3 Beav. 334 (49 E.R. 132) a judgment of Lord Langdale, M.R. pronounced in 1840 is the authority for the contention that it was. The defendant offered to sell for L 1,000. The plaintiff met that with an offer to pay L 950 and (to quote from the judgment) 'he thereby rejected the offer previously made by the Defendant. I think that it was not afterwards competent for him to revive the proposal of the Defendant, by tendering an acceptance of it.'

Stevenson v. McLean, 5 Q.B.D. 346, 49 L.J.Q.B. 701, 42 L.T. 897, 28 W.R. 916, a later case relied upon by Mr. Grant is easily distinguishable from Hyde v. Wrench as it is in fact distinguished by Lush, J. who decided it. He held that the letter there relied upon as constituting a rejection of the offer was not a new proposal but a mere enquiry which should have been answered and not treated as a rejection but the learned Judge said that if it had contained an offer it would have likened the case to Hyde v. Wrench.

Hyde v. Wrench has stood without question for 85 years. It is adopted by the text writers as a correct exposition of the law and is generally accepted and recognized as such. I think it not too much to say that it has firmly established it as a part of the law of contracts that the making of a counter-offer is a rejection of the original offer.

The plaintiff's telegram was undoubtedly a counter-offer. True, it contained an inquiry as well but that clearly was one which called for an answer only if the counter-offer was rejected. In substance it said, "I will give you $1,600 cash. If you won't take that wire your lowest cash price." In my opinion it put an end to the defendant's liability under his offer unless it was revived by his telegram in reply to it.

The real difficulty in the case, to my mind, arises out of the defendant's telegram "cannot reduce price." If this was simply a rejection of the plaintiff's counter-offer it amounts to nothing. If, however, it was a renewal of the original offer it gave the plaintiff the right to bind the defendant to it by his subsequent acceptance of it.

With some doubt I think that it was a renewal of the original offer or at any rate an intimation to the plaintiff that he was still willing to treat on the basis of it. It was, of course, a reply to the counter-offer and to the inquiry in the plaintiff's telegram. But it was more than that. The price referred to in it was unquestionably that mentioned in his letter. His statement that he could not reduce that price strikes me as having but one meaning, namely, that he was still standing by it and, therefore, still open to accept it.

There is support for this view in a judgment of the Ontario Appellate Division which I have found, In re Cowan and Boyd, 49 O.L.R. 335, 61 D.L.R. 497. That was a landlord and tenant matter. The landlord wrote the tenant offering a renewal lease at an increased rent. The tenant replied that he was paying as high a rent as he should and if the landlord would not renew at the present rental he would like an early reply as he purposed buying a house. To this the landlord replied simply saying that he would call on the tenant between two certain named dates. Before he called and without any further communication between them the tenant wrote accepting the landlord's original offer. The County Court Judge before whom the matter first came held that the tenant's reply to the landlord's offer was not a counter-offer but a mere request to modify its terms. The Appellate Division did not decide that question though from the ground on which it put its judgment it must have disagreed with the Judge below. It sustained his judgment, however, on the ground that the landlord's letter promising to call on the tenant left open the original offer for further discussion so that the tenant had the right thereafter to accept it as he did.

The landlord's letter in that case was, to my mind, much more unconvincing evidence of his willingness to stand by his original offer in the face of the tenant's rejection of it than is the telegram of the defendant in this case. That is the judgment of a very strong Court, the reasons for which were written by the late Chief Justice Meredith. If it is sound, and it is not for me to question it, a fortiori must I be right in the conclusion to which I have come.

I am, therefore, of the opinion that there was a binding contract for the sale of this land to the plaintiff of which he is entitled to specific performance. It was admitted by his counsel that if I reached this conclusion his subsequent agreement to sell the land to the defendant Williams would be of no avail as against the plaintiff's contract.

There will, therefore, be judgment for specific performance with a declaration that the plaintiff's rights under his contract have priority over those of the defendant Williams under his. The plaintiff will have his costs as agreed by the case. It is silent as to the scale but unless otherwise agreed they should be under column 3.

NOTES AND QUESTIONS:

1. *See* Restatement (Second) of Contracts §§ 35 (The Offeree's Power of Acceptance), 36 (Methods of Termination of the Power of Acceptance), 38 (Rejection), 39 (Counter-Offers), 40 (Time When Rejection or Counter-Offer Terminates the Power of Acceptance), 41 (Lapse of Time), 42 (Revocation by Communication from Offeror Received by Offeree), 43 (Indirect Communication of Revocation) (1981).

---

5. UNIFORM COMMERCIAL CODE AND THE BATTLE OF THE FORMS

NEW YORK UNIFORM COMMERCIAL CODE
§ 2-207. ADDITIONAL TERMS IN ACCEPTANCE OR CONFIRMATION
N.Y. U.C.C. LAW § 2-207 (2012).

(1) A definite and seasonable expression of acceptance or a written confirmation which is sent within a reasonable time operates as an acceptance even though it states terms additional to or different from those offered or agreed upon, unless acceptance is expressly made conditional on assent to the additional or different terms.

(2) The additional terms are to be construed as proposals for addition to the contract. Between merchants such terms become part of the contract unless:

(a) the offer expressly limits acceptance to the terms of the offer;

(b) they materially alter it; or

(c) notification of objection to them has already been given or is given within a reasonable time after notice of them is received.

(3) Conduct by both parties which recognizes the existence of a contract is sufficient to establish a contract for sale although the writings of the parties do not otherwise establish a contract. In such case the terms of the particular contract consist of those terms on which the writings of the parties agree, together with any supplementary terms incorporated under any other provisions of this Act.

C. ITOH & CO. (AMERICA) INC. V. THE JORDAN INTERNATIONAL CO.
United States Court of Appeals, Seventh Circuit
552 F.2d 1228, (1977).

SPRECHER, Circuit Judge.

The sole issue on this appeal is whether the district court properly denied a stay of the proceedings pending arbitration under Section 3 of the Federal Arbitration Act, 9 U.S.C. § 3.

I

C. Itoh & Co. (America) Inc. ("Itoh") submitted a purchase order dated August 15, 1974 for a certain quantity of steel coils to the Jordan International Company ("Jordan"). In response, Jordan sent its acknowledgment form dated August 19, 1974. On the face of Jordan's form, the following statement appears:

"Seller's acceptance is, however, expressly conditional on Buyer's assent to the additional or different terms and conditions set forth below and printed on the reverse side. If these terms and conditions are not acceptable, Buyer should notify seller at once."

One of the terms on the reverse side of Jordan's form was a broad provision for arbitration. Itoh neither expressly assented nor objected to the additional arbitration term in Jordan's form until the instant litigation.

Itoh also entered into a contract to sell the steel coils that it purchased from Jordan to Riverview Steel Corporation, Inc. ("Riverview"). The contract between Itoh and Riverview contained an arbitration term which provided in pertinent part:

"Any and all controversies arising out of or relating to this contract, or any modification, breach or cancellation thereof, except as to quality, shall be settled by arbitration. . . ."

After the steel had been delivered by Jordan and paid for by Itoh, Riverview advised Itoh that the steel coils were defective and did not conform to the standards set forth in the agreement between Itoh and Riverview; for these reasons, Riverview refused to pay Itoh for the steel. Consequently, Itoh brought the instant suit against Riverview and Jordan. Itoh alleged that Riverview had wrongfully refused to pay for the steel; as affirmative defenses, Riverview claimed that the steel was defective and that tender was improper since delivery was late. Itoh alleged that Jordan had sold Itoh defective steel and had made a late delivery of that steel.

Jordan then filed a motion in the district court requesting a stay of the proceedings pending arbitration under Section 3 of the Federal Arbitration Act, 9 U.S.C. § 3. The district court concluded that, as between Itoh and Riverview, the issue of whether the steel coils were defective was not referable to arbitration because of the "quality" exclusion in the arbitration provision of the contract between Itoh and Riverview. Since arbitration would not necessarily resolve all the issues raised by the parties, the district court, apparently assuming arguendo that there existed an agreement in writing between Jordan and Itoh to arbitrate their dispute, denied the stay pending arbitration. In the district court's opinion, sound judicial administration required that the entire litigation be resolved in a single forum; since some of the issues those relating to quality between Itoh and Riverview were not referable to arbitration, this goal could only be accomplished in the judicial forum.

It is from this denial of a stay pending arbitration that Jordan appeals.

II

Our inquiry begins with the question of whether, assuming arguendo that there existed an agreement in writing between Jordan and Itoh to arbitrate their dispute, the district court had the discretion under Section 3 of the Federal Arbitration Act, 9 U.S.C. § 3, to deny Jordan's request for a stay pending arbitration of that dispute on the ground that sound judicial administration requires resolution of the entire lawsuit in a single forum and at least some of the disputed issues between Itoh and Riverview were not referable to arbitration.

Section 3 of the federal statute provides:

> If any suit or proceeding be brought in any of the courts of the United States upon any issue referable to arbitration under an agreement in writing for such arbitration, the court in which such suit is pending, upon being satisfied that the issue involved in such suit or proceeding is referable to arbitration under such an agreement, shall on application of one of the parties stay the trial of the action until such arbitration has been had in accordance with the terms of the agreement, providing the applicant for the stay is not in default in proceeding with such arbitration.

The use of the word "shall" rather than "may" in Section 3 indicates that a district court, when presented with an application for a stay of proceedings pending arbitration, must grant the requested stay where two conditions are satisfied: (1) the issue is one which is referable to arbitration under an agreement in writing for such arbitration, and (2) the party applying for the stay is not in default in proceeding with such arbitration. . . .

III

Having concluded that the district court had no discretion under Section 3 of the Federal Arbitration Act, 9 U.S.C. § 3, to deny Jordan's timely application for a stay of the action pending arbitration if there existed an agreement in writing for such arbitration between Jordan and Itoh, the remaining issue is whether there existed such an agreement.

The pertinent facts may be briefly restated. Itoh sent its purchase order for steel coils to Jordan which contained no provision for arbitration. Subsequently, Jordan sent Itoh its acknowledgment form which included, inter alia, a broad arbitration term on the reverse side of the form. On the front of Jordan's form, the following statement also appears:

"Seller's acceptance is . . . expressly conditioned on Buyer's assent to the additional or different terms and conditions set forth below and printed on the reverse side. If these terms and conditions are not acceptable, Buyer should notify Seller at once."

After the exchange of documents, Jordan delivered and Itoh paid for the steel coils. Itoh never expressly assented or objected to the additional arbitration term in Jordan's form.

. . . . Jordan's argument is that the exchange of forms between itself and Itoh created a contract, which includes the additional arbitration term in Jordan's form.

The instant case, therefore, involves the classic "battle of the forms," and Section 2-207, not Section 2-201, furnishes the rules for resolving such a controversy. Hence, it is to Section 2-207 that we must look to determine whether a contract has been formed by the exchange of forms between Jordan and Itoh and, if so, whether the additional arbitration term in Jordan's form is to be included in that contract. See, e. g., Application of Doughboy Industries, Inc., 17 A.D.2d 216, 233 N.Y.S.2d 488 (1962); In re Tunis Manufacturing Corp., 20 UCC Rep.Serv. 284 (N.Y.Sup.Ct.1976); Tunis Manufacturing Corp. v. Mystic Mills, Inc., 40 A.D.2d 664, 337 N.Y.S.2d 150 (1972); In re Barclay Knitwear Co., 8 UCC Rep.Serv. 44 (N.Y.Sup.Ct.1970); Construction Aggregates Corp. v. Hewitt-Robins, Inc., 404 F.2d 505

(7th Cir. 1968); Valmont Industries, Inc. v. Mitsui & Co., 419 F.Supp. 1238 (D.Neb.1976); Just Born, Inc. v. Stein, Hall & Co., 13 UCC Rep.Serv. 431, 59 Pa.D&C 407 (1971); Air Products & Chemicals, Inc. v. Fairbanks Morse, Inc., 58 Wis.2d 193, 206 N.W.2d 414 (1973).

IV

Section 2-207, Additional Terms in Acceptance or Confirmation, provides:

> (1) A definite and seasonable expression of acceptance or a written confirmation which is sent within a reasonable time operates as an acceptance even though it states terms additional to or different from those offered or agreed upon, unless acceptance is expressly made conditional on assent to the additional or different terms.
>
> (2) The additional terms are to be construed as proposals for addition to the contract. Between merchants such terms become part of the contract unless:
>
> (a) the offer expressly limits acceptance to the terms of the offer;
>
> (b) they materially alter it; or
>
> (c) notification of objection to them has already been given or is given within a reasonable time after notice of them is received.
>
> (3) Conduct by both parties which recognizes the existence of a contract is sufficient to establish a contract for sale although the writings of the parties do not otherwise establish a contract. In such case the terms of the particular contract consist of those terms on which the writings of the parties agree, together with any supplementary terms incorporated under any other provisions of this Act.

Under Section 2-207 it is necessary to first determine whether a contract has been formed under Section 2-207(1) as a result of the exchange of forms between Jordan and Itoh.

At common law, "an acceptance . . . which contained terms additional to . . . those of the offer . . . constituted a rejection of the offer . . . and thus became a counter-offer." Dorton, supra, at 1166. Thus, the mere presence of the additional arbitration term in Jordan's acknowledgment form would, at common law, have prevented the exchange of documents between Jordan and Itoh from creating a contract, and Jordan's form would have automatically become a counter-offer.

Section 2-207(1) was intended to alter this inflexible common law approach to offer and acceptance:

> This section of the Code recognizes that in current commercial transactions, the terms of the offer and those of the acceptance will seldom be identical. Rather, under the current "battle of the forms," each party typically has a printed form

> drafted by his attorney and containing as many terms as could be envisioned to favor that party in his sales transactions. Whereas under common law the disparity between the fine-print terms in the parties' forms would have prevented the consummation of a contract when these forms are exchanged, Section 2-207 recognizes that in many, but not all, cases the parties do not impart such significance to the terms on the printed forms. . . . Thus, under Subsection (1), a contract . . . [may be] recognized notwithstanding the fact that an acceptance . . . contains terms additional to . . . those of the offer . . . .

Id. at 1166. See also Comment 2 to Section 2-207; Air Products & Chemicals, supra; John Thallon, supra. And it is now well-settled that the mere presence of an additional term, such as a provision for arbitration, in one of the parties' forms will not prevent the formation of a contract under Section 2-207(1). See, e. g., Dorton, supra; Valmont Industries, supra; Just Born, supra; John Thallon, supra; In re Barclay Knitwear Co., supra; In re Tunis Manufacturing Corp., supra; Mystic Mills, supra; Air Products & Chemicals, supra.

However, while Section 2-207(1) constitutes a sharp departure from the common law "mirror image" rule, there remain situations where the inclusion of an additional term in one of the forms exchanged by the parties will prevent the consummation of a contract under that section. Section 2-207(1) contains a proviso which operates to prevent an exchange of forms from creating a contract where "acceptance is expressly made conditional on assent to the additional . . . terms." In the instant case, Jordan's acknowledgment form contained the following statement:

> Seller's acceptance is . . . expressly conditional on Buyer's assent to the additional or different terms and conditions set forth below and printed on the reverse side. If these terms and conditions are not acceptable, Buyer should notify Seller at once.

The arbitration provision at issue on this appeal is printed on the reverse side of Jordan's acknowledgment, and there is no dispute that Itoh never expressly assented to the challenged arbitration term.

The Court of Appeals for the Sixth Circuit has held that the proviso must be construed narrowly:

> Although . . . [seller's] use of the words "subject to" suggests that the acceptances were conditional to some extent, we do not believe the acceptances were "expressly made conditional on [the buyer's] assent to the additional or different terms," as specifically required under the Subsection 2-207(1) proviso. In order to fall within this proviso, it is not enough that an acceptance is expressly conditional on additional or different terms; rather, an acceptance must be expressly conditional on the offeror's assent to those terms.

Dorton, supra, at 1168. In Construction Aggregates Corp. v. Hewitt-Robins, Inc., 404 F.2d 505 (7th Cir. 1968), this court found that an acceptance came within the ambit of the Section 2-207(1) proviso even though the language employed in the acceptance did not precisely track that of the proviso. Under either Construction Aggregates or Dorton, however, it is clear that the statement contained in Jordan's acknowledgment form comes within the Section 2-207(1) proviso.

Hence, the exchange of forms between Jordan and Itoh did not result in the formation of a contract under Section 2-207(1), and Jordan's form became a counteroffer. "(T)he consequence of a clause conditioning acceptance on assent to the additional or different terms is that as of the exchanged writings, there is no contract. Either party may at this point in their dealings walk away from the transaction." Duesenberg & King, supra, § 3.06(3) at 73. However, neither Jordan nor Itoh elected to follow that course; instead, both parties proceeded to performance-Jordan by delivering and Itoh by paying for the steel coils.

At common law, the "terms of the counter-offer were said to have been accepted by the original offeror when he proceeded to perform under the contract without objecting to the counter-offer." Dorton, supra, at 1166. Thus, under pre-Code law, Itoh's performance (i. e., payment for the steel coils) probably constituted acceptance of the Jordan counter-offer, including its provision for arbitration. However, a different approach is required under the Code.

Section 2-207(3) of the Code first provides that "[c]onduct by both parties which recognizes the existence of a contract is sufficient to establish a contract for sale although the writings of the parties do not otherwise establish a contract." As the court noted in Dorton, supra, at 1166:

> [W]hen no contract is recognized under Subsection 2-207(1) . . . the entire transaction aborts at this point. If, however, the subsequent conduct of the parties particularly, performance by both parties under what they apparently believe to be a contract recognizes the existence of a contract, under Subsection 2-207(3) such conduct by both parties is sufficient to establish a contract, notwithstanding the fact that no contract would have been recognized on the basis of their writings alone.

Thus, "[s]ince . . . [Itoh's] purchase order and . . . [Jordan's] counter-offer did not in themselves create a contract, Section 2-207(3) would operate to create one because the subsequent performance by both parties constituted 'conduct by both parties which recognizes the existence of a contract.'" Construction Aggregates, supra, at 509.

What are the terms of a contract created by conduct under Section 2-207(3) rather than by an exchange of forms under Section 2-207(1)? As noted above, at common law the terms of the contract between Jordan and Itoh would be the terms of the Jordan counter-offer. However, the Code has effectuated a radical departure from the common law rule. The second sentence of Section 2-207(3) provides that where, as here, a contract has been consummated by the conduct of the parties, "the terms of the particular contract consist of those terms on which the writings of the parties agree, together with any supplementary terms incorporated under any other provisions of this Act." Since it is clear that the Jordan and Itoh forms do not "agree" on arbitration, the only question which remains under the Code is whether arbitration may be considered a supplementary term incorporated under some other provision of the Code.

We have been unable to find any case authority shedding light on the question of what constitutes "supplementary terms" within the meaning of Section 2-207(3) and the Official Comments to Section 2-207 provide no guidance in this regard. We are persuaded, however, that the disputed additional terms (i.e., those terms on which the writings of the parties do not agree) which are necessarily excluded from a Subsection (3) contract by the language, "terms on which the writings of the parties agree," cannot be brought back into the contract under the guise of "supplementary terms." This conclusion has substantial support among the commentators who have addressed themselves to the issue. As two noted authorities on Article Two of the Code have stated:

> It will usually happen that an offeree-seller who returns an acknowledgment form will also concurrently or shortly thereafter ship the goods. If the responsive document [sent by the seller] contains a printed assent clause, and the goods are shipped and accepted, Subsection (3) of Section 2-207 comes into play. . . . [T]he terms on which the exchanged communications do not agree drop out of the transaction, and reference to the Code is made to supply necessary terms. . . . Rather than choosing the terms of one party over those of the other . . . it compels supplying missing terms by reference to the Code. . . .

Duesenberg & King, supra, § 3.06(4) at 73-74. Similarly, Professors White and Summers have concluded that "contract formation under subsection (3) gives neither party the relevant terms of his document, but fills out the contract with the standardized provisions of Article Two." White & Summers, supra, at 29.

Accordingly, we find that the "supplementary terms" contemplated by Section 2-207(3) are limited to those supplied by the standardized "gap-filler" provisions of Article Two. See, e. g., Section 2-308(a) ("Unless otherwise agreed . . . the place for delivery of goods is the seller's place of business or if he has none his residence"); Section 2-309(1) ("The time for shipment or delivery or any other action under a contract if not . . . agreed upon shall be a reasonable time"); Section 2-310(a) ("Unless otherwise agreed . . . payment is due at the time and place at which the buyer is to receive the goods even though the place of shipment is the place of delivery"). Since provision for arbitration is not a necessary or missing term which would be supplied by one of the Code's "gap-filler" provisions unless agreed upon by the contracting parties, there is no arbitration term in the Section 2-207(3) contract which was created by the conduct of Jordan and Itoh in proceeding to perform even though no contract had been established by their exchange of writings.

We are convinced that this conclusion does not result in any unfair prejudice to a seller who elects to insert in his standard sales acknowledgement form the statement that acceptance is expressly conditional on buyer's assent to additional terms contained therein. Such a seller obtains a substantial benefit under Section 2-207(1) through the inclusion of an "expressly conditional" clause. If he decides after the exchange of forms that the particular transaction is not in his best interest, Subsection (1) permits him to walk away from the transaction without incurring any liability so long as the buyer has not in the interim expressly assented to the additional terms. Moreover, whether or not a seller will be disadvantaged under Subsection (3) as a consequence of inserting an "expressly conditional" clause in his standard form is within his control. If the seller in fact does not intend to close a particular deal unless the additional terms are assented to, he can protect himself by not delivering the goods until such assent is forthcoming. If the seller does intend to close a deal irrespective of whether or not the buyer assents to the additional terms, he can hardly complain when the contract formed under Subsection (3) as a result of the parties' conduct is held not to include those terms. Although a seller who employs such an "expressly conditional" clause in his acknowledgement form would undoubtedly appreciate the dual advantage of not being bound to a contract under Subsection (1) if he elects not to perform and of having his additional terms imposed on the buyer under Subsection (3) in the event that performance is in his best interest, we do not believe such a result is contemplated by Section 2-207. Rather, while a seller may take advantage of an "expressly conditional" clause under Subsection (1) when he elects not to perform, he must accept the potential risk under Subsection (3) of not getting his additional terms when he elects to proceed with performance without first obtaining buyer's assent to those terms. Since the seller injected ambiguity into the transaction by inserting the "expressly conditional" clause in his form, he, and not the buyer, should bear the consequence of that ambiguity under Subsection (3).

Moreover, even were we to assume arguendo that, in a simple diversity case, a disputed additional term, while not becoming part of a Section 2-207(3) contract as a consequence of the writings exchanged by the parties (which is clearly precluded by the language of Subsection (3)), could be brought into that contract as a "supplementary term" by implication from custom and usage, the district court's denial of the stay application must still be affirmed. After the Supreme Court's decision in Prima Paint, supra, it is clear that "this action is not a simple diversity suit, but involves federal rights asserted under the Federal Arbitration Act." Commonwealth Edison Co. v. Gulf Oil Corp., 541 F.2d 1263 (7th Cir. 1976). Accordingly, "(f)ederal courts are bound to apply rules enacted by Congress with respect to matters here, a contract involving commerce over which it has legislative power." Prima Paint, supra, 388 U.S. at 406, 87 S.Ct. at 1807. Under Section 3 of the Federal Arbitration Act, 9 U.S.C. § 3, federal district courts may issue a stay order only where there is an agreement in writing for arbitration. While the arbitration provision need not be signed to come within Section 3, the Act requires that there be a written agreement to arbitrate. See Fisser v. International Bank, 282 F.2d 231 (2d Cir. 1960). As noted above, there is no written arbitration provision included in the contract created under Section 2-207(3) when Jordan and Itoh proceeded to performance.

Accordingly, for the reasons stated in this opinion, the decision of the district court is affirmed.

---

6. PRESERVATION OF THE POWER OF ACCEPTANCE

BEALL V. BEALL
Court of Special Appeals of Maryland
413 A.2d 1365 (1980).

MOORE, Judge.

. . . .

I

In 1968, the plaintiff, Carlton G. Beall, purchased a farm in Prince George's County from Pearl Beall. At that time, the property was farmed by Pearl's son, Calvin Beall. The record discloses that Carlton, the plaintiff, and Calvin were second cousins. Calvin was married to Cecelia M. Beall, the defendant herein. Carlton agreed that Calvin could continue to farm the property if he would pay the annual property taxes. Calvin and Cecelia owned and resided on a parcel of about one-half acre that was bordered on three sides by the farm bought by the plaintiff; and it is that parcel that is the subject of this dispute.

On the day that plaintiff contracted to buy Pearl's farm, he obtained a three-year option to purchase Calvin's and Cecelia's parcel for $28,000.00. The option recited a consideration of $100.00 which was paid by check. In 1971, the parties executed a new option, for five years, but on the same terms and reciting an additional $100.00 consideration.

This 1971 option was never exercised by the plaintiff, but prior to its expiration the following language was appended at the bottom of the page:

> As of October 6, 1975, we, Calvin E. Beall and Cecelia M. Beall, agree to continue this option agreement three more years Feb. 1, 1976 to Feb. 1, 1979.
> /s/ Calvin E. Beall
>
> /s/ Cecelia M. Beall.

It is this purported extension that forms the basis for plaintiff's bill of complaint seeking specific performance of the agreement. Calvin died in August 1977, and Cecelia now holds the fee simple title by right of survivorship. In letters dated May 24, 1978 and September 14, 1978, the plaintiff advised Cecelia that he was electing to exercise the option. He scheduled settlement for October 5, 1978. As the chancellor found:

> It is undisputed in this case that Mr. Carlton Beall did eventually hire attorneys to search the title, set a settlement date, attend the settlement, and was ready, willing and able to perform the contract.

Cecelia refused to attend settlement, and this suit for specific performance ensued.

At trial, after plaintiff presented his evidence, Cecelia moved to dismiss the bill of complaint. The chancellor granted the motion because she felt that the option agreements were not supported by consideration in that "no benefit . . . flowed to Cecelia Beall." In addition, as to the 1975 alleged option, the chancellor ruled:

> [T]here is no consideration recited in that extension or purported extension of the original option contract. And the one extension that had occurred in the interim, even then would also fail because there is no consideration stated in the extension. It is clear that consideration must pass for the extension each time, in some form of consideration. None is stated within the written four lines.

On appeal, the plaintiff contends that the chancellor erred in dismissing the bill of complaint and in excluding certain testimony relative to oral transactions with Calvin, the deceased husband of the defendant.

II

Under Maryland law it is clear that "an option is not a mere offer to sell, which can be withdrawn by the optionor at any time before acceptance, but a binding agreement if supported by consideration." Blondell v. Turover, 195 Md. 251, 256, 72 A.2d 697, 699 (1950). In other words, an option is an agreement to keep an offer open that requires consideration to give it its irrevocable character. Goldman v. Connecticut General Life Insurance Co., 251 Md. 575, 581, 248 A.2d 154, 158 (1968). Once the option is exercised by the optionee a binding contract is created that may be enforced through a decree commanding specific performance. Diggs v. Siomporas, 248 Md. 677, 681, 237 A.2d 725, 727 (1968); Blondell v. Turover, supra, 195 Md. at 256, 72 A.2d at 699. It is apparent, then, that an option must be supported by consideration in order to be irrevocable for the period provided in the option.

When, however, the consideration allegedly supporting an option fails or is nonexistent, the option is no longer irrevocable but rather it becomes "a mere offer to sell, which can be withdrawn by the optionor at any time before acceptance . . . ." Blondell v. Turover, supra, 195 Md. at 256, 72 A.2d at 699. The failure of consideration destroys the irrevocability of the option; it nonetheless retains its essential characteristic as an offer to buy or sell for the period stated in the option or until revoked. It has been recognized that equity will enforce a resulting contract despite lack of consideration for the option:

> While the rule that equity will enforce a contract consummated by the acceptance of an option within the time and upon the terms of the option is often stated in such a way as to suggest or imply the necessity of consideration for the option, all that is meant in most cases is that a consideration is necessary to prevent the defendant from asserting his withdrawal of the option before its acceptance by the plaintiff and before the expiration of the time fixed in the option within which acceptance could be made.

71 Am.Jur.2d, Specific Performance § 143 (1973)(footnotes omitted). See 1A Corbin on Contracts § 263 (1963). See generally Kahn v. General Development Corp., 40 Del.Ch. 83, 92, 174 A.2d 307, 312 (1961) (failure of consideration "destroyed the irrevocability of the option"). Burkhead v. Farlow, 266 N.C. 595, 597, 146 S.E.2d 802, 804 (1966) (option without consideration was "mere offer to sell which defendants might have withdrawn at any time before acceptance"); Rose v. Minis, 41 N.J.Super. 538, 543, 125 A.2d 535, 538 (1956) (option which is mere offer is "simply a naked revocable authority").

Assuming, arguendo, that the 1975 option was unsupported by consideration, it remained as an offer to sell the parcel for $28,000. The offer was open until February 1, 1979, but it was revocable at any time by action of Calvin and Cecelia Beall. As stated in the case of Holifield v. Veterans' Farm & Home Board, 218 Miss. 446, 450, 67 So.2d 456, 457 (1953):

> It is well settled that an option is not binding as a contract where there is no consideration, unless it is accepted within the time limit and before the offer is withdrawn. Since there was no consideration paid by the Veterans' Farm and Home Board and Mauldin for the option, it could have been revoked by the Holifields at any time before the Veterans' Farm and Home Board and Mauldin notified them that they intended to buy the land; but since the offer was accepted within the time limit and before withdrawal, the contract became binding upon all parties as it was thereafter supported by the consideration of the mutual promises.

This statement is generally in accord with the Maryland cases, supra.

The chancellor should, therefore, have determined whether or not there was a valid, unrevoked offer to sell the property in dispute and whether or not there was a proper acceptance of that offer sufficient to create a contract specifically enforceable in equity.[1] These issues of offer and acceptance primarily involve factual determinations that initially must be evaluated by the chancellor. As an appellate court, we are limited to a review of the chancellor's findings under the "clearly erroneous" standard. Md. Rule 1086. But our review is dependent upon the existence of factual findings on the issues material to the case. Such findings were not made below.

It was error for the chancellor to dismiss plaintiff's bill of complaint at the close of his case. A new trial, in accordance with this opinion, is necessitated.

ORDER REVERSED; CAUSE REMANDED FOR A NEW TRIAL IN ACCORDANCE WITH THIS OPINION; COSTS TO ABIDE THE FINAL RESULT.

---

[1] We express no opinion concerning the validity of the chancellor's finding that there was no consideration for the option.

RAGOSTA V. WILDER JR.
Supreme Court of Vermont
592 A.2d 367 (1991).

PECK, Justice.

. . . .

In 1985, plaintiffs became interested in purchasing "The Fork Shop" from defendant, but preliminary negotiations between the parties were fruitless. In 1987, plaintiffs learned that defendant was again considering selling the "The Fork Shop," mailed him a letter offering to purchase the property along with a check for $2,000 and began arrangements to obtain the necessary financing. By letter dated September 28, 1987, defendant returned the $2,000 check explaining that he had two properties "up for sale" and that he would not sign an acceptance to plaintiffs' offer because "that would tie up both these properties until [there was] a closing." In the letter, he also made the following counter-offer:

> I will sell you The Fork Shop and its property as listed in book 35, at page 135 of the Brookfield Land Records on 17 April 1972, for $88,000.00 (Eighty-eight thousand dollars), at anytime up until the 1st of November 1987 that you appear with me at the Randolph National Bank with said sum. At which time they will give you a certified deed to this property or to your agent as directed, providing said property has not been sold.

On October 1st, the date plaintiffs received the letter, they called defendant. The court found that during the conversation plaintiffs told defendant that "the terms and conditions of his offer were acceptable and that they would in fact prepare to accept the offer." Defendant assured plaintiffs that there was no one else currently interested in purchasing "The Fork Shop."

On October 6th, plaintiffs informed defendant that they would not close the sale on October 8th as discussed previously but that they would come to Vermont on October 10th. On October 8th, defendant called plaintiffs and informed them that he was no longer willing to sell "The Fork Shop." The trial court found that, at that time, defendant was aware plaintiffs "had processed their loan application and were prepared to close." Plaintiffs informed defendant that they would be at the Randolph National Bank at 10:00 a.m. on October 15th with the $88,000 purchase price and in fact appeared. Defendant did not. Plaintiffs claim they incurred $7,499.23 in loan closing costs.

Plaintiffs sued for specific performance arguing that defendant had contracted to sell the property to them. They alleged moreover that defendant knew they would have to incur costs to obtain financing for the purchase but assured them that the sale would go through and that they relied on his assurances.

The trial court concluded that defendant "made an offer in writing which could only be accepted by performance prior to the deadline." It concluded further that defendant could not revoke his offer on October 8th because plaintiffs, relying on the offer, had already begun performance and that defendant should be estopped from revoking the offer on a theory of equitable estoppel. It ordered defendant to convey to plaintiffs "The Fork Shop" for $88,000. This appeal followed.

I.

Plaintiffs claim that defendant's letter of September 28, 1987 created a contract to sell "The Fork Shop" to them unless the property was sold to another buyer. Rather, defendant's letter contains an offer to sell the property for $88,000, which the trial court found could only be accepted "by performance prior to the deadline," and a promise to keep the offer open unless the property were sold to another buyer. Defendant received no consideration for either promise. In fact, defendant returned plaintiffs' check for $2,000 which would have constituted consideration for the promise to keep the offer open, presumably because he did not wish to make a firm offer. Thus, the promise to keep the offer to sell open was not enforceable and, absent the operation of equitable estoppel, defendant could revoke the offer to sell the property at any time before plaintiffs accepted it. See *Buchannon v. Billings,* 127 Vt. 69, 75, 238 A.2d 638, 642 (1968) ("An option is a continuing offer, and *if supported by a consideration,* it cannot be withdrawn before the time limit.") (emphasis added).

Plaintiffs argue that the actions they undertook to obtain financing, which were detrimental to them, could constitute consideration for the promise to keep the offer to sell open. Their argument is unconvincing. Although plaintiffs are correct in stating that a detriment may constitute consideration, they ignore the rule that "[t]o constitute consideration, a performance or a return promise must be bargained for." Restatement (Second) of Contracts § 71(1) (1981). "A performance or return promise is bargained for if it is sought by the promisor in exchange for his promise and is given by the promisee in exchange for that promise." *Id.* at § 71(2). Plaintiffs began to seek financing even before defendant made a definite offer to sell the property. Whatever detriment they suffered was not in exchange for defendant's promise to keep the offer to sell open.

The trial court ruled that the offer to sell "The Fork Shop" could only be accepted by performance but concluded that in obtaining financing plaintiffs began performance and that therefore defendant could not revoke the offer to sell once plaintiffs incurred the cost of obtaining financing. Section 45 of the Restatement (Second) of Contracts provides that "[w]here an offer invites an offeree to accept by rendering a performance and does not invite a promissory acceptance, an option contract is created when the offeree tenders or begins the invited performance or tenders a beginning of it." However, "[w]hat is begun or tendered must be part of the actual performance invited in order to preclude revocation under this Section." *Id.* at comment f.

Here, plaintiffs were merely engaged in preparation for performance. The court itself found only that "plaintiffs had changed their position in order to tender performance." At most, they obtained financing and assured defendant that they would pay; plaintiffs never tendered to defendant or even began to tender the $88,000 purchase price. Thus, they never accepted defendant's offer and no contract was ever created. See *Multicare Medical Center v. State Social & Health Services,* 114 Wash.2d 572, 584, 790 P.2d 124, 131 (1990) ("under a unilateral contract, an offer cannot be accepted by promising to perform; rather, the offeree must accept, if at all, by performance, and the contract then becomes executed"). . . .*

Reversed and the cause remanded for further proceedings consistent with the principles expressed herein.

DRENNAN V. STAR PAVING CO.
Supreme Court of California
333 P.2d 757 (1958).

TRAYNOR, Justice.

Defendant appeals from a judgment for plaintiff in an action to recover damages caused by defendant's refusal to perform certain paving work according to a bid it submitted to plaintiff.

On July 28, 1955, plaintiff, a licensed general contractor, was preparing a bid on the "Monte Vista School Job" in the Lancaster school district. Bids had to be submitted before 8:00 p.m. Plaintiff testified that it was customary in that area for general contractors to receive the bids of subcontractors by telephone on the day set for bidding and to rely on them in computing their own bids. Thus on that day plaintiff's secretary, Mrs. Johnson, received by telephone between fifty and seventy-five subcontractors' bids for various parts of the school job. As each bid came in, she wrote it on a special form, which she brought into plaintiff's office. He then posted it on a master cost sheet setting forth the names and bids of all subcontractors. His own bid had to include the names of subcontractors who were to perform one-half of one per cent or more of the construction work, and he had also to provide a bidder's bond of ten per cent of his total bid of $317,385 as a guarantee that he would enter the contract if awarded the work.

Late in the afternoon, Mrs. Johnson had a telephone conversation with Kenneth R. Hoon, an estimator for defendant. He gave his name and telephone number and stated that he was bidding for defendant for the paving work at the Monte Vista School according to plans and specifications and that his bid was $7,131.60. At Mrs. Johnson's request he repeated his bid. Plaintiff listened to the bid over an extension telephone in his office and posted it on the master sheet after receiving the bid form from Mrs. Johnson. Defendant's was the lowest bid for the paving. Plaintiff computed his own bid accordingly and submitted it with the name of defendant as the subcontractor for the paving. When the bids were opened on July 28th, plaintiff's proved to be the lowest, and he was awarded the contract.

---

* Because defendant specified that the manner of acceptance would be performance, plaintiffs' argument that they accepted defendant's offer over the telephone must fail. In fact, plaintiffs admitted in their depositions that they were very worried that the property would be sold to someone else prior to closing. Thus, they should have understood that they had no enforceable contract until closing.

On his way to Los Angeles the next morning plaintiff stopped at defendant's office. The first person he met was defendant's construction engineer, Mr. Oppenheimer. Plaintiff testified: "I introduced myself and he immediately told me that they had made a mistake in their bid to me the night before, they couldn't do it for the price they had bid, and I told him I would expect him to carry through with their original bid because I had used it in compiling my bid and the job was being awarded them. And I would have to go and do the job according to my bid and I would expect them to do the same."

Defendant refused to do the paving work for less than $15,000. Plaintiff testified that he "got figures from other people" and after trying for several months to get as low a bid as possible engaged L & H Paving Company, a firm in Lancaster, to do the work for $10,948.60.

The trial court found on substantial evidence that defendant made a definite offer to do the paving on the Monte Vista job according to the plans and specifications for $7,131.60, and that plaintiff relied on defendant's bid in computing his own bid for the school job and naming defendant therein as the subcontractor for the paving work. Accordingly, it entered judgment for plaintiff in the amount of $3,817.00 (the difference between defendant's bid and the cost of the paving to plaintiff) plus costs.

Defendant contends that there was no enforceable contract between the parties on the ground that it made a revocable offer and revoked it before plaintiff communicated his acceptance to defendant.

There is no evidence that defendant offered to make its bid irrevocable in exchange for plaintiff's use of its figures in computing his bid. Nor is there evidence that would warrant interpreting plaintiff's use of defendant's bid as the acceptance thereof, binding plaintiff, on condition he received the main contract, to award the subcontract to defendant. In sum, there was neither an option supported by consideration nor a bilateral contract binding on both parties.

Plaintiff contends, however, that he relied to his detriment on defendant's offer and that defendant must therefore answer in damages for its refusal to perform. Thus the question is squarely presented: Did plaintiff's reliance make defendant's offer irrevocable?

Section 90 of the Restatement of Contracts states: "A promise which the promisor should reasonably expect to induce action or forbearance of a definite and substantial character on the part of the promisee and which does induce such action or forbearance is binding if injustice can be avoided only by enforcement of the promise." This rule applies in this state. Edmonds v. County of Los Angeles, 40 Cal.2d 642, 255 P.2d 772; Frebank Co. v. White, 152 Cal.App.2d 522, 313 P.2d 633; Wade v. Markwell & Co., 118 Cal.App.2d 410, 258 P.2d 497, 37 A.L.R.2d 1363; West v. Hunt Foods Co., 101 Cal.App.2d 597, 225 P.2d 978; Hunter v. Sparling, 87 Cal.App.2d 711, 197 P.2d 807; see 18 Cal.Jur.2d 407-408; 5 Stan.L.Rev. 783.

Defendant's offer constituted a promise to perform on such conditions as were stated expressly or by implication therein or annexed thereto by operation of law. (See 1 Williston, Contracts (3rd. ed.), § 24A, p. 56, § 61, p. 196.) Defendant had reason to expect that if its bid proved the lowest it would be used by plaintiff. It induced "action . . . of a definite and substantial character on the part of the promisee."

Had defendant's bid expressly stated or clearly implied that it was revocable at any time before acceptance we would treat it accordingly. It was silent on revocation, however, and we must therefore determine whether there are conditions to the right of revocation imposed by law or reasonably inferable in fact. In the analogous problem of an offer for a unilateral contract, the theory is now obsolete that the offer is revocable at any time before complete performance. Thus section 45 of the Restatement of Contracts provides: "If an offer for a unilateral contract is made, and part of the consideration requested in the offer is given or tendered by the offeree in response thereto, the offeror is bound by a contract, the duty of immediate performance of which is conditional on the full consideration being given or tendered within the time stated in the offer, or, if no time is stated therein, within a reasonable time." In explanation, comment b states that the "main offer includes as a subsidiary promise, necessarily implied, that if part of the requested performance is given, the offeror will not revoke his offer, and that if tender is made it will be accepted. Part performance or tender may thus furnish consideration for the subsidiary promise. Moreover, merely acting in justifiable reliance on an offer may in some cases serve as sufficient reason for making a promise binding (see § 90)."

Whether implied in fact or law, the subsidiary promise serves to preclude the injustice that would result if the offer could be revoked after the offeree had acted in detrimental reliance thereon. Reasonable reliance resulting in a foreseeable prejudicial change in position affords a compelling basis also for implying a subsidiary promise not to revoke an offer for a bilateral contract.

The absence of consideration is not fatal to the enforcement of such a promise. It is true that in the case of unilateral contracts the Restatement finds consideration for the implied subsidiary promise in the part performance of the bargained-for exchange, but its reference to section 90 makes clear that consideration for such a promise is not always necessary. The very purpose of section 90 is to make a promise binding even though there was no consideration "in the sense of something that is bargained for and given in exchange." (See 1 Corbin, Contracts 634 et seq.) Reasonable reliance serves to hold the offeror in lieu of the consideration ordinarily required to make the offer binding. In a case involving similar facts the Supreme Court of South Dakota stated that "we believe that reason and justice demand that the doctrine (of section 90) be applied to the present facts. We cannot believe that by accepting this doctrine as controlling in the state of facts before us we will abolish the requirement of a consideration in contract cases, in any different sense than an ordinary estoppel abolishes some legal requirement in its application. We are of the opinion, therefore, that the defendants in executing the agreement (which was not supported by consideration) made a promise which they should have reasonably expected would induce the plaintiff to submit a bid based thereon to the Government, that such promise did induce this action, and that injustice can be avoided only by enforcement of the promise." Northwestern Engineering Co. v. Ellerman, 69 S.D. 397, 408, 10 N.W.2d 879, 884; see also,

Robert Gordon, Inc., v. Ingersoll-Rand Co., 7 Cir., 117 F.2d 654, 661; cf. James Baird Co. v. Gimbel Bros., 2 Cir., 64 F.2d 344.

When plaintiff used defendant's offer in computing his own bid, he bound himself to perform in reliance on defendant's terms. Though defendant did not bargain for this use of its bid neither did defendant make it idly, indifferent to whether it would be used or not. On the contrary it is reasonable to suppose that defendant submitted its bid to obtain the subcontract. It was bound to realize the substantial possibility that its bid would be the lowest, and that it would be included by plaintiff in his bid. It was to its own interest that the contractor be awarded the general contract; the lower the subcontract bid, the lower the general contractor's bid was likely to be and the greater its chance of acceptance and hence the greater defendant's chance of getting the paving subcontract. Defendant had reason not only to expect plaintiff to rely on its bid but to want him to. Clearly defendant had a stake in plaintiff's reliance on its bid. Given this interest and the fact that plaintiff is bound by his own bid, it is only fair that plaintiff should have at least an opportunity to accept defendant's bid after the general contract has been awarded to him.

It bears noting that a general contractor is not free to delay acceptance after he has been awarded the general contract in the hope of getting a better price. Nor can he reopen bargaining with the subcontractor and at the same time claim a continuing right to accept the original offer. See R. J. Daum Const. Co. v. Child, Utah, 247 P.2d 817, 823. In the present case plaintiff promptly informed defendant that plaintiff was being awarded the job and that the subcontract was being awarded to defendant.

Defendant contends, however, that its bid was the result of mistake and that it was therefore entitled to revoke it. It relies on the rescission cases of M. F. Kemper Const. Co. v. City of Los Angeles, 37 Cal.2d 696, 235 P.2d 7, and Brunzell Const. Co. v. G. J. Weisbrod, Inc., 134 Cal.App.2d 278, 285 P.2d 989. See also, Lemoge Electric v. San Mateo County, 46 Cal.2d 659, 662, 297 P.2d 638. In those cases, however, the bidder's mistake was known or should have been known to the offeree, and the offeree could be placed in status quo. Of course, if plaintiff had reason to believe that defendant's bid was in error, he could not justifiably rely on it, and section 90 would afford no basis for enforcing it. Robert Gordon, Inc., v. Ingersoll-Rand, Inc., 7 Cir., 117 F.2d 654, 660. Plaintiff, however, had no reason to know that defendant had made a mistake in submitting its bid, since there was usually a variance of 160 per cent between the highest and lowest bids for paving in the desert around Lancaster. He committed himself to performing the main contract in reliance on defendant's figures. Under these circumstances defendant's mistake, far from relieving it of its obligation, constitutes an additional reason for enforcing it, for it misled plaintiff as to the cost of doing the paving. Even had it been clearly understood that defendant's offer was revocable until accepted, it would not necessarily follow that defendant had no duty to exercise reasonable care in preparing its bid. It presented its bid with knowledge of the substantial possibility that it would be used by plaintiff; it could foresee the harm that would ensue from an erroneous underestimate of the cost. Moreover, it was motivated by its own business interest. Whether or not these considerations alone would justify recovery for negligence had the case been tried on that theory (see Biakanja v. Irving, 49 Cal.2d 647, 650, 320 P.2d 16), they are persuasive that defendant's mistake should not defeat recovery under the rule of section 90 of the Restatement of Contracts. As between the subcontractor who made the bid and the general contractor who reasonably relied on it, the loss resulting from the mistake should fall on the party who caused it.

Leo F. Piazza Paving Co. v. Bebek & Brkich, 141 Cal.App.2d 226, 296 P.2d 368, 371, and Bard v. Kent, 19 Cal.2d 449, 122 P.2d 8, 139 A.L.R. 1032, are not to the contrary. In the Piazza case the court sustained a finding that defendants intended, not to make a firm bid, but only to give the plaintiff "some kind of an idea to use" in making its bid; there was evidence that the defendants had told plaintiff they were unsure of the significance of the specifications. There was thus no offer, promise, or representation on which the defendants should reasonably have expected the plaintiff to rely. The Bard case held that an option not supported by consideration was revoked by the death of the optionor. The issue of recovery under the rule of section 90 was not pleaded at the trial, and it does not appear that the offeree's reliance was "of a definite and substantial character" so that injustice could be avoided "only by the enforcement of the promise."

There is no merit in defendant's contention that plaintiff failed to state a cause of action, on the ground that the complaint failed to allege that plaintiff attempted to mitigate the damages or that they could not have been mitigated. Plaintiff alleged that after defendant's default, "plaintiff had to procur the services of the L & H Co. to perform said asphaltic paving for the sum of $10,948.60." Plaintiff's uncontradicted evidence showed that he spent several months trying to get bids from other subcontractors and that he took the lowest bid. Clearly he acted reasonably to mitigate damages. In any event any uncertainty in plaintiff's allegation as to damages could have been raised by special demurrer. Code Civ.Proc. § 430, subd. 9. It was not so raised and was therefore waived. Code Civ.Proc. § 434.

The judgment is affirmed.

GIBSON C. J., and SHENK, SCHAUER, SPENCE and McCOMB, JJ., concur.

NEW YORK UNIFORM COMMERCIAL CODE
§ 2-205. FIRM OFFERS
N.Y. U.C.C. LAW § 2-205 (2013).

An offer by a merchant to buy or sell goods in a signed writing which by its terms gives assurance that it will be held open is not revocable, for lack of consideration, during the time stated or if no time is stated for a reasonable time, but in no event may such period of irrevocability exceed three months; but any such term of assurance on a form supplied by the offeree must be separately signed by the offeror.

NOTES AND QUESTIONS:

1. *See* Restatement (Second) of Contracts §§ 25 (Option Contracts), 45 (Option Contract Created by Part Performance or Tender), 87 (Option Contract) (1981).

2. *See* U.C.C. § 2-205 (2002).

3. *See Pavel Enterprises, Inc. v. A.S. Johnson Company, Inc.*, 674 A.2d 521 (Md. 1996), *infra*.

D. MANNER, METHOD, AND MODES OF ACCEPTANCE

1. BILATERAL V. UNILATERAL

EVER-TITE ROOFING CORP. V. GREEN
Court of Appeal of Louisiana, Second Circuit
83 So. 2d 449 (1956).

AYRES, Judge.

. . . .

Defendants executed and signed an instrument June 10, 1953, for the purpose of obtaining the services of plaintiff in re-roofing their residence situated in Webster Parish, Louisiana. The document set out in detail the work to be done and the price therefor to be paid in monthly installments. This instrument was likewise signed by plaintiff's sale representative, who, however, was without authority to accept the contract for and on behalf of the plaintiff. This alleged contract contained these provisions:

> This agreement shall become binding only upon written acceptance hereof, by the principal or authorized officer of the Contractor, *or upon commencing performance of the work.* This contract is Not Subject to Cancellation. It is understood and agreed that this contract is payable at office of Ever-Tite Roofing Corporation, 5203 Telephone, Houston, Texas. It is understood and agreed that this Contract provides for attorney's fees and in no case less than ten per cent attorney's fees in the event same is placed in the hands of an attorney for collecting or collected through any court, and further provides for accelerated maturity for failure to pay any installment of principal or interest thereon when due.
>
> This written agreement is the only and entire contract covering the subject matter hereof and no other representations have been made unto Owner except these herein contained. No guarantee on repair work, partial roof jobs, or paint jobs. (Emphasis supplied.)

Inasmuch as this work was to be performed entirely on credit, it was necessary for plaintiff to obtain credit reports and approval from the lending institution which was to finance said contract. With this procedure defendants were more or less familiar and knew their credit rating would have to be checked and a report made. On receipt of the proposed contract in plaintiff's office on the day following its execution, plaintiff requested a credit report, which was made after investigation and which was received in due course and submitted by plaintiff to the lending agency. Additional information was requested by this institution, which was likewise in due course transmitted to the institution, which then gave its approval.

The day immediately following this approval, which was either June 18 or 19, 1953, plaintiff engaged its workmen and two trucks, loaded the trucks with the necessary roofing materials and proceeded from Shreveport to defendants' residence for the purpose of doing the work and performing the services allegedly contracted for the defendants. Upon their arrival at defendants' residence, the workmen found others in the performance of the work which plaintiff had contracted to do. Defendants notified plaintiff's workmen that the work had been contracted to other parties two days before and forbade them to do the work.

Formal acceptance of the contract was not made under the signature and approval of an agent of plaintiff. It was, however, the intention of plaintiff to accept the contract by commencing the work, which was one of the ways provided for in the instrument for its acceptance, as will be shown by reference to the extract from the contract quoted hereinabove. Prior to this time, however, defendants had determined on a course of abrogating the agreement and engaged other workmen without notice thereof to plaintiff.

The basis of the judgment appealed was that defendants had timely notified plaintiff before "commencing performance of work." The trial court held that notice to plaintiff's workmen upon their arrival with the materials that defendants did not desire them to commence the actual work was sufficient and timely to signify their intention to withdraw from the contract. With this conclusion we find ourselves unable to agree.

Defendants' attempt to justify their delay in thus notifying plaintiff for the reason they did not know where or how to contact plaintiff is without merit. The contract itself, a copy of which was left with them, conspicuously displayed plaintiff's name, address and telephone number. Be that as it may, defendants at no time, from June 10, 1953, until plaintiff's workmen arrived for the purpose of commencing the work, notified or attempted to notify plaintiff of their intention to abrogate, terminate or cancel the contract.

Defendants evidently knew this work was to be processed through plaintiff's Shreveport office. The record discloses no unreasonable delay on plaintiff's part in receiving, processing or accepting the contract or in commencing the work contracted to be done. No time limit was specified in the contract within which it was to be accepted or within which the work was to be begun. It was nevertheless understood between the parties that some delay would ensue before the acceptance of the contract and the commencement of the work, due to the necessity of compliance with the requirements relative to financing the job through a lending agency. The evidence as referred to hereinabove shows that plaintiff proceeded with due diligence.

The general rule of law is that an offer proposed may be withdrawn before its acceptance and that no obligation is incurred thereby. This is, however, not without exceptions. For instance, Restatement of the Law of Contracts stated:

> (1) The power to create a contract by acceptance of an offer terminates at the time specified in the offer, or, if no time is specified, at the end of a reasonable time.

> What is a reasonable time is a question of fact depending on the nature of the contract proposed, the usages of business and other circumstances of the case which the offeree at the time of his acceptance either knows or has reason to know. . . .

Therefore, since the contract did not specify the time within which it was to be accepted or within which the work was to have been commenced, a reasonable time must be allowed therefor in accordance with the facts and circumstances and the evident intention of the parties. A reasonable time is contemplated where no time is expressed. What is a reasonable time depends more or less upon the circumstances surrounding each particular case. The delays to process defendants' application were not unusual. The contract was accepted by plaintiff by the commencement of the performance of the work contracted to be done. This commencement began with the loading of the trucks with the necessary materials in Shreveport and transporting such materials and the workmen to defendants' residence. Actual commencement or performance of the work therefore began before any notice of dissent by defendants was given plaintiff. The proposition and its acceptance thus became a completed contract.

By their aforesaid acts defendants breached the contract. They employed others to do the work contracted to be done by plaintiff and forbade plaintiff's workmen to engage upon that undertaking. By this breach defendants are legally bound to respond to plaintiff in damages. . . .

For the reasons assigned, the judgment appealed is annulled, avoided, reversed and set aside and there is now judgment in favor of plaintiff, Ever-Tite Roofing Corporation, against the defendants, G. T. Green and Mrs. Jessie Fay Green, for the full sum of $311.37, with 5 per cent per annum interest thereon from judicial demand until paid, and for all costs.

Reversed and rendered.

DAVIS V. JACOBY
Supreme Court of California
34 P.2d 1026 (1934).

THE COURT

Plaintiffs appeal from a judgment refusing to grant specific performance of an alleged contract to make a will. The facts are not in dispute and are as follows:

The plaintiff Caro M. Davis was the niece of Blanche Whitehead who was married to Rupert Whitehead. Prior to her marriage in 1913 to her coplaintiff Frank M. Davis, Caro lived for a considerable time at the home of the Whiteheads, in Piedmont, California. The Whiteheads were childless and extremely fond of Caro. The record is replete with uncontradicted testimony of the close and loving relationship that existed between Caro and her aunt and uncle. During the period that Caro lived with the Whiteheads she was treated as and often referred to by the Whiteheads as their daughter. In 1913, when Caro was married to Frank Davis the marriage was arranged at the Whitehead home and a reception held there.

After the marriage Mr. and Mrs. Davis went to Mr. Davis' home in Canada, where they have resided ever since. During the period 1913 to 1931 Caro made many visits to the Whiteheads, several of them being of long duration. The Whiteheads visited Mr. and Mrs. Davis in Canada on several occasions. After the marriage and continuing down to 1931 the closest and most friendly relationship at all times existed between these two families. They corresponded frequently, the record being replete with letters showing the loving relationship.

By the year 1930 Mrs. Whitehead had become seriously ill. She had suffered several strokes and her mind was failing. Early in 1931 Mr. Whitehead had her removed to a private hospital. The doctors in attendance had informed him that she might die at any time or she might linger for many months. Mr. Whitehead had suffered severe financial reverses. He had had several sieges of sickness and was in poor health. The record shows that during the early part of 1931 he was desperately in need of assistance with his wife, and in his business affairs, and that he did not trust his friends in Piedmont. On March 18, 1931, he wrote to Mrs. Davis telling her of Mrs. Whitehead's condition and added that Mrs. Whitehead was very wistful.

> Today I endeavored to find out what she wanted. I finally asked her if she wanted to see you. She burst out crying and we had great difficulty in getting her to stop. Evidently, that is what is on her mind. It is a very difficult matter to decide. If you come it will mean that you will have to leave again, and then things may be serious. I am going to see the doctor, and get his candid opinion and will then write you again . . . . Since writing the above, I have seen the doctor, and he thinks it will help considerably if you come.

Shortly thereafter, Mr. Whitehead wrote to Caro Davis further explaining the physical condition of Mrs. Whitehead and himself. On March 24, 1931, Mr. Davis, at the request of his wife, telegraphed to Mr. Whitehead as follows:

> Your letter received. Sorry to hear Blanche not so well. Hope you are feeling better yourself. If you wish Caro to go to you can arrange for her to leave in about two weeks. Please wire me if you think it advisable for her to go.

On March 30, 1931, Mr. Whitehead wrote a long letter to Mr. Davis, in which he explained in detail the condition of Mrs. Whitehead's health and also referred to his own health. He pointed out that he had lost a considerable portion of his cash assets but still owned considerable realty, that he needed someone to help him with his wife and some friend he could trust to help him with his business affairs and suggested that perhaps Mr. Davis might come to California. He then pointed out that all his property was community property; that under his will all the property was to go to Mrs. Whitehead; that he believed that under Mrs. Whitehead's will practically everything was to go to Caro. Mr. Whitehead again wrote to Mr. Davis under date of April 9, 1931, pointing out how badly he needed someone he could trust to assist him, and giving it as his belief that if properly handled he could still save about $150,000.

He then stated:

> Having you [Mr. Davis] here to depend on and to help me regain my mind and courage would be a big thing.

Three days later, on April 12, 1931, Mr. Whitehead again wrote, addressing his letter to "Dear Frank and Caro," and in this letter made the definite offer, which offer it is claimed was accepted and is the basis of this action. In this letter he first pointed out that Blanche, his wife, was in a private hospital and that "she cannot last much longer ... my affairs are not as bad as I supposed at first. Cutting everything down I figure 150,000 can be saved from the wreck." He then enumerated the values placed upon his various properties and then continued:

> [M]y trouble was caused by my friends taking advantage of my illness and my position to skin me.
>
> Now if Frank could come out here and be with me, and look after my affairs, we could easily save the balance I mentioned, provided I dont get into another panic and do some more foolish things.
>
> The next attack will be my end, I am 65 and my health has been bad for years, so, the Drs. don't give me much longer to live. So if you can come, Caro will inherit everything and you will make our lives happier and see Blanche is provided for to the end.
>
> My eyesight has gone back on me, I can't read only for a few lines at a time. I am at the house alone with Stanley [the chauffeur] who does everything for me and is a fine fellow. Now, what I want is someone who will take charge of my affairs and see I don't lose any more. Frank can do it, if he will and cut out the booze.
>
> Will you let me hear from you as soon as possible, I know it will be a sacrifice but times are still bad and likely to be, so by settling down you can help me and Blanche and gain in the end. If I had you here my mind would get better and my courage return, and we could work things out.

This letter was received by Mr. Davis at his office in Windsor, Canada, about 9:30 A.M. April 14, 1931. After reading the letter to Mrs. Davis over the telephone, and after getting her belief that they must go to California, Mr. Davis immediately wrote Mr. Whitehead a letter, which, after reading it to his wife, he sent by air mail. This letter was lost, but there is no doubt that it was sent by Davis and received by Whitehead, in fact the trial court expressly so found. Mr. Davis testified in substance as to the contents of this letter. After acknowledging receipt of the letter of April 12, 1931, Mr. Davis unequivocally stated that he and Mrs. Davis accepted the proposition of Mr. Whitehead and both would leave Windsor to go to him on April 25th. This letter of acceptance also contained the information that the reason they could not leave prior to April 25th was that Mr. Davis had to appear in court on April 22d as one of the executors of his mother's estate. The testimony is uncontradicted and ample to support the trial court's finding that this letter was sent by Davis and received by Whitehead.

In fact under date of April 15, 1931, Mr. Whitehead again wrote to Mr. Davis and stated:

> Your letter by air mail received this a. m. Now, I am wondering if I have put you to unnecessary trouble and expense, if you are making any money don't leave it, as things are bad here . . . . You know your business and I don't and I am half crazy in the bargain, but I don't want to hurt you or Caro.
>
> Then on the other hand if I could get someone to trust and keep me straight I can save a good deal, about what I told you in my former letter.

This letter was received by Mr. Davis on April 17, 1931, and the same day Mr. Davis telegraphed to Mr. Whitehead "Cheer up—we will soon be there, we will wire you from the train."

Between April 14, 1931, the date the letter of acceptance was sent by Mr. Davis, and April 22d, Mr. Davis was engaged in closing out his business affairs, and Mrs. Davis in closing up their home and in making other arrangements to leave. On April 22, 1931, Mr. Whitehead committed suicide. Mr. and Mrs. Davis were immediately notified and they at once came to California. From almost the moment of her arrival Mrs. Davis devoted herself to the care and comfort of her aunt, and gave her aunt constant attention and care until Mrs. Whitehead's death on May 30, 1931. On this point the trial court found:

> [F]rom the time of their arrival in Piedmont, Caro M. Davis administered in every way to the comforts of Blanche Whitehead and saw that she was cared for and provided for down to the time of the death of Blanche Whitehead on May 30, 1931; during said time Caro M. Davis nursed Blanche Whitehead, cared for her and administered to her wants as a natural daughter would have done toward and for her mother.

This finding is supported by uncontradicted evidence and in fact is conceded by respondents to be correct. In fact the record shows that after their arrival in California Mr. and Mrs. Davis fully performed their side of the agreement.

After the death of Mrs. Whitehead, for the first time it was discovered that the information contained in Mr. Whitehead's letter of March 30, 1931, in reference to the contents of his and Mrs. Whitehead's wills was incorrect. By a duly witnessed will dated February 28, 1931, Mr. Whitehead, after making several specific bequests, had bequeathed all of the balance of his estate to his wife for life, and upon her death to respondents Geoff Doubble and Rupert Ross Whitehead, his nephews. Neither appellant was mentioned in his will. It was also discovered that Mrs. Whitehead by a will dated December 17, 1927, had devised all of her estate to her husband. The evidence is clear and uncontradicted that the relationship existing between Whitehead and his two nephews, respondents herein, was not nearly as close and confidential as that existing between Whitehead and appellants.

After the discovery of the manner in which the property had been devised was made, this action was commenced upon the theory that Rupert Whitehead had assumed a contractual obligation to make a will whereby "Caro Davis would inherit everything"; that he had failed to do so; that plaintiffs had fully performed their part of the contract; that damages being insufficient, *quasi* specific performance should be granted in order to remedy the alleged wrong, upon the equitable principle that equity regards that done which ought to have been done. The requested relief is that the beneficiaries under the will of Rupert Whitehead, respondents herein, be declared to be involuntary trustees for plaintiffs of Whitehead's estate.

It should also be added that the evidence shows that as a result of Frank Davis leaving his business in Canada he forfeited not only all insurance business he might have written if he had remained, but also forfeited all renewal commissions earned on past business. According to his testimony this loss was over $8,000.

The trial court found that the relationship between Mr. and Mrs. Davis and the Whiteheads was substantially as above recounted and that the other facts above stated were true; that prior to April 12, 1931, Rupert Whitehead had suffered business reverses and was depressed in mind and ill in body; that his wife was very ill; that because of his mental condition he 'was unable to properly care for or look after his property or affairs'; that on April 12, 1931, Rupert Whitehead in writing made an offer to plaintiffs that, if within a reasonable time thereafter plaintiffs would leave and abandon their said home in Windsor, and if Frank M. Davis would abandon or dispose of his said business, and if both the plaintiffs would come to Piedmont in the said county of Alameda where Rupert Whitehead then resided and thereafter reside at said place and be with or near him, and, if Frank M. Davis would thereupon and thereafter look after the business and affairs of said Rupert Whitehead until his condition improved to such an extent as to permit him so to do, and if the plaintiffs would look after and administer to the comforts of Blanche Whitehead and see that she was properly cared for until the time of her death, that, in consideration thereof, Caro M. Davis would inherit everything that Rupert Whitehead possessed at the time of his death and that by last will and testament Rupert Whitehead would devise and bequeath to Caro M. Davis all property and estate owned by him at the time of his death, other than the property constituting the community interest of Blanche Whitehead; that shortly prior to April 12, 1931, Rupert Whitehead informed plaintiffs of the supposed terms of his will and the will of Mrs. Whitehead. The court then finds that the offer of April 12th was not accepted. As already stated, the court found that plaintiffs sent a letter to Rupert Whitehead on April 14th purporting to accept the offer of April 12th, and also found that this letter was received by the Whiteheads, but finds that in fact such letter was not a legal acceptance. The court also found that the offer of April 12th was:

> 'fair and just and reasonable, and the consideration therefor, namely, the performance by plaintiffs of the terms and conditions thereof, if the same had been performed, would have been an adequate consideration for said offer and for the agreement that would have resulted from such performance; said offer was not, and said agreement would not have been, either harsh or oppressive or unjust to the heirs at law, or devisees, or legatees, of Rupert Whitehead, or to each or any of them, or otherwise.'

The court also found that plaintiffs did not know that the statements made by Whitehead in reference to the wills were not correct until after Mrs. Whitehead's death, that after plaintiffs arrived in Piedmont they cared for Mrs. Whitehead until her death and 'Blanche Whitehead was greatly comforted by the presence, companionship and association of Caro M. Davis, and by her administering to her wants.'

The theory of the trial court and of respondents on this appeal is that the letter of April 12th was an offer to contract, but that such offer could only be accepted by performance and could not be accepted by a promise to perform, and that said offer was revoked by the death of Mr. Whitehead before performance. In other words, it is contended that the offer was an offer to enter into a unilateral contract, and that the purported acceptance of April 14th was of no legal effect.

The distinction between unilateral and bilateral contracts is well settled in the law. It is well stated in section 12 of the American Institute's Restatement of the Law of Contracts as follows:

> 'A unilateral contract is one in which no promisor receives a promise as consideration for his promise. A bilateral contract is one in which there are mutual promises between two parties to the contract; each party being both a promisor and a promisee.'

This definition is in accord with the law of California. (*Chrisman v. Southern Cal. Edison Co.,* 83 Cal. App. 249 [256 Pac. 618].)

In the case of unilateral contracts no notice of acceptance by performance is required. Section 1584 of the Civil Code provides, 'Performance of the conditions of a proposal, ... is an acceptance of the proposal.' (See *Cuthill v. Peabody,* 19 Cal. App. 304 [125 Pac. 926]; *Los Angeles Traction Co. v. Wilshire,* 135 Cal. 654 [67 Pac. 1086].)

Although the legal distinction between unilateral and bilateral contracts is thus well settled, the difficulty in any particular case is to determine whether the particular offer is one to enter into a bilateral or unilateral contract. Some cases are quite clear cut. Thus an offer to sell which is accepted is clearly a bilateral contract, while an offer of a reward is a clear-cut offer of a unilateral contract which cannot be accepted by a promise to perform, but only by performance. (*Berthiaume v. Doe,* 22 Cal. App. 78 [133 Pac. 515].) Between these two extremes is a vague field where the particular contract may be unilateral or bilateral depending upon the intent of the offerer and the facts and circumstances of each case. The offer to contract involved in this case falls within this category. By the provisions of the Restatement of the Law of Contracts it is expressly provided that there is a *presumption* that the offer is to enter into a bilateral contract. Section 31 provides:

> 'In case of doubt it is presumed that an offer invites the formation of a bilateral contract by an acceptance amounting in effect to a promise by the offeree to perform what the offer requests, rather than the formation of one or more unilateral contracts by actual performance on the part of the offeree.'

Professor Williston in his Treatise on Contracts, volume 1, § 60, also takes the position that a presumption in favor of bilateral contracts exists.

In the comment following § 31 of the Restatement the reason for such presumption is stated as follows:

> 'It is not always easy to determine whether an offerer requests an act or a promise to do the act. As a bilateral contract immediately and fully protects both parties, the interpretation is favored that a bilateral contract is proposed.'

While the California cases have never expressly held that a presumption in favor of bilateral contracts exists, the cases clearly indicate a tendency to treat offers as offers of bilateral rather than of unilateral contracts. (*Roth v. Moeller,* 185 Cal. 415 [197 Pac. 62]; *Boehm v. Spreckels,* 183 Cal. 239 [191 Pac. 5]; see, also, *Wood v. Lucy, Lady Duff- Gordon,* 222 N. Y. 88 [118 N. E. 214].)

Keeping these principles in mind we are of the opinion that the offer of April 12th was an offer to enter into a bilateral as distinguished from a unilateral contract. Respondents argue that Mr. Whitehead had the right as offerer to designate his offer as either unilateral or bilateral. That is undoubtedly the law. It is then argued that from all the facts and circumstances it must be implied that what Whitehead wanted was performance and not a mere promise to perform. We think this is a *non sequitur,* in fact the surrounding circumstances lead to just the opposite conclusion. These parties were not dealing at arm's length. Not only were they related, but a very close and intimate friendship existed between them. The record indisputably demonstrates that Mr. Whitehead had confidence in Mr. and Mrs. Davis, in fact that he had lost all confidence in everyone else. The record amply shows that by an accumulation of occurrences Mr. Whitehead had become desperate, and that what he wanted was the promise of appellants that he could look to them for assistance. He knew from his past relationship with appellants that if they gave their promise to perform he could rely upon them. The correspondence between them indicates how desperately he desired this assurance. Under these circumstances he wrote his offer of April 12th, above quoted, in which he stated, after disclosing his desperate mental and physical condition, and after setting forth the terms of his offer: "*Will you let me hear from you as soon as possible*-I know it will be a sacrifice but times are still bad and likely to be, so by settling down you can help me and Blanche and gain in the end." By thus specifically requesting an immediate reply Whitehead expressly indicated the nature of the acceptance desired by him-namely, appellants' promise that they would come to California and do the things requested by him. This promise was immediately sent by appellants upon receipt of the offer, and was received by Whitehead. It is elementary that when an offer has indicated the mode and means of acceptance, an acceptance in accordance with that mode or means is binding on the offerer.

Another factor which indicates that Whitehead must have contemplated a bilateral rather than a unilateral contract, is that the contract required Mr. and Mrs. Davis to perform services until the death of both Mr. and Mrs. Whitehead. It is obvious that if Mr. Whitehead died first some of these services were to be performed after his death, so that he would have to rely on the promise of appellants to perform these services. It is also of some evidentiary force that Whitehead received the letter of acceptance and acquiesced in that means of acceptance....

For the foregoing reasons we are of the opinion that the offer of April 12, 1931, was an offer to enter into a bilateral contract which was accepted by the letter of April 14, 1931. Subsequently appellants fully performed their part of the contract. . . .

For the foregoing reasons the judgment appealed from is reversed.

Rehearing denied.

MARCHIONDO V. SCHECK
Supreme Court of New Mexico
432 P.2d 405 (1967).

. . . .

OPINION

WOOD, Judge, Court of Appeals.

The issue is whether the offeror had a right to revoke his offer to enter a unilateral contract.

Defendant, in writing, offered to sell real estate to a specified prospective buyer and agreed to pay a percentage of the sales price as a commission to the broker. The offer fixed a six-day time limit for acceptance. Defendant, in writing, revoked the offer. The revocation was received by the broker on the morning of the sixth day. Later that day, the broker obtained the offeree's acceptance.

Plaintiff, the broker, claiming breach of contract, sued defendant for the commission stated in the offer. On the above facts, the trial court dismissed the complaint.

We are not concerned with the revocation of the offer as between the offeror and the prospective purchaser. With certain exceptions (see 12 C.J.S. Brokers § 95(2), pp. 223-224), the right of a broker to the agreed compensation, or damages measured thereby, is not defeated by the refusal of the principal to complete or consummate a transaction. Southwest Motel Brokers, Inc. v. Alamo Hotels, Inc., 72 N.M. 227, 382 P.2d 707 (1963).

Plaintiff's appeal concerns the revocation of his agency. As to that revocation, the issue between the offeror and his agent is not whether defendant had the power to revoke; rather, it is whether he had the right to revoke. 1 Mechem on Agency, § 568 at 405 (2d ed. 1914).

When defendant made his offer to pay a commission upon sale of the property, he offered to enter a unilateral contract; the offer was for an act to be performed, a sale. 1 Williston on Contracts, § 13 at 23 (3rd ed. 1957); Hutchinson v. Dobson-Bainbridge Realty Co., 31 Tenn.App. 490, 217 S.W.2d 6 (1946).

Many courts hold that the principal has the right to revoke the broker's agency at any time before the broker has actually procured a purchaser. See Hutchinson v. Dobson-Bainbridge Realty Co., supra, and cases therein cited. The reason given is that until there is performance, the offeror has not received that contemplated by his offer, and there is no contract. Further, the offeror may never receive the requested performance because the offeree is not obligated to perform. Until the offeror receives the requested performance, no consideration has passed from the offeree to the offeror. Thus, until the performance is received, the offeror may withdraw the offer. Williston, supra, § 60; Hutchinson v. Dobson-Bainbridge Realty Co., supra.

Defendant asserts that the trial court was correct in applying this rule. However, plaintiff contends that the rule is not applicable where there has been part performance of the offer.

Hutchinson v. Dobson-Bainbridge Realty Co., supra, states:

> 'A greater number of courts, however, hold that part performance of the consideration may make such an offer irrevocable and that where the offeree or broker manifests his assent to the offer by entering upon performance and spending time and money in his efforts to perform, then the offer becomes irrevocable during the time stated and binding upon the principal according to its terms. . . .'

It is the action taken by the offeree which deprives the offeror of that right. Until there is action by the offeree-a partial performance pursuant to the offer-the offeror may revoke even if his offer is of an exclusive agency or an exclusive right to sell. Levander v. Johnson, 181 Wis. 68, 193 N.W. 970 (1923).

Once partial performance is begun pursuant to the offer made, a contract results. This contract has been termed a contract with conditions or an option contract. This terminology is illustrated as follows:

> 'If an offer for a unilateral contract is made, and part of the consideration requested in the offer is given or tendered by the offeree in response thereto, the offeror is bound by a contract, the duty of immediate performance of which is conditional on the full consideration being given or tendered within the time stated in the offer, or, if no time is stated therein, within a reasonable time.'

Restatement (Second) of Contracts, § 45, Tent. Draft No. 1, (approved 1964, Tent. Draft No. 2, p. vii) states:

> '(1) Where an offer invites an offeree to accept by rendering a performance and does not invite a promissory acceptance, an option contract is created when the offeree begins the invited performance or tenders part of it.

> (2) The offeror's duty of performance under any option contract so created is conditional on completion or tender of the invited performance in accordance with the terms of the offer.'

Restatement (Second) of Contracts, § 45, Tent. Draft No. 1, comment (g), says:

> 'This Section frequently applies to agency arrangements, particularly offers made to real estate brokers. . . .'

The reason for finding such a contract is stated in Hutchinson v. Dobson-Bainbridge Realty Co., supra, as follows:

> 'This rule avoids hardship to the offeree, and yet does not hold the offeror beyond the terms of his promise. It is true by such terms he was to be bound only if the requested act was done; but this implies that he will let it be done, that he will keep his offer open till the offeree who has begun can finish doing it. At least this is so where the doing of it will necessarily require time and expense. In such a case it is but just to hold that the offeree's part performance furnishes the 'acceptance' and the 'consideration' for a binding subsidiary promise not to revoke the offer, or turns the offer into a presently binding contract conditional upon the offeree's full performance.'

We hold that part performance by the offeree of an offer of a unilateral contract results in a contract with a condition. The condition is full performance by the offeree. Here, if plaintiff-offeree partially performed prior to receipt of defendant's revocation, such a contract was formed. Thereafter, upon performance being completed by plaintiff, upon defendant's failure to recognize the contract, liability for breach of contract would arise. Thus, defendant's right to revoke his offer depends upon whether plaintiff had partially performed before he received defendant's revocation. In re Ward's Estate, 47 N.M. 55, 134 P.2d 539, 146 A.L.R. 826 (1943), does not conflict with this result. Ward is clearly distinguishable because there the prospective purchaser did not complete or tender performance in accordance with the terms of the offer.

What constitutes partial performance will vary from case to case since what can be done toward performance is limited by what is authorized to be done. Whether plaintiff partially performed is a question of fact to be determined by the trial court.

The trial court denied plaintiff's requested finding concerning his partial performance. It did so on the theory that partial performance was not material. In this the trial court erred.

Because of the failure to find on the issue of partial performance, the case must be remanded to the trial court. State ex rel. Reynolds v. Board of County Comm'rs., 71 N.M. 194, 376 P.2d 976 (1962). We have not considered, and express no opinion on the question of whether there is or is not substantial evidence in the record which would support a finding one way or the other on this vital issue. Compare Geeslin v. Goodno, Inc., 75 N.M. 174, 402 P.2d 156 (1965).

The cause is remanded for findings on the issue of plaintiff's partial performance of the offer prior to its revocation, and for further proceedings consistent with this opinion and the findings so made.

It is so ordered.

NOTES AND QUESTIONS:

1. *See* Restatement (Second) of Contracts §§ 32 (Invitation of Promise or Performance), 45 (Option Contract Created by Part Performance of Tender), and 63 (Effect of Performance by Offeree Where Offer Invites Either Performance or Promise) (1981).

2. *See Cobaugh v. Klick-Lewis Inc.*, 561 A.2d 1248 (Penn. 1989).

---

2. ACCEPTANCE IN A MANNER INVITED OR REQUIRED

a. Prescriptions as to Time, Place, and Manner

TOWN OF LINDSAY V. COOKE COUNTY ELECTRIC COOPERATIVE ASSOCIATION
Supreme Court of Texas
502 S.W.2d 117 (1973).

WALKER, JUSTICE

. . . .

Petitioner was incorporated as a town in 1959. Respondent, which had been serving inhabitants of the area since 1938, prepared and submitted to the Town Council a proposed ordinance granting respondent a franchise for a period of 50 years from acceptance of the ordinance. The ordinance was enacted by the council on March 24, 1960, but was not immediately effective. The final section provided:

> Section 8: The Electric Cooperative Association shall file its written acceptance of this franchise within thirty (30) days after the passage of this ordinance, and this ordinance shall take effect and be enforced from and after its passage, approval and acceptance.

The ordinance further provided that the franchise was conditioned upon payment by respondent on April 1, 1960, and annually thereafter, of two per cent of the gross receipts from the sale of electric energy within the corporate limits during the preceding calendar year. Within a few days after March 25, 1960, respondent mailed its check for $12.45 to petitioner. The check was accompanied by a statement of the 1959 receipts from inhabitants of the town and by a voucher showing that the check was in payment of "2% Gross Receipts Tax for the Year 1960." The check was endorsed by petitioner's Secretary-Treasurer and deposited in petitioner's bank account. It was paid by the drawee bank on April 4, 1960. On April 20, 1960, the ordinance was considered at a meeting of respondent's Board of Directors, which unanimously approved the franchise agreement. The attorney retained by respondent at that time was instructed to file a formal written acceptance of the ordinance with petitioner, but there is no evidence that this was ever done.

On June 9, 1960, after expiration of the 30-day acceptance period, respondent's manager appeared before the Council and requested that the ordinance be allowed to stay in effect. No action on the matter was taken on that meeting. On June 30, 1960, the franchise ordinance was repealed and the Council at the same time ordered that the franchise tax be refunded to respondent. Petitioner thereupon issued its check for $12.45 to respondent, and the check was accepted by respondent and deposited in its bank account. In July or August, 1960, and again in 1963 and in 1970, respondent's manager appeared before the Council and requested a franchise, but the request was denied.

Under the provisions of Art. 1436a, Vernon's Ann.Tex.Civ.St., respondent was entitled to continue operating within the corporate limits and without a franchise for ten years after the date of the petitioner's incorporation. In 1970, after the expiration of the 10-year period, petitioner requested respondent to remove its poles and lines from the streets and alleys of the Town. Respondent declined to do so, and this suit followed.

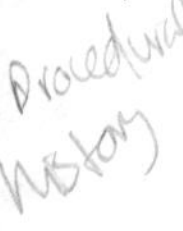

In response to the two special issues that were submitted, the jury found: (1) that the cooperative filed its written acceptance of the franchise within 30 days after March 24, 1960, and (2) respondent's payment of the gross receipts tax by writing its check with the accompanying voucher and statement was intended by both parties as an acceptance of the franchise. It was on the basis of these findings that the trial court rendered judgment for respondent. Petitioner appealed to the Court of Civil Appeals, contending that there is no evidence to support the jury's findings. The Court of Civil Appeals concluded that the issues were raised by the evidence. We do not agree.

Where, as here, an offer prescribes the time and manner of acceptance, its terms in this respect must be complied with to create a contract. The use of a different method of acceptance by the offeree will not be effectual unless the original offeror thereafter manifests his assent to the other party. See Restatement, Contracts, § 61; 1 Williston on Contracts, 3rd ed. 1957, § 76; 17 Am.Jur.2d, Contracts, § 44. Petitioner's Mayor and Secretary-Treasurer testified that there had never been a written acceptance of the franchise. While their testimony may not be conclusive, there is no evidence to the contrary. If the manner of acceptance had not been specified in the ordinance, respondent's act in paying the gross receipts tax might constitute an implied acceptance of the franchise. Its conduct in this respect was not, however, a written acceptance within the meaning of the ordinance, and the record does not suggest that petitioner assented to an implied acceptance. In our opinion there is no evidence to support the jury's findings, and the trial court erred in overruling petitioner's motion for judgment non obstante veredicto.

The judgments of the courts below are reversed, and the cause is remanded to the district court with instructions to render judgment for petitioner.

McGEE, J., notes his dissent.

LA SALLE NATIONAL BANK V. VEGA
Appellate Court of Illinois, Second District
520 N.E.2d 1129 (1988).

LINDBERG, PRESIDING JUSTICE

Plaintiff, La Salle National Bank, as trustee under Trust No. 109529, appeals from two June 22, 1987, orders of the circuit court of Du Page County. The first order granted the motion of counterplaintiff, Jerold A. Borg (Borg), for partial summary judgment. It also entered judgment on plaintiff's first amended complaint in favor of defendants, Paul Vega (Paul), as trustee under the Mel Vega Trust; Paul Vega, as independent administrator of the decedent's estate of Mel Vega (Mel); and Richard Vega (Richard), as trustee under the Marie Vega Trust. The second order denied plaintiff's petition for rehearing and dismissed both counts of plaintiff's first amended complaint (without vacating the portion of the first order entering judgment for defendants on both counts of the same first amended complaint).

Plaintiff's first amended complaint alleged the existence of a contract for the sale of real estate between it and Mel and sought specific performance of the alleged contract and damages from defendants for willfully and intentionally breaching it. Borg was permitted to intervene and filed a counterclaim naming plaintiff and defendants as counterdefendants. As finally amended, the counterclaim sought specific performance of a different contract for sale of the same real estate to Borg; a judgment declaring the alleged contract between Mel and plaintiff void and holding it for naught; and, if the alleged contract with plaintiff was "held to be a valid and enforceable contract," damages from defendants for fraud for failure to disclose the contract with plaintiff to Borg.

Borg moved for partial summary judgment (Ill.Rev.Stat.1985, ch. 110, par. 2-1,0005(d)) requesting a determination by the court that the alleged contract between plaintiff and Mel was unenforceable because it was not "signed in accordance with its terms and provisions" and because plaintiff abandoned it. The trial court granted partial summary judgment on the basis of the first ground argued by Borg.

In its verified first amended complaint, plaintiff alleged, inter alia:

> The Defendant, MEL VEGA, on March 12, 1985, in his own behalf and in behalf of all the owners of record, entered into a Real Estate Sale Contract (herein 'Contract') with the Plaintiff, a true and correct copy of said Contract is attached hereto and incorporated herein as Exhibit A.

Exhibit A is a document, drafted by counsel for plaintiff, entitled "Real Estate Sale Contract." On the first page of this document appears the date March 12, 1985, and the statement that "Attached Rider is part of this Contract." One of the Rider's provisions states:

> This contract has been executed and presented by an authorized agent for the purchaser, the beneficiaries of the La Salle National Bank, under Trust No. 109529, as Trustee aforesaid for the benefit of the Trust only and not personally. Upon execution of this contract by the Seller, this contract shall be presented to the trust for full execution. Upon the trust's execution, this contract will then be in full force and a copy of a fully executed contract

along with evidence of the earnest money deposit will be delivered back to Seller.

The document was signed by Bernard Ruekberg as the purchaser's purchasing agent and by Mel Vega (on March 19, 1985, according to the date by his signature on the Rider) as the seller but not by the trustee for the purchaser.

James Clark, an assistant vice-president in plaintiff trustee's land trust department, gave a deposition. Clark testified that there was no copy of the March 1985 contract in the relevant land trust file. Moreover, the real estate record kept by the department, which was intended to be a complete record of every document executed by the trustee (except for check endorsements), did not contain any notation of the presentation to, or the execution by, the trustee of the March 1985 contract. The trust in question was one for the Alter Group, and Clark estimated that there were 125 open trust files for the Alter Group at that time. It was conceivable that the March 1985 document had been executed and misfiled. However, counsel for plaintiff had never requested that Clark search other trust files for an executed copy of the document and had never suggested that a contract was missing from the file. On Borg's counsel's request, Clark had searched the trust department for any missing document and was unable to locate any missing contract.

Realtor Phil Bowers testified in his deposition that he had a notation that he had gone back to Mel on March 26, 1985. Bowers believed that he had then delivered to Mel an executed trust copy of the March 1985 document. However, Bowers did not have a copy of that executed document and, in fact, neither plaintiff nor any of the other deposed witnesses produced a copy of that executed document.

The trial court found, inter alia:

1. That the alleged 'Contract' which forms the basis of the claim of Plaintiff . . . is identified as Exhibit 'A' of its First Amended Complaint.

2. That the [document] contains language which provides in pertinent part. . . :

Upon execution of this Contract by the Seller, this Contract shall be presented to the trust for full execution. Upon the trust's execution, this Contract will then be in full force and a copy of a fully executed Contract along with evidence of the earnest money deposit will be delivered back to Seller.

3. That the aforesaid language is, on its own face, clear and unambiguous.

4. That the only reasonable inference to be drawn from the aforesaid language is that in the event that the Contract is not signed by the Trustee, it never will come into full force.

5. That the alleged "Contract" identified as Exhibit "A" to Plaintiff's First Amended Complaint was not signed by the Trust.

> 6. That because the aforesaid language contained in Exhibit "A" to Plaintiff's First Amended Complaint requires the signature of the Trust for the "Contract" to be in full force and because the "Contract" was not signed by the Trust, therefore, no Contract was ever formed between Mel Vega and Plaintiff. . . .

The court accordingly granted partial summary judgment for Borg and entered judgment in favor of defendants on plaintiff's complaint. . . .

We believe that the trial court correctly held that there was no genuine issue as to any material fact that no contract was ever formed between plaintiff and Mel. . . .

It has long been settled that a contract is " 'an agreement between competent parties, upon a consideration sufficient in law, to do or not to do a particular thing.' " (Steinberg v. Chicago Medical School (1977), 69 Ill.2d 320, 329, 13 Ill.Dec. 699, 704, 371 N.E.2d 634, 639, quoting People v. Dummer (1916), 274 Ill. 637, 640, 113 N.E. 934, 935). The formation of a contract requires an offer, an acceptance, and consideration. (Steinberg v. Chicago Medical School (1977), 69 Ill.2d 320, 329-30, 13 Ill.Dec. 699, 704, 371 N.E.2d 634, 639; Milanko v. Jensen (1949), 404 Ill. 261, 266-67, 88 N.E.2d 857, 859.) The trial court held that there was no genuine issue of material fact that no contract was formed because the offer was made by Mel, the offer could only be accepted by execution of the document at issue by the trust, and the document was not executed by the trust. . . .

In the case at bar, plaintiff judicially admitted that the copy of the document, not executed by the trust, was a true and correct copy of the written instrument on which its claim was founded. This withdrew from issue the question of whether the trust executed the document and dispensed with the need to prove that the trust had not.

Whether a contract was formed without execution of the document by the trust may now be considered. This requires first an analysis of the events which occurred with respect to the document in terms of offer and acceptance.

The pertinent provision of the document stated:

> This contract has been executed and presented by an authorized agent for the purchaser, the beneficiaries of the La Salle National Bank, under Trust No. 109529, as Trustee aforesaid for the benefit of the Trust only and not personally. Upon execution of this contract by the Seller, this contract shall be presented to the trust for full execution. Upon the trust's execution, this contract will then be in full force and a copy of a fully executed contract along with evidence of the earnest money deposit will be delivered back to Seller.

Thus, a specific order of events was contemplated, after which the contract would be in full force. Ruekberg (the purchasing agent) was to execute the document and present it to Mel (the seller). Then Mel was to execute it. After Mel executed it, the document was to be presented to the trust for execution. Finally, "upon the trust's execution," the contract would be in full force.

An offer is an act on the part of one person giving another person the legal power of creating the obligation called a contract. (McCarty v. Verson Allsteel Press Co. (1980), 89 Ill.App.3d 498, 507, 44 Ill.Dec. 570, 576, 411 N.E.2d 936, 942.) Where "the so-called offer is not intended to give the so-called offeree the power to make a contract there is no offer." (McCarty v. Verson Allsteel Press Co. (1980), 89 Ill.App.3d 498, 508, 44 Ill.Dec. 570, 577, 411 N.E.2d 936, 943.) From the provisions contained in the document at bar, particularly the language quoted, it is apparent that there was to be no contract (i.e., the "contract" was not to be in full force) until it was executed by the trust. Thus, Ruekberg's presentation of the document he had executed to Mel was not an offer because it did not give Mel the power to make a contract by accepting it. On the other hand, when Mel executed the document and gave it back to Ruekberg he made an offer which could be accepted by execution of the document by the trust.

An offeror has complete control over an offer and may condition acceptance to the terms of the offer. (McCarty v. Verson Allsteel Press Co. (1980), 89 Ill.App.3d 498, 509, 44 Ill.Dec. 570, 578, 411 N.E.2d 936, 944.) The language of an offer may moreover govern the mode of acceptance required, and, where an offer requires a written acceptance, no other mode may be used. (Zeller v. First National Bank & Trust Co. (1979), 79 Ill.App.3d 170, 172, 34 Ill.Dec. 473, 475, 398 N.E.2d 148, 150; Nationwide Commercial Co. v. Knox (1973), 10 Ill.App.3d 13, 15, 293 N.E.2d 638, 640; Brophy v. City of Joliet (1957), 14 Ill.App.2d 443, 453-56, 144 N.E.2d 816, 821-23.) In the case at bar, the document at issue stated clearly that the contract would be in full force upon the trust's execution. This indicates that the only mode by which Mel's offer could be accepted was execution of the document by the trust. The trust not having executed the document, there was no acceptance of the offer, and so there was no contract. E.g., Zeller v. First National Bank & Trust Co. (1979), 79 Ill.App.3d 170, 172, 34 Ill.Dec. 473, 474, 398 N.E.2d 148, 149 ("It is elementary that for a contract to exist, there must be an offer and acceptance. [Citations.]"); Moore v. Lewis (1977), 51 Ill.App.3d 388, 392, 9 Ill.Dec. 337, 342, 366 N.E.2d 594, 599 ("[A]n offer does not ripen into a contract until it is accepted").

Several contentions of plaintiff remain to be briefly addressed. Plaintiff argues that the beneficiaries to a land trust may contract and bind the trust; that Ruekberg was an agent of the beneficiaries; and that therefore Ruekberg could enter into a contract binding on the trust. Accordingly, the trust's execution was unnecessary to form a contract, but rather Ruekberg's execution as agent of the beneficiaries was sufficient. This is incorrect. Assuming arguendo that Ruekberg could enter into contracts which would bind the trust, the document at issue nonetheless could not become a contract on Ruekberg's and Mel's execution alone. This is because the document specifically provided that it would not be in force until executed by the trust and so (1) was not an offer until Mel executed it and (2) could only be accepted by execution by the trust. . . .

The judgment of the circuit court of Du Page County is accordingly affirmed.

---

b. Notice of Acceptance

HENDRICKS V. BEHEE
Missouri Court of Appeals, Southern District, Division Two
786 S.W.2d 610 (1990).

FLANIGAN, Presiding Judge.

Plaintiff Steve L. Hendricks, d/b/a Hendricks Abstract & Title Co., instituted this interpleader action, Rule 52.07, V.A.M.R., against defendants Eugene Behee, Artice Smith, and Pearl Smith. Plaintiff was the escrowee of $5,000 which had been paid by defendant Behee as a deposit accompanying Behee's offer to purchase real estate owned by defendants Artice Smith and Pearl Smith, husband and wife, in Stockton, Missouri. A dispute between Behee and the Smiths as to whether their dealings resulted in a binding contract prompted the interpleader action. Behee filed a crossclaim against the Smiths.

After a nonjury trial, the trial court awarded plaintiff $997.50 to be paid out of the $5,000 deposit. None of the parties challenges that award. The trial court awarded the balance of $4,002.50 to defendant Behee. Defendants Smith appeal.

In essence the Smiths contend that the dealings between them and Behee ripened into a contract and entitled the Smiths to the balance of $4,002.50, and that the trial court erred in ruling otherwise.

After Behee, as prospective buyer, and the Smiths, as prospective sellers, had engaged in unproductive negotiations, Behee, on March 2, 1987, made a written offer of $42,500 for the real estate and $250 for a dinner bell and flower pots. On March 3 that offer was mailed to the Smiths, who lived in Mississippi, by their real estate agent. There were two real estate agents involved.

The trial court found that both were the agents of the Smiths, and that finding has not been disputed by the Smiths in this appeal. For simplicity, the two agents will be considered in this opinion as one agent who acted on behalf of the Smiths.

On March 4 the Smiths signed the proposed agreement in Mississippi. Before Behee was notified that the Smiths had accepted the offer, Behee withdrew the offer by notifying the real estate agent of the withdrawal. That paramount fact is conceded by this statement in the Smiths' brief: "On either March 5, 6 or 7, 1987, Behee contacted [the Smiths' real estate agent] and advised her that he desired to withdraw his offer to purchase the real estate. Prior to this communication, Behee had received no notice that his offer had been accepted by the Smiths."

There is no contract until acceptance of an offer is communicated to the offeror. ACF Ind., Inc. v. Ind. Comm., 320 S.W.2d 484, 492[10] (Mo. banc 1959); Robinson v. The St. Louis Kansas City & Northern Railway Company, 75 Mo. 494, 498 (1882); Londoff v. Conrad, 749 S.W.2d 463, 465[1] (Mo.App.1988); Tri-State Motor Tr. Co., v. Ind. Comm., 509 S.W.2d 217, 226 [11] (Mo.App.1974); Lynch v. Webb City School District No. 92, 418

S.W.2d 608, 615 (Mo.App.1967); Sokol v. Hill, 310 S.W.2d 19, 20 (Mo.App.1958); 17 Am.Jur.2d Contracts § 43, p. 380; 17 C.J.S. Contracts § 45, p. 690.

An uncommunicated intention to accept an offer is not an acceptance. Thacker v. Massman Const. Co., 247 S.W.2d 623, 629-30 (Mo.1952); Medicine Shoppe Intern., Inc. v. J-Pral Corp., 662 S.W.2d 263, 269[3,4] (Mo.App.1983). When an offer calls for a promise, as distinguished from an act, on the part of the offeree, notice of acceptance is always essential. Thacker v. Massman Const. Co., supra, at 629; Daggett v. Kansas City Structural Steel Co., 334 Mo. 207, 65 S.W.2d 1036, 1039 (1933). A mere private act of the offeree does not constitute an acceptance. Lynch v. Webb City School District No. 92, supra, at 615[6]; Hunt v. Jeffries, 236 Mo.App. 476, 484, 156 S.W.2d 23, 27[3] (Mo.App.1941); 17 Am.Jur.2d Contracts § 44, p. 382. Communication of acceptance of a contract to an agent of the offeree is not sufficient and does not bind the offeror. Horton v. N.Y. Life Ins. Co., 151 Mo. 604, 620, 52 S.W. 356, 360 (1899); Sokol v. Hill, supra, at 20[1].

Unless the offer is supported by consideration, Coffman Industries, Inc. v. Gorman-Taber Co., 521 S.W.2d 763, 772 (Mo.App.1975), an offeror may withdraw his offer at any time "before acceptance and communication of that fact to him." Sokol v. Hill, supra, at 20[2]. To similar effect see National Advertising Co. v. Herold, 735 S.W.2d 74, 77 (Mo.App.1987). To be effective, revocation of an offer must be communicated to the offeree before he has accepted. Medicine Shoppe Intern., Inc. v. J-Pral Corp., supra, at 269; Rodgers v. Rodgers, 505 S.W.2d 138, 144 (Mo.App.1974); Lynch v. Webb City School District No. 92, supra, at 617; 17 Am.Jur.2d Contracts § 35, p. 374; 17 C.J.S. Contracts § 50(d), p. 712.

Notice to the agent, within the scope of the agent's authority, is notice to the principal, and the agent's knowledge is binding on the principal. Hunter v. Hunter, 327 Mo. 817, 39 S.W.2d 359, 364[10] (1931); Dace v. John Hancock Mut. Life Ins. Co., 148 S.W.2d 93, 95[1] (Mo.App.1941). See also Luker v. Moffett, 327 Mo. 929, 38 S.W.2d 1037, 1041 [6] (1931); 3 C.J.S. Agency § 432, p. 295.

Before Behee was notified that the Smiths had accepted his offer, Behee notified the agent of the Smiths that Behee was withdrawing the offer. The notice to the agent, being within the scope of her authority, was binding upon the Smiths. Behee's offer was not supported by consideration and his withdrawal of it was proper. Cases involving facts similar to those at bar include National Advertising Co. v. Herold, supra, and Sokol v. Hill, supra.

The judgment is affirmed.

HOGAN, C.J., and MAUS, J., concur.

FUJIMOTO V. RIO GRANDE PICKLE CO.
United States Court of Appeals, Fifth Circuit
414 F.2d 648 (1969).

Before GOLDBERG and MORGAN, Circuit Judges, and LIEB, District Judge.

GOLDBERG, Circuit Judge:

This appeal involves claims by George Fujimoto and Jose Bravo against the Rio Grande Pickle Company upon written contracts of employment. The questions before us are of contract formation and construction.

Rio Grande Pickle Company, a Colorado corporation engaged in the business of raising and selling cucumbers for the pickling industry, hired Fujimoto in the Spring of 1965 and Bravo in the following Fall. Both of these employees were given important jobs. Fujimoto was employed as the supervisor of the planting and growing operations, while Bravo functioned as the labor recruiter.

In order to encourage them to work with zeal and not to leave the company's employ, Rio Grande offered contracts with profit sharing bonus provisions to both Fujimoto and Bravo. Prior to the offer of the written contracts, the company had responded to the offerees' demands for more compensation by orally agreeing to pay them a salary plus a bonus of ten per cent of the company's annual profits. Bravo told the president of Rio Grande that he wanted the agreement in writing, and the president replied "I will prepare one and send you a contract in writing." The contractual documents sent to Fujimoto and Bravo did not specify how the offers could be accepted or how the acceptances should be communicated to the company. Under these circumstances Fujimoto and Bravo signed their respective contracts but did not return them to the company. Believing that they had accepted the company's offers and that they were working under the proffered bonus contracts, the two employees remained in the employ of Rio Grande until November 30, 1966.

The written contracts called for the employees to devote their best efforts to Rio Grande and promised in return that the company would pay each offeree a bonus amounting to ten per cent of the company's net profits for each fiscal year. Each employee was to agree to return half of his bonus to the company as an investment in company stock.

Partly as a consequence of projected changes in the nature of the corporation's business, Fujimoto and Bravo quit their jobs with Rio Grande on November 30, 1966. Shortly thereafter the company ceased doing business in Texas. Fujimoto and Bravo then brought this suit, claiming that they had accepted the offered contracts and that they had not received the ten per cent bonuses due them. They alleged that they were each entitled to ten per cent of the company's net profits for the fiscal year ending September 30, 1966, and ten per cent of the profits of the subsequent two months, October and November, 1966.

In answer to special interrogatories the jury found that Fujimoto and Bravo each had entered into a written contract in October, 1965. It was then determined that Fujimoto and Bravo should each recover the sum of $8,964.25 as damages for the company's breach of contract.

On appeal Rio Grande argues that there is insufficient evidence in the record to support the jury's finding that Fujimoto and Bravo had accepted the offered bonus contracts. The company further argues that even if the contracts had been accepted, the district court's judgment still should be reversed because the court erred in charging the jury as to how to compute the net profits of the corporation.

We have concluded that employment contracts were accepted and that they subsisted throughout the fiscal year ending September 30, 1966, and for two months into the following fiscal year. However, we have also concluded that the district court erred in instructing the jury on how to compute Rio Grande's net profits for the truncated period of October and November, 1966. The judgment of the district court is, therefore, affirmed in part and reversed and remanded in part.

I.

Rio Grande argues that there were no contracts because Fujimoto and Bravo did not accept the written bonus offers by signing and returning the written instruments to the company. Each contract was signed by the respective employee, but neither was returned. Thus the first issue is whether the offers, which by their terms did not specify the means by which they could be accepted, could be accepted by a mode other than the return of the signed instruments.

Professor Corbin has summarized the law on this issue as follows:

> In the first place, there is no question that the offeror can require notice of acceptance in any form that he pleases. He can require that it shall be in any language and transmitted in any manner. He may require notice to be given by a nod of the head, by flags, by wig-wag, by a smoke signal on a high hill. He may require that it be by letter, telegraph or radio, and that there shall be no contract unless and until he is himself made conscious of it.
>
> Secondly, the offeror can specify a mode of making an acceptance of his offer, without making that method exclusive of all others. If the mode that he specifies is one that may not bring home to him the knowledge that his offer has been accepted, then such knowledge by him is not a requisite. The offeror can specify a mode of acceptance without any knowledge of the law of contract and without thinking in terms of offer and acceptance at all. This will be considered below.

> Thirdly, if the offeror specifies no mode of acceptance, the law requires no more than that the mode adopted shall be in accord with the usage and custom of men in similar cases. If proof of such usage and custom is wanting or is uncertain, the court must consider probable convenience and results and then help by its decision to establish a custom for the future and a rule of law.

Corbin on Contracts § 67, p. 109 (Student Ed. 1952). See also Allied Steel & Conveyors, Inc. v. Ford Motor Company, 6 Cir. 1960, 277 F.2d 907, 910-911.

This case falls within the third of Professor Corbin's rules. Neither written offer specified a particular mode of acceptance, and there is no evidence that Rio Grande ever manifested any intent that the offers could be accepted only by the return of the signed instruments. Moreover, there is substantial and convincing evidence to the contrary. The record is replete with evidence that the company conditioned the bonus offers primarily upon the offerees remaining in the company's employment and that the employees understood that they did not have to return the signed contracts in order to have contracts under which they would each get a ten per cent bonus.

Since we have found that the return of the signed documents was not the exclusive means by which the offerees could convey their acceptances, we must now determine whether Fujimoto and Bravo in fact adequately communicated such acceptances to the company. Where, as here, the offer and surrounding circumstances are silent as to permissible modes of acceptance, the law requires only that there be some clear and unmistakable expression of the offeree's intention to accept. In the words of Professor Corbin:

> Whenever the case is such as to require a notice of acceptance, it is not enough for the offeree to express mental assent, or even to do some overt act that is not known to the offeror and is not one that constitutes a customary method of giving notice. If the overt act is one that clearly expresses an intention to accept the specific offer and is in fact known by the offeror, there is an effective acceptance. This is because the offeror has actual knowledge.

Corbin on Contracts, supra, § 67 at p. 111.

As professor Corbin indicates, the mode of expressing assent is inconsequential so long as it effectively makes known to the offeror that his offer has been accepted. One usually thinks of acceptance in terms of oral or written incantations, but in many situations acts or symbols may be equally effective communicative media. See Restatement of Contracts § 21. In the words of Chief Judge Brown in Aetna Casualty & Surety Co. v. Berry, 5 Cir. 1965, 350 F.2d 49, 54:

> That the communication from the Berry Companies to Aetna was not in words express goes only to the weight and clarity of the message, but it does not mean that no contract came into existence. Of necessity, the law has long recognized the efficacy of nonverbal communications. From the formation

> of contracts by an offeree's silence, nod, hand signal or 'x' on an order blank to the doctrine of admission by silence, the law has legally realized that to offer guidance and comment meaningfully on the full range of human conduct, cognizance must be taken of communications other than by words. Symbols for words often suffice. Lawyers and Judges live by them, as the citation to this very case may sometime demonstrate.

See also McCarty v. Langdeau, Tex.Civ.App.1960, 337 S.W.2d 407, 412 (writ ref'd n.r.e.).

In the case at bar there is substantial evidence to support the jury's finding that the company knew that the offerees had agreed to the terms of the proffered bonus contracts. Of particular importance is the fact that Fujimoto and Bravo, who had threatened to quit unless their remuneration was substantially increased, continued to work for the company for fourteen months after receiving the offers. Moreover, during this fourteen-month period they did not again express dissatisfaction with their compensation. There is also evidence that Fujimoto and Bravo discussed the bonus contracts with the company president in such circumstances and in such a manner that their assent and acceptance should have been unmistakable to him. In view of these circumstances, Rio Grande could not have been besieged with any Hamlet-like doubts regarding the existence of a contract. Since Rio Grande knew that Fujimoto and Bravo had accepted its offer, there was a valid and binding contract. See Williston on Contracts § 90 (1957). . . .

III

. . . The judgment of the district court is correct in all respect but one. The court properly held that the company's offers were accepted and that the contracts subsisted until the end of November, 1966. Contracts do not evanesce because of the perplexities in their construction, and their consequences cannot be ignored because of vexations in damage ascertainment. We hold, however, that the court should have allowed the jury a backward glance at losses carried over on the company's books from prior years. It is from this fiscal vista that the jury should have been instructed to determine Rio Grande's net profits for the October-November, 1966, period. The judgment of the district court is, therefore,

Affirmed in part and reversed and remanded in part.

---

c. Mailbox Rule

ADAMS V. LINDSELL
Court of King's Bench
106 Eng. Rep. 250 (1818).

Action for non-delivery of wool according to agreement. At the trial at the last Lent Assizes for the county of Worcester, before Burrough J. it appeared that the defendants who were dealers in wool, at St. Ives, in the county of Huntington, had, on Tuesday the 2d of September 1817, written the following letter to the plaintiff, who were woolen manufacturers residing in Bromsgrove, Worcestershire.

> We now offer you eight hundred tods of wether fleeces, of a good fair quality of our country wool, at 35s. 6d. per tod, to be delivered at Leicester, and to be paid for by two months bill in two months, and to be weighed up by your agent within fourteen days, receiving your answer in course of power.

This letter was misdirected by the defendants, to Bromsgrove, Leicestershire, in consequence of which it was not received by the plaintiffs in Worcestershire till 7 p.m. on Friday, September 5th. On that evening the plaintiffs wrote an answer, agreeing to accept the wool on the terms proposed. The course of the post between St. Ives and Bromsgrove is through London, and consequently this answer was not received till by the defendants till Tuesday, September 9th. On Monday September 8th, the defendants not having, as they expected, received an answer on Sunday September 7th, (which in case their letter had not been misdirected would have been the usual course in post,) sold the wool in question to another person. Under these circumstances, the learned Judge held, that the delay having been occasioned by the neglects of the defendants, the jury must take it, that the answer did come back in due course of post; and that then the defendants were liable for the loss that had been sustained; and the plaintiffs accordingly recovered the verdict.

Jervis having an Easter term obtained a rule nisi for a new trial on the ground that there was no binding contract between the parties.

Dauncey, Puller, and Richardson showed cause. They contended that at the moment of the acceptance of the offer of the defendants by the plaintiffs, the former became bound. And that was on the Friday evening, when there had been no change of circumstances. They were then stopped by the Court, who called upon Jervis and Campbell in support of the rule. They relied on *Payne v. Cave* [3 T.R. 148], and more particularly on *Cooke v. Oxley* [Ibid. 653]. In that case, Oxley, who had proposed to sell goods to Cooke, and given him a certain time at his request, to determine whether he would buy them or not, was held not liable to the performances of the contract, even though Cooke, within the specified time, had determined to buy them, and given Oxley notice to that effect. So here the defendants who have proposed by letter to sell this wool are not to be held liable, even though it be now admitted that the answer did come back in the due course of post. Till the plaintiffs' answer was actually received, there could be no binding contract between the parties; and before then, the defendants had retracted their offer, by selling the wool to other persons. But—

The Court said, that if that were so, no contract could ever be completed by the post. For if the defendants were not bound by their offer when accepted by the plaintiffs till the answer was received, then the plaintiffs ought not to be bound till after they had received notification that the defendants had received their answer and assented to it. And so it might go on ad infinitum. The defendants must be considered in law as making, during every instant of the time their letter was travelling, the same identical offer to the plaintiffs; and then the contract is completed by the acceptance of it by the letter. Then as to the delay in notifying the acceptance, that arises entirely from the mistake of the defendants, and it therefore must be taken against them, that the plaintiffs answer was received in course of post.

Rule discharged.

NOTES AND QUESTIONS:

1. Compare the foregoing cases with *Lewis v. Browning*, 130 Mass. 173 (1881), in which the offeror stated in a letter, "if I don't hear from you by the 18th or 20th I shall conclude 'no'," followed by an undelivered telegram sent on the 17th.

2. *See* Restatement (Second) of Contracts §§ 63 (Time When Acceptance Takes Effect), 64 (Acceptance by Telephone or Teletype), 65 (Reasonableness of Medium of Acceptance), 66 (Acceptance Must Be Properly Dispatched), and 67 (Effect of Receipt of Acceptance Improperly Dispatched) (1981).

---

3. Acceptance by Silence

DAY V. CATON
Supreme Judicial Court of Massachusetts
119 Mass. 513 (1876).

CONTRACT to recover the value of one half of a brick party wall built by the plaintiff upon and between the adjoining estates, 27 and 29 Greenwich Park, Boston.

At the trial in the Superior Court, before *Allen,* J., it appeared that, in 1871, the plaintiff, having an equitable interest in lot 29, built the wall in question, placing one half of it on the vacant lot 27, in which the defendant then had an equitable interest. The plaintiff testified that there was an express agreement on the defendant's part to pay him one half the value of the wall when the defendant should use it in building upon lot 27. The defendant denied this, and testified that he never had any conversation with the plaintiff about the wall; and there was no other direct testimony on this point.

The defendant requested the judge to rule that,

1. The plaintiff can recover in this case only upon an express agreement.

2. If the jury find there was no express agreement about the wall, but the defendant knew that the plaintiff was building upon land in which the defendant had an equitable interest, the defendant's rights would not be affected by such knowledge, and his silence and subsequent use of the wall would raise no implied promise to pay anything for the wall.

The judge refused so to rule, but instructed the jury as follows:

A promise would not be implied from the fact that the plaintiff, with the defendant's knowledge, built the wall and the defendant used it, but it might be implied from the conduct of the parties. If the jury find that the plaintiff undertook and completed the building of the wall with the expectation that the defendant would pay him for it, and the defendant had reason to know that the plaintiff was so acting with that expectation and allowed him so to act without objection, then the jury might infer a promise on the part of the defendant to pay the plaintiff.

The jury found for the plaintiff; and the defendant alleged exceptions. . . .

DEVENS, J.

The ruling that a promise to pay for the wall would not be implied from the fact that the plaintiff, with the defendant's knowledge, built the wall, and that the defendant used it, was substantially in accordance with the request of the defendant, and is conceded to have been correct. Chit. Con. (11th Am. ed.) 86. *Wells v. Banister,* 4 Mass. 514. *Knowlton v. Plantation No.* 4, 14 Maine, 20. *Davis v. School District in Bradford,* 24 Maine, 349.

The defendant, however, contends that the presiding judge incorrectly ruled that such promise might be inferred from the fact that the plaintiff undertook and completed the building of the wall with the expectation that the defendant would pay him for it, the defendant having reason to know that the plaintiff was acting with that expectation, and allowed him thus to act without objection.

The fact that the plaintiff expected to be paid for the work would certainly not be sufficient of itself to establish the existence of a contract, when the question between the parties was whether one was made. *Taft v. Dickinson,* 6 Allen 553. It must be shown that, in some manner, the party sought to be charged assented to it. If a party, however, voluntarily accepts and avails himself of valuable services rendered for his benefit, when he has the option whether to accept or reject them, even if there is no distinct proof that they were rendered by his authority or request, a promise to pay for them may be inferred. His knowledge that they were valuable, and his exercise of the option to avail himself of them, justify this inference. *Abbot v. Hermon,* 7 Greenl. 118. *Hayden v. Madison,* 7 Greenl. 76. And when one stands by in silence and sees valuable services rendered upon his real estate by the erection of a structure, (of which he must necessarily avail himself afterwards in his proper use thereof,) such silence, accompanied with the knowledge on his part that the party rendering the services expects payment therefor, may fairly be treated as evidence of an acceptance of it, and as tending to show an agreement to pay for it.

The maxim, *Qui tacet consentire videtur,* is to be construed indeed as applying only to those cases where the circumstances are such that a party is fairly called upon either to deny or admit his liability. But if silence may be interpreted as assent where a proposition is made to one which he is bound to deny or admit, so also it may be if he is silent in the face of facts which fairly call upon him to speak. *Lamb v. Bunce,* 4 M. & S. 275. *Conner v. Hackley,* 2 Met?? 613. *Preston v. American Linen Co.* 119 Mass. 400.

If a person saw day after day a laborer at work in his field doing services, which  must of necessity enure to his benefit, knowing that the laborer expected pay for his work, when it was perfectly easy to notify him if his services were not wanted, even if a request were not expressly proved, such a request, either previous to or contemporaneous with the performance of the services, might fairly be inferred. But if the fact was merely brought to his attention upon a single occasion and casually, if he had little opportunity to notify the other that he did not desire the work and should not pay for it, or could only do so at the expense of much time and trouble, the same inference might not be made. The circumstances of each case would necessarily determine whether silence with a knowledge that another was doing valuable work for his benefit, and with the expectation of payment, indicated that consent which would give rise to the inference of a contract. The question would be one for the jury, and to them it was properly submitted in the case before us by the presiding judge.

Exceptions overruled.

COLT & LORD, JJ., absent.

HOBBS V. MASSASOIT WHIP CO.
Supreme Judicial Court of Massachusetts, Essex
33 N.E. 495 (1893).

HOLMES, Justice.

This is an action for the price of eel skins sent by the plaintiff to the defendant, and kept by the defendant some months, until they were destroyed. It must be taken that the plaintiff received no notice that the defendants declined to accept the skins. The case comes before us on exceptions to an instruction to the jury that, whether there was any prior contract or not, if skins are sent to the defendant, and it sees fit, whether it has agreed to take them or not, to lie back, and to say nothing, having reason to suppose that the man who has sent them believes that it is taking them, since it says nothing about it, then, if it fails to notify, the jury would be warranted in finding for the plaintiff.

Standing alone, and unexplained, this proposition might seem to imply that one stranger may impose a duty upon another, and make him a purchaser, in spite of himself, by sending goods to him, unless he will take the trouble, and bear the expense, of notifying the sender that he will not buy. The case was argued for the defendant on that interpretation. But, in view of the evidence, we do not understand that to have been the meaning of the judge, and we do not think that the jury can have understood that to have been his meaning. The plaintiff was not a stranger to the defendant, even if there was no contract between them. He had sent eel skins in the same way four or five times before, and they had been accepted and paid for. On the defendant's testimony, it was fair to assume that if it had admitted the eel skins to be over 22 inches in length, and fit for its business, as the plaintiff testified and the jury found that they were, it would have accepted them; that this was understood by the plaintiff; and, indeed, that there was a standing offer to him for such skins.

In such a condition of things, the plaintiff was warranted in sending the defendant skins conforming to the requirements, and even if the offer was not such that the contract was made as soon as skins corresponding to its terms were sent, sending them did impose on the defendant a duty to act about them; and silence on its part, coupled with a retention of the skins for an unreasonable time, might be found by the jury to warrant the plaintiff in assuming that they were accepted, and thus to amount to an acceptance. See Bushel v. Wheeler, 15 Q.B. 442; Benj. Sales, (6th Amer.Ed.) §§ 162-164; Taylor v. Engine Co. 146 Mass. 613, 615, 16 N.E.Rep. 462. The proposition stands on the general principle that conduct which imports acceptance or assent is acceptance or assent, in the view of the law, whatever may have been the actual state of mind of the party,-a principle sometimes lost sight of in the cases. O'Donnell v. Clinton, 145 Mass. 461, 463, 14 N.E.Rep. 747; McCarthy v. Railroad Corp., 148 Mass. 550, 552, 20 N.E.Rep. 182.

Exceptions overruled.

NOTES AND QUESTIONS:

1. *See* Restatement (Second) of Contracts §§ 30 (Form of Acceptance Invited); 32 (Invitation of Promise or Performance); 50 (Acceptance of Offer Defined; Acceptance by Performance; Acceptance by Promise), 52 (Who May Accept an Offer), 53 (Acceptance by Performance; Manifestation of Intention Not to Accept); 54 (Acceptance by Performance; Necessity of Notification to Offeror); 56 (Acceptance by Promise; Necessity of Notification to Offeror); 57 (Effect of Equivocal Acceptance), 58 (Necessity of Acceptance Complying with Terms of Offer), 62 (Effect of Performance by Offeree Where Offer Invites Either Performance or Promise), 63 (Time When Acceptance Takes Effect), 65 (Reasonable Medium Of Acceptance), 66 (Acceptance Must Be Properly Dispatched), 67 (Effect of Receipt of Acceptance Improperly Dispatched), and 69 (Acceptance by Silence or Exercise of Dominion) (1981).

2. *See Bakke v. Columbia Valley Lumber Company, Inc.*, 298 P.2d 849 (Wash. Sup. Ct. 1956) (Acceptance by Silence); Moore Construction Co. v. Kuehn, 602 S.W.2d 713 (Mo. Ct. App. Eastern Dist., 1980) (Acceptance by Silence).

SECTION 5. CONSIDERATION

A. A PROMISE, PERFORMANCE, OR FORBEARANCE

HAMER V. SIDWAY
Court of Appeals of New York.
27 N.E. 256 (1891).

. . . .

APPEAL from order of the General Term of the Supreme Court in the fourth judicial department, made July 1, 1890, which reversed a judgment in favor of plaintiff entered upon a decision of the court on trial at Special Term and granted a new trial.

This action was brought upon an alleged contract.

The plaintiff presented a claim to the executor of William E. Story, Sr., for $5,000 and interest from the 6th day of February, 1875. She acquired it through several mesne assignments from William E. Story, 2d. The claim being rejected by the executor, this action was brought. It appears that William E. Story, Sr., was the uncle of William E. Story, 2d; that at the celebration of the golden wedding of Samuel Story and wife, father and mother of William E. Story, Sr., on the 20th day of March, 1869, in the presence of the family and invited guests he promised his nephew that if he would refrain from drinking, using tobacco, swearing and playing cards or billiards for money until he became twenty-one years of age he would pay him a sum of $5,000. The nephew assented thereto and fully performed the conditions inducing the promise. When the nephew arrived at the age of twenty-one years and on the 31st day of January, 1875, he wrote to his uncle informing him that he had performed his part of the agreement and had thereby become entitled to the sum of $5,000.

The uncle received the letter and a few days later and on the sixth of February, he wrote and mailed to his nephew the following letter:

> 'BUFFALO, *Feb.* 6, 1875.
>
> 'W. E. STORY, Jr.:
>
> 'DEAR NEPHEW--Your letter of the 31st ult. came to hand all right, saying that you had lived up to the promise made to me several years ago. I have no doubt but you have, for which you shall have five thousand dollars as I promised you. I had the money in the bank the day you was 21 years old that I intend for you, and you shall have the money certain. Now, Willie I do not intend to interfere with this money in any way till I think you are capable of taking care of it and the sooner that time comes the better it will please me. I would hate very much to have you start out in some adventure that you thought all right and lose this money in one year. The first five thousand dollars that I got together cost me a heap of hard work. You would hardly believe me when I tell you that to obtain this I shoved a jackplane many a day, butchered three or four years, then came to this city, and after three months' perseverence I obtained a situation in a grocery store. I opened this store early, closed late, slept in the fourth story of the building in a room 30 by 40 feet and not a human being in the building but myself. All this I done to live as cheap as I could to save something. I don't want you to take up with this kind of fare. I was here in the cholera season '49 and '52 and the deaths averaged 80 to 125 daily and plenty of small-pox. I wanted to go home, but Mr. Fisk, the gentleman I was working for, told me if I left then, after it got healthy he probably would not want me. I stayed. All the money I have saved I know just how I got it. It did not come to me in any mysterious way, and the reason I speak of this is that money got in this way stops longer with a fellow that gets it with hard knocks than it does when he finds it. Willie, you are 21 and you have many a thing to learn yet. This money you have earned much easier than I did besides acquiring good habits at the same time and you are quite welcome to the money; hope you will make good use of it. I was ten long years getting this together after I was your age. Now, hoping this will be satisfactory, I stop. One thing more. Twenty-one years ago I bought you 15 sheep. These sheep were put out to double every four years. I kept track of them the first eight years; I have not heard much about them since. Your father and grandfather promised me that they would look after them till you were of age. Have they done so? I hope they have. By this time you have between five and six hundred sheep, worth a nice little income this spring. Willie, I have said much more than I expected to; hope you can make out what I have written. To-day is the seventeenth day that I have not been out of my room, and have had the doctor as many days. Am a little better to-day; think I will get out next week. You need not mention to father, as he always worries about small matters.

Truly Yours,

'W. E. STORY.

'P. S.--You can consider this money on interest.'

The nephew received the letter and thereafter consented that the money should remain with his uncle in accordance with the terms and conditions of the letters. The uncle died on the 29th day of January, 1887, without having paid over to his nephew any portion of the said $5,000 and interest. . . .

PARKER, J.

The question which provoked the most discussion by counsel on this appeal, and which lies at the foundation of plaintiff's asserted right of recovery, is whether by virtue of a contract defendant's testator William E. Story became indebted to his nephew William E. Story, 2d, on his twenty-first birthday in the sum of five thousand dollars. The trial court found as a fact that "on the 20th day of March, 1869, . . . William E. Story agreed to and with William E. Story, 2d, that if he would refrain from drinking liquor, using tobacco, swearing, and playing cards or billiards for money until he should become 21 years of age then he, the said William E. Story, would at that time pay him, the said William E. Story, 2d, the sum of $5,000 for such refraining, to which the said William E. Story, 2d, agreed," and that he "in all things fully performed his part of said agreement."

The defendant contends that the contract was without consideration to support it, and, therefore, invalid. He asserts that the promisee by refraining from the use of liquor and tobacco was not harmed but benefited; that that which he did was best for him to do independently of his uncle's promise, and insists that it follows that unless the promisor was benefited, the contract was without consideration. A contention, which if well founded, would seem to leave open for controversy in many cases whether that which the promisee did or omitted to do was, in fact, of such benefit to him as to leave no consideration to support the enforcement of the promisor's agreement. Such a rule could not be tolerated, and is without foundation in the law. The Exchequer Chamber, in 1875, defined consideration as follows: "A valuable consideration in the sense of the law may consist either in some right, interest, profit or benefit accruing to the one party, or some forbearance, detriment, loss or responsibility given, suffered or undertaken by the other." Courts "will not ask whether the thing which forms the consideration does in fact benefit the promisee or a third party, or is of any substantial value to anyone. It is enough that something is promised, done, forborne or suffered by the party to whom the promise is made as consideration for the promise made to him." (Anson's Prin. of Con. 63.)

"In general a waiver of any legal right at the request of another party is a sufficient consideration for a promise." (Parsons on Contracts, 444.)

"Any damage, or suspension, or forbearance of a right will be sufficient to sustain a promise." (Kent, vol. 2, 465, 12th ed.)

Pollock, in his work on contracts, page 166, after citing the definition given by the Exchequer Chamber already quoted, says: "The second branch of this judicial description is really the most important one. Consideration means not so much that one party is profiting as that the other abandons some legal right in the present or limits his legal freedom of action in the future as an inducement for the promise of the first."

Now, applying this rule to the facts before us, the promisee used tobacco, occasionally drank liquor, and he had a legal right to do so. That right he abandoned for a period of years upon the strength of the promise of the testator that for such forbearance he would give him $5,000. We need not speculate on the effort which may have been required to give up the use of those stimulants. It is sufficient that he restricted his lawful freedom of action within certain prescribed limits upon the faith of his uncle's agreement, and now having fully performed the conditions imposed, it is of no moment whether such performance actually proved a benefit to the promisor, and the court will not inquire into it, but were it a proper subject of inquiry, we see nothing in this record that would permit a determination that the uncle was not benefited in a legal sense. Few cases have been found which may be said to be precisely in point, but such as have been support the position we have taken. . . .

The trial court found as a fact that "said letter was received by said William E. Story, 2d, who thereafter consented that said money should remain with the said William E. Story in accordance with the terms and conditions of said letter." And further, "That afterwards, on the first day of March, 1877, with the knowledge and consent of his said uncle, he duly sold, transferred and assigned all his right, title and interest in and to said sum of $5,000 to his wife Libbie H. Story, who thereafter duly sold, transferred and assigned the same to the plaintiff in this action.". . .

The order appealed from should be reversed and the judgment of the Special Term affirmed, with costs payable out of the estate.

All concur.

Order reversed and judgment of Special Term affirmed.

FIEGE V. BOEHM
Court of Appeals of Maryland
123 A.2d 316 (1956).

DELAPLAINE, JUDGE

This suit was brought in the Superior Court of Baltimore City by Hilda Louise Boehm against Louis Gail Fiege to recover for breach of a contract to pay the expenses incident to the birth of his bastard child and to provide for its support upon condition that she would refrain from prosecuting him for bastardy.

Plaintiff alleged in her declaration substantially as follows: (1) that early in 1951 defendant had sexual intercourse with her although she was unmarried, and as a result thereof she became pregnant, and defendant acknowledged that he was responsible for her pregnancy; (2) that on September 29, 1951, she gave birth to a female child; that defendant is the father of the child; and that he acknowledged on many occasions that he is its father; (3) that before the child was born, defendant agreed to pay all her medical and miscellaneous expenses and to compensate her for the loss of her salary caused by the child's birth, and also to pay her ten dollars per week for its support until it reached the age of 21, upon condition that she would not institute bastardy proceedings against him as long as he made the payments in accordance with the agreement; (4) that she placed the child for adoption on July 13, 1954, and she claimed the following sums: Union Memorial Hospital, $110; Florence Crittenton Home, $1,000; Dr. George Merrill, her physician, $50; medicines $70.35; miscellaneous expenses, $20.45; loss of earnings for 26 weeks, $1,105; support of the child, $1,440; total, $2,895.80; and (5) that defendant paid her only $480, and she demanded that he pay her the further sum of $2,415.80, the balance due under the agreement, but he failed and refused to pay the same.

Defendant demurred to the declaration on the ground that it failed to allege that in September, 1953, plaintiff instituted bastardy proceedings against him in the Criminal Court of Baltimore, but since it had been found from blood tests that he could not have been the father of the child, he was acquitted of bastardy. The Court sustained the demurrer with leave to amend.

Plaintiff then filed an amended declaration, which contained the additional allegation that, after the breach of the agreement by defendant, she filed a charge with the State's Attorney that defendant was the father of her bastard child; and that on October 8, 1953, the Criminal Court found defendant not guilty solely on a physician's testimony that "on the basis of certain blood tests made, the defendant can be excluded as the father of the said child, which testimony is not conclusive upon a jury in a trial court."

Defendant also demurred to the amended declaration, but the Court overruled that demurrer.

Plaintiff, a typist, now over 35 years old, who has been employed by the Government in Washington and Baltimore for over thirteen years, testified in the Court below that she had never been married, but that at about midnight on January 21, 1951, defendant, after taking her to a moving picture theater on York Road and then to a restaurant, had sexual intercourse with her in his automobile. She further testified that he agreed to pay all her medical and hospital expenses, to compensate her for loss of salary caused by the pregnancy and birth, and to pay her ten dollars per week for the support of the child upon condition that she would refrain from instituting bastardy proceedings against him. She further testified that between September 17, 1951, and May, 1953, defendant paid her a total of $480.

Defendant admitted that he had taken plaintiff to restaurants, had danced with her several times, had taken her to Washington, and had brought her home in the country; but he asserted that he had never had sexual intercourse with her. He also claimed that he did not enter into any agreement with her. He admitted, however, that he had paid her a total of

$480. His father also testified that he stated "that he did not want his mother to know, and if it were just kept quiet, kept principally away from his mother and the public and the courts, that he would take care of it."

Defendant further testified that in May, 1953, he went to see plaintiff's physician to make inquiry about blood tests to show the paternity of the child; and that those tests were made and they indicated that it was not possible that he could have been the child's father. He then stopped making payments. Plaintiff thereupon filed a charge of bastardy with the State's Attorney.

The testimony which was given in the Criminal Court by Dr. Milton Sachs, hematologist at the University Hospital, was read to the jury in the Superior Court. In recent years the blood-grouping test has been employed in criminology, in the selection of donors for blood transfusions, and as evidence in paternity cases. The Landsteiner blood-grouping test is based on the medical theory that the red corpuscles in human blood contain two affirmative agglutinating substances, and that every individual's blood falls into one of the four classes and remains the same throughout life. According to Mendel's law of inheritance, this blood individuality is an hereditary characteristic which passes from parent to child, and no agglutinating substance can appear in the blood of a child which is not present in the blood of one of its parents. The four Landsteiner blood groups, designated as AB, A, B, and O, into which human blood is divided on the basis of the compatibility of the corpuscles and serum with the corpuscles and serum of other persons, are characterized by different combinations of two agglutinogens in the red blood cells and two agglutinins in the serum. Dr. Sachs reported that Fiege's blood group was Type O, Miss Boehm's was Type B, and the infant's was Type A. He further testified that on the basis of these tests, Fiege could not have been the father of the child, as it is impossible for a mating of Type O and Type B to result in a child of Type A.

Although defendant was acquitted by the Criminal Court, the Superior Court overruled his motion for a directed verdict. In the charge to the jury the Court instructed them that defendant's acquittal in the Criminal Court was not binding upon them. The jury found a verdict in favor of plaintiff for $2,415.80, the full amount of her claim.

Defendant filed a motion for judgment n. o. v. or a new trial. The Court overruled that motion also, and entered judgment on the verdict of the jury. Defendant appealed from that judgment.

Defendant contends that, even if he did enter into the contract as alleged, it was not enforceable, because plaintiff's forbearance to prosecute was not based on a valid claim, and hence the contract was without consideration. He, therefore, asserts that the Court erred in overruling (1) his demurrer to the amended declaration, (2) his motion for a directed verdict, and (3) his motion for judgment n. o. v. or a new trial.

It was originally held at common law that a child born out of wedlock is filius nullius, and a putative father is not under any legal liability to contribute to the support of his illegitimate child, and his promise to do so is unenforceable because it is based on purely a moral obligation. Some of the courts in this country have held that, in the absence of any statutory obligation on the father to aid in the support of his bastard child, his promise to the child's mother to pay her for its maintenance, resting solely on his natural affection for it and his moral obligation to provide for it, is a promise which the law cannot enforce because of lack of sufficient consideration. Mercer v. Mercer's Adm'r, 87 Ky. 30, 7 S.W. 401; Wiggins v. Keizer, 6 Ind. 252; Davis v. Herrington, 53 Ark. 5, 13 S.W. 215. On the contrary, a few courts have stated that the natural affection of a father for his child and the moral obligation upon him to support it and to aid the woman he has wronged furnish sufficient consideration for his promise to the mother to pay for the support of the child to make the agreement enforceable at law. Birdsall v. Edgerton, 25 Wend., N.Y., 619; Todd v. Weber, 95 N.Y. 181, 47 Am.Rep. 20; Trayer v. Setzer, 72 Neb. 845, 101 N.W. 989.

However, where statutes are in force to compel the father of a bastard to contribute to its support, the courts have invariably held that a contract by the putative father with the mother of his bastard child to provide for the support of the child upon the agreement of the mother to refrain from invoking the bastardy statute against the father, or to abandon proceedings already commenced, is supported by sufficient consideration. Jangraw v. Perkins, 77 Vt. 375, 60 A. 385; Beach v. Voegtlen, 68 N.J.L. 472, 53 A. 695; Thayer v. Thayer, 189 N.C. 502, 127 S.E. 553, 39 A.L.R. 428.

In Maryland it is now provided by statute that whenever a person is found guilty of bastardy, the court shall issue an order directing such person (1) to pay for the maintenance and support of the child until it reaches the age of eighteen years, such sum as may be agreed upon, if consent proceedings be had, or in the absence of agreement, such sum as the court may fix, with due regard to the circumstances of the accused person; and (2) to give bond to the State of Maryland in such penalty as the court may fix, with good and sufficient securities, conditioned on making the payments required by the court's order, or any amendments thereof. Failure to give such bond shall be punished by commitment to the jail or the House of Correction until bond is given but not exceeding two years. Code Supp.1955, art. 12, § 8.

Prosecutions for bastardy are treated in Maryland as criminal proceedings, but they are actually civil in purpose. Kennard v. State, 177 Md. 549, 10 A.2d 710; Kisner v. State, Md., 122 A.2d 102. While the prime object of the Maryland Bastardy Act is to protect the public from the burden of maintaining illegitimate children, it is so distinctly in the interest of the mother that she becomes the beneficiary of it. Accordingly a contract by the putative father of an illegitimate child to provide for its support upon condition that bastardy proceedings will not be instituted is a compromise of civil injuries resulting from a criminal act, and not a contract to compound a criminal prosecution, and if it is fair and reasonable, it is in accord with the Bastardy Act and the public policy of the State.

Of course, a contract of a putative father to provide for the support of his illegitimate child must be based, like any other contract, upon sufficient consideration. The early English law made no distinction in regard to the sufficiency of a claim which the claimant promised to forbear to prosecute, as the consideration of a promise, other than the broad distinction between good claims and bad claims. No promise to forbear to prosecute an unfounded claim was sufficient consideration. In the early part of the Nineteenth Century, an advance was made from the criterion of the early authorities when it was held that forbearance to prosecute a suit which had already been instituted was sufficient consideration, without inquiring whether the suit would have been successful or not. Longridge v. Dorville, 5 B. & Ald. 117.

In 1867 the Maryland Court of Appeals, in the opinion delivered by Judge Bartol in Hartle v. Stahl, 27 Md. 157, 172, held: (1) that forbearance to assert a claim before institution of suit, if not in fact a legal claim, is not of itself sufficient consideration to support a promise; but (2) that a compromise of a doubtful claim or a relinquishment of a pending suit is good consideration for a promise; and (3) that in order to support a compromise, it is sufficient that the parties entering into it thought at the time that there was a bona fide question between them, although it may eventually be found that there was in fact no such question.

We have thus adopted the rule that the surrender of, or forbearance to assert, an invalid claim by one who has not an honest and reasonable belief in its possible validity is not sufficient consideration for a contract. 1 Restatement, Contracts, § 76(b). We combine the subjective requisite that the claim be bona fide with the objective requisite that it must have a reasonable basis of support. Accordingly a promise not to prosecute a claim which is not founded in good faith does not of itself give a right of action on an agreement to pay for refraining from so acting, because a release from mere annoyance and unfounded litigation does not furnish valuable consideration.

Professor Williston was not entirely certain whether the test of reasonableness is based upon the intelligence of the claimant himself, who may be an ignorant person with no knowledge of law and little sense as to facts; but he seemed inclined to favor the view that "the claim forborne must be neither absurd in fact from the standpoint of a reasonable man in the position of the claimant, nor, obviously unfounded in law to one who has an elementary knowledge of legal principles." 1 Williston on Contracts, Rev.Ed., § 135. We agree that while stress is placed upon the honesty and good faith of the claimant, forbearance to prosecute a claim is insufficient consideration if the claim forborne is so lacking in foundation as to make its assertion incompatible with honesty and a reasonable degree of intelligence. Thus, if the mother of a bastard knows that there is no foundation, either in law or fact, for a charge against a certain man that he is the father of the child, but that man  promises to pay her in order to prevent bastardy proceedings against him, the forbearance to institute proceedings is not sufficient consideration

On the other hand, forbearance to sue for a lawful claim or demand is sufficient consideration for a promise to pay for the forbearance if the party forbearing had and honest intention to prosecute litigation which is not frivolous, vexatious, or unlawful, and which he believed to be well founded. Snyder v. Cearfoss, 187 Md. 635, 643, 51 A.2d 264; Pullman Co. v. Ray, 201 Md. 268, 94 A.2d 266. Thus the promise of a woman who is expecting an illegitimate child that she will not institute bastardy proceedings against a certain man is sufficient consideration for his promise to pay for the child's support, even though it may not be certain whether the man is the father or whether the prosecution would be successful, if she makes the charge in good faith. The fact that a man accused of bastardy is forced to enter into a contract to pay for the support of his bastard child from fear of exposure and the shame that might be case upon him as a result, as well as a sense of justice to render some compensation for the injury he inflicted upon the mother, does not lessen the merit of the contract, but greatly increases it. Hook v. Pratt, 78 N.Y. 371, 34 Am.Rep. 539; Hays v. McFarlan, 32 Ga. 699, 79 Am.Dec. 317.

A case in point is Pflaum v. McClintock, 130 Pa. 369, 18 A. 734. That was an action to collect a judgment bond which the defendant signed when he was in jail to settle a fornication and bastardy case. The defendant claimed that the bond was conditioned on the support of a child expected to be born, but that he was innocent of the charge, and that in fact the obligee had not given birth to any living child, but died without issue before the judgment was entered. The Supreme Court of Pennsylvania decided that the bond was supported by a good consideration.

Another analogous case is Thompson v. Nelson, 28 Ind. 431. There the plaintiff sought to recover back money which he had paid to compromise a prosecution for bastardy. He claimed that the prosecuting witness was not pregnant and therefore the prosecution was fraudulent. It was held by the Supreme Court of Indiana, however, that the settlement of the prosecution was a good consideration for the payment of the money and it could not be recovered back, inasmuch as it appeared from the evidence that the prosecution was instituted in good faith, and at that time there was reason to believe that the prosecuting witness was pregnant, although it was found out afterwards that she was not pregnant.

Likewise, in Heaps v. Dunham, 95 Ill. 583, 590, the Supreme Court of Illinois held that a man charged with bastardy may compromise the claim with the woman who claims to be pregnant, and if the man, after being arrested, enters into a settlement not induced by fraud or oppression and gives his promissory note for the benefit of the woman and child, such a contract is supported by a good consideration. In explanation of its ruling, the Court said:

> But while there is great doubt from the evidence whether Lavina Snell was pregnant, yet so far as the charge of bastardy is concerned, as complainant voluntarily settled and gave his notes in settlement of the prosecution which had been commenced against him, he must be concluded by that settlement. When arrested on the charge he had the right to contest the case and require strict proof to sustain the charge, but under our statute a charge of this character may be settled between the prosecuting witness and defendant, and when a settlement has been made without fraud or oppression, we think it should be conclusive and binding between the parties.

In the case at bar there was no proof of fraud or unfairness. Assuming that the hematologists were accurate in their laboratory tests and findings, nevertheless plaintiff gave testimony which indicated that she made the charge of bastardy against defendant in good faith. For these reasons the Court acted properly in overruling the demurrer to the amended declaration and the motion for a directed verdict. . . .

As we have found no reversible error in the rulings and instructions of the trial Court, we will affirm the judgment entered on the verdict of the jury.

Judgment affirmed, with costs.

B. REQUIREMENT OF A BARGAIN

KIRKSEY V. KIRKSEY
Supreme Court of Alabama.
8 Ala. 131 (1845).

Error to the Circuit Court of Talladega.

ASSUMPSIT by the defendant, against the plaintiff in error. The question is presented in this Court, upon a case agreed, which shows the following facts:

The plaintiff was the wife of defendant's brother, but had for some time been a widow, and had several children. In 1840, the plaintiff resided on public land, under a contract of lease, she had held over, and was comfortably settled, and would have attempted to secure the land she lived on. The defendant resided in Talladega county, some sixty, or seventy miles off. On the 10th October, 1840, he wrote to her the following letter:

> Dear sister Antillico--Much to my mortification, I heard, that brother Henry was dead, and one of his children. I know that your situation is one of grief, and difficulty. You had a bad chance before, but a great deal worse now. I should like to come and see you, but cannot with convenience at present. . . . I do not know whether you have a preference on the place you live on, or not. If you had, I would advise you to obtain your preference, and sell the land and quit the country, as I understand it is very unhealthy, and I know society is very bad. If you will come down and see me, I will let you have a place to raise your family, and I have more open land than I can tend; and on the account of your situation, and that of your family, I feel like I want you and the children to do well.

Within a month or two after the receipt of this letter, the plaintiff abandoned her possession, without disposing of it, and removed with her family, to the residence of the defendant, who put her in comfortable houses, and gave her land to cultivate for two years, at the end of which time he notified her to remove, and put her in a house, not comfortable, in the woods, which he afterwards required her to leave.

A verdict being found for the plaintiff, for two hundred dollars, the above facts were agreed, and if they will sustain the action, the judgment is to be affirmed, otherwise it is to be reversed.

ORMOND, J.

The inclination of my mind, is, that the loss and inconvenience, which the plaintiff sustained in breaking up, and moving to the defendant's, a distance of sixty miles, is a sufficient consideration to support the promise, to furnish her with a house, and land to cultivate, until she could raise her family. My brothers, however think, that the promise on the part of the defendant, was a mere gratuity, and that an action will not lie for its breach. The judgment of the Court below must therefore be reversed, pursuant to the agreement of the parties.

MILLS v. WYMAN
SUPREME JUDICIAL COURT OF MASSACHUSETTS
20 MASS. 207 (1825).

. . . .

PARKER C. J.

General rules of law established for the protection and security of honest and fair-minded men, who may inconsiderately make promises without any equivalent, will sometimes screen men of a different character from engagements which they are bound in *foro conscientiæ* to perform. This is a defect inherent in all human systems of legislation. The rule that a mere verbal promise, without any consideration, cannot be enforced by action, is universal in its application, and cannot be departed from to suit particular cases in which a refusal to perform such a promise may be disgraceful.

The promise declared on in this case appears to have been made without any legal consideration. The kindness and services towards the sick son of the defendant were not bestowed at his request. The son was in no respect under the care of the defendant. He was twenty-five years old, and had long left his father's family. On his return from a foreign country, he fell sick among strangers, and the plaintiff acted the part of the good Samaritan, giving him shelter and comfort until he died. The defendant, his father, on being informed of this event, influenced by a transient feeling of gratitude, promises in writing to pay the plaintiff for the expenses he had incurred. But he has determined to break this promise, and is willing to have his case appear on record as a strong example of particular injustice sometimes necessarily resulting from the operation of general rules.

It is said a moral obligation is a sufficient consideration to support an express promise; and some authorities lay down the rule thus broadly; but upon examination of the cases we are satisfied that the universality of the rule cannot be supported, and that there must have been some preexisting obligation, which has become inoperative by positive law, to form a basis for an effective promise. The cases of debts barred by the statute of limitations, of debts incurred by infants, of debts of bankrupts, are generally put for illustration of the rule. Express promises founded on such preexisting equitable obligations may be enforced; there is a good consideration for them; they merely remove an impediment created by law to the recovery of debts honestly due, but which public policy protects the debtors from being compelled to pay. In all these cases there was originally a *quid pro quo;* and according to the principles of natural justice the party receiving ought to pay; but the legislature has said he shall not be coerced; then comes the promise to pay the debt that is barred, the promise of the man to pay the debt of the infant, of the discharged bankrupt to restore to his creditor what by the law he had lost. In all these cases there is a moral obligation founded upon an antecedent valuable consideration. These promises therefore have a sound legal basis. They are not promises to pay something for nothing; not naked pacts; but the voluntary revival or creation of obligation which before existed in natural law, but which had been dispensed with, not for the benefit of the party obliged solely, but principally for the public convenience. If moral obligation, in its fullest sense, is a good substratum for an express promise, it is not easy to perceive why it is not equally good to support an implied promise. What a man ought to do, generally he ought to be made to do, whether he promise or refuse. But the law of society has left most of such obligations to the *interior* forum, as the tribunal of conscience has been aptly called. Is there not a moral obligation upon every son who has become affluent by means of the education and advantages bestowed upon him by his father, to relieve that father from pecuniary embarrassment, to promote his comfort and happiness, and even to share with him his riches, if thereby he will be made happy? And yet such a son may, with impunity, leave such a father in any degree of penury above that which will expose the community in which he dwells, to the danger of being obliged to preserve him from absolute want. Is not a wealthy father under strong moral obligation to advance the interest of an obedient, well disposed son, to furnish him with the means of acquiring and maintaining a becoming rank in life, to rescue him from the horrors of debt incurred by misfortune? Yet the law will uphold him in any degree of parsimony, short of that which would reduce his son to the necessity of seeking public charity.

Without doubt there are great interests of society which justify withholding the coercive arm of the law from these duties of imperfect obligation, as they are called; imperfect, not because they are less binding upon the conscience than those which are called perfect, but because the wisdom of the social law does not impose sanctions upon them.

A deliberate promise, in writing, made freely and without any mistake, one which may lead the party to whom it is made into contracts and expenses, cannot be broken without a violation of moral duty. But if there was nothing paid or promised for it, the law, perhaps wisely, leaves the execution of it to the conscience of him who makes it. It is only when the party making the promise gains something, or he to whom it is made loses something, that the law gives the promise validity. And in the case of the promise of the adult to pay the debt of the infant, of the debtor discharged by the statute of limitations or bankruptcy, the principle is preserved by looking back to the origin of the transaction, where an equivalent is to be found. An exact equivalent is not required by the law; for there being a consideration, the parties are left to estimate its value: though here the courts of equity will step in to relieve from gross inadequacy between the consideration and the promise.

These principles are deduced from the general current of decided cases upon the subject, as well as from the known maxims of the common law. The general position, that moral obligation is a sufficient consideration for an express promise, is to be limited in its application, to cases where at some time or other a good or valuable consideration has existed.

A legal obligation is always a sufficient consideration to support either an express or an implied promise; such as an infant's debt for necessaries, or a father's promise to pay for the support and education of his minor children. But when the child shall have attained to manhood, and shall have become his own agent in the world's business, the debts he in curs [sic], whatever may be their nature, create no obligation upon the father; and it seems to follow, that his promise founded upon such a debt has no legally binding force.

The cases of instruments under seal and certain mercantile contracts, in which considerations need not be proved, do not contradict the principles above suggested. The first import a consideration in themselves, and the second belong to a branch of the mercantile law, which has found it necessary to disregard the point of consideration in respect to instruments negotiable in their nature and essential to the interests of commerce.

Instead of citing a multiplicity of cases to support the positions I have taken, I will only refer to a very able review of all the cases in the note in 3 Bos. & Pul. 249. The opinions of the judges had been variant for a long course of years upon this subject, but there seems to be no case in which it was nakedly decided, that a promise to pay the debt of a son of full age, not living with his father, though the debt were incurred by sickness which ended in the death of the son, without a previous request by the father proved or presumed, could be enforced by action. . . .

For the foregoing reasons we are all of opinion that the nonsuit directed by the Court of Common Pleas was right, and that judgment be entered thereon for costs for the defendant.

WEBB V. MCGOWIN
Court of Appeals of Alabama
168 So. 196 (1936).

BRICKEN, Presiding Judge.

This action is in assumpsit. The complaint as originally filed was amended. The demurrers to the complaint as amended were sustained, and because of this adverse ruling by the court the plaintiff took a non-suit, and the assignment of errors on this appeal are predicated upon said action or ruling of the court.

A fair statement of the case presenting the questions for decision is set out in appellant's brief, which we adopt.

> On the 3d day of August, 1925, appellant while in the employ of the W.T. Smith Lumber Company, a corporation, and acting within the scope of his employment, was engaged in clearing the upper floor of mill No. 2 of the company. While so engaged he was in the act of dropping a pine block from the upper floor of the mill to the ground below; this being the usual and ordinary way of clearing the floor, and it being the duty of the plaintiff in the course of his employment to so drop it. The block weighed about 75 pounds.
>
> As appellant was in the act of dropping the block to the ground below, he was on the edge of the upper floor of the mill. As he started to turn the block loose so that it would drop to the ground, he saw J. Greeley McGowin, testator of the defendants, on the ground below and directly under where the block would have fallen had appellant turned it loose. Had he turned it loose it would have struck McGowin with such force as to have caused him serious bodily harm or death. Appellant could have remained safely on the upper floor of the mill by turning the block loose and allowing it to drop, but had he done this the block would have fallen on McGowin and caused him serious injuries or death. The only safe and reasonable way to prevent this was for appellant to hold to the block and divert its direction in falling from the place where McGowin was standing and the only safe way to divert it so as to prevent its coming into contact with McGowin was for appellant to fall

with it to the ground below. Appellant did this, and by holding to the block and falling with it to the ground below, he diverted the course of its fall in such way that McGowin was not injured. In thus preventing the injuries to McGowin appellant himself received serious bodily injuries, resulting in his right leg being broken, the heel of his right foot torn off and his right arm broken. He was badly crippled for life and rendered unable to do physical or mental labor.

On September 1, 1925, in consideration of appellant having prevented him from sustaining death or serious bodily harm and in consideration of the injuries appellant had received, McGowin agreed with him to care for and maintain him for the remainder of appellant's life at the rate of $15 every two weeks from the time he sustained his injuries to and during the remainder of appellant's life; it being agreed that McGowin would pay this sum to appellant for his maintenance. Under the agreement McGowin paid or caused to be paid to appellant the sum so agreed on up until McGowin's death on January 1, 1934. After his death the payments were continued to and including January 27, 1934, at which time they were discontinued. Thereupon plaintiff brought suit to recover the unpaid installments accruing up to the time of the bringing of the suit.

The material averments of the different counts of the original complaint and the amended complaint are predicated upon the foregoing statement of facts.

In other words, the complaint as amended averred in substance: (1) That on August 3, 1925, appellant saved J. Greeley McGowin, appellee's testator, from death or grievous bodily harm; (2) that in doing so appellant sustained bodily injury crippling him for life; (3) that in consideration of the services rendered and the injuries received by appellant, McGowin agreed to care for him the remainder of appellant's life, the amount to be paid being $15 every two weeks; (4) that McGowin complied with this agreement until he died on January 1, 1934, and the payments were kept up to January 27, 1934, after which they were discontinued.

The action was for the unpaid installments accruing after January 27, 1934, to the time of the suit.

The principal grounds of demurrer to the original and amended complaint are: (1) It states no cause of action; (2) its averments show the contract was without consideration; (3) it fails to allege that McGowin had, at or before the services were rendered, agreed to pay appellant for them; (4) the contract declared on is void under the statute of frauds.

1. The averments of the complaint show that appellant saved McGowin from death or grievous bodily harm. This was a material benefit to him of infinitely more value than any financial aid he could have received. Receiving this benefit, McGowin became morally bound to compensate appellant for the services rendered. Recognizing his moral obligation, he expressly agreed to pay appellant as alleged in the complaint and complied with this agreement up to the time of his death; a period of more than 8 years.

Had McGowin been accidentally poisoned and a physician, without his knowledge or request, had administered an antidote, thus saving his life, a subsequent promise by McGowin to pay the physician would have been valid. Likewise, McGowin's agreement as disclosed by the complaint to compensate appellant for saving him from death or grievous bodily injury is valid and enforceable.

Where the promisee cares for, improves, and preserves the property of the promisor, though done without his request, it is sufficient consideration for the promisor's subsequent agreement to pay for the service, because of the material benefit received. Pittsburg Vitrified Paving & Building Brick Co. v. Cerebus Oil Co., 79 Kan. 603, 1,000 P. 631; Edson v. Poppe, 24 S.D. 466, 124 N.W. 441, 26 L.R.A. (N.S.) 534; Drake v. Bell, 26 Misc. 237, 55 N.Y.S. 945.

In Boothe v. Fitzpatrick, 36 Vt. 681, the court held that a promise by defendant to pay for the past keeping of a bull which had escaped from defendant's premises and been cared for by plaintiff was valid, although there was no previous request, because the subsequent promise obviated that objection; it being equivalent to a previous request. On the same principle, had the promisee saved the promisor's life or his body from grievous harm, his subsequent promise to pay for the services rendered would have been valid. Such service would have been far more material than caring for his bull. Any holding that saving a man from death or grievous bodily harm is not a material benefit sufficient to uphold a subsequent promise to pay for the service, necessarily rests on the assumption that saving life and preservation of the body from harm have only a sentimental value. The converse of this is true. Life and preservation of the body have material, pecuniary values, measurable in dollars and cents. Because of this, physicians practice their profession charging for services rendered in saving life and curing the body of its ills, and surgeons perform operations. The same is true as to the law of negligence, authorizing the assessment of damages in personal injury cases based upon the extent of the injuries, earnings, and life expectancies of those injured.

In the business of life insurance, the value of a man's life is measured in dollars and cents according to his expectancy, the soundness of his body, and his ability to pay premiums. The same is true as to health and accident insurance.

It follows that if, as alleged in the complaint, appellant saved J. Greeley McGowin from death or grievous bodily harm, and McGowin subsequently agreed to pay him for the service rendered, it became a valid and enforceable contract.

2. It is well settled that a moral obligation is a sufficient consideration to support a subsequent promise to pay where the promisor has received a material benefit, although there was no original duty or liability resting on the promisor. Lycoming County v. Union County, 15 Pa. 166, 53 Am.Dec. 575, 579, 580; Ferguson v. Harris, 39 S.C. 323, 17 S.E. 782, 39 Am.St.Rep. 731, 734; Muir v. Kane, 55 Wash. 131, 104 P. 153, 26 L.R.A. (N.S.) 519, 19 Ann.Cas. 1180; State ex rel. Bayer v. Funk, 105 Or. 134, 199 P. 592, 209 P. 113, 25 A.L.R. 625, 634; Hawkes v. Saunders, 1 Cowp. 290; In re Sutch's Estate, 201 Pa. 305, 50 A. 943; Edson v. Poppe, 24 S.D. 466, 124 N.W. 441, 26 L.R.A. (N.S.) 534; Park Falls State Bank v. Fordyce, 206 Wis. 628, 238 N.W. 516, 79 A.L.R. 1339; Baker v. Gregory, 28 Ala. 544, 65 Am.Dec. 366. In the case of State ex rel. Bayer v. Funk, supra, the court held that a moral obligation is a sufficient consideration to support an executory promise where the

promisor has received an actual pecuniary or material benefit for which he subsequently expressly promised to pay.

The case at bar is clearly distinguishable from that class of cases where the consideration is a mere moral obligation or conscientious duty unconnected with receipt by promisor of benefits of a material or pecuniary nature. Park Falls State Bank v. Fordyce, supra. Here the promisor received a material benefit constituting a valid consideration for his promise.

3. Some authorities hold that, for a moral obligation to support a subsequent promise to pay, there must have existed a prior legal or equitable obligation, which for some reason had become unenforceable, but for which the promisor was still morally bound. This rule, however, is subject to qualification in those cases where the promisor, having received a material benefit from the promisee, is morally bound to compensate him for the services rendered and in consideration of this obligation promises to pay. In such cases the subsequent promise to pay is an affirmance or ratification of the services rendered carrying with it the presumption that a previous request for the service was made. McMorris v. Herndon, 2 Bailey (S.C.) 56, 21 Am.Dec. 515; Chadwick v. Knox, 31 N.H. 226, 64 Am.Dec. 329; Kenan v. Holloway, 16 Ala. 53, 50 Am.Dec. 162; Ross v. Pearson, 21 Ala. 473.

Under the decisions above cited, McGowin's express promise to pay appellant for the services rendered was an affirmance or ratification of what appellant had done raising the presumption that the services had been rendered at McGowin's request.

4. The averments of the complaint show that in saving McGowin from death or grievous bodily harm, appellant was crippled for life. This was part of the consideration of the contract declared on. McGowin was benefited. Appellant was injured. Benefit to the promisor or injury to the promisee is a sufficient legal consideration for the promisor's agreement to pay. Fisher v. Bartlett, 8 Greenl. (Me.) 122, 22 Am.Dec. 225; State ex rel. Bayer v. Funk, supra.

5. Under the averments of the complaint the services rendered by appellant were not gratuitous. The agreement of McGowin to pay and the acceptance of payment by appellant conclusively shows the contrary.

6. The contract declared on was not void under the statute of frauds (Code 1923, § 8034). The demurrer on this ground was not well taken. 25 R.C.L. 456, 457 and 470, § 49.

The cases of Shaw v. Boyd, 1 Stew. & P. 83, and Duncan v. Hall, 9 Ala. 128, are not in conflict with the principles here announced. In those cases the lands were owned by the United States at the time the alleged improvements were made, for which subsequent purchasers from the government agreed to pay. These subsequent purchasers were not the owners of the lands at the time the improvements were made. Consequently, they could not have been made for their benefit.

From what has been said, we are of the opinion that the court below erred in the ruling complained of; that is to say, in sustaining the demurrer, and for this error the case is reversed and remanded.

SAMFORD, Judge (concurring).

The questions involved in this case are not free from doubt, and perhaps the strict letter of the rule, as stated by judges, though not always in accord, would bar a recovery by plaintiff, but following the principle announced by Chief Justice Marshall in Hoffman v. Porter, Fed.Cas. No. 6,577, 2 Brock. 156, 159, where he says, "I do not think that law ought to be separated from justice, where it is at most doubtful," I concur in the conclusions reached by the court.

WEBB V. MCGOWIN
Supreme Court of Alabama
168 So. 199 (1936).

FOSTER, Justice.

We do not in all cases in which we deny a petition for certiorari to the Court of Appeals approve the reasoning and principles declared in the opinion, even though no opinion is rendered by us. It does not always seem to be important that they be discussed, and we exercise a discretion in that respect. But when the opinion of the Court of Appeals asserts important principles or their application to new situations, and it may be uncertain whether this court agrees with it in all respects, we think it advisable to be specific in that respect when the certiorari is denied. We think such a situation here exists.

Neither this court nor the Court of Appeals has had before it questions similar to those here presented, though we have held that the state may recognize a moral obligation, and pay it or cause it to be paid by a county, or city. State v. Clements, 220 Ala. 515, 126 So. 162; Board of Revenue of Mobile v. Puckett, 227 Ala. 374, 149 So. 850; Board of Revenue of Jefferson County v. Hewitt, 206 Ala. 405(6), 90 So. 781; Moses v. Tigner (Ala.Sup.) 168 So. 194.

Those cases do not mean to affirm that the state may recompense for nice ethical obligations, or do the courteous or generous act, without a material and substantial claim to payment, though it is not enforceable by law; nor that an executory obligation may be so incurred.

The opinion of the Court of Appeals here under consideration recognizes and applies the distinction between a supposed moral obligation of the promisor, based upon some refined sense of ethical duty, without material benefit to him, and one in which such a benefit did in fact occur. We agree with that court that if the benefit be material and  substantial, and was to the person of the promisor rather than to his estate, it is within the class of material benefits which he has the privilege of recognizing and compensating either by an executed payment or an executory promise to pay. The cases are cited in that opinion. The reason is emphasized when the compensation is not only for the benefits which the promisor received, but also for the injuries either to the property or person of the promisee by reason of the service rendered.

Writ denied.

ANDERSON, C.J., and GARDNER and BOULDIN, JJ., concur.

HARRINGTON V. TAYLOR
Supreme Court of North Carolina
36 S.E.2d 227 (1945).

PER CURIAM.

The plaintiff in this case sought to recover of the defendant upon a promise made by him under the following peculiar circumstances:

The defendant had assaulted his wife, who took refuge in plaintiff's house. The next day the defendant gained access to the house and began another assault upon his wife. The defendant's wife knocked him down with an axe, and was on the point of cutting his head open or decapitating him while he was laying on the floor, and the plaintiff intervened, caught the axe as it was descending, and the blow intended for defendant fell upon her hand, mutilating it badly, but saving defendant's life.

Subsequently, defendant orally promised to pay the plaintiff her damages; but, after paying a small sum, failed to pay anything more. So, substantially, states the complaint.

The defendant demurred to the complaint as not stating a cause of action, and the demurrer was sustained. Plaintiff appealed.

The question presented is whether there was a consideration recognized by our law as sufficient to support the promise. The Court is of the opinion that, however much the defendant should be impelled by common gratitude to alleviate the plaintiff's misfortune, a humanitarian act of this kind, voluntarily performed, is not such consideration as would entitle her to recover at law.

The judgment sustaining the demurrer is

Affirmed.

NOTES AND QUESTIONS:

1. *See* Restatement (Second) of Contracts §§ 3 (Agreement Defined; Bargain Defined), 23 (Necessity That Manifestions Have Reference to Each Other), 71 (Requirement of Exchange; Types of Exchange), 72 (Exchange of Promise for Performance), 73 (Performance of a Legal Duty), 74 (Settlement of Claims), and 75 (Exchange of Promise for Promise) (1981).

2. *See* Restatement (Second) of Contracts § 86 (Promise for Benefit Received) (1981). *See also, e.g.*, California Civil Code § 1606: a "legal obligation resting upon the promisor as a moral obligation originating in some benefit conferred upon the promisor, a prejudice suffered by the promise, is also good consideration for a promise, to an extent corresponding with the extent of the obligation, but no further as otherwise."

3. *See also*, Edwin Butterfoss and H. Allen Blair, *Where is Emily Litella When You Need Her?: The Unsuccessful Effort to Craft A General Theory of Obligation of Promise for Benefit Received,* 28 Quinnipiac L. Rev. 385 (2010).

C. ADEQUACY

consideration: nominal

SCHNELL V. NELL
Supreme Court of Indiana
17 Ind. 29 (1861).

PERKINS, Justice

Action by *J. B. Nell* against *Zacharias Schnell,* upon the following instrument:

> This agreement, entered into this 13th day of *February,* 1856, between *Zach. Schnell,* of *Indianapolis, Marion* county, State of *Indiana,* as party of the first part, and *J. B. Nell,* of the same place, *Wendelin Lorenz,* of *Stilesville, Hendricks* county, State of *Indiana,* and *Donata Lorenz,* of *Frickinger, Grand Duchy of Baden, Germany,* as parties of the second part, witnesseth: The said *Zacharias Schnell* agrees as follows: whereas his wife, *Theresa Schnell,* now deceased, has made a last will and testament, in which, among other provisions, it was ordained that every one of the above named second parties, should receive the sum of $200; and whereas the said provisions of the will must remain a nullity, for the reason that no property, real or personal, was in the possession of the said *Theresa Schnell,* deceased, in her own name, at the time of her death, and all property held by *Zacharias* and *Theresa Schnell* jointly, therefore reverts to her husband; and whereas the said *Theresa Schnell* has also been a dutiful and loving wife to the said *Zach. Schnell,* and has materially aided him in the acquisition of all property, real and personal, now possessed by him; for, and in consideration of all this, and the love and respect he bears to his wife; and, furthermore, in consideration of one cent, received by him of the second parties, he, the said *Zach, Schnell,* agrees to pay the above named sums of money to the parties of the second part, to wit: $200 to the said *J. B. Nell;* $200 to the said *Wendelin Lorenz;* and $200 to the said *Donata Lorenz,* in the following installments, viz., $200 in one year from the date of these presents; $200 in two years, and $200 in three years; to be divided between the parties in equal portions of $66 2/3 each year, or as they may agree, till each one has received his full sum of $200.

And the said parties of the second part, for, and in consideration of this, agree to pay the above named sum of money [one cent], and to deliver up to said *Schnell,* and abstain from collecting any real or supposed claims upon him or his estate, arising from the said last will and testament of the said *Theresa Schnell,* deceased.

In witness whereof, the said parties have, on this 13th day of *February,* 1856, set hereunto their hands and seals.

ZACHARIAS SCHNELL	[SEAL.]
J. B. NELL	[SEAL.]
WEN. LORENZ	[SEAL.]

The complaint contained no averment of a consideration for the instrument, outside of those expressed in it; and did not aver that the one cent agreed to be paid, had been paid or tendered.

A demurrer to the complaint was overruled.

The defendant answered, that the instrument sued on was given for no consideration whatever.

He further answered, that it was given for no consideration, because his said wife, *Theresa,* at the time she made the will mentioned, and at the time of her death, owned, neither separately, nor jointly with her husband, or anyone else (except so far as the law gave her an interest in her husband's property), any property, real or personal, &c. . . .

The case turned below, and must turn here, upon the question whether the instrument sued on does express a consideration sufficient to give it legal obligation, as against *Zacharias Schnell.* It specifies three distinct considerations for his promise to pay $600:

1. A promise, on the part of the plaintiffs, to pay him one cent.

2. The love and affection he bore his deceased wife, and the fact that she had done her part, as his wife, in the acquisition of property.

3. The fact that she had expressed her desire, in the form of an inoperative will, that the persons named therein should have the sums of money specified.

The consideration of one cent will not support the promise of *Schnell.* It is true, that as a general proposition, inadequacy of consideration will not vitiate an agreement. *Baker v. Roberts,* 14 Ind. 552. But this doctrine does not apply to a mere exchange of sums of money, of coin, whose value is exactly fixed, but to the exchange of something of, in itself, indeterminate value, for money, or, perhaps, for some other thing of indeterminate value. In this case, had the one cent mentioned, been some particular one cent, a family piece, or ancient, remarkable coin, possessing an indeterminate value, extrinsic from its simple money value, a different view might be taken. As it is, the mere promise to pay six hundred dollars for one cent, even had the portion of that cent due from the plaintiff been tendered, is an unconscionable contract, void, at first blush, upon its face, if it be regarded as an earnest one. *Hardesty v. Smith,* 3 Ind. 39. The consideration of one cent is, plainly, in this case, merely nominal, and intended to be so. As the will and testament of *Schnell's* wife imposed no legal obligation upon him to discharge her bequests out of his property, and as she had none of her own, his promise to discharge them was not legally binding upon him, on that ground. A moral consideration, only, will not support a promise. Ind. Dig., p. 13. And for the same reason, a valid consideration for his promise can not be found in the fact of a compromise of a disputed claim; for where such claim is legally groundless, a promise upon a compromise of it, or of a suit upon it, is not legally binding. *Spahr v. Hollingshead,* 8 Blackf. 415. There was no mistake of law or fact in this case, as the agreement admits the will inoperative and void. The promise was simply one to make a gift. The past services of his wife, and the love and affection he had borne her, are objectionable as legal considerations for *Schnell's* promise, on two grounds: 1. They are past considerations. Ind. Dig., p. 13. 2. The fact that *Schnell* loved his wife, and that she had been industrious, constituted no consideration for his promise to pay *J. B. Nell,* and the *Lorenzes,* a sum of money. Whether, if his wife, in her lifetime, had made a bargain with *Schnell,* that, in consideration of his promising to pay, after her death, to the persons named, a sum of money, she would be industrious, and worthy of his affection, such a promise would have been valid and consistent with public policy, we need not decide. Nor is the fact that *Schnell* now venerates the memory of his deceased wife, a legal consideration for a promise to pay any third person money.

The instrument sued on, interpreted in the light of the facts alleged in the second paragraph of the answer, will not support an action. The demurrer to the answer should have been overruled. See *Stevenson v. Druley,* 4 Ind. 519.

Per Curiam.

The judgment is reversed, with costs. Cause remanded &c.

D. ILLUSORY PROMISE

AMERICAN AGRICULTURAL CHEMICAL CO. V. KENNEDY & CRAWFORD
Supreme Court of Appeals of Virginia
48 S.E. 868 (1904)

Appeal from Circuit Court, Augusta County.

. . . .

BUCHANAN, J.

The American Agricultural Chemical Company instituted its action of assumpsit against J. A. Kennedy and W. A. Crawford, partners doing business under the firm name of Kennedy & Crawford, to recover damages for the alleged breach of an agreement not under seal.

The plaintiff's cause of action, as set forth in the third count of the declaration-the only count relied on-is as follows:

"The American Agricultural Chemical Company, a corporation, complains of J. A. Kennedy and W. A. Crawford, partners doing business and trading under the firm name and style of Kennedy & Crawford, of a plea of trespass on the case in assumpsit, for this, to wit:

3rd Count. That heretofore, to wit, on the 14th day of March, 1902, in consideration that the plaintiff, at the request of the defendants, would sell and furnish to the said defendants certain fertilizer, at and for a reasonable compensation, hereinafter set out, defendants undertook, and then and there promised and contracted in writing with the said plaintiff, in the words and figures following, to wit:

> March 14, 1902.
>
> To Messrs. Kennedy & Crawford, Staunton, Augusta County, Va.: We hereby agree to ship you under the conditions and stipulations hereinafter named, and subject to the approval of the Home Office, the following fertilizers at prices and terms named below.
>
> The terms and conditions of this contract are as follows, and the prices named below are net to us in 200-lb. bags.

<table>
<tr><th>No. of Tons</th><th>Brands</th><th>Price per 2,000 lbs.</th></tr>
<tr><td rowspan="8">400
To
600</td><td>Your brands 2-10-5</td><td>$20.85</td></tr>
<tr><td>" " 2-8-5</td><td>19.85</td></tr>
<tr><td>" " 2-8-2</td><td>17.60</td></tr>
<tr><td>" " 1-8-1</td><td>14.60</td></tr>
<tr><td>" " 1-8-2</td><td>15.30</td></tr>
<tr><td>" " 10-2</td><td>12.65</td></tr>
<tr><td>" " 14</td><td>11.65</td></tr>
<tr><td>2 ½-12</td><td>21.00</td></tr>
</table>

> Goods to be delivered by us free on board cars or steamer at Staunton, Va., in car-load lots, and you are to pay freight on all shipments.
>
> All goods ordered by you under this contract shall be settled for in full on July 1, 1902, in cash for spring, and December 1, 1902, for fall.
>
> For cash payments made prior to July 1, 1902, interest will be allowed at the rate of seven (7) per cent, per annum from dates of payments to July 1, 1902.

All settlements are to be sent to us in full at the date named, and protest, demand for payment, and notice of nonpayment of any notes that may have been endorsed by you and transferred to us, are hereby waived, and you also waive all homestead and other exemptions as to any obligations growing out of this contract.

It is also agreed that you will hold in trust and separate, for the settlement of our account, all of said goods unsold and all currency, open accounts, notes, liens, mortgages, or other values received for goods sold.

This contract is subject to suspension in case of fire, accident to our works, or other causes.

We have the right to ship said goods, or any part thereof, from any factory.

We reserve the right to cancel this contract at any time we may deem proper, but in the event of such cancellation the provisions of this contract shall govern the closing of all business begun thereunder.

This contract, written and printed, constitutes the entire agreement, and no verbal understanding will be recognized.

Executed in triplicate,

The American Agricultural Chemical Company, Wm. W. Baker.

We hereby agree to take whatever fertilizers we may require for spring season 1902, not less than, as stated, tons with the privilege of taking more, if mutually agreeable, under above terms and conditions.

Name-Kennedy & Crawford. . . .

The defendants demurred to the declaration on several grounds, one of which was that the contract sued on was without consideration, and was therefore nudum pactum. This contention is based upon that clause of the written agreement which provides that "we [the plaintiffs] reserve the right to cancel this contract at any time we may deem proper, but in the event of such cancellation, the provisions of this contract shall govern the closing of all business begun thereunder."

The general rule of law is-and this seems to be conceded by the plaintiff company-that, where the consideration for the promise of one party is the promise of the other party, there must be absolute mutuality of engagement, so that each party has the right to hold the other to a positive agreement. Both parties must be bound, or neither is bound. 1 Parsons on Contracts (7th Ed.) 448-452; Clark on Contracts, 165-171; Southern Ry. Co. v. Willcox, etc., 98 Va. 222, 35 S. E. 355.

The plaintiff insists that the averments of its declaration take this case out of the general rule, upon the ground that, while the contract sued on may have lacked mutuality of obligation in its inception, yet that the plaintiff had performed and executed the contract on its part by manufacturing the fertilizer, putting it in sacks, and tendering it to the defendants, and that such performance cured any lack of mutuality in the contract in its inception, and rendered it absolutely binding. Although the contract did not bind the plaintiff to furnish the fertilizer which the defendants agreed to purchase, yet, if the defendants had actually received it, they would have been bound to pay for it; and this would be so even if the agreement in question had never been entered into. But the defendants did not receive it. The offer of the plaintiff to deliver the fertilizer which it had never bound itself to sell could not make the defendants liable in damages for refusing to receive what they, in legal contemplation, had never agreed to purchase. The defendants never having had the right to compel the plaintiff to deliver the fertilizer, the plaintiff could not by its own act make it the duty of the defendants to receive it, nor impose any liability upon them.

The promise of the defendants to purchase from the plaintiff was not a continuing offer, which, when accepted, was mutually binding upon both parties, as was the case in most of the decisions cited and relied on by the plaintiff. In those cases, while one party was not bound when the proposition of the other was made, he afterwards, before the proposition was withdrawn, either did, or bound himself to do, the thing which was the condition of the other's promise.

In discussing this class of cases, Mr. Parsons, in his work on Contracts, p. 450, after stating the general rule that a promise is not a good consideration for a promise unless there is an absolute mutuality of engagement, so that each party has the right at once to hold the other to a positive agreement, says:

> This has been doubted, from the seeming want of mutuality, in many cases of contract-as where one promises to see another paid if he will sell goods to a third person, or promises to give a certain sum if another will deliver up certain documents or securities, or if he will forbear a demand or suspend legal proceedings, or the like. Here it is said the party making the promise is bound, while the other party is at liberty to do anything or nothing. But this is a mistake. The party making the promise is bound to nothing until the promisee, within a reasonable time, engages to do, or else does or begins to do, the thing which is the condition of the first promise. Until such engagement or such doing, the promisor may withdraw his promise, because there is no mutuality, and therefore no consideration for it. But after an engagement on the part of the promisee, which is sufficient to bind him, then the promisor is bound, also, because there is now a promise for a promise, with entire mutuality of obligation. So, if the promisee begins to do the thing in a way that binds him to complete it, here, also, is mutuality of obligation. But if without any promise, while the promisee does the thing required, then the promisor is bound upon another ground. The thing done is itself a sufficient and a completed consideration, and the original promise to do something if the other party would do something is a continuing promise until the party does the thing required of him.

> A very large proportion of our most common contracts rest upon this principle. Thus in a contract of sale the proposed buyer says, 'I will give so much for these goods,' and he may withdraw his offer before it is accepted, and, if his withdrawal reaches the seller before the seller has accepted, the obligation of the buyer is extinguished; but if not withdrawn it remains a continuing offer for a reasonable time, and, if accepted within this time, both parties are bound, as by a promise for a promise. There is entire mutuality of obligation. The buyer may tender the price and demand the goods, and the seller may tender the goods and demand the price. See, also, Clark on Contracts, to the same effect, pp. 168-171.

In this case the plaintiff made a proposition to sell, which the defendants accepted, but the plaintiff's offer left it optional with it whether or not it would sell. It did not bind itself to sell. The defendants made no continuing offer to purchase. Their engagement was to purchase upon the terms and conditions stated in the plaintiff's proposition to sell. As that proposition did not bind the plaintiff to sell, there was no consideration for the defendant's promise to purchase, and, as we have seen, neither party was bound at that time. The plaintiff after that time never did any act or made any promise which bound it to complete the contract. There never was a time when the defendants had the right to tender the price and demand the fertilizer. In the absence of such obligation on the part of the plaintiff, and of such right on the part of the defendants, there never was a binding engagement between the parties which a court of law would enforce. . . .

We are of opinion that the demurrer to the declaration upon the ground discussed was properly sustained by the circuit court, and that its judgment must be affirmed.

NOTES AND QUESTIONS:

1. *See* Restatement (Second) of Contracts) §§ 2 (Promise; Promisor; Promisee; Beneficiary), 76 (Conditional Promise), 77 (Illusory and Alternative Promises), and 79 (Adequacy of Consideration; Mutuality of Obligation) (1981).

2. *See Lake Land Employment Group of Akron, LLC v. Columber*, 804 N.E.2d 27 (Ohio 2004) (Continued employment in an at-will employment relationship constitutes legally sufficient and adequate consideration to support non-competition agreement).

3. *See C.P. Cooper v. C. O. Livingston*, 19 Fla. 684 (Florida 1883) ("Our conclusion is that 'conjuring' over a sick man 'to make him well' is not a valid consideration for a promissory note; and that no man with a healthy mind would voluntarily give a note for $250 with interest at two per cent a month for services of a conjurer, who proposes to cure a lingering disease by conjury or incantation.").

4. *Compare American Agricultural Chemical Co. v. Kennedy & Crawford* with *Sylvan Crest Sand & Gravel Co. v. United States*, 150 F.2d 642, 644-5 (2nd Cir. 1945) ("It must be conceded that the cases dealing with agreements in which one party has reserved to himself an option to cancel are not entirely harmonious. Where the option is completely unrestricted some courts say that the party having the option has promised to do nothing and the contract is void for lack of mutuality. *Miami Coca-Cola Bottling Co. v. Orange Crush Co.*, 5 Cir., 296 F. 693; *Oakland Motor Car Co. v. Indiana Automobile Co.*, 7 Cir. 201 F. 499. These cases have been criticized by competent text writers and the latter case cited by this court 'with distinct lack of warmth,' as Judge Clark noted in *Bushwick-Decatur Motors v. Ford Motor Co.*, 2 Cir., 116 F.2d 675, 678. But where, as in the case at bar, the option to cancel 'does not wholly defeat consideration,' the agreement is not nudum pactum. Corbin, *The Effect of Options on Consideration*, 34 Yale L.J. 571, 585; *see Hunt v. Stimson*, 6 Cir., 23 F.2d 447; *Gurfein v. Werbelovsky*, 97 Conn. 703, 118 A. 32. A promise is not made illusory by the fact that the promissory has an option between two alternatives, if each alternative would be sufficient consideration if it alone were bargained for. A.L.I. Contracts § 79. As we have construed the agreement the United States promised by implication to take and pay for the trap rock or give notice of cancellation within a reasonable time. The alternative of giving notice was not difficult of performance, but it was a sufficient consideration to support the contract.").

5. Under U.C.C. § 2-306 (Output, Requirements and Exclusive Dealings), the Code incorporates a requirement of good faith and best efforts to save the promises from being illusory (2002).

SECTION 6. MODIFICATION AND "PRE-EXISTING DUTIES"

PINNEL'S CASE
IN THE COMMON PLEAS
Trin. 44 Eliz. Rot. 501 (1602).

Pinnell brought an action of debt on a bond against Cole, of 16£ for payment of 8£ 10 shillings the 11th day of Nov. 1600. The defendant pleaded, that he at the instance of the plaintiff, before the said day, *scil. 1 Octob. anno 44. apud W. solvit querenti 5£ 2 shillings 2 pence quas quidem 5£ 2 shillings 2 pence* the plaintiff accepted in full satisfaction of the 8£ 10 shillings. And it was resolved by the whole Court, that payment of a lesser sum on the day in satisfaction of a greater, cannot be any satisfaction for the whole because it appears to the Judges that by no possibility, a lesser sum can be a satisfaction to the plaintiff for a greater sum: but the gift of a horse, hawk, or robe, etc. in satisfaction is good. For it shall be intended that a horse, hawk, or robe, etc. might be more beneficial to the plaintiff than the money, in respect of some circumstance, or otherwise the plaintiff would not have accepted of it in satisfaction. But when the whole sum is due, by no intendment the acceptance of parcel can be a satisfaction to the plaintiff: but in the case at Bar it was resolved, that the payment and acceptance of parcel before the day in satisfaction of the whole, would be a good satisfaction in regard of circumstance of time; for peradventure parcel of it before the day would be more beneficial to him than the whole at the day, and the value of the satisfaction is not material: so if I am bound in 20£ to pay you 10£ at Westminster and you request me to pay you 5£ at the day at York, and you will accept it in full satisfaction of the whole 10£ it is good satisfaction for the whole: for the expenses to pay it at York, is sufficient satisfaction: but in this case the plaintiff had judgment for the insufficient pleading; for he did not plead that he had paid the 5£ 2 shillings 2 pence in full satisfaction (as by the law he ought) but pleaded the payment of part generally; and that the plaintiff accepted it in full satisfaction. And always the manner of the tender of the payment shall be directed byhim who made the tender or payment and not by him who accepts it. And for this cause judgment was given for the plaintiff.

See reader (g) 26 H.G. 6 Barre 37. In debt on a bond of 10£ the defendant pleaded, that one F. was bound by the said deed with him, and in the whole, and that the plaintiff had made an acquittance to F. bearing date before the obligation, and delivered after, by which acquittance he did acknowledge himself to be paid 20 shillings in full satisfaction of 10£. And it was adjudged a good bar; for if a man acknowledges himself to be satisfied by deed, it is a good bar, without any thing received.

ALASKA PACKERS' ASS'N V. DOMENICO
Circuit Court of Appeals, Ninth Circuit
117 F. 99 (1902).

ROSS, Circuit Judge.

The libel in this case was based upon a contract alleged to have been entered into between the libelants and the appellant corporation on the 22d day of May, 1900, at Pyramid Harbor, Alaska, by which it is claimed the appellant promised to pay each of the libelants, among other things, the sum of $100 for services rendered and to be rendered. In its answer the respondent denied the execution, on its part, of the contract sued upon, averred that it was without consideration, and for a third defense alleged that the work performed by the libelants for it was performed under other and different contracts than that sued on, and that, prior to the filing of the libel, each of the libelants was paid by the respondent the full amount due him thereunder, in consideration of which each of them executed a full release of all his claims and demands against the respondent.

The evidence shows without conflict that on March 26, 1900, at the city and county of San Francisco, the libelants entered into a written contract with the appellants, whereby they agreed to go from San Francisco to Pyramid Harbor, Alaska, and return, on board such vessel as might be designated by the appellant, and to work for the appellant during the fishing season of 1900, at Pyramid Harbor, as sailors and fishermen, agreeing to do "regular ship's duty, both up and down, discharging and loading; and to do any other work whatsoever when requested to do so by the captain or agent of the Alaska Packers' Association." By the terms of this agreement, the appellant was to pay each of the libelants $50 for the season, and two cents for each red salmon in the catching of which he took part.

On the 15th day of April, 1900, 21 of the libelants of the libelants signed shipping articles by which they shipped as seamen on the Two Brothers, a vessel chartered by the appellant for the voyage between San Francisco and Pyramid Harbor, and also bound themselves to perform the same work for the appellant provided for by the previous contract of March 26th; the appellant agreeing to pay them therefor the sum of $60 for the season, and two cents each for each red salmon in the catching of which they should respectively take part. Under these contracts, the libelants sailed on board the Two Brothers for Pyramid Harbor, where the appellants had about $150,000 invested in a salmon cannery. The libelants arrived there early in April of the year mentioned, and began to unload the vessel and fit up the cannery. A few days thereafter, to wit, May 19th, they stopped work in a body, and demanded of the company's superintendent there in charge $100 for services in operating the vessel to and from Pyramid Harbor, instead of the sums stipulated for in and by the contracts; stating that unless they were paid this additional wage they would stop work entirely, and return to San Francisco. The evidence showed, and the court below found, that it was impossible for the appellant to get other men to take the places of the libelants, the place being remote, the season short and just opening; so that, after endeavoring for several days without success to induce the libelants to proceed with their work in accordance with their contracts, the company's superintendent, on the 22d day of May, so far yielded to their demands as to instruct his clerk to copy the contracts executed in San Francisco, including the words "Alaska Packers' Association" at the end, substituting, for the $50 and $60 payments, respectively, of those contracts, the sum of $100, which document, so prepared, was signed by the libelants before a shipping commissioner whom they had requested to be brought from Northeast Point; the superintendent, however, testifying that he at the time told the libelants that he was without authority to enter into any such contract, or to in any way alter the contracts made between them and the company in San Francisco. Upon the return of the libelants to San Francisco at the close of the fishing season, they demanded pay in accordance with the terms of the alleged contract of May 22d, when the company denied its validity, and refused to pay other than as provided for by the contracts of March 26th and April 5th, respectively. Some of the libelants, at least, consulted counsel, and, after receiving his advice, those of them who had signed the shipping articles before the shipping commissioner at San Francisco went before that officer, and received the amount due them thereunder, executing in consideration thereof a release in full, and the others paid at the office of the company, also receipting in full for their demands.

On the trial in the court below, the libelants undertook to show that the fishing nets provided by the respondent were defective, and that it was on that account that they demanded increased wages. On that point, the evidence was substantially conflicting, and the finding of the court was against the libelants the court saying:

> 'The contention of libelants that the nets provided them were rotten and unserviceable is not sustained by the evidence. The defendants' interest required that libelants should be provided with every facility necessary to their success as fishermen, for on such success depended the profits defendant would be able to realize that season from its packing plant, and the large capital invested therein. In view of this self-evident fact, it is highly improbable that the defendant gave libelants rotten and unserviceable nets with which to fish. It follows from this finding that libelants were not justified in refusing performance of their original contract.' 112 Fed. 554.

The evidence being sharply conflicting in respect to these facts, the conclusions of the court, who heard and saw the witnesses, will not be disturbed. The Alijandro, 6 C.C.A. 54, 56 Fed. 621; The Lucy, 20 C.C.A. 660, 74 Fed. 572; The Glendale, 26 C.C.A. 500, 81 Fed. 633. The Coquitlam, 23 C.C.A. 438, 77 Fed. 744; Gorham Mfg. Co. v. Emery-Bird-Thayer Dry Goods Co., 43 C.C.A. 511, 104 Fed. 243.

The real questions in the case as brought here are questions of law, and, in the view that we take of the case, it will be necessary to consider but one of those. Assuming that the appellant's superintendent at Pyramid Harbor was authorized to make the alleged contract of May 22d, and that he executed it on behalf of the appellant, was it supported by a sufficient consideration? From the foregoing statement of the case, it will have been seen that the libelants agreed in writing, for certain stated compensation, to render their services to the appellant in remote waters where the season for conducting fishing operations is extremely short, and in which enterprise the appellant had a large amount of money invested; and, after having entered upon the discharge of their contract, and at a time when it was impossible for the appellant to secure other men in their places, the libelants, without any valid cause, absolutely refused to continue the services they were under contract to perform unless the appellant would consent to pay them more money. Consent to such a demand, under such circumstances, if given, was, in our opinion, without consideration, for the reason that it was based solely upon the libelants' agreement to render the exact services, and none other, that they were already under contract to render. The case shows that they willfully and arbitrarily broke that obligation. As a matter of course, they were liable to the appellant in damages, and it is quite probable, as suggested by the court below in its opinion, that they may have been unable to respond in damages. But we are unable to agree with the conclusions there drawn, from these facts, in these words:

> 'Under such circumstances, it would be strange, indeed, if the law would not permit the defendant to waive the damages caused by the libelants' breach, and enter into the contract sued upon,- a contract mutually beneficial to all the parties thereto, in that it gave to the libelants reasonable compensation for their labor, and enabled the defendant to employ to advantage the large capital it had invested in its canning and fishing plant.'

Certainly, it cannot be justly held, upon the record in this case, that there was any voluntary waiver on the part of the appellant of the breach of the original contract. The company itself knew nothing of such breach until the expedition returned to San Francisco, and the testimony is uncontradicted that its superintendent at Pyramid Harbor, who, it is claimed, made on its behalf the contract sued on, distinctly informed the libelants that he had no power to alter the original or to make a new contract, and it would, of course, follow that, if he had no power to change the original, he would have no authority to waive any rights thereunder. The circumstances of the present case bring it, we think, directly within the sound and just observations of the supreme court of Minnesota in the case of King v. Railway Co., 61 Minn. 482, 63 N.W. 1105:

> 'No astute reasoning can change the plain fact that the party who refuses to perform, and thereby coerces a promise from the other party to the contract to pay him an increased compensation for doing that which he is legally bound to do, takes an unjustifiable advantage of the necessities of the other party. Surely it would be a travesty on justice to hold that the party so making the promise for extra pay was estopped from asserting that the promise was without consideration. A party cannot lay the foundation of an estoppel by his own wrong, where the promise is simply a repetition of a subsisting legal promise. There can be no consideration for the promise of the other party, and there is no warrant for inferring that the parties have voluntarily rescinded or modified their contract. The promise cannot be legally enforced, although the other party has completed his contract in reliance upon it.'

In Lingenfelder v. Brewing Co., 103 Mo. 578, 15 S.W. 844, the court, in holding void a contract by which the owner of a building agreed to pay its architect an additional sum because of his refusal to otherwise proceed with the contract, said:

> 'It is urged upon us by respondents that this was a new contract. New in what? Jungenfeld was bound by his contract to design and supervise this building. Under the new promise, he was not to do anything more or

anything different. What benefit was to accrue to Wainwright? He was to receive the same service from Jungenfeld under the new, that Jungenfeld was bound to tender under the original, contract. What loss, trouble, or inconvenience could result to Jungenfeld that he had not already assumed? No amount of metaphysical reasoning can change the plain fact that Jungenfeld took advantage of Wainwright's necessities, and extorted the promise of five per cent. on the refrigerator plant as the condition of his complying with his contract already entered into. Nor had he even the flimsy pretext that Wainwright had violated any of the conditions of the contract on his part. Jungenfeld himself put it upon the simple proposition that "if he, as an architect, put up the brewery, and another company put up the refrigerating machinery, it would be a detriment to the Empire Refrigerating Company," of which Jungenfeld was president. To permit plaintiff to recover under such circumstances would be to offer a premium upon bad faith, and invite men to violate their most sacred contracts that they may profit by their own wrong. That a promise to pay a man for doing that which he is already under contract to do is without consideration is conceded by respondents. The rule has been so long imbedded in the common law and decisions of the highest courts of the various states that nothing but the most cogent reasons ought to shake it. (Citing a long list of authorities.) But it is 'carrying coals to Newcastle' to add authorities on a proposition so universally accepted, and so inherently just and right in itself. The learned counsel for respondents do not controvert the general proposition. Their contention is, and the circuit court agreed with them, that, when Jungenfeld declined to go further on his contract, the defendant then had the right to sue for damages, and not having elected to sue Jungenfeld, but having acceded to his demand for the additional compensation defendant cannot now be heard to say his promise is without consideration. While it is true Jungenfeld became liable in damages for the obvious breach of his contract, we do not think it follows that defendant is estopped from showing its promise was made without consideration. It is true that as eminent a jurist as Judge Cooley, in Goebel v. Linn, 47 Mich. 489, 11 N.W. 284, 41 Am.Rep. 723, held that an ice company which had agreed to furnish a brewery with all the ice they might need for their business from November 8, 1879, until January 1, 1881, at $1.75 per ton, and afterwards in May, 1880, declined to deliver any more ice unless the brewery would give it $3 per ton, could recover on a promissory note given for the increased price. Profound as is our respect for the distinguished judge who delivered the opinion, we are still of the opinion that his decision is not in accord with the almost universally accepted doctrine, and is not convincing; and certainly so much of the opinion as holds that the payment, by a debtor, of a part of his debt then due, would constitute a defense to a suit for the remainder, is not the law of this state, nor, do we think, of any other where the common law prevails. . . . What we hold is that, when a party merely does what he has already obligated himself to do, he cannot demand an additional compensation therefor; and although, by taking advantage of the necessities of his adversary, he obtains a promise for more, the law will regard it as nudum pactum, and will not lend its process to aid in the wrong.'

The case of Goebel v. Linn, 47 Mich. 489, 11 N.W. 284, 41 Am.Rep. 723, is one of the eight cases relied upon by the court below in support of its judgment in the present case, five of which are by the supreme court of Massachusetts, one by the supreme court of Vermont, and one other Michigan case,- that of Moore v. Locomotive Works, 14 Mich. 266. The Vermont case referred to is that of Lawrence v. Davey, 28 Vt. 264, which was one of the three cases cited by the court in Moore v. Locomotive Works, 14 Mich. 272, 273, as authority for its decision. In that case there was a contract to deliver coal at specified terms and rates. A portion of it was delivered, and plaintiff then informed the defendant that he could not deliver at those rates, and, if the latter intended to take advantage of it, he should not deliver any more; and that he should deliver no more unless the defendant would pay for the coal independent of the contract. The defendant agreed to do so, and the coal was delivered. On suit being brought for the price, the court said:

> 'Although the promise to waive the contract was after some portion of the coal sought to be recovered had been delivered, and so delivered that probably the plaintiff, if the defendant had insisted upon strict performance of the contract, could not have recovered anything for it, yet, nevertheless, the agreement to waive the contract, and the promise, and, above all, the delivery of coal after this agreement to waive the contract, and upon the faith of it, will be a sufficient consideration to bind the defendant to pay for the coal already received.'

The doctrine of that case was impliedly overruled by the supreme court of Vermont in the subsequent case of Cobb v. Cowdery, 40 Vt. 25, 94 Am.Dec. 370, where it was held that:

> 'A promise by a party to do what he is bound in law to do is not an illegal consideration, but is the same as no consideration at all, and is merely void; in other words, it is insufficient, but not illegal. Thus, if the master of a ship promise his crew an addition to their fixed wages in consideration for and as an incitement to, their extraordinary exertions during a storm, or in any other emergency of the voyage, this promise is nudum pactum; the voluntary performance of an act which it was before legally incumbent on the party to perform being in law an insufficient consideration; and so it would be in any other case where the only consideration for the promise of one party was the promise of the other party to do, or his actual doing, something which he was previously bound in law to do. Chit. Cont. (10th Am.Ed.) 51; Smith, Cont. 87; 3 Kent, Com.. 185.'

The Massachusetts cases cited by the court below in support of its judgment commence with the case of Munroe v. Perkins, 9 Pick. 305, 20 Am.Dec. 475, which really seems to be the foundation of all of the cases in support of that view. In that case, the plaintiff had agreed in writing to erect a building for the defendants. Finding his contract a losing one, he had concluded to abandon it, and resumed work on the oral contract of the defendants that, if he would do so, they would pay him what the work was worth without regard to the terms of the original contract. The court said that whether the oral contract was without consideration

> 'Depends entirely on the question whether the first contract was waived. The plaintiff having refused to perform that contract, as he might do, subjecting himself to such damages as the other parties might show they were entitled to recover, he afterward went on, upon the faith of the new promise, and finished the work. This was a sufficient consideration. If Payne and Perkins were willing to accept his relinquishment of the old contract, and proceed on a new agreement, the law, we think, would not prevent it.'

The case of Goebel v. Linn, 47 Mich. 489, 11 N.W. 284, 41 Am.Rep. 723, presented some unusual and extraordinary circumstances. But, taking it as establishing the precise rule adopted in the Massachusetts cases, we think it not only contrary to the weight of authority, but wrong on principle.

In addition to the Minnesota and Missouri cases above cited, the following are some of the numerous authorities holding the contrary doctrine: Vanderbilt v. Schreyer, 91 N.Y. 392; Ayres v. Railroad Co., 52 Iowa, 478, 3 N.W. 522; Harris v. Carter, 3 Ellis & B. 559; Frazer v. Hatton, 2 C.B.(N.S.) 512; Conover v. Stillwell, 34 N.J. Law, 54; Reynolds v. Nugent, 25 Ind. 328; Spencer v. McLean (Ind. App.) 50 N.E. 769, 67 Am.St.Rep. 271; Harris v. Harris (Colo. App.) 47 Pac. 841; Moran v. Peace, 72 Ill.App. 139; Carpenter v. Taylor (N.Y.) 58 N.E. 53; Westcott v. Mitchell (Me.) 50 Atl. 21; Robinson v. Jewett, 116 N.Y. 40, 22 N.E. 224; Sullivan v. Sullivan, 99 Cal. 187, 33 Pac. 862; Blyth v. Robinson, 104 Cal. 230, 37 Pac. 904; Skinner v. Mining Co. (C.C.) 96 Fed. 735; 1 Beach, Cont. § 166; Langd. Cont. § 54; 1 Pars.Cont. (5th Ed.) 457; Ferguson v. Harris (S.C.) 17 S.E. 782, 39 Am.St.Rep. 745.

It results from the views above expressed that the judgment must be reversed, and the cause remanded, with directions to the court below to enter judgment for the respondent, with costs. It is so ordered.

ANGEL V. MURRAY
Supreme Court of Rhode Island
322 A.2d 630 (1974).

OPINION

ROBERTS, Chief Justice.

This is a civil action brought by Alfred L. Angel and others against John E. Murray, Jr., Director of Finance of the City of Newport, the city of Newport, and James L. Maher, alleging that Maher had illegally been paid the sum of $20,000 by the Director of Finance and praying that the defendant Maher be ordered to repay the city such sum. The case was heard by a justice of the Superior Court, sitting without a jury, who entered a judgment ordering Maher to repay the sum of $20,000 to the city of Newport. Maher is now before this court prosecuting an appeal.

The record discloses that Maher has provided the city of Newport with a refuse-collection service under a series of five-year contracts beginning in 1946. On March 12, 1964, Maher and the city entered into another such contract for a period of five years commencing on July 1, 1964, and terminating on June 30, 1969. The contract provided, among other things, that Maher would receive $137,000 per year in return for collecting and removing all combustible and noncombustible waste materials generated within the city.

In June of 1967 Maher requested an additional $10,000 per year from the city council because there had been a substantial increase in the cost of collection due to an unexpected and unanticipated increase of 400 new dwelling units. Maher's testimony, which is uncontradicted, indicates the 1964 contract had been predicated on the fact that since 1946 there had been an average increase of 20 to 25 new dwelling units per year. After a public meeting of the city council where Maher explained in detail the reasons for his request and was questioned by members of the city council, the city council agreed to pay him an additional $10,000 for the year ending on June 30, 1968. Maher made a similar request again in June of 1968 for the same reasons, and the city council again agreed to pay an additional $10,000 for the year ending on June 30, 1969.

The trial justice found that each such $10,000 payment was made in violation of law. His decision, as we understand it, is premised on two independent grounds. . . . [H]e found that Maher was not entitled to extra compensation because the original contract already required him to collect all refuse generated within the city and, therefore, included the 400 additional units. . . . It appears that he based this portion of the decision upon the rule that Maher had a preexisting duty to collect the refuse generated by the 400 additional units, and thus there was no consideration for the two additional payments. . . .

II.

. . . .

A

As previously stated, the city council made two $10,000 payments. The first was made in June of 1967 for the year beginning on July 1, 1967, and ending on June 30, 1968. Thus, by the time this action was commenced in October of 1968, the modification was completely executed. That is, the money had been paid by the city council, and Maher had collected all of the refuse. Since consideration is only a test of the enforceability of executory promises, the presence or absence of consideration for the first payment is unimportant because the city council's agreement to make the first payment was fully executed at the time of the commencement of this action. See Salvas v. Jussaume, 50 R.I. 75, 145 A. 97 (1929); Young Foundation Corp. v. A. E. Ottaviano, Inc., 29 Misc.2d 302, 216 N.Y.S.2d 448, aff'd 15 A.D.2d 517, 222 N.Y.S.2d 685 (1961); Sloan v. Sloan, 66 A.2d 799 (D.C.Mun.Ct.App. 1949); Hines v. Ward Baking Co., 155 F.2d 257 (7th Cir. 1946); Julian v. Gold, 214 Cal. 74, 3 P.2d 1,0009 (1931); 1 Williston, Contracts § 130A at 543 (Jaeger 3d ed. 1957); Simpson, Contracts § 58 at 102 (2d ed. 1965). However, since both payments were made under similar circumstances, our decision regarding the second payment (Part B, infra) is fully applicable to the first payment.

B

It is generally held that a modification of a contract is itself a contract, which is unenforceable unless supported by consideration. See Simpson, supra, § 93. In Rose v. Daniels, 8 R.I. 381 (1866), this court held that an agreement by a debtor with a creditor to discharge a debt for a sum of money less than the amount due is unenforceable because it was not supported by consideration.

Rose is a perfect example of the preexisting duty rule. Under this rule an agreement modifying a contract is not supported by consideration if one of the parties to the agreement does or promises to do something that he is legally obligated to do or refrains or promises to refrain from doing something he is not legally privileged to do. See Calamari & Perillo, Contracts § 60 (1970); 1A Corbin, Contracts §§ 171-72 (1963); 1 Williston, supra, § 130; Annot., 12 A.L.R.2d 78 (1950). In Rose there was no consideration for the new agreement because the debtor was already legally obligated to repay the full amount of the debt.

Although the preexisting duty rule is followed by most jurisdictions, a small minority of jurisdictions, Massachusetts, for example, find that there is consideration for a promise to perform what one is already legally obligated to do because the new promise is given in place of an action for damages to secure performance. See Swartz v. Lieberman, 323 Mass. 109, 80 N.E.2d 5 (1948); Munroe v. Perkins, 26 Mass. (9 Pick.) 298 (1830). Swartz is premised on the theory that a promisor's forbearance of the power to breach his original agreement and be sued in an action for damages is consideration for a subsequent agreement by the promisee to pay extra compensation. This rule, however, has been widely criticized as an anomaly. See Calamari & Perillo, supra, § 61; Annot., 12 A.L.R.2d 78, 85-90 (1950).

The primary purpose of the preexisting duty rule is to prevent what has been referred to as the "hold-up game." See 1A Corbin, supra, § 171. A classic example of the "hold-up game" is found in Alaska Packers' Ass'n v. Domenico, 117 F. 99 (9th Cir. 1902). There 21 seamen entered into a written contract with Domenico to sail from San Francisco to Pyramid Harbor, Alaska. They were to work as sailors and fishermen out of Pyramid Harbor during the fishing season of 1900. The contract specified that each man would be paid $50 plus two cents for each red salmon he caught. Subsequent to their arrival at Pyramid Harbor, the men stopped work and demanded an additional $50. They threatened to return to San Francisco if Domenico did not agree to their demand. Since it was impossible for Domenico to find other men, he agreed to pay the men an additional $50. After they returned to San Francisco, Domenico refused to pay the men an additional $50. The court found that the subsequent agreement to pay the men an additional $50 was not supported by consideration because the men had a preexisting duty to work on the ship under the original contract, and thus the subsequent agreement was unenforceable.

Another example of the "hold-up game" is found in the area of construction contracts. Frequently, a contractor will refuse to complete work under an unprofitable contract unless he is awarded additional compensation. The courts have generally held that a subsequent agreement to award additional compensation is unenforceable if the contractor is only performing work which would have been required of him under the original contract. See, e.g., Lingenfelder v. Wainwright Brewing Co., 103 Mo. 578, 15 S.W. 844 (1891), which is a leading case in this area. See also cases collected in Annot., 25 A.L.R. 1450 (1923), supplemented by Annot., 55 A.L.R. 1333 (1928), and Annot., 138 A.L.R. 136 (1942); cf. Ford & Denning v. Shepard Co., 36 R.I. 497, 90 A. 805 (1914).

These examples clearly illustrate that the courts will not enforce an agreement that has been procured by coercion or duress and will hold the parties to their original contract regardless of whether it is profitable or unprofitable. However, the courts have been reluctant to apply the preexisting duty rule when a party to a contract encounters unanticipated difficulties and the other party, not influenced by coercion or duress, voluntarily agrees to pay additional compensation for work already required to be performed under the contract. For example, the courts have found that the original contract was rescinded, Linz v. Schuck, 106 Md. 220, 67 A. 286 (1907); abandoned, Connelly v. Devoe, 37 Conn. 570 (1871), or waived, Michaud v. McGregor, 61 Minn. 198, 63 N.W. 479 (1895).

Although the preexisting duty rule has served a useful purpose insofar as it deters parties from using coercion and duress to obtain additional compensation, it has been widely criticized as a general rule of law. With regard to the preexisting duty rule, one legal scholar has stated: "There has been a growing doubt as to the soundness of this doctrine as a matter of social policy. . . . In certain classes of cases, this doubt has influenced courts to refuse to apply the rule, or to ignore it, in their actual decisions. Like other legal rules, this rule is in process of growth and change, the process being more active here than in most instances. The result of this is that a court should no longer accept this rule as fully established. It should never use it as the major premise of a decision, at least without giving careful thought to the circumstances of the particular case, to the moral deserts of the parties, and to the social feelings and interests that are involved. It is certain that the rule, stated in general and all-inclusive terms, is no longer so well-settled that a court must apply it though the heavens fall." 1A Corbin, supra, § 171; see also Calamari & Perillo, supra, § 61.

The modern trend appears to recognize the necessity that courts should enforce agreements modifying contracts when unexpected or unanticipated difficulties arise during the course of the performance of a contract, even though there is no consideration for the modification, as long as the parties agree voluntarily.

Under the Uniform Commercial Code, § 2-209(1), which has been adopted by 49 states, "(a)n agreement modifying a contract (for the sale of goods) needs no consideration to be binding." See G.L.1956 (1969 Reenactment) § 6A-2-209(1). Although at first blush this section appears to validate modifications obtained by coercion and duress, the comments to this section indicate that a modification under this section must meet the test of good faith imposed by the Code, and a modification obtained by extortion without a legitimate commercial reason is unenforceable.

The modern trend away from a rigid application of the preexisting duty rule is reflected by s 89D(a) of the American Law Institute's Restatement Second of the Law of Contracts, which provides: "A promise modifying a duty under a contract not fully performed on either side is binding (a) if the modification is fair and equitable in view of circumstances not anticipated by the parties when the contract was made . . . ."

We believe that s 89D(a) is the proper rule of law and find it applicable to the facts of this case. It not only prohibits modifications obtained by coercion, duress, or extortion but also fulfills society's expectation that agreements entered into voluntarily will be enforced by the courts. See generally Horwitz, The Historical Foundations of Modern Contract Law, 87 Harv.L.Rev. 917 (1974). Section 89D(a), of course, does not compel a modification of an unprofitable or unfair contract; it only enforces a modification if the parties voluntarily agree and if (1) the promise modifying the original contract was made before the contract was fully performed on either side, (2) the underlying circumstances which prompted the modification were unanticipated by the parties, and (3) the modification is fair and equitable.

The evidence, which is uncontradicted, reveals that in June of 1968 Maher requested the city council to pay him an additional $10,000 for the year beginning on July 1, 1968, and ending on June 30, 1969. This request was made at a public meeting of the city council, where Maher explained in detail his reasons for making the request. Thereafter, the city council voted to authorize the Mayor to sign an amendment to the 1964 contract which provided that Maher would receive an additional $10,000 per year for the duration of the contract. Under such circumstances we have no doubt that the city voluntarily agreed to modify the 1964 contract.

Having determined the voluntariness of this agreement, we turn our attention to the three criteria delineated above. First, the modification was made in June of 1968 at a time when the five-year contract which was made in 1964 had not been fully performed by either party. Second, although the 1964 contract provided that Maher collect all refuse generated within the city, it appears this contract was premised on Maher's past experience that the number of refuse-generating units would increase at a rate of 20 to 25 per year. Furthermore, the evidence is uncontradicted that the 1967-1968 increase of 400 units 'went beyond any previous expectation.' Clearly, the circumstances which prompted the city council to modify the 1964 contract were unanticipated. Third, although the evidence does not indicate what proportion of the total this increase comprised, the evidence does indicate that it was a 'substantial' increase. In light of this, we cannot say that the council's agreement to pay Maher the $10,000 increase was not fair and equitable in the circumstances.

The judgment appealed from is reversed, and the cause is remanded to the Superior Court for entry of judgment for the defendants.

NOTES AND QUESTIONS:

1. *See* Restatement (Second) of Contracts §§ 82-94 (Contracts Without Consideration) (1981).

2. *See* U.C.C. § 2-209 (Modification, Rescission, and Waiver) (2002).

SECTION 7. STATUTE OF FRAUDS

A. INTRODUCTION TO THE STATUTE OF FRAUDS

Up to this point, we have examined the validity of objective manifestations of assent without regard to formalities not otherwise specified by the parties. Thus, we saw that valid contracts can and do exist with or without a writing. Nevertheless, some contracts are viewed as so susceptible to fraud that the courts require some degree of written evidence that a contract was made in order to be enforceable. It may help to trace the origins of the Statute of Frauds in order to understand the present-day requirements for satisfying the statute.

As far as it can be determined, the Statute of Frauds originated in England in 1677. At that time, the English courts had a system that precluded the parties to a contract from testifying on their on behalf. Moreover, jurors often relied on their own investigation and personal knowledge of the circumstances surrounding the case in reaching their verdict. Accordingly, the trial process was ripe for and riddled with fraud, including perjured testimony of alleged witnesses that could not be contradicted by the parties against whom the testimony was offered. Accordingly, Parliament enacted what we commonly refer to as the Statute of Frauds and other related regulations in order to gain control of juries and prevent fraudulent practices in trials. The six categories of contracts originally included in the Statute of Frauds promulgated by Parliament are contracts for the sale of interest in real property, promises made in consideration of marriage, promises to answer for the debt of another (suretyships), promises by executors or administrators to discharge the debts of the decedent's estate, promises that cannot be performed within a year, and contracts for the sale of goods over a certain amount. In 1954, England repealed the Statute of Frauds for all but two of the six categories.[3]

Virtually every American state adopted its own version of the statute of frauds early on. While the categories of contracts that fall within each state's statute vary dramatically, essentially all of the states include the original six categories. Despite Parliament's repeal of virtually all of the original Statute of Frauds, the American states continue to enforce their statutes for the six original categories, and have enlarged them to cover a variety of other contracts. As you explore the following materials, consider whether the statute of frauds is effective and worthy of preserving.

---

[3] England retained the writing requirement for suretyships and contracts for the sale of land.

SATTERFIELD V. MISSOURI DENTAL ASS'N
Missouri Court of Appeals
642 S.W.2d 110 (1982).

Before CLARK, P.J., and MANFORD and KENNEDY, JJ.

CLARK, Presiding Judge.

. . . .

The facts of the case are drawn from appellant's petition by which it is alleged that appellant was employed by the association as executive secretary from 1944 until November 11, 1979 when she was discharged. That event, she asserted, breached an oral agreement under which appellant was to have continued in her position until retirement on a date set by her. Appellant further alleged the date of retirement had been determined to be April 1981 and she had so advised the association. In addition to damages, appellant sought reinstatement to her former position. The motion to dismiss, sustained by the trial court, was based on the ground that any agreement to retain appellant in employment from November 1979 to April 1981 was not to be performed within one year and was thus required by the statute of frauds to be in writing.

In her first point, appellant contends the trial court erred in dismissing the petition because a plaintiff is under no obligation to show affirmatively by petition averments that a cause of action is not barred by the statute of frauds. The statute constitutes an affirmative defense to be pleaded by answer and, according to appellant, may not be successfully asserted on a motion to dismiss.

We first observe that plaintiff's petition here makes no particular allegation as to the form of the employment agreement, appellant having been content to plead "it was agreed and understood between plaintiff and defendant that plaintiff would serve as executive secretary of defendant until her retirement." The fact that the agreement was indeed oral was not, however, the subject of any dispute. In suggestions opposing the motion to dismiss, appellant conceded the agreement to have been oral arguing that the statute was inapplicable because the agreement could have been performed within one year.

Arguments much the same as those advanced by appellant were considered and rejected in International Plastics Development, Inc. v. Monsanto Company, 433 S.W.2d 291 (Mo. banc 1968) and State ex rel. Uthoff v. Russell, 210 S.W.2d 1017 (Mo.App.1948). Those cases hold the statute of frauds may properly be raised in a motion to dismiss for failure to state a claim if it appears the contract in question is unwritten and the plaintiff fails to plead facts which would take the contract out of the operation of the statute. In other circumstances where the pleadings raise a dispute as to whether the agreement was memorialized by a writing or where the plaintiff has raised other fact issues relevant to the applicability of the statute, a motion to dismiss would be premature until the fact questions are settled. Such was the situation in Martin v. Ray County Coal Co., 288 Mo. 241, 232 S.W. 149 (1921), cited by appellant and distinguishable on this ground.

Appellant next contends the statute of frauds was not applicable to the agreement she made to work until she decided to retire because that agreement, embracing an indefinite time period, could have been performed within one year. While it is correct that an employment contract for an indefinite period may be performed within one year by exercise of the option to terminate and such an agreement has been held not to be within the statute of frauds, Koman v. Morrissey, 517 S.W.2d 929, 935 (Mo.1974), the agreement here was not of that nature according to plaintiff's petition. She there alleged the exercise of her option to select a retirement date "which she had therefore determined to be April, 1981 and had so advised the Board of Governors of the defendant corporation." The contract on which appellant based her action was one for her continued employment until April 1981, a definite future date well beyond the limitation of one year. By setting her retirement date, which appellant was entitled to do, she established the agreement to be of definite duration obligating both parties to continue the employment and eliminating the termination option.

Appellant also argues, inexplicably, that the statute of frauds does not apply here under the exception recognized where one party to the agreement has fully performed. Apparently, she bases this contention on the fact that she rendered services from the date of the agreement until her termination, thus giving defendant the benefit of the agreement for that period of time. Of course, the cause of action here originates in a premature discharge which prevented appellant from performing the complete services her agreement contemplated. By her own allegations, the agreement would have been fully performed on her part only if she worked until retirement in April 1981. The fact that she was earlier terminated, with or without cause, does not convert partial performance into full performance such as will remove the case from the requirements of the statute of frauds. 72 Am.Jur.2d Statute of Frauds § 39 (1974); Annot., 88 A.L.R.2d 701 (1963).

Finally, appellant contends her part performance was sufficient to enable the court to enforce the contract under the "doctrine of equitable fraud" despite the statute of frauds. She cites Pointer v. Ward, 429 S.W.2d 269 (Mo.1968) as authority for this proposition.

In the last cited case, the court acknowledged the possibility, in very unusual circumstances, for a court of equity to enforce an oral contract despite the statute of frauds. Among the elements to be proved are partial performance done in reliance on the contract with a resulting change in the positions of the parties so that application of the statute of frauds would result in a grossly unjust and deep-seated wrong, constituting fraud or something akin thereto sometimes referred to as virtual fraud, constructive fraud or equitable fraud. Suffice it to say that appellant here pleaded no change in the positions of the parties based on the alleged agreement, no grossly unjust or deep-seated wrong and no act or consequence approaching fraud. The doctrine has no application to the facts as they appear in the petition. Moreover, the law is generally settled that partial performance will not remove a contract not to be performed within one year from the operation of the statute of frauds where the action is one for breach of the entire contract. Waller v. Tootle-Campbell Dry Goods Co., 59 S.W.2d 751, 754 (Mo.App.1933); Annot., 6 A.L.R.2d 1053, 1083 (1949).

The judgment is affirmed.

All concur.

NOTES AND QUESTIONS:

1. The court in *Satterfield* seems to agree, albeit in dicta, that contracts for indefinite time periods do not fall within the requirements of the statute of frauds because theoretically they are capable of being performed within a year. However, other jurisdictions disagree, determining that contracts with indefinite time periods are governed by the statute of frauds. In particular, contracts for lifetime employment are often characterized as permanent contracts in which the parties necessarily contemplated a long relationship, despite the fact that the employee could die within a year. In such jurisdictions, lifetime contracts are subject to the requirements of the statute of frauds. *E.g. McInerney v. Charter Golf*, 690 N.E.2d 1347 (Ill. 1997).

MCINTOSH V. MURPHY
Supreme Court of Hawaii
469 P.2d 177 (1970).

LEVINSON, Justice.

This case involves an oral employment contract which allegedly violates the provision of the Statute of Frauds requiring "any agreement that is not to be performed within one year from the making thereof" to be in writing in order to be enforceable. HRS § 656-1(5). In this action the plaintiff-employee Dick McIntosh seeks to recover damages from his employer, George Murphy and Murphy Motors, Ltd., for the breach of alleged one-year oral employment contract.

While the facts are in sharp conflict, it appears that defendant George Murphy was in southern California during March 1964 interviewing prospective management personnel for his Chevrolet-Oldsmobile dealerships in Hawaii. He interviewed the plaintiff twice during that time. The position of sales manager for one of the dealerships was fully discussed but no contract was entered into. In April 1964 the plaintiff received a call from the general manager of Murphy Motors informing him of possible employment within thirty days if he was still available. The plaintiff indicated his continued interest and informed the manager that he would be available. Later in April, the plaintiff sent Murphy a telegram to the effect that he would arrive in Honolulu on Sunday, April 26, 1964. Murphy then telephoned McIntosh on Saturday, April 25, 1964 to notify him that the job of assistant sales manager was open and work would begin on the following Monday, April 27, 1964. At that time McIntosh expressed surprise at the change in job title from sales manager to assistant sales manager but reconfirmed the fact that he was arriving in Honolulu the next day, Sunday. McIntosh arrived on Sunday, April 26, 1964 and began work on the following day, Monday, April 27, 1964.

As a consequence of his decision to work for Murphy, McIntosh moved some of his belongings from the mainland to Hawaii, sold other possessions, leased an apartment in Honolulu and obviously forwent any other employment opportunities. In short, the plaintiff did all those things which were incidental to changing one's residence permanently from Los Angeles to Honolulu, a distance of approximately 2200 miles. McIntosh continued working for Murphy until July 16, 1964, approximately two and one-half months, at which time he was discharged on the grounds that he was unable to close deals with prospective customers and could not train the salesmen.

At the conclusion of the trial, the defense moved for a directed verdict arguing that the oral employment agreement was in violation of the Statute of Frauds, there being no written memorandum or note thereof. The trial court ruled that as a matter of law the contract did not come within the Statute, reasoning that Murphy bargained for acceptance by the actual commencement of performance by McIntosh, so that McIntosh was not bound by a contract until he came to work on Monday, April 27, 1964. Therefore, assuming that the contract was for a year's employment, it was performable within a year exactly to the day and no writing was required for it to be enforceable. Alternatively, the court ruled that if the agreement was made final by the telephone call between the parties on Saturday, April 25, 1964, then that part of the weekend which remained would not be counted in calculating the year, thus taking the contract out of the Statute of Frauds. With commendable candor the trial judge gave as the motivating force for the decision his desire to avoid a mechanical and unjust application of the Statute.[1]

The case went to the jury on the following questions: (1) whether the contract was for a year's duration or was performable on a trial basis, thus making it terminable at the will of either party; (2) whether the plaintiff was discharged for just cause; and (3) if he was not discharged for just cause, what damages were due the plaintiff. The jury returned a verdict for the plaintiff in the sum of $12,103.40. The defendants appeal to this court on four principal grounds, three of which we find to be without merit. The remaining ground of appeal is whether the plaintiff can maintain an action on the alleged oral employment contract in light of the prohibition of the Statute of Frauds making unenforceable an oral contract that is not to be performed within one year.

I. TIME OF ACCEPTANCE OF THE EMPLOYMENT AGREEMENT

The defendants contend that the trial court erred in refusing to give an instruction to the jury that if the employment agreement was made more than one day before the plaintiff began performance, there could be no recovery by the plaintiff. The reason given was that a contract not to be performed within one year from its making is unenforceable if not in writing.

The defendants are correct in their argument that the time of acceptance of an offer is a question of fact for the jury to decide. But the trial court alternatively decided that even if the offer was accepted on the Saturday prior to the commencement of performance, the intervening Sunday and part of Saturday would not be counted in computing the year for the purposes of the Statute of Frauds. The judge stated that Sunday was a non-working day and only a fraction of Saturday was left which he would not count. In any event, there is no need to discuss the relative merits of either ruling since we base our decision in this case on the doctrine of equitable estoppel which was properly briefed and argued by both parties before this court, although not presented to the trial court.

[1] THE COURT: You make the law look ridiculous, because one day is Sunday and the man does not work on Sunday; the other day is Saturday; he is up in Fresno. He can't work down there. And he is down here Sunday night and shows up for work on Monday. To me that is a contract within a year. I don't want to make the law look ridiculous, Mr. Clause, because it is one day alter, one day too much, and that one day is a Sunday, and a non-working day.

II. ENFORCEMENT BY VIRTUE OF ACTION IN RELIANCE ON THE ORAL CONTRACT

In determining whether a rule of law can be fashioned and applied to a situation where an oral contract admittedly violates a strict interpretation of the Statute of Frauds, it is necessary to review the Statute itself together with its historical and modern functions. The Statute of Frauds, which requires that certain contracts be in writing in order to be legally enforceable, had its inception in the days of Charles II of England. Hawaii's version of the Statute is found in HRS § 656-1 and is substantially the same as the original English Statute of Frauds.

The first English Statute was enacted almost 300 years ago to prevent "many fraudulent practices, which are commonly endeavored to be upheld by perjury and subornation of perjury." 29 Car. 2, c. 3 (1677). Certainly, there were compelling reasons in those days for such a law. At the time of enactment in England, the jury system was quite unreliable, rules of evidence were few, and the complaining party was disqualified as a witness so he could neither testify on direct-examination nor, more importantly, be cross-examined. Summers, The Doctrine of Estoppel and the Statute of Frauds, 79 U.Pa.L.Rev. 440, 441 (1931). The aforementioned structural and evidentiary limitations on our system of justice no longer exist.

Retention of the Statute today has nevertheless been justified on at least three grounds: (1) the Statute still serves an evidentiary function thereby lessening the danger of perjured testimony (the original rationale); (2) the requirement of a writing has a cautionary effect which causes reflection by the parties on the importance of the agreement; and (3) the writing is an easy way to distinguish enforceable contracts from those which are not, thus chanelling certain transactions into written form.[2]

In spite of whatever utility the Statute of Frauds may still have, its applicability has been drastically limited by judicial construction over the years in order to mitigate the harshness of a mechanical application.[3] Furthermore, learned writers continue to disparage the Statute regarding it as "a statute for promoting fraud" and a "legal anachronism."[4]

Another method of judicial circumvention of the Statute of Frauds has grown out of the exercise of the equity powers of the courts. Such judicially imposed limitations or exceptions involved the traditional dispensing power of the equity courts to mitigate the "harsh" rule of law. When courts have enforced an oral contract in spite of the Statute, they

---

[2] Fuller, Consideration and Form, 41 Colum.L.Rev. 799, 800-03 (1941); Note: Statute of Frauds-The Doctrine of Equitable Estoppel and the Statute of Frauds, 66 Mich.L.Rev. 170 (1967).

[3] Thus a promise to pay the debt of another has been construed to encompass only promises made to a creditor which do not benefit the promisor (Restatement of Contracts § 184 (1932); 3 Williston, Contracts § 452 (Jaeger ed. 1960)); a promise in consideration of marriage has been interpreted to exclude mutual promises to marry (Restatement, supra § 192; 3 Williston, supra § 485); a promise not to be performed within one year means a promise not performable within one year (Restatement, supra § 198; 3 Williston, supra, § 495); a promise not to be performed within one year may be removed from the Statute of Frauds if one party has fully performed (Restatement, supra § 198; 3 Williston, supra § 504); and the Statute will not be applied where all promises involved are fully performed (Restatement, supra s 219; 3 Williston, supra § 528).

[4] Burdick, A Statute for Promoting Fraud, 16 Colum.L.Rev. 273 (1916); Willis, The Statute of Frauds-A Legal Anachronism, 3 Ind.L.J. 427, 528 (1928).

have utilized the legal labels of "part performance" or "equitable estoppels" in granting relief. Both doctrines are said to be based on the concept of estoppel, which operates to avoid unconscionable injury. 3 Williston, Contracts § 533A at 791 (Jaeger ed. 1960), Summers, supra at 443-49; Monarco v. Lo Greco, 35 Cal.2d 621, 220 P.2d 737 (1950) (Traynor, J.).

Part performance has long been recognized in Hawaii as an equitable doctrine justifying the enforcement of an oral agreement for the conveyance of an interest in land where there has been substantial reliance by the party seeking to enforce the contract. Perreira v. Perreira, 50 Haw. 641, 447 P.2d 667 (1968) (agreement to grant life estate); Vierra v. Shipman, 26 Haw. 369 (1922) (agreement to devise land); Yee Hop v. Young Sak Cho, 25 Haw. 494 (1920) (oral lease of real property). Other courts have enforced oral contracts (including employment contracts) which failed to satisfy the section of the Statute making unenforceable an agreement not to be performed within a year of its making. This has occurred where the conduct of the parties gave rise to an estoppel to assert the Statute. Oxley v. Ralston Purina Co., 349 F.2d 328 (6th Cir. 1965) (equitable estoppel); Alaska Airlines, Inc. v. Stephenson, 217 F.2d 295, 15 Alaska 272 (9th Cir. 1954) ('promissory estoppel'); Seymour v. Oelrichs, 156 Cal. 782, 106 P. 88 (1909) (equitable estoppel).

It is appropriate for modern courts to cast aside the raiments of conceptualism which cloak the true policies underlying the reasoning behind the many decisions enforcing contracts that violate the Statute of Frauds. There is certainly no need to resort to legal rubrics or meticulous legal formulas when better explanations are available. The policy behind enforcing an oral agreement which violated the Statute of Frauds, as a policy of avoiding unconscionable injury, was well set out by the California Supreme Court. In Monarco v. Lo Greco, 35 Cal.2d 621, 623, 220 P.2d 737, 739 (1950), a case which involved an action to enforce an oral contract for the conveyance of land on the grounds of 20 years performance by the promisee, the court said:

> The doctrine of estoppel to assert the statute of frauds has been consistently applied by the courts of this state to prevent fraud that would result from refusal to enforce oral contracts in certain circumstances. Such fraud may inhere in the unconscionable injury that would result from denying enforcement of the contract after one party has been induced by the other seriously to change his position in reliance on the contract . . . . See also Seymour v. Oelrichs, 156 Cal. 782, 106 P. 88 (1909) (an employment contract enforced).

In seeking to frame a workable test which is flexible enough to cover diverse factual situations and also provide some reviewable standards, we find very persuasive section 217A of the Second Restatement of Contracts.[5] That section specifically covers those situations where there has been reliance on an oral contract which falls within the Statute of Frauds. Section 217A states:

[5] Restatement (Second) of Contracts § 217A (Supp. Tentative Draft No. 4, 1969).

> (1) A promise which the promisor should reasonably expect to induce action or forbearance on the part of the promisee or a third person and which does induce the action or forbearance is enforceable notwithstanding the Statute of Frauds if injustice can be avoided only by enforcement of the promise. The remedy granted for breach is to be limited as justice requires.
>
> (2) In determining whether injustice can be avoided only by enforcement of the promise, the following circumstances are significant: (a) the availability and adequacy of other remedies, particularly cancellation and restitution; (b) the definite and substantial character of the action or forbearance in relation to the remedy sought; (c) the extent to which the action or forbearance corroborates evidence of the making and terms of the promise, or the making and terms are otherwise established by clear and convincing evidence; (d) the reasonableness of the action or forbearance; (e) the extent to which the action or forbearance was forseeable by the promisor.

We think that the approach taken in the Restatement is the proper method of giving the trial court the necessary latitude to relieve a party of the hardships of the Statute of Frauds. Other courts have used similar approaches in dealing with oral employment contracts upon which an employee had seriously relied. See Alaska Airlines, Inc. v. Stephenson, 217 F.2d 295 (9th Cir. 1954); Seymour v. Oelrichs, 156 Cal. 782, 106 P. 88 (1909). This is to be preferred over having the trial court bend over backwards to take the contract out of the Statute of Frauds. In the present case the trial court admitted just this inclination and forthrightly followed it.

There is no dispute that the action of the plaintiff in moving 2200 miles from Los Angeles to Hawaii was foreseeable by the defendant. In fact, it was required to perform his duties. Injustice can only be avoided by the enforcement of the contract and the granting of money damages. No other remedy is adequate. The plaintiff found himself residing in Hawaii without a job.

It is also clear that a contract of some kind did exist. The plaintiff performed the contract for two and one-half months receiving $3,484.60 for his services. The exact length of the contract, whether terminable at will as urged by the defendant, or for a year from the time when the plaintiff started working, was up to the jury to decide.

In sum, the trial court might have found that enforcement of the contract was warranted by virtue of the plaintiff's reliance on the defendant's promise. Naturally, each case turns on its own facts. Certainly there is considerable discretion for a court to implement the true policy behind the Statute of Frauds, which is to prevent fraud or any other type of unconscionable injury. We therefore affirm the judgment of the trial court on the ground that the plaintiff's reliance was such that injustice could only be avoided by enforcement of the contract.

Affirmed.

ABE, Justice (dissenting).

The majority of the court has affirmed the judgment of the trial court; however, I respectfully dissent.

I.

Whether alleged contract of employment came within the Statute of Frauds:

As acknowledged by this court, the trial judge erred when as a matter of law he ruled that the alleged employment contract did not come within the Statute of Frauds; however, I cannot agree that this error was not prejudicial as this court intimates.

On this issue, the date that the alleged contract was entered into was all important and the date of acceptance of an offer by the plaintiff was a question of fact for the jury to decide. In other words, it was for the jury to determine when the alleged one-year employment contract was entered into and if the jury had found that the plaintiff had accepted the offer[1] more than one day before plaintiff was to report to work, the contract would have come within the Statute of Frauds and would have been unenforceable.

II.

This court holds that though the alleged one-year employment contract came within the Statute of Frauds, nevertheless the judgment of the trial court is affirmed "on the ground that the plaintiff's reliance was such that injustice could only be avoided by enforcement of the contract."

I believe this court is begging the issue by its holding because to reach that conclusion, this court is ruling that the defendant agreed to hire the plaintiff under a one-year employment contract. The defendant has denied that the plaintiff was hired for a period of one year and has introduced into evidence testimony of witnesses that all hiring by the defendant in the past has been on a trial basis. The defendant also testified that he had hired the plaintiff on a trial basis.

Here on one hand the plaintiff claimed that he had a one-year employment contract; on the other hand, the defendant claimed that the plaintiff had not been hired for one year but on a trial basis for so long as his services were satisfactory. I believe the Statute of Frauds was enacted to avoid the consequences this court is forcing upon the defendant. In my opinion, the legislature enacted the Statute of Frauds to negate claims such as has been made by the plaintiff in this case. But this court holds that because the plaintiff in reliance of the one-year employment contract (alleged to have been entered into by the plaintiff, but denied by the defendant) has changed his position, "injustice could only be avoided by enforcement of the contract." Where is the sense of justice?

Now assuming that the defendant had agreed to hire the plaintiff under a one-year employment contract and the contract came within the Statute of Frauds, I cannot agree, as intimated by this court, that we should circumvent the Statute of Frauds by the exercise of the equity powers of courts. As to statutory law, the sole function of the judiciary is to

[1] Plaintiff testified that he accepted the offer in California over the telephone.

interpret the statute and the judiciary should not usurp legislative power and enter into the legislative field. Thus, if the Statute of Frauds is too harsh as intimated by this court, and it brings about undue hardship, it is for the legislature to amend or repeal the statute and not for this court to legislate.

KOBAYASHI, J., joins in this dissent.

YARBRO V. NEIL B. MCGINNIS EQUIPMENT CO.
Supreme Court of Arizona
420 P.2d 163 (1966).

BERNSTEIN, Vice Chief Justice.

This case is before us on an appeal from a judgment of the Superior Court of Maricopa County. The appellee, McGinnis Equipment Co., brought suit to recover payments due it pursuant to a conditional sales contract for the sale of one used Allis-Chalmers Model HD-5G tractor. The contract was negotiated in August of 1957 and called for twenty-three monthly installments of $574.00 each. The buyer, Russell, failed to make the first monthly payment, and on his suggestion a McGinnis company representative met with the appellant, Yarbro, to ask if he would help with the payments. As a result of this meeting Yarbro agreed to, and did, pay the September installment.

In the months that followed there was a continued failure on the part of Russell to make any of the monthly installment payments. During the late months of 1957 and the early months of 1958, there were numerous discussions between McGinnis Co., Russell and Yarbro relative to these monthly payments and at various times during this period, the defendant orally agreed to make some of the payments for Russell. Late in December of 1957, Yarbro gave the McGinnis Co. a check to cover one of the delinquent payments but the check was returned due to insufficient funds. In March of 1958, Yarbro agreed to bring the account of Russell current and allocated $2,378.00 of a check for this purpose. This check, however, was also returned by the bank for lack of sufficient funds.

In May, 1958 when McGinnis Co. indicated that the tractor soon would have to be repossessed, Yarbro again assured the company that it would be paid as soon as two pending real estate escrows were closed. This promised payment was not made. A similar promise was made by Yarbro in July on the strength of proceeds that were to be forthcoming from an oat crop in New Mexico but again no payment was made. An ultimatum was issued by the McGinnis Co. at the end of July, 1958 and finally steps to repossess were taken in August of 1958.

Persons at the Yarbro ranch prevented the repossession, leading to further negotiations which also provided unfruitful. The tractor was finally repossessed in January of 1959. Subsequently, the McGinnis Co. brought an action to recover the payments due under the conditional sales contract, naming Russell and Yarbro as defendants. A default judgment was entered against Russell and the only question before this court now concerns the liability of the defendant, Yarbro. The trial court found Yarbro liable for the entire balance under the conditional sales contract ($8,751.95).

The errors assigned by the defendant on this appeal are threefold. First, he contends that his promises to pay the debts of Russell, being oral, are unenforceable by reason of the Statute of Frauds. § 44-101, subsec. 2. Second, he contends that there was insufficient consideration to support the promise assuming it was otherwise enforceable. Third, he contends that if the Statute of Frauds were held to be inapplicable to this case, the judgment rendered by the trial court was excessive. The third assignment of error is based on defendant's arguments that he only promised to pay four, rather than all, of the unpaid monthly installments. We will consider these contentions separately.

A.R.S. § 44-101, commonly known as the Statute of Frauds provides:

> No action shall be brought in any court in the following cases unless the promise or agreement upon which the action is brought, or some memorandum thereof, is in writing and signed by the party to be charged, or by some person by him thereunder lawfully authorized:
>
> 2. To charge a person upon a promise to answer for the debt, default or miscarriage of another.

Although the promises made by Yarbo clearly were of the type covered in the above statute, the plaintiff contends that the leading object or primary purpose exception recognized by this court in the case of Steward v. Sirrine, 34 Ariz. 49, 267 P. 598, is applicable. Simply stated, this rule provides that where the leading object of a person promising to pay the debt of another is actually to protect his own interest, such promise if supported by sufficient consideration, is valid, even though it be oral. This rule has been adopted by a great number of states although the rationale has often been stated in varying terms. This exception to the Statute of Frauds no matter how stated, is based upon the underlying fact that the Statute does not apply to promises related to debts created at the instance, and for the benefit, of the promisor, (i.e., "original" promises) but only to those by which the debt of one party is sought to be charged upon and collected from another (i.e., "collateral" promises). Although a third party is the primary debtor, situations may arise where the promisor has a personal, immediate and pecuniary interest in the transaction, and is therefore himself a party to be benefitted by the performance of the promisee. In such cases the reason which underlies and which prompted the above statutory provision fails, and the courts will give effect to the promise. Schumm, by Whyner v. Berg, 37 Cal.2d 174, 231 P.2d 39, 21 A.L.R.2d 1051; Restatement of Contracts, § 184.

Recognizing the leading object rule as a well reasoned exception, the question remains whether the facts presently before this court make the exception applicable. There are no easy, mathematical guidelines to such a determination. To ascertain the character of the promise in question and the intention of the parties as to the nature of the liability created, regard must be had to the form of expression, the situation of the parties, and to all the circumstances of each particular case. Meinrath Brokerage Co. v. Collins-Dietz-Morris Co., 8 Cir., 298 F. 377; Amons v. Howard, 111 Okl. 195, 239 P. 217. The assumption behind the exception is that it is possible for a court to infer from the circumstances of any given case whether the "leading object" of the promisor was to become a surety for another or whether it was to secure a pecuniary advantage to himself and so, in effect, to answer for his own debt. The leading object may be inferred from that which he expected to get as the exchange for his promise. Thus, it is neither "consideration" alone (for there must be consideration to make any promise enforceable, including one of guaranty) nor "benefit" alone (for in most every guaranty situation at least some benefit will flow to the promisor-guarantor) that makes an oral promise to pay the debt of another enforceable. Rather, there must be consideration and benefit and that benefit must be the primary object of making the promise as distinguished from a benefit which is merely incidental, indirect, or remote. It is when the leading and main object of the promisor is not to become surety or guarantor of another, even though that may be the effect, but is to serve some purpose or interest of his own, that the oral promise becomes enforceable. Schumm, by Whyner v. Berg, supra.

The facts in the present case show that before the McGinnis Co. ever began its dealings with Russell, Yarbro had sought to purchase the tractor in question for himself, but that no sale had resulted because the financing institution with which the McGinnis Equipment Co. financed such deals would not accept Yarbro's credit. It was at this point that Yarbro said that he thought he could get Russell to buy the tractor. Further evidence of Yarbro's interest in the tractor comes from the fact that after its purchase he had borrowed it on a series of occasions. When repairs were needed shortly after Yarbro had made the first installment payment, the McGinnis Co. repairman found the machine on Yarbro's land. He admits that a number of times he used the tractor for jobs around his ranch, and witnesses stated at the trial that Yarbro had asked on several occasions that the McGinnis Co. not repossess the tractor because he needed it. These requests were usually in conjunction with a promise to pay what was owing on the tractor.

We have often stated that this court will not disturb the findings and judgment of the trial court when supported by substantial evidence and that all the evidence and inferences therefrom must be viewed in a manner strongest in favor of the appellees. Almada v. Ruelas, 96 Ariz. 155, 393 P.2d 254, 257; Nordale v. Fisher, 93 Ariz. 342, 380 P.2d 1003, 1006. We find that there was substantial evidence to support the trial court's conclusion that the main and leading object of Yarbro in making his promises to McGinnis Co. was not to become Russell's guarantor but rather was to serve interests of his own.

Yarbro further contends that if the oral character of the promise does not prevent its enforcement, then a failure of consideration does. We, of course, recognize that a promise must be supported by consideration or some substitute in order to be legally enforceable, but find this requirement to be fulfilled in the present instance. In Cavanagh v. Kelly, 80 Ariz. 361, 297 P.2d 1102, we held that a benefit to a promisor or a loss or detriment to the promisee is good consideration to legally support a promise. In the present case, the McGinnis Co. had a legal right to repossess the subject of its conditional sales contract, but the evidence shows that it forbore from doing so because Yarbro promised that he would pay the delinquent installment payments. This forbearance was not only a legal detriment to the McGinnis Co., but as previously noted, was a substantial benefit to Yarbro. Forbearance by a creditor to seize his debtor's property or enforce a lien against it, has often been held to be sufficient consideration to support an oral promise of guaranty when such forbearance enables the promisor to obtain an advantage or benefit. Miller v. Hanna-Logan, Inc., 95 Colo. 464, 37 P.2d 393; Kahn v. Waldman, 283 Mass. 391, 186 N.E. 587, 88 A.L.R. 699; Stephen v. Yeomans, 112 Mich. 624, 71 N.W. 159; Dybdahl v. Continental Lumber Co., 133 Wash. 81, 233 P. 10.

Thus, when the main purpose of the promisor is not to answer for the debt of another, but to obtain a substantial benefit to himself, which he actually secures as the consideration for his promise, then not only is the promise valid though oral, it is supported by good and sufficient consideration.

The defendant also contends that assuming his promise was not within the contemplation of the Statute of Frauds, the eventual judgment rendered against him was excessive. With this contention, we agree.

The trial court granted judgment in the amount of $8,751.95 which represents the entire unpaid balance of the contract purchase price reduced by the $5,000 received by the plaintiff at an auction sale of the repossessed machine. To hold Yarbro liable for the complete contract price, the evidence must indicate that his promises to pay went not only to delinquent payments but also to the remainder of the payments under the contract. The evidence, however, does not show this.

It is clear from the testimony of the creditor's agents that each time they visited Yarbro and Russell, only past due payments were requested. It is also clear from their testimony that there were no promises by Yarbro to assume future installment payments. The only evidence regarding a promise to pay in the future appears in Yarbro's own testimony on direct examination, and is as follows:

"Q. What was said by you concerning the . . . Russell obligation?"

"A. I told them that . . . if they would give me time I would pay for this tractor and take it over."

The creditors failed to make any such arrangements, and under such circumstances the above statement cannot be considered to rise to the dignity necessary to obligate the defendant to pay future installment payments. When one assumes a portion of the debt of another it does not necessarily follow that he has assumed his entire debt.

The record indicates that the last time that Yarbro was contacted prior to repossession was shortly after the July, 1958 installment came due. At this time, claiming anticipated crop proceeds for assurance, he promised to make all past due payments on the equipment. No later promises were made. Accordingly, we find Yarbro liable for the monthly installments from October 1957 through July 1958 only. The trial court judgment is reduced correspondingly.

Judgment affirmed as modified.

STRUCKMEYER, C.J., and UDALL, LOCKWOOD and McFARLAND, JJ., concur.

NOTES AND QUESTIONS:

1. In spite of the seemingly unequivocal writing requirements of the statute of frauds, courts have found various ways to mitigate the harshness of the statute's bar to enforcement of contracts. The preceding cases highlight several widely-accepted exceptions to the statute of frauds, the effect of which permits the parties to have their day in court on the underlying merits of the case.

2. Restatement (Second) of Contracts § 139 (1981) reflects the modern view that reliance or promissory estoppel may warrant enforcement of a contract that does not otherwise satisfy the requirements of the statute of frauds. This theory was discussed and adopted in *McIntosh v. Murphy*. However, courts willing to adopt this theory are all over the map in determining the appropriate remedy for reliance on a contract that does not comply with the statutory requirements. While some courts allow the parties to enforce the contract in the same manner as any other valid and enforceable contract, others limit enforcement to the extent necessary to avoid injustice. Nevertheless, many jurisdictions do not allow parties to bypass the requirements of the statute of frauds based on reliance or promissory estoppel; these jurisdictions aptly note that a reliance exception would swallow the rule, rendering it totally meaningless. For a discussion and rejection of the reliance exception, see *McInerney v. Charter Golf*, 680 N.E.2d 1347 (Ill. 1997).

B. STATUTORY APPLICATION

RESTATEMENT (SECOND) OF CONTRACTS
§ 131. GENERAL REQUISITES OF A MEMORANDUM

Unless additional requirements are prescribed by the particular statute, a contract within the Statute of Frauds is enforceable if it is evidenced by any writing, signed by or on behalf of the party to be charged, which

(a) reasonably identifies the subject matter of the contract,

(b) is sufficient to indicate that a contract with respect thereto has been made between the parties or offered by the signer to the other party, and

(c) states with reasonable certainty the essential terms of the unperformed promises in the contract.

CRABTREE V. ELIZABETH ARDEN SALES CORP.
Court of Appeals of New York
110 N.E.2d 551 (1953).

FULD, Judge.

In September of 1947, Nate Crabtree entered into preliminary negotiations with Elizabeth Arden Sales Corporation, manufacturers and sellers of cosmetics, looking toward his employment as sales manager. Interviewed on September 26th, by Robert P. Johns, executive vice-president and general manager of the corporation, who had apprised him of the possible opening, Crabtree requested a three-year contract at $25,000 a year. Explaining that he would be giving up a secure well-paying job to take a position in an entirely new field of endeavor which he believed would take him some years to master he insisted upon an agreement for a definite term. And he repeated his desire for a contract for three years to Miss Elizabeth Arden, the corporation's president. When Miss Arden finally indicated that she was prepared to offer a two-year contract, based on an annual salary of $20,000 for the first six months, $25,000 for the second six months and $30,000 for the second year, plus expenses of $5,000 a year for each of those years, Crabtree replied that that offer was "interesting." Miss Arden thereupon had her personal secretary make this memorandum on a telephone order blank that happened to be at hand:

EMPLOYMENT AGREEMENT WITH NATE CRABTREE
Date Sept. 26-1947 6: PM
At 681-5th Ave . . .
Begin 20000. 6 months 25000. 6 months 30000.
5000. per year Expense money
(2 years to make good)
Arrangement with Mr. Crabtree By Miss Arden
Present: Miss Arden Mr. John Mr. Crabtree Miss O'Leary

A few days later, Crabtree 'phoned Mr. Johns and telegraphed Miss Arden; he accepted the "invitation to join the Arden organization," and Miss Arden wired back her "welcome." When he reported for work, a "pay-roll change" card was made up and initialed by Mr. Johns, and then forwarded to the payroll department. Reciting that it was prepared on September 30, 1947, and was to be effective as of October 22d, it specified the names of the parties, Crabtree's "Job Classification" and, in addition, contained the notation that "This employee is to be paid as follows:

First six months of Employment	$20,000. per annum
Next six months of Employment	25,000. per annum
After one year of Employment	30,000. per annum

Approved by RPJ (initialed)."

After six months of employment, Crabtree received the scheduled increase from $20,000 to $25,000, but the further specified increase at the end of the year was not paid. Both Mr. Johns and the comptroller of the corporation, Mr. Carstens, told Crabtree that they would attempt to straighten out the matter with Miss Arden, and, with that in mind, the comptroller prepared another "pay-roll change" card, to which his signature is appended, noting that there was to be a "Salary increase" from $25,000 to $30,000 a year, "per contractual arrangements with Miss Arden." The latter, however, refused to approve the increase and, after further fruitless discussion, plaintiff left defendant's employ and commenced this action for breach of contract.

At the ensuing trial, defendant denied the existence of any agreement to employ plaintiff for two years, and further contended that, even if one had been made, the statute of frauds barred its enforcement. The trial court found against defendant on both issues and awarded plaintiff damages of about $14,000, and the Appellate Division, two justices dissenting, affirmed. Since the contract relied upon was not to be performed within a year, the primary question for decision is whether there was a memorandum of its terms, subscribed by defendant, to satisfy the statute of frauds, Personal Property Law, § 31.

Each of the two payroll cards the one initialed by defendant's general manager, the other signed by its comptroller unquestionably constitutes a memorandum under the statute. That they were not prepared or signed with the intention of evidencing the contract, or that they came into existence subsequent to its execution, is of no consequence, see Marks v. Cowdin, 226 N.Y. 138, 145, 123 N.E. 139, 141; Spiegel v. Lowenstein, 162 App.Div. 443, 448-449, 147 N.Y.S. 655, 658; see, also, Restatement, Contracts, §§ 209, 210, 214; it is enough, to meet the statute's demands, that they were signed with intent to authenticate the information contained therein and that such information does evidence the terms of the contract. See Marks v. Cowdin, supra, 226 N.Y. 138, 123 N.E. 139; Bayles v. Strong, 185 N.Y. 582, 78 N.E. 1099, affirming 104 App.Div. 153, 93 N.Y.S. 346; Spiegel v. Lowenstein, supra, 162 App.Div. 443, 448, 147 N.Y.S. 655, 658; see, also, 2 Corbin on Contracts (1951), pp. 732-733, 763-764; 2 Williston on Contracts (Rev. ed., 1936), pp. 1682-1683. Those two writings contain all of the essential terms of the contract the parties to it, the position that plaintiff was to assume, the salary that he was to receive except that relating to the duration of plaintiff's employment. Accordingly, we must consider whether that item, the length of the contract, may be supplied by reference to the earlier unsigned office memorandum, and, if so, whether its notation, "2 years to make good," sufficiently designates a period of employment.

The statute of frauds does not require the "memorandum . . . to be in one document. It may be pieced together out of separate writings, connected with one another either expressly or by the internal evidence of subject-matter and occasion." Marks v. Cowdin, supra, 226 N.Y. 138, 145, 123 N.E. 139, 141, see, also, 2 Williston, op cit., p. 1671; Restatement, Contracts, § 208, subd. (a). Where each of the separate writings has been subscribed by the party to be charged, little if any difficulty is encountered. See, e. g., Marks v. Cowdin, supra, 226 N.Y. 138, 144-145, 123 N.E. 139, 141. Where, however, some writings have been signed, and others have not as in the case before us there is basic disagreement as to what constitutes a sufficient connection permitting the unsigned papers to be considered as part of the statutory memorandum. The courts of some jurisdictions insist that there be a reference, of varying degrees of specificity, in the signed writing to that unsigned, and, if there is no such reference, they refuse to permit consideration of the latter in determining whether the memorandum satisfies the statute. See, e. g., Osborn v. Phelps, 19 Conn. 63; Hewett Grain & Provision Co. v. Spear, 222 Mich. 608, 193 N.W. 291. That conclusion is based upon a construction of the statute which requires that the connection between the writings and defendant's acknowledgment of the one not subscribed, appear from examination of the papers alone, without the aid of parol evidence. The other position which has gained increasing support over the years is that a sufficient connection between the papers is established simply by a reference in them to the same subject matter or transaction. See, e. g., Frost v. Alward, 176 Cal. 691, 169 P. 379; Lerned v. Wannemacher, 9 Allen, 412, 91 Mass. 412. The statute is not pressed "to the extreme of a literal and rigid logic," Marks v. Cowdin, supra, 226 N.Y. 138, 144, 123 N.E. 139, 141, and oral testimony is admitted to show the connection between the documents and to establish the acquiescence, of the party to be charged, to the contents of the one unsigned. See Beckwith v. Talbot, 95

U.S. 289, 24 L.Ed. 496; Oliver v. Hunting, 44 Ch.D. 205, 208-209; see, also, 2 Corbin, op. cit., ss 512-518; cf. Restatement, Contracts, s 208, subd. (b), par. (iii).

The view last expressed impresses us as the more sound, and, indeed although several of our cases appear to have gone the other way, see, e. g., Newbery v. Wall, 65 N.Y. 484; Wilson v. Lewiston Mill Co., 150 N.Y. 314, 44 N.E. 959 this court has on a number of occasions approved the rule, and we now definitively adopt it, permitting the signed and unsigned writings to be read together, provided that they clearly refer to the same subject matter or transaction. See, e. g., Peabody v. Speyers, 56 N.Y. 230; Raubitscheck v. Blank, 80 N.Y. 478; Peck v. Vandemark, 99 N.Y. 29, 1 N.E. 41; Coe v. Tough, 116 N.Y. 273, 22 N.E. 550; Delware Mills v. Carpenter Bros., 235 N.Y. 537, 139 N.E. 725, affirming 200 App.Div. 324, 193 N.Y.S. 201.

The language of the statute "Every agreement . . . is void, unless . . . some note or memorandum thereof be in writing, and subscribed by the party to be charged," Personal Property Law, § 31, does not impose the requirement that the signed acknowledgment of the contract must appear from the writings alone, unaided by oral testimony. The danger of fraud and perjury, generally attendant upon the admission of parol evidence, is at a minimum in a case such as this. None of the terms of the contract are supplied by parol. All of them must be set out in the various writings presented to the court, and at least one writing, the one establishing a contractual relationship between the parties, must bear the signature of the party to be charged, while the unsigned document must on its face refer to the same transaction as that set forth in the one that was signed. Parol evidence to portray the circumstances surrounding the making of the memorandum serves only to connect the separate documents and to show that there was assent, by the party to be charged, to the contents of the one unsigned. If that testimony does not convincingly connect the papers, or does not show assent to the unsigned paper, it is within the province of the judge to conclude, as a matter of law, that the statute has not been satisfied. True, the possibility still remains that, by fraud or perjury, an agreement never in fact made may occasionally be enforced under the subject matter or transaction test. It is better to run that risk, though, than to deny enforcement to all agreements, merely because the signed document made no specific mention of the unsigned writing. As the United States Supreme Court declared, in sanctioning the admission of parol evidence to establish the connection between the signed and unsigned writings. "There may be cases in which it would be a violation of reason and common sense to ignore a reference which derives its significance from such (parol) proof. If there is ground for any doubt in the matter, the general rule should be enforced. But where there is no ground for doubt, its enforcement would aid, instead of discouraging, fraud." Beckwith v. Talbot, supra, 95 U.S. 289, 292, 24 L.Ed. 496; see, also, Raubitschek v. Blank, supra, 80 N.Y. 478; Freeland v. Ritz, 154 Mass. 257, 259, 28 N.E. 226, 12 L.R.A. 561; Gall v. Brashier, 10 Cir., 169 F.2d 704, 708-709, 12 A.L.R.2d 500; 2 Corbin, op. cit. § 512, and cases there cited.

Turning to the writings in the case before us the unsigned office memo, the payroll change form initialed by the general manager Johns, and the paper signed by the comptroller Carstens it is apparent, and most patently, that all three refer on their face to the same transaction. The parties, the position to be filled by plaintiff, the salary to be paid him, are all identically set forth; it is hardly possible that such detailed information could refer to another or a different agreement. Even more, the card signed by Carstens notes that it was prepared for the purpose of a "Salary increase per contractual arrangements with Miss Arden." That certainly constitutes a reference of sorts to a more comprehensive "arrangement," and parol is permissible to furnish the explanation.

The corroborative evidence of defendant's assent to the contents of the unsigned office memorandum is also convincing. Prepared by defendant's agent, Miss Arden's personal secretary, there is little likelihood that that paper was fraudulently manufactured or that defendant had not assented to its contents. Furthermore, the evidence as to the conduct of the parties at the time it was prepared persuasively demonstrates defendant's assent to its terms. Under such circumstances, the courts below were fully justified in finding that the three papers constituted the 'memorandum' of their agreement within the meaning of the statute.

Nor can there be any doubt that the memorandum contains all of the essential terms of the contract. See N. E. D. Holding Co., v. McKinley, 246 N.Y. 40, 157 N.E. 923; Friedman & Co. v. Newman, 255 N.Y. 340, 174 N.E. 703, 73 A.L.R. 95. Only one term, the length of the employment, is in dispute. The September 26th office memorandum contains the notation, "2 years to make good." What purpose, other than to denote the length of the contract term, such a notation could have, is hard to imagine. Without it, the employment would be at will, see Martin v. New York Life Ins. Co., 148 N.Y. 117, 121, 42 N.E. 416, 417, and its inclusion may not be treated as meaningless or purposeless. Quite obviously, as the courts below decided, the phrase signifies that the parties agreed to a term, a certain and definite term, of two years, after which, if plaintiff did not "make good," he would be subject to discharge. And examination of other parts of the memorandum supports that construction. Throughout the writings, a scale of wages, increasing plaintiff's salary periodically, is set out; that type of arrangement is hardly consistent with the hypothesis that the employment was meant to be at will. The most that may be argued from defendant's standpoint is that "2 years to make good," is a cryptic and ambiguous statement. But, in such a case, parol evidence is admissible to explain its meaning. See Martocci v. Greater New York Brewery, 301 N.Y. 57, 63, 92 N.E.2d 887, 889; Marks v. Cowdin, supra, 226 N.Y. 138, 143-144, 123 N.E. 139, 140, 141; 2 Williston, op. cit., § 576; 2 Corbin, op. cit., § 527. Having in mind the relations of the parties, the course of the negotiations and plaintiff's insistence upon security of employment, the purpose of the phrase or so the trier of the facts was warranted in finding was to grant plaintiff the tenure he desired.

The judgment should be affirmed, with costs.

LOUGHRAN, C. J., and LEWIS, CONWAY, DESMOND, DYE and FROESSEL, JJ., concur.

C. UNIFORM COMMERCIAL CODE

CALIFORNIA UNIFORM COMMERCIAL CODE
§ 2201. FORMAL REQUIREMENTS; STATUTE OF FRAUDS
CAL. COM. CODE § 2201 (Deering 2012).

(1) Except as otherwise provided in this section a contract for the sale of goods for the price of five hundred dollars ($500) or more is not enforceable by way of action or defense unless there is some writing sufficient to indicate that a contract for sale has been made between the parties and signed by the party against whom enforcement is sought or by his or her authorized agent or broker. A writing is not insufficient because it omits or incorrectly states a term agreed upon but the contract is not enforceable under this paragraph beyond the quantity of goods shown in the writing.

(2) Between merchants if within a reasonable time a writing in confirmation of the contract and sufficient against the sender is received and the party receiving it has reason to know its contents, it satisfies the requirements of subdivision (1) against the party unless written notice of objection to its contents is given within 10 days after it is received.

(3) A contract which does not satisfy the requirements of subdivision (1) but which is valid in other respects is enforceable:

> (a) If the goods are to be specially manufactured for the buyer and are not suitable for sale to others in the ordinary course of the seller's business and the seller, before notice of repudiation is received and under circumstances which reasonably indicate that the goods are for the buyer, has made either a substantial beginning of their manufacture or commitments for their procurement;
>
> (b) If the party against whom enforcement is sought admits in his or her pleading, testimony, or otherwise in court that a contract for sale was made, but the contract is not enforceable under this provision beyond the quantity of goods admitted; or
>
> (c) With respect to goods for which payment has been made and accepted or which have been received and accepted (Section 2606).

(4) . . . .

JOHNSON CONTROLS, INC. V. TRW VEHICLE SAFETY SYSTEMS, INC.
United States District Court, E.D. Michigan, Southern Division
491 F. Supp. 2d 707 (2007).

OPINION AND ORDER

ZATKOFF, District Judge.

. . . .

This case involves an alleged breach of an automotive supply contract. Plaintiffs Johnson Controls, Inc., and Johnson Controls Automortriz Mexico DE RL DE CV (collectively JCI) are engaged in the business of manufacturing interior automotive component systems, notably seat assemblies. (*See* Pls.' Compl. 8.) Defendant TRW Vehicle Safety Systems, Inc. (TRW), manufactures and supplies custom made automotive parts, including components to JCI's seat assemblies.

For the last several years, JCI has ordered certain component parts from TRW for the restraint systems of two General Motors vehicle platforms: the GMT 257 and the GMT 201. For the GMT 257 parts, JCI issued Purchase Orders 910-003 (Order 003) and 910-031 (Order 031). (*See* Pls.' Ex. E, F.) For the GMT 201 parts, JCI issued Purchase Order 7002653 (Order 2653). (*See* Pls.' Ex. G.) JCI issued the purchase orders to TRW for the purchase of various parts for a period of one year. The purchase orders stated the specific price of each part but did not state the quantity. This was because JCI's need for parts depended on General Motor's production schedule. Accordingly, when JCI had a need for parts it would issue a material release to TRW, requesting that TRW ship a specified number of parts. JCI followed this practice, which is standard in the automotive industry and known as a just-in-time supply system, in order to maintain a minimum inventory. JCI would periodically revise its purchase orders, which, according to the terms incorporated therein, would supercede previous purchase orders. JCI issued the latest revisions on February 21, 2006 for purchase orders 003 and 031, and on September 5, 2006, for purchase order 2653. (*See* Pls.' Ex. E-G.)

JCI's purchase orders detail the part number, the part description and the unit price. In the column labeled quantity, the orders state "AS REL." (*See* Def.'s Ex. D, E.) The face of the orders also state:

> This purchase order is governed exclusively by Johnson Controls' Global Terms of Purchase (available at http:// johnsoncontrols.com/asg/global-terms. htm or by calling 734-254-7500, and incorporated here by reference), except as modified provided therein. Any terms and conditions appearing on the reverse side of this purchase order form do not apply and should be disregarded. All other terms are rejected. (*Id.*) JCI revises the Global Terms periodically; however, the revisions do not apply retroactively to purchase orders that have already been issued.

The Global Terms identify each purchase order as an offer for the purchase of goods and further state in bold that the "Order is limited to and conditional upon Seller's acceptance of these Terms exclusively." (Def.'s Ex. F.) The agreement formed by the Order, including the Global Terms, is binding on the parties for one year. (*See id.*) Finally, under paragraph 3, labeled "Quantity; Material Releases; Delivery," the Global Terms state:

> Quantities listed in each Order as estimated are Buyer's best estimate of the quantities of Supplies it might purchase from Seller for the contract term specified in the Order. If no other quantity is stated on the face of the Order or if the quantity is blank or states zero, "blanket," "see release" or similar term, then for consideration of U.S. $10 to be paid by Buyer upon expiration or termination of the Order, Seller grants to Buyer an irrevocable option during the term of the Order to purchase Supplies in such quantities as determined by Buyer and identified as firm orders in material authorization releases, manifests, broadcasts, or similar releases ("Material Releases") that are transmitted to Seller during the term of the Order, and Seller will supply all such Supplies at the price and other terms specified in the Order; provided that the Buyer may purchase no less than a minimum quantity of at least one piece or unit of each of the Supplies and no more than 100% of Buyer's requirements for the Supplies.... Material Releases are part of the Order, are governed by these Terms and are not independent contracts.... Buyer is not obligated to accept early deliveries, late deliveries, partial deliveries or excess deliveries.(*Id.*)

Sometime after JCI issued the purchase orders on February 21, 2006, it sent TRW material releases for the parts identified in these orders. TRW acted on the material releases and shipped the identified parts to [JIC]. According to JCI, TRW accepted JCI's offers to buy, as set forth in the purchase orders and Global Terms, when it shipped goods pursuant to the material releases JCI issued under the purchase orders. JCI further contends that a contract was formed that required TRW to supply JCI with its requirements for the parts identified in the purchase orders at the prices stated in the purchase orders for a duration of one year.

On February 23, 2006, TRW notified JCI that due to the increased cost of materials, it would be raising its prices for components sold to JCI. (*See* Pls.' Ex. H.) JCI responded that it could not pay higher prices for the parts it purchased from TRW because it could not control the pricing set by General Motors, and recommended that TRW discuss its pricing concerns directly with General Motors. (*See* Pls.' I.) In an email dated March 3, 2006, TRW notified JCI that it was objecting to the inclusion of JCI's Global Terms in the purchase orders issued on February 21, 2006. (*See* Pls.' Ex. DD.) Apparently, TRW had not been aware that the Global Terms existed prior to the issuance of the February 21, 2006 purchase orders. (*Id.*)

Less than one week later, on March 8, 2006, TRW again notified JCI that it would be increasing its prices for parts, but would honor the prices stated in JCI's purchase orders for the material releases JCI had issued as of that date. (*See* Pls.' Ex. J.) In addition, TRW indicated that unless JCI amended its purchase orders to reflect TRW's higher prices, it would cease shipping parts once its obligations under the current material releases had been fulfilled. (*See id.*) On March 10, 2006, TRW again objected to JCI's Global Terms and expressed its belief that "its supply agreements with Johnson Controls [were] binding only to the extent of [the] firm releases" that JCI issued. (Def.'s Ex. 11.)

In response to TRW's statement that intended to cease shipping parts, JCI informed TRW that the purchase orders were binding contracts that required TRW to supply JCI with parts at a fixed price for the duration of the order. (*See* Pls.' Ex. K.) JCI further stated that TRW's threat to stop shipping constituted a breach of the contracts and that if TRW stopped shipping parts General Motors would have to stop production on the affected vehicles. (*See id.*) Accordingly, JCI requested assurances from TRW that it would continue to ship parts as scheduled. (*See id.*) On March 21, 2006, TRW assured JCI that it would continue to ship parts as scheduled and rescinded the letter that threatened to stop shipment. (*See* Pls.' Ex. L.) However, ten days later, TRW sent JCI another letter notifying JCI of TRW's intent to not renew the current purchase orders once they expired. (*See* Pls.' Ex. M.) In this letter, TRW relied on a provision in JCI's Global Terms that required the seller to notify JCI of an intent to not renew a purchase order 180 days before the order is set to expire. (*See* Pls.' Ex. F.)

Throughout the summer of 2006, JCI continued to issue material releases and TRW continued to ship parts to JCI. Nevertheless, in October 2006, TRW again demanded that JCI revise its purchase orders to reflect the increased cost TRW was paying for materials. (*See* Pls.' Ex. P.) JCI informed TRW that based on the February 21, 2006, purchase orders, TRW was obligated to continue shipping parts at the current prices until February 21, 2007. (*See* Pls.' Ex. S.) Likewise, JCI expressed its belief that under the purchase order issued on September 5, 2006, TRW was obligated to continue shipping parts at the current prices until September 5, 2007. (*See id.*)

On October 11, 2006, when JCI refused to negotiate a price increase, TRW reconfirmed its intent to not renew the purchase orders and threatened to stop shipping parts as of October 29, 2006. (*See* Pls.' Ex. T.) As it had done in March, JCI demanded assurances from TRW that shipments would continue on time. (*See* Pls.' Ex. V.) This time, however, TRW stood by its threat to stop shipments. (*See* Pls.' Ex. W.) Because it did not want to damage its relationship with General Motors or cause production to cease, JCI issued revised purchase orders that reflected TRW's increased prices. (*See* Pls.' Ex. A, B, Z.) This suit followed.

JCI's complaint alleges that TRW breached the contracts embodied in Purchase Orders 003 and 031 when it threatened to stop shipping parts in October 2006. Furthermore, the complaint seeks a declaratory judgment as to Purchase Order 2653, declaring that purchase order to be a valid and enforceable contract through September 2007. . . .

IV. ANALYSIS

A. TRW's Motion for Summary Judgment

TRW's primary argument is that it did not breach the parties' contract because no enforceable contract existed. Specifically, TRW contends that the documents presented by JCI to support a contract fail the statute of frauds' requirement that a quantity term appear in the writing. TRW further argues that even if the statute of frauds is satisfied, the contract fails for lack of consideration because JCI is not obligated to purchase any parts from TRW. In response, JCI argues that the contract sufficiently states a quantity term and is not lacking in consideration under Michigan's version of the Uniform Commercial Code (UCC), MICH. COMP. LAWS §§ 440.1101 *et seq.* As explained below, the Court finds that the statute of frauds does not bar enforcement of the parties agreement but questions of fact remain as to whether the agreement is lacking in mutuality.

1. Whether the Purchase Orders Satisfy the Statute of Frauds

Michigan's statute of frauds provides:

> Except as otherwise provided in this section a contract for the sale of goods for the price of $1000.00 or more is not enforceable by way of action or defense unless there is a writing sufficient to indicate that a contract for the sale has been made between the parties and signed by the party against whom enforcement is sought or by his or her authorized agent or broker. A writing is not insufficient because it omits or incorrectly states a term agreed upon but the contract is not enforceable under this subsection beyond the quantity of goods shown in the writing.

MICH. COMP. LAWS § 440.2201(1). The writing evidencing a contract has three "definite and invariable requirements." Id. cmt 1. "First it must evidence of contract for the sale of goods; second, it must be 'signed'... and third, it must specify a quantity." Id. The Michigan Supreme Court has thus found that a quantity term must appear in the writing in order to satisfy the statute of frauds. Lorenz Supply Co. v. American Standard, Inc., 419 Mich. 610, 614, 358 N.W.2d 845 (1984). However, "[o]nce a quantity term is found to exist in the agreement, the agreement need not fail because the quantity term is not precise." In re Estate of Frost, 130 Mich.App. 556, 561, 344 N.W.2d 331 (1983). This is because the purpose of the writing requirement is "to provide a basis for believing that oral evidence which is offered rests upon a real transaction." Id. Once this purpose has been satisfied, parol evidence may be admissible to make the agreement sufficiently definite to be enforceable. Id. Accordingly, "[w]hen quantity is not precisely stated, parol evidence is admissible to show what the parties intended as the exact quantity, ... but where the writing relied upon to form the contract of sale is totally silent as to quantity, parol evidence cannot be used to supply the missing quantity term." Id. (quoting Alaska Independent Fishermen's Marketing Ass'n v. New England Fish Co., 15 Wash.App. 154, 159-60, 548 P.2d 348 (1976)) (internal quotation marks omitted). Therefore, the issue in this case is whether the writings offered by JCI as evidence of the parties' contracts contain a written quantity term.

TRW argues that the writings JCI provided do not contain a quantity term. TRW points out that the quantity column on the purchase orders either states "AS REL." or does not state anything at all. Further, TRW argues that JCI's Global Terms define "AS REL." as merely granting JCI an option to purchase parts for the duration of the order, and has no connection to quantity whatsoever. On the other hand, JCI contends that its Global Terms do contain a quantity term in that the definition of "AS REL." states that TRW grants JCI an option to purchase parts at a set price for the duration of the order so long as JCI purchases at least one part but no more than 100% of its requirements. In addition, JCI notes that the Global Terms also specifically incorporate any material releases issued under the purchase orders. JCI argues that the reference to the material releases, combined with the range of quantities qualifying the option to purchase, constitutes a written quantity term.

In order to determine the sufficiency of the writing, the Court must look to Michigan law. See Erie R.R. v. Tompkins, 304 U.S. 64, 78, 58 S.Ct. 817, 82 L.Ed. 1188 (1938). In applying Michigan law, the Court follows the law as announced by the Michigan Supreme Court. Rector v. General Motors Corp., 963 F.2d 144, 146 (6th Cir.1992). Where the Michigan Supreme Court has not decided the issue, the Court "must ascertain the state law from 'all relevant data.' " Garden City Osteopathic Hosp. v. HBE Corp., 55 F.3d 1126, 1130 (6th Cir.1995) (quoting Bailey v. V. & O Press Co., 770 F.2d 601, 604 (6th Cir.1985)). "Relevant data includes state appellate court decisions, supreme court dicta, restatements of law, law review commentaries, and [the] majority rule among other states." Orchard Group Inc. v. Konica Medical Corp., 135 F.3d 421, 427 (6th Cir.1998). While the Michigan Supreme court has clearly found that a quantity term must appear in the writing to satisfy the statute of frauds, it has not decided what is sufficient to qualify as a quantity term. Therefore, the Court will look to "all relevant data" to determine whether the writings provided in this case contain a quantity term.

The Michigan court of appeals has addressed this issue with varying results. The court first found that a quantity term must appear in the writing in Ace Concrete Prods. Co. v. Charles J. Rogers Constr. Co., 69 Mich.App. 610, 245 N.W.2d 353 (1976). Ace Concrete involved a contract between a concrete supplier and a concrete subcontractor. The supplier sent the subcontractor a letter quoting prices for concrete in connection with a specified construction contract. See id. at 611, 245 N.W.2d 353. The letter referenced the specific construction contract for which the subcontractor would need concrete, "P.C.I-13 Job 1450," and stated "[m]ay we give you the following price quote on concrete for the above job." Id. The subcontractor argued that the contract was unenforceable under the statute of frauds because it did not state a written quantity term. The court agreed, rejecting the supplier's argument that letter's reference to the construction project in combination with the quote "for the above job" revealed a requirements contract. Id. at 614, 245 N.W.2d 353. The court concluded that the quantity "must appear on the [writing] without reference to parol evidence." Id.

The court reached the opposite result in In re Estate of Frost, 130 Mich.App. 556, 344 N.W.2d 331 (1983). There, the plaintiff claimed to have had a contract with the decedent for the sale of lumber. The defendant argued that the contract was not enforceable under the statute of frauds because it did not state a quantity. The court disagreed with the defendant and found that the writing's statement that the plaintiff could take "all wood sawable" was a sufficient quantity term for the statute of frauds, analogizing the contract to an output contract. Id. at 560-61, 344 N.W.2d 331. The court stated that the statute of frauds was satisfied even though the quantity term was not precise. Id.

Similarly, in Great Northern Packaging, Inc. v. General Tire & Rubber Co., 154 Mich.App. 777, 399 N.W.2d 408 (1986), the court concluded that a term with no apparent reference to a specific quantity could satisfy the statute of frauds. In that case, the buyer issued a purchase order to buy 50 units that was later changed to a "Blanket Order" purportedly covering purchases for one year. See id. at 780, 399 N.W.2d 408. Relying on the court's holding in Frost, the court concluded that "the term 'blanket order' express[ed] a quantity term, albeit an imprecise one." Id. at 787, 399 N.W.2d 408. As the statute of frauds' purpose of providing a basis for believing a contract exists had been fulfilled, the court recognized that parol evidence should be admitted to the trier of fact to determine the precise quantity of units involved in the contract. See id.

In Acemco, Inc. v. Olympic Steel Lafayette, Inc., 2005 WL 2810716 (Mich.App.2005), the court found that the writing offered to satisfy the statute of frauds did not contain a quantity term. The writing stated that "[d]uring the term of this Agreement, the Seller agrees to sell to the Buyer such quantities of the Products as the Buyer may specify in its purchase orders, which the Buyer may deliver at its discretion." Id. at *4. The court found that the above language was not a quantity term because it specified "no quantity whatsoever." Id. The court reasoned that the language granted the buyer complete discretion to order any amount or no amount of the seller's products and concluded that " '[a]ny' quantity is in fact no quantity at all." Id. The court further rejected the seller's argument that the term "blanket" on an attached document constituted a quantity term. "Blanket" appeared on a document that described the goods to be purchased. Id. The court concluded that, unlike Great Northern, where the court held that the term "blanket order" stated a quantity, see Great Northern, 154 Mich.App. at 787, 399 N.W.2d 408, "blanket" on its own was not a quantity term. The court further explained that since the term appeared on a specifications sheet and not a purchase order, and since the term was "blanket" and not "blanket order," the writing did not contain a quantity term. See Acemco, 2005 WL 2810716.

Finally, the court in Dedoes Indus., Inc. v. Target Steel, Inc., 2005 WL 1224700 (Mich.App.2005), held that a price quote stating that the defendant "would satisfy plaintiff's steel needs" for three years did not satisfy the statute of frauds' quantity requirement. Id. *2. The court found the language referenced a time period and not a quantity. See id. Other courts have discussed Michigan's quantity requirement with differing results. Compare Busch v. Dyno Nobel, Inc., 40 Fed.Appx. 947 (6th Cir.2002) (concluding that the language "up to ten million pounds" could constitute an ambiguous quantity term), with MacSteel, Inc. v. Eramet North America, 2006 WL 3334019 (E.D.Mich.2006) (finding the term "additional material" was too indefinite to obligate the plaintiff to purchase any goods and, therefore, failed to satisfy the statute of frauds).

The Fourth Circuit also discussed this issue in Thomas J. Kline, Inc. v. Lorillard, Inc., 878 F.2d 791 (4th Cir.1989). In Lorillard, the defendant, a cigarette manufacturer, agreed to supply the plaintiff, a cigarette wholesaler, with its full line of cigarettes on a direct basis. See id. at 793. When the plaintiff began drastically increasing its orders, the defendant suspended a previous credit arrangement and demanded cash payments for purchases. The plaintiff sued and the defendant argued that the statute of frauds prevented enforcement of the alleged contract. The plaintiff contended that the terms "full line" and "direct basis" provided a quantity term in that they provided that the defendant would supply all of the plaintiff's requirements. See id. The court of appeals reviewed Maryland law and found no case in which similar terms were found to satisfy the statute of frauds quantity requirement. The court summarized those decisions:

> [I]nstructive are cases in which ambiguous terms of quantity have been deemed sufficient to prove an enforceable contract. This court, for example, recently held that quantity was adequately identified when specific language

> "referred to meeting the purchaser's needs." Barber and Ross Co. v. Lifetime Doors, Inc., 810 F.2d 1276, 1280-81 (4th Cir.1987). See also Kansas Power and Light Co. v. Burlington Northern Railroad Co., 740 F.2d 780 (10th Cir.1984) (writings mentioning possible maximum and minimum amounts of shipped coal sufficient to create requirements contract). It has been held that the words "the yarn" for "a potential program" could be sufficient written expression of quantity. O.N. Jonas Co., Inc. v. Badische Corp., 706 F.2d 1161, 1163-64 (11th Cir.1983). Courts have consistently found that words with some possible nexus to amount, including "all," "bags," or even customary terms such as lot numbers, can provide a basis for the admission of parol evidence. See also Maryland Supreme Corp. v. The Blake Co., 279 Md. 531, 369 A.2d 1017 (1977) (written phrases "for the above mentioned project" and "throughout the job" are sufficient quantity terms).

Id. at 794-95. In light of these cases, the court concluded that the terms "full line" and "direct basis" had no nexus to quantity and, therefore, did not satisfy the statute of frauds. *Id.* at 795.

The Court finds little guidance in the cases discussed above but is persuaded by the reasoning in cases such as Great Northern and Frost. The Court finds these cases provide a more reasoned analysis of the issue and are consistent with the UCC's policies as well as the commercial background of the parties and the transaction involved in this case. In contrast, the Court finds that the decisions in Ace Concrete, Acemco, and Dedoes conflict with the UCC's goals and confuse the issue of whether the quantity term is sufficiently definite to enforce the contract with the issue of whether there is a written quantity term for the purposes of satisfying the statute of frauds. See Riegel Fiber Corp. v. Anderson Gin Co., 512 F.2d 784, 789 (5th Cir.1975) (refusing to apply the statute of frauds to bar enforcement of a contract and stating that "the real issue in this case is not whether these contracts satisfy § 2-201, but whether the quantity term in the agreement the parties undeniably made-as reflected in the signed writing-is too indefinite to support judicial enforcement"). The results reached in Ace Concrete, Acemco and Dedoes minimally advance the statute of frauds' purpose to provide a basis for believing a contract exists while at the same time damaging the UCC's other substantive goals of liberally incorporating trade usage, custom and practice, course of dealing, and course of performance into parties' agreements in fact.

The UCC strives to "simplify, clarify and modernize the law governing commercial transactions ... [and] to permit the continued expansion of commercial practices through custom, usage and agreement of the parties...." MICH. COMP. LAWS § 440.1102. The "general approach" of the UCC "requires the reading of commercial background and intent into the language of any agreement and demands good faith in the performance of that agreement." MICH. COMP. LAWS § 440.2306 cmt. 1. The Court is also mindful that in determining whether a particular term is in fact a quantity term, the Court's construction of the statute of frauds' quantity requirement affects the substance and application of other code provisions. "The text of each section should be read in the light of the purpose and policy of the rule or principle in question, and also as of the Act as a whole, and the application of language should be construed narrowly or broadly, as the case may be, in conformity with the purposes and policies involved." MICH. COMP. LAWS § 440.1102 cmt. 1.

The statute of frauds expressly states that "[a] writing is not insufficient because it omits or incorrectly states a term agreed upon...." MICH. COMP. LAWS § 440.2201(1). Furthermore, "[e]ven though one or more terms are left open a contract for sale does not fail for indefiniteness if the parties have intended to make a contract and there is a reasonably certain basis for giving an appropriate remedy." MICH. COMP. LAWS § 440.2204(3). The official comment to § 2204(3) states:

> If the parties intend to enter into a binding agreement, this subsection recognizes that agreement as valid in law, despite missing terms, if there is any reasonably certain basis for granting a remedy. The test is not certainty as to what the parties were to do nor as to the exact amount of damages due the plaintiff. Nor is the fact that one or more terms are left to be agreed upon enough of itself to defeat an otherwise adequate agreement. Rather, commercial standards on the point of 'indefiniteness' are intended to be applied, this Act making provision elsewhere for missing terms needed for performance....

Id. cmt. 1 (emphasis added). To this end the code specifically contemplates contracts with indefinite quantity terms. See MICH. COMP. LAWS § 440.2306 (defining quantity in output or requirements contracts as actual good faith output or requirements). Therefore, the Court declines to analyze the purported quantity term in this case in terms of its definiteness. Whether the quantity as provided in the writing is sufficiently definite to support an enforceable contract is to be determined under the codes' substantive provisions in light of commercial standards. See Caroline N. Bruckel, The Weed and the Web: Section 2-201's Corruption of the U.C.C.'s Substantive Provisions-The Quantity Problem, 1983 U. ILL. L.REV. 811 (1983).

In the present case, the purchase orders, in combination with the Global Terms, contain a quantity term. The face of the purchase orders state "AS REL." in the column labeled quantity. There is no dispute that this term is a reference to JCI's material releases, which it issued periodically to specify the exact quantities of parts needed. The Court finds no difference between this term and those found to be sufficient in Great Northern and Frost. The purchase orders contemplate that JCI would identify specific quantities in material releases and expressly included those releases in the orders. The term "AS REL." gives some indication that JCI intended to purchase and TRW intended to sell some quantity of parts. This is all the statute of frauds requires. Interestingly, based on the reasoning in Acemco, the fact that "AS REL." was listed as the quantity and was included on actual purchase orders reinforces the conclusion that some quantity term, although indefinite, was stated in the writing. Additionally, in contrast to the terms found insufficient in Lorillard, "AS REL." does have some nexus to the notion of amount or quantity in light of the customary practice in the automotive industry of using just-in-time supply chains and material releases.

Furthermore, the fact that the Global Terms explain that "AS REL." indicates that JCI has an option to purchase supplies does not change the fact that there is some quantity term. See, e.g., R.A. Weaver & Assocs., Inc. v. Asphalt Construction, Inc., 587 F.2d 1315, 1319 (D.C.Cir.1978) (finding that a quantity term was stated in the writing even though the language stating the quantity also spoke of the grade and quality of concrete). If anything, the precise meaning of the term is ambiguous. But as the statute of frauds specifically states, the terms need not be accurately stated. In this case, the quantity could be construed as simply referencing the amount of supplies indicated in the material releases. The releases are incorporated into the purchase orders via the Global Terms and JCI is not obligated to purchase anything that exceeds the amounts stated in the material releases. On the other hand, the fact that the Global Terms referenced an option to purchase goods at a fixed price so long as JCI's orders were within a specific range of amounts could indicate that JCI was to purchase its requirements. See, e.g., Burlington Northern, 740 F.2d 780 (writings mentioning possible maximum and minimum amounts of shipped coal sufficient to create requirements contract). That this may have been a requirements contract seems reasonable in light of the practice among automotive suppliers to enter into long-term, just-in-time production arrangements that rely on a fixed price and a variable quantity, and provide flexibility to adjust to changing commercial conditions.

Based on the foregoing analysis, the Court finds that JCI's purchase orders in combination with its Global Terms contain a satisfactory quantity term for the purposes of MICH. COMP. LAWS § 440.2201. The Court concludes that a quantity term appears in the writing, albeit an ambiguous one, and that the offered writings provide a basis for believing that a contract in fact exists. Thus, the purpose of the statute of frauds has been satisfied, particularly to the extent performance has been rendered. *See* MICH. COMP. LAWS § 440.2201(3)(c) (stating that in the absence of a writing sufficient to satisfy the statute of frauds, the parties agreement is enforceable "with respect to goods for which payment has been made and accepted or which have been received and accepted"). . . .

V. CONCLUSION

In the present case, neither party has met its burden under Rule 56(c) to show the absence of a material fact for trial. The Court concludes that the statute of frauds does not bar enforcement of the parties' agreement in this case and that questions of fact remain as to whether the agreement is unenforceable for lack of consideration. Further, the Court concludes that questions of fact remain as to the nature of the parties agreement and its terms. Therefore,

IT IS ORDERED that Plaintiff's Motion for Summary Judgment is DENIED and that Defendant's Motion for Summary Judgment is DENIED.

D. MODIFICATION (AND THE STATUTE OF FRAUDS)

The statute of frauds remains a concern when parties modify their contracts. However, whether the modified agreement requires a sufficient memorandum for enforceability depends on the nature of the modifications. If the modification brings the contract within the statute of frauds, it must be in writing. Similarly, if the modified term removes the contract from the statute of frauds, it must be in writing. However, where the statute of frauds required a writing for the enforceability of the original contract and as modified the contract remains within the statute, most jurisdiction will enforce an oral modification as long as the parties did not modify any material terms.

The determination of what constitutes a material term differs from jurisdiction to jurisdiction. Some courts interpret the term "material" to mean the term that triggered the applicability of the statute of frauds. So, for contracts longer than one year in duration, such jurisdictions would require a writing for any extension of that time period. Other courts interpret the term "material" to be co-extensive with "essential" as in necessary to satisfy the requirements of a sufficient memorandum under the statute of frauds. So, for contracts involving the sale of goods of $500 or more, since the statute requires that the writing at least contain a quantity, any modification of the quantity term requires a writing in order to be enforceable. Still other jurisdictions interpret the term "material" to refer to the important terms of the underlying transaction. Under this construction, virtually every modification to a contract governed by the statute of frauds would seem to require a writing.

Even though the writing requirements for modifications are less than uniform, most jurisdictions are consistent in their treatment of the effect of unenforceable modifications. Generally speaking, when the modification is rendered unenforceable, that operates as a revival of the original unmodified contract.

For an examination of whether a modification must satisfy the requirements of the statute of frauds, see *Zemco Mfg., Inc. v. Navistar Int'l Transp. Corp.*, 186 F.3d 815 (7th Cir. 1999).

SECTION 8. PROMISSORY ESTOPPEL

RICKETTS V. SCOTHORN
Supreme Court of Nebraska
77 N.W. 365 (1898).

SULLIVAN, J.

In the district court of Lancaster county the plaintiff, Katie Scothorn, recovered judgment against the defendant, Andrew D. Ricketts, as executor of the last will and testament of John C. Ricketts, deceased. The action was based upon a promissory note, of which the following is a copy:

> May the first, 1891. I promise to pay to Katie Scothorn on demand, $2,000, to be at 6 per cent. per annum. J. C. Ricketts.

In the petition the plaintiff alleges that the consideration for the execution of the note was that she should surrender her employment as bookkeeper for Mayer Bros., and cease to work for a living. She also alleges that the note was given to induce her to abandon her occupation, and that, relying on it, and on the annual interest, as a means of support, she gave up the employment in which she was then engaged. These allegations of the petition are denied by the administrator. The material facts are undisputed. They are as follows: John C. Ricketts, the maker of the note, was the grandfather of the plaintiff. Early in May--presumably on the day the note bears date--he called on her at the store where she was working. What transpired between them is thus described by Mr. Flodene, one of the plaintiff's witnesses:

A. Well, the old gentleman came in there one morning about nine o'clock, probably a little before or a little after, but early in the morning, and he unbuttoned his vest, and took out a piece of paper in the shape of a note; that is the way it looked to me; and he says to Miss Scothorn, "I have fixed out something that you have not got to work any more." He says, "none of my grandchildren work, and you don't have to."

Q. Where was she?

A. She took the piece of paper and kissed him, and kissed the old gentleman, and commenced to cry.

It seems Miss Scothorn immediately notified her employer of her intention to quit work, and that she did soon after abandon her occupation. The mother of the plaintiff was a witness, and testified that she had a conversation with her father, Mr. Ricketts, shortly after the note was executed, in which he informed her that he had given the note to the plaintiff to enable her to quit work; that none of his grandchildren worked, and he did not think she ought to. For something more than a year the plaintiff was without an occupation, but in September, 1892, with the consent of her grandfather, and by his assistance, she secured a position as bookkeeper with Messrs. Funke & Ogden. On June 8, 1894, Mr. Ricketts died. He had paid one year's interest on the note, and a short time before his death expressed regret that he had not been able to pay the balance. In the summer or fall of 1892 he stated to his daughter, Mrs. Scothorn, that if he could sell his farm in Ohio he would pay the note out of the proceeds. He at no time repudiated the obligation. We quite agree with counsel for the defendant that upon this evidence there was nothing to submit to the jury, and that a verdict should have been directed peremptorily for one of the parties. The testimony of Flodene and Mrs. Scothorn, taken together, conclusively establishes the fact that the note was not given in consideration of the plaintiff pursuing, or agreeing to pursue, any particular line of conduct. There was no promise on the part of the plaintiff to do, or refrain from doing, anything. Her right to the money promised in the note was not made to depend upon an abandonment of her employment with Mayer Bros., and future abstention from like service. Mr. Ricketts made no condition, requirement, or request. He exacted no quid pro quo. He gave the note as a gratuity, and looked for nothing in return. So far as the evidence discloses, it was his purpose to place the plaintiff in a position of independence, where she could work or remain idle, as she might choose. The abandonment of Miss Scothorn of her position as bookkeeper was altogether voluntary. It was not an act done in fulfillment of any contract obligation assumed when she accepted the note. The instrument in suit, being given without any valuable consideration, was nothing more than a promise to make a gift in the future of the sum of money therein named. Ordinarily, such promises are not enforceable, even when put in the form of a promissory note. Kirkpatrick v. Taylor, 43 Ill. 207; Phelps v. Phelps, 28 Barb. 121; Johnston v. Griest, 85 Ind. 503; Fink v. Cox, 18 Johns. 145. But it has often been held that an action on a note given to a church, college, or other like institution, upon the faith of which money has been expended or obligations incurred, could not be successfully defended on the ground of a want of consideration. Barnes v. Perine, 12 N. Y. 18; Philomath College v. Hartless, 6 Or. 158; Thompson v. Board, 40 Ill. 379; Irwin v. Lombard University, 56 Ohio St. 9, 46 N. E. 63. In this class of cases the note in suit is nearly always spoken of as a gift or donation, but the decision is generally put on the ground that the expenditure of money or assumption of liability by the donee on the faith of the promise constitutes a valuable and sufficient consideration. It seems to us that the true reason is the preclusion of the defendant, under the doctrine of estoppel, to deny the consideration. Such seems to be the view of the matter taken by the supreme court of Iowa in the case of Simpson Centenary College v. Tuttle, 71 Iowa, 596, 33 N. W. 74, where Rothrock, J., speaking for the court, said:

> Where a note, however, is based on a promise to give for the support of the objects referred to, it may still be open to this defense [want of consideration], unless it shall appear that the donee has, prior to any revocation, entered into engagements, or made expenditures based on such promise, so that he must suffer loss or injury if the note is not paid. This is based on the equitable principle that, after allowing the donee to incur obligations on the faith that the note would be paid, the donor would be estopped from pleading want of consideration.

And in the case of Reimensnyder v. Gans, 110 Pa. St. 17, 2 Atl. 425, which was an action on a note given as a donation to a charitable object, the court said:

> The fact is that, as we may see from the case of Ryerss v. Trustees, 33 Pa. St. 114, a contract of the kind here involved is enforceable rather by way of estoppel than on the ground of consideration in the original undertaking.

It has been held that a note given in expectation of the payee performing certain services, but without any contract binding him to serve, will not support an action. Hulse v. Hulse, 84 E. C. L. 709. But when the payee changes his position to his disadvantage in reliance on the promise, a right of action does arise. McClure v. Wilson, 43 Ill. 356; Trustees v. Garvey, 53 Ill. 401.

Under the circumstances of this case, is there an equitable estoppel which ought to preclude the defendant from alleging that the note in controversy is lacking in one of the essential elements of a valid contract? We think there is. An estoppel in pais is defined to be "a right arising from acts, admissions, or conduct which have induced a change of position in accordance with the real or apparent intention of the party against whom they are alleged."

Mr. Pomeroy has formulated the following definition: "Equitable estoppel is the effect of the voluntary conduct of a party whereby he is absolutely precluded, both at law and in equity, from asserting rights which might, perhaps, have otherwise existed, either of property, of contract, or of remedy, as against another person who in good faith relied upon such conduct, and has been led thereby to change his position for the worse, and who on his part acquires some corresponding right, either of property, of contract, or of remedy." 2 Pom. Eq. Jur. 804. According to the undisputed proof, as shown by the record before us, the plaintiff was a working girl, holding a position in which she earned a salary of $10 per week, Her grandfather, desiring to put her in a position of independence, gave her the note, accompanying it with the remark that his other grandchildren did not work, and that she would not be obliged to work any longer. In effect, he suggested that she might abandon her employment, and rely in the future upon the bounty which he promised. He doubtless desired that she should give up her occupation, but, whether he did or not, it is entirely certain that he contemplated such action on her part as a reasonable and probable consequence of his gift. Having intentionally influenced the plaintiff to alter her position for the worse on the faith of the note being paid when due, it would be grossly inequitable to permit the maker, or his executor, to resist payment on the ground that the promise was given without consideration. The petition charges the elements of an equitable estoppel, and the evidence conclusively establishes them. If errors intervened at the trial, they could not have been prejudicial. A verdict for the defendant would be unwarranted.

The judgment is right, and is affirmed.

ALLEGHENY COLLEGE V. NATIONAL CHAUTAUQUA COUNTY BANK OF JAMESTOWN
Court of Appeals of New York
159 N.E. 173 (1927).

CARDOZO, C. J.

The plaintiff, Allegheny College, is an institution of liberal learning at Meadville, Pa. In June, 1921, a "drive" was in progress to secure for it an additional endowment of $1,250,000. An appeal to contribute to this fund was made to Mary Yates Johnston, of Jamestown, New York. In response thereto, she signed and delivered on June 15, 1921, the following writing:

> Estate Pledge, Allegheny College Second Century Endowment.
>
> Jamestown, N. Y., June 15, 1921.
>
> In consideration of my interest in Christian education, and in consideration of others subscribing, I hereby subscribe and will pay to the order of the treasurer of Allegheny College, Meadville, Pennsylvania, the sum of five thousand dollars; $5,000.
>
> This obligation shall become due thirty days after my death, and I hereby instruct my executor, or administrator, to pay the same out of my estate. This pledge shall bear interest at the rate of ___ per cent. per annum, payable annually, from ___ till paid. The proceeds of this obligation shall be added to the Endowment of said Institution, or expended in accordance with instructions on reverse side of this pledge.
> Name: Mary Yates Johnston,
>
> Address: 306 East 6th Street, Jamestown, N. Y.
>
> Dayton E. McClain, Witness,
>
> T. R. Courtis, Witness,
>
> To authentic signature.

On the reverse side of the writing is the following indorsement:

In loving memory this gift shall be known as the Mary Yates Johnston memorial fund, the proceeds from which shall be used to educate students preparing for the ministry, either in the United States or in the Foreign Field.

This pledge shall be valid only on the condition that the provisions of my will, now extant, shall be first met.

Mary Yates Johnston.

The subscription was not payable by its terms until 30 days after the death of the promisor. The sum of $1,000 was paid, however, upon account in December, 1923, while the promisor was alive. The college set the money aside to be held as a scholarship fund for the benefit of students preparing for the ministry. Later, in July, 1924, the promisor gave notice to the college that she repudiated the promise. Upon the expiration of 30 days following her death, this action was brought against the executor of her will to recover the unpaid balance.

The law of charitable subscriptions has been a prolific source of controversy in this state and elsewhere. We have held that a promise of that order is unenforceable like any other if made without consideration. Hamilton College v. Stewart, 1 N. Y. 581; Presbyterian Church v. Cooper, 112 N. Y. 517, 20 N. E. 352,3 L. R. A. 468, 8 Am. St. Rep. 767; Twenty-Third St. Baptist Church v. Cornell, 117 N. Y. 601, 23 N. E. 177, 6 L. R. A. 807. On the other hand, though professing to apply to such subscriptions the general law of contract, we have found consideration present where the general law of contract, at least as then declared, would have said that it was absent. Barnes v. Perine, 12 N. Y. 18; Presbyterian Soc. v. Beach, 74 N. Y. 72; Keuka College v. Ray, 167 N. Y. 96, 60 N. E. 325; cf. Eastern States League v. Vail, 97 Vt. 495, 508, 124 A. 568, 38 A. L. R. 845, and cases cited; Young Men's Christian Ass'n v. Estill, 140 Ga. 291, 78 S. E. 1075, 48 L. R. A. (N. S.) 783, Ann. Cas. 1914D, 136; Amherst Academy v. Cowles, 6 Pick. (Mass.) 427, 17 Am. Dec. 387; Ladies Collegiate Institute v. French, 16 Gray (Mass.) 196; Martin v. Meles, 179 Mass. 114, 60 N. E. 397; Robinson v. Nutt, 185 Mass. 345, 70 N. E. 198; University of Pennsylvania v. Coxe, 277 Pa. 512, 121 A. 314; Williston, Contracts, § 116.

A classic form of statement identifies consideration with detriment to the promisee sustained by virtue of the promise. Hamer v. Sidway, 124 N. Y. 538, 27 N. E. 256,12 L. R. A. 463, 21 Am. St. Rep. 693; Anson, Contracts (Corbin's Ed.) p. 116; 8 Holdsworth, History of English Law, 10. So compendious a formula is little more than a half truth. There is need of many a supplementary gloss before the outline can be so filled in as to depict the classic doctrine. "The promise and the consideration must purport to be the motive each for the other, in whole or at least in part. It is not enough that the promise induces the detriment or that the detriment induces the promise if the other half is wanting." Wisconsin & Michigan R. Co. v. Powers, 191 U. S. 379, 386, 24 S. Ct. 107, 108 (48 L. Ed. 229); McGovern v. City of New York, 234 N. Y. 377, 389, 138 N. E. 26, 25 A. L. R. 1442; Walton Water Co. v. Village of Walton, 238 N. Y. 46, 51, 143 N. E. 786; 1 Williston, Contracts, § 139; Langdell, Summary of the Law of Contracts, pp. 82-88. If A promises B to make him a gift, consideration may be lacking, though B has renounced other opportunities for betterment in the faith that the promise will be kept.

The half truths of one generation tend at times to perpetuate themselves in the law as the whole truth of another, when constant repetition brings it about that qualifications, taken once for granted, are disregarded or forgotten. The doctrine of consideration has not escaped the common lot. As far back as 1881, Judge Holmes in his lectures on the Common Law (page 292), separated the detriment, which is merely a consequence of the promise from the detriment, which is in truth the motive or inducement, and yet added that the courts "have gone far in obliterating this distinction." The tendency toward effacement has not lessened with the years. On the contrary, there has grown up of recent days a doctrine that a substitute for consideration or an exception to its ordinary requirements can be found in what is styled "a promissory estoppel." Williston, Contracts, §§ 139, 116. Whether the exception has made its way in this state to such an extent as to permit us to say that the general law of consideration has been modified accordingly, we do not now attempt to say. Cases such as Siegel v. Spear & Co., 234 N. Y. 479, 138 N. E. 414, 26 A. L. R. 1205, and De Cicco v. Schweizer, 221 N. Y. 431, 117 N. E. 807, L. R. A. 1918E, 1004, Ann. Cas. 1918C, 816, may be signposts on the road. Certain, at least, it is that we have adopted the doctrine of promissory estoppel as the equivalent of consideration in connection with our law of charitable subscriptions. So long as those decisions stand, the question is not merely whether the enforcement of a charitable subscription can be squared with the doctrine of consideration in all its ancient rigor. The question may also be whether it can be squared with doctrine of consideration as qualified by the doctrine of promissory estoppel.

We have said that the cases in this state have recognized this exception, if exception it is thought to be. Thus, in Barnes v. Perine, 12 N. Y. 18, the subscription was made without request, express or implied, that the church do anything on the faith of it. Later, the church did incur expense to the knowledge of the promisor, and in the reasonable belief that the promise would be kept. We held the promise binding, though consideration there was none except upon the theory of a promissory estoppel. In Presbyterian Society v. Beach, 74 N. Y. 72, a situation substantially the same became the basis for a like ruling. So in Roberts v. Cobb, 103 N. Y. 600, 9 N. E. 500, and Keuka College v. Ray, 167 N. Y. 96, 60 N. E. 325, the moulds of consideration as fixed by the old doctrine were subjected to a like expansion. Very likely, conceptions of public policy have shaped, more or less subconsciously, the rulings thus made. Judges have been affected by the thought that "defenses of that character" are "breaches of faith towards the public, and especially towards those engaged in the same enterprise, and an unwarrantable disappointment of the reasonable expectations of those interested." W. F. Allen, J., in Barnes v. Perine, supra, p. 24; and cf. Eastern States League v. Vail, 97 Vt. 495, 505, 124 A. 568, 38 A. L. R. 845, and cases there cited. The result speaks for itself irrespective of the motive. Decisions which have stood so long, and which are supported by so many considerations of public policy and reason, will not be overruled to save the symmetry of a concept which itself came into our law, not so much from any reasoned conviction of its justice, as from historical accidents of practice and procedure. 8 Holdsworth, History of English Law, 7 et seq. The concept survives as one of the distinctive features of our legal system. We have no thought to suggest that it is obsolete or on the way to be abandoned. As in the case of other concepts, however, the pressure of exceptions has led to irregularities of form.

It is in this background of precedent that we are to view the problem now before us. The background helps to an understanding of the implications inherent in subscription and acceptance. This is so though we may find in the end that without recourse to the innovation of promissory estoppel the transaction can be fitted within the mould of consideration as established by tradition.

The promisor wished to have a memorial to perpetuate her name. She imposed a condition that the "gift" should "be known as the Mary Yates Johnston Memorial Fund." The moment that the college accepted $1,000 as a payment on account, there was an assumption of a duty to do whatever acts were customary or reasonably necessary to maintain the memorial fairly and justly in the spirit of its creation. The college could not accept the money and hold itself free thereafter from personal responsibility to give effect to the condition. Dinan v. Coneys, 143 N. Y. 544, 547, 38 N. E. 715; Brown v. Knapp, 79 N. Y. 136; Gridley v. Gridley, 24 N. Y. 130; Grossman v. Schenker, 206 N. Y. 466, 469, 100 N. E. 39; 1 Williston, Contracts, §§ 90, 370. More is involved in the receipt of such a fund than a mere acceptance of money to be held to a corporate use. Cf. Martin v. Meles, 179 Mass. 114, 60 N. E. 397, citing Johnson v. Otterbein University, 41 Ohio St. 527, 531, and Presbyterian Church v. Cooper, 112 N. Y. 517, 20 N. E. 352,3 L. R. A. 468, 8 Am. St. Rep. 767. The purpose of the founder would be unfairly thwarted or at least inadequately served if the college failed to communicate to the world, or in any event to applicants for the scholarship, the title of the memorial. By implication it undertook, when it accepted a portion of the "gift," that in its circulars of information and in other customary ways when making announcement of this scholarship, it would couple with the announcement the name of the donor. The donor was not at liberty to gain the benefit of such an undertaking upon the payment of a part and disappoint the expectation that there would be payment of the residue. If the college had stated after receiving $1,000 upon account of the subscription, that it would apply the money to the prescribed use, but that in its circulars of information and when responding to prospective applicants it would deal with the fund as an anonymous donation, there is little doubt that the subscriber would have been at liberty to treat this statement as the repudiation of a duty impliedly assumed, a repudiation justifying a refusal to make payments in the future. Obligation in such circumstances is correlative and mutual. A case much in point is New Jersey Hospital v. Wright, 95 N. J. Law, 462, 464, 113 A. 144, where a subscription for the maintenance of a bed in a hospital was held to be enforceable by virtue of an implied promise by the hospital that the bed should be maintained in the name of the subscriber. Cf. Board of Foreign Missions v. Smith, 209 Pa. 361, 58 A. 689.A parallel situation might arise upon the endowment of a chair or a fellowship in a university by the aid of annual payments with the condition that it should commemorate the name of the founder or that of a member of his family. The university would fail to live up to the fair meaning of its promise if it were to publish in its circulars of information and elsewhere the existence of a chair or a fellowship in the prescribed subject, and omit the benefactor's name. A duty to act in ways beneficial to the promisor and beyond the application of the fund to the mere uses of the trust would be cast upon the promisee by the acceptance of the money. We do not need to measure the extent either of benefit to the promisor or of detriment to the promisee implicit in this duty. "If a person chooses to make an extravagant promise for an inadequate consideration, it is his own affair." 8 Holdsworth, History of English Law, p. 17. It was long ago said that 'when a thing is to be done by the plaintiff, be it never so small, this is a sufficient consideration to ground an action." Sturlyn v. Albany, 1587, Cro. Eliz. 67, quoted by Holdsworth, supra; cf. Walton Water Co. v. Village of Walton, 238 N. Y. 46, 51, 143 N.

E. 786. The longing for posthumous remembrance is an emotion not so weak as to justify us in saying that its gratification is a negligible good.

We think the duty assumed by the plaintiff to perpetuate the name of the founder of the memorial is sufficient in itself to give validity to the subscription within the rules that define consideration for a promise of that order. When the promisee subjected itself to such a duty at the implied request of the promisor, the result was the creation of a bilateral agreement. Williston, Contracts, §§ 60a, 68, 90, 370; Brown v. Knapp, supra;Grossman v. Schenker, supra; Williams College v. Danforth, 12 Pick. (Mass.) 541, 544; Ladies Collegiate Institute v. French, 16 Gray (Mass.) 196, 200. There was a promise on the one side and on the other a return promise, made, it is true, by implication, but expressing an obligation that had been exacted as a condition of the payment. A bilateral agreement may exist though one of the mutual promises be a promise "implied in fact," an inference from conduct as opposed to an inference from words. Williston, Contracts, §§ 90, 22a; Pettibone v. Moore, 75 Hun, 461, 464, 27 N. Y. S. 455.We think the fair inference to be drawn from the acceptance of a payment on account of the subscription is a promise by the college to do what may be necessary on its part to make the scholarship effective. The plan conceived by the subscriber will be mutilated and distorted unless the sum to be accepted is adequate to the end in view. Moreover, the time to affix her name to the memorial will not arrive until the entire fund has been collected. The college may thus thwart the purpose of the payment on account if at liberty to reject a tender of the residue. It is no answer to say that a duty would then arise to make restitution of the money. If such a duty may be imposed, the only reason for its existence must be that there is then a failure of "consideration." To say that there is a failure of consideration is to concede that a consideration has been promised, since otherwise it could not fail. No doubt there are times and situations in which limitations laid upon a promisee in connection with the use of what is paid by a subscriber lack the quality of a consideration, and are to be classed merely as conditions. Williston, Contracts, § 112; Page, Contracts, § 523. "It is often difficult to determine whether words of condition in a promise indicate a request for consideration or state a mere condition in a gratuitous promise. An aid, though not a conclusive test in determining which construction of the promise is more reasonable is an inquiry whether the happening of the condition will be a benefit to the promisor. If so, it is a fair inference that the happening was requested as a consideration." Williston, supra, § 112. Such must be the meaning of this transaction unless we are prepared to hold that the college may keep the payment on account, and thereafter nullify the scholarship which is to preserve the memory of the subscriber. The fair implication to be gathered from the whole transaction is assent to the condition and the assumption of a duty to go forward with performance. De Wolf Co. v. Harvey, 161 Wis. 535, 154 N. W. 988; Pullman Co. v. Meyer, 195 Ala. 397, 401, 70 So. 763; Braniff v. Baier, 101 Kan. 117, 165 P. 816, L. R. A. 1917E, 1036; Cf. Corbin, Offer and Acceptance, 26 Yale L. J. 169, 177, 193; McGovney, Irrevocable Offers, 27 Harv. L. R. 644; Sir Frederick Pollock, 28 L. Q. R. 100, 101. The subscriber does not say: I hand you $1,000, and you may make up your mind later, after my death, whether you will undertake to commemorate my name. What she says in effect is this: I hand you $1,000, and if you are unwilling to commemorate me, the time to speak is now. . . .

The judgment of the Appellate Division and that of the Trial Term should be reversed, and judgment ordered for the plaintiff as prayed for in the complaint, with costs in all courts.

KELLOGG, J. (dissenting).

The Chief Judge finds in the expression, "In loving memory this gift shall be known as the Mary Yates Johnston Memorial Fund," an offer on the part of Mary Yates Johnston to contract with Allegheny College. The expression makes no such appeal to me. Allegheny College was not requested to perform any act through which the sum offered might bear the title by which the offeror states that it shall be known. The sum offered was termed a "gift" by the offeror. Consequently, I can see no reason why we should strain ourselves to make it, not a gift, but a trade. Moreover, since the donor specified that the gift was made, "In consideration of my interest in Christian education, and in consideration of others subscribing," considerations not adequate in law, I can see no excuse for asserting that it was otherwise made in consideration of an act or promise on the part of the donee, constituting a sufficient quid pro quo to convert the gift into a contract obligation. To me the words used merely expressed an expectation or wish on the part of the donor and failed to exact the return of an adequate consideration. . . .

POUND, CRANE, LEHMAN, and O'BRIEN, JJ., concur with CARDOZO, C. J.
KELLOGG, J., dissents in opinion, in which ANDREWS, J., concurs.

Judgment accordingly.

KATZ V. DANNY DARE, INC.
Missouri Court of Appeals, Western District
610 S.W.2d 121 (1980).

TURNAGE, Presiding Judge.

I. G. Katz filed three suits in the Associate Division of the Circuit Court seeking pension payments for three separate time periods alleged to be due from Danny Dare, Inc. Two suits resulted in judgment in favor of Katz, but a request for a trial de novo was filed and those causes were assigned to a circuit judge for trial. The other suit pending in the Associate Division was transferred to the same circuit judge and all the cases were consolidated for trial without a jury. Judgment was entered in favor of Dare in all cases. On this appeal Katz contends the promise of pension payments made to him by Dare is binding under the Doctrine of Promissory Estoppel. Reversed and remanded.

There is little or no dispute as to the facts in this case. Katz began work for Dare in 1950 and continued in that employ until his retirement on June 1, 1975. The president of Dare was Harry Shopmaker, who was also the brother of Katz's wife. Katz worked in a variety of positions including executive vice president, sales manager, and a member of the board of directors, although he was not a member of the board at the time of his retirement. In February 1973, Katz was opening a store, operated by Dare, for business and placed a bag of money on the counter next to the cash register. A man walked in, picked up the bag of money and left. When Katz followed him and attempted to retrieve the money, Katz was struck in the head. He was hospitalized and even though he returned to work he conceded he had some difficulties. His walk was impaired and he suffered some memory loss and was not able to function as he had before. Shopmaker and others testified to many mistakes which

Katz made after his return at considerable cost to Dare. Shopmaker reached the decision that he would have to work out some agreeable pension to induce Katz to retire because he did not feel he could carry Katz as an employee. At that time Katz's earnings were about $23,000 per year.

Shopmaker began discussions with Katz concerning retirement but Katz insisted that he did not want to retire but wanted to continue working. Katz was 65 at the time of his injury and felt he could continue performing useful work for Dare to justify his remaining as an employee. However, Shopmaker persisted in his assessment that Katz was more of a liability than an asset as an employee and continued negotiating with Katz over a period of about 13 months in an effort to reach an agreement by which Katz would retire with a pension from Dare. Shopmaker first offered Katz $10,500 per year as a pension but Katz refused. Thereafter, while Katz was on vacation, Shopmaker sent Katz a letter to demonstrate how Katz could actually wind up with more take-home pay by retiring than he could by continuing as an employee. In the letter Shopmaker proposed an annual pension payable by Dare of $13,000, added the Social Security benefit which Katz and his wife would receive after retirement, and added $2,520 per year which Katz could earn for part-time employment, but not necessarily from Dare, to demonstrate that Katz would actually realize about $1,000 per year more in income by retiring with the Dare pension over what he would realize if he continued his employment. Shopmaker testified that he sent this letter in an effort to persuade Katz to retire.

Katz acceded to the offer of a pension of $13,000 per year for life, and on May 22, 1975, the board of directors of Dare unanimously approved the following resolution:

> WHEREAS, I. G. Katz has been a loyal employee of Danny Dare, Inc. and its predecessor companies for more than 25 years; and,
>
> WHEREAS, the said I. G. Katz has requested retirement because of failing health; and,
>
> WHEREAS, it has been the custom in the past for the company to retire all executives having loyally served the company for many years with a remuneration in keeping with the sum received during their last five years of employment;
>
> NOW THEN BE IT RESOLVED, That Danny Dare, Inc. pay to I. G. Katz the sum of $500.00 bi-weekly, or a total of $13,000.00 per year, so long as he shall live.

Katz retired on June 1, 1975, at age 67, and Dare began payment of the pension at the rate of $500 every other week. Katz testified that he would not have retired without the pension and relied on the promise of Dare to pay the pension when he made his decision to retire. Shopmaker testified that at the time the board resolution was passed, the board intended for Katz to rely on the resolution and to retire, but he said Katz would have been fired had he not elected to retire.

In the Fall of 1975, Katz began working for another company on 3 to 4 half-days per week. At the end of that year Shopmaker asked Katz if he could do part-time work for Dare and Katz told him he could work one-half day on Wednesdays. For the next two and one-half years Katz continued to work for Dare one-half day per week.

In July, 1978, Dare sent a semi-monthly check for $250 instead of $500. Katz sent the check back and stated he was entitled to the full $500. Thereafter Dare stopped sending any checks. Shopmaker testified that he cut off the checks to Katz because he felt Katz's health had improved to the point that he could work, as demonstrated by the part-time job he held. Katz testified the decrease was made after Shopmaker told him he would have to work one-half day for five days a week for Dare or his pension would be cut in half. Katz testified, without challenge, that he was not able to work 40 hours per week in 1978 at age 70.

The trial court entered a judgment in which some findings of fact were made. The court found that Katz based his claim on the Doctrine of Promissory Estoppel as applied in Feinberg v. Pfeiffer Company, 322 S.W.2d 163 (Mo.App.1959). The court found that Katz was not in the same situation as Feinberg had been because Katz faced the prospect of being fired if he did not accept the pension offer whereas there was no such evidence in the Feinberg case. The court found the pension from Dare did not require Katz to do anything and he was in fact free to work for another company. The court found Katz did not give up anything to which he was legally entitled when he elected to retire. The court found that since Katz had the choice of accepting retirement and a pension or being fired, that it could not be said that he suffered any detriment or significant change of position when he elected to retire. The court further found that it could not find any injustice resulting to Katz because by the time payments had been terminated, he had received about $40,000 plus a paid vacation for his wife and himself to Hawaii. The court found these were benefits he would not have received had he been fired.

Katz contends he falls within the holding in Feinberg and Dare contends that because Katz faced the alternative of accepting the pension or being fired that he falls without the holding in Feinberg.

At the outset it is interesting to note in view of the argument made by Dare that the court in Feinberg stated at p. 165:

> It is clear from the evidence that there was no contract, oral or written, as to plaintiff's length of employment, and that she was free to quit, and the defendant to discharge her, at any time.

In Feinberg the board of directors passed a resolution offering Feinberg the opportunity to retire at any time she would elect with retirement pay of $200 per month for life. Feinberg retired about two and one-half years after the resolution was passed and began to receive the retirement pay. The pay continued for about seven years when the company sent a check for $100 per month, which Feinberg refused and thereafter payments were discontinued.

The court observed that Section 90 of the Restatement of the Law of Contracts had been adopted by the Supreme Court in In Re Jamison's Estate, 202 S.W.2d 879 (Mo.1947). The court noted that one of the illustrations under § 90 was strikingly similar to the facts in Feinberg. The court applied the Doctrine of Promissory Estoppel, as articulated in § 90, and held that Feinberg had relied upon the promise of the pension when she resigned a paying position and elected to accept a lesser amount in pension. The court held it was immaterial as to whether Feinberg became unable to obtain other employment before or after the company discontinued the pension payment. The court held the reliance by Feinberg was in giving up her job in reliance on the promise of a pension. Her subsequent disability went to the prevention of injustice which is part of the Doctrine of Promissory Estoppel.

There are three elements to be satisfied to invoke the Doctrine of Promissory Estoppel. These are: (1) a promise; (2) a detrimental reliance on such promise; and (3) injustice can be avoided only by enforcement of the promise.

This court is not convinced that the alternative Shopmaker gave to Katz of either accepting the pension and retiring or be fired takes this case out of the operation of Promissory Estoppel. The fact remains that Katz was not fired, but instead did voluntarily retire, but only after the board of directors had adopted the resolution promising to pay Katz a pension of $13,000 per year for life. Thus, the same facts are present in this case as were present in Feinberg. When Katz elected to retire and give up earnings of about $23,000 per year to accept a pension of $13,000 per year, he did so as a result of a promise made by Dare and to his detriment by the loss of $10,000 per year in earnings. It is conceded Dare intended that Katz rely on its promise of a pension and Dare does not contend Katz did not in fact rely on such promise. The fact that the payments continued for about three years and that Katz at age 70 could not work full-time was unquestioned. Thus, the element that injustice can be avoided only by enforcement of the promise is present, because Katz cannot now engage in a full-time job to return to the earnings which he gave up in reliance on the pension.

Dare's argument that the threat of being fired removes this case from the operation of Promissory Estoppel is similar to an argument advanced in Trexler's Estate, 27 Pa.Dist. & Co.Rep. 4 (1936), cited with approval in Fried v. Fisher, 328 Pa. 497, 196 A. 39 (1938). In Trexler the depression had forced General Trexler to decide whether to fire several employees who had been with him for many years or place them on a pension. The General decided to promise them a pension of $50 per month and at his death, the employees filed a claim against his estate for the continuation of the payments. The court observed that the General could have summarily discharged the employees, but was loath to do this without making some provision for their old age. This was shown by the numerous conferences which the General had with his executives in considering each employee's financial situation, age and general status. The court said it was clear that the General wanted to reduce overhead and at the same time wanted to give these faithful employees some protection. The court stated it as an open question of what the General would have done if the men had not accepted his offer of a lifetime pension. The court said it would not speculate on that point but it was sufficient to observe that the men accepted the offer and received the pension. The court applied § 90 of the Restatement and held that under the Doctrine of Promissory Estoppel the estate was bound to continue the payments.

The facts in this case are strikingly similar to Trexler. Shopmaker undoubtedly wanted to reduce his overhead by reducing the amount being paid to Katz and it is true that Katz could have been summarily discharged. However, it is also true that Shopmaker refused to fire Katz, but instead patiently negotiated for about 13 months to work out a pension which Katz did agree to accept and voluntarily retired.

While Dare strenuously urges that the threat of firing effectively removed any legitimate choice on the part of Katz, the facts do not bear this out. The fact is that Katz continued in his employment with Dare until he retired and such retirement was voluntary on the part of Katz. Had Shopmaker desired to terminate Katz without any promise of a pension he could have done so and Katz would have had no recourse. However, the fact is that Shopmaker did not discharge Katz but actually made every effort to induce Katz to retire voluntarily on the promise of a pension of $13,000 per year.

Dare appears to have led the trial court into error by relying on Pitts v. McGraw-Edison Co., 329 F.2d 412 (6th Cir. 1964). Pitts was informed that the company had retired him and would pay him a certain percentage of sales thereafter. Thus, the main distinction between this case and Pitts is that Pitts did not elect to retire on the promise of any payment, but was simply informed that he had been retired by the company and the company would make payment to him. There was no promise made to Pitts on which he acted to his detriment. In addition, the court was applying the law of Tennessee and the court stated that Tennessee had not adopted § 90 of the Restatement. The court in Pitts found that Pitts had not given up anything to which he was legally entitled and was not restricted in any way in his activities after being placed in retirement by his company.

The facts in Pitts would not enable Pitts to recover under Promissory Estoppel in Missouri because there was no action taken by Pitts in reliance on a promise. The test to be applied in this case is not whether Katz gave up something to which he was legally entitled, but rather whether Dare made a promise to him on which he acted to his detriment. The legally entitled test could never be met by an employee such as Katz or Feinberg because neither could show any legal obligation on the company to promise a pension. The Doctrine of Promissory Estoppel is designed to protect those to whom a promise is made which is not legally enforcible until the requirements of the doctrine are met. Pitts is not applicable either on the facts or the law.

The trial court misapplied the law when it held that Katz was required to show that he gave up something to which he was legally entitled before he could enforce the promise of a pension made by Dare. The elements of Promissory Estoppel are present: a promise of a pension to Katz, his detrimental reliance thereon, and injustice can only be avoided by enforcing that promise. The judgment is reversed and the case is remanded with directions to enter judgment in all suits in favor of Katz for the amount of unpaid pension.

All concur.

PAVEL ENTERPRISES, INC. V. A.S. JOHNSON COMPANY, INC.
Court of Appeals of Maryland
674 A.2d 521 (1996).

KARWACKI, Judge.

In this case we are invited to adapt the "modern" contractual theory of detrimental reliance,[1] or promissory estoppel, to the relationship between general contractors and their subcontractors. Although the theory of detrimental reliance is available to general contractors, it is not applicable to the facts of this case. For that reason, and because there was no traditional bilateral contract formed, we shall affirm the trial court.

I

The National Institutes of Health [hereinafter, "NIH"], solicited bids for a renovation project on Building 30 of its Bethesda, Maryland campus. The proposed work entailed some demolition work, but the major component of the job was mechanical, including heating, ventilation and air conditioning ["HVAC"]. Pavel Enterprises Incorporated [hereinafter, "PEI"], a general contractor from Vienna, Virginia and appellant in this action, prepared a bid for the NIH work. In preparing its bid, PEI solicited sub-bids from various mechanical subcontractors. The A.S. Johnson Company [hereinafter, "Johnson"], a mechanical subcontractor located in Clinton, Maryland and the appellee here, responded with a written scope of work proposal on July 27, 1993.[2] On the morning of August 5, 1993, the day NIH opened the general contractors' bids, Johnson verbally submitted a quote of $898,000 for the HVAC component.[3] Neither party disputes that PEI used Johnson's sub-bid in computing its own bid. PEI submitted a bid of $1,585,000 for the entire project.

General contractors' bids were opened on the afternoon of August 5, 1993. PEI's bid was the second lowest bid. The government subsequently disqualified the apparent low bidder,[4] however, and in mid-August, NIH notified PEI that its bid would be accepted.

With the knowledge that PEI was the lowest responsive bidder, Thomas F. Pavel, president of PEI, visited the offices of A.S. Johnson on August 26, 1993, and met with James Kick, Johnson's chief estimator, to discuss Johnson's proposed role in the work. Pavel testified at trial to the purpose of the meeting:

[1] We prefer to use the phrase detrimental reliance, rather than the traditional nomenclature of "promissory estoppel," because we believe it more clearly expresses the concept intended. Moreover, we hope that this will alleviate the confusion which until now has permitted practitioners to confuse promissory estoppel with its distant cousin, equitable estoppel. See Note, The "Firm Offer" Problem in Construction Bids and the Need for Promissory Estoppel, 10 Wm & Mary L.Rev. 212, 214 n. 17 (1968) [hereinafter, " The Firm Offer Problem "].

[2] The scope of work proposal listed all work that Johnson proposed to perform, but omitted the price term. This is a standard practice in the construction industry. The subcontractor's bid price is then filled in immediately before the general contractor submits the general bid to the letting party.

[3] PEI alleged at trial that Johnson's bid, as well as the bids of the other potential mechanical subcontractors contained a fixed cost of $355,000 for a sub-sub-contract to "Landis and Gear Powers" [hereinafter, "Powers"]. Powers was the sole source supplier of the electric controls for the project.

[4] The project at NIH was part of a set-aside program for small business. The apparent low bidder, J.J. Kirlin, Inc. was disqualified because it was not a small business.

> I met with Mr. Kick. And the reason for me going to their office was to look at their offices, to see their facility, to basically sit down and talk with them, as I had not done, and my company had not performed business with them on a direct relationship, but we had heard of their reputation. I wanted to go out and see where their facility was, see where they were located, and basically just sit down and talk to them. Because if we were going to use them on a project, I wanted to know who I was dealing with.

Pavel also asked if Johnson would object to PEI subcontracting directly with Powers for electric controls, rather than the arrangement originally envisioned in which Powers would be Johnson's subcontractor.[5] Johnson did not object.

Following that meeting, PEI sent a fax to all of the mechanical subcontractors from whom it had received sub-bids on the NIH job. The text of that fax is reproduced:

> Pavel Enterprises, Inc.
> TO: PROSPECTIVE MECHANICAL SUBCONTRACTORS
>
> FROM: ESTIMATING DEPARTMENT
>
> REFERENCE: NIH, BLDG 30 RENOVATION

We herewith respectfully request that you review your bid on the above referenced project that was bid on 8/05/93. PEI has been notified that we will be awarded the project as J.J. Kirlin, Inc. [the original low bidder] has been found to be nonresponsive on the solicitation. We anticipate award on or around the first of September and therefor request that you supply the following information.

1. Please break out your cost for the "POWERS" supplied control work as we will be subcontracting directly to "POWERS".

2. Please resubmit your quote deleting the above referenced item.

We ask this in an effort to allow all prospective bidders to compete on an even playing field.

Should you have any questions, please call us immediately as time is of the essence.

On August 30, 1993, PEI informed NIH that Johnson was to be the mechanical subcontractor on the job. On September 1, 1993, PEI mailed and faxed a letter to Johnson formally accepting Johnson's bid. That letter read:

> Pavel Enterprises, Inc.
> September 1, 1993
>
> Mr. James H. Kick, Estimating Mngr., A.S. Johnson Company

[5] Pavel testified at trial that restructuring the arrangement in this manner would reduce the amount PEI needed to bond and thus reduce the price of the bond.

8042 Old Alexandria Ferry Road, Clinton, Maryland 20735

Re: NIH Bldg 30 HVAC Modifications IFB # 263-93-B (CM)-0422

Subject: Letter of Intent to award Subcontract

Dear Mr. Kick;

We herewith respectfully inform your office of our intent to award a subcontract for the above referenced project per your quote received on 8/05/93 in the amount of $898,000.00. This subcontract will be forwarded upon receipt of our contract from the NIH, which we expect any day. A preconstruction meeting is currently scheduled at the NIH on 9/08/93 at 10 AM which we have been requested that your firm attend.

As discussed with you, a meeting was held between NIH and PEI wherein PEI confirmed our bid to the government, and designated your firm as our HVAC Mechanical subcontractor. This action was taken after several telephonic and face to face discussions with you regarding the above referenced bid submitted by your firm.

We look forward to working with your firm on this contract and hope that this will lead to a long and mutually beneficial relationship.

Sincerely,

/s/ Thomas F. Pavel,

President

Upon receipt of PEI's fax of September 1, James Kick called and informed PEI that Johnson's bid contained an error, and as a result the price was too low. According to Kick, Johnson had discovered the mistake earlier, but because Johnson believed that PEI had not been awarded the contract, they did not feel compelled to correct the error. Kick sought to withdraw Johnson's bid, both over the telephone and by a letter dated September 2, 1993:

A.S. Johnson Co.
September 2, 1993

PEI Construction

780 West Maples Avenue, Suite 101, Vienna, Virginia 22180

Attention: Thomas Pavel, President

Reference: NIH Building 30 HVAC Modifications
Dear Mr. Pavel,

We respectfully inform you of our intention to withdraw our proposal for the above referenced project due to an error in our bid.

As discussed in our telephone conversation and face to face meeting, the management of A.S. Johnson Company was reviewing this proposal, upon which we were to confirm our pricing to you.

Please contact Mr. Harry Kick, General Manager at [telephone number deleted] for any questions you may have.

Very truly yours,

/s/ James H. Kick, Estimating Manager

PEI responded to both the September 1 phone call, and the September 2 letter, expressing its refusal to permit Johnson to withdraw.

On September 28, 1993, NIH formally awarded the construction contract to PEI. PEI found a substitute subcontractor to do the mechanical work, but at a cost of $930,000.[6] PEI brought suit against Johnson in the Circuit Court for Prince George's County to recover the $32,000 difference between Johnson's bid and the cost of the substitute mechanical subcontractor.

The case was heard by the trial court without the aid of a jury. The trial court made several findings of fact, which we summarize:

1. PEI relied upon Johnson's sub-bid in making its bid for the entire project;

2. The fact that PEI was not the low bidder, but was awarded the project only after the apparent low bidder was disqualified, takes this case out of the ordinary;

3. Prior to NIH awarding PEI the contract on September 28, Johnson, on September 2, withdrew its bid; and

4. PEI's letter to all potential mechanical subcontractors, dated August 26, 1993, indicates that there was no definite agreement between PEI and Johnson, and that PEI was not relying upon Johnson's bid.

The trial court analyzed the case under both a traditional contract theory and under a detrimental reliance theory. PEI was unable to satisfy the trial judge that under either theory that a contractual relationship had been formed.

PEI appealed to the Court of Special Appeals, raising both traditional offer and acceptance theory, and "promissory estoppel." Before our intermediate appellate court considered the case, we issued a writ of certiorari on our own motion.

---

[6] The record indicates that the substitute mechanical subcontractor used "Powers" as a sub-subcontractor and did not "break out" the "Powers" component to be directly subcontracted by PEI.

II

The relationships involved in construction contracts have long posed a unique problem in the law of contracts. A brief overview of the mechanics of the construction bid process, as well as our legal system's attempts to regulate the process, is in order.

A. CONSTRUCTION BIDDING.

Our description of the bid process in Maryland Supreme Corp. v. Blake Co., 279 Md. 531, 369 A.2d 1017 (1977) is still accurate:

> In such a building project there are basically three parties involved: the letting party, who calls for bids on its job; the general contractor, who makes a bid on the whole project; and the subcontractors, who bid only on that portion of the whole job which involves the field of its specialty. The usual procedure is that when a project is announced, a subcontractor, on his own initiative or at the general contractor's request, prepares an estimate and submits a bid to one or more of the general contractors interested in the project. The general contractor evaluates the bids made by the subcontractors in each field and uses them to compute its total bid to the letting party. After receiving bids from general contractors, the letting party ordinarily awards the contract to the lowest reputable bidder. . . .

B. THE CONSTRUCTION BIDDING CASES-AN HISTORICAL OVERVIEW.

The problem the construction bidding process poses is the determination of the precise points on the timeline that the various parties become bound to each other. The early landmark case was James Baird Co. v. Gimbel Bros., Inc., 64 F.2d 344 (2d Cir.1933). The plaintiff, James Baird Co., ["Baird"] was a general contractor from Washington, D.C., bidding to construct a government building in Harrisburg, Pennsylvania. Gimbel Bros., Inc., ["Gimbel"], the famous New York department store, sent its bid to supply linoleum to a number of bidding general contractors on December 24, and Baird received Gimbel's bid on December 28. Gimbel realized its bid was based on an incorrect computation and notified Baird of its withdrawal on December 28. The letting authority awarded Baird the job on December 30. Baird formally accepted the Gimbel bid on January 2. When Gimbel refused to perform, Baird sued for the additional cost of a substitute linoleum supplier. The Second Circuit Court of Appeals held that Gimbel's initial bid was an offer to contract and, under traditional contract law, remained open only until accepted or withdrawn. Because the offer was withdrawn before it was accepted there was no contract. Judge Learned Hand, speaking for the court, also rejected two alternative theories of the case: unilateral contract and promissory estoppel. He held that Gimbel's bid was not an offer of a unilateral contract[7] that Baird could accept by performing, i.e., submitting the bid as part of the general bid; and second, he held that the theory of promissory estoppel was limited to cases involving charitable pledges.

---

[7] A unilateral contract is a contract which is accepted, not by traditional acceptance, but by performance. 2 Williston on Contracts § 6:2 (4th ed.).

Judge Hand's opinion was widely criticized, see Note, Contracts-Promissory Estoppel, 20 Va.L.Rev. 214 (1933) [hereinafter, "Promissory Estoppel"]; Note, Contracts-Revocation of Offer Before Acceptance-Promissory Estoppel, 28 Ill.L.Rev. 419 (1934), but also widely influential. The effect of the James Baird line of cases, however, is an "obvious injustice without relief of any description." Promissory Estoppel, at 215. The general contractor is bound to the price submitted to the letting party, but the subcontractors are not bound, and are free to withdraw.[8] As one commentator described it, "If the subcontractor revokes his bid before it is accepted by the general, any loss which results is a deduction from the general's profit and conceivably may transform overnight a profitable contract into a losing deal." Franklin M. Schultz, The Firm Offer Puzzle: A Study of Business Practice in the Construction Industry, 19 U.Chi.L.Rev. 237, 239 (1952).

The unfairness of this regime to the general contractor was addressed in Drennan v. Star Paving, 333 P.2d 757, 51 Cal.2d 409 (1958). Like James Baird, the Drennan case arose in the context of a bid mistake.[9] Justice Traynor, writing for the Supreme Court of California, relied upon § 90 of the Restatement (First) of Contracts:

> A promise which the promisor should reasonably expect to induce action or forbearance of a definite and substantial character on the part of the promisee and which does induce such action or forbearance is binding if injustice can be avoided only by enforcement of the promise.
>
> Restatement (First) of Contracts § 90 (1932).[10]

Justice Traynor reasoned that the subcontractor's bid contained an implied subsidiary promise not to revoke the bid. As the court stated:

> When plaintiff [, a General Contractor,] used defendant's offer in computing his own bid, he bound himself to perform in reliance on defendant's terms. Though defendant did not bargain for the use of its bid neither did defendant make it idly, indifferent to whether it would be used or not. On the contrary it is reasonable to suppose that defendant submitted its bid to obtain the subcontract. It was bound to realize the substantial possibility that its bid

[8] Note that under the Baird line of cases, the general contractor, while bound by his offer to the letting party, is not bound to any specific subcontractor, and is free to "bid shop" prior to awarding the subcontract. Michael L. Closen & Donald G. Weiland, The Construction Industry Bidding Cases: Application of Traditional Contract, Promissory Estoppel, and Other Theories to the Relations Between General Contractors and Subcontractors, 13 J. Marshall L.Rev. 565, 583 (1980). At least one commentator argues that although potentially unfair, this system creates a necessary symmetry between general and subcontractors, in that neither party is bound. Note, Construction Contracts-The Problem of Offer and Acceptance in the General Contractor-Subcontractor Relationship, 37 U.Cinn.L.Rev. 798 (1980) [hereinafter, " The Problem of Offer and Acceptance "].

[9] Commentators have suggested that the very fact that many of these cases have arisen from bid mistake, an unusual subspecies, rather than from more typical cases, has distorted the legal system's understanding of these cases. Comment, Bid Shopping and Peddling in the Subcontract Construction Industry, 18 UCLA L.Rev. 389, 409 (1970) [hereinafter, " Bid Shopping "]. See also note, Once Around the Flag Pole: Construction Bidding and Contracts at Formation, 39 N.Y.U.L.Rev. 816, 818 (1964) [hereinafter, " Flag Pole "] (bid mistake cases generally portray general contractor as victim, but market reality is that subs are usually in weaker negotiating position).

[10] This section of the Restatement has been supplanted by the Restatement (Second) of Contracts § 90(1) (1979). That provision will be discussed, infra.

> would be the lowest, and that it would be included by plaintiff in his bid. It was to its own interest that the contractor be awarded the general contract; the lower the subcontract bid, the lower the general contractor's bid was likely to be and the greater its chance of acceptance and hence the greater defendant's chance of getting the paving subcontract. Defendant had reason not only to expect plaintiff to rely on its bid but to want him to. Clearly defendant had a stake in plaintiff's reliance on its bid. Given this interest and the fact that plaintiff is bound by his own bid, it is only fair that plaintiff should have at least an opportunity to accept defendant's bid after the general contract has been awarded to him.

Drennan, 51 Cal.2d at 415, 333 P.2d at 760. The Drennan court however did not use "promissory estoppel" as a substitute for the entire contract, as is the doctrine's usual function. Instead, the Drennan court, applying the principle of § 90, interpreted the subcontractor's bid to be irrevocable. Justice Traynor's analysis used promissory estoppel as consideration for an implied promise to keep the bid open for a reasonable time. Recovery was then predicated on traditional bilateral contract, with the sub-bid as the offer and promissory estoppel serving to replace acceptance.

The Drennan decision has been very influential. Many states have adopted the reasoning used by Justice Traynor. See, e.g., Debron Corp. v. National Homes Constr. Corp., 493 F.2d 352 (8th Cir.1974) (applying Missouri law); Reynolds v. Texarkana Constr. Co., 237 Ark. 583, 374 S.W.2d 818 (1964); Mead Assocs. Inc. v. Antonsen, 677 P.2d 434 (Colo.1984); Illinois Valley Asphalt v. J.F. Edwards Constr. Co., 45 Ill.Dec. 876, 413 N.E.2d 209, 90 Ill.App.3d 768 (Ill.Ct.App.1980); Lichtefeld-Massaro, Inc. v. R.J. Manteuffel Co., 806 S.W.2d 42 (Ky.App.1991); Constructors Supply Co. v. Bostrom Sheet Metal Works, Inc., 291 Minn. 113, 190 N.W.2d 71 (1971); E.A. Coronis Assocs. v. M. Gordon Constr. Co., 90 N.J. Super 69, 216 A.2d 246 (1966).

Despite the popularity of the Drennan reasoning, the case has subsequently come under some criticism.[11] The criticism centers on the lack of symmetry of detrimental reliance in the bid process, in that subcontractors are bound to the general, but the general is not bound to the subcontractors.[12] The result is that the general is free to bid shop,[13] bid chop,[14] and to encourage bid peddling,[15] to the detriment of the subcontractors. One commentator described the problems that these practices create:

---

[11] Home Elec. Co. v. Underdown Heating & Air Conditioning Co., 86 N.C.App. 540, 358 S.E.2d 539 (1987). See also, The Problem of Offer and Acceptance.

[12] See Williams v. Favret, 161 F.2d 822, 823 n. 1 (5th Cir.1947); Merritt-Chapman & Scott Corp. v. Gunderson Bros. Eng'g Corp., 305 F.2d 659 (9th Cir.1962). But see Electrical Constr. & Maintenance Co. v. Maeda Pac. Corp., 764 F.2d 619 (9th Cir.1985) (subcontractor rejected by general contractor could maintain an action in both traditional contract or promissory estoppel). See Bid Shopping, at 405-09 (suggesting using "promissory estoppel" to bind generals to subcontractors, as well as subs to generals, in appropriate circumstances).

[13] Bid shopping is the use of the lowest subcontractor's bid as a tool in negotiating lower bids from other subcontractors post-award.

[14] "The general contractor, having been awarded the prime contract, may pressure the subcontractor whose bid was used for a particular portion of the work in computing the overall bid on the prime contract to reduce the amount of the bid." Closen & Weiland, at 566 n. 6.

[15] An unscrupulous subcontractor can save estimating costs, and still get the job by not entering a bid or by entering an uncompetitive bid. After bid opening, this unscrupulous subcontractor, knowing the price of the low

> Bid shopping and peddling have long been recognized as unethical by construction trade organizations. These "unethical," but common practices have several detrimental results. First, as bid shopping becomes common within a particular trade, the subcontractors will pad their initial bids in order to make further reductions during post-award negotiations. This artificial inflation of subcontractor's offers makes the bid process less effective. Second, subcontractors who are forced into post-award negotiations with the general often must reduce their sub-bids in order to avoid losing the award. Thus, they will be faced with a Hobson's choice between doing the job at a loss or doing a less than adequate job. Third, bid shopping and peddling tend to increase the risk of loss of the time and money used in preparing a bid. This occurs because generals and subcontractors who engage in these practices use, without expense, the bid estimates prepared by others. Fourth, it is often impossible for a general to obtain bids far enough in advance to have sufficient time to properly prepare his own bid because of the practice, common among many subcontractors, of holding sub-bids until the last possible moment in order to avoid pre-award bid shopping by the general. Fifth, many subcontractors refuse to submit bids for jobs on which they expect bid shopping. As a result, competition is reduced, and, consequently, construction prices are increased. Sixth, any price reductions gained through the use of post-award bid shopping by the general will be of no benefit to the awarding authority, to whom these price reductions would normally accrue as a result of open competition before the award of the prime contract. Free competition in an open market is therefore perverted because of the use of post-award bid shopping.

Bid Shopping, at 394-96 (citations omitted). See also Flag Pole, at 818 (bid mistake cases generally portray general contractor as victim, but market reality is that subs are usually in weaker negotiating position); Jay M. Feinman, Promissory Estoppel and Judicial Method, 97 Harv.L.Rev. 678, 707-08 (1984). These problems have caused at least one court to reject promissory estoppel in the contractor-subcontractor relationship. Home Elec. Co. v. Underdown Heating & Air Conditioning Co., 86 N.C.App. 540, 358 S.E.2d 539 (1987). See also Note, Construction Contracts-The Problem of Offer and Acceptance in the General Contractor-Subcontractor Relationship, 37 U.Cinn.L.Re. 798 (1980). But other courts, while aware of the limitations of promissory estoppel, have adopted it nonetheless. See, e.g., Alaska Bussell Elec. Co. v. Vern Hickel Constr. Co., 688 P.2d 576 (Alaska 1984).[16]

The doctrine of detrimental reliance has evolved in the time since Drennan was decided in 1958. The American Law Institute, responding to Drennan, sought to make detrimental reliance more readily applicable to the construction bidding scenario by adding § 87. This new section was intended to make subcontractors' bids binding:

---

sub-bid, can then offer to perform the work for less money, precisely because the honest subcontractor has already paid for the estimate and included that cost in the original bid. This practice is called bid peddling.

[16] The critical literature also contains numerous suggestions that might be undertaken by the legislature to address the problems of bid shopping, chopping, and peddling. See Note, Construction Bidding Problem: Is There a Solution Fair to Both the General Contractor and Subcontractor?, 19 St. Louis L.Rev. 552, 568-72 (1975) (discussing bid depository and bid listing schemes); Flag Pole, at 825-26.

> "§ 87. Option Contract . . . .
>
> (2) An offer which the offeror should reasonably expect to induce action or forbearance of a substantial character on the part of the offeree before acceptance and which does induce such action or forbearance is binding as an option contract to the extent necessary to avoid injustice."
>
> Restatement (Second) of Contracts § 87 (1979).[17]

Despite the drafter's intention that § 87 of the Restatement (Second) of Contracts (1979) should replace Restatement (First) of Contracts § 90 (1932) in the construction bidding cases, few courts have availed themselves of the opportunity. But see, Arango Constr. Co. v. Success Roofing, Inc., 46 Wash.App. 314, 321-22, 730 P.2d 720, 725 (1986). Section 90(1) of the Restatement (Second) of Contracts (1979) modified the first restatement formulation in three ways, by: 1) deleting the requirement that the action of the offeree be "definite and substantial;" 2) adding a cause of action for third party reliance; and 3) limiting remedies to those required by justice.[18]

Courts and commentators have also suggested other solutions intended to bind the parties without the use of detrimental reliance theory. The most prevalent suggestion[19] is the use of the firm offer provision of the Uniform Commercial Code. Maryland Code (1992 Repl.Vol.), § 2-205 of the Commercial Law Article. That statute provides:

> An offer by a merchant to buy or sell goods in a signed writing which by its terms gives assurance that it will be held open is not revocable, for lack of consideration, during the time stated or if no time is stated for a reasonable time, but in no event may such period of irrevocability exceed three months; but any such term of assurance on a form supplied by the offeree must be separately signed by the offeror.

In this manner, subcontractor's bids, made in writing and giving some assurance of an intent that the offer be held open, can be found to be irrevocable.

The Supreme Judicial Court of Massachusetts has suggested three other traditional theories that might prove the existence of a contractual relationship between a general contractor and a sub: conditional bilateral contract analysis; unilateral contract analysis; and

---

[17] This provision was derived from Restatement (Second) of Contracts § 89B(2) (Tent.Drafts Nos. 1-7, 1973). There are cases that refer to the tentative drafts. See Loranger Constr. Corp. v. E.F. Hauserman Co., 384 N.E.2d 176, 179, 376 Mass. 757, 763 (1978). See also Closen & Weiland, at 593-97.

[18] Section 90 of the Restatement (First) of Contracts (1932) explains detrimental reliance as follows:"A promise which the promisor should reasonably expect to induce action or forbearance of a definite and substantial character on the part of the promisee and which does induce such action or forbearance is binding if injustice can be avoided only by enforcement of the promise."Section 90(1) of the Restatement (Second) Contracts (1979) defines the doctrine of detrimental reliance as follows:

> A promise which the promisor should reasonably expect to induce action or forbearance on the part of the promisee or a third person and which does induce such action or forbearance is binding if injustice can be avoided only by enforcement of the promise. The remedy granted for breach may be limited as justice requires.

[19] See Bid Shopping and Peddling at 399-401; Firm Offer Problem at 215; Closen & Weiland, at 604 n. 133.

unrevoked offer analysis. Loranger Constr. Corp. v. E.F. Hauserman Co., 384 N.E.2d 176, 376 Mass. 757 (1978). If the general contractor could prove that there was an exchange of promises binding the parties to each other, and that exchange of promises was made before bid opening, that would constitute a valid bilateral promise conditional upon the general being awarded the job. Loranger, 384 N.E.2d at 180, 376 Mass. at 762. This directly contrasts with Judge Hand's analysis in James Baird, that a general's use of a sub-bid constitutes acceptance conditional upon the award of the contract to the general. James Baird, 64 F.2d at 345-46.

Alternatively, if the subcontractor intended its sub-bid as an offer to a unilateral contract, use of the sub-bid in the general's bid constitutes part performance, which renders the initial offer irrevocable under the Restatement (Second) of Contracts § 45 (1979). Loranger, 384 N.E.2d at 180, 376 Mass. at 762. This resurrects a second theory dismissed by Judge Learned Hand in James Baird.

Finally, the Loranger court pointed out that a jury might choose to disbelieve that a subcontractor had withdrawn the winning bid, meaning that acceptance came before withdrawal, and a traditional bilateral contract was formed. Loranger, 384 N.E.2d at 180, 376 Mass. at 762-63.[20]

Another alternative solution to the construction bidding problem is no longer seriously considered-revitalizing the common law seal. William Noel Keyes, Consideration Reconsidered-The Problem of the Withdrawn Bid, 10 Stan.L.Rev. 441, 470 (1958). Because a sealed option contract remains firm without consideration this alternative was proposed as a solution to the construction bidding problem.[21]

It is here that the state of the law rests.

III

If PEI is able to prove by any of the theories described that a contractual relationship existed, but Johnson failed to perform its end of the bargain, then PEI will recover the $32,000 in damages caused by Johnson's breach of contract. Alternatively, if PEI is unable to prove the existence of a contractual relationship, then Johnson has no obligation to PEI. We will test the facts of the case against the theories described to determine if such a relationship existed.

The trial court held, and we agree, that Johnson's sub-bid was an offer to contract and that it was sufficiently clear and definite. We must then determine if PEI made a timely and valid acceptance of that offer and thus created a traditional bilateral contract, or in the absence of a valid acceptance, if PEI's detrimental reliance served to bind Johnson to its sub-bid. We examine each of these alternatives, beginning with traditional contract theory.[22]

[20] For an excellent analysis of the Loranger case, see Closen & Weiland at 597-603.

[21] Of course, general contractors could require their subcontractors to provide their bids under seal. The fact that they do not is testament to the lack of appeal this proposal holds.

[22] Because they were not raised, either below or in this Court, we need not address the several methods in which a court might interpret a subcontractor's bid as a firm, and thus irrevocable, offer. Nevertheless, for the benefit of bench and bar [eds. - and the student], we review those theories as applied to this case. First, PEI could have

A. TRADITIONAL BILATERAL CONTRACT

The trial judge found that there was not a traditional contract binding Johnson to PEI. A review of the record and the trial judge's findings make it clear that this was a close question. On appeal however, our job is to assure that the trial judge's findings were not clearly erroneous. Maryland Rule 8-131(c). This is an easier task.

The trial judge rejected PEI's claim of bilateral contract for two separate reasons: 1) that there was no meeting of the minds; and 2) that the offer was withdrawn prior to acceptance. Both need not be proper bases for decision; if either of these two theories is not clearly erroneous, we must affirm.

There is substantial evidence in the record to support the judge's conclusion that there was no meeting of the minds. PEI's letter of August 26, to all potential mechanical subcontractors, reproduced supra, indicates, as the trial judge found, that PEI and Johnson "did not have a definite, certain meeting of the minds on a certain price for a certain quantity of goods...." Because this reason is itself sufficient to sustain the trial judge's finding that no contract was formed, we affirm.

Alternatively, we hold, that the evidence permitted the trial judge to find that Johnson revoked its offer prior to PEI's final acceptance. We review the relevant chronology. Johnson made its offer, in the form of a sub-bid, on August 5. On September 1, PEI accepted. Johnson withdrew its offer by letter dated September 2. On September 28, NIH awarded the contract to PEI. Thus, PEI's apparent acceptance came one day prior to Johnson's withdrawal.

The trial court found, however, "that before there was ever a final agreement reached with the contract awarding authorities, that Johnson made it clear to [PEI] that they were not going to continue to rely on their earlier submitted bid." Implicit in this finding is the judge's understanding of the contract. Johnson's sub-bid constituted an offer of a contingent contract. PEI accepted that offer subject to the condition precedent of PEI's receipt of the award of the contract from NIH. Prior to the occurrence of the condition precedent, Johnson was free to withdraw. See 2 Williston on Contracts § 6:14 (4th ed.). On September 2, Johnson exercised that right to revoke.[23] The trial judge's finding that

---

purchased an option, thus supplying consideration for making the offer irrevocable. This did not happen. Second, Johnson could have submitted its bid as a sealed offer. Md.Code (1995 Repl.Vol.), § 5-102 of the Courts & Judicial Proceedings Article. An offer under seal supplants the need for consideration to make an offer firm. This did not occur in the instant case. The third method of Johnson's offer becoming irrevocable is by operation of Md.Code (1992 Repl.Vol.), § 2-205 of the Commercial Law Article. We note that Johnson's sub-bid was made in the form of a signed writing, but without further evidence we are unable to determine if the offer "by its terms gives assurance that it will be held open" and if the sub-bid is for "goods" as that term is defined by Md.Code (1994 Repl.Vol.), § 2-105(1) of the Commercial Law Article and by decisions of this Court, including Anthony Pools v. Sheehan, 295 Md. 285, 455 A.2d 434 (1983) and Burton v. Artery Co., 279 Md. 94, 367 A.2d 935 (1977).

[23] We have also considered the possibility that Johnson's offer was not to enter into a contingent contract. This is unlikely because there is no incentive for a general contractor to accept a non-contingent contract prior to contract award but it would bind the general to purchase the subcontractor's services even if the general did not receive the award. Moreover, PEI's September 1 letter clearly "accepted" Johnson's offer subject to the award from NIH. If Johnson's bid was for a non-contingent contract, PEI's response substantially varied the offer and

withdrawal proceeded valid final acceptance is therefore logical and supported by substantial evidence in the record. It was not clearly erroneous, so we shall affirm.

B. DETRIMENTAL RELIANCE

PEI's alternative theory of the case is that PEI's detrimental reliance binds Johnson to its bid. We are asked, as a threshold question, if detrimental reliance applies to the setting of construction bidding. Nothing in our previous cases suggests that the doctrine was intended to be limited to a specific factual setting. The benefits of binding subcontractors outweigh the possible detriments of the doctrine.[24]

This Court has decided cases based on detrimental reliance as early as 1854,[25] and the general contours of the doctrine are well understood by Maryland courts. The historical development of promissory estoppel, or detrimental reliance, in Maryland has mirrored the development nationwide. It was originally a small exception to the general consideration requirement, and found in "cases dealing with such narrow problems as gratuitous agencies and bailments, waivers, and promises of marriage settlement." Jay M. Feinman, Promissory Estoppel and Judicial Method, 97 Harv.L.Rev. 678, 680 (1984). The early Maryland cases applying "promissory estoppel" or detrimental reliance primarily involve charitable pledges.

The leading case is Maryland Nat'l Bank v. United Jewish Appeal Fed'n of Greater Washington, 286 Md. 274, 407 A.2d 1130 (1979), where this Court's opinion was authored by the late Judge Charles E. Orth, Jr. In that case, a decedent, Milton Polinger, had pledged $200,000 to the United Jewish Appeal ["UJA"]. The UJA sued Polinger's estate in an attempt to collect the money promised them. Judge Orth reviewed four prior decisions of this Court[26] and determined that Restatement (First) of Contracts § 90 (1932) applied. Id. at 281, 407 A.2d at 1134. Because the Court found that the UJA had not acted in a "definite or substantial" manner in reliance on the contribution, no contract was found to have been created. Id. at 289-90, 407 A.2d at 1138-39.

Detrimental reliance doctrine has had a slow evolution from its origins in disputes over charitable pledges, and there remains some uncertainty about its exact dimensions.[27] Two cases from the Court of Special Appeals demonstrate that confusion.

---

was therefore a counter-offer, not an acceptance. Post v. Gillespie, 219 Md. 378, 385-86, 149 A.2d 391, 395-96 (1959); 2 Williston on Contracts § 6:13 (4th ed.).

[24] General contractors, however, should not assume that we will also adopt the holdings of our sister courts who have refused to find general contractors bound to their subcontractors. See, e.g., N. Litterio & Co. v. Glassman Constr. Co., 319 F.2d 736 (D.C.Cir.1963).

[25] Gittings v. Mayhew, 6 Md. 113 (1854).

[26] The cases reviewed were Gittings v. Mayhew, 6 Md. 113 (1854); Erdman v. Trustees Eutaw M.P. Ch., 129 Md. 595, 99 A. 793 (1917); Sterling v. Cushwa & Sons, 170 Md. 226, 183 A. 593 (1936); and American University v. Collings, 190 Md. 688, 59 A.2d 333 (1948).

[27] Other cases merely acknowledged the existence of a doctrine of "promissory estoppel," but did not comment on the standards for the application of this doctrine. See, e.g., Chesapeake Supply & Equip. Co. v. Manitowoc Eng'g Corp., 232 Md. 555, 566, 194 A.2d 624, 630 (1963).

The first, Snyder v. Snyder, 79 Md.App. 448, 558 A.2d 412 (1989), arose in the context of a suit to enforce an antenuptial agreement. To avoid the statute of frauds, refuge was sought in the doctrine of "promissory estoppel."[28] The court held that "promissory estoppel" requires a finding of fraudulent conduct on the part of the promisor. See also Friedman & Fuller v. Funkhouser, 107 Md.App. 91, 666 A.2d 1298 (1995).

The second, Kiley v. First Nat'l Bank, 102 Md.App. 317, 649 A.2d 1145 (1994), the court stated that "[i]t is unclear whether Maryland continues to adhere to the more stringent formulation of promissory estoppel, as set forth in the original Restatement of Contracts, or now follows the more flexible view found in the Restatement (Second) Contracts." Id. at 336, 649 A.2d at 1154.

To resolve these confusions we now clarify that Maryland courts are to apply the test of the Restatement (Second) of Contracts § 90(1) (1979), which we have recast as a four-part test:

1. a clear and definite promise;

2. where the promisor has a reasonable expectation that the offer will induce action or forbearance on the part of the promisee;

3. which does induce actual and reasonable action or forbearance by the promisee; and

4. causes a detriment which can only be avoided by the enforcement of the promise.[29]

---

[28] Section 139 of the Restatement (Second) of Contracts (1979) provides that detrimental reliance can remove a case from the statute of frauds:

> Enforcement by Virtue of Action in Reliance
>
> (1) A promise which the promisor should reasonably expect to induce action or forbearance on the part of the promisee or a third person and which does induce the action or forbearance is enforceable notwithstanding the Statute of Frauds if injustice can be avoided only by enforcement of the promise. The remedy granted for breach is to be limited as justice requires.
>
> (2) In determining whether injustice can be avoided only by enforcement of the promise, the following circumstances are significant:
>
> (a) the availability and adequacy of other remedies, particularly cancellation and restitution;(b) the definite and substantial character of the action or forbearance in relation to the remedy sought;(c) the extent to which the action or forbearance corroborates evidence of the making and terms of the promise, or the making and terms are otherwise established by clear and convincing evidence;(d) the reasonableness of the action or forbearance;(e) the extent to which the action or forbearance was foreseeable by the promisor.

[29] This comports with the formulation given by the United States District Court for the District of Maryland in Union Trust Co. of Md. v. Charter Medical Corp., 663 F.Supp. 175, 178 n. 4 (D.Md.1986) aff'd w/o opinion, 823 F.2d 548 (4th Cir.1987).We have adopted language of the Restatement (Second) of Contracts (1979) because we believe each of the three changes made to the previous formulation were for the better. As discussed earlier, the first change was to delete the requirement that the action of the offeree be "definite and substantial." Although the Court of Special Appeals in Kiley v. First Nat'l Bank, 102 Md.App. 317, 336, 649 A.2d 1145, 1154 (1994) apparently presumed this to be a major change from the "stringent" first restatement to the "more flexible" second restatement, we perceive the language to have always been redundant. If the reliance is not "substantial and definite" justice will not compel enforcement.

The decisions in Snyder v. Snyder, 79 Md.App. 448, 558 A.2d 412 (1989) and Friedman & Fuller v. Funkhouser, 107 Md.App. 91, 666 A.2d 1298 (1995) to the extent that they required a showing of fraud on the part of the offeree are therefore disapproved.

In a construction bidding case, where the general contractor seeks to bind the subcontractor to the sub-bid offered, the general must first prove that the subcontractor's sub-bid constituted an offer to perform a job at a given price. We do not express a judgment about how precise a bid must be to constitute an offer, or to what degree a general contractor may request to change the offered scope before an acceptance becomes a counter-offer. That fact-specific judgment is best reached on a case-by-case basis. In the instant case, the trial judge found that the sub-bid was sufficiently clear and definite to constitute an offer, and his finding was not clearly erroneous.

Second, the general must prove that the subcontractor reasonably expected that the general contractor would rely upon the offer. The subcontractor's expectation that the general contractor will rely upon the sub-bid may dissipate through time.[30]

In this case, the trial court correctly inquired into Johnson's belief that the bid remained open, and that consequently PEI was not relying on the Johnson bid. The judge found that due to the time lapse between bid opening and award, "it would be unreasonable for offers to continue." This is supported by the substantial evidence. James Kick testified that although he knew of his bid mistake, he did not bother to notify PEI because J.J. Kirlin, Inc., and not PEI, was the apparent low bidder. The trial court's finding that Johnson's reasonable expectation had dissipated in the span of a month is not clearly erroneous.

As to the third element, a general contractor must prove that he actually and reasonably relied on the subcontractor's sub-bid. We decline to provide a checklist of potential methods of proving this reliance, but we will make several observations. First, a showing by the subcontractor, that the general contractor engaged in "bid shopping," or actively encouraged "bid chopping," or "bid peddling" is strong evidence that the general did not rely on the sub-bid. Second, prompt notice by the general contractor to the subcontractor that the general intends to use the sub on the job, is weighty evidence that the general did rely on the bid.[31] Third, if a sub-bid is so low that a reasonably prudent general contractor would not rely upon it, the trier of fact may infer that the general contractor did not in fact rely upon the erroneous bid.

In this case, the trial judge did not make a specific finding that PEI failed to prove its reasonable reliance upon Johnson's sub-bid. We must assume, however, that it was his conclusion based on his statement that "the parties did not have a definite, certain meeting of the minds on a certain price for a certain quantity of goods and wanted to renegotiate...." The August 26, 1993, fax from PEI to all prospective mechanical subcontractors, is evidence supporting this conclusion. Although the finding that PEI did not rely on Johnson's bid was indisputably a close call, it was not clearly erroneous.

---

[30] We expect that evidence of "course of dealing" and "usage of the trade," see Restatement (Second) of Contracts §§ 219-223 (1979), will provide strong indicies of the reasonableness of a subcontractor's expectations.

[31] Prompt notice and acceptance also significantly dispels the possibility of bid shopping, bid chopping, and bid peddling.

Finally, as to the fourth prima facie element, the trial court, and not a jury, must determine that binding the subcontractor is necessary to prevent injustice. This element is to be enforced as required by common law equity courts-the general contractor must have "clean hands." This requirement includes, as did the previous element, that the general did not engage in bid shopping, chopping or peddling, but also requires the further determination that justice compels the result. The fourth factor was not specifically mentioned by the trial judge, but we may infer that he did not find this case to merit an equitable remedy.

Because there was sufficient evidence in the record to support the trial judge's conclusion that PEI had not proven its case for detrimental reliance, we must, and hereby do, affirm the trial court's ruling.

IV

In conclusion, we emphasize that there are different ways to prove that a contractual relationship exists between a general contractor and its subcontractors. Traditional bilateral contract theory is one. Detrimental reliance can be another. However, under the evidence in this case, the trial judge was not clearly erroneous in deciding that recovery by the general contractor was not justified under either theory.

JUDGMENT AFFIRMED, WITH COSTS.

NOTES AND QUESTIONS:

1. *See* Restatement (Second) of Contracts §§ 2 (Promise; Promisor; Promisee; Beneficiary), 4 (How a Promise May Be Made), 5 (Terms of Promise, Agreement, or Contract), 87(2) (Option Contract), and 90 (Promise Reasonably Inducing Action or Forbearance) (1981).

CHAPTER THREE

DEFENSES

No court will lend its aid to a man who founds his cause of action upon an immoral or an illegal act . . . .[*]

Lord Mansfield, 1775.

SECTION 1. INCAPACITY

Recall that one of the requirements for a validly formed and enforceable contract is that all parties have the requisite capacity, the notion being only those with the ability to understand the import of their acts should be bound by their contractual undertakings. Generally, everyone is presumed to have the capacity and power to contract. However, certain classifications warrant special treatment under the law. Among those are children (or minors) and mentally incompetent.

A. INFANCY

The minority incapacity doctrine provides, with certain exceptions, anyone under the age of majority may disaffirm his contracts at his election. The long-accepted rationale for this doctrine has been that children lack the ability to understand and appreciate the consequences of their acts, and thus should not be inextricably bound by the consequences of their youthful follies. Moreover, the rationale posits that because of their lack of capacity to understand the nature of their acts, children are vulnerable to overreaching by adults who would otherwise take advantage of their naivete.

STERNLIEB V. NORMANDIE NATIONAL SECURITIES CORP.
Court of Appeals of New York
188 N.E. 726 (1934).

CRANE, Judge.

Again we have the troublesome question arising from the repudiation by a young gentleman, just under twenty-one, of his contract of purchase. On the 21st day of September, 1929, the plaintiff purchased from the defendant five shares of the capital stock of the Bank of United States and of the Bankus Corporation, for which he paid $990. In his complaint he alleges that he was under twenty-one years of age. After the stock had dropped in value until it was worthless, this young plaintiff further alleges that on the 14th day of September, 1932, he notified the defendant that he rescinded his purchase, and that he was ready to tender and return the certificates.

[*] *Holman v. Johnson*, 98 Eng. Rep. 1120, 1121 (K.B. 1775).

In its answer the defendant as a defense alleges that the plaintiff falsely and fraudulently represented and warranted to the defendant before and at the time of purchase he was over twenty-one years of age, and that the defendant relied upon these statements in parting with the stock.

The action was brought in the Municipal Court of the city of New York. The plaintiff moved to strike out the defense. The motion was denied, and affirmed, on appeal, by the Appellate Term. The Appellate Division, however, reversed this action of the two lower courts and has certified to this court the following question: "Is the separate and distinct defense set forth in the answer herein sufficient in law?"

That young men, nearly twenty-one years of age, actively engaged in business, can at will revoke any or all of their business transactions and obligations, thereby causing loss to innocent parties dealing with them, upon the assumption or even the assurance that they were of age, has not appealed to some courts, and has been adopted without much enthusiasm by others. This state from the earliest days has followed the common-law doctrine, adopted at a time when young men were not so actively engaged in trade and in lucrative occupations as at present. The opportunities for making a living by barter and sale were not so numerous for them as now.

At common law a male infant attains his majority when he becomes twenty-one years of age, and all unexecuted contracts made by him before that date, except for necessaries, while not absolutely void, are voidable at his election. In an action upon a contract made by an infant, he is not estopped from pleading his infancy by any representation as to his age made by him to induce another person to contract with him. International Text Book Co. v. Connelly, 206 N. Y. 188, 99 N. E. 722, 42 L. R. A. (N. S.) 1115. Neither could the infant be sued for damages in tort by reason of any false representations made in inducing or procuring the contract. For his torts generally, where they have no basis in any contract relation, an infant is liable, just as any other person would be, but the doctrine is equally well settled that a matter arising *ex contractu*, though infected with fraud, cannot be changed into a tort, in order to charge an infant, by a change of the remedy. Collins v. Gifford, 203 N. Y. 465, 96 N. E. 721, 38 L. R. A. (N. S.) 202, Ann. Cas. 1913A, 969. The only difference between an executory and an executed contract appears to be, that in the former the infant may disaffirm at any time short of the period of the statute of limitations, unless by some act he has ratified the contract, whereas in the latter, he must disaffirm within a reasonable time after becoming of age, or his silence will be considered a ratification.

This case pertains to an executed contract for the purchase of stock which the plaintiff has disaffirmed within a reasonable time. The distinction which the appellant would have us make between these well-established authorities and the present case is the fact that the infant is here the plaintiff seeking relief from the courts and should do equity before obtaining relief. That is, while as a defendant the courts will protect him from further liability on his contracts, they will not aid him in getting back money or property which will give him profit or gain through his fraudulent representations regarding his age. This was the view taken by the Appellate Division of the Second Department in Falk v. MacMasters, 197 App. Div. 357, 188 N. Y. S. 795.

This court, however, has not gone so far. The nearest approach to the point is Rice v. Butler, 160 N. Y. 578, 55 N. E. 275, 47 L. R. A. 303, 73 Am. St. Rep. 703. In that case the infant was a plaintiff seeking to recover installments paid upon a bicycle which he offered to return. The court recognized the right of the infant to rescind his bargain and get back his money, insisting, however, that he must pay for the use of, or wear and tear on, the machine. The defendant was allowed to deduct this from the money paid by the infant.

The same principle was followed in Myers v. Hurley Motor Co., 273 U. S. 18, 47 S. Ct. 277, 71 L. Ed. 515, 50 A. L. R. 1181, where it was held that a contract made by an infant, induced by his fraudulent representations of his age, may be disaffirmed by him and an action maintained to recover money paid under it. However, the infant must do equity and make restitution, not only of the profits and advantages which he has received, if possible, but also for the use or deterioration of property, if it is to be returned to the defendant. In that case, a young man, twenty years of age, represented that he was twenty-four, and contracted to buy a Hudson touring car, on which he had made certain installment payments. After becoming of age, he disaffirmed his contract and demanded the return of the money paid, offering to return the car. The Supreme Court held while he was entitled to the relief asked, the defendant was also entitled to recoup out of the infant's money damages for deterioration of the car, or the value of its use. In Rice v. Butler, supra, there was no allegation or proof of false and fraudulent representations as to his age by the infant. In Myers v. Hurley Motor Co., supra, the fraud was part of the defense. We do not see how the allegation of fraud justifies any distinction of principle. It is a mere element or feature of the case. The fundamental principle is the same, whether the infant be plaintiff or defendant. He may repudiate and rescind his contract upon becoming of age, whether he has made false representations regarding his years or not, and in any instance, the party with whom he had his dealings is entitled to recoup under certain circumstances.

That the false representation regarding age does not prevent rescission, even when the infant be the plaintiff, is the holding of the courts in the majority of our states. . . .

Some of the state courts, however, have taken a different view, and find that fraudulent representations regarding age estop an infant from maintaining an action for relief. Pinnacle Motor Co. v. Daugherty, 231 Ky. 626, 21 S.W. (2d) 1001; La Rosa v. Nichols, 92 N. J. Law, 375, 105 A. 201, 6 A. L. R. 412; Tuck v. Payne, 159 Tenn. 192, 17 S.W.(2d) 8.

Like so many questions of policy, there is much to be said upon both sides, and the necessities of one period of time are not always those of another. The law, from time out of mind, has recognized that infants must be protected from their own folly and improvidence. It is not always flattering to our young men in college and in business, between the ages of eighteen and twenty-one, to refer to them as infants, and yet this is exactly what the law considers them in their mental capacities and abilities to protect themselves in ordinary transactions and business relationships. That many young people under twenty-one years of age are improvident and reckless is quite evident, but these defects in judgment are by no means confined to the young. There is another side to the question. As long as young men and women, under twenty-one years of age, having the semblance and appearance of adults, are forced to make a living and enter into business transactions, how are the persons dealing with them to be protected if the infant's word cannot be taken or recognized at law? Are business men to deal with young people at their peril? Well, the law is as it is, and the duty of this court is to give force and effect to the decisions as we find them. . . .

We, therefore, conclude that the law of this state, in accordance with the trend of most of the authorities, is to the effect that the defense pleaded in the answer is insufficient and was properly stricken out by the Appellate Division.

The order should, therefore, be affirmed, with costs.

POUND, C. J., and LEHMAN, KELLOGG, O'BRIEN, HUBBS, and CROUCH, JJ., concur.

Order affirmed.

NOTES AND QUESTIONS:

1. As the *Sternlieb* court points out, the minority incapacity doctrine requires adults deal with minors at their own peril. The minor's ability to disaffirm a contract is a one-way street, meaning that the adult on the other end of the transaction does not have a corresponding right to disaffirm the contract if the minor is perfectly content to live with it. Despite the *Sternlieb's* court's recognition that "infants" under the age of 21 are improvident and reckless, in the early 1970s most jurisdictions lowered the age of majority to 18 to coincide with the lowering of the voting age and the military draft age.

2. Are the policies outlined before the *Sternlieb* case being furthered in light of the facts?

3. What are the exceptions to the rule regarding minors' liabilities for their contracts?

4. How should fraudulent misrepresentations of age factor into the minority incapacity doctrine?

VALENCIA V. WHITE
Court of Appeals of Arizona, Division 2
654 P.2d 287 (1982).

BIRDSALL, Judge.

The appellee, Valencia, commenced this action in the trial court seeking an injunction to prohibit the sale of his truck-tractor, upon which the appellant, White, claimed an artisan's lien (A.R.S. § 33-1021 et seq.), and for return of the tractor. He alleged fraud in Count Two of his complaint, and the return of a trailer and damages for loss of use of his tractor resulting from the alleged fraud in Count Three. The trial court dismissed Counts Two and Three at the conclusion of the appellee's evidence, and no cross-appeal has been taken.

The appellants (hereinafter referred to as appellant) filed a counterclaim alleging that the appellee owed $13,783 on open account for repairs to his tractor, trailer and other trucking business vehicles. Counts Two and Three of the counterclaim sought alternative quantum meruit relief and a lien on the tractor.

In his reply to the counterclaim, in addition to denying the open account liability, the appellee asserted that he lacked the capacity to contract because of his minority. Actually, the original complaint filed November 10, 1977, was filed by the appellee's mother as his guardian ad litem and the appellee was substituted as plaintiff sometime after he became 18 on November 20, 1977.

The trial to the court without a jury resulted in the following judgment:

> The above-referenced matter being under advisement, the undersigned now finds and ORDERS as follows:
>
> 1. That the Plaintiff was a minor at the time the parties entered into the contract at issue and as such may repudiate the contract if the contract was not for necessities.
>
> 2. That the services provided by the Defendant to the Plaintiff minor were performed for the benefit of the Plaintiff's business.
>
> 3. That the Plaintiff owned a business but his support was provided by his parents and as such the contract was not entered into for necessities.
>
> 4. That the services not being for necessities, the minor may therefore repudiate the contract. The case cited by the Defendant, Porter v. Wilson, 106 N.G. (sic, N.H.) 270, 209 A.2d 730, 12 A.L.R.3d 1247 is the minority view and is not followed in Arizona. Worman Motor Co. v. Hill, 54 Ariz. 227 [, 94] P.2d [865] (1939).
>
> 5. That the law provides the Court must restore the parties as close as possible to the status quo.
>
> 6. That the minor will be restored to his original position by the Defendant returning the Seven Thousand One Hundred ($7,100.00) and No/100 Dollars which the Plaintiff paid to the Defendant.
>
> 7. The Defendant cannot be fully restored to his original position because the engine upon which he performed services has been damaged by the minor's acts. As a result thereof, the disassembled engine presently in the possession of the Defendant may be retained by the Defendant as a restoration to the status quo.
>
> 8. The minor cannot recover for his loss of business since these are contractual remedies which cannot be recovered without the existence of a contract.
>
> 9. The contract being disaffirmed, the Defendant cannot recover on his counterclaim.

The Plaintiff is, therefore, awarded judgment against the Defendant in the amount of Seven Thousand One Hundred ($7,100.00) and No/100 Dollars plus taxable costs incurred herein.

We reverse and remand.

The questions presented on appeal are (1) whether a minor who owns and successfully operates a business may disaffirm contracts for necessary expenses of that business and (2) if he may so disaffirm, what are the rights between the parties?

. . . . Turning now to the issues raised by the appellant, we commence with a factual background. The appellee was a sophomore in high school, 17 years old, when his father established him in the trucking business in 1976 by giving him two truck-tractor semi-trailer rigs. The appellee hired drivers, secured jobs hauling produce and managed the business at a profit, as much as $26,000 in 1978. The appellee was single and lived at home with his parents, although his father left the home in December, 1976. He was furnished his food, clothing, and housing during his minority by his parents (his father continued to support the family although not living in the home).

The appellant owned and operated a garage in Nogales for the repair of motor vehicles, including large trucks and trailers. He serviced and repaired the appellee's equipment from 1976 to July, 1977, when their disagreements commenced. In December, 1976, the appellee brought in one of his trucks with a major engine problem and the appellant agreed to replace its GMC engine with a Cummins to be built by the appellant. The charge for this engine, approximately $10,700, was the major item on the open account. The engine was installed and the truck was delivered to the appellee in May, 1977. He experienced troubles with this truck shortly thereafter and returned it to the appellant. The evidence was in conflict as to whether the new engine, other mechanical defects, or misuse, caused this breakdown. The trial court found that the minor's acts caused the damage to the engine. Since there is evidence to support this finding of fact it is binding on appeal. K & K Mfg., Inc. v. Union Bank, 129 Ariz. 7, 628 P.2d 44 (App.1981). Periodic payments by the appellee on the account totaled $7,100, resulting in a balance of about $12,900 owing to the appellant except for the disaffirmance of the contract.

After the commencement of the action the truck and trailer were returned to the appellee, but the appellant retained the damaged engine, which had been disassembled for repair, and the radiator and transmission, which had been removed from the truck in order to determine what was wrong with the engine.

The appellant first argues that the garage bill was a necessity and the appellee cannot disaffirm. We disagree.

The trial court found that the services performed for the appellee by the appellant were not necessities of the minor. Whether contracts of a minor are for necessities is ultimately a question of fact if there is some reasonable basis upon which the goods or services furnished could be considered necessaries. 42 Am.Jur.2d Infants § 68; Haynie v. Dicus, 210 Ark. 1092, 199 S.W.2d 954 (1947). Where the contract is for a purpose benefiting the minor's employment or business there is a question to be decided upon the particular facts and circumstances of each case. See Annot. 56 A.L.R.3d 1335 § 4, p. 1345; Bancredit, Inc. v. Bethea, 65 N.J.Super. 538, 168 A.2d 250 (1961). Although the judgment does not expressly state whether this finding was intended to be one of fact or law, we will consider it to be a finding of fact, and the record supports the finding. Since the appellee was provided board, room, clothing, medical needs and education, it was not necessary that he engage in business. We cannot fault this reasoning. The appellant argues that Worman Motor Co. v. Hill, 54 Ariz. 227, 94 P.2d 865, 124 A.L.R. 1363 (1939) contains language supporting his position:

> The evidence does not show for what purpose the plaintiff used the automobile. It does not even show what his employment was. In the oral argument, as we recall, his business was stated to be that of picking cotton. But, even so, the evidence fails to show the car was necessary for him to go to and from his work, or for what purpose it was being used. For all we know, it may have been used only as a pleasure car. 54 Ariz. at 236-237, 94 P.2d 865.

These observations of the supreme court follow a quotation from Braham & Co. v. Zittel, 232 App.Div. 406, 250 N.Y.S. 44 (1931), which recognizes the rule we have already stated, i.e., whether an item is a necessity for a minor must be determined on the facts of each case, and then states there was no evidence in that case to support the minor's need. The Arizona Supreme Court merely found the same lack of record in Worman.

The appellant next contends the filing of the complaint ratified the contract. Again we disagree. In the complaint the appellee alleged his minority and alleged that the lien claimed on the tractor "is null and void" because he was a minor and incapable of contracting. In his reply to the counterclaim, he again alleged lack of capacity to contract because of minority. Although the complaint arose out of the contract, the appellee did not seek to enforce the contract or gain any benefits from it.

The appellant argues further that claims for attorney fees in each count of the complaint, pursuant to A.R.S. § 12-341.01, constitute a ratification. Since the complaint arises out of the contract these claims may properly be made. Amphitheater Public Schools v. Eastman, 117 Ariz. 559, 574 P.2d 47 (1977). Even if the contract is disaffirmed, this is an action arising out of a contract. There has been no ratification.

The appellant's last contention concerns the trial court's attempt to restore the parties to a "status quo" after disaffirmance. He argues that requiring him to return monies paid on the account and refusing to allow him any remuneration for the services performed was error. We agree.

The trial court correctly recognized that the New Hampshire case of Porter v. Wilson, 106 N.H. 270, 209 A.2d 730, 13 A.L.R.3d 1247 (1965), adopts a minority view that a minor who disaffirms a contract may be held liable for benefits received even though they are not necessaries and even though the benefits cannot be returned in kind. The court in Porter held that the minor must pay for legal services furnished him in a guardianship matter, and his liability was the reasonable value of such services that were of benefit to him and not the amount he had agreed to pay or that had been charged. The matter was remanded to the trial court to determine that amount, which we understand could still be the same amount charged if the trial court found that was the reasonable value of those services.

The New Hampshire court itself recognized that this "benefit rule" represents a minority view but found that it was a doctrine which has received approval of those who have given the matter serious consideration, citing 2 Williston on Contracts § 238, p. 43 (3d Ed. Jaeger 1959):

> In some states the ordinary rule prevailing in regard to necessaries has been extended so far as to hold an infant bound by his contracts, where he fails to restore what he has received under them to the extent of the benefit actually derived by him from what he has received from the other party to the transaction. This seems to offer a flexible rule which will prevent imposition upon the infant and also tend to prevent the infant from imposing to any serious degree upon others.

Except for the citation of Williston and a 1933 note at 81 U.Pa.L.Rev. 731, Porter relies only upon prior New Hampshire cases. The benefit rule has also been followed in Minnesota. Berglund v. American Multigraph Sales Co., 135 Minn. 67, 160 N.W. 191 (1916); Kelly v. Furlong, 194 Minn. 465, 261 N.W. 460 (1935). Both of these Minnesota decisions are cited with approval in Worman Motor Co. v. Hill, supra. The trial court concluded that Worman followed the majority rule that the minor must account only for property that he still has in his possession and notwithstanding that he has wasted, consumed or destroyed it, he can recover what he has paid. See Whitman v. Allen, 123 Me. 1, 121 A. 160, 36 A.L.R. 776 (1923). We understand Worman to have adopted instead the minority rule and aligned Arizona with Minnesota and New Hampshire. In Worman the minor traded his Plymouth for a Ford and financed the balance. The trade-in allowance of the Plymouth was $275. The minor then sold his equity in the Ford for $45, with the purchaser assuming the minor's financing obligation. The trial court gave the minor judgment for $275 when he disaffirmed the transaction. (The Plymouth had been sold by Worman.) The supreme court reduced the judgment by $45, the amount received by the minor. The Worman trial court had used the majority rule-since the minor no longer had the Ford he was not required to account for it and was entitled to the value of his Plymouth which the dealer could not return. However, the supreme court found he had benefited by $45 which, upon disaffirmance, he should not be entitled to keep.

If there is any doubt that Arizona adopted the then minority rule and we are thus deciding a case of first impression, we would be persuaded that the rule which requires a minor to account for the benefit he has received is much the better rule. The Court of Appeals of Ohio has observed that:

> At a time when we see young persons between 18 and 21 years of age demanding and assuming more responsibilities in their daily lives; when we see such persons emancipated, married, and raising families; when we see such persons charged with the responsibility for committing crimes; when we see such persons being sued in tort claims for acts of negligence; when we see such persons subject to military service; when we see such persons engaged in business and acting in almost all other respects as an adult, it

> seems timely to re-examine the case law pertaining to contractual rights and responsibilities of infants to see if the law as pronounced and applied by the courts should be redefined. Haydocy Pontiac, Inc. v. Lee, 19 Ohio App.2d 217, 250 N.E.2d 898, 900 (1969).

Other state courts have adopted the Minnesota rule in varying degrees. See Pankas v. Bell, 413 Pa. 494, 198 A.2d 312, 17 A.L.R.3d 855 (1964) (minor enjoined from violating covenant not to compete); Scalone v. Talley Motors, Inc., 3 App.Div.2d 674, 158 N.Y.S.2d 615 (1957) (minor held liable for depreciation of the property in his possession); Sacco v. Schallus, 11 N.J.Super. 197, 78 A.2d 143 (1950) (minor required to make an accounting in a partnership dissolution); See Also Annot. 12 A.L.R.3d 1174. Under the trial court's judgment in the instant case the appellant is not only precluded from recovering for parts and labor furnished the appellee in his going, successful business, he is required to repay monies paid to him on account of those services. In return he is only permitted to retain a disassembled engine that was damaged by the appellee's acts.

No evidence suggests that the appellant took advantage of the appellee because of his age, lack of experience or judgment. Likewise no evidence suggests that the contract was disadvantageous to the appellee. Absent such evidence, the rule adopted in Worman must be properly applied.

In order to properly apply the rule in this case the trial court should have determined what benefits, if any, the minor actually received from the entire transaction. The only evidence presented in this regard is that the reasonable value of the parts and labor, including the Cummins engine, was $19,998.76. The parts and labor furnished the minor by the appellant were of benefit to him in that amount. The repair of the minor's business vehicles enabled him to successfully operate his trucking business. In addition to showing the profits from that business the evidence shows he purchased a pickup truck and a dragster from those profits. Obviously the parts and labor cannot be returned in kind to the appellant. Likewise the Cummins engine, having been damaged by acts attributable to the minor, cannot be returned in anywhere near the same condition as when it was acquired from the appellant. See 42 Am.Jur.2d Infants § 104, p. 103; Dobbs, Remedies § 13.4; Berglund v. American Multigraph Sales Co., supra.

We find that to restore both parties to a status quo, the disassembled engine and the other parts in the possession of the appellant should be returned to the appellee; that the appellee received benefits having a value to him of $19,998.76; that the $7,100 paid by the appellee should be credited against the value of the benefits, leaving a balance of $12,898.71 which the appellee must pay to the appellant.

We reverse and remand with directions to enter judgment in favor of the appellants and against the appellee, in that amount and to order the return of the engine and other parts to the appellee.

HOWARD, C.J., and LILLIAN S. FISHER, Superior Court Judge, concur.

NOTES AND QUESTIONS:

1. Note the different approaches regarding the minor's liability for restitution following dissaffirmance of a contract. Which is the better approach?

2. *See* Restatement (Second) of Contracts § 14 (Infants) (1981).

3. For further examination of the minority incapacity doctrine, *see* Juanda Lowder Daniel, *Virtually Mature: Examining the Policy of Minors' Incapacity to Contract Through the Cyberscope*, 43 GONZ. L. REV. 239 (2008).

B. MENTAL INCAPACITY

SIMMONS FIRST NATIONAL BANK V. LUZADER
Supreme Court of Arkansas
438 S.W.2d 25 (1969).

HARRIS, Chief Justice.

This appeal involves the validity of a written contract entered into by N.F. Yarbrough and his nephew and his wife, Dewey Luzader and Anna Pearl Luzader, apellees herein. The instrument provided that the Luzaders should have $12,000.00, which was on deposit with the Southern Federal Savings and Loan Association in Pine Bluff, if appellees gave him a home until his death. A factual background is as follows:

Yarbrough's wife died on September 19, 1966, Mr. Yarbrough being 84 years of age at that time. On the day following Mrs. Yarbrough's death, and also a few days later, Yarbrough, together with his brother, Claude, went to the Southern Federal office for the purpose of transferring savings accounts. Yarbrough held four or more such accounts, which totaled more than $49,000.00. One account, in the amount of $7,000.00, was placed entirely in the brother's name. Remaining accounts were changed to require the signatures of both brothers in order to make withdrawals. Subsequently, Frank (N. F.) Yarbrough returned to the Southern Federal office on one other occasion to discuss the accounts with the company secretary.

Yarbrough had long expressed the desire to live with the Luzaders in the event of the death of his wife, and he went to the Luzader home at Leola, Grant County, Arkansas, three days after the funeral of Mrs. Yarbrough. On October 25, Mr. Yarbrough, accompanied by Anna Pearl, went to the office of Pierce A. Reeder, postmaster at Leola, and a contract was handed to Reeder, Mrs. Luzader requesting the postmaster to "notarize" it. Reeder testified that he read it, and concluded that it should be drawn up in a form where it could be witnessed by two other people.[1] When Mrs. Luzader left to find two persons, Reeder typed up the agreement, and made it ready for signatures. The postmaster testified that he copied the paper handed him, and added the part about the presence of witnesses. Mr. Yarbrough then executed the typed contract, and the two witnesses signed their names.[2]

---

[1] Reeder was under the impression that the instrument was a will.

[2] "When and if Dewey Luzader and his wife, Anna Pearl Luzader gives me a home until my death, it is understood that they shall have the sum of Twelve Thousand Dollars ($12,000.00) of my money on account in

On December 5, 1966, Mr. Luzader petitioned the Probate Court for the appointment of a guardian for Yarbrough, the allegations being that the latter was incompetent, because of senility and old age. On December 9, the court held Yarbrough incompetent, and appointed Simmons First National Bank of Pine Bluff as guardian. At this hearing, Claude Yarbrough relinquished the interest in his brother's savings accounts, and the court awarded appellees the sum of $150.00 per month for keeping the old man. Yarbrough died on August 21, 1967, and appellant bank was named administrator of the estate. The Luzaders filed a claim for $12,000.00 based on the written contract heretofore mentioned. The bank refused to allow this claim, but on hearing, same was allowed by the Probate Court. From the judgment allowing the claim in the amount of $12,000.00, the bank brings this appeal. For reversal, it is asserted that the court erred in holding that the administrator had failed to overcome the presumption of Yarbrough's competency, and it is also alleged that the contract was unenforceable for failure of consideration.

All parties agree that the document in question was not a conveyance, or will, but was a contract. The court, in its written opinion at the conclusion of the case, held that the bank had 'failed to overcome the presumption of competency that follows the execution of a written instrument.' Appellant disputes that there is such a presumption, and points out that the Chancellor cited no case in support thereof. We disagree with this argument. In Dalton v. Polster, 200 Ark. 168, 138 S.W.2d 64, this court said:

> Having pleaded her incompetency, the burden was on appellants to show it. Incompetency is never presumed, but the contrary is.[3]

In Harris v. Harris, 236 Ark. 676, 370 S.W.2d 121, we commented:

> There is a presumption of law that every man is sane, fully competent and capable of understanding the nature and effect of his contracts.

. . . . As a matter of proving the mental incompetency of Yarbrough, appellant relies upon the testimony of Claude Yarbrough, the brother of the deceased, Connie Haner, a niece of N. F. Yarbrough, and Hattie Bea Blaser, Secretary of the Southern Federal Savings and Loan Association of Pine Bluff. Mrs. Haner testified that she probably saw Yarbrough twice between the time of his wife's death and the execution of the contract with the Luzaders. When interrogated as to her uncle's mental condition at the time of his wife's death, she replied:

> Just like he always was the last few years. Just a little, well, you'd have to know Uncle Frank to know him. He was just sort of here and there.

Mrs. Haner said that he could remember some things pretty well, but could not remember others; that he had "been like that for years." When asked if he had an understanding of the nature and extent of his property, the witness said:

---

the Southern Federal Loan and Savings at Pine Bluff, Arkansas or wherever it may be at the time of my death. Signed this 25th day of October 1966. Signed /s/ N. F. YarbroughIn the presence of the following witnesses and in the presence of each other on this 25th day of October 1966./s/ Olen Biggs Leola/s/ Austin Lamb Leola"

[3] Our Emphasis.

> Well, he knew he had his money and we talked about it and different things like that. He liked to talk about his money to me. . . . He didn't know how much he had, really. He didn't know that, no.

She said that in April, 1967, a relative had died, and she talked to her uncle in Gurdon; that he told her at that time that he wanted to go to Pine Bluff, and get his money out of the bank, because Anna Pearl had written a paper that would give her $12,000.00, and he didn't want her to have it. She also said that he desired to move back to Pine Bluff. The witness made clear that she was not saying that her uncle had been compelled to sign the paper. 'He said that she wrote out a paper and I signed it that I would give her this money.' Mrs. Haner did agree that Yarbrough had been anxious to live with his nephew and wife at the time of the death of his wife.

Claude C. Yarbrough lives in Little Rock. He testified that he went to the N. F. Yarbrough home in Pine Bluff the morning after Mrs. Yarbrough's death, and "he (N. F. Yarbrough) told me, as he had previously, that he wanted to sign over all of his savings in my name." They went to the Southern Federal Savings and Loan Association, and $7,000.00 was transferred to the witness; the balance was not transferred, because he did not have the "deposit slips." N. F. Yarbrough did not know where these were located, but a stepdaughter, who arrived the next day from Illinois, produced them, the balance amounting to about $42,000.00. The Yarbroughs returned to the savings and loan office, and these amounts were placed in joint accounts for the two brothers, with right of survivorship; during their lifetime, the money could not be drawn out without both signatures. Claude testified that his brother did not know how much money he had with the savings and loan, and he said that N. F. argued with the secretary of the association that he only had $21,000.00. The witness stated that N. F.'s mind was "bad then," and it kept deteriorating until he was completely blank the last month or two of his life. While Claude testified that, at the probate hearing, he agreed to turn over all of these accounts to the guardian, it appeared on cross-examination that he might have been a little reluctant to do so.

The strongest evidence offered by appellant was that of Hattie Bea Blaser, the secretary for the savings and loan association. She said that N. F. Yarbrough, accompanied by Claude, came to the office on September 20, and informed her that his wife had passed away the night before, and he would like to transfer his money to his brother's name. She told him that he would need his pass book and certificates of deposit, and he then asked how much money he had. After checking the accounts, Mrs. Blaser advised that there was $42,000.00 in four different accounts. Referring to the deceased, the witness stated:

> . . . I've known him for several years. He was a peculiar person in a certain sense. One account he would carry in a different name. One would be Newton F. and one would be in N. Frank Yarbrough or N. F. Yarbrough. He always, you know, in opening a new account, would use his name in a different manner.

Mrs. Blaser said that he didn't seem to have any idea of how much he had on deposit, and that it was her personal opinion that he didn't understand the effect of transferring the accounts. She added that, for the last three or four years, N. F. Yarbrough had not been as alert as she had known him to be in years past; that for the last two years, there never was a time when he knew what he was doing. She later modified this statement, saying that, during that period, she did not believe him able to take care of a business matter.

Mrs. Luzader testified that Yarbrough came to Leola to live with the Luzader family three days after his wife's death; that he died on August 21, 1967, in a hospital, after suffering a stroke on July 7. She detailed the necessary duties in taking care of Mr. Yarbrough, who, after a few months, lost control over his bodily functions. Appellee said that sometimes the bathroom would have to be cleaned two or three times a morning, and that this lack of control was evidenced in the family automobile; that it was difficult to get Yarbrough to a barber and back home without changing his clothes; that her 16-year-old son would bathe him, and they would dress him. She said that Yarbrough was happy in the home, but embarrassed.

Mrs. Luzader testified that she received the $150.00 per month allowed by the probate court for Mr. Yarbrough's maintenance, and that Yarbrough paid her an additional $150.00 per month from his railroad retirement check after the first of the year, 1967.

Glenn Paul Luzader, the son, testified that on one occasion, when they were sitting in the den, he heard his Uncle Frank tell his mother that Yarbrough wanted her to have the $12,000.00 after he passed away.

Iona Jones, daughter of the Luzaders, testified that she had many times, as a child, heard her uncle express the desire to live with her parents if he out-lived his wife; he did not want to go to a home for old folks. She said that she would visit on weekends following his move to Leola, and that he had told her that he was very thankful that he didn't have to go to a rest home, but could spend the rest of his life with her folks.

Evelyn Smith, the housekeeper, had been going to the Luzader home one day per week for years, but after Yarbrough moved in, Mrs. Smith worked two days per week. She said that she helped Mrs. Luzader rearrange the furniture, giving Mr. Yarbrough the bedroom closest to the bathroom, and that she had many conversations with him while she was ironing. Mrs. Smith stated that he would mention that he did not want to go to a rest home, and that he wanted Mrs. Luzader to have a part of his savings.[4]

We agree with the Chancellor that the evidence was insufficient to establish the incompetency of Mr. Yarbrough. It is noticeable that no medical evidence was introduced that Yarbrough was incompetent, though, according to Mrs. Blaser, he appeared, in her opinion, to have been unable to attend to business matters for the last two years before his death. Medical testimony of incompetency, though certainly not essential, is important and

[4] H. B. Atwood, trust officer for Simmons First National Bank, produced a letter which he had received from Mrs. Martha Frances Grothe Lyche, a stepdaughter of N. F. Yarbrough, in which she said that her mother and stepfather did not want to be placed in a nursing home; that Mr. Yarbrough had always desired to live with the Luzaders, and that the Luzaders were giving him a good home. The introduction of the letter was objected to as hearsay, and the Chancellor reserved his ruling. He never did pass upon the admissibility of the evidence, but apparently did not consider it, since it is not mentioned in a rather lengthy opinion rendered by the trial court.

potent evidence in this type of case, and, in Harwell v. Garrett, 239 Ark. 551, 393 S.W.2d 256, we emphasized that not a single medical witness testified that Frank Garrett was incompetent.

The fact that Yarbrough did not seem to understand the result of a joint account, or did not know just how much money he had, is, in our view, of no great significance under the circumstances of this case. We daresay there are many people in their 80's, who have but little knowledge of business affairs, and who have difficulty in remembering details. Certainly, Claude Yarbrough must have considered that his brother was competent to make the changes in the accounts, or he would not have permitted this to be done. It would appear, according to the testimony of Mrs. Blaser, that N. F. Yarbrough had acted peculiarly for a number of years. She mentioned that each time he opened an account, he would use a different version of his own name, but peculiarities do not establish one's mental incompetence. In Harwell v. Garrett, supra, in quoting from Volume 1, Page on Wills, § 12.37, we said:

> The fact that the testator was filthy, forgetful and eccentric, or that he was miserly and filthy, or that he was blasphemous, filthy, believed in witchcraft, and had dogs eat at the same table with him or that he was filthy, frequently refused to eat, and would lie in bed with his clothes on for two weeks at a time, or that he would leave his home only at night, and would count or recount his money, or that he was high tempered and violent, or was irritable and profane, or that testator thought that others were plotting against him and was afraid to go out in the dark, or that he was inattentive when spoken to and mumbled when trying to talk, does not establish lack of capacity.

It is readily apparent that Mr. Yarbrough's acts in no wise compared with the language just quoted, and we have many times said that being forgetful and eccentric does not establish lack of mental capacity.

Of course, it is necessary that appellant show the lack of Yarbrough's mental capacity to enter into the contract at the time this instrument was executed. Here, there is not one line of evidence relative to that point offered by the appellant; in fact, the only effort was an attempt to show that Yarbrough was mentally deficient thirty-eight days before he signed the agreement. In Petree v. Petree, 211 Ark. 654, 201 S.W.2d 1009, Mrs. Anna Petree executed a contract on June 22, 1942. Lay evidence was offered that she was not able to transact business in June, 1942, and medical evidence was offered to the same effect, although the doctor so testifying did not examine Mrs. Petree thoroughly until September or October of that year. The physician stated that her condition had not come on suddenly; however, he was unwilling to testify that she was incompetent in June. We held Mrs. Petree competent. In the instant litigation, we reiterate that there is not one iota of evidence to the effect that Mr. Yarbrough was mentally incompetent in October, 1966.

This court has said that mental weakness, though not to the extent of making one incapable of executing a deed, may cause a person to be more susceptible to fraud, duress, or undue influence, and that when that mental incapacity is coupled with any of those conditions, a contract may be voidable. Cain v. Mitchell, 179 Ark. 556, 17 S.W.2d 282. Here again, there is no proof of fraud, duress or undue influence. One paragraph in appellant's brief is devoted to the argument of undue influence, and this is based upon a comment by Mrs. Blaser that it was her personal feeling that Yarbrough was easily influenced by anyone close to him. It hardly seems necessary to state that that testimony comes nowhere near establishing that Mrs. Luzader exercised undue influence upon the uncle.

It is argued that appellees were well paid for their services in taking care of Mr. Yarbrough by virtue of the fact that they received $300.00 per month. One hundred and fifty dollars ($150.00) of this was allowed by the Probate Court, and the other $150.00 was paid to Mrs. Luzader by Yarbrough from his retirement check. Appellant says that certainly Mr. Yarbrough did not contemplate, in agreeing that they should receive $12,000.00, that appellees would also receive $300.00 each month; that accordingly, the consideration for the agreement fails. We do not know what Mr. Yarbrough contemplated, but the evidence certainly indicates that he was quite devoted to the Luzaders.

It is established by the evidence, in fact, undisputed, that Mr. Yarbrough had a strong aversion to being placed in a nursing, or old folks, home; he expressed the desire many time to live with his nephew and wife. It is likewise established that the Luzaders took care of Mr. Yarbrough, as they agreed to do; in other words, they carried out their part of the agreement....

We find no reversible error.

Affirmed.

NOTES AND QUESTIONS

1. As with the minority incapacity doctrine, the law protects the mentally incompetent from the consequences of his or her acts. The justification for this doctrine is rooted in the requirement of a "meeting of the minds" at the time of contracting, which cannot occur without two competent minds. However, unlike the minority incapacity doctrine, contracts made by mentally incompetent persons may be voidable or void *ab initio*, depending the circumstances. Uniformly, jurisdictions treat as void any contract made by a person subject to a judicial declaration of incompetency. Many jurisdictions treat the judicial declaration as conclusive at all times following the pronouncement of incompetency until terminated by a judicial declaration of restoration. However, in some jurisdictions, a judicial declaration of incompetency serves as a rebuttable presumption of incompetency for contracts made after the judicial declaration.

2. For persons not subject to a judicial declaration of incompetency, most jurisdictions treat contracts made while mentally incompetent as voidable at the option of the incompetent person. However, establishing that a person had a mental defect that impaired his or her capacity to contract can be problematic. Traditionally, many jurisdictions made this determination based on a cognitive test – whether, at the time of contracting, the person understood the nature and consequences of his acts. Later on, some jurisdictions adopted, either in lieu of or in addition to the cognitive test, the volitional test – whether the person had the ability to control his or her actions.

3. Read Restatement (Second) of Contracts §15 (1981). The Restatement reflects an either/or inquiry of mental capacity under both the cognitive test and the volitional test, adding to the volitional inquiry whether the other person has reason to know of such condition. In addition, Restatement §15 includes equitable considerations based on fairness, knowledge of incompetency by the other party and potential hardship to the other party that would result from disaffirming the contract. Most jurisdictions seem to take into account such equitable considerations in the course of determining whether to allow the incompetent to disaffirm the contract.

C. INTOXICATION

VAN HORN V. PERSINGER
Kansas City Court of Appeals, Missouri
215 S.W. 930 (1919).

ELLISON, J.

Plaintiff's action is replevin whereby he seeks to recover the tools and implements of a barber shop, spoken of in evidence as a "barber shop" valued at $325. No bond was given, and the property remained in defendant's possession. Plaintiff was successful both in the justice court and the circuit court, where it was taken on appeal.

The evidence tended to show that defendant was the owner of a barber shop which he sold to plaintiff for $650, on the 1st of September, 1918; that he claimed to have bought it back in a little over a month afterwards for $150 and assuming a debt of plaintiff for $78. Plaintiff denied any knowledge of the latter purchase.

There was abundant evidence tending to show that shortly after plaintiff's purchase from defendant the former became a helpless drunkard, and that, when defendant claimed to have purchased the shop back from him, he was too far gone in his drunken condition to be aware of what he was doing.

On becoming capable for business, plaintiff found defendant in possession claiming to be the owner, and he thereupon denied his title and instituted this action. The chief ground of complaint against the judgment is that, before plaintiff could maintain the action, he should have restored to defendant the consideration paid him for the shop. It does not appear in evidence that plaintiff has the consideration defendant claims to have paid him. The jury must have found that he did not, since they were instructed, at the request of defendant, that if they believed he did, and that he never returned it, the verdict would be for defendant. Under this instruction the jury must have refused to believe that defendant paid plaintiff any money at the time he claimed to have made the purchase while plaintiff was helplessly intoxicated.

There is no foundation for defendant's point that the instructions for plaintiff were inconsistent with the one for defendant just referred to. They did not direct a verdict for plaintiff on any hypothesis submitted. They merely correctly declared, in substance, that, if plaintiff was so drunk at the time of the alleged sale to defendant that he was bereft of understanding and incapable of caring for himself, then the sale was of no effect and, as against plaintiff, transferred no right of property or possession. One of plaintiff's instructions used the word "void" in referring to the sale. Ordinarily "voidable" is the appropriate word but as to this case, in view of plaintiff's insistence that he did not sell to defendant and his instituting the action, the use of the word "void" was not material error.

Referring again to defendant's point that before plaintiff can maintain an action for the property he must restore to defendant the consideration received, we recognize the law that, if one does not intend to be bound by a contract of sale made when he is too drunk to understand what he is doing, he should, when restored to his senses, return the consideration he received (Eaton v. Perry, 29 Mo. 96, 98), yet there is this qualification to be borne in mind, viz., that he must still have that consideration when he recovers his mental responsibility, otherwise if it pass from him when incapable of knowing what became of it, so that he cannot restore it, he would be deprived of the law which has for its object protection to his weakness.

Incapable drunkards and infants are alike in the respect here considered, and the rule applicable to one may well be applied to the other; and, as to the latter, it is well settled that, before he can be denied the right of avoiding his contract on the ground of not restoring the consideration, he must have it at the time he reaches his majority. In the first and third of those cases, it is said that, if the infant has lost or squandered the consideration, he may avoid the contract without returning the consideration or its equivalent

We think the judgment for the right party, and that it should be affirmed.

All concur.

SECTION 2. MISUNDERSTANDING AND MISTAKE

A. MISUNDERSTANDING

RAFFLES V. WICHELHAUS
Court of Exchequer
159 Eng. Rep. 375 (1864).

Declaration. For that it was agreed between the plaintiff and the defendants, to wit, at Liverpool, that the plaintiff should sell to the defendants, and the defendants buy of the plaintiff, certain goods, to wit, 125 bales of Surat cotton, guaranteed middling fair merchant's Dhollorah, to arrive ex "Peerless" from Bombay; and that the cotton should be taken from the quay, and that the defendants would pay the plaintiff for the same at a certain rate, to wit, at the rate of 17 1/2 d. per pound, within a certain time then agreed upon after the arrival of the said goods in England. Averments: that the said goods did arrive by the said ship from Bombay in England, to wit, at Liverpool, and the plaintiff was then and there ready, and willing and offered to deliver the said goods to the defendants, &c. Breach: that the defendants refused to accept the said goods or pay the plaintiff for them.

Plea. That the said ship mentioned in the said agreement was meant and intended by the defendants to be the ship called the "Peerless," which sailed from Bombay, to wit, in October; and that the plaintiff was not ready and willing and did not offer to deliver to the defendants any bales of cotton which arrived by the last mentioned ship, but instead thereof was only ready and willing and offered to deliver to the defendants 125 bales of Surat cotton which arrived by another and different ship, which was also called the "Peerless," and which sailed from Bombay, to wit, in December.

Demurrer, and joinder therein.

Milward, in support of the demurrer. The contract was for the sale of a number of bales of cotton of a particular description, which the plaintiff was ready to deliver. It is immaterial by what ship the cotton was to arrive, so that it was a ship called the "Peerless." The words "to arrive ex' Peerless,"' only mean that if the vessel is lost on the voyage, the contract is to be at an end. [Pollock, C. B. It would be a question for the jury whether both parties meant the same ship called the "Peerless."] That would be so if the contract was for the sale of a ship called the "Peerless"; but it is for the sale of cotton on board a ship of that name. [Pollock, C. B. The defendant only bought that cotton which was to arrive by a particular ship. It may as well be said, that if there is a contract for the purchase of certain goods in warehouse A., that is satisfied by the delivery of goods of the same description in warehouse B.] In that case there would be goods in both warehouses; here it does not appear that the plaintiff had any goods on board the other "Peerless." [Martin, B. It is imposing on the defendant a contract different from that which he entered into. Pollock, C. B. It is like a contract for the purchase of wine coming from a particular estate in France or Spain, where there are two estates of that name.] The defendant has no right to contradict by parol evidence a written contract good upon the face of it. He does not impute misrepresentation or fraud, but only says that he fancied the ship was a different one. Intention is of no avail, unless stated at the time of the contract. [Pollock, C. B. One vessel sailed in October and the other in December.] The time of sailing is no part of the contract.

Mellish (Cohen with him), in support of the plea. There is nothing on the face of the contract to shew that any particular ship called the "Peerless" was meant; but the moment it appears that two ships called the "Peerless" were about to sail from Bombay there is a latent ambiguity, and parol evidence may be given for the purpose of shewing that the defendant meant one "Peerless," and the plaintiff another. That being so, there was no consenus ad idem, and therefore no binding contract. He was then stopped by the Court.

Per Curiam. There must be judgment for the defendants.
Pollock, C. B., Martin, B., and Pigott, B.
Judgment for the defendants.

RESTATEMENT (SECOND) OF CONTRACTS
§ 20. EFFECT OF MISUNDERSTANDING

(1) There is no manifestation of mutual assent to an exchange if the parties attach materially different meanings to their manifestations and

(a) Neither party knows or has reason to know the meaning attached by the other; or

(b) Each party knows or each party has reason to know the meaning attached by the other.

(2) The manifestations of the parties are operative in accordance with the meaning attached to them by one of the parties if

(a) that party does not know of any different meaning attached by the other, and the other knows the meaning attached by the first party; or

(b) that party has no reason to know of any different meaning attached by the other, and the other has reason to know the meaning attached by the first party.

NOTES AND QUESTIONS:

1. In line with Restatement (Second) of Contracts § 20 (1981), only a material misunderstanding will render a contract unenforceable. The cases that follow explore the concept of materiality under the doctrine of mistake.

2. It merits noting the discussion of parol evidence in *Raffles*. We will return to this case when we explore the parameters of contract interpretation.

3. Are *misunderstanding* and *mistake* one and the same?

B. MUTUAL MISTAKE

SHERWOOD V. WALKER
Supreme Court of Michigan
33 N.W. 919 (1887).

MORSE, J.

Replevin for a cow. Suit commenced in justice's court; judgment for plaintiff; appealed to circuit court of Wayne county, and verdict and judgment for plaintiff in that cour. The defendants bring error, and set out 25 assignments of the same.

The main controversy depends upon the construction of a contract for the sale of the cow. The plaintiff claims that the title passed, and bases his action upon such claim. The defendants contend that the contract was executory, and by its terms no title to the animal was acquired by plaintiff. The defendants reside at Detroit, but are in business at Walkerville, Ontario, and have a farm at Greenfield, in Wayne county, upon which were some blooded cattle supposed to be barren as breeders. The Walkers are importers and breeders of polled Angus cattle. The plaintiff is a banker living at Plymouth, in Wayne county. He called upon the defendants at Walkerville for the purchase of some of their stock, but found none there that suited him. Meeting one of the defendants afterwards, he was informed that they had a few head upon their Greenfield farm. He was asked to go out and look at them, with the statement at the time that they were probably barren, and would not breed. May 5, 1886, plaintiff went out to Greenfield, and saw the cattle. A few days thereafter, he called upon one of the defendants with the view of purchasing a cow, known as "Rose 2d of Aberlone." After considerable talk, it was agreed that defendants would telephone Sherwood at his home in Plymouth in reference to the price. The second morning after this talk he was called up by telephone, and the terms of the sale were finally agreed upon. He was to pay five and one-half cents per pound, live weight, fifty pounds shrinkage.

He was asked how he intended to take the cow home, and replied that he might ship her from King's cattle-yard. He requested defendants to confirm the sale in writing, which they did by sending him the following letter:

> WALKERVILLE, May 15, 1886.
>
> T.C. Sherwood, President, etc.-DEAR SIR: We confirm sale to you of the cow Rose 2d of Aberlone, lot 56 of our catalogue, at five and half cents per pound, less fifty pounds shrink. We inclose herewith order on Mr. Graham for the cow. You might leave check with him, or mail to us here, as you prefer.
>
> Yours, truly, HIRAM WALKER & SONS.

The order upon Graham inclosed [*sic*] in the letter read as follows:

> WALKERVILLE, May 15, 1886.
>
> George Graham: You will please deliver at King's cattle-yard to Mr. T.C. Sherwood, Plymouth, the cow Rose 2d of Aberlone, lot 56 of our catalogue. Send halter with the cow, and have her weighed.
>
> Yours truly, HIRAM WALKER & SONS.

On the twenty-first of the same month the plaintiff went to defendants' farm at Greenfield, and presented the order and letter to Graham, who informed him that the defendants had instructed him not to deliver the cow. Soon after, the plaintiff tendered to Hiram Walker, one of the defendants, $80, and demanded the cow. Walker refused to take the money or deliver the cow. The plaintiff then instituted this suit. After he had secured possession of the cow under the writ of replevin, the plaintiff caused her to be weighed by the constable who served the writ, at a place other than King's cattle-yard. She weighed 1,420 pounds.

When the plaintiff, upon the trial in the circuit court, had submitted his proofs showing the above transaction, defendants moved to strike out and exclude the testimony from the case, for the reason that it was irrelevant and did not tend to show that the title to the cow passed, and that it showed that the contract of sale was merely executory. The court refused the motion, and an exception was taken. The defendants then introduced evidence tending to show that at the time of the alleged sale it was believed by both the plaintiff and themselves that the cow was barren and would not breed; that she cost $850 [*sic*]*, and if not barren would be worth from $750 to $1,000; that after the date of the letter, and the order to Graham, the defendants were informed by said Graham that in his judgment the cow was with calf, and therefore they instructed him not to deliver her to plaintiff, and on the twentieth of May, 1886, telegraphed plaintiff what Graham thought about the cow being with calf, and that consequently they could not sell her. The cow had a calf in the month of October following. On the nineteenth of May, the plaintiff wrote Graham as follows:

* Eds. It appears that the court meant $80.

PLYMOUTH, May 19, 1886.

Mr. George Graham, Greenfield-DEAR SIR: I have bought Rose or Lucy from Mr. Walker, and will be there for her Friday morning, nine or ten o'clock. Do not water her in the morning.

Yours, etc., T.C. SHERWOOD.

Plaintiff explained the mention of the two cows in this letter by testifying that, when he wrote this letter, the order and letter of defendants was at his home, and, writing in a hurry, and being uncertain as to the name of the cow, and not wishing his cow watered, he thought it would do no harm to name them both, as his bill of sale would show which one he had purchased. Plaintiff also testified that he asked defendants to give him a price on the balance of their herd at Greenfield, as a friend thought of buying some, and received a letter dated May 17, 1886, in which they named the price of five cattle, including Lucy, at $90, and Rose 2d at $80. When he received the letter he called defendants up by telephone, and asked them why they put Rose 2d in the list, as he had already purchased her. They replied that they knew he had, but thought it would make no difference if plaintiff and his friend concluded to take the whole herd.

The foregoing is the substance of all the testimony in the case.

. . . The defendants submitted a number of requests [for jury instructions] which were refused. The substance of them [was] . . . that if the defendants only agreed to sell a cow that would not breed, then the barrenness of the cow was a condition precedent to passing title, and plaintiff cannot recover. The court also charged the jury that it was immaterial whether the cow was with calf or not. . . .

The refusal to deliver the cow grew entirely out of the fact that, before the plaintiff called upon Graham for her, they discovered she was not barren, and therefore of greater value than they had sold her for. . . .

It appears from the record that both parties supposed this cow was barren and would not breed, and she was sold by the pound for an insignificant sum as compared with her real value if a breeder. She was evidently sold and purchased on the relation of her value for beef, unless the plaintiff had learned of her true condition, and concealed such knowledge from the defendants. Before the plaintiff secured the possession of the animal, the defendants learned that she was with calf, and therefore of great value, and undertook to rescind the sale by refusing to deliver her. The question arises whether they had a right to do so. The circuit judge ruled that this fact did not avoid the sale and it made no difference whether she was barren or not. I am of the opinion that the court erred in this holding. I know that this is a close question, and the dividing line between the adjudicated cases is not easily discerned. But it must be considered as well settled that a party who has given an apparent consent to a contract of sale may refuse to execute it, or he may avoid it after it has been completed, if the assent was founded, or the contract made, upon the mistake of a material fact,-such as the subject-matter of the sale, the price, or some collateral fact materially inducing the agreement; and this can be done when the mistake is mutual. 1 Benj. Sales, §§ 605, 606; Leake, Cont. 339; Story, Sales, (4th Ed.) §§ 377, 148. See, also, Cutts v. Guild, 57 N.Y. 229;

Harvey v. Harris, 112 Mass. 32; Gardner v. Lane, 9 Allen, 492, 12 Allen, 44; Huthmacher v. Harris' Adm'rs, 38 Pa.St. 491; Byers v. Chapin, 28 Ohio St. 300; Gibson v. Pelkie, 37 Mich. 380, and cases cited; Allen v. Hammond, 11 Pet. 63-71.

If there is a difference or misapprehension as to the substance of the thing bargained for; if the thing actually delivered or received is different in substance from the thing bargained for, and intended to be sold,-then there is no contract; but if it be only a difference in some quality or accident, even though the mistake may have been the actuating motive to the purchaser or seller, or both of them, yet the contract remains binding. "The difficulty in every case is to determine whether the mistake or misapprehension is as to the substance of the whole contract, going, as it were, to the root of the matter, or only to some point, even though a material point, an error as to which does not affect the substance of the whole consideration." Kennedy v. Panama, etc., Mail Co., L.R. 2 Q.B. 580, 587. It has been held, in accordance with the principles above stated, that where a horse is bought under the belief that he is sound, and both vendor and vendee honestly believe him to be sound, the purchaser must stand by his bargain, and pay the full price, unless there was a warranty.

It seems to me, however, in the case made by this record, that the mistake or misapprehension of the parties went to the whole substance of the agreement. If the cow was a breeder, she was worth at least $750; if barren, she was worth not over $80. The parties would not have made the contract of sale except upon the understanding and belief that she was incapable of breeding, and of no use as a cow. It is true she is now the identical animal that they thought her to be when the contract was made; there is no mistake as to the identity of the creature. Yet the mistake was not of the mere quality of the animal, but went to the very nature of the thing. A barren cow is substantially a different creature than a breeding one. There is as much difference between them for all purposes of use as there is between an ox and a cow that is capable of breeding and giving milk. If the mutual mistake had simply related to the fact whether she was with calf or not for one season, then it might have been a good sale, but the mistake affected the character of the animal for all time, and for its present and ultimate use. She was not in fact the animal, or the kind of animal, the defendants intended to sell or the plaintiff to buy. She was not a barren cow, and, if this fact had been known, there would have been no contract. The mistake affected the substance of the whole consideration, and it must be considered that there was no contract to sell or sale of the cow as she actually was. The thing sold and bought had in fact no existence. She was sold as a beef creature would be sold; she is in fact a breeding cow, and a valuable one. The court should have instructed the jury that if they found that the cow was sold, or contracted to be sold, upon the understanding of both parties that she was barren, and useless for the purpose of breeding, and that in fact she was not barren, but capable of breeding, then the defendants had a right to rescind, and to refuse to deliver, and the verdict should be in their favor.

The judgment of the court below must be reversed, and a new trial granted, with costs of this court to defendants.

CAMPBELL, C.J., and CHAMPLIN, J., concurred.

SHERWOOD, J., (dissenting.)

I do not concur in the opinion given by my brethren in this case. I think the judgments before the justice and at the circuit were right. I agree with my Brother MORSE that the contract made was not within the statute of frauds, and the payment for the property was not a condition precedent to the passing of the title from the defendants to the plaintiff. And I further agree with him that the plaintiff was entitled to a delivery of the property to him when the suit was brought, unless there was a mistake made which would invalidate the contract, and I can find no such mistake. . . . .

As has already been stated by my brethren, the record shows that the plaintiff is a banker and farmer as well, carrying on a farm, and raising the best breeds of stock, and lived in Plymouth, in the county of Wayne, 23 miles from Detroit; that the defendants lived in Detroit, and were also dealers in stock of the higher grades; that they had a farm at Walkerville, in Canada, and also one in Greenfield in said county of Wayne, and upon these farms the defendants kept their stock. . . . In the spring of 1886 the plaintiff . . . was informed that they had none at Walkerville, "but had a few head left on their farm in Greenfield, and asked the plaintiff to go and see them, stating that in all probability they were sterile and would not breed." . . . [T]he plaintiff . . . went out and looked at the defendants' cattle at Greenfield, and found one called "Rose, Second," which he wished to purchase, and the terms were finally agreed upon . . . . The record further shows that the defendants, when they sold the cow, believed the cow was not with calf, and barren; that from what the plaintiff had been told by defendants (for it does not appear he had any other knowledge or facts from which he could form an opinion) he believed the cow was farrow, but still thought she could be made to breed. The foregoing shows the entire interview and treaty between the parties as to the sterility and qualities of the cow sold to the plaintiff. The cow had a calf in the month of October.

There is no question but that the defendants sold the cow representing her of the breed and quality they believed the cow to be, and that the purchaser so understood it. And the buyer purchased her believing her to be of the breed represented by the sellers, and possessing all the qualities stated, and even more. He believed she would breed. There is no pretense that the plaintiff bought the cow for beef, and there is nothing in the record indicating that he would have bought her at all only that he thought she might be made to breed. Under the foregoing facts,-and these are all that are contained in the record material to the contract,-it is held that because it turned out that the plaintiff was more correct in his judgment as to one quality of the cow than the defendants, and a quality, too, which could not by any possibility be positively known at the time by either party to exist, the contract may be annulled by the defendants at their pleasure. I know of no law, and have not been referred to any, which will justify any such holding, and I think the circuit judge was right in his construction of the contract between the parties.

It is claimed that a mutual mistake of a material fact was made by the parties when the contract of sale was made. There was no warranty in the case of the quality of the animal. When a mistaken fact is relied upon as ground for rescinding, such fact must not only exist at the time the contract is made, but must have been known to one or both of the parties. Where there is no warranty, there can be no mistake of fact when no such fact exists, or, if in existence, neither party knew of it, or could know of it; and that is precisely this case. If the owner of a Hambletonian horse had speeded him, and was only able to make him go a mile in three minutes, and should sell him to another, believing that was his greatest speed, for $300, when the purchaser believed he could go much faster, and made the purchase for that sum, and a few days thereafter, under more favorable circumstances, the horse was driven a mile in 2 min. 16 sec., and was found to be worth $20,000, I hardly think it would be held, either at law or in equity, by any one, that the seller in such case could rescind the contract. The same legal principles apply in each case.

In this case neither party knew the actual quality and condition of this cow at the time of the sale. The defendants say, or rather said, to the plaintiff, "they had a few head left on their farm in Greenfield, and asked plaintiff to go and see them, stating to plaintiff that in all probability they were sterile and would not breed." Plaintiff did go as requested, and found there these cows, including the one purchased, with a bull. The cow had been exposed, but neither knew she was with calf or whether she would breed. The defendants thought she would not, but the plaintiff says that he thought she could be made to breed, but believed she was not with calf. The defendants sold the cow for what they believed her to be, and the plaintiff bought her as he believed she was, after the statements made by the defendants. No conditions whatever were attached to the terms of sale by either party. It was in fact as absolute as it could well be made, and I know of no precedent as authority by which this court can alter the contract thus made by these parties in writing,-interpolate in it a condition by which, if the defendants should be mistaken in their belief that the cow was barren, she could be returned to them and their contract should be annulled. It is not the duty of courts to destroy contracts when called upon to enforce them, after they have been legally made. There was no mistake of any material fact by either of the parties in the case as would license the vendors to rescind. There was no difference between the parties, nor misapprehension, as to the substance of the thing bargained for, which was a cow supposed to be barren by one party, and believed not to be by the other. As to the quality of the animal, subsequently developed, both parties were equally ignorant, and as to this each party took his chances. If this were not the law, there would be no safety in purchasing this kind of stock.

I entirely agree with my brethren that the right to rescind occurs whenever "the thing actually delivered or received is different in substance from the thing bargained for, and intended to be sold; but if it be only a difference in some quality or accident, even though the misapprehension may have been the actuating motive" of the parties in making the contract, yet it will remain binding. In this case the cow sold was the one delivered. What might or might not happen to her after the sale formed no element in the contract. The case of Kennedy v. Panama Mail Co., L.R. 2 Q.B. 587, and the extract cited therefrom in the opinion of my brethren, clearly sustains the views I have taken. See, also, Smith v. Hughes, L.R. 6 Q.B. 597; Carter v. Crick, 4 Hurl. & N. 416.

According to this record, whatever the mistake was, if any, in this case, it was upon the part of the defendants, and while acting upon their own judgment. It is, however, elementary law, and very elementary, too, "that the mistaken party, without any common understanding with the other party in the premises as to the quality of an animal, is remediless if he is injured through his own mistake." Leake, Cont. 338; Torrance v. Bolton, L.R. 8 Ch. 118; Smith v. Hughes, L.R. 6 Q.B. 597. . . .

In this case, if either party had superior knowledge as to the qualities of this animal to the other, certainly the defendants had such advantage. I understand the law to be well settled that "there is no breach of any implied confidence that one party will not profit by his superior knowledge as to facts and circumstances" actually within the knowledge of both, because neither party reposes in any such confidence unless it be specially tendered or required, and that a general sale does not imply warranty of any quality, or the absence of any; and if the seller represents to the purchaser what he himself believes as to the qualities of an animal, and the purchaser buys relying upon his own judgment as to such qualities, there is no warranty in the case, and neither has a cause of action against the other if he finds himself to have been mistaken in judgment.

The only pretense for avoiding this contract by the defendants is that they erred in judgment as to the qualities and value of the animal. I think the principles adopted by Chief Justice CAMPBELL in Williams v. Spurr completely cover this case, and should have been allowed to control in its decision. See 24 Mich. 335. See, also, Story, Sales, §§ 174, 175, 382, and Benj. Sales, § 430. The judgment should be affirmed.

WOOD V. BOYNTON
Supreme Court of Wisconsin
25 N.W. 42 (1885).

TAYLOR, J.

This action was brought in the circuit court for Milwaukee county to recover the possession of an uncut diamond of the alleged value of $1,000. The case was tried in the circuit court, and after hearing all the evidence in the case, the learned circuit judge directed the jury to find a verdict for the defendants. The plaintiff excepted to such instruction, and, after a verdict was rendered for the defendants, moved for a new trial upon the minutes of the judge. The motion was denied, and the plaintiff duly excepted, and after judgment was entered in favor of the defendants, appealed to this court. The defendants are partners in the jewelry business. On the trial it appeared that on and before the twenty-eighth of December, 1883, the plaintiff was the owner of and in the possession of a small stone of the nature and value of which she was ignorant; that on that day she sold it to one of the defendants for the sum of one dollar. Afterwards it was ascertained that the stone was a rough diamond, and of the value of about $700. After hearing this fact the plaintiff tendered the defendants the one dollar, and ten cents as interest, and demanded a return of the stone to her. The defendants refused to deliver it, and therefore she commenced this action.

The plaintiff testified to the circumstances attending the sale of the stone to Mr. Samuel B. Boynton, as follows:

> The first time Boynton saw that stone he was talking about buying the topaz, or whatever it is, in September or October. I went into the store to get a little pin mended, and I had it in a small box,--the pin,--a small ear-ring; . . . this stone, and a broken sleeve-button were in the box. Mr. Boynton turned to give me a check for my pin. I thought I would ask him what the stone was, and I took it out of the box and asked him to please tell me what that was.

> He took it in his hand and seemed some time looking at it. I told him I had been told it was a topaz, and he said it might be. He says, "I would buy this; would you sell it?" I told him I did not know but what I would. What would it be worth? And he said he did not know; he would give me a dollar and keep it as a specimen, and I told him I would not sell it; and it was certainly pretty to look at. He asked me where I found it, and I told him in Eagle. He asked about how far out, and I said right in the village, and I went out. Afterwards, and about the twenty-eighth of December, I needed money pretty badly, and thought every dollar would help, and I took it back to Mr. Boynton and told him I had brought back the topaz, and he says, "Well, yes; what did I offer you for it?" and I says, "One dollar;" and he stepped to the change drawer and gave me the dollar, and I went out. In another part of her testimony she says: Before I sold the stone I had no knowledge whatever that it was a diamond. I told him that I had been advised that it was probably a topaz, and he said probably it was. The stone was about the size of a canary bird's egg, nearly the shape of an egg,--worn pointed at one end; it was nearly straw color,--a little darker.

She also testified that before this action was commenced she tendered the defendants $1.10, and demanded the return of the stone, which they refused. This is substantially all the evidence of what took place at and before the sale to the defendants, as testified to by the plaintiff herself. She produced no other witness on that point.

The evidence on the part of the defendant is not very different from the version given by the plaintiff, and certainly is not more favorable to the plaintiff. Mr. Samuel B. Boynton, the defendant to whom the stone was sold, testified that at the time he bought this stone, he had never seen an uncut diamond; had seen cut diamonds, but they are quite different from the uncut ones; "he had no idea this was a diamond, and it never entered his brain at the time." Considerable evidence was given as to what took place after the sale and purchase, but that evidence has very little if any bearing, upon the main point in the case.

This evidence clearly shows that the plaintiff sold the stone in question to the defendants, and delivered it to them in December, 1883, for a consideration of one dollar. By such sale the title to the stone passed by the sale and delivery to the defendants. . . . The only question in the case is whether there was anything in the sale which entitled the vendor (the appellant) to rescind the sale and so revest the title in her. The only reasons we know of for rescinding a sale and revesting the title in the vendor so that he may maintain an action at law for the recovery of the possession against his vendee are (1) that the vendee was guilty of some fraud in procuring a sale to be made to him; (2) that there was a mistake made by the vendor in delivering an article which was not the article sold,--a mistake in fact as to the identity of the thing sold with the thing delivered upon the sale. This last is not in reality a rescission of the sale made, as the thing delivered was not the thing sold, and no title ever passed to the vendee by such delivery.

In this case, upon the plaintiff's own evidence, there can be no just ground for alleging that she was induced to make the sale she did by any fraud or unfair dealings on the part of Mr. Boynton. Both were entirely ignorant at the time of the character of the stone and of its intrinsic value. Mr. Boynton was not an expert in uncut diamonds, and had made no examination of the stone, except to take it in his hand and look at it before he made the offer of one dollar, which was refused at the time, and afterwards accepted without any comment or further examination made by Mr. Boynton. The appellant had the stone in her possession for a long time, and it appears from her own statement that she had made some inquiry as to its nature and qualities. If she chose to sell it without further investigation as to its intrinsic value to a person who was guilty of no fraud or unfairness which induced her to sell it for a small sum, she cannot repudiate the sale because it is afterwards ascertained that she made a bad bargain. Kennedy v. Panama, etc., Mail Co., L. R. 2 Q. B. 580. There is no pretense of any mistake as to the identity of the thing sold. It was produced by the plaintiff and exhibited to the vendee before the sale was made, and the thing sold was delivered to the vendee when the purchase price was paid. Kennedy v. Panama, etc., Mail Co., supra., 587; Street v. Blay, 2 Barn. & Adol. 456; Gompertz v. Bartlett, 2 El. & Bl. 849; Gurney v. Womersley, 4 El. & Bl. 133; Ship's Case, 2 De G. J. & S. 544. Suppose the appellant had produced the stone, and said she had been told it was a diamond, and she believed it was, but had no knowledge herself as to its character or value, and Mr. Boynton had given her $500 for it, could he have rescinded the sale if it had turned out to be a topaz or any other stone of very small value? Could Mr. Boynton have rescinded the sale on the ground of mistake? Clearly not, nor could he rescind it on the ground that there had been a breach of warranty, because there was no warranty, nor could he rescind it on the ground of fraud, unless he could show that she falsely declared that she had been told it was a diamond, or, if she had been so told, still she knew it was not a diamond. See Street v. Blay, supra.

It is urged, with a good deal of earnestness, on the part of the counsel for the appellant that, because it has turned out that the stone was immensely more valuable than the parties at the time of the sale supposed it was, such fact alone is a ground for the rescission of the sale, and that fact was evidence of fraud on the part of the vendee. Whether inadequacy of price is to be received as evidence of fraud, even in a suit in equity to avoid a sale, depends upon the facts known to the parties at the time the sale is made. When this sale was made the value of the thing sold was open to the investigation of both parties, neither knowing its intrinsic value, and, so far as the evidence in this case shows, both supposed that the price paid was adequate. How can fraud be predicated upon such a sale, even though after investigation showed that the intrinsic value of the thing sold was hundreds of times greater than the price paid? It certainly shows no such fraud as would authorize the vendor to rescind the contract and bring an action at law to recover the possession of the thing sold. Whether that fact would have any influence in an action in equity to avoid the sale we need not consider. See Stettheimer v. Killip, 75 N. Y. 287; Etting v. Bank of U. S., 11 Wheat. 59.

We can find nothing in the evidence from which it could be justly inferred that Mr. Boynton, at the time he offered the plaintiff one dollar for the stone, had any knowledge of the real value of the stone, or that he entertained even a belief that the stone was a diamond. It cannot, therefore, be said that there was a suppression of knowledge on the part of the defendant as to the value of the stone which a court of equity might seize upon to avoid the sale. The following cases show that, in the absence of fraud or warranty, the value of the property sold, as compared with the price paid, is no ground for a rescission of a sale. Wheat v. Cross, 31 Md. 99; Lambert v. Heath, 15 Mees. & W. 487; Bryant v. Pember, 45 Vt. 487; Kuelkamp v. Hidding, 31 Wis. 503-511. However unfortunate the plaintiff may have been in selling this valuable stone for a mere nominal sum, she has failed entirely to make out a case either of fraud or mistake in the sale such as will entitle her to a rescission of such sale so as to recover the property sold in an action at law.

The judgment of the circuit court is affirmed.

LENAWEE CO. BOARD OF HEALTH v. MESSERLY
Supreme Court of Michigan
331 N.W.2d 203 (1982).

RYAN, Justice.

In March of 1977, Carl and Nancy Pickles, appellees, purchased from appellants, William and Martha Messerly, a 600-square-foot tract of land upon which is located a three-unit apartment building. Shortly after the transaction was closed, the Lenawee County Board of Health condemned the property and obtained a permanent injunction which prohibits human habitation on the premises until the defective sewage system is brought into conformance with the Lenawee County sanitation code.

We are required to determine whether appellees should prevail in their attempt to avoid this land contract on the basis of mutual mistake and failure of consideration. We conclude that the parties did entertain a mutual misapprehension of fact, but that the circumstances of this case do not warrant rescission.

I

The facts of the case are not seriously in dispute. In 1971, the Messerlys acquired approximately one acre plus 600 square feet of land. A three-unit apartment building was situated upon the 600-square-foot portion. The trial court found that, prior to this transfer, the Messerlys' predecessor in title, Mr. Bloom, had installed a septic tank on the property without a permit and in violation of the applicable health code. The Messerlys used the building as an income investment property until 1973 when they sold it, upon land contract, to James Barnes who likewise used it primarily as an income-producing investment.

Mr. and Mrs. Barnes, with the permission of the Messerlys, sold approximately one acre of the property in 1976, and the remaining 600 square feet and building were offered for sale soon thereafter when Mr. and Mrs. Barnes defaulted on their land contract. Mr. and Mrs. Pickles evidenced an interest in the property, but were dissatisfied with the terms of the Barnes-Messerly land contract. Consequently, to accommodate the Pickleses' preference to enter into a land contract directly with the Messerlys, Mr. and Mrs. Barnes executed a quit-claim deed which conveyed their interest in the property back to the Messerlys. After inspecting the property, Mr. and Mrs. Pickles executed a new land contract with the Messerlys on March 21, 1977. It provided for a purchase price of $25,500. A clause was added to the end of the land contract form which provides:

> 17. Purchaser has examined this property and agrees to accept same in its present condition. There are no other or additional written or oral understandings.

Five or six days later, when the Pickleses went to introduce themselves to the tenants, they discovered raw sewage seeping out of the ground. Tests conducted by a sanitation expert indicated the inadequacy of the sewage system. The Lenawee County Board of Health subsequently condemned the property and initiated this lawsuit in the Lenawee Circuit Court against the Messerlys as land contract vendors, and the Pickleses, as vendees, to obtain a permanent injunction proscribing human habitation of the premises until the property was brought into conformance with the Lenawee County sanitation code. The injunction was granted, and the Lenawee County Board of Health was permitted to withdraw from the lawsuit by stipulation of the parties.

When no payments were made on the land contract, the Messerlys filed a cross-complaint against the Pickleses seeking foreclosure, sale of the property, and a deficiency judgment. Mr. and Mrs. Pickles then counterclaimed for rescission against the Messerlys, and filed a third-party complaint against the Barneses, which incorporated, by reference, the allegations of the counterclaim against the Messerlys. In count one, Mr. and Mrs. Pickles alleged failure of consideration. Count two charged Mr. and Mrs. Barnes with willful concealment and misrepresentation as a result of their failure to disclose the condition of the sanitation system. Additionally, Mr. and Mrs. Pickles sought to hold the Messerlys liable in equity for the Barneses' alleged misrepresentation. The Pickleses prayed that the land contract be rescinded.

After a bench trial, the court concluded that the Pickleses had no cause of action against either the Messerlys or the Barneses as there was no fraud or misrepresentation. This ruling was predicated on the trial judge's conclusion that none of the parties knew of Mr. Bloom's earlier transgression or of the resultant problem with the septic system until it was discovered by the Pickleses, and that the sanitation problem was not caused by any of the parties. The trial court held that the property was purchased "as is," after inspection and, accordingly, its "negative . . . value cannot be blamed upon an innocent seller." Foreclosure was ordered against the Pickleses, together with a judgment against them in the amount of $25,943.09.

Mr. and Mrs. Pickles appealed from the adverse judgment. The Court of Appeals unanimously affirmed the trial court's ruling with respect to Mr. and Mrs. Barnes but, in a two-to-one decision, reversed the finding of no cause of action on the Pickleses' claims against the Messerlys. Lenawee County Board of Health v. Messerly, 98 Mich.App. 478, 295 N.W.2d 903 (1980). It concluded that the mutual mistake[5] between the Messerlys and the Pickleses went to a basic, as opposed to a collateral, element of the contract, and that the parties intended to transfer income-producing rental property but, in actuality, the vendees paid $25,500 for an asset without value.[7]

---

[5] Mr. and Mrs. Pickles did not allege mutual mistake as a ground for rescission in their pleadings. However, the trial court characterized their failure of consideration argument as mutual mistake resulting in failure of consideration. . . . Since the mutual mistake issue was dispositive in the Court of Appeals, we find its consideration necessary to a proper determination of this case.

[7] The trial court found that the only way that the property could be put to residential use would be to pump and haul the sewage, a method which is economically unfeasible, as the cost of such a disposal system amounts to double the income generated by the property. There was speculation by the trial court that the adjoining land might be utilized to make the property suitable for residential use, but, in the absence of testimony directed at that point, the court refused to draw any conclusions. The trial court and the Court of Appeals both found that the property was valueless, or had a negative value.

We granted the Messerlys' application for leave to appeal. 411 Mich. 900 (1981).

II

We must decide initially whether there was a mistaken belief entertained by one or both parties to the contract in dispute and, if so, the resultant legal significance.

A contractual mistake "is a belief that is not in accord with the facts". 1 Restatement Contracts, 2d, § 151, p 383. The erroneous belief of one or both of the parties must relate to a fact in existence at the time the contract is executed. Richardson Lumber Co. v. Hoey, 219 Mich. 643, 189 N.W. 923 (1922); Sherwood v. Walker, 66 Mich. 568, 580, 33 N.W. 919 (1887) (Sherwood, J., dissenting). That is to say, the belief which is found to be in error may not be, in substance, a prediction as to a future occurrence or non-occurrence. Henry v. Thomas, 241 Ga. 360, 245 S.E.2d 646 (1978); Hailpern v. Dryden, 154 Colo. 231, 389 P.2d 590 (1964). But see Denton v. Utley, 350 Mich. 332, 86 N.W.2d 537 (1957).

The Court of Appeals concluded, after a de novo review of the record, that the parties were mistaken as to the income-producing capacity of the property in question. 98 Mich.App. 487-488, 295 N.W.2d 903. We agree. The vendors and the vendees each believed that the property transferred could be utilized as income-generating rental property. All of the parties subsequently learned that, in fact, the property was unsuitable for any residential use. . . .

An examination of the record reveals that the septic system was defective prior to the date on which the land contract was executed. The Messerlys' grantor installed a nonconforming septic system without a permit prior to the transfer of the property to the Messerlys in 1971. Moreover, virtually undisputed testimony indicates that, assuming ideal soil conditions, 2,500 square feet of property is necessary to support a sewage system adequate to serve a three-family dwelling. Likewise, 750 square feet is mandated for a one-family home. Thus, the division of the parcel and sale of one acre of the property by Mr. and Mrs. Barnes in 1976 made it impossible to remedy the already illegal septic system within the confines of the 600-square-foot parcel.

Appellants do not dispute these underlying facts which give rise to an inference contrary to their contentions.

Having determined that when these parties entered into the land contract they were laboring under a mutual mistake of fact, we now direct our attention to a determination of the legal significance of that finding.

A contract may be rescinded because of a mutual misapprehension of the parties, but this remedy is granted only in the sound discretion of the court. Harris v. Axline, 323 Mich. 585, 36 N.W.2d 154 (1949). Appellants argue that the parties' mistake relates only to the quality or value of the real estate transferred, and that such mistakes are collateral to the agreement and do not justify rescission, citing A & M Land Development Co. v. Miller, 354 Mich. 681, 94 N.W.2d 197 (1959). . . .

Appellees contend, on the other hand, that in this case the parties were mistaken as to the very nature of the character of the consideration and claim that the pervasive and essential quality of this mistake renders rescission appropriate. They cite in support of that view Sherwood v. Walker, 66 Mich. 568, 33 N.W. 919 (1887), the famous "barren cow" case. In that case, the parties agreed to the sale and purchase of a cow which was thought to be barren, but which was, in reality, with calf. When the seller discovered the fertile condition of his cow, he refused to deliver her. In permitting rescission, the Court stated:

> It seems to me, however, in the case made by this record, that the mistake or misapprehension of the parties went to the whole substance of the agreement. If the cow was a breeder, she was worth at least $ 750; if barren, she was worth not over $ 80. The parties would not have made the contract of sale except upon the understanding and belief that she was incapable of breeding, and of no use as a cow. It is true she is now the identical animal that they thought her to be when the contract was made; there is no mistake as to the identity of the creature. Yet the mistake was not of the mere quality of the animal, but went to the very nature of the thing. A barren cow is substantially a different creature than a breeding one. There is as much difference between them for all purposes of use as there is between an ox and a cow that is capable of breeding and giving milk. If the mutual mistake had simply related to the fact whether she was with calf or not for one season, then it might have been a good sale; but the mistake affected the character of the animal for all time, and for her present and ultimate use. She was not in fact the animal, or the kind of animal, the defendants intended to sell or the plaintiff to buy. She was not a barren cow, and, if this fact had been known, there would have been no contract. The mistake affected the substance of the whole consideration, and it must be considered that there was no contract to sell or sale of the cow as she actually was. The thing sold and bought had in fact no existence. She was sold as a beef creature would be sold; she is in fact a breeding cow, and a valuable one.
>
> The court should have instructed the jury that if they found that the cow was sold, or contracted to be sold, upon the understanding of both parties that she was barren, and useless for the purpose of breeding, and that in fact she was not barren, but capable of breeding, then the defendants had a right to rescind, and to refuse to deliver, and the verdict should be in their favor. 66 Mich 577-578.

As the parties suggest, the foregoing precedent arguably distinguishes mistakes affecting the essence of the consideration from those which go to its quality or value, affording relief on a per se basis for the former but not the latter. See, e.g., Lenawee County Board of Health v. Messerly, 98 Mich.App. 478, 492, 295 N.W.2d 903 (1980) (Mackenzie, J., concurring in part).

However, the distinctions which may be drawn from Sherwood and A & M Land Development Co. do not provide a satisfactory analysis of the nature of a mistake sufficient to invalidate a contract. Often, a mistake relates to an underlying factual assumption which, when discovered, directly affects value, but simultaneously and materially affects the essence of the contractual consideration. It is disingenuous to label such a mistake collateral. McKay v. Coleman, 85 Mich. 60, 48 N.W. 203 (1891). Corbin, Contracts (One Vol ed.), § 605, p. 551.

Appellant and appellee both mistakenly believed that the property which was the subject of their land contract would generate income as rental property. The fact that it could not be used for human habitation deprived the property of its income-earning potential and rendered it less valuable. However, this mistake, while directly and dramatically affecting the property's value, cannot accurately be characterized as collateral because it also affects the very essence of the consideration. "The thing sold and bought [income generating rental property] had in fact no existence." Sherwood v. Walker, 66 Mich. 578, 33 N.W. 919.

We find that the inexact and confusing distinction between contractual mistakes running to value and those touching the substance of the consideration serves only as an impediment to a clear and helpful analysis for the equitable resolution of cases in which mistake is alleged and proven. Accordingly, the holdings of A & M Land Development Co. and Sherwood with respect to the material or collateral nature of a mistake are limited to the facts of those cases.

Instead, we think the better-reasoned approach is a case-by-case analysis whereby rescission is indicated when the mistaken belief relates to a basic assumption of the parties upon which the contract is made, and which materially affects the agreed performances of the parties. Denton v. Utley, 350 Mich. 332, 86 N.W.2d 537 (1957); Farhat v. Rassey, 295 Mich. 349, 294 N.W. 707 (1940); Richardson Lumber Co. v. Hoey, 219 Mich. 643, 189 N.W. 923 (1922). 1 Restatement Contracts, 2d, § 152, p. 385-386.[11] Rescission is not available, however, to relieve a party who has assumed the risk of loss in connection with the mistake. Denton v. Utley, 350 Mich. 344-345, 86 N.W.2d 537; Farhat v. Rassey, 295 Mich. 352, 294 N.W. 707; Corbin, Contracts (One Vol ed.), § 605, p. 552; 1 Restatement Contracts, 2d, §§ 152, 154, pp. 385-386, 402-406.[12]

All of the parties to this contract erroneously assumed that the property transferred by the vendors to the vendees was suitable for human habitation and could be utilized to generate rental income. The fundamental nature of these assumptions is indicated by the fact that their invalidity changed the character of the property transferred, thereby frustrating, indeed precluding, Mr. and Mrs. Pickles' intended use of the real estate. Although the Pickleses are disadvantaged by enforcement of the contract, performance is advantageous to the Messerlys, as the property at issue is less valuable absent its income-earning potential.

[11] [T]he second edition was published subsequent to the issuance of the lower court opinion and the filing of the briefs with this Court. Thus, we take it upon ourselves to refer to the latest edition to aid us in our resolution of this case.Section 152 delineates the legal significance of a mistake. "§ 152. When Mistake of Both Parties Makes a Contract Voidable"(1) Where a mistake of both parties at the time a contract was made as to a basic assumption on which the contract was made has a material effect on the agreed exchange of performances, the contract is voidable by the adversely affected party unless he bears the risk of the mistake under the rule stated in § 154."(2) In determining whether the mistake has a material effect on the agreed exchange of performances, account is taken of any relief by way of reformation, restitution, or otherwise."

[12] "§ 154. When a Party Bears the Risk of a Mistake" A party bears the risk of a mistake when "(a) the risk is allocated to him by agreement of the parties, or (b) he is aware, at the time the contract is made, that he has only limited knowledge with respect to the facts to which the mistake relates but treats his limited knowledge as sufficient, or (c) the risk is allocated to him by the court on the ground that it is reasonable in the circumstances to do so."

Nothing short of rescission can remedy the mistake. Thus, the parties' mistake as to a basic assumption materially affects the agreed performances of the parties.

Despite the significance of the mistake made by the parties, we reverse the Court of Appeals because we conclude that equity does not justify the remedy sought by Mr. and Mrs. Pickles.

Rescission is an equitable remedy which is granted only in the sound discretion of the court. Harris v. Axline, 323 Mich. 585, 36 N.W.2d 154 (1949); Hathaway v. Hudson, 256 Mich. 694, 239 N.W. 859 (1932). A court need not grant rescission in every case in which the mutual mistake relates to a basic assumption and materially affects the agreed performance of the parties.

In cases of mistake by two equally innocent parties, we are required, in the exercise of our equitable powers, to determine which blameless party should assume the loss resulting from the misapprehension they shared.[13] Normally that can only be done by drawing upon our "own notions of what is reasonable and just under all the surrounding circumstances."[14]

Equity suggests that, in this case, the risk should be allocated to the purchasers. We are guided to that conclusion, in part, by the standards announced in § 154 of the Restatement of Contracts 2d, for determining when a party bears the risk of mistake. See fn 12. Section 154(a) suggests that the court should look first to whether the parties have agreed to the allocation of the risk between themselves. While there is no express assumption in the contract by either party of the risk of the property becoming uninhabitable, there was indeed some agreed allocation of the risk to the vendees by the incorporation of an "as is" clause into the contract which, we repeat, provided:

> Purchaser has examined this property and agrees to accept same in its present condition. There are no other or additional written or oral understandings.

That is a persuasive indication that the parties considered that, as between them, such risk as related to the "present condition" of the property should lie with the purchaser. If the "as is" clause is to have any meaning at all, it must be interpreted to refer to those defects which were unknown at the time that the contract was executed.[15] Thus, the parties themselves assigned the risk of loss to Mr. and Mrs. Pickles.

---

[13] This risk-of-loss analysis is absent in both A & M Land Development Co. and Sherwood, and this omission helps to explain, in part, the disparate treatment in the two cases. Had such an inquiry been undertaken in Sherwood, we believe that the result might have been different. Moreover, a determination as to which party assumed the risk in A & M Land Development Co. would have alleviated the need to characterize the mistake as collateral so as to justify the result denying rescission. Despite the absence of any inquiry as to the assumption of risk in those two leading cases, we find that there exists sufficient precedent to warrant such an analysis in future cases of mistake.

[14] Hathaway v. Hudson, 256 Mich. 702, 239 N.W. 859, quoting 9 C.J., p. 1161.

[15] An "as is" clause waives those implied warranties which accompany the sale of a new home, Tibbitts v. Openshaw, 18 Utah 2d 442, 425 P.2d 160 (1967), or the sale of goods. M.C.L. § 440.2316(3)(a); M.S.A. § 19.2316(3)(a). Since implied warranties protect against latent defects, an "as is" clause will impose upon the purchaser the assumption of the risk of latent defects, such as an inadequate sanitation system, even when there are no implied warranties.

We conclude that Mr. and Mrs. Pickles are not entitled to the equitable remedy of rescission and, accordingly, reverse the decision the Court of Appeals.

WILLIAMS, C.J., and COLEMAN, FITZGERALD, KAVANAGH and LEVIN, JJ., concur. RILEY, J., not participating.

C. UNILATERAL MISTAKE

Traditionally, courts have not granted relief from a contract where only one party was mistaken about the basic assumption upon which he agreed to terms of a contract. Recall the case of *Drennan v. Star Paving* discussed in Chapter 2. There, defendant subcontractor alleged, as an alternative defense, that its bid for the paving work was the result of a mistake and thereby the resulting contract between it and the general contractor should be rescinded. In rejecting this defense, the court noted:

> Plaintiff, however, had no reason to know that defendant had made a mistake in submitting its bid, since there was usually a variance of 160 per cent between the highest and lowest bids for paving in the desert around Lancaster. He committed himself to performing the main contract in reliance on defendant's figures. Under these circumstances defendant's mistake, far from relieving it of its obligation, constitutes an additional reason for enforcing it, for it misled plaintiff as to the cost of doing the paving. Even had it been clearly understood that defendant's offer was revocable until accepted, it would not necessarily follow that defendant had no duty to exercise reasonable care in preparing its bid. It presented its bid with knowledge of the substantial possibility that it would be used by plaintiff; it could foresee the harm that would ensue from an erroneous underestimate of the cost. Moreover, it was motivated by its own business interest.... As between the subcontractor who made the bid and the general contractor who reasonably relied on it, the loss resulting from the mistake should fall on the party who caused it. 333 P.2d at 761

Modernly courts are more inclined to consider the request. Consider the following cases:

DONNOVAN V. RRL CORP.
Supreme Court of California
27 P.3d 702 (2001).

GEORGE, C.J.

. . . .

I

While reading the April 26, 1997, edition of the Costa Mesa Daily Pilot, a local newspaper, plaintiff noticed a full-page advertisement placed by defendant. The advertisement promoted a "PRE-OWNED COUP-A-RAMA SALE!/ 2-DAY PRE-OWNED SALES EVENT" and listed, along with 15 other used automobiles, a 1995 Jaguar XJ6

Vanden Plas. The advertisement described the color of this automobile as sapphire blue, included a vehicle identification number, and stated a price of $25,995. The name Lexus of Westminster was displayed prominently in three separate locations in the advertisement, which included defendant's address along with a small map showing the location of the dealership. The following statements appeared in small print at the bottom of the advertisement: "All cars plus tax, lic., doc., smog & bank fees. On approved credit. Ad expires 4/27/97[.]"

Also on April 26, 1997, plaintiff visited a Jaguar dealership that offered other 1995 Jaguars for sale at $8,000 to $10,000 more than the price specified in defendant's advertisement. The following day, plaintiff and his spouse drove to Lexus of Westminster and observed a blue Jaguar displayed on an elevated ramp. After verifying that the identification number on the sticker was the same as that listed in defendant's April 26 Daily Pilot advertisement, they asked a salesperson whether they could test drive the Jaguar. Plaintiff mentioned that he had seen the advertisement and that the price "looked really good." The salesperson responded that, as a Lexus dealer, defendant might offer better prices for a Jaguar automobile than would a Jaguar dealer. At that point, however, neither plaintiff nor the salesperson mentioned the specific advertised price.

After the test drive, plaintiff and his spouse discussed several negative characteristics of the automobile, including high mileage, an apparent rust problem, and worn tires. In addition, it was not as clean as the other Jaguars they had inspected. Despite these problems, they believed that the advertised price was a very good price and decided to purchase the vehicle. Plaintiff told the salesperson, "Okay. We will take it at your price, $26,000." When the salesperson did not respond, plaintiff showed him the advertisement. The salesperson immediately stated, "That's a mistake."

After plaintiff asked to speak with an individual in charge, defendant's sales manager also told plaintiff that the price listed in the advertisement was a mistake. The sales manager apologized and offered to pay for plaintiff's fuel, time, and effort expended in traveling to the dealership to examine the automobile. Plaintiff declined this offer and expressed his belief that there had been no mistake. Plaintiff stated that he could write a check for the full purchase price as advertised. The sales manager responded that he would not sell the vehicle at the advertised price. Plaintiff then requested the sales price. After performing some calculations, and based upon defendant's $35,000 investment in the automobile, the sales manager stated that he would sell it to plaintiff for $37,016. Plaintiff responded, "No, I want to buy it at your advertised price, and I will write you a check right now." The sales manager again stated that he would not sell the vehicle at the advertised price, and plaintiff and his spouse left the dealership.

Plaintiff subsequently filed this action against defendant for breach of contract, fraud, and negligence. In addition to testimony consistent with the facts set forth above, the following evidence was presented to the municipal court, which acted as the trier of fact.

Defendant's advertising manager compiles information for placement in advertisements in several local newspapers, including the Costa Mesa Daily Pilot. Defendant's advertisement published in the Saturday, April 19, 1997, edition of the Daily Pilot listed a 1995 Jaguar XJ6 Vanden Plas but did not specify a price for that automobile; instead, the word "Save" appeared in the space where a price ordinarily would have appeared. The following Thursday afternoon, defendant's sales manager instructed the advertising manager to delete the 1995 Jaguar from all advertisements and to substitute a 1994 Jaguar XJ6 with a price of $25,995. The advertising manager conveyed the new information to a representative of the Daily Pilot that same afternoon.

Because of typographical and proofreading errors made by employees of the Daily Pilot, however, the newspaper did not replace the description of the 1995 Jaguar with the description of the 1994 Jaguar, but did replace the word "Save" with the price of $25,995. Thus, the Saturday, April 26, edition of the Daily Pilot erroneously advertised the 1995 Jaguar XJ6 Vanden Plas at a price of $25,995. The Daily Pilot acknowledged its error in a letter of retraction sent to defendant on April 28. No employee of defendant reviewed a proof sheet of the revised Daily Pilot advertisement before it was published, and defendant was unaware of the mistake until plaintiff attempted to purchase the automobile.

Except for the 1995 Jaguar XJ6 Vanden Plas, defendant intended to sell each vehicle appearing in the April 26, 1997, Daily Pilot advertisement at the advertised price. Defendant's advertisements in the April 26 editions of several other newspapers correctly listed the 1994 Jaguar XJ6 with a price of $25,995. In May 1997, defendant's advertisements in several newspapers listed the 1995 Jaguar XJ6 Vanden Plas for sale at $37,995. Defendant subsequently sold the automobile for $38,399.

The municipal court entered judgment for defendant. . . . After the close of evidence and presentation of argument, the municipal court concluded as a matter of law that a newspaper advertisement for an automobile generally constitutes a valid contractual offer that a customer may accept by tendering payment of the advertised price. . . . Nevertheless, the municipal court held that in the present case there was no valid offer because defendant's unilateral mistake of fact vitiated or negated contractual intent. The court made factual findings that defendant's mistake regarding the advertisement was made in good faith and was not intended to deceive the public. The municipal court also found that plaintiff was unaware of the mistake before it was disclosed to him by defendant's representatives.

Plaintiff appealed from the judgment to the appellate department of the superior court (Cal. Rules of Court, rule 121), limiting his contentions to the breach of contract claim. The appellate department reversed the judgment for defendant and directed the municipal court to calculate plaintiff's damages. Relying upon the public policies underlying Vehicle Code section 11713.1, subdivision (e), the appellate department concluded that the advertisement constituted an offer capable of acceptance by tender of the advertised price. Section 11713.1, subdivision (e), provides that it is a violation of the Vehicle Code for a dealer to "[f]ail to sell a vehicle to any person at the advertised total price ... while the vehicle remains unsold, unless the advertisement states the advertised total price is good only for a specified time and the time has elapsed." The appellate department further concluded that defendant bore the risk of the mistaken transmission of its offer, because plaintiff was unaware of the mistake.

The appellate department of the superior court certified the appeal to the Court of Appeal, which ordered the case transferred to it for hearing and decision. (Cal. Rules of Court, rules 62(a), 63(a).) Like the appellate department, the Court of Appeal reversed the judgment of the municipal court and held that defendant's advertisement constituted a contractual offer that invited acceptance by the act of tendering the advertised price, which plaintiff performed. Acknowledging that the question was close, however, the Court of Appeal reasoned that Vehicle Code section 11713.1, subdivision (e), "tips the scale in favor of ... construing the advertisement as an offer ...." The court disagreed with the municipal court's conclusion that defendant's unilateral mistake of fact, unknown to plaintiff at the time he tendered the purchase price, precluded the existence of a valid offer. With regard to the contention that defendant should not bear the risk of an error resulting solely from the negligence of the newspaper, the Court of Appeal made a factual finding based upon the appellate record (Code Civ. Proc., § 909) that defendant's failure to review a proof sheet for the Daily Pilot advertisement constituted negligence that contributed to the placement of the erroneous advertisement.

We granted defendant's petition for review and requested that the parties include in their briefing a discussion of the effect, if any, of California Uniform Commercial Code division 2, chapter 2, sections 2201-2210, upon the present case.

II

An essential element of any contract is the consent of the parties, or mutual assent. (Civ.Code, §§ 1550, subd. 2, 1565, subd. 2.) Mutual assent usually is manifested by an offer communicated to the offeree and an acceptance communicated to the offeror. (1 Witkin, Summary of Cal. Law (9th ed. 1987) Contracts, § 128, p. 153 (hereafter Witkin).) " ' "An offer is the manifestation of willingness to enter into a bargain, so made as to justify another person in understanding that his assent to that bargain is invited and will conclude it." ' [Citations.]" (City of Moorpark v. Moorpark Unified School Dist. (1991) 54 Cal.3d 921, 930, 1 Cal.Rptr.2d 896, 819 P.2d 854 (Moorpark).) The determination of whether a particular communication constitutes an operative offer, rather than an inoperative step in the preliminary negotiation of a contract, depends upon all the surrounding circumstances. (1 Corbin, Contracts (rev. ed.1993) § 2.2, p. 105.) The objective manifestation of the party's assent ordinarily controls, and the pertinent inquiry is whether the individual to whom the communication was made had reason to believe that it was intended as an offer. (1 Witkin, supra, Contracts, § 119, p. 144; 1 Farnsworth, Contracts (2d ed.1998) § 3.10, p. 237.)

In the present case, the municipal court ruled that newspaper advertisements for automobiles generally constitute offers that can be accepted by a customer's tender of the purchase price. Its conclusion that defendant's advertisement for the 1995 Jaguar did not constitute an offer was based solely upon the court's factual determination that the erroneous price in the advertisement was the result of a good faith mistake. . . .

This court has not previously applied the common law rules upon which defendant relies, including the rule that advertisements generally constitute invitations to negotiate rather than offers. Plaintiff observes that such rules governing the construction of advertisements have been criticized on the ground that they are inconsistent with the reasonable expectations of consumers and lead to haphazard results. (See Eisenberg, Expression Rules in Contract Law and Problems of Offer and Acceptance (1994) 82 Cal. L.Rev. 1127, 1166-1172.) Plaintiff urges this court to reject the black-letter advertising rule.

In the present case, however, we need not consider the viability of the black-letter rule regarding the interpretation of advertisements in general. Like the Court of Appeal, we conclude that a licensed automobile dealer's advertisement for the sale of a particular vehicle at a specific price-when construed in light of Vehicle Code section 11713.1, subdivision (e)-reasonably justifies a consumer's understanding that the dealer intends the advertisement to constitute an offer and that the consumer's assent to the bargain is invited and will conclude it. . . .

As one commentator has observed, legislation can affect consumer expectations and cause reasonable individuals to regard certain retail advertisements for the sale of goods as offers to complete a bargain. (1 Corbin, Contracts, supra, § 2.4, p. 118.) By authorizing disciplinary action against a licensed automobile dealer that fails to sell a vehicle at the advertised price, section 11713.1(e) creates a reasonable expectation on the part of consumers that the dealer intends to make an offer to sell at that price, and that the consumer can accept the offer by paying the price specified in the advertisement. Interpreted in light of the regulatory obligations imposed upon dealers, an advertisement for a particular automobile at a specific price constitutes an objective manifestation of the dealer's willingness to enter into a bargain on the stated terms, and justifies the consumer's understanding that his or her assent to the bargain is invited and will conclude it. Such an advertisement therefore constitutes an offer that is accepted when a consumer tenders the advertised price.[1] . . .

IV

Having concluded that defendant's advertisement for the sale of the Jaguar automobile constituted an offer that was accepted by plaintiff's tender of the advertised price . . . we next consider whether defendant can avoid enforcement of the contract on the ground of mistake.

A party may rescind a contract if his or her consent was given by mistake. (Civ.Code, § 1689, subd. (b)(1).) A factual mistake by one party to a contract, or unilateral mistake, affords a ground for rescission in some circumstances. . . .

Under the first Restatement of Contracts, unilateral mistake did not render a contract voidable unless the other party knew of or caused the mistake. (1 Witkin, supra, Contracts, § 370, p. 337; see Rest., Contracts, § 503.) In Germain etc. Co. v. Western Union etc. Co. (1902) 137 Cal. 598, 602, 70 P. 658, this court endorsed a rule similar to that of the first Restatement. Our opinion indicated that a seller's price quotation erroneously transcribed and delivered by a telegraph company contractually could bind the seller to the incorrect price, unless the buyer knew or had reason to suspect that a mistake had been made. Some decisions of the Court of Appeal have adhered to the approach of the original Restatement. (See, e.g., Conservatorship of O'Connor (1996) 48 Cal.App.4th 1076, 1097-1098, 56 Cal.Rptr.2d 386, and cases cited therein.) Plaintiff also advocates this approach and contends

[1] Of course, the consumer's tender of payment must be in a form that is commercially acceptable (see Cal. U. Com.Code, § 2511), and other legal requirements necessary to complete the transaction must be satisfied, such as execution of a formal written agreement containing the required statutory disclosures, and proper delivery of the certificate of ownership and registration (see Veh.Code, § 5600).

that rescission is unavailable to defendant, because plaintiff was unaware of the mistaken price in defendant's advertisement when he accepted the offer.

The Court of Appeal decisions reciting the traditional rule do not recognize that in M.F. Kemper Const. Co. v. City of L.A. (1951) 37 Cal.2d 696, 701, 235 P.2d 7 (Kemper), we acknowledged but rejected a strict application of the foregoing Restatement rule regarding unilateral mistake of fact. The plaintiff in Kemper inadvertently omitted a $301,769 item from its bid for the defendant city's public works project-approximately one-third of the total contract price. After discovering the mistake several hours later, the plaintiff immediately notified the city and subsequently withdrew its bid. Nevertheless, the city accepted the erroneous bid, contending that rescission of the offer was unavailable for the plaintiff's unilateral mistake.

Our decision in Kemper recognized that the bid, when opened and announced, resulted in an irrevocable option contract conferring upon the city a right to accept the bid, and that the plaintiff could not withdraw its bid unless the requirements for rescission of this option contract were satisfied. (Kemper, supra, 37 Cal.2d at pp. 700, 704, 235 P.2d 7.) We stated: "Rescission may be had for mistake of fact if the mistake is material to the contract and was not the result of neglect of a legal duty, if enforcement of the contract as made would be unconscionable, and if the other party can be placed in statu quo. [Citations.]" (Id. at p. 701, 235 P.2d 7.) Although the city knew of the plaintiff's mistake before it accepted the bid, and this circumstance was relevant to our determination that requiring the plaintiff to perform at the mistaken bid price would be unconscionable (id. at pp. 702-703, 235 P.2d 7), we authorized rescission of the city's option contract even though the city had not known of or contributed to the mistake before it opened the bid.

Similarly, in Elsinore Union etc. Sch. Dist. v. Kastorff (1960) 54 Cal.2d 380, 6 Cal.Rptr. 1, 353 P.2d 713 (Elsinore), we authorized the rescission of an erroneous bid even where the contractor had assured the public agency, after the agency inquired, that his figures were accurate, and where the agency already had accepted the bid before it was aware of the mistake. In this situation, the other party clearly had no reason to know of the contractor's mistake before it accepted the bid.

The decisions in Kemper and Elsinore establish that California law does not adhere to the original Restatement's requirements for rescission based upon unilateral mistake of fact-i.e., only in circumstances where the other party knew of the mistake or caused the mistake. Consistent with the decisions in Kemper and Elsinore, the Restatement Second of Contracts authorizes rescission for a unilateral mistake of fact where "the effect of the mistake is such that enforcement of the contract would be unconscionable." (Rest.2d Contracts, § 153, subd. (a).)[19] The comment following this section recognizes "a growing willingness to allow avoidance where the consequences of the mistake are so grave that enforcement of the contract would be unconscionable." (Id., com. a, p. 394.) Indeed, two of the illustrations recognizing this additional ground for rescission in the Restatement Second

[19] Section 153 of the Restatement Second of Contracts states: "Where a mistake of one party at the time a contract was made as to a basic assumption on which he made the contract has a material effect on the agreed exchange of performances that is adverse to him, the contract is voidable by him if he does not bear the risk of the mistake under the rule stated in § 154, and [¶] (a) the effect of the mistake is such that enforcement of the contract would be unconscionable, or [¶] (b) the other party had reason to know of the mistake or his fault caused the mistake."

of Contracts are based in part upon this court's decisions in Kemper and Elsinore. (Rest.2d Contracts, § 153, com. c, illus. 1, 3, pp. 395, 396, and Reporter's Note, pp. 400-401; see also Schultz v. County of Contra Costa (1984) 157 Cal.App.3d 242, 249-250, 203 Cal.Rptr. 760 [applying Rest.2d Contracts,§153, subd. (a),], disagreed with on another ground in Van Petten v. County of San Diego (1995) 38 Cal.App.4th 43, 50-51, 44 Cal.Rptr.2d 816; 1 Witkin, supra, Contracts, § 370, p. 337 [reciting the rule of the same Restatement provision].) Although the most common types of mistakes falling within this category occur in bids on construction contracts, section 153 of the Restatement Second of Contracts is not limited to such cases. (Rest.2d Contracts, § 153, com. b, p. 395.)

Because the rule in section 153, subdivision (a), of the Restatement Second of Contracts, authorizing rescission for unilateral mistake of fact where enforcement would be unconscionable, is consistent with our previous decisions, we adopt the rule as California law. As the author of one treatise recognized more than 40 years ago, the decisions that are inconsistent with the traditional rule "are too numerous and too appealing to the sense of justice to be disregarded." (3 Corbin, Contracts (1960) § 608, p. 675, fn. omitted.) We reject plaintiff's contention and the Court of Appeal's conclusion that, because plaintiff was unaware of defendant's unilateral mistake, the mistake does not provide a ground to avoid enforcement of the contract.

Having concluded that a contract properly may be rescinded on the ground of unilateral mistake of fact as set forth in section 153, subdivision (a), of the Restatement Second of Contracts, we next consider whether the requirements of that provision, construed in light of our previous decisions, are satisfied in the present case. Where the plaintiff has no reason to know of and does not cause the defendant's unilateral mistake of fact, the defendant must establish the following facts to obtain rescission of the contract: (1) the defendant made a mistake regarding a basic assumption upon which the defendant made the contract; (2) the mistake has a material effect upon the agreed exchange of performances that is adverse to the defendant; (3) the defendant does not bear the risk of the mistake; and (4) the effect of the mistake is such that enforcement of the contract would be unconscionable. We shall consider each of these requirements below.

A significant error in the price term of a contract constitutes a mistake regarding a basic assumption upon which the contract is made, and such a mistake ordinarily has a material effect adverse to the mistaken party. (See, e.g., Elsinore, supra, 54 Cal.2d at p. 389, 6 Cal.Rptr. 1, 353 P.2d 713 [7 percent error in contract price]; Lemoge Electric v. County of San Mateo (1956) 46 Cal.2d 659, 661-662, 297 P.2d 638 [6 percent error]; Kemper, supra, 37 Cal.2d at p. 702, 235 P.2d 7 [28 percent error]; Brunzell Const. Co. v. G.J. Weisbrod, Inc. (1955) 134 Cal.App.2d 278, 286, 285 P.2d 989 [20 percent error]; Rest.2d Contracts, § 152, com. b, illus. 3, p. 387 [27 percent error].) In establishing a material mistake regarding a basic assumption of the contract, the defendant must show that the resulting imbalance in the agreed exchange is so severe that it would be unfair to require the defendant to perform. (Rest.2d Contracts, § 152, com. c, p. 388.) Ordinarily, a defendant can satisfy this requirement by showing that the exchange not only is less desirable for the defendant, but also is more advantageous to the other party. (Ibid.)

Measured against this standard, defendant's mistake in the contract for the sale of the Jaguar automobile constitutes a material mistake regarding a basic assumption upon which it made the contract. Enforcing the contract with the mistaken price of $25,995 would require defendant to sell the vehicle to plaintiff for $12,000 less than the intended advertised price of $37,995-an error amounting to 32 percent of the price defendant intended. The exchange of performances would be substantially less desirable for defendant and more desirable for plaintiff. Plaintiff implicitly concedes that defendant's mistake was material.

The parties and amici curiae vigorously dispute, however, whether defendant should bear the risk of its mistake. Section 154 of the Restatement Second of Contracts states: "A party bears the risk of a mistake when [¶] (a) the risk is allocated to him by agreement of the parties, or [¶] (b) he is aware, at the time the contract is made, that he has only limited knowledge with respect to the facts to which the mistake relates but treats his limited knowledge as sufficient, or [¶] (c) the risk is allocated to him by the court on the ground that it is reasonable in the circumstances to do so." Neither of the first two factors applies here. Thus, we must determine whether it is reasonable under the circumstances to allocate to defendant the risk of the mistake in the advertisement.

Civil Code section 1577, as well as our prior decisions, instructs that the risk of a mistake must be allocated to a party where the mistake results from that party's neglect of a legal duty. (Kemper, supra, 37 Cal.2d at p. 701, 235 P.2d 7.)[20] It is well established, however, that ordinary negligence does not constitute neglect of a legal duty within the meaning of Civil Code section 1577. (Kemper, supra, 37 Cal.2d at p. 702, 235 P.2d 7.) For example, we have described a careless but significant mistake in the computation of the contract price as the type of error that sometimes will occur in the conduct of reasonable and cautious businesspersons, and such an error does not necessarily amount to neglect of legal duty that would bar equitable relief. (Ibid.; see also Sun 'n Sand, Inc. v. United California Bank (1978) 21 Cal.3d 671, 700-701, 148 Cal.Rptr. 329, 582 P.2d 920 (plur. opn. of Mosk, J.); Elsinore, supra, 54 Cal.2d at pp. 388-389, 6 Cal.Rptr. 1, 353 P.2d 713.)

A concept similar to neglect of a legal duty is described in section 157 of the Restatement Second of Contracts, which addresses situations in which a party's fault precludes relief for mistake. Only where the mistake results from "a failure to act in good faith and in accordance with reasonable standards of fair dealing" is rescission unavailable. (Rest.2d Contracts, § 157.) This section, consistent with the California decisions cited in the preceding paragraph, provides that a mistaken party's failure to exercise due care does not necessarily bar rescission under the rule set forth in section 153.

"The mere fact that a mistaken party could have avoided the mistake by the exercise of reasonable care does not preclude ... avoidance ... [on the ground of mistake]. Indeed, since a party can often avoid a mistake by the exercise of such care, the availability of relief would be severely circumscribed if he were to be barred by his negligence. Nevertheless, in extreme cases the mistaken party's fault is a proper ground for denying him relief for a mistake that he otherwise could have avoided.... [T]he rule is stated in terms of good faith

[20] Civil Code section 1577 does not include language regarding allocation of the risk of mistake to one party, but rather excludes from the definition of "mistake of fact" any mistake resulting from the neglect of a legal duty.

and fair dealing.... [A] failure to act in good faith and in accordance with reasonable standards of fair dealing during pre-contractual negotiations does not amount to a breach. Nevertheless, under the rule stated in this Section, the failure bars a mistaken party from relief based on a mistake that otherwise would not have been made. During the negotiation stage each party is held to a degree of responsibility appropriate to the justifiable expectations of the other. The terms 'good faith' and 'fair dealing' are used, in this context, in much the same sense as in ... Uniform Commercial Code § 1-203." (Rest.2d Contracts, § 157, com. a, pp. 416-417, italics added.) Section 1201, subdivision (19), of the California Uniform Commercial Code defines "good faith," as used in section 1203 of that code, as "honesty in fact in the conduct or transaction concerned."

. . . Plaintiff contends that section 11713.1(e) imposes a legal duty upon licensed automobile dealers to ensure that their advertisements containing sale prices are accurate. As established above, section 11713.1(e) provides that it is a violation of the Vehicle Code for a dealer to "[f]ail to sell a vehicle to any person at the advertised total price ... while the vehicle remains unsold, unless the advertisement states the advertised total price is good only for a specified time and the time has elapsed." Plaintiff also relies upon Vehicle Code section 11713, subdivision (a), which provides that a licensed dealer shall not "[m]ake or disseminate ... in any newspaper ... any statement which is untrue or misleading and which is known, or which by the exercise of reasonable care should be known, to be untrue or misleading ...." According to plaintiff, defendant's alleged violation of the duties arising from these statutes also constitutes the neglect of a legal duty within the meaning of Civil Code section 1577.

Even if we were to conclude that the foregoing statutes impose a duty of care upon automobile dealers to ensure that prices in an advertisement are accurate, a violation of such a duty would not necessarily preclude the availability of equitable relief. Our prior decisions instruct that the circumstance that a statute imposes a duty of care does not establish that the violation of such a duty constitutes "the neglect of a legal duty" (Civ.Code, § 1577) that would preclude rescission for a unilateral mistake of fact. . . .

In a related claim, plaintiff contends that section 11713.1(e) imposes upon automobile dealers an absolute obligation to sell a vehicle at the advertised price-notwithstanding any mistake regarding the price, or the circumstances under which the mistake was made-and that this statute therefore supplants the common law regarding rescission of contracts and eliminates the defense of mistake. Allowing automobile dealers to avoid contracts because of carelessness in proofreading advertisements, plaintiff asserts, would undermine the legislative intent and public policy favoring the protection of consumers and ensuring accuracy in advertisements.

Plaintiff's contention regarding the effect of section 11713.1(e) upon the common law is inconsistent with our prior decisions. In Moorpark, supra, 54 Cal.3d 921, 1 Cal.Rptr.2d 896, 819 P.2d 854, we held that a statute supplying the parameters for the price term of a contract, and requiring one party to perform certain acts as part of the process of making the contract, "does not remove the contract-making process from the purview of the common law unless the Legislature intends to occupy the field." (Id. at p. 929, 1 Cal.Rptr.2d 896, 819 P.2d 854.) Our decision in Moorpark indicated that where a statutory scheme neither explicitly defines an offer nor, by the breadth of its regulation, implicitly supplants the common law of contracts, general common law principles govern the question whether an effective legal offer has been made. (Id. at p. 930, 1 Cal.Rptr.2d 896, 819 P.2d 854.)

Section 11713.1(e) does not eliminate mistake as a ground for rescission of the contract, as plaintiff contends. The statute is part of a regulatory scheme that subjects licensed dealers to potential discipline for a violation of the duties set forth therein. As in Moorpark, supra, 54 Cal.3d 921, 1 Cal.Rptr.2d 896, 819 P.2d 854, nothing in section 11713.1(e) or the regulatory scheme reflects a legislative intent completely to remove the contract-making process from the purview of the common law. At most, section 11713.1(e) reflects an intent to supplement contract law by establishing a ceiling for the price term of a contract for the sale of an advertised vehicle. Therefore, the common law, including the law governing mistake, remains applicable. . . .

As in the foregoing cases, if we were to accept plaintiff's position that section 11713.1(e), by requiring a dealer to sell a vehicle at the advertised price, necessarily precludes relief for mistake, and that the dealer always must be held to the strict terms of a contract arising from an advertisement, we would be holding that the dealer intended to assume the risk of all typographical errors in advertisements, no matter how serious the error and regardless of the circumstances in which the error was made. For example, if an automobile dealer proofread an advertisement but, through carelessness, failed to detect a typographical error listing a $75,000 automobile for sale at $75, the defense of mistake would be unavailable to the dealer.[21]

The trial court expressed a similar concern when it posed the following hypothetical to plaintiff.

> The perennial mistakes in ads are infinite. You can move the decimal point over two, three places, so you are selling a $1,000,000 item for $100, any ridiculous example you can think of.
>
> If your theory is correct, that a printout would constitute an unconditional offer to sell, would that same result be attained if we had one of these mistakes, where some printer, instead of printing a million, left off some of the zeros, put in a thousand, and you are selling a million dollar yacht, and it came out to a thousand dollars, would a person be entitled, under your theory of the law, to say here's my thousand bucks, and I would like to sail away?

Consistent with his contention that the violation of section 11713.1(e) constitutes the neglect of a legal duty, plaintiff responded that the answer to the court's hypothetical is "yes." Plaintiff reiterated his position in this regard at oral argument in this court.[22]

---

[21] Pursuant to Civil Code section 1577 and the Restatement Second of Contracts section 157, the neglect of a legal duty amounting to a breach of the duty of good faith and fair dealing bars relief from mistake, whether or not the other party has reason to know of the mistake.

[22] In addition, if we were to accept plaintiff's position that Vehicle Code section 11713.1(e) imposes an absolute contractual obligation upon dealers to sell a vehicle at the advertised price to any person-notwithstanding any legal justification for refusing to do so-a dealer would be required to enter into a sales contract with an individual who obviously lacks the mental capacity to contract. (See Civ.Code, §§ 38, 1556, 1557.) And, under plaintiff's view of the statute, a dealer would be required to sell a vehicle at an erroneous price mistakenly broadcast by a

Giving such an effect to section 11713.1(e), however, "is contrary to common sense and ordinary business understanding and would result in the loss of heretofore well-established equitable rights to relief from certain types of mistake." (Kemper, supra, 37 Cal.2d at p. 704, 235 P.2d 7.) Although this statute obviously reflects an important public policy of protecting consumers from injury caused by unscrupulous dealers who publish deceptive advertisements (see Ford Dealers Assn. v. Department of Motor Vehicles (1982) 32 Cal.3d 347, 356, 185 Cal.Rptr. 453, 650 P.2d 328), and establishes that automobile dealers that violate the statute can suffer the suspension or revocation of their licenses, there is no indication in the statutory scheme that the Legislature intended to impose such an absolute contractual obligation upon automobile dealers who make an honest mistake. Therefore, absent evidence of bad faith, the violation of any obligation imposed by this statute does not constitute the neglect of a legal duty that precludes rescission for unilateral mistake of fact.

The municipal court made an express finding of fact that "the mistake on the part of [defendant] was made in good faith[;] it was an honest mistake, not intended to deceive the public ...." The Court of Appeal correctly recognized that "[w]e must, of course, accept the trial court's finding that there was a 'good faith' mistake that caused the error in the advertisement." The evidence presented at trial compellingly supports this finding.

Defendant regularly advertises in five local newspapers. Defendant's advertising manager, Crystal Wadsworth, testified that ordinarily she meets with Kristen Berman, a representative of the Daily Pilot, on Tuesdays, Wednesdays, and Thursdays to review proof sheets of the advertisement that will appear in the newspaper the following weekend. When Wadsworth met with Berman on Wednesday, April 23, 1997, defendant's proposed advertisement listed a 1995 Jaguar XJ6 Vanden Plas without specifying a price, as it had the preceding week. On Thursday, April 24, a sales manager instructed Wadsworth to substitute a 1994 Jaguar XJ6 with a price of $25,995. The same day, Wadsworth met with Berman and conveyed to her this new information. Wadsworth did not expect to see another proof sheet reflecting this change, however, because she does not work on Friday, and the Daily Pilot goes to press on Friday and the edition in question came out on Saturday, April 26.

Berman testified that the revised advertisement was prepared by the composing department of the Daily Pilot. Berman proofread the advertisement, as she does all advertisements for which she is responsible, but Berman did not notice that it listed the 1995 Jaguar XJ6 Vanden Plas for sale at $25,995, instead of listing the 1994 Jaguar at that price. Both Berman and Wadsworth first learned of the mistake on Monday, April 28, 1997. Defendant's sales manager first became aware of the mistake after plaintiff attempted to purchase the automobile on Sunday, April 27. Berman confirmed in a letter of retraction that Berman's proofreading error had led to the mistake in the advertisement.

Defendant's erroneous advertisement in the Daily Pilot listed 16 used automobiles for sale. Each of the advertisements prepared for several newspapers in late April 1997, except for the one in the Daily Pilot, correctly identified the 1994 Jaguar XJ6 for sale at a price of $25,995. In May 1997, defendant's advertisements in several newspapers listed the

radio announcer, even though the dealer would have had no opportunity to correct the announcer's error before it was made. Pursuant to analogous consumer protection legislation, an unintentional publication of a false or misleading advertisement does not result in statutory liability. . . .

1995 Jaguar XJ6 Vanden Plas for sale at $37,995, and defendant subsequently sold the automobile for $38,399. Defendant had paid $35,000 for the vehicle.

Evidence at trial established that defendant adheres to the following procedures when an incorrect advertisement is discovered. Defendant immediately contacts the newspaper and requests a letter of retraction. Copies of any erroneous advertisements are provided to the sales staff, the error is explained to them, and the mistake is circled in red and posted on a bulletin board at the dealership. The sales staff informs customers of any advertising errors of which they are aware.

No evidence presented at trial suggested that defendant knew of the mistake before plaintiff attempted to purchase the automobile, that defendant intended to mislead customers, or that it had adopted a practice of deliberate indifference regarding errors in advertisements. Wadsworth regularly reviews proof sheets for the numerous advertisements placed by defendant, and representatives of the newspapers, including the Daily Pilot, also proofread defendant's advertisements to ensure they are accurate. Defendant follows procedures for notifying its sales staff and customers of errors of which it becomes aware. The uncontradicted evidence established that the Daily Pilot made the proofreading error resulting in defendant's mistake.

Defendant's fault consisted of failing to review a proof sheet reflecting the change made on Thursday, April 24, 1997, and/or the actual advertisement appearing in the April 26 edition of the Daily Pilot-choosing instead to rely upon the Daily Pilot's advertising staff to proofread the revised version. Although, as the Court of Appeal found, such an omission might constitute negligence, it does not involve a breach of defendant's duty of good faith and fair dealing that should preclude equitable relief for mistake. In these circumstances, it would not be reasonable for this court to allocate the risk of the mistake to defendant. . . .

The final factor defendant must establish before obtaining rescission based upon mistake is that enforcement of the contract for the sale of the 1995 Jaguar XJ6 Vanden Plas at $25,995 would be unconscionable. Although the standards of unconscionability warranting rescission for mistake are similar to those for unconscionability justifying a court's refusal to enforce a contract or term, the general rule governing the latter situation (Civ.Code, § 1670.5) is inapplicable here, because unconscionability resulting from mistake does not appear at the time the contract is made. (Rest.2d Contracts, § 153, com. c, p. 395; 1 Witkin, supra, Contracts, § 370, pp. 337-338.)

An unconscionable contract ordinarily involves both a procedural and a substantive element: (1) oppression or surprise due to unequal bargaining power, and (2) overly harsh or one-sided results. (Armendariz v. Foundation Health Psychcare Services, Inc. (2000) 24 Cal.4th 83, 114, 99 Cal.Rptr.2d 745, 6 P.3d 669.) Nevertheless, " 'a sliding scale is invoked which disregards the regularity of the procedural process of the contract formation, that creates the terms, in proportion to the greater harshness or unreasonableness of the substantive terms themselves.' [Citations.]" (Ibid.) For example, the Restatement Second of Contracts states that "[i]nadequacy of consideration does not of itself invalidate a bargain, but gross disparity in the values exchanged may be an important factor in a determination that a contract is unconscionable and may be sufficient ground, without more, for denying specific performance." (Rest.2d Contracts, § 208, com. c, p. 108.) In ascertaining whether rescission is warranted for a unilateral mistake of fact, substantive unconscionability often will constitute the determinative factor, because the oppression and surprise ordinarily results from the mistake-not from inequality in bargaining power. Accordingly, even though defendant is not the weaker party to the contract and its mistake did not result from unequal bargaining power, defendant was surprised by the mistake, and in these circumstances overly harsh or one-sided results are sufficient to establish unconscionability entitling defendant to rescission. . . .

In the present case, enforcing the contract with the mistaken price of $25,995 would require defendant to sell the vehicle to plaintiff for $12,000 less than the intended advertised price of $37,995-an error amounting to 32 percent of the price defendant intended. Defendant subsequently sold the automobile for slightly more than the intended advertised price, suggesting that that price reflected its actual market value. Defendant had paid $35,000 for the 1995 Jaguar and incurred costs in advertising, preparing, displaying, and attempting to sell the vehicle. Therefore, defendant would lose more than $9,000 of its original investment in the automobile. Plaintiff, on the other hand, would obtain a $12,000 windfall if the contract were enforced, simply because he traveled to the dealership and stated that he was prepared to pay the advertised price.

These circumstances are comparable to those in our prior decisions authorizing rescission on the ground that enforcing a contract with a mistaken price term would be unconscionable. Defendant's 32 percent error in the price exceeds the amount of the errors in cases such as Kemper and Elsinore. For example, in Elsinore, supra, 54 Cal.2d at page 389, 6 Cal.Rptr. 1, 353 P.2d 713, we authorized rescission for a $6,500 error in a bid that was intended to be $96,494-a mistake of approximately 7 percent in the intended contract price. As in the foregoing cases, plaintiff was informed of the mistake as soon as defendant discovered it. Defendant's sales manager, when he first learned of the mistake in the advertisement, explained the error to plaintiff, apologized, and offered to pay for plaintiff's fuel, time, and effort expended in traveling to the dealership to examine the automobile. Plaintiff refused this offer to be restored to the status quo. Like the public agencies in Kemper and Elsinore, plaintiff should not be permitted to take advantage of defendant's honest mistake that resulted in an unfair, one-sided contract. (Cf. Drennan v. Star Paving Co. (1958) 51 Cal.2d 409, 415-416, 333 P.2d 757 [no rescission of mistaken bid where other party detrimentally altered his position in reasonable reliance upon the bid and could not be restored to the status quo].).

. . . Accordingly, section 11713.1(e) does not undermine our determination that, under the circumstances, enforcement of the contract for the sale of the 1995 Jaguar XJ6 Vanden Plas at the $25,995 mistaken price would be unconscionable. The other requirements for rescission on the ground of unilateral mistake have been established. Defendant entered into the contract because of its mistake regarding a basic assumption, the price. The $12,000 loss that would result from enforcement of the contract has a material effect upon the agreed exchange of performances that is adverse to defendant. Furthermore, defendant did not neglect any legal duty within the meaning of Civil Code section 1577 or breach any duty of good faith and fair dealing in the steps leading to the formation of the contract. Plaintiff refused defendant's offer to compensate him for his actual losses in responding to the advertisement. "The law does not penalize for negligence beyond requiring compensation for the loss it has caused." (3 Corbin, Contracts, supra, § 609, p. 684.) In this situation, it would not be reasonable for this court to allocate the risk of the mistake to defendant.

Having determined that defendant satisfied the requirements for rescission of the contract on the ground of unilateral mistake of fact, we conclude that the municipal court correctly entered judgment in defendant's favor.

V

The judgment of the Court of Appeal is reversed.

KENNARD, J., CHIN, J., and BROWN, J., concur.

Dissenting Opinion by WERDEGAR, J.

Although I agree with the majority's conclusion that an enforceable contract was formed between the parties, I respectfully dissent from the majority's grant of contractual rescission to defendant RRL Corporation, relief that is both unsolicited and procedurally irregular. As the majority implicitly acknowledges, defendant did not seek in the trial court to rescind its contract with plaintiff. (Maj. opn., ante, 109 Cal.Rptr.2d at p. 821, fn. 5, 27 P.3d at p. 714, fn. 5.) But the majority neglects to note, further, that at no point on appeal or on review in this court has defendant argued for rescission; defendant's position throughout has been, instead, that no contract was formed between plaintiff and itself. Thus, neither the petition for review nor the answer, which ordinarily delimit the issues to be briefed in this court (Cal. Rules of Court, rule 29.3(c)), so much as mentions rescission. Even at oral argument, counsel for defendant resisted the suggestion that he was seeking rescission, viewing that position as a concession that a contract had been formed, although counsel did eventually agree he "would be pleased to prevail on any theory."

. . . For these reasons, I dissent.

M.J. McGOUGH CO. v. JANE LAMB MEMORIAL HOSPITAL
United States District Court, S.D. of Iowa
302 F. Supp. 482 (1969).

STEPHENSON, Chief Judge.

. . . .

The controversy herein arises from the competitive bidding on a hospital improvement proposed by Jane Lamb Memorial Hospital, a nonprofit Iowa corporation. On or about January 2, 1968, the Hospital published an invitation for bids on this improvement. M. J. McGough Company, a Minnesota corporation, accepted said invitation and submitted a bid along with a bid bond from The Continental Insurance Company in the amount of $100,000. The bid of M. J. McGough was submitted shortly before the opening time of 2:00 p.m., on February 16, 1968. The bids were opened by the Chairman of the Board of Trustees of Jane Lamb Memorial Hospital, Mr. Clark Depue III, at 2:00 p.m., and recorded as follows:

M. J. McGough Co., St. Paul	$1,957,000
Knutson Construction Co., Minneapolis	2,120,643
Steenberg Construction Co., St. Paul	2,185,000
Rinderknecht Construction Co., Cedar Rapids	2,264,000
O. Jorgenson & Sons Construction Co., Clinton	2,322,064
Lovering Construction Co., St. Paul	2,326,380
Universal Construction Co., Kansas City, Mo.	2,500,000
Ringland-Johnson-Crowley Co., Inc., Clinton	2,557,837
Priester Construction Co., Davenport	2,611,000

These figures were relayed to Mr. J. H. McGough, President of M. J. McGough Company, by a representative present at the opening. Mr. McGough was immediately concerned over the ten percent (10%) difference between his low bid and the next lowest bid of Knutson Construction Company.[24] Feeling a serious mistake had been made in the compilation of his bid, therefore, Mr. McGough called his representative at the opening and instructed him to request that he be allowed to withdraw his bid. This request was transmitted to Mr. Depue at approximately 2:45 p.m. while the Board was still analyzing the bids received. Shortly thereafter Mr. McGough spoke with Mr. Depue by telephone and Mr. Depue requested a letter explaining the circumstances of the mistake and a written request to withdraw. Mr. McGough and his staff then began checking the papers relating to this bid and discovered an error in the amount of $199,800. The circumstances surrounding the error were set out in a letter dated February 16, 1968, directed to Milton Holmgrain, the hospital administrator. In the letter Mr. McGough offered to "submit to you immediately all of our records relating to this project for verification of this error." In spite of this the Board of Trustees, without further communication with M. J. McGough Company, at its meeting on February 22, 1968, passed a "Resolution of Intent" to the effect that the Board intended to accept the bid of M. J. McGough Company subject to obtaining the approval of the Division of Hospital Services of the Iowa State Department of Health and the U.S. Public Health Service.

Thereafter, the parties communicated a number of times by telephone, letter and in person on the matter. At all times M. J. McGough Company sought the withdrawal of its bid and offered to produce its papers to verify the error in its bid. Likewise, the representatives of Jane Lamb Memorial Hospital continuously sought to hold M. J. McGough Company to its original bid. Upon the refusal of M. J. McGough Company to execute the contract and other necessary documents, however, the contract was awarded to the next lowest bidder, Knutson Construction Company.

On April 11, 1968, M. J. McGough Company filed a complaint in this Court seeking to have its bid declared rescinded and the surety, The Continental Insurance Company, be released from liability on the bond. On that same date Jane Lamb Memorial Hospital filed a complaint in this court against M. J. McGough Company and The Continental Insurance

[24] By his testimony at trial Mr. McGough explained that Knutson Construction Company was known in the trade as a notoriously low bidder.

Company seeking damages in the amount of $190,156.58.[25] These claims are consolidated for decision herein.

The circumstances surrounding the mistake in the bid of M. J. McGough Company are not seriously disputed. The majority of the subcontractor bids used in computing the bid of M. J. McGough Company were received on February 16, 1968, the day of the opening. It is the accepted practice and custom among subcontractors to refrain from submitting their final sub-bids until the day of the opening and, then, only within a matter of hours before the actual opening of bids.[26] The final sub-bids were received by telephone in the offices of M. J. McGough Company in St. Paul, Minnesota, between 10:30 a.m. and 1:00 p.m. on February 16, 1968. The sub-bids were recorded as they were phoned in on a slip of paper. Mr. McGough received the sub-bid of Artcraft Interiors, Inc., during this period of frenzied activity, and although he correctly recorded it on the slip of paper as $222,000, he verbally called it to an employee who recorded it as $22,200. This erroneous figure was, subsequently, transposed by the employee on the recapitulation sheet and used in computing the final bid of M. J. McGough Company. It was not until after the opening of bids, when Mr. McGough sought to check their figures, that the mistake was discovered.

By the overwhelming weight of authority a contractor may be relieved from a unilateral mistake in his bid by rescission under the proper circumstances. See generally, Annot., 52 A.L.R.2d 792 (1957). The prerequisites for obtaining such relief are: (1) the mistake is of such consequence that enforcement would be unconscionable; (2) the mistake must relate to the substance of the consideration; (3) the mistake must have occurred regardless of the exercise of ordinary care; (4) it must be possible to place the other party in status quo. See e.g., Peerless Casualty Co. v. Housing Authority, 228 F.2d 376 (5th Cir. 1955) . . . . It is also generally required that the bidder give prompt notification of the mistake and his intention to withdraw. . . .

Applying the criteria for rescission for a unilateral mistake to the circumstances in this case, it is clear that M. J. McGough Company and his surety, The Continental Insurance Company, are entitled to equitable relief. The notification of mistake was promptly made, and Mr. McGough made every possible effort to explain the circumstances of the mistake to the authorities of Jane Lamb Memorial Hospital. Although Jane Lamb Memorial Hospital argues to the contrary, the Court finds that notification of the mistake was received before acceptance of the bid. The mere opening of the bids did not constitute the acceptance of the lowest bid. O. C. Kinney, Inc. v. Paul Hardeman, Inc., 151 Colo. 571, 379 P.2d 628 (1963). Likewise, the acceptance by the Board of Trustees on February 22, 1968, being conditional, was not effective. Peerless Casualty Co. v. Housing Authority, supra; Lexington Housing Authority v. Continental Cas. Co., 210 F.Supp. 732, 735 (W.D.Tenn.1962). Furthermore, it is generally held that acceptance prior to notification does not bar the right to equitable relief from a mistake in the bid. See, e.g., James T. Taylor and Son, Inc. v. Arlington Ind. School

[25] Jane Lamb Memorial Hospital arrived at this amount by adding the difference ($179,393) between the M. J. McGough Company bid and the Knutson Construction Company bid plus the amount of increased architect's fees ($10,763.58), which are based on a percentage of the total price.

[26] . . . The reasoning for this custom was stated in Berkeley Unified School Dist. of Alameda County v. James I. Barnes Const. Co., 123 F.Supp. 924, footnote 1 (N.D.Cal.1954), as follows: 'Subcontractors generally wait as long as possible before placing their bids with a contractor in order to prevent the contractor from having the time in which to obtain a lower bid from some other subcontractor.'

Dist., supra; School Dist. of Scottsbluff v. Olson Const. Co., supra; Kutsche v. Ford, 222 Mich. 442, 192 N.W. 714 (1922); Annot., 52 A.L.R.2d 792, at 803 (1957).

The mistake in this case was an honest error made in good faith. While a mistake in and of itself indicates some degree of lack of care or negligence, under the circumstances here there was not such a lack of care as to bar relief. . . .

The mistake here was a simple clerical error. To allow Jane Lamb Memorial Hospital to take advantage of this mistake would be unconscionable. This is especially true in light of the fact that they had actual knowledge of the mistake before the acceptance of the bid. Mount St. Mary's College v. Aetna Casualty & Surety, supra; Berkeley Unified School Dist. v. Barnes Const. Co., 123 F.Supp. 924 (N.D.Cal.1954); M. F. Kemper Const. Co. v. City of Los Angeles, supra. Nor can it be seriously contended that a $199,800 error, amounting to approximately 10% Of the bid, does not relate directly to the substance of the consideration. Furthermore, Jane Lamb Memorial Hospital has suffered no actual damage by the withdrawal of the bid of M. J. McGough Company. The Hospital has lost only what it sought to gain by taking advantage of M. J. McGough Company's mistake. St. Nicholas Church v. Kropp, supra; Kutsche v. Ford, supra. Equitable considerations will not allow the recovery of the loss of bargain in this situation.

Under the facts before the Court, therefore, M. J. McGough Company will be allowed to rescind its bid and be relieved from any liability thereon. The Continental Insurance Company, surety on the bid bond, is likewise relieved from liability. See, e.g., Peerless Casualty Co. V. Housing Authority, supra; State ex rel. Arkansas State Highway Commission v. Ottinger, 232 Ark. 35, 334 S.W.2d 694 (1960); see generally Annot., 52 A.L.R.2d 792, at 807 (1957).

As a final matter, the Court notes that Jane Lamb Memorial Hospital relies heavily on the provisions on the bid which provides:

> The bidder agrees that this bid shall be good and may not be withdrawn for a period of 45 calendar days after the scheduled closing time for receiving bids.

It is also provided by Government regulations pursuant to the Hill-Burton Act, under which this project was to be financed, as follows:

> Withdrawal of Bids.- Bids may be withdrawn on written or telegraphic request received from bidders prior to the time fixed for opening. Negligence on the part of the bidder in preparing the bid confers no right for the withdrawal of the bid after it has been opened.

It is sufficient to say that provisions such as these have been considered many times in similar cases, and have never been held effective when equitable considerations dictate otherwise. Peerless Casualty Co. v. Housing Authority, supra . . . .

Based on equitable principles, therefore, judgment will be entered in favor of M. J. McGough Company and against Jane Lamb Memorial Hospital. Due to the factual situation out of which this litigation arose and the reasons for which relief has been granted to M. J. McGough Company, the Court deems it to be in the best interests of justice that each party bear its own costs.

It is ordered that the bid submitted by M. J. McGough Company to Jane Lamb Memorial Hospital on February 16, 1968, be and is hereby declared rescinded. It is further declared hereby that no enforceable contract exists between M. J. McGough Company and Jane Lamb Memorial Hospital. The surety on the bid bond, The Continental Insurance Company, is hereby released from further liability thereon. Each party will bear its own costs.

NOTES AND QUESTIONS:

1. Revisit the question of whether a *misunderstanding* and a *mistake* are the same thing. Can you articulate the difference?

2. Another form of mistake, commonly referred to a scrivener's error, occurs in the process of reducing the agreement to writing. Here, the parties mutually agreed on the terms, however the writing mistakenly reflected something other than parties' actual agreement. A written contract may be reformed to reflect the parties' actual agreement upon a showing based on clear and convincing evidence that the mistake existed at the time the writing was executed, the mistake was mutual and common to all parties, and the parties intended to say one thing but the writing reflected something else. For a discussion of whether a party is entitled to reformation of a written agreement, see *Sedlacek v. Sedlacek*, 246 N.E.2d 6 (Ill. App. 1969).

SECTION 3. MISREPRESENTATION/FRAUD

A. MISREPRESENTATION

YARBOROUGH V. BACK
Court of Civil Appeals of Texas
561 S.W.2d 593 (1978).

REYNOLDS, Justice.

. . . .

Texas residents Neville Back, the owner of a sixteen-year-old stallion named Poco Pine Back, and M. W. Yarborough conversed in the spring of 1975 concerning Yarborough's lease of the stallion. On or about 11 June 1975, Yarborough paid Back $2,000 and Back released Poco Pine Back to Yarborough's son. Yarborough secured and mailed an attorney-prepared written agreement to Back, who had gone to New Mexico. Back signed and returned the agreement to Yarborough.

By the agreement, dated 26 June 1975 and executed by both parties, Yarborough leased Poco Pine Back for the balance of the year for the $2,000 paid with an option Yarborough could exercise before 1 January 1976 to purchase the stallion for $10,000, less the $2,000 paid for the lease. The agreement did not mention insurance.

Poco Pine Back died uninsured some four and one-half months after Yarborough took possession of him. No fault for the death is attributed to Yarborough.

Back grounded his suit on fraud, pleading false representations by Yarborough upon which he reasonably relied and by which he was induced to enter into the written contract. The representations pleaded were: Yarborough's "telling Plaintiff (Back) that the stallion would be covered by insurance in the event of loss by death of the stallion;" and Yarborough told Back's agent, when the contract was prepared without the insurance provision, "that the stallion was at that time already insured against loss by death for the amount of $25,000.00 by insurance purchased by Defendant (Yarborough)."

The matter of insurance coverage was in dispute at the trial before the court. Back testified that insurance was discussed before the agreement was finalized, and that he would not have agreed to lease Poco Pine Back if Yarborough had not told him "that he was going to get insurance on the horse." Yarborough testified that the first time insurance was mentioned was after the signed agreement was sent back to him; that Back requested insurance and Yarborough said he would turn it over to his insurance agent to see if he could get the horse insured.

There is Back's testimony that he wanted $8,000 insurance made in his name, and Yarborough said he would get insurance, before Poco Pine Back was released to Yarborough. Yet, Back released the stallion on or about 11 June 1975 to Yarborough's son after the son "told me his daddy was having his insurance agent work on it (the insurance)."

Back developed testimony that when he received the written agreement in New Mexico, he called his granddaughter, who was taking care of his ranch in Texas, and asked about the insurance. She then talked with Yarborough over a period of some two weeks. Yarborough first told her his insurance agent was working on it and then told her the horse was insured for $25,000. She reported to Back. However, Yarborough denied that he ever said the horse was insured.

Back was not asked, nor did he state, specifically whether he signed the written agreement before or after he was told the stallion was insured. His only testimony in this regard was developed in cross-examination as follows:

> Q. When you noticed in the lease agreement that there wasn't any mention of insurance, why did you sign it?
>
> A. I had talked to my granddaughter at home and she had talked to him, and he assured her he was working on getting the insurance.

The parties stipulated that Yarborough attempted to get insurance. It was Yarborough's testimony that his insurance agent was unable to find a company that would insure Poco Pine Back.

To be entitled to judgment on his pleadings, Back had the burden to prove and secure findings, either express or presumed, that he was induced by fraud on the part of Yarborough to enter into the written contract. See Dallas Joint Stock Land Bank of Dallas v. Harrison, 138 Tex. 84, 156 S.W.2d 963, 967 (1941). Preliminarily to rendering judgment for Back in the amount of $6,000, the trial court advised counsel by letter of "conclusions" made from the testimony. The parties dispute whether the "conclusions" constitute findings of fact; but, in any event, the court expressed no finding on reliance. Nevertheless, an essential element of fraud is that the false statement(s) must have been relied upon. Davidson v. Commercial Nat. Bank of Brady, 59 S.W.2d 949, 953 (Tex.Civ.App. Austin 1933, writ ref'd).

At the outset, it must be noted that the first pleaded representation by Yarborough "that the stallion would be covered by insurance" (emphasis added) is nothing more than a promise to be performed in the future. At such, it does not constitute actionable fraud even if it was made to induce a contract and thereafter was not fulfilled, Cassel v. West, 98 S.W.2d 437, 439 (Tex.Civ.App. Amarillo 1936, writ ref'd), unless the promise was made with a present intention not to perform. Stanfield v. O'Boyle, 462 S.W.2d 270, 272 (Tex.1971). Of course, the failure to fulfill the promise does not, by itself, even raise the issue of a present intention not to perform, Turner v. Biscoe, 141 Tex. 197, 171 S.W.2d 118, 119 (1943), which is completely negated by the stipulation that Yarborough attempted to secure insurance.

The query, then, is whether there is any proof that Back contracted in reliance on the pleaded false representation "that the stallion was at that time already insured" (emphasis added). Neither Back nor anyone else testified that he relied on that representation in entering into the contract. The only evidence directly bearing on the matter is Back's testimony quoted above, the sense of which is that he signed the agreement because his granddaughter had been assured that Yarborough "was working on getting the insurance." This testimony is neither evidence of probative force, nor the proper basis for a reasonable inference, that Back entered into the contract through reliance on the representation that Poco Pine Back was then insured.

There being no evidence in support of an essential element of the pleaded cause of action, a take-nothing judgment should have been rendered.

By their briefs, the parties have joined the issue whether the judgment is sustainable on the theory of breach of contract. In lieu of an extended discussion of the diverse positions taken, it suffices to state that Back, having pleaded only fraud, cannot recover on the unpleaded ground of breach of contract. Starr v. Ferguson, 140 Tex. 80, 166 S.W.2d 130, 132 (1942).

The judgment of the trial court is reversed, and judgment is here rendered that Neville Back take nothing by his cause of action asserted against M. W. Yarborough. Rule 434, Texas Rules of Civil Procedure.

NOTES AND QUESTIONS:

1. There must be a misrepresentation of a fact presumably in existence at the time of the assertion - the promise to be performed in the future is not a misrepresentation of a present fact. It is not a false statement unless it is made with the present intent not to perform. Additionally, there must be reliance on such a misrepresented fact for it to operate as a defense. *See Martin v. Ohio State Univ. Found.*, 742 N.E.2d 1198 (10th Dist. 2000) (stating that when a person makes his promise of future action, occurrence, or conduct which at the time it is made the promisor has no intention of keeping, the requisite misrepresentation of an existing fact is said to be found in the lie as to the promisor's existing mental attitude and present intent). *See also U.S. v. Heatley*, 39 F. Supp. 2d 287 (S.D.N.Y. 1998) (citing Restatement (Second) of Contracts § 164(1)).

HALPERT V. ROSENTHAL
Supreme Court of Rhode Island
267 A.2d 730 (1970).

KELLEHER, Justice.

This is a civil action wherein the plaintiff vendor seeks damages for the breach by the defendant vendee of a contract for the sale of real estate. The defendant filed a counterclaim in which he sought the return of his deposit. A jury trial was held in the Superior Court. The jury found for the defendant and judgment followed. The case is before us on the plaintiff's appeal.

On February 21, 1967, the parties hereto entered into a real estate agreement whereby plaintiff agreed to convey a one-family house located in Providence on the southeasterly corner of Wayland and Upton Avenues to defendant for the sum of $54,000. The defendant paid a deposit of $2,000 to plaintiff. The agreement provided for the delivery of the deed and the payment of the balance of the purchase price by June 30, 1967.

On May 17, 1967, a termite inspection was made of the premises, and it was discovered that the house was inhabited by termites. The defendant then notified plaintiff that, because of the termite infestation, he was not going to purchase the property. The defendant did not appear for the title closing which plaintiff had scheduled for June 30, 1967.

The plaintiff immediately commenced this suit. Her complaint prayed for specific performance or monetary damages. When the case came on for trial, the property had been sold to another buyer for the sum of $35,000. The plaintiff then sought to recover from defendant the $19,000 difference between the selling price called for in the sales agreement and the actual selling price. The defendant in his answer alleged that plaintiff and her agent had, during the preagreement negotiation, intentionally misrepresented the house as being free of termites. The defendant's counterclaim sought the return of the $2,000 deposit.

At the conclusion of the presentation of all the evidence, plaintiff made a motion for a directed verdict on the issue of the alleged fraudulent misrepresentations. The trial justice reserved decision on the motion and submitted the case to the jury. After the jury's verdict, he denied the motion. . . .

Since we consider only the evidence favorable to defendant, we shall set forth defendant's version of three different occasions in 1967 when the alleged misrepresentations relative to absence of any termites were made.

> 1. In early February, defendant and his wife inspected the Halpert home. They asked the agent about termites and he told them that there was no termite problem and that he had never experienced any termite problem with any of the houses he sold in the East Side section of Providence.
>
> 2. Later on in February, defendant, his wife, his sister-in-law and his brother-in-law met plaintiff. The brother-in-law inquired about the presence of termites; plaintiff said that there were no termites in the house.
>
> 3. When defendant was about to sign the purchase and sales agreement, he asked plaintiff's real estate agent whether it might not be advisable if the home be inspected for termites before the agreement was signed. The agent told defendant that such a step was unnecessary because there were no termite problems in the house.

The plaintiff contends that any statements or representations attributed to her or her agent were qualified in that when asked about the termites, they replied that to the best of their knowledge or experience the Wayland Avenue property was termite free. What she overlooks is that in our consideration of the correctness of the denial of her motion for a direction, we can consider only that evidence and the reasonable inferences flowing therefrom which favor defendant. We do not weigh the evidence to determine whether her or her agent's representations were qualified or unqualified.

In contending that she was entitled to a directed verdict, plaintiff contends that to sustain the charge of fraudulent misrepresentation, some evidence had to be produced showing that either she or her agent knew at the time they said there were no termites in the house, that such a statement was untrue. Since the representations made to defendant were made in good faith, she argues that, as a matter of law, defendant could not prevail on his counterclaim.

The defendant concedes that there was no evidence which shows that plaintiff or her agent knowingly made false statements as to the existence of the termites but he maintains that an innocent misrepresentation of a material fact is grounds for rescission of a contract where, as here, a party relies to his detriment on the misrepresentation.

We affirm the denial of the motion for a directed verdict.

. . . The distinction between a claim for damages for intentional deceit and a claim for rescission is well defined. Deceit is a tort action, and it requires some degree of culpability on the misrepresenter's part. Prosser, Law of Torts (3d ed.) s 100. An individual who sues in an action of deceit based on fraud has the burden of proving that the defendant in making the statements knew they were false and intended to deceive him. Cliftex Clothing Co. v. DiSanto, 88 R.I. 338, 148 A.2d 273; Conti v. Walter Winters, Inc., 86 R.I. 456, 136 A.2d 622. On the other hand, a suit to rescind an agreement induced by fraud sounds in contract. It is this latter aspect of fraud that we are concerned with in this case, and the pivotal issue before us is whether an innocent misrepresentation of a material fact warrants the granting of a claim for rescission. We believe that it does.

When he denied plaintiff's motion, the trial justice indicated that a false, though innocent, misrepresentation of a fact made as though of one's knowledge may be the basis for the rescission of a contract. While this issue is one of first impression in this state, it is clear that the trial judge's action finds support in the overwhelming weight of decisionand textual authority which has established the rule that where one induces another to enter into a contract by means of a material misrepresentation, the latter may rescind the contract. It does not matter if the representation was "innocent" or fraudulent.

In 12 Williston, supra, § 1500 at 400-01, Professor Jaeger states:

> It is not necessary, in order that a contract may be rescinded for fraud or misrepresentation, that the party making the misrepresentation should have known that it was false. Innocent misrepresentation is sufficient, for though the representation may have been made innocently, it would be unjust and inequitable to permit a person who has made false representations, even innocently, to retain the fruits of a bargain induced by such representations.

This statement of law is in accord with Restatement of Contracts, § 476 at 908 which states:

> Where a party is induced to enter into a transaction with another party that he was under no duty to enter into by means of the latter's fraud or material misrepresentation, the transaction is voidable as against the latter . . . .

Misrepresentation is defined as

> . . . any manifestation by words or other conduct by one person to another that, under the circumstances, amounts to an assertion not in accordance with the facts. Restatement of Contracts, § 470 at 890-91.

The comment following this section explains that a misrepresentation may be innocent, negligent or known to be false. A misrepresentation becomes material when it becomes likely to affect the conduct of a reasonable man with reference to a transaction with another person. Restatement of Contracts, § 470(2) at 891. Section 28 of Restatement of Restitution is also in accord with this proposition of law that a transaction can be rescinded for innocent misrepresentation of a material fact. In addition, many courts have also adopted this rule including the following: Lehnhardt v. City, 105 Ariz. 142, 460 P.2d 637; Prudential Ins. Co. v. Anaya, 78 N.M. 101, 428 P.2d 640; Lanners v. Whitney, 247 Or. 223, 428 P.2d 398; Hudspeth v. Zorn, (Mo.) 292 S.W.2d 271; Keeton Packing Co. v. State, (Tex.Civ.App.) 437 S.W.2d 20; Chesapeake Homes, Inc. v. McGrath, 249 Md. 480, 240 A.2d 245; Yorke v. Taylor, 332 Mass. 368, 124 N.E.2d 912; Whipp v. Iverson, 43 Wis.2d 166, 168 N.W.2d 201; Seneca Wire & Mfg. Co. v. A. B. Leach & Co., 247 N.Y. 1, 159 N.E. 700; Berger v. Pittsburgh Auto Equipment Co., 387 Pa. 61, 127 A.2d 334.

In Ham v. Hart, 58 N.M. 550, 273 P.2d 748, the court in holding that the honesty and good faith of the person making misrepresentations is immaterial, quoted the following excerpt from 1 Story Equity Jurisprudence § 272 (14 ed.):

> Whether the party thus misrepresenting a material fact knew it to be false, or made the assertion without knowing whether it were true or false, is wholly immaterial; for the affirmation of what one does not know or believe to be true is equally in morals and law as unjustifiable as the affirmation of what is known to be positively false. And even if the party innocently misrepresents a material fact by mistake, it is equally conclusive; for it operates as a surprise and imposition upon the other party. 58 N.M. at 552, 273 P.2d at 749.

It is true that some courts require proof of knowledge of the falsity of the misrepresentation before a contract may be invalidated. Wilkinson v. Appleton, 28 Ill.2d 184, 190 N.E.2d 727; Classic Bowl, Inc. v. AMF Pinspotters, Inc., 6 Cir., 403 F.2d 463; Southern Roofing & Petroleum Co. v. Aetna Ins. Co., D.C., 293 F.Supp. 725. However, the weight of authority follows the view that the misrepresenter's good faith is immaterial. We believe this view the better one.

A misrepresentation, even though innocently made, may be actionable, if made and relied on as a positive statement of fact. The question to be resolved in determining whether a wrong committed as the result of an innocent misrepresentation may be rectified is succinctly stated in 12 Williston, supra, § 1510 at 462 as follows:

> When a defendant has induced another to act by representations false in fact although not dishonestly made, and damage has directly resulted from the action taken, who should bear the loss?

The question we submit is rhetorical. The answer is obvious. Simple justice demands that the speaker be held responsible. Accordingly, we hold that here defendant vendee could maintain his counterclaim. . . .

Before leaving this phase of plaintiff's appeal, we think it appropriate that we allude to the tendency of many courts to equate an innocent misrepresentation with some species of fraud. Usually the word "fraud"connotes a conscious dishonest conduct on the part of the misrepresenter. Fraud, however, is not present if the speaker actually believes that what he states as the truth is the truth. We believe that it would be better if an innocent misrepresentation was not described as some specie of fraud. Unqualified statements imply certainty. Reliance is more likely to be placed on a positive statement of fact than a mere expression of opinion or a qualified statement. The speaker who uses the unqualified statement does so at his peril. The risk of falsity is his. If he is to be liable for what he states, the liability is imposed because he is to be held strictly accountable for his words. Responsibility for an innocent misrepresentation should be recognized for what it is-an example of absolute liability rather than as many courts have said, an example of constructive fraud. See 12 Williston, supra, § 1510; 1 Harper and James, The Law of Torts § 7.7. . . .

The appeal of the plaintiff is denied and dismissed, and the case is remanded to the Superior Court for entry of judgment thereon.

B. PASSIVE CONCEALMENT

SWINTON V. WHITINSVILLE SAVINGS BANK
Supreme Judicial Court of Massachusetts
42 N.E.2d 808 (1942).

QUA, Justice.

The declaration alleges that on or about September 12, 1938, the defendant sold the plaintiff a house in Newton to be occupied by the plaintiff and his family as a dwelling; that at the time of the sale the house 'was infested with termites, an insect that is most dangerous and destructive to buildings'; that the defendant knew the house was so infested; that the plaintiff could not readily observe this condition upon inspection; that "knowing the internal destruction that these insects were creating in said house," the defendant falsely and fraudulently concealed from the plaintiff its true condition; that the plaintiff at the time of his purchase had no knowledge of the termites, exercised due care thereafter, and learned of them about August 30, 1940; and that, because of the destruction that was being done and the dangerous condition that was being created by the termites, the plaintiff was put to great expense for repairs and for the installation of termite control in order to prevent the loss and destruction of said house.

There is no allegation of any false statement or representation, or of the uttering of a half truth which may be tantamount to a falsehood. There is no intimation that the defendant by any means prevented the plaintiff from acquiring information as to the condition of the house. There is nothing to show any fiduciary relation between the parties, or that the plaintiff stood in a position of confidence toward or dependence upon the defendant. So far as appears the parties made a business deal at arm's length. The charge is concealment and nothing more; and it is concealment in the simple sense of mere failure to reveal, with nothing to show any peculiar duty to speak. The characterization of the concealment as false and fraudulent of course adds nothing in the absence of further allegations of fact. Province Securities Corp. v. Maryland Casualty Co., 269 Mass. 75, 92, 168 S.E. 252.

If this defendant is liable on this declaration every seller is liable who fails to disclose any nonapparent defect known to him in the subject of the sale which materially reduces its value and which the buyer fails to discover. Similarly it would seem that every buyer would be liable who fails to disclose any nonapparent virtue known to him in the subject of the purchase which materially enhances its value and of which the seller is ignorant. See Goodwin v. Agassiz, 283 Mass. 358, 186 N.E. 659. The law has not yet, we believe, reached the point of imposing upon the frailties of human nature a standard so idealistic as this. That the particular case here stated by the plaintiff possesses a certain appeal to the moral sense is scarcely to be denied. Probably the reason is to be found in the facts that the infestation of buildings by termites has not been common in Massachusetts and constitutes a concealed risk against which buyers are off their guard. But the law cannot provide special rules for termites and can hardly attempt to determine liability according to the varying probabilities of the existence and discovery of different possible defects in the subjects of trade. The rule of nonliability for bare nondisclosure has been stated and followed by this court in Matthews v. Bliss, 22 Pick. 48, 52, 53; Potts v. Chapin, 133 Mass. 276; Van Houten v. Morse, 162 Mass. 414, 38 N.E. 705, 26 L.R.A. 430, 44 Am.St.Rep. 373; Phinney v. Friedman, 224 Mass. 531, 533, 113 N.E. 285; Windram Mfg. Co. v. Boston Blacking Co., 239 Mass. 123, 126, 131 N.E. 454, 17 A.L.R. 669; Wellington v. Rugg, 243 Mass. 30, 35, 36, 136 N.E. 831, and Brockton Olympia Realty Co. v. Lee, 266 Mass. 550, 561, 165 N.E. 873. It is adopted in the American Law Institute's Restatement of Torts, § 551. See Williston on Contracts, Rev.Ed., §§ 1497, 1498, 1499.

The order sustaining the demurrer is affirmed, and judgment is to be entered for the defendant. Keljikian v. Star Brewing Co., 303 Mass. 53, 55-63, 20 N.E.2d 465.

So ordered.

C. ACTIVE CONCEALMENT

JENKINS V. MCCORMICK
Supreme Court of Kansas
339 P.2d 8 (1959).

JACKSON, Justice.

In the district court, the appellee filed a suit against the appellant and in her petition alleged that she had purchased a newly constructed house from the defendant who was a contractor; that there was a latent defect in the floor of the basement apartment; that the defendant knew of such defect and fraudulently concealed the same to the damage of the plaintiff. Plaintiff sought damages because of the alleged fraudulent concealment in a total of $1,145.61. . . .

. . . The principal allegations of the petition attacked are found in paragraphs 5 through 10 and read as follows:

> 5. That the making and execution of said written agreement and the performance thereof by plaintiff, according to its terms, as above set forth, were procured by the fraud and deceit of defendant, exercised upon plaintiff for the purpose of procuring said making, execution and performance through the wilful concealment of certain matter and the wilfully false representations and statements made to plaintiff.
>
> 6. Plaintiff further states that said duplex had been newly constructed by defendant and was sold to plaintiff as a newly built house; that said duplex contained a basement apartment the floor of which was asphalt tile laid on concrete; that at the time of said sales contract said asphalt basement floor appeared to be smooth and in good shape.
>
> 7. That for the purpose of inducing plaintiff to make, execute and perform said written agreement defendant deceived plaintiff as follows:

> That said house contained a basement apartment the floor of which was asphalt tile *layed* on concrete; that the defendant well knew that the concrete in the basement floor had been allowed by him to set and dry without being smoothed and properly *trowled*; that nevertheless the defendant placed asphalt tile over this cement floor and the defendant, a contractor, knew or should have known that the said asphalt tile would crack and come loose in a short length of time; that defendant knew that these floor defects were concealed from plaintiff; that defendant concealed said facts from plaintiff by suppressing defendant's knowledge of the same and by failing to inform plaintiff that said basement floor was latently defective and that defendant concealed said facts from plaintiff for the sole purposing of inducing plaintiff to make, execute and perform said written agreement.
>
> 8. That at all times herein mentioned defendant carefully concealed from plaintiff that said basement concrete floor was improperly constructed although defendant knew the same and knew plaintiff was unable to ascertain the same by inspection; that defendant was in a superior position to plaintiff to ascertain this knowledge in that he had seen the cement floor prior to putting the asphalt tile onto it.
>
> 9. That plaintiff was wholly deceived by defendant, said concealment of said fact and was thereby induced to make, execute, and perform said written agreement.
>
> 10. That plaintiff would not have made, executed or performed said written agreement if plaintiff had knowledge of said floor defects which were hidden from plaintiff and which plaintiff could not reasonably have discovered.

In the balance of the petition, plaintiff alleges that the entire basement asphalt tile floor broke up within two weeks after the house was purchased and then alleges her damages suffered because of the alleged defect and asks judgment therefor.

The defendant seems to urge that the demurrer should have been sustained to the above petition on the ground of the old rule of *caveat emptor*. He cites numerous cases in the application of that rule, none of which seem to apply to the situation alleged in the instant petition. Here we have the builder of a house effectively concealing a known defect caused by his own workmanship. In such a situation, the rule of *caveat emptor* does not apply, and such concealment amounts to fraud upon the purchaser.

In 23 Am.Jur. 857, § 80, it is said:

> There is much authority to the effect that if one party to a contract or transaction has superior knowledge, or knowledge which is not within the fair and reasonable reach of the other party and which he could not discover by the exercise of reasonable diligence, or means of knowledge which are not open to both parties alike, he is under a legal obligation to speak, and his silence constitutes fraud, especially when the other party relies upon him to

> communicate to him the true state of facts to enable him to judge of the expediency of the bargain.
>
> Again in 37 C.J.S. Fraud § 16b, p. 246, it is said:
>
> The rule that when the parties deal at arm's length and their relations are not confidential silence is not fraud is particularly true where the facts are equally within the means of knowledge of both parties or peculiarly within the knowledge of one party and of such a nature that the other has no right to expect information. *If the fact concealed is peculiarly within the knowledge of one party and of such a nature that the other party is justified in assuming its nonexistence, there is a duty of disclosure, and deliberate suppression of such fact is fraud.* (Italics supplied.)

See especially the recent case of Dargue v. Chaput, 166 Neb. 69, 88 N.W.2d 148, and also McWilliam v. Barnes, 172 Kan. 701, 242 P.2d 1063; Nairn v. Ewalt, 51 Kan. 355, Syl. ¶2, 32 P. 1110; Downing v. Wimble, 97 Vt. 390, 123 A. 433, and Deardorf v. Rosenbusch, 201 Okl. 420, 206 P. 2d 996.

There is no question raised in this case, but that plaintiff has a right to affirm the contract of sale and sue for damages caused by the alleged fraudulent concealment (McWilliams v. Barnes, supra). From what has been said, it appears the district court did not err in overruling the demurrer to the petition, and that the order should be affirmed. It is so ordered.

STAMBOVSKY V. ACKLEY
Supreme Court, Appellate Division, New York
169 A.D.2d 254 (1991).

RUBIN, Justice.

Plaintiff, to his horror, discovered that the house he had recently contracted to purchase was widely reputed to be possessed by poltergeists, reportedly seen by defendant seller and members of her family on numerous occasions over the last nine years. Plaintiff promptly commenced this action seeking rescission of the contract of sale. Supreme Court reluctantly dismissed the complaint, holding that plaintiff has no remedy at law in this jurisdiction.

The unusual facts of this case, as disclosed by the record, clearly warrant a grant of equitable relief to the buyer who, as a resident of New York City, cannot be expected to have any familiarity with the folklore of the Village of Nyack. Not being a "local," plaintiff could not readily learn that the home he had contracted to purchase is haunted. Whether the source of the spectral apparitions seen by defendant seller are parapsychic or psychogenic, having reported their presence in both a national publication ("Readers' Digest") and the local press (in 1977 and 1982, respectively), defendant is estopped to deny their existence and, as a matter of law, the house is haunted. More to the point, however, no divination is required to conclude that it is defendant's promotional efforts in publicizing her close encounters with these spirits which fostered the home's reputation in the community. In 1989, the house was included in a five-home walking tour of Nyack and described in a November 27th newspaper article as "a riverfront Victorian (with ghost)." The impact of the reputation thus created goes to the very essence of the bargain between the parties, greatly impairing both the value of the property and its potential for resale. The extent of this impairment may be presumed for the purpose of reviewing the disposition of this motion to dismiss the cause of action for rescission (Harris v. City of New York, 147 A.D.2d 186, 188-189, 542 N.Y.S.2d 550) and represents merely an issue of fact for resolution at trial.

While I agree with Supreme Court that the real estate broker, as agent for the seller, is under no duty to disclose to a potential buyer the phantasmal reputation of the premises and that, in his pursuit of a legal remedy for fraudulent misrepresentation against the seller, plaintiff hasn't a ghost of a chance, I am nevertheless moved by the spirit of equity to allow the buyer to seek rescission of the contract of sale and recovery of his downpayment. New York law fails to recognize any remedy for damages incurred as a result of the seller's mere silence, applying instead the strict rule of caveat emptor. Therefore, the theoretical basis for granting relief, even under the extraordinary facts of this case, is elusive if not ephemeral.

"Pity me not but lend thy serious hearing to what I shall unfold" (William Shakespeare, Hamlet, Act I, Scene V [Ghost]).

From the perspective of a person in the position of plaintiff herein, a very practical problem arises with respect to the discovery of a paranormal phenomenon: "Who you gonna' call?" as the title song to the movie "Ghostbusters" asks. Applying the strict rule of caveat emptor to a contract involving a house possessed by poltergeists conjures up visions of a psychic or medium routinely accompanying the structural engineer and Terminix man on an inspection of every home subject to a contract of sale. It portends that the prudent attorney will establish an escrow account lest the subject of the transaction come back to haunt him and his client-or pray that his malpractice insurance coverage extends to supernatural disasters. In the interest of avoiding such untenable consequences, the notion that a haunting is a condition which can and should be ascertained upon reasonable inspection of the premises is a hobgoblin which should be exorcised from the body of legal precedent and laid quietly to rest.

It has been suggested by a leading authority that the ancient rule which holds that mere non-disclosure does not constitute actionable misrepresentation "finds proper application in cases where the fact undisclosed is patent, or the plaintiff has equal opportunities for obtaining information which he may be expected to utilize, or the defendant has no reason to think that he is acting under any misapprehension" (Prosser, Law of Torts § 106, at 696 [4th ed., 1971]). However, with respect to transactions in real estate, New York adheres to the doctrine of caveat emptor and imposes no duty upon the vendor to disclose any information concerning the premises (London v. Courduff, 141 A.D.2d 803, 529 N.Y.S.2d 874) unless there is a confidential or fiduciary relationship between the parties (Moser v. Spizzirro, 31 A.D.2d 537, 295 N.Y.S.2d 188, affd., 25 N.Y.2d 941, 305 N.Y.S.2d 153, 252 N.E.2d 632; IBM Credit Fin. Corp. v. Mazda Motor Mfg. (USA) Corp., 152 A.D.2d 451, 542 N.Y.S.2d 649) or some conduct on the part of the seller which constitutes "active concealment" (see, 17 East 80th Realty Corp. v. 68th Associates, 173 A.D.2d 245, 569 N.Y.S.2d 647 [dummy ventilation system constructed by seller]; Haberman v. Greenspan, 82 Misc.2d 263, 368 N.Y.S.2d 717 [foundation cracks covered by seller]). Normally, some affirmative misrepresentation (e.g., Tahini Invs., Ltd. v. Bobrowsky, 99

A.D.2d 489, 470 N.Y.S.2d 431 [industrial waste on land allegedly used only as farm]; Jansen v. Kelly, 11 A.D.2d 587, 200 N.Y.S.2d 561 [land containing valuable minerals allegedly acquired for use as campsite]) or partial disclosure (Junius Constr. Corp. v. Cohen, 257 N.Y. 393, 178 N.E. 672 [existence of third unopened street concealed]; Noved Realty Corp. v. A.A.P. Co., 250 App.Div. 1, 293 N.Y.S. 336 [escrow agreements securing lien concealed]) is required to impose upon the seller a duty to communicate undisclosed conditions affecting the premises (contra, Young v. Keith, 112 A.D.2d 625, 492 N.Y.S.2d 489 [defective water and sewer systems concealed]).

Caveat emptor is not so all-encompassing a doctrine of common law as to render every act of non-disclosure immune from redress, whether legal or equitable. "In regard to the necessity of giving information which has not been asked, the rule differs somewhat at law and in equity, and while the law courts would permit no recovery of damages against a vendor, because of mere concealment of facts under certain circumstances, yet if the vendee refused to complete the contract because of the concealment of a material fact on the part of the other, equity would refuse to compel him so to do, because equity only compels the specific performance of a contract which is fair and open, and in regard to which all material matters known to each have been communicated to the other" (Rothmiller v. Stein, 143 N.Y. 581, 591-592, 38 N.E. 718 [emphasis added]). Even as a principle of law, long before exceptions were embodied in statute law (see, e.g., UCC 2-312, 2-313, 2-314, 2-315; 3-417[2][e]), the doctrine was held inapplicable to contagion among animals, adulteration of food, and insolvency of a maker of a promissory note and of a tenant substituted for another under a lease (see, Rothmiller v. Stein, supra, at 592-593, 38 N.E. 718 and cases cited therein). Common law is not moribund. Ex facto jus oritur (law arises out of facts). Where fairness and common sense dictate that an exception should be created, the evolution of the law should not be stifled by rigid application of a legal maxim.

The doctrine of caveat emptor requires that a buyer act prudently to assess the fitness and value of his purchase and operates to bar the purchaser who fails to exercise due care from seeking the equitable remedy of rescission (see, e.g., Rodas v. Manitaras, 159 A.D.2d 341, 552 N.Y.S.2d 618). For the purposes of the instant motion to dismiss the action pursuant to CPLR 3211(a)(7), plaintiff is entitled to every favorable inference which may reasonably be drawn from the pleadings (Arrington v. New York Times Co., 55 N.Y.2d 433, 442, 449 N.Y.S.2d 941, 434 N.E.2d 1319; Rovello v. Orofino Realty Co., 40 N.Y.2d 633, 634, 389 N.Y.S.2d 314, 357 N.E.2d 970), specifically, in this instance, that he met his obligation to conduct an inspection of the premises and a search of available public records with respect to title. It should be apparent, however, that the most meticulous inspection and the search would not reveal the presence of poltergeists at the premises or unearth the property's ghoulish reputation in the community. Therefore, there is no sound policy reason to deny plaintiff relief for failing to discover a state of affairs which the most prudent purchaser would not be expected to even contemplate (see, Da Silva v. Musso, 53 N.Y.2d 543, 551, 444 N.Y.S.2d 50, 428 N.E.2d 382).

The case law in this jurisdiction dealing with the duty of a vendor of real property to disclose information to the buyer is distinguishable from the matter under review. The most salient distinction is that existing cases invariably deal with the physical condition of the premises (e.g., London v. Courduff, supra [use as a landfill]; Perin v. Mardine Realty Co., 5 A.D.2d 685, 168 N.Y.S.2d 647 affd. 6 N.Y.2d 920, 190 N.Y.S.2d 995, 161 N.E.2d 210 [sewer line crossing adjoining property without owner's consent]), defects in title (e.g., Sands v. Kissane, 282 App.Div. 140, 121 N.Y.S.2d 634 [remainderman]), liens against the property (e.g., Noved Realty Corp. v. A.A.P. Co., supra), expenses or income (e.g., Rodas v. Manitaras, supra [gross receipts]) and other factors affecting its operation. No case has been brought to this court's attention in which the property value was impaired as the result of the reputation created by information disseminated to the public by the seller (or, for that matter, as a result of possession by poltergeists).

Where a condition which has been created by the seller materially impairs the value of the contract and is peculiarly within the knowledge of the seller or unlikely to be discovered by a prudent purchaser exercising due care with respect to the subject transaction, nondisclosure constitutes a basis for rescission as a matter of equity. Any other outcome places upon the buyer not merely the obligation to exercise care in his purchase but rather to be omniscient with respect to any fact which may affect the bargain. No practical purpose is served by imposing such a burden upon a purchaser. To the contrary, it encourages predatory business practice and offends the principle that equity will suffer no wrong to be without a remedy.

Defendant's contention that the contract of sale, particularly the merger or "as is" clause, bars recovery of the buyer's deposit is unavailing. Even an express disclaimer will not be given effect where the facts are peculiarly within the knowledge of the party invoking it (Danann Realty Corp. v Harris, 5 N.Y.2d 317, 322; Tahini Invs. v Bobrowsky, supra). Moreover, a fair reading of the merger clause reveals that it expressly disclaims only representations made with respect to the physical condition of the premises and merely makes general reference to representations concerning "any other matter or things affecting or relating to the aforesaid premises." As broad as this language may be, a reasonable interpretation is that its effect is limited to tangible or physical matters and does not extend to paranormal phenomena. Finally, if the language of the contract is to be construed as broadly as defendant urges to encompass the presence of poltergeists in the house, it cannot be said that she has delivered the premises "vacant" in accordance with her obligation under the provisions of the contract rider.

To the extent New York law may be said to require something more than “mere concealment” to apply even the equitable remedy of rescission, the case of Junius Construction Corporation v. Cohen, 257 N.Y. 393, 178 N.E. 672, supra, while not precisely on point, provides some guidance. In that case, the seller disclosed that an official map indicated two as yet unopened streets which were planned for construction at the edges of the parcel. What was not disclosed was that the same map indicated a third street which, if opened, would divide the plot in half. The court held that, while the seller was under no duty to mention the planned streets at all, having undertaken to disclose two of them, he was obliged to reveal the third (see also, Rosenschein v. McNally, 17 A.D.2d 834, 233 N.Y.S.2d 254).

In the case at bar, defendant seller deliberately fostered the public belief that her home was possessed. Having undertaken to inform the public at large, to whom she has no legal relationship, about the supernatural occurrences on her property, she may be said to owe no less a duty to her contract vendee. It has been remarked that the occasional modern cases which permit a seller to take unfair advantage of a buyer's ignorance so long as he is not actively misled are "singularly unappetizing" (Prosser, Law of Torts § 106, at 696 [4th ed. 1971]). Where, as here, the seller not only takes unfair advantage of the buyer's ignorance but has created and perpetuated a condition about which he is unlikely to even inquire, enforcement of the contract (in whole or in part) is offensive to the court's sense of equity. Application of the remedy of rescission, within the bounds of the narrow exception to the doctrine of caveat emptor set forth herein, is entirely appropriate to relieve the unwitting purchaser from the consequences of a most unnatural bargain.

Accordingly, the judgment of the Supreme Court, New York County (Edward H. Lehner, J.), entered April 9, 1990, which dismissed the complaint pursuant to CPLR 3211(a)(7), should be modified, on the law and the facts and in the exercise of discretion, and the first cause of action seeking rescission of the contract reinstated, without costs.

Judgment, Supreme Court, New York County (Edward H. Lehner, J.), entered on April 9, 1990, modified, on the law and the facts and in the exercise of discretion, and the first cause of action seeking rescission of the contract reinstated, without costs.

All concur except MILONAS, J.P. and SMITH, J., who dissent in an opinion by SMITH, J.

SMITH, Justice (dissenting).

I would affirm the dismissal of the complaint by the motion court.

Plaintiff seeks to rescind his contract to purchase defendant Ackley's residential property and recover his down payment. Plaintiff alleges that Ackley and her real estate broker, defendant Ellis Realty, made material misrepresentations of the property in that they failed to disclose that Ackley believed that the house was haunted by poltergeists. Moreover, Ackley shared this belief with her community and the general public through articles published in Reader's Digest (1977) and the local newspaper (1982). In November 1989, approximately two months after the parties entered into the contract of sale but subsequent to the scheduled October 2, 1989 closing, the house was included in a five-house walking tour and again described in the local newspaper as being haunted.

Prior to closing, plaintiff learned of this reputation and unsuccessfully sought to rescind the $650,000 contract of sale and obtain return of his $32,500 down payment without resort to litigation. The plaintiff then commenced this action for that relief and alleged that he would not have entered into the contract had he been so advised and that as a result of the alleged poltergeist activity, the market value and resaleability of the property was greatly diminished. Defendant Ackley has counterclaimed for specific performance.

"It is settled law in New York that the seller of real property is under no duty to speak when the parties deal at arm's length. The mere silence of the seller, without some act or conduct which deceived the purchaser, does not amount to a concealment that is actionable as a fraud (see Perin v. Mardine Realty Co., Inc., 5 A.D.2d 685, 168 N.Y.S.2d 647, aff'd., 6 N.Y.2d 920, 190 N.Y.S.2d 995, 161 N.E.2d 210; Moser v. Spizzirro, 31 A.D.2d 537, 295 N.Y.S.2d 188, aff'd., 25 N.Y.2d 941, 305 N.Y.S.2d 153, 252 N.E.2d 632). The buyer has the duty to satisfy himself as to the quality of his bargain pursuant to the doctrine of caveat emptor, which in New York State still applies to real estate transactions." London

v. Courduff, 141 A.D.2d 803, 804, 529 N.Y.S.2d 874, app. dism'd., 73 N.Y.2d 809, 537 N.Y.S.2d 494, 534 N.E.2d 332 (1988).

The parties herein were represented by counsel and dealt at arm's length. This is evidenced by the contract of sale which, inter alia, contained various riders and a specific provision that all prior understandings and agreements between the parties were merged into the contract, that the contract completely expressed their full agreement and that neither had relied upon any statement by anyone else not set forth in the contract. There is no allegation that defendants, by some specific act, other than the failure to speak, deceived the plaintiff. Nevertheless, a cause of action may be sufficiently stated where there is a confidential or fiduciary relationship creating a duty to disclose and there was a failure to disclose a material fact, calculated to induce a false belief. County of Westchester v. Welton Becket Assoc., 102 A.D.2d 34, 50-51, 478 N.Y.S.2d 305, aff'd., 66 N.Y.2d 642, 495 N.Y.S.2d 364, 485 N.E.2d 1029 (1985). However, plaintiff herein has not alleged and there is no basis for concluding that a confidential or fiduciary relationship existed between these parties to an arm's length transaction such as to give rise to a duty to disclose. In addition, there is no allegation that defendants thwarted plaintiff's efforts to fulfill his responsibilities fixed by the doctrine of caveat emptor. See London v. Courduff, supra, 141 A.D.2d at 804, 529 N.Y.S.2d 874.

Finally, if the doctrine of caveat emptor is to be discarded, it should be for a reason more substantive than a poltergeist. The existence of a poltergeist is no more binding upon the defendants than it is upon this court.

Based upon the foregoing, the motion court properly dismissed the complaint.

D. OPINION

VOKES V. ARTHUR MURRAY, INC.
District Court of Appeal of Florida, Second District
212 So. 2d 906 (1968).

PIERCE, Judge.

. . . .

Defendant Arthur Murray, Inc., a corporation, authorizes the operation throughout the nation of dancing schools under the name of "Arthur Murray School of Dancing" through local franchised operators, one of whom was defendant J. P. Davenport whose dancing establishment was in Clearwater.

Plaintiff Mrs. Audrey E. Vokes, a widow of 51 years and without family, had a yen to be "an accomplished dancer" with the hopes of finding "new interest in life." So, on February 10, 1961, a dubious fate, with the assist of a motivated acquaintance, procured her to attend a "dance party" at Davenport's "School of Dancing" where she whiled away the pleasant hours, sometimes in a private room, absorbing his accomplished sales technique, during which her grace and poise were elaborated upon and her rosy future as "an excellent dancer" was painted for her in vivid and glowing colors. As an incident to this interlude, he sold her eight 1/2-hour dance lessons to be utilized within one calendar month therefrom, for the sum of $14.50 cash in hand paid, obviously a baited "comeon."

Thus she embarked upon an almost endless pursuit of the terpsichorean art during which, over a period of less than sixteen months, she was sold fourteen "dance courses" totalling in the aggregate 2302 hours of dancing lessons for a total cash outlay of $31,090.45, all at Davenport's dance emporium. All of these fourteen courses were evidenced by execution of a written 'Enrollment Agreement-Arthur Murray's School of Dancing' with the addendum in heavy black print, "No one will be informed that you are taking dancing lessons. Your relations with us are held in strict confidence," setting forth the number of "dancing lessons" and the "lessons in rhythm sessions" currently sold to her from time to time, and always of course accompanied by payment of cash of the realm.

These dance lesson contracts and the monetary consideration therefor of over $31,000 were procured from her by means and methods of Davenport and his associates which went beyond the unsavory, yet legally permissible, perimeter of "sales puffing" and intruded well into the forbidden area of undue influence, the suggestion of falsehood, the suppression of truth, and the free exercise of rational judgment, if what plaintiff alleged in her complaint was true. From the time of her first contact with the dancing school in February, 1961, she was influenced unwittingly by a constant and continuous barrage of flattery, false praise, excessive compliments, and panegyric encomiums, to such extent that it would be not only inequitable, but unconscionable, for a Court exercising inherent chancery power to allow such contracts to stand.

She was incessantly subjected to overreaching blandishment and cajolery. She was assured she had "grace and poise;" that she was "rapidly improving and developing in her dancing skill;" that the additional lessons would "make her a beautiful dancer, capable of dancing with the most accomplished dancers;" that she was "rapidly progressing in the development of her dancing skill and gracefulness," etc., etc. She was given "dance aptitude tests" for the ostensible purpose of "determining" the number of remaining hours instructions needed by her from time to time.

At one point she was sold 545 additional hours of dancing lessons to be entitled to award of the "Bronze Medal" signifying that she had reached "the Bronze Standard," a supposed designation of dance achievement by students of Arthur Murray, Inc.

Later she was sold an additional 926 hours in order to gain the "Silver Medal," indicating she had reached "the Silver Standard," at a cost of $12,501.35.

At one point, while she still had to her credit about 900 unused hours of instructions, she was induced to purchase an additional 24 hours of lessons to participate in a trip to Miami at her own expense, where she would be "given the opportunity to dance with members of the Miami Studio."

She was induced at another point to purchase an additional 123 hours of lessons in order to be not only eligible for the Miami trip but also to become "a life member of the Arthur Murray Studio," carrying with it certain dubious emoluments, at a further cost of $1,752.30.

At another point, while she still had over 1,000 unused hours of instruction she was induced to buy 151 additional hours at a cost of $2,049.00 to be eligible for a "Student Trip to Trinidad," at her own expense as she later learned.

Also, when she still had 1100 unused hours to her credit, she was prevailed upon to purchase an additional 347 hours at a cost of $4,235.74, to qualify her to receive a "Gold Medal" for achievement, indicating she had advanced to "the Gold Standard."

On another occasion, while she still had over 1200 unused hours, she was induced to buy an additional 175 hours of instruction at a cost of $2,472.75 to be eligible "to take a trip to Mexico."

Finally, sandwiched in between other lesser sales promotions, she was influenced to buy an additional 481 hours of instruction at a cost of $6,523.81 in order to "be classified as a Gold Bar Member, the ultimate achievement of the dancing studio."

All the foregoing sales promotions, illustrative of the entire fourteen separate contracts, were procured by defendant Davenport and Arthur Murray, Inc., by false representations to her that she was improving in her dancing ability, that she had excellent potential, that she was responding to instructions in dancing grace, and that they were developing her into a beautiful dancer, whereas in truth and in fact she did not develop in her dancing ability, she had no "dance aptitude," and in fact had difficulty in "hearing that musical beat." The complaint alleged that such representations to her "were in fact false and known by the defendant to be false and contrary to the plaintiff's true ability, the truth of plaintiff's ability being fully known to the defendants, but withheld from the plaintiff for the sole and specific intent to deceive and defraud the plaintiff and to induce her in the purchasing of additional hours of dance lessons." It was averred that the lessons were sold to her "in total disregard to the true physical, rhythm, and mental ability of the plaintiff." In other words, while she first exulted that she was entering the "spring of her life," she finally was awakened to the fact there was "spring" neither in her life nor in her feet.

The complaint prayed that the Court decree the dance contracts to be null and void and to be cancelled, that an accounting be had, and judgment entered against, the defendants "for that portion of the $31,090.45 not charged against specific hours of instruction given to the plaintiff." The Court held the complaint not to state a cause of action and dismissed it with prejudice. We disagree and reverse.

The material allegations of the complaint must, of course, be accepted as true for the purpose of testing its legal sufficiency. Defendants contend that contracts can only be rescinded for fraud or misrepresentation when the alleged misrepresentation is as to a material fact, rather than an opinion, prediction or expectation, and that the statements and representations set forth at length in the complaint were in the category of "trade puffing," within its legal orbit.

It is true that "generally a misrepresentation, to be actionable, must be one of fact rather than of opinion." Tonkovich v. South Florida Citrus Industries, Inc., Fla.App.1966, 185 So.2d 710; Kutner v. Kalish, Fla.App.1965, 173 So.2d 763. But this rule has significant qualifications, applicable here. It does not apply where there is a fiduciary relationship between the parties, or where there has been some artifice or trick employed by the representor, or where the parties do not in general deal at "arm's length" as we understand the phrase, or where the representee does not have equal opportunity to become apprised of the truth or falsity of the fact represented. 14 Fla.Jur. Fraud and Deceit, s 28; Kitchen v.

Long, 1914, 67 Fla. 72, 64 So. 429. As stated by Judge Allen of this Court in Ramel v. Chasebrook Construction Company, Fla.App.1961, 135 So.2d 876:

> . . . A statement of a party having . . . superior knowledge may be regarded as a statement of fact although it would be considered as opinion if the parties were dealing on equal terms.

It could be reasonably supposed here that defendants had "superior knowledge" as to whether plaintiff had "dance potential" and as to whether she was noticeably improving in the art of terpsichore. And it would be a reasonable inference from the undenied averments of the complaint that the flowery eulogiums heaped upon her by defendants as a prelude to her contracting for 1944 additional hours of instruction in order to attain the rank of the Bronze Standard, thence to the bracket of the Silver Standard, thence to the class of the Gold Bar Standard, and finally to the crowning plateau of a Life Member of the Studio, proceeded as much or more from the urge to "ring the cash register" as from any honest or realistic appraisal of her dancing prowess or a factual representation of her progress.

Even in contractual situations where a party to a transaction owes no duty to disclose facts within his knowledge or to answer inquiries respecting such facts, the law is if he undertakes to do so he must disclose the Whole truth. Ramel v. Chasebrook Construction Company, supra; Beagle v. Bagwell, Fla.App.1964, 169 So.2d 43. From the face of the complaint, it should have been reasonably apparent to defendants that her vast outlay of cash for the many hundreds of additional hours of instruction was not justified by her slow and awkward progress, which she would have been made well aware of if they had spoken the "whole truth.". . .

We repeat that where parties are dealing on a contractual basis at arm's length with no inequities or inherently unfair practices employed, the Courts will in general "leave the parties where they find themselves." But in the case sub judice, from the allegations of the unanswered complaint, we cannot say that enough of the accompanying ingredients, as mentioned in the foregoing authorities, were not present which otherwise would have barred the equitable arm of the Court to her. In our view, from the showing made in her complaint, plaintiff is entitled to her day in Court.

It accordingly follows that the order dismissing plaintiff's last amended complaint with prejudice should be and is reversed.

Reversed.

LILES, C.J., and MANN, J., concur

SECTION 4. DURESS AND UNDUE INFLUENCE

A. DURESS

AUSTIN INSTRUMENTS, INC. V. LORAL CORPORATION
Court of Appeals of New York
272 N.E.2d 533 (1971).

FULD, Chief Judge.

. . . .

In July of 1965, Loral was awarded a $6,000,000 contract by the Navy for the production of radar sets. The contract contained a schedule of deliveries, a liquidated damages clause applying to late deliveries and a cancellation clause in case of default by Loral. The latter thereupon solicited bids for some 40 precision gear components needed to produce the radar sets, and awarded Austin a subcontract to supply 23 such parts. That party commenced delivery in early 1966.

In May, 1966, Loral was awarded a second Navy contract for the production of more radar sets and again went about soliciting bids. Austin bid on all 40 gear components but, on July 15, a representative from Loral informed Austin's president, Mr. Krauss, that his company would be awarded the subcontract only for those items on which it was low bidder. The Austin officer refused to accept an order for less than all 40 of the gear parts and on the next day he told Loral that Austin would cease deliveries of the parts due under the existing subcontract unless Loral consented to substantial increases in the prices provided for by that agreement-both retroactively for parts already delivered and prospectively on those not yet shipped-and placed with Austin the order for all 40 parts needed under Loral's second Navy contract. Shortly thereafter, Austin did, indeed, stop delivery. After contacting 10 manufacturers of precision gears and finding none who could produce the parts in time to meet its commitments to the Navy,[1] Loral acceded to Austin's demands; in a letter dated July 22, Loral wrote to Austin that "We have feverishly surveyed other sources of supply and find that because of the prevailing military exigencies, were they to start from scratch as would have to be the case, they could not even remotely begin to deliver on time to meet the delivery requirements established by the Government. . . . Accordingly, we are left with no choice or alternative but to meet your conditions."

Loral thereupon consented to the price increases insisted upon by Austin under the first subcontract and the latter was awarded a second subcontract making it the supplier of all 40 gear parts for Loral's second contract with the Navy.[2] Although Austin was granted until September to resume deliveries, Loral did, in fact, receive parts in August and was able to produce the radar sets in time to meet its commitments to the Navy on both contracts. After Austin's last delivery under the second subcontract in July, 1967, Loral notified it of its intention to seek recovery of the price increases.

---

[1] The best reply Loral received was from a vendor who stated he could commence deliveries sometime in October.

[2] Loral makes no claim in this action on the second subcontract.

On September 15, 1967, Austin instituted this action against Loral to recover an amount in excess of $17,750 which was still due on the second subcontract. On the same day, Loral commenced an action against Austin claiming damages of some $22,250-the aggregate of the price increases under the first subcontract-on the ground of economic duress. The two actions were consolidated and, following a trial, Austin was awarded the sum it requested and Loral's complaint against Austin was dismissed on the ground that it was not shown that "it could not have obtained the items in question from other sources in time to meet its commitment to the Navy under the first contract." A closely divided Appellate Division affirmed (35 A.D.2d 387, 316 N.Y.S.2d 528, 532). There was no material disagreement concerning the facts; as Justice Steuer stated in the course of his dissent below, "(t)he facts are virtually undisputed, nor is there any serious question of law. The difficulty lies in the application of the law to these facts." (35 A.D.2d 392, 316 N.Y.S.2d 534.)

The applicable law is clear and, indeed, is not disputed by the parties. A contract is voidable on the ground of duress when it is established that the party making the claim was forced to agree to it by means of a wrongful threat precluding the exercise of his free will. (See Allstate Med. Labs., Inc. v. Blaivas, 20 N.Y.2d 654, 282 N.Y.S.2d 268, 229 N.E.2d 50; Kazaras v. Manufacturers Trust Co., 4 N.Y.2d 930, 175 N.Y.S.2d 172, 151 N.E.2d 356; Adams v. Irving Nat. Bank, 116 N.Y. 606, 611, 23 N.E. 7, 9; see, also, 13 Williston, Contracts (3d ed., 1970), s 1603, p. 658.) The existence of economic duress or business compulsion is demonstrated by proof that "immediate possession of needful goods is threatened" (Mercury Mach. Importing Corp. v. City of New York, 3 N.Y.2d 418, 425, 165 N.Y.S.2d 517, 520, 144 N.E.2d 400) or, more particularly, in cases such as the one before us, by proof that one party to a contract has threatened to breach the agreement by withholding goods unless the other party agrees to some further demand. (See, e.g., Du Pont de Nemours & Co. v. J. T. Hass Co., 303 N.Y. 785, 103 N.E.2d 896; Gallagher Switchboard Corp. v. Heckler Elec. Co., 36 Misc.2d 225, 232 N.Y.S.2d 590; see, also, 13 Williston, Contracts (3d ed., 1970), § 1617, p. 705.) However, a mere threat by one party to breach the contract by not delivering the required items, though wrongful, does not in itself constitute economic duress. It must also appear that the threatened party could not obtain the goods from another source of supply and that the ordinary remedy of an action for breach of contract would not be adequate.

We find without any support in the record the conclusion reached by the courts below that Loral failed to establish that it was the victim of economic duress. On the contrary, the evidence makes out a classic case, as a matter of law, of such duress.

It is manifest that Austin's threat-to stop deliveries unless the prices were increased-deprived Loral of its free will. As bearing on this, Loral's relationship with the Government is most significant. As mentioned above, its contract called for staggered monthly deliveries of the radar sets, with clauses calling for liquidated damages and possible cancellation on default. Because of its production schedule, Loral was, in July, 1966, concerned with meeting its delivery requirements in September, October and November, and it was for the sets to be delivered in those months that the withheld gears were needed. Loral had to plan ahead, and the substantial liquidated damages for which it would be liable, plus the threat of default, were genuine possibilities. Moreover, Loral did a substantial portion of its business with the Government, and it feared that a failure to deliver as agreed upon would jeopardize its chances for future contracts. These genuine concerns do not merit the label "self-imposed, undisclosed and subjective" which the Appellate Division majority placed upon them. It was perfectly reasonable for Loral, or any other party similarly placed, to consider itself in an emergency, duress situation.

Austin, however, claims that the fact that Loral extended its time to resume deliveries until September negates its alleged dire need for the parts. A Loral official testified on this point that Austin's president told him he could deliver some parts in August and that the extension of deliveries was a formality. In any event, the parts necessary for production of the radar sets to be delivered in September were delivered to Loral on September 1, and the parts needed for the October schedule were delivered in late August and early September. Even so, Loral had to "work . . . around the clock" to meet its commitments. Considering that the best offer Loral received from the other vendors it contacted was commencement of delivery sometime in October, which, as the record shows, would have made it late in its deliveries to the Navy in both September and October, Loral's claim that it had no choice but to accede to Austin's demands is conclusively demonstrated.

We find unconvincing Austin's contention that Loral, in order to meet its burden, should have contacted the Government and asked for an extension of its delivery dates so as to enable it to purchase the parts from another vendor. Aside from the consideration that Loral was anxious to perform well in the Government's eyes, it could not be sure when it would obtain enough parts from a substitute vendor to meet its commitments. The only promise which it received from the companies it contacted was for Commencement of deliveries, not full supply, and, with vendor delay common in this field, it would have been nearly impossible to know the length of the extension it should request. It must be remembered that Loral was producing a needed item of military hardware. Moreover, there is authority for Loral's position that nonperformance by a subcontractor is not an excuse for default in the main contract. (See, e.g., McBride & Wachtel, Government Contracts, § 35.10, (11).) In light of all this, Loral's claim should not be held insufficiently supported because it did not request an extension from the Government.

Loral, as indicated above, also had the burden of demonstrating that it could not obtain the parts elsewhere within a reasonable time, and there can be no doubt that it met this burden. The 10 manufacturers whom Loral contacted comprised its entire list of "approved vendors" for precision gears, and none was able to commence delivery soon enough.[6] As Loral was producing a highly sophisticated item of military machinery requiring parts made to the strictest engineering standards, it would be unreasonable to hold that Loral should have gone to other vendors, with whom it was either unfamiliar or dissatisfied, to procure the needed parts. As Justice Steuer noted in his dissent, Loral "contacted all the manufacturers whom it believed capable of making these parts" (35 A.D.2d at p. 393, 316 N.Y.S.2d at p. 534), and this was all the law requires.

It is hardly necessary to add that Loral's normal legal remedy of accepting Austin's breach of the contract and then suing for damages would have been inadequate under the circumstances, as Loral would still have had to obtain the gears elsewhere with all the concomitant consequences mentioned above. In other words, Loral actually had no choice,

[6] Loral, as do many manufacturers, maintains a list of "approved vendors," that is, vendors whose products, facilities, techniques and performance have been inspected and found satisfactory.

when the prices were raised by Austin, except to take the gears at the 'coerced' prices and then sue to get the excess back.

Austin's final argument is that Loral, even if it did enter into the contract under duress, lost any rights it had to a refund of money by waiting until July, 1967, long after the termination date of the contract, to disaffirm it. It is true that one who would recover moneys allegedly paid under duress must act promptly to make his claim known. (See Oregon Pacific R.R. Co. v. Forrest, 128 N.Y. 83, 93, 28 N.E. 137, 139; Port Chester Elec. Constr. Corp. v. Hastings Terraces, 284 App.Div. 966, 967, 134 N.Y.S.2d 656, 658.) In this case, Loral delayed making its demand for a refund until three days after Austin's last delivery on the second subcontract. Loral's reason-for waiting until that time-is that it feared another stoppage of deliveries which would again put it in an untenable situation. Considering Austin's conduct in the past, this was perfectly reasonable, as the possibility of an application by Austin of further business compulsion still existed until all of the parts were delivered.

In sum, the record before us demonstrates that Loral agreed to the price increases in consequence of the economic duress employed by Austin. Accordingly, the matter should be remanded to the trial court for a computation of its damages.

The order appealed from should be modified, with costs, by reversing so much thereof as affirms the dismissal of defendant Loral Corporation's claim and, except as so modified, affirmed.

BERGAN, Judge (dissenting).

Whether acts charged as constituting economic duress produce or do not produce the damaging effect attributed to them is normally a routine type of factual issue.

Here the fact question was resolved against Loral both by the Special Term and by the affirmance at the Appellate Division. It should not be open for different resolution here.

In summarizing the Special Term's decision and its own, the Appellate Division decided that "the conclusion that Loral acted deliberately and voluntarily, without being under immediate pressure of incurring severe business reverses, precludes a recovery on the theory of economic duress" (35 A.D.2d 387, 391, 316 N.Y.S.2d 528, 532).

When the testimony of the witnesses who actually took part in the negotiations for the two disputing parties is examined, sharp conflicts of fact emerge. Under Austin's version the request for a renegotiation of the existing contract was based on Austin's contention that Loral had failed to carry out an understanding as to the items to be furnished under that contract and this was the source of dissatisfaction which led both to a revision of the existing agreement and to entering into a new one.

This is not necessarily and as a matter of law to be held economic duress. On this appeal it is needful to look at the facts resolved in favor of Austin most favorably to that party. Austin's version of events was that a threat was not made but rather a request to accommodate the closing of its plant for a customary vacation period in accordance with the general understanding of the parties.

Moreover, critical to the issue of economic duress was the availability of alternative suppliers to the purchaser Loral. The demonstration is replete in the direct testimony of Austin's witnesses and on cross-examination of Loral's principal and purchasing agent that the availability of practical alternatives was a highly controverted issue of fact. On that issue of fact the explicit findings made by the Special Referee were affirmed by the Appellate Division. Nor is the issue of fact made the less so by assertion that the facts are undisputed and that only the application of equally undisputed rules of law is involved.

Austin asserted and Loral admitted on cross-examination that there were many suppliers listed in a trade registry but that Loral chose to rely only on those who had in the past come to them for orders and with whom they were familiar. It was, therefore, at least a fair issue of fact whether under the circumstances such conduct was reasonable and made what might otherwise have been a commercially understandable renegotiation an exercise of duress.

The order should be affirmed.

BURKE, SCILEPPI and GIBSON, JJ., concur with FULD, C.J.
BERGAN, J., dissents and votes to affirm in a separate opinion in which BREITEL and JASEN, JJ., concur.

Ordered accordingly.

TOTEM MARINE TUG & BARGE V. ALYESKA PIPELINE SERVICE COMPANY
Supreme Court of Alaska
584 P.2d 15 (1978).

BURKE, Justice.

. . . .

The following summary of events is derived from the materials submitted in the summary judgment proceedings below.

Totem is a closely held Alaska corporation which began operations in March of 1975. Richard Stair, at all times relevant to this case, was vice-president of Totem. In June of 1975, Totem entered into a contract with Alyeska under which Totem was to transport pipeline construction materials from Houston, Texas, to a designated port in southern Alaska, with the possibility of one or two cargo stops along the way. In order to carry out this contract, which was Totem's first, Totem chartered a barge (the "Marine Flasher") and an ocean-going tug (the "Kirt Chouest"). These charters and other initial operations costs were made possible by loans to Totem from Richard Stair individually and Pacific, Inc., a corporation of which Stair was principal stockholder and officer, as well as by guarantees by Stair and Pacific.

By the terms of the contract, Totem was to have completed performance by approximately August 15, 1975. From the start, however, there were numerous problems which impeded Totem's performance of the contract. For example, according to Totem, Alyeska represented that approximately 1,800 to 2,100 tons of regular uncoated pipe were to be loaded in Houston, and that perhaps another 6,000 or 7,000 tons of materials would be put on the barge at later stops along the west coast. Upon the arrival of the tug and barge in Houston, however, Totem found that about 6,700 to 7,200 tons of coated pipe, steel beams and valves, haphazardly and improperly piled, were in the yard to be loaded. This situation called for remodeling of the barge and extra cranes and stevedores, and resulted in the loading taking thirty days rather than the three days which Totem had anticipated it would take to load 2,000 tons. The lengthy loading period was also caused in part by Alyeska's delay in assuring Totem that it would pay for the additional expenses, bad weather and other administrative problems.

The difficulties continued after the tug and barge left Houston. It soon became apparent that the vessels were travelling more slowly than anticipated because of the extra load. In response to Alyeska's complaints and with its verbal consent, on August 13, 1975, Totem chartered a second tug, the "N. Joseph Guidry." When the "Guidry" reached the Panama Canal, however, Alyeska had not yet furnished the written amendment to the parties' contract. Afraid that Alyeska would not agree to cover the cost of the second tug, Stair notified the "Guidry" not to go through the Canal. After some discussions in which Alyeska complained of the delays and accused Totem of lying about the horsepower of the first tug, Alyeska executed the amendment on August 21, 1975.

By this time the "Guidry" had lost its preferred passage through the Canal and had to wait two or three additional days before it could go through. Upon finally meeting, the three vessels encountered the tail of a hurricane which lasted for about eight or nine days and which substantially impeded their progress.

The three vessels finally arrived in the vicinity of San Pedro, California, where Totem planned to change crews and refuel. On Alyeska's orders, however, the vessels instead pulled into port at Long Beach, California. At this point, Alyeska's agents commenced off-loading the barge, without Totem's consent, without the necessary load survey, and without a marine survey, the absence of which voided Totem's insurance. After much wrangling and some concessions by Alyeska, the freight was off-loaded. Thereafter, on or about September 14, 1975, Alyeska terminated the contract. Although there was talk by an Alyeska official of reinstating the contract, the termination was affirmed a few days later at a meeting at which Alyeska officials refused to give a reason for the termination.

Following termination of the contract, Totem submitted termination invoices to Alyeska and began pressing the latter for payment. The invoices came to something between $260,000 and $300,000. An official from Alyeska told Totem that they would look over the invoices but that they were not sure when payment would be made perhaps in a day or perhaps in six to eight months. Totem was in urgent need of cash as the invoices represented debts which the company had incurred on 10-30 day payment schedules. Totem's creditors were demanding payment and according to Stair, without immediate cash, Totem would go bankrupt. Totem then turned over the collection to its attorney, Roy Bell, directing him to advise Alyeska of Totem's financial straits. Thereafter, Bell met with Alyeska officials in Seattle, and after some negotiations, Totem received a settlement offer from Alyeska for $97,500. On November 6, 1975, Totem, through its president Stair, signed an agreement releasing Alyeska from all claims by Totem in exchange for $97,500.

On March 26, 1976, Totem, Richard Stair, and Pacific filed a complaint against Alyeska, which was subsequently amended. In the amended complaint, the plaintiffs sought to rescind the settlement and release on the ground of economic duress and to recover the balance allegedly due on the original contract. In addition, they alleged that Alyeska had wrongfully terminated the contract and sought miscellaneous other compensatory and punitive damages.

Before filing an answer, Alyeska moved for summary judgment against the plaintiffs on the ground that Totem had executed a binding release of all claims against Alyeska and that as a matter of law, Totem could not prevail on its claim of economic duress. In opposition, plaintiffs contended that the purported release was executed under duress in that Alyeska wrongfully terminated the contract; that Alyeska knew that Totem was faced with large debts and impending bankruptcy; that Alyeska withheld funds admittedly owed knowing the effect this would have on plaintiffs and that plaintiffs had no alternative but to involuntarily accept the $97,500 in order to avoid bankruptcy. Plaintiffs maintained that they had thus raised genuine issues of material fact such that trial was necessary, and that Alyeska was not entitled to judgment as a matter of law. Alyeska disputed the plaintiffs' assertions.

On November 30, 1976, the superior court granted the defendant's motion for summary judgment. This appeal followed. . . .

II

As was noted above, a court's initial task in deciding motions for summary judgment is to determine whether there exist genuine issues of material fact. In order to decide whether such issues exist in this case, we must examine the doctrine allowing avoidance of a release on grounds of economic duress.

This court has not yet decided a case involving a claim of economic duress or what is also called business compulsion. At early common law, a contract could be avoided on the ground of duress only if a party could show that the agreement was entered into for fear of loss of life or limb, mayhem or imprisonment. 13 Williston on Contracts, § 1601 at 649 (3d ed. Jaeger 1970). The threat had to be such as to overcome the will of a person of ordinary firmness and courage. Id., s 1602 at 656. Subsequently, however, the concept has been broadened to include myriad forms of economic coercion which force a person to involuntarily enter into a particular transaction. The test has come to be whether the will of the person induced by the threat was overcome rather than that of a reasonably firm person. Id., s 1602 at 657.

At the outset it is helpful to acknowledge the various policy considerations which are involved in cases involving economic duress. Typically, those claiming such coercion are attempting to avoid the consequences of a modification of an original contract or of a settlement and release agreement. On the one hand, courts are reluctant to set aside agreements because of the notion of freedom of contract and because of the desirability of having private dispute resolutions be final. On the other hand, there is an increasing recognition of the law's role in correcting inequitable or unequal exchanges between parties of disproportionate bargaining power and a greater willingness to not enforce agreements which were entered into under coercive circumstances.

There are various statements of what constitutes economic duress, but as noted by one commentator, "The history of generalization in this field offers no great encouragement for those who seek to summarize results in any single formula." Dawson, Economic Duress An Essay in Perspective, 45 Mich.L.Rev. 253, 289 (1947). Section 492(b) of the Restatement of Contracts defines duress as:

> any wrongful threat of one person by words or other conduct that induces another to enter into a transaction under the influence of such fear as precludes him from exercising free will and judgment, if the threat was intended or should reasonably have been expected to operate as an inducement.

Professor Williston states the basic elements of economic duress in the following manner:

> 1. The party alleging economic duress must show that he has been the victim of a wrongful or unlawful act or threat, and
> 2. Such act or threat must be one which deprives the victim of his unfettered will.
>
> 13 Williston on Contracts, § 1617 at 704 (footnotes omitted).

Many courts state the test somewhat differently, eliminating use of the vague term "free will," but retaining the same basic idea. Under this standard, duress exists where: (1) one party involuntarily accepted the terms of another, (2) circumstances permitted no other alternative, and (3) such circumstances were the result of coercive acts of the other party. Undersea Engineering & Construction Co. v. International Telephone & Telegraph Corp., 429 F.2d 543, 550 (9th Cir. 1970); Urban Plumbing and Heating Co. v. United States, 408 F.2d 382, 389, 187 Ct.Cl. 15 (1969); W. R. Grimshaw Co. v. Nevil C. Withrow Co., 248 F.2d 896, 904 (8th Cir. 1957); Fruhauf Southwest Garment Co. v. United States, 111 F.Supp. 945, 951, 126 Ct.Cl. 51 (1953). The third element is further explained as follows:

> In order to substantiate the allegation of economic duress or business compulsion, the plaintiff must go beyond the mere showing of reluctance to accept and of financial embarrassment. There must be a showing of acts on the part of the defendant which produced these two factors. The assertion of duress must be proven by evidence that the duress resulted from defendant's wrongful and oppressive conduct and not by the plaintiff's necessities. W. R. Grimshaw Co., supra, 111 F.Supp. at 904.

As the above indicates, one essential element of economic duress is that the plaintiff show that the other party by wrongful acts or threats, intentionally caused him to involuntarily enter into a particular transaction. Courts have not attempted to define exactly what constitutes a wrongful or coercive act, as wrongfulness depends on the particular facts in each case. This requirement may be satisfied where the alleged wrongdoer's conduct is criminal or tortious but an act or threat may also be considered wrongful if it is wrongful in the moral sense. Restatement of Contracts, § 492, comment (g); Gerber v. First National Bank of Lincolnwood, 30 Ill.App.3d 776, 332 N.E.2d 615, 618 (1975); Fowler v. Mumford, 48 Del. 282, 9 Terry 282, 102 A.2d 535, 538 (Del.Supr.1954).

In many cases, a threat to breach a contract or to withhold payment of an admitted debt has constituted a wrongful act. Hartsville Oil Mill v. United States, 271 U.S. 43, 49, 46 S.Ct. 389, 391, 70 L.Ed. 822, 827 (1926); Austin Instrument, Inc. v. Loral Corp., 29 N.Y.2d 124, 324 N.Y.S.2d 22, 25, 272 N.E.2d 533, 535 (1971); Capps v. Georgia-Pacific Corporation, 253 Or. 248, 453 P.2d 935 (1969); See also 13 Williston, supra, § 1616A at 701. Implicit in such cases is the additional requirement that the threat to breach the contract or withhold payment be done in bad faith. See Louisville Title Insurance Co. v. Surety Title & Guaranty Co., 60 Cal.App.3d 781, 132 Cal.Rptr. 63, 76, 79 (1976); Restatement (Second) of Contracts, § 318 comment (e).

Economic duress does not exist, however, merely because a person has been the victim of a wrongful act; in addition, the victim must have no choice but to agree to the other party's terms or face serious financial hardship. Thus, in order to avoid a contract, a party must also show that he had no reasonable alternative to agreeing to the other party's terms, or, as it is often stated, that he had no adequate remedy if the threat were to be carried out. First National Bank of Cincinnati v. Pepper, 454 F.2d 626, 632-33 (2d Cir. 1972); Austin Instrument, supra, 324 N.Y.S.2d at 25, 272 N.E.2d at 535; Capps, supra; Ross Systems v. Linden Dari-Delite, Inc., 35 N.J. 329, 173 A.2d 258, 261 (1961); Leeper v. Beltrami, 53 Cal.2d 195, 1 Cal.Rptr. 12, 19, 347 P.2d 12, 19 (1959); Tri-State Roofing Company of Uniontown v. Simon, 187 Pa.Super. 17, 142 A.2d 333, 335-36 (1958). What constitutes a reasonable alternative is a question of fact, depending on the circumstances of each case. An available legal remedy, such as an action for breach of contract, may provide such an alternative. First National Bank of Cincinnati, supra; Austin Instrument, supra; Tri-State Roofing, supra. Where one party wrongfully threatens to withhold goods, services or money from another unless certain demands are met, the availability on the market of similar goods and services or of other sources of funds may also provide an alternative to succumbing to the coercing party's demands. Austin Instrument, supra; Tri-State Roofing, supra. Generally, it has been said that "(t)he adequacy of the remedy is to be tested by a practical standard which takes into consideration the exigencies of the situation in which the alleged victim finds himself." Ross Systems, 173 A.2d at 262. See also First National Bank of Cincinnati, supra at 634; Dalzell, Duress By Economic Pressure I, 20 N. Carolina L.Rev. 237, 240 (1942).

An available alternative or remedy may not be adequate where the delay involved in pursuing that remedy would cause immediate and irreparable loss to one's economic or business interest. For example, in Austin Instrument, supra, and Gallagher Switchboard Corp. v. Heckler Electric Co., 36 Misc.2d 225, 232 N.Y.S.2d 590 (N.Y.Sup.Ct.1962), duress was found in the following circumstances: A subcontractor threatened to refuse further delivery under a contract unless the contractor agreed to modify the existing contract between the parties. The contractor was unable to obtain the necessary materials elsewhere without delay, and if it did not have the materials promptly, it would have been in default on its main contract with the government. In each case such default would have had grave economic consequences for the contractor and hence it agreed to the modifications. In both, the courts found that the alternatives to agreeing to the modification were inadequate (I. e., suing for breach of contract or obtaining the materials elsewhere) and that modifications therefore were signed under duress and voidable.

Professor Dalzell, in Duress By Economic Pressure II, 20 N. Carolina L.Rev. 340, 370 (1942), notes the following with regard to the adequacy of legal remedies where one party refuses to pay a contract claim:

> Nowadays, a wait of even a few weeks in collecting on a contract claim is sometimes serious or fatal for an enterprise at a crisis in its history. The business of a creditor in financial straits is at the mercy of an unscrupulous debtor, who need only suggest that if the creditor does not care to settle on the debtor's own hard terms, he can sue. This situation, in which promptness in payment is vastly more important than even approximate justice in the settlement terms, is too common in modern business relations to be ignored by society and the courts. . . .

III

Turning to the instant case, we believe that Totem's allegations, if proved, would support a finding that it executed a release of its contract claims against Alyeska under economic duress. Totem has alleged that Alyeska deliberately withheld payment of an acknowledged debt, knowing that Totem had no choice but to accept an inadequate sum in settlement of that debt; that Totem was faced with impending bankruptcy; that Totem was unable to meet its pressing debts other than by accepting the immediate cash payment offered by Alyeska; and that through necessity, Totem thus involuntarily accepted an inadequate settlement offer from Alyeska and executed a release of all claims under the contract. If the release was in fact executed under these circumstances, we think that under the legal principles discussed above that this would constitute the type of wrongful conduct and lack of alternatives that would render the release voidable by Totem on the ground of economic duress. We would add that although Totem need not necessarily prove its allegation that Alyeska's termination of the contract was wrongful in order to sustain a claim of economic duress, the events leading to the termination would be probative as to whether Alyeska exerted any wrongful pressure on Totem and whether Alyeska wrongfully withheld payment from Totem. . . .

Our examination of the materials presented by Totem in opposition to Alyeska's motion for summary judgment leads us to conclude that Totem has made a sufficient factual showing as to each of the elements of economic duress to withstand that motion. There is no doubt that Alyeska disputes many of the factual allegations made by Totem[7] and drawing all inferences in favor of Totem, we believe that genuine issues of material fact exist in this case such that trial is necessary. Admittedly, Totem's showing was somewhat weak in that, for example, it did not produce the testimony of Roy Bell, the attorney who represented Totem in the negotiations leading to the settlement and release. At trial, it will probably be necessary for Totem to produce this evidence if it is to prevail on its claim of duress. However, a party opposing a motion for summary judgment need not produce all of the evidence it may have at its disposal but need only show that issues of material fact exist. 10 C. Wright and A. Miller, Federal Practice and Procedure: Civil, § 2727 at 546 (1973).

[7] For example, Alyeska has denied that it ever admitted to owing any particular sum to Totem and has disputed the truthfulness of Totem's assertions of impending bankruptcy. Other factual issues which remain unresolved include whether or not Alyeska knew of Totem's financial situation after termination of the contract and whether Alyeska did in fact threaten by words or conduct to withhold payment unless Totem agreed to settle.

Therefore, we hold that the superior court erred in granting summary judgment for appellees and remand the case to the superior court for trial in accordance with the legal principles set forth above. . . .

REVERSED and REMANDED.

B. UNDUE INFLUENCE

ODORIZZI V. BLOOMFIELD SCHOOL DISTRICT
District Court of Appeal, Second District, California
246 Cal. App. 2d 123 (1966).

FLEMING, J.

Appeal from a judgment dismissing plaintiff's amended complaint on demurrer.

Plaintiff Donald Odorizzi was employed during 1964 as an elementary school teacher by defendant Bloomfield School District and was under contract with the district to continue to teach school the following year as a permanent employee. On June 10 he was arrested on criminal charges of homosexual activity, and on June 11 he signed and delivered to his superiors his written resignation as a teacher, a resignation which the district accepted on June 13. In July the criminal charges against Odorizzi were dismissed under Penal Code section 995, and in September he sought to resume his employment with the district. On the district's refusal to reinstate him he filed suit for declaratory and other relief.

Odorizzi's amended complaint asserts his resignation was invalid because obtained through duress, fraud, mistake, and undue influence and given at a time when he lacked capacity to make a valid contract. Specifically, Odorizzi declares he was under such severe mental and emotional strain at the time he signed his resignation, having just completed the process of arrest, questioning by the police, booking, and release on bail, and having gone for 40 hours without sleep, that he was incapable of rational thought or action. While he was in this condition and unable to think clearly, the superintendent of the district and the principal of his school came to his apartment. They said they were trying to help him and had his best interests at heart, that he should take their advice and immediately resign his position with the district, that there was no time to consult an attorney, that if he did not resign immediately the district would suspend and dismiss him from his position and publicize the proceedings, his "aforedescribed arrest" and cause him "to suffer extreme embarrassment and humiliation"; but that if he resigned at once the incident would not be publicized and would not jeopardize his chances of securing employment as a teacher elsewhere. Odorizzi pleads that because of his faith and confidence in their representations they were able to substitute their will and judgment in place of his own and thus obtain his signature to his purported resignation. A demurrer to his amended complaint was sustained without leave to amend.

By his complaint plaintiff in effect seeks to rescind his resignation pursuant to Civil Code, section 1689, on the ground that his consent had not been real or free within the meaning of Civil Code, section 1567, but had been obtained through duress, menace, fraud, undue influence, or mistake. A pleading under these sections is sufficient if, stripped of its conclusions, it sets forth sufficient facts to justify legal relief. (Gogerty v. Coachella Valley Junior College Dist., 57 Cal.2d 727, 731 [21 Cal.Rptr. 806, 371 P.2d 582]; Krug v. Meeham, 109 Cal.App.2d 274, 277 [240 P.2d 732].) In our view the facts in the amended complaint are insufficient to state a cause of action for duress, menace, fraud, or mistake, but they do set out sufficient elements to justify rescission of a consent because of undue influence. We summarize our conclusions on each of these points.

No duress or menace has been pleaded. Duress consists in unlawful confinement of another's person, or relatives, or property, which causes him to consent to a transaction through fear. (Civ. Code, § 1569.) Duress is often used interchangeably with menace (Leeper v. Beltrami, 53 Cal.2d 195, 203 [1 Cal.Rptr. 12, 347 P.2d 12, 77 A.L.R.2d 803]), but in California menace is technically a threat of duress or a threat of injury to the person, property, or character of another. (Civ. Code, § 1570; Rest., Contracts, §§ 492, 493.) We agree with respondent's contention that neither duress nor menace was involved in this case, because the action or threat in duress or menace must be unlawful, and a threat to take legal action is not unlawful unless the party making the threat knows the falsity of his claim. (Leeper v. Beltrami, 53 Cal.2d 195, 204 [1 Cal.Rptr. 12, 347 P.2d 12, 77 A.L.R.2d 803].) The amended complaint shows in substance that the school representatives announced their intention to initiate suspension and dismissal proceedings under Education Code, sections 13403, 13408 et seq. at a time when the filing of such proceedings was not only their legal right but their positive duty as school officials. (Ed. Code, § 13409; Board of Education v. Weiland, 179 Cal.App.2d 808 [4 Cal.Rptr. 286].) Although the filing of such proceedings might be extremely damaging to plaintiff's reputation, the injury would remain incidental so long as the school officials acted in good faith in the performance of their duties. (Schumm v. Berg, 37 Cal.2d 174, 185-186 [231 P.2d 39, 21 A.L.R.2d 1051].) Neither duress nor menace was present as a ground for rescission.

Nor do we find a cause of action for fraud, either actual or constructive. (Civ. Code, §§ 1571 to 1574.) Actual fraud involves conscious misrepresentation, or concealment, or non- disclosure of a material fact which induces the innocent party to enter the contract. (Civ. Code, § 1572; Pearson v. Norton, 230 Cal.App.2d 1, 7 [40 Cal.Rptr. 634]; Rest., Contracts, § 471.) A complaint for fraud must plead misrepresentation, knowledge of falsity, intent to induce reliance, justifiable reliance, and resulting damage. (Sixta v. Ochsner, 187 Cal.App.2d 485, 489 [9 Cal.Rptr. 617]; Zinn v. Ex-Cell-O Corp., 148 Cal.App.2d 56, 68 [306 P.2d 1017].) While the amended complaint charged misrepresentation, it failed to assert the elements of knowledge of falsity, intent to induce reliance, and justifiable reliance. A cause of action for actual fraud was therefore not stated. (Norkin v. United States Fire Ins., 237 Cal.App.2d 435 [47 Cal.Rptr. 15].)

Constructive fraud arises on a breach of duty by one in a confidential or fiduciary relationship to another which induces justifiable reliance by the latter to his prejudice. (Civ. Code, § 1573.) Plaintiff has attempted to bring himself within this category, for the amended complaint asserts the existence of a confidential relationship between the school superintendent and principal as agents of the defendant, and the plaintiff. (9) Such a confidential relationship may exist whenever a person with justification places trust and confidence in the integrity and fidelity of another. (Vai v. Bank of America, 56 Cal.2d 329, 338 [15 Cal.Rptr. 71, 364 P.2d 247]; Pryor v. Bistline, 215 Cal.App.2d 437, 446 [30

Cal.Rptr. 376].) Plaintiff, however, sets forth no facts to support his conclusion of a confidential relationship between the representatives of the school district and himself, other than that the parties bore the relationship of employer and employee to each other. Under prevailing judicial opinion no presumption of a confidential relationship arises from the bare fact that parties to a contract are employer and employee; rather, additional ties must be brought out in order to create the presumption of a confidential relationship between the two. (Annot., 100 A.L.R. 875.) The absence of a confidential relationship between employer and employee is especially apparent where, as here, the parties were negotiating to bring about a termination of their relationship. In such a situation each party is expected to look after his own interests, and a lack of confidentiality is implicit in the subject matter of their dealings. We think the allegations of constructive fraud were inadequate.

As to mistake, the amended complaint fails to disclose any facts which would suggest that consent had been obtained through a mistake of fact or of law. The material facts of the transaction were known to both parties. Neither party was laboring under any misapprehension of law of which the other took advantage. The discussion between plaintiff and the school district representatives principally attempted to evaluate the probable consequences of plaintiff's predicament and to predict the future course of events. The fact that their speculations did not forecast the exact pattern which events subsequently took does not provide the basis for a claim that they were acting under some sort of mistake. The doctrine of mistake customarily involves such errors as the nature of the transaction, the identity of the parties, the identity of the things to which the contract relates, or the occurrence of collateral happenings. (Rest., Contracts, § 502, com. e.) Errors of this nature were not present in the case at bench.

However, the pleading does set out a claim that plaintiff's consent to the transaction had been obtained through the use of undue influence.

Undue influence, in the sense we are concerned with here, is a shorthand legal phrase used to describe persuasion which tends to be coercive in nature, persuasion which overcomes the will without convincing the judgment. (Estate of Ricks, 160 Cal. 467, 480-482 [117 P. 539].) The hallmark of such persuasion is high pressure, a pressure which works on mental, moral, or emotional weakness to such an extent that it approaches the boundaries of coercion. In this sense, undue influence has been called overpersuasion. (Kelly v. McCarthy, 6 Cal.2d 347, 364 [57 P.2d 118].) Misrepresentations of law or fact are not essential to the charge, for a person's will may be overborne without misrepresentation. By statutory definition undue influence includes "taking an unfair advantage of another's weakness of mind, or ... taking a grossly oppressive and unfair advantage of another's necessities or distress." (Civ. Code, § 1575.) While most reported cases of undue influence involve persons who bear a confidential relationship to one another, a confidential or authoritative relationship between the parties need not be present when the undue influence involves unfair advantage taken of another's weakness or distress. (Wells Fargo Bank v. Brady, 116 Cal.App.2d 381, 398 [254 P.2d 71]; Buchmayer v. Buchmayer, 68 Cal.App.2d 462, 467 [157 P.2d 9].)

We paraphrase the summary of undue influence given the jury by Sir James P. Wilde in Hall v. Hall, L.R. 1, P. & D. 481, 482 (1868):

> To make a good contract a man must be a free agent. Pressure of whatever sort which overpowers the will without convincing the judgment is a species of restraint under which no valid contract can be made. Importunity or threats, if carried to the degree in which the free play of a man's will is overborne, constitute undue influence, although no force is used or threatened. A party may be led but not driven, and his acts must be the offspring of his own volition and not the record of someone else's.

In essence undue influence involves the use of excessive pressure to persuade one vulnerable to such pressure, pressure applied by a dominant subject to a servient object. In combination, the elements of undue susceptibility in the servient person and excessive pressure by the dominating person make the latter's influence undue, for it results in the apparent will of the servient person being in fact the will of the dominant person.

Undue susceptibility may consist of total weakness of mind which leaves a person entirely without understanding (Civ. Code, § 38); or, a lesser weakness which destroys the capacity of a person to make a contract even though he is not totally incapacitated (Civ. Code, § 39; Peterson v. Ellebrecht, 205 Cal.App.2d 718, 721-722 [23 Cal.Rptr. 349]); or, the first element in our equation, a still lesser weakness which provides sufficient grounds to rescind a contract for undue influence (Civ. Code, § 1575; Faulkner v. Beatty, 161 Cal.App.2d 547, 551 [327 P.2d 41]; Stewart v. Marvin, 139 Cal.App.2d 769, 775 [294 P.2d 114]). Such lesser weakness need not be long-lasting nor wholly incapacitating, but may be merely a lack of full vigor due to age (Wells Fargo Bank v. Brady, 116 Cal.App.2d 381, 397-398 [254 P.2d 71]), physical condition (Weger v. Rocha, 138 Cal.App. 109, 114-115 [32 P.2d 417]), emotional anguish (Moore v. Moore, 56 Cal. 89, 93; 81 Cal. 195, 197-198 [22 P. 589, 874]), or a combination of such factors. The reported cases have usually involved elderly, sick, senile persons alleged to have executed wills or deeds under pressure. (Malone v. Malone, 155 Cal.App.2d 161 [317 P.2d 65] [constant importuning of a senile husband]; Stewart v. Marvin, 139 Cal.App.2d 769 [294 P.2d 114] [persistent nagging of elderly spouse].) In some of its aspects this lesser weakness could perhaps be called weakness of spirit. But whatever name we give it, this first element of undue influence resolves itself into a lessened capacity of the object to make a free contract.

In the present case plaintiff has pleaded that such weakness at the time he signed his resignation prevented him from freely and competently applying his judgment to the problem before him. Plaintiff declares he was under severe mental and emotional strain at the time because he had just completed the process of arrest, questioning, booking, and release on bail and had been without sleep for forty hours. It is possible that exhaustion and emotional turmoil may wholly incapacitate a person from exercising his judgment. As an abstract question of pleading, plaintiff has pleaded that possibility and sufficient allegations to state a case for rescission.

Undue influence in its second aspect involves an application of excessive strength by a dominant subject against a servient object. Judicial consideration of this second element in undue influence has been relatively rare, for there are few cases denying persons who persuade but do not misrepresent the benefit of their bargain. Yet logically, the same legal consequences should apply to the results of excessive strength as to the results of undue weakness. Whether from weakness on one side, or strength on the other, or a combination of the two, undue influence occurs whenever there results "that kind of influence or supremacy of one mind over another by which that other is prevented from acting according to his own wish or judgment, and whereby the will of the person is overborne and he is induced to do or forbear to do an act which he would not do, or would do, if left to act freely." (Webb v. Saunders, 79 Cal.App.2d 863, 871 [181 P.2d 43].) Undue influence involves a type of mismatch which our statute calls unfair advantage. (Civ. Code, § 1575.) Whether a person of subnormal capacities has been subjected to ordinary force or a person of normal capacities subjected to extraordinary force, the match is equally out of balance. If will has been overcome against judgment, consent may be rescinded.

The difficulty, of course, lies in determining when the forces of persuasion have overflowed their normal banks and become oppressive flood waters. There are second thoughts to every bargain, and hindsight is still better than foresight. Undue influence cannot be used as a pretext to avoid bad bargains or escape from bargains which refuse to come up to expectations. A woman who buys a dress on impulse, which on critical inspection by her best friend turns out to be less fashionable than she had thought, is not legally entitled to set aside the sale on the ground that the saleswoman used all her wiles to close the sale. A man who buys a tract of desert land in the expectation that it is in the immediate path of the city's growth and will become another Palm Springs, an expectation cultivated in glowing terms by the seller, cannot rescind his bargain when things turn out differently. If we are temporarily persuaded against our better judgment to do something about which we later have second thoughts, we must abide the consequences of the risks inherent in managing our own affairs. (Estate of Anderson, 185 Cal. 700, 706-707 [198 P. 407].)

However, overpersuasion is generally accompanied by certain characteristics which tend to create a pattern. The pattern usually involves several of the following elements: (1) discussion of the transaction at an unusual or inappropriate time, (2) consummation of the transaction in an unusual place, (3) insistent demand that the business be finished at once, (4) extreme emphasis on untoward consequences of delay, (5) the use of multiple persuaders by the dominant side against a single servient party, (6) absence of third-party advisers to the servient party, (7) statements that there is no time to consult financial advisers or attorneys. If a number of these elements are simultaneously present, the persuasion may be characterized as excessive. The cases are illustrative:

Moore v. Moore, 56 Cal. 89, 93, and 81 Cal. 195 [22 P. 589, 874]. The pregnant wife of a man who had been shot to death on October 30 and buried on November 1 was approached by four members of her husband's family on November 2 or 3 and persuaded to deed her entire interest in her husband's estate to his children by a prior marriage. In finding the use of undue influence on Mrs. Moore, the court commented: "It was the second day after her late husband's funeral. It was at a time when she would naturally feel averse to transacting any business, and she might reasonably presume that her late husband's brothers would not apply to her at such a time to transact any important business, unless it was of a nature that would admit of no delay. And as it would admit of delay, the only reason which we can discover for their unseemly haste is, that they thought that she would be more likely to comply with their wishes then than at some future time, after she had recovered from the shock which she had then so recently experienced. If for that reason they selected that time for the accomplishment of their purpose, it seems to us that they not only took, but that they designed to take, an unfair advantage of her weakness of mind. If they did not, they probably can explain why they selected that inappropriate time for the transaction of business which might have been delayed for weeks without injury to anyone. In the absence of any explanation, it appears to us that the time was selected with reference to just that condition of mind which she alleges that she was then in.

"Taking an unfair advantage of another's weakness of mind is undue influence, and the law will not permit the retention of an advantage thus obtained. (Civ. Code, § 1575.)"

Weger v. Rocha, 138 Cal.App. 109 [32 P.2d 417]. Plaintiff, while confined in a cast in a hospital, gave a release of claims for personal injuries for a relatively small sum to an agent who spent two hours persuading her to sign. At the time of signing plaintiff was in a highly nervous and hysterical condition and suffering much pain, and she signed the release in order to terminate the interview. The court held that the release had been secured by the use of undue influence.

Fyan v. McNutt (1934) 266 Mich. 406 [254 N.W. 146]. At issue was the validity of an agreement by Mrs. McNutt to pay Fyan, a real estate broker, a 5 percent commission on all moneys received from the condemnation of Mrs. McNutt's land. Earlier, Fyan had secured an option from Mrs. McNutt to purchase her land for his own account and offer it for sale as part of a larger parcel to Wayne County for an airport site. On July 25 Fyan learned from the newspapers that the county would probably start condemnation proceedings rather than obtain an airport site by purchase. Fyan, with four others, arrived at Mrs. McNutt's house at 1 a.m. on July 26 with the commission agreement he wanted her to sign. Mrs. McNutt protested being awakened at that hour and was reluctant to sign, but Fyan told her he had to have the paper in Detroit by morning, that the whole airport proposition would fall through if she did not sign then and there, that there wasn't time to wait until morning to get outside advice. In holding the agreement invalid the Michigan Supreme Court said: "The late hour of the night at which her signature was secured over her protest and plea that she be given until the next day to consider her action, the urge of the moment, the cooperation of the others present in their desire to obtain a good price for their farm lands, the plaintiff's anxiety over the seeming weakness of his original option, all combined to produce a situation in which, to say the least, it is doubtful that the defendant had an opportunity to exercise her own free will. . . . A valid contract can be entered into only when there is a meeting of the minds of the parties under circumstances conducive to a free and voluntary execution of the agreement contemplated. It must be conceived in good faith and come into existence under circumstances that do not deprive the parties of the exercise of their own free will."

The difference between legitimate persuasion and excessive pressure, like the difference between seduction and rape, rests to a considerable extent in the manner in which the parties go about their business. For example, if a day or two after Odorizzi's release on bail the superintendent of the school district had called him into his office during business hours and directed his attention to those provisions of the Education Code compelling his leave of absence and authorizing his suspension on the filing of written charges, had told him that the district contemplated filing written charges against him, had pointed out the alternative of resignation available to him, had informed him he was free to consult counsel or any adviser he wished and to consider the matter overnight and return with his decision the next day, it is extremely unlikely that any complaint about the use of excessive pressure could ever have been made against the school district.

But, according to the allegations of the complaint, this is not the way it happened, and if it had happened that way, plaintiff would never have resigned. Rather, the representatives of the school board undertook to achieve their objective by overpersuasion and imposition to secure plaintiff's signature but not his consent to his resignation through a high-pressure carrot-and-stick technique-under which they assured plaintiff they were trying to assist him, he should rely on their advice, there wasn't time to consult an attorney, if he didn't resign at once the school district would suspend and dismiss him from his position and publicize the proceedings, but if he did resign the incident wouldn't jeopardize his chances of securing a teaching post elsewhere.

Plaintiff has thus pleaded both subjective and objective elements entering the undue influence equation and stated sufficient facts to put in issue the question whether his free will had been overborne by defendant's agents at a time when he was unable to function in a normal manner. It was sufficient to pose "... the ultimate question ... whether a free and competent judgment was merely influenced, or whether a mind was so dominated as to prevent the exercise of an independent judgment." (Williston on Contracts, § 1625 [rev. ed.]; Rest., Contracts, § 497, com. c.) The question cannot be resolved by an analysis of pleading but requires a finding of fact.

We express no opinion on the merits of plaintiff's case, or the propriety of his continuing to teach school (Ed. Code, § 13403), or the timeliness of his rescission (Civ. Code, § 1691). We do hold that his pleading, liberally construed, states a cause of action for rescission of a transaction to which his apparent consent had been obtained through the use of undue influence.

The judgment is reversed.

Roth, P. J., and Herndon, J., concurred.

KASE V. FRENCH
Supreme Court of South Dakota
325 N.W.2d 678 (1982).

WOLLMAN, Justice.

This is an appeal from a judgment in an action brought by the administrator of the estate Olivia M. McWilliams, deceased, (appellant) against Kenneth and Betty French to vacate a contract for deed and to recover various cash transfers allegedly obtained through undue influence. The trial court upheld the validity of the contract for deed and the cash transfers, holding that no confidential relationship existed at the time of the sale and that no undue influence resulted from the confidential relationship that subsequently did develop. We affirm.

A widow in her eighties, Mrs. McWilliams lived in a large, somewhat rundown two-story house in Rapid City. As she had a fourth-grade education and no business experience, her nephew, Charles Bruggeman, had been assisting her in the conduct of her business affairs. There was no dispute, however, that Mrs. McWilliams was mentally competent. Mr. and Mrs. Bruggeman visited Mrs. McWilliams frequently and regularly ran errands for her even though they lived in Belle Fourche.

Charles Bruggeman was named as one of several beneficiaries in Mrs. McWilliams' original will. She gave him a general power of attorney in 1969 and added his name to her checking account and certificates of deposit. One year later she revoked this power of attorney. He continued to assist her with her business affairs, however, and their relationship continued on the same basis as before this revocation. Mrs. McWilliams also executed a new will in 1970 in which she left her entire estate to various branches of medical research.

Mr. and Mrs. French moved to Rapid City in 1971, where they purchased a small neighborhood grocery store. They delivered groceries as part of their service. In 1972 Mr. French delivered an order of groceries to Mrs. McWilliams. As he made her acquaintance he was struck by her resemblance to his grandmother. He commented upon this to Mrs. French and suggested to her that she also make Mrs. McWilliams' acquaintance. Once the two women met, a friendship quickly developed between them. Soon after their meeting, Mrs. French stopped by to see Mrs. McWilliams and found that she had injured herself in a fall. From that time on Mrs. French called on Mrs. McWilliams daily and started to help her with household work and other chores. About a month after meeting, Mrs. French told Mrs. McWilliams that she need never be lonely again because they, the Frenches, would take care of her for the rest of her life.

During the latter part of 1972 or early in 1973, the Frenches suggested to Mrs. McWilliams that she move to a dwelling that was less dilapidated. They testified that Mrs. McWilliams countered with the suggestion that they buy her home and fix an apartment in it for her. Within a few months, and after the Frenches had the property appraised (at $35,000), it was agreed that Mrs. McWilliams would sell her property, consisting of two lots, the home, a separate dwelling called the annex, and the personal property and fixtures in the home and the annex, to the Frenches for $40,000. There was to be no downpayment, and the purchase price was to be paid, with interest at the rate of one percent per year, in monthly payments over a period of twenty years ($184 per month) beginning two years after the date of sale. Mrs. McWilliams was to continue to occupy an apartment in the house, rent free, for two years.

Either Mrs. French or Mrs. McWilliams asked Mr. Eugene Christol, Mrs. McWilliams' attorney, to go to the McWilliams home to discuss the impending transaction. Both the Frenches and Mrs. McWilliams participated in this conversation and related the terms of the sale already agreed to. Mr. Christol attempted to dissuade Mrs. McWilliams from selling her property under terms so inadequate to provide for her support and expenses for the rest of her life. He explained to her that one of the shortcomings of the proposed transaction was that the interest rate was not proper. In addition, he reminded her that other parties had expressed interest in buying her property at a far higher price. Mr. Christol testified that this advice made no impression on Mrs. McWilliams and that it appeared to him that her mind was set to transact the sale under those terms in spite of his advice and warnings. He testified that he asked Mr. Bruggeman to also try to persuade Mrs. McWilliams to change the terms of the transaction. Mr. Bruggeman testified that he reminded his aunt of a previous offer for her property of $90,000. (Neither Mr. Christol nor Mr. Bruggeman, however, was able to document any offers at trial.) Mr. Bruggeman was also unable to convince Mrs. McWilliams to take a second look at the terms and was informed by Mrs. McWilliams that she no longer needed him to take care of her business because the Frenches would do that for her. Eventually, Mr. Christol prepared a contract for deed according to the terms specified by Mrs. McWilliams and the Frenches. Very shortly thereafter Mrs. McWilliams removed Mr. Bruggeman's name from all her bank, savings and loan accounts, and certificates of deposit, and opened a joint account with the Frenches. Mr. Bruggeman continued to visit his aunt but no longer counseled her on her business affairs.

Mr. French testified that although Mrs. McWilliams did not want any interest, she thought that such an interest-free arrangement would not be legal. He further testified that Mrs. McWilliams suggested one percent interest because she was aware of one percent government loans available after the 1972 Rapid City flood and therefore thought that one percent would be legal. The Frenches' testimony reveals that they were aware that the going interest rate in Rapid City at the time of the sale ranged from six to eight percent. Neither Mr. nor Mrs. French informed Mrs. McWilliams of this fact.

The trial court found that a confidential relationship existed between Mrs. McWilliams and the Frenches only following the sale of her residence to the Frenches. Appellant contends that this finding was clearly erroneous. We agree.

"A confidential relationship 'exists whenever trust and confidence is reposed by the testator in the integrity and fidelity of another.' " Matter of Heer's Estate, 316 N.W.2d 806, 810 (S.D.1982) (quoting In re Estate of Hobelsberger, 85 S.D. 282, 291, 181 N.W.2d 455, 460 (1970)). "[A] [c]onfidential relationship is not restricted to any particular association of persons. It exists whenever there is trust and confidence, regardless of its origin." Hyde v. Hyde, 78 S.D. 176, 186, 99 N.W.2d 788, 793 (1959). "Such a confidential relation exists between two persons when one has gained the confidence of the other and purports to act or advise with the other's interest in mind." Schwartzle v. Dale, 74 S.D. 467, 471, 54 N.W.2d 361, 363 (1952).

In the light of the contacts Mr. and Mrs. French had with Mrs. McWilliams and of the fact that the promise to take care of Mrs. McWilliams was made prior to the sale of her home, we conclude that a confidential relationship existed between Mrs. McWilliams and the Frenches at the time of the sale of the property.

The existence of a confidential relation requires the dominant party "to exercise the utmost good faith and to refrain from obtaining any advantage at the expense of the confiding party." Hyde v. Hyde, supra, 78 S.D. at 186, 99 N.W.2d at 793. In Davies v. Toms, 75 S.D. 273, 281, 63 N.W.2d 406, 410 (1954), an action to set aside a deed, this court stated:

While ... the "burden of proof" never shifts from the one who undertakes to set aside a deed on the ground of undue influence, there is a burden that does transfer over to the other side when evidence offered shows a relationship of trust and confidence.... The latter type burden this court has called the "burden of going forward with the evidence." ... [T]he burden then rested on appellants to show that they took no unfair advantage of their dominant position....

The Frenches were therefore under a duty to go forward with the evidence and show that the transaction was free from undue influence. Hyde v. Hyde, supra. See also Niles v. Lee, 31 S.D. 234, 140 N.W. 259 (1913). During cross-examination as well as during the presentation of their witnesses, the Frenches, in fact, went forward with evidence as required by our decisions. Thus we are satisfied that the failure of the trial court to make the proper finding on the issue of the existence of a confidential relationship does not require reversal of the judgment.

The indicia of undue influence are: person susceptible to undue influence, opportunity to exert undue influence and effect wrongful purpose, disposition to do so for improper purpose, and result clearly showing effect of undue influence. Matter of Estate of Landeen, 264 N.W.2d 521 (S.D.1978); In re Rowlands' Estate, 70 S.D. 419, 18 N.W.2d 290 (1945). The trial court concluded that "at all times [Mrs. McWilliams] enjoyed good health, was able to care for herself, was mentally alert and competent to the time of her death, was a strong-willed person and independent in her thinking, and was not weak willed or easily influenced." The record supports this finding. Even appellant in his brief describes Mrs. McWilliams as a "strong willed and stubborn old lady, [who] was not about to take advice."

We cannot say that the contract for deed clearly shows the effect of undue influence. The Frenches called as a witness the realtor who had appraised the property at $35,000. While the interest and downpayment terms were certainly favorable to the Frenches, Mrs. McWilliams received the favorable term of being able to live rent free in an apartment for two years. Although the promise to take care of Mrs. McWilliams for the rest of her life was not incorporated into the contract for deed, Mrs. McWilliams did, in fact, live with Mr. and Mrs. French rent free for one and a half years. Also, when Mrs. McWilliams was later placed in a nursing home, Mrs. French signed an agreement which made her the responsible party in the event of problems with payment.

This court has recognized the presence of independent legal advice as an important factor to be considered in determining whether undue influence exists. Davies v. Toms, supra; In re Daly's Estate, 59 S.D. 403, 240 N.W. 342 (1932). Appellant attempts to undermine the importance of the advice of Mrs. McWilliams' attorney, Mr. Christol, because his advice was neither accepted nor acted upon. Appellant characterizes Mr. Christol's role as one of a draftsman who simply reduced to writing what was already agreed upon. We cannot agree with this characterization. Mr. Christol had been the attorney for Mrs. McWilliams since 1965. He had also given legal advice to her deceased husband and sister. His advice to Mrs. McWilliams was anything other than perfunctory. Cf. Black v. Gardner, 320 N.W.2d 153 (S.D.1982). When Mr. and Mrs. French and Mrs. McWilliams informed Mr. Christol of the terms of their proposed contract, Mr. Christol explained to Mrs. McWilliams why he thought the contract would be a poor business agreement for her. He delayed in writing the contract and called Mr. Bruggeman to inform him of his opinion of the proposed contract. Merely because Mrs. McWilliams chose not to follow Mr. Christol's advice does not destroy the importance of her having received that advice.

The trial court found that the Frenches had neither taken unfair advantage of Mrs. McWilliams nor exerted undue influence upon her in any of their dealings. Given the trial court's opportunity to judge the credibility of the Frenches on the basis of their courtroom demeanor and testimony, we cannot say that this finding is clearly erroneous. SDCL 15-6-52(a); In re Estate of Hobelsberger, supra.

Appellant contends that he is entitled to judgment against the Frenches for all money received from Mrs. McWilliams after the contract for deed transaction. Our review of the record satisfies us that the trial court's treatment of this aspect of appellant's case also finds support in the evidence and thus should not be set aside.

The judgment is affirmed.

FOSHEIM, C.J., and DUNN, and MORGAN, JJ., concur.
HENDERSON, J., dissents.

HENDERSON, Justice (dissenting).

ACTION

This action to vacate a contract for deed and cash transfers, being equitable in nature, is on meritorious appeal to this Court. The majority opinion permits the Frenches to enrich themselves at the expense of an elderly lady, Mrs. McWilliams (her estate), thereby weakening the safeguards which courts of equity have historically employed to protect the weak. I dissent as the evidence does not disclose that the Frenches were the Good Samaritans they professed themselves to be unto Mrs. McWilliams nor to the South Dakota courts. Rather, the factual history reflects that the Frenches took advantage of Mrs. McWilliams by gaining her confidence, placing themselves in a fiduciary relationship, abusing that confidential and fiduciary relationship, profiting exceedingly when they were in a dominant position as compared to the dependent position of Mrs. McWilliams, and by garnering most of her earthly possessions and home before she died. By this dissent, I sustain and defend her cause.

There are three principal issues to this appeal which are recited and treated below with supporting reasons and authorities. . . .

ISSUES

1) Did a confidential relationship exist as between Mrs. McWilliams and the Frenches at the time of the real estate transaction by which Mrs. McWilliams contracted to sell her home in Rapid City to the Frenches? Yes. . . .

2) At the time of the real estate transaction, and conceding that a confidential relationship existed between the Frenches and Mrs. McWilliams, did the Frenches meet their burden of

proof that (a) they took no unfair advantage of their dominant position and (b) that they did not unduly profit at the expense of Mrs. McWilliams? No. . . .

3) The trial court found that a confidential relationship existed subsequent to the sale of Mrs. McWilliams' home to the Frenches. Is the estate of Mrs. McWilliams entitled to a judgment for approximately $31,456.09 constituting money in the form of "gifts", money which the Frenches obtained from Mrs. McWilliams when this confidential relationship existed? Yes. . . .

I.

[The dissent agrees with the majority's finding of a confidential relationship at the time of sale.]

II.

At the time of the real estate transaction, Mrs. McWilliams was a widow of 83 years of age with a fourth-grade education and no business experience. Undeniably, she was lonely. She apparently had no close acquaintances or relatives in Rapid City and her two nephews lived in Belle Fourche, one of whom was close to her. The Frenches were in the prime of life, Kenneth French being 47 and Betty French 48 years of age. Mr. French was a businessman.

Concerning the sale of Mrs. McWilliams' home to the Frenches, the majority opinion notes: "Neither Mr. nor Mrs. French informed Mrs. McWilliams of this fact" (that the going interest rate in Rapid City at the time of the sale ranged from six to eight percent). Notwithstanding this observation, the majority opinion finds no wrongdoing on the house sale. The majority opinion fails to recognize that once it has been established that the Frenches were in a confidential or fiduciary relationship, they owed a duty to divulge a fair rate of interest to her. McClintock On Equity at 224 (1948), tells us: "An intentional, active concealment of a fact of which the other party is known to be ignorant has the same effect as a false statement, but mere nondisclosure does not invalidate the transaction, unless some previous relationship or transaction between them has imposed some obligation to make disclosure." McClintock further states at 225: "The principle that a party can keep silent with respect to matters of which he knows the other is ignorant applies only when the parties are dealing at arm's length. Where there is such a relationship between them, or such relationship has recently existed, as to justify the mistaken party in relying upon the other for information with respect to the transaction, the latter must make full disclosure." The Frenches failed to make full disclosure. During the course of trial, witness Lewis Rohrer submitted a summary, duly received into evidence, reflecting that monthly payments on $40,000.00 amortized over 20 years at 8% interest would amount to $334.58 per month or $150.58 more than the monthly payments of $184.00 provided for by the contract. Such computation reflects a difference of $36,139.20, which the Frenches would pay under an 8% interest rate as compared to a 1% interest rate under the contract. This offends one's sense of good morals and fair dealings and should require a court of equity to act in response thereto. This unfair interest rate was known to the Frenches, they who said they would take care of her the rest of her life and who said she would never be lonely again. Yes, and they who "would see that she had money." As the record indicates, the Frenches, a few years earlier, had paid 6 3/4% interest on their loan to get into the grocery business. These facts, these figures, demonstrate that the Frenches took unfair advantage of Mrs. McWilliams and that they profited handsomely at her expense. For people who were going to do good (to her), they did very well. Mrs. French admitted, under oath, that neither she nor her husband ever suggested to Mrs. McWilliams that the 1% interest rate was not a fair rate or the going rate of interest. . . .

Seemingly, the majority opinion would instill the Frenches' position with a defense because Mr. Christol's advice was sought. But the majority opinion fails to recognize that this is only a defense when the advice is sought and acted upon, and not when the advice is given and then rejected by a closed mind. As in Davies, cited in the majority opinion, "[h]er mind was made up." 75 S.D. at 279, 63 N.W.2d at 409. This case supports my position that the advice given implies at least an apparent open-mindedness on the part of the recipient, and Mrs. McWilliams did not have an open mind. I further believe that language found in In Re Daly's Estate, 59 S.D. 403, 240 N.W. 342 (1932) (Daly), supports my position that the rejected advice of Mr. Christol does not obliterate or soften the overreaching of the Frenches. Daly quotes from Jones' Commentaries on Evidence, vol. 2, § 190:

. . . As indicated in Dibel v. Meredith, 233 Iowa 545, 10 N.W.2d 28, 30 (1943) (Dibel), a confidential relationship (in the instant case, it was fiduciary as well) was explained "[i]n law it has been defined or described as any relation existing between parties to a transaction wherein one of the parties is duty bound to act with the utmost good faith for the benefit of the other party." Here, the Frenches did not act in good faith for Mrs. McWilliams; they acted for themselves. In Matter of Estate of Herm, 284 N.W.2d 191, 200 (Iowa 1979), the Supreme Court of Iowa approved of its language in Dibel and further expressed: "Where such a confidential relationship exists, a transaction by which the one having the advantage profits at the expense of the other will be held presumptively fraudulent and voidable." I disagree with the conclusion of the majority opinion that the Frenches took no unfair advantage of their dominant position. The results of their efforts patently establish unfair advantage.

III.

Of the $31,456.09 that the Frenches obtained from Mrs. McWilliams, the Frenches maintain this accumulation was a series of gifts except for the first $4,000.00 they obtained from her.

When the Frenches put Mrs. McWilliams into the nursing home against her wishes and left her crying and confused, she was apparently given a check for $11,200.00. Ostensibly, this was in repayment of a $4,000.00 note and a refund of the proceeds of the sales of Harding County land, plus interest thereon. The trial court found a confidential relationship between Mrs. McWilliams and the Frenches, but confined this finding to all times subsequent to the sale of the home. Mrs. French took Mrs. McWilliams to various banks and savings and loan associations where Mrs. McWilliams had money on deposit, for the express purpose of having Mrs. McWilliams withdraw money from her accounts to turn the money over to the Frenches. In this, the confidential relationship was used and abused and the gifts are presumptively fraudulent and voidable and the Frenches have failed to overcome this presumption. . . .

36A C.J.S. *Fiduciary* § 389 (1961) provides:

> It is a doctrine repeatedly announced that courts of equity will scrutinize with the most jealous vigilance transactions between parties occupying fiduciary relations toward each other, and particularly any transaction between the parties by which the dominant party secures any profit or advantage at the expense of the person under his influence.
>
> Transactions between parties to a fiduciary relation are presumptively fraudulent and void, and will be stricken down unless their fairness is established by clear and convincing proof, and the burden of proof is on the party asserting validity with respect thereto.

. . . As a fiduciary, the Frenches had no right to breach or abuse their relationship with Mrs. McWilliams. See Dobbs, Law of Remedies at 680 (1973). I would reverse and direct that the trial court enter a judgment voiding the unconscionable contract for sale and further direct the trial court to credit the Frenches for the money expended in the repair, remodeling, and improvement of the real property. Furthermore, I would reverse and direct the trial court to restore unto the estate all inter vivos gifts plus interest, believing that a court of equity will not suffer a wrong to be committed without fashioning a remedy. This well could include the appointment of a referee to take evidence to establish the necessary arithmetic calculations to put the court's judgment into effect. See McClintock on Equity at 76.

SECTION 5. UNCONSCIONABILITY

WILLIAMS V. WALKER-THOMAS FURNITURE CO.
United States Court of Appeals, District of Columbia Circuit
350 F.2d 445 (1965).

J. SKELLY WRIGHT, Circuit Judge:

Appellee, Walker-Thomas Furniture Company, operates a retail furniture store in the District of Columbia. During the period from 1957 to 1962 each appellant in these cases purchased a number of household items from Walker-Thomas, for which payment was to be made in installments. The terms of each purchase were contained in a printed form contract which set forth the value of the purchased item and purported to lease the item to appellant for a stipulated monthly rent payment. The contract then provided, in substance, that title would remain in Walker-Thomas until the total of all the monthly payments made equaled the stated value of the item, at which time appellants could take title. In the event of a default in the payment of any monthly installment, Walker-Thomas could repossess the item.

The contract further provided that "the amount of each periodical installment payment to be made by (purchaser) to the Company under this present lease shall be inclusive of and not in addition to the amount of each installment payment to be made by (purchaser) under such prior leases, bills or accounts; and all payments now and hereafter made by (purchaser) shall be credited pro rata on all outstanding leases, bills and accounts due the Company by (purchaser) at the time each such payment is made." The effect of this rather obscure provision was to keep a balance due on every item purchased until the balance due on all items, whenever purchased, was liquidated. As a result, the debt incurred at the time of purchase of each item was secured by the right to repossess all the items previously purchased by the same purchaser, and each new item purchased automatically became subject to a security interest arising out of the previous dealings.

On May 12, 1962, appellant Thorne purchased an item described as a Daveno, three tables, and two lamps, having total stated value of $391.10. Shortly thereafter, he defaulted on his monthly payments and appellee sought to replevy all the items purchased since the first transaction in 1958. Similarly, on April 17, 1962, appellant Williams bought a stereo set of stated value of $514.95.[1] She too defaulted shortly thereafter, and appellee sought to replevy all the items purchased since December, 1957. The Court of General Sessions granted judgment for appellee. The District of Columbia Court of Appeals affirmed, and we granted appellants' motion for leave to appeal to this court.

Appellants' principal contention, rejected by both the trial and the appellate courts below, is that these contracts, or at least some of them, are unconscionable and, hence, not enforceable. In its opinion in Williams v. Walker-Thomas Furniture Company, 198 A.2d 914, 916 (1964), the District of Columbia Court of Appeals explained its rejection of this contention as follows:

> Appellant's second argument presents a more serious question. The record reveals that prior to the last purchase appellant had reduced the balance in her account to $164. The last purchase, a stereo set, raised the balance due to $678. Significantly, at the time of this and the preceding purchases, appellee was aware of appellant's financial position. The reverse side of the stereo contract listed the name of appellant's social worker and her $218 monthly stipend from the government. Nevertheless, with full knowledge that appellant had to feed, clothe and support both herself and seven children on this amount, appellee sold her a $514 stereo set.
>
> We cannot condemn too strongly appellee's conduct. It raises serious questions of sharp practice and irresponsible business dealings. A review of the legislation in the District of Columbia affecting retail sales and the pertinent decisions of the highest court in this jurisdiction disclose, however, no ground upon which this court can declare the contracts in question contrary to public policy. We note that were the Maryland Retail Installment Sales Act, Art. 83 §§ 128-153, or its equivalent, in force in the District of Columbia, we could grant appellant appropriate relief. We think Congress should consider corrective legislation to protect the public from such exploitive contracts as were utilized in the case at bar.

---

[1] At the time of this purchase her account showed a balance of $164 still owing from her prior purchases. The total of all the purchases made over the years in question came to $1,800. The total payments amounted to $1,400.

We do not agree that the court lacked the power to refuse enforcement to contracts found to be unconscionable. In other jurisdictions, it has been held as a matter of common law that unconscionable contracts are not enforceable. While no decision of this court so holding has been found, the notion that an unconscionable bargain should not be given full enforcement is by no means novel. In Scott v. United States, 79 U.S. (12 Wall.) 443, 445, 20 L.Ed. 438 (1870), the Supreme Court stated:

> . . . If a contract be unreasonable and unconscionable, but not void for fraud, a court of law will give to the party who sues for its breach damages, not according to its letter, but only such as he is equitably entitled to. . . .

Since we have never adopted or rejected such a rule, the question here presented is actually one of first impression.

Congress has recently enacted the Uniform Commercial Code, which specifically provides that the court may refuse to enforce a contract which it finds to be unconscionable at the time it was made. 28 D.C.CODE § 2-302 (Supp. IV 1965). The enactment of this section, which occurred subsequent to the contracts here in suit, does not mean that the common law of the District of Columbia was otherwise at the time of enactment, nor does it preclude the court from adopting a similar rule in the exercise of its powers to develop the common law for the District of Columbia. In fact, in view of the absence of prior authority on the point, we consider the congressional adoption of § 2-302 persuasive authority for following the rationale of the cases from which the section is explicitly derived. Accordingly, we hold that where the element of unconscionability is present at the time a contract is made, the contract should not be enforced.

Unconscionability has generally been recognized to include an absence of meaningful choice on the part of one of the parties together with contract terms which are unreasonably favorable to the other party. Whether a meaningful choice is present in a particular case can only be determined by consideration of all the circumstances surrounding the transaction. In many cases the meaningfulness of the choice is negated by a gross inequality of bargaining power. The manner in which the contract was entered is also relevant to this consideration. Did each party to the contract, considering his obvious education or lack of it, have a reasonable opportunity to understand the terms of the contract, or were the important terms hidden in a maze of fine print and minimized by deceptive sales practices? Ordinarily, one who signs an agreement without full knowledge of its terms might be held to assume the risk that he has entered a one-sided bargain. But when a party of little bargaining power, and hence little real choice, signs a commercially unreasonable contract with little or no knowledge of its terms, it is hardly likely that his consent, or even an objective manifestation of his consent, was ever given to all the terms. In such a case the usual rule that the terms of the agreement are not to be questioned[9] should be abandoned and

[9] This rule has never been without exception. In cases involving merely the transfer of unequal amounts of the same commodity, the courts have held the bargain unenforceable for the reason that 'in such a case, it is clear, that the law cannot indulge in the presumption of equivalence between the consideration and the promise.' 1 WILLISTON, CONTRACTS § 115 (3d ed. 1957).

the court should consider whether the terms of the contract are so unfair that enforcement should be withheld.[10]

In determining reasonableness or fairness, the primary concern must be with the terms of the contract considered in light of the circumstances existing when the contract was made. The test is not simple, nor can it be mechanically applied. The terms are to be considered 'in the light of the general commercial background and the commercial needs of the particular trade or case."[11] Corbin suggests the test as being whether the terms are "so extreme as to appear unconscionable according to the mores and business practices of the time and place." 1 CORBIN, op. cit. supra Note 2.[12] We think this formulation correctly states the test to be applied in those cases where no meaningful choice was exercised upon entering the contract.

Because the trial court and the appellate court did not feel that enforcement could be refused, no findings were made on the possible unconscionability of the contracts in these cases. Since the record is not sufficient for our deciding the issue as a matter of law, the cases must be remanded to the trial court for further proceedings.

So ordered.

DANAHER, Circuit Judge (dissenting):

The District of Columbia Court of Appeals obviously was as unhappy about the situation here presented as any of us can possibly be. Its opinion in the Williams case, quoted in the majority text, concludes: "We think Congress should consider corrective legislation to protect the public from such exploitive contracts as were utilized in the case at bar."

My view is thus summed up by an able court which made no finding that there had actually been sharp practice. Rather the appellant seems to have known precisely where she stood.

There are many aspects of public policy here involved. What is a luxury to some may seem an outright necessity to others. Is public oversight to be required of the expenditures of relief funds? A washing machine, e.g., in the hands of a relief client might become a fruitful source of income. Many relief clients may well need credit, and certain business establishments will take long chances on the sale of items, expecting their pricing policies will afford a degree of protection commensurate with the risk. Perhaps a remedy when necessary will be found within the provisions of the "Loan Shark" law, D.C.CODE §§ 26-601 et seq. (1961).

---

[10] See the general discussion of 'Boiler-Plate Agreements' in LLEWELLYN, THE COMMON LAW TRADITION 362-371 (1960).

[11] Comment, Uniform Commercial Code § 2-307.

[12] See Henningsen v. Bloomfield Motors, Inc., supra Note 2; Mandel v. Liebman, 303 N.Y. 88, 100 N.E.2d 149 (1951). The traditional test as stated in Greer v. Tweed, supra Note 3, 13 Abb.Pr.,N.S., at 429, is 'such as no man in his senses and not under delusion would make on the one hand, and as no honest or fair man would accept, on the other.'

I mention such matters only to emphasize the desirability of a cautious approach to any such problem, particularly since the law for so long has allowed parties such great latitude in making their own contracts. I dare say there must annually be thousands upon thousands of installment credit transactions in this jurisdiction, and one can only speculate as to the effect the decision in these cases will have.[1]

I join the District of Columbia Court of Appeals in its disposition of the issues.

WEAVER V. AMERICAN OIL CO.
Supreme Court of Indiana
276 N.E.2d 144 (1971).

ARTERBURN, Chief Justice.

In this case the appellee oil company presented to the appellant-defendant leasee, a filling station operator, a printed form contract as a lease to be signed, by the defendant, which contained, in addition to the normal leasing provisions, a "hold harmless" clause which provided in substance that the leasee operator would hold harmless and also indemnify the oil company for any negligence of the oil company occurring on the leased premises. The litigation arises as a result of the oil company's own employee spraying gasoline over Weaver and his assistant and causing them to be burned and injured on the leased premises. This action was initiated by American Oil and Hoffer (Appellees) for a declaratory judgment to determine the liability of appellant Weaver, under the clause in the lease. The trial court entered judgment holding Weaver liable under the lease.

Clause three (3) of the lease reads as follows:

> Lessor, its agents and employees shall not be liable for any loss, damage, injuries, or other casualty of whatsoever kind or by whomsoever caused to the person or property of anyone (including Lessee) on or off the premises, arising out of or resulting from Lessee's use, possession or operation thereof, or from defects in the premises whether apparent or hidden, or from the installation existence, use, maintenance, condition, repair, alteration, removal or replacement of any equipment thereon, whether due in whole or in part to negligent acts or omissions of Lessor, its agents or employees; and Lessee for himself, his heirs, executors, administrators, successors and assigns, hereby agrees to indemnify and hold Lessor, its agents and employees, harmless from and against all claims, demands, liabilities, suits or actions (including all reasonable expenses and attorneys' fees incurred by or imposed on the Lessor in connection therewith) for such loss, damage, injury or other casualty. Lessee also agrees to pay all reasonable expenses and attorneys' fees incurred by Lessor in the event that Lessee shall default under the provisions of this paragraph.

---

[1] However the provision ultimately may be applied or in what circumstances, D.C.CODE § 28-2-301 (Supp. IV, 1965) did not become effective until January 1, 1965.

It will be noted that this lease clause not only exculpated the leasor oil company from its liability for its negligence, but also compelled Weaver to indemnify them for any damages or loss incurred as a result of its negligence. The appellate court held the exculpatory clause invalid, 261 N.E.2d 99, but the indemnifying clause valid, 262 N.E.2d 663. In our opinion, both these provisions must be read together since one may be used to effectuate the result obtained through the other. We find no ground for any distinction and we therefore grant the petition to transfer the appeal to this court.

This is a contract, which was submitted (already in printed form) to a party with lesser bargaining power. As in this case, it may contain unconscionable or unknown provisions which are in fine print. Such is the case now before this court.

The facts reveal that Weaver had left high school after one and a half years and spent his time, prior to leasing the service station, working at various skilled and unskilled labor oriented jobs. He was not one who should be expected to know the law or understand the meaning of technical terms. The ceremonious activity of signing the lease consisted of nothing more than the agent of American Oil placing the lease in front of Mr. Weaver and saying "sign," which Mr. Weaver did. There is nothing in the record to indicate that Weaver read the lease; that the agent asked Weaver to read it; or that the agent, in any manner, attempted to call Weaver's attention to the "hold harmless" clause in the lease. Each year following, the procedure was the same. A salesman, from American Oil, would bring the lease to Weaver, at the station, and Weaver would sign it. The evidence showed that Weaver had never read the lease prior to signing and that the clauses in the lease were never explained to him in a manner from which he could grasp their legal significance. The leases were prepared by the attorneys of American Oil Company, for the American Oil Company, and the agents of the American Oil Company never attempted to explain the conditions of the lease nor did they advise Weaver that he should consult legal counsel, before signing the lease. The superior bargaining power of American Oil is patently obvious and the significance of Weaver's signature upon the legal document amounted to nothing more than a mere formality to Weaver for the substantial protection of American Oil.

Had this case involved the sale of goods it would have been termed an "unconscionable contract" under sec. 2-302 of the Uniform Commercial Code as found in Burns' Ind.Stat. sec. 19-2-302, IC 1971, 26-1-2-302. The statute reads as follows:

> 19-2-302. Unconscionable contract or clause.-If the court as a matter of law find the contract or any clause of the contract to have been unconscionable at the time it was made the court may refuse to enforce the contract, or it may enforce the remainder of the contract without the unconscionable clause, or it may so limit the application of any unconscionable clause as to avoid any unconscionable result.
>
> (2) When it is claimed or appears to the court that the contract or any clause thereof may be unconscionable the parties shall be afforded a reasonable opportunity to present evidence as to its commercial setting, purpose and effect to aid the court in making the determination. (Acts 1963, ch. 317, sec. 2-302 p. 539)

According to the Comment to Official Text, the basic test of unconscionability is whether, in light of the general commercial background and the commercial needs of the particular trade or case, the clauses involved are so one-sided as to be unconscionable under the circumstances existing at the time of the making of the contract. Subsection two makes it clear that it is proper for the court to hear evidence upon these questions.

> An "unconscionable contract" has been defined to be such as no sensible man not under delusion, duress or in distress would make, and such as no honest and fair man would accept. There exists here an "inequality so strong, gross and manifest that it is impossible to state it to a man of common sense without producing an exclamation at the inequality of it." "Where the inadequacy of the price is so great that the mind revolts at it the court will lay hold on the slightest circumstances of oppression or advantage to rescind the contract."
>
> It is not the policy of the law to restrict business dealings or to relieve a party of his own mistakes of judgment, but where one party has taken advantage of another's necessities and distress to obtain an unfair advantage over him, and the latter, owing to his condition, has encumbered himself with a heavy liability or an onerous obligation for the sake of a small or inadequate present gain, there will be relief granted.

Stiefler v. McCullough (1933), 97 Ind.App. 123, 174 N.E. 823.

The facts of this case reveal that in exchange for a contract which, if the clause in question is enforceable, may cost Mr. Weaver potentially thousands of dollars in damages for negligence of which he was not the cause, Weaver must operate the service station seven days a week for long hours, at a total yearly income of $5,000-$6,000. The evidence also reveals that the clause was in fine print and contained no title heading which would have identified it as an indemnity clause. It seems a deplorable abuse of justice to hold a man of poor education, to a contract prepared by the attorneys of American Oil, for the benefit of American Oil which was presented to Weaver on a "take it or leave it basis."

Justice Frankfurther of the United States Supreme Court spoke on the question of inequality of bargaining power in his dissenting opinion in United States v. Bethlehem Steel Corp. (1942), 315 U.S. 289, 326, 62 S.Ct. 581, 599, 86 L.Ed. 855, 876.

> (I)t is said that familiar principles would be outraged if Bethlehem were denied recovery on these contracts. But is there any principle which is more familiar or more firmly embedded in the history of Anglo-American law than the basic doctrine that the courts will not permit themselves to be used as instruments of inequity and injustice? Does any principle in our law have more universal application than the doctrine that courts will not enforce transactions in which the relative positions of the parties are such that one has unconscionably taken advantage of the necessities of the other?

> These principles are not foreign to the law of contracts. Fraud and physical duress are not the only grounds upon which courts refuse to enforce contracts. The law is not so primitive that it sanctions every injustice except brute force and downright fraud. More specifically, the courts generally refuse to lend themselves to the enforcement of a "bargain" in which one party has unjustly taken advantage of the economic necessities of the other . . . .

The traditional contract is the result of free bargaining of parties who are brought together by the play of the market, and who meet each other on a footing of approximate economic equality. In such a society there is no danger that freedom of contract will be a threat to the social order as a whole. But in present-day commercial life the standardized mass contract has appeared. It is used primarily by enterprises with strong bargaining power and position. The weaker party, in need of the good or services, is frequently not in a position to shop around for better terms, either because the author of the standard contract has a monopoly (natural or artificial) or because all competitors use the same clauses. . . .

When a party can show that the contract, which is sought to be enforced, was in fact an unconscionable one, due to a prodigious amount of bargaining power on behalf of the stronger party, which is used to the stronger party's advantage and is unknown to the lesser, party, causing a great hardship and risk on the lesser party, the contract provision, or the contract as a whole, if the provision is not separable, should not be enforceable on the grounds that the provision is contrary to public policy. The party seeking to enforce such a contract has the burden of showing that the provisions were explained to the other party and came to his knowledge and there was in fact a real and voluntary meeting of the minds and not merely an objective meeting.

Unjust contract provisions have been found unenforceable, in the past, on the grounds of being contrary to public policy, where a party has a greater superior bargaining position. In Pennsylvania Railroad Co. v. Kent (1964), 136 Ind.App. 551, 198 N.E.2d 615, Judge Hunter, speaking for the court said that although the proposition that "parties may enter into such contractual arrangement as they may desire may be conceded in the general sense; when, however, such special agreement may result in affecting the public interest and thereby contravene public policy, the abrogation of the rules governing common carriers must be zealously guarded against."

We do not mean to say or infer that parties may not make contracts exculpating one of his negligence and providing for indemnification, but it must be done knowingly and willingly as in insurance contracts made for that very purpose.

It is the duty of the courts to administer justice and that role is not performed, in this case, by enforcing a written instrument, not really an agreement of the parties as shown by the evidence here, although signed by the parties. The parole [*sic*] evidence rule must yield to the equities of the case. The appeal is transferred to this court and the judgment of the trial court is reversed with direction to enter judgment for the appellant.

GIVAN, DeBRULER and HUNTER, JJ., concur.
PRENTICE, J., dissents, with opinion.

My opinion is diametrically opposed to those of both the majority herein and of the Appellate Court as set forth in 261 N.E.2d 99, and 262 N.E.2d 663. There is no law to support the decisions of the Appellate Court and, since I contend there are no facts to support the majority opinion of this Court, it, therefore, is necessary to burden this record by setting forth not only the special findings of fact of the trial court but also to add, arguendo, the additional findings that the defendant (appellant) contends were either admitted or proved. . . .

Upon the foregoing, the trial court stated conclusions of law and rendered judgment for the plaintiffs (appellees). The conclusions, in substance, were that the law was with the plaintiffs and that the exculpatory and indemnifying provisions of the lease between the plaintiff and defendant, American, were enforceable against the defendant.

The decisions of the Appellate Court would not enforce the exculpatory agreement upon the theory that, although this Court has consistently refused to void exculpatory provisions as contrary to public policy, their burdens being unusual and considerable, they should not be enforced unless it appears that the party who assumes the burden under the clause was aware of it and understood its far reaching implications. The burden of proving such awareness, or lack of it, would vary depending upon the relative bargaining positions of the parties. The indemnity provision, however, was held enforceable, by reason of the availability of insurance rendering the risk manageable.

The facts as found, are that although the defendant never read the lease, he had ample opportunity to do so and to obtain counsel. A general rule in effect not only in Indiana but elsewhere, is that a person who signs a contract, without bothering to read the same, will be bound by its terms. Welsh v. Kelly-Springfield Tire Co. (1938), 213 Ind. 188, 12 N.E.2d 254; Walb Construction Co. v. Chipman (1931), 202 Ind. 434, 175 N.E. 132; Givan v. Masterson (1898), 152 Ind. 127, 51 N.E. 237; Keller v. Orr (1886), 106 Ind. 406, 7 N.E. 195.

Without regard to whether or not he was aware of its contents, a person will be relieved of his obligations under a contract under circumstances falling into two main categories: (a) where the contract is not enforceable because of occurrences or omissions (fraud, concealment, etc.) surrounding its execution and where (2) the contract it not enforceable because of the nature or subject of the contract (illegality of subject matter). The Appellate Court would have us recognize a third category and excuse performance, at least as to harsh provisions, without a showing that he was aware of and understood the contract provisions and their implications, with the burden of proof upon such issues to vary depending upon the relative bargaining positions of the parties. The objective of such a rule is laudable, but I think it, nevertheless, totally unworkable. . . .

Chief Justice Arterburn, speaking for a majority of this Court, has concluded that the defendant was in an inferior position with respect to the lease and treats the lease as we might treat an adhesion contract. I find justification for neither. An adhesion contract is one that has been drafted unilaterally by the dominant party and then presented on a "take it or leave it" basis to the weaker party, who has no real opportunity to bargain about its terms. (Restatement 2d, Conflict of Law § 332 a, Comment e) (17 C.J.S. Contracts § 10, p. 581.) Here we have a printed form contract prepared by American. There was great disparity between the economic positions of American and Defendant; and Defendant was a man of limited educational and business background. However, there is nothing from which we can find or infer that the printed lease provisions were not subject to negotiation or that, with respect to this particular lease, Defendant was not in a bargaining position equal to that of American. The fact that Defendant did not avail himself of the opportunity to read the agreement but elected to accept it as presented does not warrant the inference that his only options were to "take it or leave it." That the "hold harmless" clause was or might have been in small print, as suggested by the majority, can hardly have significance in light of the claim and finding that the defendant did not read any portion of the document. . . .

I would accept transfer of this cause, set aside the decision of the Appellate Court, as modified, and affirm the decision of the trial court.

NOTES AND QUESTIONS:

1. In *Weaver*, the contract contained a hold harmless or exculpatory division, as well as an indemnification provision. What is the effect of each of these provisions?

2. Take note of the court's discussion of the requirements for an enforceable exculpatory provision. Does this opinion require a contracting party to explain contractual provisions or otherwise make sure the other party fully understands the effect of each provision of the contract?

3. We will revisit the perimeters of valid and enforceable exculpatory clauses in connection with the Illegality and Public Policy section of Chapter Four.

SECTION 6. ILLEGALITY AND PUBLIC POLICY

COWAN V. MILBOURNE
Exchequer Chamber
L.R. 2 Ex. 236 (1867).

Action (in the Court of Passage, Liverpool) for breach of a contract to let rooms to the defendant. The first and third counts of the declaration related to contracts to let to the defendant the St. Anne's Assembly Rooms, Liverpool, for the purpose of lectures, which were to be delivered there on the 20th of January and the 3d of February, 1867; and the second count related to a contract to let the same rooms to the defendant for the purpose of a ball and tea-party on the 29th of January.

To these counts the defendant, amongst other pleas, pleaded, fourthly, that, after making the alleged agreements respectively, the defendant was informed, and learned for the first time, that the plaintiff intended (as he did in fact intend) to use the rooms for certain irreligious, blasphemous, and illegal lectures or entertainments; whereupon the defendant, within a reasonable time, after satisfying himself as to the truth of the premises, gave notice to the plaintiff that he could not permit the plaintiff the use of the rooms for the purposes aforesaid, and thereupon notified to the plaintiff not to incur any further or other expense in relation thereto; and in like manner, and within such reasonable time as aforesaid, tendered and paid to the plaintiff the amount of the moneys which the plaintiff had paid him for the intended use of the rooms; and that his refusal to permit the plaintiff under the said circumstances, and for the said purposes, to use the rooms was the breach complained of.

The defendant, by his seventh plea, also relied upon the provisions of 21 Geo. 3, c. 49, § 1.

Issue.

At the trial the following facts appeared in evidence: —

In December, 1865, the plaintiff, who was secretary to the Liverpool Secular Society, hired of the defendant, through defendant's son, the rooms in question, for Sunday, the 20th of January, for the purpose of having lectures delivered there in advancement of the views of the society. He did not communicate to the defendant the subjects of the lectures, nor that they were to be delivered in connection with the society. He afterwards hired the same rooms for the delivery of lectures on Sunday, the 3d of February, and for a ball and tea-party in memory of Tom Paine, on the 29th of January the subjects of the lectures for the morning, afternoon, and evening of the 20th of January were advertised by placards as "The Soul: its Nature and Destination;" "The Character and Teachings of Christ: the former Defective, the latter Misleading;" "Bible Morality and Bible Science;" and those of the lectures for the 3d of February as "The Sceptical Tendency of Bishop Butler's Analogy;" "The Bible shown to be no more Inspired than any other Book, with a Refutation of Modern Theories thereon." "Catholicism, Protestantism, and Secularism: which contains most Truth, and which is best calculated to benefit Humanity?"

On the 17th of January the plaintiff received from the defendant's son a letter written the day previous, complaining of an evening lecture having been advertised, and alleging that the rooms were only let for the morning and afternoon, but making no complaint of the subject of the lectures; and on the 19th of January the plaintiff received from the defendant's attorney a letter of that date, entirely refusing the use of the rooms, but not assigning any reason.

The plaintiff, having attempted without success to obtain possession of the rooms on the days in question, brought this action for breach of the several contracts.

It appeared upon the evidence of the chief constable of Liverpool, who was called for the defendant, that the defendant's refusal was caused by his interference, and by his threatened opposition to a renewal of the license attached to the rooms.

The learned judge ruled that the lectures announced were blasphemous and illegal, and that the plaintiff could not therefore recover on the agreement for the Sundays (20th of January and 3d of February), but that he might recover on the agreement relating to the tea-party of the 29th of January; and a verdict for one farthing damages was found for the plaintiff on the second count, and a verdict was entered for the defendant on the first and third counts, with leave to the plaintiff (under 16 & 17 Vict. c. xxi. s. 45) to move this court to enter a verdict for the plaintiff for the £10 on each of those counts.

Littler moved accordingly.

BRAMWELL, B.[1]

I am of the same opinion, and I will state my grounds. I think that the plaintiff was about to use the rooms for an unlawful purpose, because he was about to use them for the purpose of, "by teaching or advised speaking," "denying the Christian religion to be true, or the Holy Scriptures of the Old and New Testament to be of divine authority." That he intended to use the rooms for the purposes declared by the statute to be unlawful is perfectly clear, for he proposed to show that the character of Christ was defective, and His teaching misleading, and that the Bible was no more inspired than any other book. That being so, his purpose was unlawful; and if the defendant had known his purpose at the time of the refusal, he clearly would not have been bound to let the plaintiff occupy them, for, if he would, he would then have been compelled to do a thing in pursuance of an illegal purpose. Neither if he had let the plaintiff into possession could he, for the same reason, have recovered the price for their letting. . . . Now it appears that the plaintiff here was going to use the rooms for an unlawful purpose; he therefore could not enforce the contract for that purpose, and therefore the defendant was not bound, though he did not know the fact. It is strange there should be so much difficulty in making it understood that a thing may be unlawful, in the sense that the law will not aid it, and yet that the law will not immediately punish it. If that only were unlawful to which a penalty is attached, the consequence would be that, inasmuch as no penalty is provided by the law for prostitution, a contract having prostitution for its object would be valid in a court of law. The rule must be refused, and I do not regret the result, and on this ground, that this placard must have given great pain to many of those who read it.

BOVARD V. AMERICAN HORSE ENTERPRISES, INC.
Court of Appeal, Third District, California
201 Cal. App. 3d 832 (1988).

PUGLIA, P. J.

Robert Bovard appeals from the judgment dismissing his supplemental complaint against defendants, American Horse Enterprises, Inc., and James T. Ralph. Bovard contends the trial court erroneously concluded the contract upon which his action was founded was illegal and void as contrary to public policy; alternatively, he contends it is the law of the case that the contract does not violate public policy. Ralph cross-appeals, challenging the trial court's postjudgment order striking his memorandum of costs and taxing costs. We shall affirm the judgment and post-judgment order.[1]

I

This is the second appeal in this case. Our unpublished opinion disposing of the first appeal sets out much of the relevant procedural history of this dispute:

---

[1] Kelly, C. B., and Martin, B., delivered concurring opinions.

[1] Ralph separately appeals from an order dismissing his cross-complaint to the supplemental complaint. Ralph's appeal has been consolidated with Bovard's. In the unpublished part of this opinion we uphold the trial court's ruling that the cross-complaint was premised upon the void contract and affirm the judgment of dismissal accordingly.

"In two actions later consolidated, plaintiff Bovard separately sued defendants Ralph and American Horse Enterprises, Inc. a corporation . . . to recover on promissory notes executed by defendants in connection with Ralph's purchase of the corporation in 1978."

. . . The trial court severed the supplemental complaint from the cross-complaint (see fn. 1, ante, p. 836) and from the consolidated action on the promissory notes. The supplemental complaint went to trial before a jury. On the third day of trial, Bovard testified as to the nature of the business conducted by American Horse Enterprises, Inc., at the time the corporation was sold to Ralph. Bovard explained the corporation made jewelry and drug paraphernalia, which consisted of "roach clips" and "bongs" used to smoke marijuana and tobacco. At that point the trial court excused the jury and asked counsel to prepare arguments on the question whether the contract for sale of the corporation was illegal and void.

The following day, after considering the arguments of counsel, the trial court dismissed the supplemental complaint. The court found that the corporation predominantly produced paraphernalia used to smoke marijuana and was not engaged significantly in jewelry production, and that Bovard had recovered the corporate machinery through self-help. The parties do not challenge these findings. The court acknowledged that the manufacture of drug paraphernalia was not itself illegal in 1978 when Bovard and Ralph contracted for the sale of American Horse Enterprises, Inc. However, the court concluded a public policy against the manufacture of drug paraphernalia was implicit in the statute making the possession, use and transfer of marijuana unlawful. (See Health & Saf. Code, §§ 11357, 11358, 11359, 11360.)[2] The trial court held the consideration for the contract was contrary to the policy of express law, and the contract was therefore illegal and void. Finally, the court found the parties were in pari delicto and thus with respect to their contractual dispute should be left as the court found them.

II

"The consideration of a contract must be lawful within the meaning of section sixteen hundred and sixty-seven." (Civ. Code, § 1607.) "That is not lawful which is: 1. Contrary to an express provision of law; 2. Contrary to the policy of express law, though not expressly prohibited; or, 3. Otherwise contrary to good morals." (Civ. Code, § 1667.) "If any part of a single consideration for one or more objects, or of several considerations for a single object, is unlawful, the entire contract is void." (Civ. Code, § 1608.)

The trial court concluded the consideration for the contract was contrary to the policy of the law as expressed in the statute prohibiting the possession, use and transfer of marijuana. (1a) Whether a contract is contrary to public policy is a question of law to be determined from the circumstances of the particular case. (Kallen v. Delug (1984) 157 Cal.App.3d 940, 951 [203 Cal.Rptr. 879]; Russell v. Soldinger (1976) 59 Cal.App.3d 633, 642 [131 Cal.Rptr. 145].) Here, the critical facts are not in dispute. (2) Whenever a court

[2] The manufacture of drug paraphernalia, including bongs and roach clips, was made criminal effective January 1, 1983, by Statutes 1982, chapter 1278, sections 1 and 2, pages 4725-4728, which enacted Health and Safety Code sections 11014.5 and 11364.7. (See A&B Cattle Co. v. City of Escondido (1987) 192 Cal.App.3d 1032, 1036-1037, 1042 [238 Cal.Rptr. 580].) In addition, Sacramento County made criminal the manufacture of drug paraphernalia by ordinance in July 1980.

becomes aware that a contract is illegal, it has a duty to refrain from entertaining an action to enforce the contract. (Russell v. Soldinger, supra; Santoro v. Carbone (1972) 22 Cal.App.3d 721, 732 [99 Cal.Rptr. 488], disapproved on another ground in Liodas v. Sahadi (1977) 19 Cal.3d 278, 287 [137 Cal.Rptr. 635, 562 P.2d 316].) (3) Furthermore the court will not permit the parties to maintain an action to settle or compromise a claim based on an illegal contract. (Union Collection Co. v. Buckman (1907) 150 Cal. 159, 165 [88 P. 708]; see also First Nat. Bk. v. Thompson (1931) 212 Cal. 388, 405 [298 P. 808].)

The question whether a contract violates public policy necessarily involves a degree of subjectivity. Therefore, "... courts have been cautious in blithely applying public policy reasons to nullify otherwise enforceable contracts. This concern has been graphically articulated by the California Supreme Court as follows: "It has been well said that public policy is an unruly horse, astride of which you are carried into unknown and uncertain paths, . . . While contracts opposed to morality or law should not be allowed to show themselves in courts of justice, yet public policy requires and encourages the making of contracts by competent parties upon all valid and lawful considerations, and courts so recognizing have allowed parties the widest latitude in this regard; and, unless it is entirely plain that a contract is violative of sound public policy, a court will never so declare." The power of the courts to declare a contract void for being in contravention of sound public policy is a very delicate and undefined power, and, like the power to declare a statute unconstitutional, should be exercised only in cases free from doubt. " [Citation.] ... "No court ought to refuse its aid to enforce a contract on doubtful and uncertain grounds. (4) The burden is on the defendant to show that its enforcement would be in violation of the settled public policy of this state, or injurious to the morals of its people." [Citation.]"' (Moran v. Harris (1982) 131 Cal.App.3d 913, 919-920 [182 Cal.Rptr. 519, 28 A.L.R.4th 655], quoting Stephens v. Southern Pacific Co. (1895) 109 Cal. 86, 89-90 [41 P. 783].)

Bovard places great reliance on Moran v. Harris, supra, 131 Cal.App. 3d 913, to support his argument the trial court erred in finding the contract violative of public policy. In Moran, two lawyers entered into a fee splitting agreement relative to a case referred by one to the other. The agreement was made in 1972, 10 months before the adoption of a rule of professional conduct prohibiting such agreements. In 1975, the attorney to whom the case had been referred settled the case, but then refused to split the attorney's fees with the referring attorney. (Id., at pp. 916-917.) The trial court held the fee splitting contract violated public policy. The appellate court reversed, noting the rule of professional conduct had been amended effective January 1, 1979, to permit fee splitting agreements; thus there was no statute or rule prohibiting fee splitting agreements either at the time the attorneys' contract was formed or after January 1, 1979, during the pendency of the action to enforce the fee splitting contract. Therefore, the court held there was no basis for a finding that the contract violated public policy. (Id., at pp. 920-921.)

Here, in contrast to Moran, there is positive law on which to premise a finding of public policy, although the trial court did not find the manufacture of marijuana paraphernalia against public policy on the basis of the later enacted ordinance or statute prohibiting such manufacture. (1b)(See fn. 3.) Rather, the court's finding was based on a statute prohibiting the possession, use and transfer of marijuana which long antedated the parties' contract.[3]

Moran suggests factors to consider in analyzing whether a contract violates public policy: "Before labeling a contract as being contrary to public policy, courts must carefully inquire into the nature of the conduct, the extent of public harm which may be involved, and the moral quality of the conduct of the parties in light of the prevailing standards of the community. [Citations.]" (Id., at p. 920.)

These factors are more comprehensively set out in the Restatement Second of Contracts section 178:

> (1) A promise or other term of an agreement is unenforceable on grounds of public policy if legislation provides that it is unenforceable or the interest in its enforcement is clearly outweighed in the circumstances by a public policy against the enforcement of such terms.
>
> (2) In weighing the interest in the enforcement of a term, account is taken of (a) the parties' justified expectations, (b) any forfeiture that would result if enforcement were denied, and (c) any special public interest in the enforcement of the particular term.
>
> (3) In weighing a public policy against enforcement of a term, account is taken of (a) the strength of that policy as manifested by legislation or judicial decisions, (b) the likelihood that a refusal to enforce the term will further that policy, (c) the seriousness of any misconduct involved and the extent to which it was deliberate, and (d) the directness of the connection between that misconduct and the term.

Applying the Restatement test to the present circumstances, we conclude the interest in enforcing this contract is very tenuous. Neither party was reasonably justified in expecting the government would not eventually act to geld American Horse Enterprises, a business harnessed to the production of paraphernalia used to facilitate the use of an illegal drug. Moreover, although voidance of the contract imposed a forfeiture on Bovard, he did recover the corporate machinery, the only assets of the business which could be used for lawful purposes, i.e., to manufacture jewelry. Thus, the forfeiture was significantly mitigated if not negligible. Finally, there is no special public interest in the enforcement of this contract, only the general interest in preventing a party to a contract from avoiding a debt.

On the other hand, the Restatement factors favoring a public policy against enforcement of this contract are very strong. As we have explained, the public policy against manufacturing paraphernalia to facilitate the use of marijuana is strongly implied in the statutory prohibition against the possession, use, etc., of marijuana, a prohibition which dates back at least to 1929. (See Stats. 1929, ch. 216, § 1, p. 380.) Obviously, refusal to enforce the instant contract will further that public policy not only in the present circumstances but

[3] "In determining whether the subject of a given contract violates public policy, courts must rely on the state of the law as it existed at the time the contract was made. [Citations.]" (Moran v. Harris, supra, 131 Cal.App.3d at p. 918.)

by serving notice on manufacturers of drug paraphernalia that they may not resort to the judicial system to protect or advance their business interests. Moreover, it is immaterial that the business conducted by American Horse Enterprises was not expressly prohibited by law when Bovard and Ralph made their agreement since both parties knew that the corporation's products would be used primarily for purposes which were expressly illegal. We conclude the trial court correctly declared the contract contrary to the policy of express law and therefore illegal and void. . . .

The judgment dismissing the supplemental complaint, the order striking the memorandum of costs and taxing costs, and the judgment dismissing the cross-complaint are affirmed. The parties are to bear their own costs on appeal.

Evans, J., and Sims, J., concurred.

THORPE V. CARTE
Court of Appeals of Maryland
250 A.2d 618 (1969).

HAMMOND, Chief Judge.

Bernard C. Thorpe, a contractor, and his wife, the appellants (hereinafter collectively called Thorpe), owned a tract of land in Montgomery County which they desired to sell. Holmead, Frey and Associates had furnished Thorpe enginerring and surveying services. Mr. Frey of that firm told Thorpe he thought he could find a buyer from a group he knew who "had been in it big" and Thorpe told him to "go ahead." Frey, who was unlicensed as a real estate salesman or broker, brought Eisenstadt, a licensed salesman and an employee of the appellee Ross J. Carte., a licensed broker, who trades as the Ross J. Carte Real Estate Co., to meet Thorpe. As a result, on July 21, 1965, Thorpe gave Carte an exclusive listing agreement which provided for a commission of 6% to Carte. Four days later Thorpe executed a contract to sell his property which was executed also by the purchaser and by Eisenstadt on behalf of Carte. The contract in the part here pertinent provided: "The Sellers recognize Ross J. Carte Real Estate Co. -65% & Holmead, Frey & Assoc. -35% as the Agent negotiating this Contract and agree to pay 6% commission for services rendered . . . ." The sale was not consummated because Thorpe had agreed in the contract that it was to depend on his having certain covenants restricting building on the property removed and he was unsuccessful in his efforts in court to remove them. . . .

Carte sued Thorpe for 65% of 6% of the contract price. . . . Summary judgment was entered for $ 49,040 in favor of Carte against Thorpe. [Defendant appeals].

The licensing and regulation of real estate brokers and salesmen are provided for under the Subtitle "Real Estate Brokers" by §§ 212 to 232 of Art. 56 of the Code (1968 Repl.Vol.). In Smirlock v. Potomac Development Corporation, 235 Md. 195, 202-203, 200 A.2d 922, we decided that a broker, licensed in another State but not in Maryland could not recover a commission on an agreement made in this State for the sale of property here. In establishing the basis for the holding, Chief Judge Brune for the Court analyzed the various defining and regulatory sections of the Subtitle "Real Estate Brokers" in Art. 56 of the Code

(1957) and pertinent prior decisions, including Bernstein v. Real Estate Comm., 221 Md. 221, 156 A.2d 657, appeal dismissed 363 U.S. 419, 80 S.Ct. 1257, 4 L.Ed.2d 1515; Buffington v. Wentz, 228 Md. 33, 178 A.2d 417; Baliles v. Bryant, 207 Md. 332, 114 A.2d 601, and Glaser v. Shostack, 213 Md. 383, 131 A.2d 724, and held that though none of those cases decided the matter they pointed definitely to "the view that the Real Estate Brokers License law is a regulatory enactment for the protection of the public (as) the statute itself makes clear," and added:

> We now hold that the Real Estate Brokers subtitle of Art. 56 of the Code (1957, as amended) is a regulation for the benefit of the public.
>
> It follows, we think, that § 228 is, as it purports to be, bar to the appellant's action for commissions. Goldsmith v. Manufacturers' Liability Ins. Co., 132 Md. 283, 103 A. 627; Snodgrass v. Immler, 232 Md. 416, 194 A.2d 103. In Snodgrass we held that provisions pertaining to the licensing of architects (Code (1957), Art. 43, ss 515, 516) were of a regulatory nature for the protection of the public and barred a suit by a person not licensed thereunder on a contract calling for compensation for his architectural services. In Goldsmith, which involved the licensing of insurance agents, a purpose to protect the public was also held to be present and a suit for commissions by an unlicensed agent was similarly held barred. As was said in Goldsmith (132 Md. at 286, 103 A. at 628), quoted in Snodgrass, 232 Md. at 421-422, 194 A.2d 103):
>
> . . . a contract entered into by an unlicensed person engaged in a trade, business or profession, required to be licensed, and made in the course of such trade, business, or profession, cannot be enforced by such person, if it appears that the license required by the statute is, in whole or in part, for the protection of the public, and to prevent improper persons from engaging in such trade, business, or profession. See also 12 Am.Jur.2d Brokers, § 178, par. 2.' (235 Md. at 202-203, 200 A.2d 926)

Section 227 of Art. 56 in terms makes it unlawful for any real estate broker, or real estate salesman, to pay any compensation, in money or other valuable thing, to any person other than a licensed real estate broker . . . or real estate salesman "for the rendering of any service, or the doing of any of the acts by this subtitle forbidden to be rendered or performed by other than licensees," and § 228 prohibits recovery in any court of this State by any person unlicensed at "the time of offering to perform any such act or service or procuring any promise or contract for the payment of compensation for any such contemplated act or service,". . . "for any act done or service rendered," the doing of which is prohibited to other than real estate licensees.

We have no doubt that Carte violated §§ 227 and 228. Under the exclusive listing agreement Carte was to receive a commission of 6% of the sales price. He orally agreed that this 6% commission was to be divided between him and Holmead, Frey. He did not physically receive the full commission and then in turn give Holmead, Frey 35% thereof; he orally (and later in writing) agreed that he and Holmead, Frey would be joint obligees under a single contractual provision and that Thorpe, rather than he would do the dividing of the agreed upon commission to which he otherwise would have been entitled in full.

We see the effect of this contract to be the same as if Carte had received the commission and then himself split it. What one does by another he does himself and the intents and purposes of §§ 227 and 228 could not be effectuated if a broker could do by manifestly obvious indirection what he is forbidden to do directly. Compare Gilbert v. Edwards (Ct.App.Mo.), 276 S.W.2d 611. Carte's contract to split his commission with Holmead, Frey violated ss 227 and 228 and was illegal. "Any bargain is illegal if either the formation or the performance thereof is prohibited by constitution or statute." 2 Restatement Contracts § 580. Generally a party to an illegal bargain cannot recover either damages for its breach or, after rescission, the performance he has rendered or its value. 2 Restatement Contracts § 598. Comment a under § 598 says:

> (T)he rule of public policy that forbids an action for damages for breach of such an agreement is not based on the impropriety of compelling the defendant to pay the damages. That in itself would generally be a desirable thing. When relief is denied it is because the plaintiff is a wrongdoer, and to such a person the law denies relief. Courts do not wish to aid a man who founds his cause of action upon his own immoral or illegal act. If from the plaintiff's own statement or otherwise it appears that the bargain forming the basis of the action is opposed to public policy or transgresses statutory prohibitions, the courts ordinarily give him no assistance. The court's refusal is not for the sake of the defendant, but because it will not aid such a plaintiff.

. . . Where the statute involved is (a) one for the protection of the public against incompetence and dishonesty, as is the Maryland statute, and (b) there is a single contract for the payment of real estate commissions in part to an unlicensed person and in part to a licensed person and the licensed person's suit for part of the commission necessarily reveals the statutorily forbidden participation in the deal of an unlicensed person with the consent of the licensee, almost all courts have held that because the contract is illegal the licensed obligee will not be permitted to recover. Payne v. Volkman, 183 Wis. 412, 198 N.W. 438; Kemmerer v. Roscher, 9 Wis.2d 60, 100 N.W.2d 314; Wise v. Radis, 74 Cal.App. 765, 242 P. 90; Weber v. Tonini, 151 Cal.App.2d 168, 311 P.2d 132; Davis v. Jouganatos, 81 Nev. 333, 402 P.2d 985; Harris v. McKay (Dist.Ct.App.Fla.), 176 So.2d 572; Frieman v. Greaves, 80 Ohio App. 341, 74 N.E.2d 860; Brandenburger & Marx v. Heimberg (N.Y.City Mun.Ct.), 34 N.Y.S.2d 935; Wasson v. Hartt (Civ.App.Tex.), 244 S.W.2d 258, writ of error refused. The cases are collected in an annotation, Real Estate Brokers-License, in 8 A.L.R.3d 523, 531, et seq.

Summary judgment should have been entered for Thorpe for costs.

Judgment reversed and judgment for costs entered in favor of appellants against the appellee.

THE CASE OF MONOPOLIES
Court of King's Bench
77 E.R. 1260 (1601).

Edward Darcy, Esquire, a groom of the Privy Chamber to Queen Elizabeth brought an action on the case against T. Allein, haberdasher, of London, and declared, that Queen Elizabeth, 13 Junii, anno 30 Eliz. intending that her subjects being able men to exercise husbandry, should apply themselves thereunto, and that they should not employ themselves in making playing cards, which had not been any ancient manual occupation within this realm, and that by making such a multitude of cards, card-playing was become more frequent and especially among servants and apprentices, and poor artificers; and to the end her subjects might apply themselves to more lawful and necessary trades; by her letters patent under the Great Seal of the same date granted to Ralph Bowes, Esq. full power, licence and authority, by himself, his servants, factors, and deputies, to provide and buy in any parts beyond the sea, all such playing cards as he thought good, and to import them into this realm, and to sell and utter them within the same, and that he, his servants, factors, and deputies, should have and enjoy the whole trade, traffic, and merchandize, of all playing cards: and by the same letters patent further granted, that the said Ralph Bowes, his servants, factors, and deputies, and none other should have the making of playing cards within the realm, to have and to hold for twelve years; and by the same letters patent, the Queen charged and commanded, that no person or persons besides the said Ralph Bowes, &c. should bring any cards within the realm during those twelve years, nor should buy, sell, or offer to be sold within the said realm, within the said term, any playing cards, nor should make, or cause to be made any playing cards within the said realm, upon pain of the Queen's highest displeasure, and of such fine and punishment as offenders in the case of voluntary contempt deserve. And afterwards the said Queen, 11 Aug. anno 40 Eliz. by her letters patent reciting the former grants made to Ralph Bowes, granted the plaintiff, his executors, and administrators, and their deputies, &c. the same privileges, authorities, and other the said premises, for twenty-one years after the end of the former term, rendering to the Queen 100 marks per annum; and further granted to him a seal to mark the cards. And further declared, that after the end of the said term of twelve years, s. 30 Junii, an. 42 Eliz. the plaintiff caused to be made 400 grosses of cards for the necessary uses of the subjects, to be sold within this realm, and had expended in making them 5000 £., and that the defendant knowing of the said grant and prohibition in the plaintiff's letters patent, and other the premises, 15 Martii, anno 44 Eliz. without the Queen's licence, or the plaintiff's, &c. at Westminster caused to be made 80 grosses of playing cards, and as well those, as 100 other grosses of playing cards, none of which were made within the realm, or imported within the realm by the plaintiff, or his servants, factors, or deputies, &c. nor marked with his seal, he had imported within the realm, and them had sold and uttered to sundry persons unknown, and shewed some in certain, wherefore the plaintiff could not utter his playing cards, &c. *Contra formam prædict' literar' patentium, et in contemptum dictæ dominæ Reginæ*, whereby the plaintiff was disabled to pay his farm, to the plaintiff's damages. The defendant, except to one half gross pleaded not guilty, and as to that pleaded, that the City of London is an ancient city, and that within the same, from time whereof, &c. there has been a society of Haber-dashers, and that within the said city there was a custom, *quod quælibet persona de societate illa, usus fuit et consuerit emere rendere, et libere merchandizare omnem rem et omnes res merchandizabiles infra hoc regnum Angliæ de quocunque, vel quibuscunque personis, &c.* and pleaded, that he was *civis et liber homo de civitate et societate illa* , and sold the said half gross of playing cards, being made within the realm, &c. as he lawfully might; upon which the plaintiff demurred in law.

. . . . And in the Case two general questions were moved and argued at the Bar, arising upon the two distinct grants in the said Letters Patents, *viz*

1. If the said Grant to the Plaintiff of the sole making of Cards within the Realm were good or not?

2. If the License or dispensation to have the sole importation of Foreign Cards granted to the Plaintiff, were available or not in law? . . .

As to the first question it was argued on the plaintiff's side, that the said grant of the sole making of playing cards within the realm, was good for three reasons. 1. Because the said playing cards were not any merchandize, or thing concerning trade of any necessary use, but things of vanity, and the occasion of loss of time, and decrease of the substance of many, the loss of the service and work of servants, causes of want, which is the mother of woe and destruction, and therefore it belongs to the Queen (who is *parens patriæ, et paterfamilias totius regni* , and as it is said in 20 H. 7. fol. 4. *Capitalis Justiciarius Angliæ*) to take away the great abuse, and to take order for the moderate and convenient use of them. 2. In matters of recreation and pleasure, the Queen has a prerogative given her by the law to take such order for such moderate use of them as seems good to her. 3. The Queen, in regard of the great abuse of them, and of the cheat put upon her subjects by reason of them, might utterly suppress them, and by consequence without injury done to any one, might moderate and tolerate them at her pleasure. And the reason of the law which gives the King these prerogatives in matters of recreation and pleasure was, because the greatest part of mankind are inclinable to exceed in them; and upon these grounds divers cases were put, *sc.* that no subject can make a park, chace, or warren within his own land, for his recreation or pleasure, without the King's grant or licence; and if he does it of his own head, in a *quo warranto* , they shall be seised into the King's hands, as it is held in 3 E. 2. Action sur le Statute Br. 48. and 30 E. 3. Rot. Pat. The King granted to another all the wild swans betwixt London Bridge and Oxford. . . .

As to the first, it was argued to the contrary by the defendant's counsel, and resolved by Popham, Chief Justice, *et per totam Curiam* , that the said grant to the plaintiff of the sole making of cards within the realm was utterly void , and that for two reasons:—1. That it is a monopoly, and against the common law. 2. That it is against divers Acts of Parliament. Against the common law for four reasons:—1. All trades, as well mechanical as others, which prevent idleness (the bane of the commonwealth) and exercise men and youth in labour, for the maintenance of themselves and their families, and for the increase of their substance, to serve the Queen when occasion shall require, are profitable for the commonwealth, and therefore the grant to the plaintiff to have the sole making of them is against the common law, and the benefit and liberty of the subject, and therewith agrees Fortescue in Laudibus legum Angliæ, cap. 26.

. . . . The sole trade of any mechanical artifice, or any other monopoly, is not only a damage and prejudice to those who exercise the same trade, but also to all other subjects, for the end of all these monopolies is for the private gain of the patentees; and although provisions and cautions are added to moderate them, yet *res profecto stulta est nequitiæ modus* , it is mere folly to think that there is any measure in mischief or wickedness: and, therefore, there are three inseparable incidents to every monopoly against the commonwealth, *sc.* 1. That the price of the same commodity will be raised, for he who has the sole selling of any commodity, may and will make the price as he pleases: and this word *Monopolium, dicitur quod est, cum unus solus aliquod genus mercaturæ universum emit, pretium ad suum libitum statuens* . And the poet saith; *omnia Castor emit, sic fit ut omnia vendat* . And it appears by the writ of *ad quod damnum* , F. N. B. 222 a. that every gift or grant from the King has this condition, either expressly or tacitly annexed to it, *Illa quod patria per donationem illam magis solito non oneretur seu gravetur* , and therefore every grant made in grievance or prejudice of the subject is void; and 13 H. 4. 14 b. the King's grant which tends to the charge and prejudice of the subject is void. The 2d incident to a monopoly is, that after the monopoly granted, the commodity is not so good and merchantable as it was before: for the patentee having the sole trade, regards only his private benefit, and not the common wealth. 3. It tends to the impoverishment of divers artificers and others, who before, by the labour of their hands in their art or trade, had maintained themselves and their families, who now will of necessity be constrained to live in idleness and beggary; *vide* Fortescue *ubi supra:* and the common law, in this point, agrees with the equity of the law of God, as appears in Deut. cap. xxiv. ver. 6. *Non accipies loco pignoris inferiorem et superiorem molam, quia animam suam apposuit tibi;* you shall not take in pledge the nether and upper millstone, for that is his life; by which it appears, that every man's trade maintains his life, and therefore he ought not to be deprived or dispossessed of it, no more than of his life: and it agrees also with the civil law; . . . . The Queen was deceived in her grant; for the Queen, as by the preamble appears, intended it to be for the weal public, and it will be employed for the private gain of the patentee, and for the prejudice of the weal public; moreover the Queen meant that the abuse should be taken away, which shall never be by this patent, but *potius* the abuse will be increased for the private benefit of the patentee, and therefore as it is said in 21 E. 3. 47. in the *Earl of Kent's case* , this grant is void *jure regio.* 4. This grant is *primæ impressionis* , for no such was ever seen to pass by letters patent under the Great Seal before these days, and therefore it is a dangerous innovation, as well without any precedent, or example, as without authority of law, or reason. . . .

And it is true *quod privilegia quæ re vera sunt in præjudicium reipublicæ, magis tamen speciosa habent frontispicia, et boni publici pratertum, quam bonæ et legales concessiones, sed prætextu liciti non debet admitti illicitum* . And our lord the King that now is, in a book which he in zeal to the law and justice commanded to be printed anno 1610, intituled, "A Declaration of His Majesty's Pleasure, &c." p. 13. has published, that monopolies are things against the laws of this realm: and therefore expressly commands, that no suitor presume to move him to grant any of them, &c.

VALLEY MEDICAL SPECIALISTS V. FARBER
Supreme Court of Arizona
982 P. 2d 1277 (1999).

FELDMAN, Justice.

. . . .

FACTS AND PROCEDURAL HISTORY

In 1985, Valley Medical Specialists ("VMS"), a professional corporation, hired Steven S. Farber, D.O., an internist and pulmonologist who, among other things, treated AIDS and HIV-positive patients and performed brachytherapy-a procedure that radiates the inside of the lung in lung cancer patients. Brachytherapy can only be performed at certain hospitals that have the necessary equipment. A few years after joining VMS, Dr. Farber became a shareholder and subsequently a minority officer and director. In 1991, the three directors, including Dr. Farber, entered into new stock and employment agreements. The employment agreement contained a restrictive covenant, the scope of which was amended over time.

In 1994, Dr. Farber left VMS and began practicing within the area defined by the restrictive covenant, which at that time read as follows:

> The parties recognize that the duties to be rendered under the terms of this Agreement by the Employee are special, unique and of an extraordinary character. The Employee, in consideration of the compensation to be paid to him pursuant to the terms of this Agreement, expressly agrees to the following restrictive covenants:
>
> (a) The Employee shall not, directly or indirectly:
>
> (i) Request any present or future patients of the Employer to curtail or cancel their professional affiliation with the Employer;
>
> (ii) Either separately, jointly, or in association with others, establish, engage in, or become interested in, as an employee, owner, partner, shareholder or otherwise, or furnish any information to, work for, or assist in any manner, anyone competing with, or who may compete with the Employer in the practice of medicine.
>
> (iii) Disclose the identity of any past, present or future patients of the Employer to any other person, firm or corporation engaged in a medical practice the same as, similar to or in general competition with the medical services provided by the Employer.
>
> (iv) Either separately, jointly or in association with others provide medical care or medical assistance for any person or persons who were patients or [sic] Employer during the period that Employee was in the hire of Employer.

. . .

(d) *The restrictive covenants set forth herein shall continue during the term of this Agreement and for a period of three (3) years after the date of termination, for any reason, of this Agreement. The restrictive covenants set forth herein shall be binding upon the Employee in that geographical area encompassed within the boundaries measured by a five (5) mile radius of any office maintained or utilized by Employer at the time of execution of the Agreement or at any time thereafter.*

(e) The Employee agrees that a violation on his part of any covenant set forth in this Paragraph 17 will cause such damage to the Employer as will be irreparable and for that reason, that Employee further agrees that the Employer shall be entitled, as a matter of right, and upon notice as provided in Paragraph 20 hereof, to an injunction from any court of competent jurisdiction, restraining any further violation of said covenants by Employee, his corporation, employees, partners or agents. Such right to injunctive remedies shall be in addition to and cumulative with any other rights and remedies the Employer may have pursuant to this Agreement or law, including, specifically with regard to the covenants set forth in subparagraph 17(a) above, the recovery of liquidated damages equal to forty percent (40%) of the gross receipts received for medical services provided by the Employee, or any employee, associate, partner, or corporation of the Employee during the term of this Agreement and for a period of three (3) years after the date of termination, for any reason, of this Agreement. The Employee expressly acknowledges and agrees that the covenants and agreement contained in this Paragraph 17 are minimum and reasonable in scope and are necessary to protect the legitimate interest of the Employer and its goodwill.

(Emphasis added.)

VMS filed a complaint against Dr. Farber seeking (1) preliminary and permanent injunctions enjoining Dr. Farber from violating the restrictive covenant, (2) liquidated damages for breach of the employment agreement, and (3) damages for breach of fiduciary duty, conversion of patient files and confidential information, and intentional interference with contractual and/or business relations.

Following six days of testimony and argument, the trial court denied VMS's request for a preliminary injunction, finding that the restrictive covenant violated public policy or, alternatively, was unenforceable because it was too broad. Specifically, the court found that: any covenant over six months would be unreasonable; the five-mile radius from each of the three VMS offices was unreasonable because it covered a total of 235 square miles; and the restriction was unreasonable because it did not provide an exception for emergency medical aid and was not limited to pulmonology.

The court of appeals reversed, concluding that a modified covenant was reasonable. . . .

DISCUSSION

. . . .

B. History of restrictive covenants

A brief reference to basic principles is appropriate. Historically, covenants not to compete were viewed as restraints of trade and were invalid at common law. Ohio Urology, Inc. v. Poll, 72 Ohio App.3d 446, 594 N.E.2d 1027, 1031 (1991); see generally Harlan M. Blake, Employee Agreements not to Compete, 73 HARV. L. REVV. 625 (1960); Serena L. Kafker, Golden Handcuffs: Enforceability of Noncompetition Clauses in Professional Partnership Agreements of Accountants, Physicians, and Attorneys, 31 AM. BUS. L J. 31, 33 (1993). Eventually, ancillary restraints, such as those incident to employment or partnership agreements, were enforced under the rule of reason. See RESTATEMENT (SECOND) OF CONTRACTS § 188 (hereinafter "RESTATEMENT"). Given the public interest in doctor-patient relationships, the validity of restrictive covenants between physicians was carefully examined long ago in Mandeville v. Harman:

> The rule is not that a limited restraint is good, but that it may be good. It is valid when the restraint is reasonable; and the restraint is reasonable when it imposes no shackle upon the one party which is not beneficial to the other.
>
> The authorities are uniform that such contracts are valid when the restraint they impose is reasonable, and the test to be applied, ... is this: To consider whether the restraint is such only as to afford a fair protection to the interest of the party in favor of whom it is given, and not so large as to interfere with the interest of the public. Whatever restraint is larger than the necessary protection of the party can be of no benefit to either; it can only be oppressive, and, if oppressive, it is, in the eye of the law, unreasonable and void, on the ground of public policy, as being injurious to the interests of the public.

42 N.J. Eq. 185, 7 A. 37, 38-39 (1886) (citations omitted); see also Karlin v. Weinberg, 77 N.J. 408, 390 A.2d 1161, 1165 (1978).

To be enforced, the restriction must do more than simply prohibit fair competition by the employee. Bryceland, 160 Ariz. at 216, 772 P.2d at 39. In other words, a covenant not to compete is invalid unless it protects some legitimate interest beyond the employer's desire to protect itself from competition. Amex Distrib. Co. v. Mascari, 150 Ariz. 510, 518, 724 P.2d 596, 604 (App.1986). The legitimate purpose of post-employment restraints is "to prevent competitive use, for a time, of information or relationships which pertain peculiarly to the employer and which the employee acquired in the course of the employment." Blake, supra, 73 HARV. L. REVV. at 647. Despite the freedom to contract, the law does not favor restrictive covenants. Ohio Urology, Inc., 594 N.E.2d at 1031. This disfavor is particularly strong concerning such covenants among physicians because the practice of medicine affects the public to a much greater extent. Id. In fact, "[f]or the past 60 years, the American Medical Association (AMA) has consistently taken the position that noncompetition agreements between physicians impact negatively on patient care." Paula Berg, Judicial

Enforcement of Covenants not to Compete Between Physicians: Protecting Doctors' Interests at Patients' Expense, 45 RUTGERS L. REV. 1, 6 (1992).

C. Level of scrutiny-public policy considerations

We first address the level of scrutiny that should be afforded to this restrictive covenant. Dr. Farber argues that this contract is simply an employer-employee agreement and thus the restrictive covenant should be strictly construed against the employer. See Amex Distrib. Co., 150 Ariz. at 514, 724 P.2d at 600 (noting employer-employee restrictive covenants are disfavored and strictly construed against the employer). This was the approach taken by the trial court. VMS contends that this is more akin to the sale of a business; thus, the noncompete provision should not be strictly construed against it. See id. (courts more lenient in enforcing restrictive covenants connected to sale of business because of need to effectively transfer goodwill). Finding the agreement here not on all fours with either approach, the court of appeals applied a standard "somewhere between" the two. Valley Med. Specialists, 190 Ariz. at 566, 950 P.2d at 1187.

Although this agreement is between partners, it is more analogous to an employer-employee agreement than a sale of a business. See RESTATEMENT § 188 cmt. h ("A rule similar to that applicable to an employee or agent applies to a partner who makes a promise not to compete that is ancillary to the partnership agreement or to an agreement by which he disposes of his partnership interest."). Many of the concerns present in the sale of a business are not present or are reduced where, as here, a physician leaves a medical group, even when that physician is a partner. When a business is sold, the value of that business's goodwill usually figures significantly into the purchase price. The buyer therefore deserves some protection from competition from the former owner. See Kafker, supra, 31 AM. BUS. L.J. at 33. A restraint accompanying the sale of a business is necessary for the buyer to get the full goodwill value for which it has paid. Blake, supra, 73 HARV. L. REVV. at 647.

It is true that in this case, unlike typical employer-employee agreements, Dr. Farber may not have been at a bargaining disadvantage, which is one of the reasons such restrictive covenants are strictly construed. See, e.g., Rash v. Toccoa Clinic Med. Assocs., 253 Ga. 322, 320 S.E.2d 170, 172-73 (1984). Unequal bargaining power may be a factor to consider when examining the hardship on the departing employee. But in cases involving the professions, public policy concerns may outweigh any protectable interest the remaining firm members may have. Thus, this case does not turn on the hardship to Dr. Farber.

By restricting a physician's practice of medicine, this covenant involves strong public policy implications and must be closely scrutinized. See Peairs, 164 Ariz. at 60, 790 P.2d at 758; Ohio Urology, Inc., 594 N.E.2d at 1032 (restrictive covenant in medical context "strictly construed in favor of professional mobility and access to medical care and facilities"). Although stopping short of banning restrictive covenants between physicians, the American Medical Association ("AMA") "discourages" such covenants, finding they are not in the public interest.

. . . In addition, the AMA recognizes that free choice of doctors is the right of every patient, and free competition among physicians is a prerequisite of optimal care and ethical practice. See AMA Opinions, Section 9.06; Ohio Urology, Inc., 594 N.E.2d at 1030.

For similar reasons, restrictive covenants are prohibited between attorneys. See Dwyer v. Jung, 133 N.J.Super. 343, 336 A.2d 498, 501 (Ct. Ch. Div.), aff'd, 137 N.J.Super. 135, 348 A.2d 208 (App.Div.1975); Cohen v. Lord, Day & Lord, 75 N.Y.2d 95, 551 N.Y.S.2d 157, 550 N.E.2d 410, 410-11 (1989). In 1969, the American Bar Association adopted a code of professional conduct that contained a disciplinary rule prohibiting restrictive covenants between attorneys. See Berg, supra, 45 RUTGERS L. REV. at 37. . . .

Restrictive covenants between lawyers limit not only their professional autonomy but also the client's freedom to choose a lawyer. See ER 5.6 cmt. We do not, of course, enact ethical rules for the medical profession, but given the view of the AMA to which we have previously alluded, we believe the principle behind prohibiting restrictive covenants in the legal profession is relevant.

Commercial standards may not be used to evaluate the reasonableness of lawyer restrictive covenants. Strong public policy considerations preclude their applicability. In that sense lawyer restrictions are injurious to the public interest. A client is always entitled to be represented by counsel of his own choosing. The attorney-client relationship is consensual, highly fiduciary on the part of counsel, and he may do nothing which restricts the right of the client to repose confidence in any counsel of his choice. No concept of the practice of law is more deeply rooted. Dwyer, 336 A.2d at 500.

We therefore conclude that the doctor-patient relationship is special and entitled to unique protection. It cannot be easily or accurately compared to relationships in the commercial context. In light of the great public policy interest involved in covenants not to compete between physicians, each agreement will be strictly construed for reasonableness.[1]

D. Reasonableness of covenant

Reasonableness is a fact-intensive inquiry that depends on the totality of the circumstances. Bryceland, 160 Ariz. at 217, 772 P.2d at 40 ("Each case hinges on its own particular facts."); Olliver/Pilcher Ins., 148 Ariz. at 532, 715 P.2d at 1220. A restriction is unreasonable and thus will not be enforced: (1) if the restraint is greater than necessary to protect the employer's legitimate interest; or (2) if that interest is outweighed by the hardship to the employee and the likely injury to the public. See RESTATEMENT § 188 cmt. a.; see also Blake, supra, 73 HARV. L. REVV. at 648-49; Ferdinand S. Tinio, Annotation, Validity and Construction of Contractual Restrictions on Right of Medical Practitioner to Practice, Incident to Partnership Agreement, 62 A.L.R.3d 970, 984 (1975). Thus, in the present case, the reasonableness inquiry requires us to examine the interests of the employer, employee, patients, and public in general. See 62 A.L.R.3d at 976; see also Peairs, 164 Ariz. at 57, 790 P.2d at 755; Amex Distrib. Co., 150 Ariz. at 514, 724 P.2d at 600 (accommodating right to work, right to contract, and public's right to competition); see generally Blake, supra. Balancing these competing interests is no easy task and no exact formula can be used. See RESTATEMENT § 188 cmt. a. . . .

---

[1] Dr. Farber asks us to hold restrictive covenants in the medical profession void per se as against public policy. Finding the present covenant unreasonable and thus unenforceable by injunction, we need not and do not address that contention.

E. VMS's protectable interest

VMS contends, and the court of appeals agreed, that it has a protectable interest in its patients and referral sources. In the commercial context, it is clear that employers have a legitimate interest in retaining their customer base. See, e.g., Bryceland, 160 Ariz. at 217, 772 P.2d at 40. "The employer's point of view is that the company's clientele is an asset of value which has been acquired by virtue of effort and expenditures over a period of time, and which should be protected as a form of property." Blake, supra, 73 HARV. L. REVV. at 654. In the medical context, however, the personal relationship between doctor and patient, as well as the patient's freedom to see a particular doctor, affects the extent of the employer's interest. See Ohio Urology Inc., 594 N.E.2d at 1031-32. "The practice of a physician is a thing so purely personal, depending so absolutely on the confidence reposed in his personal skill and ability, that when he ceases to exist it necessarily ceases also...." Mandeville, 7 A. at 40-41 (holding medical practice's patient base is not protectable interest); see also Berg, supra, 45 RUTGERS L. REV. at 17.

Even in the commercial context, the employer's interest in its customer base is balanced with the employee's right to the customers. Where the employee took an active role and brought customers with him or her to the job, courts are more reluctant to enforce restrictive covenants. Blake, supra, 73 HARV. L. REVV. at 664, 667. Dr. Farber was a pulmonologist. He did not learn his skills from VMS. Restrictive covenants are designed to protect an employer's customer base by preventing "a skilled employee from leaving an employer and, based on his skill acquired from that employment, luring away the employer's clients or business while the employer is vulnerable-that is-before the employer has had a chance to replace the employee with someone qualified to do the job." Bryceland, 160 Ariz. at 217, 772 P.2d at 40. These facts support the trial judge's conclusion that VMS's interest in protecting its patient base was outweighed by other factors.

We agree with VMS, however, that it has a protectable interest in its referral sources. See Medical Specialists, Inc. v. Sleweon, 652 N.E.2d 517, 523 (Ind.App.1995) ("Clearly, the continued success of [a specialty] practice, which is dependent upon patient referrals, is a legitimate interest worthy of protection."); Ballesteros v. Johnson, 812 S.W.2d 217, 223 (Mo.App.1991).

F. Scope of the restrictive covenant

The restriction cannot be greater than necessary to protect VMS's legitimate interests. A restraint's scope is defined by its duration and geographic area. The frequency of contact between doctors and their patients affects the permissible length of the restraint. Blake, supra, 73 HARV. L. REVV. at 659. The idea is to give the employer a reasonable amount of time to overcome the former employee's loss, usually by hiring a replacement and giving that replacement time to establish a working relationship. Id. Even in the commercial context, "[w]hen the restraint is for the purpose of protecting customer relationships, its duration is reasonable only if it is no longer than necessary for the employer to put a new man on the job and for the new employee to have a reasonable opportunity to demonstrate his effectiveness to the customers." Amex Distrib. Co., 150 Ariz. at 518, 724 P.2d at 604 (quoting Blake, supra, 73 HARV. L. REVV. at 677).

In this case, the trial judge found that the three-year period was an unreasonable duration because all of the experts agree that the practice of pulmonology entails treating patients with chronic conditions which require more hospital care than office care and which requires regular contact with the treating physician at least once within each six-month period so that any provision over six months is onerous and unnecessary to protect VMS's economic interests where virtually all of Dr. Farber's VMS patients had an opportunity by late 1994 or early 1995 (Farber left September 12, 1994) to decide which pulmonologist ... they would consult for their ongoing treatment[.]

On this record, we cannot say this factual finding was clearly erroneous. The three-year duration is unreasonable.

The activity prohibited by the restraint also defines the covenant's scope. The restraint must be limited to the particular speciality of the present employment. See Blake, supra, 73 HARV. L. REVV. at 676. On its face, the restriction here is not limited to internal medicine or even pulmonology. It precludes any type of practice, even in fields that do not compete with VMS. Thus, we agree with the trial judge that this restriction is too broad. Compare Peairs, 164 Ariz. at 56, 790 P.2d at 754 (upholding injunction that enforced restrictive covenant preventing doctor from practicing only orthopaedic medicine and orthopaedic surgery).

G. Public policy

The court of appeals held that the restrictive covenant does not violate public policy, pointing out that the record contains nothing to suggest there will be a lack of pulmonologists in the restricted area if Dr. Farber is precluded from practicing there. Even if we assume other pulmonologists will be available to cover Dr. Farber's patients, we disagree with this view. It ignores the significant interests of individual patients within the restricted area. Kafker, supra, 31 AM. BUS. L.J. at 39-40. A court must evaluate the extent to which enforcing the covenant would foreclose patients from seeing the departing physician if they desire to do so. See Karlin, 390 A.2d at 1170; see also AMA Opinions, Section 9.06.

Concluding that patients' right to see the doctor of their choice is entitled to substantial protection, VMS's protectable interests here are comparatively minimal. See Berg, supra, 45 RUTGERS L. REV. at 15-36. The geographic scope of this covenant encompasses approximately 235 square miles, making it very difficult for Dr. Farber's existing patients to continue treatment with him if they so desire. After six days of testimony, the trial judge concluded that this restrictive covenant was unreasonably broad and against public policy. Specifically, the judge found:

> (1) the three year duration was unreasonable because pulmonology patients typically require contact with the treating physician once every six months. Thus, a restriction over six months is unnecessary to protect VMS's economic interests. Patients would have had opportunity within approximately six months to decide which doctor to see for continuing treatment;

(2) the five mile radius was unreasonable because with the three offices, the restriction covered more than 235 square miles;

(3) the restriction was unreasonable because it did not expressly provide for an exception for emergency medical treatment;

(4) the restriction was overly broad because it is not limited to pulmonology;

(5) the covenant violates public policy because of the sensitive and personal nature of the doctor-patient relationship.

Given the facts and the principles discussed, that finding is well supported factually and legally.

H. Severance-the blue pencil rule

This contract contains a severance clause. The court of appeals accepted a stipulation by VMS that the restriction would not prohibit Dr. Farber from treating HIV-positive and AIDS patients or from performing brachytherapy. On its face, however, the restriction is broader than that, restricting him from providing "medical care or medical assistance for any person or persons who were patients or [sic] Employer during the period that Employee was in the hire of Employer." Arizona courts will "blue pencil" restrictive covenants, eliminating grammatically severable, unreasonable provisions. See Amex Distrib. Co., 150 Ariz. at 514, 724 P.2d at 600; Olliver/Pilcher Ins., 148 Ariz. at 533, 715 P.2d at 1221 ("If it is clear from its terms that a contract was intended to be severable, the court can enforce the lawful part and ignore the unlawful part."). Here, however, the modifications go further than cutting grammatically severable portions. The court of appeals, in essence, rewrote the agreement in an attempt to make it enforceable. This goes too far. "Where the severability of the agreement is not evident from the contract itself, the court cannot create a new agreement for the parties to uphold the contract." Olliver/Pilcher Ins., 148 Ariz. at 533, 715 P.2d at 1221.

Even the blue pencil rule has its critics. For every agreement that makes its way to court, many more do not. Thus, the words of the covenant have an in terrorem effect on departing employees. See Blake, supra, 73 HARV. L. REVV. at 682-83. Employers may therefore create ominous covenants, knowing that if the words are challenged, courts will modify the agreement to make it enforceable. Id. Although we will tolerate ignoring severable portions of a covenant to make it more reasonable, we will not permit courts to add terms or rewrite provisions. . . .

CONCLUSION

We hold that the restrictive covenant between Dr. Farber and VMS cannot be enforced. Valley Medical Specialists' interest in enforcing the restriction is outweighed by the likely injury to patients and the public in general. See RESTATEMENT § 188. In so holding, we need not reach the question of the hardship imposed on Dr. Farber. The public policy implications here are enough to invalidate this particular agreement. We stop short of holding that restrictive covenants between physicians will never be enforced, but caution that such restrictions will be strictly construed.

Dr. Farber listed in his petition for review several issues "presented to, but not decided by, the court of appeals." Valley Medical Specialists' response also contained "additional issues if the court accepts review." None of the issues were briefed in this court. We thus remand to the court of appeals for a determination of those issues that are capable of decision and still need to be decided.

THOMAS A. ZLAKET, Chief Justice, and CHARLES E. JONES, Vice Chief Justice, FREDERICK J. MARTONE, Justice, and RUTH V. McGREGOR, Justice, concur.

NOTES AND QUESTIONS:

1. Another type of contractual provision that garners a great deal of scrutiny is a hold harmless or exculpatory clause. By including such a provision in a contract, one party attempts to exempt herself from liability in tort for harm caused by her own conduct. Revisit the case of *Weaver v. American Oil*, discussed under the unconscionability material, where the court acknowledged that such provisions can be enforceable but prescribed strict standards for enforceability. Generally speaking, exculpatory clauses are enforceable to limit liability for a party's negligent conduct. However, a party is not permitted to escape liability for her own intentional, reckless or grossly negligent conduct. Moreover, the party seeking to enforce the provision must establish that the agreement was made knowingly and voluntarily.

In some cases, public policy prohibits a party from exempting herself from liability for negligent conduct. In *Tunkl v. Regents of the University of California*, 60 Cal.2d 92 (1963), the California Supreme Court enumerated and discussed the following six factors in determining whether an exculpatory provision violates public policy:

a. Whether the transaction concerns a business suitable for public regulation;

b. Whether the party seeking exculpation is engaged in performance of service of great importance and practical necessity to the public;

c. Whether the party generally purports to be willing to perform such service to any member of public;

d. Whether the party has a decisive advantage of bargaining strength;

e. Whether the party uses a standardized adhesion form making no provision for the payment of additional reasonable fees to obtain protection against negligence; and

f. Whether the person or property of the other party is placed in the control of party seeking exculpation and subject to risk of carelessness.

Typically, the types of relationships in which exculpatory clauses are deemed violative of public policy include landlord-tenant, employer-employee, and common carriers-passengers. Moreover, professional licensees are often included in this group. On the other hand, exculpatory clauses often are enforced in contracts involving activities with inherent risk of injury.

CHAPTER FOUR

PERFORMANCE, BREACH, AND EXCUSES

Laws too gentle are seldom obeyed; too severe, seldom executed.[*]

Benjamin Franklin

SECTION 1. SCOPE AND TERMS

A. HISTORICAL DEVELOPMENT

EVANS V. ROE
Court of Common Pleas
7 L.C.R.P. 138 (1872).

. . . .

THE declaration stated that the plaintiff and defendants agreed that the plaintiff should serve the defendants, and that the defendants should retain and employ the plaintiff in their service in a certain capacity, to wit, that of a foreman, at certain wages and salary, to wit, 2l. per week and a house to live in, for a certain time, to wit, for one year; that the plaintiff resided and was received into the service of the defendants under and in pursuance of the agreement, and that he did all things necessary on his part to entitle him to be continued in such service until the same was duly determined; yet the defendants, during the said period of service, and before the same was duly determined, dismissed the plaintiff from the said service, and put an end to the relation created by the said agreement, and had from thence hitherto refused to continue the plaintiff in their service or find him a house to live in, whereby the plaintiff was deprived of the wages and advantages which he would have derived from the service, &c.

The defendants pleaded a denial of the contract as alleged; and, further, that it was part of the terms of the agreement that the defendants might determine and put an end to the service and dismiss the plaintiff from it at the expiration of a week after giving the plaintiff notice of their intention so to do; that the defendants gave the plaintiff one week's notice of their intention to determine and put an end to the service and dismiss him from it; and that, at the expiration of a week after the giving of such notice, the defendants determined and put an end to the service and dismissed the plaintiff from it, as they lawfully might, &c. Issue thereon.

The cause was tried before Blackburn, J., at the last assizes at Croydon. The plaintiff, who had formerly carried on the trade of a shoddy maker in Gloucestershire, applied to the defendants, rag-merchants at Mitcham, who contemplated entering into the shoddy trade, for employment, and they agreed to engage the plaintiff as foreman, upon the terms mentioned in the following memorandum, which was drawn up in duplicate by one of the defendants, and one part signed by each of the parties:--

[*] Benjamin Franklin (1706 – 1790).

April 13, 1871. Messrs. James Thorne Roe & Co., Mitcham.

I hereby agree to accept the situation as foreman of the works of Messrs. J. T. Roe & Co., flock and shoddy manufacturers, &c., and to do all that lays in my power to serve them faithfully, and promote the welfare of the said firm, on my receiving a salary of two pounds per week and house to live in from 19th April, 1871.

Before signing the agreement, the plaintiff asked the defendants if the engagement was to be understood to be an engagement for a year, and one of the defendants answered, "Yes, certainly." The reason why the service was to commence at a future day was that the plaintiff had to bring his family from Gloucestershire. A house was hired by the defendants for the plaintiff for one year from the 19th of April. The plaintiff remained in the service of the defendants and in the occupation of the house until the 3rd of June, when they gave him a week's wages, and dismissed him.

On the part of the defendants it was objected that, upon the true construction of the memorandum, the hiring was a weekly one, and therefore determinable by a week's notice or payment of a week's wages; and that, assuming the evidence of what passed by parol at the time of signing the agreement to be admissible, the contract was void by the Statute of Frauds, inasmuch as it was not to be performed within a year.

The learned judge left it to the jury to say whether, taking the parol evidence and the writing together, it was really agreed that the hiring should be terminable at a week's notice, or was for a year, reserving leave to defendants to move to enter a nonsuit, on the ground that "the writing of the 13th of April, 1871, was conclusive against the plaintiff, and that, the contract being within the Statute of Frauds, extrinsic evidence was not admissible." The jury found that the hiring was for a year, and returned a verdict for the plaintiff, damages 30l.

Oppenheim, in Michaelmas Term last, obtained a rule nisi accordingly. . . .

Joyce shewed cause. The case is not within the Statute of Frauds. The true construction of the memorandum of the 13th of April is, that the hiring is a hiring for one year from that day, but that the payment of salary is to commence from the 19th, and the occupation of the house to be from the same day; or, it may be that the service and salary were to commence on the 13th of April, and the occupation of the house from the 19th. If the period of service was left in doubt upon the face of the memorandum, it was competent to the plaintiff to supplement it by parol.

Oppenheim, in support of the rule. The terms of the hiring can only be gathered from the written contract; oral evidence was not admissible to vary it: Marshall v. Lynn;[1] Giraud v. Richmond.[2] And there is nothing on the face of the memorandum to shew that it was otherwise than a weekly hiring, at weekly wages: Rex v Newton Toney;[3] Rex v. Dodderhill.[4]

[1] 6 M. & W. 109.
[2] 2 C. B. 835.
[3] 2 T. R. 453.
[4] 3 M. & S. 243.

BYLES, J.

Independently of any reference to the Statute of Frauds, the contract declared upon in this case is a written contract clearly defining all the terms of the bargain. It is in terms a weekly hiring and a weekly service at weekly wages; and it cannot be varied by anything which passed at the time by parol, or, as I should think, by anything which might have passed afterwards.

BRETT, J.

The agreement being in writing, oral evidence was not admissible to vary it. We must gather the intention of the parties from the writing and the writing only. The rule to be deduced from the cases cited shews that this was a weekly hiring; and the plaintiff should have been nonsuited.

GROVE, J.

It would render written agreements useless if conversations which take place at the time could be let in to vary them. The service was to commence from the 19th. On both grounds therefore I agree that the rule should be absolute. . . .

Rule absolute.

GERMAIN FRUIT CO. V. J.K. ARMSBY CO.
Supreme Court of California
96 P. 319 (1908).

PER CURIAM.

The appeals in this case, of which there are two, were originally presented to the district court of appeal for the Second Appellate District, but, the judges thereof being unable to agree in a judgment therein, the appeals were ordered to this court for disposition. Accompanying such order are the opinions filed by the respective judges of the district court of appeal. One of said opinions is as follows:

> Judgment was for plaintiff and both parties appeal. In view of the conclusion reached and the order made, it is deemed advisable to consider the two appeals together. Plaintiff's appeal (No. 149) is from an order denying its motion to vacate and set aside the judgment in the cause and to enter a different judgment, increasing the amount thereof. Defendant's appeal No. 154 is from the whole judgment and from an order denying its motion for a new trial. The action was brought to recover damages for breach of warranty of quality of dried apricots sold by defendant to plaintiff. The damages claimed ($1,748.22) were alleged in the amended complaint to be $1,126.47 for the loss actually sustained by the breach complained of, and $621.75, profits which plaintiff alleges it would have made if the goods had been as warranted. The contract between the parties, which was reduced to writing,

was silent as to any warranty of the goods, but parol evidence was admitted by the court, on behalf of plaintiff, for the purpose of establishing that the sale was made upon an express warranty by sample. It is claimed by defendant that this was error, and that the findings upon which the judgment is based are unsupported without this parol evidence.

The findings material here show: The plaintiff purchased a lot of dried apricots from defendant to be resold in the markets in cities east of the Rocky Mountains. The defendant, knowing such purpose, warranted said fruit to be according to certain samples delivered to plaintiff. The fruit was in Pomona and the sale took place in Los Angeles and plaintiff relied upon such samples for quality and weight (the number of boxes being given) and had no opportunity to inspect the bulk of the fruit. Plaintiff paid to defendant the full amount of the purchase price, to wit, $4,352.25, and delivery for shipment was made f. o. b cars at Pomona, as agreed. Plaintiff, without examination, shipped the fruit to the city of Philadelphia for sale, where its representative, on inspection, discovered it to be inferior in quality to the samples shown, and light in weight. After notice to defendant and the refusal of the latter to take any action in the matter, plaintiff sold the apricots in the market at Philadelphia for $3,225.78 over and above the freight and usual and necessary expenses of making the sale, which was the best price obtainable for such apricots. Had the apricots been of the quality of the samples exhibited to plaintiff, they could and would have been sold by it in Philadelphia for the sum of $4,974, in excess of freight and expenses of sale. As an inference from these facts, the court finds that by reason of such breach of warranty plaintiff has been damaged in the sum of $1,748.22; $1,126.47 being actual loss and $621.75 being the profits which would have been made on resale if the apricots had been as warranted. Judgment is then given for $1,126.47 and denied as to the $621.75, profits. Argumentatively, and as a conclusion of law based on specific findings made, the reason for not including the 'profits' in the judgment is stated by the court in its findings to be "that defendant did not have notice that plaintiff intended to sell said apricots in any specific market, or at any definite price." Plaintiff claims that on the findings of fact made it was entitled to a judgment for $1,748.22.

Plaintiff's Appeal (No. 149).

Considering first the plaintiff's appeal (No. 149), which involves but one question and must be determined from the judgment roll, we are of the opinion that the segregation of the damages into actual loss and profits in such a case as this is not necessary under the statute. "Speculative" profits are one thing and that portion of the price of goods having an actual value in the market above what was paid for them is another. The goods delivered in Philadelphia were actually worth only $3,225.78 over and above freight and expenses of sale. Had they been according to sample, they would have been of the value of $4,974 over freight and expenses at the same place. That is, the same quantity of apricots purchased by plaintiff of defendant of the

> quality of the samples shown were actually worth $4,974 in Philadelphia at the time the ones delivered to plaintiff by defendant were sold for the smaller sum named. There is nothing "speculative" about these differences of value. The findings to this effect are express, and may be considered independent of the finding upon the theory of a resale which also fixes the last-mentioned value at the same amount ($4,974) for that purpose. Defendant sold goods to plaintiff which it knew the latter would have no opportunity to inspect until they reached some Eastern market. The court finds Philadelphia to be one of the places that must be included in the term "Eastern market." The inspection at that place disclosed goods worth $3,225.78. instead of $4,974. The reason for the difference was the failure and breach of defendant's warranty. If there had been any element of special additional damage by reason of plaintiff's inability to make good some contract of sale made by it, at the time of, or prior to, the purchase from defendant, and the fulfillment of such contract had been dependent upon the goods being up to sample, notice to defendant of such special sale at a definite price would have been necessary in order to hold it for such special damages. No damages are asked here for profits on a contract for resale at an advanced price. Damages for breach of an obligation are measured by the amount which will compensate the party aggrieved for all the detriment proximately caused thereby, or which in the ordinary course of things will be likely to result therefrom. Civ. Code, § 3300. "The detriment caused by the breach of a warranty of the quality of personal property is deemed to be the excess, if any, of the value which the property would have had at the time to which the warranty referred, if it had been complied with, over its actual value at that time." Civ. Code, § 3313. . . .

The damages which plaintiff sues for in this case may all be recovered as general damages, and it is not necessary that the "profits" be specially alleged. . . . As the conclusion reached on defendant's appeal will require a new trial of the case, it is not necessary for us to consider whether or not the amended complaint and the findings of fact would support the judgment here indicated as proper on the case made. The foregoing opinion will suffice to guide the parties as to all matters affected by this appeal, if a new trial be had. By the opinion filed in appeal No. 154, it being held that the evidence was insufficient to support the findings made in the case, it would be idle to make an order overruling the trial court's action in denying plaintiff's motion. This appeal, therefore must be governed by the order made in No. 154.

Defendant's Appeal (No. 154).

The real question to be determined on this appeal relates to the admissibility of the parol evidence to affect the terms of the writing executed by the parties at the time said dried apricots were sold. This writing was as follows:

> Los Angeles, Cal., Oct. 19, 1901.
>
> This agreement made by and between the J. K. Armsby Co. and the Germain Fruit Company, Witnesseth:

That the said J. K. Armsby Co. has this day sold and the said Germain Fruit Company has this day bought twenty-five hundred boxes apricots, more or less, consisting of:

Lot A	287 boxes
Lot K	104 boxes
Lot C	1400 boxes
Lot E	715 boxes

at seven (7) cents per pound plus one per cent net cash f. o. b. cars at Pomona, on surrender of bill of lading; shipment to be made during the month of October, 1901.

Signed in duplicate.

The J. K. Armsby Company

By A. B. Miner.

Germain Fruit Company,

By Eugene Germain.

Measured by the criterion that the completeness of a written contract, as a full expression of the parties, is the writing itself, the writing appears upon its face to contain all the necessary elements of a complete contract of sale. The description of the property sold is admittedly incorrect, and it contains no express warranty of quality of the goods sold, but contracts of sale may be complete without the latter. The contract calls for apricots, while the evidence shows and both parties admit that dried apricots were the subject of the agreement. It is conceded that this defect of description may be supplied by parol. Respondent contends that the same rule warrants the introduction of parol evidence to determine what apricots were intended to be described by lot "A," lot "K," lot "C," and lot "E," and also to identify them by sample. There is no question as to the former proposition, and in a proper case and under proper circumstances the latter would no doubt be true. For instance, if the fruit itself, the label on the box, the package, or the method of packing were peculiar, or so different in character from other fruit or packages of dried apricots, as generally prepared for market, that the sample box would serve to identify or aid in identifying the goods from which the box was taken, such evidence might be admissible for the purpose of identifying the subject-matter of the written contract. "Lot A, 287 boxes," does not so clearly describe the goods sold as to preclude the admission of evidence for purposes of identification, if necessary. . . .

No effort, however, was made to show such circumstances as would warrant the introduction of the samples or the testimony in relation thereto upon this theory. If the facts had been such as to make the evidence proper upon this theory alone, the purpose of its introduction should have been limited so as to exclude its consideration in connection with the question of warranty of quality. On the contrary, the very purpose of its introduction was apparently to add to the written contract of sale another term, a parol warranty of quality by sample. The court permitted the introduction of parol evidence as to sample, and applied it on the theory that it was competent proof of a warranty. It expressly found such a warranty, and the judgment for damages rests upon its breach. There is no other evidence to support the finding, except the inferences to be drawn from plaintiff's Exhibit 5. This was a receipted bill showing on its face words and figures, which taken with plaintiff's explanation of them served to corroborate plaintiff's testimony that the sale was made by sample. Alone it was insufficient as evidence in writing to justify a finding to that effect. The finding and judgment therefore rest on the parol evidence.

It is urged by respondent in support of the court's action that an ambiguity or uncertainty appearing in the language of the instrument by the use of the terms "Lot A, 287 boxes," etc., the matter is open for explanation by parol evidence; and that such ambiguity or uncertainty may as well be removed by showing the term was intended to mean "according to sample A" as by showing that it was intended to mean some certain pile of 287 boxes marked "A," or designated as "A" in some other manner for purposes of description or identification. In other words, that the term being ambiguous, there is no good reason why such ambiguity may not be resolved upon the assumption of an ambiguity in expressing the warranty as well as upon the theory of an ambiguity in description. There is much weight in this contention. We must, however, bear in mind that the law permits no new term to be introduced into a written contract by parol, while it does permit such evidence for the purpose of making certain an ambiguous description or for purposes of identification. To hold that the words, "Lot A, 287 boxes," considered either in their ordinary use or as used in a commercial way, relate to warranty rather than identification, would do violence to the use of language. It would amount to what the rule does not permit even in cases of description the supplying by parol of something not expressed in the instrument in any manner. Neither the grammatical construction of the language used in the contract nor the definition given to the word "lot" by the lexicographers justifies attributing to it a meaning which imports quality or warranty. While from the parol evidence introduced the inference may be drawn that the parties intended the sale should be on a warranty by sample, we cannot permit any bias or knowledge of the fact to lend weight to the construction of the instrument. Admitting that such was the intention, an examination of the writing shows that, if this were the case, there was an entire failure to embody such intention in the contract. The language used was unfit and inappropriate to express a warranty of quality by sample or otherwise, being language importing description and identity only. "Lot" is not an ambiguous word of warranty, but a word used solely to describe and identify. All definitions of the word display its derivation from "share, portion or parcel." See Century Dictionary. There are well-considered cases holding that an express warranty can be proven by parol evidence where the contract of sale is silent in this respect. The decisions in these cases are based upon the principle that a warranty is not one of the essential elements of a sale, but is a mere collateral undertaking. Chapin v. Dobson, 78 N. Y. 74, 34 Am. Dec. 512.

This view, however, is not in harmony with the cases upon which the latest declarations of the law on this subject by our Supreme Court rest. In Thompson v. Libby, 34 Minn. 377, 26 N. W. 2, it is said: "When made, a warranty is a part of the contract of sale. The common sense of men would say, and correctly so, that when, on a sale of personal property a warranty is given, it is one of the terms of the sale and not a separate and independent contract." To justify the admission of parol evidence on the ground that it is collateral, it must relate to a subject distinct from that to which the writing relates. Where the written sale contains no warranty or expresses the warranty that is given by the vendor, parol evidence is inadmissible to prove the existence of the warranty in the former case or to extend it in the latter. Johnson v. Powers, 65 Cal. 181, 3 Pac 625, citing Benj on Sales, 621. "If it [the writing] imports on its face to be a complete expression of the whole agreement,-that is, contains such language as imports a complete legal obligation-it is to be presumed that the parties have introduced into it every material item and term; and parol evidence cannot be admitted to add another term to the agreement, although the writing contains nothing on the particular one to which parol evidence is directed. The rule forbids to add by parol when the writing is silent, as well as to vary where it speaks." Harrison v. McCormick, 89 Cal. 330, 26 Pac. 830, 23 Am. St. Rep 469; citing Thompson v. Libby supra, and Naumberg v. Young, 44 N. J. Law, 331, 43 Am. Rep. 380.

The effect and limitations of Guidery v. Green, 95 Cal. 630, 30 Pac 786, and Sivers v. Sivers, 97 Cal. 518, and the cases citing them, have been clearly distinguished in Bradford Inv. Co. v. Joost, 117 Cal. 204, 48 Pac. 1083, and they are not authority here. See, also, Board of Education v. Grant, 118 Cal. 44, 50 Pac. 5. The rule declared in Harrison v. McCormick was affirmed in Gardiner v. McDonogh, 147 Cal. 313, 81 Pac. 964, and finds abundant support elsewhere. Wilson v. New U. S. Co., 20 C. C. A. 241, 73 Fed. 994; Union Selling Co. v. Jones, 63 C. C. A. 224, 128 Fed. 672; Day Leather Co. v. Michigan Leather Co., 141 Mich. 533, 104 N. W. 797.

Even Mr. Wigmore, who in his work on Evidence argues most strenuously for an extension of the rule relating to the admission of parol evidence, so that, what he calls "all the terms of the contract" may be considered by the court, recognizes a distinction in the application of the rule to the matter of warranty and its application to matters of description. Sections 2401, 2434, and 2465. We cannot help suggesting, however, that in his discussion on this subject Mr. Wigmore has not given sufficient weight to the possibility, or rather probability, that the extension urged might result in the admission not only of "all the terms of the contract," but some additional ones, and, in rare cases, might even result in removing from the written contract some of the most important terms that had been formally, carefully, and intentionally put down therein. To hold parties to diligence and care in reducing their negotiations to writing, and to hold the writing to be subject to attack only by specific allegations of fraud or mistake, appears to be the better rule, and is now supported by the weight of authority. Like the statute of frauds, this rule is founded upon long and convincing experience that written evidence is more certain and accurate than "slippery memory."

So long as the rule is applied, the actual contract made can be preserved without fear of its being affected in its terms by the frailties of an interested human recollection. That sometimes the written contract does not include all the terms intended by reason of neglect or oversight, and injustice is thereby done in particular cases, does not justify the abandonment of the rule. To construe it away is to destroy one of the greatest barriers against fraud and perjury. Without specially indicating the rulings to which this opinion is applicable, it is sufficient to say that the admission of testimony to show a sale by sample for the purpose of establishing an express warranty of quality of the appricots sold was error. The finding of such a warranty was without competent evidence to sustain it, and the case was tried on an erroneous theory inconsistent with the rule declared in Gardiner v. McDonogh, supra.

The other points made by appellant on this appeal need not be considered further than they come within the reasoning in appeal No. 149.

We are satisfied that the foregoing opinion correctly states the law applicable to the points presented on both appeals, and we adopt it as the opinion of this court.

The judgment and order appealed from are reversed.

SHAW, J. concurring in part, dissenting in part.

I concur in the judgment, on the authority of the decision in Gardiner v. McDonogh, 147 Cal. 313, 81 Pac. 964. I do not agree to all that is said in the opinion adopted by the court, as I understand it. I can conceive of a sale of goods in bulk, of varying quality, in which the different qualities might be represented by samples shown to the purchaser, the goods being absent, and in which an estimate would be made by the seller of the quantities of each kind comprised in the whole bulk corresponding to the samples shown, the samples being marked as "lot A," "lot B," etc. In such a case a writing, such as that here in question, purporting to agree to sell "500 boxes lot A, and 600 boxes lot B" if construed with reference to the circumstances attending its execution, would properly be held to mean that a sale was made of 500 boxes of the quality of the sample marked as lot A and 600 boxes of the quality of the sample marked as lot B. Such evidence would, in my opinion, be competent to point the meaning of the writing. I do not understand that the opinion intends to express anything contrary to this, but I think some of its language might be so understood. The evidence admitted by the court below and here held incompetent, however, shows a mere sale by sample, and, according to that evidence, the designations "lot A," etc., refer to certain lots stored in a warehouse, and not to the respective samples exhibited to the purchaser. The case falls precisely within the rule established in Gardiner v. McDonogh, which is now to be considered as the settled rule of this court.

B. DEFINING THE SCOPE OF THE AGREEMENT

1. The Parol Evidence Rule

RESTATEMENT (SECOND) OF CONTRACTS
§ 213. EFFECT OF INTEGRATED AGREEMENT ON PRIOR AGREEMENTS (PAROL EVIDENCE RULE)

a. A binding integrated agreement discharges prior agreements to the extent that it is inconsistent with them.

b. A binding completely integrated agreement discharges prior agreements to the extent that they are within its scope.

c. An integrated agreement that is not binding or that is voidable and avoided does not discharge a prior agreement. But an integrated agreement even though not binding, may be effective to render inoperative a term which would have been part of the agreement if it had not been integrated.

TENNESSEE UNIFORM COMMERCIAL CODE
§ 47-2-202. FINAL WRITTEN EXPRESSION: PAROL OR EXTRINSIC EVIDENCE
TENN. CODE ANN. § 47-2-202 (2012).

Terms with respect to which the confirmatory memoranda of the parties agree or which are otherwise set forth in a writing intended by the parties as a final expression of their agreement with respect to such terms as are included therein may not be contradicted by evidence of any prior agreement or of a contemporaneous oral agreement but may be explained or supplemented:

(a) By course of performance, course of dealing or usage of trade, pursuant to § 47-1-303; and

(b) By evidence of consistent additional terms unless the court finds the writing to have been intended also as a complete and exclusive statement of the terms of the agreement.

LURIA BROS. & CO. V. PIELET BROS. SCRAP IRON & METAL, INC.
United States Court of Appeals, Seventh Circuit
600 F.2d 103 (1979).

FAIRCHILD, Chief Judge.

This is a diversity action for breach of contract. Most of the events giving rise to this litigation occurred in Illinois and we accept the parties' assumption that Illinois law is applicable. The action below was tried before a jury which returned a verdict in the amount of $600,000, having found that a contract for the purchase of barge scrap steel existed between plaintiff, Luria Brothers & Co., Inc. (hereinafter referred to as "Luria") and defendant, Pielet Brothers Scrap Iron & Metal, Inc. (hereinafter referred to as "Pielet"), and that Luria was damaged as a consequence of Pielet's failure to deliver. Defendant appeals, arguing among other things that no enforceable agreement was ever made, and therefore, plaintiff was not entitled to damages. We affirm.

A consideration of the issues requires a statement of the facts in some detail. Luria, in its capacity as both a broker and a dealer is in the business of buying, selling, and processing scrap metal. Pielet is in the same business. The parties had done business with each other on a number of occasions prior to the transaction giving rise to this litigation. In fact, Lawrence Bloom, who represented Pielet in this matter had formerly been employed by Luria as a scrap trader.

Most of the facts surrounding the subject transaction are not in dispute and were stipulated to at trial. In mid-September, 1973, Bloom, a vice-president of Pielet, telephoned Richard Fechheimer, a vice-president of Luria. Bloom informed Fechheimer that Pielet might offer a substantial quantity of scrap metal for sale. Bloom inquired as to whether Luria would be interested in purchasing the metal and Fechheimer said that it would be. Subsequent telephone conversations took place between Bloom and Fechheimer in which price quotations and other matters were discussed. The quantity was to be 35,000 net tons of scrap steel from old barges cut into sections measuring five feet by five feet by twenty feet. The shipment date was to be on or before December 31, 1973. The price was set at $42 per net ton if Luria took delivery in Houston or $49 if Luria took delivery in Brownsville (Texas). This transaction was unusual in two respects. First, the amount of scrap involved was much larger than that in a typical scrap transaction. Secondly, while the type or grade of scrap was not unusual, the dimensions were. Luria intended to process the scrap for resale as "No. 1 heavy melting" scrap by reducing it to a size that would fit into a steel furnace, generally in pieces at least 1/4 inch thick and not more than 5 feet long by 18 inches wide. . . .

On September 24, 1973, Bloom caused to be prepared a sales confirmation relating to the scrap transaction between Pielet and Luria. The following information was typed on the confirmation form:

Quantity: Thirty-five thousand (35,000) net tons

Material: Steel barges cut 5' X 5' X 20' free of non metallics

Price: $42.00 per net ton F.O.B. Shipping point barge Houston, Texas or $49.00 per net ton delivered Brownsville, Texas

Shipment: On or before December 31, 1973

Terms: 90% Advance on receipt of surveyor's weights and bill of lading

Bloom signed the sales confirmation and mailed the original and one copy to Forlani. The copy bore the printed words "confirmation copy." The following words are printed at the bottom of both the original and the confirmation copy of Pielet's confirmation form:

PLEASE SIGN AND RETURN THE COPY OF THIS CONFIRMATION FOR OUR FILES. FAILURE TO RETURN COPY DOES NOT VOID CONTRACT.

Neither Forlani nor any officer or other employee of Luria ever signed or returned the confirmation copy to Bloom or anyone else at Pielet.

In the ordinary course of business when Luria makes a purchase of scrap, information regarding the purchase is typed or written on its own purchase confirmation form. On or about October 4, 1973, Forlani caused to be prepared a purchase confirmation containing the same terms as in Pielet's form, except with respect to the delivery date and mode of shipment. The delivery date typed on the form was by October 31, 1973 and the mode of shipment appeared to be left to the discretion of Luria. On the reverse side of this form are printed standard terms including ones referring to warranties, insurance, and taxes, as well as one stating "This order constitutes the entire contract between the parties." The original and one copy of this form are sent to the seller. These bear in red letters the words "RETURN ACCEPTANCE COPY IMMEDIATELY" in the lower right hand corner. There were no other words on this document to indicate any condition as to the existence of a contract.

Forlani sent the original and a copy of the October 4th purchase confirmation to Bloom. Bloom testified that upon receipt of this document, he immediately or shortly thereafter called Forlani to inform him that the Luria confirmation was erroneous with respect to delivery date and mode of shipment. Forlani agreed that the confirmation was erroneous in these two particulars. Bloom asked Forlani to send him an amendment correcting these errors, but Forlani never did. Neither Bloom nor any other officer or employee of Pielet ever signed or returned the acceptance copy to Luria.

During late October and November, Forlani called Bloom several times to ask why Pielet had not begun to deliver the steel. Although the delivery date stated in Pielet's confirmation form and orally agreed upon was on or before December 31, 1973, it is "common trade practice" to space deliveries out during the contract period, especially where the quantity involved is very large. On December 3, 1973, Forlani wrote a letter to Pielet saying Luria had not receiving notification of shipment and requesting that prompt attention be given. On February 6, 1974 representatives of Luria met with Bloom. Bloom stated he was having trouble with his supplier, and further mentioned that his supplier could not obtain the propane necessary for the torches used to cut the barges. On February 13, a week after the meeting, Luria wrote a letter to Bloom to make it clear that the matter had to be resolved. Luria never received a reply and Pielet never delivered the scrap. Luria filed its complaint in the district court on April 25, 1974.

I.

Appellant first argues on this appeal that the evidence is insufficient to establish the existence of a contract, oral or otherwise. Given the facts of this case, we disagree.

The Uniform Commercial Code, which governs this case, specifically states that "a contract for sale of goods may be made in any manner sufficient to show agreement, including conduct by both parties which recognizes the existence of such a contract."[1] U.C.C. § 2-204(1) (Ill.Rev.Stat. Ch. 26, § 2-204 (1973)). . . .

[The court discussed some of the evidence supporting a finding of "meeting of the minds."]

Luria also relied on U.C.C. § 2-207(3) to establish the existence of a contract. That section provides that "Conduct by both parties which recognizes the existence of a contract is sufficient to establish a contract for sale although the writings of the parties do not otherwise establish a contract . . ." Appellant's conduct following the exchange of confirmatory memoranda is entirely consistent with the existence of a contract. Bloom continued to make excuses for non-delivery as late as the February 6, 1974 meeting and there is no evidence that during that time he ever denied the existence of an enforceable agreement.

In light of the above, we think a jury could readily find that a contract existed between the parties.

II.

Next, Pielet contends that even if the evidence is sufficient to establish the existence of a binding contract between the parties, it was error for the district court to exclude evidence that the sales contract was expressly conditional upon Pielet obtaining the scrap metal from a particular supplier. In an offer of proof, Bloom testified that in their first conversation in September, he told Fechheimer "I was doing business with people that I had never heard of, that they were fly-by-night people, that I was worried about shipment and if I didn't get shipment, I didn't want any big hassle, but if I got the scrap, he would get it." . . .

In excluding this offered testimony, the district court relied on the Uniform Commercial Code's parol evidence rule, § 2-202 (Ill.Rev.Stat. Ch. 26, § 2-202), which provides:

[1] The Uniform Commercial Code has been adopted in Illinois and is identical to the 1972 official text of the code.

> Terms with respect to which the confirmatory memoranda of the parties agree or which are otherwise set forth in a writing intended by the parties as a final expression of their agreement with respect to such terms as are included therein may not be contradicted by evidence of any prior agreement or of a contemporaneous oral agreement but may be explained or supplemented
>
> (a) By course of dealing or usage of trade (§ 1-205) or by course of performance (§ 2-208); and
>
> (b) By evidence of consistent additional terms unless the court finds the writing to have been intended also as a complete and exclusive statement of the terms of the agreement.

The determination that the writings of the parties were intended to be a final expression of their agreement is to be made by the trial court. In light of Luria's acceptance of the terms stated in the Pielet writing, we agree with the district court's conclusion that the Pielet sales confirmation brought § 2-202 into play to bar Bloom's testimony.

Nevertheless, Pielet contends that § 2-202 is not applicable to this case. According to Pielet, Luria sued on an oral contract and therefore the parol evidence rule is not applicable because the writings of the parties were not the basis of the action but only collateral to it.

It is true that although these writings were relied on to satisfy the Code's Statute of Frauds, § 2-201, and to exclude parol evidence, Luria had to go outside these writings to prove to the jury the existence of an enforceable sales contract. But the writings are insufficient in themselves only because of two differing terms and are directly related to the contract sought to be proved.

As noted in 1 Anderson, UNIFORM COMMERCIAL CODE § 2-202:3 (2d 1970), § 2-202 of the Code

> extends (the operation of the parol evidence rule) to some degree to writings which are not the complete contract of the parties. The code itself refers to this fact in § 2-207(3) which provides that where a contract is established by the conduct of the parties, the terms of the contract consist, at least, of those terms on which the writings agree even though "the writings of the parties do not otherwise establish a contract.

In a case construing Illinois law, the court in Jones & McKnight Corp. v. Birdsboro Corporation, 320 F.Supp. 39 (N.D.Ill., E.D.1970) noted that where the existence of a sales contract was clear (in that case because of the actual delivery of goods and payment), § 2-202 "obviates the necessity of determining . . . whether the contract was oral or written." Id. at 42. Evidence of an alleged prior oral agreement cannot be used to contradict the terms on which the writings of the parties agree.

In this case, of course, the existence of a sales contract was in issue. At first glance, it is troublesome that Luria was allowed to introduce testimony of the September conversations between the parties to help establish its case while Pielet was denied the opportunity to introduce statements made in the course of those same conversations. However, the fairness of this result becomes clear upon examination of why it was necessary for Luria to use parol evidence to prove the existence of the sales contract. Pielet's sales confirmation and Luria's purchase confirmation differed on two important terms, delivery date and mode of shipment. Luria used undisputed parol evidence that there had been a "meeting of the minds" as to these terms prior to the confirmatory memoranda to support its position that these two discrepancies were due to inadvertence and clerical error on Luria's part rather than disagreement between the parties. If the writings had agreed on these two important terms, Pielet would be hard pressed to argue that no contract for sale existed. In fact, Bloom testified that had the Luria purchase confirmation been correct on these points he would have signed and returned it. (Trans. at 67.) Allowing one party to use parol evidence to clarify a mistake in a writing, does not open the flood gates to any and all parol evidence bearing on the agreement.[5]

Having found § 2-202 applicable, the next question is whether the excluded evidence contradicts or is inconsistent with the terms of the writings. Pielet argues that the offered testimony did not "contradict" but instead "explained or supplemented" the writings with "consistent additional terms." For this contention, Pielet relies upon Hunt Foods & Industries, Inc. v. Doliner, 26 A.D.2d 41, 270 N.Y.S.2d 937 (1966). In reversing the trial court's summary judgment for plaintiff, the court in Hunt held that evidence of an oral condition precedent did not contradict the terms of a written stock option which was unconditional on its face. Therefore evidence of the condition precedent should not have been barred by U.C.C. § 2-202. "In a sense any oral provision which would prevent the ripening of the obligations of a writing is inconsistent with the writing. But that obviously is not the sense in which the word is used. (Citation omitted.) To be inconsistent the term must contradict or negate a term of the writing." Id. at 43, 270 N.Y.S.2d at 940. This reasoning in Hunt was followed in Michael Schiavone & Sons, Inc. v. Securalloy Co., 312 F.Supp. 801 (D.Conn.1970). In that case, the court found that parol evidence that the quantity in a sales contract was "understood to be up to 500 tons cannot be said to be inconsistent with the terms of the written contract which specified the quantity as '500 Gross Ton.' " Id. at 804.

The narrow view of inconsistency espoused in these two cases has been criticized. In Snyder v. Herbert Greenbaum & Assoc., Inc., 38 Md.App. 144, 380 A.2d 618 (1977), the court held that parol evidence of a contractual right to unilateral rescission was inconsistent with a written agreement for the sale and installation of carpeting. The court defined "inconsistency" as used in § 2-202(b) as "the absence of reasonable harmony in terms of the language *and* respective obligations of the parties." Id. at 623 (emphasis in original) (citing U.C.C. § 1-205(4)). See also Southern Concrete v. Mableton Contractors, 407 F.Supp. 581 (N.D.Ga.1975), Aff'd memo., 569 F.2d 1154 (5th Cir. 1978).

---

[5] Pielet cites McCormick on Evidence § 56 (2d ed. 1972) for the proposition that once one party has introduced part of a conversation, the other party automatically has the right to introduce the remainder of the conversation relating to the same subject. This is a general rule of evidence based on materiality and relevance. The parol evidence rule, on the other hand, is a rule of substantive law. Evidence is excluded not because it is not credible or not relevant but because of a policy favoring the reliability of written representations of the terms of a contract.

We adopt this latter view of inconsistency and reject the view expressed in Hunt. Where writings intended by the parties to be a final expression of their agreement call for an unconditional sale of goods, parol evidence that the seller's obligations are conditioned upon receiving the goods from a particular supplier is inconsistent and must be excluded.

Had there been some additional reference such as "per our conversation" on the written confirmation indicating that oral agreements were meant to be incorporated into the writing, the result might have been different. See Ralston Purina v. Rooker, 346 So.2d 901 (Miss.1977), distinguishing Paymaster Oil Mill Company v. Mitchell, 319 So.2d 652 (Miss.1975).

We also note that Comment 3 of the Official Comment to § 2-202 provides, among other things:

> If the additional terms are such that, if agreed upon, they would certainly have been included in the document in the view of the court, then evidence of their alleged making must be kept from the trier of fact.

Pielet makes much of the fact that this transaction was an unusual one due to the size and the amount of scrap involved. Surely a term relieving Pielet of its obligations under the contract in the event its supplier failed it would have been included in the Pielet sales confirmation. . . .

The judgment appealed from is affirmed.

NOTES AND QUESTIONS:

1. Do you see any inconsistency in the court's finding that the parties' agreement was based on their conduct, not the exchange of forms, and the ultimate conclusion that the parol evidence rule applies?

2. In *Luria Bros.*, what term of the writing is contradicted by the alleged prior agreement?

BETACO, INC. V. CESSNA AIRCRAFT CO.
United States Court of Appeals, Seventh Circuit
32 F.3d 1126 (1994).

ROVNER, Circuit Judge.

Betaco, Inc. ("Betaco") agreed in 1990 to purchase a six-passenger CitationJet from the Cessna Aircraft Company ("Cessna"). Betaco's decision was based in part on Cessna's representation in a cover letter accompanying the purchase agreement that the new jet was "much faster, more efficient and has more range than the popular Citation I," a model with which Betaco was familiar. After advancing $150,000 toward the purchase of the new plane, Betaco became convinced that the CitationJet would not have a greater range than the Citation I with a full passenger load and decided to cancel the purchase. When Cessna refused to return Betaco's deposit, Betaco filed suit in diversity claiming, inter alia, that Cessna had breached an express warranty that the CitationJet had a greater range than the

Citation I. The district court rejected Cessna's contention that the purchase agreement signed by the parties was a fully integrated document that precluded Betaco's attempt to rely on this warranty. A jury concluded that the cover letter's representation as to the range of the plane did amount to an express warranty and that Cessna had breached this warranty, and Betaco was awarded damages of $150,000 with interest. We reverse the district court's entry of partial summary judgment in favor of Betaco on the threshold integration issue, concluding that a question of fact exists as to the parties' intent that can be resolved only after a factual hearing before the district court.

I. BACKGROUND

A. Facts

Betaco is a Delaware corporation headquartered in Indiana; it is a holding company that acquires aircraft for sale or lease to other companies and also for the personal use of J. George Mikelsons, the company owner. Betaco leases aircraft to Execujet and also to American Transair, an airline that Mikelsons founded in 1973 and of which he is the chairman and chief executive. Both companies interlock with Betaco. Mikelsons is himself an experienced pilot.

In late 1989, Betaco became interested in a new aircraft known as the CitationJet to be manufactured by Cessna, a Kansas corporation. Mikelsons contacted Cessna and asked for information about the forthcoming plane. On January 25, 1990, Cessna forwarded to Mikelsons a packet of materials accompanied by a cover letter which read as follows:

> Dear Mr. Mikelsons:
>
> We are extremely pleased to provide the material you requested about the phenomenal new CitationJet.
>
> Although a completely new design, the CitationJet has inherited all the quality, reliability, safety and economy of the more than 1600 Citations before it. At 437 miles per hour, the CitationJet is much faster, more efficient, and has more range than the popular Citation I. And its luxurious first-class cabin reflects a level of comfort and quality found only in much larger jets.
>
> And you get all this for less than an ordinary turbo-prop!
>
> If you have questions or need additional information about the CitationJet, please give me a call. I look forward to discussing this exciting new airplane with you.
>
> Sincerely,
>
> Robert T. Hubbard
> Regional Manager

. . . Enclosed with Hubbard's letter was a twenty-three page brochure providing general information about the CitationJet, including estimates of the jet's anticipated range and performance at various fuel and payload weights. A purchase agreement was also enclosed. The preliminary specifications attached and incorporated into that agreement as "Exhibit A" indicated that the CitationJet would have a full fuel range of 1,500 nautical miles, plus or minus four percent, under specified conditions.

Mikelsons signed the purchase agreement on January 29, 1990 and returned it to Cessna, whose administrative director, Ursula Jarvis, added her signature on February 8, 1990. The agreement occupied both sides of a single sheet of paper. As completed by the parties, the front side reflected a purchase price of $2.495 million and a preliminary delivery date of March, 1994, with Betaco reserving the right to opt for an earlier delivery in the event one were possible. The payment terms required Betaco to make an initial deposit of $50,000 upon execution of the contract, a second deposit of $100,000 when Cessna gave notice that the first prototype had been flown, and a third deposit of $125,000 at least six months in advance of delivery. The balance was to be paid when the plane was delivered. The agreement expressly incorporated the attached preliminary specifications, although Cessna reserved the right to revise them "whenever occasioned by product improvements or other good cause as long as such revisions do not result in a reduction in performance standards." Item number 9 on the front page stated:

> The signatories to this Agreement verify that they have read the complete Agreement, understand its contents and have full authority to bind and hereby do bind their respective parties.

Following this provision, in a final paragraph located just above the signature lines (written in capital lettering that distinguished this provision from the preceding provisions), the agreement stated:

> **PURCHASER AND SELLER ACKNOWLEDGE AND AGREE BY EXECUTION OF THIS AGREEMENT THAT THE TERMS AND CONDITIONS ON REVERSE SIDE HEREOF ARE EXPRESSLY MADE PART OF THIS AGREEMENT.** EXCEPT FOR THE EXPRESS TERMS OF SELLER'S WRITTEN LIMITED WARRANTIES PERTAINING TO THE AIRCRAFT, WHICH ARE SET FORTH IN THE SPECIFICATION (EXHIBIT A), SELLER MAKES NO REPRESENTATIONS OR WARRANTIES EXPRESS OR IMPLIED, OF MERCHANTABILITY, FITNESS FOR ANY PARTICULAR PURPOSE, OR OTHERWISE WHICH EXTEND BEYOND THE FACE HEREOF OR THEREOF. THE WRITTEN LIMITED WARRANTIES OF SELLER ACCOMPANYING ITS PRODUCT ARE IN LIEU OF ANY OTHER OBLIGATION OR LIABILITY WHATSOEVER BY REASON OF THE MANUFACTURE, SALE, LEASE OR USE OF THE WARRANTED PRODUCTS AND NO PERSON OR ENTITY IS AUTHORIZED TO MAKE ANY REPRESENTATIONS OR WARRANTIES OR TO ASSUME ANY OBLIGATIONS ON BEHALF OF SELLER. THE REMEDIES OF REPAIR OR REPLACEMENT SET FORTH IN SELLER'S WRITTEN LIMITED WARRANTIES ARE THE ONLY

> REMEDIES UNDER SUCH WARRANTIES OR THIS AGREEMENT. IN NO EVENT SHALL SELLER BE LIABLE FOR ANY INCIDENTAL OR CONSEQUENTIAL DAMAGES, INCLUDING, WITHOUT LIMITATION, LOSS OF PROFITS OR GOODWILL, LOSS OF USE, LOSS OF TIME, INCONVENIENCE, OR COMMERCIAL LOSS. THE ENGINES AND ENGINE ACCESSORIES ARE SEPARATELY WARRANTED BY THEIR MANUFACTURER AND ARE EXPRESSLY EXCLUDED FROM THE LIMITED WARRANTIES OF SELLER. **THE LAWS OF SOME STATES DO NOT PERMIT CERTAIN LIMITATIONS ON WARRANTIES OR REMEDIES. IN THE EVENT THAT SUCH A LAW APPLIES, THE FOREGOING EXCLUSIONS AND LIMITATIONS ARE AMENDED INSOFAR AND ONLY INSOFAR, AS REQUIRED BY SAID LAW.** (emphasis in original).

. . . On the reverse side, the agreement included the following integration clause among its "General Terms":

> This agreement is the only agreement controlling this purchase and sale, express or implied, either verbal or in writing, and is binding on Purchaser and Seller, their heirs, executors, administrators, successors or assigns. This Agreement, including the rights of Purchaser hereunder, may not be assigned by Purchaser except to a wholly-owned subsidiary or successor in interest by name change or otherwise and then only upon the prior written consent of Seller. Purchaser acknowledges receipt of a written copy of this Agreement which may not be modified in any way except by written agreement executed by both parties.

. . . In early 1992, Paul Ruley and another Betaco employee visited Cessna's facilities in order to select the radio and navigational equipment to be installed in the plane. In the course of his work as an administrator for Execujet and American Transair, Ruley assesses the suitability of aircraft for particular charter flights based on the distance, passenger load, fuel, aircraft weight, and runway requirements. After his visit to Cessna, Ruley completed some calculations concerning the CitationJet and showed them to Mikelsons. By Ruley's estimate, the new jet would have a greater range than its predecessor, the Citation I, when carrying three to five passengers; but with a full passenger load of six (plus two crew members), the CitationJet would have a range no greater than or slightly less than that of the Citation I. Ruley also believed that the new plane would not meet the full fuel range of 1,500 nautical miles set forth in the preliminary specifications.

After seeing Ruley's numbers, Mikelsons contacted Cessna in March or April 1992. The testimony at trial was in conflict as to exactly what Cessna personnel told Mikelsons about the range of the new plane. In any case, Mikelsons was not satisfied that the CitationJet would live up to his expectations and decided to cancel the purchase. On April 16, 1992, Mick Hoveskeland of Cessna wrote to Mikelsons accepting the cancellation and offering to apply Betaco's deposit toward the purchase of another aircraft. Cessna subsequently refused Betaco's demand for a return of the deposit, however, invoking the contract's proviso that "all cash deposits shall be retained by [Cessna] not as a forfeiture but as liquidated damages for default if this Agreement is canceled or terminated by [Betaco] for any cause whatsoever . . . . " Betaco proceeded to file this suit.

B. Proceedings Below

Betaco filed a three-count complaint against Cessna on May 12, 1992. In Count I, Betaco alleged that Cessna had breached the warranty contained in the preliminary specifications that the CitationJet would have a full fuel range of 1,500 nautical miles, plus or minus four percent. In Count II, Betaco alleged that Cessna had also expressly warranted by way of the cover letter accompanying the purchase agreement that the CitationJet would have a range greater than that of the Citation I, and that Cessna had breached this warranty as well. . . .

At the completion of discovery, the parties filed cross-motions for partial summary judgment on Count II. Betaco asked the Court to find as a matter of law that Cessna had expressly warranted that the CitationJet would have a range greater than the range of the Citation I. Cessna asked the Court to find that the purchase agreement was a fully integrated document that excluded any warranties not set forth within the agreement itself.

The district court granted partial summary judgment in favor of Betaco on Count II. The court found that Hubbard's January 25, 1990 cover letter to Mikelsons did, in fact, contain an express warranty to the effect that the range of the CitationJet would exceed the range of the Citation I. The court then considered whether the purchase agreement was a fully integrated document that would rule out extrinsic evidence concerning such an independent express warranty. Although the court acknowledged that the terms of the agreement declared it to be fully integrated and disclaimed any express warranties beyond its four corners, the court nonetheless concluded that the parties did not intend the contract to be the sole and exclusive reflection of their agreement. The court reasoned that Hubbard's representation as to the range of the CitationJet vis à vis the Citation I was not the type of term that would necessarily have been included in the contract itself; it was not, for example, so central to the agreement that Betaco would have insisted that it be written into the pre-printed purchase agreement. At the same time, the fact that the representation had been made in the cover letter accompanying the purchase agreement (which Mikelsons signed shortly after he received it) suggested to the court that the parties considered that representation to be the basis of their bargain. Finally, the court noted that the purchase agreement had not been the subject of extensive negotiation, and that Mikelsons had simply signed it without first seeking the counsel of an attorney. "Not only does this tend to excuse Betaco for failing to have the representations [as to the relative range of the jet] included in the Purchase Agreement, but it minimizes the impact of the warranty limitation and contract integration clauses in the Purchase Agreement." Mem.Op. at 8. . . .

The case proceeded to trial on Counts I and II. In the midst of trial, the court granted Cessna's motion to reconsider the summary judgment ruling on Count II to the extent of allowing the jury to decide whether the representation in Hubbard's letter amounted to a warranty. The jury subsequently found in Betaco's favor on Count II, concluding that Hubbard's letter did contain a warranty that the CitationJet's range exceeded that of the Citation I and that Cessna had breached this warranty. . . . The district court subsequently entered judgment in Betaco's favor on Count II and ordered Cessna to pay damages of

$150,000 (the amount of the deposit), prejudgment interest of $17,630.14, and post-judgment interest at the rate of 3.54 percent.

II. ANALYSIS

The sole issue before us is whether the district court erred in concluding that the contract signed by Betaco and Cessna was not a fully integrated contract containing a complete and exclusive statement of the parties' agreement. Cessna does not challenge the jury's determination that Hubbard's representation as to the relative range of the CitationJet constituted an express warranty. Rather, Cessna's contention is that because the purchase agreement was, contrary to the district court's determination, fully integrated, Betaco was precluded from attempting to establish any additional warranty via extrinsic evidence (in this case, Hubbard's cover letter). Both parties agree that we should look to Kansas law in resolving this issue; their contract contains a provision that both the agreement and the parties' legal relationship shall be determined in accordance with Kansas commercial law, including the Uniform Commercial Code ("U.C.C.") as adopted by the Kansas legislature. . . .

The provision of the U.C.C. that is central to this case is U.C.C. section 2-202, found at section 84-2-202 of the Kansas Statutes:

> Final written expression: Parol or extrinsic evidence. Terms with respect to which the confirmatory memoranda of the parties agree or which are otherwise set forth in a writing intended by the parties as a final expression of their agreement with respect to such terms as are included therein may not be contradicted by evidence of any prior agreement or of a contemporaneous oral agreement but may be explained or supplemented
>
> (a) by course of dealing or usage of trade (section 84-1-205) or by course of performance (section 84-2-208); and
>
> (b) by evidence of consistent additional terms unless the court finds the writing to have been intended also as a complete and exclusive statement of the terms of the agreement.

Kan.Stat.Ann. § 84-2-202. The parties agree that they intended the signed purchase contract as a final expression of the terms set forth within its four corners. Betaco, however, has relied on Hubbard's cover letter as evidence of a "consistent additional term" of the agreement. Section 2-202(b) bars that evidence (and thus Betaco's claim for breach of the warranty in Hubbard's letter) if the parties intended the signed contract to be the "complete and exclusive" statement of their agreement.

An initial question arises as to the appropriate standard of review. Cessna urges us to review the district court's decision de novo, whereas Betaco contends that the court's ruling was a factual determination that we may review for clear error only.

Although the rule set forth in section 2-202 is superficially a rule of evidence, Kansas does not treat it as such: " 'The parol evidence rule is not a rule of evidence, but of substantive law. Its applicability is for the court to determine, and, when the result is reached it is a conclusion of substantive law.' " In re Estate of Goff, 191 Kan. 17, 379 P.2d 225, 234 (1963) (quoting Phipps v. Union Stock Yards Nat'l Bank, 140 Kan. 193, 34 P.2d 561, 563 (1934)); see also Prophet v. Builders, Inc., 204 Kan. 268, 462 P.2d 122, 125 (1969); Willner v. University of Kansas, 848 F.2d 1020, 1022 (10th Cir.1988) (per curiam), cert. denied, 488 U.S. 1011, 109 S.Ct. 797, 102 L.Ed.2d 788 (1989). We have likewise treated the rule as a substantive one, and have accordingly considered the determination of whether or not an agreement was completely integrated to be a legal determination subject to de novo review. Merk v. Jewel Food Stores, 945 F.2d 889, 893 (7th Cir.1991), cert. denied, 504 U.S. 914, 112 S.Ct. 1951, 118 L.Ed.2d 555 (1992); Calder v. Camp Grove State Bank, 892 F.2d 629, 632 (7th Cir.1990) (applying Illinois law).

Betaco correctly points out, however, that insofar as this determination turns on the intent of the contracting parties, it poses a factual question. See Willner, 848 F.2d at 1022 n. 3; Transamerica Oil Corp. v. Lynes, Inc., 723 F.2d 758, 763 (10th Cir.1983). Thus, in cases where the integration assessment amounts to "a predominantly factual inquiry, revolving around the unwritten intentions of the parties instead of interpretation of a formal integration clause," courts have treated the district court's determination as a finding of fact subject to review only for clear error. Northwest Cent. Pipeline Corp. v. JER Partnership, 943 F.2d 1219, 1225 (10th Cir.1991); Transamerica Oil, 723 F.2d at 763; see also In re Pearson Bros. Co., 787 F.2d 1157, 1161 (7th Cir.1986) ("When a court interpreting a contract goes beyond the four corners of the contract and considers extrinsic evidence, the court's determination of the parties' intent is a finding of fact.").

Yet, in this case, the district court decided the question on summary judgment. Essentially, the court determined that the evidence before it could only be construed in one way, and that Betaco was entitled to judgment as a matter of law on the integration issue. Thus, the precise question before us is not who should prevail ultimately on the integration issue, but whether it was appropriate to enter partial summary judgment in favor of Betaco and against Cessna on the matter. Our review of that particular determination is of course, de novo, as it would be in any other appeal from the grant of summary judgment. . . . We examine the record in the light most favorable to Cessna, granting it the benefit of all reasonable inferences that may be drawn from the evidence. . . .

The familiar rule of contractual interpretation is that absent an ambiguity, the intent of the parties is to be determined from the face of the contract, without resort to extrinsic evidence. . . . Yet, the drafters of section 2-202 rejected any presumption that a written contract sets forth the parties' entire agreement. See Kan.Stat.Ann. § 84-2-202, Official U.C.C. Comment (1); Mid Continent Cabinetry, Inc. v. George Koch Sons, Inc., 1991 WL 151074, at (D.Kan. July 11, 1991). Instead, in ascertaining whether the parties intended their contract to be completely integrated, a court looks beyond the four corners of the document to the circumstances surrounding the transaction, "including the words and actions of the parties." Burge v. Frey, 545 F.Supp. 1160, 1170 (D.Kan.1982). Mid Continent Cabinetry identifies the relevant considerations:

> The focus is on the intent of the parties. Sierra Diesel Injection Service v. Burroughs Corp., 890 F.2d 108, 112 (9th Cir.1989). Section 2-202 does not offer any tests for determining if the parties intended their written agreement to be integrated. Comment three to § 2-202 offers one measure of when a statement is complete and exclusive: "If the additional terms are such that, if agreed upon, they would certainly have been included in the document in the view of the court, then evidence of their alleged making must be kept from the trier of fact." The courts have looked to several factors, not just the writing, in deciding if the writing is integrated. These factors include merger or integration clauses, B. Clark & C. Smith, The Law of Product Warranties 4.04[1] and [2] at 4-37-4-40 (1984) (1990 Supp.); disclaimer clauses, see, e.g., St. Croix Printing Equipment, Inc. v. Rockwell Intern. Corp., [428 N.W.2d 877, 880 (Minn.App.1988)]; the nature and scope of prior negotiations and any alleged extrinsic terms, J. White and R. Summers, Uniform Commercial Code § 2-10 at 108 (3d ed. 1988); and the sophistication of the parties, Sierra Diesel Injection Service, 890 F.2d at 112.

1991 WL 151074, at *8. See also Transamerica Oil, 723 F.2d at 763; Ray Martin Painting, Inc. v. Ameron, Inc., 638 F.Supp. 768, 773 (D.Kan.1986).

We look first to the warranty limitation and integration clauses of the purchase agreement, as these speak directly to the completeness and exclusivity of the contract. The warranty limitation clause states that "[e]xcept for the express terms of seller's written limited warranties pertaining to the aircraft, which are set forth in the specification (Exhibit A), [Cessna] makes no representations or warranties express or implied, of merchantability, fitness for any particular purpose, or otherwise *which extend beyond the face hereof or thereof*." (Emphasis supplied.) The clause goes on to admonish the buyer that no individual is authorized to make representations or warranties on behalf of Cessna. On its face, this clause might be construed to disavow the types of representations found in Hubbard's letter to Mikelsons. However, as a general rule, express warranties, once made, cannot be so easily disclaimed. Section 2-316(1) of the Kansas U.C.C. provides that "subject to the provisions of this article on parol or extrinsic evidence (K.S.A. § 84-2-202), negation or limitation [of an express warranty] is inoperative to the extent such construction is unreasonable." Kan.Stat.Ann. § 84-2-316(1); see L.S. Heath & Son, Inc. v. AT & T Info. Sys., Inc., 9 F.3d 561, 570 (7th Cir.1993); Transamerica Oil, 723 F.2d at 762. The commentary explains that the purpose of this provision is to "protect a buyer from unexpected and unbargained language of disclaimer." Kans.Stat.Ann. 84-2-316(1), Official U.C.C. Comment (1); see also Kan.Stat.Ann. 84-2-313, Official U.C.C. Comment (4), Kansas Comment 1983; Hemmert Agric. Aviation, Inc. v. Mid-Continent Aircraft Corp., 663 F.Supp. 1546, 1553 (D.Kan.1987); Ray Martin Painting, 638 F.Supp. at 772-73. On the other hand, the disclaimer rule is, by its express terms, subject to the provisions of section 2-202 (see Kan.Stat.Ann. 84-2-316(1) & Kansas Comment 1983); thus, if the signed contract is deemed fully integrated, the plaintiff is precluded from attempting to establish any express warranty outside the signed contract. Jordan v. Doonan Truck & Equip., Inc., 220 Kan. 431, 552 P.2d 881, 884 (1976); Ray Martin Painting, 638 F.Supp. at 774; see also Jack Richards Aircraft Sales, Inc. v. Vaughn, 203 Kan. 967, 457 P.2d 691, 696 (1969); Prophet, 462 P.2d at 125-26.

We thus turn to the integration clause of the contract. Although not dispositive, "the presence of a merger clause is strong evidence that the parties intended the writing to be the complete and exclusive agreement between them...." L.S. Heath & Son, Inc., 9 F.3d at 569 (citing Sierra Diesel, 890 F.2d at 112; R. Anderson, Uniform Commercial Code, § 2-202:25 (1983)); see also Ray Martin Painting, 638 F.Supp. at 773-74. Here the clause states that "[t]his agreement is the *only* agreement controlling this purchase and sale, express or implied, either verbal or in writing, and is binding on Purchaser and Seller" and that the agreement "may not be modified in any way except by written agreement executed by both parties." (Emphasis supplied.)[2] The language is simple and straightforward; and Betaco does not suggest that a reasonable buyer would find it difficult to comprehend. On the other hand, Betaco does note, as the district court did (Mem.Op. at 8), that this was, like most other provisions in the contract, a pre-printed clause that was not the subject of negotiation by the parties. Yet, that fact alone does not render the provision unenforceable. See Northwestern Nat'l Ins. Co. v. Donovan, 916 F.2d 372, 377 (7th Cir.1990). The clause was not buried in fine print, nor was it written so as to be opaque. See id. It was relegated to the back of the contract rather than the front, but the front page admonished the signatories in bold, capitalized lettering that the terms on the back were part of the agreement, and although the reverse side contained a number of provisions, they were neither so many nor so complicated that the reader would have given up before he or she reached the integration clause. Mikelsons signed the contract, and there is no dispute that he had the opportunity to review it in as much detail as he wished before signing it. Under these circumstances, the integration provision should have come as no surprise to Betaco. Compare Transamerica Oil, 723 F.2d at 763 (where plaintiff's order was taken over telephone, document that plaintiff received and signed upon delivery did not constitute fully integrated agreement); Hemmert, 663 F.Supp. at 1553 (same). In our view, therefore, the clause is strong evidence that the parties intended and agreed for the signed contract to be the complete embodiment of their agreement.

The district court focused on another circumstance that courts frequently consider in assessing the degree to which a contract is integrated: is the term contained in a purported warranty outside the contract one that the parties would have included in the contract itself had they intended it to be part of the agreement? U.C.C. § 2-202, Official Comment (3); Mid-Continent Cabinetry, 1991 WL 151074, at *8. The court thought that Hubbard's representation as to the relative range of the CitationJet was not such a term, although neither the court nor Betaco has cited any evidence in the record to support that proposition. The court did note that "[t]he representation made by Mr. Hubbard was not so formally presented nor central to the purchase that Mr. Mikelsons of Betaco would most likely have insisted it be included, especially where the Purchase Agreement was a standard form. The representation did not include the word 'warranty,' a red flag that might have clued a non-attorney into the necessity of including it in the Purchase Agreement." Mem.Op. at 7. Our analysis is somewhat different on this score, however.

---

[2] Betaco points out that the integration clause purports only to disavow other agreements, not other warranties. We do not find the distinction persuasive, however. The essence of the integration inquiry, after all, is whether the parties intended their written contract to embody the entirety of their agreement; if so, extrinsic evidence of an additional warranty that Cessna purportedly made cannot be admitted. Thus, although the integration clause speaks in terms of agreements rather than warranties, if it is given effect and the signed purchase contract is deemed to be a fully integrated agreement, it effectively operates so as to preclude the plaintiff from relying on purported warranties beyond the four corners of that agreement.

We are not persuaded that the range of the aircraft was not something that certainly would be included in the agreement. On the contrary, the specifications made part of the contract do contain an express representation as to the range of the CitationJet, and, in fact, it was that warranty that formed the basis for Count I of Betaco's complaint.[3] In that sense, an extraneous reference to the range of the aircraft arguably is less like a supplemental term on a subject as to which the contract is otherwise silent, and more like a potentially conflicting term that section 2-202 would explicitly exclude from admission into evidence. See generally Souder v. Tri-County Refrigeration Co., 190 Kan. 207, 373 P.2d 155, 159-60 (1962) (noting the distinction between using extrinsic evidence to explain or supplement the contract and using it to vary the terms of the agreement).[4]

The context of the representation does not alter our analysis in this regard. It may well be, as the district court emphasized, that because the statement as to the relative range of the CitationJet was contained in the cover letter accompanying the purchase agreement, Mr. Mikelsons may have given it more weight than he would a more isolated statement. Mem.Op. at 7. At the same time, as the court pointed out, the reference was informal, without language that might alert the reader that the contract should include a comparable provision. Id. But in our view, one might just as readily infer from this that the contents of the letter were not meant to supplement the purchase agreement. Recall the wording of the passage on which Betaco relies: "At 437 miles per hour, the CitationJet is much faster, more efficient, and has more range than the popular Citation I." Like the balance of the letter, this statement is long on adjectives and short on details-how much faster? how much more efficient? how much more range?. . . Consider, in contrast, the following excerpt from the specifications incorporated into the purchase agreement:

2. ESTIMATED PERFORMANCE (Preliminary)

Conditions:

All estimated performance data are based on a standard aircraft and International Standard Atmosphere. Takeoff and landing field lengths are based on level, hard surface, dry runways with zero wind.

---

[3] The informational brochure enclosed with the agreement also contains a number of references to the plane's estimated range at various loads. Betaco has not alleged that any of these estimates were inaccurate. However, the brochure did contain a page listing in highly cursory fashion (less than fifty words) the purported "Benefits" of owning a CitationJet (App. 141), including a "substantial increase over the Citation I" in "performance" and "operating efficiency." In its complaint, Betaco cited this document along with Hubbard's letter in support of the Count II breach of warranty claim, but Betaco does not rely on it here.

[4] In footnote 6 of its opinion, the district court misappropriates the dissent's explanation of the parol evidence rule in Intercorp., Inc. v. Pennzoil Co., 877 F.2d 1524 (11th Cir.1989). There, Judge Henderson noted that evidence of oral or written terms outside the four corners of the contract traditionally has been excluded " 'not because doubt exists concerning the terms' reliability, but rather because the terms are irrelevant, since the parties superseded them in the final integrated writing.' " Id. at 1537 (quoting M. Metzger, The Parol Evidence Rule: Promissory Estoppel's Next Conquest?, 36 Vand.L.Rev. 1383, 1390 (1983)). The district court found this language particularly pertinent to the case at bar, pointing out that "there is no doubt as to the reliability of the additional terms [in Hubbard's letter] because they are in writing." Mem.Op. at 6-7 n. 6. Yet, Judge Henderson's point is that the extrinsic terms, reliable or otherwise, are irrelevant where the parties record their agreement in a final, integrated writing. The very purpose of the parol evidence rule is to honor final, integrated agreements signed by autonomous parties, and excluding extraneous terms achieves that purpose. See 877 F.2d at 1537.

Range +/- 4% (Includes Takeoff, Climb, Cruise at 41,000 Feet, Descent and 45-Minute Reserve)	At 10,000 lbs (4536 kg) TOGW 1500 nautical miles (2779 km) with full fuel
Stall Speed (Landing Configuration)	81 knots (150 km/hr) (93 MPH) CAS at 9500 lbs (4309 kg)
Maximum Altitude	41,000 ft (12,497 m)
Single Engine Climb Rate (Sea Level, ISA, 10,000 lbs)	1070 feet per minute
Takeoff Runway Length (Sea Level, ISA, Balanced Field Length per FAR 25)	2960 ft (902 m) at 10,000 lbs (4536 kg)
Landing Runway Length (Sea Level, ISA, per FAR 25)	2800 ft (854 m) at 9500 lbs (4309 kg)
Cruising Speed +/- 3% (Maximum Cruise Thrust, ISA Conditions at 35,000 Feet)	380 kts (704 km/hr) (437 mph) TAS at 8500 lbs (3856 kg) cruise weight

. . . This summary of the aircraft's performance capabilities is, in stark contrast to the letter, quite precise and quite explicit about the assumptions underlying each of the estimates. Given the marked difference in style and detail between these specifications and the indeterminate braggadocio in the cover letter, we find it somewhat implausible that the parties might have considered the "more range" reference to be part of their agreement yet failed to include it in the purchase contract with the level of specificity characteristic of that document.

Finally, we do not find it particularly significant that Mikelsons did not consult a lawyer before signing the purchase agreement. Again, the contract was neither lengthy nor obtuse. Nor was this a contract of adhesion. These were two seemingly sophisticated parties entering into a commercial agreement, and Mikelsons' significant experience as a pilot, as an airline executive, and as a purchaser of an earlier model of the Citation aircraft surely went a long way toward balancing whatever advantage Cessna may have enjoyed as the drafter of the agreement. See Bowers Mfg. Co. v. Chicago Mach. Tool Co., 117 Ill.App.3d 226, 72 Ill.Dec. 756, 761, 453 N.E.2d 61, 66 (1983) ("the courts are less reluctant to hold educated businessmen to the terms of contracts to which they have entered than consumers dealing with skilled corporate sellers") (quoted with approval in Ray Martin Painting, 638 F.Supp. at 773); see also Binks Mfg. Co. v. National Presto Indus., Inc., 709 F.2d 1109, 1116 (7th Cir.1983). Furthermore, there is no evidence that the contract was tainted by fraud, mutual mistake, or any other circumstance that would call into question the binding nature of the agreement. See generally Prophet, 462 P.2d at 126. That Betaco chose not to have the contract reviewed by an attorney before Mikelsons signed it does not, standing alone, permit Betaco to escape the operation of the terms it signed on to, including the integration clause. As the Kansas Supreme Court has stated:

> This court follows the general rule that a contracting party is under a duty to learn the contents of a written contract before signing it. Sutherland v. Sutherland, 187 Kan. 599, 610, 358 P.2d 776 (1961). We have interpreted this duty to include the duty to obtain a reading and explanation of the contract, and we have held that the negligent failure to do so will estop the contracting party from avoiding the contract on the ground of ignorance of its contents. Maltby v. Sumner, 169 Kan. 417, Syl. 5, 219 P.2d 395 (1950). As a result of this duty, a person who signs a written contract is bound by its terms regardless of his or her failure to read and understand its terms. Rosenbaum v. Texas Energies, Inc., 241 Kan. 295, 736 P.2d 888, 891-92 (1987). Accord Albers v. Nelson, 248 Kan. 575, 809 P.2d 1194, 1197 (1991); Washington v. Claassen, 218 Kan. 577, 545 P.2d 387, 390-91 (1976); see also Paper Express, Ltd. v. Pfankuch Maschinen GmbH, 972 F.2d 753, 757 (7th Cir.1992); Northwestern Nat'l Ins. Co. v. Donovan, supra, 916 F.2d at 378.

That we would make this assumption should come as no surprise to Betaco, for in signing the contract, Mikelsons also assented to its provision that "[t]he signatories to this Agreement verify that they have read the complete Agreement, understand its contents and have full authority to bind and hereby do bind their respective parties."

The circumstances identified by the district court do not, in sum, establish as a matter of law that the purchase agreement was not fully integrated and that extrinsic evidence of additional, consistent terms was therefore admissible. Nor has Betaco identified anything more in the record that would support partial summary judgment in its favor on this question. The district court's decision to grant partial summary judgment in favor of Betaco and against Cessna therefore must be reversed, and the jury's verdict (which was based upon the extrinsic evidence admitted pursuant to the district court's summary judgment ruling) must be vacated.

Two options remain for us at this juncture: we may reverse the denial of Cessna's cross-motion for partial summary judgment and deem the signed purchase agreement fully integrated as a matter of law (thus entitling Cessna to judgment on Count II) or, in the event we detect factual disputes that preclude this determination on summary judgment, remand the case for a bench hearing (as the applicability of section 2-202 is, as we have noted above, a question for the court rather than the jury). We are somewhat surprised to note that although the parties ask us to draw diametrically opposed conclusions from the evidence bearing on the integration issue, neither has ever (either on appeal or in the district court) suggested that a factual hearing might be necessary in order to resolve their dispute. Instead, both parties appear confident that the issue can simply be decided one way or the other based on the summary judgment record presented to the district court.

If the only evidence offered on the question of whether the parties meant the signed purchase agreement to be fully integrated had been the two documents on which the district court relied-the agreement itself (and in particular, the warranty limitation and integration clauses of that agreement) along with the cover letter from Hubbard-we might be inclined to agree that no hearing was necessary to assess the parties' intent. The purchase agreement contains, as we have discussed above, a straightforward integration clause which, coupled with the express disclaimer of other warranties, suggests that the parties' understanding did not extend beyond the four corners of the signed contract. Against that, the very casual nature of the cover letter's remark attributing "more range" to the new CitationJet than its predecessor is, at best, only weak evidence to the contrary, particularly when the contract itself addresses the range of the new aircraft in quite specific terms. Thus, we would be most reluctant to hold that Hubbard's letter, standing alone, would provide enough support for the notion that the contract was not a complete reflection of the parties' understanding to avoid summary judgment.

But there is a bit more to the evidence that Betaco tendered. In a brief affidavit, Mikelsons offered the following background averments regarding Hubbard's "more range" remark:

> 3. In late 1989 and prior to my receipt of Robert Hubbard's letter of January 25, 1990, and my execution of the Purchase Agreement dated January 29, 1990, I had several telephone conversations with Mr. Hubbard and other Cessna representatives who were aware of my interest in possibly purchasing a CitationJet.
>
> 4. During those conversations, I expressed the requirement that the CitationJet have or possess greater range (that is, available flying distance) than the Cessna Citation I which Betaco owned and that I occasionally flew. The Cessna representatives assured me that the range of the CitationJet was greater than the range of the Citation I.
>
> 5. I specifically relied on the verbal representations and statements of Cessna representatives and Robert Hubbard's letter confirming his prior verbal representation that the range of the CitationJet was greater than that of the Citation I when I executed the Purchase Agreement.

. . . Again to our surprise, neither party has so much as mentioned these averments in the briefing, but we find them to be significant. In part they bear on a question that the jury has already decided-did Cessna expressly warrant that the CitationJet had a range greater than the Citation I's? . . . But they also bear in part on whether the purchase agreement, although it did address the range of the CitationJet, set forth the parties' entire understanding as to the range capabilities of the plane, particularly as compared to the earlier model. If, in fact, there were substantial discussions preceding Betaco's commitment to the purchase of the CitationJet focusing specifically on the range of the new jet vis à vis the

Citation I, one might infer that the signed agreement did not, ultimately, embody the complete agreement between the parties. In that respect, the case could be viewed as being more like Transamerica Oil, for example, where the court concluded that the parties' agreement extended beyond the signed "Sales and Service Invoice" to include the representations that the plaintiff had seen in trade journals and the assurances that the seller had given it over the telephone prior to the purchase. 723 F.2d at 761, 763. We do not mean to suggest that the evidence ought to be viewed in that way, of course. Although Mikelsons' affidavit appears to characterize Hubbard's letter as the culmination of prior discussions about the range of the new plane, the wording of the letter is far more consistent with that of a standard promotional letter than a confirmation of prior discussions concerning what Betaco contends was an essential contract term. Moreover, as we have noted, Mikelsons was an apparently sophisticated businessman who had the opportunity to review the contract at length before deciding to purchase, very much in contrast to the situation in Transamerica Oil. Still, as we consider the merits of Cessna's cross-motion for summary judgment, we must take care to give Betaco the benefit of every reasonable inference that may be drawn from the record. Construed favorably to Betaco, we believe that Mikelsons' affidavit raises a question of fact as to whether the parties considered the purchase contract to be the complete and exclusive statement of their agreement.

Both parties seem to have forgotten that where competing inferences may be drawn from facts that are otherwise undisputed, summary judgment is improper. See Texas Refrigeration Supply, Inc. v. FDIC, 953 F.2d 975, 982 (5th Cir.1992) (citing Phillips Oil Co. v. OKC Corp., 812 F.2d 265, 274 n. 15 (5th Cir.), cert. denied, 484 U.S. 851, 108 S.Ct. 152, 98 L.Ed.2d 107 (1987)); see generally Sarsha v. Sears, Roebuck & Co., 3 F.3d 1035, 1041 (7th Cir.1993) (collecting cases). Just as we believe that plausible inferences from the record rendered partial summary judgment in Betaco's favor on the integration issue improper, so we believe that contrary inferences preclude summary judgment in favor of Cessna. We therefore remand the case for a hearing in which the district judge will sit as a finder of fact and decide, based on whatever evidence the parties choose to submit, whether the parties intended the purchase agreement to be the complete embodiment of their understanding or not. In the event the court answers this question in the affirmative, of course, the rule set forth in section 2-202 would bar Betaco's warranty claim and compel the entry of final judgment in Cessna's favor on Count II of the complaint. We express no opinion as to the appropriate outcome of this hearing; that is a matter for the district court to decide based on the totality of the circumstances and the resolution of the competing inferences that the evidence permits.

III. CONCLUSION

Because we find that the record before the court on summary judgment was reasonably subject to contrary assessments of whether the parties intended their signed contract to be the complete embodiment of their agreement, we REVERSE the entry of partial summary judgment against Cessna on this question and VACATE the final judgment subsequently entered in favor of Betaco on Count II of the complaint. The case is REMANDED for a factual hearing before the bench on the integration issue and for appropriate disposition based on the outcome of that hearing. . . .

NOTES AND QUESTIONS:

1. What, if any, effect does the presence of the integration clause have on the issue of full versus partial integration?

2. The court preliminarily discusses whether the parol evidence rule is procedural or substantive. Why does this matter in a federal court proceeding?

3. What, if any, importance should be attached to the parties' stipulation that the signed purchase contract was a final expression of the terms set forth in the document? Why didn't this automatically bar introduction of any prior statement? Should this particular statement be barred in light of such stipulation and the express terms of the writing?

---

2. "Exceptions"*

MITCHILL V. LATH
Court of Appeals of New York
160 N.E. 646 (1928).

ANDREWS, Justice.

In the fall of 1923 the Laths owned a farm. This they wished to sell. Across the road, on land belonging to Lieutenant Governor Lunn, they had an icehouse which they might remove. Mrs. Mitchill looked over the land with a view to its purchase. She found the icehouse objectionable. Thereupon "the defendants orally promised and agreed, for and in consideration of the purchase of their farm by the plaintiff, to remove the said icehouse in the spring of 1924." Relying upon this promise, she made a written contract to buy the property for $8,400, for cash and mortgage and containing various provisions usual in such papers. Later receiving a deed, she entered into possession, and has spent considerable sums in improving the property for use as a summer residence. The defendants have not fulfilled their promise as to the icehouse, and do not intend to do so. We are not dealing, however, with their moral delinquencies. The question before us is whether their oral agreement may be enforced in a court of equity.

This requires a discussion of the parol evidence rule - a rule of law which defines the limits of the contract to be construed. Glackin v. Bennett, 226 Mass. 316, 115 N. E. 490. It is more than a rule of evidence, and oral testimony, even if admitted, will not control the written contract (O'Malley v. Grady, 222 Mass. 202, 109 N. E. 829), unless admitted without objection (Brady v. Nally, 151 N. Y. 258, 45 N. E. 547). It applies, however, to attempts to modify such a contract by parol. It does not affect a parol collateral contract distinct from and independent of the written agreement. It is, at times, troublesome to draw the line. Williston, in his work on Contracts (section 637) points out the difficulty. "Two entirely distinct contracts," he says, "each for a separate consideration, may be made at the same time, and will be distinct legally. Where, however, one agreement is entered into wholly or partly in consideration of the simultaneous agreement to enter into another, the transactions

---

* Although contract scholars typically refer to the following doctrines as "exceptions," the authors would argue that these "exceptions" are "distinctions without a difference," ultimately amounting to a monument of nothingness.

are necessarily bound together. . . . Then if one of the agreements is oral and the other in writing, the problem arises whether the bond is sufficiently close to prevent proof of the oral agreement." That is the situation here. It is claimed that the defendants are called upon to do more than is required by their written contract in connection with the sale as to which it deals.

The principle may be clear, but it can be given effect by no mechanical rule. As so often happens it is a matter of degree, for, as Prof. Williston also says, where a contract contains several promises on each side it is not difficult to put any one of them in the form of a collateral agreement. If this were enough, written contracts might always be modified by parol. Not form, but substance, is the test.

In applying this test, the policy of our courts is to be considered. We have believed that the purpose behind the rule was a wise one, not easily to be abandoned. Notwithstanding injustice here and there, on the whole it works for good. Old precedents and principles are not to be lightly cast aside, unless it is certain that they are an obstruction under present conditions. New York has been less open to arguments that would modify this particular rule, than some jurisdictions elsewhere. Thus in Eighmie v. Taylor, 98 N. Y. 288, it was held that a parol warranty might not be shown, although no warranties were contained in the writing.

Under our decisions before such an oral agreement as the present is received to vary the written contract, at least three conditions must exist: (1) The agreement must in form be a collateral one; (2) it must not contradict express or implied provisions of the written contract; (3) it must be one that parties would not ordinarily be expected to embody in the writing, or, put in another way, an inspection of the written contract, read in the light of surrounding circumstances, must not indicate that the writing appears "to contain the engagements of the parties, and to define the object and measure the extent of such engagement." Or, again, it must not be so clearly connected with the principal transaction as to be part and parcel of it.

The respondent does not satisfy the third of these requirements. It may be, not the second. We have a written contract for the purchase and sale of land. The buyer is to pay $8,400 in the way described. She is also to pay her portion of any rents, interest on mortgages, insurance premiums, and water meter charges. She may have a survey made of the premises. On their part, the sellers are to give a full covenant deed of the premises as described, or as they may be described by the surveyor, if the survey is had, executed, and acknowledged at their own expense; they sell the personal property on the farm and represent they own it; they agree that all amounts paid them on the contract and the expense of examining the title shall be a lien on the property; they assume the risk of loss or damage by fire until the deed is delivered; and they agree to pay the broker his commissions. Are they to do more? Or is such a claim inconsistent with these precise provisions? It could not be shown that the plaintiff was to pay $500 additional. Is it also implied that the defendants are not to do anything unexpressed in the writing?

That we need not decide. At least, however, an inspection of this contract shows a full and complete agreement, setting forth in detail the obligations of each party. On reading it, one would conclude that the reciprocal obligations of the parties were fully detailed. Nor would his opinion alter if he knew the surrounding circumstances. The presence of the icehouse, even the knowledge that Mrs. Mitchill thought it objectionable, would not lead to the belief that a separate agreement existed with regard to it. Were such an agreement made it would seem most natural that the inquirer should find it in the contract. Collateral in form it is found to be, but it is closely related to the subject dealt with in the written agreement - so closely that we hold it may not be proved.

Where the line between the competent and the incompetent is narrow the citation of authorities is of slight use. Each represents the judgment of the court on the precise facts before it. How closely bound to the contract is the supposed collateral agreement is the decisive factor in each case. But reference may be made to Johnson v. Oppenheim, 55 N. Y. 280, 292; Thomas v. Scutt, 127 N. Y. 133, 27 N. E. 961; Eighmie v. Taylor, 98 N. Y. 288; Stowell v. Greenwich Ins. Co., 163 N. Y. 298, 57 N. E. 480; Newburger v. American Surety Co., 242 N. Y. 134, 151 N. E. 155; Love v. Hamel, 59 App. Div. 360, 69 N. Y. S. 251; Daly v. Piza, 105 App. Div. 496, 94 N. Y. S. 154; Seitz v. Brewer's Refrigerating Co., 141 U. S. 510, 12 S. Ct. 46, 35 L. Ed. 837; American Locomotive Co. v. National Wholesale Grocery Co., Inc., 226 Mass. 314, 115 N. E. 404, L. R. A. 1917D, 1125; Doyle v. Dixon, 12 Allen (Mass.) 576. Of these citations, Johnson v. Oppenheim and the two in the Appellate Division relate to collateral contracts said to have been the inducing cause of the main contract. They refer to leases. A similar case is Wilson v. Deen, 74 N. Y. 531. All hold that an oral stipulation, said to have been the inducing cause for the subsequent execution of the lease itself, concerning some act to be done by the landlord, or some condition as to the leased premises, might not be shown. In principle they are not unlike the case before us. Attention should be called also to Taylor v. Hopper, 62 N. Y. 649, where it is assumed that eivdence of a parol agreement to remove a barn, which was an inducement to the sale of lots, was improper.

We do not ignore the fact that authorities may be found that would seem to support the contention of the appellant. Such are Erskine v. Adeane (1873) L. R. 8 Ch. App. 756, and Morgan v. Griffith (1871) L. R. 6 Exch. 70, where, although there was a written lease a collateral agreement of the landlord to reduce the game was admitted. In this state, Wilson v. Deen might lead to the contrary result. Neither are they approved in New Jersey. Naumberg v. Young, 44 N. J. Law, 331, 43 Am. Rep. 380. Nor in view of later cases in this court can Batterman v. Pierce, 3 Hill, 171, be considered an authority. A line of cases in Massachusetts, of which Durkin v. Cobleigh, 156 Mass. 108, 30 N. E. 474, 17 L. R. A. 270, 32 Am. St. Rep. 436, is an example, have to do with collateral contracts made before a deed is given. But the fixed form of a deed makes it inappropriate to insert collateral agreements, however closely connected with the sale. This may be cause for an exception. Here we deal with the contract on the basis of which the deed to Mrs. Mitchill was given subsequently, and we confine ourselves to the question whether its terms may be modified.

Finally there is the case of Chapin V. Dobson, 78 N. Y. 74, 76, 34 Am. Rep. 512. This is acknowledged to be on the border line and is rarely cited except to be distinguished. Assuming the premises, however, the court was clearly right. There was nothing on the face of the written contract, it said, to show that it intended to express the entire agreement. And there was a finding, sustained by evidence, that there was an entire contract, only part of which was reduced to writing. This being so, the contract as made might be proved.

It is argued that what we have said is not applicable to the case as presented. The collateral agreement was made with the plaintiff. The contract of sale was with her husband, and no assignment of it from him appears. Yet the deed was given to her. It is evident that here was a transaction in which she was the principal from beginning to end. We must treat the contract as if in form, as it was in fact, made by her.

Our conclusion is that the judgment of the Appellate Division and that of the Special Term should be reversed and the complaint dismissed, with costs in all courts.

LEHMAN, J. (dissenting).

I accept the general rule as formulated by Judge ANDREWS. I differ with him only as to its application to the facts shown in the record. The plaintiff contracted to purchase land from the defendants for an agreed price. A formal written agreement was made between the sellers and the plaintiff's husband. It is on its face a complete contract for the conveyance of the land. It describes the property to be conveyed. It sets forth the purchase price to be paid. All the conditions and terms of the conveyance to be made are clearly stated. I concede at the outset that parol evidence to show additional conditions and terms of the conveyance would be inadmissible. There is a conclusive presumption that the parties intended to integrate in that written contract every agreement relating to the nature or extent of the property to be conveyed, the contents of the deed to be delivered, the consideration to be paid as a condition precedent to the delivery of the deeds, and indeed all the rights of the parties in connection with the land. The conveyance of that land was the subject-matter of the written contract, and the contract completely covers that subject.

The parol agreement which the court below found the parties had made was collateral to, yet connected with, the agreement of purchase and sale. It has been found that the defendants induced the plaintiff to agree to purchase the land by a promise to remove an icehouse from land not covered by the agreement of purchase and sale. No independent consideration passed to the defendants for the parol promise. To that extent the written contract and the alleged oral contract are bound together. The same bond usually exists wherever attempt is made to prove a parol agreement which is collateral to a written agreement. Hence "the problem arises whether the bond is sufficiently close to prevent proof of the oral agreement." See Judge ANDREWS' citation from Williston on Contracts, § 637.

Judge ANDREWS has formulated a standard to measure the closeness of the bond. Three conditions, at least, must exist before an oral agreement may be proven to increase the obligation imposed by the written agreement. I think we agree that the first condition that the agreement "must in form be a collateral one" is met by the evidence. I concede that this condition is met in most cases where the courts have nevertheless excluded evidence of the collateral oral agreement. The difficulty here, as in most cases, arises in connection with the two other conditions.

The second condition is that the "parol agreement must not contradict express or implied provisions of the written contract." Judge ANDREWS voices doubt whether this condition is satisfied. The written contract has been carried out. The purchase price has been paid; conveyance has been made; title has passed in accordance with the terms of the written contract. The mutual obligations expressed in the written contract are left unchanged by the alleged oral contract. When performance was required of the written contract, the obligations of the parties were measured solely by its terms. By the oral agreement the plaintiff seeks to hold the defendants to other obligations to be performed by them thereafter upon land which was not conveyed to the plaintiff. The assertion of such further obligation is not inconsistent with the written contract, unless the written contract contains a provision, express or implied, that the defendants are not to do anything not expressed in the writing. Concededly there is no such express provision in the contract, and such a provision may be implied, if at all, only if the asserted additional obligation is "so clearly connected with the principal transaction as to be part and parcel of it," and is not "one that the parties would not ordinarily be expected to embody in the writing." The hypothesis so formulated for a conclusion that the asserted additional obligation is inconsistent with an implied term of the contract is that the alleged oral agreement does not comply with the third condition as formulated by Judge ANDREWS. In this case, therefore, the problem reduces itself to the one question whether or not the oral agreement meets the third condition.

I have conceded that upon inspection the contract is complete. "It appears to contain the engagements of the parties, and to define the object and measure the extent of such engagement;" it constitutes the contract between them, and is presumed to contain the whole of that contract. Eighmie v. Taylor, 98 N. Y. 288. That engagement was on the one side to convey land; on the other to pay the price. The plaintiff asserts further agreement based on the same consideration to be performed by the defendants after the conveyance was complete, and directly affecting only other land. It is true, as Judge ANDREWS points out, that "the presence of the icehouse, even the knowledge that Mrs. Mitchill though it objectionable, would not lead to the belief that a separate agreement existed with regard to it"; but the question we must decide is whether or not, assuming an agreement was made for the removal of an unsightly icehouse from one parcel of land as an inducement for the purchase of another parcel, the parties would ordinarily or naturally be expected to embody the agreement for the removal of the icehouse from one parcel in the written agreement to convey the other parcel. Exclusion of proof of the oral agreement on the ground that it varies the contract embodied in the writing may be based only upon a finding or presumption that the written contract was intended to cover the oral negotiations for the removal of the icehouse which lead up to the contract of purchase and sale. To determine what the writing was intended to cover, "the document alone will not suffice. What it was intended to cover cannot be known till we know what there was to cover. The question being whether certain subjects of negotiation were intended to be covered, we must compare the writing and the negotiations before we can determine whether they were in fact covered." Wigmore on Evidence (2d Ed.) § 2430.

The subject-matter of the written contract was the conveyance of land. The contract was so complete on its face that the conclusion is inevitable that the parties intended to embody in the writing all the negotiations covering at least the conveyance. The promise by the defendants to remove the icehouse from other land was not connected with their obligation to convey except that one agreement would not have been made unless the other was also made. The plaintiff's assertion of a parol agreement by the defendants to remove the icehouse was completely established by the great weight of evidence. It must prevail unless that agreement was part of the agreement to convey and the entire agreement was embodied in the writing.

The fact that in this case the parol agreement is established by the overwhelming weight of evidence is, of course, not a factor which may be considered in determining the competency or legal effect of the evidence. Hardship in the particular case would not justify the court in disregarding or emasculating the general rule. It merely accentuates the outlines of our problem. The assumption that the parol agreement was made is no longer obscured by any doubts. The problem, then, is clearly whether the parties are presumed to have intended to render that parol agreement legally ineffective and nonexistent by failure to embody it in the writing. Though we are driven to say that nothing in the written contract which fixed the terms and conditions of the stipulated conveyance suggests the existence of any further parol agreement, an inspection of the contract, though it is complete on its face in regard to the subject of the conveyance, does not, I think, show that it was intended to embody negotiations or agreements, if any, in regard to a matter so loosely bound to the conveyance as the removal of an icehouse from land not conveyed.

The rule of integration undoubtedly frequently prevents the assertion of fraudulent claims. Parties who take the precaution of embodying their oral agreements in a writing should be protected against the assertion that other terms of the same agreement were not integrated in the writing. The limits of the integration are determined by the writing, read in the light of the surrounding circumstances. A written contract, however complete, yet covers only a limited field. I do not think that in the written contract for the conveyance of land here under consideration we can find an intention to cover a field so broad as to include prior agreements, if any such were made, to do other acts on other property after the stipulated conveyance was made.

In each case where such a problem is presented, varying factors enter into its solution. Citation of authority in this or other jurisdictions is useless, at least without minute analysis of the facts. The analysis I have made of the decisions in this state leads me to the view that the decision of the courts below is in accordance with our own authorities and should be affirmed.

CARDOZO, C. J., and POUND, KELLOGG and O'BRIEN, JJ., concur with ANDREWS, J.
LEHMAN, J., dissents in opinion in which CRANE, J., concurs.

Judgment accordingly.

NOTES AND QUESTIONS:

1. For an analysis of how the collateral matter exception applies, *see Lee v. Joseph E. Seagram & Sons, Inc.*, 552 F.2d 447 (2d Cir. 1977).

PYM V. CAMPBELL
Queen's Bench
6 Ellis & Blackburn 370 (1856).

. . . .

First count. That defendants agreed to purchase of the plaintiff, for 800l., three eighth parts of the benefits to accrue from an invention of plaintiff's. General averments of readiness to convey, and tender of a conveyance of the three eighths. Breach: that defendants refused to accept them. Counts for shares in inventions bargained and sold, and on accounts stated. Pleas. 1st, to first count: That defendants did not agree. 9th, to the other counts: Never indebted. It is not necessary to notice the other seven pleas.

On the trial, before Lord Campbell C.J., at the Sittings at Guildhall after last Hilary term, the plaintiff was called as a witness. He produced and gave in evidence a paper of which the following is a copy.

> 500£ for a quarter share. 300£ for one eighth, and 50£ to be paid to Mr. Sadler. No other shares to be sold without mutual consent for three months. London, 17th January 1854.
>
> One eighth. R. J. R. Campbell.
> John Pym.
> One eighth. J. T. Mackenzie.
> One eighth. R. P. Pritchard.
>
> With reference to the above agreement and in consideration of the sum of five pounds paid me I engage, within two days from this date, to execute the legal documents, to the satisfaction of your solicitors, to complete your title to the respective interests against your names in my Crushing, Washing and Amalgamating Machine.
>
> London. 17 January 1854.
> JOHN PYM.

He gave evidence that he was inventor of a machine which he wished to sell through the instrumentality of one Sadler, who had introduced the defendants to him; that, after some negotiations, the defendant Campbell drew out the above paper, which both plaintiff and defendants then signed, and which plaintiff took away.

The defendants gave evidence that, in the course of the negotiations with the plaintiff, they had got so far as to agree on the price at which the invention should be purchased if bought at all, and had appointed a meeting at which the plaintiff was to explain his invention to two engineers appointed by the defendants, when, if they approved, the machine should be bought. At the appointed time the defendants and two engineers of the names of Fergusson and Abernethie attended; but the plaintiff did not come; and the engineers went away. Shortly after they were gone the plaintiff arrived. Fergusson was found, and expressed a favourable opinion; but Abernethie could not then be found. It was then proposed that, as the parties were all present, and might find it troublesome to meet again, an agreement should be then drawn up and signed, which, if Abernethie approved of the invention, should be the agreement, but, if Abernethie did not approve, should not be one. Abernethie did not approve of the invention when he saw it; and the defendants contended that there was no bargain.

The Lord Chief Justice told the jury that, if they were satisfied that, before the paper was signed, it was agreed amongst them all that it should not operate as an agreement until Abernethie approved of the invention, they should find for the defendant on the pleas denying the agreement. Verdict for the defendants.

Thomas Serjt., in the ensuing term, obtained a rule nisi for a new trial on the ground of misdirection.

Watson and Manisty now . . . shewed cause. The direction was correct. When parties have signed an instrument in writing as the record of their contract, it is not competent to them to shew by evidence that the contract really was something different from that contained in the writing; and therefore in this case, if the defendants had signed this as an agreement, they could not have shewn that the agreement was subject to a condition. But they may shew that the writing was signed on the terms that it should be merely void till a condition was fulfilled; for that shews there never was a contract; *Davies* v. *Jones* (17 Com. B. 625). So, where the holder of a bill writes his name on it and hands it over, that is no indorsement if it was done on the terms that it should not operate as an indorsement till a condition is fulfilled; *Bell* v. *Lord Ingestre* (12 Q. B. 317), *Marston* v. *Allen*. . . . It is true that a deed cannot be delivered as an escrow to the party (Co. Litt. 36, a): but that is for purely technical reasons, inapplicable to parol contracts.

Thomas Serjt. and J. H. Hodgson, contrà. The very object of reducing a contract to writing and signing it is to prevent all disputes as to the terms of the contract. Here the attempt is to shew by parol that the agreement to take this invention was subject to a condition that Abernethie approved; while the writing is silent as to that. *Davies* v. *Jones* (17 Com. B. 625) proceeded on the ground that the instrument was imperfect; the cases as to bills of exchange proceed upon the necessity that there should be a delivery to make an indorsement.

ERLE J.

I think that this rule ought to be discharged. The point made is that this is a written agreement, absolute on the face of it, and that evidence was admitted to shew it was conditional: and if that had been so it would have been wrong. But I am of opinion that the evidence shewed that in fact there was never any agreement at all. The production of a paper purporting to be an agreement by a party, with his signature attached, affords a strong presumption that it is his written agreement; and, if in fact he did sign the paper animo contrahendi, the terms contained in it are conclusive, and cannot be varied by parol evidence: but in the present case the defence begins one step earlier: the parties met and expressly stated to each other that, though for convenience they would then sign the memorandum of the terms, yet they were not to sign it as an agreement until Abernethie was consulted. I grant the risk that such a defence may be set up without ground; and I agree that a jury should therefore always look on such a defence with suspicion: but, if it be proved that in fact the paper was signed with the express intention that it should not be an agreement, the other party cannot fix it as an agreement upon those so signing. [The distinction in point of law is that evidence to vary the terms of an agreement in writing is not admissible, but evidence to shew that there is not an agreement at all is admissible.

CROMPTON J.

I also think that the point in this case was properly left to the jury. If the parties had come to an agreement, though subject to a condition not shewn in the agreement, they could not shew the condition, because the agreement on the face of the writing would have been absolute, and could not be varied: but the finding of the jury is that this paper was signed on the terms that it was to be an agreement if Abernethie approved of the invention, not otherwise. I know of no rule of law to estop parties from shewing that a paper, purporting to be a signed agreement, was in fact signed by mistake, or that it was signed on the terms that it should not be an agreement till money was paid, or something else done. When the instrument is under seal it cannot be a deed until there is a delivery; and when there is a delivery that estops the parties to the deed; that is a technical reason why a deed cannot be delivered as an escrow to the other party. But parol contracts, whether by word of mouth or in writing, do not estop. There is no distinction between them, except that where there is a writing it is the record of the contract. The decision in *Davis v. Jones* (17 Com. B. 625) is, I think, sound law, and proceeds on a just distinction: the parties may not vary a written agreement; but they may shew that they never came to an agreement at all, and that the signed paper was never intended to be the record of the terms of the agreement; for they never had agreeing minds. Evidence to shew that does not vary an agreement, and is admissible.

LORD CAMPBELL C.J.

I agree. No addition to or variation from the terms of a written contract can be made by parol: but in this case the defence was that there never was any agreement entered into. Evidence to that effect was admissible; and the evidence given in this case was overwhelming. It was proved in the most satisfactory manner that before the paper was signed it was explained to the plaintiff that the defendants did not intend the paper to be an agreement till Abernethie had been consulted, and found to approve of the invention; and that the paper was signed before he was seen only because it was not convenient to the defendants to remain. The plaintiff assented to this, and received the writing on those terms. That being proved, there was no agreement.

(Wightman J., not having heard the whole argument, gave no opinion.)

Rule discharged.

NOTES AND QUESTIONS:

1. In *PYM v. Campbell*, the court points out that while evidence purporting to vary the terms of an agreement is not admissible under the parol evidence rule, evidence that would establish that no agreement exists is admissible. This distinction is crucial, and continues to serve as a major exception to the parol evidence rule. Under this theory, parties routinely proffer evidence of avoidance doctrines (e.g. mistake, fraud, etc.) to show that the purported contract should not be enforced. Such evidence is not barred by the parol evidence rule.

C. INTERPRETATION

As promised, we now return to the following case, previously discussed under Misunderstanding.

RAFFLES V. WICHELHAUS
Court of Exchequer
159 E.R. 375 (1864).

. . . .

Declaration. For that it was agreed between the plaintiff and the defendants, to wit, at Liverpool, that the plaintiff should sell to the defendants, and the defendants buy of the plaintiff, certain goods, to wit, 125 bales of Surat cotton, guaranteed middling fair merchant's Dhollorah, to arrive ex "Peerless" from Bombay; and that the cotton should be taken from the quay, and that the defendants would pay the plaintiff for the same at a certain rate, to wit, at the rate of 17 1/2 d. per pound, within a certain time then agreed upon after the arrival of the said goods in England. Averments: that the said goods did arrive by the said ship from Bombay in England, to wit, at Liverpool, and the plaintiff was then and there ready, and willing and offered to deliver the said goods to the defendants, &c. Breach: that the defendants refused to accept the said goods or pay the plaintiff for them.

Plea. That the said ship mentioned in the said agreement was meant and intended by the defendants to be the ship called the "Peerless," which sailed from Bombay, to wit, in October; and that the plaintiff was not ready and willing and did not offer to deliver to the defendants any bales of cotton which arrived by the last mentioned ship, but instead thereof was only ready and willing and offered to deliver to the defendants 125 bales of Surat cotton which arrived by another and different ship, which was also called the "Peerless," and which sailed from Bombay, to wit, in December.

Demurrer, and joinder therein.

MILWARD, in support of the demurrer.

The contract was for the sale of a number of bales of cotton of a particular description, which the plaintiff was ready to deliver. It is immaterial by what ship the cotton was to arrive, so that it was a ship called the "Peerless." The words "to arrive ex ' Peerless,"' only mean that if the vessel is lost on the voyage, the contract is to be at an end. [Pollock, C. B. It would be a question for the jury whether both parties meant the same ship called the "Peerless."] That would be so if the contract was for the sale of a ship called the "Peerless"; but it is for the sale of cotton on board a ship of that name. [Pollock, C. B. The defendant only bought that cotton which was to arrive by a particular ship. It may as well be said, that if there is a contract for the purchase of certain goods in warehouse A., that is satisfied by the delivery of goods of the same description in warehouse B.] In that case there would be goods in both warehouses; here it does not appear that the plaintiff had any goods on board the other "Peerless." [Martin, B. It is imposing on the defendant a contract different from that which he entered into. Pollock, C. B. It is like a contract for the purchase of wine coming from a particular estate in France or Spain, where there are two estates of that name.] The defendant has no right to contradict by parol evidence a written contract good upon the face of it. He does not impute misrepresentation or fraud, but only says that he fancied the ship was a different one. Intention is of no avail, unless stated at the time of the contract. [Pollock, C. B. One vessel sailed in October and the other in December.] The time of sailing is no part of the contract.

MELLISH (Cohen with him), in support of the plea. There is nothing on the face of the contract to shew that any particular ship called the "Peerless" was meant; but the moment it appears that two ships called the "Peerless" were about to sail from Bombay there is a latent ambiguity, and parol evidence may be given for the purpose of shewing that the defendant meant one "Peerless," and the plaintiff another. That being so, there was no consensus ad idem, and therefore no binding contract. He was then stopped by the Court.

PER CURIAM. There must be judgment for the defendants.

Judgment for the defendants.

FRIGALIMENT IMPORTING CO. V. B.N.S. INT'L
United States District Court S.D. New York
190 F. Supp. 116 (1960).

FRIENDLY, Circuit Judge.

The issue is, what is chicken? Plaintiff says "chicken" means a young chicken, suitable for broiling and frying. Defendant says "chicken" means any bird of that genus that meets contract specifications on weight and quality, including what it calls "stewing chicken" and plaintiff pejoratively terms "fowl." Dictionaries give both meanings, as well as some others not relevant here. To support its, plaintiff sends a number of volleys over the net; defendant essays to return them and adds a few serves of its own. Assuming that both parties were acting in good faith, the case nicely illustrates Holmes' remark "that the making of a contract depends not on the agreement of two minds in one intention, but on the agreement of two sets of external signs- not on the parties' having meant the same thing but on their having said the same thing." The Path of the Law, in Collected Legal Papers, p. 178. I have concluded that plaintiff has not sustained its burden of persuasion that the contract used "chicken" in the narrower sense.

The action is for breach of the warranty that goods sold shall correspond to the description, New York Personal Property Law, McKinney's Consol. Laws, c. 41, § 95. Two contracts are in suit.

In the first, dated May 2, 1957, defendant, a New York sales corporation, confirmed the sale to plaintiff, a Swiss corporation, of:

US Fresh Frozen Chicken, Grade A, Government Inspected, Eviscerated 2 1/2-3 lbs. and 1 1/2-2 lbs. each all chicken individually wrapped in cryovac, packed in secured fiber cartons or wooden boxes, suitable for export.

75,000 lbs. 2 1/2-3 lbs........ @$33.00
25,000 lbs. 1 1/2-2 lbs........ @$36.50
per 100 lbs. FAS New York

Scheduled May 10, 1957 pursuant to instructions from Penson & Co., New York.

The second contract, also dated May 2, 1957, was identical save that only 50,000 lbs. of the heavier "chicken" were called for, the price of the smaller birds was $37 per 100 lbs., and shipment was scheduled for May 30. The initial shipment under the first contract was short but the balance was shipped on May 17. When the initial shipment arrived in Switzerland, plaintiff found, on May 28, that the 2 1/2-3 lbs. birds were not young chicken suitable for broiling and frying but stewing chicken or "fowl"; indeed, many of the cartons and bags plainly so indicated. Protests ensued. Nevertheless, shipment under the second contract was made on May 29, the 2 1/2-3 lbs. birds again being stewing chicken. Defendant stopped the transportation of these at Rotterdam.

This action followed. Plaintiff says that, notwithstanding that its acceptance was in Switzerland, New York law controls under the principle of Rubin v. Irving Trust Co., 1953, 305 N.Y. 288, 305, 113 N.E.2d 424, 431; defendant does not dispute this, and relies on New York decisions. I shall follow the apparent agreement of the parties as to the applicable law.

Since the word "chicken" standing alone is ambiguous, I turn first to see whether the contract itself offers any aid to its interpretation. Plaintiff says the 1 1/2-2 lbs. birds necessarily had to be young chicken since the older birds do not come in that size, hence the 2 1/2-3 lbs. birds must likewise be young. This is unpersuasive- a contract for "apples" of two different sizes could be filled with different kinds of apples even though only one species came in both sizes. Defendant notes that the contract called not simply for chicken but for "US Fresh Frozen Chicken, Grade A, Government Inspected." It says the contract thereby incorporated by reference the Department of Agriculture's regulations, which favor its interpretation; I shall return to this after reviewing plaintiff's other contentions.

The first hinges on an exchange of cablegrams which preceded execution of the formal contracts. The negotiations leading up to the contracts were conducted in New York between defendant's secretary, Ernest R. Bauer, and a Mr. Stovicek, who was in New York for the Czechoslovak government at the World Trade Fair. A few days after meeting Bauer at the fair, Stovicek telephoned and inquired whether defendant would be interested in exporting poultry to Switzerland. Bauer then met with Stovicek, who showed him a cable from plaintiff dated April 26, 1957, announcing that they "are buyer" of 25,000 lbs. of chicken 2 1/2-3 lbs. weight, Cryovac packed, grade A Government inspected, at a price up to 33¢ per pound, for shipment on May 10, to be confirmed by the following morning, and were interested in further offerings. After testing the market for price, Bauer accepted, and Stovicek sent a confirmation that evening. Plaintiff stresses that, although these and subsequent cables between plaintiff and defendant, which laid the basis for the additional quantities under the first and for all of the second contract, were predominantly in German, they used the English word "chicken"; it claims this was done because it understood "chicken" meant young chicken whereas the German word, "Huhn," included both "Brathuhn" (broilers) and "Suppenhuhn" (stewing chicken), and that defendant, whose officers were thoroughly conversant with German, should have realized this. Whatever force this argument might otherwise have is largely drained away by Bauer's testimony that he asked Stovicek what kind of chickens were wanted, received the answer "any kind of chickens," and then, in German, asked whether the cable meant "Huhn" and received an affirmative response. . . .

Plaintiff's next contention is that there was a definite trade usage that "chicken" meant "young chicken." Defendant showed that it was only beginning in the poultry trade in 1957, thereby bringing itself within the principle that "when one of the parties is not a member of the trade or other circle, his acceptance of the standard must be made to appear" by proving either that he had actual knowledge of the usage or that the usage is "so generally known in the community that his actual individual knowledge of it may be inferred." 9 Wigmore, Evidence (3d ed. § 1940) 2464. Here there was no proof of actual knowledge of the alleged usage; indeed, it is quite plain that defendant's belief was to the contrary. In order to meet the alternative requirement, the law of New York demands a showing that "the usage is of so long continuance, so well established, so notorious, so universal and so reasonable in itself, as that the presumption is violent that the parties contracted with reference to it, and made it a part of their agreement." Walls v. Bailey, 1872, 49 N.Y. 464, 472-473.

Plaintiff endeavored to establish such a usage by the testimony of three witnesses and certain other evidence. Strasser, resident buyer in New York for a large chain of Swiss cooperatives, testified that "on chicken I would definitely understand a broiler." However, the force of this testimony was considerably weakened by the fact that in his own transactions the witness, a careful businessman, protected himself by using "broiler" when that was what he wanted and "fowl" when he wished older birds. Indeed, there are some indications, dating back to a remark of Lord Mansfield, Edie v. East India Co., 2 Burr. 1216, 1222 (1761), that no credit should be given "witnesses to usage, who could not adduce instances in verification." 7 Wigmore, Evidence (3d ed. 1940), § 1954; see McDonald v. Acker, Merrall & Condit Co., 2d Dept.1920, 192 App.Div. 123, 126, 182 N.Y.S. 607. While Wigmore thinks this goes too far, a witness' consistent failure to rely on the alleged usage deprives his opinion testimony of much of its effect. Niesielowski, an officer of one of the companies that had furnished the stewing chicken to defendant, testified that "chicken" meant "the male species of the poultry industry. That could be a broiler, a fryer or a roaster," but not a stewing chicken; however, he also testified that upon receiving defendant's inquiry for "chickens," he asked whether the desire was for "fowl or frying chickens" and, in fact, supplied fowl, although taking the precaution of asking defendant, a day or two after plaintiff's acceptance of the contracts in suit, to change its confirmation of its order from "chickens," as defendant had originally prepared it, to "stewing chickens." Dates, an employee of Urner-Barry Company, which publishes a daily market report on the poultry trade, gave it as his view that the trade meaning of "chicken" was "broilers and fryers." In addition to this opinion testimony, plaintiff relied on the fact that the Urner-Barry service, the Journal of Commerce, and Weinberg Bros. & Co. of Chicago, a large supplier of poultry, published quotations in a manner which, in one way or another, distinguish between "chicken," comprising broilers, fryers and certain other categories, and "fowl," which, Bauer acknowledged, included stewing chickens. This material would be impressive if there were nothing to the contrary. However, there was, as will now be seen.

Defendant's witness Weininger, who operates a chicken eviscerating plant in New Jersey, testified "Chicken is everything except a goose, a duck, and a turkey. Everything is a chicken, but then you have to say, you have to specify which category you want or that you are talking about." Its witness Fox said that in the trade "chicken" would encompass all the various classifications. Sadina, who conducts a food inspection service, testified that he would consider any bird coming within the classes of "chicken" in the Department of Agriculture's regulations to be a chicken. The specifications approved by the General Services Administration include fowl as well as broilers and fryers under the classification "chickens." Statistics of the Institute of American Poultry Industries use the phrases 'Young chickens' and "Mature chickens," under the general heading "Total chickens." and the Department of Agriculture's daily and weekly price reports avoid use of the word "chicken" without specification.

Defendant advances several other points which it claims affirmatively support its construction. Primary among these is the regulation of the Department of Agriculture, 7 C.F.R. § 70.300-70.370, entitled, "Grading and Inspection of Poultry and Edible Products Thereof." and in particular 70.301 which recited:

> *Chickens.* The following are the various classes of chickens:
> (a) Broiler or fryer . . .
> (b) Roaster . . .
> (c) Capon . . .
> (d) Stag . . .
> (e) Hen or stewing chicken or fowl . . .
> (f) Cock or old rooster . . .

Defendant argues, as previously noted, that the contract incorporated these regulations by reference. Plaintiff answers that the contract provision related simply to grade and Government inspection and did not incorporate the Government definition of "chicken," and also that the definition in the Regulations is ignored in the trade. However, the latter contention was contradicted by Weininger and Sadina; and there is force in defendant's argument that the contract made the regulations a dictionary, particularly since the reference to Government grading was already in plaintiff's initial cable to Stovicek.

Defendant makes a further argument based on the impossibility of its obtaining broilers and fryers at the 33¢ price offered by plaintiff for the 2 1/2-3 lbs. birds. There is no substantial dispute that, in late April, 1957, the price for 2 1/2-3 lbs. broilers was between 35 and 37¢ per pound, and that when defendant entered into the contracts, it was well aware of this and intended to fill them by supplying fowl in these weights. It claims that plaintiff must likewise have known the market since plaintiff had reserved shipping space on April 23, three days before plaintiff's cable to Stovicek, or, at least, that Stovicek was chargeable with such knowledge. It is scarcely an answer to say, as plaintiff does in its brief, that the 33¢ price offered by the 2 1/2-3 lbs. "chickens" was closer to the prevailing 35¢ price for broilers than to the 30¢ at which defendant procured fowl. Plaintiff must have expected defendant to make some profit- certainly it could not have expected defendant deliberately to incur a loss.

Finally, defendant relies on conduct by the plaintiff after the first shipment had been received. On May 28 plaintiff sent two cables complaining that the larger birds in the first shipment constituted "fowl." Defendant answered with a cable refusing to recognize plaintiff's objection and announcing "We have today ready for shipment 50,000 lbs. chicken 2 1/2-3 lbs. 25,000 lbs. broilers 1 1/2-2 lbs.," these being the goods procured for shipment under the second contract, and asked immediate answer "whether we are to ship this merchandise to you and whether you will accept the merchandise." After several other cable exchanges, plaintiff replied on May 29 "Confirm again that merchandise is to be shipped since resold by us if not enough pursuant to contract chickens are shipped the missing quantity is to be shipped within ten days stop we resold to our customers pursuant to your contract chickens grade A you have to deliver us said merchandise we again state that we shall make you fully responsible for all resulting costs."[2] Defendant argues that if plaintiff was sincere in thinking it was entitled to young chickens, plaintiff would not have allowed the shipment under the second contract to go forward, since the distinction between broilers and chickens drawn in defendant's cablegram must have made it clear that the larger birds would not be broilers. However, plaintiff answers that the cables show plaintiff was insisting on delivery of young chickens and that defendant shipped old ones at its peril. Defendant's point would be highly relevant on another disputed issue- whether if liability were established, the measure of damages should be the difference in market value of broilers and stewing chicken in New York or the larger difference in Europe, but I cannot give it weight on the issue of interpretation. Defendant points out also that plaintiff proceeded to deliver some of the larger birds in Europe, describing them as "poulets"; defendant argues that it was only when plaintiff's customers complained about this that plaintiff developed the idea that "chicken" meant "young chicken." There is little force in this in view of plaintiff's immediate and consistent protests.

When all the evidence is reviewed, it is clear that defendant believed it could comply with the contracts by delivering stewing chicken in the 2 1/2-3 lbs. size. Defendant's subjective intent would not be significant if this did not coincide with an objective meaning of "chicken." Here it did coincide with one of the dictionary meanings, with the definition in the Department of Agriculture Regulations to which the contract made at least oblique reference, with at least some usage in the trade, with the realities of the market, and with what plaintiff's spokesman had said. Plaintiff asserts it to be equally plain that plaintiff's own subjective intent was to obtain broilers and fryers; the only evidence against this is the material as to market prices and this may not have been sufficiently brought home. In any event it is unnecessary to determine that issue. For plaintiff has the burden of showing that "chicken" was used in the narrower rather than in the broader sense, and this it has not sustained.

This opinion constitutes the Court's findings of fact and conclusions of law. Judgment shall be entered dismissing the complaint with costs.

---

[2] These cables were in German; 'chicken', 'broilers' and, on some occasions, 'fowl,' were in English.

PACIFIC GAS & ELECTRIC CO. V. G.W. THOMAS DRAYAGE & RIGGING CO.
Supreme Court of California
442 P.2d 641 (1968).

TRAYNOR, Chief Justice.

Defendant appeals from a judgment for plaintiff in an action for damages for injury to property under an indemnity clause of a contract.

In 1960 defendant entered into a contract with plaintiff to furnish the labor and equipment necessary to remove and replace the upper metal cover of plaintiff's steam turbine. Defendant agreed to perform the work "at (its) own risk and expense" and to "indemnify" plaintiff "against all loss, damage, expense and liability resulting from . . . injury to property, arising out of or in any way connected with the performance of this contract." Defendant also agreed to procure not less than $50,000 insurance to cover liability for injury to property. Plaintiff was to be an additional named insured, but the policy was to contain a cross-liability clause extending the coverage to plaintiff's property.

During the work the cover fell and injured the exposed rotor of the turbine. Plaintiff brought this action to recover $25,144.51, the amount it subsequently spent on repairs. During the trial it dismissed a count based on negligence and thereafter secured judgment on the theory that the indemnity provision covered injury to all property regardless of ownership.

Defendant offered to prove by admissions of plaintiff's agents, by defendant's conduct under similar contracts entered into with plaintiff, and by other proof that in the indemnity clause the parties meant to cover injury to property of third parties only and not to plaintiff's property. . . . Although the trial court observed that the language used was "the classic language for a third party indemnity provision" and that "one could very easily conclude that . . . its whole intendment is to indemnify third parties," it nevertheless held that the "plain language" of the agreement also required defendant to indemnify plaintiff for injuries to plaintiff's property. Having determined that the contract had a plain meaning, the court refused to admit any extrinsic evidence that would contradict its interpretation.

When a court interprets a contract on this basis, it determines the meaning of the instrument in accordance with the ". . . extrinsic evidence of the judge's own linguistic education and experience." (3 Corbin on Contracts (1960 ed.) (1964 Supp. § 579, p. 225, fn. 56).) The exclusion of testimony that might contradict the linguistic background of the judge reflects a judicial belief in the possibility of perfect verbal expression. (9 Wigmore on Evidence (3d ed. 1940) § 2461, p. 187.) This belief is a remnant of a primitive faith in the inherent potency[2] and inherent meaning of words.[3]

---

[2] E.g., 'The elaborate system of taboo and verbal prohibitions in primitive groups; the ancient Egyptian myth of Khern, the apotheosis of the word, and of Thoth, the Scribe of Truth, the Giver of Words and Script, the Master of Incantations; the avoidance of the name of God in Brahmanism, Judaism and Islam; totemistic and protective names in mediaeval Turkish and Finno-Ugrian languages; the misplaced verbal scruples of the 'Pre cieuses'; the Swedish peasant custom of curing sick cattle smitten by witchcraft, by making them swallow a page torn out of the psalter and put in dough. . . .' from Ullman, The Principles of Semantics (1963 ed.) 43. (See also Ogden and Richards, The Meaning of Meaning (rev. ed. 1956) pp. 24-47.)

The test of admissibility of extrinsic evidence to explain the meaning of a written instrument is not whether it appears to the court to be plain and unambiguous on its face, but whether the offered evidence is relevant to prove a meaning to which the language of the instrument is reasonably susceptible. . . .

A rule that would limit the determination of the meaning of a written instrument to its four-corners merely because it seems to the court to be clear and unambiguous, would either deny the relevance of the intention of the parties or presuppose a degree of verbal precision and stability our language has not attained.

Some courts have expressed the opinion that contractual obligations are created by the mere use of certain words, whether or not there was any intention to incur such obligations.[4] Under this view, contractual obligations flow, not from the intention of the parties but from the fact that they used certain magic words. Evidence of the parties' intention therefore becomes irrelevant.

In this state, however, the intention of the parties as expressed in the contract is the source of contractual rights and duties.[5] A court must ascertain and give effect to this intention by determining what the parties meant by the words they used. Accordingly, the exclusion of relevant, extrinsic evidence to explain the meaning of a written instrument could be justified only if it were feasible to determine the meaning the parties gave to the words from the instrument alone.

If words had absolute and constant referents, it might be possible to discover contractual intention in the words themselves and in the manner in which they were arranged. Words, however, do not have absolute and constant referents. "A word is a symbol of thought but has no arbitrary and fixed meaning like a symbol of algebra or chemistry, . . ." (Pearson v. State Social Welfare Board (1960) 54 Cal.2d 184, 195, 5 Cal.Rptr. 553, 559, 353 P.2d 33, 39.) The meaning of particular words or groups of words varies with the ". . . verbal context and surrounding circumstances and purposes in view of the linguistic education and experience of their users and their hearers or readers (not excluding judges). . . . A word has no meaning apart from these factors; much less does it have an objective meaning, one true meaning." (Corbin, The Interpretation of Words and the Parol Evidence Rule (1965) 50 Cornell L.Q. 161, 187.) Accordingly, the meaning of a writing ". . . can only be found by interpretation in the light of all the circumstances that reveal the sense in which the writer used the words. The exclusion of parol evidence regarding such circumstances merely because the words do not appear ambiguous to the reader can easily lead to the attribution to a written instrument of a meaning that was never intended. (Citations

---

[3] "Rerum enim vocabula immutabilia sunt, homines mutabilia," (Words are unchangeable, men changeable) from Dig. XXXIII, 10, 7, s 2, de sup. leg. as quoted in 9 Wigmore on Evidence, op. cit. supra, § 2461, p. 187.

[4] "A contract has, strictly speaking, nothing to do with the personal, or individual, intent of the parties. A contract is an obligation attached by the mere force of law to certain acts of the parties, usually words, which ordinarily accompany and represent a known intent." (Hotchkiss v. National City Bank of New York (S.D.N.Y.1911) 200 F. 287, 293. See also C. H. Pope & Co. v. Bibb Mfg. Co. (2d Cir. 1923) 290 F. 586, 587; see 4 Williston on Contracts (3d ed. 1961) § 612, pp. 577-578, § 613, p. 583.)

[5] "A contract must be so interpreted as to give effect to the mutual intention of the parties as it existed at the time of contracting, so far as the same is ascertainable and lawful." (Civ.Code, § 1636; see also Code Civ.Proc. § 1859; Universal Sales Corp. v. Cal. Press Mfg. Co. (1942) 20 Cal.2d 751, 760, 128 P.2d 665; Lemm v. Stillwater Land & Cattle Co. (1933) 217 Cal. 474, 480, 19 P.2d 785.)

omitted.)" (Universal Sales Corp. v. Cal. Press Mfg. Co., supra, 20 Cal.2d 751, 776, 128 P.2d 665, 679 (concurring opinion). . . .

Although extrinsic evidence is not admissible to add to, detract from, or vary the terms of a written contract, these terms must first be determined before it can be decided whether or not extrinsic evidence is being offered for a prohibited purpose. The fact that the terms of an instrument appear clear to a judge does not preclude the possibility that the parties chose the language of the instrument to express different terms. That possibility is not limited to contracts whose terms have acquired a particular meaning by trade usage,[6] but exists whenever the parties' understanding of the words used may have differed from the judge's understanding.

Accordingly, rational interpretation requires at least a preliminary consideration of all credible evidence offered to prove the intention of the parties.[7] (Civ.Code, § 1647; Code Civ.Proc. § 1860; see also 9 Wigmore on Evidence, op. cit. supra, § 2470, fn. 11, p. 227.) Such evidence includes testimony as to the "circumstances surrounding the making of the agreement . . . including the object, nature and subject matter of the writing . . ." so that the court can "place itself in the same situation in which the parties found themselves at the time of contracting." (Universal Sales Corp. v. Cal. Press Mfg. Co., supra, 20 Cal.2d 751, 761, 128 P.2d 665, 671; Lemm v. Stillwater Land & Cattle Co., supra, 217 Cal. 474, 480-481, 19 P.2d 785.) If the court decides, after considering this evidence, that the language of a contract, in the light of all the circumstances, is "fairly susceptible of either one of the two interpretations contended for . . . ." (Balfour v. Fresno C. & I. Co. (1895) 109 Cal. 221, 225, 44 P. 876, 877; . . .extrinsic evidence relevant to prove either of such meanings is admissible.[8]

In the present case the court erroneously refused to consider extrinsic evidence offered to show that the indemnity clause in the contract was not intended to cover injuries to plaintiff's property. Although that evidence was not necessary to show that the indemnity clause was reasonably susceptible of the meaning contended for by defendant, it was nevertheless relevant and admissible on that issue. Moreover, since that clause was

---

[6] Extrinsic evidence of trade usage or custom has been admitted to show that the term "United Kingdom" in a motion picture distribution contract included Ireland (Ermolieff v. R.K.O. Radio Pictures (1942) 19 Cal.2d 543, 549-552, 122 P.2d 3); that the word "ton" in a lease meant a long ton or 2,240 pounds and not the statutory ton of 2,000 pounds (Higgins v. Cal. Petroleum, etc., Co. (1898) 120 Cal. 629, 630-632, 52 P. 1080); that the word 'stubble' in a lease included not only stumps left in the ground but everything 'left on the ground after the harvest time' (Callahan v. Stanley (1881) 57 Cal. 476, 477-479); that the term "north" in a contract dividing mining claims indicated a boundary line running along the "magnetic and not the true meridian" (Jenny Lind Co. v. Bower & Co. (1858) 11 Cal. 194, 197-199) and that a form contract for purchase and sale was actually an agency contract (Body-Steffner Co. v. Flotill Products (1944) 63 Cal.App.2d 555, 558-562, 147 P.2d 84). See also Code Civ.Proc. § 1861; Annot., 89 A.L.R. 1228; Note (1942) 30 Cal.L.Rev. 679.)

[7] When objection is made to any particular item of evidence offered to prove the intention of the parties, the trial court may not yet be in a position to determine whether in the light of all of the offered evidence, the item objected to will turn out to be admissible as tending to prove a meaning of which the language of the instrument is reasonably susceptible or inadmissible as tending to prove a meaning of which the language is not reasonably susceptible. In such case the court may admit the evidence conditionally by either reserving its ruling on the objection or by admitting the evidence subject to a motion to strike. (See Evid.Code, § 403.)

[8] Extrinsic evidence has often been admitted in such cases on the stated ground that the contract was ambiguous (e.g., Universal Sales Corp. v. Cal. Press Mfg. Co., supra, 20 Cal.2d 751, 761, 128 P.2d 665). This statement of the rule is harmless if it is kept in mind that the ambiguity may be exposed by extrinsic evidence that reveals more than one possible meaning.

reasonably susceptible of that meaning, the offered evidence was also admissible to prove that the clause had that meaning and did not cover injuries to plaintiff's property.[9] Accordingly, the judgment must be reversed. . . .

The judgment is reversed.

PETERS, MOSK, BURKE, SULLIVAN, and PEEK, JJ., concur.
McCOMB, J., dissents.

NOTES AND QUESTIONS:

1. See *Nanakuli Paving & Rock Co. v. Shell Oil Co.*, 664 F.2d 772 (1981), for its discussion of course of performance under UCC §1-303.

---

[9] The court's exclusion of extrinsic evidence in this case would be error even under a rule that excluded such evidence when the instrument appeared to the court to be clear and unambiguous on its face. The controversy centers on the meaning of the word "indemnify" and the phrase "all loss, damage, expense and liability." The trial court's recognition of the language as typical of a third party indemnity clause and the double sense in which the word "indemnify" is used in statutes and defined in dictionaries demonstrate the existence of an ambiguity. (Compare Civ.Code, § 2772, "Indemnity is a contract by which one engages to save another from a legal consequence of the conduct of one of the parties, or of some other person," with Civ.Code, § 2527, "Insurance is a contract whereby by one undertakes to indemnify another against loss, damage, or liability, arising from an unknown or contingent event." Black's Law Dictionary (4th ed. 1951) defines "indemnity" as "A collateral contract or assurance, by which one person engages to secure another against an anticipated loss or to prevent him from being damnified by the legal consequences of an act or forbearance on the part of one of the parties or of some third person." Stroud's Judicial Dictionary (2d ed. 1903) defines it as a "Contract . . .to indemnify against a liability. . . ." One of the definitions given to "indemnify" by Webster's Third New Internat. Dict. (1961 ed.) is "to exempt from incurred penalties or liabilities.")Plaintiff's assertion that the use of the word "all" to modify "loss, damage, expense and liability" dictates an all inclusive interpretation is not persuasive. If the word 'indemnify' encompasses only third-party claims, the word "all" simply refers to all such claims. The use of the words "loss," "damage," and "expense" in addition to the word "liability" is likewise inconclusive. These words do not imply an agreement to reimburse for injury to an indemnitee's property since they are commonly inserted in third-party indemnity clauses, to enable an indemnitee who settles a claim to recover from his indemnitor without proving his liability. (Carpenter Paper Co. v. Kellogg (1952) 114 Cal.App.2d 640, 651, 251 P.2d 40. Civ.Code, § 2778, provides: "1. Upon an indemnity against liability . . . the person indemnified is entitled to recover upon becoming liable; 2. Upon an indemnity against claims, or demands, or damages, or costs . . . the person indemnified is not entitled to recover without payment thereof; . . . .")The provision that defendant perform the work "at his own risk and expense" and the provisions relating to insurance are equally inconclusive. By agreeing to work at its own risk defendant may have released plaintiff from liability for any injuries to defendant's property arising out of the contract's performance, but this provision did not necessarily make defendant an insurer against injuries to plaintiff's property. Defendant's agreement to procure liability insurance to cover damages to plaintiff's property does not indicate whether the insurance was to cover all injuries or only injuries caused by defendant's negligence.

SECTION 2. IMPLIED TERMS

A. IMPLIED COVENANT OF GOOD FAITH AND FAIR DEALING

WOOD v. LUCY, LADY DUFF-GORDON
Court of Appeals of New York
118 N.E. 214 (1917).

CARDOZO, Justice.

The defendant styles herself "a creator of fashions." Her favor helps a sale. Manufacturers of dresses, millinery, and like articles are glad to pay for a certificate of her approval. The things which she designs, fabrics, parasols, and what not, have a new value in the public mind when issued in her name. She employed the plaintiff to help her to turn this vogue into money. He was to have the exclusive right, subject always to her approval, to place her indorsements on the designs of others. He was also to have the exclusive right to place her own designs on sale, or to license others to market them. In return she was to have one-half of "all profits and revenues" derived from any contracts he might make. The exclusive right was to last at least one year from April 1, 1915, and thereafter from year to year unless terminated by notice of 90 days. The plaintiff says that he kept the contract on his part, and that the defendant broke it. She placed her indorsement on fabrics, dresses, and millinery without his knowledge, and withheld the profits. He sues her for the damages, and the case comes here on demurrer.

The agreement of employment is signed by both parties. It has a wealth of recitals. The defendant insists, however, that it lacks the elements of a contract. She says that the plaintiff does not bind himself to anything. It is true that he does not promise in so many words that he will use reasonable efforts to place the defendant's indorsements and market her designs. We think, however, that such a promise is fairly to be implied. The law has outgrown its primitive stage of formalism when the precise word was the sovereign talisman, and every slip was fatal. It takes a broader view today. A promise may be lacking, and yet the whole writing may be "instinct with an obligation," imperfectly expressed (Scott, J., in McCall Co. v. Wright, 133 App. Div. 62, 117 N. Y. Supp. 775; Moran v. Standard Oil Co., 211 N. Y. 187, 198, 105 N. E. 217). If that is so, there is a contract.

The implication of a promise here finds support in many circumstances. The defendant gave an exclusive privilege. She was to have no right for at least a year to place her own indorsements or market her own designs except through the agency of the plaintiff. The acceptance of the exclusive agency was an assumption of its duties. Phoenix Hermetic Co. v. Filtrine Mfg. Co., 164 App. Div. 424, 150 N. Y. Supp. 193; W. G. Taylor Co. v. Bannerman, 120 Wis. 189, 97 N. W. 918; Mueller v. Mineral Spring Co., 88 Mich. 390, 50 N. W. 319. We are not to suppose that one party was to be placed at the mercy of the other. Hearn v. Stevens & Bro., 111 App. Div. 101, 106, 97 N. Y. Supp. 566; Russell v. Allerton, 108 N. Y. 288, 15 N. E. 391. Many other terms of the agreement point the same way. We are told at the outset by way of recital that: "The said Otis F. Wood possesses a business organization adapted to the placing of such indorsements as the said Lucy, Lady Duff-Gordon, has approved."

The implication is that the plaintiff's business organization will be used for the purpose for which it is adapted. But the terms of the defendant's compensation are even more significant. Her sole compensation for the grant of an exclusive agency is to be one-half of all the profits resulting from the plaintiff's efforts. Unless he gave his efforts, she could never get anything. Without an implied promise, the transaction cannot have such business "efficacy, as both parties must have intended that at all events it should have." Bowen, L. J., in the Moorcock, 14 P. D. 64, 68. But the contract does not stop there. The plaintiff goes on to promise that he will account monthly for all moneys received by him, and that he will take out all such patents and copyrights and trade-marks as may in his judgment be necessary to protect the rights and articles affected by the agreement. It is true, of course, as the Appellate Division has said, that if he was under no duty to try to market designs or to place certificates of indorsement, his promise to account for profits or take out copyrights would be valueless. But in determining the intention of the parties the promise has a value. It helps

to enforce the conclusion that the plaintiff had some duties. His promise to pay the defendant one-half of the profits and revenues resulting from the exclusive agency and to render accounts monthly was a promise to use reasonable efforts to bring profits and revenues into existence. For this conclusion the authorities are ample. . . . .

The judgment of the Appellate Division should be reversed, and the order of the Special Term affirmed, with costs in the Appellate Division and in this court.

CUDDEBACK, McLAUGHLIN, and ANDREWS, JJ., concur. HISCOCK, C. J., and CHASE and CRANE, JJ., dissent.

Order reversed, etc.

LOCKE V. WARNER BROS, INC.
Court of Appeal, Second District, California
57 Cal. App. 4th 354 (1997).

KLEIN, Presiding Judge.

Plaintiffs and appellants Sondra Locke (Locke) and Caritas Films, a California corporation (Caritas) (sometimes collectively referred to as Locke) appeal a judgment following a grant of summary judgment in favor of defendant and respondent Warner Bros., Inc. (Warner).

The essential issue presented is whether triable issues of material fact are present which would preclude summary judgment.

We conclude triable issues are present with respect to whether Warner breached its development deal with Locke by categorically refusing to work with her . . . . The judgment therefore is reversed as to the second . . . cause . . . of action and otherwise is affirmed.

Factual and Procedural Background

1. *Locke's dispute with Eastwood.*

In 1975, Locke came to Warner to appear with Clint Eastwood in The Outlaw Josey Wales (Warner Bros. 1976). During the filming of the movie, Locke and Eastwood began a personal and romantic relationship. For the next dozen years, they lived in Eastwood's Los Angeles and Northern California homes. Locke also appeared in a number of Eastwood's films. In 1986, Locke made her directorial debut in Ratboy (Warner Bros. 1986).

In 1988, the relationship deteriorated, and in 1989 Eastwood terminated it. Locke then brought suit against Eastwood, alleging numerous causes of action. That action was resolved by a November 21, 1990, settlement agreement and mutual general release. Under said agreement, Eastwood agreed to pay Locke additional compensation in the sum of $450,000 "on account of past employment and Locke's contentions" and to convey certain real property to her.

2. *Locke's development deal with Warner.*

According to Locke, Eastwood secured a development deal for Locke with Warner in exchange for Locke's dropping her case against him. Contemporaneously with the Locke/Eastwood settlement agreement, Locke entered into a written agreement with Warner, dated November 27, 1990. It is the Locke/Warner agreement which is the subject of the instant controversy.

The Locke/Warner agreement had two basic components. The first element states Locke would receive $250,000 per year for three years for a "non-exclusive first look deal." It required Locke to submit to Warner any picture she was interested in developing before submitting it to any other studio. Warner then had 30 days either to approve or reject a submission.

The second element of the contract was a $750,000 "pay or play" directing deal. The provision is called "pay or play" because it gives the studio a choice: It can either "play" the director by using the director's services, or pay the director his or her fee.

Unbeknownst to Locke at the time, Eastwood had agreed to reimburse Warner for the cost of her contract if she did not succeed in getting projects produced and developed. Early in the second year of the three-year contract, Warner charged $975,000 to an Eastwood film, Unforgiven (Warner Bros. 1992).

Warner paid Locke the guaranteed compensation of $1.5 million under the agreement. In accordance with the agreement, Warner also provided Locke with an office on the studio lot and an administrative assistant. However, Warner did not develop any of Locke's proposed projects or hire her to direct any films. Locke contends the development deal was a sham, that Warner never intended to make any films with her, and that Warner's sole motivation in entering into the agreement was to assist Eastwood in settling his litigation with Locke.

3. *Locke's action against Warner.*

On March 10, 1994, Locke filed suit against Warner, alleging four causes of action. . . .

The second cause of action alleged that Warner breached the contract by refusing to consider Locke's proposed projects and thereby deprived her of the benefit of the bargain of the Warner/Locke agreement.

Warner answered, denied each and every allegation and asserted various affirmative defenses.

4. *Warner's motion for summary judgment and opposition thereto.*

On January 6, 1995, Warner filed a motion for summary judgment. Warner contended it did not breach its contract with Locke because it did consider all the projects she presented, and the studio's decision not to put any of those projects into active development or "hand" Locke a script which it already owned was not a breach of any express or implied contractual duty. Warner asserted the odds are slim a producer can get a project into development and even slimmer a director will be hired to direct a film. During the term of Locke's deal, Warner had similar deals with numerous other producers and directors, who fared no better than Locke. . . .

In opposing summary judgment, Locke contended Warner breached the agreement in that it had no intention of accepting any project regardless of its merits. Locke also asserted Warner committed fraud by entering into the agreement without any intention of approving any project with Locke or allowing Locke to direct another film.

Locke's opposition papers cited the deposition testimony of Joseph Terry, who recounted a conversation he had with Bob Brassel, a Warner executive, regarding Locke's projects. Terry had stated to Brassel:

> "Well, Bob, this woman has a deal on the lot. She's a director that you want to work with. You have a deal with her.... I've got five here that she's interested in." And then I would get nothing. ... I was told [by Brassel], "Joe, we're not going to work with her," and then, "That's Clint's deal." And that's something I just completely did not understand.

Similarly, the declaration of Mary Wellnitz stated: She worked with Locke to set up projects at Warner, without success. Shortly after she began her association with Locke, Wellnitz submitted a script to Lance Young, who at the time was a senior vice-president of production at Warner. After discussing the script, Young told Wellnitz,

> Mary, I want you to know that I think Sondra is a wonderful woman and very talented, but, if you think I can go down the hall and tell Bob Daly that I have a movie I want to make with her he would tell me to forget it. They are not going to make a movie with her here.

5. *Trial court's ruling.*

On February 17, 1995, the trial court granted summary judgment in favor of Warner. Thereafter, the trial court signed an extensive order granting summary judgment. The order stated:

> Under the contract, Warner had no obligation either to put into development any of the projects submitted to the studio for its consideration, or to "hand off" to Locke any scripts for her to direct that it previously had acquired from someone else. The implied covenant of good faith and fair dealing cannot be imposed to create a contract different from the one the parties negotiated for themselves. Warner had the option to pass on each project Locke submitted. Warner was not required to have a "good faith" or "fair" basis for declining to exercise its right to develop her material. Such a requirement would be improper and unworkable. A judge or jury cannot and should not substitute its judgment for a film studio's when the studio is making the creative decision of whether to develop or produce a proposed motion picture. Such highly subjective artistic and business decisions are not proper subjects for judicial review. Moreover, Warner had legitimate commercial and artistic reasons for declining to develop the projects Locke submitted. . . .

Locke filed a timely notice of appeal from the judgment.

Contentions

Locke contends: The trial court erred by granting Warner's motion for summary judgment based on its conclusion there were no disputed issues of material fact; the trial court erred in weighing the evidence, resolving doubts against Locke, the nonmoving party, and adopting only those inferences favorable to Warner where the evidence supported contrary inferences; and the trial court committed reversible error first by failing to make any findings or evidentiary rulings and then by adopting Warner's defective ruling.

Discussion

. . . .

2. *A triable issue exists as to whether Warner breached its contract with Locke by failing to evaluate Locke's proposals on their merits.*

. . . As indicated, the second cause of action alleged Warner breached the contract by "refusing to consider the projects prepared by [Locke] and depriving [Locke] of the benefit of the bargain of the Warner-Locke agreement."[3]

---

[3] Contrary to Warner's contention Locke is raising an unpled claim for breach of the implied covenant of good faith and fair dealing, the second cause of action for breach of contract adequately alleges Warner deprived Locke of the benefit of the bargain of the development deal by refusing to consider her projects. Such conduct by Warner, if proven, would amount to a breach of the covenant, implied "in every contract that neither party will do anything which will injure the right of the other to receive the benefits of the agreement. [Citation.]" . . . .

In granting summary judgment on this claim, the trial court ruled "[a] judge or jury cannot and should not substitute its own judgment for a film studio's when the studio is making the creative decision of whether to develop or produce a proposed motion picture. Such highly-subjective artistic and business decisions are not proper subjects for judicial review."

The trial court's ruling missed the mark by failing to distinguish between Warner's right to make a subjective creative decision, which is not reviewable for reasonableness, and the requirement the dissatisfaction be bona fide or genuine.

a. *General principles.*

. . ."'[W]here a contract confers on one party a discretionary power affecting the rights of the other, a duty is imposed to exercise that discretion in good faith and in accordance with fair dealing.' [Citations.]" (Perdue v. Crocker National Bank (1985) 38 Cal.3d 913, 923 [216 Cal.Rptr. 345, 702 P.2d 503]; accord, Kendall v. Ernest Pestana, Inc. (1985) 40 Cal.3d 488, 500 [220 Cal.Rptr. 818, 709 P.2d 837].) It is settled that in " 'every contract there is an implied covenant that neither party shall do anything which will have the effect of destroying or injuring the right of the other party to receive the fruits of the contract....'" (Kendall, supra, at p. 500; accord, Waller, v. Truck Ins. Exchange, Inc., supra, 11 Cal.4th at p. 36.)

Therefore, when it is a condition of an obligor's duty that he or she be subjectively satisfied with respect to the obligee's performance, the subjective standard of *honest satisfaction* is applicable. . . .

> Where the contract involves matters of fancy, taste or judgment, the promisor is the sole judge of his satisfaction. If he asserts *in good faith* that he is not satisfied, there can be no inquiry into the reasonableness of his attitude. [Citations.] Traditional examples are employment contracts ... and agreements to paint a portrait, write a literary or scientific article, or produce a play or vaudeville act. [Citations.]

In such cases, "the promisor's determination that he is not satisfied, *when made in good faith*, has been held to be a defense to an action on the contract. [Citations.]" (Mattei v. Hopper (1958) 51 Cal.2d 119, 123 [330 P.2d 625], italics added.)

. . . . Therefore, the trial court erred in deferring entirely to what it characterized as Warner's "creative decision" in the handling of the development deal. If Warner acted in bad faith by categorically rejecting Locke's work and refusing to work with her, irrespective of the merits of her proposals, such conduct is not beyond the reach of the law.

b. *Locke presented evidence from which a trier of fact reasonably could infer Warner breached the agreement by refusing to consider her proposals in good faith.*

Merely because Warner paid Locke the guaranteed compensation under the agreement does not establish Warner fulfilled its contractual obligation. As pointed out by Locke, the value in the subject development deal was not merely the guaranteed payments under the agreement, but also the opportunity to direct and produce films and earn additional sums, and most importantly, the opportunity to promote and enhance a career.

Unquestionably, Warner was entitled to reject Locke's work based on its subjective judgment, and its creative decision in that regard is not subject to being second-guessed by a court. However, bearing in mind the requirement that subjective dissatisfaction must be an honestly held dissatisfaction, the evidence raises a triable issue as to whether Warner breached its agreement with Locke by not considering her proposals on their merits.

As indicated, the deposition testimony of Joseph Terry recounted a conversation he had with Bob Brassel, a Warner executive, regarding Locke's projects. In that conversation, Brassel stated " 'Joe, we're not going to work with her,' and then, 'That's Clint's deal.' "

Similarly, the declaration of Mary Wellnitz recalled a conversation she had with Lance Young, a senior vice-president of production at Warner. After discussing the script with Wellnitz, Young told her: "Mary, I want you to know that I think Sondra is a wonderful woman and very talented, but, if you think I can go down the hall and tell Bob Daly that I have a movie I want to make with her he would tell me to forget it. They are not going to make a movie with her here."

The above evidence raises a triable issue of material fact as to whether Warner breached its contract with Locke by categorically refusing to work with her, irrespective of the merits of her proposals. While Warner was entitled to reject Locke's proposals based on its subjective dissatisfaction, the evidence calls into question whether Warner had an honest or good faith dissatisfaction with Locke's proposals, or whether it merely went through the motions of purporting to "consider" her projects.

c. *No merit to Warner's contention Locke seeks to rewrite the instant agreement to limit Warner's discretionary power.*

Warner argues that while the implied covenant of good faith and fair dealing is implied in all contracts, it is limited to assuring compliance with the express terms of the contract and cannot be extended to create obligations not contemplated in the contract. . . .

This principle is illustrated in Carma Developers (Cal.), Inc. v. Marathon Development California, Inc. (1992) 2 Cal.4th 342, 351-352 [6 Cal.Rptr.2d 467, 826 P.2d 710], wherein the parties entered into a lease agreement which stated that if the tenant procured a potential sublessee and asked the landlord for consent to sublease, the landlord had the right to terminate the lease, enter into negotiations with the prospective sublessee, and appropriate for itself all profits from the new arrangement. Carma recognized "[t]he covenant of good faith finds particular application in situations where one party is invested with a discretionary power affecting the rights of another." (Id., at p. 372.) The court expressed the view that "[s]uch power must be exercised in good faith." (Ibid.) At the same time, Carma upheld the right of the landlord under the express terms of the lease to freely exercise its discretion to terminate the lease in order to claim for itself-and deprive the tenant of-the appreciated rental value of the premises. (*Id.*, at p. 376.)

In this regard, Carma stated: "We are aware of no reported case in which a court has held the covenant of good faith may be read to prohibit a party from doing that which is expressly permitted by an agreement. On the contrary, as a general matter, implied terms should never be read to vary express terms. [Citations.] 'The general rule [regarding the covenant of good faith] is plainly subject to the exception that the parties may, by express provisions of the contract, grant the right to engage in the very acts and conduct which would otherwise have been forbidden by an implied covenant of good faith and fair dealing.... This is in accord with the general principle that, in interpreting a contract "an implication ... should not be made when the contrary is indicated in clear and express words." 3 Corbin, Contracts, § 564, p. 298 (1960).... *As to acts and conduct authorized by the express provisions of the contract*, no covenant of good faith and fair dealing can be implied which forbids such acts and conduct. And if defendants were given the right to do what they did by the express provisions of the contract there can be no breach.' [Citation.]" (Carma Developers (Cal.), Inc. v. Marathon Development California, Inc., supra, 2 Cal.4th at p. 374, italics added.).

In Third Story Music, Inc. v. Waits (1995) 41 Cal.App.4th 798, 801 [48 Cal.Rptr.2d 747], the issue presented was "whether a promise to market music, or to refrain from doing so, at the election of the promisor is subject to the implied covenant of good faith and fair dealing where substantial consideration has been paid by the promisor."

In that case, Warner Communications obtained from Third Story Music (TSM) the worldwide right to manufacture, sell, distribute and advertise the musical output of singer/songwriter Tom Waits. . . . The agreement also specifically stated that Warner Communications " 'may at our election refrain from any or all of the foregoing.' " . . . TSM sued Warner Communications for contract damages based on breach of the implied covenant of good faith and fair dealing, claiming Warner Communications had impeded TSM's receiving the benefit of the agreement. . . . Warner Communications demurred to the complaint, alleging the clause in the agreement permitting it to " 'at [its] election refrain' from doing anything to profitably exploit the music is controlling and precludes application of any implied covenant." . . . The demurrer was sustained on those grounds. . . .

The reviewing court affirmed, holding the implied covenant was unavailing to the plaintiff. . . .Because the agreement *expressly* provided Warner Communications had the right to *refrain* from marketing the Waits recordings, the implied covenant of good faith and fair dealing did not limit the discretion given to Warner Communications in that regard. . . .

Warner's reliance herein on Third Story Music, Inc., is misplaced. The Locke/Warner agreement did not give Warner the express right to refrain from working with Locke. Rather, the agreement gave Warner *discretion* with respect to developing Locke's projects. The implied covenant of good faith and fair dealing obligated Warner to exercise that discretion honestly and in good faith.

In sum, the Warner/Locke agreement contained an implied covenant of good faith and fair dealing, that neither party would frustrate the other party's right to receive the benefits of the contract. . . . Whether Warner violated the implied covenant and breached the contract by categorically refusing to work with Locke is a question for the trier of fact. . . .

Disposition

The judgment is reversed with respect to the second . . . cause . . . of action . . . . Locke to recover costs on appeal.

Kitching, J., and Aldrich, J., concurred. . . .

B. The U.C.C. and Implied Terms

Consistent with the common law requirements of good faith and fair dealing, U.C.C. § 1-304 specifically provides that every contract and duty within the purview of the U.C.C. contains an obligation of good faith. This provision precludes a party from invoking rights under the U.C.C. to the extent he has not acted in good faith.

In addition to the implied duty of good faith, Article 2 contains a myriad of implied terms that govern the parties' transaction to the extent the contract does not provide otherwise. As discussed in the formation material, these implied terms often save the parties' agreement from defects due to indefiniteness, as well as provide a set of default rules or gap fillers. Among the numerous gap filler provisions contained in Article 2 are Open Price Terms (§ 2-305); Output, Requirements and Exclusive Dealings (§ 2-306); Absence of Specified Place for Delivery (§ 2-308); and Absence of Specific Time Provisions (§ 2-309). Accordingly, it is critical that the parties have an understanding of the gap filler provisions contained in the U.C.C. in order to make an informed decision about whether to specifically negate the operation of such default rules by including in their contract express provisions addressing matters otherwise governed by the default rules.

SECTION 3. WARRANTIES UNDER THE UCC

A. EXPRESS WARRANTIES

ROYAL BUSINESS MACHINES, INC. V. LORRAINE CORP.
United States Court of Appeals, Seventh Circuit
633 F.2d 34 (1980).

BAKER, District Judge.

This is an appeal from a judgment of the district court entered after a bench trial awarding Michael L. Booher and Lorraine Corp. (Booher) $1,171,216.16 in compensatory and punitive damages against Litton Business Systems, Inc. and Royal Business Machines, Inc. (Royal). The judgment further awarded Booher attorneys' fees of $156,800.00. It denied, for want of consideration, the recovery by Royal of a $596,921.33 indebtedness assessed against Booher earlier in the proceedings in a summary judgment. The judgment also granted Royal a set-off of $12,020.00 for an unpaid balance due on computer typewriters.

The case arose from commercial transactions extending over a period of 18 months between Royal and Booher in which Royal sold and Booher purchased 114 RBC I and 14 RBC II plain paper copying machines. In mid-August 1976, Booher filed suit against Royal in the Indiana courts claiming breach of warranties and fraud. On September 1, 1976, Royal sued Booher on his financing agreements in the district court and also removed the state litigation to the district court where the cases were consolidated.

The issues in the cases arise under Indiana common law and under the U.C.C. as adopted in Indiana, Ind.Code § 26-1-2-102 et seq. (1976). The contentions urged by Royal on appeal are that:

> (1) substantial evidence does not support the findings that Royal made certain express warranties or that it breached any express warranty and, as a matter of law, no warranties were made . . . .
>
> We reverse and remand for a new trial on the grounds set forth in this opinion.

EXPRESS WARRANTIES

We first address the question whether substantial evidence on the record supports the district court's findings that Royal made and breached express warranties to Booher. The trial judge found that Royal Business Machines made and breached the following express warranties:

> (1) that the RBC Model I and II machines and their component parts were of high quality;
>
> (2) that experience and testing had shown that frequency of repairs was very low on such machines and would remain so;
>
> (3) that replacement parts were readily available;
>
> (4) that the cost of maintenance for each RBC machine and cost of supplies was and would remain low, no more than 1/2 cent per copy;
>
> (5) that the RBC machines had been extensively tested and were ready to be marketed;
>
> (6) that experience and reasonable projections had shown that the purchase of the RBC machines by Mr. Booher and Lorraine Corporation and the leasing of the same to customers would return substantial profits to Booher and Lorraine;
>
> (7) that the machines were safe and could not cause fires; and

(8) that service calls were and would be required for the RBC Model II machine on the average of every 7,000 to 9,000 copies, including preventive maintenance calls.

Substantial evidence supports the court's findings as to Numbers 5, 7, 8, and the maintenance aspect of Number 4, but, as a matter of law, Numbers 1, 2, 3, 6, and the cost of supplies portion of Number 4 cannot be considered express warranties.

Paraphrasing U.C.C. § 2-313 as adopted in Indiana,[1] an express warranty is made up of the following elements: (a) an affirmation of fact or promise, (b) that relates to the goods, and (c) becomes a part of the basis of the bargain between the parties. When each of these three elements is present, a warranty is created that the goods shall conform to the affirmation of fact or to the promise.

The decisive test for whether a given representation is a warranty or merely an expression of the seller's opinion is whether the seller asserts a fact of which the buyer is ignorant or merely states an opinion or judgment on a matter of which the seller has no special knowledge and on which the buyer may be expected also to have an opinion and to exercise his judgment. . . . General statements to the effect that goods are "the best," . . . or are "of good quality," . . . or will "last a lifetime" and be "in perfect condition," . . . are generally regarded as expressions of the seller's opinion or "the puffing of his wares" and do not create an express warranty.

No express warranty was created by Royal's affirmation that both RBC machine models and their component parts were of high quality. This was a statement of the seller's opinion, the kind of "puffing" to be expected in any sales transaction, rather than a positive averment of fact describing a product's capabilities to which an express warranty could attach. . . .

Similarly, the representations by Royal that experience and testing had shown that the frequency of repair was "very low" and would remain so lack the specificity of an affirmation of fact upon which a warranty could be predicated. These representations were statements of the seller's opinion.

---

[1] Ind. Code § 26-1-2-313 (1976) provides:

(1) Express warranties by the seller are created as follows:

(a) any affirmation of fact or promise made by the seller to the buyer which relates to the goods and becomes part of the basis of the bargain creates an express warranty that the goods shall conform to the affirmation or promise.

(b) any description of the goods which is made part of the basis of the bargain creates an express warranty that the goods shall conform to the description.

(c) any sample or model which is made part of the basis of the bargain creates an express warranty that the whole of the goods shall conform to the sample or model.

(2) It is not necessary to the creation of an express warranty that the seller use formal words such as "warrant" or "guarantee" or that he had a specific intention to make a warranty, but an affirmation merely of the value of the goods or a statement purporting to be merely the seller's opinion or commendation of the goods does not create a warranty.

The statement that replacement parts were readily available is an assertion of fact, but it is not a fact that relates to the goods sold as required by Ind.Code § 26-1-2-313(1)(a) and is not an express warranty to which the goods were to conform. Neither is the statement about the future costs of supplies being 1/2 cent per copy an assertion of fact that relates to the goods sold, so the statement cannot constitute the basis of an express warranty.

It was also erroneous to find that an express warranty was created by Royal's assurances to Booher that purchase of the RBC machines would bring him substantial profits. Such a representation does not describe the goods within the meaning of U.C.C. § 2-313(1)(b), nor is the representation an affirmation of fact relating to the goods under U.C.C. § 2-313(1)(a). It is merely sales talk and the expression of the seller's opinion. See Regal Motor Products v. Bender, 102 Ohio App. 447, 139 N.E.2d 463, 465 (1956) (representation that goods were "readily saleable" and that the demand for them would create a market was not a warranty). . . .

On the other hand, the assertion that the machines could not cause fires is an assertion of fact relating to the goods, and substantial evidence in the record supports the trial judge's findings that the assertion was made by Royal to Booher.[2] The same may be said for the assertion that the machines were tested and ready to be marketed. See Bemidji Sales Barn v. Chatfield, 312 Minn. 11, 250 N.W.2d 185 (1977) (seller's representation that cattle "had been vaccinated for shipping fever and were ready for the farm" constituted an express warranty). . . . The record supports the district court's finding that Royal represented that the machines had been tested.[3]

Michael Booher testified at trial that Tom Gavel had assured Booher the Royal Bond Copier machine had been tested: "He (Gavel) said, 'They have been well tested,' and said, 'They are great machines.' " (Tr. Vol. III, p. 292).

Booher also testified that Jack Airey, a Royal representative, had stated at a promotional meeting that the RBC II had been extensively tested and was ready to market: "They (Royal) were now ready to market it (RBC II); that it had been extensively tested." . . .

As for findings 8 and the maintenance portion of Number 4, Royal's argument that those statements relate to predictions for the future and cannot qualify as warranties is unpersuasive. An expression of future capacity or performance can constitute an express warranty. In Teter v. Shultz, 110 Ind.App. 541, 39 N.E.2d 802, 804 (1942), the Indiana courts held that a seller's statement that dairy cows would give six gallons of milk per day was an affirmation of fact by the seller relating to the goods. It was not a statement of value nor was it merely a statement of the seller's opinion. The Indiana courts have also found that

---

[2] Michael Booher testified at trial that in February or March of 1975 he called the service department at Royal Typewriter Company and spoke with either Bruce Lewis, national service manager, or with Joe Miller. Booher testified that he told the Royal representative that he had received a report of a fire in an RBC I machine at a customer's office. Booher then testified, "They told me that that couldn't happen." (Tr. Vol. IV, pp. 457-59). For a discussion of whether the assertions about fires, maintenance, and service calls became part of the basis of the bargain, see infra, pp. 44-45.

[3] The trial court's findings speak of "RBC machines" with reference to the testing warranty. The court's specific findings, however, refer only to the RBC II machine. On retrial, it would clarify matters if the specific machine intended were named.

an express warranty was created by a seller's representation that a windmill was capable of furnishing power to grind 20 to 30 bushels of grain per hour in a moderate wind and with a very light wind would pump an abundance of water. . . . Further, in General Supply and Equipment Co. v. Phillips, supra, the Texas courts upheld the following express warranties made by a seller of roof panels: (1) that tests show no deterioration in 5 years of normal use; (2) that the roofing panels won't turn black or discolor ... even after years of exposure; and (3) that the panels will not burn, rot, rust, or mildew. Snow's Laundry and Dry Cleaning v. Georgia Power Co., 61 Ga.App. 402, 6 S.E.2d 159 (1959), impliedly recognized that a warranty as to future gas consumption following installation of gas equipment was possible. In holding that no warranty was created in that particular case, the Georgia court noted: "The statements made by Spencer were denominated by him as estimates, nowhere did he warrant or guarantee that the gas consumption would not exceed $230.50 per month." . . .

Whether a seller affirmed a fact or made a promise amounting to a warranty is a question of fact reserved for the trier of fact. . . . Substantial evidence in the record supports the finding that Royal made the assertion to Booher that maintenance cost for the machine would run 1/2 cent per copy and that this assertion was not an estimate but an assertion of a fact of performance capability.

Gavel testified by deposition taken on May 27, 1977, which was admitted into evidence at trial, that he told Booher that service costs for the RBC I machine would be half a cent (Gavel Dep., p. 28). He further testified in reference to the costs quoted to dealers on the RBC II machines that "(n)obody ever implied they were estimates" . . . .

Finding Number 8, that service calls on the RBC II would be required every 7,000 to 9,000 copies, relates to performance capability and could constitute the basis of an express warranty. There is substantial evidence in the record to support the finding that this assertion was also made.

While substantial evidence supports the trial court's findings as to the making of those four affirmations of fact or promises, the district court failed to make the further finding that they became part of the basis of the bargain. Ind.Code § 26-1-2-313(1) (1976). While Royal may have made such affirmations to Booher, the question of his knowledge or reliance is another matter.[7]

Cf. Woodruff v. Clark County Farm Bureau Coop. Ass'n, 153 Ind.App. 31, 286 N.E.2d 188 (1972) where the court stated: "Whether such assertions (statements by the seller) constituted express warranties and whether (the buyer) relied upon these assertions are material issues of fact to be determined by the trier of fact." . . .

[7] The requirement that a statement be part of the basis of the bargain in order to constitute an express warranty "is essentially a reliance requirement and is inextricably intertwined with the initial determination as to whether given language may constitute an express warranty since affirmations, promises and descriptions tend to become a part of the basis of the bargain. It was the intention of the drafters of the U.C.C. not to require a strong showing of reliance. In fact, they envisioned that all statements of the seller become part of the basis of the bargain unless clear affirmative proof is shown to the contrary. See Official Comments 3 and 8 to U.C.C. § 2-313." . . . (Citation Omitted).

> (F)or all practical purposes it is suggested that no great change was wrought by the Code. Whether one speaks of reliance or basis of the bargain, little difference exists between the two. In neither case should the statement be required to have been the sole factor leading the buyer to purchase. In either case, the statement should, at least, be one of such factors. What is really crucial is whether the statement was made as an affirmation of fact, the goods did not live up to the statement, and the defect was not so apparent that the buyer could not be held to have discovered it for himself. . . . (Citation omitted).

This case is complicated by the fact that it involved a series of sales transactions between the same parties over approximately an 18-month period and concerned two different machines. The situations of the parties, their knowledge and reliance, may be expected to change in light of their experience during that time. An affirmation of fact which the buyer from his experience knows to be untrue cannot form a part of the basis of the bargain. . . . Therefore, as to each purchase, Booher's expanding knowledge of the capacities of the copying machines would have to be considered in deciding whether Royal's representations were part of the basis of the bargain. The same representations that could have constituted an express warranty early in the series of transactions might not have qualified as an express warranty in a later transaction if the buyer had acquired independent knowledge as to the fact asserted.

The trial court did not indicate that it considered whether the warranties could exist and apply to each transaction in the series. Such an analysis is crucial to a just determination. Its absence renders the district court's findings insufficient on the issue of the breach of express warranties.

Since a retrial on the questions of the breach of express warranties and the extent of damages is necessary, we offer the following observations. The court must consider whether the machines were defective upon delivery. Breach occurs only if the goods are defective upon delivery and not if the goods later become defective through abuse or neglect. . . .

In considering the promise relating to the cost of maintenance, the district court should determine at what stage Booher's own knowledge and experience prevented him from blindly relying on the representations of Royal. A similar analysis is needed in examining the representation concerning fire hazard in the RBC I machines. The court also should determine when that representation was made. If not made until February 1975, the representation could not have been the basis for sales made prior to that date. . . .

For the foregoing reasons the judgment of the district court is reversed, and the cause is remanded for a new trial on the remaining issues outlined herein. Each party is to bear its own costs.

NOTES AND QUESTIONS:

1. In *Royal Business Machines, Inc.*, 633 F.2d 34 (7th Cir. 1980), the court discussed the creation of warranties for the purpose of determining whether a breach occurred. We will return to this case later to explore additional issues related to a buyer's rights and obligations once a breach has been established.

DAUGHTREY V. ASHE
Supreme Court of Virginia
413 S.E.2d 336 (1992).

WHITING, Justice.

In this dispute between the buyers and the sellers of a diamond bracelet, the principal issues arise under the Uniform Commercial Code-Sales. Code §§ 8.2-101 through 8.2-725. Specifically, they are: (1) whether the sellers' appraisal statement of the grade of diamonds on the bracelet is a description of the goods under Code § 8.2-313(1)(b), and therefore an express warranty; and (2) whether such a statement made the description "a part of the basis of the bargain" under Code § 8.2-313(1)(b), and therefore an express warranty, when the buyers did not know of the warranty until some time after the purchase price was paid and the bracelet was delivered.

In conformity with familiar appellate principles, we state the evidence in the light most favorable to the sellers, who prevailed in the trial court.

In October 1985, W. Hayes Daughtrey consulted Sidney Ashe (Ashe), a jeweler, about the purchase of a diamond bracelet as a Christmas gift for his wife, Fenton C. Daughtrey. Ashe exhibited, and offered to sell, a diamond bracelet to Daughtrey for $15,000. Although Ashe "knew" and "classified" the bracelet diamonds as v.v.s. grade (v.v.s. is one of the highest ratings in a quality classification system employed by gemologists and jewelers), he merely described the diamonds as "nice" in his conversation with Daughtrey. Ashe told Daughtrey that if he was later dissatisfied with the bracelet, he would refund the purchase price upon its return.

When Daughtrey later telephoned Ashe and told him he would buy the bracelet, Ashe had Adele Ashe, his business associate, complete an appraisal form which he signed. The form contained the following pertinent language:

> The following represents our estimate for insurance purposes only, of the present retail replacement cost of identical items, and not necessarily the amounts that might be obtained if the articles were offered for sale . . . .

DESCRIPTION	**APPRAISED VALUE**
platinum diamond bracelet, set with 28 brilliant full ct diamonds weighing a total of 10 carats. H color and v.v.s. quality.	$25,000.00

(Emphasis added.)

When Daughtrey came with his daughter to close the sale, he showed the bracelet to his daughter and then paid Ashe for it. As Ashe was counting the money, Daughtrey handed the bracelet to Adele Ashe, who put it in a box together with the appraisal and delivered the box to Daughtrey. Daughtrey later gave the bracelet to his wife as a Christmas present.

In February 1989, Daughtrey discovered that the diamonds were not of v.v.s. quality when another jeweler looked at the bracelet. Shortly thereafter, Daughtrey complained to Ashe, who refused to replace the bracelet with one mounted with diamonds of v.v.s. quality but offered to refund the purchase price upon return of the bracelet. Because the value of diamonds generally had increased in the meantime, Daughtrey declined Ashe's offer.

On May 8, 1989, Daughtrey and his wife filed this specific performance suit against Sidney Ashe and Adele Ashe t/a Ashe Jewelers (the Ashes) to compel them to replace the bracelet with one mounted with v.v.s. diamonds or pay appropriate damages. After hearing the evidence, the trial court found that the diamonds "were of substantially lesser grade" than v.v.s. Nevertheless, because it concluded that the Daughtreys had not proven that "the appraisal was a term or condition of the sale nor a warranty upon which [they] relied in the purchase of the bracelet," the court denied relief for breach of warranty. The Daughtreys appeal.

First, we consider whether Ashe's statement of the grade of the diamonds was an express warranty. Code § 8.2-313 provides in pertinent part:

> (1) Express warranties by the seller are created as follows: . . . .
>
> (b) any description of the goods which is made part of the basis of the bargain creates an express warranty that the goods shall conform to the description.

The Ashes argue that the statement in the appraisal form is not an express warranty for two reasons.

First, they say the "appraisal on its face stated that it was 'for insurance purposes only.'" However, we think that the balance of the emphasized language in the appraisal form demonstrates that the limiting language relates *only* to the statement of the *appraised value.* Therefore, Ashe's description of the grade of the diamonds should be treated as any other statement he may have made about them.

Second, the Ashes contend that Ashe's statement of the grade of the diamonds is a mere opinion and, thus, cannot qualify as an express warranty under Code § 8.2-313(2). Code § 8.2-313(2) provides:

> It is not necessary to the creation of an express warranty that the seller use formal words such as "warrant" or "guarantee" or that he have a specific intention to make a warranty, but an affirmation merely of the value of the goods or a statement purporting to be merely the seller's opinion or commendation of the goods does not create a warranty.

The Ashes rely principally upon a North Carolina case construing the identical code section from the North Carolina Uniform Commercial Code. *Hall v. T.L. Kemp Jewelry, Inc.*, 71 N.C.App. 101, 104, 322 S.E.2d 7, 10 (1984) (jeweler's assurance of value of jewels mere opinion under N.C.Gen.Stat. § 25-2-313, not warranty). However, here, Ashe did more than give a mere opinion of the value of the goods; he specifically described them as diamonds of "H color and v.v.s. quality."

Ashe did not qualify his statement as a mere opinion. And, if one who has superior knowledge makes a statement about the goods sold and does not qualify the statement as his opinion, the statement will be treated as a statement of fact. . . .

Nor does it matter that the opinions of other jewelers varied in minor respects. All of them said, and the trial judge found, that the diamonds were of a grade substantially less than v.v.s.

Clearly, Ashe intended to sell Daughtrey v.v.s. diamonds. He testified that he used only the term "nice" diamonds but "[n]ever mentioned vvs because [Daughtrey] didn't know anything about vvs." Later, Ashe testified that "I know when I sold the bracelet and I classified it as vvs, I knew it was vvs."

Given these considerations, we conclude that Ashe's description of the goods was more than his opinion; rather, he intended it to be a statement of a fact. Therefore, the court erred in holding that the description was not an express warranty under Code § 8.2-313(2).

Next, the Ashes maintain that because the description of the diamonds as v.v.s. quality was not discussed, Daughtrey could not have relied upon Ashe's warranty and, thus, it cannot be treated as "a part of the basis of the bargain."

In our opinion, the "part of the basis of the bargain" language of Code § 8.2-313(1)(b) does not establish a buyer's reliance requirement. Instead, this language makes a seller's description of the goods that is not his mere opinion a representation that defines his obligation. . . .

Our construction of Code § 8.2-313, containing language identical to § 2-313 of the Uniform Commercial Code, is supported by a consideration of the following pertinent portions of the Official Comment to the Uniform Commercial Code section:

> The present section deals with affirmations of fact by the seller, descriptions of the goods . . . exactly as any other part of a negotiation which ends in a contract is dealt with. No specific intention to make a warranty is necessary if any of these factors is made part of the basis of the bargain. In actual practice affirmations of fact made by the seller about the goods during a bargain are regarded as a part of the description of those goods; hence *no particular reliance* on such statements need be shown in order to weave them into the fabric of the agreement. Rather, any fact which is to take such affirmations, once made, out of the agreement requires clear affirmative proof. The issue normally is one of fact. Official Comment 3 (emphasis added).
>
> In view of the principle that *the whole purpose of the law of warranty is to determine what it is that the seller has in essence agreed to sell,* the policy is adopted of those cases which refuse except in unusual circumstances to recognize a material deletion of the seller's obligation. Thus, a contract is normally a contract for a sale of something describable and described.
>
> . . . . Official Comment 4 (emphasis added).
>
> Paragraph (1)(b) makes specific some of the principles set forth above when a description of the goods is given by the seller.
>
> . . . . Official Comment 5.
>
> *The precise time when words of description or affirmation are made . . . is not material. The sole question is whether the language [is] fairly to be regarded as part of the contract.* If language is used after the closing of the deal (as when the buyer when taking delivery asks and receives an additional assurance), the warranty becomes a modification, and need not be supported by consideration, if it is otherwise reasonable and in order (Section 2-209). Official Comment 7 (emphasis added).
>
> Concerning affirmations of value or a seller's opinion or commendation under subsection (2), the *basic question* remains the same: *What statements of the seller have in the circumstances and in objective judgment become part of the basis of the bargain*? As indicated above, all of the statements of the seller do so unless good reason is shown to the contrary. The provisions of subsection (2) are included, however, since common experience discloses that some statements or predictions cannot fairly be viewed as entering into the bargain. Official Comment 8 (emphasis added).

We conclude from the language used in Code § 8.2-313 and the Official Comment thereto that the drafters of the Uniform Commercial Code intended to modify the traditional requirement of buyer reliance on express warranties. Such a requirement was contained in the following pertinent language of the earlier Uniform Sales Act § 12: "[a]ny affirmation of fact or any promise by the seller relating to the goods is an express warranty if the natural tendency of such affirmation or promise is to *induce* the buyer to purchase the goods, and if the buyer purchases the goods *relying thereon.*" (Emphasis added.) We note that "induce" and "reliance" appear nowhere in Code § 8.2-313, as contrasted with the reference to buyer reliance in the subsequent section, Code § 8.2-315, dealing with an implied warranty of fitness for a particular purpose.

Hence, the seller's representation need only be "a part of the basis of the bargain," as set forth in Code § 8.2-313(1)(b). The term "bargain" is not defined in the Code, but it is used in the following definition of "agreement" as

> the bargain of the parties in fact as found in their language or by implication from other circumstances.... Whether an agreement has legal consequences is determined by the provisions of this act, if applicable; otherwise by the law of contracts as provided in Code § 8.1-103. (Compare "Contract"). Code § 8.1-201(3).
>
> The word "'Contract' means the total legal obligation which results from the parties' agreement as affected by this act and any other applicable rules of law. (Compare "Agreement.")" Code § 8.1-201(11).

Ashe introduced no evidence of any factor that would take his affirmation of the quality of the diamonds out of the agreement. Therefore, his affirmation was "a part of the basis of the bargain." Accordingly, we hold that the Daughtreys are entitled to recover for their loss of bargain, and that the court erred in ruling to the contrary.

Therefore, we will reverse the judgment of the trial court and remand the case for further proceedings to ascertain the Daughtreys' damages.

Reversed and remanded.

COMPTON, Justice, dissenting.

The seller supplied an appraisal form "for insurance purposes only" so that the buyer could obtain adequate replacement coverage. Because I do not believe that this representation was a "part of the basis of the bargain," Code § 8.2-313(1)(b), I would affirm the judgment of the trial court.

NOTES AND QUESTIONS:

1. Read U.C.C. § 2-313 (Express Warranties By Affirmation, Promise, Description, Sample) (2002).

2. Recall the case of *Germain Fruit Co. v. J.K. Armsby Co.*, 96 P. 319 (Calif. 1908), discussed in connection with the parol evidence material, where the buyer's claim was premised on an express warranty by sample.

B. IMPLIED WARRANTIES

WEBSTER V. BLUE SHIP TEA ROOM, INC.
Supreme Judicial Court of Massachusetts
198 N.E.2d 309 (1964).

REARDON, Justice.

This is a case which by its nature evokes earnest study not only of the law but also of the culinary traditions of the Commonwealth which bear so heavily upon its outcome. It is an action to recover damages for personal injuries sustained by reason of a breach of implied warranty of food served by the defendant in its restaurant. An auditor, whose findings of fact were not to be final, found for the plaintiff. On a retrial in the Superior Court before a judge and jury, in which the plaintiff testified, the jury returned a verdict for her. The defendant is here on exceptions to the refusal of the judge (1) to strike certain portions of the auditor's report, (2) to direct a verdict for the defendant, and (3) to allow the defendant's motion for the entry of a verdict in its favor under leave reserved.

The jury could have found the following facts: On Saturday, April 25, 1959, about 1 P. M., the plaintiff, accompanied by her sister and her aunt, entered the Blue Ship Tea Room operated by the defendant. The group was seated at a table and supplied with menus.

This restaurant, which the plaintiff characterized as "quaint," was located in Boston "on the third floor of an old building on T Wharf which overlooks the ocean."

The plaintiff, who had been born and brought up in New England (a fact of some consequence), ordered clam chowder and crabmeat salad. Within a few minutes she received tidings to the effect that "there was no more clam chowder," whereupon she ordered a cup of fish chowder. Presently, there was set before her "a small bowl of fish chowder." She had previously enjoyed a breakfast about 9 A.M. which had given her no difficulty. "The fish chowder contained haddock, potatoes, milk, water and seasoning. The chowder was milky in color and not clear. The haddock and potatoes were in chunks" (also a fact of consequence). "She agitated it a little with the spoon and observed that it was a fairly full bowl . . . . It was hot when she got it, but she did not tip it with her spoon because it was hot . . . but stirred it in an up and under motion. She denied that she did this because she was looking for something, but it was rather because she wanted an even distribution of fish and potatoes." "She started to eat it, alternating between the chowder and crackers which were on the table with . . . [some] rolls. She ate about 3 or 4 spoonfuls then stopped. She looked at the spoonfuls as she was eating. She saw equal parts of liquid, potato and fish as she spooned it into her mouth. She did not see anything unusual about it. After 3 or 4 spoonfuls she was aware that something had lodged in her throat because she couldn't swallow and couldn't clear her throat by gulping and she could feel it." This misadventure led to two esophagoscopies at the Massachusetts General Hospital, in the second of which, on April 27, 1959, a fish bone was found and removed. The sequence of events produced injury to the plaintiff which was not insubstantial.

We must decide whether a fish bone lurking in a fish chowder, about the ingredients of which there is no other complaint, constitutes a breach of implied warranty under applicable provisions of the Uniform Commercial Code,[1] the annotations to which are not helpful on this point. As the judge put it in his charge, "Was the fish chowder fit to be eaten and wholesome? . . . [N]obody is claiming that the fish itself wasn't wholesome. . . . But the bone of contention here-I don't mean that for a pun-but was this fish bone a foreign substance that made the fish chowder unwholesome or not fit to be eaten?"

The plaintiff has vigorously reminded us of the high standards imposed by this court where the sale of food is involved (see Flynn v. First Natl. Stores Inc., 296 Mass. 521, 523, 6 N.E.2d 814) and has made reference to cases involving stones in beans (Friend v. Childs Dining Hall Co., 231 Mass. 65, 120 N.E. 407, 5 A.L.R. 1100), trichinae in pork (Holt v. Mann, 294 Mass. 21, 22, 200 N.E. 403), and to certain other cases, here and elsewhere, serving to bolster her contention of breach of warranty.

The defendant asserts that here was a native New Englander eating fish chowder in a "quaint" Boston dining place where she had been before; that "[f]ish chowder, as it is served and enjoyed by New Englanders, is a hearty dish, originally designed to satisfy the appetites of our seamen and fishermen"; that "[t]his court knows well that we are not talking of some insipid broth as is customarily served to convalescents." We are asked to rule in such fashion that no chef is forced "to reduce the pieces of fish in the chowder to miniscule size in an effort to ascertain if they contained any pieces of bone." "In so ruling," we are told (in the defendant's brief), "the court will not only uphold its reputation for legal knowledge and acumen, but will, as loyal sons of Massachusetts, save our world-renowned fish chowder from degenerating into an insipid broth containing the mere essence of its former stature as a culinary masterpiece." Notwithstanding these passionate entreaties we are bound to examine with detachment the nature of fish chowder and what might happen to it under varying interpretations of the Uniform Commercial Code.

Chowder is an ancient dish preexisting even "the appetites of our seamen and fishermen." It was perhaps the common ancestor of the "more refined cream soups, purées, and bisques." Berolzheimer, The American Woman's Cook Book (Publisher's Guild Inc., New York, 1941) p. 176. The word "chowder" comes from the French "chaudière," meaning a "cauldron" or "pot." "In the fishing villages of Brittany . . . 'faire la chaudière' means to supply a cauldron in which is cooked a mess of fish and biscuit with some savoury condiments, a hodge-podge contributed by the fishermen themselves, each of whom in return receives his share of the prepared dish. The Breton fishermen probably carried the custom to Newfoundland, long famous for its chowder, whence it has spread to Nova Scotia, New Brunswick, and New England." A New English Dictionary (MacMillan and Co., 1893) p. 386. Our literature over the years abounds in references not only to the delights of

[1] (1) Unless excluded or modified by section 2-316, a warranty that the goods shall be merchantable is implied in a contract for their sale if the seller is a merchant with respect to goods of that kind. Under this section the serving for value of food or drink to be consumed either on the premises or elsewhere is a sale. (2) Goods to be merchantable must at least be such as . . . (c) are fit for the ordinary purposes for which such goods are used . . . . G.L. c. 106, § 2-314. . . .

chowder but also to its manufacture. A namesake of the plaintiff, Daniel Webster, had a recipe for fish chowder which has survived into a number of modern cookbooks[2] and in which the removal of fish bones is not mentioned at all. One old time recipe recited in the New English Dictionary study defines chowder as "A dish made of fresh fish (esp. cod) or clams, stewed with slices of pork or bacon, onions, and biscuit. 'Cider and champagne are sometimes added.'" Hawthorne, in The House of the Seven Gables (Allyn and Bacon, Boston, 1957) p. 8, speaks of "[a] codfish of sixty pounds, caught in the bay, [which] had been dissolved into the rich liquid of a chowder." A chowder variant, cod "Muddle," was made in Plymouth in the 1890s by taking "a three or four pound codfish, head added. Season with salt and pepper and boil in just enough water to keep from burning. When cooked, add milk and piece of butter."[3] The recitation of these ancient formulae suffices to indicate that in the construction of chowders in these parts in other years, worries about fish bones played no role whatsoever. This broad outlook on chowders has persisted in more modern cookbooks. "The chowder of today is much the same as the old chowder. . . ." The American Woman's Cook Book, supra, p. 176. The all embracing Fannie Farmer states in a portion of her recipe, fish chowder is made with a "fish skinned, but head and tail left on. Cut off head and tail and remove fish from backbone. Cut fish in 2-inch pieces and set aside. Put head, tail, and backbone broken in pieces, in stewpan; add 2 cups cold water and bring slowly to boiling point . . . ." The liquor thus produced from the bones is added to the balance of the chowder. Farmer, The Boston Cooking School Cook Book (Little Brown Co., 1937) p. 166.

Thus, we consider a dish which for many long years, if well made, has been made generally as outlined above. It is not too much to say that a person sitting down in New England to consume a good New England fish chowder embarks on a gustatory adventure which may entail the removal of some fish bones from his bowl as he proceeds. We are not inclined to tamper with age old recipes by any amendment reflecting the plaintiff's view of the effect of the Uniform Commercial Code upon them. We are aware of the heavy body of case law involving foreign substances in food, but we sense a strong distinction between them and those relative to unwholesomeness of the food itself, e. g., tainted mackerel (Smith v. Gerrish, 256 Mass. 183, 152 N.E. 318), and a fish bone in a fish chowder. Certain Massachusetts cooks might cavil at the ingredients contained in the chowder in this case in that it lacked the heartening lift of salt pork. In any event, we consider that the joys of life in New England include the ready availability of fresh fish chowder. We should be prepared to cope with the hazards of fish bones, the occasional presence of which in chowders is, it seems to us, to be anticipated, and which, in the light of a hallowed tradition, do not impair their fitness or merchantability. While we are buoyed up in this conclusion by Shapiro v. Hotel Statler Corp., 132 F.Supp. 891 (S.D.Cal.), in which the bone which afflicted the

---

[2] "Take a cod of ten pounds, well cleaned, leaving on the skin. Cut into pieces one and a half pounds thick, preserving the head whole. Take one and a half pounds of clear, fat salt pork, cut in thin slices. Do the same with twelve potatoes. Take the largest pot you have. Fry out the pork first, then take out the pieces of pork, leaving in the drippings. Add to that three parts of water, a layer of fish, so as to cover the bottom of the pot; next a layer of potatoes, then two tablespoons of salt, 1 teaspoon of pepper, then the pork, another layer of fish, and the remainder of the potatoes. Fill the pot with water to cover the ingredients. Put over a good fire. Let the chowder boil twenty-five minutes. When this is done have a quart of boiling milk ready, and ten hard crackers split and dipped in cold water. Add milk and crackers. Let the whole boil five minutes. The chowder is then ready to be first-rate if you have followed the directions. An onion may be added if you like the flavor." "This chowder," he adds, "is suitable for a large fishing party." Wolcott, The Yankee Cook Book (Coward-McCann, Inc., New York City, 1939) p. 9.

[3] Atwood, Receipts for Cooking Fish (Avery & Doten, Plymouth, 1896) p. 8.

plaintiff appeared in "Hot Barquette of Seafood Mornay," we know that the United States District Court of Southern California, situated as are we upon a coast, might be expected to share our views. We are most impressed, however, by Allen v. Grafton, 170 Ohio St. 249, 164 N.E.2d 167, where in Ohio, the Midwest, in a case where the plaintiff was injured by a piece of oyster shell in an order of fried oysters, Mr. Justice Taft (now Chief Justice) in a majority opinion held that "the possible presence of a piece of oyster shell in or attached to an oyster is so well known to anyone who eats oysters that we can say as a matter of law that one who eats oysters can reasonably anticipate and guard against eating such a piece of shell . . . ." (P. 259 of 170 Ohio St., p. 174 of 164 N.E.2d.) [sic]

Thus, while we sympathize with the plaintiff who has suffered a peculiarly New England injury, the order must be

Exceptions sustained.

Judgment for the defendant.

AMBASSADOR STEEL CO. V. EWALD STEEL CO.
Court of Appeals of Michigan
190 N.W.2d 275 (1971).

FITZGERALD, Judge.

This is an appeal by leave granted from a circuit court order affirming a judgment of the common pleas court for $1,055.78 in favor of plaintiff in an action in assumpsit. Plaintiff appeals the judgment as inadequate.

Plaintiff and defendant are both merchants in the business of the sale of steel. On or about October 4 and 5, 1966, plaintiff sold a certain amount of steel to defendant. The purchase price of the steel was $9,856.44, of which defendant paid $4,107.60, leaving an unpaid balance of $5,748.84. Plaintiff brought an action in the common pleas court to recover the balance due, waiving all amounts over $5,000 so as to bring the matter within the jurisdiction of that court.

Defendant admitted the purchase price of the steel, but claimed a set-off, alleging that plaintiff breached its implied warranty of merchantability in that plaintiff failed to supply defendant with "commercial quality" steel, that is, steel with a carbon content of 1010 to 1020. The defect came to light when the company to whom the defendant in turn sold the steel informed defendant that the steel cracked after being welded on to railroad cars. As a result of this, defendant's customer charged back its losses to defendant. Defendant thus claimed the set-off against plaintiff.

The trial court allowed defendant to set off the entire amount of the charge-back, with the exception of a claim for overhead, and entered a judgment for plaintiff in the amount of $1,055.78. Plaintiff appealed to the circuit court, contending the judgment was inadequate. The circuit court affirmed, plaintiff applied for leave to appeal to this court and we granted it.

Plaintiff on appeal raises four issues which will be dealt with Seriatim.

The first issue can be stated in the following form:

As between dealers in steel, is there an implied warranty that the steel is merchantable for the purpose for which it is used, where plaintiff was not advised by defendant of the use to which the steel was to be put?

Plaintiff contends on appeal that because defendant did not inform plaintiff of the purposes for which the steel was to be used, defendant cannot claim that it was not fit for the purpose for which it was used. Defendant, however, appears to be relying on a different implied warranty, that of merchantability, and not that of particular fitness.

Section 2-314 of the Uniform Commercial Code provides, in part:

> (1) Unless excluded or modified . . ., a warranty that the goods shall be merchantable is implied in a contract for their sale if the seller is a merchant with respect to goods of that kind. . . .
>
> (2) Goods to be merchantable must be at least such as
>
> (a) pass without objection in the trade under the contract description; and
>
> (b) . . .
>
> (c) are fit for the ordinary purposes for which such goods are used; and
>
> (d) run, within the variations permitted by the agreement, of even kind, quality and quantity within each unit and among all units involved; and
>
> (e) . . .
>
> (f) . . .
>
> (3) Unless excluded or modified . . . , other implied warranties may arise from course of dealing or usage of trade. (M.C.L.A. § 440.2314 (Stat.Ann.1964 Rev. § 19.2314)).

This section is further explained in the Comments of National Conference of Commissioners following the section, which states:

> 2. The question when the warranty is imposed turns basically on the meaning of the terms of the agreement as recognized in the trade. Goods delivered under an agreement made by a merchant in a given line of trade must be of a quality comparable to that generally acceptable in that line of trade under the description or other designation of the goods used in the agreement.

Thus, unless there is an exclusion or modification, when, as here, a merchant sells such goods, an implied warranty arises that the goods would pass without objection in the trade under the contract description; also, that they are fit for the ordinary purposes for which the goods are used.

The implied warranty of merchantability is decidedly different from the implied warranty for a particular purpose that arises under M.C.L.A. § 440.2315 (Stat.Ann.1964 Rev. § 19.2315). The particular purpose warranty is defined by the official UCC comment as:

> 2. A "Particular purpose" differs from the ordinary purpose for which the goods are used in that it envisages a specific use by the buyer which is peculiar to the nature of his business whereas the ordinary purposes for which goods are used are those envisaged in the concept of merchantability and go to uses which are customarily made of the goods in question. For example, shoes are generally used for the purpose of walking upon ordinary ground, but a seller may know that a particular pair was selected to be used for climbing mountains.

It appears, then, that the warranty of merchantability warrants that the goods sold are of average quality within the industry, whereas a warranty of fitness for a particular purpose warrants that the goods sold are fit for the purposes for which they are intended. The latter is also further qualified by the requirement that the seller must know, at the time of sale, the particular purpose for which the goods are required and also that the buyer is relying on the seller to select or furnish suitable goods.

In the instant case, it is undisputed that the plaintiff was not made aware of the purpose for which the steel was to be used. Therefore, the implied warranty of fitness for a particular purpose did not arise under M.C.L.A. § 440.2315 (Stat.Ann.1964 Rev. § 19.2315).

The question then becomes whether or not the steel sold by plaintiff to defendant was subject to the implied warranty of merchantability under M.C.L.A. § 440.2314 (Stat.Ann.1964 Rev. § 19.2314). Although defendant sold the goods to a third party, M.C.L.A. § 440.2314 (Stat.Ann.1964 Rev. § 19.2314) Comment 1 states that the warranty of merchantability applies to goods sold for resale as well as those for sale. And, as we previously stated, Comment 2 of the same section states that the question of when the warranty is imposed turns basically on the meaning of the terms as recognized in the trade.

M.C.L.A. § 440.1205(2) (Stat.Ann.1964 Rev. § 19.1205(2)) defines a usage of trade as:

> any practice or method of dealing having such regularity of observance in a place, vocation or trade as to justify an expectation that it will be observed with respect to the transaction in question.

M.C.L.A. § 440.1205(3) (Stat.Ann.1964 Rev. § 19.1205(3)) provides,

> A course of dealing between parties and any usage of trade in the vocation in which they are engaged or of which they are or should be aware give particular meaning to and supplement or qualify terms of an agreement.

Testimony in the transcript indicates that defendant made no specific request concerning the particular quality of steel they ordered. However, there was also ample testimony below to the effect that when an order is placed without specification as to the particular quality desired, custom and usage of the steel business is that a "commercial quality" steel, that is, steel with a carbon content between 1010 and 1020, is to be used. Further testimony was to the effect that if one desired steel other than "commercial quality" it must be specified in the order, according to local custom and usage. The testimony indicated that the steel sold by plaintiff to defendant was not within the commercial range, thus the steel cracked after being welded. Therefore, plaintiff breached the implied warranty of merchantability in selling to defendant steel of a different quality than ordinarily sold in the custom and usage of the steel business, and not fit for the ordinary purposes for which such goods are used. M.C.L.A. § 440.2314 (Stat.Ann.1964 Rev. § 19.2314).

Plaintiff raises the point that they were not notified of the purpose to which the steel was to be put. Apparently plaintiff implies that the use made of the steel was a particular purpose and thus not an ordinary purpose. We have already held that plaintiff is not liable for any implied warranty for fitness for a particular purpose. Furthermore, we need not decide whether this was a particular purpose, because the quality of steel that should have been delivered under the general warranty of merchantability, but was not, was sufficient to satisfy the use in the instant case.

Plaintiff also raises the contention that there can be no implied warranty because defendant did not inspect the goods. Plaintiff cites Salzman v. Maldaver (1946), 315 Mich. 403, 24 N.W.2d 161, to support this contention.

Salzman suggests that one who buys an article that is subject to his inspection, but does not inspect it, cannot later claim breach of an implied warranty. However, Salzman was decided under the Uniform Sales Act, C.L.1929, § 9454 (Stat.Ann. § 19.255), which was superseded by the U.C.C. The pertinent part of the U.C.C. is M.C.L.A. § 440.2316(3)(b) (Stat.Ann.1964 Rev. § 19.2316(3)) (b)) which provides:

> When the buyer before entering into the contract has examined the goods or the sample or model as fully as he desired or has refused to examine the goods there is no implied warranty with regard to defects which an examination ought in the circumstances to have revealed to him.

Thus, under the above section it appears that the buyer must have in fact examined the goods, not the case here, or must have refused a demand by the seller that he do so, also not the case here. Additionally, the section applies only to defects that would have been revealed upon examination. There is testimony in the record indicating that in order to have discovered the defect in the steel, a test for carbon content, not merely an examination, would have had to have been made. Thus, a reasonable examination would not have revealed the defects in the steel. We therefore hold that M.C.L.A. § 440.2316(3)(b) (Stat.Ann.1964 Rev. § 19.2316(3)(b)) did not exclude or modify the implied warranty of merchantability in the instant case. . . .

Therefore, the lower court should be, and hereby is, affirmed. Costs to appellees.

TYSON V. CIBA-GEIGY CORP.
Court of Appeals of North Carolina
347 S.E.2d 473 (1986).

HEDRICK, Chief Judge.

. . . .

Plaintiff assigns as error the trial court's granting of defendants' motions for directed verdict. Plaintiff first argues in support of this assignment of error that the evidence is sufficient for the jury to find that Ciba-Geigy breached an express warranty on the Dual 8E label that the product was reasonably fit for the purposes referred to in the directions for use. This argument is without merit. The label attached to the Dual 8E delivered to plaintiff contained the following express warranty: "CIBA-GEIGY warrants that this product conforms to the chemical description on the label and is reasonably fit for the purposes referred to in the Directions for Use." Under the "Directions for Use" the label instructs, "In soybeans, it [Dual 8E] may be applied alone or in combination with Sencor, Lexone, or Lorox in water or fluid fertilizer with conventional ground sprayers." The label also contains tables describing the necessary amount of Dual 8E per acre when using Dual 8E alone or in conjunction with Sencor, Lexone or Lorox. The label does not contain directions for mixing Dual 8E with Paraquat and a surfactant. Vance Tyson testified that he mixed the Dual 8E with Paraquat and a surfactant and that he did not mix the Dual 8E in accordance with the directions for use on the label. The record contains no evidence tending to show that the Dual 8E was not fit for the purposes referred to in the directions for use, and thus there is no evidence that this express warranty was breached by Ciba-Geigy. . . .

Plaintiff argues that he presented sufficient evidence for the jury to find that Farm Chemical breached express warranties relating to the effectiveness of Dual 8E, to kill crabgrass in the no-till cultivation of soybeans. Plaintiff contends that the statements of the sales representative of Farm Chemical that the Dual 8E, when mixed with Paraquat and a surfactant, would "do a good job" created an express warranty.

G.S. 25-2-313(1)(a) provides that "[a]ny affirmation of fact or promise made by the seller to the buyer which relates to the goods and becomes part of the basis of the bargain creates an express warranty that the goods shall conform to the affirmation or promise." A salesman's expression of his opinion in "the puffing of his wares" does not create an express warranty. . . . Thus, statements such as "supposed to last a lifetime" and "in perfect condition" do not create an express warranty. *Id.* Similarly, the statement made by the salesman in the present case that the Dual 8E would "do a good job" is a mere expression of opinion and did not create an express warranty.

Finally, plaintiff contends that the trial court erred in granting defendant Farm Chemical's motion for directed verdict on the issue of breach of implied warranty. We agree with this contention. G.S. 25-2-315 defines implied warranty of fitness for particular purpose as follows:

> Where the seller at the time of contracting has reason to know any particular purpose for which the goods are required and that the buyer is relying on the seller's skill or judgment to select or furnish suitable goods, there is unless excluded or modified under the next section [§ 25-2-316] an implied warranty that the goods shall be fit for such purpose.

The evidence in the present case, when considered in the light most favorable to plaintiff, tends to show that plaintiff contacted defendant Farm Chemical to order the herbicides Lasso and Lorox, for the no-till cultivation of soybeans. He spoke with Mr. Gregory, an employee of Farm Chemical, on the telephone and told him that he was planning the no-till cultivation of soybeans on 145 acres of his land and described the type of soil on the land. Mr. Gregory gave Dual 8E a good recommendation and told plaintiff that it would "do a good job," would be less expensive to use than the chemicals he had used the previous year and would also be less risky to use on plaintiff's type of land. He further told plaintiff that Dual 8E could be mixed with Paraquat and a surfactant to replace Lasso and Lorox. He also told plaintiff the amount of Dual 8E per acre that he should use. Plaintiff testified that based upon Mr. Gregory's recommendation and his past business dealings with Farm Chemical, he decided to use Dual 8E and ordered thirty-five gallons from Farm Chemical. Vance Tyson testified that he mixed the chemicals in accordance with Mr. Gregory's instructions, but that the Dual 8E was ineffective in killing crabgrass. Plaintiff also introduced evidence tending to show that Dual 8E must be mixed with Sencor, Lexone or Lorox and either Ortho Paraquat CL or Roundup. This evidence is sufficient to support a finding that the seller, Farm Chemical, had reason to know of the particular purpose, the no-till cultivation of soybeans, for which the product was required and that plaintiff was relying on its recommendation when he ordered the Dual 8E. There is no evidence in the record indicating that defendant Farm Chemical disclaimed any warranties relating to the Dual 8E. Thus, the evidence in the record is sufficient for a jury to find that Farm Chemical made an implied warranty relating to the fitness of the Dual 8E for plaintiff's purpose and that this warranty was breached. We hold, therefore, that the trial court erred in directing a verdict for defendant Farm Chemical on the issue of breach of an implied warranty of fitness for particular purpose. . . .

For the foregoing reasons, directed verdict for defendant Ciba-Geigy Corporation is affirmed. Directed verdict for defendant Farm Chemical is reversed and remanded for a new trial with respect to plaintiff's claim for breach of an implied warranty of fitness for particular purpose as to defendant Farm Chemical and any and all damages resulting therefrom.

Affirmed in part, reversed in part.

WEBB and WELLS, JJ., concur.

MISSISSIPPI UNIFORM COMMERCIAL CODE
§ 75-2-312. WARRANTY OF TITLE AND AGAINST INFRINGEMENT; BUYER'S OBLIGATION AGAINST INFRINGEMENT
MISS. CODE ANN. § 75-2-312 (2011)

(1) Subject to subsection (2) there is in a contract for sale a warranty by the seller that

(a) The title conveyed shall be good, and its transfer rightful; and

(b) The goods shall be delivered free from an security interest or other lien or encumbrance of which the buyer at the time of contracting has no knowledge.

(2) A warranty under subsection (1) will be excluded or modified only by a specific language or by circumstances which give the buyer reason to know that the person selling does not claim title in himself or that he is purporting to sell only such right or title as he or a third person may have.

(3) Unless otherwise agreed a seller who is a merchant regularly dealing in goods of the kind warrants that the goods shall be delivered free of the rightful claim of any third person by way of infringement or the like but a buyer who furnishes specifications to the seller must hold the seller harmless against any such claim which arises out of compliance with the specifications.

C. EXCLUSION OR MODIFICATION OF WARRANTIES

OFFICE SUPPLY CO. V. BASIC/FOUR CORP.
United States District Court, E.D. Wisconsin
538 F. Supp. 776 (1982).

REYNOLDS, Chief Judge.

This is an action for damages brought pursuant to 28 U.S.C. § 1332. The plaintiff Office Supply Co., Inc. ("Office Supply") is a corporation located in Racine, Wisconsin, which sells office supplies. The defendant Basic/Four Corporation ("Basic/Four") is a California corporation which manufactures and sells computer hardware and software. In 1975, Office Supply purchased computer hardware and leased computer software from Basic/Four. Office Supply claims that the system was defective and caused it to suffer substantial losses. It seeks compensation for "lost customers, income, good will and executive time and incurred additional hardware and software expense, office form expense, personnel expense and maintenance expense, all to its damage in the sum of $186,000 plus reasonable interest since April, 1975." . . .

On January 31, 1975, the plaintiff's president, James F. Bruno, signed a contract for the purchase of computer hardware from the defendant and of computer software which was intended to control order processing, inventory control, sales analysis, and accounts receivable.[1] Mr. Bruno mailed the contract to the defendant, and it was accepted by the defendant's assistant treasurer, R. C. Trost, on February 7, 1975. On April 1, 1975, the hardware was installed. In a letter dated May 22, 1975, the defendant advised the plaintiff that the warranty on the hardware would expire on July 1, 1975. The input of data on the software programs took longer to complete, and for a period of time the plaintiff ran parallel operations on the computer and manually as a check on the accuracy of the software applications. In a letter dated October 6, 1975, Mr. Bruno advised Basic/Four:

> All of the applications anticipated by our company in agreeing to acquire our BASIC/FOUR System are complete and the system appears to be satisfactory. This fulfills your contractual obligation.
>
> Although the applications programs appear to be operating satisfactorily, some 'defects' might become apparent (sic) later. (Defects might comprise misinterpretation of data, mishandling of a keyboarding error, or a confusing operator instruction-but would not include anything beyond the scope of the system design specification.) It is my understanding that you warrant your programs, when used in accordance with Basic/Four operating instructions, to be free from 'defects' for a period of ninety days, and that you will correct such 'defects' promptly when they are brought to your attention. (Exhibit E to defendant's memorandum in support of motion for summary judgment, filed December 15, 1981.)

Basic/Four took the position that its warranty on the software expired on January 6, 1976. As to complaints received after that date from Office Supply, it did continue to work with Office Supply in an effort to correct any claimed defects in the computer system. Office Supply also hired Ted Templeton, an independent programmer with a company called Computer Methods, Inc., who was recommended by Basic/Four, to work on its Basic/Four system starting some time after Basic/Four advised that the warranty period was over. The record established that Mr. Templeton made some modifications in the Basic/Four software. He also added at least one new program, the ABC program which involved inventory control, to the system. Starting in January 1978, Office Supply also hired a programmer, Marc Jerome, as a fulltime employee. He found what he claims were three major defects in the software system. The record establishes that two of those defects were in programs which Basic/Four did not supply to the plaintiff. The third defect was in the UJ portion of the Basic/Four accounts receivable program, but there is no evidence that the defect arose in the UJ program until after July 1976, which was after the end of the ninety-day period during which Basic/Four continued to warrant its software applications to be free from defects.

The plaintiff's vice president, David Carlson, testified during his deposition that starting at the end of October 1975 and continuing through early 1978, approximately 20% of the customer accounts were out of balance and the Basic/Four system performed up to 78% of expectation for Office Supply (Tr. at 50-51 and 63). Since February 1978, when Marc Jerome finished correcting the defects in the system, Carlson testified that it has performed up to 100% of expectation (Tr. at 46). The plaintiff's president, James Bruno, testified that the system only performed up to 50% of expectation prior to 1978 (Tr. at 114),

[1] The sale of the software was technically in lease form for reasons related to copyright protection. No one has contended that the technical lease arrangement has any significance to application of the UCC.

that the accounts receivable first went out of balance on the October 1975 monthly statement printed during the first week of November 1975 (Tr. at 43), that it printed through for the first time in February 1976 (Tr. at 135), but that thereafter the accounts receivable problem continued on an intermittent basis until it was corrected by Marc Jerome in early 1978 (Tr. at 87, 132-134, 136, and 142). Both men testified that there were also problems with the hardware but that those problems were always corrected by Sorbus, a service corporation related to Basic/Four with which Office Supply had a hardware maintenance contract, with only a very few minimal extra charges not covered by the monthly maintenance charges. . . .

On June 17, 1980, Office Supply commenced its action against Basic/Four.

The portion of the Office Supply-Basic/Four contract dealing with the purchase of the hardware is a straightforward document. It describes on the front of the document the computer model and features and the purchase price. Additional terms and conditions of sale are set forth on the reverse. In relevant part it provides on the reverse that it constitutes the entire agreement and understanding between the parties, that it shall be governed by the law of California, and as to warranties and remedies for breach of warranty:

> 3. For ninety (90) days after the Equipment is installed . . . the Seller warrants the Equipment to be free from defects in material, workmanship, and operating failure from ordinary use, and the Seller's liability is limited solely to correcting any such defect or failure without charge. . . .

In italic print paragraph 3 also states:

> The warranties contained in this Agreement are in lieu of all other warranties, express or implied, including any regarding merchantability or fitness for a particular purpose, arising out of or in connection with any Equipment (or the delivery, use or performance thereof). The Seller will not be liable . . . (b) for loss of profits or other incidental or consequential damages . . . .

The portion of the contract dealing with the lease of the software is not as clearly drafted. On its first page, which is page 3 of the contract, it states:

> This Addendum to the Agreement for the Purchase of BASIC/FOUR Equipment, dated as of the 31 day of January 1975, between Basic/Four Corporation and Office Supply Inc. is hereby incorporated therein and made a part thereof.

Page 3 describes the program applications and their price. Additional terms and conditions are set forth on the reverse side. As to warranties and limitation of remedies, paragraph 3 provides:

> The Seller believes that the programming being furnished hereunder is accurate and reliable and when programming accomplishes the results set forth in the "Design Specifications," to be agreed to by the Seller and the Purchaser, such programming will be considered completed.

Paragraph 3 continues in italics:

> However, the amounts to be paid to the Seller under this Agreement and this Addendum do not include any assumption of risk, and the Seller disclaims any and all liability for incidental or consequential damages arising out of the delivery, use or operation of the programs provided herein.
>
> If the purchaser, without the written consent of the Seller, makes any modification to the programming or any deviations from the operating instructions or violates the provisions of paragraph 2, all warranties set forth herein cease immediately.
>
> All warranties set forth herein are in lieu of all other warranties, express or implied, including any regarding merchantability or fitness for a particular purpose, arising out of or in connection with any program (or the delivery, use or performance thereof).

The contract also contains a fourteen-page description of the program applications.

The parties agree that the contract is a sales contract, that the choice of law provision which it contains is valid, and consequently that the parties' rights and liabilities are governed by the Uniform Commercial Code ("UCC") as adopted in California. They agree about very little else.

The defendant contends in its motion for summary judgment that this action is barred by the applicable statute of limitations, that the warranty disclaimer and damage limitation provisions in the contract are valid and binding and therefore the plaintiff is entitled to no relief, and that the plaintiff's second cause of action, which is based not on the UCC but on a negligence tort theory, does not state a cognizable claim. The plaintiff's summary judgment motion consists of a denial of each of those contentions and arguments favoring the application of contrary rules of law at the ultimate trial of this action.

Each of the defendant's contentions, along with the arguments as to the applicable legal principles raised by the plaintiff in opposing defendant's summary judgment motion, is discussed separately below. . . .

Disclaimer of Warranties

The Office Supply-Basic/Four contract specifically provides that it constitutes the entire agreement and understanding between the parties. That being so, parol evidence is not admissible under California law to vary the terms of the agreement. Aplications, Inc. v. Hewlitt-Packard Co., 501 F.Supp. 129 (S.D.N.Y.1980). The language of the contract must be interpreted in an effort to determine the intent of the contracting parties. S. M. Wilson & Company v. Smith International, Inc., 587 F.2d 1363 (9th Cir. 1978).

If there are no exclusions or modifications in the contract, every sales contract governed by the UCC contains an implied warranty of merchantability and, if the seller has reason to know of a particular purpose for which the goods are required, an implied warranty of fitness for a particular purpose. Section 2315, Cal.Comm.Code. Express warranties are created if the seller makes an affirmation of fact or promise to the buyer and the affirmation becomes part of the bargain between the parties. Section 2313, Cal.Comm.Code. Thus, any express warranties must be found in the language of the contract. Implied warranties, in contrast, will be held to exist unless they are specifically excluded.

With regard to the computer hardware, the contract expressly warrants the hardware to be free from defects in material, workmanship, and operating failure from ordinary use for ninety days after installation. (Page 2, paragraph 3.)

With regard to the computer software, the most reasonable interpretation of the contract is that the same ninety-day warranty of material, workmanship, and operating failure applies, dating from the time when the "programming accomplishes the results set forth in the 'Design Specifications'" (page 4, paragraph 3), which in this case was on October 6, 1975, when plaintiff's president so advised the defendant.

The plaintiff contends that the language just quoted is a warranty of future performance, and that in fact the programming did not accomplish the desired results until 1978. Courts have been parsimonious in finding warranties of future performance where there is no explicit language in the contract creating such a warranty. Standard Alliance Industries, Inc. v. Black Clawson Company, 587 F.2d 813, 820 (6th Cir. 1978). For example, a representation as to the performance ability of an existing product will not be construed as an explicit warranty of future performance ability of the product. Jones & Laughlin Steel Corporation v. Johns-Manville Sales Corporation, 626 F.2d 280, 291 (3d Cir. 1980) (interpreting California law). Section 2316(1), Cal.Comm.Code, provides in part:

> (1) Words or conduct relevant to the creation of an express warranty and words or conduct tending to negate or limit warranty shall be construed wherever reasonable as consistent with each other . . . .

The first page of the software addendum (page 3 of the contract) provides that it is incorporated within and made a part of the hardware purchase agreement. That agreement contains the ninety-day express warranty provision which, as a result of the incorporation, also applies to the software purchase. In light of the ninety-day express warranty, the most reasonable construction of the software addendum language regarding the results to be accomplished by the programming is that the completion of the programming and installation of all of the bargained-for applications starts the running of the ninety-day warranty period, and not that the applications are warranted to run perfectly once their installation is apparently successfully completed.

The UCC allows contracting parties to exclude or modify all implied warranties. There is no correlative requirement that if implied warranties are excluded, express warranties must be given. Thus it is permissible, for example, to exclude all implied warranties and to provide for a ninety-day express warranty limited to repair or replacement of defective goods. . . .

In order to make an effective waiver of implied warranties, the provisions of § 2316(2), Cal.Comm.Code, must be followed:

> . . . to exclude or modify the implied warranty of merchantability or any part of it the language must mention merchantability and in case of a writing must be conspicuous, and to exclude or modify any implied warranty of fitness the exclusion must be by a writing and conspicuous. . . .

There is no dispute that the language contained in the contract was in this case sufficient to waive all implied warranties. The issue is whether the disclaimer was "conspicuous." Section 1201(10), Cal.Comm.Code, provides:

> (10) "Conspicuous." A term or clause is conspicuous when it is so written that a reasonable person against whom it is to operate ought to have noticed it. A printed heading in capitals (as: NONNEGOTIABLE BILL OF LADING) is conspicuous. Language in the body of a form is "conspicuous" if it is in larger or other contrasting type or color. But in a telegram any stated term is "conspicuous." Whether a term or clause is "conspicuous" or not is for decision by the court.

Basic/Four points out that it disclaimed the implied warranties not once but twice, and that the disclaimers were written in italicized print, in contrast to the regular print used on the rest of the contract. Nevertheless, the disclaimers are not conspicuous. In Dorman v. International Harvester Company, 46 Cal.App.3d 11, 120 Cal.Rptr. 516 (1975), the California court of appeals noted that under pre-Code California law, disclaimers of warranty are strictly construed, and, applying the code, it found that an attempted disclaimer written in only slightly contrasting print and without a heading adequate to call the buyer's attention to the disclaimer clause was not effective. That decision controls in this case. The two disclaimers in the Office Supply-Basic/Four contract are on the reverse sides of the first two pages of the contract. They are not positioned close to the buyer's signature line. The contracts are printed on pale green paper and the disclaimers are set forth in print which, although italicized, is only slightly contrasting with the remainder of the contract. There are no headings noting the disclaimers of warranty. Since there is only "'some slight contrasting set-off'" and there is "'only a slight contrast with the balance of the instrument,'" Dorman, supra, 120 Cal.Rptr. at 522, quoting Woodruff v. Clark County Farm Bureau Coop. Assn. (1972), 153 Ind.App. 31, 286 N.E.2d 188, 198, quoting in turn Greenspun v. American Adhesives, Inc., 320 F.Supp. 442 (E.D.Pa.1970), therefore, the disclaimers are not conspicuous.

Discussion of the effectiveness of the disclaimer provisions in the contract does not end with the finding of lack of conspicuousness. In their treatise Uniform Commercial Code s 12-5 at 444 (2d ed. 1980), Messrs. White and Summers note "with apprehension" the growing number of cases which hold that if a buyer is actually aware of a warranty disclaimer, then the disclaimer is effective even if not conspicuous. See also 73 A.L.R.3d, "Construction and Effect of UCC § 2-316(2) Providing that Implied Warranty Disclaimer must be 'Conspicuous,'" § 5(b), pointing out the same line of cases. The Official Comment to UCC § 2-316 states that the section is designed "to protect a buyer from unexpected and unbargained language of disclaimer." Pointing to that language, the Court in Dorman, supra, 120 Cal.Rptr. at 521-522, indicated that California will follow the trend:

> . . . (W)e must rely predominantly on the official comments to sections 2316 and 1201, subdivision (1), and to foreign law. The official comment to subdivision (10) of section 1201 states that the "test (of conspicuousness) is whether attention can reasonably be expected to be called to (the disclaimer provision)." (Cf. Gray v. Zurich Insurance Co., 65 Cal.2d 263, 271, 54 Cal.Rptr. 104, 419 P.2d 168.) We must examine this comment in the light of the official comment to section 2316, which states: "This section is designed principally to deal with those frequent clauses in sales contracts which seek to exclude [all warranties, express or implied.] It seeks to protect a buyer from unexpected and unbargained language of disclaimer by denying effect to such language when inconsistent with language of express warranty and permitting the exclusion of implied warranties only by conspicuous language or other circumstances which protect the buyer from surprise." (Emphasis added.) In other words, section 2316 seeks to protect the buyer from the situation where the salesman's "pitch," advertising brochures, or large print in the contract, giveth, and the disclaimer clause-in fine print-taketh away.

The Dorman Court also noted that under pre-Code California law as well, a provision disclaiming implied warranties "was ineffectual unless the buyer assented to the provision or was charged with notice of the disclaimer before the bargain was completed." Id., 120 Cal.Rptr. at 521.

James Bruno testified during his deposition taken on November 3, 1980, that before he purchased the Basic/Four system, he spent approximately two months comparing it with other systems (Tr. at 10), and that he drew up a written comparison of the Basic/Four and Qantel systems, including their guarantees. Basic/Four, 90 days; and Qantel had one year." (Tr. at 30.) He read the back of the contract before he signed it (Tr. at 52-53), when he received the contract from Basic/Four he made out a list of questions to ask Basic/Four before signing and one subject on his list was the ninety-day guarantee (Tr. at 77-78), and before he signed he showed the warranty provision in the contract to someone he knew in the data processing field (Tr. at 81-82). He discussed the warranties with Basic/Four before signing and tried to have them modified:

> Q Did you read the provisions of the warranty?
>
> A Yes.
>
> Q And did you discuss those provisions with Basic/Four, or with someone from Basic/Four?
>
> A Yes.
>
> Q And what was said to you about those provisions?

A That that was the condition that I had to accept.

Q All right. And was that discussion before or after the contract was signed?

A I would say before.

Q . . . did you call up Darryl Bannister, for example, and say I want to buy this system but I refuse to agree to the warranty provisions in the contract?

A Well, I argued with him, but it was to no avail. Nothing. (Tr. at 84-85.)

He also was aware of the warranty limitations before he signed the contract:

Q Well, were you aware of the provisions of that warranty before you signed the contract?

A That there were limitations?

Q That there are limitations to the warranty? Were you aware of that?

A Certainly.

Q You were?

A Yes. (Tr. at 87.)

That testimony establishes that the warranty disclaimers were neither unexpected nor unbargained for, and that, consequently, under Dorman, they should be enforced. . . .

ORDER

For the foregoing reasons. . . .

IT IS FURTHER ORDERED that the defendant's motion for summary judgment is granted, and that judgment be entered dismissing this action with prejudice and awarding costs to the defendant.

NOTES AND QUESTIONS:

1. For a valid disclaimer of implied warranties of quality under U.C.C. § 2-316(3), see *Schneider v. Miller*, 597 N.E.2d 175 (Ohio Ct. App. 1991).

SECTION 4. EXCUSES FOR NONPERFORMANCE

Once the terms of a contract are ascertained, it is then necessary to determine when a party's duty to perform arises, whether another's party's failure to perform relieves the first party of his duty to perform, and whether less than full performance of either party constitutes a breach. Thus, we turn our attention to these matters.

A. COVENANTS AND CONDITIONS GENERALLY

In order to establish a claim for breach of contract, it is necessary for the aggrieved party to establish that the other party had a duty that was not performed. In some cases, the duty arose by virtue of the making of the contract, without anything else having to occur. In others, the duty is tied to the occurrence of some other event. To go even further, in some cases, the complaining party had a duty to ensure that the other event occurred; in others cases, no such duty existed. Accordingly, it is necessary to ascertain the nature of the duties undertaken by the parties in order to determine if and when performance was due, as well as whether nonperformance constitutes a breach.

Covenants or contractual undertakings give rise to duties in the form of promises, and the failure to perform such duties generally gives rise to liability for such nonperformance. Compare and contrast a covenant with a condition: "[A]n event, not certain to occur, [but] which must occur . . . before [a party's] performance under a contract becomes due."*

1. EXPRESS CONDITIONS

HOWARD V. FEDERAL CROP INSURANCE CORP.
United States Court of Appeals, Fourth Circuit
540 F.2d 695 (1976).

WIDENER, Circuit Judge:

Plaintiff-appellants sued to recover for losses to their 1973 tobacco crop due to alleged rain damage. The crops were insured by defendant-appellee, Federal Crop Insurance Corporation (FCIC). Suits were brought in a state court in North Carolina and removed to the United States District Court. The three suits are not distinguishable factually so far as we are concerned here and involve identical questions of law. They were combined for disposition in the district court and for appeal. The district court granted summary judgment for the defendant and dismissed all three actions. We remand for further proceedings. Since we find for the plaintiffs as to the construction of the policy, we express no opinion on the procedural questions.

Federal Crop Insurance Corporation, an agency of the United States, in 1973, issued three policies to the Howards, insuring their tobacco crops, to be grown on six farms, against weather damage and other hazards.

* Restatement (Second) of Contracts § 224 (1981).

The Howards (plaintiffs) established production of tobacco on their acreage, and have alleged that their 1973 crop was extensively damaged by heavy rains, resulting in a gross loss to the three plaintiffs in excess of $35,000. The plaintiffs harvested and sold the depleted crop and timely filed notice and proof of loss with FCIC, but, prior to inspection by the adjuster for FCIC, the Howards had either plowed or disked under the tobacco fields in question to prepare the same for sowing a cover crop of rye to preserve the soil. When the FCIC adjuster later inspected the fields, he found the stalks had been largely obscured or obliterated by plowing or disking and denied the claims, apparently on the ground that the plaintiffs had violated a portion of the policy which provides that the stalks on any acreage with respect to which a loss is claimed shall not be destroyed until the corporation makes an inspection.

The holding of the district court is best capsuled in its own words:

> The inquiry here is whether compliance by the insureds with this provision of the policy was a condition precedent to the recovery. The court concludes that it was and that the failure of the insureds to comply worked a forfeiture of benefits for the alleged loss.[1]

There is no question but that apparently after notice of loss was given to defendant, but before inspection by the adjuster, plaintiffs plowed under the tobacco stalks and sowed some of the land with a cover crop, rye. The question is whether, under paragraph 5(f) of the tobacco endorsement to the policy of insurance, the act of plowing under the tobacco stalks forfeits the coverage of the policy. Paragraph 5 of the tobacco endorsement is entitled Claims. Pertinent to this case are subparagraphs 5(b) and 5(f), which are as follows:

> 5(b) It shall be a condition precedent to the payment of any loss that the insured establish the production of the insured crop on a unit and that such loss has been directly caused by one or more of the hazards insured against during the insurance period for the crop year for which the loss is claimed, and furnish any other information regarding the manner and extent of loss as may be required by the Corporation . . . .

> 5(f) The tobacco stalks on any acreage of tobacco of types 11a, 11b, 12, 13, or 14 with respect to which a loss is claimed shall not be destroyed until the Corporation makes an inspection . . . .

The arguments of both parties are predicated upon the same two assumptions. First, if subparagraph 5(f) creates a condition precedent, its violation caused a forfeiture of plaintiffs' coverage. Second, if subparagraph 5(f) creates an obligation (variously called a promise or covenant) upon plaintiffs not to plow under the tobacco stalks, defendant may recover from plaintiffs (either in an original action, or, in this case, by a counterclaim, or as a matter of defense) for whatever damage it sustained because of the elimination of the stalks.

[1] The district court also relied upon language in subparagraph 5(b), infra, which required as a condition precedent to payment that the insured, in addition to establishing his production and loss from an insured case, "furnish any other information regarding the manner and extent of loss as may be required by the Corporation." The court construed the preservation of the stalks as such "information." We see no language in the policy or connection in the record to indicate this is the case.

However, a violation of subparagraph 5(f) would not, under the second premise, standing alone, cause a forfeiture of the policy.

Generally accepted law provides us with guidelines here. There is a general legal policy opposed to forfeitures. United States v. One Ford Coach, 307 U.S. 219, 226, 59 S.Ct. 861, 83 L.Ed. 1249 (1939); Baca v. Commissioner of Internal Revenue, 326 F.2d 189, 191 (5th Cir. 1963). Insurance policies are generally construed most strongly against the insurer. Henderson v. Hartford Accident & Indemnity Co., 268 N.C. 129, 150 S.E.2d 17, 19 (1966). When it is doubtful whether words create a promise or a condition precedent, they will be construed as creating a promise. Harris and Harris Const. Co. v. Crain and Denbo, Inc., 256 N.C. 110, 123 S.E.2d 590, 595 (1962). The provisions of a contract will not be construed as conditions precedent in the absence of language plainly requiring such construction. Harris, 123 S.E.2d at 596. And Harris, at 123 S.E.2d 590, 595, cites Jones v. Palace Realty Co., 226 N.C. 303, 37 S.E.2d 906 (1946), and Restatement of the Law, Contracts, § 261.

Plaintiffs rely most strongly upon the fact that the term "condition precedent" is included in subparagraph 5(b) but not in subparagraph 5(f). It is true that whether a contract provision is construed as a condition or an obligation does not depend entirely upon whether the word "condition" is expressly used. Appleman, Insurance Law and Practice (1972), vol. 6A, s 4144. However, the persuasive force of plaintiffs' argument in this case is found in the use of the term "condition precedent" in subparagraph 5(b) but not in subparagraph 5(f). Thus, it is argued that the ancient maxim to be applied is that the expression of one thing is the exclusion of another.

The defendant places principal reliance upon the decision of this court in Fidelity-Phenix Fire Insurance Company v. Pilot Freight Carriers, 193 F.2d 812, 31 A.L.R.2d 839 (4th Cir. 1952). Suit there was predicated upon a loss resulting from theft out of a truck covered by defendant's policy protecting plaintiff from such a loss. The insurance company defended upon the grounds that the plaintiff had left the truck unattended without the alarm system being on. The policy contained six paragraphs limiting coverage. Two of those imposed what was called a "condition precedent." They largely related to the installation of specified safety equipment. Several others, including paragraph 5, pertinent in that case, started with the phrase, "It is further warranted." In paragraph 5, the insured warranted that the alarm system would be on whenever the vehicle was left unattended. Paragraph 6 starts with the language: "The assured agrees, by acceptance of this policy, that the foregoing conditions precedent relate to matters material to the acceptance of the risk by the insurer." Plaintiff recovered in the district court, but judgment on its behalf was reversed because of a breach of warranty of paragraph 5, the truck had been left unattended with the alarm off. In that case, plaintiff relied upon the fact that the words "condition precedent" were used in some of the paragraphs but the word "warranted" was used in the paragraph in issue. In rejecting that contention, this court said that "warranty" and "condition precedent" are often used interchangeably to create a condition of the insured's promise, and "(m)anifestly the terms 'condition precedent' and 'warranty' were intended to have the same meaning and effect." 193 F.2d at 816.

Fidelity-Phenix thus does not support defendant's contention here. Although there is some resemblance between the two cases, analysis shows that the issues are actually entirely different. Unlike the case at bar, each paragraph in Fidelity-Phenix contained either the term "condition precedent" or the term "warranted." We held that, in that situation, the two terms had the same effect in that they both involved forfeiture. That is well established law. See Appleman, Insurance Law and Practice (1972), vol. 6A, § 4144. In the case at bar, the term "warranty" or "warranted" is in no way involved, either in terms or by way of like language, as it was in Fidelity-Phenix. The issue upon which this case turns, then, was not involved in Fidelity-Phenix.

The Restatement of the Law of Contracts states:

> § 261. INTERPRETATION OF DOUBTFUL WORDS AS PROMISE OR CONDITION.
>
> Where it is doubtful whether words create a promise or an express condition, they are interpreted as creating a promise; but the same words may sometimes mean that one party promises a performance and that the other party's promise is conditional on that performance.

Two illustrations (one involving a promise, the other a condition) are used in the Restatement:

> 2. A, an insurance company, issues to B a policy of insurance containing promises by A that are in terms conditional on the happening of certain events. The policy contains this clause: "provided, in case differences shall arise touching any loss, the matter shall be submitted to impartial arbitrators, whose award shall be binding on the parties." This is a promise to arbitrate and does not make an award a condition precedent of the insurer's duty to pay.
>
> 3. A, an insurance company, issues to B an insurance policy in usual form containing this clause: "In the event of disagreement as to the amount of loss it shall be ascertained by two appraisers and an umpire. The loss shall not be payable until 60 days after the award of the appraisers when such an appraisal is required." This provision is not merely a promise to arbitrate differences but makes an award a condition of the insurer's duty to pay in case of disagreement . . . .

We believe that subparagraph 5(f) in the policy here under consideration fits illustration 2 rather than illustration 3. Illustration 2 specifies something to be done, whereas subparagraph 5(f) specifies something not to be done. Unlike illustration 3, subparagraph 5(f) does not state any conditions under which the insurance shall "not be payable," or use any words of like import. We hold that the district court erroneously held, on the motion for summary judgment, that subparagraph 5(f) established a condition precedent to plaintiffs' recovery which forfeited the coverage.

From our holding that defendant's motion for summary judgment was improperly allowed, it does not follow the plaintiffs' motion for summary judgment should have been granted, for if subparagraph 5(f) be not construed as a condition precedent, there are other questions of fact to be determined. At this point, we merely hold that the district court erred in holding, on the motion for summary judgment, that subparagraph 5(f) constituted a condition precedent with resulting forfeiture.

The explanation defendant makes for including subparagraph 5(f) in the tobacco endorsement is that it is necessary that the stalks remain standing in order for the Corporation to evaluate the extent of loss and to determine whether loss resulted from some cause not covered by the policy. However, was subparagraph 5(f) inserted because without it the Corporation's opportunities for proof would be more difficult, or because they would be impossible? Plaintiffs point out that the Tobacco Endorsement, with subparagraph 5(f), was adopted in 1970, and crop insurance goes back long before that date. Nothing is shown as to the Corporation's prior 1970 practice of evaluating losses. Such a showing might have a bearing upon establishing defendant's intention in including 5(f). Plaintiffs state, and defendant does not deny, that another division of the Department of Agriculture, or the North Carolina Department, urged that tobacco stalks be cut as soon as possible after harvesting as a means of pest control. Such an explanation might refute the idea that plaintiffs plowed under the stalks for any fraudulent purpose. Could these conflicting directives affect the reasonableness of plaintiffs' interpretation of defendant's prohibition upon plowing under the stalks prior to adjustment?

We express no opinion on these questions because they were not before the district court and are mentioned to us largely by way of argument rather than from the record. No question of ambiguity was raised in the court below or here and no question of the applicability of paragraph 5(c) to this case was alluded to other than in the defendant's pleadings, so we also do not reach those questions. Nothing we say here should preclude FCIC from asserting as a defense that the plowing or disking under of the stalks caused damage to FCIC if, for example, the amount of the loss was thereby made more difficult or impossible to ascertain whether the plowing or disking under was done with bad purpose or innocently. To repeat, our narrow holding is that merely plowing or disking under the stalks does not of itself operate to forfeit coverage under the policy.

The case is remanded for further proceedings not inconsistent with this opinion.

VACATED AND REMANDED.

NATIONAL FUEL GAS DISTRIB. CORP. V. HARTFORD FIRE INS. CO.
Supreme Court of New York, Appellate Division
28 A.D.3d. 1169 (2006).

. . . .

MEMORANDUM: Plaintiff commenced this action to recover on a $3.8 million surety bond issued by Hartford Fire Insurance Company (defendant) to guarantee the payment obligations of a now bankrupt entity, Iroquois Energy Management, LLC (Iroquois), under a service agreement entered into between Iroquois and plaintiff. . . . [I]n appeal No. 1, defendant appeals and plaintiff cross-appeals from a subsequent order denying defendant's cross motion for summary judgment dismissing the first and second causes of action and granting in part plaintiff's cross motion for partial summary judgment. We address only the order in appeal No. 1 . . . . We modify the order in appeal No. 1 by granting defendant's cross motion and dismissing the first and second causes of action of the second amended complaint.

We conclude that the notice requirement set forth in paragraph or proviso 4 of the bond creates a condition precedent to defendant's obligation and plaintiff's recovery under the bond. The notice requirement follows the word "PROVIDED," which indicates the creation of a condition . . . . In addition, the notice requirement is listed among a number of other conditions for recovery under the bond. Under the circumstances, we conclude that the notice requirement is an express condition that "must be literally performed" or satisfied before defendant "is obliged to perform" its obligations under the bond (Oppenheimer & Co. v Oppenheim, Appel, Dixon & Co., 86 NY2d 685, 690 [1995]). We are mindful of the "interpretative preference" favoring construction of contractual "language as embodying a promise or constructive condition rather than an express condition . . . especially . . . when a finding of express condition would increase the risk of forfeiture by the obligee" (id. at 691, citing Restatement [Second] of Contracts § 227 [1]). We note, however, that such "interpretative preference" "cannot be employed if 'the occurrence of the event as a condition is expressed in unmistakable language' " (id., quoting Restatement [Second] of Contracts § 229, Comment a, at 185), or where "the event is within the obligee's control or the circumstances indicate that [it] has assumed the risk" (Restatement [Second] of Contracts § 227 [1]). Here, the requirement that plaintiff provide notice, as specified by the bond, was entirely within its control. Moreover, the language requiring notice may not be construed as a covenant or promise inasmuch as plaintiff is not a signatory to the bond and therefore made no promises thereunder.

We conclude as a matter of law that plaintiff failed to comply with the requirement that it "notify [defendant] in writing within five (5) business days if [Iroquois] is in default, partially or in full, and that [plaintiff] has made a determination to grant an extension of time for payment by [Iroquois]." The record establishes as a matter of law that, from April 2000 on, Iroquois was continually in default on its obligations to plaintiff and that plaintiff continually extended Iroquois's time for payment, but that plaintiff did not provide notice of default and extension of time for payment until August 1, 2000. As a matter of law, plaintiff's failure to comply with the condition in a timely manner defeats plaintiff's right to recover on the bond. . . . Finally, we conclude that there is no support in the record for plaintiff's contention that the performance of the condition, which existed for defendant's benefit, was waived or excused by defendant . . . .

NOTES AND QUESTIONS:

1. But see *Bright v. Ganas*, 189 A. 427 (Md. 1937), for a decision where the court strains to find a forfeiture based on an implied condition.

2. Revisit the definitions and effects of covenants and conditions. While the preceding cases tend to discuss covenants and conditions as if they are mutually exclusive, the definitions and effects of each actually make it clear that contractual undertakings can, and often times are, both. Thus, students are cautioned not to think of contractual duties as one or the other. Instead, the inquiry should be whether the failure to perform a contractual undertaking solely gives rise to contractual liability by the nonperforming party, or whether it also results in the nonperforming party forfeiting his right to demand performance by the other party.

3. Frequently, conditions are identified as either conditions precedent, meaning the event must occur before a dependent duty arises, or conditions subsequent, meaning a duty already exists but is subject to termination if the event does or does not occur. The difference between the two largely turns on to whom the burden of proving the occurrence of the condition will be assigned.* For our purposes, the distinction has little or no significance in that either the event occurred and the duty exists or it did not and the duty does not exist.

4. Read *Burger King Corp. v. Family Dining*, 426 F. Supp. 485 (E.D. Penn. 1977). How does the issue of forfeiture impact the outcome of the case?

---

2. IMPLIED AND CONSTRUCTIVE CONDITIONS

Again, revisit the definition and effect of a condition. While some conditions are expressly agreed to by the parties, whether the parties intended for the failure of the condition to operate as a forfeiture may not be clear from the parties' expressions. In other cases, while the parties may not express agreement on a condition, it may be inferred by the subject matter of the contract, prior dealings or common practice. Still others are supplied by the court in the interpretation process in order to avoid an inequitable result. As you read the following group of cases, ask yourself the following: What condition is the court reviewing; how did it arise; and what is the effect of nonoccurrence?

a. Order of Performance

KINGSTON V. PRESTON
King's Bench
99 Eng. Rep. 437 (1773).

It was an action of debt, for non-performance of covenants contained in certain articles of agreement between the plaintiff and the defendant. The declaration stated; -That, by articles made the 24th of March, 1770, the plaintiff, for the considerations therein-after mentioned, covenanted, with the defendant, to serve him for one year and a quarter next ensuing, as a covenant-servant, in his trade of a silk-mercer, at £200 a year, and in consideration of the premises, the defendant covenanted, that at the end of the year and a quarter, he would give up his business of a mercer to the plaintiff, and a nephew of the defendant, or some other person to be nominated. by the defendant, and give up to them his stock in trade, at a fair valuation; and that, between the young traders, deeds of partnership should be executed for 14 years, and from and immediately after the execution of the said deeds, the defendant would permit the said young traders to carry on the said business in the defendant's house. Then the declaration stated a covenant by the plaintiff, that he would accept the business and stock in trade, at a fair valuation, with the defendant's nephew, or such other person, &c. and execute such deeds of partnership, and, further, that the plaintiff should, and would, at, and before, the sealing and delivery of the deeds, cause and procure

---

* *See Gray v. Gardner*, 17 Mass. 188 (1821).

good and sufficient security to be given to the defendant, to be approved of by the defendant, for the payment of £250 monthly, to the defendant, in lieu of a moiety of the monthly produce of the stock in trade, until the value of the stock should be reduced to £4000. Then the plaintiff averred, that he had performed, and been ready to perform, his covenants, and assigned for breach on the part of the defendant, that he had refused to surrender and give up his business, at the end of the said year and a quarter.

The defendant pleaded, 1. That the plaintiff did not offer sufficient security; and, 2. That he did not give sufficient security for the payment of the £250, &c.-And the plaintiff demurred generally to both pleas.-On the part of the plaintiff, the case was argued by Mr. Buller, who contended, that the covenants were mutual and independant [sic], and, therefore, a plea of the breach of one of the covenants to be performed by the plaintiff was no bar to an action for a breach by the defendant of one of which he had bound himself to perform, but that the defendant might have his remedy for the breach by the plaintiff, in a separate action. On the other side, Mr. Grose insisted, that the covenants were dependant in their nature, and, therefore, performance must be alleged: the security to be given for the money, was manifestly the chief object of the transaction, and it would be highly unreasonable to construe the agreement, so as to oblige the defendant to give up a beneficial business, and valuable stock in trade, and trust to the plaintiff's personal security, (who might, and, indeed, was admitted to be worth nothing,) for the performance of his part.-In delivering the judgment of the Court, Lord Mansfield expressed himself to the following effect: There are three kinds of covenants: 1. Such as are called mutual and independant [sic], where either party may recover damages from the other, for the injury he may have received by a breach of the covenants in his favour [sic], and where it is no excuse for the defendant, to allege a breach of the covenants on the part of the plaintiff. 2. There are covenants which are conditions and dependant, in which the performance of one depends on the prior performance of another, and, therefore, till this prior condition is performed, the other party is not liable to an action on his covenant. 3. There is also a third sort of covenants, which are mutual conditions to be performed at the same time; and, in these, if one party whs [sic] ready, and offered, to perform his part, and the other neglected, or refused, to perform his, he who was ready, and offered, has fulfilled his engagement, and may maintain an action for the default of the other; though it is not certain that either is obliged to do the first act.-His Lordship then proceeded to say, that the dependance [sic], or independance [sic], of covenants, was to be collected from the evident sense and meaning of the parties, and, that, however transposed they might be in the deed, their precedency [sic] must depend on the order of time in which the intent of the transaction requires their performance. That, in the case before the Court, it would be the greatest injustice if the plaintiff should prevail: the essence of the agreement was, that the defendant should not trust to the personal security of the plaintiff, but, before he delivered up his stock and business, should have good security for the payment of the money. The giving such security, therefore, must necessarily be a condition precedent.-Judgment was accordingly given for the defendant, because the part to be performed by the plaintiff was clearly a condition precedent.

NOTES & QUESTIONS:

1. *See* Restatement (Second) of Contracts § 234 (1981). For which of the three types of covenants described in *Kingston v. Preston* does this section reflect a preference?

2. Read U.C.C. § 2-507(1) and U.C.C. § 2-511(1). Compare these two sections with Restatement (Second) of Contracts § 234 (1981).

---

b. Time of the Essence

CATER V. SHERBURNE CORP.
Supreme Court of Vermont
315 A.2d 870 (1974).

SHANGRAW, Chief Justice.

This is an appeal by the defendant from a judgment of the Rutland County Court. The subject matter of the litigation is work done and materials furnished by the plaintiff in connection with a development of the defendant's near Sherburne Mountain. The plaintiff claimed that he was not fully paid for labor and materials furnished under written contracts . . . . The defendant claimed defective performance and payment for everything due, and asserted a counterclaim for expense necessitated by plaintiff's alleged failure to fulfill contractual commitments. The Court found that the plaintiff was in substantial compliance under his contracts, that the defendant had no right to terminate the contracts, and that the defendant's counterclaim was without foundation. . . . The defendant corporation has appealed.

The facts as found by the Court are, in substance, as follows:

There were four written contracts between the parties covering (a) the furnishing and placing of gravel on one road, (b) the drilling and blasting of rock on various residential roads, (c) road construction, and (d) the cutting and grubbing of a gondola lift-line. The contracts called for weekly progress payments based upon work completed with a provision for retaining 10% until ten days after final acceptance. The billings from the plaintiff to the defendant amounted to $52,571.25, of which $41,368.05 was paid by the defendant. The difference between the $52,571.25 billed, and $41,368.05 paid, comprised $4,596.45 retained by the defendant under its holdback provision, and adjustments claimed by the defendant of $6,606.75. The Court found that adjustments in the amount of $4,747.25 was improperly taken by the defendant and that amount was decreed to the plaintiff. In addition the Court found that the plaintiff was entitled to all the retainage held by the defendant.

As to the defendant's contention that the plaintiff's performance was unsatisfactory and, in particular, that the plaintiff failed to abide by the completion schedules in the contracts, the Court found that on the whole, the plaintiff rendered substantial performance under the contracts without major complaints from the defendant up to the time it terminated the contracts. The Court found further, that time was not of the essence of the contracts, that many of the delays were due to the directions of the defendant in constantly shifting the plaintiff's activities from one contract to another, and that other delays were financial in origin, in that the plaintiff had difficulty meeting his outstanding obligations because of payments withheld by the defendant without justification. . . .

Defendant claims the Court erred in its ruling that the plaintiff was in substantial compliance under his contracts and in its finding that the plaintiff was entitled to recover certain sums under the gondola lift-line contract. . . .

The defendant's primary contention is that the Court's ruling that the plaintiff was in substantial compliance under his contracts is error. The contention is that this ruling was based on the erroneous conclusion that time was not of the essence of the contracts, and that as time was of the essence and plaintiff failed to perform within the time specified, plaintiff was not in substantial compliance and defendant is entitled to the amounts withheld as retainage.

Where time is of the essence, performance on time is a constructive condition of the other party's duty, usually the duty to pay for the performance rendered . . . . Time may be made of the essence of a contract by a stipulation to that effect . . . , or by any language that expressly provides that the contract will be void if performance is not within a specified time. . . . Where the parties have not expressly declared their intention, the determination as to whether time is of the essence depends on the intention of the parties, the circumstances surrounding the transaction, and the subject matter of the contract. . . .

As a general rule, time is not of the essence in a building or construction contract in the absence of an express provision making it such. 13 Am.Jur.2d Building and Construction Contracts § 47.

> Construction contracts are subject to many delays for innumerable reasons, the blame for which may be difficult to assess. The structure . . . becomes part of the land and adds to the wealth of its owner. Delays are generally foreseen as probable; and the risks thereof are discounted . . . The complexities of the work, the difficulties commonly encountered, the custom of men in such cases, all these lead to the result that performance at the agreed time by the contractor is not of the essence. 3A A. Corbin, Contracts § 720, at 377 (1960).

We conclude, then, that time was not of the essence of any of the contracts considered here. None of the four contracts included express language making time of the essence, and we can find nothing in the circumstances surrounding these contracts what would lift them out of the operation of the general rule. Two of the contracts called for completion dates and forfeitures for non-completion on schedule, but the inclusion of dates in construction contracts does not make time of the essence. Moreover, the inclusion of penalty or forfeiture provisions for non-completion on schedule is strong evidence that time is not of the essence and that performance on time is not a condition of the other party's duty to accept and pay for the performance rendered . . . .

Ordinarily, in contracts where time is not of the essence, a failure to complete the work within the specified time will not terminate the contract, but it will subject the contractor to damages for the delay. . . . However, in this case, most of the delays were due to the actions of the defendant corporation in constantly shifting the plaintiff's activities from one contract to another, . . . and in improperly withholding the plaintiff's payments. . . Delay in the performance of a contract will, as a rule be excused where it is caused by the act or default of the opposite party . . .or by the act or default of persons for whose conduct the opposite party is responsible. . . . Where this is the case, the contractor will not be held liable, under a provision for liquidated damages or otherwise, for his non-compliance with the terms of the contract; . . . and his non-compliance will not be considered a breach. . . . An obligation of good faith and fair dealing is an implied term in every contract . . . and a party may not obstruct, hinder, or delay a contractor's work and then seek damages for the delay thus occasioned.

Defendant also disputes the Court's conclusions with respect to the gondola lift-line contract. Defendant informed the plaintiff in April, 1968, that no more progress payments would be made on the gondola contract. At that time, plaintiff had completed a substantial portion of the contracted work, but had not yet invoiced it. After defendant's notice, plaintiff continued to work on the lift-line, but was forced to stop for financial reasons. Defendant claims that the plaintiff is not entitled to recover for work done or invoiced after the notice concerning termination of payments.

Defendant's April notice concerned only the progress payments due the plaintiff. It was not a notice of contract termination. In the absence of a total disavowal of the contract, failure of payment does not require an immediate cessation of performance. Williams v. Carter, 129 Vt. 619, 285 A.2d 735 (1971). The contracts between the plaintiff and the defendant were not terminated until June of 1968. The termination was without legal justification, and the plaintiff is entitled to recover the contract price for all work done before the termination date. . . .

. . . The Court's finding and conclusions are therefore correct.

Judgment affirmed.

---

c. Satisfaction Clauses

HUTTON V. MONOGRAMS PLUS, INC.
Court of Appeals of Ohio, Second District
604 N.E.2d 200 (1992).

WOLFF, Judge.

Monogram Plus, Inc. ("MPI") appeals from a summary judgment rendered in favor of David D. Hutton. In granting the summary judgment, the trial court determined that, as a matter of law, a satisfaction clause contained in a franchise agreement executed by MPI and Hutton called for Hutton's subjective satisfaction as to what qualified as "suitable financing."

The following facts are largely undisputed.

On August 4, 1989, Hutton and MPI executed a franchise agreement wherein MPI sold a monogramming franchise to Hutton. Hutton purchased the MPI franchise for $25,000. The terms of the agreement specified that MPI granted a nonexclusive ten-year license to Hutton to operate an MPI store. Pursuant to the agreement, Hutton was obligated to market and promote the retail sale of monogrammed items such as T-shirts, fleece wear, and jackets. On August 17, 1989, Hutton and MPI executed an addendum to the franchise agreement. The addendum supplemented the franchise agreement, providing in part that if Hutton were "unable . . . to obtain financing suitable to him" within ninety days of signing the franchise agreement, he would then be entitled to a refund of the $25,000 franchise fee. Hutton was responsible for the drafting of the addendum.

There were two primary areas of expenditure involved in the funding of the monogramming enterprise: the "start up" costs, and the purchase or lease of a Meistergram 800 XLC computerized monogramming machine. The purchase or lease of the monogramming machine represented a critical component of the required financing because the entire operation revolved around the application of monograms to imprintable items of clothing.

After executing the franchise agreement and addendum, Hutton obtained a $26,000 loan from Star Bank to cover the start-up costs of the business operation. The loan was secured by a mortgage executed by Hutton and his wife Pamela against their residence.

To facilitate the lease or purchase of the monogramming machine, MPI issued a franchise offering circular to Hutton. The circular, which MPI was required to provide under Ohio law, estimated that the total cost of an MPI franchise varied between $32,420 and $36,720, with an additional $9,150 to $31,150 cost for construction. The fee paid by Hutton accounted for $25,000 of the $36,720 total estimated franchise cost. The circular also estimated that the monogramming machine could be leased for $520, excluding taxes, per month for sixty months, or purchased at a cost of $21,000.

After receiving the circular, Hutton spoke with MPI representative Pam Totty, who functioned as a liaison between Dennis Hanley, MPI's financial director, and MPI franchisees. One of Totty's duties in this capacity was to assist MPI franchisees in securing leases for monogramming equipment. On November 20, 1989, Totty notified Hutton that she had secured a sixty-month lease through United Leasing Corporation. The monthly lease payments totaled [sic] $751.01, excluding taxes, with a total equipment cost of $45,060.60 over the life of the lease. The lease also required Hutton to make a ten percent down payment on the purchase price, which was listed at $24,751. Since Hutton considered these terms to be substantially less advantageous than the terms offered in the MPI circular, he rejected the financing. He then requested Totty to submit his application to Trinity Leasing despite the fact that she had told him that he did not meet Trinity's minimum leasing qualifications. At Hutton's insistence, Totty submitted his application to Trinity, which subsequently rejected it due to Hutton's inadequate financial position. When Totty notified Hutton that the application had been rejected, she recommended that he pursue other avenues of financing. In order to help Hutton obtain financing from other sources, Dennis Hanley prepared a financial statement for Hutton which Hutton then submitted with a loan application to Society Bank in December 1989. This application was rejected because of insufficient collateral.

On January 1, 1990, Hutton wrote to Larry Meyer, MPI's president, requesting a refund of the $25,000 franchise fee due to the difficulty he had experienced in securing financing. This request was denied. On March 5, 1990, Hutton filed a three-count complaint against MPI. In the first count, Hutton sought to recover the franchise fee . . . .

MPI counterclaimed on April 9, 1990, alleging, *inter alia,* that Hutton had breached the franchise agreement by failing to perform his obligations pursuant to the franchise agreement. According to MPI, Hutton's breach caused MPI to lose the opportunity to offer Hutton's franchise to others as well as the loss of a weekly royalty fee of six percent of Hutton's gross sales and one percent of the gross revenues payable to MPI as an advertising fee. MPI also sought attorney fees to which it alleged it was entitled under the terms of the franchise agreement.

Hutton moved for summary judgment on June 1, 1990, arguing that the language of the addendum clearly and unambiguously gave him the sole right to determine what financing was suitable to him. He claimed that since he failed to find financing which was in fact suitable to him, he was entitled as a matter of law to the return of the $25,000 franchise fee. In support of his motion, Hutton offered his sworn affidavit as well as the notice of the rejection of his loan application by Society Bank and excerpts from MPI's franchise circular. In rebuttal, MPI offered the affidavits of Pam Totty, Dennis Hanley, and Roger Guertin, the vice-president of Trinity Leasing. MPI also attached a copy of Hutton's response to MPI's interrogatories, which Hutton had filed on June 21, 1991.

There was a dispute over whether Hutton's father-in-law, Charles Allport, was a potential source of financing. Interrogatory No. 9 requested Hutton to:

> Describe in detail the terms and conditions of any financing agreements and/or arrangements, and/or any support agreements and/or arrangements, between yourself and Charles Allport.

Hutton responded that there was no such arrangement between himself and Allport. However, in Paragraph 5 of Dennis Hanley's affidavit, Hanley averred that Hutton had represented to him that if the $26,000 loan was insufficient, he could obtain whatever additional funds were needed from his father-in-law. Hanley also averred in Paragraph 6 that he had had various conversations with Allport wherein Allport referred to himself as an investor in Hutton's franchise. Hanley swore that Allport's conduct was consistent with Hutton's representations that Allport would supply additional funding for the franchise if necessary.

The trial court entered judgment on August 3, 1991, granting Hutton's motion. . . .

Key to the trial court's determination was its finding that the language of the addendum was clear and unambiguous. Based on this finding the court concluded that:

> The $25,000 franchise fee was refundable if within 90 days Plaintiff was unable to obtain financing suitable *to him.* [Emphasis *sic.*] Defendants [*sic*] chose to live with the subjective language employed in the agreement and did not specify any steps Plaintiff would have to take in order to satisfy the

condition. The language did not require the Plaintiff to accept any available financing, nor did it require the Plaintiff to exhaust all possible options in an effort to obtain financing. As a consequence Defendants [*sic*] must live with the agreement entered. This Court finds that the Plaintiff's efforts to obtain financing were adequate pursuant to the terms of the agreement in that the first available financing method was clearly out of line with the terms suggested by the Defendant company. The second attempt to obtain financing with a firm which often participates in leasing agreements with franchisees of the Defendant rejected Plaintiff's application without consideration because the Plaintiff did not meet the necessary requirements. The third attempt Plaintiff made to obtain financing through a local bank was rejected because Plaintiff did not have enough collateral. Plaintiff is not required to search endlessly when it seems further efforts will meet with similar results.

MPI has appealed, raising a single assignment of error as follows:

The entry of summary judgment in the plaintiff's favor upon the claim asserted in the 'first branch' of the complaint, and against the defendant upon its counterclaim, was error.

MPI advances two arguments in support of this assignment.

I. THE ADDENDUM LANGUAGE IS AMBIGUOUS

MPI first argues that the language of the addendum was ambiguous wherein it predicated Hutton's right to a refund upon his ability to secure financing which was "suitable to him." According to MPI, these words were susceptible to three interpretations. "Suitable to him" could mean that the financing had to be "suitable as determined by Hutton," "suitable *for* Hutton," or "suitable for Hutton's needs." We agree with the trial court's holding that the language of the addendum created no ambiguity. However, this does not dispose of the appeal because a question of interpretation remains.

Contract clauses which make the duty of performance of one of the parties conditional upon his satisfaction are generally referred to as "satisfaction clauses." These clauses have been divided by the courts into two categories, and have been interpreted in accordance with the category. Mattei v. Hopper (1958), 51 Cal.2d 119, 121, 330 P.2d 625, 626.

Where the satisfaction clause requires satisfaction as to such matters as commercial value or quality, operative fitness, or mechanical utility, dissatisfaction cannot be claimed unreasonably. In these contracts, an objective standard is applied to the satisfaction clause and the test is whether the performance would satisfy a reasonable person. Id.; Cranetex, Inc. v. Precision Crane & Rigging of Houston, Inc. (1988), 760 S.W.2d 298, 301-302.

If, on the other hand, the satisfaction clause relates to matters involving fancy, personal taste, or judgment, then a subjective standard is applied, and the test is whether the party is actually satisfied. Id. Although application of a subjective standard to a satisfaction clause would seem to give the obligor virtually unlimited latitude to avoid his duty of performance, such is not the case. In these situations, courts impose the limitation that the obligor act in good faith. Mattei, supra, 51 Cal.2d at 121, 330 P.2d at 626. Thus, under the subjective standard, the promisor can avoid the contract as long as he is genuinely, albeit unreasonably, dissatisfied. Which standard applies in a given transaction is a matter of the actual or constructive intent of the parties, which, in turn, is a function of the express language of the contract, or the subject matter of the contract. Kadner v. Shields (1971), 20 Cal.App.3d 251, 262-263, 97 Cal.Rptr. 742, 751-752.

This court has previously held that an objective standard applies to contracts containing satisfaction clauses. Enterprise Roofing v. Howard Investment (1957), 105 Ohio App. 502, 505, 6 O.O.2d 232, 233, 152 N.E.2d 807, 810. However, we neither explained why an objective standard applied in that case nor distinguished between those contracts which require a subjective assessment of satisfaction by a court and those which require an objective assessment. This distinction is critical to the disposition of this appeal. Although we did not address this distinction in our holding in Enterprise Roofing, we did not say that an objective standard applies to every satisfaction clause in every contract.

The Hamilton County Court of Appeals has twice recently considered contracts containing satisfaction clauses. In Superior Die & Eng. v. Gen. Chain & Mfg. Corp. (Aug. 15, 1984), Hamilton App. No. C-830748, unreported, 1984 WL 6958, the court cited Enterprise Roofing and held that "where performance is to be measured by the satisfaction of a party to a contract, the general view has been that an objective standard of reasonableness will apply to assess the sufficiency of performance." Superior Die also recognized that an exception existed where the subject matter of the contract involved individual taste, personal convenience, or individual preference. Id. at fn. 1. The court reached the same result in Loft v. Sibcy-Cline Realtors (Dec. 13, 1989), Hamilton App. No. C-880446, unreported, 1989 WL 149667, relying on Enterprise Roofing and Superior Die.

In addition to considering these Ohio cases, we find it helpful to examine how other jurisdictions have considered the question of whether to apply an objective or subjective standard in determining whether the trial court applied the correct standard.

As to the appropriate standard, other jurisdictions have categorized satisfaction clauses in the same manner as did Kadner v. Shields, supra. For example, a subjective standard governs when the language of the contract expressly calls for the application of such a standard. An example of such language is found in Ard Dr. Pepper Bottling Co. v. Dr. Pepper Co. (C.A.5, 1953), 202 F.2d 372.

Ard dealt with a satisfaction clause contained in a commercial licensing agreement which granted to Ard the exclusive license to bottle Dr. Pepper soda in a designated territory. The satisfaction clause at issue reserved Dr. Pepper Co.'s right to rescind Ard's license if Ard did not faithfully promote the sale of the Dr. Pepper product to Dr. Pepper Co.'s satisfaction. The satisfaction clause at issue was as follows:

> (e) To at all times loyally and faithfully promote the sale of and secure thorough distribution of Dr. Pepper throughout every part of said territory and to all dealers therein, and to develop an increase in volume of sales of

> Dr. Pepper satisfactory to the Grantor. And in this connection, the Grantee agrees, represents and guarantees that the said territory included in this license, and every part thereof, and all dealers therein, ca-, [sic] and will be fully covered, solicited and worked by the Grantee in a systemkatic [sic] and business-like manner now, and at all times hereafter while this license agreement remains in effect.
>
> The determination and judgment of Dr. Pepper Company as to whether or not this clause is being complied with when made in good faith, shall be sole, exclusive and final, and such determination by the Dr. Pepper Company that this clause is not being complied with shall . . . be grounds for forfeiture of this license. . . .
>
> (k)5. That in case of the violation of any one or more of the terms or provisions of this license agreement by the Grantee or in the event Grantee fails, within the judgment of the Grantor, to faithfully comply with provisions as above set out, then Grantor shall be entitled to cancel or terminate this license upon giving written notice mailed to Grantee by registered mail and addressed to his last known place of business, and upon notice being given of such cancellation as herein provided, this license agreement and all rights hereunder shall be terminated and at an end, provided, however, that in the event of the termination of this license agreement as herein provided, or in any other manner, such termination shall not release the Grantee from the payment of any amount which may then be owing to Grantor. And upon any termination of this license agreement Grantee shall discontinue the use of the name of "Dr. Pepper" and the bottling of said product. The judgment and determination of Dr. Pepper Company when made in good faith, as to the failure of Grantee to comply with any of the terms of this license, shall be, and is hereby, made conclusive and final. . . . Id. at 374-375.

The decision in Ard to measure Dr. Pepper Co.'s satisfaction according to a subjective standard rested upon the construction of the contract terms which gave Dr. Pepper Co. the right to revoke Ard's license. The circuit court, agreeing with the district court's judgment, found that the contract expressly provided that absent bad faith, Dr. Pepper Co.'s judgment on the matter was conclusive. Id. at 376. The contract expressly made Dr. Pepper Co. the sole arbiter of satisfaction, circumscribed only by the exercise of its good faith judgment. Thus, the express language of the contract implicated a subjective standard of satisfaction.

In this case, we are not presented with an Ard-like situation where the contract language clearly mandated that Hutton's satisfaction be assessed subjectively. Nowhere in the addendum does it state, as it did in the Ard contract, quoted supra, that Hutton's judgment as to the suitability of financing was to be "sole, exclusive or final." Nor did it impose a "good faith" limitation on his judgment. (Even if Hutton's satisfaction as to the financing were to be assessed subjectively, he was still required to present evidence that he was, in good faith, dissatisfied with the available financing. Since Hutton presented no evidence as to the genuineness of his dissatisfaction, the court should not have, for this additional reason, granted summary judgment in his favor.)

The addendum contained only a general satisfaction clause. The fact that a contract contains a general satisfaction clause, without more, does not mandate the application of a subjective standard. Absent express contract language, courts have looked to the nature of the contract as an indicator of which standard governs. In these cases, there still is no clear line of demarcation. Generally, the subjective standard applies to contracts involving matters of aesthetic taste, feasibility of operation, or management, regardless of financial impact. The objective standard of the reasonable person is generally applied where commercial or financial matters are involved. Kadner, supra, 20 Cal.App.3d at 263, 97 Cal.Rptr. at 752; Cranetex, Inc. v. Precision Crane & Rigging of Houston, Inc., supra; Mattei v. Hopper, supra. This is not to say that a subjective standard is always inapplicable to a contract involving commercial transactions. Mattei v. Hopper, supra.

Mattei involved an action for breach of contract by a purchaser against a vendor who failed to convey real estate in accordance with the terms of a deposit receipt executed by the parties. The real estate was to be developed into a commercial shopping center. The concluding paragraph of the deposit receipt contained a satisfaction clause which conditioned the purchaser's tender of the payment of the balance of the purchase price upon a bank's obtaining leases for the tenants of the shopping center which were satisfactory to the purchaser. The purchaser complied with the preliminary terms of the deposit receipt, but the vendor repudiated the contract while the purchaser was in the process of obtaining the leases. The purchaser secured satisfactory leases and offered payment of the balance due on the contract. The vendor refused to tender the deed. The precise issue in Mattei was whether the condition of the purchaser's "satisfaction," which satisfaction the court determined was to be scrutinized on a subjective basis, rendered the agreement illusory and unsupported by consideration, and thus unenforceable against the vendor.

While recognizing that an objective standard generally applied where the condition called for satisfaction as to commercial value or quality, as was the case therein, the California Supreme Court nevertheless applied a subjective standard. The court so concluded because application of an objective standard was impracticable under the facts presented:

> [I]t would seem that the factors involved in determining whether a lease is satisfactory to the lessor are too numerous and varied to permit the application of a reasonable man standard as envisioned by this line of cases. Illustrative of some of the factors which would have to be considered in this case are the duration of the leases, their provisions for renewal options, if any, their covenants and restrictions, the amounts of the rentals, the financial responsibility of the lessees, and the character of the lessees' businesses.
> This multiplicity of factors which must be considered in evaluating a lease shows that this case more appropriately falls within the second line of authorities dealing with 'satisfaction' clauses, being those involving fancy, taste, or judgment. Where the question is one of judgment, the promisor's determination that he is not satisfied, when made in good faith, has been held to be a defense to an action on the contract. (Citations omitted.) Id., 51 Cal.2d at 123, 330 P.2d at 627.

Such a holding is consistent with the view taken by the Restatement of the Law 2d, Contracts (1981), Section 228, which states:

> When it is a condition of an obligor's duty that he be satisfied with respect to the obligee's performance . . . and it is practicable to determine whether a reasonable person in the position of the obligor would be satisfied, an interpretation is preferred under which the condition occurs if such a reasonable person in the position of the obligor would be satisfied. (Emphasis added.)

(The California Supreme Court rejected the vendor's contention that the subjective nature of the purchaser's satisfaction rendered the argument unenforceable.)

In this case, the evidence fails to establish that it would have been impracticable to apply an objective standard to the addendum. Hutton presented no evidence of impracticability. Indeed, he only presented evidence and argument as to the unambiguous nature of the addendum's language, resting his motion on the alleged inherently subjective nature of the language. Therefore, absent evidence of impracticability, we consider whether the nature of the contract indicated which standard controlled. We find Kadner v. Shields, supra, to be instructive.

Kadner involved a breach of contract action stemming from a dispute over a real estate sale. The buyers had agreed to purchase a luxury tract home in Beverly Hills subject to their satisfaction with the terms and conditions of an encumbrance they were to assume which was contained in an escrow agreement. If they were dissatisfied with the terms of the encumbrance, the escrow agreement stated that they were entitled to the return of their partial down payment. Id., 20 Cal.App.3d at 254, 97 Cal.Rptr. at 745. In reversing the trial court's judgment which held that the buyers' approval had to be measured according to a subjective standard, the court of appeals examined when satisfaction is measured by an objective standard and by a subjective standard. The court held that:

> Which test is to be used in a given transaction is a matter of actual or constructive (legally presumed) intent of the parties. . . . The choice can be settled of course by explicit language in the instrument. We feel that that is lacking in the instant case. So it is one of constructive intent. The absence of such explicitness in the instant case militates against a judicial decision in favor of the subjective personal judgment criterion in two ways: . . . In the absence of a specific expression in the instrument or a clear indication from the nature of the subject matter, the preference of the law is for the less arbitrary standard of the reasonable man. Id., 20 Cal.App.3d at 262-263, 97 Cal.Rptr. at 751-752.

In this case, the franchise agreement was clearly commercial in nature and pertained to matters of financial concern. Without express language to the contrary, or evidence of impracticability, the commercial nature of the contract, without more, dictated that Hutton's satisfaction had to be measured objectively.

There was nothing unique about this commercial contract that would implicate a subjective assessment of Hutton's satisfaction. Indeed, this contract presents a classic example of an arm's-length business transaction in which reasonable business concerns, relevant to the financing of equipment, dictated the terms of the contract.

Based on the foregoing analysis, we hold that, in the absence of express language to the contrary, or evidence of impracticability of application, an objective standard governs satisfaction clauses in contracts which involve commercial and financial matters. Accordingly, we conclude that the trial court improperly applied a subjective standard in assessing Hutton's satisfaction.

II. GENUINE ISSUES OF MATERIAL FACT EXIST AS TO WHETHER HUTTON WAS "UNABLE" TO LOCATE FINANCING SUITABLE TO HIM.

This argument requires us to determine whether the trial court correctly found that there was no genuine issue of material fact as to Hutton's *inability* to locate financing. This poses a discrete query separate from the issue of the *suitability* of available financing. In their briefs, the parties agree that even if the satisfaction clause were assessed according to a subjective standard, a separate "good faith" standard would govern the determination of whether Hutton was *able* to secure financing. The good faith inquiry focuses on whether Hutton exerted a reasonable effort to locate suitable financing. The following undisputed facts are relevant to this inquiry.

Hutton admitted that he could obtain financing from at least United Leasing. MPI had negotiated the lease terms with United Leasing on Hutton's behalf. Hutton refused to accept the United Leasing proposal in part because the monthly lease cost was almost $200 more than the monthly cost set forth in MPI's franchise circular. Aside from the United Leasing proposal, Hutton explored only two other avenues of financing. He first requested that MPI submit a lease application to Trinity Leasing despite his knowledge that he did not qualify for such financing under Trinity's leasing guidelines. Trinity denied his application. Hutton then submitted an application to Society Bank of Dayton which was prepared with Dennis Hanley's assistance. The application was rejected due to insufficient collateral.

The trial court apparently concluded that these efforts were sufficient to obviate any genuine issue of fact as to whether Hutton was able to locate financing. While we agree with the court's observation that Hutton "[was] not required to search endlessly when it seem[ed] further efforts [would] meet with similar results," we do not agree these efforts conclusively established that Hutton exerted a good faith effort to secure financing. Indeed, we identify two issues of material fact based on this uncontroverted evidence. The issues are whether contacting only one bank and only one other leasing institution constituted a reasonable effort to secure suitable financing, and whether Hutton could claim he made a reasonable attempt to secure suitable leasing with United Leasing and Trinity Leasing when MPI, not Hutton, arranged the United Leasing lease, and when Hutton knew before submitting an application to Trinity that he did not meet Trinity's leasing criteria.

Moreover, the record also contains critical, disputed evidence which precluded summary judgment. The affidavit of MPI's financial director, Dennis Hanley, contained evidence that Hutton told Hanley he could, in fact, have obtained the necessary financing from his father-in-law, Charles Allport. Hanley's affidavit also contained evidence that Allport had repeatedly represented himself to Hanley as one of Hutton's franchise investors. In his response to MPI's interrogatories, Hutton steadfastly denied any such arrangement existed. This conflicting evidence, without more, was sufficient to create a genuine issue of fact as to Hutton's ability to obtain satisfactory financing and to thus render summary judgment inappropriate.

The assignment of error is sustained.

The judgment of the trial court will be reversed. The matter will be remanded for further proceedings consistent with this opinion.

Judgment accordingly.

BROGAN, J., concurs.

FAIN, P.J., concurs in the judgment.

Although I concur in the judgment of the court, I would apply a subjective standard in determining whether reasonable minds could reach different conclusions as to whether Hutton was unable to obtain financing "suitable to him."

I find Judge Wolff's analysis of this issue to be excellent, but I would reach a different conclusion. There are many variables to consider in determining whether financing is "suitable." Besides the duration of the loan and the interest rate, there are (i) the scope and extent of the definitions of acts of default; (ii) the consequences of acts of default, which can range from modest to punitive; and (iii) the extent of personal collateral required for the loan. In my view, the many and diverse implications of the terms of possible financing packages makes this case similar to Mattei v. Hopper (1958), 51 Cal.2d 119, 330 P.2d 625, in which it was held to be impractical to apply an objective test for a contracting party's satisfaction.

Although I would employ a subjective test, I nevertheless agree that reasonable minds could reach different conclusions whether "suitable" financing was available to Hutton. There was some evidence that Hutton had refused MPI's help in seeking possible sources of financing, and there was some evidence, albeit controverted, that Hutton's father-in-law was a possible source of financing. In my view, reasonable minds could have reached different conclusions whether Hutton acted in good faith in declaring that no suitable financing was available to him. Therefore, I join in the judgment of this court reversing the summary judgment rendered in Hutton's favor, and remanding this cause to the trial court for further proceedings.

NOTES AND QUESTIONS:

1. For different treatments of conditions related to timing of payment, *see Gulf Construction Co. v. Self*, 676 S.W.2d 624 (Tex. Ct. App. 1984) and *MidAmerica Construction Management v. Mastech North America*, No. CIV-03-1561-R, 2004 WL 5434662 (W.D. Okla. June 16, 2004).

B. ANTICIPATORY REPUDIATION

1. GENERALLY

HOCHSTER V. DE LA TOUR
Court of Queen's Bench
118 Eng. Rep. 922 (1853).

. . . .

Cur. adv. vult.

Lord Campbell C.J. now delivered the judgment of the Court.

On this motion in arrest of judgment, the question arises, Whether, if there be an agreement between A. and B., whereby B. engages to employ A. on and from a future day for a given period of time, to travel with him into a foreign country as a courier, and to start with him in that capacity on that day, A. being to receive a monthly salary during the continuance of such service, B. may, before the day, refuse to perform the agreement and break and renounce it, so as to entitle A. before the day to commence an action against B. to recover damages for breach of the agreement; A. having been ready and willing to perform it, till it was broken and renounced by B. The defendant's counsel very powerfully contended that, if the plaintiff was not contented to dissolve the contract, and to abandon all remedy upon it, he was bound to remain ready and willing to perform it till the day when the actual employment as courier in the service of the defendant was to begin; and that there could be no breach of the agreement, before that day, to give a right of action. But it cannot be laid down as a universal rule that, where by agreement an act is to be done on a future day, no action can be brought for a breach of the agreement till the day for doing the act has arrived. If a man promises to marry a woman on a future day, and before that day marries another woman, he is instantly liable to an action for breach of promise of marriage; *Short* v. *Stone* (8 Q. B. 358). If a man contracts to execute a lease on and from a future day for a certain term, and, before that day, executes a lease to another for the same term, he may be immediately sued for breaking the contract; *Ford* v. *Tiley* (6 B. & C. 325). So, if a man contracts to sell and deliver specific goods on a future day, and before the day he sells and delivers them to another, he is immediately liable to an action at the suit of the person with whom he first contracted to sell and deliver them; *Bowdell* v. *Parsons* (10 East, 359). One reason alleged in support of such an action is, that the defendant has, before the day, rendered it impossible for him to perform the contract at the day: but this does not necessarily follow; for, prior to the day fixed for doing the act, the first wife may have died, a surrender of the lease executed might be obtained, and the defendant might have repurchased the goods so as to be in a situation to sell and deliver them to the plaintiff. Another reason may be, that, where there is a contract to do an act on a future day, there is a relation constituted between the parties in the meantime by the contract, and that they impliedly promise that in the meantime neither will do any thing to the prejudice of the other inconsistent with that relation. As an example, a man and woman engaged to marry are affianced to one another during the period between the time of the engagement and the celebration of the marriage. In this very case, of traveller and courier, from the day of the hiring till the day when the employment was to begin, they were engaged to each other; and it seems to be a breach of an implied contract if either of them renounces the engagement.

This reasoning seems in accordance with the unanimous decision of the Exchequer Chamber in *Elderton* v. *Emmens*,[1] which we have followed in subsequent cases in this Court. The declaration in the present case, in alleging a breach, states a great deal more than a passing intention on the part of the defendant which he may repent of, and could only be proved by evidence that he had utterly renounced the contract, or done some act which rendered it impossible for him to perform it. If the plaintiff has no remedy for breach of the contract unless he treats the contract as in force, and acts upon it down to the 1st June 1852, it follows that, till then, he must enter into no employment which will interfere with his promise "to start with the defendant on such travels on the day and year," and that he must then be properly equipped in all respects as a courier for a three months' tour on the continent of Europe. But it is surely much more rational, and more for the benefit of both parties, that, after the renunciation of the agreement by the defendant, the plaintiff should be at liberty to consider himself absolved from any future performance of it, retaining his right to sue for any damage he has suffered from the breach of it. Thus, instead of remaining idle and laying out money in preparations which must be useless, he is at liberty to seek service under another employer, which would go in mitigation of the damages to which he would otherwise be entitled for a breach of the contract. It seems strange that the defendant, after renouncing the contract, and absolutely declaring that he will never act under it, should be permitted to object that faith is given to his assertion, and that an opportunity is not left to him of changing his mind. If the plaintiff is barred of any remedy by entering into an engagement inconsistent with starting as a courier with the defendant on the 1st June, he is prejudiced by putting faith in the defendant's assertion: and it would be more consonant with principle, if the defendant were precluded from saying that he had not broken the contract when he declared that he entirely renounced it. Suppose that the defendant, at the time of his renunciation, had embarked on a voyage for Australia, so as to render it physically impossible for him to employ the plaintiff as a courier on the continent of Europe in the months of June, July and August 1852: according to decided cases, the action might have been brought before the 1st June; but the renunciation may have been founded on other facts, to be given in evidence, which would equally have rendered the defendant's performance of the contract impossible. The man who wrongfully renounces a contract into which he has deliberately entered cannot justly complain if he is immediately sued for a compensation in damages by the man whom he has injured: and it seems reasonable to allow an option to the injured party, either to sue immediately, or to wait till the time when the act was to be done, still holding it as prospectively binding for the exercise of this option, which may be advantageous to the innocent party, and cannot be prejudicial to the wrongdoer. An argument against the action before the 1st of June is urged from the difficulty of calculating the damages: but this argument is equally strong against an action before the 1st of September, when the three months would expire. In either case, the jury in assessing the damages would be justified in looking to all that had happened, or was likely to happen, to increase or mitigate the loss of the plaintiff down to the day of trial. . . .

Judgment for plaintiff.

---

[1] 6 Com. B. 160. Affirmed in Dom. Proc.; Emmens v. Elderton , 4 H. L. Ca.

TRUMAN L. FLATT & SONS CO. V. SCHUPF
Appellate Court of Illinois, Fourth District
649 N.E.2d 990 (1995).

Presiding Justice KNECHT delivered the opinion of the court:

Plaintiff Truman L. Flatt & Sons Co., Inc., filed a complaint seeking specific performance of a real estate contract made with defendants Sara Lee Schupf, Ray H. Neiswander, Jr., and American National Bank and Trust Company of Chicago (American), as trustee under trust No. 23257. Defendants filed a motion for summary judgment, which the trial court granted. Plaintiff now appeals from the trial court's grant of the motion for summary judgment. We reverse and remand.

In March 1993, plaintiff and defendants entered a contract in which defendants agreed to sell plaintiff a parcel of land located in Springfield, Illinois. The contract stated the purchase price was to be $160,000. The contract also contained the following provisions:

> 1. This transaction shall be closed on or before June 30, 1993, or upon approval of the relief requested from the Zoning Code of the City of Springfield, Illinois, whichever first occurs ("Closing Date"). The closing is subject to contingency set forth in paragraph 14. . . .
>
> 14. This Contract to Purchase Real Estate is contingent upon the Buyer obtaining, within one hundred twenty (120) days after the date hereof, amendment of, or other sufficient relief of, the Zoning Code of the City of Springfield to permit the construction and operation of an asphalt plant. In the event the City Council of the City of Springfield denies the request for such use of the property, then this contract shall be voidable at Buyer's option and if Buyer elects to void this contract Buyer shall receive a refund of the earnest money paid.

On May 21, plaintiff's attorney sent a letter to defendants' attorney informing him of substantial public opposition plaintiff encountered at a public meeting concerning its request for rezoning. The letter concluded:

> The day after the meeting all of the same representatives of the buyer assembled and discussed our chances for successfully pursuing the re-zoning request. Everyone who was there was in agreement that our chances were zero to none for success. As a result, we decided to withdraw the request for rezoning, rather than face almost certain defeat.
>
> The bottom line is that we are still interested in the property, but the property is not worth as much to us a 35-acre parcel zoned I-1, as it would be if it were zoned I-2. At this juncture, I think it is virtually impossible for anyone to get that property re-zoned I-2, especially to accommodate the operation of an asphalt plant. In an effort to keep this thing moving, my clients have authorized me to offer your clients the sum of $142,500.00 for the property, which they believe fairly represents its value with its present

> zoning classification. Please check with your clients and advise whether or not that revision in the contract is acceptable. If it is, I believe we can accelerate the closing and bring this matter to a speedy conclusion. Your prompt attention will be appreciated. Thanks.

Defendants' attorney responded in a letter dated June 9, the body of which stated, in its entirety:

> In reply to your May 21 letter, be advised that the owners of the property in question are not interested in selling the property for $142,500 and, accordingly, the offer is not accepted.
>
> I regret that the zoning reclassification was not approved.

Plaintiff's attorney replied back in a letter dated June 14, the body of which stated, in its entirety:

> My clients received your letter of June 9, 1993[,] with some regret, however upon some consideration they have elected to proceed with the purchase of the property as provided in the contract. At your convenience please give me a call so that we can set up a closing date.

After this correspondence, plaintiff's attorney sent two more brief letters to defendants' attorney, dated June 23 and July 6, each requesting information concerning the status of defendants' preparation for fulfillment of the contract. Defendants' attorney replied in a letter dated July 8. The letter declared it was the defendants' position plaintiff's failure to waive the rezoning requirement and elect to proceed under the contract at the time the rezoning was denied, coupled with the new offer to buy the property at less than the contract price, effectively voided the contract. Plaintiff apparently sent one more letter in an attempt to convince defendants to honor the contract, but defendants declined. Defendants then arranged to have plaintiff's earnest money returned.

Plaintiff filed a complaint for specific performance and other relief against defendants and American, asking the court to direct defendants to comply with the terms of the contract. Defendants responded by filing a "motion to strike, motion to dismiss or, in the alternative, motion for summary judgment." The motion for summary judgment sought summary judgment on the basis plaintiff repudiated the contract.

Prior to the hearing on the motions, plaintiff filed interrogatories requesting, among other things, information concerning the current status of the property. Defendants' answers to the interrogatories stated defendants had no knowledge of any third party's involvement in a potential sale of the property, defendants had not made any offer to sell the property to anyone, no one had made an offer to purchase the property or discussed the possibility of purchasing the property, and defendants had not sold the property to, received any offer from, or discussed a sale of the property with, any other trust member.

After a hearing on the motions, the trial court granted the defendants' motion for summary judgment without explaining the basis for its ruling. Plaintiff filed a post-trial motion to vacate the judgment. The trial court denied the post-trial motion, declaring defendants' motion for summary judgment was granted because plaintiff had repudiated the contract. Plaintiff now appeals the trial court's grant of summary judgment, arguing the trial court erred because (1) it did not repudiate the contract, and (2) even if it did repudiate the contract, it timely retracted that repudiation. . . .

Plaintiff first argues summary judgment was improper because the trial court erred in finding plaintiff had repudiated the contract.

> The doctrine of anticipatory repudiation requires a clear manifestation of an intent not to perform the contract on the date of performance. . . . That intention must be a definite and unequivocal manifestation that he will not render the promised performance when the time fixed for it in the contract arrives. [Citation.] Doubtful and indefinite statements that performance may or may not take place are not enough to constitute anticipatory repudiation. (In re Marriage of Olsen (1988), 124 Ill.2d 19, 24, 123 Ill.Dec. 980, 982, 528 N.E.2d 684, 686.)

These requirements exist because "[a]nticipatory breach is not a remedy to be taken lightly." (Olsen, 124 Ill.2d at 25, 123 Ill.Dec. at 983, 528 N.E.2d at 687.) The Restatement (Second) of Contracts adopts the view of the Uniform Commercial Code (UCC) and states "language that under a fair reading 'amounts to a statement of intention not to perform except on conditions which go beyond the contract' constitutes a repudiation. Comment 2 to Uniform Commercial Code § 2-610." (Restatement (Second) of Contracts § 250, Comment b, at 273 (1981).) Whether an anticipatory repudiation occurred is a question of fact and the judgment of the trial court thereon will not be disturbed unless it is against the manifest weight of evidence. . . .

As can be seen, whether a repudiation occurred is determined on a case-by-case basis, depending on the particular language used. Both plaintiff and defendants, although they cite Illinois cases discussing repudiation, admit the cited Illinois cases are all factually distinguishable from the case at hand because none of those cases involved a request to change a term in the contract. According to the commentators, a suggestion for modification of the contract does not amount to a repudiation. (J. Calamari & J. Perillo, Contracts § 12-4, at 524-25 n. 74 (3d ed. 1987) (hereinafter Calamari). . . . Plaintiff also cites cases in other jurisdictions holding a request for a change in the price term of a contract does not constitute a repudiation. . . . Defendants attempt to distinguish these cases by arguing here, under the totality of the language in the letter and the circumstances surrounding the letter, the request by plaintiff for a decrease in price clearly implied a threat of nonperformance if the price term was not modified. We disagree.

The language in the May 21 letter did not constitute a clearly implied threat of nonperformance. First, although the language in the May 21 letter perhaps could be read as implying plaintiff would refuse to perform under the contract unless the price was modified, given the totality of the language in the letter, such an inference is weak. More important, even if such an inference were possible, Illinois law requires a repudiation be manifested clearly and unequivocally. Plaintiff's May 21 letter at most created an *ambiguous implication* whether performance would occur. Indeed, during oral argument defense counsel conceded the May 21 letter was "ambiguous" on whether a repudiation had occurred. This is insufficient to constitute a repudiation under well-settled Illinois law. Therefore, the trial court erred in declaring the May 21 letter anticipatorily repudiated the real estate contract as a matter of law.

Moreover, even if plaintiff had repudiated the contract, the trial court erred in granting summary judgment on this basis because plaintiff timely retracted its repudiation. Only one published decision has discussed and applied Illinois law regarding retraction of an anticipatory repudiation, Refrigeradora Del Noroeste, S.A. v. Appelbaum (1956), 138 F.Supp. 354 (holding the repudiating party has the power of retraction unless the injured party has brought suit or otherwise materially changed position), aff'd in part & rev'd in part on other grounds (1957), 248 F.2d 858. The Restatement (Second) of Contracts states:

> The effect of a statement as constituting a repudiation under § 250 or the basis for a repudiation under § 251 is nullified by a retraction of the statement if notification of the retraction comes to the attention of the injured party before he materially changes his position in reliance on the repudiation or *indicates* to the other party that he considers the repudiation to be final. (Emphasis added.) (Restatement (Second) of Contracts § 256(1), at 293 (1981).)

The UCC adopts the same position:

> Retraction of Anticipatory Repudiation. (1) Until the repudiating party's next performance is due he can retract his repudiation unless the aggrieved party has since the repudiation cancelled or materially changed his position or otherwise *indicated* that he considers the repudiation final. (Emphasis added.) (810 ILCS 5/2-611(1) (West 1992).)

Professors Calamari and Perillo declare section 2-611 of the UCC:

> . . . is in general accord with the common law rule that an anticipatory repudiation may be retracted until the other party has commenced an action thereon or has otherwise changed his position. The Code is explicit that no other act of reliance is necessary where the aggrieved party indicates 'that he considers the repudiation final.' (Emphasis added.) (Calamari § 12.7, at 528.)

"The majority of the common law cases appear to be in accord with this position." (Calamari § 12.7, at 528 n. 93.) Other commentators are universally in accord. Professor Farnsworth states: "The repudiating party can prevent the injured party from treating the contract as terminated by retracting before the injured party has acted in response to it." (Emphasis added.) (2 E. Farnsworth, Contracts § 8.22, at 482 (1990).) Professor Corbin declares one who has anticipatorily repudiated his contract has the power of retraction until the aggrieved party has materially changed his position in reliance on the repudiation. (4 A. Corbin, Corbin on Contracts § 980, at 930-31 (1951) (hereinafter Corbin).) Corbin goes on to say the assent of the aggrieved party is necessary for retraction only when the repudiation is no longer merely anticipatory, but has become an actual breach at the time performance is due. (4 Corbin § 980, at 935.) Williston states an anticipatory repudiation can be retracted by the repudiating party "unless the other party has, before the withdrawal, manifested an election to rescind the contract, or changed his position in reliance on the repudiation." (Emphasis added.) 11 W. Jaeger, Williston on Contracts § 1335, at 180 (3d ed. 1968) (hereinafter Williston).

Defendants completely avoid discussion of the common-law right to retract a repudiation other than to say Illinois is silent on the issue. Defendants then cite Stonecipher v. Pillatsch (1975), 30 Ill.App.3d 140, 332 N.E.2d 151, . . . as well as Williston § 1337, at 185-86. These authorities stand for the proposition that after an anticipatory repudiation, the aggrieved party is entitled to choose to treat the contract as rescinded or terminated, to treat the anticipatory repudiation as a breach by bringing suit or otherwise changing its position, or to await the time for performance. The UCC adopts substantially the same position. (810 ILCS 5/2-610 (West 1992).) Defendants here assert they chose to treat the contract as rescinded, as they had a right to do under well-settled principles of law.

Plaintiff admits the law stated by defendants is well settled, and admits if the May 21 letter was an anticipatory breach, then defendants had the right to treat the contract as being terminated or rescinded. However, plaintiff points out defendants' assertions ignore the great weight of authority, discussed earlier, which provides a right of the repudiating party to retract the repudiation before the aggrieved party has chosen one of its options allowed under the common law and listed in Stonecipher, Builder's Concrete, and Leazzo. Plaintiff argues defendants' letter of June 9 failed to treat the contract as rescinded, and absent notice or other manifestation defendants were pursuing one of their options, plaintiff was free to retract its repudiation. Plaintiff is correct.

Defendants' precise theory that plaintiff should not be allowed to retract any repudiation in this instance is ambiguous and may be given two interpretations. The first is Illinois should not follow the common-law rule allowing retraction of an anticipatory repudiation before the aggrieved party elects a response to the repudiation. This theory warrants little discussion, because the rule is well settled. Further, defendants have offered no public policy reason to disallow retraction of repudiation other than the public interest in upholding the "sanctity of the contract."

The second possible interpretation of defendants' precise theory is an aggrieved party may treat the contract as terminated or rescinded without notice or other indication being given to the repudiating party, and once such a decision is made by the aggrieved party, the repudiating party no longer has the right of retraction. It is true no notice is required to be given to the repudiating party if the aggrieved party materially changes its position as a result of the repudiation. (See, e.g., Calamari § 12-7, at 528 n. 92, citing Bu-Vi-Bar Petroleum Corp. v. Krow (10th Cir.1930), 40 F.2d 488, 493.) Here, however, the defendants admitted in their answers to plaintiff's interrogatories they had not entered another agreement to sell the property, nor even discussed or considered the matter with another party. Defendants had not changed their position at all, nor do defendants make any attempt to so argue. As can be seen from the language of the Restatement, the UCC, and the commentators, shown earlier, they are in accord that where the aggrieved party has not otherwise undergone a material change in position, the aggrieved party must indicate to the other party it is electing to treat the contract as rescinded. This can be accomplished either by bringing suit, by notifying the repudiating party, or by in some other way manifesting an election to treat the contract as rescinded. Prior to such indication, the repudiating party is free to retract its repudiation. The Restatement (Second) of Contracts provides the following illustrations:

> 2. On February 1, A contracts to supply B with natural gas for one year beginning on May 1, payment to be made each month. On March 1, A repudiates. On April 1, before B has taken any action in response to the repudiation, A notifies B that he retracts his repudiation. B's duties under the contract are not discharged, and B has no claim against A. . . .
>
> 4. The facts being otherwise as stated in Illustration 2, on March 15, B *notifies* A that he cancels the contract. B's duties under the contract are discharged and B has a claim against A for damages for total breach . . . . (Emphasis added.) Restatement (Second) of Contracts § 256, Comments *a, c* (1981).

This rule makes sense as well. If an aggrieved party could treat the contract as rescinded or terminated without notice or other indication to the repudiating party, the rule allowing retraction of an anticipatory repudiation would be eviscerated. No repudiating party ever would be able to retract a repudiation, because after receiving a retraction, the aggrieved party could, if it wished, simply declare it had already decided to treat the repudiation as a rescission or termination of the contract. Defendants' theory would effectively rewrite the common-law rule regarding retraction of anticipatory repudiation so that the repudiating party may retract an anticipatory repudiation only upon assent from the aggrieved party. This is not the common-law rule, and we decline to adopt defendants' proposed revision of it.

Applying the actual common-law rule to the facts here, plaintiff sent defendants a letter dated June 14, which clearly and unambiguously indicated plaintiff intended to perform under the contract. However, defendants did not notify plaintiff, either expressly or impliedly, of an intent to treat the contract as rescinded until July 8. Nor is there anything in the record demonstrating any indication to plaintiff, prior to July 8, of an intent by defendants to treat the contract as rescinded or terminated. Thus, assuming plaintiff's May 21 request for a lower purchase price constituted an anticipatory repudiation of the contract, plaintiff successfully retracted that repudiation in the letter dated June 14 because defendants had not yet materially changed their position or indicated to plaintiff an intent to treat the contract as rescinded. Therefore, because plaintiff had timely retracted any alleged repudiation of the contract, the trial court erred in granting summary judgment for defendants on the basis plaintiff repudiated the contract. Defendants were not entitled to judgment as a matter of law.

The trial court's grant of summary judgment for defendants is reversed, and the cause is remanded.

Reversed and remanded.

NOTES & QUESTIONS:

1. Read UCC §§ 2-610 and 2-611. Compare and contrast the doctrine of anticipatory repudiation under UCC and at common law.

HOPE'S ARCHITECTURAL PRODUCTS V. LUNDY'S CONSTRUCTION
United States District Court, Kansas
781 F.Supp. 711 (1991).

LUNGSTRUM, District Judge.

This case presents a familiar situation in the field of construction contracts. Two parties, who disagreed over the meaning of their contract, held their positions to the brink, with litigation and loss the predictable result of the dispute. What is rarely predictable, however, (and what leads to a compromise resolution of many construction disputes when cool heads hold sway) is which party will ultimately prevail. The stakes become winner-take-all.

Plaintiff Hope's Architectural Products (Hope's) is a New York corporation that manufactures and installs custom window fixtures. Defendant Lundy's Construction (Lundy's) is a Kansas corporation that contracted to buy windows from Hope's for a school remodeling project. Defendant Bank IV Olathe (Bank IV) is a national banking organization with its principal place of business in Kansas. Bank IV acted as surety for a statutory bond obtained by Lundy's for the remodeling project.

Hope's contends that Lundy's breached the contract to buy windows, entitling Hope's to damages in the amount of the contract price of $55,000. Hope's also contends that Bank IV wrongfully refused to pay Hope's on the bond when Lundy's breached the contract. Hope's has sued for breach of contract, and in the alternative, for recovery under the theory of *quantum meruit.* A trial to the Court was held December 4 and 5, 1991. Two issues emerged as pivotal to the resolution of this case: (1) when was delivery of the windows due, and (2) if delivery was late, could Hope's lawfully suspend performance and demand certain assurances, (including ultimately, a demand for prepayment in full) that Lundy's would not back charge for the late delivery under the authority of K.S.A. § 84-2-609? Because the Court finds that a determination of these issues leads to the conclusion that Hope's was the party in breach of this contract, the plaintiff's request for relief is denied.

I. FACTS

The following findings of fact are entered pursuant to Fed.R.Civ.P. 52. On June 13, 1988, defendant Lundy's entered into a contract with the Shawnee Mission School District as general contractor for the construction of an addition to the Rushton Elementary School. Lundy's provided a public works bond in connection with the Rushton project as required by K.S.A. § 60-1111 (1983). The purpose of the bond was to insure that Lundy's paid any outstanding indebtedness it incurred in the construction of the project. The statutory bond was secured through defendant Bank IV.

Plaintiff Hope's is a manufacturer of custom-built windows. The initial contact between Hope's and Lundy's occurred through Mr. Richard Odor, a regional agent for Hope's in Kansas City. On June 29, 1988, Hope's contracted with Lundy's to manufacture ninety-three windows for the Rushton project. The contract price, including the cost of labor and materials for the windows, was $55,000.

Although the contract included a term pertaining to the time for delivering the windows, there is some controversy over the meaning of this provision. Even under the most favorable interpretation to Hope's, however, delivery was due twelve to fourteen weeks after Hope's received approved shop drawings from Lundy's on July 18. Thus, delivery was due no later than October 24, 1988.

During the late summer and fall of 1988, several discussions took place between Hope's and Lundy's concerning when the windows would be delivered to the job site. Production of the windows was delayed by events that, according to the testimony of Mr. Odor, were not the fault of Lundy's. On September 27, 1988, Mark Hannah, vice president of Lundy's, wrote to Hope's requesting that installation of the windows begin by October 19, and be completed by October 26. On October 14 Hannah again wrote to Hope's, threatening to withhold "liquidated damages" from the contract price if Hope's did not comply with these deadlines. Although there was no provision in the contract for liquidated damages, Hope's did not make any response to the October 14 letter.

The windows were shipped from Hopes' New York plant to Kansas City on October 28. Delivery to the Rushton site was anticipated on November 4. On November 1, Hannah called Hopes' office in New York to inquire about the windows. He spoke to Kathy Anderson, Hopes' customer service manager. The substance of this conversation is disputed. Hope's claims that Hannah threatened a back charge of $11,000 (20% of the contract price) for late delivery of the windows. Hannah testified, however, that although the possibility of a back charge was discussed, no specific dollar amount was mentioned. Hannah specifically denies that he threatened to withhold $11,000 from the contract.

After her conversation with Hannah, Anderson immediately informed Chris Arvantinos, vice president of Hope's, of the threatened back charge. Arvantinos called Hannah to discuss the back charge, but he does not recall hearing Hannah mention the $11,000 figure. Arvantinos requested that Hannah provide assurances that Lundy's would not back charge Hope's, but Hannah was unwilling to provide such assurances.

In a letter written on November 2, Arvantinos informed Hannah that Hope's was suspending delivery of the windows until Lundy's provided assurances that there would be no back charge. Hannah received this letter on the morning of November 3, shortly before Mr. Odor visited Hannah at Lundy's. Odor, who had spoken with Arvantinos about the back charge, issued a new demand that Lundy's had to meet before Hope's would deliver the windows. He gave Hannah an invoice for the full amount of the contract price, demanding prepayment before the windows would be delivered.

Odor set out three ways that Lundy's could meet this demand: (1) payment of the contract price in full by cashier's check; (2) placement of the full contract price in an escrow account until the windows were installed; or (3) delivery of the full contract amount to the architect to hold until the windows were installed. All three options required Lundy's to come up with $55,000 before the windows would be delivered. Hannah believed that the demand presented by Odor superseded the letter from Arvantinos he received earlier that morning.

Hannah informed Odor that there was no way for Lundy's to get an advance from the school district at that time to comply with Hopes' request. The meeting ended, Lundy's did not prepay, and Hope's did not deliver the windows. On November 7, 1988, Lundy's terminated the contract with Hope's. Thereafter, Lundy's obtained an alternate supplier of the windows.

On February 15, 1989, Hope's notified defendant Bank IV of Lundy's failure to pay the contract price and demanded payment from Bank IV on the public works bond. Bank IV refused to pay Hopes' claim. This action was filed by Hope's on March 20, 1989. Jurisdiction of the matter rests with this Court pursuant to 28 U.S.C. § 1332.

II. DISCUSSION

At the outset, the Court concludes that the Uniform Commercial Code (UCC) governs this transaction. Article 2 of the UCC applies to transactions in goods. K.S.A. § 84-2-102 (1983). The contract at issue in this case involved a mixed goods/services transaction. Whether the UCC applies to hybrid transactions such as this depends upon " 'whether their predominant factor, their thrust, their purpose, reasonably stated, is the rendition of service, with goods incidentally involved ... or is a transaction of sale, with labor incidentally involved.' " Systems Design & Management Information, Inc. v. Kansas City Post Office Employees Credit Union, 14 Kan.App.2d 266, 270-71, 788 P.2d 878 (1990). If the UCC applies, it applies to all facets of the transaction. . . . The transaction at issue in this case primarily involved a sale of windows, with installation and manufacturing services provided as an incidental component. Therefore, the UCC applies.

A. *Plaintiff's Contract Claim Against Defendant Lundy's*

This case turns on the resolution of two central and interrelated issues: (1) when was delivery due under the contract, and (2) could Hope's lawfully demand the assurances it demanded from Lundy's under K.S.A. § 84-2-609.[2] If the demands for assurances were proper, then Hope's would have been justified in suspending its performance and withholding delivery and Lundy's failure to provide assurances and subsequent termination of the contract amounted to a total breach. If, however, the demands for assurances were not proper under 84-2-609 then Hope's breached the contract by wrongfully withholding delivery of the windows and Lundy's was entitled to cancel the contract. The delivery date

[2] Section 2-609 provides:84-2-609. Right to adequate assurance of performance.

> (1) ... When reasonable grounds for insecurity arise with respect to the performance of either party the other may in writing demand adequate assurance of due performance and until he receives such assurance may if commercially reasonable suspend any performance for which he has not already received the agreed return.
> (2) Between merchants the reasonableness of grounds for insecurity and the adequacy of any assurance offered shall be determined according to commercial standards.

issue is addressed first because the matter of whether or not Hope's was already in breach for late delivery goes directly to the propriety of its demand for assurances.

1. Delivery Date

Even under Hopes' interpretation of the delivery term, delivery of the windows was not timely.[3] At trial, Chris Arvantinos, Hopes' vice president, testified that Hope's committed to deliver the windows twelve to fourteen weeks after July 18, 1988, the day Hope's received approved shop drawings. This would make delivery due between October 10 and October 24. In fact, the windows did not arrive in Kansas City until November 4, fifteen and one-half weeks after July 18. Hope's claims that this delay was "immaterial" and did not excuse Lundy's from its duties under the contract. Hope's is unable to cite any controlling authority to support this argument, however. Moreover, this argument misses the point. Even if an "immaterial" delay did not excuse future performance by Lundy's, no performance was due from Lundy's until the windows were delivered to the job site, which never occurred.

Hope's also argues, almost in passing, that the delay was caused by problems that were outside of its control, thus excusing Hope's from responsibility for the late delivery. Under a clause in the contract, Hope's disclaimed responsibility "for delayed shipments and deliveries occasioned by strikes, fires, accidents, delays of common carriers or other causes beyond our control...." (Plaintiff's exhibit 11, 3). During the course of production, Hope's experienced problems with its "bonderizing" and prime paint system, which resulted in a delay in production of approximately two weeks. (Defendants' exhibit 403). Hope's produced no evidence at trial, however, to show that this was a matter which was beyond its control. Moreover, it is interesting to note that Hope's did not contemporaneously seek from Lundy's any extension of the delivery date under this provision or notify Lundy's that it might result in a delay beyond October 24. It appears that reference to this clause is more of an afterthought born of litigation than a bona fide excuse for modifying the delivery date.

Hope's also contends that a three to four day delay resulted when Lundy's asked for a change in the design of the windows to include "weep holes" after production had already begun. However, Hopes' representative, Odor, testified that nothing Lundy's did delayed Hopes' manufacturing. Moreover, even accounting for this delay, Hope's was a week late delivering the windows.

---

[3] "Delivery" is defined by Black's Law Dictionary as " [t]he act by which the res or substance thereof is placed within the actual or constructive possession or control of another.... What constitutes delivery depends largely on the intent of the parties." Black's Law Dictionary 385 (5th ed.1979). In this case, the parties bargained for more than mere shipment of the windows. Arvantinos testified that Hope's committed to delivering the windows to the job site between October 10 and October 24. Thus, delivery was to occur under the parties' agreement when the windows arrived in Kansas City and were available for installation at the Rushton job site.

2. Section 2-609 Demand for Assurances

The framework for judging demands for assurances under 84-2-609 was set forth in LNS Investment Co., Inc. v. Phillips 66 Co., 731 F.Supp. 1484, 1487 (D.Kan.1990):

> To suspend its performance pursuant to [84-2-609], defendant must (1) have had reasonable grounds for insecurity regarding plaintiff's performance under the contract, (2) have demanded in writing adequate assurance of plaintiff's future performance and (3) have not received from plaintiff such assurance.

White and Summers note that what constitutes a "reasonable ground" for insecurity and an "adequate assurance" are fact questions. J. White & R. Summers, Uniform Commercial Code § 6-2, at 236 (3d ed. 1988). Reasonableness and adequacy are determined according to commercial standards when, as is the case here, the parties are merchants. K.S.A. § 84-2-609(2) (1983).

Although nothing in the record indicates that Hope's expressly claimed any rights under 84-2-609 during the course of this transaction, Hope's asserted at trial that the October 14 letter from Lundy's demanding delivery by October 16 and threatening liquidated damages gave Hope's reasonable grounds for insecurity. Delivery was not due until October 24 under Hopes' version of the parties' agreement, and Lundy's had no right to demand performance early, let alone broach the withholding of liquidated damages. This letter might have justified a demand for assurances under 84-2-609. However, Hope's made no such demand after receiving the letter. Instead of invoking its rights under 84-2-609, Hope's chose not to respond at all to Lundy's threat of liquidated damages. This event merely came and went without any legal consequence.

Hope's in effect invoked its rights under 84-2-609 in response to Lundys' threat of a back charge during the November 1 phone conversations. Two separate demands for assurances were made in response to this threat. Initially, Chris Arvantinos demanded assurances that Lundy's would not back charge Hope's for the delayed shipment in a telephone conversation with Mark Hannah later in the day on November 1. Arvantinos memorialized this demand in a letter composed on that day and mailed on the second of November. In their telephone conversation, Hannah refused to provide assurances that Lundy's would not back charge Hope's.

Hope's made a second demand for assurances on November 3, when Richard Odor presented Hopes' invoice to Hannah demanding payment in full. Thus, Hope's demanded assurances that it would not be back charged on November 1, and when that demand was refused, Hope's made a second demand on November 3. The Court finds that Hope's was not entitled to invoke 84-2-609 on either occasion.

When Hope's made its first demand for assurances on November 1, it was already in breach of the parties' agreement. Delivery of the windows was due by October 24, but the windows did not arrive in Kansas City until November 4. A party already in breach is not entitled to invoke section 2-609 by demanding assurances. United States v. Great Plains Gasification Associates, 819 F.2d 831, 835 (8th Cir.1987); cf. Sumner v. Fel-Air, Inc., 680

P.2d 1109 (Alaska 1984) (2-609 does not apply after a breach has already occurred). To hold otherwise would allow a party to avoid liability for breaching its contract by invoking 2-609 to extract from the nonbreaching party an assurance that no damages will be sought for the breach. A nonbreaching party in need of prompt performance could be coerced into giving up its right to damages for the breach by giving in to the demands in order to receive the needed performance. This Court refuses to endorse such a result.

The assurances which Hope's demanded, moreover, were excessive. "What constitutes 'adequate assurance' is to be determined by factual conditions; the seller must exercise good faith and observe commercial standards; his satisfaction must be based upon reason and must not be arbitrary or capricious." Richmond Leasing Co. v. Capital Bank, N.A., 762 F.2d 1303, 1310 (5th Cir.1985). "If the assurances he demands are more than 'adequate' and the other party refuses to accede to the excessive demands, the court may find that the demanding party was in breach or a repudiator." J. White & R. Summers, supra, § 6-2, at 236.

Lundy's argues that Hopes' demand for assurances in the November 2 letter from Arvantinos was overly broad and unreasonable. The letter informed Lundy's that Hope's would not deliver the windows to the job site until it received assurances that it would not "be backcharged or otherwise held responsible for liquidated damages, delay charges *or any extra costs on account of time of delivery of the windows.*" (Plaintiff's exhibit 23) (emphasis added). When this demand was made, the windows had not yet arrived in Kansas City. Therefore, the parties did not know at this time whether the proper quantity of windows had been shipped, whether the windows were the correct size, or whether they otherwise met Lundy's specifications. If there were any nonconformities in the shipment, there could have been another delay in the time of delivery while Hope's corrected the problem. Yet, Hope's demanded a blanket assurance that it would not be held responsible for *any extra costs* incurred because of "time of delivery of the windows." This demand was overly broad on its face and unreasonable under 84-2-609.

The assurances Hope's demanded on November 3 were also excessive. In his meeting with Mark Hannah, Richard Odor insisted that Lundy's prepay the contract price, deliver a cashier's check to the architect, or place the full contract price in an escrow account before the windows would be delivered. Yet, Lundy's never gave any indication that it was unable or unwilling to pay the amount it owed to Hope's when the windows were delivered and the bond stood as security for Lundy's obligation. Such a demand was unreasonable and amounted to a breach by Hope's. See Pittsburgh-Des Moines Steel v. Brookhaven Manor Water Co., 532 F.2d 572, 578-82 (7th Cir.1976) (demanding under 2-609 a personal guarantee of payment from a shareholder, or that other party escrow the entire amount of the contract price before it was due, absent any showing of an inability to pay, was unreasonable); Scott v. Crown, 765 P.2d 1043 (Colo.Ct.App.1988) (demanding payment in full before it was due was unreasonable demand under 2-609 and amounted to anticipatory breach). The payment terms under the contract were "Progress payments by the 10th of each month covering 90% of the total value of materials delivered and installation performed during the previous month with final payment upon completion of our [Hopes'] work.". . . By demanding prepayment, Hope's essentially attempted to rewrite this term of the contract. Pittsburgh-Des Moines Steel, 532 F.2d at 578-82 (2-609 may not be used to force a contract modification); Scott, 765 P.2d 1043 (same).

Although Hope's contends that a threatened back charge of $11,000 for a one week delay in shipment justified its demand for prepayment, the Court is not persuaded that Lundy's made any specific demand for $11,000. The testimony on this issue was controverted, but only Kathy Anderson, Hopes' customer service manager, testified, in a perfunctory manner, that an $11,000 back charge was threatened. Mark Hannah specifically denied making such a demand. Neither Chris Arvantinos nor Richard Odor testified to recalling receiving such a demand. There was also testimony at trial from one witness for Hope's that the threatened back charge was in the amount of $5,000. The Court is not persuaded that Lundy's went beyond making unspecified threats of a back charge for possible damages it would incur because of Hopes' delay.

By threatening to withhold damages from the contract price, Lundy's was merely exercising its rights under K.S.A. § 84-2-717,[4] which entitles a buyer to deduct from the amount owing on the contract any damages from the seller's breach. See, e.g., Patel v. Telerent Leasing Corp., 574 So.2d 3 (Miss.1990); Teeman v. Jurek, 312 Minn. 292, 251 N.W.2d 698 (1977). Giving notice of its intention to avail itself of a legal right did not indicate that Lundy's was unwilling or unable to perform under the contract. Indeed, the very nature of the right invoked by Lundy's manifests an intention that it would continue performing and pay the contract price due, less damages caused by Hopes' delay. Thus, the demand for prepayment was unreasonably excessive when there was no indication that Lundy's would not pay Hope's when performance was due.

Both Hopes' delay in delivering the windows and Hopes' excessive demands entitled Lundy's to treat Hope's as in breach and to cancel the contract, which it did on November 7, 1988. K.S.A. § 84-2-711 (1983) ("Where the seller fails to make delivery or repudiates ... the buyer may cancel...."). Thus, Hope's is not entitled to recover under its claim for breach of contract.

B. *Plaintiff's Quantum Meruit Claim*

Hope's also claims that it is entitled to compensation from Lundy's under the theory of *quantum meruit*. "*Quantum meruit,*" which literally means "as much as he deserves," is a phrase used often in older cases to describe an equitable doctrine premised on the theories of unjust enrichment and restitution. Black's Law Dictionary 1119 (5th ed.1979). Recovery was allowed under this theory when a benefit had been received by a party and it would be inequitable to allow the party to retain it. E. Farnsworth, Contracts § 2.20, at 103 n. 4 (2d ed.1990). Instead of labeling it quantum meruit, courts today speak in terms of restitution. See Pioneer Operations Co. v. Brandeberry, 14 Kan.App.2d 289, 789 P.2d 1182 (1990).

To recover in restitution, a breaching plaintiff must have conferred a benefit on the nonbreaching party. See Walker v. Ireton, 221 Kan. 314, 559 P.2d 340 (1977) (right to restitution limited to expenditures or services that benefitted other party); Restatement (Second) of Contracts § 374 (1979). The burden is on the breaching party to prove the extent of the benefit conferred, and doubts will be resolved against him. Restatement (Second) of Contracts § 374 comment b (1977).

[4] 84-2-717. Deduction of damages from the price. The buyer on notifying the seller of his intentions to do so may deduct all or any part of the damages resulting from any breach of the contract from any part of the price still due under the same contract. K.S.A. § 84-2-717 (1983).

In this case, Hope's conferred no benefit on Lundy's. The windows manufactured by Hope's were never used in the Rushton project, and the Court is not persuaded that the installation advice provided by Christiansen Steel Erection for Hope's improved the project. Hope's admits that the only labor it claims to have provided at the Rushton job site was consultation work performed by Christiansen Steel Erection, a company Hope's subcontracted with to install the windows. Mike and John Christiansen visited the job site on several occasions to advise Lundy's on how to prepare the window openings for installation. The advice they provided, however, related to the installation of windows that were never used on the project. When Lundy's canceled its contract with Hope's, it obtained an alternate supplier of a different type of windows. These windows did not require the same careful preparation of the window openings as the Hope's windows. Lundy's job foreman testified that the Christiansens' advice became moot when the alternate supplier was obtained. "[A] party's expenditures in preparation for performance that do not confer a benefit on the other party do not give rise to a restitution interest." Restatement (Second) of Contracts § 370 comment a (1977). Thus, because no benefit was conferred upon Lundy's, Hope's has no valid claim to restitution.

III. CONCLUSION

After careful consideration of the facts and law, this Court holds that Hope's breached the contract in question. Therefore, defendant Lundy's was entitled to cancel its performance and defendant Bank IV was not obligated to pay Hope's under the statutory bond.

IT IS THEREFORE ORDERED that plaintiff's claims for relief are hereby denied, and judgment is entered in favor of defendants.

IT IS SO ORDERED.

NOTES & QUESTIONS:

1. In order to allow the aggrieved party to pursue remedies for breach immediately, the prospective nonperformance must rise to the level of a material breach of the entire contract. This is true both at common law and under the U.C.C.

---

2. EXCEPTIONS

COBB V. PACIFIC MUTUAL LIFE INSURANCE CO.
Supreme Court of California
51 P.2d 84 (1935).

SEAWELL, Justice.

Plaintiff and respondent, Augustus M. Cobb, will be referred to, when not designated by name, as the insured or respondent. The Pacific Mutual Life Insurance Company, a corporation, will be referred to as the company, or as insurer, or as appellant. Respondent, Cobb, brought this action against the Pacific Mutual Life Insurance Company, corporation, upon two policies of insurance issued by said company to insured, Cobb, during the month of August, 1929. One of said policies was upon the life of the insured, and therefore it is only collaterally involved in the action. The other, No. 5603198, known as noncancelable income policy, is the policy which furnishes the bases of the action and it is brought to our attention by this appeal. By its terms the company obligated itself to pay indemnity on account of disability resulting from sickness or accidental means, at the rate of $250 per month for the period throughout when such disability 'consists of continuous, necessary and total loss of all business time.'

Said two policies above mentioned are in fact reissues of an original policy issued by said company to respondent, Cobb, on March 15, 1926. Said original policy was not only a life policy, but it also contained a provision known as a business, permanent total disability provision, which provided for health indemnity payment in a lump or gross sum of $15,000 in the event the insured should become totally, continuously, and irrevocably disabled as a result of sickness. The original policy of 1926 insured against two elements of risk, to wit, death and health disability. In 1929 two separate policies were issued to take the place of the 1926 policy; one being issued solely upon the life of the insured and the other-No. 5603198, which forms the basis of the judgment hereinbeing issued as a noncancelable income policy, providing for the payment of health indemnity at the rate of $250 per month "for the period throughout which disability described above [in said policy] consists of continuous, necessary and total loss of business time. . . ." The original policy was canceled upon the issuance and acceptance of the 1929 policies. The main difference between the indemnity provisions of the 1926 and 1929 policies is apparent. The carlier one provided that said policy would fully mature upon either the death of the holder or upon total and irreparable disability suffered by the insured, payable in a gross or lump sum. The policy of August, 1929, in effect at the time of breach, provided for monthly payments of $250 so long as the insured should remain physically disabled to the extent expressly stated therein. Two and one-half years after the 1929 indemnity policy was issued, the insured became wholly, permanently, and incurably disabled from the disease known as encephalitis or sleeping sickness. That the disabling effects of said disease has rendered the insured totally and permanently incapacitated within the terms of the policy and constitutes a continuous loss of "business time," and that its course is progressive and cannot be cured or arrested, is conclusively established by all of the medical testimony in the case, and this prognosis of the medical experts is not disputed by either of the parties to the action. This being true, the insured was entitled to receive a monthly payment of $250 per month, provided he had made no fraudulent misrepresentations nor withheld any material information from the company's medical examiner as to the state of his health or made any statement as to facts which were not true and which, if fully and truthfully given, would have probably caused said company to reject said applicant as not being an acceptable or desirable risk. The insured became totally disabled so as to suffer the loss of all business time on March 14, 1932. Proper notice as to disability was given to the company and demand was made for monthly indemnity at the rate of $250 per month as provided in the contract of insurance, but the company repudiated its contract by giving notice of rescission and by refusing to pay any amount thereunder, claiming fraudulent representations and the suppression of material information bearing on the state of health of the insured during a definite period of time both immediately before and on the day he was examined and interrogated by the examining physician on behalf of the company on matters affecting his health and physical condition. The company's repudiation was complete and absolute, as it was made by written notice offering to restore all the premiums it had received from the insured, with interest, which amount it afterwards deposited in court. Said repudiation was again set up by its cross-complaint, wherein it sought rescission and prayed for a cancellation of the policy on the ground that it had been fraudulently procured. Quoting from Williston on Contracts, volume 3, § 1325, citing sustaining authorities, it is said: "So denying the validity of the contract between the parties, or insisting that its meaning or legal effect are different in a material particular from the true meaning or effect, coupled with the assertion, express or implied in fact, that performance will be made only according to the erroneous interpretation," amounts to total repudiation. In the instant case the validity of the contract was vigorously assailed by the company. The contract of insurance having been repudiated, the insured filed his complaint containing three counts. The prayer of the first, as set forth in paragraph 1, asks for indemnity at the rate of $250 per month, and paragraph 2 thereof prays for judgment in the gross sum of plaintiff's life expenctancy, amounting to $54,270. The second cause of action prays for indemnity at the rate of $250 per month as in said policy provided, but does not make any claim for damages caused by a breach of the policy. It is a straight action on the contract. The third cause of action is grounded upon the policy of 1926, and judgment is asked at the rate of $250 for three months, plus the aggregate gross sum of $15,000 as provided in said 1926 policy. This policy was superseded by policy No. 5603198, issued in 1929.

Upon the trial of the case, the jury rendered a verdict in favor of the insured, and in the words of the verdict assessed "his damages in the amount of the present worth of payments of $250 per month for a life expectancy of fifteen years." According to the American mortality tables, the life expectancy of a person in reasonably good health of the age of the insured was a fraction above eighteen years. The trial court, treating the verdict of the jury as advisory, found that the policy and contract of insurance had been repudiated by the insurer without legal cause, and adopted the terms of the policy for the payment of monthly indemnity at the rate of $250 per month during the period of disability, and decreed that the contract had been breached and that the insured was entitled to be indemnified in damages for "the present worth of the sum of $250 per month for the period of plaintiff's life expectancy of fifteen years and that the present worth of said sum was $30,830." Judgment was accordingly entered in said sum, together with interest thereon a the rate of 7 per centum per annum from the 19th of May, 1932, together with plaintiff's costs of suit. . . .

An appeal was taken from said judgment by the insurer to the District Court of Appeal, Second Appellate District, Division 2 (Scott, Justice pro tem., delivering the opinion of the court), and that portion of the judgment which applied the doctrine of anticipatory breach to the case and consequently allowed the insured a judgment for a sum equal to the present value of the monthly payments for the length of time that the insured at the time of the trial would be reasonably expected to live (fifteen years) was reversed and the insured was remitted to the amount of the accrued installments. The finding that the policy had not been fraudulently or wrongfully procured was sustained. . . .

The single question presented by this appeal is whether the doctrine of anticipatory breach is applicable to a policy of insurance which provides for payment of installments of indemnity for disabilities in the manner herein set forth, even though the insurer repudiates the contract on the grounds that it would not have issued the policy had the appellant given truth ful answers to the medical examiner and full information germane to the condition of his health, and which, if so given, may have reasonably resulted in his rejection as an insurable risk.

The rule as accepted by this state is decisively stated in a number of decisions of this court, the most recent of which (February 20, 1935), is Brix v. People's Mutual Life Insurance Co., 41 P.(2d) 537, 541. In that case the insurance company by way of cross-complaint alleged that the policy upon which the action was brought was procured by the insured by means of material false representations made by the insured, and because of such it prayed for its cancellation and rescission. The court made findings against the company on the allegations of misrepresentations; thus taking notice of the issue of repudiation. The court have judgment for plaintiff at the rate of $100 per month during the remainder of his life. The judgment was modified on appeal by striking therefrom the portion which gave to plaintiff $100 per month for the remainder of his life. The decision nowhere recognizes the right of the insured to obtain judgment for future benefits either in monthly payments or for a gross sum. On this branch of the law we said:

> The books are filled with cases in which actions have been brought to recover upon insurance policies similar to the one here involved in which the insured has attempted to recover judgment not only for accrued payments, but has also sought an adjudication as to installments not yet due. While the decisions upon the right of the plaintiff in such character of actions to recover for installments which have not yet accrued are not entirely uniform, the great weight of authority is to the effect that, in such actions, recovery cannot be had for any installments falling due in the future. . . . In Atkinson v. Railroad Employees Mutual Relief Society, supra [160 Tenn. 158], 22 S.W.(2d) 631, 634, the court declared the law as follows: "While the benefit certificate issued to complainant constitutes an entire contract, the obligation thereby cast upon the society is severable, with a right of action accruing to the holder for each benefit installment payable and in default. (Citing suthorities.) So it is generally held that, in an action at law for breach of a contract of insurance, payable in weekly or periodic installments, only those installments in default at the time suit was brought may be recovered." (Citing authorities.)

Howard v. Benefit Ass'n of Railway Employees, 239 Ky. 465, 39 S.W.(2d) 657, 81 A. L. R. 375, is directly in point. It is there held that, upon repudiation by an insurer of its obligation under a health insurance policy to make stipulated monthly payments so long as the insured shall continuously suffer total disability, the insured may not treat the entire contract as breached and sue for gross damages based upon his alleged expectancy of life. The annotation (81 A. L. R. 379) contains the statement that "the decision is supported by a substantial number of authorities holding that judgment cannot be rendered in favor of the insured for instalments of indemnity not accrued at the date of the judgment." A number of the decisions of our sister state courts supporting this doctrine are listed and a brief synopsis of said cases is set forth. We are mindful that there are many decisions which hold to the contrary view. It would be an interminable and delicate task to attempt even to sketch the origin, development, and application of the doctrine of anticipatory damages for the breach of contracts, taking either the leading English case of Hochster v. De La Tour, 2 E. & B. 678, or the leading American case of Roehm v. Horst, 178 U. S. 1, 20 S. Ct. 780, 44 L. Ed. 953, as a guide. Both have been criticized by some very eminent law writers, but they are nevertheless accepted as firmly establishing the doctrine which awards damages for the wrongful deprivation of future benefits. The difficulty lies not so much in the elucidation of the doctrine as it does with a knowledge as to the time and things to which it should be applied. There can be no anticipatory breach of a unilateral contract. Williston on Contracts, vol. 3, § 1328. In volume 1, Restatement of Contracts, California Annotations, page 178, § 318, the rule is thus stated: "In unilateral contracts for payment in instalments after default of one or more no repudiation can amount to an anticipatory breach of the rest of the instalments not yet due"-citing a list of California decisions. It is also the law that a bilateral contract becomes unilateral when the promisee has fully performed. In the case at bar the promisee had fully performed. He was exempt from future performance so far as dues or assessments were concerned. The fact that he was required or requested to submit to reasonable future medical examinations or furnish an occasional health report is too trivial and inconsequential to be regarded as an unperformed obligation on the part of the insured. He was therefore within the exception stated in the rule which holds that no repudiation can amount to an anticipatory breach of the rest of the installments not yet due. There is yet another obstacle in the way of plaintiff's right to recover future benefits in a gross sum, even under the theory advanced by him. He did not rely solely upon the right of election to declare a breach of the contract, but, as above noticed, in one count of his complaint he affirmed the contract and prayed for judgment in accordance therewith. This alone would be sufficient to hold him to an action on the contract.

The principle upon which the right to declare a contract at an end without a provision to do so and to sue for a breach of contract differ so fundamentally and widely from a contract of indemnity to pay a definite fixed sum in money during health disability that doctrine of anticipatory breach would seem to be an inept and in many cases an unjust doctrine to invoke.

The action is based upon contract for the payment of money, not unlike a promissory note providing for installments or the payment of rent. The installments as they become due are but debts. Yet, if the insurer in good faith and with color of right challenges the good faith of the insured and fails to prevail in an action, he is required to pay a large gross amount, athough the insured is suffering from a permanent progressive disease and will not probably live the period of expectancy that a person in normal health would live.

To apply to this case the principle contended for by the insured would, in effect, penalize the company for asserting its defense if it did not prevail in a controversial matter even if made in good faith and with color of reason, notwithstanding the fact that the insured expressly agreed that "the falsity of any statement in the application materially affecting either the acceptance of the risk or the hazard assumed . . . or made with the intent to deceive, shall bar all right to recovery under this contract." It is admitted that there is some authority for the application of this rule in cases so clearly within the doctrine of anticipatory breach that there is no room for question, but at best it is a drastic rule and should not be applied to a contract in which the parties impliedly recognize the right of contest.

The insured urges the application of the doctrine on the theory that, if the company becomes unfriendly or hostile to the insured, it may compel him to bring an action on every installment falling due, possibly for the purpose of harassing the insured, thereby causing a multiplicity of actions. It would seem that a reasonably sound business policy would of itself be a sufficient consideration to deter an insurer against practices which could not do otherwise than bring discredit to it. Besides, the law ought to be able to offer relief where compensation is willfully and contumaciously withheld. In the instant case, however, the situation cannot occur. It is admitted that the insured is totally and incurably ill with a progressive and totally incapacitative disease. The decision as to the validity of the contract has become final, and there is nothing left to be done but the payment of the indemnity as expressly provided by the parties thereto.

The tendency of this court has consistently been opposed to the application of the doctrine of anticipatory damages to cases involving fixed installment money payments which arise in the manner set forth in the contract herein. There is ample authority in other jurisdictions which sustains our conclusion, and it is true that there are also a number of decisions holding the contrary view.

The cause is remanded to the trial court, with leave to respondent, Cobb, to file a supplemental complaint including all payments due, and interest thereon, at the time of filing the complaint herein. That portion of the judgment which allows respondent damages for breach of said contract for the present worth of the sum of $250 per month for plaintiff's life expectancy of fifteen years, estimated to be the gross sum of $30,830, is reversed. In all other respects the judgment is affirmed. Let proceedings be had consistent with the views expressed and conclusions reached by this decision.

We concur: WASTE, C. J.; SHENK, J.; CURTIS, J.; THOMPSON, J.

NOTES & QUESTIONS:

1. For a discussion of the pitfalls of the exception for unilateral contracts, see the dissent in the similarly decided case of *Greguhn v. Mutual of Omaha Ins. Co.*, 461 P.2d 285 (Utah 1969).

2. *See Pollack v. Pollack*, 46 S.W.2d 282 (Tex. Com. App. 1932) for a rejection of this exception for unilateral contracts.

C. SUBSTANTIAL PERFORMANCE AND MATERIAL BREACH

You may recall the "Reading pipe" case from our earlier studying of damages. In that case, a contractor sued the home owner for payment due on a construction contract. Even though the house was not constructed in strict compliance with the written specifications that all wrought iron pipe be Reading manufacture, the court determined that the contractor nevertheless was entitled to recover the balance due on the construction contract. We now return to the Reading Pipe case in the context of performance and breach to further explore the basis upon which the contractor was entitled to payment.

JACOB & YOUNGS V. KENT
Court of Appeals of New York
129 N.E. 889 (1921).

CARDOZO, Justice.

The plaintiff built a country residence for the defendant at a cost of upwards of $77,000, and now sues to recover a balance of $3,483.46, remaining unpaid. The work of construction ceased in June, 1914, and the defendant then began to occupy the dwelling. There was no complaint of defective performance until March, 1915. One of the specifications for the plumbing work provides that--

> All wrought-iron pipe must be well galvanized, lap welded pipe of the grade known as "standard pipe" of Reading manufacture.

The defendant learned in March, 1915, that some of the pipe, instead of being made in Reading, was the product of other factories. The plaintiff was accordingly directed by the architect to do the work anew. The plumbing was then encased within the walls except in a few places where it had to be exposed. Obedience to the order meant more than the substitution of other pipe. It meant the demolition at great expense of substantial parts of the completed structure. The plaintiff left the work untouched, and asked for a certificate that the final payment was due. Refusal of the certificate was followed by this suit.

The evidence sustains a finding that the omission of the prescribed brand of pipe was neither fraudulent nor willful. It was the result of the oversight and inattention of the plaintiff's subcontractor. Reading pipe is distinguished from Cohoes pipe and other brands only by the name of the manufacturer stamped upon it at intervals of between six and seven feet. Even the defendant's architect, though he inspected the pipe upon arrival, failed to notice the discrepancy. The plaintiff tried to show that the brands installed, though made by other manufacturers, were the same in quality, in appearance, in market value, and in cost as the brand stated in the contract-that they were, indeed, the same thing, though manufactured in another place. The evidence was excluded, and a verdict directed for the defendant. The Appellate Division reversed, and granted a new trial.

We think the evidence, if admitted, would have supplied some basis for the inference that the defect was insignificant in its relation to the project. The courts never say that one who makes a contract fills the measure of his duty by less than full performance. They do say, however, that an omission, both trivial and innocent, will sometimes be atoned for by allowance of the resulting damage, and will not always be the breach of a condition to be followed by a forfeiture . . . . The distinction is akin to that between dependent and independent promises, or between promises and conditions. . . . Some promises are so plainly independent that they can never by fair construction be conditions of one another. . . . Others are so plainly dependent that they must always be conditions. Others, though dependent and thus conditions when there is departure in point of substance, will be viewed as independent and collateral when the departure is insignificant. . . . Considerations partly of justice and partly of presumable intention are to tell us whether this or that promise shall be placed in one class or in another. The simple and the uniform will call for different remedies from the multifarious and the intricate. The margin of departure within the range of normal expectation upon a sale of common chattels will vary from the margin to be expected upon a contract for the construction of a mansion or a "skyscraper." There will be harshness sometimes and oppression in the implication of a condition when the thing upon which labor has been expended is incapable of surrender because united to the land, and equity and reason in the implication of a like condition when the subject-matter, if defective, is in shape to be returned. From the conclusion that promises may not be treated as dependent to the extent of their uttermost minutiae without a sacrifice of justice, the progress is a short one to the conclusion that they may not be so treated without a perversion of intention. Intention not otherwise revealed may be presumed to hold in contemplation the reasonable and probable. If something else is in view, it must not be left to implication. There will be no assumption of a purpose to visit venial faults with oppressive retribution.

Those who think more of symmetry and logic in the development of legal rules than of practical adaptation to the attainment of a just result will be troubled by a classification where the lines of division are so wavering and blurred. Something, doubtless, may be said on the score of consistency and certainty in favor of a stricter standard. The courts have balanced such considerations against those of equity and fairness, and found the latter to be the weightier. The decisions in this state commit us to the liberal view, which is making its way, nowadays, in jurisdictions slow to welcome it. . . . Where the line is to be drawn between the important and the trivial cannot be settled by a formula. "In the nature of the case precise boundaries are impossible." 2 Williston on Contracts, § 841. The same omission may take on one aspect or another according to its setting. Substitution of equivalents may not have the same significance in fields of art on the one side and in those of mere utility on the other. Nowhere will change be tolerated, however, if it is so dominant or pervasive as in any real or substantial measure to frustrate the purpose of the contract. . . . There is no general license to install whatever, in the builder's judgment, may be regarded as "just as good." . . . The question is one of degree, to be answered, if there is doubt, by the triers of the facts . . . , and, if the inferences are certain, by the judges of the law . . . . We must weigh the purpose to be served, the desire to be gratified, the excuse for deviation from the letter, the cruelty of enforced adherence. Then only can we tell whether literal fulfillment is to be implied by law as a condition. This is not to say that the parties are not free by apt and certain words to effectuate a purpose that performance of every term shall be a condition of recovery. That question is not here. This is merely to say that the law will be slow to impute the purpose, in the silence of the parties, where the significance of the default is grievously out of proportion to the oppression of the forfeiture. The willful transgressor must accept the penalty of his transgression. . . . For him there is no occasion to mitigate the rigor of implied conditions. The transgressor whose default is unintentional and trivial may hope for mercy if he will offer atonement for his wrong. . . .

In the circumstances of this case, we think the measure of the allowance is not the cost of replacement, which would be great, but the difference in value, which would be either nominal or nothing. Some of the exposed sections might perhaps have been replaced at moderate expense. The defendant did not limit his demand to them, but treated the plumbing as a unit to be corrected from cellar to roof. In point of fact, the plaintiff never reached the stage at which evidence of the extent of the allowance became necessary. The trial court had excluded evidence that the defect was unsubstantial, and in view of that ruling there was no occasion for the plaintiff to go farther with an offer of proof. We think, however, that the offer, if it had been made, would not of necessity have been defective because directed to difference in value. It is true that in most cases the cost of replacement is the measure. The owner is entitled to the money which will permit him to complete, unless the cost of completion is grossly and unfairly out of proportion to the good to be attained. When that is true, the measure is the difference in value. Specifications call, let us say, for a foundation built of granite quarried in Vermont. On the completion of the building, the owner learns that through the blunder of a subcontractor part of the foundation has been built of granite of the same quality quarried in New Hampshire. The measure of allowance is not the cost of reconstruction. "There may be omissions of that which could not afterwards be supplied exactly as called for by the contract without taking down the building to its foundations, and at the same time the omission may not affect the value of the building for use or otherwise, except so slightly as to be hardly appreciable." Handy v. Bliss, 204 Mass. 513, 519, 90 N. E. 864, 134. . . The rule that gives a remedy in cases of substantial performance with compensation for defects of trivial or inappreciable importance has been developed by the courts as an instrument of justice. The measure of the allowance must be shaped to the same end.

The order should be affirmed, and judgment absolute directed in favor of the plaintiff upon the stipulation, with costs in all courts.

McLAUGHLIN, J.

I dissent. The plaintiff did not perform its contract. Its failure to do so was either intentional or due to gross neglect which, under the uncontradicted facts, amounted to the same thing, nor did it make any proof of the cost of compliance, where compliance was possible.

Under its contract it obligated itself to use in the plumbing only pipe (between 2,000 and 2,500 feet) made by the Reading Manufacturing Company. The first pipe delivered was about 1,000 feet and the plaintiff's superintendent then called the attention of the foreman of the subcontractor, who was doing the plumbing, to the fact that the specifications annexed to the contract required all pipe used in the plumbing to be of the Reading Manufacturing Company. They then examined it for the purpose of ascertaining whether this delivery was of that manufacture and found it was. Thereafter, as pipe was required in the progress of the work, the foreman of the subcontractor would leave word at its shop that he wanted a specified number of feet of pipe, without in any way indicating of what manufacture. Pipe would thereafter be delivered and installed in the building, without any examination whatever. Indeed, no examination, so far as appears, was made by the plaintiff, the subcontractor, defendant's architect, or any one else, of any of the pipe except the first delivery, until after the building had been completed. Plaintiff's architect then refused to give the certificate of completion, upon which the final payment depended, because all of the pipe used in the plumbing was not of the kind called for by the contract. After such refusal, the subcontractor removed the covering or insulation from about 900 feet of pipe which was exposed in the basement, cellar, and attic, and all but 70 feet was found to have been manufactured, not by the Reading Company, but by other manufacturers, some by the

Cohoes Rolling Mill Company, some by the National Steel Works, some by the South Chester Tubing Company, and some which bore no manufacturer's mark at all. The balance of the pipe had been so installed in the building that an inspection of it could not be had without demolishing, in part at least, the building itself.

I am of the opinion the trial court was right in directing a verdict for the defendant. The plaintiff agreed that all the pipe used should be of the Reading Manufacturing Company. Only about two-fifths of it, so far as appears, was of that kind. If more were used, then the burden of proving that fact was upon the plaintiff, which it could easily have done, since it knew where the pipe was obtained. The question of substantial performance of a contract of the character of the one under consideration depends in no small degree upon the good faith of the contractor. If the plaintiff had intended to, and had, complied with the terms of the contract except as to minor omissions, due to inadvertence, then he might be allowed to recover the contract price, less the amount necessary to fully compensate the defendant for damages caused by such omissions . . . But that is not this case. It installed between 2,000 and 2,500 feet of pipe, of which only 1,000 feet at most complied with the contract. No explanation was given why pipe called for by the contract was not used, nor that any effort made to show what it would cost to remove the pipe of other manufacturers and install that of the Reading Manufacturing Company. The defendant had a right to contract for what he wanted. He had a right before making payment to get what the contract called for. It is no answer to this suggestion to say that the pipe put in was just as good as that made by the Reading Manufacturing Company, or that the difference in value between such pipe and the pipe made by the Reading Manufacturing Company would be either "nominal or nothing." Defendant contracted for pipe made by the Reading Manufacturing Company. What his reason was for requiring this kind of pipe is of no importance. He wanted that and was entitled to it. It may have been a mere whim on his part, but even so, he had a right to this kind of pipe, regardless of whether some other kind, according to the opinion of the contractor or experts, would have been "just as good, better, or done just as well." He agreed to pay only upon condition that the pipe installed were made by that company and he ought not to be compelled to pay unless that condition be performed. . . . The rule, therefore, of substantial performance, with damages for unsubstantial omissions, has no application. . . .

What was said by this court in Smith v. Brady, supra, is quite applicable here:

> I suppose it will be conceded that every one has a right to build his house, his cottage or his store after such a model and in such style as shall best accord with his notions of utility or be most agreeable to his fancy. The specifications of the contract become the law between the parties until voluntarily changed. If the owner prefers a plain and simple Doric column, and has so provided in the agreement, the contractor has no right to put in its place the more costly and elegant Corinthian. If the owner, having regard to strenght and durability, has contracted for walls of specified materials to be laid in a particular manner, or for a given number of joists and beams, the builder has no right to substitute his own judgment or that of others. Having departed from the agreement, if performance has not been waived by the other party, the law will not allow him to allege that he has made as good a building as the one he engaged to erect. He can demand payment only upon and according to the terms of his contract, and if the conditions on which

> payment is due have not been performed, then the right to demand it does not exist. To hold a different doctrine would be simply to make another contract, and would be giving to parties an encouragement to violate their engagements, which the just policy of the law does not permit. (17 N. Y. 186, 72 Am. Dec. 422).

I am of the opinion the trial court did not err in ruling on the admission of evidence or in directing a verdict for the defendant.

For the foregoing reasons I think the judgment of the Appellate Division should be reversed and the judgment of the Trial Term affirmed.

HISCOCK, C. J., and HOGAN and CRANE, JJ., concur with CARDOZO, J.
POUND and ANDREWS, JJ., concur with McLAUGHLIN, J.

Order affirmed, etc.

NOTES & QUESTIONS:

1. *Jacob & Youngs v. Kent,* 129 N.E. 889 (1921), illustrates that substantial performance is aptly regarded as the counterpart to economic waste. If the deficient performance is deemed trivial and innocent, the measure of damages for such breach will be limited to the diminution in value resulting from the deficient performance. More importantly, the substantial performance doctrine satisfies the constructive condition of performance by the contractor, thereby triggering the homeowner's duty to pay and avoiding a forfeiture of the contract price by the breaching contractor. For a further explanation of how the doctrines of substantial performance and economic waste relate, see Daniel & Marshall, *Avoiding Economic Waste in Contract Damages: Myths, Misunderstanding, and Malcontent*, 85 Neb. L. Rev. 875, 881.

2. What, if any, significance is found in the court's acknowledgement that the parties are free to make performance of every contract term a condition of recovery "by apt and certain words"? *See Oppenheimer v. Oppenheim, Appel, Dixon & Co.*, 660 N.E.2d 415, 418-419 (N.Y. 1995).

GROVES V. JOHN WUNDER CO.
Supreme Court of Minnesota
286 N.W. 235 (1939).

STONE, Justice.

Action for breach of contract. Plaintiff got judgment for a little over $15,000. Sorely disappointed by that sum, he appeals.

In August, 1927, S. J. Groves & Sons Company, a corporation (hereinafter mentioned simply as Groves), owned a tract of 24 acres of Minneapolis suburban real estate. It was served or easily could be reached by railroad trackage. It is zoned as heavy industrial property. But for lack of development of the neighborhood its principal value thus far may have been in the deposit of sand and gravel which it carried. The Groves company had a plant on the premises for excavating and screening the gravel. Nearby defendant owned and was operating a similar plant.

In August, 1927, Groves and defendant made the involved contract. For the most part it was a lease from Groves, as lessor, to defendant, as lessee; its term seven years. Defendant agreed to remove the sand and gravel and to leave the property "at a uniform grade, substantially the same as the grade now existing at the roadway . . . on said premises, and that in stripping the overburden . . . it will use said overburden for the purpose of maintaining and establishing said grade."

Under the contract defendant got the Groves screening plant. The transfer thereof and the right to remove the sand and gravel made the consideration moving from Groves to defendant, except that defendant incidentally got rid of Groves as a competitor. On defendant's part it paid Groves $105,000. So that from the outset, on Groves' part the contract was executed except for defendant's right to continue using the property for the stated term. (Defendant had a right to renewal which it did not exercise.)

Defendant breached the contract deliberately. It removed from the premises only "the richest and best of the gravel" and wholly failed, according to the findings, "to perform and comply with the terms, conditions, and provisions of said lease . . . with respect to the condition in which the surface of the demised premises was required to be left." Defendant surrendered the premises, not substantially at the grade required by the contract "nor at any uniform grade." Instead, the ground was "broken, rugged, and uneven." Plaintiff sues as assignee and successor in right of Groves.

As the contract was construed below, the finding is that to complete its performance 288,495 cubic yards of overburden would need to be excavated, taken from the premises, and deposited elsewhere. The reasonable cost of doing that was found to be upwards of $60,000. But, if defendant had left the premises at the uniform grade required by the lease, the reasonable value of the property on the determinative date would have been only $12,160. The judgment was for that sum, including interest, thereby nullifying plaintiff's claim that cost of completing the contract rather than difference in value of the land was the measure of damages. The gauge of damage adopted by the decision was the difference between the market value of plaintiff's land in the condition it was when the contract was made and what it would have been if defendant had performed. The one question for us arises upon plaintiff's assertion that he was entitled, not to that difference in value, but to the reasonable cost to him of doing the work called for by the contract which defendant left undone.

Defendant's breach of contract was wilful. There was nothing of good faith about it. Hence, that the decision below handsomely rewards bad faith and deliberate breach of contract is obvious. That is not allowable. Here the rule is well settled, and has been since Elliott v. Caldwell, 43 Minn. 357, 45 N.W. 845, 9 L.R.A. 52, that, where the contractor wilfully and fraudulently varies from the terms of a construction contract, he cannot sue thereon and have the benefit of the equitable doctrine of substantial performance. That is the rule generally. See Annotation, "Wilful or intentional variation by contractor from terms of contract in regard to material or work as affecting measure of damages," 6 A.L.R. 137.

Jacob & Youngs, Inc. v. Kent, 230 N.Y. 239, 243, 244, 129 N.E. 889, 891, 23 A.L.R. 1429, is typical. It was a case of substantial performance of a building contract. (This case is distinctly the opposite.) Mr. Justice Cardozo, in the course of his opinion, stressed the distinguishing features. "Nowhere," he said, "will change be tolerated, however, if it is so dominant or pervasive as in any real or substantial measure to frustrate the purpose of the contract." Again, "the willful transgressor must accept the penalty of his transgression." . . .

The judgment must be reversed with a new trial to follow.

So ordered. . . .

O.W. GRUN ROOFING & CONSTRUCTION CO. V. COPE
Court of Civil Appeals of Texas
529 S.W.2d 258 (1975).

CADENA, Justice.

Plaintiff, Mrs. Fred M. Cope, sued defendant, O. W. Grun Roofing & Construction Co., to set aside a mechanic's lien filed by defendant and for damages in the sum of $1,500.00 suffered by plaintiff as a result of the alleged failure of defendant to perform a contract calling for the installation of a new roof on plaintiff's home. Defendant, in addition to a general denial, filed a cross-claim for $648.00, the amount which plaintiff agreed to pay defendant for installing the roof, and for foreclosure of the mechanic's lien on plaintiff's home.

Following trial to a jury, the court below entered judgment awarding plaintiff $122.60 as damages for defendant's failure to perform the contract; setting aside the mechanic's lien; and denying defendant recovery on its cross-claim. It is from this judgment that defendant appeals.

The jury found (1) defendant failed to perform his contract in a good and workmanlike manner; (2) defendant did not substantially perform the contract; (3) plaintiff received no benefits from the labor performed and the materials furnished by defendant; the reasonable cost of performing the contract in a good and workmanlike manner would be $777.60. Although the verdict shows the cost of proper performance to be $777.60, the judgment describes this finding as being in the amount of $770.60, and the award of $122.60 to plaintiff is based on the difference between $770.60 and the contract price of $648.00. . . .

The only questions . . . which we can consider under defendant's first point are that there is no evidence to support the finding that defendant did not perform in a good and workmanlike manner and that the evidence establishes as a matter of law that defendant substantially performed the contract. In considering these "no evidence" points, we look only to the evidence supporting the verdict. . . .

The written contract required defendant to install a new roof on plaintiff's home for $648.00. The contract describes the color of the shingles to be used as "russet glow," which defendant defined as a "brown varied color." Defendant acknowledges that it was his obligation to install a roof of uniform color.

After defendant had installed the new roof, plaintiff noticed that it had streaks which she described as yellow, due to a difference in color or shade of some of the shingles. Defendant agreed to remedy the situation and he removed the nonconforming shingles. However, the replacement shingles do not match the remainder, and photographs introduced in evidence clearly show that the roof is not of a uniform color. Plaintiff testified that her roof has the appearance of having been patched, rather than having been completely replaced. According to plaintiff's testimony, the yellow streaks appeared on the northern, eastern and southern sides of the roof, and defendant only replaced the non-matching shingles on the northern and eastern sides, leaving the southern side with the yellow streaks still apparent. The result is that only the western portion of the roof is of uniform color.

When defendant originally installed the complete new roof, it used 24 "squares" of shingles. In an effort to achieve a roof of uniform color, five squares were ripped off and replaced. There is no testimony as to the number of squares which would have to be replaced on the southern, or rear, side of the house in order to eliminate the original yellow streaks. Although there is expert testimony to the effect that the disparity in color would not be noticeable after the shingles have been on the roof for about a year, there is testimony to the effect that, although some nine or ten months have elapsed since defendant attempted to achieve a uniform coloration, the roof is still "streaky" on three sides. One of defendant's experts testified that if the shingles are properly applied the result will be a "blended" roof rather than a streaked roof.

In view of the fact that the disparity in color has not disappeared in nine or ten months, and in view of the fact that there is testimony to the effect that it would be impossible to secure matching shingles to replace the nonconforming ones, it can reasonably by inferred that a roof or uniform coloration can be achieved only by installing a completely new roof.

The evidence is undisputed that the roof is a substantial roof and will give plaintiff protection against the elements.

The principle which allows recovery for part performance in cases involving dependent promises may be expressed by saying that a material breach or a breach which goes to the root of the matter or essence of the contract defeats the promisor's claim despite his part performance, or it may be expressed by saying that a promisor who has substantially performed is entitled to recover, although he has failed in some particular to comply with his agreement. The latter mode of expressing the rule is generally referred to as the doctrine of substantial performance and is especially common in cases involving building contracts, although its application is not restricted to such contracts.

It is difficult to formulate definitive rule for determining whether the contractor's performance, less than complete, amounts to "substantial performance," since the question is one of fact and of degree, and the answer depends on the particular facts of each case. But, although the decisions furnish no rule of thumb, they are helpful in suggesting guidelines. One of the most obvious factors to be considered is the extent of the nonperformance. The deficiency will not be tolerated if it is so pervasive as to frustrate the purpose of the contract in any real or substantial sense. The doctrine does not bestow on a contractor a license to install whatever is, in his judgment, "just as good." The answer is arrived at by weighing the purpose to be served, the desire to be gratified, the excuse for deviating from the letter of the contract and the cruelty of enforcing strict adherence or of compelling the promisee to receive something less than for which he bargained. Also influential in many cases is the ratio of money value of the tendered performance and of the promised performance. In most cases the contract itself at least is an indication of the value of the promised performance, and courts should have little difficulty in determining the cost of curing the deficiency. But the rule cannot be expressed in terms of a fraction, since complete reliance on a mathematical formula would result in ignoring other important factors, such as the purpose which the promised performance was intended to serve and the extent to which the nonperformance would defeat such purpose, or would defeat it if not corrected. See, generally, 3A Corbin, Contracts §§ 700-07 (1960).

Although definitions of "substantial performance" are not always couched in the same terminology and, because of the facts involved in a particular case, sometimes vary in the recital of the factors to be considered, the following definition by the Commission of Appeals in Atkinson v. Jackson Bros., 270 S.W. 848, 851 (Tex.Comm.App.1925), is a typical recital of the constituent elements of the doctrine:

> To constitute substantial compliance the contractor must have in good faith intended to comply with the contract, and shall have substantially done so in the sense that the defects are not pervasive, do not constitute a deviation from the general plan contemplated for the work, and are not so essential that the object of the parties in making the contract and its purpose cannot, without difficulty, be accomplished by remedying them. Such performance permits only such omissions or deviations from the contract as are inadvertent and unintentional, are not due to bad faith, do not impair the structure as a whole, and are remediable without doing material damage to other parts of the building in tearing down and reconstructing. (Citation Omitted).

What was the general plan contemplated for the work in this case? What was the object and purpose of the parties? It is clear that, despite the frequency with which the courts speak of defects that are not "pervasive," which do not constitute a "deviation from the general plan," and which are "not so essential that the object of the parties in making the contract and its purpose cannot, without difficulty, be accomplished by remedying them," when an attempt is made to apply the general principles to a particular case difficulties are encountered at the outset. Was the general plan to install a substantial roof which would serve the purpose which roofs are designed to serve? Or, rather, was the general plan to install a substantial roof of uniform color? Was the object and purpose of the contract merely to furnish such a roof, or was it to furnish such a roof which would be of a uniform color? It should not come as a shock to anyone to adopt a rule to the effect that a person has, particularly with respect to his home, to choose for himself and to contract for something which exactly satisfies that choice, and not to be compelled to accept something else. In the matter of homes and their decoration, as much as, if not more than, in many other fields, mere taste or preference, almost approaching whimsy, may be controlling with the homeowner, so that variations which might, under other circumstances, be considered trifling, may be inconsistent with that "substantial performance" on which liability to pay must be predicated. Of mere incompleteness or deviations which may be easily supplied or remedied after the contractor has finished his work, and the cost of which to the owner is not excessive and readily ascertainable, present less cause for hesitation in concluding that the performance tendered constitutes substantial performance, since in such cases the owner can obtain complete satisfaction by merely spending some money and deducting the amount of such expenditure from the contract price.

In the case before us there is evidence to support the conclusion that plaintiff can secure a roof of uniform coloring only by installing a completely new roof. We cannot say, as a matter of law, that the evidence establishes that in this case that a roof which so lacks uniformity in color as to give the appearance of a patch job serves essentially the same purpose as a roof of uniform color which has the appearance of being a new roof. We are not prepared to hold that a contractor who tenders a performance so deficient that it can be remedied only by completely redoing and work for which the contract called has established, as a matter of law, that he has substantially performed his contractual obligation. . . .

Finally, defendant argues that it was entitled to judgment at least on the theory of quantum meruit on its cross claim because the evidence establishes as a matter of law that defendant installed a good weatherproof roof which was guaranteed for 15 years, and that such roof was installed properly in accordance with factory specifications and was of use and benefit to plaintiff.

The evidence does not conclusively establish that the shingles were properly installed. There is evidence to the effect that if shingles of this type are properly installed the result will be a roof which "blends," rather than a roof with clearly discordant streaks. In any event, the evidence does not conclusively establish that plaintiff has received any benefit from defendant's defective performance. As already pointed out, there is evidence that plaintiff will have to install a completely new roof. Because of defendant's deficient performance, plaintiff is not in a position which requires that she pay for a new roof.

π not need to pay for new roof

Nor does the evidence conclusively establish that plaintiff accepted the claimed benefit. She complained immediately and has expressed dissatisfaction at all times. We cannot infer an acceptance from the fact that plaintiff continued to live in the house. She was living in the house before defendant installed the new roof, and we know of no rule which would require that, in order to avoid a finding of implied acceptance, plaintiff was obligated to move out of her home.

The judgment of the trial court is affirmed.

NOTES AND QUESTIONS:

1. Read Restatement (Second) of Contracts § 241 (1981) and note the factors commonly considered in determining whether a breach will be deemed material. For a discussion of such factors, see *Milner Hotels, Inc. v. Norfolk & Western Ry. Co.*, 822 F. Supp. 341 (S.D.W.V. 1993).

2. A determination that a breach is material is another way of stating that the deficient performance did not meet the standard of substantial performance.

RAMIREZ V. AUTOSPORT
Supreme Court of New Jersey
440 A.2d 1345 (1982).

POLLOCK, Justice.

This case raises several issues under the Uniform Commercial Code ("the Code" and "UCC") concerning whether a buyer may reject a tender of goods with minor defects and whether a seller may cure the defects. We consider also the remedies available to the buyer, including cancellation of the contract. The main issue is whether plaintiffs, Mr. and Mrs. Ramirez, could reject the tender by defendant, Autosport, of a camper van with minor defects and cancel the contract for the purchase of the van.

The trial court ruled that Mr. and Mrs. Ramirez rightfully rejected the van and awarded them the fair market value of their trade-in van. The Appellate Division affirmed in a brief per curiam decision which, like the trial court opinion, was unreported. We affirm the judgment of the Appellate Division.

I

Following a mobile home show at the Meadowlands Sports Complex, Mr. and Mrs. Ramirez visited Autosport's showroom in Somerville. On July 20, 1978 the Ramirezes and Donald Graff, a salesman for Autosport, agreed on the sale of a new camper and the trade-in of the van owned by Mr. and Mrs. Ramirez. Autosport and the Ramirezes signed a simple contract reflecting a $14,100 purchase price for the new van with a $4,700 trade-in allowance for the Ramirez van, which Mr. and Mrs. Ramirez left with Autosport. After further allowance for taxes, title and documentary fees, the net price was $9,902. Because Autosport needed two weeks to prepare the new van, the contract provided for delivery on or about August 3, 1978.

On that date, Mr. and Mrs. Ramirez returned with their checks to Autosport to pick up the new van. Graff was not there so Mr. White, another salesman, met them. Inspection disclosed several defects in the van. The paint was scratched, both the electric and sewer hookups were missing, and the hubcaps were not installed. White advised the Ramirezes not to accept the camper because it was not ready.

Mr. and Mrs. Ramirez wanted the van for a summer vacation and called Graff several times. Each time Graff told them it was not ready for delivery. Finally, Graff called to notify them that the camper was ready. On August 14 Mr. and Mrs. Ramirez went to Autosport to accept delivery, but workers were still touching up the outside paint. Also, the camper windows were open, and the dining area cushions were soaking wet. Mr. and Mrs. Ramirez could not use the camper in that condition, but Mr. Leis, Autosport's manager, suggested that they take the van and that Autosport would replace the cushions later. Mrs. Ramirez counteroffered to accept the van if they could withhold $2,000, but Leis agreed to no more than $250, which she refused. Leis then agreed to replace the cushions and to call them when the van was ready.

On August 15, 1978 Autosport transferred title to the van to Mr. and Mrs. Ramirez, a fact unknown to them until the summer of 1979. Between August 15 and September 1, 1978 Mrs. Ramirez called Graff several times urging him to complete the preparation of the van, but Graff constantly advised her that the van was not ready. He finally informed her that they could pick it up on September 1.

When Mr. and Mrs. Ramirez went to the showroom on September 1, Graff asked them to wait. And wait they did-for one and a half hours. No one from Autosport came forward to talk with them, and the Ramirezes left in disgust.

On October 5, 1978 Mr. and Mrs. Ramirez went to Autosport with an attorney friend. Although the parties disagreed on what occurred, the general topic was whether they should proceed with the deal or Autosport should return to the Ramirezes their trade-in van. Mrs. Ramirez claimed they rejected the new van and requested the return of their trade-in. Mr. Lustig, the owner of Autosport, thought, however, that the deal could be salvaged if the parties could agree on the dollar amount of a credit for the Ramirezes. Mr. and Mrs. Ramirez never took possession of the new van and repeated their request for the return of their trade-in. Later in October, however, Autosport sold the trade-in to an innocent third party for $4,995. Autosport claimed that the Ramirez' van had a book value of $3,200 and claimed further that it spent $1,159.62 to repair their van. By subtracting the total of those two figures, $4,159.62, from the $4,995.00 sale price, Autosport claimed a $600-700 profit on the sale.

On November 20, 1978 the Ramirezes sued Autosport seeking, among other things, rescission of the contract. Autosport counterclaimed for breach of contract.

II

Our initial inquiry is whether a consumer may reject defective goods that do not conform to the contract of sale. The basic issue is whether under the UCC, adopted in New Jersey as N.J.S.A. 12A:1-101 et seq., a seller has the duty to deliver goods that conform precisely to the contract. We conclude that the seller is under such a duty to make a "perfect tender" and that a buyer has the right to reject goods that do not conform to the contract. That conclusion, however, does not resolve the entire dispute between buyer and seller. A more complete answer requires a brief statement of the history of the mutual obligations of buyers and sellers of commercial goods.

In the nineteenth century, sellers were required to deliver goods that complied exactly with the sales agreement. See Filley v. Pope, 115 U.S. 213, 220, 6 S.Ct. 19, 21, 29 L.Ed. 372, 373 (1885) (buyer not obliged to accept otherwise conforming scrap iron shipped to New Orleans from Leith, rather than Glasgow, Scotland, as required by contract); Columbian Iron Works & Dry-Dock Co. v. Douglas, 84 Md. 44, 47, 34 A. 1118, 1120-1121 (1896) (buyer who agreed to purchase steel scrap from United States cruisers not obliged to take any other kind of scrap). That rule, known as the "perfect tender" rule, remained part of the law of sales well into the twentieth century. By the 1920's the doctrine was so entrenched in the law that Judge Learned Hand declared "(t)here is no room in commercial contracts for the doctrine of substantial performance." Mitsubishi Goshi Kaisha v. J. Aron & Co., Inc., 16 F.2d 185, 186 (2 Cir. 1926).

The harshness of the rule led courts to seek to ameliorate its effect and to bring the law of sales in closer harmony with the law of contracts, which allows rescission only for material breaches. . . . The chief objection to the continuation of the perfect tender rule was that buyers in a declining market would reject goods for minor nonconformities and force the loss on surprised sellers. . . .

To the extent that a buyer can reject goods for any nonconformity, the UCC retains the perfect tender rule. Section 2-106 states that goods conform to a contract "when they are in accordance with the obligations under the contract." N.J.S.A. 12A:2-106. Section 2-601 authorizes a buyer to reject goods if they "or the tender of delivery fail in any respect to conform to the contract." N.J.S.A. 12A:2-601. The Code, however, mitigates the harshness of the perfect tender rule and balances the interests of buyer and seller. . . . The Code achieves that result through its provisions for revocation of acceptance and cure. N.J.S.A. 12A:2-608, 2-508.

Initially, the rights of the parties vary depending on whether the rejection occurs before or after acceptance of the goods. Before acceptance, the buyer may reject goods for any nonconformity. N.J.S.A. 12A:2-601. Because of the seller's right to cure, however, the buyer's rejection does not necessarily discharge the contract. N.J.S.A. 12A:2-508. Within the time set for performance in the contract, the seller's right to cure is unconditional. . . . Underlying the right to cure in both kinds of contracts is the recognition that parties should be encouraged to communicate with each other and to resolve their own problems. . . .

The rights of the parties also vary if rejection occurs after the time set for performance. After expiration of that time, the seller has a further reasonable time to cure if he believed reasonably that the goods would be acceptable with or without a money allowance. N.J.S.A. 12A:2-508(2). The determination of what constitutes a further reasonable time depends on the surrounding circumstances, which include the change of position by and the amount of inconvenience to the buyer. N.J.S.A. 12A:2-508, Official Comment 3. Those circumstances also include the length of time needed by the seller to correct the nonconformity and his ability to salvage the goods by resale to others. . . . Thus, the Code balances the buyer's right to reject nonconforming goods with a "second chance" for the seller to conform the goods to the contract under certain limited circumstances. N.J.S.A. 12A:2-508, New Jersey Study Comment 1.

After acceptance, the Code strikes a different balance: the buyer may revoke acceptance only if the nonconformity substantially impairs the value of the goods to him. N.J.S.A. 12A:2-608. . . . This provision protects the seller from revocation for trivial defects. . . . It also prevents the buyer from taking undue advantage of the seller by allowing goods to depreciate and then returning them because of asserted minor defects. . . . Because this case involves rejection of goods, we need not decide whether a seller has a right to cure substantial defects that justify revocation of acceptance. See Pavesi v. Ford Motor Co., 155 N.J.Super. 373, 378, 382 A.2d 954 (App.Div.1978) (right to cure after acceptance limited to trivial defects) and White & Summers, supra, § 8-4 at 319 n.76 (open question as to the relationship between § 2-608 and 2-508).

. . . . [W]e conclude that the perfect tender rule is preserved to the extent of permitting a buyer to reject goods for any defects. . . .

Although the complaint requested rescission of the contract, plaintiffs actually sought not only the end of their contractual obligations, but also restoration to their pre-contractual position. That request incorporated the equitable doctrine of restitution, the purpose of which is to restore plaintiff to as good a position as he occupied before the contract. Corbin, supra, § 1102 at 455. In UCC parlance, plaintiffs' request was for the cancellation of the contract and recovery of the price paid. N.J.S.A. 12A:2-106(4), 2-711.

General contract law permits rescission only for material breaches, and the Code restates "materiality" in terms of "substantial impairment." See Herbstman v. Eastman Kodak Co., supra, 68 N.J. at 9, 342 A.2d 181; id. at 15, 342 A.2d 181 (Conford, J., concurring). The Code permits a buyer who rightfully rejects goods to cancel a contract of sale. N.J.S.A. 12A:2-711. Because a buyer may reject goods with insubstantial defects, he also may cancel the contract if those defects remain uncured. Otherwise, a seller's failure to cure minor defects would compel a buyer to accept imperfect goods and collect for any loss caused by the nonconformity. N.J.S.A. 12A:2-714.

Although the Code permits cancellation by rejection for minor defects, it permits revocation of acceptance only for substantial impairments. That distinction is consistent with other Code provisions that depend on whether the buyer has accepted the goods. Acceptance creates liability in the buyer for the price, N.J.S.A. 12A:2-709(1), and precludes rejection. N.J.S.A. 12A:2-607(2); N.J.S.A. 12A:2-606, New Jersey Study Comment 1. Also, once a buyer accepts goods, he has the burden to prove any defect. N.J.S.A. 12A:2-607(4); White & Summers, supra, § 8-2 at 297. By contrast, where goods are rejected for not conforming to the contract, the burden is on the seller to prove that the nonconformity was corrected. Miron v. Yonkers Raceway, Inc., 400 F.2d 112, 119 (2 Cir. 1968).

Underlying the Code provisions is the recognition of the revolutionary change in business practices in this century. The purchase of goods is no longer a simple transaction in which a buyer purchases individually-made goods from a seller in a face-to-face transaction. Our economy depends on a complex system for the manufacture, distribution, and sale of goods, a system in which manufacturers and consumers rarely meet. Faceless manufacturers mass-produce goods for unknown consumers who purchase those goods from merchants exercising little or no control over the quality of their production. In an age of assembly lines, we are accustomed to cars with scratches, television sets without knobs and other products with all kinds of defects. Buyers no longer expect a "perfect tender." If a merchant sells defective goods, the reasonable expectation of the parties is that the buyer will return those goods and that the seller will repair or replace them.

Recognizing this commercial reality, the Code permits a seller to cure imperfect tenders. Should the seller fail to cure the defects, whether substantial or not, the balance shifts again in favor of the buyer, who has the right to cancel or seek damages. N.J.S.A. 12A:2-711. In general, economic considerations would induce sellers to cure minor defects.

See generally Priest, supra, 91 Harv.L.Rev. 973-974. Assuming the seller does not cure, however, the buyer should be permitted to exercise his remedies under N.J.S.A. 12A:2-711. The Code remedies for consumers are to be liberally construed, and the buyer should have the option of cancelling if the seller does not provide conforming goods. See N.J.S.A. 12A:1-106.

To summarize, the UCC preserves the perfect tender rule to the extent of permitting a buyer to reject goods for any nonconformity. Nonetheless, that rejection does not automatically terminate the contract. A seller may still effect a cure and preclude unfair rejection and cancellation by the buyer. N.J.S.A. 12A:2-508, Official Comment 2; N.J.S.A. 12A:2-711, Official Comment 1.

III

The trial court found that Mr. and Mrs. Ramirez had rejected the van within a reasonable time under N.J.S.A. 12A:2-602. The court found that on August 3, 1978 Autosport's salesman advised the Ramirezes not to accept the van and that on August 14, they rejected delivery and Autosport agreed to replace the cushions. Those findings are supported by substantial credible evidence, and we sustain them. See Rova . . . . Although the trial court did not find whether Autosport cured the defects within a reasonable time, we find that Autosport did not effect a cure. Clearly the van was not ready for delivery during August, 1978 when Mr. and Mrs. Ramirez rejected it, and Autosport had the burden of proving that it had corrected the defects. Although the Ramirezes gave Autosport ample time to correct the defects, Autosport did not demonstrate that the van conformed to the contract on September 1. In fact, on that date, when Mr. and Mrs. Ramirez returned at Autosport's invitation, all they received was discourtesy.

On the assumption that substantial impairment is necessary only when a purchaser seeks to revoke acceptance under N.J.S.A. 12A:2-608, the trial court correctly refrained from deciding whether the defects substantially impaired the van. The court properly concluded that plaintiffs were entitled to “rescind”-i.e., to “cancel”-the contract. . . .

For the preceding reasons, we affirm the judgment of the Appellate Division.

For affirmance-Chief Justice WILENTZ and Justices PASHMAN, CLIFFORD, SCHREIBER, HANDLER, POLLOCK and O'HERN-7.

For reversal -None.

NOTES AND QUESTIONS:

1. Despite the seemingly harsh outcome of the perfect tender rule in single delivery situations, remnants of the substantial performance doctrine are still found in installment contracts for the sale of goods. *See* U.C.C. § 2-612 (“Installment contract”; Breach).

D. IMPOSSIBILITY, IMPRACTICABILITY, FRUSTRATION OF PURPOSE

TAYLOR V. CALDWELL
Queen's Bench
122 Eng. Rep. 309 (1863).

. . . .

The declaration alleged that by an agreement, bearing date the 27th May, 1861, the defendants agreed to let, and the plaintiffs agreed to take, on the terms therein stated, The Surrey Gardens and Music Hall, Newington, Surrey, for the following days, that is to say, Monday the 17th June, 1861, Monday the 15th July, 1861, Monday the 5th August, 1861, and Monday the 19th August, 1861, for the purpose of giving a series of four grand concerts and day and night fêtes, at the Gardens and Hall on those days respectively, at the rent or sum of 100£. for each of those days. It then averred the fulfilment of conditions &c., on the part of the plaintiffs; and breach by the defendants, that they did not nor would allow the plaintiffs to have the use of The Surrey Music Hall and Gardens according to the agreement, but wholly made default therein, &c.; whereby the plaintiffs lost divers moneys paid by them for printing advertisements of and in advertising the concerts, and also lost divers sums expended and expenses incurred by them in preparing for the concerts and otherwise in relation thereto, and on the faith of the performance by the defendants of the agreement on their part, and had been otherwise injured, &c. . . .

On the trial, before Blackburn J., at the London Sittings after Michaelmas Term, 1861, it appeared that the action was brought on the following agreement:--

> Royal Surrey Gardens,
> 27th May, 1861.
>
> Agreement between Messrs. Caldwell & Bishop, of the one part, and Messrs. Taylor & Lewis of the other part, whereby the said Caldwell & Bishop agree to let, and the said Taylor & Lewis agree to take, on the terms hereinafter stated, The Surrey Gardens and Music Hall, Newington, Surrey, for the following days, viz.:--for the purpose of giving a series of four grand concerts and day and night fêtes at the said Gardens and Hall on those days respectively at the rent or sum of 100£ for each of the said days. The said Caldwell & Bishop agree to find and provide at their own sole expense, on each of the aforesaid days, for the amusement of the public and persons then in the said Gardens and Hall, an efficient and organised military and quadrille band, the united bands to consist of from thirty-five to forty members; al fresco entertainments of various descriptions; coloured minstrels, fireworks and full illuminations; a ballet or divertissement, if permitted; a wizard and Grecian statues; tight rope performances; rifle galleries; air gun shooting; Chinese and Parisian games; boats on the lake, and (weather permitting) aquatic sports, and all and every other entertainment as given nightly during the months and times above mentioned. And the said Caldwell & Bishop also agree that the before mentioned united bands shall be present and assist at each of the said concerts, from its commencement until 9 o'clock at night; that they will, one

week at least previous to the above mentioned dates, underline in bold type in all their bills and advertisements that Mr. Sims Reeves and other artistes will sing at the said gardens on those dates respectively, and that the said Taylor & Lewis shall have the right of placing their boards, bills and placards in such number and manner (but subject to the approval of the said Caldwell & Bishop) in and about the entrance to the said gardens, and in the said grounds, one week at least previous to each of the above mentioned days respectively, all bills so displayed being affixed on boards. And the said Caldwell & Bishop also agree to allow dancing on the new circular platform after 9 o'clock at night, but not before. And the said Caldwell & Bishop also agree not to allow the firework display to take place till a 1/4 past 11 o'clock at night. And, lastly, the said Caldwell & Bishop agree that the said Taylor & Lewis shall be entitled to and shall be at liberty to take and receive, as and for the sole use and property of them the said Taylor & Lewis, all moneys paid for entrance to the Gardens, Galleries and Music Hall and firework galleries, and that the said Taylor & Lewis may in their own discretion secure the patronage of any charitable institution in connection with the said concerts. And the said Taylor & Lewis agree to pay the aforesaid respective sum of 100£. in the evening of the said respective days by a crossed cheque, and also to find and provide, at their own sole cost, all the necessary artistes for the said concerts, including Mr. Sims Reeves, God's will permitting. (Signed)

J. CALDWELL .
Witness CHAS. BISHOP .
(Signed) S. Denis.

On the 11th June the Music Hall was destroyed by an accidental fire, so that it became impossible to give the concerts. Under these circumstances a verdict was returned for the plaintiff, with leave reserved to enter a verdict for the defendants on the second and third issues.

Petersdorff Serjt., in Hilary Term, 1862, obtained a rule to enter a verdict for the defendants generally.

The rule was argued, in Hilary Term, 1863 (January 28th); before Cockburn C.J., Wightman, Crompton and Blackburn JJ. . . .

The judgment of the Court was now delivered by Blackburn J. In this case the plaintiffs and defendants had, on the 27th May, 1861, entered into a contract by which the defendants agreed to let the plaintiffs have the use of The Surrey Gardens and Music Hall on four days then to come, viz., the 17th June, 15th July, 5th August and 19th August, for the purpose of giving a series of four grand concerts, and day and night fêtes at the Gardens and Hall on those days respectively; and the plaintiffs agreed to take the Gardens and Hall on those days, and pay 100£ for each day.

The . . . agreement then proceeds to set out various stipulations between the parties as to what each was to supply for these concerts and entertainments, and as to the manner in which they should be carried on. The effect of the whole is to shew that the existence of the Music Hall in the Surrey Gardens in a state fit for a concert was essential for the fulfilment of the contract,--such entertainments as the parties contemplated in their agreement could not be given without it.

After the making of the agreement, and before the first day on which a concert was to be given, the Hall was destroyed by fire. This destruction, we must take it on the evidence, was without the fault of either party, and was so complete that in consequence the concerts could not be given as intended. And the question we have to decide is whether, under these circumstances, the loss which the plaintiffs have sustained is to fall upon the defendants. The parties when framing their agreement evidently had not present to their minds the possibility of such a disaster, and have made no express stipulation with reference to it, so that the answer to the question must depend upon the general rules of law applicable to such a contract.

There seems no doubt that where there is a positive contract to do a thing, not in itself unlawful, the contractor must perform it or pay damages for not doing it, although in consequence of unforeseen accidents, the performance of his contract has become unexpectedly burthensome or even impossible. The law is so laid down in 1 Roll. Abr. 450, Condition (G), and in the note (2) to *Walton* v. *Waterhouse* (2 Wms. Saund. 421 a. 6th ed.), and is recognised as the general rule by all the Judges in the much discussed case of *Hall* v. *Wright* (E. B. & E. 746). But this rule is only applicable when the contract is positive and absolute, and not subject to any condition either express or implied: and there are authorities which, as we think, establish the principle that where, from the nature of the contract, it appears that the parties must from the beginning have known that it could not be fulfilled unless when the time for the fulfilment of the contract arrived some particular specified thing continued to exist, so that, when entering into the contract, they must have contemplated such continuing existence as the foundation of what was to be done; there, in the absence of any express or implied warranty that the thing shall exist, the contract is not to be construed as a positive contract, but as subject to an implied condition that the parties shall be excused in case, before breach, performance becomes impossible from the perishing of the thing without default of the contractor.

There seems little doubt that this implication tends to further the great object of making the legal construction such as to fulfil the intention of those who entered into the contract. For in the course of affairs men in making such contracts in general would, if it were brought to their minds, say that there should be such a condition. . . .

There is a class of contracts in which a person binds himself to do something which requires to be performed by him in person; and such promises, e.g. promises to marry, or promises to serve for a certain time, are never in practice qualified by an express exception of the death of the party; and therefore in such cases the contract is in terms broken if the promisor dies before fulfilment. Yet it was very early determined that, if the performance is personal, the executors are not liable; *Hyde* v. *The Dean of Windsor* (Cro. Eliz. 552, 553). See 2 Wms. Exors. 1560, 5th ed., where a very apt illustration is given. "Thus," says the learned author, "if an author undertakes to compose a work, and dies before completing it, his executors are discharged from this contract: for the undertaking is merely personal in its nature, and, by the intervention of the contractor's death, has become impossible to be performed." For this he cites a dictum of Lord Lyndhurst in *Marshall* v. *Broadhurst* (1 Tyr. 348, 349), and a case mentioned by Patteson J. in *Wentworth* v. *Cock* (10 A. & E. 42, 45-46). In *Hall* v. *Wright* (E. B. & E. 746, 749), Crompton J., in his judgment, puts another case. "Where a contract depends upon personal skill, and the act of God renders it impossible, as, for instance, in the case of a painter employed to paint a picture who is struck blind, it may be that the performance might be excused."

It seems that in those cases the only ground on which the parties or their executors, can be excused from the consequences of the breach of the contract is, that from the nature of the contract there is an implied condition of the continued existence of the life of the contractor, and, perhaps in the case of the painter of his eyesight. In the instances just given, the person, the continued existence of whose life is necessary to the fulfilment of the contract, is himself the contractor, but that does not seem in itself to be necessary to the application of the principle; as is illustrated by the following example. In the ordinary form of an apprentice deed the apprentice binds himself in unqualified terms to "serve until the full end and term of seven years to be fully complete and ended," during which term it is covenanted that the apprentice his master "faithfully shall serve," and the father of the apprentice in equally unqualified terms binds himself for the performance by the apprentice of all and every covenant on his part. (See the form, 2 Chitty on Pleading, 370, 7th ed. by Greening.) It is undeniable that if the apprentice dies within the seven years, the covenant of the father that he shall perform his covenant to serve for seven years is not fulfilled, yet surely it cannot be that an action would lie against the father? Yet the only reason why it would not is that he is excused because of the apprentice's death. . . .

It may, we think, be safely asserted to be now English law, that in all contracts of loan of chattels or bailments if the performance of the promise of the borrower or bailee to return the things lent or bailed, becomes impossible because it has perished, this impossibility (if not arising from the fault of the borrower or bailee from some risk which he has taken upon himself) excuses the borrower or bailee from the performance of his promise to redeliver the chattel. . . .

In none of these cases is the promise in words other than positive, nor is there any express stipulation that the destruction of the person or thing shall excuse the performance; but that excuse is by law implied, because from the nature of the contract it is apparent that the parties contracted on the basis of the continued existence of the particular person or chattel. In the present case, looking at the whole contract, we find that the parties contracted on the basis of the continued existence of the Music Hall at the time when the concerts were to be given; that being essential to their performance.

We think, therefore, that the Music Hall having ceased to exist, without fault of either party, both parties are excused, the plaintiffs from taking the gardens and paying the money, the defendants from performing their promise to give the use of the Hall and Gardens and other things. Consequently the rule must be absolute to enter the verdict for the defendants.

Rule absolute.

KRELL V. HENRY
Court of Appeal
2 K.B. 740 (1903).

. . . .

The plaintiff, Paul Krell, sued the defendant, C. S. Henry, for 50£., being the balance of a sum of 75£., for which the defendant had agreed to hire a flat at 56A, Pall Mall on the days of June 26 and 27, for the purpose of viewing the processions to be held in connection with the coronation of His Majesty. The defendant denied his liability, and counter-claimed for the return of the sum of 25£, which had been paid as a deposit, on the ground that, the processions not having taken place owing to the serious illness of the King, there had been a total failure of consideration for the contract entered into by him.

The facts, which were not disputed, were as follows. The plaintiff on leaving the country in March, 1902, left instructions with his solicitor to let his suite of chambers at 56A, Pall Mall on such terms and for such period (not exceeding six months) as he thought proper. On June 17, 1902, the defendant noticed an announcement in the windows of the plaintiff's flat to the effect that windows to view the coronation processions were to be let. The defendant interviewed the housekeeper on the subject, when it was pointed out to him what a good view of the processions could be obtained from the premises, and he eventually agreed with the housekeeper to take the suite for the two days in question for a sum of 75£.

On June 20 the defendant wrote the following letter to the plaintiff's solicitor:--

> I am in receipt of yours of the 18th instant, inclosing form of agreement for the suite of chambers on the third floor at 56A, Pall Mall, which I have agreed to take for the two days, the 26th and 27th instant, for the sum of 75l. For reasons given you I cannot enter into the agreement, but as arranged over the telephone I inclose herewith cheque for 25£ as deposit, and will thank you to confirm to me that I shall have the entire use of these rooms during the days (not the nights) of the 26th and 27th instant. You may rely that every care will be taken of the premises and their contents. On the 24th inst. I will pay the balance, viz., 50£, to complete the 75£ agreed upon.

On the same day the defendant received the following reply from the plaintiff's solicitor:--

> I am in receipt of your letter of to-day's date inclosing cheque for 25£ deposit on your agreeing to take Mr. Krell's chambers on the third floor at 56A, Pall Mall for the two days, the 26th and 27th June, and I confirm the agreement that you are to have the entire use of these rooms during the days (but not the nights), the balance, 50£, to be paid to me on Tuesday next the 24th instant.

The processions not having taken place on the days originally appointed, namely, June 26 and 27, the defendant declined to pay the balance of 50£ alleged to be due from him under the contract in writing of June 20 constituted by the above two letters. Hence the present action.

Darling J., on August 11, 1902, held, upon the authority of Taylor v. Caldwell and The Moorcock, that there was an implied condition in the contract that the procession should take place, and gave judgment for the defendant on the claim and counter-claim.

The plaintiff appealed.

Spencer Bower, K.C., and *Holman Gregory*, for the plaintiff.

In the contract nothing is said about the coronation procession, but it is admitted that both parties expected that there would be a procession, and that the price to be paid for the rooms was fixed with reference to the expected procession. Darling J. held that both the claim and the counter-claim were governed by Taylor v. Caldwell, and that there was an implied term in the contract that the procession should take place. It is submitted that the learned judge was wrong. If he was right, the result will be that in every case of this kind an unremunerated promisor will be in effect an insurer of the hopes and expectations of the promisee.

Taylor v. Caldwell purports to be founded on two passages in the Digest. But other passages in the Digest are more directly in point, and shew that the implied condition is that there shall not be a physical extinction of the subject-matter of the contract. . . .

Duke, K.C., and *Ricardo*, for the defendant.

The question is, What was the bargain? The defendant contends that it was a bargain with an implied condition that the premises taken were premises in front of which a certain act of State would take place by Royal Proclamation. A particular character was thus impressed upon the premises; and when that character ceased to be impressed upon them the contract was at an end. It is through nobody's fault, but through an unforeseen misfortune that the premises lost that character. The price agreed to be paid must be regarded: it is equivalent to many thousands a year. What explanation can be given of that, except that it was agreed to be paid for the purpose of enabling the defendant to see the procession? It was the absolute assumption of both parties when entering into the contract that the procession would pass.

The principle of Taylor v. Caldwell- namely, that a contract for the sale of a particular thing must not be construed as a positive contract, but as subject to an implied condition that, when the time comes for fulfillment, the specified thing continues to exist - exactly applies. The certainty of the coronation and consequent procession taking place was the basis of this contract. Both parties bargained upon the happening of a certain event the occurrence of which gave the premises a special character with a corresponding value to the defendant; but as the condition failed the premises lost their adventitious value. There has been such a change in the character of the premises which the plaintiff agreed the defendant should occupy as to deprive them of their value. When the premises become unfit for the purpose for which they were taken the bargain is off: Taylor v. Caldwell, the principle of which case was adopted by the Court of Appeal in Nickoll v. Ashton. What was in contemplation here was not that the defendant should merely go and sit in the room, but that he should see a procession which both parties regarded as an inevitable event. There was an implied warranty or condition founded on the presumed intention of the parties, and upon reason: The Moorcock. No doubt the observations of the Court in that case were addressed to a totally different subject-matter, but the principle laid down was exactly as stated in Taylor v. Caldwell and Nickoll v. Ashton. In Hamlyn v. Wood it was held that in a contract there must be a reasonable implication in order to give the transaction such efficacy as both parties intended it to have, and that without such implication the consideration would fail. In the case of a demise, collateral bargains do not arise; but here there is an agreement, and what has to be done is to ascertain the meaning and intention the parties had in entering into it.

[STIRLING L.J. In Appleby v. Myers there was a contract to supply certain machinery to a building, but before the completion of the contract the building was burnt down; and it was held that both parties were excused from performance of the contract.]

In that case the contract had been partly performed; but the defendant's case is stronger than that. When, as here, the contract is wholly executory and the subject-matter fails, the contract is at an end.

[STIRLING L.J. In Baily v. De Crespigny, where the performance of a covenant was rendered impossible by an Act of Parliament, it was held that the covenantor was discharged.

VAUGHAN WILLIAMS L.J. In Howell v. Coupland the contract was held to be subject to an implied condition that the parties should be excused if performance became impossible through the perishing of the subject-matter.]

That applies here: it is impossible for the plaintiff to give the defendant that which he bargained for, and, therefore, there is a total failure of consideration.

To sum up, the basis of the contract is that there would be a procession - that is to say, it is a contract based upon a certain thing coming into existence: there is a condition precedent that there shall be a procession. But for the mutual expectation of a procession upon the days mentioned there would have been no contract whatever. The basis of the contract was also the continuance of a thing in a certain condition; for on June 20 the rooms were capable of being described as a place from which to view a procession on two particular days; whereas when those days arrived the rooms were no longer capable of being so described.

Holman Gregory replied.

Cur. adv. vult.

Aug. 11. VAUGHAN WILLIAMS L.J. read the following written judgment:-- The real question in this case is the extent of the application in English law of the principle of the Roman law which has been adopted and acted on in many English decisions, and notably in the case of Taylor v. Caldwell. That case at least makes it clear that "where, from the nature of the contract, it appears that the parties must from the beginning have known that it could not be fulfilled unless, when the time for the fulfilment of the contract arrived, some particular specified thing continued to exist, so that when entering into the contract they must have contemplated such continued existence as the foundation of what was to be done; there, in the absence of any express or implied warranty that the thing shall exist, the contract is not to be considered a positive contract, but as subject to an implied condition that the parties shall be excused in case, before breach, performance becomes impossible from the perishing of the thing without default of the contractor." Thus far it is clear that the principle of the Roman law has been introduced into the English law. The doubt in the present case arises as to how far this principle extends. The Roman law dealt with obligationes de certo corpore. Whatever may have been the limits of the Roman law, the case of Nickoll v. Ashton makes it plain that the English law applies the principle not only to cases where the performance of the contract becomes impossible by the cessation of existence of the thing which is the subject-matter of the contract, but also to cases where the event which renders the contract incapable of performance is the cessation or non-existence of an express condition or state of things, going to the root of the contract, and essential to its performance. It is said, on the one side, that the specified thing, state of things, or condition the continued existence of which is necessary for the fulfilment of the contract, so that the parties entering into the contract must have contemplated the continued existence of that thing, condition, or state of things as the foundation of what was to be done under the contract, is limited to things which are either the subject-matter of the contract or a condition or state of things, present or anticipated, which is expresssly mentioned in the contract. But, on the other side, it is said that the condition or state of things need not be expressly specified, but that it is sufficient if that condition or state of things clearly appears by extrinsic evidence to have been assumed by the parties to be the foundation or basis of the contract, and the event which causes the impossibility is of such a character that it cannot reasonably be supposed to have been in the contemplation of the contracting parties when the contract was made. In such a case the contracting parties will not be held bound by the general words which, though large enough to include, were not used with reference to a possibility of a particular event rendering performance of the contract impossible. I do not think that the principle of the civil law as introduced into the English law is limited to cases in which the event causing the impossibility of performance is the destruction or non-existence of some thing which is the subject-matter of the contract or of some condition or state of things expressly specified as a condition of it. I think that you first have to ascertain, not necessarily from the terms of the contract, but, if required, from necessary inferences, drawn from surrounding circumstances recognised by both contracting parties, what is the substance of the contract, and then to ask the question whether that substantial contract needs for its foundation the assumption of the existence of a particular state of things. If it does, this will limit the operation of the general words, and in such case, if the contract becomes impossible of performance by reason of the non-existence of the state of things assumed by both contracting parties as the foundation of the contract, there will be no breach of the contract thus limited. Now what are the facts of the present case? The contract is contained in two letters of June 20 which passed between the defendant and the plaintiff's agent, Mr. Cecil Bisgood. These letters do not mention the coronation, but speak merely of the taking of Mr. Krell's chambers, or, rather, of the use of them, in the daytime of June 26 and 27, for the sum of 75£, 25£ then paid, balance 50£ to be paid on the 24th. But the affidavits, which by agreement between the parties are to be taken as stating the facts of the case, shew that the plaintiff exhibited on his premises, third floor, 56A, Pall Mall, an announcement to the effect that windows to view the Royal coronation procession were to be let, and that the defendant was induced by that announcement to apply to the housekeeper on the premises, who said that the owner was willing to let the suite of rooms for the purpose of seeing the Royal procession for both days, but not nights, of June 26 and 27. In my judgment the use of the rooms was let and taken for the purpose of seeing the Royal procession. It was not a demise of the rooms, or even an agreement to let and take the rooms. It is a licence to use rooms for a particular purpose and none other. And in my judgment the taking place of those processions on the days proclaimed along the proclaimed route, which passed 56A, Pall Mall, was regarded by both contracting parties as the foundation of the contract; and I think that it cannot reasonably be supposed to have been in the contemplation of the contracting parties, when the contract was made, that the coronation would not be held on the proclaimed days, or the processions not take place on those days along the proclaimed route; and I think that the words imposing on the defendant the obligation to accept and pay for the use of the rooms for the named days, although general and unconditional, were not used with reference to the possibility of the particular contingency which afterwards occurred. It was suggested in the course of the argument that if the occurrence, on the proclaimed days, of the coronation and the procession in this case were the foundation of the contract, and if the general words are thereby limited or qualified, so that in the event of the non-occurrence of the coronation and procession along the proclaimed route they would discharge both parties from further performance of the contract, it would follow that if a cabman was engaged to take some one to Epsom on Derby Day at a suitable enhanced price for such a journey, say 10£, both parties to the contract would be discharged in the contingency of the race at Epsom for some reason becoming impossible; but I do not think this follows, for I do not think that in the cab case the happening of the race would be the foundation of the contract. No doubt the purpose of the engager would be to go to see the Derby, and the price would be proportionately high; but the cab had no special qualifications for the purpose which led to the selection of the cab for this particular occasion. Any other cab would have done as well. Moreover, I think that, under the cab contract, the hirer, even if the race went off, could have said, "Drive me to Epsom; I will pay you the agreed sum; you have nothing to do with the purpose for which I hired the cab," and that if the cabman refused he would have been guilty of a breach of contract, there being nothing to qualify his promise to drive the hirer to Epsom on a particular day. Whereas in the case of the coronation, there is not merely the purpose of the hirer to see the coronation procession, but it is the coronation procession and the relative position of the rooms which is the basis of the contract as much for the lessor as the hirer; and I think that if the King, before the coronation day and after the contract, had died, the hirer could not have insisted on having the rooms on the days named. It could not in the cab case be reasonably said that seeing the Derby race was the foundation of the contract, as it was of the licence in this case. Whereas in the present case, where the rooms were offered and taken, by reason of their peculiar suitability from the position of the rooms for a view of the coronation procession, surely the view of the coronation procession was the foundation of the contract, which is a very different thing from the purpose of the man who engaged the cab - namely, to see the race - being held to be the foundation of the contract. Each case must be judged by its own circumstances. In each case one must ask oneself, first, what, having regard to all the circumstances, was the foundation of the contract? Secondly, was the performance of the contract prevented? Thirdly, was the event which prevented the performance of the contract of such a character that it cannot reasonably be said to have been in the contemplation of the parties at the date of the contract? If all these questions are answered in the affirmative (as I think they should be in this case), I think both parties are discharged from further performance of the contract. I think that the coronation procession was the foundation of this contract, and that the non-happening of it prevented the performance of the contract; and, secondly, I think that the non-happening of the procession, to use the words of Sir James Hannen in Baily v. De Crespigny, was an event "of such a character that it cannot reasonably be supposed to have been in the contemplation of the contracting parties when the contract was made, and that they are not to be held bound by general words which, though large enough to include, were not used with reference to the possibility of the particular contingency which afterwards happened." The test seems to be whether the event which causes the impossibility was or might have been anticipated and guarded against. It seems difficult to say, in a case where both parties anticipate the happening of an event, which anticipation is the foundation of the contract, that either party must be taken to have anticipated, and ought to have guarded against, the event which prevented the performance of the contract. In both Jackson v. Union Marine Insurance Co. and Nickoll v. Ashton the parties might have anticipated as a possibility that perils of the sea might delay the ship and frustrate the commercial venture: in the former case the carriage of the goods to effect which the charterparty was entered into; in the latter case the sale of the goods which were to be shipped on the steamship which was delayed. But the Court held in the former case that the basis of the contract was that the ship would arrive in time to carry out the contemplated commercial venture, and in the latter that the steamship would arrive in time for the loading of the goods the subject of the sale. I wish to observe that cases of this sort are very different from cases where a contract or warranty or representation is implied, such as was implied in The Moorcock, and refused to be implied in Hamlyn v. Wood. But The Moorcock is of importance in the present case as shewing that whatever is the suggested implication - be it condition, as in this case, or warranty or representation - one must, in judging whether the implication ought to be made, look not only at the words of the contract, but also at the surrounding facts and the knowledge of the parties of those facts. There seems to me to be ample authority for this proposition. Thus in Jackson v. Union Marine Insurance Co., in the Common Pleas, the question whether the object of the voyage had been frustrated by the delay of the ship was left as a question of fact to the jury, although there was nothing in the charterparty defining the time within which the charterers were to supply the cargo of iron rails for San Francisco, and nothing on the face of the charterparty to indicate the importance of time in the venture; and that was a case in which, as Bramwell B. points out in his judgment at p. 148, Taylor v. Caldwell was a strong authority to support the conclusion arrived at in the judgment - that the ship not arriving in time for the voyage contemplated, but at such time as to frustrate the commercial venture, was not only a breach of the contract but discharged the charterer, though he had such an excuse that no action would lie. And, again, in Harris v. Dreesman the vessel had to be loaded, as no particular time was mentioned, within a reasonable time; and, in judging of a reasonable time, the Court approved of evidence being given that the defendants, the charterers, to the knowledge of the plaintiffs, had no control over the colliery from which both parties knew that the coal was to come; and that, although all that was said in the charterparty was that the vessel should proceed to Spital Tongue's Spout (the spout of the Spital Tongue's Colliery), and there take on board from the freighters a full and complete cargo of coals, and five tons of coke, and although there was no evidence to prove any custom in the port as to loading vessels in turn. Again it was held in Mumford v. Gething that, in construing a written contract of service under which A. was to enter the employ of B., oral evidence is admissible to shew in what capacity A. was to serve B. See also Price v. Mouat. The rule seems to be that which is laid down in Taylor on Evidence, vol. ii. s. 1082: "It may be laid down as a broad and distinct rule of law that extrinsic evidence of every material fact which will enable the Court to ascertain the nature and qualities of the subject-matter of the instrument, or, in other words, to identify the persons and things to which the instrument refers, must of necessity be received." And Lord Campbell in his judgment says: "I am of opinion that, when there is a contract for the sale of a specific subject-matter, oral evidence may be received, for the purpose of shewing what that subject-matter was, of every fact within the knowledge of the parties before and at the time of the contract." See per Campbell C.J., Macdonald v. Longbottom. It seems to me that the language of Willes J. in Lloyd v. Guibert points in the same direction. I myself am clearly of opinion that in this case, where we have to ask ourselves whether the object of the contract was frustrated by the non-happening of the coronation and its procession on the days proclaimed, parol evidence is admissible to shew that the subject of the contract was rooms to view the coronation procession, and was so to the knowledge of both parties. When once this is established, I see no difficulty whatever in the case. It is not essential to the application of the principle of Taylor v. Caldwell that the direct subject of the contract should perish or fail to be in existence at the date of performance of the contract. It is sufficient if a state of things or condition expressed in the contract and essential to its performance perishes or fails to be in existence at that time. In the present case the condition which fails and prevents the achievement of that which was, in the contemplation of both parties, the foundation of the contract, is not expressly mentioned either as a condition of the contract or the purpose of it; but I think for the reasons which I have given that the principle of Taylor v. Caldwell ought to be applied. This disposes of the plaintiff's claim for 50£ unpaid balance of the price agreed to be paid for the use of the rooms. The defendant at one time set up a cross-claim for the return of the 25£. he paid at the date of the contract. As that claim is now withdrawn it is unnecessary to say anything about it. I have only to add that the facts of this case do not bring it within the principle laid down in Stubbs v. Holywell Ry. Co.; that in the case of contracts falling directly within the rule of Taylor v. Caldwell the subsequent impossibility does not affect rights already acquired, because the defendant had the whole of June 24 to pay the balance, and the public announcement that the coronation and processions would not take place on the proclaimed days was made early on the morning of the 24th, and no cause of action could accrue till the end of that day. I think this appeal ought to be dismissed.

ROMER L.J.

With some doubt I have also come to the conclusion that this case is governed by the principle on which Taylor v. Caldwell was decided, and accordingly that the appeal must be dismissed. The doubt I have felt was whether the parties to the contract now before us could be said, under the circumstances, not to have had at all in their contemplation the risk that for some reason or other the coronation processions might not take place on the days fixed, or, if the processions took place, might not pass so as to be capable of being viewed from the rooms mentioned in the contract; and whether, under this contract, that risk was not undertaken by the defendant. But on the question of fact as to what was in the contemplation of the parties at the time, I do not think it right to differ from the conclusion arrived at by Vaughan Williams L.J., and (as I gather) also arrived at by my brother Stirling. This being so, I concur in the conclusions arrived at by Vaughan Williams L.J. in his judgment, and I do not desire to add anything to what he has said so fully and completely.

STIRLING L.J.

Said he had had an opportunity of reading the judgment delivered by Vaughan Williams L.J., with which he entirely agreed. Though the case was one of very great difficulty, he thought it came within the principle of Taylor v. Caldwell.

Representation

Solicitors: Cecil Bisgood; M. Grunebaum.

Appeal dismissed. (W. C. D.)

CHASE PRECAST CORP. V. JOHN J. PAONESSA CO.
Supreme Court of Massachusetts, Worcester
566 N.E.2d 603 (1991).

LYNCH, Justice.

. . . .

The claim of the plaintiff, Chase Precast Corporation (Chase), arises from the cancellation of its contracts with Paonessa to supply median barriers in a highway reconstruction project of the Commonwealth. Chase brought an action to recover its anticipated profit on the amount of median barriers called for by its supply contracts with Paonessa but not produced. Paonessa brought a cross action against the Commonwealth for indemnification in the event it should be held liable to Chase. After a jury-waived trial, a Superior Court judge ruled for Paonessa on the basis of impossibility of performance.[2] Chase and Paonessa cross appealed. The Appeals Court affirmed, noting that the doctrine of frustration of purpose more accurately described the basis of the trial judge's decision than the doctrine of impossibility. Chase Precast Corp. v. John J. Paonessa Co., 28 Mass.App.Ct. 639, 554 N.E.2d 868 (1990). We agree. We allowed Chase's application for further appellate review, and we now affirm.

The pertinent facts are as follows. In 1982, the Commonwealth, through the Department of Public Works (department), entered into two contracts with Paonessa for resurfacing and improvements to two stretches of Route 128. Part of each contract called for replacing a grass median strip between the north and southbound lanes with concrete surfacing and precast concrete median barriers. Paonessa entered into two contracts with Chase under which Chase was to supply, in the aggregate, 25,800 linear feet of concrete median barriers according to the specifications of the department for highway construction. The quantity and type of barriers to be supplied were specified in two purchase orders prepared by Chase.

---

[2] The judge also ruled that the Department of Public Works had the right to cancel the order for median barriers under its general contracts with Paonessa, particularly under subsection 4.06 of those contracts. See note 6, infra.

The highway reconstruction began in the spring of 1983. By late May, the department was receiving protests from angry residents who objected to use of the concrete median barriers and removal of the grass median strip. Paonessa and Chase became aware of the protest around June 1. On June 6, a group of about 100 citizens filed an action in the Superior Court to stop installation of the concrete median barriers and other aspects of the work. On June 7, anticipating modification by the department, Paonessa notified Chase by letter to stop producing concrete barriers for the projects. Chase did so upon receipt of the letter the following day. On June 17, the department and the citizens' group entered into a settlement which provided, in part, that no additional concrete median barriers would be installed. On June 23, the department deleted the permanent concrete median barriers item from its contracts with Paonessa.

Before stopping production on June 8, Chase had produced approximately one-half of the concrete median barriers called for by its contracts with Paonessa, and had delivered most of them to the construction sites. Paonessa paid Chase for all that it had produced, at the contract price. Chase suffered no out-of-pocket expense as a result of cancellation of the remaining portion of barriers.

This court has long recognized and applied the doctrine of impossibility as a defense to an action for breach of contract. See, e.g., Boston Plate & Window Glass Co. v. John Bowen Co., 335 Mass. 697, 141 N.E.2d 715 (1957); Baetjer v. New England Alcohol Co., 319 Mass. 592, 66 N.E.2d 798 (1946); Butterfield v. Byron, 153 Mass. 517, 27 N.E. 667 (1891). Under that doctrine, "where from the nature of the contract it appears that the parties must from the beginning have contemplated the continued existence of some particular specified thing as the foundation of what was to be done, then, in the absence of any warranty that the thing shall exist ... the parties shall be excused ... [when] performance becomes impossible from the accidental perishing of the thing without the fault of either party." Boston Plate & Window Glass Co., supra, 335 Mass. at 700, 141 N.E.2d 715, quoting Hawkes v. Kehoe, 193 Mass. 419, 423, 79 N.E. 766 (1907).

On the other hand, although we have referred to the doctrine of frustration of purpose in a few decisions, we have never clearly defined it. See Mishara Constr. Co. v. Transit-Mixed Concrete Corp., 365 Mass. 122, 128-129, 310 N.E.2d 363 (1974); Essex-Lincoln Garage, Inc. v. Boston, 342 Mass. 719, 721-722, 175 N.E.2d 466 (1961); Baetjer v. New England Alcohol Co., supra, 319 Mass. at 602, 66 N.E.2d 798. Other jurisdictions have explained the doctrine as follows: when an event neither anticipated nor caused by either party, the risk of which was not allocated by the contract, destroys the object or purpose of the contract, thus destroying the value of performance, the parties are excused from further performance. See Howard v. Nicholson, 556 S.W.2d 477, 482 (Mo.Ct.App.1977); Perry v. Champlain Oil Co., 101 N.H. 97, 134 A.2d 65 (1957); Lloyd v. Murphy, 25 Cal.2d 48, 153 P.2d 47 (1944).

In Mishara Constr. Co., supra, 365 Mass. at 129, 310 N.E.2d 363, we called frustration of purpose a "companion rule" to the doctrine of impossibility. Both doctrines concern the effect of supervening circumstances upon the rights and duties of the parties. The difference lies in the effect of the supervening event. Under frustration, "[p]erformance remains possible but the expected value of performance to the party seeking to be excused has been destroyed by [the] fortuitous event...."[3] Lloyd v. Murphy, supra, 25 Cal.2d at 53, 153 P.2d 47. The principal question in both kinds of cases remains "whether an unanticipated circumstance, the risk of which should not fairly be thrown on the promisor, has made performance vitally different from what was reasonably to be expected." See Lloyd, supra at 54, 153 P.2d 47 (frustration); Mishara Constr. Co., supra, 365 Mass. at 129, 310 N.E.2d 363 (impossibility).

Since the two doctrines differ only in the effect of the fortuitous supervening event, it is appropriate to look to our cases dealing with impossibility for guidance in treating the issues that are the same in a frustration of purpose case.[4] The trial judge's findings with regard to those issues are no less pertinent to application of the frustration defense because they were considered relevant to the defense of impossibility.

Another definition of frustration of purpose is found in the Restatement (Second) of Contracts § 265 (1981):

> Where, after a contract is made, a party's principal purpose is substantially frustrated without his fault by the occurrence of an event the non-occurrence of which was a basic assumption on which the contract was made, his remaining duties to render performance are discharged, unless the language or the circumstances indicate the contrary.

This definition is nearly identical to the defense of "commercial impracticability," found in the Uniform Commercial Code, G.L. c. 106, § 2-615 (1988 ed.),[5] which this court, in Mishara Constr. Co., supra at 127-128, 310 N.E.2d 363, held to be consistent with the common law of contracts regarding impossibility of performance. It follows, therefore, that the Restatement's formulation of the doctrine is consistent with this court's previous treatment of impossibility of performance and frustration of purpose.

Paonessa bore no responsibility for the department's elimination of the median barriers from the projects. Therefore, whether it can rely on the defense of frustration turns on whether elimination of the barriers was a risk allocated by the contracts to Paonessa. Mishara Constr. Co., supra, 365 Mass. at 129, 310 N.E.2d 363, articulates the relevant test:

---

[3] Clearly frustration of purpose is a more accurate label for the defense argued in this case than impossibility of performance, since, as the Appeals Court pointed out, "[p]erformance was not literally impossible. Nothing prevented Paonessa from honoring its contract to purchase the remaining sections of median barrier, whether or not the [department] would approve their use in the road construction." 28 Mass.App.Ct. 639, 644 n. 5, 554 N.E.2d 868 (1990).

[4] Those issues include the foreseeability of the supervening event, allocation of the risk of occurrence of the event, and the degree of hardship to the promisor. Compare Mishara Constr. Co., supra, 365 Mass. at 128-130, 310 N.E.2d 363, and Boston Plate & Window Glass Co., supra, 335 Mass. at 700-701, 141 N.E.2d 715 with Howard, supra at 482-483, and Perry, supra, 101 N.H. at 98-100, 134 A.2d 65. See also 18 S. Williston, Contracts §§ 1935, 1954 (1978 & Supp.1990).

[5] That section states that performance is excused when it has been made "impracticable by the occurrence of a contingency the non-occurrence of which was a basic assumption on which the contract was made." G.L. c. 106, § 2-615.

> The question is, given the commercial circumstances in which the parties dealt: Was the contingency which developed one which the parties could reasonably be thought to have foreseen as a real possibility which could affect performance? Was it one of that variety of risks which the parties were tacitly assigning to the promisor by their failure to provide for it explicitly? If it was, performance will be required. If it could not be so considered, performance is excused.

This is a question for the trier of fact. Id. at 127, 130, 310 N.E.2d 363.

Paonessa's contracts with the department contained a standard provision allowing the department to eliminate items or portions of work found unnecessary.[6] The purchase order agreements between Chase and Paonessa do not contain a similar provision. This difference in the contracts does not mandate the conclusion that Paonessa assumed the risk of reduction in the quantity of the barriers. It is implicit in the judge's findings that Chase knew the barriers were for department projects. The record supports the conclusion that Chase was aware of the department's power to decrease quantities of contract items. The judge found that Chase had been a supplier of median barriers to the department in the past. The provision giving the department the power to eliminate items or portions thereof was standard in its contracts. See Standard Specifications for Highways and Bridges, Commonwealth of Massachusetts Department of Public Works § 4.06 (1973). The judge found that Chase had furnished materials under and was familiar with the so-called "Unit Price Philosophy" in the construction industry, whereby contract items are paid for at the contract unit price for the quantity of work actually accepted. Finally, the judge's finding that "[a]ll parties were well aware that lost profits were not an element of damage in either of the public works projects in issue" further supports the conclusion that Chase was aware of the department's power to decrease quantities, since the term prohibiting claims for anticipated profit is part of the same sentence in the standard provision as that allowing the engineer to eliminate items or portions of work.

In Mishara Constr. Co., supra at 130, 310 N.E.2d 363, we held that, although labor disputes in general cannot be considered extraordinary, whether the parties in a particular case intended performance to be carried out, even in the face of a labor difficulty, depends on the facts known to the parties at the time of contracting with respect to the history of and prospects for labor difficulties. In this case, even if the parties were aware generally of the department's power to eliminate contract items, the judge could reasonably have concluded that they did not contemplate the cancellation for a major portion of the project of such a

---

[6] The contracts contained the following provision:

> 4.06 Increased or Decreased Contract Quantities.
>
> When the accepted quantities of work vary from the quantities in the bid schedule, the Contractor shall accept as payment in full, so far as contract items are concerned, payment at the original contract unit prices for the accepted quantities of work done.
>
> The Engineer may order omitted from the work any items or portions of work found unnecessary to the improvement and such omission shall not operate as a waiver of any condition of the Contract nor invalidate any of the provisions thereof, nor shall the Contractor have any claim for anticipated profit.
>
> No allowance will be made for any increased expenses, loss of expected reimbursement therefor or from any other cause.

widely used item as concrete median barriers, and did not allocate the risk of such cancellation.[7]

Our opinion in Chicopee Concrete Serv., Inc. v. Hart Eng'g Co., 398 Mass. 476, 498 N.E.2d 121 (1986), does not lead to a different conclusion. Although we held there that a provision of a prime contract requiring city approval of subcontractors was not incorporated by reference into the subcontract, id. at 478, 498 N.E.2d 121, we nevertheless stated that, if the record had supported the conclusion that the subcontractor knew, or at least had notice of, the approval clause, the result might have been different. Id. at 478-479, 498 N.E.2d 121.[8] . . . .

Judgment affirmed.

E. WAIVER, ESTOPPEL AND OTHER JUSTIFICATIONS

MOE V. JOHN DEERE CO.
Supreme Court of South Dakota
516 N.W.2d 332 (1994).

MOSES, Circuit Judge.

This is an appeal by Ted Moe (Moe) from a summary judgment granted by Third Judicial Circuit Court in favor of John Deere Company (Deere) and Day County Implement Company (Implement). We reverse.

FACTS

On September 29, 1983, Moe bought a farm tractor from Day County Equipment in Watertown, South Dakota. He purchased a John Deere D8850 for a cash price of $121,268.00. In financing the transaction, Moe traded in two old tractors for the amount of $77,543.00 and agreed to pay the $59,802.40 difference in five equal installments of

---

[7] The judge did not explicitly find that cancellation of the barriers was not contemplated and that the risk of their elimination was not allocated by the contracts. However, the judge's decision imports every finding essential to sustain it if there is evidence to support it. Mailer v. Mailer, 390 Mass. 371, 373, 455 N.E.2d 1211 (1983).

[8] This court held in John Soley & Sons v. Jones, 208 Mass. 561, 566-567, 95 N.E. 94 (1911), that, where by its terms the prime contract could be cancelled if the defendant was not making sufficient progress on the work, and the plaintiff knew of the article of cancellation, nevertheless, even if it was mutually understood that the defendant did not intend to perform unless the prime contract remained in force, the defendant was not relieved from performance on the ground of impossibility where it failed to provide for the risk of cancellation in its contract with the plaintiff. To the extent that holding is contrary to our decision in this case, we decline to follow it, and refer to our adoption in Mishara Constr. Co., supra, 365 Mass. at 130, 310 N.E.2d 363, of the following statement: "Rather than mechanically apply any fixed rule of law, where the parties themselves have not allocated responsibility, justice is better served by appraising all of the circumstances, the part the various parties played, and thereon determining liability," quoting Badhwar v. Colorado Fuel & Iron Corp., 138 F.Supp. 595, 607 (S.D.N.Y.1955), aff'd, 245 F.2d 903 (2d Cir.1957). See West Los Angeles Inst. for Cancer Research v. Mayer, 366 F.2d 220, 225 (9th Cir.1966), cert. denied, 385 U.S. 1010, 87 S.Ct. 718, 17 L.Ed.2d 548 (1967) ("foreseeability of the frustrating event is not alone enough to bar rescission if it appears that the parties did not intend the promisor to assume the risk of its occurrence").

$11,960.48 each due on October 1st for the years 1984, 1985, 1986, 1987 and 1988. After the contract was completed it was assigned to Deere on September 30, 1983.

Moe was two months late in paying his first installment. Rather than paying $11,960.48 on October 1, 1984, Moe paid $12,212.87 on December 3, 1984. On October 1, 1985, Moe was again unable to timely pay his second installment. Deere waived full payment and extended the time in which Moe was to make this payment. On January 13, 1986, Moe made a partial payment in the amount of $6,200.00, over three months late. Moe and Deere agreed that Moe was to pay a second amount on March 1, 1986 in the amount of $6,350.17 to complete the second installment. On March 10, 1986, Deere sent a notice to Moe indicating that Moe's second installment was past due and that he had until March 20, 1986 to pay $6,389.48 to bring his account current. Again Moe missed this payment deadline.

Deere did not follow up on the delinquent payment until a representative from Deere contacted Moe sometime in May or the first part of June 1986, over seven months after the second installment was originally due. Deere's representative and Moe agreed that Moe would pay $2,000.00 of the $6,389.48 plus interest owing to Deere and Deere would allow Moe to pay the balance when he started to harvest. Deere's representative and Moe failed to specify the due date for either the $2,000.00 payment or when the balance was due. Moe had no further conversations with the representative from Deere about the $2,000.00 until after Deere repossessed the tractor on July 30, 1986.

Moe, who was in Oklahoma at the time of repossession, did not receive any notice from Deere's representative that the tractor was going to be repossessed because his payments were delinquent. Deere reassigned Moe's contract to Implement following the repossession. On August 1, 1986, Deere mailed from Minneapolis, Minnesota a certified letter dated July 31, 1986 to Moe which indicated that Deere "[found] it necessary to gain possession of the equipment involved." This letter apparently was returned to Deere undelivered to Moe. Thus, Deere hand-addressed a new letter and sent it to Moe who picked it up on August 18, 1986. The letter indicated:

> We intend to reassign your contract to the above named dealer. Once we reassign it, two weeks from the date of this letter, you will contact them on all matters concerning the disposition of the equipment or the amount owed under the contract. They intend to dispose of said collateral by public or private sale. If you wish to redeem this equipment, you must pay to John Deere Company $37,591.20 plus any expenses incurred from this repossession, in cash certified funds, before we reassign the contract.
>
> We hope you will be able to pay this amount within the prescribed period. If you have any questions regarding this matter please contact us. M.K. Mehus, Manager Financial Services.

Implement sold the tractor on August 19, 1986 for $44,000.00. Implement paid Deere in full on the contract and applied the proceeds to the debt and turned over the excess proceeds to Moe's lender by mailing two (2) checks totalling $2,616.77 to the Farmers and Merchants Bank on December 1, 1986.

Moe sued Deere and Implement on the following causes of action: (1) wrongful repossession; (2) fraudulent repossession; (3) commercially unreasonable sale; and (4) failure to account for the surplus.

Deere moved for partial summary judgment on the third and fourth issues of commercially unreasonable sale and failure to account for surplus. The trial court granted Deere's motion. Then, Deere moved for summary judgment on the first and second issues of wrongful repossession and fraudulent repossession. On February 5, 1993, the trial court issued an order granting Deere's summary judgment motion on both issues. Moe appeals. . . .

ISSUE

DO GENUINE ISSUES OF MATERIAL FACT AS TO WHETHER MOE WAS IN "DEFAULT" PRECLUDE THE GRANTING OF SUMMARY JUDGMENT?

We recognized in First Nat. Bank of Black Hills v. Beug, 400 N.W.2d 893, 896 (S.D.1987), that "[t]he term 'default' is not defined in the Uniform Commercial Code, thus we must look to other sources for a definition." Id. at 895. Then, we turned to hornbook law for a definition of default:

> Default' triggers the secured creditor's rights under Part Five of Article Nine. But what is "default?" Article Nine does not define the word; instead it leaves this to the parties and to any scraps of common law lying around. Apart from the modest limitations imposed by the unconscionability doctrine and the requirement of good faith, default is 'whatever the security agreement says it is. Id. at 896 (quoting J. White & R. Summers, Uniform Commercial Code § 26-22 at 1085-86 (2d ed. 1980)).

Several jurisdictions recognize that the determination of default is not a matter of law for the court to decide. Whether a breach or a default exists is a question of fact. . . .

Here, the promissory note provided a definition of default:

> The borrower shall be in default upon the occurrence of any one or more of the following events: (1) the Borrower shall fail to pay, when due, any amount required hereunder, or any other indebtedness of the borrower to the Lender of any third parties; (2) the Borrower shall be in default in the performance of any covenant or obligation under the line of credit or equivalent agreement for future advances (if applicable) or any document or agreement related thereto; (3) any warranty or representation made by the Borrower shall prove false or misleading in any respect; (4) the Borrower or any Guarantor of this promissory note shall liquidate, merge dissolve, terminate its existence, suspend business operations, die (if individual), have a receiver appointed for all or any part of its property, make an assignment for the benefit of creditors, or file or have filed against it any petition under any existing or future bankruptcy or insolvency law; (5) any change that occurs in the condition or affairs (financial or otherwise) of the Borrower or any Guarantor of this promissory note which, in the opinion of the lender,

> impairs, the Lender's security or increases its risk with respect to this promissory note or (6) an event of default shall occur under any agreements intended to secure the repayment of this promissory note. Unless prohibited by law, the Lender may, at its option, declare the entire unpaid balance of principal and interest immediately due and payable without notice or demand at any time after default as such term is defined in this paragraph.

Technically, there was a breach of the security agreement and the promissory note when Moe did not make his payment on October 1, 1984, but instead paid it on December 3, 1984. One could find Moe in default, and under SDCL 57A-9-503, Deere would have had a right to repossess the tractor. However, Deere's right to a default or remedies under breach of contract can be modified or waived by the conduct of the parties.

The trial court's memorandum opinion indicated that "The terms of the written contract should control. Further the 'course of dealing' between the parties is not persuasive." However, here there is a question of fact. Did the oral statements and conduct of the parties modify the written agreement? In Alaska Statebank v. Fairco Fin., 674 P.2d 288 (Alaska 1983), the issue was if the parties' oral statements and conduct between September 15, 1978 and November 6, 1978 modified the written agreement so that pre-possession notice was required. The court held:

> [M]odification of a written contract may be effected either through subsequent conduct or oral agreements. Whether a modification has occurred is a question of fact. The superior court found that the parties had agreed to such modification, "[g]iven the course of dealings between the parties...." Id. at 292 (quoting Nat. Bank of Alaska v. J.B.L. & K. of Alaska, Inc., 546 P.2d 579, 586-87 (Alaska 1976)).

See SDCL 53-8-7 (1990); See also South Dakota Pattern Jury Instruction No. 47-16 for Modification of a Written Contract by Subsequent Oral Agreement.

The record reveals through affidavits and depositions that the oral statements and conduct of the parties herein between October 1, 1984 and July 30, 1986 appear to modify the written agreement. Deere sent notice to Moe that he had until March 20, 1986 to pay $6,389.48 including late charges. Moe admits that in May or the first week of June 1986 he agreed to pay the March installment in two parts. He agreed to pay $2,000.00 with the balance due in August 1986 when he commenced his wheat harvest. There was no date certain by which Moe was to pay the $2,000.00. In determining if there was a default on the part of Moe in complying with this contract, all statements and conduct of the parties are essential in determining whether there was an oral modification or waiver of the promissory note or security agreement by John Deere.

WHETHER A NON-WAIVER CLAUSE IN THIS CONTRACT IS ENFORCEABLE?

The second issue that needs to be addressed is whether the "non-waiver clause" is enforceable in this contract. Deere's brief refers to this clause as an "anti-waiver" clause but we will refer to it as a "non-waiver" clause. See Lewis v. National City Bank, 814 F.Supp. 696, 699 (N.D.Ill.1993) (referring to the clause dealing with waiver provisions as a "non-waiver" clause). The security agreement between Moe and Deere contained the following provisions:

> In the event of default (as defined on the reverse side hereof), holder may take possession of the Goods and exercise any other remedies provided by law.
>
> This contract shall be in default if I (we) shall fail to pay any installment when due....
>
> In any such event (default) the holder may immediately and without notice declare the entire balance of this contract due and payable together with reasonable expenses incurred in realizing on the security interest granted hereunder, including reasonable attorney's fees.
>
> Waiver or condonation of any breach or default shall not constitute a waiver of any other or subsequent breach or default.
>
> We now turn to other jurisdictions' interpretations of the "non-waiver" clause.

Courts have adopted two basic rules for interpreting situations where repeated late payments have been accepted by a creditor who has the contractual (i.e., "non-waiver" clauses) and the statutory right (i.e., SDCL 57A-9-503) to repossess the collateral without notice. Some courts have held that the acceptance of late payments does not waive or otherwise affect the right of a creditor to repossess without notice after subsequent late payment defaults. Westinghouse Credit Corp. v. Shelton, 645 F.2d 869 (10th Cir.1981) . . . . Other courts have imposed a duty on the creditor to notify the debtor that strict compliance with the time for payment will be required in the future or else the contract remedies may be invoked. See, e.g., Cobb v. Midwest Recovery Bureau Co., 295 N.W.2d 232 (Minn.1980); . . . Nevada Nat. Bank v. Huff, 94 Nev. 506, 582 P.2d 364, 369 (1978) . . . .

Deere urges us to adopt the position that the acceptance of late payments does not waive or otherwise affect the right of a creditor to repossess without notice after subsequent late payment defaults stating to do so would mean that the "non-waiver" clause is a nullity.

A majority of states who have considered the issue adhere to the general rule that "a secured party who has not insisted upon strict compliance in the past, who has accepted late payments as a matter of course, must, before he may validly rely upon such a clause to declare a default and effect repossession, give notice to the debtor ... that strict compliance with the terms of the contract will be demanded henceforth if repossession is to be avoided." Huff, 582 P.2d at 369 (citations omitted) (emphasis in original).

The basis for imposing this duty on the secured party is that the secured party is estopped from asserting his contract rights because his conduct has induced the debtor's justified reliance in believing that late payments were acceptable. SDCL 57A-1-103 preserves the law of estoppel. The acts which induced reliance are the repeated acceptance of late payments. The reliance is evidenced by the continual pattern of irregular and late payments.

The debtor has the right to rely on the continuation of the course of performance and that right to rely is sufficient to satisfy the reliance element. See Waters, supra. This right to rely is supported by the policy of the Uniform Commercial Code which encourages the continual development of "commercial practices through, custody, usage, and agreement between the parties." See U.C.C. § 1-102(2) or SDCL 57A-1-102(2). South Dakota's adaptation of the Uniform Commercial Code is found in Title 57A of the South Dakota Code. The purpose of Title 57A is found in SDCL 57A-1-102 and states in pertinent part as follows:

> (1) This title shall be liberally construed and applied to promote its underlying purposes and polices.
>
> (2) Underlying purposes and polices of this title are
>
> (a) To simplify, clarify and modernize the law governing commercial transactions;
>
> (b) To permit the continued expansion of commercial practices, through custom, usage and agreement of the parties; SDCL 57A-1-102(1)-(2) (1988).

The Uniform Commercial Code should be liberally construed and applied to promote its underlying purposes and policies. First Nat. Bank v. John Deere Co., 409 N.W.2d 664 (S.D.1987).

Adopting the rule that a creditor must give pre-possession notice upon modification of a contract results in both the debtor and the creditor being protected. The debtor would be protected from surprise and from a damaging repossession by being forewarned that late payments would no longer be acceptable. Likewise, the creditor would be protected utilizing the device of "one letter." The creditor can totally preserve his remedies so that if the account continues in default, repossession could be pursued as provided in the contract without further demand or notice. It is recognized that this rule does place the creditor in a slightly worse position because if a creditor sends out a letter to preserve his rights and then once again accepts late payments another notice would be required. The second notice would be required because the acceptance of the late payment after the initial letter could again act as a waiver of the rights asserted in the letter.

We hold that the repeated acceptance of late payments by a creditor who has the contractual right to repossess the property imposes a duty on the creditor to notify the debtor that strict compliance with the contract terms will be required before the creditor can lawfully repossess the collateral.

The dispositive issue is if the plaintiff was in default. Whether a default exists is a factual question not properly resolved on a motion for summary judgment. Defendant's right to repossess turns on this default. Therefore what constitutes a "breach of the peace" when repossessing collateral is premature at this time. We reverse this order and the judgment of the circuit court and remand for trial.

MILLER, C.J., and HENDERSON and SABERS, JJ., concur.
WUEST, J., concurs in result and concurs specially.
MOSES, Circuit Judge, for AMUNDSON, J., disqualified. . . .

NOTES AND QUESTIONS:

1. Prevention: In addition to waiver and estoppel, a party may be excused from performance if such performance is prevented by the conduct of the other party. For a discussion of the circumstances giving rise to this excuse, read *Sullivan v. Bullock*, 864 P.2d 184 (Idaho Ct. App. 1993).

2. Impossibility: As previously discussed under Defenses and Other Doctrines of Avoidance, impossibility may serve as an excuse for nonperformance. In such cases, the impossibility of performance by one party may also excuse the other party's performance. Read *Shaw v. Mobil Oil Corp.*, 535 P.2d 756 (Or. 1975) for a discussion of the mutual availability of this excuse.

CHAPTER FIVE

REMEDIES

*One of the many evil effects of the confusion between legal and moral ideas . . . is that theory is apt to get the cart before the horse, and to consider the right or the duty as something existing apart from and independent of the consequences of its breach, to which certain sanctions are added afterward.**

Justice O.W. Holmes

SECTION 1. INTRODUCTION

At this point, we digress to discuss mechanisms for enforcing a contract. Although it may seem premature to discuss remedies before defenses, an examination of the policies behind contractual remedies, as well as the types of relief available to a party to redress another's incomplete, defective, or nonperformance, will provide insight for the material that follows. The basic premise behind contractual remedies is an aggrieved party should receive a substitute for the performance they expected under the contract. To that end, the goal is to compensate for the missed performance. However, what is adequate compensation for the missed performance depends on what you are trying to achieve. Consider the following:

A. Sportsco entered into a contract with Builder for the construction of a sports complex for $100,000. Sportsco then entered into a separate contract with a local sports team whereby the team agreed to rent the sports complex for a year for $50,000. Builder failed to build the sports complex.

B. Writer entered into a contract with Publisher in which Publisher agreed to publish, market and distribute Writer's manuscript. In return writer would be paid royalties in the amount of 30% of the sales. Publisher refused to perform.

C. Seller entered into a contract with Buyer for the sale of a residence for $200,000. Buyer refused to go through with the purchase. Accordingly, Seller paid $200 to re-advertise the property and subsequently sold it to another buyer for $180,000.

For each scenario, consider what kinds of things should be taken into account in determining an appropriate substitute for the missed performance. Should the nonperforming party be ordered to perform as promised? Will money suffice to compensate for the missed performance? If so, how are we to determine how much money is appropriate?

---

* Justice O.W. Holmes *The Path of the Law*, 10 HARV. L. REV. 457, 458 (1897).

Should the reason for the nonperformance matter in determining the appropriateness of a remedy? Obviously, not all breaches are caused by the same set of circumstances. Some are caused by circumstances beyond the control of the breaching party. Others stem from a conscious decision by the breaching party that it would be better off if it did not go through with the deal. Still others are the result of concerted effort to adversely affect the other party. Recall the discussion regarding moral versus economic approaches to a contractual arrangement. From a morality standpoint, if a party promises to render performance under a contract, he should be required to do so, not only by his conscience, but by the force of the law. From an economic standpoint, if one party would be better off by not performing and the other party can be adequately compensated for the missed performance, there is little to be gained by requiring performance under the contract.

Now, consider the following underpinnings in Contract Law:

1. The primary goal of contractual remedies is not to punish the breaching party but to compensate the aggrieved party for the missed performance.[1]

2. In determining the appropriateness of a remedy to redress a breach, we should be careful to avoid putting the aggrieved party in a better position than he or she would have occupied had the contract been fully performed.[2]

As you study the materials in this chapter, ask yourself, "What is the desired goal in redressing the incomplete performance, and what is the best method for doing this?"

RESTATEMENT (SECOND) OF CONTRACTS
§ 344. PURPOSES OF REMEDIES

Judicial remedies under the rules stated in this Restatement serve to protect one or more of the following interests of a promisee:

(a) his "expectation interest," which is his interest in having the benefit of his bargain by being put in as good a position as he would have been in had the contract been performed,

(b) his "reliance interest," which is his interest in being reimbursed for loss caused by reliance on the contract by being put in as good a position as he would have been in had the contract not been made, or

(c) his "restitution interest," which is his interest in having restored to him any benefit that he has conferred on the other party.

---

[1] See E. Allan Farnsworth, Contracts s. 12.8, at 760 (4th ed. 2004).

[2] See id.

TEXAS BUSINESS & COMMERCIAL CODE
§ 1.305. REMEDIES TO BE LIBERALLY ADMINISTERED.
TEX. BUS. & COM. CODE § 1.305 (2011).

(a) The remedies provided by this title must be liberally administered to the end that the aggrieved party may be put in as good a position as if the other party had fully performed but neither consequential or special damages nor penal damages may be had except as specifically provided in [the Uniform Commercial Code] or by other rule of law.

(b) Any right or obligation declared by this title is enforceable by action unless the provision declaring it specifies a different and limited effect.

SECTION 2. DAMAGES

A. MEASURING EXPECTATION DAMAGES

HAWKINS V. MCGEE
Supreme Court of New Hampshire
146 A. 641 (1929).

BRANCH, J.

The operation in question consisted in the removal of a considerable quantity of scar tissue from the palm of the plaintiff's right hand and the grafting of skin taken from the plaintiff's chest in place thereof. The scar tissue was the result of a severe burn caused by contact with an electric wire, which the plaintiff received about nine years before the time of the transactions here involved. There was evidence to the effect that before the operation was performed the plaintiff and his father went to the defendant's office, and that the defendant, in answer to the question, "How long will the boy be in the hospital?" replied, "Three or four days, not over four; then the boy can go home and it will be just a few days when he will go back to work with a good hand." Clearly this and other testimony to the same effect would not justify a finding that the doctor contracted to complete the hospital treatment in three or four days or that the plaintiff would be able to go back to work within a few days thereafter. The above statements could only be construed as expressions of opinion or predictions as to the probable duration of the treatment and plaintiff's resulting disability, and the fact that these estimates were exceeded would impose no contractual liability upon the defendant. The only substantial basis for the plaintiff's claim is the testimony that the defendant also said before the operation was decided upon, "I will guarantee to make the hand a hundred per cent perfect hand or a hundred per cent good hand." The plaintiff was present when these words were alleged to have been spoken, and, if they are to be taken at their face value, it seems obvious that proof of their utterance would establish the giving of a warranty in accordance with his contention.

The defendant argues, however, that, even if these words were uttered by him, no reasonable man would understand that they were used with the intention of entering "into any contractual relation whatever," and that they could reasonably be understood only "as his expression in strong language that he believed and expected that as a result of the operation he would give the plaintiff a very good hand." It may be conceded, as the defendant contends, that, before the question of the making of a contract should be submitted to a jury, there is a preliminary question of law for the trial court to pass upon, i. e. "whether the words could possibly have the meaning imputed to them by the party who founds his case upon a certain interpretation," but it cannot be held that the trial court decided this question erroneously in the present case. It is unnecessary to determine at this time whether the argument of the defendant, based upon "common knowledge of the uncertainty which attends all surgical operations," and the improbability that a surgeon would ever contract to make a damaged part of the human body "one hundred per cent perfect," would, in the absence of countervailing considerations, be regarded as conclusive, for there were other factors in the present case which tended to support the contention of the plaintiff. There was evidence that the defendant repeatedly solicited from the plaintiff's father the opportunity to perform this operation, and the theory was advanced by plaintiff's counsel in cross-examination of defendant that he sought an opportunity to "experiment on skin grafting," in which he had had little previous experience. If the jury accepted this part of plaintiff's contention, there would be a reasonable basis for the further conclusion that, if defendant spoke the words attributed to him, he did so with the intention that they should be accepted at their face value, as an inducement for the granting of consent to the operation by the plaintiff and his father, and there was ample evidence that they were so accepted by them. The question of the making of the alleged contract was properly submitted to the jury.

The substance of the charge to the jury on the question of damages appears in the following quotation: "If you find the plaintiff entitled to anything, he is entitled to recover for what pain and suffering he has been made to endure and for what injury he has sustained over and above what injury he had before." To this instruction the defendant seasonably excepted. By it, the jury was permitted to consider two elements of damage: (1) Pain and suffering due to the operation; and (2) positive ill effects of the operation upon the plaintiff's hand. Authority for any specific rule of damages in cases of this kind seems to be lacking, but, when tested by general principle and by analogy, it appears that the foregoing instruction was erroneous.

"By 'damages,' as that term is used in the law of contracts, is intended compensation for a breach, measured in the terms of the contract." Davis v. New England Cotton Yarn Co., 77 N. H. 403, 404, 92 A. 732, 733. The purpose of the law is "to put the plaintiff in as good a position as he would have been in had the defendant kept his contract." 3 Williston Cont. § 1338; Hardie-Tynes Mfg. Co. v. Easton Cotton Oil Co., 150 N. C. 150, 63 S. E. 676, 134 Am. St. Rep. 899. The measure of recovery "is based upon what the defendant should have given the plaintiff, not what the plaintiff has given the defendant or otherwise expended." 3 Williston Cont. § 1341. "The only losses that can be said fairly to come within the terms of a contract are such as the parties must have had in mind when the contract was made, or such as they either knew or ought to have known would probably result from a failure to comply with its terms." Davis v. New England Cotton Yarn Co., 77 N. H. 403, 404, 92 A. 732, 733, Hurd v. Dunsmore, 63 N. H. 171.

The present case is closely analogous to one in which a machine is built for a certain purpose and warranted to do certain work. In such cases, the usual rule of damages for breach of warranty in the sale of chattels is applied, and it is held that the measure of damages is the difference between the value of the machine, if it had corresponded with the warranty and its actual value, together with such incidental losses as the parties knew, or ought to have known, would probably result from a failure to comply with its terms. Hooper v. Story, 155 N. Y. 171, 175, 49 N. E. 773; Adams Hardware Co. v. Wimbish, 201 Ala. 548, 78 So. 902 . . . .

The rule thus applied is well settled in this state. "As a general rule, the measure of the vendee's damages is the difference between the value of the goods as they would have been if the warranty as to quality had been true, and the actual value at the time of the sale, including gains prevented and losses sustained, and such other damages as could be reasonably anticipated by the parties as likely to be caused by the vendor's failure to keep his agreement, and could not by reasonable care on the part of the vendee have been avoided." Union Bank v. Blanchard, 65 N. H. 21, 23, 18 A. 90, 91; Hurd v. Dunsmore, supra; Noyes v. Blodgett, 58 N. H. 502; P. L. ch. 166, § 69, subd. 7. We therefore conclude that the true measure of the plaintiff's damage in the present case is the difference between the value to him of a perfect hand or a good hand, such as the jury found the defendant promised him, and the value of his hand in its present condition, including any incidental consequences fairly within the contemplation of the parties when they made their contract. 1 Sutherland, Damages (4th Ed.) § 92. Damages not thus limited, although naturally resulting, are not to be given.

The extent of the plaintiff's suffering does not measure this difference in value. The pain necessarily incident to a serious surgical operation was a part of the contribution which the plaintiff was willing to make to his joint undertaking with the defendant to produce a good hand. It was a legal detriment suffered by him which constituted a part of the consideration given by him for the contract. It represented a part of the price which he was willing to pay for a good hand, but it furnished no test of the value of a good hand or the difference between the value of the hand which the defendant promised and the one which resulted from the operation.

It was also erroneous and misleading to submit to the jury as a separate element of damage any change for the worse in the condition of the plaintiff's hand resulting from the operation, although this error was probably more prejudicial to the plaintiff than to the defendant. Any such ill effect of the operation would be included under the true rule of damages set forth above, but damages might properly be assessed for the defendant's failure to improve the condition of the hand, even if there were no evidence that its condition was made worse as a result of the operation.

It must be assumed that the trial court, in setting aside the verdict, undertook to apply the same rule of damages which he had previously given to the jury, and, since this rule was erroneous, it is unnecessary for us to consider whether there was any evidence to justify his finding that all damages awarded by the jury above $500 were excessive.

Defendant's requests for instructions were loosely drawn, and were properly denied. A considerable number of issues of fact were raised by the evidence, and it would have been extremely misleading to instruct the jury in accordance with defendant's request No. 2, that "the only issue on which you have to pass is whether or not there was a special contract between the plaintiff and the defendant to produce a perfect hand." Equally inaccurate was defendant's request No. 5, which reads as follows: "You would have to find, in order to hold the defendant liable in this case, that Dr. McGee and the plaintiff both understood that the doctor was guaranteeing a perfect result from this operation." If the defendant said that he would guarantee a perfect result, and the plaintiff relied upon that promise, any mental reservations which he may have had are immaterial. The standard by which his conduct is to be judged is not internal, but external. Woburn Bank v. Woods, 77 N. H. 172, 89 A. 491; McConnell v. Lamontagne, 82 N. H. 423, 425, 134 A. 718; Eleftherion v. Great Falls Mfg. Co. 83 N. H., 146 A. 172.

Defendant's request No. 7 was as follows: "If you should get so far as to find that there was a special contract guaranteeing a perfect result, you would still have to find for the defendant unless you also found that a further operation would not correct the disability claimed by the plaintiff." In view of the testimony that the defendant had refused to perform a further operation, it would clearly have been erroneous to give this instruction. The evidence would have justified a verdict for an amount sufficient to cover the cost of such an operation, even if the theory underlying this request were correct.

It is unlikely that the questions now presented in regard to the argument of plaintiff's counsel will arise at another trial, and therefore they have not been considered.

New trial.

LEINGANG V. CITY OF MANDAN WEED BOARD
Supreme Court of North Dakota
468 N.W.2d 397 (1991).

LEVINE, Justice.

Robert Leingang appeals from an award of damages for breach of contract. The issue is whether the trial court used the appropriate measure of damages. We hold it did not, and reverse and remand.

The City of Mandan Weed Board awarded Leingang a contract to cut weeds on lots with an area greater than 10,000 square feet. Another contractor received the contract for smaller lots. During 1987, Leingang discovered that the Weed Board's agent was improperly assigning large lots to the small-lot contractor. Leingang complained and the weed board assigned some substitute lots to him.

Leingang brought a breach of contract action in small claims court and the City removed the action to county court. The City admitted that it had prevented Leingang's performance under the contract and that the contract price for the lost work was $1,933.78. A bench trial was held to assess the damages suffered by Leingang.

At trial, Leingang argued that the applicable measure of damages was the contract price less the costs of performance he avoided due to the breach. Leingang testified that the total gas, oil, repair and replacement blade expenses saved when he was prevented from cutting the erroneously assigned lots was $211.18.

The City argued that to identify Leingang's damages for net profits, some of Leingang's overhead expenses should be attributed to the weed cutting contract and deducted from the contract price. The City offered testimony about the profitability of businesses in Mandan and testimony from Leingang's competitor about the profitability of a weed cutting business in Mandan. The City also offered Leingang's 1986 and 1987 federal tax returns. Based on the Schedule C-"Profit or Loss From Business"-in those returns, the City argued that Leingang attributed considerably more expenses to the business of cutting weeds than he had testified he had avoided.

The trial court adopted what it called a "modified net profit" approach as the measure of damages. It derived a profit margin of 20% by subtracting four categories of expenses reported on Leingang's Schedule C, and attributed to the weed-cutting business, from the weed-cutting income reported to the IRS. The trial court selected insurance, repairs, supplies, and car and truck expenses as costs attributed to the weed-cutting business. Applying the profit margin of 20% to the contract price, the trial court deducted 80% from the contract price as expenses and awarded Leingang $368.59 plus interest. Leingang appeals.

Leingang contends that the method used by the trial court to derive net profits was improper because it did not restrict the expenses that are deductible from the contract price to those which would have been incurred but for the breach of the contract, i.e., those expenses Leingang did not have to pay because the City kept him from doing the work. We agree.

For a breach of contract, the injured party is entitled to compensation for the loss suffered, but can recover no more than would have been gained by full performance. NDCC §§ 32-03-09, 32-03-36. Our law thus incorporates the notion that contract damages should give the nonbreaching party the benefit of the bargain by awarding a sum of money that will put that person in as good a position as if the contract had been performed. See generally 22 Am.Jur.2d Damages § 45 (1988). Where the contract is for service and the breach prevents the performance of that service, the value of the contract consists of two items: (1) the party's reasonable expenditures toward performance, including costs paid, material wasted, and time and services spent on the contract, and (2) the anticipated profits. Welch Mfg. Co. v. Herbst Dept. Store, 53 N.D. 42, 204 N.W. 849, 854 (1925). Thus, a party is entitled to recover for the detriment caused by the defendant's breach, including lost profits if they are reasonable and not speculative . . . .

Where a plaintiff offers evidence estimating anticipated profits with reasonable certainty, they may be awarded. See King Features Synd. v. Courrier, 241 Iowa 870, 43 N.W.2d 718 (1950). In King Features, the plaintiff proved the value of its anticipated profits by reducing the contract price by the amount it would have spent to perform. The court held that this proof was reasonably certain. In quantifying the costs of performance, the plaintiff did not deduct "overhead" expenses because the evidence established that those expenses were constant whether or not the contract was performed. 43 N.W.2d at 725-26.

The King Features approach fulfills the Welch Mfg. requirement that a plaintiff be compensated for all the detriment caused by the breach. Under King Features, constant overhead expenses are not deducted from the contract price because they are expenses the plaintiff had to pay whether or not the contract was breached. The King Features approach compensates plaintiff for constant overhead expenses by allowing an award of the contract price, reduced only by expenses actually saved because the contract did not have to be performed. The remaining contract proceeds are available to pay constant expenses. See also Buono Sales, Inc. v. Chrysler Motors Corp., 449 F.2d 715, 720 (3d Cir.1971) [because fixed expenses must be paid from the sum remaining after costs of performance are deducted, further reducing contract price by fixed expenses would not fully, or fairly, compensate plaintiff].

Neither side argues that lost profits are not calculable here. Instead, each urges a different method for computing lost profits. In measuring Leingang's anticipated profits, the trial court erroneously calculated a "net profit" margin by deducting general costs of doing business including insurance, repairs, supplies, and car and truck expenses, without determining whether these costs remained constant regardless of the City's breach and whether they were, therefore, not to be deducted from the contract price. King Features, 43 N.W.2d at 726. The reduction from the contract price of a portion of the "fixed," or constant expenses, effectively required Leingang to pay that portion twice. See Buono Sales, Inc., 449 F.2d at 720.

We reverse the judgment and remand for a new trial on the issue of damages.

NOTES AND QUESTIONS:

1. Read U.C.C. §§ 2-706 (Seller's Resale Including Contract for Resale); 2-708 (Seller's Damages for Non-acceptance or Repudiation); 2-709 (Action for the Price); 2-712 ("Cover"; Buyer's Procurement of Substitute Goods); 2-713 (Buyer's Damages for Non-delivery or Repudiation); and 2-714 (Buyer's Damages for Breach in Regard to Accepted Goods). How do these code sections compare with the expectancy measure of damages? We will return to these provisions when we examine U.C.C. damages.

RESTATEMENT (SECOND) OF CONTRACTS
§ 347. MEASURE OF DAMAGES IN GENERAL

Subject to the limitations stated in §§ 350-53, the injured party has a right to damages based on his expectation interest as measured by

(a) the loss in the value to him of the other party's performance caused by its failure or deficiency, plus

(b) any other loss, including incidental or consequential loss, caused by the breach, less

(c) any cost or other loss that he has avoided by not having to perform.

JACOB & YOUNGS, INC. V. KENT
Court of Appeals of New York
230 N.Y. 239 (1921).

CARDOZO, J.

The plaintiff built a country residence for the defendant at a cost of upwards of $77,000, and now sues to recover a balance of $3,483.46, remaining unpaid. The work of construction ceased in June, 1914, and the defendant then began to occupy the dwelling. There was no complaint of defective performance until March, 1915. One of the specifications for the plumbing work provides that "all wrought iron pipe must be well galvanized, lap welded pipe of the grade known as 'standard pipe' of Reading manufacture." The defendant learned in March, 1915, that some of the pipe, instead of being made in Reading, was the product of other factories. The plaintiff was accordingly directed by the architect to do the work anew. The plumbing was then encased within the walls except in a few places where it had to be exposed. Obedience to the order meant more than the substitution of other pipe. It meant the demolition at great expense of substantial parts of the completed structure. The plaintiff left the work untouched, and asked for a certificate that the final payment was due. Refusal of the certificate was followed by this suit.

The evidence sustains a finding that the omission of the prescribed brand of pipe was neither fraudulent nor willful. It was the result of the oversight and inattention of the plaintiff's subcontractor. Reading pipe is distinguished from Cohoes pipe and other brands only by the name of the manufacturer stamped upon it at intervals of between six and seven feet. Even the defendant's architect, though he inspected the pipe upon arrival, failed to notice the discrepancy. The plaintiff tried to show that the brands installed, though made by other manufacturers, were the same in quality, in appearance, in market value and in cost as the brand stated in the contract--that they were, indeed, the same thing, though manufactured in another place. The evidence was excluded, and a verdict directed for the defendant. The Appellate Division reversed, and granted a new trial.

We think the evidence, if admitted, would have supplied some basis for the inference that the defect was insignificant in its relation to the project. The courts never say that one who makes a contract fills the measure of his duty by less than full performance. They do say, however, that an omission, both trivial and innocent, will sometimes be atoned for by allowance of the resulting damage, and will not always be the breach of a condition to be followed by a forfeiture . . . .

Where the line is to be drawn between the important and the trivial cannot be settled by a formula. "In the nature of the case precise boundaries are impossible" (2 Williston on Contracts, sec. 841). The same omission may take on one aspect or another according to its setting. Substitution of equivalents may not have the same significance in fields of art on the one side and in those of mere utility on the other. Nowhere will change be tolerated, however, if it is so dominant or pervasive as in any real or substantial measure to frustrate the purpose of the contract. There is no general license to install whatever, in the builder's judgment, may be regarded as "just as good." The question is one of degree, to be answered, if there is doubt, by the triers of the facts (Crouch v. Gutmann; Woodward v. Fuller, supra), and, if the inferences are certain, by the judges of the law (Easthampton L. & C. Co., Ltd., v. Worthington, supra). We must weigh the purpose to be served, the desire to be gratified, the excuse for deviation from the letter, the cruelty of enforced adherence. Then only can we tell whether literal fulfilment is to be implied by law as a condition. This is not to say that the parties are not free by apt and certain words to effectuate a purpose that performance of every term shall be a condition of recovery. That question is not here. This is merely to say that the law will be slow to impute the purpose, in the silence of the parties, where the significance of the default is grievously out of proportion to the oppression of the forfeiture. The willful transgressor must accept the penalty of his transgression (Schultze v. Goodstein, 180 N. Y. 248, 251; Desmond-Dunne Co. v. Friedman-Doscher Co., 162 N. Y. 486, 490). For him there is no occasion to mitigate the rigor of implied conditions. The transgressor whose default is unintentional and trivial may hope for mercy if he will offer atonement for his wrong (Spence v. Ham, supra).

In the circumstances of this case, we think the measure of the allowance is not the cost of replacement, which would be great, but the difference in value, which would be either nominal or nothing . . . . It is true that in most cases the cost of replacement is the measure (Spence v. Ham, supra). The owner is entitled to the money which will permit him to complete, unless the cost of completion is grossly and unfairly out of proportion to the good to be attained. When that is true, the measure is the difference in value. Specifications call, let us say, for a foundation built of granite quarried in Vermont. On the completion of the building, the owner learns that through the blunder of a subcontractor part of the foundation has been built of granite of the same quality quarried in New Hampshire. The measure of allowance is not the cost of reconstruction. "There may be omissions of that which could not afterwards be supplied exactly as called for by the contract without taking down the building to its foundations, and at the same time the omission may not affect the value of the building for use or otherwise, except so slightly as to be hardly appreciable" (Handy v. Bliss, 204 Mass. 513, 519. Cf. Foeller v. Heintz, 137 Wis. 169, 178; Oberlies v. Bullinger, 132 N. Y. 598, 601; 2 Williston on Contracts, sec. 805, p. 1541). The rule that gives a remedy in cases of substantial performance with compensation for defects of trivial or inappreciable importance, has been developed by the courts as an instrument of justice. The measure of the allowance must be shaped to the same end.

The order should be affirmed, and judgment absolute directed in favor of the plaintiff upon the stipulation, with costs in all courts.

GROVES V. JOHN WUNDER CO.
Supreme Court of Minnesota
205 Minn. 163 (1939).

STONE, Justice.

Action for breach of contract. Plaintiff got judgment for a little over $15,000. Sorely disappointed by that sum, he appeals.

In August, 1927, S. J. Groves & Sons Company, a corporation (hereinafter mentioned simply as Groves), owned a tract of 24 acres of Minneapolis suburban real estate.

It was served or easily could be reached by railroad trackage. It is zoned as heavy industrial property. But for lack of development of the neighborhood its principal value thus far may have been in the deposit of sand and gravel which it carried. The Groves company had a plant on the premises for excavating and screening the gravel. Nearby defendant owned and was operating a similar plant.

In August, 1927, Groves and defendant made the involved contract. For the most part it was a lease from Groves, as lessor, to defendant, as lessee; its term seven years. Defendant agreed to remove the sand and gravel and to leave the property 'at a uniform grade, substantially the same as the grade now existing at the roadway . . . on said premises, and that in stripping the overburden . . . it will use said overburden for the purpose of maintaining and establishing said grade.'

Under the contract defendant got the Groves screening plant. The transfer thereof and the right to remove the sand and gravel made the consideration moving from Groves to defendant, except that defendant incidentally got rid of Groves as a competitor. On defendant's part it paid Groves $105,000. So that from the outset, on Groves' part the contract was executed except for defendant's right to continue using the property for the stated term. (Defendant had a right to renewal which it did not exercise.)

Defendant breached the contract deliberately. It removed from the premises only "the richest and best of the gravel" and wholly failed, according to the findings, "to perform and comply with the terms, conditions, and provisions of said lease . . . with respect to the condition in which the surface of the demised premises was required to be left." Defendant surrendered the premises, not substantially at the grade required by the contract "nor at any uniform grade." Instead, the ground was "broken, rugged, and uneven." Plaintiff sues as assignee and successor in right of Groves.

As the contract was construed below, the finding is that to complete its performance 288,495 cubic yards of overburden would need to be excavated, taken from the premises, and deposited elsewhere. The reasonable cost of doing that was found to be upwards of $60,000. But, if defendant had left the premises at the uniform grade required by the lease, the reasonable value of the property on the determinative date would have been only $12,160. The judgment was for that sum, including interest, thereby nullifying plaintiff's claim that cost of completing the contract rather than difference in value of the land was the measure of damages. The gauge of damage adopted by the decision was the difference between the market value of plaintiff's land in the condition it was when the contract was made and what it would have been if defendant had performed. The one question for us arises upon plaintiff's assertion that he was entitled, not to that difference in value, but to the reasonable cost to him of doing the work called for by the contract which defendant left undone.

Defendant's breach of contract was wilful. There was nothing of good faith about it. Hence, that the decision below handsomely rewards bad faith and deliberate breach of contract is obvious. That is not allowable. Here the rule is well settled, and has been since Elliott v. Caldwell, 43 Minn. 357, 45 N.W. 845, 9 L.R.A. 52, that, where the contractor wilfully and fraudulently varies from the terms of a construction contract, he cannot sue thereon and have the benefit of the equitable doctrine of substantial performance. That is the rule generally. See Annotation, "Wilful or intentional variation by contractor from terms of contract in regard to material or work as affecting measure of damages," 6 A.L.R. 137.

Jacob & Youngs, Inc. v. Kent, 230 N.Y. 239, 243, 244, 129 N.E. 889, 891, 23 A.L.R. 1429, is typical. It was a case of substantial performance of a building contract. (This case is distrinctly the opposite.) Mr. Justice Cardozo, in the course of his opinion, stressed the distinguishing features. "Nowhere," he said, "will change be tolerated, however, if it is so dominant or pervasive as in any real or substantial measure to frustrate the purpose of the contract." Again, "the willful transgressor must accept the penalty of his transgression."

In reckoning damages for breach of a building or construction contract, the law aims to give the disappointed promisee, so far as money will do it, what he was promised. 9 Am.Jur. Building and Construction Contracts, § 152. It is so ruled by a long line of decisions in this state, beginning with Carli v. Seymour, Sabin & Co., 26 Minn. 276, 3 N.W. 348, where the contract was for building a road. There was a breach. Plaintiff was held entitled to recover what it would cost to complete the grading as contemplated by the contract. For our other similar cases, see 2 Dunnell, Minn. Dig. (2 ed. & Supp.) §§ 2561, 2565.

Never before, so far as our decisions show, has it even been suggested that lack of value in the land furnished to the contractor who had bound himself to improve it any escape from the ordinary consequences of a breach of the contract.

A case presently as interesting as any of our own, is Sassen v. Haegle, 125 Minn. 441, 147 N.W. 445, 446, 52 L.R.A.,N.S., 1176. The defendant, lessee of a farm, had agreed to haul and spread manure. He removed it, but spread it elsewhere than on the leased farm. Plaintiff had a verdict, but a new trial was ordered for error in the charge as to the measure of damages. The point was thus discussed by Mr. Justice Holt [125 Minn. page 443, 147 N.W. page 446, 52 L.R.A.,N.S., 1176]: "But it is also true that the landlord had a perfect right to stipulate as to the disposal of the manure or as to the way in which the farm should be worked, and the tenant cannot evade compliance by showing that the farm became more valuable or fertile by omitting the agreed work or doing other work. Plaintiff's pleading and proof was directed to the reasonable value of performing what defendant agreed but failed to perform. Such reasonable cost or value was the natural and proximate damages. The question is not whether plaintiff made a wise or foolish agreement. He had a right to have it performed as made, and the resulting damage, in case of failure, is the reasonable cost of performance. Whether such performance affects the value of the farm was no concern of defendant."

Even in case of substantial performance in good faith, the resulting defects being remediable, it is error to instruct that the measure of damage is "the difference in value between the house as it was and as it would have been if constructed according to contract." The "correct doctrine" is that the cost of remedying the defect is the "proper" measure of damages. Snider v. Peters Home Building Co., 139 Minn. 413, 414, 416, 167 N.W. 108.

Value of the land (as distinguished from the value of the intended product of the contract, which ordinarily will be equivalent to its reasonable cost) is no proper part of any measure of damages for wilful breach of a building contract. The reason is plain.

The summit from which to reckon damages from trespass to real estate is its actual value at the moment. The owner's only right is to be compensated for the deterioration in value caused by the tort. That is all he has lost. But not so if a contract to improve the same land has been breached by the contractor who refuses to do the work, especially where, as here, he has been paid in advance. The summit from which to reckon damages for that wrong is the hypothetical peak of accomplishment (not value) which would have been reached had the work been done as demanded by the contract.

The owner's right to improve his property is not trammeled by its small value. It is his right to erect thereon structures which will reduce its value. If that be the result, it can be of no aid to any contractor who declines performance. As said long ago in Chamberlain v. Parker, 45 N.Y. 569, 572: "A man may do what he will with his own, and if he chooses to erect a monument to his caprice or folly on his premises, and employs and pays another to do it, it does not lie with a defendant who has been so employed and paid for building it, to say that his own performance would not be beneficial to the plaintiff." To the same effect is Restatement, Contracts, § 346, p. 576, Illustrations of Subsection (1), par. 4.

To diminish damages recoverable against him in proportion as there is presently small value in the land would favor the faithless contractor. It would also ignore and so defeat plaintiff's right to contract and build for the future. To justify such a course would require more of the prophetic vision than judges possess. This factor is important when the subject matter is trackage property in the margin of such an area of population and industry as that of the Twin Cities.

The objective of this contract of present importance was the improvement of real estate. That makes irrelevant the rules peculiar to damages to chattels, arising from tort or breach of contract. Crowley v. Burns Boiler & Mfg. Co., 100 Minn. 178, 187, 110 N.W. 969, 973, dealt with a breach of contract for the sale of a steam boiler. The court observed: "If the application of a particular rule for measuring damages to given facts results in more than compensation, it is at once apparent that the wrong rule has been adopted."

That is unquestioned law, but for its correct application there must be ascertainment of the loss for which compensation is to be reckoned. In tort, the thing lost is money value, nothing more. But under a construction contract, the thing lost by a breach such as we have here is a physical structure or accomplishment, a promised and paid for alteration in land. That is the "injury" for which the law gives him compensation. Its only appropriate measure is the cost of performance.

It is suggested that because of little or no value in his land the owner may be unconscionably enriched by such a reckoning. The answer is that there can be no unconscionable enrichment, no advantage upon which the law will frown, when the result is but to give one party to a contract only what the other has promised; particularly where, as here, the delinquent has had full payment for the promised performance.

It is said by the Restatement, Contracts, § 346, comment b: "Sometimes defects in a completed structure cannot be physically remedied without tearing down and rebuilding, at a cost that would be imprudent and unreasonable. The law does not require damages to be measured by a method requiring such economic waste. If no such waste is involved, the cost of remedying the defect is the amount awarded as compensation for failure to render the promised performance."

The "economic waste" declaimed against by the decisions applying that rule has nothing to do with the value in money of the real estate, or even with the product of the contract. The waste avoided is only that which would come from wrecking a physical structure, completed, or nearly so, under the contract. The cases applying that rule go no further. Illustrative are Buchholz v. Rosenberg, 163 Wis. 312, 156 N.W. 946; Burmeister v. Wolfgram, 175 Wis. 506, 185 N.W. 517. Absent such waste, as it is in this case, the rule of the Restatement, Contracts, § 346, is that "the cost of remedying the defect is the amount awarded as compensation for failure to render the promised performance." That means that defendants here are liable to plaintiff for the reasonable cost of doing what defendants promised to do and have wilfully declined to do. . . .

The judgment must be reversed with a new trial to follow.

So ordered.

PEEVYHOUSE V. GARLAND COAL & MINING CO.
Supreme Court of Oklahoma
382 P.2d 109 (1962).

JACKSON, Justice.

In the trial court, plaintiffs Willie and Lucille Peevyhouse sued the defendant, Garland Coal and Mining Company, for damages for breach of contract. Judgment was for plaintiffs in an amount considerably less than was sued for. Plaintiffs appeal and defendant cross-appeals.

In the briefs on appeal, the parties present their argument and contentions under several propositions; however, they all stem from the basic question of whether the trial court properly instructed the jury on the measure of damages.

Briefly stated, the facts are as follows: plaintiffs owned a farm containing coal deposits, and in November, 1954, leased the premises to defendant for a period of five years for coal mining purposes. A "stripmining" operation was contemplated in which the coal would be taken from pits on the surface of the ground, instead of from underground mine shafts. In addition to the usual covenants found in a coal mining lease, defendant specifically agreed to perform certain restorative and remedial work at the end of the lease period. It is unnecessary to set out the details of the work to be done, other than to say that it would involve the moving of many thousands of cubic yards of dirt, at a cost estimated by expert witnesses at about $29,000.00. However, plaintiffs sued for only $25,000.00.

During the trial, it was stipulated that all covenants and agreements in the lease contract had been fully carried out by both parties, except the remedial work mentioned above; defendant conceded that this work had not been done.

Plaintiffs introduced expert testimony as to the amount and nature of the work to be done, and its estimated cost. Over plaintiffs' objections, defendant thereafter introduced expert testimony as to the "diminution in value" of plaintiffs' farm resulting from the failure of defendant to render performance as agreed in the contract-that is, the difference between the present value of the farm, and what its value would have been if defendant had done what it agreed to do.

At the conclusion of the trial, the court instructed the jury that it must return a verdict for plaintiffs, and left the amount of damages for jury determination. On the measure of damages, the court instructed the jury that it might consider the cost of performance of the work defendant agreed to do, "together with all of the evidence offered on behalf of either party."

It thus appears that the jury was at liberty to consider the "diminution in value" of plaintiffs' farm as well as the cost of "repair work" in determining the amount of damages.

It returned a verdict for plaintiffs for $5000.00-only a fraction of the "cost of performance," but more than the total value of the farm even after the remedial work is done.

On appeal, the issue is sharply drawn. Plaintiffs contend that the true measure of damages in this case is what it will cost plaintiffs to obtain performance of the work that was not done because of defendant's default. Defendant argues that the measure of damages is the cost of performance "limited, however, to the total difference in the market value before and after the work was performed."

It appears that this precise question has not heretofore been presented to this court. In Ardizonne v. Archer, 72 Okl. 70, 178 P. 263, this court held that the measure of damages for breach of a contract to drill an oil well was the reasonable cost of drilling the well, but here a slightly different factual situation exists. The drilling of an oil well will yield valuable geological information, even if no oil or gas is found, and of course if the well is a producer, the value of the premises increases. In the case before us, it is argued by defendant with some force that the performance of the remedial work defendant agreed to do will add at the most only a few hundred dollars to the value of plaintiffs' farm, and that the damages should be limited to that amount because that is all plaintiffs have lost.

Plaintiffs rely on Groves v. John Wunder Co., 205 Minn. 163, 286 N.W. 235, 123 A.L.R. 502. In that case, the Minnesota court, in a substantially similar situation, adopted the "cost of performance" rule as-opposed to the "value" rule. The result was to authorize a jury to give plaintiff damages in the amount of $60,000, where the real estate concerned would have been worth only $12,160, even if the work contracted for had been done.

It may be observed that Groves v. John Wunder Co., supra, is the only case which has come to our attention in which the cost of performance rule has been followed under circumstances where the cost of performance greatly exceeded the diminution in value resulting from the breach of contract . . . .

Defendant relies principally upon Sandy Valley & E. R. Co., v. Hughes, 175 Ky. 320, 194 S.W. 344; Bigham v. Wabash-Pittsburg Terminal Ry. Co., 223 Pa. 106, 72 A. 318; and Sweeney v. Lewis Const. Co., 66 Wash. 490, 119 P. 1108. These were all cases in which, under similar circumstances, the appellate courts followed the "value" rule instead of the "cost of performance" rule. Plaintiff points out that in the earliest of these cases (Bigham) the court cites as authority on the measure of damages an earlier Pennsylvania tort case, and that the other two cases follow the first, with no explanation as to why a measure of damages ordinarily followed in cases sounding in tort should be used in contract cases. Nevertheless, it is of some significance that three out of four appellate courts have followed the diminution in value rule under circumstances where, as here, the cost of performance greatly exceeds the diminution in value.

The explanation may be found in the fact that the situations presented are artificial ones. It is highly unlikely that the ordinary property owner would agree to pay $29,000 (or its equivalent) for the construction of "improvements" upon his property that would increase its value only about ($300) three hundred dollars. The result is that we are called upon to apply principles of law theoretically based upon reason and reality to a situation which is basically unreasonable and unrealistic.

In Groves v. John Wunder Co., supra, in arriving at its conclusions, the Minnesota court apparently considered the contract involved to be analogous to a building and construction contract, and cited authority for the proposition that the cost of performance or completion of the building as contracted is ordinarily the measure of damages in actions for damages for the breach of such a contract.

In an annotation following the Minnesota case beginning at 123 A.L.R. 515, the annotator places the three cases relied on by defendant (Sandy Valley, Bigham and Sweeney) under the classification of cases involving "grading and excavation contracts."

We do not think either analogy is strictly applicable to the case now before us. The primary purpose of the lease contract between plaintiffs and defendant was neither "building and construction" nor "grading and excavation." It was merely to accomplish the economical recovery and marketing of coal from the premises, to the profit of all parties. The special provisions of the lease contract pertaining to remedial work were incidental to the main object involved.

Even in the case of contracts that are unquestionably building and construction contracts, the authorities are not in agreement as to the factors to be considered in determining whether the cost of performance rule or the value rule should be applied. The American Law Institute's Restatement of the Law, Contracts, Volume 1, Sections 346(1)(a)(i) and (ii) submits the proposition that the cost of performance is the proper measure of damages "if this is possible and does not involve unreasonable economic waste"; and that the diminution in value caused by the breach is the proper measure "if construction and completion in accordance with the contract would involve unreasonable economic waste." (Emphasis supplied.) In an explanatory comment immediately following the text, the Restatement makes it clear that the "economic waste" referred to consists of the destruction of a substantially completed building or other structure. Of course no such destruction is involved in the case now before us.

On the other hand, in McCormick, Damages, Section 168, it is said with regard to building and construction contracts that ". . . in cases where the defect is one that can be repaired or cured without undue expense" the cost of performance is the proper measure of damages, but where ". . . the defect in material or construction is one that cannot be remedied without an expenditure for reconstruction disproportionate to the end to be attained" (emphasis supplied) the value rule should be followed. The same idea was expressed in Jacob & Youngs, Inc. v. Kent, 230 N.Y. 239, 129 N.E. 889, 23 A.L.R. 1429, as follows:

> The owner is entitled to the money which will permit him to complete, unless the cost of completion is grossly and unfairly out of proportion to the good to be attained. When that is true, the measure is the difference in value. . . .

It thus appears that the prime consideration in the Restatement was "economic waste"; and that the prime consideration in McCormick, Damages, and in Jacob & Youngs, Inc. v. Kent, supra, was the relationship between the expense involved and the 'end to be attained'-in other words, the "relative economic benefit."

In view of the unrealistic fact situation in the instant case, and certain Oklahoma statutes to be hereinafter noted, we are of the opinion that the "relative economic benefit" is a proper consideration here. This is in accord with the recent case of Mann v. Clowser, 190 Va. 887, 59 S.E.2d 78, where, in applying the cost rule, the Virginia court specifically noted that "[T]he defects are remediable from a practical standpoint and the costs are not grossly disproportionate to the results to be obtained" (Emphasis supplied).

23 O.S.1961 §§ 96 and 97 provide as follows:

> § 96. . . . Notwithstanding the provisions of this chapter, no person can recover a greater amount in damages for the breach of an obligation, than he would have gained by the full performance thereof on both sides . . . .
>
> § 97. . . . Damages must, in all cases, be reasonable, and where an obligation of any kind appears to create a right to unconscionable and grossly oppressive damages, contrary to substantial justice no more than reasonable damages can be recovered.

Although it is true that the above sections of the statute are applied most often in tort cases, they are by their own terms, and the decisions of this court, also applicable in actions for damages for breach of contract. It would seem that they are peculiarly applicable here where, under the "cost of performance" rule, plaintiffs might recover an amount about nine times the total value of their farm. Such would seem to be "unconscionable and grossly oppressive damages, contrary to substantial justice" within the meaning of the statute. Also, it can hardly be denied that if plaintiffs here are permitted to recover under the "cost of performance" rule, they will receive a greater benefit from the breach than could be gained from full performance, contrary to the provisions of § 96. . . .

We therefore hold that where, in a coal mining lease, lessee agrees to perform certain remedial work on the premises concerned at the end of the lease period, and thereafter the contract is fully performed by both parties except that the remedial work is not done, the measure of damages in an action by lessor against lessee for damages for breach of contract is ordinarily the reasonable cost of performance of the work; however, where the contract provision breached was merely incidental to the main purpose in view, and where the economic benefit which would result to lessor by full performance of the work is grossly disproportionate to the cost of performance, the damages which lessor may recover are limited to the diminution in value resulting to the premises because of the non-performance.

We believe the above holding is in conformity with the intention of the Legislature as expressed in the statutes mentioned, and in harmony with the better-reasoned cases from the other jurisdictions where analogous fact situations have been considered. It should be noted that the rule as stated does not interfere with the property owner's right to "do what he will with his own" Chamberlain v. Parker, 45 N.Y. 569), or his right, if he chooses, to contract for "improvements" which will actually have the effect of reducing his property's value. Where such result is in fact contemplated by the parties, and is a main or principal purpose of those contracting, it would seem that the measure of damages for breach would ordinarily be the cost of performance.

The above holding disposes of all of the arguments raised by the parties on appeal.

Under the most liberal view of the evidence herein, the diminution in value resulting to the premises because of non-performance of the remedial work was $300.00. After a careful search of the record, we have found no evidence of a higher figure, and plaintiffs do not argue in their briefs that a greater diminution in value was sustained. It thus appears that the judgment was clearly excessive, and that the amount for which judgment should have been rendered is definitely and satisfactorily shown by the record . . . .

We are of the opinion that the judgment of the trial court for plaintiffs should be, and it is hereby, modified and reduced to the sum of $300.00, and as so modified it is affirmed.

WELCH, DAVISON, HALLEY, and JOHNSON, JJ., concur.
WILLIAMS, C. J., BLACKBIRD, V. C. J., and IRWIN and BERRY, JJ., dissent.

IRWIN, Justice (dissenting).

By the specific provisions in the coal mining lease under consideration, the defendant agreed as follows:

> . . . '7b Lessee agrees to make fills in the pits dug on said premises on the property line in such manner that fences can be placed thereon and access had to opposite sides of the pits.
>
> 'c Lessee agrees to smooth off the top of the spoil banks on the above premises.

'7d Lessee agrees to leave the creek crossing the above premises in such a condition that it will not interfere with the crossings to be made in pits as set out in 7b....

'7f Lessee further agrees to leave no shale or dirt on the high wall of said pits....

Following the expiration of the lease, plaintiffs made demand upon defendant that it carry out the provisions of the contract and to perform those covenants contained therein.

Defendant admits that it failed to perform its obligations that it agreed and contracted to perform under the lease contract and there is nothing in the record which indicates that defendant could not perform its obligations. Therefore, in my opinion defendant's breach of the contract was wilful and not in good faith.

Although the contract speaks for itself, there were several negotiations between the plaintiffs and defendant before the contract was executed. Defendant admitted in the trial of the action, that plaintiffs insisted that the above provisions be included in the contract and that they would not agree to the coal mining lease unless the above provisions were included.

In consideration for the lease contract, plaintiffs were to receive a certain amount as royalty for the coal produced and marketed and in addition thereto their land was to be restored as provided in the contract.

Defendant received as consideration for the contract, its proportionate share of the coal produced and marketed and in addition thereto, the *right to use* plaintiffs' land in the furtherance of its mining operations.

The cost for performing the contract in question could have been reasonably approximated when the contract was negotiated and executed and there are no conditions now existing which could not have been reasonably anticipated by the parties. Therefore, defendant had knowledge, when it prevailed upon the plaintiffs to execute the lease, that the cost of performance might be disproportionate to the value or benefits received by plaintiff for the performance.

Defendant has received its benefits under the contract and now urges, in substance, that plaintiffs' measure of damages for its failure to perform should be the economic value of performance to the plaintiffs and not the cost of performance.

If a peculiar set of facts should exist where the above rule should be applied as the proper measure of damages, (and in my judgment those facts do not exist in the instant case) before such rule should be applied, consideration should be given to the benefits received or contracted for by the party who asserts the application of the rule.

Defendant did not have the right to mine plaintiffs' coal or to use plaintiffs' property for its mining operations without the consent of plaintiffs. Defendant had knowledge of the benefits that it would receive under the contract and the approximate cost of performing the contract. With this knowledge, it must be presumed that defendant thought that it would be to its economic advantage to enter into the contract with plaintiffs and that it would reap benefits from the contract, or it would have not entered into the contract.

Therefore, if the value of the performance of a contract should be considered in determining the measure of damages for breach of a contract, the value of the benefits received under the contract by a party who breaches a contract should also be considered. However, in my judgment, to give consideration to either in the instant action, completely rescinds and holds for naught the solemnity of the contract before us and makes an entirely new contract for the parties.

In Goble v. Bell Oil & Gas Co., 97 Okl. 261, 223 P. 371, we held:

"Even though the contract contains harsh and burdensome terms which the court does not in all respects approve, it is the province of the parties in relation to lawful subject matter to fix their rights and obligations, and the court will give the contract effect according to its expressed provisions, unless it be shown by competent evidence proof that the written agreement as executed is the result of fraud, mistake, or accident."

In Cities Service Oil Co. v. Geolograph Co. Inc., 208 Okl. 179, 254 P.2d 775, we said:

"While we do not agree that the contract as presently written is an onerous one, we think the short answer is that the folly or wisdom of a contract is not for the court to pass on."

In Great Western Oil & Gas Company v. Mitchell, Okl., 326 P.2d 794, we held:

"The law will not make a better contract for parties than they themselves have seen fit to enter into, or alter it for the benefit of one party and to the detriment of the others; the judicial function of a court of law is to enforce a contract as it is written."

I am mindful of Title 23 O.S.1961 § 96, which provides that no person can recover a greater amount in damages for the breach of an obligation than he could have gained by the full performance thereof on both sides, except in cases not applicable herein. However, in my judgment, the above statutory provision is not applicable here.

In my judgment, we should follow the case of Groves v. John Wunder Company, 205 Minn. 163, 286 N.W. 235, 123 A.L.R. 502, which defendant agrees "that the fact situation is apparently similar to the one in the case at bar," and where the Supreme Court of Minnesota held:

"The owner's or employer's damages for such a breach (i. e. breach hypothesized in 2d syllabus) are to be measured, not in respect to the value of the land to be improved, but by the reasonable cost of doing that which the contractor promised to do and which he left undone."

The hypothesized breach referred to states that where the contractor's breach of a contract is wilful, that is, in bad faith, he is not entitled to any benefit of the equitable doctrine of substantial performance.

In the instant action defendant has made no attempt to even substantially perform. The contract in question is not immoral, is not tainted with fraud, and was not entered into through mistake or accident and is not contrary to public policy. It is clear and unambiguous and the parties understood the terms thereof, and the approximate cost of fulfilling the obligations could have been approximately ascertained. There are no conditions existing now which could not have been reasonably anticipated when the contract was negotiated and executed. The defendant could have performed the contract if it desired. It has accepted and reaped the benefits of its contract and now urges that plaintiffs' benefits under the contract be denied. If plaintiffs' benefits are denied, such benefits would inure to the direct benefit of the defendant.

Therefore, in my opinion, the plaintiffs were entitled to specific performance of the contract and since defendant has failed to perform, the proper measure of damages should be the cost of performance. Any other measure of damage would be holding for naught the express provisions of the contract; would be taking from the plaintiffs the benefits of the contract and placing those benefits in defendant which has failed to perform its obligations; would be granting benefits to defendant without a resulting obligation; and would be completely rescinding the solemn obligation of the contract for the benefit of the defendant to the detriment of the plaintiffs by making an entirely new contract for the parties.

I therefore respectfully dissent to the opinion promulgated by a majority of my associates.

NOTES AND QUESTIONS:

1. What is the "economic waste" doctrine? Does the economic waste doctrine protect the aggrieved party's expectancy interest? *See* Juanda Lowder Daniel and Kevin Scott Marshall, *Avoiding Economic Waste in Contract Damages: Myths, Misunderstandings, and Malcontent*, 85 NEB. L. REV. 875 (2007).

2. Consider Restatement (Second) of Contracts § 348(2) (Alternatives to Loss in Value of Performances) (1981):

> If a breach results in defective or unfinished construction and the loss in value to the injured party is not proved with sufficient certainty, he may recover damages based on:
>
> (a) the diminution in the market price of the property caused by the breach, or
>
> (b) the reasonable cost of completing performance or of remedying the defects if that cost is not clearly disproportionate to the probable loss in value to him.

3. Do you see any difference between this section and the economic waste doctrine as crafted by *Jacobs & Young* and *Peevyhouse*?

B. THE RELIANCE INTEREST

DPJ CO. V. FEDERAL DEPOSIT INSURANCE CORP.
United States Court of Appeals, First Circuit
30 F.3d 247 (1st Cir. 1994).

BOUDIN, Circuit Judge.

DPJ Company Limited Partnership ("DPJ") is a Massachusetts real estate developer. On February 12, 1988, it entered into a commitment letter agreement with the Bank of New England. Subject to various conditions being satisfied, the agreement contemplated the creation of a three-year $2.5 million line of credit on which DPJ could draw to finance primary steps in land development ventures (e.g., deposits, option payments, and architectural and engineering services).

The commitment letter provided that the creation of the line of credit-an event called the "closing" (as in "closing" a deal)-would occur after DPJ met various requirements, such as the delivery to the bank of certain documents, appraisals, and the like. DPJ also had to pay a non-refundable loan commitment fee of $31,250 immediately. In satisfying the conditions, DPJ spent a total of $180,072.37 in commitment fees, closing costs, legal fees, survey costs, points, environmental reports and other such items.

The line of credit was "closed" on July 23, 1988. Between that time and January 6, 1991, DPJ borrowed approximately $500,000 from the bank pursuant to the line of credit. The bank failed on January 6, 1991. On February 1, 1991, the bank's receiver, the Federal Deposit Insurance Corporation, disaffirmed the line of credit agreement pursuant to its statutory authority to repudiate contracts of failed banks. 12 U.S.C. § 1821(e)(1). Although the FDIC may repudiate such contracts, the injured party may under the statute sue the FDIC as receiver for damages for breach of contract; but, with certain exceptions, the injured party may recover only "actual direct compensatory damages," 12 U.S.C. § 1821(e)(3)(A)(i), and may not recover inter alia "damages for lost profits or opportunities." Id. § 1821(e)(3)(B)(ii).

On May 22, 1991, DPJ filed an administrative claim with the FDIC to recover the costs and expenses it incurred pursuant to the commitment letter mentioned to obtain the line of credit. 12 U.S.C. § 1821(d)(5). The FDIC disallowed the claim. DPJ then brought suit in the district court to recover its claimed damages. Id. § 1821(d)(6)(A). Both sides moved for summary judgment.

The district court entered a decision on September 10, 1993, denying recovery to DPJ. The court concluded that DPJ was "really seek[ing] to recoup its closing costs as compensation for its lost borrowing opportunity resulting from the FDIC's disaffirmance." In substance, the court held that the "loss of borrowing capability" does not constitute "actual direct compensatory damages." In support of its decision it cited and relied upon Judge Zobel's decision in FDIC v. Cobblestone Corp., 1992 WL 333961 (D.Mass. Oct. 28, 1992). DPJ then appealed to this court.

The critical statutory phrases-"actual direct compensatory damages" and "lost profits and opportunities"-have been the recurrent subject of litigation. See, e.g., Howell v. FDIC, 986 F.2d 569 (1st Cir.1993); Lawson v. FDIC, 3 F.3d 11 (1st Cir.1993). We have read the limitation of recovery to compensatory damages, and the exclusion barring lost profits or opportunities, against the background of Congress' evident purpose: "to spread the pain," in a situation where the assets are unlikely to cover all claims, by placing policy-based limits on what can be recouped as damages for repudiated contracts. Howell, 986 F.2d at 572; Lawson, 3 F.3d at 16.

Contract damages are often calculated to place the injured party in the position that that party would have enjoyed if the other side had fulfilled its part of the bargain. Subject to various limitations, lost profits and opportunities are sometimes recovered under such a "benefit of the bargain" calculation. A. Farnsworth, Contracts § 12.14 (2d ed. 1990); C. McCormick, Damages, § 25 (1935). Yet where an injured claimant cannot recover the full benefit of the bargain-for example, because profits cannot be proved with sufficient certainty-there is an alternative, well-established contract damage theory:

> [O]ne who fails to meet the burden of proving prospective profits is not necessarily relegated to nominal damages. If one has relied on the contract, one can usually meet the burden of proving with sufficient certainty the extent of that reliance.... One can then recover damages based on reliance, with deductions for any benefit received through salvage or otherwise.

Farnsworth, supra, § 12.16, at 928 (emphasis added).

As McCormick has explained, "[t]his recovery is strictly upon the contract," McCormick, supra, § 142 at 583. It is not a remedy for unjust enrichment, nor is it rescission of the contract. It is a contract damage computation that "conform[s] to the more general aim of awarding compensation in all cases, and [it] departs from the standard of value of performance only because of the difficulty in applying the [latter standard]." Id. at 583-84. See generally In re Las Colinas, Inc., 453 F.2d 911, 914 (1st Cir.1971) (citing numerous authorities), cert. denied, 405 U.S. 1067, 92 S.Ct. 1502, 31 L.Ed.2d 797 (1972).

Subject to common-law limitations, to which we shall return in due course, expenditures by DPJ in fulfilling its part of the bargain can properly be recovered as compensatory damages under this alternative reliance theory. Certainly damages so computed do not offend the terms of the federal statute. The FDIC does not dispute that the $180,072.37 in costs and expenses were "actual" expenditures. And, as they were apparently made to fulfill specific stipulations laid down by the bank, the resulting damages can fairly be described as "direct," a term normally used to filter out damages that are causally remote, unforeseeable or both. Farnsworth, supra, at §§ 12.14-12.15.

Similarly, DPJ's expenditures are not, by any stretch of literal language, "lost profits or opportunities." One might argue that since lost profits and opportunities are unrecoverable, the recovery of reliance damages would also offend the policy of the statute. But the policy underlying the statutory ban on lost profits and opportunities is Congress' apparent view that these benefits have, in some measure, an aspect of being windfall gains. This same policy is reflected in the disallowance of punitive or exemplary damages, 12 U.S.C. § 1821(e)(3)(B)(i), and damages for future rent when the FDIC disaffirms a lease and surrenders property previously leased by the bank. Id. § 1821(e)(4)(B).

There is normally no windfall involved in the recovery of reliance damages. DPJ is seeking to recapture money actually spent under the commitment letter agreement to obtain a line of credit that the FDIC has now repudiated. Whether or not one shares Congress' belief that "lost profits and opportunities" are a special category of damages which should be disfavored, that policy is not even remotely offended by returning DPJ its out-of-pocket expenditures which, because of the FDIC's repudiation, have made DPJ's own expenditures (at least in part) fruitless.

The district court called DPJ's claim one to recover for a "lost opportunity" since the breach of contract deprived DPJ of the opportunity to secure further loans. This could be so if, as in Cobblestone, DPJ were claiming profits that would have been realized through further loans.[1] It might be arguably so (we do not decide the point) if DPJ was claiming as damages the cost of securing a substitute line of credit. But reliance damages do not compensate for a lost opportunity; they merely restore to the claimant what he or she spent before the opportunity was withdrawn.

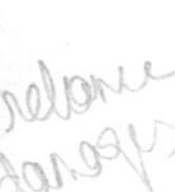

In sum, DPJ has claimed reliance damages in this case and we hold that reliance damages-or at least those claimed by DPJ-are "actual direct compensatory damages," are not compensation for "lost profits and opportunities," and are not barred by Cobblestone. Construction of the quoted statutory phrases is, of course, a matter of federal law, and the concept of reliance damages has long been recognized both in federal litigation, Rumsey Mfg. Corp. v. United States Hoffman Mach. Corp., 187 F.2d 927, 931-32 (2d Cir.1951) (L. Hand), and in Massachusetts. Air Technology Corp. v. General Elec. Co., 347 Mass. 613, 199 N.E.2d 538, 549 n. 19 (1964).

When we turn to the final issues in this case-the common-law limitations on reliance damages-the choice of governing law is more debatable. The underlying obligation on which DPJ sues is a contract created by Massachusetts law. Federal law imposes statutory limits on the damages that may be awarded against the FDIC when it repudiates the contract. Whether the nuances and qualifications that shape reliance damages should be decided under Massachusetts law, federal law or conceivably both is an interesting question. It need not be answered here, because Massachusetts' view of reliance damages does not appear to depart

[1] In Cobblestone, the company took the position that it had lost approximately $5 million because the FDIC repudiated a line of credit used by Cobblestone to finance equipment that it expected to lease to customers. We agree with the denial of such a lost-profits recovery in Cobblestone, but think the decision quite distinguishable.

from general practice. We turn, then, to possible common-law limitations on DPJ's recovery of reliance damages in this case.

First, because reliance damages seek to measure the injured party's "cost of reliance" on the breached contract, "an injured party cannot recover for costs incurred before that party made the contract." Farnsworth, supra, § 12.16, at 928 n. 2. The FDIC in this case argues that, at the time DPJ made its expenditures, the bank had no obligation to make a loan at all, for that obligation arose only after the bank later made a discretionary judgment to "close" the transaction and establish the line of credit. Farnsworth, supra, § 12.16, at 928 n. 2. The FDIC concludes that DPJ's pre-loan expenditures were not made in reliance upon the line of credit promise but were made in order to secure it.

This will not wash. The commitment letter was itself an agreement that gave rise, upon the satisfying of conditions, to the bank's obligation to create and maintain DPJ's line of credit. Whether the bank reserved for itself the discretion to refuse to close (e.g., if dissatisfied with the documents submitted to it), the DPJ expenditures were made pursuant to the agreement and so "in preparing to perform and in part performance" by DPJ. McCormick, supra, § 142, at 583. As a practical matter, companies do not normally spend almost $200,000 in satisfying loan conditions without very good reason to expect that the loan itself will be approved. Thus, we think it is unrealistic to separate the expenditures by DPJ from the bank's promise to provide the line of credit and to make loans pursuant to it.

Second, where full performance of a contract would have given claimant no benefit, or at least less than the reliance damages claimed, this fact may justify limiting or disallowing reliance damages. The notion is that claimant should on no account get more than would have accrued if the contract had been performed. Farnsworth, supra, § 12.16, at 930 & nn. 11-14 (citing cases). Prior to the bank's closing, DPJ had borrowed only $500,000; DPJ in turn says that it was preparing to borrow further on its line of credit when the FDIC put an end to the opportunity. If it has not waived the issue, on remand the FDIC might conceivably try to show that DPJ would in fact not have borrowed further on the line of credit and, therefore, that DPJ had in fact received everything it would have received had FDIC not disaffirmed the line of credit agreement.

Third, a reliance recovery may be reduced to the extent that the breaching party can prove that a "deduction" is appropriate "for any benefit received [by the claimant] for salvage or otherwise." Farnsworth, supra, § 12.16, at 928-29 & nn. 1, 3 & 7 (citing cases). Compare Restatement (Second), Contracts § 349 (benefits not mentioned). It is an intriguing question whether, assuming that the issue is open, there should be any deduction for the benefit already received by DPJ by virtue of the $500,000 in loans actually made and, if so, how that deduction should be measured.

These are by no means easy issues to resolve in the abstract. On the one hand the FDIC could argue, if it has not waived the issue, that DPJ received some portion of benefits promised by the agreement, such as 20 per cent of the potential loan amount ($500,000 out of $2.5 million) or the availability of credit for two and one half of the promised three years. On the other hand DPJ might have arguments as to why no equitable offset is proper. Neither side has briefed the relatively sparse caselaw pertaining to a possible deduction for benefits received where reliance damages are claimed.

There is no indication that the FDIC argued in the district court that DPJ would assuredly have declined to borrow further on the line of credit or that a deduction from the amount claimed should be made to account for benefit received. Certainly no such arguments have been made in this court. If the FDIC does press such arguments on remand, the district court can determine whether the arguments have been waived by a failure to assert them in a timely manner.

The judgment of the district court is vacated and the matter remanded for further proceedings consistent with this opinion.

NOTES AND QUESTIONS:

1. For a different view on recovery of pre-contract expenses, *see Anglia Television, Ltd v. Reed*, 3 All Eng. Rep. 690 (1971).

2. Is an aggrieved party entitled to recover consequential and incidentals as reliance damages? *See Sullivan v. O'Connor*, 296 N.E.2d 183 (Mass. 1973).

3. *See* Restatement (Second) of Contracts § 349 (Damages Based on Reliance Interest) (1981).

C. LIMITATIONS ON THE RECOVERY

1. CERTAINTY

ESPN, INC. V. OFFICE OF THE COMMISSIONER OF BASEBALL
United States District Court, S.D. New York
76 F. Supp. 2d 416 (1999).

SCHEINDLIN, District Judge.

On October 15, 1999, ESPN, Inc. ("ESPN") and the Office of the Commissioner of Baseball ("Baseball") moved in limine to preclude the admission of certain evidence and argument at their forthcoming trial. Ten separate motions-five by ESPN and five by Baseball-were fully submitted on October 29, 1999. Six of the motions were resolved by opinion dated November 22, 1999. Three of the motions were resolved from the bench during a hearing on November 23, 1999. The final motion, ESPN's motion in limine to preclude damages evidence, is the subject of this Opinion and Order.

I. ESPN's Motion in Limine to Preclude Damages Evidence

In my November 22 opinion, I ruled that ESPN breached its 1996 telecasting agreement ("1996 Agreement") with Baseball when it preempted six baseball games scheduled for Sunday nights in September 1998 and September 1999 without the prior written approval of Baseball. See ESPN, Inc. v. Office of Commissioner of Baseball, 1999

WL 1063241, 99 Civ. 3225, slip op. at 38-39 (S.D.N.Y. Nov. 23, 1999).[1] ESPN broadcast NFL football games rather than the previously scheduled baseball games on those six nights.

Baseball claims that it has been damaged in an amount "believed to exceed millions of dollars" as a result of ESPN's breach of the 1996 Agreement. Baseball attributes its damages to an alleged loss of:

(1) national television exposure;
(2) promotional opportunities and ratings;

(3) value of the "Sunday Night Baseball" television package;

(4) prestige;

(5) potential sponsorships; and

(6) the future value of all of Baseball's national telecast packages

Because Baseball received full payment from ESPN under the contract, it may only seek extra-contractual damages stemming from the six preemptions.

By its motion, ESPN seeks to preclude Baseball from introducing testimony or other evidence of its alleged monetary damages. ESPN contends that "there is no factual basis to support any claim for monetary damages arising from these perceived injuries, and that such claims are the product of speculation and guesswork." ESPN's Memorandum in Support of Its Motion in Limine to Preclude Damages Evidence ("ESPN MIL") at 2. Baseball argues that it has made the "requisite showing of damage" and therefore it is "entitled to have the opportunity to prove its damages at trial." Baseball's Response to Plaintiff's Motion to Preclude Damages ("BB Op.") at 10.

II. Legal Standard

It is well-settled under New York law that

> [a] plaintiff seeking compensatory damages has the burden of proof and should present to the court a proper basis for ascertaining the damages [it] seeks to recover. They must be susceptible of ascertainment in some manner other than by mere conjecture or guesswork.

Dunkel v. McDonald, 272 A.D. 267, 70 N.Y.S.2d 653, 656 (1st Dep't 1947), aff'd, 298 N.Y. 586, 81 N.E.2d 323 (1948).

. . . Although it is true that "[w]hen the existence of damage is certain, and the only uncertainty is as to its amount, the plaintiff will not be denied recovery of substantial damages," but even then the plaintiff must show "a stable foundation for a reasonable estimate" of damages . . . .

---

[1] The facts of the case are set forth in the November 23 opinion and will not be repeated here.

With respect to damages for loss of goodwill, business reputation or future profits, the proof requirements are much more stringent. . . . Not only must the claimant prove the fact of loss with certainty, but the "loss must be 'reasonably certain in amount.' " . . . "In other words, the damages may not be merely possible speculative or imaginary but must be reasonably certain and directly traceable to the breach, not remote or the result of other intervening causes." Beeland Interests, Inc. v. Armstrong, 1999 WL 813266 at *17, 95 Civ. 8132 (S.D.N.Y. Oct. 12, 1999) (dismissing claim for lost profits where plaintiff failed to prove "both the fact and amount of lost profits with reasonable certainty").

III. Baseball's Proffered Damages Evidence

During discovery, ESPN served Baseball with interrogatories regarding its claims for monetary damages. Among other things, ESPN asked Baseball to "state the amount of monetary damages you seek in this action and explain the basis for the computation of your claim." ESPN Interrogatory No. 6, Ex. A to Lobenfeld Aff. at 7. Baseball responded as follows:

> Baseball has not quantified the amount of damages it has sustained by reason of ESPN's willful refusal to carry [baseball] games as required by the 1996 Agreement. A quantification of those damages, however real, is extremely complex and for that reason Baseball insisted, and ESPN agreed, in the 1996 Agreement that ESPN would produce and distribute the telecasts and that its failure to do so could be specifically enforced, without regard to the need for Baseball to prove irreparable harm. At its essence the damages, believed to exceed millions of dollars, are attributable to [loss of national television exposure; promotional opportunities and ratings; value of the "Sunday Night Baseball" television package; prestige; potential sponsorships; and the future value of all of Baseball's national telecast packages]. Id. at 7-8.[2]

Nowhere in its response does Baseball set forth any specific dollar amount of monetary damages other than its estimate that damages are "believed to exceed millions of dollars." Nor does Baseball set forth any method of calculating its alleged damages.

As the following excerpts demonstrate, Baseball's 30(b)(6) witness on the topic of damages, Baseball's President Paul Beeston, was equally speculative and vague regarding the alleged harm caused by ESPN's breach.

---

[2] Baseball's interrogatory response is quite revealing. Baseball concedes that it had agreed that in the event of a breach it would seek "specific[ ] enforce[ment]" without the need to prove "irreparable harm." Baseball's failure to seek that specific enforcement is puzzling and leads one to question whether it really wanted the games aired, or whether it really wanted an excuse to renegotiate a contract which it no longer found sufficiently lucrative. On the other hand, ESPN's behavior is also suspect. In the November 22 opinion, I held that ESPN should not have engaged in self-help but should have sought judicial intervention as to whether Baseball's failure to grant permission to broadcast football in place of baseball games was unreasonable. ESPN's failure leads one to question whether the fear of an adverse ruling, and the accompanying loss of millions of dollars in revenues, caused ESPN to choose the option of intentionally breaching its contract.

Q: Has Baseball quantified any of the damages it alleges in this case?

A: No, we have not quantified it to the extent of a specific dollar, no.

Q: Has Baseball made any calculations as to any specific element of its alleged damages?

A: We have not.

Q: Is there a reason why Baseball has not done any calculation of its damages in this case?

A: No. We just believe it's significant. We believe that the case speaks for itself at the present time, and we have not worked out what the dollars are of the damages.

9/27/99 Deposition of Paul Beeston ("Beeston Dep.") at 6-7. . . .

Q: [W]hat's the basis for your belief that Baseball's alleged damages exceed millions of dollars?

A: Based on what we have right here and what we've said what we've [g]ot here going forward. I don't have anything specific, as I said.

Q: [I]f somebody suggested to you that they believed you're right, Baseball was damaged but it's only a hundred thousand dollars, would you be able to point me to anything to say it's not a hundred thousand dollars, it's a million dollars?

A: Specifically I won't be able to say this is what it is, try this calculation and that's the way it works out, no.

Id. at 28. . . .

Q: Can you point to anything specific as evidence that ESPN's [breach] has made Baseball less valuable in any way?

A: "Specifically, no if you're asking for one example that I could give you...."

Q: You say you think it probably hurt you. Are you able to point to us specifically-

A: No, I said I cannot.

Id. at 10-11.

Not once during his deposition did Beeston offer a concrete example of harm or monetary loss stemming from ESPN's breach. Baseball's expert witness, Robert J. Wussler, was similarly unable to cite specific examples of loss. During his deposition, Wussler testified as follows:

> Q: Are you aware of any money that Baseball lost as a result of those three games?
>
> A: No I'm not.
>
> Q: And the same thing is true in '99, same question with respect to '99?
>
> A: They've lost in perception. It's very hard to evaluate dollars and perception.
>
> Q: I'm not going to ask you about perception. You are not aware of any dollars lost, correct?
>
> A: I'm not.
>
> 10/15/99 Deposition of Robert J. Wussler at 92-93. . . .
>
> Q: Again, just so I'm clear, are you aware of 5 cents of advertising revenue that Baseball lost as a result of the three games being [not shown on ESPN]–
>
> A: No I'm not.
>
> Id. at 107. . . .
>
> Q: I take it you are not aware of any lost sponsors or lost advertisers; is that correct?
>
> A: That is correct.
>
> Id. at 108.

Finally, on November 23, this Court held oral argument on ESPN's motion to preclude damages evidence. During that argument, this Court specifically asked counsel for Baseball whether Baseball had any "concrete proof of monetary harm." See Transcript of 11/23/99 Hearing ("11/23/99 Tr.") at 23. In response, counsel for Baseball merely reiterated the entirely subjective and speculative assertion that Baseball "feel[s] this was very dilatory [sic] to our position and denigrated our product and cost us in the marketplace and otherwise." Id. at 28. Counsel for Baseball was unable to show "any loss of sponsorship, any loss of advertising, [or] any loss of ancillary sales or ticket sales." Id. at 36. As counsel for Baseball conceded: "We have not shown specific losses your Honor, we agree with you there. What we have said is we believe it did affect us." Id.[3]

---

[3] At the end of oral argument, counsel for Baseball set forth, for the very first time, an alternate theory of damages. Baseball proposed that damages be calculated according to the amount it would have sought had ESPN

IV. Discussion

As the above-quoted testimony and answers to ESPN's interrogatories demonstrate, there can be no question that Baseball has failed to adequately demonstrate either the fact of damages or the amount of damages. Put simply, Baseball's subjective belief that the amount of damages is "significant"-no matter how fervent-does not meet any of the required proofs set forth under New York law. Baseball has not cited a single lost promotional opportunity, sponsor or advertising dollar stemming from ESPN's breach. Nor has Baseball set forth any evidence of a decrease in ratings or box office ticket sales. Although damage to Baseball's prestige and future value are difficult to prove, such difficulty does not allow Baseball to proceed with speculative claims of damages. To the contrary, under New York law, a claim of damages for loss of reputation and future profits must be "reasonably certain." . . .

Baseball's damages claim is based on nothing more than its own vague assertions that it was "hurt." Baseball cites no specific examples of monetary damage, nor does it proffer a method for calculating such damages. The proffered unsupported allegations are simply inadequate to sustain a claim for damages under New York law, and therefore ESPN's motion to preclude damages evidence is granted.

V. Nominal Damages and Materiality

Although Baseball is not entitled to an award of money damages, it may still receive nominal damages. "[I]t is a well-settled tenet of contract law that even if the breach of contract caused no loss or if the amount of the loss cannot be proven with sufficient certainty, the injured party is entitled to recover as nominal damages a small sum fixed without regard to the amount of the loss, if any." Hirsch Elec. Co. v. Community Servs., Inc., 145 A.D.2d 603, 536 N.Y.S.2d 141, 142-43 (2d Dep't 1988); see also Contemporary Mission, 557 F.2d at 926 (when the existence of damage is speculative "plaintiff is limited to the recovery of nominal damages").[4] Accordingly, I will instruct the jury that if Baseball proves its breach of damages claim, it is entitled to an award of nominal damages.[5]

Baseball's ability to recover only nominal damages does not impede its ability to present testimony and evidence regarding the materiality of ESPN's breach. Materiality goes to the essence of the contract. That is, a breach is material if it defeats the object of the parties in making the contract and "deprive[s] the injured party of the benefit that it justifiably expected." Farnsworth, Contracts § 8.16 (3d ed.1999). Materiality does not depend upon the amount of provable money damages, it depends upon whether the

asked Baseball to "sell the right to dump [Baseball] onto [another channel]." 11/23/99 Tr. at 30. In other words, Baseball seeks to calculate damages based on a hypothetical negotiation or sale of the six preempted games.Regardless of the merits of Baseball's alternate theory, I reject it as a basis for the calculation of damages. Baseball's failure to mention this alternate theory of damages until six days before trial-months after the close of discovery and weeks after the submission of pre-trial motions-bars it from presenting such a theory at trial.

4 Although unable to prove monetary damage, there is no question that Baseball was harmed by virtue of ESPN's breach. Baseball was entitled to the broadcast of six baseball games during September 1998 and September 1999. When ESPN failed to broadcast those games, ESPN was harmed regardless of whether it can prove any monetary damage.

5 Although ESPN breached the 1996 Agreement when it preempted baseball games without Baseball's approval, in order for Baseball to prove its breach of contract claim, it must first demonstrate that it substantially performed under the contract.

nonbreaching party lost the benefit of its bargain. Thus, although Baseball is only entitled to nominal damages, it may still present evidence and argument to the effect that ESPN's breach was material . . . .

VII. Conclusion

For the reasons set forth above, Baseball is precluded from presenting damages evidence at trial and is only entitled to seek an award of nominal damages.

KENFORD COMPANY V. COUNTY OF ERIE
Court of Appeals of New York
67 N.Y.2d 257 (1986).

Per Curiam

The issue in this appeal is whether a plaintiff, in an action for breach of contract, may recover loss of prospective profits for its contemplated 20-year operation of a domed stadium which was to be constructed by defendant County of Erie (County).

On August 8, 1969, pursuant to a duly adopted resolution of its legislature, the County of Erie entered into a contract with Kenford Company, Inc. (Kenford) and Dome Stadium, Inc. (DSI) for the construction and operation of a domed stadium facility near the City of Buffalo. The contract provided that construction of the facility by the County would commence within 12 months of the contract date and that a mutually acceptable 40-year lease between the County and DSI for the operation of said facility would be negotiated by the parties and agreed upon within three months of the receipt by the County of preliminary plans, drawings and cost estimates. It was further provided that in the event a mutually acceptable lease could not be agreed upon within the three-month period, a separate management contract between the County and DSI, as appended to the basic agreement, would be executed by the parties, providing for the operation of the stadium facility by DSI for a period of 20 years from the completion of the stadium and its availability for use.

Although strenuous and extensive negotiations followed, the parties never agreed upon the terms of a lease, nor did construction of a domed facility begin within the one-year period or at any time thereafter. A breach of the contract thus occurred and this action was commenced in June 1971 by Kenford and DSI.

Prolonged and extensive pretrial and preliminary proceedings transpired throughout the next 10 years, culminating with the entry of an order which affirmed the grant of summary judgment against the County on the issue of liability and directed a trial limited to the issue of damages . . . . The ensuing trial ended some nine months later with a multimillion dollar jury verdict in plaintiffs' favor. An appeal to the Appellate Division resulted in a modification of the judgment. That court reversed portions of the judgment awarding damages for loss of profits and for certain out-of-pocket expenses incurred, and directed a new trial upon other issues . . . . On appeal to this court, we are concerned only with that portion of the verdict which awarded DSI money damages for loss of prospective profits during the 20-year period of the proposed management contract, as appended to the basic contract. That portion of the verdict was set aside by the Appellate Division and the cause of action dismissed. The court concluded that the use of expert opinion to present statistical projections of future business operations involved the use of too many variables to provide a rational basis upon which lost profits could be calculated and, therefore, such projections were insufficient as a matter of law to support an award of lost profits. We agree with this ultimate conclusion, but upon different grounds.

Loss of future profits as damages for breach of contract have been permitted in New York under long-established and precise rules of law. First, it must be demonstrated with certainty that such damages have been caused by the breach and, second, the alleged loss must be capable of proof with reasonable certainty. In other words, the damages may not be merely speculative, possible or imaginary, but must be reasonably certain and directly traceable to the breach, not remote or the result of other intervening causes . . . . In addition, there must be a showing that the particular damages were fairly within the contemplation of the parties to the contract at the time it was made . . . . If it is a new business seeking to recover for loss of future profits, a stricter standard is imposed for the obvious reason that there does not exist a reasonable basis of experience upon which to estimate lost profits with the requisite degree of reasonable certainty . . . .

These rules must be applied to the proof presented by DSI in this case. We note the procedure for computing damages selected by DSI was in accord with contemporary economic theory and was presented through the testimony of recognized experts. Such a procedure has been accepted in this State and many other jurisdictions . . . . DSI's economic analysis employed historical data, obtained from the operation of other domed stadiums and related facilities throughout the country, which was then applied to the results of a comprehensive study of the marketing prospects for the proposed facility in the Buffalo area. The quantity of proof is massive and, unquestionably, represents business and industry's most advanced and sophisticated method for predicting the probable results of contemplated projects. Indeed, it is difficult to conclude what additional relevant proof could have been submitted by DSI in support of its attempt to establish, with reasonable certainty, loss of prospective profits. Nevertheless, DSI's proof is insufficient to meet the required standard.

The reason for this conclusion is twofold. Initially, the proof does not satisfy the requirement that liability for loss of profits over a 20-year period was in the contemplation of the parties at the time of the execution of the basic contract or at the time of its breach . . . . Indeed, the provisions in the contract providing remedy for a default do not suggest or provide for such a heavy responsibility on the part of the County. In the absence of any provision for such an eventuality, the commonsense rule to apply is to consider what the parties would have concluded had they considered the subject. The evidence here fails to demonstrate that liability for loss of profits over the length of the contract would have been in the contemplation of the parties at the relevant times.

Next, we note that despite the massive quantity of expert proof submitted by DSI, the ultimate conclusions are still projections, and as employed in the present day commercial world, subject to adjustment and modification. We of course recognize that any projection cannot be absolute, nor is there any such requirement, but it is axiomatic that the degree of certainty is dependent upon known or unknown factors which form the basis of the ultimate conclusion. Here, the foundations upon which the economic model was created undermine the certainty of the projections. DSI assumed that the facility was completed, available for use and successfully operated by it for 20 years, providing professional sporting events and other forms of entertainment, as well as hosting meetings, conventions and related commercial gatherings. At the time of the breach, there was only one other facility in this country to use as a basis of comparison, the Astrodome in Houston. Quite simply, the multitude of assumptions required to establish projections of profitability over the life of this contract require speculation and conjecture, making it beyond the capability of even the most sophisticated procedures to satisfy the legal requirements of proof with reasonable certainty.

The economic facts of life, the whim of the general public and the fickle nature of popular support for professional athletic endeavors must be given great weight in attempting to ascertain damages 20 years in the future. New York has long recognized the inherent uncertainties of predicting profits in the entertainment field in general . . . and, in this case, we are dealing, in large part, with a new facility furnishing entertainment for the public. It is our view that the record in this case demonstrates the efficacy of the principles set forth by this court in Cramer v Grand Rapids Show Case Co., 223 NY 63 (1918) principles to which we continue to adhere. In so doing, we specifically reject the "rational basis" test enunciated in Perma Research & Dev. Co. v Singer Co. (542 F2d 111, cert denied 429 US 987) and adopted by the Appellate Division.

Accordingly, that portion of the order of the Appellate Division being appealed from should be affirmed . . . .

NOTES AND QUESTIONS:

1. *See* Restatement (Second) of Contracts § 352 (Uncertainty as a Limitation on Damages) (1981).

2. *See* Kevin S. Marshall and Kurt J. Beron, *Statistics and the Law: Proving a Case for Lost Profits*, 2 TEX. WESLEYAN L. REV. 467 (1996).

3. What effect, if any, should the fact that the aggrieved party is a new business have on the showing of certainty in damages? *See Barbier v. Barry*, 345 S.W.2d 557, 563 (Tex. Civ. App. 1961) (prospective profits generally not recoverable for new and unestablished business because such profits are not "susceptible of being established by proof to degree of certainty which the law demands."). Compare *The Drews Company, Inc. v. Ledwith-Wolfe Associates, Inc.*, 371 S.E.2d 532, 534 (S.C. 1988) ("Modern cases, however, reflect the willingness of this Court and our Court of Appeals to view the new business rule as a rule of evidentiary sufficiency rather than an automatic bar to recovery of lost profits for a new business.").

---

2. FORESEEABILITY

HADLEY V. BAXENDALE
Court of Exchequer
156 Eng. Rep. 145 (1854).

At the trial before Crompton, J., at the last Gloucester Assizes, it appeared that the plaintiffs carried on an extensive business as millers at Gloucester; and that, on the 11th of May, their mill was stopped by a breakage of the crank shaft by which the mill was worked.

The steam-engine was manufactured by Messrs. Joyce & Co., the engineers, at Greenwich, and it became necessary to send the shaft as a pattern for a new one to Greenwich. The fracture was discovered on the 12th, and on the 13th the plaintiffs sent one of their servants to the office of the defendants, who are the well-known carriers trading under the name of Pickford & Co., for the purpose of having the shaft carried to Greenwich. The plaintiffs' servant told the clerk that the mill was stopped, and that the shaft must be sent immediately; and in answer to the inquiry when the shaft would be taken, the answer was, that if it was sent up by twelve o'clock any day, it would be delivered at Greenwich on the following day. On the following day the shaft was taken by the defendants, before noon, for the purpose of being conveyed to Greenwich, and the sum of 2l. 4s. was paid for its carriage for the whole distance; at the same time the defendants' clerk was told that a special entry, if required, should be made to hasten its delivery. The delivery of the shaft at Greenwich was delayed by some neglect; and the consequence was, that the plaintiffs did not receive the new shaft for several days after they would otherwise have done, and the working of their mill was thereby delayed, and they thereby lost the profits they would otherwise have received.

On the part of the defendants, it was objected that these damages were too remote, and that the defendants were not liable with respect to them. The learned Judge left the case generally to the jury, who found a verdict with 25£ damages beyond the amount paid into Court.

Whateley, in last Michaelmas Term, obtained a rule nisi for a new trial, on the ground of misdirection. . . .

ALDERSON, B.

We think that there ought to be a new trial in this case; but, in so doing, we deem it to be expedient and necessary to state explicitly the rule which the Judge, at the next trial, ought, in our opinion, to direct the jury to be governed by when they estimate the damages.

It is, indeed, of the last importance that we should do this; for, if the jury are left without any definite rule to guide them, it will, in such cases as these, manifestly lead to the greatest injustice. The Courts have done this on several occasions; and, in Blake v. Midland Railway Company (18 Q. B. 93), the Court granted a new trial on this very ground, that the rule had not been definitely laid down to the jury by the learned Judge at Nisi Prius.

"There are certain established rules," this Court says, in Alder v. Keighley (15 M. & W. 117), "according to which the jury ought to find." And the Court, in that case, adds: "and here there is a clear rule, that the amount which would have been received if the contract had been kept, is the measure of damages if the contract is broken."

Now we think the proper rule in such a case as the present is this:-Where two parties have made a contract which one of them has broken, the damages which the other party ought to receive in respect of such breach of contract should be such as may fairly and reasonably be considered either arising naturally, i.e., according to the usual course of things, from such breach of contract itself, or such as may reasonably be supposed to have been in the contemplation of both parties, at the time they made the contract, as the probable result of the breach of it. Now, if the special circumstances under which the contract was actually made were communicated by the plaintiffs to the defendants, and thus known to both parties, the damages resulting from the breach of such a contract, which they would reasonably contemplate, would be the amount of injury which would ordinarily follow from a breach of contract under these special circumstances so known and communicated. But, on the other hand, if these special circumstances were wholly unknown to the party breaking the contract, he, at the most, could only be supposed to have had in his contemplation the amount of injury which would arise generally, and in the great multitude of cases not affected by any special circumstances, from such a breach of contract. For, had the special circumstances been known, the parties might have specially provided for the breach of contract by special terms as to the damages in that case; and of this advantage it would be very unjust to deprive them. Now the above principles are those by which we think the jury ought to be guided in estimating the damages arising out of any breach of contract. It is said, that other cases such as breaches of contract in the non-payment of money, or in the not making a good title to land, are to be treated as exceptions from this, and as governed by a conventional rule. But as, in such cases, both parties must be supposed to be cognisant of that well-known rule, these cases may, we think, be more properly classed under the rule above enunciated as to cases under known special circumstances, because there both parties may reasonably be presumed to contemplate the estimation of the amount of damages according to the conventional rule. Now, in the present case, if we are to apply the principles above laid down, we find that the only circumstances here communicated by the plaintiffs to the defendants at the time the contract was made, were, that the article to be carried was the broken shaft of a mill, and that the plaintiffs were the millers of that mill. But how do these circumstances shew reasonably that the profits of the mill must be stopped by an unreasonable delay in the delivery of the broken shaft by the carrier to the third person? Suppose the plaintiffs had another shaft in their possession put up or putting up at the time, and that they only wished to send back the broken shaft to the engineer who made it; it is clear that this would be quite consistent with the above circumstances, and yet the unreasonable delay in the delivery would have no effect upon the intermediate profits of the mill. Or, again, suppose that, at the time of the delivery to the carrier, the machinery of the mill had been in other respects defective, then, also, the same results would follow. Here it is true that the shaft was actually sent back to serve as a model for a new one, and that the want of a new one was the only cause of the stoppage of the mill, and that the loss of profits really arose from not sending down the new shaft in proper time, and that this arose from the delay in delivering the broken one to serve as a model. But it is obvious that, in the great multitude of cases of millers sending off broken shafts to third persons by a carrier under ordinary circumstances, such consequences would not, in all probability, have occurred; and these special circumstances were here never communicated by the plaintiffs to the defendants. It follows, therefore, that the loss of profits here cannot reasonably be considered such a consequence of the breach of contract as could have been fairly and reasonably contemplated by both the parties when they made this contract. For such loss would neither have flowed naturally from the breach of this contract in the great multitude of such cases occurring under ordinary circumstances, nor were the special circumstances, which, perhaps, would have made it a reasonable and natural consequence of such breach of contract, communicated to or known by the defendants. The Judge ought, therefore, to have told the jury, that, upon the facts then before them, they ought not to take the loss of profits into consideration at all in estimating the damages. There must therefore be a new trial in this case.

Rule absolute.

NOTES AND QUESTIONS:

1. Read U.C.C. § 2-715 (Buyer's Incidental and Consequential Damages) (2002). Is foreseeability also a requirement for U.C.C. damages?

2. *See* Restatement (Second) of Contracts § 351 (Unforseeability and Related Limitations on Damages) (1981).

---

3. AVOIDABILITY

ROCKINGHAM COUNTY V. LUTEN BRIDGE CO.
Circuit Court of Appeals, Fourth Circuit
35 F.2d 301 (1929).

PARKER, Circuit Judge.

This was an action at law instituted in the court below by the Luten Bridge Company, as plaintiff, to recover of Rockingham county, North Carolina, an amount alleged to be due under a contract for the construction of a bridge. The county admits the execution and breach of the contract, but contends that notice of cancellation was given the bridge company before the erection of the bridge was commenced, and that it is liable only for the damages which the company would have sustained, if it had abandoned construction at that time. The judge below refused to strike out an answer filed by certain members of the board of commissioners of the county, admitting liability in accordance with the prayer of the complaint, allowed this pleading to be introduced in evidence as the answer of the county, excluded evidence offered by the county in support of its contentions as to notice of cancellation and damages, and instructed a verdict for plaintiff for the full amount of its claim. From judgment on this verdict the county has appealed.

The facts out of which the case arises, as shown by the affidavits and offers of proof appearing in the record, are as follows: On January 7, 1924, the board of commissioners of Rockingham county voted to award to plaintiff a contract for the construction of the bridge in controversy. Three of the five commissioners favored the awarding of the contract and two opposed it. Much feeling was engendered over the matter, with the result that on February 11, 1924, W. K. Pruitt, one of the commissioners who had voted in the affirmative, sent his resignation to the clerk of the superior court of the county. The clerk received this resignation on the same day, and immediately accepted same and noted his acceptance thereon. Later in the day, Pruitt called him over the telephone and stated that he wished to withdraw the resignation, and later sent him written notice to the same effect. The clerk, however, paid no attention to the attempted withdrawal, and proceeded on the next day to appoint one W. W. Hampton as a member of the board to succeed him.

After his resignation, Pruitt attended no further meetings of the board, and did nothing further as a commissioner of the county. Likewise Pratt and McCollum, the other two members of the board who had voted with him in favor of the contract, attended no further meetings. Hampton, on the other hand, took the oath of office immediately upon his appointment and entered upon the discharge of the duties of a commissioner. He met regularly with the two remaining members of the board, Martin and Barber, in the courthouse at the county seat, and with them attended to all of the business of the county. Between the 12th of February and the first Monday in December following, these three attended, in all, 25 meetings of the board.

At one of these meetings, a regularly advertised called meeting held on February 21st, a resolution was unanimously adopted declaring that the contract for the building of the bridge was not legal and valid, and directing the clerk of the board to notify plaintiff that it refused to recognize same as a valid contract, and that plaintiff should proceed no further thereunder. This resolution also rescinded action of the board theretofore taken looking to the construction of a hard-surfaced road, in which the bridge was to be a mere connecting link. The clerk duly sent a certified copy of this resolution to plaintiff.

At the regular monthly meeting of the board on March 3d, a resolution was passed directing that plaintiff be notified that any work done on the bridge would be done by it at its own risk and hazard, that the board was of the opinion that the contract for the construction of the bridge was not valid and legal, and that, even if the board were mistaken as to this, it did not desire to construct the bridge, and would contest payment for same if constructed. A copy of this resolution was also sent to plaintiff. At the regular monthly meeting on April 7th, a resolution was passed, reciting that the board had been informed that one of its members was privately insisting that the bridge be constructed. It repudiated this action on the part of the member and gave notice that it would not be recognized. At the September meeting, a resolution was passed to the effect that the board would pay no bills presented by plaintiff or any one connected with the bridge. At the time of the passage of the first resolution, very little work toward the construction of the bridge had been done, it being estimated that the total cost of labor done and material on the ground was around $1,900; but, notwithstanding the repudiation of the contract by the county, the bridge company continued with the work of construction.

On November 24, 1924, plaintiff instituted this action against Rockingham county, and against Pruitt, Pratt, McCollum, Martin, and Barber, as constituting its board of commissioners. Complaint was filed, setting forth the execution of the contract and the doing of work by plaintiff thereunder, and alleging that for work done up until November 3, 1924, the county was indebted in the sum of $18,301.07. On November 27th, three days after the filing of the complaint, and only three days before the expiration of the term of office of the members of the old board of commissioners, Pruitt, Pratt, and McCollum met with an attorney at the county seat, and, without notice to or consultation with the other members of the board, so far as appears, had the attorney prepare for them an answer admitting the allegations of the complaint. This answer, which was filed in the cause on the following day, did not purport to be an answer of the county, or of its board of commissioners, but of the three commissioners named.

On December 1, 1924, the newly elected board of commissioners held its first meeting and employed attorneys to defend the action which had been instituted by plaintiff against the county . . . .

At the trial, plaintiff, over the objection of the county, was allowed to introduce in evidence, the answer filed by Pruitt, Pratt, and McCollum, the contract was introduced, and proof was made of the value under the terms of the contract of the work done up to November 3, 1924. The county elicited on cross-examination proof as to the state of the work at the time of the passage of the resolutions to which we have referred. It then offered these resolutions in evidence, together with evidence as to the resignation of Pruitt, the acceptance of his resignation, and the appointment of Hampton; but all of this evidence was excluded, and the jury was instructed to return a verdict for plaintiff for the full amount of its claim. The county preserved exceptions to the rulings which were adverse to it, and contends that there was error on the part of the judge below in denying the motion to strike out the answer filed by Pruitt, Pratt, and McCollum; in allowing same to be introduced in evidence; in excluding the evidence offered of the resignation of Pruitt, the acceptance of his resignation, and the appointment of Hampton, and of the resolutions attempting to cancel the contract and the notices sent plaintiff pursuant thereto; and in directing a verdict for plaintiff in accordance with its claim.

As the county now admits the execution and validity of the contract, and the breach on its part, the ultimate question in the case is one as to the measure of plaintiff's recovery, and the exceptions must be considered with this in mind. Upon these exceptions, three principal questions arise for our consideration, viz. . . . . And (3) whether plaintiff, if the notices are to be deemed action by the county, can recover under the contract for work done after they were received, or is limited to the recovery of damages for breach of contract as of that date . . . .

Coming, then, to the third question- i.e., as to the measure of plaintiff's recovery- we do not think that, after the county had given notice, while the contract was still executory, that it did not desire the bridge built and would not pay for it, plaintiff could proceed to build it and recover the contract price. It is true that the county had no right to rescind the contract, and the notice given plaintiff amounted to a breach on its part; but, after plaintiff had received notice of the breach, it was its duty to do nothing to increase the damages flowing therefrom. If A enters into a binding contract to build a house for B, B, of course, has no right to rescind the contract without A's consent. But if, before the house is built, he decides that he does not want it, and notifies A to that effect, A has no right to proceed with the building and thus pile up damages. His remedy is to treat the contract as broken when he receives the notice, and sue for the recovery of such damages, as he may have sustained from the breach, including any profit which he would have realized upon performance, as well as any other losses which may have resulted to him. In the case at bar, the county decided not to build the road of which the bridge was to be a part, and did not build it. The bridge, built in the midst of the forest, is of no value to the county because of this change of circumstances. When, therefore, the county gave notice to the plaintiff that it would not proceed with the project, plaintiff should have desisted from further work. It had no right thus to pile up damages by proceeding with the erection of a useless bridge.

The contrary view was expressed by Lord Cockburn in Frost v. Knight, L.R. 7 Ex. 111, but, as pointed out by Prof. Williston (Williston on Contracts, vol. 3, p. 2347), it is not in harmony with the decisions in this country. The American rule and the reasons supporting it are well stated by Prof. Williston as follows:

> There is a line of cases running back to 1845 which holds that, after an absolute repudiation or refusal to perform by one party to a contract, the other party cannot continue to perform and recover damages based on full performance. This rule is only a particular application of the general rule of damages that a plaintiff cannot hold a defendant liable for damages which need not have been incurred; or, as it is often stated, the plaintiff must, so far as he can without loss to himself, mitigate the damages caused by the defendant's wrongful act. The application of this rule to the matter in question is obvious. If a man engages to have work done, and afterwards repudiates his contract before the work has been begun or when it has been only partially done, it is inflicting damage on the defendant without benefit to the plaintiff to allow the latter to insist on proceeding with the contract. The work may be useless to the defendant, and yet he would be forced to pay the full contract price. On the other hand, the plaintiff is interested only in the profit he will make out of the contract. If he receives this it is equally advantageous for him to use his time otherwise.

The leading case on the subject in this country is the New York case of Clark v. Marsiglia, 1 Denio (N.Y.) 317, 43 Am.Dec. 670. In that case defendant had employed plaintiff to paint certain pictures for him, but countermanded the order before the work was finished. Plaintiff, however, went on and completed the work and sued for the contract price. In reversing a judgment for plaintiff, the court said:

> The plaintiff was allowed to recover as though there had been no countermand of the order; and in this the court erred. The defendant, by requiring the plaintiff to stop work upon the paintings, violated his contract, and thereby incurred a liability to pay such damages as the plaintiff should sustain. Such damages would include a recompense for the labor done and materials used, and such further sum in damages as might, upon legal principles, be assessed for the breach of the contract; but the plaintiff had no right, by obstinately persisting in the work, to make the penalty upon the defendant greater than it would otherwise have been.

And the rule as established by the great weight of authority in America is summed up in the following statement in 6 R.C.L. 1029, which is quoted with approval by the Supreme Court of North Carolina in the recent case of Novelty Advertising Co. v. Farmers' Mut. Tobacco Warehouse Co., 186 N.C. 197, 119 S.E. 196, 198:

> While a contract is executory a party has the power to stop performance on the other side by an explicit direction to that effect, subjecting himself to such damages as will compensate the other party for being stopped in the performance on his part at that stage in the execution of the contract. The party thus forbidden cannot afterwards go on and thereby increase the damages, and then recover such damages from the other party. The legal right of either party to violate, abandon, or renounce his contract, on the usual terms of compensation to the other for the damages which the law recognizes and allows, subject to the jurisdiction of equity to decree specific performance in proper cases, is universally recognized and acted upon.

This is in accord with the earlier North Carolina decision of Heiser v. Mears, 120 N.C. 443, 27 S.E. 117, in which it was held that, where a buyer countermands his order for goods to be manufactured for him under as executory contract, before the work is completed, it is notice to the seller that he elects to rescind his contract and submit to the legal measure of damages, and that in such case the seller cannot complete the goods and recover the contract price. See, also, Kingman & Co. v. Western Mfg. Co. (C.C.A. 8th) 92 F. 486; Davis v. Bronson, 2 N.D. 300, 50 N.W. 836, 16 L.R.A. 655 and note, 33 Am.St.Rep. 783, and note; Richards v. Manitowoc & Northern Traction Co., 140 Wis. 85, 121 N.W. 837, 133 Am.St.Rep. 1063.

We have carefully considered the cases . . . upon which plaintiff relies; but we do not think that they are at all in point . . . . It follows that there was error in directing a verdict for plaintiff for the full amount of its claim. The measure of plaintiff's damage, upon its appearing that notice was duly given not to build the bridge, is an amount sufficient to compensate plaintiff for labor and materials expended and expense incurred in the part performance of the contract, prior to its repudiation, plus the profit which would have been realized if it had been carried out in accordance with its terms.

Our conclusion, on the whole case, is that there was error in failing to strike out the answer of Pruitt, Pratt, and McCollum, and in admitting same as evidence against the county, in excluding the testimony offered by the county to which we have referred, and in directing a verdict for plaintiff. The judgment below will accordingly be reversed, and the case remanded for a new trial.

Reversed.

NOTES AND QUESTIONS:

1. Read U.C.C. § 2-715 (Buyer's Incidental and Consequential Damages) (2002). How does Avoidability factor into U.C.C. damages?

2. *See* Restatement (Second) of Contracts § 350 (Avoidability as a Limitation on Damages) (1981).

PARKER V. TWENTIETH CENTURY-FOX FILM CORP.
Supreme Court of California
474 P.2d 689 (1970).

BURKE, J.

Defendant Twentieth Century-Fox Film Corporation appeals from a summary judgment granting to plaintiff the recovery of agreed compensation under a written contract for her services as an actress in a motion picture. As will appear, we have concluded that the trial court correctly ruled in plaintiff's favor and that the judgment should be affirmed.

Plaintiff is well known as an actress, and in the contract between plaintiff and defendant is sometimes referred to as the "Artist." Under the contract, dated August 6, 1965, plaintiff was to play the female lead in defendant's contemplated production of a motion picture entitled "Bloomer Girl." The contract provided that defendant would pay plaintiff a minimum "guaranteed compensation" of $53,571.42 per week for 14 weeks commencing May 23, 1966, for a total of $750,000. Prior to May 1966 defendant decided not to produce the picture and by a letter dated April 4, 1966, it notified plaintiff of that decision and that it would not "comply with our obligations to you under" the written contract.

By the same letter and with the professed purpose "to avoid any damage to you," defendant instead offered to employ plaintiff as the leading actress in another film tentatively entitled "Big Country, Big Man" (hereinafter, "Big Country"). The compensation offered was identical, as were 31 of the 34 numbered provisions or articles of the original contract.[1] Unlike "Bloomer Girl," however, which was to have been a musical production, "Big Country" was a dramatic "western type" movie. "Bloomer Girl" was to have been filmed in California; "Big Country" was to be produced in Australia. Also, certain terms in the proffered contract varied from those of the original.[2] Plaintiff was given one week within which to accept; she did not and the offer lapsed. Plaintiff then commenced this action seeking recovery of the agreed guaranteed compensation.

The complaint sets forth two causes of action. The first is for money due under the contract; the second, based upon the same allegations as the first, is for damages resulting from defendant's breach of contract. Defendant in its answer admits the existence and validity of the contract, that plaintiff complied with all the conditions, covenants and promises and stood ready to complete the performance, and that defendant breached and "anticipatorily repudiated" the contract. It denies, however, that any money is due to plaintiff either under the contract or as a result of its breach, and pleads as an affirmative defense to both causes of action plaintiff's allegedly deliberate failure to mitigate damages, asserting that she unreasonably refused to accept its offer of the leading role in "Big Country."

---

[1] Among the identical provisions was the following found in the last paragraph of Article 2 of the original contract: "We [defendant] shall not be obligated to utilize your [plaintiff's] services in or in connection with the Photoplay hereunder, our sole obligation, subject to the terms and conditions of this Agreement, being to pay you the guaranteed compensation herein provided for."

[2] Article 29 of the original contract specified that plaintiff approved the director already chosen for "Bloomer Girl" and that in case he failed to act as director plaintiff was to have approval rights of any substitute director. Article 31 provided that plaintiff was to have the right of approval of the "Bloomer Girl" dance director, and Article 32 gave her the right of approval of the screenplay. Defendant's letter of April 4 to plaintiff, which contained both defendant's notice of breach of the "Bloomer Girl" contract and offer of the lead in "Big Country," eliminated or impaired each of those rights. It read in part as follows: "The terms and conditions of our offer of employment are identical to those set forth in the 'BLOOMER GIRL' Agreement, Articles 1 through 34 and Exhibit A to the Agreement, except as follows:"1. Article 31 of said Agreement will not be included in any contract of employment regarding 'BIG COUNTRY, BIG MAN' as it is not a musical and it thus will not need a dance director."2. In the 'BLOOMER GIRL' agreement, in Articles 29 and 32, you were given certain director and screenplay approvals and you had preapproved certain matters. Since there simply is insufficient time to negotiate with you regarding your choice of director and regarding the screenplay and since you already expressed an interest in performing the role in 'BIG COUNTRY, BIG MAN,' we must exclude from our offer of employment in 'BIG COUNTRY, BIG MAN' any approval rights as are contained in said Articles 29 and 32; however, we shall consult with you respecting the director to be selected to direct the photoplay and will further consult with you with respect to the screenplay and any revisions or changes therein, provided, however, that if we fail to agree ... the decision of ... [defendant] with respect to the selection of a director and to revisions and changes in the said screenplay shall be binding upon the parties to said agreement."

Plaintiff moved for summary judgment under Code of Civil Procedure section 437c, the motion was granted, and summary judgment for $750,000 plus interest was entered in plaintiff's favor. This appeal by defendant followed.

The familiar rules are that the matter to be determined by the trial court on a motion for summary judgment is whether facts have been presented which give rise to a triable factual issue. The court may not pass upon the issue itself. Summary judgment is proper only if the affidavits or declarations in support of the moving party would be sufficient to sustain a judgment in his favor and his opponent does not by affidavit show facts sufficient to present a triable issue of fact. The affidavits of the moving party are strictly construed, and doubts as to the propriety of summary judgment should be resolved against granting the motion. Such summary procedure is drastic and should be used with caution so that it does not become a substitute for the open trial method of determining facts.

As stated, defendant's sole defense to this action which resulted from its deliberate breach of contract is that in rejecting defendant's substitute offer of employment plaintiff unreasonably refused to mitigate damages.

The general rule is that the measure of recovery by a wrongfully discharged employee is the amount of salary agreed upon for the period of service, less the amount which the employer affirmatively proves the employee has earned or with reasonable effort might have earned from other employment.... However, before projected earnings from other employment opportunities not sought or accepted by the discharged employee can be applied in mitigation, the employer must show that the other employment was comparable, or substantially similar, to that of which the employee has been deprived; the employee's rejection of or failure to seek other available employment of a different or inferior kind may not be resorted to in order to mitigate damages . . . .

In the present case defendant has raised no issue of reasonableness of efforts by plaintiffs to obtain other employment; the sole issue is whether plaintiff's refusal of defendant's substitute offer of "Big Country" may be used in mitigation. Nor, if the "Big Country" offer was of employment different or inferior when compared with the original "Bloomer Girl" employment, is there an issue as to whether or not plaintiff acted reasonably in refusing the substitute offer. Despite defendant's arguments to the contrary, no case cited or which our research has discovered holds or suggests that reasonableness is an element of a wrongfully discharged employee's option to reject, or fail to seek, different or inferior employment lest the possible earnings therefrom be charged against him in mitigation of damages.[5]

---

[5] Instead, in each case the reasonableness referred to was that of the efforts of the employee to obtain other employment that was not different or inferior; his right to reject the latter was declared as an unqualified rule of law. Thus, Gonzales v. Internat. Assn. of Machinists, supra., 213 Cal.App.2d 817, 823-824, holds that the trial court correctly instructed the jury that plaintiff union member, a machinist, was required to make "such efforts as the average [member of his union] desiring employment would make at that particular time and place" (italics added); but, further, that the court properly rejected defendant's offer of proof of the availability of other kinds of employment at the same or higher pay than plaintiff usually received and all outside the jurisdiction of his union, as plaintiff could not be required to accept different employment or a nonunion job.In Harris v. Nat. Union etc. Cooks, Stewards, supra., 116 Cal.App.2d 759, 761, the issues were stated to be, inter alia, whether comparable employment was open to each plaintiff employee, and if so whether each plaintiff made a reasonable effort to secure such employment. It was held that the trial court properly sustained an objection to an offer to prove a

Applying the foregoing rules to the record in the present case, with all intendments in favor of the party opposing the summary judgment motion-here, defendant-it is clear that the trial court correctly ruled that plaintiff's failure to accept defendant's tendered substitute employment could not be applied in mitigation of damages because the offer of the "Big Country" lead was of employment both different and inferior, and that no factual dispute was presented on that issue. The mere circumstance that "Bloomer Girl" was to be a musical review calling upon plaintiff's talents as a dancer as well as an actress, and was to be produced in the City of Los Angeles, whereas "Big Country" was a straight dramatic role in a "Western Type" story taking place in an opal mine in Australia, demonstrates the difference in kind between the two employments; the female lead as a dramatic actress in a western style motion picture can by no stretch of imagination be considered the equivalent of or substantially similar to the lead in a song-and-dance production.

Additionally, the substitute "Big Country" offer proposed to eliminate or impair the director and screenplay approvals accorded to plaintiff under the original "Bloomer Girl" contract (see fn. 2, ante), and thus constituted an offer of inferior employment. No expertise or judicial notice is required in order to hold that the deprivation or infringement of an employee's rights held under an original employment contract converts the available "other employment" relied upon by the employer to mitigate damages, into inferior employment which the employee need not seek or accept.

In view of the determination that defendant failed to present any facts showing the existence of a factual issue with respect to its sole defense-plaintiff's rejection of its substitute employment offer in mitigation of damages-we need not consider plaintiff's further contention that for various reasons, including the provisions of the original contract set forth in footnote 1, ante, plaintiff was excused from attempting to mitigate damages.

The judgment is affirmed.

McComb, J., Peters, J., Tobriner, J., Kaus, J., and Roth, J., concurred.

---

custom of accepting a job in a lower rank when work in the higher rank was not available, as "The duty of mitigation of damages... does not require the plaintiff 'to seek or to accept other employment of a different or inferior kind." (P. 764 [5].)See also: Lewis v. Protective Security Life Ins. Co. (1962) 208 Cal.App.2d 582, 584 [25 Cal.Rptr. 213]: " honest effort to find similar employment...." (Italics added.) de la Falaise v. Gaumont-British Picture Corp., supra., 39 Cal.App.2d 461, 469: "reasonable effort." Erler v. Five Points Motors, Inc. (1967) 249 Cal.App.2d 560, 562 [57 Cal.Rptr. 516]: Damages may be mitigated "by a showing that the employee, by the exercise of reasonable diligence and effort, could have procured comparable employment ...." (Italics added.) Savitz v. Gallaccio (1955) 179 Pa.Super. 589 [118 A.2d 282, 286]; Atholwood Dev. Co. v. Houston (1941) 179 Md. 441 [19 A.2d 706, 708]; Harcourt & Co. v. Heller (1933) 250 Ky. 321 [62 S.W.2d 1056]; Alaska Airlines, Inc. v. Stephenson (1954) 217 F.2d 295, 299 [15 Alaska 272]; United Protective Workers v. Ford Motor Co. (7th Cir. 1955) 223 F.2d 49, 52 [48 A.L.R.2d 1285]; Chisholm v. Preferred Bankers' Life Assur. Co. (1897) 112 Mich. 50 [70 N.W. 415]; each of which held that the reasonableness of the employee's efforts, or his excuses for failure, to find other similar employment was properly submitted to the jury as a question of fact. NB: Chisholm additionally approved a jury instruction that a substitute offer of the employer to work for a lesser compensation was not to be considered in mitigation, as the employee was not required to accept it. Williams v. National Organization, Masters, etc. (1956) 384 Pa. 413 [120 A.2d 896, 901 [13]]: "Even assuming that plaintiff...could have obtained employment in ports other than...where he resided, legally he was not compelled to do so in order to mitigate his damages." (Italics added.)

SULLIVAN, Acting Chief Justice (dissenting).

The basic question in this case is whether or not plaintiff acted reasonably in rejecting defendant's offer of alternate employment. The answer depends upon whether that offer (starring in "Big Country, Big Man") was an offer of work that was substantially similar to her former employment (starring in "Bloomer Girl") or of work that was of a different or inferior kind. To my mind this is a factual issue which the trial court should not have determined on a motion for summary judgment. The majority have not only repeated this error but have compounded it by applying the rules governing mitigation of damages in the employer-employee context in a misleading fashion. Accordingly, I respectfully dissent.

The familiar rule requiring a plaintiff in a tort or contract action to mitigate damages embodies notions of fairness and socially responsible behavior which are fundamental to our jurisprudence. Most broadly stated, it precludes the recovery of damages which, through the exercise of due diligence, could have been avoided. Thus, in essence, it is a rule requiring reasonable conduct in commercial affairs. This general principle governs the obligations of an employee after his employer has wrongfully repudiated or terminated the employment contract. Rather than permitting the employee simply to remain idle during the balance of the contract period, the law requires him to make a reasonable effort to secure other employment.[1] He is not obliged, however, to seek or accept any and all types of work which may be available. Only work which is in the same field and which is of the same quality need be accepted.[2]

Over the years the courts have employed various phrases to define the type of employment which the employee, upon his wrongful discharge, is under an obligation to accept. Thus in California alone it has been held that he must accept employment which is "substantially similar" . . . .

For reasons which are unexplained, the majority cite several of these cases yet select from among the various judicial formulations which contain one particular phrase, "Not of a different or inferior kind," with which to analyze this case. I have discovered no historical or theoretical reason to adopt this phrase, which is simply a negative restatement of the affirmative standards set out in the above cases, as the exclusive standard. Indeed, its emergence is an example of the dubious phenomenon of the law responding not to rational judicial choice or changing social conditions, but to unrecognized changes in the language of opinions or legal treatises. However, the phrase is a serviceable one and my concern is not with its use as the standard but rather with what I consider its distortion.

---

[1] The issue is generally discussed in terms of a duty on the part of the employee to minimize loss. The practice is long-established and there is little reason to change despite Judge Cardozo's observation of its subtle inaccuracy. 'The servant is free to accept employment or reject it according to his uncensored pleasure. What is meant by the supposed duty is merely this: That if he unreasonably reject, he will not be heard to say that the loss of wages from then on shall be deemed the jural consequence of the earlier discharge. He has broken the chain of causation, and loss resulting to him thereafter is suffered through his own act.' (McClelland v. Climax Hosiery Mills (1930) 252 N.Y. 347, 359, 169 N.E. 605, 609, concurring opinion.)

[2] This qualification of the rule seems to reflect the simple and humane attitude that it is too severe to demand of a person that he attempt to find and perform work for which he has no training or experience. Many of the older cases hold that one need not accept work in an inferior rank or position nor work which is more menial or arduous. This suggests that the rule may have had its origin in the bourgeois fear of resubmergence in lower economic classes.

. . . It has never been the law that the mere existence of differences between two jobs in the same field is sufficient, as a matter of law, to excuse an employee wrongfully discharged from one from accepting the other in order to mitigate damages. Such an approach would effectively eliminate any obligation of an employee to attempt to minimize damage arising from a wrongful discharge. The only alternative job offer an employee would be required to accept would be an offer of his former job by his former employer.

Although the majority appear to hold that there was a difference "in kind" between the employment offered plaintiff in "Bloomer Girl" and that offered in "Big Country" (opn. at p. 10), an examination of the opinion makes crystal clear that the majority merely point out differences between the two Films (an obvious circumstance) and then apodically assert that these constitute a difference in the Kind of Employment. The entire rationale of the majority boils down to this: that the "mere circumstances" that "Bloomer Girl" was to be a musical review while "Big Country" was a straight drama "demonstrates the difference in kind" since a female lead in a western is not "the equivalent of or substantially similar to" a lead in a musical. This is merely attempting to prove the proposition by repeating it. It shows that the vehicles for the display of the star's talents are different but it does not prove that her employment as a star in such vehicles is of necessity different In kind and either inferior or superior.

I believe that the approach taken by the majority (a superficial listing of differences with no attempt to assess their significance) may subvert a valuable legal doctrine.[5] The inquiry in cases such as this should not be whether differences between the two jobs exist (there will always be differences) but whether the differences which are present are substantial enough to constitute differences in the Kind of employment or, alternatively, whether they render the substitute work employment of an Inferior kind.

It seems to me that This inquiry involves, in the instant case at least, factual determinations which are improper on a motion for summary judgment. Resolving whether or not one job is substantially similar to another or whether, on the other hand, it is of a different or inferior kind, will often (as here) require a critical appraisal of the similarities and differences between them in light of the importance of these differences to the employee. This necessitates a weighing of the evidence, and it is precisely this undertaking which is forbidden on summary judgment.

This is not to say that summary judgment would never be available in an action by an employee in which the employer raises the defense of failure to mitigate damages. No case has come to my attention, however, in which summary judgment has been granted on the issue of whether an employee was obliged to accept available alternate employment. Nevertheless, there may well be cases in which the substitute employment is so manifestly of a dissimilar or inferior sort, the declarations of the plaintiff so complete and those of the defendant so conclusionary and inadequate that no factual issues exist for which a trial is required. This, however, is not such a case.

---

[5] The values of the doctrine of mitigation of damages in this context are that it minimizes the unnecessary personal and social (e.g., nonproductive use of labor, litigation) costs of contractual failure. If a wrongfully discharged employee can, through his own action and without suffering financial or psychological loss in the process, reduce the damages accruing from the breach of contract, the most sensible policy is to require him to do so. I fear the majority opinion will encourage precisely opposite conduct.

It is not intuitively obvious, to me at least, that the leading female role in a dramatic motion picture is a radically different endeavor from the leading female role in a musical comedy film. Nor is it plain to me that the rather qualified rights of director and screenplay approval contained in the first contract are highly significant matters either in the entertainment industry in general or to this plaintiff in particular. Certainly, none of the declarations introduced by plaintiff in support of her motion shed any light on these issues. Nor do they attempt to explain why she declined the offer of starring in "Big Country, Big Man." Nevertheless, the trial court granted the motion, declaring that these approval rights were "critical" and that their elimination altered "the essential nature of the employment."

The plaintiff's declarations were of no assistance to the trial court in its effort to justify reaching this conclusion on summary judgment. Instead, it was forced to rely on judicial notice of the definitions of "motion picture," "screenplay" and "director" (Evid.Code, § 451, subd. (e)) and then on judicial notice of practices in the film industry which were purportedly of "common knowledge." (Evid.Code, § 451, subd. (f) or § 452, subd. (g).) This use of judicial notice was error. Evidence Code section 451, subdivision (e) was never intended to authorize resort to the dictionary to solve essentially factual questions which do not turn upon conventional linguistic usage. More important, however, the trial court's notice of "facts commonly known" violated Evidence Code section 455, subdivision (a). Before this section was enacted there were no procedural safeguards affording litigants an opportunity to be heard as to the propriety of taking judicial notice of a matter or as to the tenor of the matter to be noticed. Section 455 makes such an opportunity (which may be an element of due process, see Evid.Code, § 455, Law Revision Com. Comment (a)) mandatory and its provisions should be scrupulously adhered to. "Judicial notice can be a valuable tool in the adversary system for the lawyer as well as the court" (Kongsgaard, Judicial Notice (1966) 18 Hastings L.J. 117, 140) and its use is appropriate on motions for summary judgment. Its use in this case, however, to determine on summary judgment issues fundamental to the litigation without complying with statutory requirements of notice and hearing is a highly improper effort to "cut the Gordion knot of involved litigation."

The majority do not confront the trial court's misuse of judicial notice. They avoid this issue through the expedient of declaring that neither judicial notice nor expert opinion (such as that contained in the declarations in opposition to the motion) is necessary to reach the trial court's conclusion. Something, however, clearly Is needed to support this conclusion. Nevertheless, the majority make no effort to justify the judgment through an examination of the plaintiff's declarations. Ignoring the obvious insufficiency of these declarations, the majority announce that "the deprivation or infringement of an employee's rights held under an original employment contract" changes the alternate employment offered or available into employment of an inferior kind.

I cannot accept the proposition that an offer which eliminates Any contract right, regardless of its significance, is, as a matter of law, an offer of employment of an inferior kind. Such an absolute rule seems no more sensible than the majority's earlier suggestion that the mere existence of differences between two jobs is sufficient to render them employment of different kinds. Application of such per se rules will severely undermine the principle of mitigation of damages in the employer-employee context.

I remain convinced that the relevant question in such cases is whether or not a particular contract provision is so significant that its omission create employment of an inferior kind. This question is, of course, intimately bound up in what I consider the ultimate issue: whether or not the employee acted reasonably. This will generally involve a factual inquiry to ascertain the importance of the particular contract term and a process of weighing the absence of that term against the countervailing advantages of the alternate employment. In the typical case, this will mean that summary judgment must be withheld.

In the instant case, there was nothing properly before the trial court by which the importance of the approval rights could be ascertained, much less evaluated. Thus, in order to grant the motion for summary judgment, the trial court misused judicial notice. In upholding the summary judgment, the majority here rely upon per se rules which distort the process of determining whether or not an employee is obliged to accept particular employment in mitigation of damages.

I believe that the judgment should be reversed so that the issue of whether or not the offer of the lead role in "Big Country, Big Man" was of employment comparable to that of the lead role in "Bloomer Girl" may be determined at trial.

NOTES AND QUESTIONS:

1. Recall *Jacob & Youngs, Inc. v. Kent*, 230 N.Y. 239, 245 (Ct. of App. 1921) ("The rule that gives a remedy in cases of substantial performance with compensation for defects of trivial or inappreciable importance, has been developed by the courts as an instrument of justice. The measure of the allowance must be shaped to the same end.").

2. *See* Restatement (Second) of Contracts § 350 (Avoidability as a Limitation on Damages) (1981).

3. Read U.C.C. §§ 2-704 (Seller's Right to Identify Goods to the Contract Notwithstanding Breach or to Salvage Unfinished Goods), 2-715 (Buyer's Incidental and Consequential Damages). How does avoidability factor into U.C.C. damages?

SECTION 3. EQUITABLE REMEDIES

A. SPECIFIC PERFORMANCE

VAN WAGNER ADVERTISING V. S & M ENTERPRISES
Court of Appeals of New York
67 N.Y.2d 186 (1986).

Kaye, J.

Specific performance of a contract to lease "unique" billboard space is properly denied when damages are an adequate remedy to compensate the tenant and equitable relief would impose a disproportionate burden on the defaulting landlord. However, owing to an error in the assessment of damages, the order of the Appellate Division should be modified so as to remit the matter to Supreme Court, New York County, for further proceedings with respect to damages.

By agreement dated December 16, 1981, Barbara Michaels leased to plaintiff, Van Wagner Advertising, for an initial period of three years plus option periods totaling seven additional years space on the eastern exterior wall of a building on East 36th Street in Manhattan. Van Wagner was in the business of erecting and leasing billboards, and the parties anticipated that Van Wagner would erect a sign on the leased space, which faced an exit ramp of the Midtown Tunnel and was therefore visible to vehicles entering Manhattan from that tunnel.

In early 1982 Van Wagner erected an illuminated sign and leased it to Asch Advertising, Inc. for a three-year period commencing March 1, 1982. However, by agreement dated January 22, 1982, Michaels sold the building to defendant S & M Enterprises. Michaels informed Van Wagner of the sale in early August 1982, and on August 19, 1982 S & M sent Van Wagner a letter purporting to cancel the lease as of October 18 pursuant to section 1.05 . . . .

Trial Term declared the lease "valid and subsisting" and found that the "demised space is unique as to location for the particular advertising purpose intended by Van Wagner and Michaels, the original parties to the Lease." However, the court declined to order specific performance in light of its finding that Van Wagner "has an adequate remedy at law for damages." Moreover, the court noted that specific performance "would be inequitable in that its effect would be disproportionate in its harm to the defendant and its assistance to plaintiff." Concluding that "[t]he value of the unique qualities of the demised space has been fixed by the contract Van Wagner has with its advertising client, Asch for the period of the contract," the court awarded Van Wagner the lost revenues on the Asch sublease for the period through trial, without prejudice to a new action by Van Wagner for subsequent damages if S & M did not permit Van Wagner to reoccupy the space. On Van Wagner's motion to resettle the judgment to provide for specific performance, the court adhered to its judgment.

On cross appeals the Appellate Division affirmed, without opinion. We granted both parties leave to appeal.

Van Wagner seeks specific performance of the contract, S & M urges that money damages are adequate but that the amount of the award was improper.[2]

---

[2] We note that the parties' contentions regarding the remedy of specific performance in general, mirror a scholarly debate that has persisted throughout our judicial history, reflecting fundamentally divergent views about the quality of a bargained-for promise. While the usual remedy in Anglo-American law has been damages, rather than compensation "in kind" (see,Holmes,The Path of the Law,10 Harv L Rev 457, 462 [1897]; Holmes, The Common Law, at 299-301 [1881]; and Gilmore, The Death of Contract, at 14-15), the current trend among commentators appears to favor the remedy of specific performance (see, Farnsworth,Legal Remedies for Breach of Contract, 70 Colum L Rev 1145, 1156 [1970]; Linzer,On the Amorality of Contract Remedies--Efficiency, Equity, and the Second Restatement,81 Colum L Rev 111 [1981]; and Schwartz,The Case for Specific Performance, 89 Yale LJ 271 [1979]), but the view is not unanimous(see,Posner, Economic Analysis of Law § 4.9, at 89-90 [2d ed 1977]; Yorio,In Defense of Money Damages for Breach of Contract,82 Colum L Rev 1365 [1982]).

Whether or not to award specific performance is a decision that rests in the sound discretion of the trial court, and here that discretion was not abused. Considering first the nature of the transaction, specific performance has been imposed as the remedy for breach of contracts for the sale of real property . . . but the contract here is to lease rather than sell an interest in real property. While specific performance is available, in appropriate circumstances, for breach of a commercial or residential lease, specific performance of real property leases is not in this State awarded as a matter of course . . . .

Van Wagner argues that specific performance must be granted in light of the trial court's finding that the "demised space is unique as to location for the particular advertising purpose intended." The word "uniqueness" is not, however, a magic door to specific performance. A distinction must be drawn between physical difference and economic interchangeability. The trial court found that the leased property is physically unique, but so is every parcel of real property and so are many consumer goods. Putting aside contracts for the sale of real property, where specific performance has traditionally been the remedy for breach, uniqueness in the sense of physical difference does not itself dictate the propriety of equitable relief.

By the same token, at some level all property may be interchangeable with money. Economic theory is concerned with the degree to which consumers are willing to substitute the use of one good for another (see, Kronman,Specific Performance, 45 U. Chi. L. Rev. 351, 359), the underlying assumption being that "every good has substitutes, even if only very poor ones," and that "all goods are ultimately commensurable" (id.). Such a view, however, could strip all meaning from uniqueness, for if all goods are ultimately exchangeable for a price, then all goods may be valued. Even a rare manuscript has an economic substitute in that there is a price for which any purchaser would likely agree to give up a right to buy it, but a court would in all probability order specific performance of such a contract on the ground that the subject matter of the contract is unique.

The point at which breach of a contract will be redressable by specific performance thus must lie not in any inherent physical uniqueness of the property but instead in the uncertainty of valuing it: "What matters, in measuring money damages, is the volume, refinement, and reliability of the available information about substitutes for the subject matter of the breached contract. When the relevant information is thin and unreliable, there is a substantial risk that an award of money damages will either exceed or fall short of the promisee's actual loss. Of course this risk can always be reduced--but only at great cost when reliable information is difficult to obtain. Conversely, when there is a great deal of consumer behavior generating abundant and highly dependable information about substitutes, the risk of error in measuring the promisee's loss may be reduced at much smaller cost. In asserting that the subject matter of a particular contract is unique and has no established market value, a court is really saying that it cannot obtain, at reasonable cost, enough information about substitutes to permit it to calculate an award of money damages without imposing an unacceptably high risk of undercompensation on the injured promisee. Conceived in this way, the uniqueness test seems economically sound." (45 U Chi L Rev, at 362.) This principle is reflected in the case law . . . and is essentially the position of the Restatement (Second) of Contracts, which lists "the difficulty of proving damages with reasonable certainty" as the first factor affecting adequacy of damages (Restatement [Second] of Contracts § 360 [a]).

Thus, the fact that the subject of the contract may be "unique as to location for the particular advertising purpose intended" by the parties does not entitle a plaintiff to the remedy of specific performance.

Here, the trial court correctly concluded that the value of the "unique qualities" of the demised space could be fixed with reasonable certainty and without imposing an unacceptably high risk of undercompensating the injured tenant. Both parties complain: Van Wagner asserts that while lost revenues on the Asch contract may be adequate compensation, that contract expired February 28, 1985, its lease with S & M continues until 1992, and the value of the demised space cannot reasonably be fixed for the balance of the term. S & M urges that future rents and continuing damages are necessarily conjectural, both during and after the Asch contract, and that Van Wagner's damages must be limited to 60 days--the period during which Van Wagner could cancel Asch's contract without consequence in the event Van Wagner lost the demised space. S & M points out that Van Wagner's lease could remain in effect for the full 10-year term, or it could legitimately be extinguished immediately, either in conjunction with a bona fide sale of the property by S & M, or by a reletting of the building if the new tenant required use of the billboard space for its own purposes. Both parties' contentions were properly rejected.

First, it is hardly novel in the law for damages to be projected into the future. Particularly where the value of commercial billboard space can be readily determined by comparisons with similar uses--Van Wagner itself has more than 400 leases--the value of this property between 1985 and 1992 cannot be regarded as speculative. Second, S & M having successfully resisted specific performance on the ground that there is an adequate remedy at law, cannot at the same time be heard to contend that damages beyond 60 days must be denied because they are conjectural. If damages for breach of this lease are indeed conjectural, and cannot be calculated with reasonable certainty, then S & M should be compelled to perform its contractual obligation by restoring Van Wagner to the premises. Moreover, the contingencies to which S & M points do not, as a practical matter, render the calculation of damages speculative. While S & M could terminate the Van Wagner lease in the event of a sale of the building, this building has been sold only once in 40 years; S & M paid several million dollars, and purchased the building in connection with its plan for major development of the block. The theoretical termination right of a future tenant of the existing building also must be viewed in light of these circumstances. If any uncertainty is generated by the two contingencies, then the benefit of that doubt must go to Van Wagner and not the contract violator. Neither contingency allegedly affecting Van Wagner's continued contractual right to the space for the balance of the lease term is within its own control; on the contrary, both are in the interest of S & M . . . . Thus, neither the need to project into the future nor the contingencies allegedly affecting the length of Van Wagner's term render inadequate the remedy of damages for S & M's breach of its lease with Van Wagner.

The trial court, additionally, correctly concluded that specific performance should be denied on the ground that such relief "would be inequitable in that its effect would be disproportionate in its harm to defendant and its assistance to plaintiff" . . . . It is well settled that the imposition of an equitable remedy must not itself work an inequity, and that specific performance should not be an undue hardship . . . . This conclusion is "not within the absolute discretion of the Supreme Court" . . . . Here, however, there was no abuse of discretion; the finding that specific performance would disproportionately harm S & M and benefit Van Wagner has been affirmed by the Appellate Division and has support in the proof regarding S & M's projected development of the property.

While specific performance was properly denied, the court erred in its assessment of damages. Our attention is drawn to two alleged errors.

First, both parties are dissatisfied with the award of lost profits on the Asch contract: Van Wagner contends that the award was too low because it failed to take into account incidental damages such as sign construction, and S & M asserts that it was too high because it failed to take into account offsets against alleged lost profits such as painting costs. Both arguments are precluded. Although the trial was not bifurcated or limited to the issue of liability, the Asch contract was placed in evidence and neither party chose to submit additional proof of incidental damages or other expenses for that period. Nor--as is evident from the judgment--did the trial court understand that any separate presentations would be made as to damages for that period. Based on the Asch contract indicating revenues, and the lease indicating expenses, the trial court properly calculated Van Wagner's lost profits. Having found that the value of the space was fixed by the Asch contract for the entire period of that contract, however, the court erred in awarding the lost revenues only through November 23, 1983. Damages should have been awarded for the duration of the Asch contract.

Second, the court fashioned relief for S & M's breach of contract only to the time of trial, and expressly contemplated that "[i]f defendant continues to exclude plaintiff from the leased space action for continuing damages may be brought." In requiring Van Wagner to bring a multiplicity of suits to recover its damages the court erred. Damages should have been awarded through the expiration of Van Wagner's lease.

Accordingly, the order of the Appellate Division should be modified, with costs to plaintiff, and the case remitted to Supreme Court, New York County, for further proceedings in accordance with this opinion and, as so modified, affirmed.

CENTEX HOMES CORP. V. BOAG
Superior Court of New Jersey, Chancery Division
320 A.2d 194 (1974).

GELMAN, J.S.C . . .

Plaintiff Centex Homes Corporation (Centex) is engaged in the development and construction of a luxury high-rise condominium project in the Boroughs of Cliffside Park and Fort Lee. The project when completed will consist of six 31-story buildings containing in excess of 3600 condominium apartment units, together with recreational buildings and facilities, parking garages and other common elements associated with this form of residential development. As sponsor of the project Centex offers the condominium apartment units for sale to the public and has filed an offering plan covering such sales with the appropriate regulatory agencies of the States of New Jersey and New York.

On September 13, 1972 defendants Mr. & Mrs. Eugene Boag executed a contract for the purchase of apartment unit No. 2019 in the building under construction and known as "Winston Towers 200." The contract purchase price was $73,700, and prior to signing the contract defendants had given Centex a deposit in the amount of $525. At or shortly after signing the contract defendants delivered to Centex a check in the amount of $6,870 which, together with the deposit, represented approximately 10% of the total purchase of the apartment unit. Shortly thereafter Boag was notified by his employer that he was to be transferred to the Chicago, Illinois, area. Under date of September 27, 1972 he advised Centex that he "would be unable to complete the purchase" agreement and stopped payment on the $6,870 check. Centex deposited the check for collection approximately two weeks after receiving notice from defendant, but the check was not honored by defendants' bank. On August 8, 1973 Centex instituted this action in Chancery Division for specific performance of the purchase agreement or, in the alternative, for liquidated damages in the amount of $6,870. The matter is presently before this court on the motion of Centex for summary judgment.

Both parties acknowledge, and our research has confirmed, that no court in this State or in the United States has determined in any reported decision whether the equitable remedy of specific performance will lie for the enforcement of a contract for the sale of a condominium apartment. The closest decision on point is Silverman v. Alcoa Plaza Associates, 37 A.D.2d 166, 323 N.Y.S.2d 39 (App.Div.1971), which involved a default by a contract-purchaser of shares of stock and a proprietary lease in a cooperative apartment building. The seller, who was also the sponsor of the project, retained the deposit and sold the stock and the lease to a third party for the same purchase price. The original purchaser thereafter brought suit to recover his deposit, and on appeal the court held that the sale of shares of stock in a cooperative apartment building, even though associated with a proprietary lease, was a sale of personalty and not of an interest in real estate. Hence, the seller was not entitled to retain the contract deposit as liquidated damages.

As distinguished from a cooperative plan of ownership such as involved in Silverman, under a condominium housing scheme each condominium apartment unit constitutes a separate parcel of real property which may be dealt with in the same manner as any real estate. Upon closing of title the apartment unit owner receives a recordable deed which confers upon him the same rights and subjects him to the same obligations as in the case of traditional forms of real estate ownership, the only difference being that the condominium owner receives in addition an undivided interest in the common elements associated with the building and assigned to each unit . . . .

Centex urges that since the subject matter of the contract is the transfer of a fee interest in real estate, the remedy of specific performance is available to enforce the agreement under principles of equity which are well-settled in this state . . . .

The principle underlying the specific performance remedy is equity's jurisdiction to grant relief where the damage remedy at law is inadequate. The text writers generally agree that at the time this branch of equity jurisdiction was evolving in England, the presumed uniqueness of land as well as its importance to the social order of that era led to the conclusion that damages at law could never be adequate to compensate for the breach of a contract to transfer an interest in land. Hence specific performance became a fixed remedy in this class of transactions. See 11 Williston on Contracts (3d ed. 1968) § 1418A; 5A Corbin on Contracts § 1143 (1964). The judicial attitude has remained substantially unchanged and is expressed in Pomeroy as follows:

> . . . in applying this doctrine the courts of equity have established the further rule that in general the legal remedy of damages is inadequate in all agreements for the sale or letting of land, or of any estate therein; and therefore in such class of contracts the jurisdiction is always exercised, and a specific performance granted, unless prevented by other and independent equitable considerations which directly affect the remedial right of the complaining party. . . (1 Pomeroy, Equity Jurisprudence (5th ed. 1941), § 221(b)).

While the inadequacy of the damage remedy suffices to explain the origin of the vendee's right to obtain specific performance in equity, it does not provide a Rationale for the availability of the remedy at the instance of the vendor of real estate. Except upon a showing of unusual circumstances or a change in the vendor's position, such as where the vendee has entered into possession, the vendor's damages are usually measurable, his remedy at law is adequate and there is no jurisdictional basis for equitable relief . . . The early English precedents suggest that the availability of the remedy in a suit by a vendor was an outgrowth of the equitable concept of mutuality, I.e., that equity would not specifically enforce an agreement unless the remedy was available to both parties . . . .

So far as can be determined from our decisional law, the mutuality of remedy concept has been the prop which has supported equitable jurisdiction to grant specific performance in actions by vendors of real estate. The earliest reported decision in this State granting specific performance in favor of a vendor is Rodman v. Zilley, 1 N.J.Eq. 320 (Ch.1831), in which the vendee (who was also the judgment creditor) was the highest bidder at an execution sale. In his opinion Chancellor Vroom did not address himself to the question whether the vendor had an adequate remedy at law. The first reported discussion of the question occurs in Hopper v. Hopper, 16 N.J.Eq. 147 (Ch.1863), which was an action by a vendor to compel specific performance of a contract for the sale of land. In answer to the contention that equity lacked jurisdiction because the vendor had an adequate legal remedy, Chancellor Green said (at p. 148);

> It constitutes no objection to the relief prayed for, that the application is made by the vendor to enforce the payment of the purchase money, and not by the vendee to compel a delivery of the title. The vendor has not a complete remedy at law. Pecuniary damages for the breach of the contract is not what the complainant asks, or is entitled to receive at the hands of a court of equity. He asks to receive the price stipulated to be paid in lieu of the land. The doctrine is well established that the remedy is mutual, and that the vendor may maintain his bill in all cases where the purchaser could sue for a specific performance of the agreement.

No other Rationale has been offered by our decisions subsequent to Hopper, and specific performance has been routinely granted to vendors without further discussion of the underlying jurisdictional issue.

Our present Supreme Court has squarely held, however, that mutuality of remedy is not an appropriate basis for granting or denying specific performance. Fleischer v. James Drug Store, 1 N.J. 138, 62 A.2d 383 (1948); see also, Restatement, Contracts § 372; 11 Williston, Contracts (3d ed. 1968), § 1433. The test is whether the obligations of the contract are mutual and not whether each is entitled to precisely the same remedy in the event of a breach. In Fleischer plaintiff sought specific performance against a cooperative buying and selling association although his membership contract was terminable by him on 60 days' notice. Justice Heher said:

> And the requisite mutuality is not wanting. The contention Contra rests upon the premise that, although the corporation "can terminate the contract only in certain restricted and unusual circumstances, any 'member' may withdraw at any time by merely giving notice."
>
> Clearly, there is mutuality of obligation, for until his withdrawal complainant is under a continuing obligation of performance in the event of performance by the corporation. It is not essential that the remedy of specific performance be mutual . . . . The modern view is that the rule of mutuality of remedy is satisfied if the decree of specific performance operates effectively against both parties and gives to each the benefit of a mutual obligation . . . .
>
> The fact that the remedy of specific enforcement is available to one party to a contract is not in itself a sufficient reason for making the remedy available to the other; but it may be decisive when the adequacy of damages is difficult to determine and there is no other reason for refusing specific enforcement. Restatement, Contracts (1932), sections 372, 373. It is not necessary, to serve the ends of equal justice, that the parties shall have identical remedies in case of breach. (at 149, 62 A.2d at 388).

The disappearance of the mutuality of remedy doctrine from our law dictates the conclusion that specific performance relief should no longer be automatically available to a vendor of real estate, but should be confined to those special instances where a vendor will otherwise suffer an economic injury for which his damage remedy at law will not be adequate, or where other equitable considerations require that the relief be granted. Cf. Dover Shopping Center, Inc. v. Cushman's Sons, Inc., 63 N.J.Super. 384, 394, 164 A.2d 785 (App.Div.1960). As Chancellor Vroom noted in King v. Morford, 1 N.J.Eq. 274, 281-282 (Ch.Div.1831), whether a contract should be specifically enforced is always a matter resting in the sound discretion of the court and

> . . . considerable caution should be used in decreeing the specific performance of agreements . . . and the court is bound to see that it really does the complete justice which it aims at, and which is the ground of its jurisdiction.

Here the subject matter of the real estate transaction-a condominium apartment unit-has no unique quality but is one of hundreds of virtually identical units being offered by a developer for sale to the public. The units are sold by means of sample, in this case model apartments, in much the same manner as items of personal property are sold in the market place. The sales prices for the units are fixed in accordance with schedule filed by Centex as part of its offering plan, and the only variance as between apartments having the same floor plan (of which six plans are available) is the floor level or the bulding location within the project. In actuality, the condominium apartment units, regardless of their realty label, share the same characteristics as personal property.

From the foregoing one must conclude that the damages sustained by a condominium sponsor resulting from the breach of the sales agreement are readily measurable and the damage remedy at law is wholly adequate. No compelling reasons have been shown by Centex for the granting of specific performance relief and its complaint is therefore dismissed as to the first count.

Centex also seeks money damages pursuant to a liquidated damage clause in its contract with the defendants. It is sufficient to note only that under the language of that clause (which was authored by Centex) liquidated damages are limited to such moneys as were paid by defendant at the time the default occurred. Since the default here consisted of the defendant's stopping payment of his check for the balance of the down-payment, Centex's liquidated damages are limited to the retention of the 'moneys paid' prior to that date, or the initial $525 deposit. Accordingly, the second count of the complaint for damage relief will also be dismissed.

THE CASE OF MARY CLARK, A WOMAN OF COLOR
Supreme Court of Indiana.
1 Blackf. 122 (1821).

HOLMAN, J.

In obedience to a writ of habeas corpus, issued by the Knox Circuit Court, G. W. Johnson brought before that Court the body of Mary Clark, (a woman of color,) said to be illegally detained by him; and assigned as the cause of her detention, that she was his servant by indenture, executed at Vincennes, in this State, on the 24th of October, 1816: which indenture is set out in the return, regularly executed and acknowledged, by which the said Mary (being a free woman) voluntarily bound herself to serve him as an indented servant and house maid for 20 years. This cause of detention was deemed sufficient by the Circuit Court, and said Mary remanded to the custody of the said Johnson. She has appealed to this Court.

This application of Mary Clark to be discharged from her state of servitude, clearly evinces that the service she renders to the obligee is involuntary; and the Constitution, having determined that there shall be no involuntary servitude in this State, seems at the first view to settle this case in favor of the appellant. But a question still remains, whether her service, although involuntary in fact, shall not be considered voluntary by operation of law, being performed under an indenture voluntarily executed. This indenture is a writing obligatory. The clause in the 7th section of the 11th article of the Constitution, that provides that no indenture hereafter executed by any negro or mulatto without the bounds of this State, shall be of any validity within this State, has no bearing on it. An indenture executed by a negro or mulatto out of this State, is by virtue of this provision, absolutely void; and can be set up neither as a demand for the services therein specified, nor as a remuneration in damages for a non-performance. But the Constitution, having confirmed the liberty of all our citizens, has considered them as possessing equal right and ability to contract, and, without any reference to the color of the contracting parties, has given equal validity to all their contracts when executed within the State. We shall, therefore, discard all distinctions that might be drawn from the color of the appellant, and consider this indenture as a writing obligatory, and test it, in all its bearings, by the principles that are applicable to all cases of a similar nature. It is a covenant for personal service, and the obligee requires a specific performance. It may be laid down as a general rule, that neither the common law nor the statutes in force in this State recognize the coercion of a specific performance of contracts. The principal, if not the only exceptions to this general rule, are statutory provisions, few, if any, of which are applicable to this State, and none of them has any bearing on this case . . . . The case of soldiers and sailors depends on national policy, and cannot be used in the elucidation of matters of private right.

There are some covenants that may be specially enforced in equity; but they are of a very different nature from the contract before us. They are mostly covenants for the conveyance of real estate, and in no case have any relation to the person. But if the law were silent, the policy of enforcing a specific performance of a covenant of this nature, would settle this question. Whenever contracting parties disagree about the performance of their contract, and a Court of justice of necessity interposes to settle their different rights, their feelings become irritated against each other, and the losing party feels mortified and degraded in being compelled to perform for the other what he had previously refused, and the more especially if that performance will place him frequently in the presence or under the direction of his adversary. But this state of degradation, this irritation of feeling, could be in no other case so manifestly experienced, as in the case of a common servant, where the master would have a continual right of command, and the servant be compelled to a continual obedience. Many covenants, the breaches of which are only remunerated in damages, might be specially performed, either by a third person at a distance from the adversary, or in a short space of time. But a covenant for service, if performed at all, must be performed under the eye of the master; and might, as in the case before us, require a number of years. Such a performance, if enforced by law, would produce a state of servitude as degrading and demoralizing in its consequences, as a state of absolute slavery; and if enforced under a government like ours, which acknowledges a personal equality, it would be productive of a state of feeling more discordant and irritating than slavery itself. Consequently, if all other contracts were specifically enforced by law, it would be impolitic to extend the principle to contracts for personal service . . . . But it is not the master who in this case applies for legal aid. He has not appealed to a Court of justice to obtain a specific performance of this indenture. All he asks from the constituted authorities is, that they would withhold their assistance from his servant. Does this alter the case in his favor? Is it more consistent with good policy, that a man possessing the power, should be left to enforce a specific performance of a contract in his own behalf, than that the officers of justice, on a full consideration of his case, should enforce it for him? These questions are not only easily answered in the negative, but their reverse is unquestionably true. Deplorable indeed would be the state of society, if the obligee in every contract had a right to seize the person of the obligor, and force him to comply with his undertaking. In contracts for personal service, the exercise of such a right would be most alarming in its consequences. If a man, contracting to labor for another a day, a month, a year, or a series of years, were liable to be taken by his adversary, and compelled to perform the labor, it would either put a stop to all such contracts, or produce in their performance a state of domination in the one party, and abject humiliation in the other. We may, therefore, unhesitatingly conclude, that when the law will not directly coerce a specific performance, it will not leave a party to exercise the law of the strong, and coerce it in his own behalf. A state of servitude thus produced, either by direct or permissive coercion, would not be considered voluntary either in fact or in law. It presents a case where legal intendment can have no operation. While the appellant remained in the service of the obligee without complaint, the law presumes that her service was voluntarily performed; but her application to the Circuit Court to be discharged from the custody of her master, establishes the fact that she is willing to serve no longer; and, while this state of the will appears, the law cannot, by any possibility of intendment, presume that her service is voluntary

. . . . The appellant in this case is of legal age to regulate her own conduct; she has a right to the exercise of volition; and, having declared her will in respect to the present service, the law has no intendment that can contradict that declaration. We must take the fact as it appears, and declare the law accordingly. The fact then is, that the appellant is in a state of involuntary servitude; and we are bound by the constitution, the supreme law of the land, to discharge her therefrom.

Per Curiam.

The judgment is reversed with costs, and the woman discharged. . . .

B. INJUNCTIONS

WALGREEN CO. V. SARA CREEK PROPERTY
United States Court of Appeals, Seventh Circuit
966 F.2d 273 (7th Cir. 1992).

POSNER, Circuit Judge.

This appeal from the grant of a permanent injunction raises fundamental issues concerning the propriety of injunctive relief . . . . The essential facts are simple. Walgreen has operated a pharmacy in the Southgate Mall in Milwaukee since its opening in 1951. Its current lease, signed in 1971 and carrying a 30-year, 6-month term, contains, as had the only previous lease, a clause in which the landlord, Sara Creek, promises not to lease space in the mall to anyone else who wants to operate a pharmacy or a store containing a pharmacy . . . .

In 1990, fearful that its largest tenant-what in real estate parlance is called the "anchor tenant"-having gone broke was about to close its store, Sara Creek informed Walgreen that it intended to buy out the anchor tenant and install in its place a discount store operated by Phar-Mor Corporation, a "deep discount" chain, rather than, like Walgreen, just a "discount" chain. Phar-Mor's store would occupy 100,000 square feet, of which 12,000 would be occupied by a pharmacy the same size as Walgreen's. The entrances to the two stores would be within a couple of hundred feet of each other.

Walgreen filed this diversity suit for breach of contract against Sara Creek and Phar-Mor and asked for an injunction against Sara Creek's letting the anchor premises to Phar-Mor. After an evidentiary hearing, the judge found a breach of Walgreen's lease and entered a permanent injunction against Sara Creek's letting the anchor tenant premises to Phar-Mor until the expiration of Walgreen's lease. He did this over the defendants' objection that Walgreen had failed to show that its remedy at law-damages-for the breach of the exclusivity clause was inadequate. Sara Creek had put on an expert witness who testified that Walgreen's damages could be readily estimated, and Walgreen had countered with evidence from its employees that its damages would be very difficult to compute, among other reasons because they included intangibles such as loss of goodwill.

Sara Creek reminds us that damages are the norm in breach of contract as in other cases. Many breaches, it points out, are "efficient" in the sense that they allow resources to be moved into a more valuable use. Perhaps this is one-the value of Phar-Mor's occupancy of the anchor premises may exceed the cost to Walgreen of facing increased competition. If so, society will be better off if Walgreen is paid its damages, equal to that cost, and Phar-Mor is allowed to move in rather than being kept out by an injunction. That is why injunctions are not granted as a matter of course, but only when the plaintiff's damages remedy is inadequate .... Walgreen's is not, Sara Creek argues; the projection of business losses due to increased competition is a routine exercise in calculation. Damages representing either the present value of lost future profits or (what should be the equivalent . . .) the diminution in the value of the leasehold have either been awarded or deemed the proper remedy in a number of reported cases for breach of an exclusivity clause in a shopping-center lease .... Why, Sara Creek asks, should they not be adequate here?

Sara Creek makes a beguiling argument that contains much truth, but we do not think it should carry the day. For if, as just noted, damages have been awarded in some cases of breach of an exclusivity clause in a shopping-center lease, injunctions have been issued in others. The choice between remedies requires a balancing of the costs and benefits of the alternatives. The task of striking the balance is for the trial judge, subject to deferential appellate review in recognition of its particularistic, judgmental, fact-bound character. As we said in an appeal from a grant of a preliminary injunction . . . "The question for us [appellate judges] is whether the [district] judge exceeded the bounds of permissible choice in the circumstances, not what we would have done if we had been in his shoes." Roland Machinery Co. v. Dresser Industries, Inc., 749 F.2d 380, 390 (7th Cir.1984).

The plaintiff who seeks an injunction has the burden of persuasion-damages are the norm, so the plaintiff must show why his case is abnormal. But when, as in this case, the issue is whether to grant a permanent injunction, not whether to grant a temporary one, the burden is to show that damages are inadequate ....

The benefits of substituting an injunction for damages are twofold. First, it shifts the burden of determining the cost of the defendant's conduct from the court to the parties. If it is true that Walgreen's damages are smaller than the gain to Sara Creek from allowing a second pharmacy into the shopping mall, then there must be a price for dissolving the injunction that will make both parties better off. Thus, the effect of upholding the injunction would be to substitute for the costly processes of forensic fact determination the less costly processes of private negotiation. Second, a premise of our free-market system, and the lesson of experience here and abroad as well, is that prices and costs are more accurately determined by the market than by government. A battle of experts is a less reliable method of determining the actual cost to Walgreen of facing new competition than negotiations between Walgreen and Sara Creek over the price at which Walgreen would feel adequately compensated for having to face that competition.

That is the benefit side of injunctive relief but there is a cost side as well. Many injunctions require continuing supervision by the court, and that is costly . . . . Some injunctions are problematic because they impose costs on third parties . . . . A more subtle cost of injunctive relief arises from the situation that economists call "bilateral monopoly," in which two parties can deal only with each other: the situation that an injunction creates. The sole seller of widgets selling to the sole buyer of that product would be an example. But so will be the situation confronting Walgreen and Sara Creek if the injunction is upheld. Walgreen can "sell" its injunctive right only to Sara Creek, and Sara Creek can "buy" Walgreen's surrender of its right to enjoin the leasing of the anchor tenant's space to Phar-Mor only from Walgreen. The lack of alternatives in bilateral monopoly creates a bargaining range, and the costs of negotiating to a point within that range may be high. Suppose the cost to Walgreen of facing the competition of Phar-Mor at the Southgate Mall would be $1 million, and the benefit to Sara Creek of leasing to Phar-Mor would be $2 million. Then at any price between those figures for a waiver of Walgreen's injunctive right both parties would be better off, and we expect parties to bargain around a judicial assignment of legal rights if the assignment is inefficient. R.H. Coase, "The Problem of Social Cost," 3 J. Law & Econ. 1 (1960). But each of the parties would like to engross as much of the bargaining range as possible-Walgreen to press the price toward $2 million, Sara Creek to depress it toward $1 million. With so much at stake, both parties will have an incentive to devote substantial resources of time and money to the negotiation process. The process may even break down, if one or both parties want to create for future use a reputation as a hard bargainer; and if it does break down, the injunction will have brought about an inefficient result. All these are in one form or another costs of the injunctive process that can be avoided by substituting damages.

The costs and benefits of the damages remedy are the mirror of those of the injunctive remedy. The damages remedy avoids the cost of continuing supervision and third-party effects, and the cost of bilateral monopoly as well. It imposes costs of its own, however, in the form of diminished accuracy in the determination of value, on the one hand, and of the parties' expenditures on preparing and presenting evidence of damages, and the time of the court in evaluating the evidence, on the other.

The weighing up of all these costs and benefits is the analytical procedure that is or at least should be employed by a judge asked to enter a permanent injunction, with the understanding that if the balance is even the injunction should be withheld. The judge is not required to explicate every detail of the analysis and he did not do so here, but as long we are satisfied that his approach is broadly consistent with a proper analysis we shall affirm; and we are satisfied here. The determination of Walgreen's damages would have been costly in forensic resources and inescapably inaccurate. The lease had ten years to run. So Walgreen would have had to project its sales revenues and costs over the next ten years, and then project the impact on those figures of Phar-Mor's competition, and then discount that impact to present value. All but the last step would have been fraught with uncertainty.

It is difficult to forecast the profitability of a retail store over a decade, let alone to assess the impact of a particular competitor on that profitability over that period. Of course one can hire an expert to make such predictions . . . and if injunctive relief is infeasible the expert's testimony may provide a tolerable basis for an award of damages. We cited cases in which damages have been awarded for the breach of an exclusivity clause in a shopping-center lease. But they are awarded in such circumstances not because anyone thinks them a clairvoyant forecast but because it is better to give a wronged person a crude remedy than none at all . . . . Sara Creek presented evidence of what happened (very little) to Walgreen when Phar-Mor moved into other shopping malls in which Walgreen has a pharmacy, and it was on the right track in putting in comparative evidence. But there was a serious question whether the other malls were actually comparable to the Southgate Mall, so we cannot conclude, in the face of the district judge's contrary conclusion, that the existence of comparative evidence dissolved the difficulties of computing damages in this case. Sara Creek complains that the judge refused to compel Walgreen to produce all the data that Sara Creek needed to demonstrate the feasibility of forecasting Walgreen's damages. Walgreen resisted, on grounds of the confidentiality of the data and the cost of producing the massive data that Sara Creek sought. Those are legitimate grounds; and the cost (broadly conceived) they expose of pretrial discovery, in turn presaging complexity at trial, is itself a cost of the damages remedy that injunctive relief saves.

Damages are not always costly to compute, or difficult to compute accurately. In the standard case of a seller's breach of a contract for the sale of goods where the buyer covers by purchasing the same product in the market, damages are readily calculable by subtracting the contract price from the market price and multiplying by the quantity specified in the contract. But this is not such a case and here damages would be a costly and inaccurate remedy; and on the other side of the balance some of the costs of an injunction are absent and the cost that is present seems low. The injunction here . . . is a simple negative injunction-Sara Creek is not to lease space in the Southgate Mall to Phar-Mor during the term of Walgreen's lease-and the costs of judicial supervision and enforcement should be negligible.

To summarize, the judge did not exceed the bounds of reasonable judgment in concluding that the costs (including forgone benefits) of the damages remedy would exceed the costs (including forgone benefits) of an injunction. We need not consider whether, as intimated by Walgreen, exclusivity clauses in shopping-center leases should be considered presumptively enforceable by injunctions. Although we have described the choice between legal and equitable remedies as one for case-by-case determination, the courts have sometimes picked out categories of case in which injunctive relief is made the norm. The best-known example is specific performance of contracts for the sale of real property.

The rule that specific performance will be ordered in such cases as a matter of course is a generalization of the considerations discussed above. Because of the absence of a fully liquid market in real property and the frequent presence of subjective values (many a homeowner, for example, would not sell his house for its market value), the calculation of damages is difficult; and since an order of specific performance to convey a piece of property does not create a continuing relation between the parties, the costs of supervision and enforcement if specific performance is ordered are slight. The exclusivity clause in

Walgreen's lease relates to real estate, but we hesitate to suggest that every contract involving real estate should be enforceable as a matter of course by injunctions.

AFFIRMED.

LUMLEY V. WAGNER
Lord Chancellor's Court
42 Eng. Rep. 687 (1852).

[The bill in this suit was filed on the 22d April 1852, by Benjamin Lumley, the lessee of Her Majesty's Theatre, against Johanna Wagner . . . it stated that in November 1851 Joseph Bacher, as the agent of . . . Johanna Wagner, came to and concluded at Berlin an agreement in writing . . . as follows:

"The undersigned Mr. Benjamin Lumley, possessor of Her Majesty's Theatre at London, and of the Italian Opera at Paris, of the one part, and Mademoiselle Johanna Wagner, cantatrice of the Court of His Majesty the King of Prussia, with the consent of her father, Mr. A. Wagner, residing at Berlin, of the other part, have concerted and concluded the following contract: --First, Mademoiselle Johanna Wagner binds herself to sing three months at the theatre of Mr. Lumley, Her Majesty's, at London, to date from the 1st of April 1852 . . . ."

"Mademoiselle Wagner engages herself not to use her talents at any other threatre, nor in any concert or reunion, public or private, without the written authorization of Mr. Lumley."

The bill then stated that J. and A. Wagner subsequently made another engagement with the Defendant F. Gye, by which it was agreed that the Defendant J. Wagner should, for a larger sum than that stipulated by the agreement with the Plaintiff, sing at the Royal Italian Opera, Covent Garden, and abandon the agreement with the Plaintiff . . . .

The bill prayed that the Defendants Johanna Wagner and Albert Wagner might be restrained from violating or committing any breach of the last article of the agreement; that the Defendant Johanna Wagner might be restrained from singing and performing or singing at the Royal Italian Opera, Covent Garden, or at any other theatre or place without the sanction or permission in writing of the Plaintiff during the existence of the agreement with the Plaintiff] . . . .

THE LORD CHANCELLOR.

The question which I have to decide in the present case arises out of a very simple contract, the effect of which is, that the Defendant Johanna Wagner should sing at Her Majesty's Theatre for a certain number of nights, and that she should not sing elsewhere (for that is the true construction) during that period. As I understand the points taken by the Defendant's counsel in support of this appeal they in effect come to this, namely, that a Court of Equity ought not to grant an injunction except in cases connected with specific performance, or where the injunction being to compel a party to forbear from committing an act (and not to perform an act), that injunction will complete the whole of the agreement remaining unexecuted . . . .

The present is a mixed case, consisting not of two correlative acts to be done--one by the Plaintiff, and the other by the Defendants, which state of facts may have and in some cases has introduced a very important difference-but of an act to be done by J. Wagner alone, to which is superadded a negative stipulation on her part to abstain from the commission of any act which will break in upon her affirmative covenant; the one being ancillary to, concurrent and operating together with, the other. The agreement to sing for the Plaintiff during three months at his theatre, and during that time not to sing for anybody else, is not a correlative contract, it is in effect one contract; and though beyond all doubt this Court could not interfere to enforce the specific performance of the whole of this contract, yet in all sound construction, and according to the true spirit of the agreement, the engagement to perform for three months at one theatre must necessarily exclude the right to perform at the same time at another theatre. It was clearly intended that J. Wagner was to exert her vocal abilities to the utmost to aid the theatre to which she agreed to attach herself. I am of opinion that if she had attempted, even in the absence of any negative stipulation, to perform at another theatre, she would have broken the spirit and true meaning of the contract as much as she would now do with reference to the contract into which she has actually entered.

Wherever this Court has not proper jurisdiction to enforce specific performance, it operates to bind men's consciences, as far as they can be bound, to a true and literal performance of their agreements; and it will not suffer them to depart from their contracts at their pleasure, leaving the party with whom they have contracted to the mere chance of any damages which a jury may give. The exercise of this jurisdiction has, I believe, had a wholesome tendency towards the maintenance of that good faith which exists in this country to a much greater degree perhaps than in any other; and although the jurisdiction is not to be extended, yet a Judge would desert his duty who did not act up to what his predecessors have handed down as the rule for his guidance in the administration of such an equity.

It was objected that the operation of the injunction in the present case was mischievous, excluding the Defendant J. Wagner from performing at any other theatre while this Court had no power to compel her to perform at Her Majesty's Theatre. It is true that I have not the means of compelling her to sing, but she has no cause of complaint if I compel her to abstain from the commission of an act which she has bound herself not to do, and thus possibly cause her to fulfil her engagement. The jurisdiction which I now exercise is wholly within the power of the Court, and being of opinion that it is a proper case for interfering, I shall leave nothing unsatisfied by the judgment I pronounce. The effect, too, of the injunction in restraining J. Wagner from singing elsewhere may, in the event of an action being brought against her by the Plaintiff, prevent any such amount of vindictive damages being given against her as a jury might probably be inclined to give if she had carried her talents and exercised them at the rival theatre: the injunction may also, as I have said, tend to the fulfillment of her engagement; though, in continuing the injunction, I disclaim doing indirectly what I cannot do directly . . . .

NOTES AND QUESTIONS:

1. Historically, the decision of whether to grant equitable relief rests within the sound discretion of the court. *See Eastern Motors Inns, Inc. v. Ricci*, 565 A.2d 1265, 1268 (R.I. 1989). What other considerations should the court take into account in deciding whether to issue a decree of specific performance? *See New York Football Giants, Inc. v. Los Angeles Chargers Football Club, Inc.*, 291 F.2d 471 (5th Cir. 1961) (quoting the ancient maxim "he who comes into equity must come with clean hands."). *But see Houston Oilers, Inc. v. Neeley*, 361 F.2d 36 (10th Cir. 1966) (". . . [b]ut the doctrine does not exclude all wrongdoers from a court of equity nor should it be applied in every case where the conduct of a party may be considered unconscionable or inequitable.").

SECTION 4. RESTITUTION

We now explore the remedial protection of the parties' restitutionary interest, which can be legal or equitable in nature. As a legal remedy, it serves as an alternative measure of damages for breach of contract. As an equitable remedy, it serves as an independent theory of recovery to avoid unjust enrichment, regardless of whether an enforceable contract exists. As you examine the following cases and material, consider what showing the requesting party must make to recover his restitutionary interests.

RESTATEMENT (SECOND) OF CONTRACTS
§ 371. MEASURE OF RESTITUTION INTEREST

If a sum of money is awarded to protect a party's restitution interest, it may as justice requires be measured by either

(a) the reasonable value to the other party of what he received in terms of what it would have cost him to obtain it from a person in the claimant's position, or

(b) the extent to which the other party's property has been increased in value or his other interests advanced.

A. RESTITUTION FOR BREACH OF CONTRACT

UNITED STATES V. ALGERNON BLAIR, INC.
United States Court of Appeals, Fourth Circuit
479 F.2d 638 (4th Cir. 1973).

CRAVEN, Circuit Judge:

May a subcontractor, who justifiably ceases work under a contract because of the prime contractor's breach, recover in quantum meruit the value of labor and equipment already furnished pursuant to the contract irrespective of whether he would have been entitled to recover in a suit on the contract? We think so, and, for reasons to be stated, the decision of the district court will be reversed.

The subcontractor, Coastal Steel Erectors, Inc., brought this action under the provisions of the Miller Act, 40 U.S.C.A. § 270a et seq., in the name of the United States against Algernon Blair, Inc., and its surety, United States Fidelity and Guaranty Company. Blair had entered a contract with the United States for the construction of a naval hospital in Charleston County, South Carolina. Blair had then contracted with Coastal to perform certain steel erection and supply certain equipment in conjunction with Blair's contract with the United States. Coastal commenced performance of its obligations, supplying its own cranes for handling and placing steel. Blair refused to pay for crane rental, maintaining that it was not obligated to do so under the subcontract. Because of Blair's failure to make payments for crane rental, and after completion of approximately 28 percent of the subcontract, Coastal terminated its performance. Blair then proceeded to complete the job with a new subcontractor. Coastal brought this action to recover for labor and equipment furnished.

The district court found that the subcontract required Blair to pay for crane use and that Blair's refusal to do so was such a material breach as to justify Coastal's terminating performance. This finding is not questioned on appeal. The court then found that under the contract the amount due Coastal, less what had already been paid, totaled approximately $37,000. Additionally, the court found Coastal would have lost more than $37,000 if it had completed performance. Holding that any amount due Coastal must be reduced by any loss it would have incurred by complete performance of the contract, the court denied recovery to Coastal. While the district court correctly stated the "'normal' rule of contract damages,"[1] we think Coastal is entitled to recover in quantum meruit.

In United States for Use of Susi Contracting Co. v. Zara Contracting Co., 146 F.2d 606 (2d Cir. 1944), a Miller Act action, the court was faced with a situation similar to that involved here-the prime contractor had unjustifiably breached a subcontract after partial performance by the subcontractor. The court stated:

> For it is an accepted principle of contract law, often applied in the case of construction contracts, that the promisee upon breach has the option to forego any suit on the contract and claim only the reasonable value of his performance.
>
> 146 F.2d at 610.

The Tenth Circuit has also stated that the right to seek recovery under quantum meruit in a Miller Act case is clear. Quantum meruit recovery is not limited to an action against the prime contractor but may also be brought against the Miller Act surety, as in this case. Further, that the complaint is not clear in regard to the theory of a plaintiff's recovery does not preclude recovery under quantum meruit. Narragansett Improvement Co. v. United States, 290 F.2d 577 (1st Cir. 1961). A plaintiff may join a claim for quantum meruit with a claim for damages from breach of contract.

[1] Fuller & Perdue, The Reliance Interest in Contract Damages, 46 Yale L.J. 52 (1936); Restatement of Contracts § 333 (1932).

In the present case, Coastal has, at its own expense, provided Blair with labor and the use of equipment. Blair, who breached the subcontract, has retained these benefits without having fully paid for them. On these facts, Coastal is entitled to restitution in quantum meruit.

> The "restitution interest," involving a combination of unjust impoverishment with unjust gain, presents the strongest case for relief. If, following Aristotle, we regard the purpose of justice as the maintenance of an equilibrium of goods among members of society, the restitution interest presents twice as strong a claim to judicial intervention as the reliance interest, since if A not only causes B to lose one unit but appropriates that unit to himself, the resulting discrepancy between A and B is not one unit but two.
>
> Fuller & Perdue, The Reliance Interest in Contract Damages, 46 Yale L.J. 52, 56 (1936).[6]

The impact of quantum meruit is to allow a promisee to recover the value of services he gave to the defendant irrespective of whether he would have lost money on the contract and been unable to recover in a suit on the contract. Scaduto v. Orlando, 381 F.2d 587, 595 (2d Cir. 1967). The measure of recovery for quantum meruit is the reasonable value of the performance, Restatement of Contracts § 347 (1932); and recovery is undiminished by any loss which would have been incurred by complete performance. 12 Williston on Contracts § 1485, at 312 (3d ed. 1970). While the contract price may be evidence of reasonable value of the services, it does not measure the value of the performance or limit recovery.[7] Rather, the standard for measuring the reasonable value of the services rendered is the amount for which such services could have been purchased from one in the plaintiff's position at the time and place the services were rendered.

Since the district court has not yet accurately determined the reasonable value of the labor and equipment use furnished by Coastal to Blair, the case must be remanded for those findings. When the amount has been determined, judgment will be entered in favor of Coastal, less payments already made under the contract. Accordingly, for the reasons stated above, the decision of the district court is reversed and remanded with instructions.

---

[6] This case also comes within the requirements of the Restatements for recovery in quantum meruit. Restatement of Restitution § 107 (1937); Restatement of Contracts §§ 347-357 (1932).

[7] Scaduto v. Orlando, 381 F.2d 587, 595-596 (2d Cir. 1967); St. Paul-Mercury Indem. Co. v. United States ex rel. Jones, 238 F.2d 917, 924 (10th Cir. 1956); United States for Use of Susi Contracting Co. v. Zara Contracting Co., 146 F.2d 606, 610-611 (2d Cir. 1944).It should be noted, however, that in suits for restitution there are many cases permitting the plaintiff to recover the value of benefits conferred on the defendant, even though this value exceeds that of the return performance promised by the defendant. In these cases it is no doubt felt that the defendant's breach should work a forfeiture of his right to retain the benefits of an advantageous bargain.Fuller & Perdue, supra at 77.

B. THE BREACHING PLAINTIFF

BRITTON V. TURNER
Supreme Court of New Hampshire
6 N.H. 481 (1834).

. . . .

PARKER, J. delivered the opinion of the court.

It may be assumed, that the labor performed by the plaintiff, and for which he seeks to recover a compensation in this action, was commenced under a special contract to labor for the defendant the term of one year, for the sum of one hundred and twenty dollars, and that the plaintiff has labored but a portion of that time, and has voluntarily failed to complete the entire contract.

It is clear, then, that he is not entitled to recover upon the contract itself, because the service, which was to entitle him to the sum agreed upon, has never been performed.

But the question arises, can the plaintiff, under these circumstances, recover a reasonable sum for the service he has actually performed, under the count in quantum meruit.

Upon this, and questions of a similar nature, the decisions to be found in the books are not easily reconciled.

It has been held, upon contracts of this kind for labor to be performed at a specified price, that the party who voluntarily fails to fulfil the contract by performing the whole labor contracted for, is not entitled to recover any thing for the labor actually performed, however much he may have done towards the performance, and this has been considered the settled rule of law upon this subject.

That such rule in its operation may be very unequal, not to say unjust, is apparent.

A party who contracts to perform certain specified labor, and who breaks his contract in the first instance, without any attempt to perform it, can only be made liable to pay the damages which the other party has sustained by reason of such non performance, which in many instances may be trifling--whereas a party who in good faith has entered upon the performance of his contract, and nearly completed it, and then abandoned the further performance--although the other party has had the full benefit of all that has been done, and has perhaps sustained no actual damage--is in fact subjected to a loss of all which has been performed, in the nature of damages for the non fulfilment of the remainder, upon the technical rule, that the contract must be fully performed in order to a recovery of any part of the compensation.

By the operation of this rule, then, the party who attempts performance may be placed in a much worse situation than he who wholly disregards his contract, and the other party may receive much more, by the breach of the contract, than the injury which he has sustained by such breach, and more than he could be entitled to were he seeking to recover damages by an action.

The case before us presents an illustration. Had the plaintiff in this case never entered upon the performance of his contract, the damage could not probably have been greater than some small expense and trouble incurred in procuring another to do the labor which he had contracted to perform. But having entered upon the performance, and labored nine and a half months, the value of which labor to the defendant as found by the jury is $95, if the defendant can succeed in this defence, he in fact receives nearly five sixths of the value of a whole year's labor, by reason of the breach of contract by the plaintiff a sum not only utterly disproportionate to any probable, not to say possible damage which could have resulted from the neglect of the plaintiff to continue the remaining two and an half months, but altogether beyond any damage which could have been recovered by the defendant, had the plaintiff done nothing towards the fulfilment of his contract.

Another illustration is furnished in Lantry v. Parks, 8 Cowen, 83. There the defendant hired the plaintiff for a year, at ten dollars per month. The plaintiff worked ten and an half months, and then left saying he would work no more for him. This was on Saturday--on Monday the plaintiff returned, and offered to resume his work, but the defendant said he would employ him no longer. The court held that the refusal of the defendant on Saturday was a violation of his contract, and that he could recover nothing for the labor performed.

There are other cases, however, in which principles have been adopted leading to a different result.

It is said, that where a party contracts to perform certain work, and to furnish materials, as, for instance, to build a house, and the work is done, but with some variations from the mode prescribed by the contract, yet if the other party has the benefit of the labor and materials he should be bound to pay so much as they are reasonably worth. . . .

A different doctrine seems to have been holden in Ellis v. Hamlen, 3 Taunt. 52, and it is apparent, in such cases, that if the house has not been built in the manner specified in the contract, the work has not been done. The party has no more performed what he contracted to perform, than he who has contracted to labor for a certain period, and failed to complete the time.

It is in truth virtually conceded in such cases that the work has not been done, for if it had been, the party performing it would be entitled to recover upon the contract itself, which it is held he cannot do.

Those cases are not to be distinguished, in principle, from the present, unless it be in the circumstance, that where the party has contracted to furnish materials, and do certain labor, as to build a house in a specified manner, if it is not done according to the contract, the party for whom it is built may refuse to receive it--elect to take no benefit from what has been performed--and therefore if he does receive, he shall be bound to pay the value--

whereas in a contract for labor, merely, from day to day, the party is continually receiving the benefit of the contract under an expectation that it will be fulfilled, and cannot, upon the breach of it, have an election to refuse to receive what has been done, and thus discharge himself from payment.

But we think this difference in the nature of the contracts does not justify the application of a different rule in relation to them.

The party who contracts for labor merely, for a certain period, does so with full knowledge that he must, from the nature of the case, be accepting part performance from day to day, if the other party commences the performance, and with knowledge also that the other may eventually fail of completing the entire term.

If under such circumstances he actually receives a benefit from the labor performed, over and above the damage occasioned by the failure to complete, there is as much reason why he should pay the reasonable worth of what has thus been done for his benefit, as there is when he enters and occupies the house which has been built for him, but not according to the stipulations of the contract, and which he perhaps enters, not because he is satisfied with what has been done, but because circumstances compel him to accept it such as it is, that he should pay for the value of the house. . . .

It is as "hard upon the plaintiff to preclude him from recovering at all, because he has failed as to part of his entire undertaking," where his contract is to labor for a certain period, as it can be in any other description of contract, provided the defendant has received a benefit and value from the labor actually performed.

We hold then, that where a party undertakes to pay upon a special contract for the performance of labor, or the furnishing of materials, he is not to be charged upon such special agreement until the money is earned according to the terms of it, and where the parties have made an express contract the law will not imply and raise a contract different from that which the parties have entered into, except upon some farther transaction between the parties. . . .

But if, where a contract is made of such a character, a party actually receives labor, or materials, and thereby derives a benefit and advantage, over and above the damage which has resulted from the breach of the contract by the other party, the labor actually done, and the value received, furnish a new consideration, and the law thereupon raises a promise to pay to the extent of the reasonable worth of such excess. This may be considered as making a new case, one not within the original agreement, and the party is entitled to "recover on his new case, for the work done, not as agreed, but yet accepted by the defendant." 1 Dane's Abr. 224.

If on such failure to perform the whole, the nature of the contract be such that the employer can reject what has been done, and refuse to receive any benefit from the part performance, he is entitled so to do, and in such case is not liable to be charged, unless he has before assented to and accepted of what has been done, however much the other party may have done towards the performance. He has in such case received nothing, and having contracted to receive nothing but the entire matter contracted for, he is not bound to pay, because his express promise was only to pay on receiving the whole, and having actually received nothing the law cannot and ought not to raise an implied promise to pay. But where the party receives value--takes and uses the materials, or has advantage from the labor, he is liabe to pay the reasonable worth of what he has received. 1 Camp. 38, Farnsworth v. Garrard. And the rule is the same whether it was received and accepted by the assent of the party prior to the breach, under a contract by which, from its nature, he was to receive labor, from time to time until the completion of the whole contract; or whether it was received and accepted by an assent subsequent to the performance of all which was in fact done. If he received it under such circumstances as precluded him from rejecting it afterwards, that does not alter the case--it has still been received by his assent.

The amount, however, for which the employer ought to be charged, where the laborer abandons his contract, is only the reasonable worth, or the amount of advantage he receives upon the whole transaction, (6 N.H. 15, Wadleigh v. Sutton) and, in estimating the value of the labor, the contract price for the service cannot be exceeded. 7 Green. 78 ; 4 Wendell, 285, Dubois v. Delaware & Hudson Canal Company; 7 Wend. 121, Koon v. Greenman.

If a person makes a contract fairly he is entitled to have it fully performed, and if this is not done he is entitled to damages. He may maintain a suit to recover the amount of damage sustained by the non performance.

The benefit and advantage which the party takes by the labor, therefore, is the amount of value which he receives, if any, after deducting the amount of damage; and if he elects to put this in defence he is entitled so to do, and the implied promise which the law will raise, in such case, is to pay such amount of the stipulated price for the whole labor, as remains after deducting what it would cost to procure a completion of the residue of the service, and also any damage which has been sustained by reason of the non fulfilment of the contract.

If in such case it be found that the damages are equal to, or greater than the amount of the labor performed, so that the employer, having a right to the full performance of the contract, has not upon the whole case received a beneficial service, the plaintiff cannot recover.

This rule, by binding the employer to pay the value of the service he actually receives, and the laborer to answer in damages where he does not complete the entire contract, will leave no temptation to the former to drive the laborer from his service, near the close of his term, by ill treatment, in order to escape from payment; nor to the latter to desert his service before the stipulated time, without a sufficient reason; and it will in most instances settle the whole controversy in one action, and prevent a multiplicity of suits and cross actions. . . .

Applying the principles thus laid down, to this case, the plaintiff is entitled to judgment on the verdict.

The defendant sets up a mere breach of the contract in defence of the action, but this cannot avail him. He does not appear to have offered evidence to show that he was damnified by such breach, or to have asked that a deduction should be made upon that account. The direction to the jury was therefore correct, that the plaintiff was entitled to recover as much as the labor performed was reasonably worth, and the jury appear to have allowed a pro rata compensation, for the time which the plaintiff labored in the defendant's service.

As the defendant has not claimed or had any adjustment of damages, for the breach of the contract, in this action, if he has actually sustained damage he is still entitled to a suit to recover the amount. . . .

Judgment on the verdict.

C. RESTITUTION WHEN THERE IS NO CONTRACT: QUASI-CONTRACT

MAGLICA V. MAGLICA
California Court of Appeals
66 Cal. App. 4th 442 (1998).

SILLS, P. J.

I. Introduction

This case forces us to confront the legal doctrine known as "quantum meruit" in the context of a case about an unmarried couple who lived together and worked in a business solely owned by one of them. Quantum meruit is a Latin phrase, meaning "as much as he deserves,"[1] and is based on the idea that someone should get paid for beneficial goods or services which he or she bestows on another.[2]

The trial judge instructed the jury that the reasonable value of the plaintiff's services was either the value of what it would have cost the defendant to obtain those services from someone else or the "value by which" he had "benefitted [sic] as a result" of those services. The instruction allowed the jury to reach a whopping number in favor of the plaintiff-$84 million-because of the tremendous growth in the value of the business over the years.

As we explain later, the finding that the couple had no contract in the first place is itself somewhat suspect because certain jury instructions did not accurately convey the law concerning implied-in-fact contracts. However, assuming that there was indeed no contract, the quantum meruit award cannot stand. The legal test for recovery in quantum meruit is not

---

[1] See Black's Law Dictionary (5th ed. 1979) page 1119, column 1.

[2] See, e.g., Earhart v. William Low Co. (1979) 25 Cal.3d 503, 518 [158 Cal.Rptr. 887, 600 P.2d 1344] ("Where one person renders services at the request of another and the latter obtains benefits from the services, the law ordinarily implies a promise to pay for the services."); Palmer v. Gregg (1967) 65 Cal.2d 657, 660 [56 Cal.Rptr. 97, 422 P.2d 985] ("The measure of recovery in quantum meruit is the reasonable value of the services rendered, provided they were of direct benefit to the defendant."); Hedging Concepts, Inc. v. First Alliance Mortgage Co. (1996) 41 Cal.App.4th 1410, 1419 [49 Cal.Rptr.2d 191] ("A quantum meruit or quasi-contractual recovery rests upon the equitable theory that a contract to pay for services rendered is implied by law for reasons of justice ....").

the value of the benefit, but value of the services (assuming, of course, that the services were beneficial to the recipient in the first place). In this case the failure to appreciate that fine distinction meant a big difference. People who work for businesses for a period of years and then walk away with $84 million do so because they have acquired some equity in the business, not because $84 million is the going rate for the services of even the most workaholic manager. In substance, the court was allowing the jury to value the plaintiff's services as if she had made a sweetheart stock option deal-yet such a deal was precisely what the jury found she did not make. So the $84 million judgment cannot stand.

On the other hand, plaintiff was hindered in her ability to prove the existence of an implied-in-fact contract by a series of jury instructions which may have misled the jury about certain of the factors which bear on such contracts. The instructions were insufficiently qualified. They told the jury flat out that such facts as a couple's living together or holding themselves out as husband and wife or sharing a common surname did not mean that they had any agreement to share assets. That is not exactly correct. Such factors can, indeed, when taken together with other facts and in context, show the existence of an implied-in-fact contract. At most the jury instructions should have said that such factors do not by themselves necessarily show an implied-in-fact contract. Accordingly, when the case is retried, the plaintiff will have another chance to prove that she indeed had a deal for a share of equity in the defendant's business.

II. Facts

The important facts in this case may be briefly stated. Anthony Maglica, a Croatian immigrant, founded his own machine shop business, Mag Instrument, in 1955. He got divorced in 1971 and kept the business. That year he met Claire Halasz, an interior designer. They got on famously, and lived together, holding themselves out as man and wife-hence Claire began using the name Claire Maglica-but never actually got married. And, while they worked side by side building the business, Anthony never agreed-or at least the jury found Anthony never agreed-to give Claire a share of the business. When the business was incorporated in 1974 all shares went into Anthony's name. Anthony was the president and Claire was the secretary. They were paid equal salaries from the business after incorporation. In 1978 the business began manufacturing flashlights, and, thanks in part to some great ideas and hard work on Claire's part (e.g., coming out with a purse-sized flashlight in colors), the business boomed. Mag Instrument, Inc., is now worth hundreds of millions of dollars.

In 1992 Claire discovered that Anthony was trying to transfer stock to his children but not her, and the couple split up in October. In June 1993 Claire sued Anthony for, among other things, breach of contract, breach of partnership agreement, fraud, breach of fiduciary duty and quantum meruit. The case came to trial in the spring of 1994. The jury awarded $84 million for the breach of fiduciary duty and quantum meruit causes of action, finding that $84 million was the reasonable value of Claire's services.

III. Discussion

A. The Jury's Finding That There Was No Agreement to Hold Property for One Another Meant There Was No Breach of Fiduciary Duty

. . . .

B. Quantum Meruit Allows Recovery for the Value of Beneficial Services, Not the Value by Which Someone Benefits From Those Services

The absence of a contract between Claire and Anthony, however, would not preclude her recovery in quantum meruit: As every first year law student knows or should know, recovery in quantum meruit does not require a contract. (See 1 Witkin, Summary of Cal. Law (9th ed. 1987) Contracts, § 112, p. 137; see, e.g., B.C. Richter Contracting Co. v. Continental Cas. Co. (1964) 230 Cal.App.2d 491, 499-500 [41 Cal.Rptr. 98].)[4]

The classic formulation concerning the measure of recovery in quantum meruit is found in Palmer v. Gregg, supra, 65 Cal.2d 657. Justice Mosk, writing for the court, said: "The measure of recovery in quantum meruit is the reasonable value of the services rendered provided they were of direct benefit to the defendant." (Id. at p. 660, italics added; see also Producers Cotton Oil Co. v. Amstar Corp. (1988) 197 Cal.App.3d 638, 659 [242 Cal.Rptr. 914].)

The underlying idea behind quantum meruit is the law's distaste for unjust enrichment. If one has received a benefit which one may not justly retain, one should "restore the aggrieved party to his [or her] former position by return of the thing or its equivalent in money." (1 Witkin, Summary of Cal. Law, supra, Contracts, § 91, p. 122.)

The idea that one must be benefited by the goods and services bestowed is thus integral to recovery in quantum meruit; hence courts have always required that the plaintiff have bestowed some benefit on the defendant as a prerequisite to recovery. (See Earhart v. William Low Co., supra, 25 Cal.3d 503, 510 [explaining origins of quantum meruit recovery in actions for recovery of money tortiously retained; law implied an obligation to restore " 'benefit,' unfairly retained by the defendant"].)

But the threshold requirement that there be a benefit from the services can lead to confusion, as it did in the case before us. It is one thing to require that the defendant be benefited by services, it is quite another to measure the reasonable value of those services by the value by which the defendant was "benefited" as a result of them. Contract price and the reasonable value of services rendered are two separate things; sometimes the reasonable value of services exceeds a contract price. (See B. C. Richter Contracting Co. v. Continental Cas. Co., supra, 230 Cal.App.2d at p. 500.) And sometimes it does not.

[4] The doctrine can become trickier when an actual contract is involved. (See Hedging Concepts, Inc. v. First Alliance Mortgage Co., supra, 41 Cal.App.4th 1410, 1419-1420 [quantum meruit recovery cannot conflict with terms of actual contract between parties, lest the court in effect impose its own ideas of a fair deal on the parties].)

At root, allowing quantum meruit recovery based on "resulting benefit" of services rather than the reasonable value of beneficial services affords the plaintiff the best of both contractual and quasi-contractual recovery. Resulting benefit is an open-ended standard, which, as we have mentioned earlier, can result in the plaintiff obtaining recovery amounting to de facto ownership in a business all out of reasonable relation to the value of services rendered. After all, a particular service timely rendered can have, as Androcles was once pleasantly surprised to discover in the case of a particular lion, disproportionate value to what it would cost on the open market.

The facts in this court's decision in Passante v. McWilliam (1997) 53 Cal.App.4th 1240 [62 Cal.Rptr.2d 298] illustrate the point nicely. In Passante, the attorney for a fledgling baseball card company gratuitously arranged a needed loan for $100,000 at a crucial point in the company's history; because the loan was made the company survived and a grateful board promised the attorney a 3 percent equity interest in the company. The company eventually became worth more than a quarter of a billion dollars, resulting in the attorney claiming $33 million for his efforts in arranging but a single loan. This court would later conclude, because of the attorney's duty to the company as an attorney, that the promise was unenforceable. (See id. at pp. 1247-1248.) Interestingly enough, however, the one cause of action the plaintiff in Passante did not sue on was quantum meruit; while this court opined that the attorney should certainly get paid "something" for his efforts, a $33 million recovery in quantum meruit would have been too much. Had the services been bargained for, the going price would likely have been simply a reasonable finder's fee. (See id. at p. 1248.)

The jury instruction given here allows the value of services to depend on their impact on a defendant's business rather than their reasonable value. True, the services must be of benefit if there is to be any recovery at all; even so, the benefit is not necessarily related to the reasonable value of a particular set of services. Sometimes luck, sometimes the impact of others makes the difference. Some enterprises are successful; others less so. Allowing recovery based on resulting benefit would mean the law imposes an exchange of equity for services, and that can result in a windfall-as in the present case-or a serious shortfall in others. Equity-for-service compensation packages are extraordinary in the labor market, and always the result of specific bargaining. To impose such a measure of recovery would make a deal for the parties that they did not make themselves. If courts cannot use quantum meruit to change the terms of a contract which the parties did make (see Hedging Concepts, Inc. v. First Alliance Mortgage Co., supra, 41 Cal.App.4th at p. 1420), it follows that neither can they use quantum meruit to impose a highly generous and extraordinary contract that the parties did not make.

Telling the jury that it could measure the value of Claire's services by "[t]he value by which Defendant has benefited as a result of [her] services" was error. It allowed the jury to value Claire's services as having bought her a de facto ownership interest in a business whose owner never agreed to give her an interest. On remand, that part of the jury instruction must be dropped. . . .

D. Certain Jury Instructions May Have Misled the Jury Into Finding There Was No Implied Contract When in Fact There Was One

As we have shown, the quantum meruit damage award cannot stand in the wake of the jury's finding that Claire and Anthony had no agreement to share the equity in Anthony's business. But the validity of that very finding itself is challenged in Claire's protective cross-appeal, where she attacks a series of five jury instructions, specially drafted and proferred by Anthony. These instructions are set out in the margin.[11] We agree with Claire that it was error for the trial court to give three of these five instructions. The three instructions are so infelicitously worded that they might have misled the jury into concluding that evidence which can indeed support a finding of an implied contract could not.

The problem with the three instructions is this: They isolate three uncontested facts about the case: (1) living together, (2) holding themselves out to others as husband and wife, (3) providing services "such as" being a constant companion and confidant-and, seriatim, tell the jury that these facts definitely do not mean[13] there was an implied contract. True, none of these facts by themselves and alone necessarily compels the conclusion that there was an implied contract. But that does not mean that these facts cannot, in conjunction with all the facts and circumstances of the case, establish an implied contract. In point of fact, they can.

Unlike the "quasi-contractual" quantum meruit theory which operates without an actual agreement of the parties, an implied-in-fact contract entails an actual contract, but one manifested in conduct rather than expressed in words. (See Silva v. Providence Hospital of Oakland (1939) 14 Cal.2d 762, 773 [97 P.2d 798] ["The true implied contract, then, consists of obligations arising from a mutual agreement and intent to promise where the agreement and promise have not been expressed in words."]; McGough v. University of San Francisco (1989) 214 Cal.App.3d 1577, 1584 [263 Cal.Rptr. 404] ["An implied-in-fact contract is one whose existence and terms are manifested by conduct."]; 1 Witkin, Summary of Cal. Law, supra, Contracts, § 11, p. 46 ["The distinction between express and implied in fact contracts relates only to the manifestation of assent; both types are based upon the expressed or apparent intention of the parties."].)[14]

---

[11] Here are the five:"1. No Contract Results From Parties Holding Themselves out as Husband and Wife"You cannot find an agreement to share property or form a partnership from the fact that the parties held themselves out as husband and wife. The fact that unmarried persons live together as husband and wife and share a surname does not mean that they have any agreement to share earnings or assets."2. No Implied Contract From Living Together"You cannot find an implied contract to share property or form a partnership simply from the fact that the parties lived together[.]"3. Creation of an Implied Contract"... The fact the parties are living together does not change any of the requirements for finding an express or implied contract between the parties."4. Companionship Does Not Constitute Consideration"Providing services such as a constant companion and confidant does not constitute the consideration required by law to support a contract to share property, does not support any right of recovery and such services are not otherwise compensable."5. Obligations Imposed by Legal Marriage"In California, there are various obligations imposed upon parties who become legally and formally married. These obligations do not arise under the law merely by living together without a formal and legal marriage."

[13] The first instruction says "does not" mean there is an agreement, the second says the jury "cannot find" an "implied" agreement, and the fourth says "does not support any right."

[14] Because an implied-in-fact contract can be found where there is no expression of agreement in words, the line between an implied-in-fact contract and recovery in quantum meruit-where there may be no actual agreement at all-is fuzzy indeed. We will not attempt, in dicta, to clear up that fuzziness here. Suffice to say that because quantum meruit is a theory which implies a promise to pay for services as a matter of law for reasons of justice (Hedging Concepts, Inc. v. First Alliance Mortgage Co., supra, 41 Cal.App.4th at p. 1419), while implied-in-fact contracts are predicated on actual agreements, albeit not ones expressed in words (Silva v. Providence Hospital

In Alderson v. Alderson (1986) 180 Cal.App.3d 450, 461 [225 Cal.Rptr. 610], the court observed that a number of factors, including

- direct testimony of an agreement;
- holding themselves out socially as husband and wife;
- the woman and her children's taking the man's surname;
- pooling of finances to purchase a number of joint rental properties;
- joint decisionmaking in rental property purchases;
- rendering bookkeeping services for, paying the bills on, and collecting the rents of those joint rental properties; and
- the nature of title taken in those rental properties

could all support a finding there was an implied agreement to share the rental property acquisitions equally.

We certainly do not say that living together, holding themselves out as husband and wife, and being companions and confidants, even taken together, are sufficient in and of themselves to show an implied agreement to divide the equity in a business owned by one of the couple. However, Alderson clearly shows that such facts, together with others bearing more directly on the business and the way the parties treated the equity and proceeds of the business, can be part of a series of facts which do show such an agreement. The vice of the three instructions here is that they affirmatively suggested that living together, holding themselves out, and companionship could not, as a matter of law, even be part of the support for a finding of an implied agreement. That meant the jury could have completely omitted these facts when considering the other factors which might also have borne on whether there was an implied contract.

On remand, the three instructions should not be given. The jury should be told, rather, that while the facts that a couple live together, hold themselves out as married, and act as companions and confidants toward each other do not, by themselves, show an implied agreement to share property, those facts, when taken together and in conjunction with other facts bearing more directly on the alleged arrangement to share property, can show an implied agreement to share property.

Disposition

The judgment is reversed. The case is remanded for a new trial. At the new trial the jury instructions identified in this opinion as erroneous shall not be given. In the interest of justice both sides will bear their own costs on appeal.

---

of Oakland, supra, 14 Cal.2d at p. 773; McGough v. University of San Francisco, supra, 214 Cal.App.3d at p. 1584), recovery in quantum meruit is necessarily a different theory than recovery on an implied-in-fact contract. (Cf. 1 Witkin, Summary of Cal. Law, supra, Contracts, § 112, pp. 137-138 [noting uncertainty created by decisions which were not clear about whether quantum meruit was based on implied-in-law or implied-in-fact contracts].)Neither do we address the quantum of proof necessary to support recovery on a quantum meruit theory or attempt to divine the dividing line between services which may be so gratuitously volunteered under circumstances in which there can be no reasonable expectation of payment and services which do qualify for recovery in quantum meruit. These matters have not been briefed and may be left for another day.

NOTES AND QUESTIONS:

1. Recall the alternative measures of restitution interest set out in Restatement (Second) of Contracts §371 (1981). Is this court's ruling in line with the modern view expressed in that section?

2. *See* Restatement (Second) of Contracts §§ 371 (Measure of Restitution Interest) and 373 (Restitution When Other Party Is in Breach) (1981).

3. *See* Restatement (Second) of Contracts § 374 (Restitution in Favor of Party in Breach) (1981).

SECTION 5. REMEDIES UNDER THE UNIFORM COMMERCIAL CODE

VERMONT UNIFORM COMMERCIAL CODE
§ 1-305 REMEDIES TO BE LIBERALLY ADMINISTERED.
VT. STAT. ANN. 9A § 1-305 (2011).

(a) The remedies provided by . . . must be liberally administered to the end that the aggrieved party may be put in as good a position as if the other party had fully performed but neither consequential or special damages nor penal damages may be had except as specifically provided in [the Uniform Commercial Code] or by other rule of law.

A. BUYER'S DAMAGES

MISSISSIPPI UNIFORM COMMERCIAL CODE
§ 75-2-711. BUYER'S REMEDIES IN GENERAL; BUYER'S SECURITY INTEREST IN REJECTED GOODS.
MISS. CODE. ANN. § 75-2-711 (2011).

(1) Where the seller fails to make delivery or repudiates or the buyer rightfully rejects or justifiably revokes acceptance then with respect to any goods involved, and with respect to the whole if the breach goes to the whole contract (Section 2-612) [Section 75-2-612], the buyer may cancel and whether or not he has done so may in addition to recovering so much of the price as has been paid

(a) "cover" and have damages under the Section 75-2-712 as to all the goods affected whether or not they have been identified to the contract; or

(b) recover damages for non-delivery as provided in this Article (Section 2-713) [Section 75-2-713].

(2) Where the seller fails to deliver or repudiates the buyer may also

(a) if the goods have been identified recover them as provided in this Article (Section 2-502) [Section 75-2-502]; or

(b) in a proper case obtain specific performance or replevy the goods as provided in this Article (Section 2-716) [Section 75-2-716].

(3) On rightful rejection or justifiable revocation of acceptance a buyer has a security interest in goods in his possession or control for any payments made on their price and any expenses reasonably incurred in their inspection, receipt, transportation, care and custody and may hold such goods and resell them in like manner as an aggrieved seller (Section 2-706) [Section 75-2-706].

JEWELL-RUNG AGENCY, INC. V. THE HADDAD ORGANIZATION, LTD.
United States District Court, S.D. New York
814 F. Supp. 337 (1993).

ROBERT P. PATTERSON, Jr., District Judge.

Plaintiff Jewell-Rung Agency, Inc. ("Jewell-Rung"), seeks damages in excess of $350,000 for the defendant's alleged breach of contract. Defendant The Haddad Organization, Ltd. ("Haddad"), moves for summary judgment on the issue of damages . . . For the reasons set forth below, . . . Defendant's motion for summary judgment is denied.

BACKGROUND

Jewell-Rung is a Canadian corporation engaged in the business of importing and selling men's clothing at wholesale. Haddad is a New York corporation that manufactures men's outerwear sold under the "Lakeland" label.

In 1990, Jewell-Rung ordered samples of Lakeland men's outerwear from Haddad so that it might seek orders for this clothing from Canadian retailers. Haddad supplied Jewell-Rung with the ordered samples, which Jewell-Rung used to obtain orders from customers in Canada.

In January of 1991, Jewell-Rung placed an initial purchase order with Haddad for 2,325 garments of Lakeland men's outerwear, having a total listed price of approximately $250,000 in American currency, for the Fall 1991 season. By February 1991, Plaintiff had taken orders for 372 of these garments at a wholesale price of $107,506 in Canadian currency.

According to Jewell-Rung's Complaint, Haddad accepted its purchase order in January 1991 with the understanding that Jewell-Rung would obtain an exclusive distributorship of Lakeland outerwear in Canada, but Haddad, after accepting the order, granted a third party, Olympic Pant and Sportswear Co. ("Olympic"), the exclusive right to sell, manufacture, and market Lakeland outerwear throughout Canada. Plaintiff alleges that Haddad's acceptance of its January 1991 purchase order created a binding contract, which Haddad subsequently breached by failing to fill the purchase order and entering into its exclusive distributorship agreement with Olympic. Plaintiff further alleges that because it did not learn of Haddad's alleged breach until February of 1991, it was unable to fill its customers' orders for Lakeland goods for the Fall 1991 season or to obtain a substitute line of men's outerwear and, as a result, sustained over $350,000 in damages.

For the purposes of this summary judgment motion only, Defendant Haddad concedes that its acceptance of Jewell-Rung's January 1991 purchase order created a binding contract and that Haddad's agreement with Olympic constituted a breach of that contract. . . .

DISCUSSION

. . . .

II. MOTION FOR SUMMARY JUDGMENT

. . . .

Haddad moves for summary judgment on the issue of damages only. More specifically, Haddad asks this Court to rule that (1) Jewell-Rung's failure to mitigate damages bars any recovery; (2) Jewell-Rung's refusal to cover prohibits recovery of consequential damages; and, in the alternative, (3) any recovery of lost profits should be limited to the profits derived from the confirmed orders placed with Jewell-Rung at the time of the alleged breach of contract.

A. The availability of damages in general

New York's Uniform Commercial Code provides that a buyer may recover damages for a seller's breach of a contract of sale by either of two methods. N.Y.U.C.C. § 2-711(1). The buyer may either "cover" and obtain damages under N.Y.U.C.C. § 2-712, or recover damages for non-delivery as provided under N.Y.U.C.C. § 2-713.

It is undisputed that Jewell-Rung, the buyer in this case, did not "cover" and may seek damages under section 2-713 only. This section provides that "the measure of damages for non-delivery or repudiation by the seller is the difference between the market price at the time when the buyer learned of the breach and the contract price together with any incidental and consequential damages ..., but less expenses saved in consequence of the seller's breach."

Haddad asserts that at the time when Jewell-Rung learned of the alleged breach of contract, Olympic offered to sell Jewell-Rung Lakeland outerwear to fill all of its orders at the contract price to which Jewell-Rung and Haddad had agreed. According to Haddad, the market price of the goods at the time when the buyer learned of the breach was therefore equivalent to the contract price, and the buyer is deemed to have suffered no damage under section 2-713.

Plaintiff has, however, demonstrated the existence of a genuine issue of fact as to whether Olympic actually offered to supply Jewell-Rung with the same goods at the same price agreed upon by Haddad . . . .

Haddad's argument boils down to an assertion that Plaintiff's failure to effect cover bars recovery of damages under section 2-713. However, the Uniform Commercial Code makes clear that "cover" is an alternative to the relief authorized under section 2-713, see N.Y.U.C.C. § 2-711(1), and that failure of a buyer to effect cover "does not bar him from any other remedy." Id. at § 2-712(3). "Recovery of damages based on market price fluctuation under Section 2-713 is not ... contingent upon the buyer's attempting to cover." Kashi v. Gratsos, 790 F.2d 1050, 1056 (2d Cir.1986). Accordingly, Plaintiff's failure to purchase substitute goods from Olympic or any other seller does not preclude recovery of damages for Haddad's alleged breach of contract.

B. The availability of consequential damages

Haddad maintains that Jewell-Rung's failure to effect cover bars it from recovering consequential damages. Although N.Y.U.C.C. § 2-712(3) explicitly states that "[f]ailure of the buyer to effect cover ... does not bar him from any other remedy," the Official Comment to this section of the Uniform Commercial Code cautions that it must be read in conjunction with section 2-715(2)(a). See N.Y.U.C.C. § 2-712 Official Comment at 645 (McKinney 1964). Section 2-715(2)(a) limits consequential damages to losses "which could not reasonably be prevented by cover or otherwise."

As previously stated, Jewell-Rung does not dispute that it did not attempt to effect cover. However, a genuine issue of material fact exists as to whether Jewell-Rung's failure to seek cover was reasonable under the circumstances.

Jewell-Rung provides several reasons why it did not seek cover. In explaining why it did not buy goods from Olympic, Jewell-Rung states that it had the following concerns: that its customers would not be satisfied with the quality of Lakeland goods manufactured by Olympic, which specializes in the production of lower-priced clothing for discounters and department stores . . . that supplying its customers with outerwear manufactured by Olympic for the Fall 1991 season would provide Olympic with an entree to those customers for all of the next season's goods . . . and that purchasing goods from Olympic would place it at the complete mercy of a competitor for the timely supply of goods.

Jewell-Rung further points out that it had no source other than Olympic for Lakeland goods, which were not fungible but were "branded goods, manufactured from specific patterns and specific styles." . . . in addition, Jewell-Rung alleges that substitutions for Lakeland goods were not available that late in the purchasing cycle, and that it was in fact unable to find a replacement line for two seasons.

Based upon the reasons put forth by Jewell-Rung for its failure to cover, this Court cannot say at this time that such failure to cover was unreasonable as a matter of law . . . .

Accordingly, the defendant's motion for summary judgment is also denied insofar as it seeks to bar recovery for consequential damages.

C. Limitation on recovery of lost profits

In the alternative, Haddad asserts that any lost profits awarded to Jewell-Rung should be limited to those derived from confirmed orders placed by Jewell-Rung's customers at the time of the alleged breach.

Under New York law, recovery of lost profits has three prerequisites. First, the party seeking lost profits must demonstrate "with certainty that such damages have been caused by the breach and, second, the alleged loss must be capable of proof with reasonable certainty." Kenford Co. v. County of Erie, 67 N.Y.2d 257, 502 N.Y.S.2d 131, 132, 493 N.E.2d 234, 235

(1986). Third, "there must be a showing that the particular damages were fairly within the contemplation of the parties to the contract at the time it was made." Id....

Before any evidence of lost profits is presented in this matter, Haddad asks the Court to rule as a matter of law that lost profits, with the exception of anticipated payments for garments already ordered by retailers at the time of breach, are incapable of proof with reasonable certainty. Haddad makes two arguments in support of this position.

First, Haddad cites Texpor Traders, 720 F.Supp. at 1114, Wullschleger & Co. v. Jenny Fashions, Inc., 618 F.Supp. 373, 378 (S.D.N.Y.1985), and Harbor Hill Lithographing Corp. v. Dittler Bros., Inc., 76 Misc.2d 145, 348 N.Y.S.2d 920, 924 (Sup.Ct.Nassau Cty.1973), for the proposition that in the case of a wholesaler, lost profits are restricted to those pertaining to confirmed orders of resale. None of these cases comes close to establishing such a per se rule. Each case merely limits recovery of lost profits after the plaintiff has presented evidence and failed to demonstrate a reasonable basis for calculating lost profits other than those derived from confirmed orders that were in place at the time of breach.

Second, Haddad maintains that lost profits are rarely appropriate where the injured party is a new business because such damages are by nature highly speculative. When a "new business" seeks to recover lost profits, "a stricter standard" of proof is required "for the obvious reason that there does not exist a reasonable basis of experience upon which to estimate lost profits with the requisite degree of reasonable certainty." Kenford Co., 502 N.Y.S.2d at 132, 493 N.E.2d at 235; accord Care Travel Co., 944 F.2d at 993. This heightened standard of proof for new businesses indicates that new ventures will have difficulty demonstrating lost profits; it does not mean that new businesses should be denied an opportunity to present their evidence of such damages at trial.

Whether Jewell-Rung is in fact a "new business" within the meaning of Kenford Co. is itself unclear. It is new to the business of selling Lakeland products in Canada, but its experience as a wholesaler of men's clothing in Canada is evidence of its viability as an enterprise and could, for example, yield evidence as to previous patterns of profit on resale of similar lines of clothing.

Accordingly, Defendant's request to limit recovery of lost profits to confirmed orders of resale is denied at this time.

CONCLUSION

For the reasons set forth above . . . Defendant's motion for summary judgment is denied.

IT IS SO ORDERED.

---

1. BREACH OF WARRANTY

AM/PM FRANCHISE ASS'N. V. ATLANTIC RICHFIELD CO.
Supreme Court of Pennsylvania
584 A.2d 915 (1990).

CAPPY, Justice.

Before us is an appeal by members of a franchisee association from an order of the Superior Court of Pennsylvania at No. 01958 Philadelphia 1987, issued April 14, 1988, affirming the order of the Court of Common Pleas at No. 157 November Term 1986, dated June 16, 1987, sustaining defendant's preliminary objections in the nature of a demurrer and dismissing the action.

We granted allocatur to determine whether the named appellants ("plaintiffs") have alleged sufficient facts to sustain a cause of action when they aver that the gasoline they purchased from the appellee ("ARCO") was not in conformance with the warranties made and resulted in their suffering economic harm. In making such a determination, we address the question of whether such damages constitute a "loss of good will," and whether good will damages are too speculative as a matter of law to permit recovery. For the reasons set forth herein, we find that the plaintiffs have alleged sufficient facts to entitle them to proceed with their claim and that the damages claimed are not good will nor so speculative as to deny them an attempt at recovery. We reverse the decision of the Superior Court in part and affirm in part.

PROCEDURAL HISTORY

ARCO filed preliminary objections in the nature of a demurrer to Appellants' complaint, claiming that the damages sought by Appellants stemmed from a loss of good will, which are speculative and not recoverable as a matter of law. Additionally, the defendants claim that the plaintiffs should not be entitled to recover under a tort theory.

The trial court sustained ARCO's preliminary objections and dismissed Appellants' complaint.

The Superior Court affirmed the ruling of the trial court, holding that under current Pennsylvania law, damages sought for the breach of warranty claims due to a loss of good will are not recoverable as they have traditionally been considered to be too speculative. Additionally, the Superior Court held that the plaintiff was not entitled to recover in tort, finding that the duty of the parties to act in good faith arises under contract and not tort principles.

In the dissent to the opinion of the Superior Court, Judge Brosky remarked that the majority characterizes the claim as one for loss of good will, while he "view[s] appellants' claim as a request for lost profits occasioned by appellee's delivery of an unmerchantable product." 373 Pa.Super. 572, 580, 542 A.2d 90, 94 (1988). Additionally, Judge Brosky disagreed with the characterization of the loss as speculative, stating "[a]lthough calculating damages may have been a problem in the past, and in certain cases, may still be a problem, I cannot see that it presents a problem here.... Further, a comparison of the business profits before and after the delivery of the unmerchantable gasoline should prove to be enlightening." Id. at 581, 542 A.2d at 94-95.

FACTUAL HISTORY

The Plaintiffs claim to represent a class of over 150 franchisees of ARCO that operated AM/PM Mini Markets in Pennsylvania and New York during a three and one-half year period.

ARCO entered into franchise agreements with the plaintiffs which were comprised of a premises lease, a lessee dealer gasoline agreement, and an AM/PM mini-market agreement. The products agreement mandated that the franchisees sell only ARCO petroleum products.

The complaint sets forth the following facts: ARCO began experimenting with its formula for unleaded gasoline and provided its franchisees with an unleaded gasoline blended with oxinol, consisting of 4.5% methanol and 4.5% gasoline grade tertiary butyl alcohol (hereinafter "the oxinol blend") from early 1982 through September 30, 1985.

During this three and a half year period, the franchisees were required to sell the oxinol blend to their clients who desired unleaded gasoline. The franchisees were given no opportunity to buy regular unleaded gasoline from ARCO during that period.

Plaintiffs claim that numerous purchasers of the oxinol blend gasoline experienced poor engine performance and physical damage to fuel system components. Specifically, plaintiffs claim that the oxinol gasoline permitted an excess accumulation of alcohol and/or water which interfered with the efficiency of gasoline engines and, in certain vehicles, caused swelling of plastic or rubber components in the fuel delivery system and resulted in engine damage. The plaintiffs claim that the gasoline did not conform to ARCO's warranties about the product.

As the problems with the oxinol blend became known, the plaintiffs claim to have suffered a precipitous drop in the volume of their business and an attendant loss of profits. Specifically, plaintiffs point to the rise in sales from 1973 until 1982, when sales began to fall dramatically; allegedly due to defective oxinol blend gasoline.

In their complaint, plaintiffs allege three counts of Breach of Warranty, Breach of Implied Duty, Misrepresentation, and Exemplary Damages. They request damages for "lost profits, consequential and incidental damages."

DISCUSSION

The point at which we start our inquiry is the Uniform Commercial Code ("the U.C.C."), codified at 13 Pa.C.S. § 1101 et seq. Section 2714, entitled "Damages of buyer for breach in regard to accepted goods" is one of the governing provisions in the case before us,[2] and provides, in pertinent part:

> (b) Measure of damages for breach of warranty.-The measure of damages for breach of warranty is the difference at the time and place of acceptance between the value of the goods accepted and the value they would have had if they had been as warranted, unless special circumstances show proximate damages of a different amount.
>
> (c) Incidental and consequential damages.-In a proper case any incidental and consequential damages under section 2715 (relating to incidental and consequential damages of buyer) may also be recovered.

Section 2715 is entitled "Incidental and Consequential Damages of Buyer" and provides, in pertinent part:

> (a) Incidental damages.-Incidental damages resulting from the breach of the seller include:
>
> (3) any other reasonable expenses incident to the delay or other breach.[3]
>
> (b) Consequential damages.-Consequential damages resulting from the breach of the seller include:
>
> (1) any loss resulting from general or particular requirements and needs of which the seller at the time of contracting had reason to know and which could not reasonably be prevented by cover or otherwise.[4]

Pursuant to the provisions of the U.C.C., plaintiffs are entitled to seek "general" damages, so-called, under section 2714(b), and consequential damages as provided by section 2714(c).

There has been substantial confusion in the courts and among litigants about what consequential damages actually are and what types of consequential damages are available in a breach of warranty case. Where a buyer in the business of reselling goods can prove that a breach by the seller has caused him to lose profitable resales, the buyer's lost profits

---

[2] The plaintiffs claim they have accepted gasoline which allegedly does not conform to the warranty. Thus, we believe § 2714 is one of the governing provisions.

[3] The incidental damage provision is aimed at reimbursing the buyer for expenses incurred in rightfully rejecting goods, or in connection with effecting cover. We have not quoted all the sections included in the subtitle of Incidental Damages. The courts below have not addressed the claim for incidental damages, nor have the parties to the litigation.

[4] Another section of the Consequential Damages section includes a provision addressing injury to person or property; a matter which is not before us.

constitute a form of consequential damages.[5] We now hold that in addition to general damages, there are three types of lost profit recoverable as consequential damages that may flow from a breach of warranty: (1) loss of primary profits; (2) loss of secondary profits; and (3) a loss of good will damages (or prospective damages, as they are sometimes termed).

In order to alleviate the confusion that has developed concerning the various damages, we use an example to help illustrate the different types.

General damages in the case of accepted goods (such as occurred here) are the actual difference in value between the goods as promised and the goods as received. Thus, suppose a buyer bought five hundred tires from a wholesaler that were to be delivered in good condition, and in that condition would be worth $2,500. The tires were delivered with holes in them which rendered them worthless. The buyer would be entitled to $2,500 from the seller-the difference between the value of the tires as warranted and the value of the tires as received; those would be the general damages.

Consequential damages are generally understood to be other damages which naturally and proximately flow from the breach and include three types of lost profit damages: (1) lost primary profits; (2) lost secondary profits; and (3) loss of prospective profits, also commonly referred to as good will damages.

Lost primary profits are the difference between what the buyer would have earned from reselling the goods in question had there been no breach and what was earned after the breach occurred. Thus, if the buyer of the tires proved that he would have resold the tires for $5,000, he would be able to claim an additional $2,500 for loss of tire profits; the difference between what he would have earned from the sale of the tires and what he actually did earn from the sale (or lack of sales) from the tires.

If the buyer of the tires also sold, for example, hubcaps with every set of tires, he would also suffer a loss of hubcap profits. These types of damages are what we term “loss of secondary profits.”

If the buyer's regular customers were so disgruntled about the defective tires that they no longer frequented the buyer's business and began to patronize a competitor's business, the buyer would have suffered a “loss of good will” beyond the direct loss of profits from the nonconforming goods; his future business would be adversely affected as a result of the defective tires. Thus, good will damages refer to profits lost on future sales rather than on sales of the defective goods themselves.

While this example provides a simple framework to understand the different types of possible damages in a breach of warranty case, it does not encompass the myriad of circumstances in which a claim for damages can arise, nor does it specify which of these different damages have been allowed in Pennsylvania.

---

[5] See, generally, U.C.C. § 2-715, comment 6 (1978).

In addition to recognizing general damages under § 2714 of the Code, Pennsylvania allows consequential damages in the form of lost profits to be recovered. See, e.g., Kassab v. Central Soya, 432 Pa. 217, 246 A.2d 848 (1968); Delahanty v. First Pennsylvania Bank N.A., 318 Pa.Super. 90, 464 A.2d 1243 (1983); Frank B. Bozzo, Inc. v. Electric Weld Division, 283 Pa.Super. 35, 423 A.2d 702, aff'd, 495 Pa. 617, 435 A.2d 176 (1981). See also National Controls Corporation v. National Semiconductor Corporation, 833 F.2d 491 (3d Cir.1987) and Kunststoffwerk Alfred Huber v. R.J. Dick, Inc., 621 F.2d 560 (3d Cir.1980).

Pennsylvania has, however, disallowed good will damages; finding them to be too speculative to permit recovery. In the cases disallowing good will damages, part of the reason we found them too speculative is that the damages were not contemplated by the parties at the time the contract was made.

In 1977, this court had occasion to re-examine sections 2714 and 2715 of the Uniform Commercial Code in the case of R.I. Lampus Co. v. Neville Cement Products Corp., 474 Pa. 199, 378 A.2d 288 (1977). Before the Lampus case, we required the party seeking consequential damages in the form of lost profits to show that there were "special circumstances" indicating that such damages were actually contemplated by the parties at the time they entered into the agreement. This rule, termed the "tacit-agreement" test, "permit[ed] the plaintiff to recover damages arising from special circumstances only if 'the defendant fairly may be supposed to have assumed consciously, or to have warranted the plaintiff reasonably to suppose that it assumed, [such liability] when the contract was made.' " R.I. Lampus Co., supra, at 207, 378 A.2d at 291 (1977). (cites omitted) (brackets in original), quoting from J. White & R. Summers, Uniform Commercial Code (1972).

In Lampus, we overruled the restrictive "tacit-agreement" test and replaced it with the "reason to know" test; which requires that "[i]f a seller knows of a buyer's general or particular requirements and needs, that seller is liable for the resulting consequential damages whether or not that seller contemplated or agreed to such damages." Id. at 209, 378 A.2d at 292 (1977) (emphasis supplied).[6] Thus, in order to obtain consequential damages, the plaintiff need only prove that the damages were reasonably foreseeable at the time the agreement was entered into.[7]

Turning to the case at hand, we must determine whether the plaintiffs have alleged sufficient facts to permit them to proceed with a claim for consequential damages.

We note initially that the standard of review for preliminary objections is a limited one. As we stated in Vattimo v. Lower Bucks Hosp., Inc., 502 Pa. 241, 465 A.2d 1231, 1232-33 (1983):

All material facts set forth in the complaint as well as all inferences reasonably deducible therefrom are admitted as true for [the purpose of this review.] Clevenstein v. Rizzuto, 439 Pa. 397, 266 A.2d 623 (1970). The question presented by the demurrer is whether, on the facts averred, the law says with certainty that no recovery is possible. Hoffman v. Misericordia Hospital of Philadelphia, 439 Pa. 501, 267 A.2d 867 (1970). Where

---

[6] Lampus is in accord with section 2-715 of the U.C.C., comment 2 (1978), which states; "[t]he 'tacit agreement' test for the recovery of consequential damages is rejected."

[7] Accord; U.C.C. § 2-715, comment 3 (1978).

a doubt exists as to whether a demurrer should be sustained, this doubt should be resolved in favor of overruling it. Birl v. Philadelphia Electric Co., 402 Pa. 297, 167 A.2d 472 (1960).

In this complaint, the plaintiffs have alleged, inter alia: that ARCO expressly warranted through its agreements, mailgrams and brochures that its oxinol gasoline was of high quality, better for the environment and would not damage new or older automobiles; that the oxinol gasoline was not merchantable because it damaged engines; that it was not fit for the ordinary purpose for which it was intended; that ARCO knew that the plaintiffs were relying on the skill of the defendants to select or furnish suitable gasoline; that ARCO's actions constituted a breach of express warranties which resulted in harm to the plaintiffs in the form of lost profits, incidental and consequential damages.

Based on our standard of review as set forth above, we believe that the plaintiffs have set forth sufficient facts in their complaint to state a cause of action under the breach of warranty counts.

The plaintiffs seek lost profits, incidental and consequential damages.[8] The defendants and the lower courts, however, considered these damages to be lost good will. We believe that the lower courts and the defendants are in error in categorizing all the claimed damages as good will damages. We address separately the different types of damages claimed.

LOSS OF PROFITS FOR GASOLINE SALES

The first claim the plaintiff makes for damages is for the profits lost from the sales of gasoline. The plaintiffs claim that the breach of warranty by the defendant concerning the gasoline caused the plaintiffs to lose sales during a three and one half year period while they received nonconforming gasoline from ARCO. In the case of Kassab v. Central Soya, 432 Pa. 217, 246 A.2d 848 (1968), we permitted lost profits for cattle sales when the plaintiff showed that the defective feed caused harm to their cattle, causing the public to stop buying their cattle. The allegation here is similar. When the gasoline buying public discovered that the gasoline was defective, many stopped purchasing ARCO gasoline.

Employing the reasoning of Kassab and taking it one step further, we believe that the plaintiffs here are entitled to show that the gasoline buying community did not buy their gasoline from 1982 through 1985 because of the reasonable belief that the gasoline was defective and would harm their engines. The lost gasoline sales are comparable to the lost cattle sales in Kassab. The distinction between the two cases is that the Kassabs had bought the feed all at one time and thus all their livestock was affected. The instant plaintiffs bought their gasoline in regular intervals and could only earn a profit on what they could sell per month. The defendant's argument-that the plaintiffs sold all the gasoline they bought-misses the point. While they may have sold every gallon, they sold significantly fewer gallons during the period that ARCO allegedly delivered nonconforming gasoline. Thus, during this

[8] The plaintiffs claim "lost profits, incidental and consequential damages." As we noted herein, however, "lost profits" are a type of consequential damage; not a separate category of damages.

period, the plaintiffs' lost sales were just as directly attributable to the defective gasoline as the lost profits were attributable to the defective tires in the example we used previously.[9]

Thus, if prior to the manufacture of defective gasoline the plaintiffs sold 100,000 gallons per month every month and then as a result of the defective gasoline, they sold only 60,000 gallons per month every month until ARCO discontinued that gasoline, then the plaintiffs have lost the profits they would have received on 40,000 gallons per month for the three year claimed period.[10] Lost profits are, in fact, the difference between what the plaintiff actually earned and what they would have earned had the defendant not committed the breach. Because the gasoline was allegedly not in conformance with the warranties, the plaintiffs may be entitled to lost profits for the gasoline on a breach of warranty theory. The lost gasoline sales are what we have termed "loss of primary profits," and they are recoverable pursuant to § 2715 of the U.C.C. upon proper proof.

We note, furthermore, that the remedy of cover was unavailable to the plaintiffs. Section 2715 of the U.C.C. limits a plaintiff's ability to recover when he could have prevented such damage "by cover or otherwise." Pursuant to the code, cover is defined as the buyer's purchase of substitute goods at a commercially reasonable price. The buyer can recover from the seller the difference between the contract price and the cost of goods bought as cover. 13 Pa.C.S. § 2712, defining "cover" and damages recoverable, provides, in pertinent part:

> (a) Right and manner of cover.-After a breach within section 2711 (relating to remedies of buyer in general; security interest of buyer in rejected goods) the buyer may "cover" by making in good faith and without unreasonable delay any reasonable purchase of or contract to purchase goods in substitution for those due from the seller.

The plaintiffs here, by their allegations, could not "cover;" they were contractually required to purchase all their gasoline from ARCO. In effect, they had to accept the allegedly nonconforming gasoline and had no possible way to avoid the attendant loss of profits. Thus, since they could not cover, the only remedy that was available to them was to file suit.[11]

Furthermore, we note that Section 1106 of the U.C.C. provides:

> [t]he remedies provided by this title shall be liberally administered to the end that the aggrieved party may be put in as good a position as if the other party had fully performed but neither consequential or special nor penal damages

---

[9] The current case, unlike the tire example, involves a requirements contract rather than a fixed quantity agreement. In a requirement contract, profits lost during the period of time in which the seller supplies nonconforming goods constitute lost primary profits. The Code does not require that the buyer prove he would have purchased the same amount as usually required, for § 2715 permits the buyer to mitigate his damages by "cover or otherwise." Thus the buyer need not buy his usual amount of goods and then be unable to sell them before he can claim a loss of profits.

[10] The figures used are representational only and do not represent any claims made by the plaintiffs.

[11] The comment to the Code for the section relating to cover states; 1. "[t]he definition of "cover ... envisages a series of contracts or sales, as well as a single contract or sale; goods not identical with those involved but commercially usable as reasonable substitutes under the circumstances...."

may be had except as specifically provided in this title or by other rule of law. (emphasis supplied).

The Code itself compels us to be liberal in our interpretation of the types of damages we permit. We would therefore allow the plaintiffs to proceed with their claims for lost gasoline profits during the period ARCO supplied allegedly nonconforming gasoline.

LOSS OF PROFITS FOR ITEMS OTHER THAN GASOLINE SALES

The plaintiffs allege that in addition to a loss of profits for sales of gasoline, they had a concomitant loss of sales for other items that they sold in their mini-marts during the period of time that ARCO supplied nonconforming gasoline. Their rationale is that when the number of customers buying gasoline decreased, so did the number of customers buying items at the mini-mart. In other words, related facets of their business suffered as a result of the defective gasoline. This type of injury is what we characterize as "loss of secondary profits;" meaning that the sales of other products suffered as a result of the breach of warranty. This court has not had an opportunity to address whether these types of damages are recoverable.

In the case before us, the essence of plaintiffs' allegations is that customers frequent the mini-marts because it is convenient to do so at the time they purchase gasoline. Customers of the mini-mart are foremost gasoline buying patrons; gasoline is their primary purchase and sundries are their incidental purchases. Here, the plaintiffs claim that the primary product sales so affected the incidental sales as to create a loss in other aspects of their business. It is reasonable to assume that if the gasoline sales dropped dramatically, there was a ripple effect on the mini-mart sales. Additionally, when a primary product does not conform to the warranty, we believe that it is foreseeable that there will be a loss of secondary profits. Thus, permitting these damages would correspond with the requirement of foreseeability as set forth in Lampus, supra, and the Code. It is much less foreseeable to assume there will be a loss of secondary profits when the nonconforming products are not the primary ones. We believe that unless it is a primary product that does not conform to the warranty, the causal relationship between the breach and the loss is too attenuated to permit damages for the loss of secondary profits.[12]

We also find that the fact situation before us presents a further problem in that the plaintiffs were not able to mitigate the harm in any way by buying substitute goods or "cover." Thus, the plaintiffs' primary product was defective and they were unable to remedy the situation by buying gasoline from another supplier.

[12] As with all cases involving breach of warranty, the plaintiff is charged with the burden of proving that the defendant's breach is the proximate cause of the harm suffered. Thus, in order to proceed with their case, the plaintiffs here must prove that the alleged nonconformance of the gasoline caused both their loss of gasoline sales as well as their loss of mini-mart sales. This requirement is an arduous one and we render no opinion as to whether the plaintiffs can meet this burden. However, we note that this is for the trial court, in its wisdom, to decide whether the plaintiffs have met the threshold of proof to submit the case to the factfinder.

We find that the present case presents compelling reasons for permitting damages for loss of secondary profits. Henceforth, in a breach of warranty case, when a primary product of the plaintiff is alleged to be nonconforming and the plaintiff is unable to cover by purchasing substitute goods, we hold that upon proper proof, the plaintiff should be entitled to sue for loss of secondary profits.[13]

LOSS OF GOOD WILL

Historically, Pennsylvania has disallowed recovery for loss of good will damages or prospective profits in breach of warranty cases. The cases generally relied upon for this proposition are Michelin Tire Co. v. Schulz, 295 Pa. 140, 145 A. 67 (1929); Harry Rubin & Sons, Inc. v. Consolidated Pipe Co. of America, 396 Pa. 506, 153 A.2d 472 (1959); and Kassab v. Central Soya, 432 Pa. 217, 246 A.2d 848 (1968).

The defendant and the lower courts rely on these cases for the proposition that the plaintiffs claims are for "good will damages" and thus too speculative as a matter of law to permit recovery. While this analysis is seductive in its simplicity, it ignores the nuances of each of these cases and the effect R.I. Lampus Co. v. Neville Cement Products Corp., has had on this area of law.

In fact, in the case of Rubin & Sons, supra, the court remarked "[i]ndeed if such were the holding [permitting good will damages], damages which the parties never contemplated would seem to be involved in every contract of sale." Id. at 513, 153 A.2d at 477.

With the advent of the Lampus "reason-to-know" test-which is a test of foreseeability-the holdings under each of these cases have much less precedential effect, since the Lampus test is much less restrictive than the tacit-agreement test.

Although the plaintiffs do not style their claim as one for good will damages, the Superior Court, the trial court, and the defendant have all characterized the claim for lost profits in this case as good will damages. What actually constitutes good will damages has caused much consternation to the courts and litigants. We in fact have serious doubts that the plaintiffs are even seeking good will damages. However, in order to determine that issue in the case before us, we must first discuss what good will damages are and whether they are allowable.

As one commentator aptly noted, "[l]oss of good will is a mercurial concept and, as such, is difficult to define. In a broad sense, it refers to a loss of future profits."[14] Other jurisdictions have considered loss of good will to be a loss of profits and reputation among customers.[15] Generally, good will refers to the reputation that businesses have built over the course of time that is reflected by the return of customers to purchase goods and the

[13] What constitutes a "primary product" will be dependent on the facts of each case. However, we would define a "primary product" as an item upon which the aggrieved party relies for a substantial amount of its revenue. The plaintiff must show that without that product, his business would be severely incapacitated.

[14] Anderson, Incidental and Consequential Damages, 7 J.L. & Com. 327, 420 (1987).

[15] Texsun Feed Yards, Inc. v. Ralston Purina Co., 447 F.2d 660 (5th Cir.1971).

attendant profits that accompanies such sales. Thus the phrase "good will damages" is coextensive with prospective profits and loss of business reputation.

Secondly, we must decide when good will damages arise in a breach of warranty situation. Essentially, damage to good will in a case in which the seller supplies a quantity dictated by the buyer's requirements arises only after the seller has ceased providing nonconforming goods-or the buyer has purchased substitute goods. Damage to good will in this case would refer to the loss of business sales that occurred after the buyer was able to provide acceptable goods to his customers; it does not refer to the period of time during which he is forced to sell the nonconforming goods.

Thirdly, we must address whether good will damages are too speculative to permit recovery, as we held in Michelin, Rubin & Sons, supra, and Kassab, supra. Although we disallowed good will damages in those cases, they are not recent. They were written in a time when business was conducted on a more simple basis, where market studies and economic forecasting were unexplored sciences.

We are now in an era in which computers, economic forecasting, sophisticated marketing studies and demographic studies are widely used and accepted. As such, we believe that the rationale for precluding prospective profits under the rubric of "too speculative" ignores the realities of the marketplace and the science of modern economics. We believe that claims for prospective profits should not be barred ab initio. Rather, plaintiffs should be given an opportunity to set forth and attempt to prove their damages.

Twenty years ago, the Third Circuit Court of Appeals noted in a case disallowing claims for prospective profits that damages once considered speculative may not be in the future:

> This is not to say we approve the Pennsylvania view or believe it will be the Pennsylvania position in the future [prohibiting good will damages]. Considering the advances made in techniques of market analysis and the use of highly sophisticated computers it may be that lost profits of this nature are no more speculative than lost profits from the destruction of a factory or hotel, and perhaps Pennsylvania will reconsider the reason for its rule in a future case.

Neville Chemical Co. v. Union Carbide Corp., 422 F.2d 1205, 1227 (1970).

We believe the time has come to reconsider that rule. In doing so, we find our position on recovery for good will damages (or prospective profits) to be out of step with modern day business practices and techniques, as well as the law of other jurisdictions.[16] As

[16] Many state and federal courts now allow good will damages. See, e.g., R.E.B., Inc. v. Ralston Purina Co., 525 F.2d 749 (10th Cir.1975); Consolidated Data Terminals v. Applied Digital Data Systems, Inc., 708 F.2d 385 (9th Cir.1983); Roundhouse v. Owens Illinois, Inc. 604 F.2d 990 (6th Cir.1979); Texsun Feed Yards, Inc. v. Ralston Purina Co., 447 F.2d 660 (5th Cir.1971); Isenberg v. Lemon, 84 Ariz. 340, 327 P.2d 1016 (1958); Delano Growers' Cooperative Winery v. Supreme Wine Co., 393 Mass. 666, 473 N.E.2d 1066 (1985); Hydraform Products Corp. v. American Steel & Aluminum Corp., 127 N.H. 187, 498 A.2d 339 (1985); Adams v. J.I. Case Co., 125 Ill.App.2d 388, 261 N.E.2d 1 (1970); Robert T. Donaldson, Inc. v. Aggregate Surfacing Corp., 47

noted by Professor Anderson in his well-crafted article on incidental and consequential damages,

> [t]o date, only the Pennsylvania courts have categorically denied recovery for loss of goodwill under any circumstances, an issue which has been oft-litigated in Pennsylvania. If one removes the Pennsylvania cases from the count, a significant majority of the cases have allowed for the recovery of lost goodwill in proper circumstances.[17]

Furthermore, our rule has been repeatedly criticized by other courts and commentators.[18] In reviewing our case law on the issue of prospective profits, we have not had a significant case come before us since Kassab was decided in 1968. Since that time, astronauts have walked on the moon, engineers have developed computers capable of amazing feats and biomedical engineers and physicians have made enormous strides in organ transplantation and replacement. It is evident that the world of 1990 is not the same world as it was in 1929 when the Michelin case was decided, nor even the same world as it was in 1968 when Kassab was decided. While these rapid technological developments have not been without their concomitant problems, they have made possible many things that were not possible before; including the calculation of prospective profits.[19] For these reasons, we overrule Michelin, supra, Rubin & Sons, Inc., supra, and Kassab, supra, to the extent they prohibit a plaintiff from alleging a claim for damage to good will as a matter of law.

See also, Massachusetts Bonding & Insurance Co. v. Johnston & Harder, Inc., 343 Pa. 270, 22 A.2d 709 (1941); Hahn v. Andrews, 182 Pa.Super. 338, 126 A.2d 519 (1956); Bolus v. United Penn Bank, 363 Pa.Super. 247, 525 A.2d 1215 (1987).

In these cases, this court has recognized that although proof of prospective damages might be difficult, such difficulty should not operate as an absolute bar to the claim itself:

Compensation for breach of contract cannot be justly refused because proof of the exact amount of loss is not produced, for there is judicial recognition of the difficulty or even impossibility of the production of such proof. What the law does require in cases of this character is that the evidence shall with a fair degree of probability establish a basis for the assessment of damages. Massachusetts Bonding & Insurance Co. v. Johnston & Harder, Inc., 343 Pa. 270, 280, 22 A.2d 709, 714 (1941).

A.D.2d 852, 366 N.Y.S.2d 194 (1975), appeal dismissed, 37 N.Y.2d 793, 375 N.Y.S.2d 106, 337 N.E.2d 612 (1975); Sol-O-Lite Laminating Corp. v. Allen, 223 Ore. 80, 353 P.2d 843 (1960).

[17] Anderson, Incidental and Consequential Damages, 7 J.L. & Com. 327, 421 (1987).

[18] See, e.g., Neville Chemical Co. v. Union Carbide Corp., 422 F.2d 1205, 1227 (3d Cir.1970); Comment, Loss of Goodwill and Business Reputation as Recoverable Elements of Damages Under Uniform Commercial Code § 2-715-The Pennsylvania Experience, 75 Dick.L.Rev. 63, (1970); Peters, Remedies for Breach of Contracts, 73 Yale L.J. 199, 276-77 (1963).

[19] Further curiosity is engendered by our extensive history of allowing claims for loss of prospective profits in breach of contract case. In Wilson v. Wernwag, 217 Pa. 82, 66 A. 242 (1907), this court said:An examination of the well-considered cases will show that prospective profits may be recovered for the breach of a contract whenever they are susceptible of proof. They have been rejected by the courts as damages only because of the failure to prove them with sufficient certainty and definitiveness. There can be no good reason why they should not be recovered when they are capable of definite estimation." Id., at 94, 66 A., at 246.

The problem of proof in these breach of contract cases is really no different from the problems of proof in breach of warranty cases. In our attempt to craft law that is internally consistent as well as historically consistent, we must strive to reconcile differences as they become apparent. As such, we see no legitimate reason to prohibit prospective damages in breach of warranty cases when we never have in breach of contract cases.

Inextricably entwined with the issue of speculation is the difficulty in proving the damages are causally related to the breach. As we stated earlier, difficulty in proving causation should not operate as a bar to permitting plaintiffs to claim the damages. Furthermore, we note that pursuant to our case law and the Uniform Commercial Code, damages need not be proved with mathematical certainty. As long as the plaintiffs can provide a reasonable basis from which the jury can calculate damages, they will be permitted to pursue their case.

Thus, we now hold that plaintiffs should be entitled to try to prove good will damages; provided they are able to introduce sufficient evidence (1) to establish that the such profits were causally related to a breach of warranty and (2) to provide the trier of fact with a reasonable basis from which to calculate damages.[20]

Turning to the facts of this case, we note that the plaintiffs have made no claim for good will damages, since none was incurred; ARCO having cured the breach by stopping the supply of the nonconforming gasoline. The damages claimed are only for the period of time that the plaintiffs were forced to purchase the gasoline with oxinol. Thus, we reverse the decision of the lower courts in holding that the plaintiffs' claim was for good will damages.

CONCLUSION

We now hold that there are three types of lost profits recoverable as consequential damages available under § 2714 and § 2715 of the Uniform Commercial Code: (1) loss of primary profits; (2) loss of secondary profits; and (3) good will damages, defined as a loss of prospective profits or business reputation. While this categorization of damages represents a new direction for the court, we believe it is the better direction.

As a final note, we do not find that this case should be decided on tort principles, but on warranty principles. The relationship between the parties is of a contractual nature and should be decided on contractual principles. For that reason, we uphold the decision of the court below dismissing the tort claims. Additionally, we do not believe that our case law or the Uniform Commercial Code authorizes a legitimate claim for exemplary damages and thus affirm the lower court's dismissal of such claim. Accordingly, we reverse the decision

[20] There are a number of different ways that damages may be removed from the realm of speculation and be submitted to the jury with a rational basis from which the amount can be inferred. As long as the method of proof provides the jury with "a reasonable basis" for calculating damages, the issue should be submitted to the trier of fact. This is the approach taken by most jurisdictions. See, e.g., Eastman Kodak Co. v. Southern Photo Materials Co., 273 U.S. 359, 47 S.Ct. 400, 71 L.Ed. 684 (1927); Macdonald v. Winfield Corp., 93 F.Supp. 153 (E.D.Pa.1950); Schatz v. Abbott Labs. Inc., 51 Ill.2d 143, 281 N.E.2d 323 (1972); Hawkins v. Jamrog, 277 Mass. 540, 179 N.E. 224 (1931); Apex Metal Stamping Co. v. Alexander & Sawyer, Inc., 48 N.J.Super. 476, 138 A.2d 568 (1958).

of the lower courts with respect to the breach of warranty claims and remand the case for proceedings consistent with the opinion.

It is so ordered.

B. SELLER'S DAMAGES

OHIO REVISED CODE
§ 1302.77. SELLER'S REMEDIES IN GENERAL (UCC 2-703).
Ohio Rev. Code Ann. § 1302.77 (LexisNexis 2012).

Where the buyer wrongfully rejects or revokes acceptance of goods or fails to make a payment due on or before delivery or repudiates with respect to a part or the whole, then with respect to any goods directly affected and, if the breach is of the whole contract under section 1302.70 of the Revised Code [Section 2-612], then also with respect to the whole undelivered balance, the aggrieved seller may:

(a) withhold delivery of such goods;

(b) stop delivery by any bailee as hereafter provided in section 1302.79 of the Revised Code [Section 2-705];

(c) proceed under under section 1302.78 of the Revised Code respecting goods still unidentified to the contract;

(d) resell and recover damages as provided in section 1302.80 of the Revised Code [Section 2-706];

(e) recover damages for non-acceptance as provided in section 1302.82 of the Revised Code [Section 2-708] or in a proper case the price as provided in section 1302.83 of the Revised Code [Section 2-709];

(f) cancel.

BAII BANKING CORP. V. ATLANTIC RICHFIELD CO.
United States District Court, S.D. New York
1992 WL 209287 (S.D.N.Y.) (1992).

KEENAN, District Judge:

Introduction

Before the Court is the motion in limine of defendant/third-party plaintiff Atlantic Richfield Company, Inc. ("ARCO"). ARCO seeks an order precluding the introduction of evidence concerning the sales by plaintiff BAII Banking Corporation ("BAII") of the inventory of gasoline BAII acquired from its predecessor in interest, Will Petroleum, Inc. ("Will") . . . . For the reasons set forth below, the motion is denied.

Background

This case was the subject of an opinion and order dated September 27, 1990, in which the Court denied defendant's motion for summary judgment. While familiarity with that opinion is assumed, the Court will briefly describe the facts of the case necessary to frame the issues before the Court on this motion.

Plaintiff BAII is a banking corporation engaged in the business of financing petroleum product transactions. Will Petroleum ("Will") is a petroleum trading concern which used the plaintiff to finance petroleum transactions. Defendant ARCO is a corporation engaged in the business of buying and selling petroleum products.

This suit arises out of a transaction between the plaintiff, Will, and the defendant. In November of 1985, the defendant agreed to purchase approximately 30,000 metric tons of unleaded blending gasoline from Will. Will planned to purchase the gasoline from Move Oil Trading AG, of Zug, Switzerland ("Move"), then have it loaded onto a ship, the Jo Lonn, to be transported to New York.

At the same time Will was involved in a separate but similar transaction for which it sought financing from the plaintiff. On the same day that it undertook to purchase the gasoline that fueled this dispute, it agreed to a separate purchase of gasoline, which was to be loaded in Constanza onto another ship, the Ultrasea. This purchase was not made from Move, but from Oilman Handels GmbH of Hamburg, West Germany.

On November 14, 1985, the plaintiff agreed to issue a letter of credit to Will to finance the Ultrasea sale. That letter of credit was issued on an unsold basis, which meant that the buyer of the gasoline from Will was not specified. According to the plaintiff, the following then transpired:

> Because the letter of credit was issued on an unsold basis, Will was required to post ten percent cash margin with BAII by the following business day. If, prior to that time, Will provided BAII with a sale of the cargo to a buyer that would post a letter of credit or issue an acceptable purchase confirmation, BAII would release Will from its obligation to post margin.

By November 15, Will had neither posted margin money nor provided an acceptable buyer, and the letter of credit No. (IC-12345) remained undrawn. It appeared that the letter of credit could not be drawn on for several days, because the Ultrasea had not arrived at the loading port as expected and was forced to wait for an available berth. At the same time, Will wished to load the product it had purchased from Move onto the Jo Lonn (which was ready for loading), and needed financing to do so. . . .

At this point in the narrative, the parties have different versions of what transpired and the meaning of certain events. What is clear is that the letter of credit, apparently issued by the plaintiff to finance the Ultrasea purchase, was amended to finance the Jo Lonn purchase.

In mid-December 1985, Will and defendant extended the time for delivery of and payment for the gasoline from the Jo Lonn to January 17, 1986. The defendant sent the plaintiff a confirmatory telex on December 17, indicating the new payment date.

Between December 17 and December 20, the cargo of the Jo Lonn was unloaded and placed into storage at Stolt Outerbrigde Terminal in Perth Amboy, New Jersey. The parties agree that between December 20 and January 17 the plaintiff permitted a portion of the cargo of the Jo Lonn to be distributed to customers other than the defendant. Defendant points to the release of a large portion of the Jo Lonn cargo as an indication that the parties had terminated whatever agreement they had entered into before the defendant's performance was due. Plaintiff, in contrast, asserts that after the mid-December modification, Will was no longer obligated to deliver the exact cargo that was originally slated for the defendant. Instead, plaintiff insists that industry custom dictates that "the seller is permitted to deliver any product that conforms to the contract's quantity and quality specifications."

Will filed for bankruptcy in federal district court in Texas soon after these events took place. Plaintiff, however, had previously perfected a security interest in Will's claims against the defendants. BAII also obtained from the bankruptcy court an order abandoning to BAII Will's entire inventory of gasoline, including that which BAII alleges ARCO was obliged to buy. BAII held the inventory for some weeks, during which time the market price of gasoline apparently declined. BAII sold the Will inventory in a series of private sales that ended in April, 1986. Joint Pretrial Order page 16, ¶ 21. BAII appears to contend that it realized an average price of less that 40 cents per gallon in reselling Will's inventory.

Discussion

BAII seeks to have its damages measured by calculating the difference between the contract price on the ARCO-Will deal and the average price BAII realized on selling Will's inventory several weeks after the alleged breach. In support of that measure of damages, BAII will need to introduce at trial evidence concerning the circumstances of the sale of the Will inventory and the commercial reasonableness of the sale. ARCO argues that BAII's proposed measure of damages is precluded by law, and that the evidence should be excluded. ARCO argues that the issue should be decided now to facilitate trial preparation and to save trial time.

The remedies of a seller of goods such as BAII to recover are provided for in U.C.C. § 2-703. § 2-703(d) provides that a seller, after the buyer breaches the contract of sale, may resell the goods and recover damages as provided for in § 2-706.

Under § 2-706, the measure of damages is the difference between the contract price and the price obtained on the resale of goods identified to the contract. To rely on § 2-706, the seller must satisfy two requirements: (1) the goods resold must have been "reasonably identified to the broken contract," and (2) "every aspect of the sale including the method, manner, time, place and terms must be commercially reasonable." The question on this motion is whether BAII has met these requirements. BAII argues that if a seller cannot meet the standards of § 2-706, the measure of damages is that provided for in § 2-708: "the difference between market price at the time and place for tender and the unpaid contract price together with any incidental damages." U.C.C. § 2-708.

The Court of Appeals for the Second Circuit examined the identification and commercial reasonableness issues in Apex Oil Corp. v. Belcher Co. of New York, Inc., 855 F.2d 997 (2d Cir.1988). The district court had permitted a jury to apply § 2706, and the Second Circuit reversed.

On the question of identification of goods to a contract, the Court in Apex held that "at least with respect to fungible goods, identification for the purposes of a resale transaction does not necessarily require that the resold goods be the exact goods that were rejected or repudiated." Id. at 1002.

On the question of commercial reasonableness, the Second Circuit reasoned that the object of resale is simply determination of the seller's damages. Therefore, the timing of the resale is crucial to a determination of whether the resale price is a reasonable measure of the seller's damages. Apex, 855 F.2d at 1006. In Apex, the Second Circuit held that the seller's six-week delay was commercially unreasonable as a matter of law. Judge Winter reasoned that

> [t]he rule that a "resale should be made as soon as practicable after ... breach," ... should be stringently applied where, as here, the resold goods are not those originally identified to the contract. In such circumstances, of course, there is a significant risk that the seller, who may perhaps have already disposed of the original goods without suffering any loss, has identified new goods for resale in order to minimize the real price and thus to maximize damages. Id. at 1007.

ARCO argues that Apex makes it clear the BAII cannot meet the standards of § 2-706 as a matter of law, and that therefore the Court should exclude evidence of issues related to the resale. In Apex, the cargo was resold after six weeks; ARCO points out that the resale in this case was delayed more two months.

ARCO's motion is denied because the Court concludes that whether the resale was commercially reasonable is a question of fact and that evidence on that issue must be placed before the finder of fact at trial. The facts giving rise to the Apex decision are different from the situation before the Court. For example, gasoil, unlike the home heating oil cargo in

Apex, does not have a clearly defined and readily identifiable market price. Moreover, the Court accepts BAII's representation that it would need to introduce for other purposes evidence which would be excluded if ARCO's motion were granted.

Conclusion

For the reasons set forth above, ARCO's motion is denied.

SO ORDERED

NOTES AND QUESTIONS:

1. What should the trier-of-fact consider in determining commercial reasonableness?

2. Revisit U.C.C. § 2-704(2) (2002). Does a seller have a duty to mitigate damages where buyer repudiates?

---

1. LOST VOLUME SELLER

TERADYNE, INC. V. TELEDYNE INDUSTRIES, INC.
United States Court of Appeals, First Circuit
676 F.2d 865 (1st Cir. 1982).

WYZANSKI, Senior District Judge.

In this diversity action, Teradyne, Inc. sued Teledyne Industries, Inc. and its subsidiary for damages pursuant to § 2-708(2) of the UCC, Mass.Gen.Laws c. 106 s 2-708(2) (hereafter "§ 2-708(2)").[1] Teledyne does not dispute the facts that it is bound as a buyer under a sales contract with Teradyne, that it broke the contract, and that Teradyne's right to damages is governed by § 2-708(2). The principal dispute concerns the calculation of damages.

If the measure of damages provided in subsection (1) is inadequate to put the seller in as good a position as performance would have done then the measure of damages is the profit (including reasonable overhead) which the seller would have made from full performance by the buyer, together with any incidental damages provided in this Article (section 2-710), due allowance for costs reasonably incurred and due credit for payments or proceeds of resale.

---

[1] Section 2-708(1) and (2) of the Uniform Commercial Code, Mass.Gen.Laws c. 106 § 2-708(1) and (2) provide:Seller's Damages for Non-acceptance or Repudiation. (1) Subject to subsection (2) and to the provisions of this Article with respect to proof of market price (section 2-723), the measure of damages for non-acceptance or repudiation by the buyer is the difference between the market price at the time and place for tender and the unpaid contract price together with any incidental damages provided in this Article (section 2-710), but less expenses saved in consequence of the buyer's breach.

The district court referred the case to a master whose report the district court approved and made the basis of the judgment here on appeal.

The following facts, derived from the master's report, are undisputed.

On July 30, 1976 Teradyne, Inc. ("the seller"), a Massachusetts corporation, entered into a Quantity Purchase Contract ("the contract") which, though made with a subsidiary, binds Teledyne Industries, Inc., a California corporation ("the buyer"). That contract governed an earlier contract resulting from the seller's acceptance of the buyer's July 23, 1976 purchase order to buy at the list price of $98,400 (which was also its fair market value) a T-347A transistor test system ("the T-347A"). One consequence of such governance was that the buyer was entitled to a $984 discount from the $98,400 price.

The buyer canceled its order for the T-347A when it was packed ready for shipment scheduled to occur two days later. The seller refused to accept the cancellation.

The buyer offered to purchase instead of the T-347A a $65,000 Field Effects Transistor System ("the FET") which would also have been governed by "the contract." The seller refused the offer.

After dismantling, testing, and reassembling at an estimated cost of $614 the T-347A, the seller, pursuant to an order that was on hand prior to the cancellation, sold it for $98,400 to another purchaser (hereafter "resale purchaser").

Teradyne would have made the sale to the resale purchaser even if Teledyne had not broken its contract. Thus if there had been no breach, Teradyne would have made two sales and earned two profits rather than one.

The seller was a volume seller of the equipment covered by the July 23, 1976 purchase order. The equipment represented standard products of the seller and the seller had the means and capacity to duplicate the equipment for a second sale had the buyer honored its purchase order.

Teradyne being of the view that the measure of damages under § 2-708(2) was the contract price less ascertainable costs saved as a result of the breach-see Jericho Sash and Door Company, Inc. v. Building Erectors, Inc., 362 Mass. 871, 872, 286 N.E.2d 343, (1972) (hereafter "Jericho")-offered as evidence of its cost prices its Inventory Standards Catalog ("the Catalog")-a document which was prepared for tax purposes not claimed to have been illegitimate, but which admittedly disclosed "low inventory valuations." Relying on that Catalog, Teradyne's Controller, McCabe, testified that the only costs which the seller saved as a result of the breach were:

Direct labor costs associate with production	$ 3,301
Material charges	17,045
Sales commission on one T-347A	492
Expense	1,800
Total	$22,638

McCabe admitted that he had not included as costs saved the labor costs of employees associated with testing, shipping, installing, servicing, or fulfilling 10-year warranties on the T-347A (although he acknowledged that in forms of accounting for purposes other than damage suits the costs of those employees would not be regarded as "overhead"). His reason was that those costs would not have been affected by the production of one machine more or less. McCabe also admitted that he had not included fringe benefits which amounted to 12% in the case of both included and excluded labor costs.

During McCabe's direct examination, he referred to the 10-K report which Teradyne had filed with the SEC. On cross-examination McCabe admitted that the 10-K form showed that on average the seller's revenues were distributed as follows:

Profit	9%
"Selling and administrative" expense	26%
Interest	1%
"Cost of sales and engineering" (including substantial research and development costs incidental to a high technology business)	64%

He also admitted that the average figures applied to the T-347A.

Teledyne contended that the 10-K report was a better index of lost profits than was the Catalog. The master disagreed and concluded that the more appropriate formula for calculating Teradyne's damages under § 2-708(2) was the one approved in Jericho, supra - " 'gross profit' including fixed costs but not costs saved as a result of the breach." He then stated:

> In accordance with the statutory mandate that the remedy "be liberally administered to the end that the aggrieved party may be put in as good a position as if the other party had fully performed," M.G.L. c. 106 § 1-106(1), I find that the Plaintiff has met its burden of proof of damages, and has established the accuracy of its direct costs and the ascertainability of its variable costs with reasonable certainty and "whatever definiteness and accuracy the facts permit." Comment 1 to § 1-106(1) of the UCC.

In effect, this was a finding that Teradyne had saved only $22,638 as a result of the breach. Subtracting that amount and also the $984 quantity discount from the original contract price of $98,400, the master found that the lost "profit (including reasonable overhead)" was $74,778. To that amount the master added $614 for "incidental damages" which Teradyne incurred in preparing the T-347A for its new customer. Thus he found that Teradyne's total s 2-708(2) damages amounted to $75,392.

The master declined to make a deduction from the $75,392 on account of the refusal of the seller to accept the buyer's offer to purchase an FET tester in partial substitution for the repudiated T-347A.

At the time of the reference to the master, the court, without securing the agreement of the parties, had ordered that the master's costs should be paid by them in equal parts.

Teradyne filed a motion praying that the district court (1) should adopt the master's report allowing it to recover $75,392, and (2) should require Teledyne to pay all the master's costs. The district court, without opinion, entered a judgment which grants the first prayer and denies the second. Teledyne appealed from the first part of the judgment; Teradyne appealed from the second part.

The parties are agreed that § 2-708(2) applies to the case at bar. Inasmuch as this conclusion is not plain from the text, we explain the reasons why we concur in that agreement.

Section 2-708(2) applies only if the damages provided by § 2-708(1) are inadequate to put the seller in as good a position as performance would have done. Under § 2-708(1) the measure of damages is the difference between unpaid contract price and market price. Here the unpaid contract price was $97,416 and the market price was $98,400. Hence no damages would be recoverable under § 2-708(1). On the other hand, if the buyer had performed, the seller (1) would have had the proceeds of two contracts, one with the buyer Teledyne and the other with the "resale purchaser" and (2) it seems would have had in 1976-7 one more T-347A sale.

A literal reading of the last sentence of § 2-708(2)-providing for "due credit for payments or proceeds of resale"-would indicate that Teradyne recovers nothing because the proceeds of the resale exceeded the price set in the Teledyne-Teradyne contract. However, in light of the statutory history of the subsection, it is universally agreed that in a case where after the buyer's default a seller resells the goods, the proceeds of the resale are not to be credited to the buyer if the seller is a lost volume seller[2]-that is, one who had there been no breach by the buyer, could and would have had the benefit of both the original contract and the resale contract.[3]

Thus, despite the resale of the T-347A, Teradyne is entitled to recover from Teledyne what s 2-708(2) calls its expected "profit (including reasonable overhead)" on the broken Teledyne contract.[4]

---

[2] The term "lost volume seller" was apparently coined by Professor Robert J. Harris in his article A Radical Restatement of the Law of Seller's Damages: Sales Act and Commercial Code Results Compared, 18 Stan.L.Rev. 66 (1965). The terminology has been widely adopted. See Famous Knitwear Corp. v. Drug Fair Inc., 493 F.2d 251, 254 n.5 (4th Cir. 1974); Snyder v. Herbert Greenbaum & Assoc. Inc., 38 Md.App. 144, 157, 380 A.2d 618, 624 (1977); Publicker Industries, Inc. v. Roman Ceramics Corp., 652 F.2d 340, 346 (3rd Cir. 1981). See Restatement (Second) Contracts s 347 Comment f; J. White and R. Summers, Uniform Commercial Code, 2d ed. (1980) (hereafter "White and Summers") s 7-9, particularly p. 276 first full paragraph.

[3] Famous Knitwear Corp. v. Drug Fair Inc., supra, 493 F.2d at 254 n.7; Snyder v. Herbert Greenbaum & Assoc. Inc., supra, 380 A.2d 625-626; Neri v. Retail Marine Corp., 30 N.Y.2d 393, 399, 334 N.Y.S.2d 165, 285 N.E.2d 311, 314 (1972). See White and Summers, s 7-13, particularly 284-285.

[4] Ibid. White and Summers at pp. 284-285 give the following suppositious case which parallels the instant case. Boeing is able to make and sell in one year 100 airplanes. TWA contracts to buy the third plane off the assembly line, but it breaks the contract and Boeing resells the plane to Pan Am which had already agreed to buy the fourth plane. Because of the breach Boeing sells only 99 aircraft during the year. White and Summers say that the right result, despite the words of s 2-708(2), is that Boeing recovers from TWA both the net profit and the overhead components of the TWA contract price, no credit being given for any part of the proceeds Boeing received from its sale to Pan Am.We do not agree with the third sentence in the following Comment f to Restatement (Second) Contract s 347 insofar as it indicates that a volume seller like Teradyne may recover from a defaulting buyer only the lost net profit on the original contract.

Lost volume. Whether a subsequent transaction is a substitute for the broken contract sometimes raises difficult questions of fact. If the injured party could and would have entered into the subsequent contract, even if the contract had not been broken, and could have had the benefit of both, he can be said to have "lost volume" and the subsequent transaction is not a substitute for the broken contract. The injured party's damages are then based on the net profit that he has lost as a result of the broken contract. Since entrepreneurs try to operate at optimum capacity, however, it is possible that an additional transaction would not have been profitable and that the injured party would not have chosen to expand his business by undertaking it had there been no breach. It is sometime assumed that he would have done so, but the question is one of fact to be resolved according to the circumstances of each case. See illustration 16. See also Uniform Commercial Code § 2-708(2). (Emphasis added.)

Limiting the volume seller's recovery to lost net profit does not permit the recovery of reasonable overhead for which provision is specifically made in the text of § 2-708(2). The reason for the allowance of overhead is set forth in Vitex Mfg. Corp. v. Caribtex Corp., 377 F.2d 795, 799 (3rd Cir. 1967) (hereafter "Vitex"):..... as the number of transaction(s) over which overhead can be spread becomes smaller, each transaction must bear a greater portion or allocate share of the fixed overhead cost. Suppose a company has fixed overhead of $10,000 and engages in five similar transactions; then the receipts of each transaction would bear $2000 of overhead expense. If the company is now forced to spread this $10,000 over only four transactions, then the overhead expense per transaction will rise to $2500, significantly reducing the profitability of the four remaining transactions. Thus, where the contract is between businessmen familiar with commercial practices, as here, the breaching party should reasonably foresee that his breach will not only cause a loss of "clear" profit, but also a loss in that the profitability of other transactions will be reduced. Resolute Ins. Co. v. Percy Jones, Inc., 198 F.2d 309 (C.A.10, 1952); Cf. In re Kellett Aircraft Corp., 191 F.2d 231 (C.A.3, 1951). Vitex represents the law of Massachusetts. F. A. Bartlett Tree Expert Co. v. Hartney, 308 Mass. 407, 412, 32 N.E.2d 237 (1941); Roblin Hope Industries Inc. v. J. A. Sullivan Corp., Mass.App.Ct.Adv.Sh. (1980) 2229, 2232, 413 N.E.2d 1134.

Teledyne not only "does not dispute that damages are to be calculated pursuant to § 2-708(2)" but concedes that the formula used in Jericho Sash & Door Co. v. Building Erectors Inc., 362 Mass. 871, 286 N.E.2d 343 (1972), for determining lost profit including overhead-that is, the formula under which direct costs of producing and selling manufactured goods are deducted from the contract price in order to arrive at "profit (including reasonable overhead)" as that term is used in § 2-708(2)-"is permissible provided all variable expenses are identified."[5]

[5] We concur in the view that Massachusetts law determines whether a particular formula for calculating damages under a Massachusetts statute is permissible. Salemme v. Ristaino, 587 F.2d 81, 87 (1st Cir. 1978). But we are not certain that the Jericho court purported to declare that in every s 2-708(2) case the use of the formula would be permissible.An examination of the original record in Jericho shows that the seller offered evidence of the contract price and of virtually all the expenses that were saved by him as a result of the breach, but he did not offer evidence showing separate figures for profit and for overhead. The trier of fact allowed as damages the contract price less the direct costs because "as a general principle, it may be stated that the loss will be measured by the contract price less those costs and expenses directly attributable to the performance of the contract." On appeal, the Massachusetts Supreme Judicial Court stated that "The sole question presented is whether the trial judge erred in allowing damages for 'profit (including reasonable overhead),' under G.L. c. 106, s 2-708(2), in the absence of evidence showing separate figures for profit and for overhead." Inspection of the briefs reveals

In light of the concession made in Teledyne's brief, we need not determine whether in a case where reasonableness of overhead was an issue the Massachusetts courts would distinguish Jericho, or would declare that if part or all of a particular item is not recoverable as "reasonable overhead" it is nonetheless recoverable as part of "the profit ... which the seller would have made from full performance," or would permit the use of the formula and leave it to the trier of fact to decide whether the results which flowed from its application were credible.

What Teledyne contends is that all variable costs were not identified because the cost figures came from a catalog, prepared for tax purposes, which did not fully reflect all direct costs. The master found that the statement of costs based on the catalog was reliable and that Teledyne's method of calculating costs based on the 10-K statements was not more accurate. Those findings are not clearly erroneous and therefore we may not reverse the judgment on the ground that allegedly the items of cost which were deducted are unreliable. Fed.R.Civ.P. 52(a); Merrill Trust Co. v. Bradford, 507 F.2d 467, 468 (1st Cir. 1974); Van Alen v. Dominick & Dominick, Inc., 560 F.2d 547, 551 (2d Cir. 1977).

Teledyne's more significant objection to Teradyne's and the master's application of the Jericho formula in the case at bar is that neither of them made deductions on account of the wages paid to testers, shippers, installers, and other Teradyne employees who directly handled the T-347A, or on account of the fringe benefits amounting in the case of those and other employees to 12 per cent of wages. Teradyne gave as the reason for the omission of the wages of the testers, etc. that those wages would not have been affected if each of the testers, etc. handled one product more or less. However, the work of those employees entered as directly into producing and supplying the T-347A as did the work of a fabricator of a T-347A. Surely no one would regard as "reasonable overhead" within § 2-708(2) the wages of a fabricator of a T-347A even if his wages were the same whether he made one product more or less. We conclude that the wages of the testers, etc. likewise are not part of overhead and as a "direct cost" should have been deducted from the contract price. A fortiori fringe benefits amounting to 12 per cent of wages should also have been deducted as direct costs. Taken together we cannot view these omitted items as what Jericho called "relatively insignificant items." We, therefore, must vacate the district court's judgment. In accordance with the procedure followed in Publicker Industries, Inc. v. Roman Ceramics Corp., 603 F.2d 1065, 1072-3 (3rd Cir. 1979) and Famous Knitwear Corp. v. Drug Fair, Inc., 493 F.2d 251, 255-256 (4th Cir. 1974), we remand this case so that with respect to the omitted direct labor costs specified above the parties may offer further evidence and the court may make findings "with whatever definiteness and accuracy the facts permit, but no more." Jericho, p. 872, 286 N.E.2d 343.

There are two other matters which may properly be dealt with before the case is remanded to the district court.

---

that that statement is not accurate. Other questions were presented. But the parties nowhere raised the issue whether the method-contract price less direct costs-which was proper as a general principle would be proper where the seller had expenses which were not direct costs (say, for example, a rental charge, or an executive officer's salary, or research expenses) which either were in excess of a reasonable amount or were not properly regarded as overhead reasonably related to the goods covered by the contract.

mitigate

Teledyne contends that Teradyne was required to mitigate damages by acceptance of Teledyne's offer to purchase instead of the T-347A the FET system.

That point is without merit.

The meaning of Teledyne's offer was that if Teradyne would forego its profit-loss claim arising out of Teledyne's breach of the T-347A contract, Teledyne would purchase another type of machine which it was under no obligation to buy. The seller's failure to accept such an offer does not preclude it from recovering the full damages to which it would otherwise be entitled. As Restatement (Second) Contracts, § 350 Comment c indicates, there is no right to so-called mitigation of damages where the offer of a substitute contract "is conditioned on surrender by the injured party of his claim for breach." "One is not required to mitigate his losses by accepting an arrangement with the repudiator if that is made conditional on his surrender of his rights under the repudiated contract." 5 Corbin, Contracts 2nd (1964) § 1043 at 274. Acc. Campfield v. Sauer, 189 F. 576 (6th Cir. 1911); Stanspec Corp. v. Jelco, Inc., 464 F.2d 1184, 1187 (10th Cir. 1972). Teradyne acted in a commercially reasonable manner in refusing to accept Teledyne's offer.

Teradyne's appeal from the second part of the district court's judgment is on the ground that it was an abuse of discretion for the district court without equitable cause not to impose on Teledyne all the master's costs and to leave Teradyne, the prevailing party, with the burden of half of those costs.

We hold that the district court's order, made at the time the case was referred to the master, which provided for an equal payment of costs, was merely a temporary method of financing the master. The court retained its power at the end of the case to determine who should ultimately bear the master's costs.

Generally it is an abuse of discretion for a district court without cause to charge the prevailing party the costs of the reference to a master. See Popeil Brothers, Inc. v. Schick Electric, Inc., 516 F.2d 772, 774 (7th Cir. 1975); Chemical Bank & Trust Co. v. Prudence-Bonds Corp., 207 F.2d 67, 77-78 (2nd Cir. 1953).

As the matter stood when the district judge denied Teradyne's motion to require Teledyne to pay all the master's costs, while Teradyne had not prevailed on all the issues presented in its complaint which sought a recovery of $98,400, it had recovered $75,392 by prevailing on all the issues finally submitted to the master. However, as a result of the present opinion that $75,392 recovery will be reduced by an unpredictable amount. Under these circumstances, we deem it appropriate to vacate the part of the judgment denying Teradyne's motion, and we remand the case to allow the district court after it has decided how much to deduct from the $75,392 recovery to determine afresh how the master's costs should be allocated. In making its determination the district court may exercise a reasonable discretion. It is not required to impose all the master's costs on Teledyne on the theory that since Teradyne recovered a substantial part of what it sought, it was the prevailing party. If it so chooses, the district court may adopt some other approach-for example, an allocation of the master's costs by reference to the ratio of the amount which Teradyne finally recovers to the amount it originally sought in the complaint or to the amount it sought when the case was submitted to the master.

The district court's judgment is vacated and the case is remanded to the district court to proceed in accordance with this opinion.

---

2. CONTRACT PRICE

IDAHO CODE
§ 28-2-709. ACTION FOR THE PRICE.
IDAHO CODE ANN. § 28-2-709 (2011).

(1) When the buyer fails to pay the price as it becomes due the seller may recover, together with any incidental damages under the next section, the price

(a) of goods accepted or of conforming goods lost or damaged within a commercially reasonable time after risk of their loss has passed to the buyer; and

(b) of goods identified to the contract if the seller is unable after reasonable effort to resell them at a reasonable price or the circumstances reasonably indicate that such effort will be unavailing.

(2) Where the seller sues for the price he must hold for the buyer any goods which have been identified to the contract and are still in his control except that if resale becomes possible he may resell them at any time prior to the collection of the judgment. The net proceeds of any such resale must be credited to the buyer and payment of the judgment entitles him to any goods no resold.

(3) After the buyer has wrongfully rejected or revoked acceptance of the goods or has failed to make a payment due or has repudiated (section 28-2-610), a seller who is held not entitled to the price under this section shall nevertheless be awarded damages for non-acceptance under the preceding section.

C. EQUITABLE DOCTRINES: SPECIFIC PERFORMANCE, RESTITUTION & REPLEVIN

1. SPECIFIC PERFORMANCE

LACLEDE GAS CO. V. AMOCO OIL CO.
United States Court of Appeals, Eighth Circuit
522 F.2d 33 (8th Cir. 1975).

ROSS, Circuit Judge.

The Laclede Gas Company (Laclede), a Missouri corporation, brought this diversity action alleging breach of contract against the Amoco Oil Company (Amoco), a Delaware corporation. It sought relief in the form of a mandatory injunction prohibiting the continuing breach or, in the alternative, damages. The district court held a bench trial on the issues of whether there was a valid, binding contract between the parties and whether, if there was such a contract, Amoco should be enjoined from breaching it. It then ruled that the "contract is invalid due to lack of mutuality" and denied the prayer for injunctive relief. The court made no decision regarding the requested damages. Laclede Gas Co. v. Amoco Oil Co., 385 F.Supp. 1332, 1336 (E.D.Mo.1974). This appeal followed, and we reverse the district court's judgment.

On September 21, 1970, Midwest Missouri Gas Company (now Laclede), and American Oil Company (now Amoco), the predecessors of the parties to this litigation, entered into a written agreement which was designed to provide central propane gas distribution systems to various residential developments in Jefferson County, Missouri, until such time as natural gas mains were extended into these areas. The agreement contemplated that as individual developments were planned the owners or developers would apply to Laclede for central propane gas systems. If Laclede determined that such a system was appropriate in any given development, it could request Amoco to supply the propane to that specific development. This request was made in the form of a supplemental form letter, as provided in the September 21 agreement; and if Amoco decided to supply the propane, it bound itself to do so by signing this supplemental form.

Once this supplemental form was signed the agreement placed certain duties on both Laclede and Amoco. Basically, Amoco was to "(i)nstall, own, maintain and operate . . . storage and vaporization facilities and any other facilities necessary to provide (it) with the capability of delivering to (Laclede) commercial propane gas suitable . . . for delivery by (Laclede) to its customers' facilities." Amoco's facilities were to be "adequate to provide a continuous supply of commercial propane gas at such times and in such volumes commensurate with (Laclede's) requirements for meeting the demands reasonably to be anticipated in each Development while this Agreement is in force." Amoco was deemed to be "the supplier," while Laclede was "the distributing utility."

For its part Laclede agreed to "(i)nstall, own, maintain and operate all distribution facilities" from a "point of delivery" which was defined to be "the outlet of (Amoco) header piping." Laclede also promised to pay Amoco "the Wood River Area Posted Price for propane plus four cents per gallon for all amounts of commercial propane gas delivered" to it under the agreement.

Since it was contemplated that the individual propane systems would eventually be converted to natural gas, one paragraph of the agreement provided that Laclede should give Amoco 30 days written notice of this event, after which the agreement would no longer be binding for the converted development.

Another paragraph gave Laclede the right to cancel the agreement. However, this right was expressed in the following language:

> This Agreement shall remain in effect for one (1) year following the first delivery of gas by (Amoco) to (Laclede) hereunder. Subject to termination as provided in Paragraph 11 hereof (dealing with conversions to natural gas), this Agreement shall automatically continue in effect for additional periods of one (1) year each unless (Laclede) shall, not less than 30 days prior to the expiration of the initial one (1) year period or any subsequent one (1) year period, give (Amoco) written notice of termination.

There was no provision under which Amoco could cancel the agreement.

For a time the parties operated satisfactorily under this agreement, and some 17 residential subdivisions were brought within it by supplemental letters. However, for various reasons, including conversion to natural gas, the number of developments under the agreement had shrunk to eight by the time of trial. These were all mobile home parks.

During the winter of 1972-73 Amoco experienced a shortage of propane and voluntarily placed all of its customers, including Laclede, on an 80% Allocation basis, meaning that Laclede would receive only up to 80% of its previous requirements. Laclede objected to this and pushed Amoco to give it 100% of what the developments needed. Some conflict arose over this before the temporary shortage was alleviated.

Then, on April 3, 1973, Amoco notified Laclede that its Wood River Area Posted Price of propane had been increased by three cents per gallon. Laclede objected to this increase also and demanded a full explanation. None was forthcoming. Instead Amoco merely sent a letter dated May 14, 1973, informing Laclede that it was "terminating" the September 21, 1970, agreement effective May 31, 1973. It claimed it had the right to do this because "the Agreement lacks 'mutuality.' "[1]

The district court felt that the entire controversy turned on whether or not Laclede's right to "arbitrarily cancel the Agreement" without Amoco having a similar right rendered the contract void "for lack of mutuality" and it resolved this question in the affirmative. We disagree with this conclusion and hold that settled principles of contract law require a reversal.

I.

A bilateral contract is not rendered invalid and unenforceable merely because one party has the right to cancellation while the other does not. There is no necessity "that for each stipulation in a contract binding the one party there must be a corresponding stipulation binding the other." James B. Berry's Sons Co. v. Monark Gasoline & Oil Co., 32 F.2d 74, 75 (8th Cir. 1929). Accord, Boland v. Shell Oil Co., 71 F.Supp. 649, 651 (E.D.Mo.1947) (Missouri law); Zeppenfeld v. Morgan, 168 S.W.2d 971, 975 (Mo.Ct.App.1943); Banner Creamery Co. v. Judy, 47 S.W.2d 129, 131 (Mo.App.1932).

The important question in the instant case is whether Laclede's right of cancellation rendered all its other promises in the agreement illusory so that there was a complete failure of consideration. This would be the result had Laclede retained the right of immediate cancellation at any time for any reason. 1 S. Williston, Law of Contracts § 104, at 400-401 (3d ed. 1957). However, Professor Williston goes on to note:

[1] While Amoco sought to repudiate the agreement, it resumed supplying propane to the subdivisions on February 1, 1974, under the mandatory allocation guidelines promulgated by the Federal Energy Administration under the Federal Mandatory Allocation Program for propane. It is agreed that this is now being done under the contract.

> Since the courts . . . do not favor arbitrary cancellation clauses, the tendency is to interpret even a slight restriction on the exercise of the right of cancellation as constituting such legal detriment as will satisfy the requirement of sufficient consideration; for example, where the reservation of right to cancel is for cause, or by written notice, or after a definite period of notice, or upon the occurrence of some extrinsic event, or is based on some other objective standard. Id. § 105, at 418-419 (footnotes omitted).

Professor Corbin agrees and states simply that when one party has the power to cancel by notice given for some stated period of time, "the contract should never be held to be rendered invalid thereby for lack of 'mutuality' or for lack of consideration." 1A A. Corbin, Corbin on Contracts § 164 at 83 (1963). The law of Missouri appears to be in conformity with this general contract rule that a cancellation clause will invalidate a contract only if its exercise is unrestricted. Phillips Petroleum Co. v. Rau Const. Co., 130 F.2d 499, 501 (8th Cir.), cert. denied, 317 U.S. 685, 63 S.Ct. 260, 87 L.Ed. 549 (1942), (Missouri law); Boland v. Shell Oil Co., supra, 71 F.Supp. at 651-652; Bevins v. Harris, 380 S.W.2d 345, 352 (Mo.1964); National Refining Co. v. Cox, 227 Mo.App. 778, 57 S.W.2d 778, 781 (1933).

Here Laclede's right to terminate was neither arbitrary nor unrestricted. It was limited by the agreement in at least three ways. First, Laclede could not cancel until one year had passed after the first delivery of propane by Amoco. Second, any cancellation could be effective only on the anniversary date of the first delivery under the agreement. Third, Laclede had to give Amoco 30 days written notice of termination. These restrictions on Laclede's power to cancel clearly bring this case within the rule.

A more difficult issue in this case is whether or not the contract fails for lack of "mutuality of consideration" because Laclede did not expressly bind itself to order all of its propane requirements for the Jefferson County subdivisions from Amoco.

While there is much confusion over the meaning of the terms "mutuality" or "mutuality of obligation" as used by the courts in describing contracts, 1 S. Williston, supra, § 105A, at 420-421; 1A A. Corbin, supra, § 152, at 2-3, our use of this concept here is best described by Professor Williston:

Sometimes the question involved where mutuality is discussed is whether one party to the transaction can by fair implication be regarded as making any promise; but this is simply an inquiry whether there is consideration for the other party's promise. 1 S. Williston, supra, § 105A, at 423. (Footnote omitted.) As stated by the Missouri Supreme Court:

> Mutuality of contract means that an obligation rests upon each party to do or permit to be done something in consideration of the act or promise of the other; that is, neither party is bound unless both are bound.
>
> Aden v. Dalton, 341 Mo. 454, 107 S.W.2d 1070, 1073 (1937), quoting Gillen v. Bayfield, 329 Mo. 681, 46 S.W.2d 571, 575 (1935). (Emphasis supplied.) See Middleton v. Holecroft, 270 S.W.2d 90, 92 (Mo.App.1954).

We are satisfied that, while Laclede did not expressly promise to purchase all the propane requirements for the subdivisions from Amoco, a practical reading of the contract provisions reveals that this was clearly the intent of the parties. In making this determination we are mindful of three pertinent rules of contract law. First, the contract herein consisted of both the September 21, 1970, agreement and the supplemental letter agreements, for a contract may be made up of several documents. State ex rel. Foster v. Griffin, 246 S.W.2d 396, 398 (Mo.App.1952). Second, "the consideration for a contract will not be held uncertain if by the application of the usual tests of construction, the court can reasonably discover to what the parties agreed." Burger v. City of Springfield, 323 S.W.2d 777, 783 (Mo.1959). Finally, "(w)here an agreement is susceptible of two constructions, one of which renders the contract invalid and the other sustains its validity, the latter construction is preferred." Perbal v. Dazor Manufacturing Corp., 436 S.W.2d 677, 689 (Mo.1968).

Once Amoco had signed the supplemental letter agreement, thereby making the September 21 agreement applicable to any given Jefferson County development, it was bound to be the propane supplier for that subdivision and to provide a continuous supply of the gas sufficient to meet Laclede's reasonably anticipated needs for that development. It was to perform these duties until the agreement was cancelled by Laclede or until natural gas distribution was extended to the development.[2]

For its part, Laclede bound itself to purchase all the propane required by the particular development from Amoco. This commitment was not expressly written out, but it necessarily follows from an intelligent, practical reading of the agreement.

Laclede was to "(i)nstall, own, maintain and operate all distribution facilities from the point of delivery as defined in Paragraph 3(b) . . . ." Paragraph 3(b) provided: "the point of delivery shall be at the outlet of (Amoco) header piping." Also under Paragraph 3(b) Amoco was to own and operate all the facilities on the bulk side of that header piping. Laclede thus bound itself to buy all its requirements from Amoco by agreeing to attach its distribution lines to Amoco's header piping; and even if a change of suppliers could be made under the contract, Laclede could not own and operate a separate distribution system hooked up to some other supplier's propane storage tanks without substantially altering the supply route to its distribution system or making a very substantial investment in its own storage equipment and site. As a practical matter, then, Laclede is bound to buy all the propane it distributes from Amoco in any subdivision to which the supplemental agreement applies and for which the distribution system has been established.

When analyzed in this manner, it can be seen that the contract herein is simply a so-called "requirements contract." Such contracts are routinely enforced by the courts where, as here, the needs of the purchaser are reasonably foreseeable and the time of performance is reasonably limited. Cold Blast Transp. Co. v. Kansas City Bolt & Nut Co., 114 F. 77, 81 (8th Cir. 1902); Great Eastern Oil Co. v. DeMert & Dougherty, 350 Mo. 535, 166 S.W.2d 490, 493 (1942); Cantrell v. Knight, 72 S.W.2d 196, 199-200 (Mo.Ct.App.1934); 1 S. Williston, supra, § 104A; 1A A. Corbin, supra, § 156.

---

[2] The evidence indicates that Laclede contemplates converting all of the subdivisions within 10 to 15 years, although it could not and would not commit itself to this timeframe.

We conclude that there is mutuality of consideration within the terms of the agreement and hold that there is a valid, binding contract between the parties as to each of the developments for which supplemental letter agreements have been signed.

II.

Since he found that there was no binding contract, the district judge did not have to deal with the question of whether or not to grant the injunction prayed for by Laclede. He simply denied this relief because there was no contract. Laclede Gas Co. v. Amoco Oil Co., supra, 385 F.Supp. at 1336.

Generally the determination of whether or not to order specific performance of a contract lies within the sound discretion of the trial court. Landau v. St. Louis Public Service Co., 364 Mo. 1134, 273 S.W.2d 255, 259 (1954). However, this discretion is, in fact, quite limited; and it is said that when certain equitable rules have been met and the contract is fair and plain "specific performance goes as a matter of right." Miller v. Coffeen, 365 Mo. 204, 280 S.W.2d 100, 102 (1955), quoting, Berberet v. Myers, 240 Mo. 58, 77, 144 S.W. 824, 830 (1912). (Emphasis omitted.)

With this in mind we have carefully reviewed the very complete record on appeal and conclude that the trial court should grant the injunctive relief prayed. We are satisfied that this case falls within that category in which specific performance should be ordered as a matter of right. See Miller v. Coffeen, supra, 280 S.W.2d at 102.

Amoco contends that four of the requirements for specific performance have not been met. Its claims are: (1) there is no mutuality of remedy in the contract; (2) the remedy of specific performance would be difficult for the court to administer without constant and long-continued supervision; (3) the contract is indefinite and uncertain; and (4) the remedy at law available to Laclede is adequate. The first three contentions have little or no merit and do not detain us for long.

There is simply no requirement in the law that both parties be mutually entitled to the remedy of specific performance in order that one of them be given that remedy by the court. Beets v. Tyler, 365 Mo. 895, 290 S.W.2d 76, 80 (1956); Rice v. Griffith, 349 Mo. 373, 161 S.W.2d 220, 225 (1942).

While a court may refuse to grant specific performance where such a decree would require constant and long-continued court supervision, this is merely a discretionary rule of decision which is frequently ignored when the public interest is involved. See, e. g., Joy v. St. Louis, 138 U.S. 1, 47, 11 S.Ct. 243, 34 L.Ed. 843 (1891); Western Union Telegraph Co. v. Pennsylvania Co., 129 F. 849, 869 (3d Cir. 1904); Municipal Gas Co. v. Lone Star Gas Co., 259 S.W. 684, 690-691 (Tex.Civ.App.1924), aff'd, 117 Tex. 331, 3 S.W.2d 790 (1928).

Here the public interest in providing propane to the retail customers is manifest, while any supervision required will be far from onerous.

Section 370 of the Restatement of Contracts (1932) provides:

> Specific enforcement will not be decreed unless the terms of the contract are so expressed that the court can determine with reasonable certainty what is the duty of each party and the conditions under which performance is due.

We believe these criteria have been satisfied here. As discussed in part I of this opinion, as to all developments for which a supplemental agreement has been signed, Amoco is to supply all the propane which is reasonably foreseeably required, while Laclede is to purchase the required propane from Amoco and pay the contract price therefor. The parties have disagreed over what is meant by "Wood River Area Posted Price" in the agreement, but the district court can and should determine with reasonable certainty what the parties intended by this term and should mold its decree, if necessary accordingly.[3] Likewise, the fact that the agreement does not have a definite time of duration is not fatal since the evidence established that the last subdivision should be converted to natural gas in 10 to 15 years. This sets a reasonable time limit on performance and the district court can and should mold the final decree to reflect this testimony.

It is axiomatic that specific performance will not be ordered when the party claiming breach of contract has an adequate remedy at law. Jamison Coal & Coke Co. v. Goltra, 143 F.2d 889, 894 (8th Cir.), cert. denied, 323 U.S. 769, 65 S.Ct. 122, 89 L.Ed. 615 (1944). This is especially true when the contract involves personal property as distinguished from real estate.

However, in Missouri, as elsewhere, specific performance may be ordered even though personalty is involved in the "proper circumstances." Mo.Rev.Stat. s 400.2-716(1); Restatement of Contracts, supra, § 361. And a remedy at law adequate to defeat the grant of specific performance "must be as certain, prompt, complete, and efficient to attain the ends of justice as a decree of specific performance." National Marking Mach. Co. v. Triumph Mfg. Co., 13 F.2d 6, 9 (8th Cir. 1926). Accord, Snip v. City of Lamar, 239 Mo.App. 824, 201 S.W.2d 790, 798 (1947).

One of the leading Missouri cases allowing specific performance of a contract relating to personalty because the remedy at law was inadequate is Boeving v. Vandover, 240 Mo.App. 117, 218 S.W.2d 175, 178 (1949). In that case the plaintiff sought specific performance of a contract in which the defendant had promised to sell him an automobile. At that time (near the end of and shortly after World War II) new cars were hard to come by, and the court held that specific performance was a proper remedy since a new car "could not be obtained elsewhere except at considerable expense, trouble or loss, which cannot be estimated in advance."

We are satisfied that Laclede has brought itself within this practical approach taken by the Missouri courts. As Amoco points out, Laclede has propane immediately available to it under other contracts with other suppliers. And the evidence indicates that at the present time propane is readily available on the open market. However, this analysis ignores the fact that the contract involved in this lawsuit is for a long-term supply of propane to these

[3] The record indicates that Laclede has now accepted Amoco's interpretation and has agreed that "Wood River Area Posted Price" means Amoco's posted price for propane at its Wood River refinery.

subdivisions. The other two contracts under which Laclede obtains the gas will remain in force only until March 31, 1977, and April 1, 1981, respectively; and there is no assurance that Laclede will be able to receive any propane under them after that time. Also it is unclear as to whether or not Laclede can use the propane obtained under these contracts to supply the Jefferson County subdivisions, since they were originally entered into to provide Laclede with propane with which to "shave" its natural gas supply during peak demand periods.[4] Additionally, there was uncontradicted expert testimony that Laclede probably could not find another supplier of propane willing to enter into a long-term contract such as the Amoco agreement, given the uncertain future of worldwide energy supplies. And, even if Laclede could obtain supplies of propane for the affected developments through its present contracts or newly negotiated ones, it would still face considerable expense and trouble which cannot be estimated in advance in making arrangements for its distribution to the subdivisions.

Specific performance is the proper remedy in this situation, and it should be granted by the district court.[5]

CONCLUSION

For the foregoing reasons the judgment of the district court is reversed and the cause is remanded for the fashioning of appropriate injunctive relief in the form of a decree of specific performance as to those developments for which a supplemental agreement form has been signed by the parties.

---

2. RESTITUTION FOR BREACHING BUYER

OHIO REVISED CODE
§ 1302.92. (UCC 2-718) LIQUIDATION OR LIMITATION OF DAMAGES; DEPOSITS.
Ohio Rev. Code Ann. § 1302.92 (LexisNexis 2012).

(A) . . . .

(B) Where the seller justifiably withholds delivery of goods because of the buyer's breach, the buyer is entitled to restitution of any amount by which the usm of his payments exceeds

(1) the amount to which the seller is entitled by virtue of terms liquidating the seller's damages in accordance with subsection (A), or

(2) in the absence of such terms, twenty per cent of the value of the total performance for which the buyer is obligated under the contract or $500, whichever is smaller.

(C) The buyer's right to restitution under subsection (B) is subject to offset to the extent that the seller establishes

---

[4] During periods of cold weather, when demand is high, Laclede does not receive enough natural gas to meet all this demand. It, therefore, adds propane to the natural gas it places in its distribution system. This practice is called "peak shaving."

[5] In fashioning its decree the district court must take into account any relevant rules and regulations promulgated under the Federal Mandatory Allocation Program.

(1) a right to recover damages under the provisions of this Article other than subsection (A), and

(2) the amount or value of any benefits received by the buyer directly or indirectly by reason of the contract.

(D) . . . .

---

3. REPLEVIN

MONTANA CODE
§ 30-2-716. BUYER'S RIGHT TO SPECIFIC PERFORMANCE OR REPLEVIN.
MONT. CODE ANN. § § 30-2-716 (2011).

. . . . (3) The buyer has a right to maintain an action for the recovery of goods identified to the contract if after reasonable effort the buyer is unable to effect cover for such goods or the circumstances reasonably indicate that such effort will be unavailing or if the goods have been shipped under reservation and satisfaction of the security interest in them has been made or tendered. In the case of goods bought for personal, family, or household purposes, the buyer's right to maintain an action for recovery of the goods vests upon acquisition of a special property, even if the seller had not then repudiated or failed to deliver.

SECTION 6. PUNITIVE DAMAGES

HIBSCHMAN PONTIAC, INC. V. BATCHELOR
Supreme Court of Indiana
362 N.E.2d 845 (1977).

GIVAN, Chief Justice.

Batchelor brought an action for breach of contract and oppressive conduct by Hibschman Pontiac, Inc. and General Motors Corporation. A trial before a jury resulted in a verdict for Batchelor and against Hibschman Pontiac and General Motors Corporation in the amount of $1,500.00. Further, the jury assessed punitive damages against Hibschman Pontiac, Inc. in the amount of $15,000.00.

The Court of Appeals, Third District, reversed the grant of punitive damages. See 340 N.E.2d 377. Batchelor now petitions for transfer.

The record reveals the following evidence: Prior to buying the Pontiac GTO automobile involved in this case, Batchelor inquired of the salesman, the service manager and the vice president as to the quality of Hibschman Pontiac's service department, as it was important that any deficiencies in the car be corrected. The salesman and the service manager responded that the service department at Hibschman Pontiac was above average. Jim Hibschman, the vice president, assured him that he would personally see that any difficulties would be corrected. Batchelor stated that he relied on the statements of the three men and ordered a 1969 GTO Pontiac automobile.

When Batchelor picked up his new car he discovered several problems with it. As requested by the service manager of Hibschman Pontiac, Batchelor made a list of his complaints and brought the car in for repair a few days later. The service manager attached the list to a work order but did not list the deficiencies on the work order. Later the manager called Batchelor and said that the car was ready. When he picked up the car Batchelor noticed that several items on the list had not been touched. Batchelor testified that there were many occasions when he took the car to Hibschman Pontiac for repairs and the service manager told him that the defects had been fixed when in fact they were not fixed. Batchelor testified that the service manager knew the defects were not corrected, but represented to him that the defects were corrected. Batchelor stated that he relied on the service manager's statements and took the car on several trips, only to have it break down. Some of the deficiencies resulted in abnormal wear of the car and breakdowns after the warranty period had expired.

Batchelor testified that he had taken the car in for repairs five times before he had owned it a month but that the defects had not been corrected. Batchelor had taken the car in 12 times during the warranty period for overnight repair and at least 20 times in all during the period. During the warranty period Batchelor lost use of the car approximately 45 days while it was at Hibschman Pontiac.

Batchelor had appealed to Jim Hibschman on several occasions to take care of his car. Hibschman replied that he realized the repairs were not effected properly but that Hibschman Pontiac would "do everything to get you happy." On another occasion Jim Hibschman responded they had done all they could with the car but that Batchelor was just a particular, habitual complainer whom they could not satisfy and "I would rather you would just leave and not come back. We are going to have to write you off as a bad customer."

On several occasions Batchelor attempted to see Dan Shaules, an area service representative from Pontiac Division, about the car but was kept waiting so long that he had to leave without seeing him. Batchelor did see Shaules in Buchanan, Michigan, when he took the car to an authorized Pontiac dealer there after the warranty had expired. Shaules inspected the car and told Batchelor to return the car to Hibschman Pontiac for repairs.

Hugh Haverstock, the owner of the garage where several of the deficiencies where corrected after the expiration of the warranty, testified that Batchelor was a good customer and paid his bills. He stated that an average transmission man could have corrected the problem with the transmission and that a problem with the timing chain was discovered and corrected when a tune up lasted only 800 miles. Haverstock stated that the difference in value of the car without defects and with the defects it had was approximately $1,500.00. Haverstock testified that when a person complains about problems with cars that have not been fixed by dealerships, word gets out and others do not want to work on the cars.

Arnold Miexel, the service manager for Hibschman Pontiac during the time in question, testified that his representation to Batchelor regarding Hibschman Pontiac service department was based on the fact that the mechanics were factory trained and that he had received no complaints regarding their work. He further stated that he could not check the work of the mechanics. Miexel testified that if their work was unsatisfactory it was done over but no work order was written for it. He stated that it was possible Batchelor made complaints about the car, but the defects were not corrected. The warranty expired and, as a consequence, later work was not considered under warranty.

Dan Shaules testified that Miexel was an average service manager. He testified that not all of the deficiencies in the car were corrected properly. He further stated that if any defects in the car were brought to their attention within the warranty period, items would be corrected if necessary after the warranty had expired.

Appellant first argues that there was insufficient evidence to permit the issue of punitive damages to go to the jury and that the court should have rendered a directed verdict on the issue of punitive damages on behalf of Hibschman Pontiac. This Court has recently dealt with the question of punitive damages in a contract action. In Vernon Fire & Casualty Ins. Co. v. Sharp (1976), Ind., 349 N.E.2d 173, the majority restated the general provision that punitive damages are not recoverable in contract actions and went on to state exceptions to this rule. Where the conduct of a party, in breaching his contract, independently establishes the elements of a common law tort, punitive damages may be awarded for the tort.

Punitive damages may be awarded in addition to compensatory damages "whenever the elements of fraud, malice, gross negligence or oppression mingle in the controversy." (emphasis supplied.) Vernon Fire & Casualty Ins. Co. v. Sharp, supra, Ind., 349 N.E.2d 173, 180, quoting Taber v. Hutson (1854), 5 Ind. 322.

Further, where a separate tort accompanies the breach or the elements of tort mingle with the breach, it must appear that the public interest will be served by the deterrent effect of the punitive damages. Vernon Fire & Casualty Ins. Co. v. Sharp, supra.

Appellant urges that the evidence presented does not indicate tortious conduct of any sort on its part. While a reasonable inference could be made from the evidence that appellant merely attempted to fulfill its contract and to do no more than that contract required, it is also reasonable to infer that Hibschman Pontiac acted tortiously and in willful disregard of the right of Batchelor. This Court has often stated the maxim that it will not reweigh the evidence nor determine the credibility of witnesses, but will sustain a verdict if there is any evidence of probative value to support it. Moore v. Waitt (1973), Ind.App., 298 N.E.2d 456; Smart and Perry Ford Sales, Inc. v. Weaver (1971), 149 Ind.App. 693, 274 N.E.2d 718.

A corporation can act only through its agents, and their acts, when done within the scope of their authority, are attributable to the corporation. Soft Water Utilities, Inc. v. Lefevre (1974), Ind.App., 308 N.E.2d 395.

Here, the jury could reasonably have found elements of fraud, malice, gross negligence or oppression mingled into the breach of warranty. The evidence showed that requested repairs were not satisfactorily completed although covered by the warranty and capable of correction. Some of these defects were clearly breaches of warranty. Paint was bubbled, the radio never worked properly, the hood and bumper were twisted and misaligned, the universal joints failed, the transmission linkage was improperly adjusted, the timing chain was defective causing improper tune-ups and the carburetor was defective, among other things. Batchelor took the car to the defendant with a list of defects on numerous occasions and picked up the car when told it was "all ready to go." It was reasonable to infer that the defendant's service manager represented repairs to have been made when he knew that the work had not been done and that in reliance on his representations, Batchelor drove the car on trips and had breakdowns. Before purchasing the car Batchelor was given special representations on the excellence of Hibschman's service department, and the jury could find that Batchelor relied on these in buying the car from the defendant. After having brought the car in on numerous occasions, Batchelor was told by Jim Hibschman, "I would rather you would just leave and not come back. We are going to have to write you off as a bad customer." And he was told by one of Hibschman's mechanics that, "If you don't get on them and get this fixed, they will screw you around and you will never get it done." From these statements the jury could infer that the defendant was attempting to avoid making certain repairs by concealing them during the period of the warranty. Batchelor gave the defendant numerous opportunities to repair the car and the defendant did not do so; instead he tried to convince Batchelor that the problems were not with the car, but rather with Batchelor. We are of the opinion that in this case the jury could have found there was cogent proof to establish malice, fraud, gross negligence and oppressive conduct.

Although fraudulent conduct was not alleged in the complaint, evidence on the subject was admitted. Any inconsistency between the pleadings and proof will be resolved in favor of the proof at trial. Ayr-Way Stores, Inc. v. Chitwood (1973), 261 Ind. 86, 300 N.E.2d 335; Vernon Fire & Casualty Ins. Co. v. Sharp, supra. Thus there was probative evidence supporting the claim for punitive damages. The trial court did not err in denying a directed verdict as to that issue. See Jordanich v. Gerstbauer (1972), 153 Ind.App. 416, 287 N.E.2d 784.

Appellant next presents a collective argument for three issues: whether there was sufficient evidence to support an award for punitive damages in the amount of $15,000; whether the award of $15,000 punitive damages bears a reasonable relationship to the actual damages; and whether punitive damages of $15,000 is excessive in this case.

Appellant here urges that there was no evidence presented concerning its worth or ability to pay. In Physicians Mutual Ins. Co. v. Savage (1973), 156 Ind.App. 283, 296 N.E.2d 165, the Court of Appeals held that the assessment of punitive damages in the amount of $50,000 'was not excessive when considered in relation to the evidence available to the trial court.' The opinion noted that included in the evidence was a statement of net worth of the defendant. In Manning v. Lynn Immke Buick, Inc. (1971), 28 Ohio App.2d 203, 276 N.E.2d 253, the court held that where punitive damages are to be assessed, the wealth of the defendant may be shown so that the jury will assess damages that will punish him. Such a rule is based on the theory that it will take a greater amount of penalty to dissuade a rich person than a poor person from oppressive conduct. However there appears to be no requirement that evidence of worth be submitted in cases of punitive damages.

Indiana has followed a rule that punitive damages in a proper case may be assessed by the jury within their sound discretion guided by proper instructions given by the court. Murphy Auto Sales v. Coomer (1953), 123 Ind.App. 709, 112 N.E.2d 589. There is no rule that the amount of punitive damages must be within a certain ratio to compensatory damages, although in the case of Bangert v. Hubbard (1955), 127 Ind.App. 579, 126 N.E.2d 778, a malicious prosecution suit, the court held that punitive damages of $10,500, being 105 times the compensatory damages, was so excessive as to indicate that the verdict was given under the influence of passion and prejudice. In Lou Leventhal Auto Co. v. Munns (1975), Ind.App., 328 N.E.2d 734, the Court of Appeals held that punitive damages in the amount of $1,500 was not excessive, although it was 50 times greater than the compensatory damages proven. That case involved an action to replevin an automobile wrongfully repossessed by a dealer. As noted by Judge Lowdermilk, the high ratio of punitive damages to compensatory damages "alone is not conclusive of an improper award. The amount here awarded is not so large as to appear the result of passion or prejudice, and is therefore not excessive." 328 N.E.2d at 742.

In the case at bar, although it was within the province of the jury to assess punitive damages, the amount in this case is so high as to violate the "first blush" rule as set out in City of Indianapolis v. Stockes (1914), 182 Ind. 31, 105 N.E. 477:

> Damages are not (to be) considered excessive unless at first blush they appear to be outrageous and excessive or it is apparent that some improper element was taken into account by the jury in determining the amount.

For the above reasons transfer is granted and the cause is remanded to the trial court with instruction to order a remittitur of $7,500 of the punitive damages. In the event the remittitur is not made, the trial court shall order a new trial. The trial court is in all other matters affirmed.

NOTES AND QUESTIONS:

1. *See* Restatement (Second) of Contracts § 355 (1981). Is this section consistent with the last case?

SECTION 7. DAMAGES BY AGREEMENT

JAQUITH V. HUDSON
Supreme Court of Michigan
5 Mich. 123 (1858).

Error to Wayne Circuit Court.

The action was by Jaquith against Hudson, upon a promissory note for one thousand dollars, given by the latter to the former, April 15th, 1855, and payable twelve months after date. Defendant pleaded the general issue, and gave notice that, on the trial he would prove that, previous to said 15th day of April, 1855, plaintiff and defendant had been and were partners in trade, at Trenton, in said county of Wayne, under the name of Hudson & Jaquith;

that, on that day the copartnership was dissolved, and the parties then entered into an agreement, of which the following is a copy:

"This article of agreement, made and entered into between Austin E. Jaquith, of Trenton, Wayne county, and state of Michigan, of the first part, and Jonathan Hudson, of Trenton, county of Wayne, and state of Michigan, of the second part, Witnesseth, That the said Austin E. Jaquith agrees to sell, and by these presents does sell and convey unto the said Jonathan Hudson, his heirs and assigns, all his right, title, and interest in the stock of goods now owned by the firm of Hudson and Jaquith, together with all the notes, books, book accounts, moneys, deposits, debts, dues, and demands, as well as all assets that in anywise belong to the said firm of Hudson & Jaquith; and that the copartnership that has existed between the said firm of Hudson & Jaquith is hereby dissolved; and that the said Austin E. Jaquith, by these presents, agrees that he will not engage in the mercantile business, in Trenton, for himself, or in connection with any other one, for the space of three years from this date, upon the forfeiture of the sum of one thousand dollars, to be collected by the said Hudson as his damages . . . .

Trenton, April, 1855. AUSTIN E. JAQUITH. [L. S.]
JONATHAN HUDSON [L. S.]

Witnesses: ARTHUR EDWARDS. ARTHUR EDWARDS JR.

. . . No evidence was given to show any damage sustained by the defendant, by reason of plaintiff's again engaging in business in Trenton. . . .

The court was then asked by plaintiff's counsel to charge the jury, as follows: . . .

That, even if the agreement set up was, in the opinion of the jury, properly delivered, as between the parties, the defendant can not recoup any damages against the plaintiff, except upon evidence showing that some damage was actually sustained by him; that the clause in the agreement as to damages, can not, of itself, and in the absence of evidence, operate to the reduction of the claim of the plaintiff, as the sum fixed in the agreement is in the the nature of a penalty, and not liquidated damages; and no damages can be recovered under it except such as are proven."

The court refused so to charge; and plaintiff excepted. . . .

The court further charged the jury, that it was not necessary for the defendant to prove any actual damage under the plaintiff's breach of the said agreement, as the damages therein fixed were liquidated damages, and not a penalty.

The issue was then submitted to the jury on the evidence, who found a verdict for the plaintiff in the sum of eighteen dollars and eight cents, allowing the defendant the sum of one thousand dollars mentioned in the agreement. . . .

CHRISTIANCY J.:

[The court briefly discussed and dismissed plaintiff's claim that the alleged agreement never became operative]. . . .

The second exception raises the single question, whether the sum of $1,000, mentioned in the covenant of Jaquith not to go into business in Trenton, is to be construed as a penalty, or as stipulated damages--the plaintiff in error insisting it should be construed as the former, the defendant as the latter.

We shall not attempt here to analyze all the decided cases upon the subject, which were read and cited upon the argument, and which, with others, have been examined. It is not to be denied that there is some conflict, and more confusion, in the cases; judges have been long and constantly complaining of the confusion and want of harmony in the decisions upon this subject. But, while no one can fail to discover a very great amount of apparent conflict, still it will be found, on examination, that most of the cases, however conflicting in appearance, have yet been decided according to the justice and equity of the particular case. And while there are some isolated cases (and they are but few), which seem to rest upon no very intelligible principle, it will be found, we think, that the following general principles may be confidently said to result from, and to reconcile, the great majority of the cases, both in England and in this country:

First. The law, following the dictates of equity and natural justice, in cases of this kind, adopts the principle of just compensation for the loss or injury actually sustained; considering it no greater violation of this principle to confine the injured party to the recovery of less, than to enable him, by the aid of the court to extort more. It is the application, in a court of law, of that principle long recognized in courts of equity, which, disregarding the penalty of the bond, gives only the damages actually sustained. This principle may be stated, in other words, to be, that courts of justice will not recognize or enforce a contract, or any stipulation of a contract, clearly unjust and unconscionable; a principle of common sense and common honesty so obviously in accordance with the dictates of justice and sound policy, as to make it rather matter of surprise that courts of law had not always, and in all cases, adopted it to the same extent as courts of equity. And, happily for the purposes of justice, the tendency of courts of law seems now to be towards the full recognition of the principle, in all cases.

This principle of natural justice, the courts of law, following courts of equity, have, in this class of cases, adopted as the law of the contract; and they will not permit the parties by express stipulation, or any form of language, however clear the intent, to set it aside; on the familiar ground, "conventus privatorum non potest publico juri derogare."

But the court will apply this principle, and disregard the express stipulation of parties, only in those cases where it is obvious from the contract before them, and the whole subject matter, that the principle of compensation has been disregarded, and that to carry out the express stipulation of the parties, would violate this principle, which alone the court recognizes as the law of the contract.

The violation, or disregard of this principle of compensation, may appear to the court in various ways--from the contract, the sum mentioned, and the subject matter. Thus, where a large sum (say one thousand dollars) is made payable solely in consequence of the non-payment of a much smaller sum (say one hundred dollars), at a certain day; or where the contract is for the performance of several stipulations of very different degrees of importance, and one large sum is made payable on the breach of any one of them, even the most trivial, the damages for which can, in no reasonable probability, amount to that sum; in the first case, the court must see that the real damage is readily computed, and that the principle of compensation has been overlooked, or purposely disregarded; in the second case, though there may be more difficulty in ascertaining the precise amount of damage, yet, as the contract exacts the same large sum for the breach of a trivial or comparatively unimportant stipulation, as for that of the most important, or of all of them together, it is equally clear that the parties have wholly departed from the idea of just compensation, and attempted to fix a rule of damages which the law will not recognize or enforce.

We do not mean to say that the principle above stated as deducible from the cases, is to be found generally announced in express terms, in the language of the courts; but it will be found, we think, to be necessarily implied in, and to form the only rational foundation for, all that large class of cases which have held the sum to be in the nature of a penalty, notwithstanding the strongest and most explicit declarations of the parties that it was intended as stipulated and ascertained damages.

It is true, the courts in nearly all these cases profess to be construing the contract with reference to the intention of the parties, as if for the purpose of ascertaining and giving effect to that intention; yet it is obvious, from these cases, that wherever it has appeared to the court, from the face of the contract and the subject matter, that the sum was clearly too large for just compensation, here, while they will allow any form of words, even those expressing the direct contrary, to indicate the intent to make it a penalty, yet no form of words, no force of language, is competent to the expression of the opposite intent. Here, then, is an intention incapable of expression in words; and as all written contracts must be expressed in words, it would seem to be a mere waste of time and effort to look for such an intention in such a contract. And as the question is between two opposite intents only, and the negation of the one necessarily implies the existence of the other, there would seem to be no room left for construction with reference to the intent. It must, then, be manifest that the intention of the parties in such cases is not the governing consideration.

But some of the cases attempt to justify this mode of construing the contract with reference to the intent, by declaring, in substance, that though the language is the strongest which could be used to evince the intention in favor of stipulated damages, still, if it appear clearly, by reference to the subject matter, that the parties have made the stipulation without reference to the principle of just compensation, and so excessive as to be out of all proportion to the actual damage, the court must hold that they could not have intended it as stipulated damages, though they have so expressly declared . . . .

Now this, it is true, may lead to the same result in the particular case, as to have placed the decision upon the true ground, viz., that though the parties actually intended the sum to be paid, as the damages agreed upon between them, yet it being clearly unconscionable, the court would disregard the intention, and refuse to enforce the stipulation. But, as a rule of construction, or interpretation of contracts, it is radically vicious, and tends to a confusion of ideas in the construction of contracts generally. It is this, more than anything else, which has produced so much apparent conflict in the decisions upon this whole subject of penalty and stipulated damages. It sets at defiance all rules of interpretation, by denying the intention of the parties to be what they, in the most unambiguous terms, have declared it to be, and finds an intention directly opposite to that which is clearly expressed—"divinatio, non interpretatio est, quœ omnino recedit a litera."

Again, the attempt to place this question upon the intention of the parties, and to make this the governing consideration, necessarily implies that, if the intention to make the sum stipulated damages should clearly appear, the court would enforce the contract according to that intention. To test this, let it be asked, whether, in such a case, if it were admitted that the parties actually intended the sum to be considered as stipulated damages, and not as a penalty, would a court of law enforce it for the amount stipulated? Clearly, they could not, without going back to the technical and long exploded doctrine which gave the whole penalty of the bond, without reference to the damages actually sustained. They would thus be simply changing the names of things, and enforcing, under the name of stipulated damages, what in it own nature is but a penalty.

The real question in this class of cases will be found to be, not what the parties intended, but whether the sum is, in fact, in the nature of a penalty; and this is to be determined by the magnitude of the sum, in connection with the subject matter, and not at all by the words or the understanding of the parties. The intention of the parties can not alter it. While courts of law gave the penalty of the bond, the parties intended the payment of the penalty as much as they now intend the payment of stipulated damages; it must, therefore, we think, be very obvious that the actual intention of the parties, in this class of cases, and relating to this point, is wholly immaterial; and though the courts have very generally professed to base their decisions upon the intention of the parties, that intention is not, and can not, be made the real basis of these decisions. In endeavoring to reconcile their decisions with the actual intention of the parties, the courts have sometimes been compelled to use language wholly at war with any idea of interpretation, and to say "that the parties must be considered as not meaning exactly what they say:" May it not be said, with at least equal propriety, that the courts have sometimes said what they did not exactly mean?

The foregoing remarks are all to be confined to that class of cases where it was clear, from the sum mentioned and the subject matter, that the principle of compensation had been disregarded.

But, secondly, there are great numbers of cases, where, from the nature of the contract and the subject matter of the stipulation, for the breach of which the sum is provided, it is apparent to the court that the actual damages for a breach are uncertain in their nature, difficult to be ascertained, or impossible to be estimated with certainty, by reference to any pecuniary standard, and where the parties themselves are more intimately acquainted with all the peculiar circumstances, and therefore better able to compute the actual or probable damages, than courts or juries, from any evidence which can be brought before them. In all such cases, the law permits the parties to ascertain for themselves, and to provide in the contract itself, the amount of the damages which shall be paid for the breach. In permitting this, the law does not lose sight of the principle of compensation, which is the law of the contract, but merely adopts the computation or estimate of the damages made by the parties, as being the best and most certain mode of ascertaining the actual damage, or what sum will amount to a just compensation. The reason, therefore, for allowing the parties to ascertain for themselves the damages in this class of cases, is the same which denies the right in the former class of cases; viz., the courts adopt the best and most practicable mode of ascertaining the sum which will produce just compensation.

In this class of cases, where the law permits the parties to ascertain and fix the amount of damages in the contract, the first inquiry obviously is, whether they have done so in fact? And here, the intention of the parties is the governing consideration; and in ascertaining this intention, no merely technical effect will be given to the particular words relating to the sum, but the entire contract, the subject matter, and often the situation of the parties with respect to each other and to the subject matter, will be considered. Thus, though the word "penalty" be used . . . or "forfeit" . . . or "forfeit and pay" . . . it will still be held to be stipulated damages, if, from the whole contract, the subject matter, and situation of the parties, it can be gathered that such was their intention. And in proportion as the difficulty of ascertaining the actual damage by proof is greater or less, where this difficulty grows out of the nature of such damages, in the like proportion is the presumption more or less strong that the parties intended to fix the amount.

It remains only to apply these principles to the case before us. It is contended by the plaintiff in error, that the payment of the one thousand dollars mentioned in the covenant of Jaquith is not made dependent solely upon the breach of the stipulation not to go into business in Trenton, but that it applies equally--first, to the agreement to sell to Hudson his interest in the goods; second, to sell his interest in the books, notes, accounts, etc.; and, third, to the agreement to dissolve the partnership. But we can perceive no ground for such a construction. The language in reference to the sale of the interest in the goods, books, notes, accounts, etc., and that in reference to the dissolution, is not that of a sale in futuro, nor for the dissolution of the partnership at a future period, but it is that of a present sale and a present dissolution--"does hereby sell," and "the copartnership is hereby dissolved," is the language of the instrument. It is plain, from this language, from the subject matter, and from all the acts of the parties, that these provisions were to take, and did take immediate effect. There could be no possible occasion to provide any penalty or stipulated damages for the non-performance of these stipulations, because this sale and dissolution would already have been accomplished the moment the contract took effect for any purpose; and, until it took effect, the stipulation for the one thousand dollars could not take effect, or afford any security, nor would Hudson be bound or need the security. But it remained to provide for the future. If Jaquith were to be at liberty to set up a rival store in the same village, it might seriously affect the success of Hudson's business; and we are bound to infer, from the whole scope of this contract, that Hudson would never have agreed to pay the consideration mentioned in it, nor to have entered into the contract at all, but for the stipulation of Jaquith "that he will not engage in the mercantile business in Trenton, for himself or in connection with any other one, for the space of three years from this date, upon the forfeiture of the sum of one thousand dollars, to be collected by said Hudson as his damages." This stipulation of Jaquith not to go into business, is the only one on his part which looks to the future; and it is to this, alone, that the language in reference to the one thousand dollars applies. Any other construction would do violence to the language, and be at war with the whole subject matter.

The damages to arise from the breach of this covenant, from the nature of the case, must be not only uncertain in their nature, but impossible to be exhibited in proof, with any reasonable degree of accuracy, by any evidence which could possibly be adduced. It is easy to see that while the damages might be very heavy, it would be very difficult clearly to prove any. Their nature and amount could be better estimated by the parties themselves, than by witnesses, courts, or juries. It is, then, precisely one of that class of cases in which it has always been recognized as peculiarly appropriate for the parties to fix and agree upon the damages for themselves. In such a case, the language must be very clear to the contrary, to overcome the inference of intent (so to fix them), to be drawn from the subject matter and the situation of the parties; because, it is difficult to suppose, in such a case, that the party taking the stipulation intended it only to cover the amount of damages actually to be proved, as he would be entitled to the latter without the mention of any sum in the contract, and he must also be supposed to know that his actual damages, from the nature of the case, are not susceptible of legal proof to any thing approaching their actual extent. That the parties actually intended, in this case, to fix the amount to be recovered, is clear from the language itself, without the aid of a reference to the subject matter, "upon the forfeiture of the sum of one thousand dollars, to be collected by the said Hudson as his damages." It is manifest from this language that it was intended Hudson should "collect," or, in other words, receive this amount, and that it should be for his damages for the breach of the stipulation. This language is stronger than "forfeit and pay," or "under the penalty of," as these might be supposed to have reference to the form of the penal part of a bond, or to the form of action upon it, and not to the actual "collection" of the money.

It is, therefore, very clear, from every view we have been able to take of this case, that it was competent and proper for the parties to ascertain and fix for themselves the amount of damages for the breach complained of, and equally clear that they have done so in fact. From the uncertain nature of the damages, we cannot say that the sum in this case exceeds the actual damages, or that the principle of compensation has been violated. Indeed, it would have been perhaps difficult to discover a violation of this principle had the sum in this case been more than it now is; though, doubtless, even in such cases as the present, if the sum stated were so excessive as clearly to exceed all reasonable apprehension of actual loss or injury for the breach, we should be compelled to disregard the intention of the parties, and treat the sum only as a penalty to cover the actual damages to be exhibited in proof. In this case the party must be held to the amount stipulated in his contract.

The second exception, therefore, is not well taken; the court properly refused to charge as requested, and no error appearing in the record, the judgment of the Circuit Court for the county of Wayne must be affirmed.

The other justices concurred.

LAKE RIVER CORP. V. CARBORUNDUM CO.
United States Court of Appeals, Seventh Circuit.
769 F.2d 1284 (7th Cir. 1985)

POSNER, Circuit Judge.

This diversity suit between Lake River Corporation and Carborundum Company requires us to consider questions of Illinois commercial law, and in particular to explore the fuzzy line between penalty clauses and liquidated-damages clauses.

Carborundum manufactures "Ferro Carbo," an abrasive powder used in making steel. To serve its midwestern customers better, Carborundum made a contract with Lake River by which the latter agreed to provide distribution services in its warehouse in Illinois.

Lake River would receive Ferro Carbo in bulk from Carborundum, "bag" it, and ship the bagged product to Carborundum's customers. The Ferro Carbo would remain Carborundum's property until delivered to the customers.

Carborundum insisted that Lake River install a new bagging system to handle the contract. In order to be sure of being able to recover the cost of the new system ($89,000) and make a profit of 20 percent of the contract price, Lake River insisted on the following minimum-quantity guarantee:

> In consideration of the special equipment [i.e., the new bagging system] to be acquired and furnished by LAKE-RIVER for handling the product, CARBORUNDUM shall, during the initial three-year term of this Agreement, ship to LAKE-RIVER for bagging a minimum quantity of [22,500 tons]. If, at the end of the three-year term, this minimum quantity shall not have been shipped, LAKE-RIVER shall invoice CARBORUNDUM at the then prevailing rates for the difference between the quantity bagged and the minimum guaranteed.

If Carborundum had shipped the full minimum quantity that it guaranteed, it would have owed Lake River roughly $533,000 under the contract.

After the contract was signed in 1979, the demand for domestic steel, and with it the demand for Ferro Carbo, plummeted, and Carborundum failed to ship the guaranteed amount. When the contract expired late in 1982, Carborundum had shipped only 12,000 of the 22,500 tons it had guaranteed. Lake River had bagged the 12,000 tons and had billed Carborundum for this bagging, and Carborundum had paid, but by virtue of the formula in the minimum-guarantee clause Carborundum still owed Lake River $241,000-the contract price of $533,000 if the full amount of Ferro Carbo had been shipped, minus what Carborundum had paid for the bagging of the quantity it had shipped.

When Lake River demanded payment of this amount, Carborundum refused, on the ground that the formula imposed a penalty. At the time, Lake River had in its warehouse 500 tons of bagged Ferro Carbo, having a market value of $269,000, which it refused to release unless Carborundum paid the $241,000 due under the formula. Lake River did offer to sell the bagged product and place the proceeds in escrow until its dispute with Carborundum over the enforceability of the formula was resolved, but Carborundum rejected the offer and trucked in bagged Ferro Carbo from the East to serve its customers in Illinois, at an additional cost of $31,000.

Lake River brought this suit for $241,000, which it claims as liquidated damages. Carborundum counterclaimed for the value of the bagged Ferro Carbo when Lake River impounded it and the additional cost of serving the customers affected by the impounding. The theory of the counterclaim is that the impounding was a conversion, and not as Lake River contends the assertion of a lien. The district judge, after a bench trial, gave judgment for both parties. Carborundum ended up roughly $42,000 to the good: $269,000 + $31,000-$241,000-$17,000, the last figure representing prejudgment interest on Lake River's damages. (We have rounded off all dollar figures to the nearest thousand.) Both parties have appealed. . . .

The hardest issue in the case is whether the formula in the minimum-guarantee clause imposes a penalty for breach of contract or is merely an effort to liquidate damages. Deep as the hostility to penalty clauses runs in the common law, see Loyd, Penalties and Forfeitures, 29 Harv.L.Rev. 117 (1915), we still might be inclined to question, if we thought ourselves free to do so, whether a modern court should refuse to enforce a penalty clause where the signator is a substantial corporation, well able to avoid improvident commitments. Penalty clauses provide an earnest of performance. The clause here enhanced Carborundum's credibility in promising to ship the minimum amount guaranteed by showing that it was willing to pay the full contract price even if it failed to ship anything. On the other side it can be pointed out that by raising the cost of a breach of contract to the contract breaker, a penalty clause increases the risk to his other creditors; increases (what is the same thing and more, because bankruptcy imposes "deadweight" social costs) the risk of bankruptcy; and could amplify the business cycle by increasing the number of bankruptcies in bad times, which is when contracts are most likely to be broken. But since little effort is made to prevent businessmen from assuming risks, these reasons are no better than makeweights.

A better argument is that a penalty clause may discourage efficient as well as inefficient breaches of contract. Suppose a breach would cost the promisee $12,000 in actual damages but would yield the promisor $20,000 in additional profits. Then there would be a net social gain from breach. After being fully compensated for his loss the promisee would be no worse off than if the contract had been performed, while the promisor would be better off by $8,000. But now suppose the contract contains a penalty clause under which the promisor if he breaks his promise must pay the promisee $25,000. The promisor will be discouraged from breaking the contract, since $25,000, the penalty, is greater than $20,000, the profits of the breach; and a transaction that would have increased value will be forgone.

On this view, since compensatory damages should be sufficient to deter inefficient breaches (that is, breaches that cost the victim more than the gain to the contract breaker), penal damages could have no effect other than to deter some efficient breaches. But this overlooks the earlier point that the willingness to agree to a penalty clause is a way of making the promisor and his promise credible and may therefore be essential to inducing some value-maximizing contracts to be made. It also overlooks the more important point that the parties (always assuming they are fully competent) will, in deciding whether to include a penalty clause in their contract, weigh the gains against the costs-costs that include the possibility of discouraging an efficient breach somewhere down the road-and will include the clause only if the benefits exceed those costs as well as all other costs.

On this view the refusal to enforce penalty clauses is (at best) paternalistic-and it seems odd that courts should display parental solicitude for large corporations. But however this may be, we must be on guard to avoid importing our own ideas of sound public policy into an area where our proper judicial role is more than usually deferential. The responsibility for making innovations in the common law of Illinois rests with the courts of Illinois, and not with the federal courts in Illinois. And like every other state, Illinois, untroubled by academic skepticism of the wisdom of refusing to enforce penalty clauses against sophisticated promisors, see, e.g., Goetz & Scott, Liquidated Damages, Penalties and the Just Compensation Principle, 77 Colum.L.Rev. 554 (1977), continues steadfastly to insist on the distinction between penalties and liquidated damages. To be valid under Illinois law a liquidation of damages must be a reasonable estimate at the time of contracting of the likely damages from breach, and the need for estimation at that time must be shown by reference to the likely difficulty of measuring the actual damages from a breach of contract after the breach occurs. If damages would be easy to determine then, or if the estimate greatly exceeds a reasonable upper estimate of what the damages are likely to be, it is a penalty.

The distinction between a penalty and liquidated damages is not an easy one to draw in practice but we are required to draw it and can give only limited weight to the district court's determination. Whether a provision for damages is a penalty clause or a liquidated-damages clause is a question of law rather than fact, and unlike some courts of appeals we do not treat a determination by a federal district judge of an issue of state law as if it were a finding of fact, and reverse only if persuaded that clear error has occurred, though we give his determination respectful consideration.

Mindful that Illinois courts resolve doubtful cases in favor of classification as a penalty, we conclude that the damage formula in this case is a penalty and not a liquidation of damages, because it is designed always to assure Lake River more than its actual damages. The formula-full contract price minus the amount already invoiced to Carborundum-is invariant to the gravity of the breach. When a contract specifies a single sum in damages for any and all breaches even though it is apparent that all are not of the same gravity, the specification is not a reasonable effort to estimate damages; and when in addition the fixed sum greatly exceeds the actual damages likely to be inflicted by a minor breach, its character as a penalty becomes unmistakable. This case is within the gravitational field of these principles even though the minimum-guarantee clause does not fix a single sum as damages.

Suppose to begin with that the breach occurs the day after Lake River buys its new bagging system for $89,000 and before Carborundum ships any Ferro Carbo. Carborundum would owe Lake River $533,000. Since Lake River would have incurred at that point a total cost of only $89,000, its net gain from the breach would be $444,000. This is more than four times the profit of $107,000 (20 percent of the contract price of $533,000) that Lake River expected to make from the contract if it had been performed: a huge windfall.

Next suppose (as actually happened here) that breach occurs when 55 percent of the Ferro Carbo has been shipped. Lake River would already have received $293,000 from Carborundum. To see what its costs then would have been (as estimated at the time of contracting), first subtract Lake River's anticipated profit on the contract of $107,000 from the total contract price of $533,000. The difference-Lake River's total cost of performance-is $426,000. Of this, $89,000 is the cost of the new bagging system, a fixed cost. The rest ($426,000-$89,000 = $337,000) presumably consists of variable costs that are roughly proportional to the amount of Ferro Carbo bagged; there is no indication of any other fixed costs. Assume, therefore, that if Lake River bagged 55 percent of the contractually agreed quantity, it incurred in doing so 55 percent of its variable costs, or $185,000. When this is added to the cost of the new bagging system, assumed for the moment to be worthless except in connection with the contract, the total cost of performance to Lake River is $274,000. Hence a breach that occurred after 55 percent of contractual performance was complete would be expected to yield Lake River a modest profit of $19,000 ($293,000-$274,000). But now add the "liquidated damages" of $241,000 that Lake River claims, and the result is a total gain from the breach of $260,000, which is almost two and a half times the profit that

Lake River expected to gain if there was no breach. And this ignores any use value or salvage value of the new bagging system, which is the property of Lake River-though admittedly it also ignores the time value of money; Lake River paid $89,000 for that system before receiving any revenue from the contract.

To complete the picture, assume that the breach had not occurred till performance was 90 percent complete. Then the "liquidated damages" clause would not be so one-sided, but it would be one-sided. Carborundum would have paid $480,000 for bagging. Against this, Lake River would have incurred its fixed cost of $89,000 plus 90 percent of its variable costs of $337,000, or $303,000. Its total costs would thus be $392,000, and its net profit $88,000. But on top of this it would be entitled to "liquidated damages" of $53,000, for a total profit of $141,000-more than 30 percent more than its expected profit of $107,000 if there was no breach.

The reason for these results is that most of the costs to Lake River of performing the contract are saved if the contract is broken, and this saving is not reflected in the damage formula. As a result, at whatever point in the life of the contract a breach occurs, the damage formula gives Lake River more than its lost profits from the breach-dramatically more if the breach occurs at the beginning of the contract; tapering off at the end, it is true. Still, over the interval between the beginning of Lake River's performance and nearly the end, the clause could be expected to generate profits ranging from 400 percent of the expected contract profits to 130 percent of those profits. And this is on the assumption that the bagging system has no value apart from the contract. If it were worth only $20,000 to Lake River, the range would be 434 percent to 150 percent.

Lake River argues that it would never get as much as the formula suggests, because it would be required to mitigate its damages. This is a dubious argument on several grounds. First, mitigation of damages is a doctrine of the law of court-assessed damages, while the point of a liquidated-damages clause is to substitute party assessment; and that point is blunted, and the certainty that liquidated-damages clauses are designed to give the process of assessing damages impaired, if a defendant can force the plaintiff to take less than the damages specified in the clause, on the ground that the plaintiff could have avoided some of them. It would seem therefore that the clause in this case should be read to eliminate any duty of mitigation, that what Lake River is doing is attempting to rewrite the clause to make it more reasonable, and that since actually the clause is designed to give Lake River the full damages it would incur from breach (and more) even if it made no effort to find a substitute use for the equipment that it bought to perform the contract, this is just one more piece of evidence that it is a penalty clause rather than a liquidated-damages clause.

But in any event mitigation would not mitigate the penal character of this clause. If Carborundum did not ship the guaranteed minimum quantity, the reason was likely to be-the reason was-that the steel industry had fallen on hard times and the demand for Ferro Carbo was therefore down. In these circumstances Lake River would have little prospect of finding a substitute contract that would yield it significant profits to set off against the full contract price, which is the method by which it proposes to take account of mitigation. At argument Lake River suggested that it might at least have been able to sell the new bagging equipment to someone for something, and the figure $40,000 was proposed. If the breach occurred on the first day when performance under the contract was due and Lake River promptly sold the bagging equipment for $40,000, its liquidated damages would fall to $493,000. But by the same token its costs would fall to $49,000. Its profit would still be $444,000, which as we said was more than 400 percent of its expected profit on the contract. The penal component would be unaffected.

With the penalty clause in this case compare the liquidated-damages clause in Arduini v. Board of Education, supra, which is representative of such clauses upheld in Illinois. The plaintiff was a public school teacher whose contract provided that if he resigned before the end of the school year he would be docked 4 percent of his salary. This was a modest fraction of the contract price. And the cost to the school of an untimely resignation would be difficult to measure. Since that cost would be greater the more senior and experienced the teacher was, the fact that the liquidated damages would be greater the higher the teacher's salary did not make the clause arbitrary. Even the fact that the liquidated damages were the same whether the teacher resigned at the beginning, the middle, or the end of the school year was not arbitrary, for it was unclear how the amount of actual damages would vary with the time of resignation. Although one might think that the earlier the teacher resigned the greater the damage to the school would be, the school might find it easier to hire a replacement for the whole year or a great part of it than to bring in a replacement at the last minute to grade the exams left behind by the resigning teacher. Here, in contrast, it is apparent from the face of the contract that the damages provided for by the "liquidated damages" clause are grossly disproportionate to any probable loss and penalize some breaches much more heavily than others regardless of relative cost.

We do not mean by this discussion to cast a cloud of doubt over the "take or pay" clauses that are a common feature of contracts between natural gas pipeline companies and their customers. Such clauses require the customer, in consideration of the pipeline's extending its line to his premises, to take a certain amount of gas at a specified price-and if he fails to take it to pay the full price anyway. The resemblance to the minimum-guarantee clause in the present case is obvious, but perhaps quite superficial. Neither party has mentioned take-or-pay clauses, and we can find no case where such a clause was even challenged as a penalty clause-though in one case it was argued that such a clause made the damages unreasonably low. See National Fuel Gas Distribution Corp. v. Pennsylvania Public Utility Comm'n, 76 Pa.Commw. 102, 126-27 n. 8, 464 A.2d 546, 558 n. 8 (1983). If, as appears not to be the case here but would often be the case in supplying natural gas, a supplier's fixed costs were a very large fraction of his total costs, a take-or-pay clause might well be a reasonable liquidation of damages. In the limit, if all the supplier's costs were incurred before he began supplying the customer, the contract revenues would be an excellent measure of the damages from breach. But in this case, the supplier (Lake River, viewed as a supplier of bagging services to Carborundum) incurred only a fraction of its costs before performance began, and the interruption of performance generated a considerable cost saving that is not reflected in the damage formula.

The fact that the damage formula is invalid does not deprive Lake River of a remedy. The parties did not contract explicitly with reference to the measure of damages if the agreed-on damage formula was invalidated, but all this means is that the victim of the breach is entitled to his common law damages. See, e.g., Restatement, Second, Contracts § 356, comment a (1981). In this case that would be the unpaid contract price of $241,000 minus the costs that Lake River saved by not having to complete the contract (the variable costs on the other 45 percent of the Ferro Carbo that it never had to bag). The case must be remanded to the district judge to fix these damages. . . .

The judgment of the district court is affirmed in part and reversed in part, and the case is returned to that court to redetermine both parties' damages in accordance with the principles in this opinion . . . .

Affirmed in Part, Reversed in Part, and Remanded.

NOTES AND QUESTIONS:

1. Read U.C.C. § 2-718(1) (Liquidation or Limitations of Damage; Deposits) (2002) and Restatement (Second) of Contracts § 356 (Liquidated Damages and Penalties) (1981). Is there a difference between the common law and Article 2's approach to liquidated damages?

2. Read U.C.C. § 2-719 (Contractual Modification or Limitation of Remedy) (2002), which allows the parties to limit the types of remedies available. *NEC Technologies, Inc. v. Nelson*, 478 S.E.2d 769 (1996) included in Chapter 4 discusses the operation of U.C.C. § 2-719 in consumer transactions.

3. *See also* Restatement (Second) of Contracts § 195 (Term Exempting from Liability for Harm Caused Intentionally, Recklessly or Negligently) (1981).

CHAPTER SIX

THIRD PARTIES

*For kindness begets kindness evermore, but he from whose mind fades the memory of benefits, noble is he no more.**

Sophocles

SECTION 1. THIRD PARTY BENEFICIARIES

A. CLASSES OF THIRD PARTY BENEFICIARIES

LAWRENCE V. FOX
Court of Appeals of New York
20 N.Y. 268 (1859).

. . . .

APPEAL from the Superior Court of the city of Buffalo. On the trial before Mr. Justice MASTEN, it appeared by the evidence of a bystander, that one Holly, in November, 1857, at the request of the defendant, loaned and advanced to him $300, stating at the time that he owed that sum to the plaintiff for money borrowed of him, and had agreed to pay it to him the then next day; that the defendant in consideration thereof, at the time of receiving the money, promised to pay it to the plaintiff the then next day. Upon this state of facts the defendant moved for a nonsuit, upon three several grounds, viz.: That there was no proof tending to show that Holly was indebted to the plaintiff; that the agreement by the defendant with Holly to pay the plaintiff was void for want of consideration, and that there was no privity between the plaintiff and defendant. The court overruled the motion, and the counsel for the defendant excepted. The cause was then submitted to the jury, and they found a verdict for the plaintiff for the amount of the loan and interest, $344.66, upon which judgment was entered; from which the defendant appealed to the Superior Court, at general term, where the judgment was affirmed, and the defendant appealed to this court. The cause was submitted on printed arguments.

H. GRAY, J.

[The court first discussed the competency of the evidence of Holly's indebtedness to Lawrence.]

. . . . But it is claimed that notwithstanding this promise was established by competent evidence, it was void for the want of consideration. It is now more than a quarter of a century since it was settled by the Supreme Court of this State--in an able and pains-taking opinion by the late Chief Justice SAVAGE, in which the authorities were fully

* Sophocles (496 – 406 B.C.).

examined and carefully analysed--that a promise in all material respects like the one under consideration was valid; and the judgment of that court was unanimously affirmed by the Court for the Correction of Errors. (Farley v. Cleaveland, 4 Cow., 432; same case in error, 9 id., 639.) In that case one Moon owed Farley and sold to Cleaveland a quantity of hay, in consideration of which Cleaveland promised to pay Moon's debt to Farley; and the decision in favor of Farley's right to recover was placed upon the ground that the hay received by Cleaveland from Moon was a valid consideration for Cleaveland's promise to pay Farley, and that the subsisting liability of Moon to pay Farley was no objection to the recovery. The fact that the money advanced by Holly to the defendant was a loan to him for a day, and that it thereby became the property of the defendant, seemed to impress the defendant's counsel with the idea that because the defendant's promise was not a trust fund placed by the plaintiff in the defendant's hands, out of which he was to realize money as from the sale of a chattel or the collection of a debt, the promise although made for the benefit of the plaintiff could not enure to his benefit. The hay which Cleaveland delivered to Moon was not to be paid to Farley, but the debt incurred by Cleaveland for the purchase of the hay, like the debt incurred by the defendant for money borrowed, was what was to be paid. That case has been often referred to by the courts of this State, and has never been doubted as sound authority for the principle upheld by it. (Barker v. Buklin, 2 Denio, 45; Hudson Canal Company v. The Westchester Bank, 4 id., 97.) It puts to rest the objection that the defendant's promise was void for want of consideration. The report of that case shows that the promise was not only made to Moon but to the plaintiff Farley. In this case the promise was made to Holly and not expressly to the plaintiff; and this difference between the two cases presents the question, raised by the defendant's objection, as to the want of privity between the plaintiff and defendant. As early as 1806 it was announced by the Supreme Court of this State, upon what was then regarded as the settled law of England, "That where one person makes a promise to another for the benefit of a third person, that third person may maintain an action upon it." Schermerhorn v. Vanderheyden (1 John. R., 140), has often been re-asserted by our courts and never departed from. . . . In Hall v. Marston the court say: "It seems to have been well settled that if A promises B for a valuable consideration to pay C, the latter may maintain assumpsit for the money;" and in Brewer v. Dyer, the recovery was upheld, as the court said,

> upon the principle of law long recognized and clearly established, that when one person, for a valuable consideration, engages with another, by a simple contract, to do some act for the benefit of a third, the latter, who would enjoy the benefit of the act, may maintain an action for the breach of such engagement; that it does not rest upon the ground of any actual or supposed relationship between the parties as some of the earlier cases would seem to indicate, but upon the broader and more satisfactory basis, that the law operating on the act of the parties creates the duty, establishes a privity, and implies the promise and obligation on which the action is founded.

. . . . In this case the defendant, upon ample consideration received from Holly, promised Holly to pay his debt to the plaintiff; the consideration received and the promise to Holly made it as plainly his duty to pay the plaintiff as if the money had been remitted to him for that purpose, and as well implied a promise to do so as if he had been made a trustee of property to be converted into cash with which to pay. The fact that a breach of the duty imposed in the one case may be visited, and justly, with more serious consequences than in the other, by no means disproves the payment to be a duty in both. The principle illustrated by the example so frequently quoted (which concisely states the case in hand) "that a promise made to one for the benefit of another, he for whose benefit it is made may bring an action for its breach," has been applied to trust cases, not because it was exclusively applicable to those cases, but because it was a principle of law, and as such applicable to those cases. It was also insisted that Holly could have discharged the defendant from his promise, though it was intended by both parties for the benefit of the plaintiff, and therefore the plaintiff was not entitled to maintain this suit for the recovery of a demand over which he had no control. It is enough that the plaintiff did not release the defendant from his promise, and whether he could or not is a question not now necessarily involved; but if it was, I think it would be found difficult to maintain the right of Holly to discharge a judgment recovered by the plaintiff upon confession or otherwise, for the breach of the defendant's promise; and if he could not, how could he discharge the suit before judgment, or the promise before suit, made as it was for the plaintiff's benefit and in accordance with legal presumption accepted by him (Berley v. Taylor, 5 Hill, 577-584, et seq.), until his dissent was shown. The cases cited, and especially that of Farley v. Cleaveland, establish the validity of a parol promise; it stands then upon the footing of a written one. Suppose the defendant had given his note in which, for value received of Holly, he had promised to pay the plaintiff and the plaintiff had accepted the promise, retaining Holly's liability. Very clearly Holly could not have discharged that promise, be the right to release the defendant as it may. No one can doubt that he owes the sum of money demanded of him, or that in accordance with his promise it was his duty to have paid it to the plaintiff; nor can it be doubted that whatever may be the diversity of opinion elsewhere, the adjudications in this State, from a very early period, approved by experience, have established the defendant's liability; if, therefore, it could be shown that a more strict and technically accurate application of the rules applied, would lead to a different result (which I by no means concede), the effort should not be made in the face of manifest justice.

The judgment should be affirmed.

JOHNSON, Ch. J., DENIO, SELDEN, ALLEN and STRONG, Js., concurred. . . .

COMSTOCK, J. (Dissenting.)

The plaintiff had nothing to do with the promise on which he brought this action. It was not made to him, nor did the consideration proceed from him. If he can maintain the suit, it is because an anomaly has found its way into the law on this subject. In general, there must be privity of contract. The party who sues upon a promise must be the promisee, or he must have some legal interest in the undertaking. In this case, it is plain that Holly, who loaned the money to the defendant, and to whom the promise in question was made, could at any time have claimed that it should be performed to himself personally. He had lent the money to the defendant, and at the same time directed the latter to pay the sum to the plaintiff. This direction he could countermand, and if he had done so, manifestly the defendant's promise to pay according to the direction would have ceased to exist. The plaintiff would receive a benefit by a complete execution of the arrangement, but the arrangement itself was between other parties, and was under their exclusive control. If the defendant had paid the money to Holly, his debt would have been discharged thereby. So Holly might have released the demand or assigned it to another person, or the parties might have annulled the promise now in question, and designated some other creditor of Holly as the party to whom the money should be paid. It has never been claimed, that in a case thus situated, the right of a third person to sue upon the promise rested on any sound principle of law. We are to inquire whether the rule has been so established by positive authority. . . .

GROVER, J., also dissented.

Judgment affirmed.

EX PARTE STAMEY
Supreme Court of Alabama
776 So. 2d. 85 (2000).

HOUSTON, Justice.

. . . .

In December 1996, the Stameys contracted with Hallmont Homes, Inc., which is operated by Jarod Hall and Gaylon Hall, to purchase land and a mobile home. The contract also included assurances that Hallmont would prepare a foundation for the mobile home and would install a septic system and a light pole. The Stameys claim that the septic system and the light pole were never installed. The Stameys had borrowed money from Green Tree to pay for these purchases and installations. Included in the financing agreement between Green Tree and the Stameys was this arbitration provision:

> ARBITRATION: ALL DISPUTES, CLAIMS OR CONTROVERSIES ARISING FROM OR RELATING TO THIS CONTRACT OR THE PARTIES THERETO SHALL BE RESOLVED BY BINDING ARBITRATION BY ONE ARBITRATOR SELECTED BY YOU WITH MY CONSENT. THIS AGREEMENT IS MADE PURSUANT TO A TRANSACTION IN INTERSTATE COMMERCE AND SHALL BE GOVERNED BY THE FEDERAL ARBITRATION ACT AT 9 U.S.C. SECTION 1. JUDGMENT UPON THE AWARD RENDERED MAY BE ENTERED IN ANY COURT HAVING JURISDICTION. . . . THE PARTIES VOLUNTARILY AND KNOWINGLY WAIVE ANY RIGHT THEY HAVE TO A JURY TRIAL, EITHER PURSUANT TO ARBITRATION UNDER THIS CLAUSE OR PURSUANT TO A COURT ACTION BY YOU (AS PROVIDED HEREIN). . . .

Dr. Bernard Eichold II, in his capacity as health officer of Mobile County, sued for injunctive relief against the Stameys, alleging that their property was in violation of state health laws-specifically, his complaint alleged a violation concerning the septic system on the Stameys' property. The Stameys filed an answer, along with a third-party complaint against Hallmont and Jarod Hall and Gaylon Hall (hereinafter all collectively referred to as "Hallmont"), and Green Tree, alleging conversion, fraud, and breach of contract. The Stameys contend that Hallmont and/or Green Tree caused the problem with the septic system for which the Stameys were sued. Hallmont and Green Tree both moved the trial court to compel arbitration of the claims asserted against them. Hallmont was not a signatory to the arbitration agreement. The trial court granted the motions to compel. . . .

It is undisputed that the Stameys voluntarily and knowingly entered into the arbitration agreement with Green Tree. We have reviewed the Stameys' arguments concerning the arbitration provision as they relate to their claims against Green Tree, and we find them to be without merit. See Northcom, Ltd. v. James, 694 So.2d 1329 (Ala.1997), and Ex parte Isbell, 708 So.2d 571 (Ala.1997). Green Tree presented the trial court evidence showing that the transaction on which the Stameys' claims are based involved interstate commerce. Exhibits to the Stameys' petition show that the Green Tree office the Stameys dealt with is located in Pensacola, Florida, and the Stameys acknowledged in the security agreement they signed that the contract involves a transaction in interstate commerce. Therefore, the trial court properly granted Green Tree's motion to compel arbitration.

While the Stameys' contract with Green Tree contains an arbitration agreement, neither the sale contract between the Stameys and Hallmont nor any other document to which Hallmont was a signatory contained an arbitration agreement. Hallmont's motion to compel arbitration was based on the arbitration provision in the contract between Green Tree and the Stameys.

Normally, in order to have a valid arbitration provision, there must be an agreement to arbitrate, and if no agreement exists, then a party cannot be forced to submit a dispute to arbitration. See First Options of Chicago, Inc. v. Kaplan, 514 U.S. 938, 115 S.Ct. 1920, 131 L.Ed.2d 985 (1995). The question whether one has assented to an arbitration provision is governed by ordinary principles of a state's common law and statutory law governing the formation of contracts. See Volt Info. Sciences, Inc. v. Board of Trustees of Leland Stanford Jr. Univ., 489 U.S. 468, 109 S.Ct. 1248, 103 L.Ed.2d 488 (1989). Assent to arbitrate is usually to be manifested through a party's signature on the contract containing the arbitration provision. However, both Federal courts and Alabama courts have enforced exceptions to this rule, so as to allow a nonsignatory, and even one who is not a party, as to a particular contract, to enforce an arbitration provision within that same contract. Two such exceptions apply to the present case. The first is an exception under a theory of equitable estoppel for claims that are so "intimately founded in and intertwined with" the claims made against a party that is a signatory to the contract. See Sunkist Soft Drinks, Inc. v. Sunkist Growers, Inc., 10 F.3d 753, 757 (11th Cir.1993) (quoting McBro Planning & Dev. Co. v. Triangle Elec. Constr. Co., 741 F.2d 342, 344 (11th Cir.1984)); see also Ex parte Napier, 723 So.2d 49 (Ala.1998); Ex parte Gates, 675 So.2d 371 (Ala.1996). The second exception arises from a third-party-beneficiary theory that affords the third party all the rights and benefits, as well as the burdens, of that contract, including those associated with arbitration. See Ex parte Dyess, 709 So.2d 447 (Ala.1997); Ex parte Warren, 718 So.2d 45 (Ala.1998); Georgia Power Co. v. Partin, 727 So.2d 2 (Ala.1998); Infiniti of Mobile, Inc. v. Office, 727 So.2d 42 (Ala.1999); Colonial Sales-Lease-Rental, Inc. v. Target Auction & Land Co., 735 So.2d 1161 (Ala.1999); see also McPheeters v. McGinn, Smith & Co., 953 F.2d 771 (2d Cir.1992); O'Connor v. R.F. Lafferty & Co., 965 F.2d 893 (10th Cir.1992); In re Prudential Ins. Co. of America Sales Practice Litigation All Agent Actions, 133 F.3d 225 (3d Cir.1998); MS Dealer Service Corp. v. Franklin, 177 F.3d 942 (11th Cir.1999). . . .

II. *Third-party-Beneficiary Exception*

The exception for third-party beneficiaries of a contract also applies in this case. This exception can arise out of at least two different sets of facts. The first occurs when a third-party beneficiary-a nonsignatory to the contract-is attempting to resist arbitration. In that situation, this Court has held that the third-party beneficiary cannot both claim the benefit of the contract and avoid the arbitration provision contained within that contract. Dyess, 709 So.2d at 451; Warren, 718 So.2d at 47 n. 4.

The second fact situation is the one present in this case-a nonsignatory third-party beneficiary attempts to enforce the arbitration provision against a signatory to the contract. In these situations where "a nonsignatory to an agreement is a third-party beneficiary ... he is able to enforce the agreement." O'Connor, 965 F.2d at 901.

Therefore, if Hallmont is a third-party beneficiary, then it should be able to enforce the arbitration provision included in the contract between the Stameys and Green Tree. Thus, we must determine whether Hallmont is a third-party beneficiary of that contract.

A party claiming to be a third-party beneficiary, "must establish that the contracting parties intended, upon execution of the contract, to bestow a direct, as opposed to an incidental, benefit upon the third party." Weathers Auto Glass, Inc. v. Alfa Mut. Ins. Co., 619 So.2d 1328, 1329 (Ala.1993) (quoted in Dyess, 709 So.2d at 450.) In other words, Hallmont must show that the Stameys and Green Tree intended for Hallmont to receive a direct benefit from the financing contract. This issue will be determined with almost the same analysis as the estoppel issue-the intent of the parties as indicated by the language used. However, while we looked to the language of only the arbitration provision to answer the estoppel question, in order to determine the third-party beneficiary question we look to the language of the entire financing contract between the Stameys and Green Tree. We conclude that they did intend for Hallmont to receive a direct benefit.

The financing contract is a standard contract that provides for a secured transaction in which Green Tree received a security interest in the manufactured home and in which Green Tree would pay Hallmont for the manufactured home on behalf of the Stameys. In other words, this contract allows Green Tree to pay the obligation of the Stameys to Hallmont. The section of the contract entitled "ITEMIZATION OF THE AMOUNT FINANCED" sets out the amounts that were to be "paid on [the Stameys'] behalf." Included in this chart are the amounts that were paid on behalf of the Stameys to Hallmont for the cost of the manufactured home, the cost of the land, and the cost of the installations.

Furthermore, the language of the contract clearly shows that the parties contemplated Hallmont as a third-party beneficiary. The last section of the contract states:

> WAIVER OF JURY TRIAL: I HEREBY WAIVE ANY RIGHT TO A TRIAL BY JURY THAT I HAVE IN ANY SUBSEQUENT LITIGATION *BETWEEN ME AND THE SELLER*, OR ME AND ANY ASSIGNEE OF THE SELLER, WHERE SUCH LITIGATION ARISES OUT OF, IS RELATED TO, OR IS IN CONNECTION WITH ANY PROVISION OF THIS AGREEMENT, WHETHER THE AGREEMENT IS ASSERTED AS

> RELATED TO, OR IS IN CONNECTION WITH ANY PROVISION OF THIS AGREEMENT, WHETHER THE AGREEMENT IS ASSERTED AS THE BASIS FOR A CLAIM, COUNTERCLAIM OR CROSS CLAIM, OR A DEFENSE TO A CLAIM, COUNTERCLAIM OR CROSS CLAIM. (Emphasis added.)

By this section, the Stameys clearly waived the right to a jury trial, not against Green Tree, but against Hallmont-"the seller."

The language of the two sections mentioned in the two preceding paragraphs clearly indicates an intent on behalf of the Stameys and Green Tree to benefit Hallmont through the financing contract. Therefore, we conclude that Hallmont is a third-party beneficiary of the financing contract and that it has all the rights that exist under that contract. As a result, Hallmont can enforce the arbitration agreement set out in that contract. See Dyess, 709 So.2d 447; O'Connor, 965 F.2d 893; MS Dealer Serv. Corp., 177 F.3d at 947.

III. Conclusion

Hallmont has the right to enforce the arbitration agreement, under either the equitable estoppel theory or the third-party-beneficiary theory. Furthermore, we have reviewed the other issues raised by the Stameys with respect to their claims against Hallmont, and we find them to be without merit.

The trial court properly submitted the Stameys' claims against both Green Tree and Hallmont to arbitration.

WRIT DENIED.

HOOPER, C.J., and MADDOX, SEE, LYONS, BROWN, and ENGLAND, JJ., concur.
COOK, J., concurs in the result.
JOHNSTONE, J., dissents.

SEAVER V. RANSOM
Court of Appeals of New York
120 N. E. 639 (1918).

POUND, J.

Judge Beman and his wife were advanced in years. Mrs. Beman was about to die. She had a small estate consisting of a house and lot in Malone and little else. Judge Beman drew his wife's will according to her instructions. It gave $1,000 to plaintiff, $500 to one sister, plaintiff's mother, and $100 each to another sister and her son, the use of the house to her husband for life, remainder to the American Society for the Prevention of Cruelty to Animals. She named her husband as residuary legatee and executor. Plaintiff was her niece, thirty-four years old, in ill health, sometimes a member of the Beman household. When the will was read to Mrs. Beman she said that it was not as she wanted it; she wanted to leave the house to plaintiff. She had no other objection to the will, but her strength was waning and although the judge offered to write another will for her, she said she was afraid she would not hold out long enough to enable her to sign it. So the judge said if she would sign the will he would leave plaintiff enough in his will to make up the difference. He avouched the promise by his uplifted hand with all solemnity and his wife then executed the will. When he came to die it was found that his will made no provision for the plaintiff.

This action was brought and plaintiff recovered judgment in the trial court on the theory that Beman had obtained property from his wife and induced her to execute the will in the form prepared by him by his promise to give plaintiff $6,000, the value of the house, and that thereby equity impressed his property with a trust in favor of plaintiff. Where a legatee promises the testator that he will use property given him by the will for a particular purpose, a trust arises. (O'Hara v. Dudley, 95 N. Y. 403; Trustees of Amherst College v. Ritch, 151 N. Y. 282; Ahrens v. Jones, 169 N. Y. 555.) Beman received nothing under his wife's will but the use of the house in Malone for life. Equity compels the application of property thus obtained to the purpose of the testator, but equity cannot so impress a trust except on property obtained by the promise. Beman was bound by his promise, but no property was bound by it; no trust in plaintiff's favor can be spelled out.

An action on the contract for damages or to make the executors trustees for performance stands on different ground. (Farmers Loan & Trust Co. v. Mortimer, 219 N. Y. 290, 294, 295.) The Appellate Division properly passed to the consideration of the question whether the judgment could stand upon the promise made to the wife, upon a valid consideration, for the sole benefit of plaintiff. The judgment of the trial court was affirmed by a return to the general doctrine laid down in the great case of Lawrence v. Fox (20 N. Y. 268) which has since been limited as herein indicated.

Contracts for the benefit of third persons have been the prolific source of judicial and academic discussion. (Williston, Contracts for the Benefit of a Third Person, 15 Harvard Law Review, 767; Corbin, Contracts for the Benefit of Third Persons, 27 Yale Law Review, 1008.) The general rule, both in law and equity (Phalen v. U. S. Trust Co., 186 N. Y. 178, 186), was that privity between a plaintiff and a defendant is necessary to the maintenance of an action on the contract. The consideration must be furnished by the party to whom the promise was made. The contract cannot be enforced against the third party and, therefore, it cannot be enforced by him. On the other hand, the right of the beneficiary to sue on a contract made expressly for his benefit has been fully recognized in many American jurisdictions, either by judicial decision or by legislation, and is said to be "the prevailing rule in this country." (Hendrick v. Lindsay, 93 U. S. 143; Lehow v. Simonton, 3 Col. 346.) It has been said that "the establishment of this doctrine has been gradual, and is a victory of practical utility over theory, of equity over technical subtlety." (Brantly on Contracts [2d ed.], p. 253.) The reasons for this view are that it is just and practical to permit the person for whose benefit the contract is made to enforce it against one whose duty it is to pay. Other jurisdictions still adhere to the present English rule (7 Halsbury's Laws of England, 342, 343; Jenks' Digest of English Civil Law, § 229) that a contract cannot be enforced by or against a person who is not a party. (Exchange Bank v. Rice, 107 Mass. 37; but see, also, Forbes v. Thorpe, 209 Mass. 570; Gardner v. Denison, 217 Mass. 492.) In New York the right of the beneficiary to sue on contracts made for his benefit is not clearly or simply defined. It is at present confined, first, to cases where there is a pecuniary obligation running from the promisee to the beneficiary; "a legal right founded upon some obligation of the promisee in the third party to adopt and claim the promise as made for his benefit." (Farley v. Cleveland, 4 Cow. 432; Lawrence v. Fox, supra; Garnsey v. Rogers, 47 N. Y. 233; Vrooman v. Turner, 69 N. Y. 280; Lorillard v. Clyde, 122 N. Y. 498; Durnherr v. Rau, 135 N. Y. 219; Townsend v. Rackham, 143 N. Y. 516; Sullivan v. Sullivan, 161 N. Y. 554.) Secondly, to cases where the contract is made for the benefit of the wife (Buchanan v. Tilden, 158 N. Y. 109; Bouton v. Welch, 170 N. Y. 554), affianced wife (De Cicco v. Schweizer, 221 N. Y. 431), or child (Todd v. Weber, 95 N. Y. 181, 193; Matter of Kidd, 188 N. Y. 274) of a party to the contract. The close relationship cases go back to the early King's Bench case (1677), long since repudiated in England, of Dutton v. Poole (2 Lev. 210; s. c., 1 Ventris, 318, 332). (Schemerhorn v. Vanderheyden, 1 Johns. 139.) The natural and moral duty of the husband or parent to provide for the future of wife or child sustains the action on the contract made for their benefit. "This is the farthest the cases in this state have gone," says Cullen, J., in the marriage settlement case of Borland v. Welch (162 N. Y. 104, 110).

The right of the third party is also upheld in, thirdly, the public contract cases (Little v. Banks, 85 N. Y. 258; Pond v. New Rochelle Water Co., 183 N. Y. 330; Smyth v. City of New York, 203 N. Y. 106; Farnsworth v. Boro Oil & Gas Co., 216 N. Y. 40, 48; Rigney v. N. Y. C. & H. R. R. R. Co., 217 N. Y. 31; Matter of International Ry. Co. v. Rann, 224 N. Y. 83; cf. German Alliance Ins. Co. v. Home Water Supply Co., 226 U. S. 220) where the municipality seeks to protect its inhabitants by covenants for their benefit and, fourthly, the cases where, at the request of a party to the contract, the promise runs directly to the beneficiary although he does not furnish the consideration. (Rector, etc., v. Teed, 120 N. Y. 583; F. N. Bank of Sing Sing v. Chalmers, 144 N. Y. 432, 439; Hamilton v. Hamilton, 127 App. Div. 871, 875.) It may be safely said that a general rule sustaining recovery at the suit of the third party would include but few classes of cases not included in these groups, either categorically or in principle.

The desire of the childless aunt to make provision for a beloved and favorite niece differs imperceptibly in law or in equity from the moral duty of the parent to make testamentary provision for a child. The contract was made for the plaintiff's benefit. She alone is substantially damaged by its breach. The representatives of the wife's estate have no interest in enforcing it specifically. It is said in Buchanan v. Tilden that the common law imposes moral and legal obligations upon the husband and the parent not measured by the necessaries of life. It was, however, the love and affection or the moral sense of the husband and the parent that imposed such obligations in the cases cited rather than any common-law duty of husband and parent to wife and child. If plaintiff had been a child of Mrs. Beman, legal obligation would have required no testamentary provision for her, yet the child could have enforced a covenant in her favor identical with the covenant of Judge Beman in this case. (De Cicco v. Schweizer, supra.) The constraining power of conscience is not regulated by the degree of relationship alone. The dependent or faithful niece may have a stronger claim than the affluent or unworthy son. No sensible theory of moral obligation denies arbitrarily to the former what would be conceded to the latter. We might consistently either refuse or allow the claim of both, but I cannot reconcile a decision in favor of the wife in Buchanan v. Tilden based on the moral obligations arising out of near relationship with a decision against the niece here on the ground that the relationship is too remote for equity's ken. No controlling authority depends upon so absolute a rule. In Sullivan v. Sullivan (supra) the grandniece lost in a litigation with the aunt's estate founded on a certificate of deposit payable to the aunt "or in case of her death to her niece," but what was said in that case of the relations of plaintiff's intestate and defendant does not control here, any more than what was said in Durnherr v. Rau (supra) on the relation of husband and wife, and the inadequacy of mere moral duty, as distinguished from legal or equitable obligation, controlled the decision in Buchanan v. Tilden. Borland v. Welch (supra) deals only with the rights of volunteers under a marriage settlement not made for the benefit of collaterals.

Kellogg, P. J., writing for the court below well said: "The doctrine of Lawrence v. Fox is progressive, not retrograde. The course of the late decisions is to enlarge, not to limit the effect of that case." The court in that leading case attempted to adopt the general doctrine that any third person, for whose direct benefit a contract was intended, could sue on it. The head note thus states the rule. Finch, J., in Gifford v. Corrigan (117 N. Y. 257, 262) says that the case rests upon that broad proposition; Edward T. Bartlett, J., in Pond v. New Rochelle Water Co. (183 N. Y. 330, 337) calls it "the general principle;" but Vrooman v. Turner (supra) confined its application to the facts on which it was decided. "In every case in which an action has been sustained," says Allen, J., "there has been a debt or duty owing by the promisee to the party claiming to sue upon the promise." (69 N. Y. 285.) As late as Townsend v. Rackham (143 N. Y. 516, 523) we find Peckham, J., saying that "to maintain the action by the third person there must be this liability to him on the part of the promisee." Buchanan v. Tilden went further than any case since Lawrence v. Fox in a desire to do justice rather than to apply with technical accuracy strict rules calling for a legal or equitable obligation. In Embler v. Hartford Steam Boiler Inspection & Ins. Co. (158 N. Y. 431) it may at least be said that a majority of the court did not avail themselves of the opportunity to concur with the views expressed by Gray, J.,--who wrote the dissenting opinion in Buchanan v. Tilden,--to the effect that an employee could not maintain an action on an insurance policy issued to the employer, which covered injuries to employees.

In Wright v. Glen Telephone Co. (48 Misc. Rep. 192, 195) the learned presiding justice who wrote the opinion in this case said, at Trial Term: "The right of a third person to recover upon a contract made by other parties for his benefit must rest upon the peculiar circumstances of each case rather than upon the law of some other case." "The case at bar is decided upon its peculiar facts." (Edward T. Bartlett, J., in Buchanan v. Tilden.) But, on principle, a sound conclusion may be reached. If Mrs. Beman had left her husband the house on condition that he pay the plaintiff $6,000 and he had accepted the devise, he would have become personally liable to pay the legacy and plaintiff could have recovered in an action at law against him, whatever the value of the house. (Gridley v. Gridley, 24 N. Y. 130; Brown v. Knapp, 79 N. Y. 136, 143; Dinan v. Coneys, 143 N. Y. 544, 547; Blackmore v. White, [1899] 1 Q. B. 293, 304.) That would be because the testatrix had in substance bequeathed the promise to plaintiff and not because close relationship or moral obligation sustained the contract. The distinction between an implied promise to a testator for the benefit of a third party to pay a legacy and an unqualified promise on a valuable consideration to make provision for the third party by will is discernible but not obvious. The tendency of American authority is to sustain the gift in all such cases and to permit the donee-beneficiary to recover on the contract. (Matter of Edmundson's Estate, [1918, Pa.] 103 Atl. Rep. 277.) The equities are with the plaintiff and they may be enforced in this action, whether it be regarded as an action for damages or an action for specific performance to convert the defendants into trustees for plaintiff's benefit under the agreement.

The judgment should be affirmed, with costs.

HOGAN, CARDOZO and CRANE, JJ., concur; HISCOCK, Ch. J., COLLIN and ANDREWS, JJ., dissent.

Judgment affirmed.

NOTES & QUESTIONS:

1. For creative uses of the third party beneficiary theory, see *Blair v. Anderson*, 325 A.2d 94 (Del. 1974) and *Bain v. Gillispie*, 357 N.W.2d 47 (Iowa Ct. App. 1984).

KOCH V. CONSOLIDATED EDISON CO.
Court of Appeals of New York
62 N.Y.2d 548 (1984).

JONES, Judge.

The determination made in a prior action that Con Edison was grossly negligent in connection with the 1977 blackout in the City of New York is binding and conclusive on Con Edison in this action. Although plaintiffs may recover damages for physical injury to persons and property directly resulting from the service interruption, including damages resulting from looting and vandalism by rioters, they may not recover damages for additional expenditures, occasioned by the blackout, made by plaintiffs in the performance of their governmental functions, nor may they recover for loss of revenues assertedly attributable to the blackout.

On July 13, 1977 at approximately 9:36 p.m. there was a complete failure of electrical service in the City of New York except for an area in the Borough of Queens which was supplied by the Long Island Lighting Company. The blackout lasted for approximately 25 hours with power not being completely restored until approximately 10:40 p.m. on July 14.

The present action was instituted on September 7, 1978 by the City of New York and 14 public benefit corporations to recover damages allegedly sustained as a result of Con Edison's gross negligence and reckless and willful conduct with respect to the blackout.

Plaintiffs moved for partial summary judgment with respect to Con Edison's liability for gross negligence "on the ground that, under the doctrine of collateral estoppel, a prior determination in another lawsuit (Food Pageant, Inc. v. Consolidated Edison Co., Inc., Supreme Court, Bronx County, Index No. 16971/77)[1] that the July 13-14, 1977 electric power failure . . . resulted from the gross negligence of the defendant Consolidated Edison, is conclusive and binding on the defendant Consolidated Edison in this action." Con Edison thereupon made a cross motion for partial summary judgment, so far as pertinent for the

---

[1] When this case reached our court we upheld the jury verdict which found Con Edison to have been grossly negligent in causing the 1977 blackout and which awarded plaintiff grocery store chain damages in the sum of $40,500 for food spoilage and loss of business. (Food Pageant v. Consolidated Edison Co., 54 N.Y.2d 167, 445 N.Y.S.2d 60, 429 N.E.2d 738).

purposes of the present appeal, (1) dismissing plaintiffs' claims based on Con Edison's contracts with the Power Authority of the State of New York (PASNY) because "plaintiffs are neither parties nor third-party beneficiaries of those contracts" . . . .

Special Term granted plaintiffs' motion and denied Con Edison's motion as described above. The Appellate Division, 95 A.D.2d 988, 465 N.E.2d 99, affirmed, without opinion, and granted both plaintiffs and Con Edison leave to appeal to our court. We modify the determination at the Appellate Division. . . .

We reject, too, Con Edison's argument that because the city and the other plaintiffs associated with it were customers of PASNY and not direct customers of Con Edison, they are not entitled to recover against Con Edison. In 1974 a new section, "§ 1001-a. Emergency Provisions For The Metropolitan Area of the City of New York," was added to the Public Authorities Law (L. 1974, ch. 369, § 2). Pursuant to the authorization of that section, in December, 1974 and December, 1975 PASNY acquired from Con Edison two partially completed generating units (the Astoria 6 and the Indian Point 3 Units). The underlying legislation and both acquisitions anticipated that Con Edison would continue to provide transmission and delivery of the electricity produced in the two plants. In conformity with that expectation, a service agreement was entered into by PASNY and Con Edison for delivery of power and energy from the Astoria 6 Unit and the Indian Point 3 Unit, in which was recited Con Edison's willingness, by use of its existing facilities, to assist PASNY in serving the needs of the Astoria-Indian Point customers, and Con Edison became obligated to provide the same quality of service to PASNY's customers as it did to its own customers and under Con Edison's regular tariff schedules. In a simultaneously executed "Contract for the Sale of Power and Energy", Con Edison agreed to provide sufficient energy to meet the requirements of PASNY's affected customers.

Against this background we have no difficulty in concluding that all the plaintiffs were third-party beneficiaries of the agreements between PASNY and Con Edison. They were precisely the consumers for whose benefit the legislation was enacted and the agreements made between PASNY and Con Edison.

To be distinguished are our holdings in Moch Co. v. Rensselaer Water Co., 247 N.Y. 160, 159 N.E. 896 [contract between water company and city to supply water for fire hydrants did not create a duty to member of the public] and Kornblut v. Chevron Oil Co., 62 A.D.2d 831, 407 N.Y.S.2d 498, affd. on opn. below 48 N.Y.2d 853, 424 N.Y.S.2d 429, 400 N.E.2d 368 [contract with Thruway Authority to provide repair services did not create duty to members of the public]. In neither of those cases did the operative contract provide that the service was to be rendered other than for the contracting party, city or authority. Moreover, in Moch we noted the distinction between the agreement of the water company, there in issue, to furnish water at the hydrants and the agreement of the water company to provide direct service to members of the public at their homes and factories (247 NY, at pp. 164, 166, 159 N.E. 896). In the present instance, the purpose of the enabling legislation was expressly stated to be "To preserve reliability of electric service in the metropolitan area of the city of New York" (Public Authorities Law, § 1001-a, subd. 1), and the service agreement contained the express obligation to "operate and maintain all the facilities necessary to deliver power to Astoria-Indian Point Customers [which included plaintiffs] in accordance with good utility operating practice." Indeed, the essence of the responsibility of a public utility is to provide services to the consuming public. . . .

COOKE, C.J., and JASEN, WACHTLER, MEYER, SIMONS and KAYE, JJ., concur.

Order modified, without costs, in accordance with the opinion herein and, as so modified, affirmed. Cross appeal by plaintiffs dismissed, without costs. Question certified answered in the negative.

NOTES AND QUESTIONS:

1. For a determination that a member of the public was not an intended third party beneficiary of a public contract, *see H.R. Moch Co. v. Rensselaer Water Co.*, 159 N.E. 896 (N.Y. 1928).

B. RIGHTS AND DEFENSES

BD. OF EDUC. OF COMMUNITY SCHOOL DIST. NO. 220 V. VILLAGE OF HOFFMAN ESTATES
Appellate Court of Illinois, First District
467 N.E.2d 1064 (1984).

SULLIVAN, Justice:

Defendant Village of Hoffman Estates (Village) appeals from the granting of summary judgment for plaintiff Board of Education of Community School District No. 220 (District) in an action seeking a declaration of District 220's rights as a beneficiary under the terms of certain annexation agreements. The sole question before us is whether District 220 acquired any rights under the agreements which could not be altered by subsequent amendment mutually agreed to by the contracting parties.

The facts of the case are largely undisputed. In 1975, two groups of developers (Owners), desiring to have certain tracts of land annexed to the Village, entered into annexation agreements with the Village. Each agreement provided in relevant part that the Owners would pay to the Village "the sum of $135 per residential unit as developed." The funds paid were to be held in escrow "for the benefit of education," and the agreements further provided that during the 5-year period following execution of the agreements, the parties thereto would use their best efforts to cause the area annexed to be included within the boundaries of School District 15. If, at any time during the prescribed period, their efforts were successful, the funds were to be paid to School District 15. If, however, their efforts were unsuccessful, then at the end of the 5-year period the escrowed funds were to be paid to District 220.

The Owners and the Village were not successful in their attempts to have the area in question included within the boundaries of District 15, and shortly before the expiration of the 5-year period, they amended their agreements, extending the period to 9 years and providing that they would use their best efforts to cause the area to be included within the boundaries of "School Districts 15 or 54." Again, if their efforts were unsuccessful, then at the end of the 9-year period the funds were to be paid to District 220. At all pertinent times, the land which is the subject of the annexation agreements has been within the boundaries of District 220, and it has provided free education for the children residing in that area, as it is required to do under the Illinois School Code. (Ill.Rev.Stat.1981, ch. 122, par. 10-20.12.) The funds required by the agreements have been paid and are currently being held in escrow.

After the 5-year period prescribed by the original annexation agreements expired, District 220 brought the instant action seeking a declaration that it was presently entitled to receive the escrowed funds on the ground that it was a donee beneficiary of the contracts between the Owners and the Village, and that the contracting parties had no power to alter the terms of their agreements without its consent. The trial court granted summary judgment for District 220, ruling that, as a matter of law, execution of the agreements created a vested right, subject to divestment, in District 220, and that the purported amendments were therefore ineffective. Since the 5-year period had elapsed, and the "divesting condition subsequent," *i.e.,* inclusion of the land within the boundaries of School District 15, had not occurred, the trial court ordered that the escrowed funds be paid to District 220. This appeal followed.

OPINION

The issue presents us with the question of when the rights of a third-party beneficiary under a contract become "vested"; that is, at what point is the third-party's right to demand performance irrevocable and unamendable. The parties herein are in agreement that District 220's status is that of a donee beneficiary, since the promise made for its benefit was a gift rather than a means of repaying some debt owed it by the Village. This point being conceded, the sole issue is whether the Owners and the Village retained any right to amend that portion of their agreements which conferred a benefit upon District 220.

It is established that third-party beneficiaries have enforceable rights under contracts made for their benefit. (See, e.g., Carson Pirie Scott & Co. v. Parrett (1931), 346 Ill. 252, 178 N.E. 498 (creditor beneficiary); Riepe v. Schmidt (1916), 199 Ill.App. 129 (donee beneficiary).) However, we are aware of only one case directly concerned with the question of subsequent revocation or amendment. In Bay v. Williams (1884), 112 Ill. 91, 1 N.E. 340, Bay purchased land from Newman and Sissons, promising as partial consideration therefore to pay certain notes owed by them to Williams. Subsequently, Sissons agreed to release Bay from that promise. When Williams sought to recover from Bay, he asserted the release as a defense, and the supreme court, in a divided opinion, held that the promise to pay "invests the person for whose use it is made with an immediate interest and right, as though the promise had been made to him. This being true, the person who procures the promise has no legal right to release or discharge the person who made the promise, from his liability to the beneficiary." (112 Ill. 91, 97, 1 N.E. 340, 342-43.) Subsequent cases, relying on Bay, have stated that the rights of a creditor beneficiary become vested immediately upon execution of the contract (see, e.g., Town & Country Bank of Springfield v. James M. Canfield Contracting Co. (1977), 55 Ill.App.3d 91, 12 Ill.Dec. 826, 370 N.E.2d 630; Pliley v. Phifer (1954), 1 Ill.App.2d 398, 117 N.E.2d 678), although none of those cases involved an attempted rescission or modification of an original agreement. It appears that the same rule is applied to contracts made for the benefit of a donee beneficiary (see, e.g., Joslyn v. Joslyn (1944), 386 Ill. 387, 54 N.E.2d 475), but it seems to be based more on an analogy to the law of trusts or gifts than to the law of contracts. We are aware that this rule is contrary to that expressed in the Restatement (Second) of Contracts, which states that, in the absence of language in the contract making the rights of a third-party beneficiary irrevocable, "the promisor and promisee retain power to discharge or modify the duty by subsequent agreement" until such time as the beneficiary, without notice of the discharge or modification, "materially changes his position in justifiable reliance on the promise or brings suit on it or manifests assent to it at the request of the promisor or the promisee." (Restatement (Second) of Contracts § 311 (1979).) Furthermore, it appears that the majority of jurisdictions have now adopted the rule as set forth in the Restatement (see 17 Am.Jur.2d Contracts § 317 (1964); 17A C.J.S. Contracts § 373 (1963), and cases cited therein), perhaps on the theory that the parties to a contract should remain free to amend or rescind their agreement so long as there is no detriment to a third party who has provided no consideration for the benefit received.

In the instant case, the Village does not contend that we should alter the rule established 100 years ago in Bay v. Williams, a rule which apparently has not been considered in the light of modern trends in the law of contracts, and we therefore need not express our views thereon. Instead, the Village asserts that the above rule is inapplicable where, as here, there are two possible beneficiaries of the promise, and the ultimate beneficiary could not be determined until certain specified events occurred. Under those circumstances, it maintains, no rights could have vested in District 220, since it was not assured of being a beneficiary of the promise, and the parties should therefore be free to alter their agreement. It is District 220's position that the right became vested as soon as the Owners and the Village executed the agreements, although the right was subject to divestment. Therefore, it posits, no amendment was possible. Unfortunately, although both sides cite several cases which purportedly support their arguments, none of the cases involve a situation even remotely analogous to the facts before us. All of the cases cited involved a single, identifiable beneficiary, whereas here, there are quite obviously two possible beneficiaries.

In considering this issue, we begin with the premise, accepted by most commentators, that a third-party beneficiary contract may exist even if the beneficiary is not named, not identifiable, or not yet in existence, so long as the beneficiary is identifiable or in existence when the time for performance arrives. These same commentators note, however, that such beneficiaries have no vested rights until they are identified, and that contracts made for their benefit may therefore be rescinded or modified by the parties thereto until such time as the beneficiaries are identified. (See e.g., J. Calamari & J. Perillo, Contracts § 17-9 (2d ed. 1977); 4 Corbin, Contracts § 781 (1951); L. Simpson, Contracts § 122 (2d ed. 1965). See also 17A C.J.S. Contracts § 373 (1963).) We have indicated that such agreements are valid in Illinois, as where a contract provides that final payment will be withheld until a general contractor provides proof that all materialmen and subcontracts have been paid. (See Town & Country Bank of Springfield v. James M. Canfield Contracting Co. (1977), 55 Ill.App.3d 91, 12 Ill.Dec. 826, 370 N.E.2d 630.) Clearly, under such contracts, the third-party beneficiaries are not identifiable until they provide materials or service, and it could never be seriously contended that they had any vested rights prior to that time which would preclude the contracting parties from modifying the agreement.

Our courts have never considered the question of modification or rescission under similar facts, although the few cases from other jurisdictions which have addressed the issue indicate that until the third-party beneficiary is identified, no vested rights arise. In Stanfield v. W.C. McBride, Inc. (1939), 149 Kan. 567, 88 P.2d 1002, Stanfield was awarded judgment for injuries he suffered when struck by an automobile owned by Miller-Morgan Motor Co. (Miller-Morgan) and driven with its consent by an employee of W.C. McBride, Inc. (McBride). McBride paid the judgment, then sought to recover from Miller-Morgan's insurer, claiming that its employee was covered under the omnibus clause of Miller-Morgan's automobile policy. The evidence disclosed that the omnibus clause had been stricken from the policy eight days before the accident occurred, and the court ruled that while McBride's employee was a potential third-party beneficiary under the contract of insurance, he had no vested rights thereunder until such time as he became identified as an actual beneficiary, and the parties to the contract were free to modify or rescind their agreement prior to that time. Accord, Winchester v. Sipp (1960), 252 Iowa 156, 106 N.W.2d 55.

Similar reasoning is evident in Associated Teachers of Huntington, Inc. v. Board of Education, Union Free School, District No. 3, Town of Huntington (1973), 33 N.Y.2d 229, 306 N.E.2d 791, 351 N.Y.S.2d 670. There, a contract between the association and the school board provided that sabbatical leaves would be granted to as many as 3% of the staff per school term. Twenty-one teachers submitted applications, and it was understood that not all could be granted leave. Prior to considering the applications, the school board stated that, due to financial considerations, no leaves would be granted, and the association brought an action to enforce the agreement. The court noted that the individual teachers had no vested rights, since none was assured of being granted leave and the third-party beneficiaries under the contract had not yet been identified. However, the court went on to hold that the association, as promisee, had a right to enforce the contract.

While the cases cited are not directly on point, we believe that they are analogous. Here, although two entities are named in the contract, it could not be ascertained until certain events occurred which would be the third-party beneficiary. Thus, while it is true that the field of potential beneficiaries is much smaller than in the above-cited cases, ultimately-by the terms of the contract-there could be only one beneficiary of the funds held in escrow "for the benefit of education," and that beneficiary could not be identified until the time for performance arose; i.e., until the land was included within the boundaries of School District 15 or 5 years elapsed, whichever event occurred first. It does not appear to us that District 220 was any more certain to be the beneficiary than was District 15 or that it had any greater claim to the funds than did District 15. District 220 points out that during that 5-year period, it was providing education for the children residing in the area, and apparently asserts that we may conclude from that fact that the phrase "for the benefit of education" meant "for the benefit of District 220." We disagree. District 220, in providing education for the children, was doing what it is required to do under the School Code, a duty which it might have had for only a short time should the school boundaries have changed. It appears to us from the language of the contract that the parties thereto intended to confer a benefit on whichever school district would be serving the area over the long term, and they apparently hoped that that district would be District 15 rather than District 220.

Based on the clear language of the contract, it is our view that District 220 was merely a potential beneficiary of the promise to pay certain specified sums for the benefit of education, and the undisputed facts establish that the actual beneficiary of the promise had not yet been identified at the time the Village and the Owners modified their agreement. Since neither school district was identified as the beneficiary, neither had a vested right under the contract, and we hold that under those circumstances the parties were free to modify their agreement.

For the foregoing reasons, the order of the trial court is reversed, and the cause remanded for further proceedings not inconsistent with the views expressed herein.

Reversed and remanded.

LORENZ and PINCHAM, JJ., concur.

OLSON V. ETHERIDGE
Supreme Court of Illinios
686 N.E.2d 563 (1997).

Justice BILANDIC delivered the opinion of the court:

Bay v. Williams, 112 Ill. 91, 1 N.E. 340 (1884), established the rule in Illinois that the rights of a third-party beneficiary in a contract are subject to immediate vesting and, once vested, cannot be altered or extinguished through a later agreement of the contracting parties without the assent of the beneficiary. Bay, 112 Ill. at 96-97, 1 N.E. 340. We are here called upon to determine the continued validity of the Bay rule.

The four plaintiffs in this case are third-party beneficiaries of a promise contained in a contract entered into by the appellant and another party. The circuit court of Bureau County awarded summary judgment to the plaintiffs based on Bay. The appellate court affirmed. We now reverse this award of summary judgment and remand for further proceedings, for the reasons set forth below.

FACTS

The facts are not in dispute. The four plaintiffs, Karen Olson, Nancy Stites, Cheryl Stevenson, and Carolin Polson, were the owners of Heitzler, Inc., a John Deere dealership in Walnut, Illinois. In 1979 they sold all the stock in Heitzler, Inc., to a group of three buyers, including Dean Etheridge, for $350,000 pursuant to the terms of a stock purchase agreement and a corresponding promissory note, hereinafter referred to as Agreement I and Note I. Agreement I and Note I obligated the buyers to make annual payments to the plaintiffs on December 1 of each year, along with 9% interest, and provided remedies to the plaintiffs in the event of a default. The buyers' payments were to be made directly to the plaintiffs' checking account at a bank in Walnut (the Walnut Bank). The buyers also pledged the shares of stock as security for the unpaid balance of the purchase price, with the shares to be held in an escrow account at the Walnut Bank until the debt was satisfied. The three buyers changed the corporate name of Heitzler, Inc., to Woodley Implement, Inc., and continued operation of the business.

Nearly four years later, in August of 1983, Dean Etheridge and the appellant, August Engelhaupt, executed a written agreement wherein Etheridge sold one-half of his stock in the corporation to Engelhaupt, hereinafter referred to as Agreement II. In Agreement II, Engelhaupt agreed "to assume" one-half of Etheridge's liability and obligation under Agreement I, which included the obligation to satisfy Note I. In exchange, Etheridge assigned one-half of his rights in Agreement I over to Engelhaupt. This assignment of rights was made subject to the terms of Agreement I. The entirety of Agreement I was incorporated by reference into Agreement II.

Agreement II obligated Engelhaupt to make annual payments on December 1 of each year, along with 9% interest, directly to the Walnut Bank. These payments were to be credited toward Etheridge's balance due to the plaintiffs under Agreement I and Note I. Specifically, under the terms of Agreement II, Engelhaupt agreed to pay a total purchase price of $88,900 for the corporate shares, as follows: $9,000 down, with the balance to be paid in the December 1 installments. A corresponding promissory note, hereinafter called Note II, was executed along with Agreement II for the remaining purchase price of $79,900. Note II reiterated the same payment schedule contained in Agreement II. Note II also stated that Engelhaupt's payments were to be made to the Walnut Bank "or at such other place as, from time to time, may be designated in writing."

From 1983 through 1985, Engelhaupt apparently made the payments due under Agreement II and Note II to the Walnut Bank, although the record is silent on this matter. On February 10, 1986, Etheridge directed Engelhaupt to pay the amount then due on Note II to another creditor of Etheridge, the Citizens First National Bank of Princeton (Princeton Bank). Sometime prior, Etheridge had assigned all his interest in Agreement II and Note II over to Princeton Bank as collateral security for another debt of Etheridge's.

Also on February 10, 1986, Engelhaupt and Princeton Bank entered into a written agreement entitled "Agreement Providing for Payment of Note," hereinafter referred to as Agreement III. Engelhaupt, in Agreement III, agreed "to satisfy the remaining indebtedness due on" Note II, by paying $83,385 to Princeton Bank. Princeton Bank agreed that this payment of $83,385 constituted full payment of Note II. Engelhaupt also paid Princeton Bank an extra $100 and, in exchange, Princeton Bank assigned to Engelhaupt all its interest in Agreement II. Etheridge concurrently executed a document ratifying Agreement III and transferring any remaining interest that he had in Agreement II over to Engelhaupt. No one disputes the fact that Engelhaupt paid Princeton Bank $83,485 on February 10, 1986.

In March of 1986 the plaintiffs filed a complaint against the original purchasers of the corporation, including Etheridge, and against Engelhaupt. The counts against the original purchasers charged that they had defaulted on Agreement I and Note I. Count V was directed against Engelhaupt. In count V, the plaintiffs asserted that they were intended third-party beneficiaries of Agreement II, the contract entered into between Etheridge and Engelhaupt. The plaintiffs claimed that, as third-party beneficiaries of Agreement II, they were entitled to enforce it. They requested the circuit court to enter a judgment against Engelhaupt for the sum of $76,500 plus interest and attorney fees. The plaintiffs asserted that $76,500 was the principal sum which remained owing under Agreement II.

Engelhaupt filed an answer to the plaintiffs' complaint and raised an affirmative defense. Engelhaupt first argued that the plaintiffs were not intended third-party beneficiaries of Agreement II. Alternatively, Engelhaupt argued that, even if the plaintiffs were intended third-party beneficiaries, any rights that they had under Agreement II were terminated before they brought suit. Specifically, Engelhaupt claimed that all his obligations under Agreement II and Note II were discharged by the actions taken between him, Etheridge, and Princeton Bank on February 10, 1986.

Ultimately, the circuit court granted the plaintiffs' motion for summary judgment against Engelhaupt on count V in the amount of $159,375.08 (representing principal and accrued interest) plus $22,000 in attorney fees.

Engelhaupt appealed, and the appellate court affirmed. No. 3-95-0903 (unpublished order under Supreme Court Rule 23). The appellate court held that, as a matter of law, Agreement II conferred intended third-party beneficiary status on the plaintiffs. The appellate court reached this conclusion because Agreement II(1) incorporates by reference Agreement I; (2) states that Engelhaupt assumed one-half of Etheridge's liability and obligation under Agreement I; (3) contains a payment schedule identical to that in Agreement I; and (4) required Engelhaupt to make his payments directly to the plaintiffs' account. The appellate court further reasoned that the fact that Note II allowed for altering the place of payment was irrelevant because the terms of Agreement II precisely set forth the rights and obligations of the parties.

The appellate court next rejected Engelhaupt's claim that his obligations to the plaintiffs as third-party beneficiaries under Agreement II and Note II were discharged by the actions taken between him, Etheridge, and Princeton Bank on February 10, 1986. The appellate court determined that Bay v. Williams, 112 Ill. 91, 1 N.E. 340 (1884), was dispositive of this issue. Bay established the rule in Illinois that third-party beneficiary rights are subject to immediate vesting and, once vested, cannot subsequently be altered or extinguished through a later agreement of the original parties to the contract. Bay, 112 Ill. at 96-97, 1 N.E. 340. Applying the Bay rule, the appellate court concluded that the plaintiffs' third-party beneficiary rights in Agreement II vested immediately upon Etheridge's and Engelhaupt's execution of that agreement. Once this vesting occurred, Etheridge and Engelhaupt were powerless to modify the terms of Agreement II in a manner detrimental to the plaintiffs without their consent. The appellate court therefore affirmed the circuit court's grant of summary judgment in favor of the plaintiffs and against Engelhaupt.

One appellate court justice specially concurred in the judgment. He acknowledged that Bay is controlling precedent, but stated his belief that the Bay rule is antiquated and should be replaced by the modern approach as articulated in the Restatement (Second) of Contracts.

We allowed Engelhaupt's petition for leave to appeal (155 Ill.2d R. 315(a)) to determine whether Bay remains good law.

ANALYSIS

As a preliminary matter, we note that Engelhaupt does not challenge the appellate court's initial holding that the plaintiffs are intended third-party beneficiaries of Agreement II. We therefore accept that holding as correct for purposes of this appeal because the waiver doctrine applies. See 155 Ill.2d R. 341(e)(7).

Engelhaupt's appeal focuses on the appellate court's rejection of his claim that he is not subject to liability to the plaintiffs because all his obligations under Agreement II and Note II were discharged by the actions taken between him, Etheridge, and Princeton Bank on February 10, 1986. The actions pointed to by Engelhaupt are his $83,385 payment to Princeton Bank on Note II, and Princeton Bank's agreement that this constituted full payment; and his $100 payment to Princeton Bank for Agreement II, and Princeton Bank's and Etheridge's assignments of all their interests in Agreement II over to Engelhaupt. Engelhaupt concedes that the vesting rule in Bay commands a contrary conclusion, but argues that the Bay rule should be replaced with the vesting rule set forth in section 311 of the Restatement (Second) of Contracts (1981). According to Engelhaupt, if section 311 is applied, the summary judgment entered in favor of the plaintiffs was improper because questions of material fact remain to be determined.

An award of summary judgment is appropriate when there is no genuine issue of material fact and the moving party is entitled to judgment as a matter of law. Purtill v. Hess, 111 Ill.2d 229, 240, 95 Ill.Dec. 305, 489 N.E.2d 867 (1986). Although summary judgment is to be encouraged as an aid in the expeditious disposition of a lawsuit, it is a drastic measure and should be granted only when the movant's right to judgment is free from doubt. Reed v. Bascon, 124 Ill.2d 386, 393, 125 Ill.Dec. 259, 530 N.E.2d 417 (1988). A reviewing court conducts de novo review in an appeal from a summary judgment ruling. Outboard Marine Corp. v. Liberty Mutual Insurance Co., 154 Ill.2d 90, 102, 180 Ill.Dec. 691, 607 N.E.2d 1204 (1992).

Before addressing the parties' arguments, we briefly summarize third-party beneficiary law. The well-established rule in Illinois is that if a contract is entered into for the direct benefit of a third person, the third person may sue for a breach of the contract in his or her own name, even though the third person is a stranger to the contract and the consideration. Joslyn v. Joslyn, 386 Ill. 387, 400, 54 N.E.2d 475 (1944); Carson Pirie Scott & Co. v. Parrett, 346 Ill. 252, 257, 178 N.E. 498 (1931). This principle of law is widely accepted throughout the United States, because allowing a third-party beneficiary to sue the promisor directly is said to be manifestly just and practical. See 17A Am.Jur.2d Contracts §§ 435, 437 (2d ed.1991). In cases such as this one, it increases judicial efficiency by removing the privity requirement, under which the beneficiary must sue the promisee, who then in turn must sue the promisor.

An important corollary to this principle is that the promisor may assert against the beneficiary any defense that the promisor could assert against the promisee if the promisee were suing on the contract. See J. Calamari & J. Perillo, Contracts § 17-10, at 711 (3d ed.1987). This is because the third-party beneficiary's rights stem from a contract to which the beneficiary is not a party. Accordingly, the promisor in this case, Engelhaupt, may assert against the plaintiffs-beneficiaries any defense that he could assert against the promisee,

Etheridge, if Etheridge were suing him on Agreement II. Engelhaupt here asserts the defense that all his obligations under Agreement II and Note II were discharged when he made full payment to Princeton Bank on Note II and obtained assignments of both Princeton Bank's and Etheridge's interests in Agreement II.

The plaintiffs maintain, however, that Engelhaupt is not entitled to assert this defense against them because their rights as third-party beneficiaries had "vested." The vesting doctrine is an exception to the above rule that the promisor may assert against the beneficiary any defense that the promisor could assert against the promisee. See J. Calamari & J. Perillo, Contracts § 17-11, at 715 (3d ed.1987); J. Calamari & J. Perillo, Contracts § 17-8, at 624 (2d ed.1977). Under this doctrine, once a third-party beneficiary's rights vest, the original contracting parties cannot modify or discharge those rights without the beneficiary's assent. The "question of vesting arises only where the promisor and the promisee purport to vary or discharge the rights of the beneficiary"; otherwise, "the topic of vesting is irrelevant." J. Calamari & J. Perillo, Contracts § 17-11, at 715 (3d ed.1987). Before proceeding, then, we must determine in this case what rights the plaintiffs are asserting under Agreement II, and whether Engelhaupt and Etheridge attempted to vary or discharge those rights.

The plaintiffs here are asserting third-party beneficiary rights in Agreement II. In particular, they claim that they are the beneficiaries of Engelhaupt's promise in Agreement II "to assume" one-half of Etheridge's obligation to pay the plaintiffs under Agreement I and Note I. This assumption by Engelhaupt of one-half of Etheridge's obligation to pay is a classic example of a delegation. Unlike an assignment, which involves only a transfer of rights, a delegation involves the appointment of another to perform one's duties. See In re Marriage of LaShelle, 213 Ill.App.3d 730, 735, 157 Ill.Dec. 726, 572 N.E.2d 1190 (1991) ("Rights are assigned; duties are delegated"); J. Calamari & J. Perillo, Contracts § 18-1, at 722 (3d ed.1987). When a duty is delegated, the delegating party continues to remain liable for performance. See J. Calamari & J. Perillo, Contracts § 18-25, at 757 (3d ed.1987). The effects of this delegation are as follows: Etheridge remains liable to the plaintiffs under Agreement I and Note I, while Engelhaupt is liable to the plaintiffs under the third-party beneficiary theory. The plaintiffs therefore have a claim against both Etheridge and Engelhaupt, but are entitled to only one satisfaction. See J. Calamari & J. Perillo, Contracts § 18-26, at 758 (3d ed.1987). Thus, in count V, the plaintiffs are asserting their rights as third-party beneficiaries to payment from Engelhaupt, as provided for in Agreement II.

The next inquiry is whether Engelhaupt and Etheridge attempted to modify or discharge the plaintiffs' rights to payment as provided for in Agreement II. The undisputed facts show that Etheridge, after entering into Agreement II and Note II with Engelhaupt, later assigned all his interest in Agreement II and Note II over to Princeton Bank as collateral security for another debt. As Etheridge's assignee, Princeton Bank stood in Etheridge's shoes, thereby obtaining no better rights than those Etheridge had. See Wetherell v. Thirty-First Street Building & Loan Ass'n, 153 Ill. 361, 365, 39 N.E. 143 (1894); U.S. Air, Inc. v. Prestige Tours, Inc., 159 Ill.App.3d 150, 155, 111 Ill.Dec. 164, 512 N.E.2d 68 (1987) ("It is hornbook law that an assignee stands in the shoes of the assignor and can enforce only those claims that the assignor could enforce"). Engelhaupt and Princeton Bank then entered into yet another agreement, Agreement III. Under the terms of Agreement III, Engelhaupt agreed to satisfy the remaining indebtedness due on Note II, by paying $83,385 to Princeton

Bank, and Princeton Bank agreed that this payment constituted full payment of Note II. Engelhaupt also paid Princeton Bank an extra $100 and, in exchange, Princeton Bank assigned to Engelhaupt all the Bank's interest in Agreement II. We find that, through these actions, Engelhaupt and Etheridge's assignee did attempt to discharge the plaintiffs' rights to payment as beneficiaries of Agreement II and Note II. Etheridge's assignee claimed Engelhaupt's payments for itself, while purporting to modify and discharge the plaintiffs' rights to those payments. Indeed, Engelhaupt's constant assertion throughout these proceedings has been that the above actions constitute a discharge, by satisfaction, of all his obligations under Agreement II and Note II. The vesting doctrine therefore applies because Engelhaupt and Etheridge's assignee purported to discharge the plaintiffs' rights to payment under Agreement II and Note II.

We now turn to the primary issue in this case: how vesting should be defined in this context. The plaintiffs urge application of the vesting rule declared in Bay. Engelhaupt, on the other hand, asks us to apply the vesting rule set forth in section 311 of the Second Restatement of Contracts.

In Bay, 112 Ill. 91, 1 N.E. 340, Williams sold land to Newman and Sissons in exchange for a down payment and promissory notes payable in installments. Newman and Sissons then sold the land to Bay. The deed tendered to Bay contained an express promise by Bay to pay the balance due on the promissory notes executed by Williams and Newman and Sissons. Bay later obtained a release of his obligation to pay Williams from Sissons. Newman went bankrupt without giving Bay a release. Williams exercised her power of foreclosure and sold the land, but was left being owed $3,559 on the notes. She sued Bay for that amount as third-party beneficiary of the deed between Newman and Sissons and Bay.

Bay argued that he was absolved from his promise to pay the promissory notes by Sissons' release. He proposed three different theories: (1) that third-party beneficiary rights do not vest until suit is brought; (2) that third-party beneficiary rights do not vest until the beneficiary relies upon or accepts the promisor's promise; and (3) that the promisor's promise to pay is a mere indemnity, which cannot be reached until the promisee is insolvent or on some other equitable ground. This court in Bay rejected these views, holding:

> [The promisor's] promise invests the person for whose use it is made with an immediate interest and right, as though the promise had been made to him. This being true, the person who procures the promise has no legal right to release or discharge the person who made the promise, from his liability to the beneficiary. Having the right, it is under the sole control of the person for whose benefit it is made,-as much so as if made directly to him. Bay, 112 Ill. at 97, 1 N.E. 340.

Consequently, Bay established the rule in Illinois that third-party beneficiary rights vest immediately and cannot be altered or extinguished through a later agreement of the original parties to the contract, unless the beneficiary assents.

Engelhaupt urges us to replace the Bay rule with the "modern view" as set forth in section 311 of the Second Restatement. Section 311, entitled "Variation of a Duty to a Beneficiary," stands in direct contrast to Bay. It provides that, in the absence of language in a contract making the rights of a third-party beneficiary irrevocable, the parties to the contract "retain power to discharge or modify the duty by subsequent agreement," without the third-party beneficiary's assent, at any time until the third-party beneficiary, without notice of the discharge or modification, materially changes position in justifiable reliance on the promise, brings suit on the promise or manifests assent to the promise at the request of the promisor or promisee. Restatement (Second) of Contracts § 311 (1981).

Section 311 now represents the majority view on the subject of vesting. Karo v. San Diego Symphony Orchestra Ass'n, 762 F.2d 819 (9th Cir.1985) (applying California law); see, e.g., Bridgman v. Curry, 398 N.W.2d 167 (Iowa 1986); Detroit Bank & Trust Co. v. Chicago Flame Hardening Co., 541 F.Supp. 1278 (N.D.Ind.1982) (applying Indiana law); see also 17A Am.Jur.2d Contracts § 461, at 482-83 (2d ed.1991) (and cases cited therein); 17A C.J.S. Contracts § 373 (1963). In contrast, the immediate vesting rule as set forth in Bay represents the minority view, followed by only a handful of states. See 17A Am.Jur.2d Contracts § 461, at 483 (2d ed.1991) (and cases cited therein).

Engelhaupt maintains that we should adopt section 311. He asserts that section 311 represents the majority rule on vesting because it better conforms to modern commercial practices and general principles of contract law. According to Engelhaupt, parties should remain free to modify or discharge their contracts as they see fit, without the assent of a third-party beneficiary, subject only to the three exceptions provided for in section 311. Section 311 makes sense, Engelhaupt contends, because third-party beneficiaries should not be able to enforce contracts for which they do not give any consideration, unless they demonstrate some detriment or act of faith in reliance on the contract.

Engelhaupt asserts that the superiority of the Restatement approach over the Bay rule is demonstrated by the facts present in this case. As he explains, the plaintiffs here freely chose to extend credit to Etheridge, who was then bound to pay them under Agreement I and Note I. Etheridge and Engelhaupt then freely contracted with each other that Engelhaupt would make one-half of Etheridge's payments to the plaintiffs, in Agreement II and Note II. The plaintiffs, however, were not bound to accept Engelhaupt's promise to pay in Agreement II and Note II in replacement of Etheridge's promise to pay in Agreement I and Note I, and did not do so. Consequently, the plaintiffs' contractual remedies against Etheridge in the event of Etheridge's nonpayment under Agreement I remained intact. Engelhaupt asserts that, in this situation, he and Etheridge should not be forever barred from modifying or discharging their agreement without the plaintiffs' assent, which is precisely what Bay mandates. Rather, Engelhaupt asserts, the third-party beneficiary plaintiffs should be found to have obtained vested rights in his and Etheridge's contract only if they meet one of the circumstances set forth in section 311.

Finding Engelhaupt's arguments persuasive, we hereby adopt the vesting rule set forth in section 311 of the Second Restatement. The rationale underlying section 311's vesting rule is that "parties to a contract should remain free to amend or rescind their agreement so long as there is no detriment to a third party who has provided no consideration for the benefit received." Board of Education of Community School District No. 220 v. Village of Hoffman Estates, 126 Ill.App.3d 625, 628, 81 Ill.Dec. 942, 467 N.E.2d 1064 (1984). This rationale is compelling. Moreover, we find this rationale to be consistent with the general principles running throughout contract law. Contract law generally favors the freedom to contract. Contract law also allows for equitable remedies where the facts compel such a result.

In contrast, the immediate vesting rule of Bay curtails the freedom to contract. It provides, in essence, that every promise which benefits a third-party beneficiary carries with it another term, implied at law, that the parties to the contract are prohibited from modifying or discharging the promise that benefits the beneficiary, without the beneficiary's assent. We do not believe that the modern law of contracts should always imply such a term. To do so can work a great injustice upon the parties involved in a particular case. Although, as the plaintiffs contend, the Bay rule is clear and easy to apply, this does not persuade us to retain it. Our concern is that the rule of law we expound best serves the pursuit of justice, not that it is the easiest rule of law for courts to apply.

We note, moreover, that the plaintiffs' argument against adoption of the Restatement rule is not persuasive. They maintain that the Restatement position has fluctuated so much over the past century that it is not stable. We do not agree with this characterization. In fact, the Restatement position regarding creditor beneficiaries, such as the plaintiffs, is essentially the same as it has always been. Under the original Restatement, the rights of creditor beneficiaries vested once the beneficiary brought suit or otherwise materially changed position in reliance on the promise. Restatement of Contracts §§ 142, 143 (1932). Today, creditor beneficiaries are called intended beneficiaries, and their rights vest once the beneficiary brings suit on the promise, materially changes position in justifiable reliance on the promise or manifests assent to the promise at the request of the promisor or promisee. Restatement (Second) of Contracts §§ 302, 311 (1981). As to donee beneficiaries, the original Restatement provided that their rights vested immediately. Restatement of Contracts §§ 142, 143 (1932). This was changed after substantial criticism. See J. Calamari & J. Perillo, Contracts § 17-9, at 626 (2d ed.1979). Now donee beneficiaries are also classified as intended beneficiaries, and their rights vest as in the same manner stated above. Restatement (Second) of Contracts §§ 302, 311 (1981). Even were we to agree with the plaintiffs' characterization of the Restatement view as unstable, however, this would not impact our decision. We find the current Restatement position on vesting to be consistent with general principles underlying contract law. This court is free to reject any later revisions of the Restatement.

In conclusion, we adopt the vesting rule set forth in section 311 of the Second Restatement. Bay is hereby overruled. The circuit court awarded summary judgment to the plaintiffs based on the Bay rule. The circuit court did not consider the plaintiffs' motion for summary judgment in the context of the vesting rule of section 311. We therefore reverse this award of summary judgment for the plaintiffs and remand to the circuit court for further proceedings, consistent with section 311's vesting rule.

The plaintiffs contend, however, that reversal is not warranted because, even applying section 311, summary judgment in their favor was proper. According to the plaintiffs, they materially changed their position to their detriment in justifiable reliance on Agreement II, brought timely suit on Agreement II, and appropriately manifested their assent to Agreement II. The plaintiffs certainly are entitled to raise these arguments on remand. If, on remand, the plaintiffs establish any of these facts, then their rights have vested under section 311. These arguments, however, provide us with no basis to affirm the summary judgment awarded to the plaintiffs based on Bay. Engelhaupt must be given the opportunity to present facts and argument pertinent to section 311's application.

The plaintiffs also assert that it is inequitable to apply section 311 to their case. They ask us to "fashion an appropriate decree in equity . . . that leaves to them, without further delay or expense, the benefits of Bay." They assert that it is inequitable for this court to prolong these proceedings by changing the law applicable to their case. They further assert that they have "clean hands," while Engelhaupt, Etheridge, and Princeton Bank do not.

We do not agree with the plaintiffs that it is inequitable to apply section 311's vesting rule to their case. As we explained above, section 311 is superior to the Bay rule precisely because it allows for consideration of the particular facts involved in a situation. We note, moreover, that it remains to be determined in this case who has clean hands and who does not. Consequently, this request is denied. . . .

CONCLUSION

For the reasons stated, the appellate court's affirmance of the circuit court's award of summary judgment for the plaintiffs and against Engelhaupt based on *Bay* is reversed. The remainder of the appellate court's rulings are affirmed. The circuit court's award of summary judgment for the plaintiffs and against Engelhaupt is reversed. The circuit court's denial of relief on Engelhaupt's third-party complaint against Princeton Bank is affirmed. Lastly, the circuit court's award of summary judgment to Princeton Bank on its counterclaim against Engelhaupt is affirmed. This cause is remanded to the circuit court of Bureau County for further proceedings not inconsistent with this opinion.

Appellate court judgment affirmed in part and reversed in part; circuit court judgment affirmed in part and reversed in part; cause remanded.

NOTES AND QUESTIONS:

1. As noted in *Olson v. Etheridge*, 686 N.E.2d 563 (1997), third party beneficiary rights stem from the contract itself; thus, the beneficiary is subject to all defenses that the promisor could have asserted against the promisee if the promisee sued on the contract. Restatement (Second) of Contracts § 309 (1981) echoes this same principle by specifying that the beneficiary is subject to the same infirmities as the promisee.

2. Whether and when a third party beneficiary's rights under the contract vests determines whether the original parties can adversely impact the rights of the beneficiary by modifying or discharging their contractual obligations without the consent of the beneficiary. Both *Olson v. Etheridge*, 686 N.E.2d 563 (1997), and *Board of Education of Community School Dist. No. 220 v. Village of Hoffman Estates*, 467 N.E.2d 1064 (1984), embraced the rule as set forth in Restatement (Second) of Contracts § 311 (Variation of a Duty to a Beneficiary) (1981) requiring some indicia of detriment to the beneficiary prior to notice of the alleged discharge or modification.

SECTION 2. ASSIGNMENT AND DELAGATION

You cannot escape the responsibility of tomorrow by evading it today.[*]

Abraham Lincoln

A. GENERALLY

This chapter deals with additional situations involving strangers to the original contract. However, unlike third party beneficiaries, in this chapter the strangers will be introduced after the original contract is made.

Under what circumstances is a party entitled to enforce his contract against someone with whom he has no privity? Similarly, is a party to a contract required to perform its contractual duties to someone other than the party with whom he contracted? Finally, when one of the original parties subsequently transfers his duties to another, is the original party still liable to the other contracting party for any nonperformance? These are some of the questions that will be explored in the assignments and delegations material.

When one of the original contracting parties purports to transfer his right to receive benefits under the contract to a stranger to the original transaction, this is referred to as an *assignment*. In this case, the original contracting party transferring his rights is the *assignor*; the stranger to whom he transfers such rights is the *assignee*; and the other original contracting party that now owes a duty to the stranfer is the *obligor*.

However, when one of the original contracting parties purports to transfer his duty to perform some aspect of the contract to a stranger to the original transaction, this is called a *delegation*. Here, the original contracting party delegating his duty to another is the *delegator*; the stranger to whom he delegates such duty is the *delegatee*; and the other original contracting party that now is entitled to performance from the stranger is the *obligee*.

As you review the following material, you will notice various references to U.C.C. Article 9. Although that article generally applies to secured transactions, it also governs many commercial assignments of rights to payment.[1]

---

[*] Abraham Lincoln (1809 - 1865).

[1] U.C.C. § 9-102(a)(2) and §§ 9-109(a), (d).

1. GENERAL EFFECT OF ASSIGNMENT AND DELEGATION

MACKE CO. V. PIZZA OF GAITHERSBURG, INC.
Court of Appeals of Maryland
270 A.2d 645 (1970).

SINGLEY, Judge.

The appellees and defendants below, Pizza of Gaithersburg, Inc.; Pizzeria, Inc.; The Pizza Pie Corp., Inc. and Pizza Oven, Inc., four corporations under the common ownership of Sidney Ansell, Thomas S. Sherwood and Eugene Early and the same individuals as partners or proprietors (the Pizza Shops) operated at six locations in Montgomery and Prince George's Counties. The appellees had arranged to have installed in each of their locations cold drink vending machines owned by Virginia Coffee Service, Inc., and on 30 December 1966, this arrangement was formalized at five of the locations, by contracts for terms of one year, automatically renewable for a like term in the absence of 30 days' written notice. A similar contract for the sixth location, operated by Pizza of Gaithersburg, Inc., was entered into on 25 July 1967.

On 30 December 1967, Virginia's assets were purchased by The Macke Company (Macke) and the six contracts were assigned to Macke by Virginia. In January, 1968, the Pizza Shops attempted to terminate the five contracts having the December anniversary date, and in February, the contract which had the July anniversary date.

Macke brought suit in the Circuit Court for Montgomery County against each of the Pizza Shops for damages for breach of contract. From judgments for the defendants, Macke has appealed.

The lower court based the result which it reached on two grounds: first, that the Pizza Shops, when they contracted with Virginia, relied on its skill, judgment and reputation, which made impossible a delegation of Virginia's duties to Macke; and second, that the damages claimed could not be shown with reasonable certainty. These conclusions are challenged by Macke.

In the absence of a contrary provision-and there was none here-rights and duties under an executory bilateral contract may be assigned and delegated, subject to the exception that duties under a contract to provide personal services may never be delegated, nor rights be assigned under a contract where delectus personae was an ingredient of the bargain.[1] 4 Corbin on Contracts § 865 (1951) at 434; 6 Am.Jur.2d, Assignments s 11 (1963) at 196. Crane Ice Cream Co. v. Terminal Freezing & Heating Co., 147 Md. 588, 128 A. 280 (1925) held that the right of an individual to purchase ice under a contract which by its terms reflected a knowledge of the individual's needs and reliance on his credit and responsibility could not be assigned to the corporation which purchased his bursiness. In Eastern Advertising Co. v. McGaw & Co., 89 Md. 72, 42 A. 923 (1899), our predecessors held that

[1] Like all generalizations, this one is subject to an important exception. Uniform Commercial Code § 9-318 makes ineffective a term in any contract prohibiting the assignment of a contract right: i. e., a right to payment. Compare Restatement, Contracts § 151(c) (1932).

an advertising agency could not delegate its duties under a contract which had been entered into by an advertiser who had relied on the agency's skill, judgment and taste.

The six machines were placed on the appellees' premises under a printed "Agreement-Contract" which identified the "customer," gave its place of business, described the vending machine, and then provided:

TERMS

1. The Company will install on the Customer's premises the above listed equipment and will maintain the equipment in good operating order and stocked with merchandise.

2. The location of this equipment will be such as to permit accessibility to persons desiring use of same. This equipment shall remain the property of the Company and shall not be moved from the location at which installed, except by the Company.

3. For equipment requiring electrity and water, the Customer is responsible for electrical receptacle and water outlet within ten (10) feet of the equipment location. The Customer is also responsible to supply the Electrical Power and Water needed.

4. The Customer will exercise every effort to protect this equipment from abuse or damage.

5. The Company will be responsible for all licenses and taxes on the equipment and sale of products.

6. This Agreement-Contract is for a term of one (1) year from the date indicated herein and will be automatically renewed for a like period, unless thirty (30) day written notice is given by either party to terminate service.

7. Commission on monthly sales will be paid by the Company to the Customer at the following rate: . . . .

The rate provided in each of the agreements was "30% of Gross Receipts to $300.00 monthly (,) 35% over ($)300.00," except for the agreement with Pizza of Gaithersburg, Inc., which called for "40% of Gross Receipts."

We cannot regard the agreements as contracts for personal services. They were either a license or concession granted Virginia by the appellees, or a lease of a portion of the appellees' premises, with Virginia agreeing to pay a percentage of gross sales as a license or concession fee or as rent, see Charlotte Coca-Cola Bottling Co. v. Shaw, 232 N.C. 307, 59 S.E.2d 819 (1950) and Herbert's Laurel-Ventura, Inc. v. Laurel Ventura Holding Corp., 58 Cal.App.2d 684, 138 P.2d 43, 46-47 (1943), and were assignable by Virginia unless they imposed on Virginia duties of a personal or unique character which could not be delegated, S

& L Vending Corp. v. 52 Thompkins Ave. Restaurant, Inc., 26 A.D.2d 935, 274 N.Y.S.2d 697 (1966).

The appellees earnestly argue that they had dealt with Macke before and had chosen Virginia because they preferred the way it conducted its business. Specifically, they say that service was more personalized, since the president of Virginia kept the machines in working order, that commissions were paid in cash, and that Virginia permitted them to keep keys to the machines so that minor adjustments could be made when needed. Even if we assume all this to be true, the agreements with Virginia were silent as to the details of the working arrangements and contained only a provision requiring Virginia to "install . . . the above listed equipment and . . . maintain the equipment in good operating order and stocked with merchandise." We think the Supreme Court of California put the problem of personal service in proper focus a century ago when it upheld the assignment of a contract to grade a San Francisco street:

> All painters do not paint portraits like Sir Joshua Reynolds, nor landscapes like Claude Lorraine, nor do all writers write dramas like Shakespeare or fiction like Dickens. Rare genius and extraordinary skill are not transferable, and contracts for their employment are therefore personal, and cannot be assigned. But rare genius and extraordinary skill are not indispensable to the workmanlike digging down of a sand hill or the filling up of a depression to a given level, or the construction of brick sewers with manholes and covers, and contracts for such work are not personal, and may be assigned. Taylor v. Palmer, 31 Cal. 240 at 247-248 (1866).

See also Devlin v. Mayor, Aldermen and Commonalty of the City of New York, 63 N.Y. 8, at 17 (1875). Moreover, the difference between the service the Pizza Shops happened to be getting from Virginia and what they expected to get from Macke did not mount up to such a material change in the performance of obligations under the agreements as would justify the appellees' refusal to recognize the assignment. Crane Ice Cream Co. v. Terminal Freezing & Heating Co., supra, 147 Md. 588, 128 A. 280.

In support of the proposition that the agreements were for personal services, and not assignable, the Pizza Shops rely on three Supreme Court cases, Burck v. Taylor, 152 U.S. 634, 14 S.Ct. 696, 38 L.Ed. 578 (1894); Delaware County Comm'r v. Diebold Safe & Lock Co., 133 U.S. 473, 10 S.Ct. 399, 33 L.Ed. 674 (1890); and Arkansas Valley Smelting Co. v. Belden Mining Co., 127 U.S. 379, 8 S.Ct. 1308, 32 L.Ed. 246 (1888), all of which were cited with approval by our predecessors in Tarr v. Veasey, 125 Md. 199, 207, 93 A. 428 (1915). We find none of these cases persuasive. Burck held that the contractor for the state capitol in Texas, who was prohibited by the terms of his contract from assigning it without the state's consent, could not make a valid assignment of his right to receive three-fourths of the proceeds. In Delaware County, Diebold Safe and Lock, which was a subcontractor in the construction of a county jail, was barred from recovering from the county commissioners for its work on the theory that there had been a partial assignment of the construction contract by the prime contractor, which had never been assented to by the commissioners. This result must be limited to the facts: i. e., to the subcontractor's right to recover under the assignment, and not to the contractor's right to delegate. See Taylor v. Palmer and Devlin v. Mayor, Aldermen and Commonalty of the City of New York, both supra. Arkansas Valley, which held invalid an attempt to assign a contract for the purchase of ore, is clearly distinguishable, because of a contract provision which stipulated that payment for the ore was to be made after delivery, based on an assay to be made by the individual purchaser named in the contract. The court concluded that this was a confidence imposed in the individual purchaser's credit and responsibility and that his rights under the contract could not be transferred to another. Tarr v. Veasey involved a situation where duties were delegated to one person and rights assigned to another and our predecessors held the rights not to be assignable, because of the parties' intention that duties and rights were interdependent.

We find more apposite two cases which were not cited by the parties. In The British Waggon Co. & The Parkgate Waggon Co. v. Lea & Co., 5 Q.B.D. 149 (1880), Parkgate Waggon Company, a lessor of railway cars, who had agreed to keep the cars "in good and substantial repair and working order," made an assignment of the contract to British Waggon Company. When British Waggon Company sued for rent, the lessee contended that the assignment had terminated the lease. The court held that the lessee remained bound under the lease, because there was no provision making performance of the lessor's duty to keep in repair a duty personal to it or its employees.

Except for the fact that the result has been roundly criticized, see Corbin, supra, at 448-49, the Pizza Shops might have found some solace in the facts found in Boston Ice Co. v. Potter, 123 Mass. 28 (1877). There, Potter, who had dealt with the Boston Ice Company, and found its service unsatisfactory, transferred his business to Citizens' Ice Company. Later, Citizens' sold out to Boston, unbeknown to Potter, and Potter was served by Boston for a full year. When Boston attempted to collect its ice bill, the Massachusetts court sustained Potter's demurrer on the ground that there was no privity of contract, since Potter had a right to choose with whom he would deal and could not have another supplier thrust upon him. Modern authorities do not support this result, and hold that, absent provision to the contrary, a duty may be delegated, as distinguished from a right which can be assigned, and that the promisee cannot rescind, if the quality of the performance remains materially the same.

Restatement, Contracts § 160(3) (1932) reads, in part:

> Performance or offer of performance by a person delegated has the same legal effect as performance or offer of performance by the person named in the contract, unless,
>
> (a) performance by the person delegated varies or would vary materially from performance by the person named in the contract as the one to perform, and there has been no . . . assent to the delegation . . . .

In cases involving the sale of goods, the Restatement rule respecting delegation of duties has been amplified by Uniform Commercial Code § 2-210(5), Maryland Code (1957, 1964 Repl.Vol.) Art 95B § 2-210(5), which permits a promisee to demand assurances from the party to whom duties have been delegated. See also, "The Uniform Commercial Code and Contract Law: Some Selected Problems," 105 U. of Pa.L.R. 837, at 913-16 (1957); Noblett v. General Electric Credit Corp., 400 F.2d 442 (10th Cir., 1968), cert. denied 393 U.S. 935, 89 S.Ct. 295, 21 L.Ed.2d 271 (1968).

As we see it, the delegation of duty by Virginia to Macke was entirely permissible under the terms of the agreements. In so holding, we do not put ourselves at odds with Eastern Advertising Co. v. McGaw, supra, 89 Md. 72, 42 A. 923. for in that case, the agreement with the agency contained a provision that "the advertising cards were to be subject to the approval of Eastern Advertising Company as to style and contents," at 82, 42 A. at 923, which the court found to import that reliance was being placed on the agency's skill, judgment and taste, at 88, 42 A. 923. . . .

Judgment reversed as to liability; judgment entered for appellant for costs, on appeal and below; case remanded for a new trial on the question of damages.

SALLY BEAUTY CO., INC. V. NEXXUS PRODUCTS, INC.
United States Court of Appeals, Seventh Circuit
801 F.2d 1001 (1986).

CUDAHY, Circuit Judge.

Nexxus Products Company ("Nexxus") entered into a contract with Best Barber & Beauty Supply Company, Inc. ("Best"), under which Best would be the exclusive distributor of Nexxus hair care products to barbers and hair stylists throughout most of Texas. When Best was acquired by and merged into Sally Beauty Company, Inc. ("Sally Beauty"), Nexxus cancelled the agreement. Sally Beauty is a wholly-owned subsidiary of Alberto-Culver Company ("Alberto-Culver"), a major manufacturer of hair care products and a competitor of Nexxus'. Sally Beauty claims that Nexxus breached the contract by cancelling; Nexxus asserts by way of defense that the contract was not assignable or, in the alternative, not assignable to Sally Beauty. The district court granted Nexxus' motion for summary judgment, ruling that the contract was one for personal services and therefore not assignable. We affirm on a different theory-that this contract could not be assigned to the wholly-owned subsidiary of a direct competitor under section 2-210 of the Uniform Commercial Code.

I.

Only the basic facts are undisputed and they are as follows. Prior to its merger with Sally Beauty, Best was a Texas corporation in the business of distributing beauty and hair care products to retail stores, barber shops and beauty salons throughout Texas. Between March and July 1979, Mark Reichek, Best's president, negotiated with Stephen Redding, Nexxus' vice-president, over a possible distribution agreement between Best and Nexxus. Nexxus, founded in 1979, is a California corporation that formulates and markets hair care products. Nexxus does not market its products to retail stores, preferring to sell them to independent distributors for resale to barbers and beauticians. On August 2, 1979, Nexxus executed a distributorship agreement with Best, in the form of a July 24, 1979 letter from Reichek, for Best, to Redding, for Nexxus:

Dear Steve:

It was a pleasure meeting with you and discussing the distribution of Nexus [sic] Products. The line is very exciting and we feel we can do a substantial job with it-especially as the exclusive distributor in Texas (except El Paso).

If I understand the pricing structure correctly, we would pay $1.50 for an item that retails for $5.00 (less 50%, less 40% off retail), and Nexus will pay the freight charges regardless of order size. This approach to pricing will enable us to price the items in the line in such a way that they will be attractive and profitable to the salons.

Your offer of assistance in promoting the line seems to be designed to simplify the introduction of Nexus Products into the Texas market. It indicates a sincere desire on your part to assist your distributors. By your agreeing to underwrite the cost of training and maintaining a qualified technician in our territory, we should be able to introduce the line from a position of strength. I am sure you will let us know at least 90 days in advance should you want to change this arrangement.

By offering to provide us with the support necessary to conduct an annual seminar (ie. mailers, guest artisit [sic]) at your expense, we should be able to reenforce our position with Nexus users and introduce the product line to new customers in a professional manner.

To satisfy your requirement of assured payment for merchandise received, each of our purchase orders will be accompanied by a Letter of Credit that will become negotiable when we receive the merchandise. I am sure you will agree that this arrangement is fairest for everybody concerned.

While we feel confident that we can do an outstanding job with the Nexus line and that the volume we generate will adequately compensate you for your continued support, it is usually best to have an understanding should we no longer be distributing Nexus Products-either by our desire or your request. Based on our discussions, cancellation or termination of Best Barber & Beauty Supply Co., Inc. as a distributor can only take place on the anniversary date of our original appointment as a distributor-and then only with 120 days prior notice. If Nexus terminates us, Nexus will buy back all of our inventory at cost and will pay the freight charges on the returned merchandise.

Steve, we feel that the Nexus line is exciting and very promotable. With the program outlined in this letter, we feel it can be mutually profitable and look forward to a long and successful business relationship. If you agree that this letter contains the details of our understanding regarding the distribution of

Nexus Products, please sign the acknowledgment below and return one copy of this letter to me.

Very truly yours,

/s/ Mark E. Reichek

President

Acknowledged /s/ Stephen Redding Date 8/2/79.

In July 1981 Sally Beauty acquired Best in a stock purchase transaction and Best was merged into Sally Beauty, which succeeded to Best's rights and interests in all of Best's contracts. Sally Beauty, a Delaware corporation with its principal place of business in Texas, is a wholly-owned subsidiary of Alberto-Culver. Sally Beauty, like Best, is a distributor of hair care and beauty products to retail stores and hair styling salons. Alberto-Culver is a major manufacturer of hair care products and, thus, is a direct competitor of Nexxus in the hair care market.[1]

Shortly after the merger, Redding met with Michael Renzulli, president of Sally Beauty, to discuss the Nexxus distribution agreement. After the meeting, Redding wrote Renzulli a letter stating that Nexxus would not allow Sally Beauty, a wholly-owned subsidiary of a direct competitor, to distribute Nexxus products:

> As we discussed in New Orleans, we have great reservations about allowing our NEXXUS Products to be distributed by a company which is, in essence, a direct competitor. We appreciate your argument of autonomy for your business, but the fact remains that you are totally owned by Alberto-Culver.
>
> Since we see no way of justifying this conflict, we cannot allow our products to be distributed by Sally Beauty Company.

In August 1983 Sally Beauty commenced this action by filing a complaint in the Northern District of Illinois, claiming that Nexxus had . . . breached the distribution agreement. . . . Nexxus filed a motion for summary judgment on the breach of contract claim. . . .

The district court . . . granted Nexxus' motion for summary judgment. . . .

II.

Sally Beauty's breach of contract claim alleges that by acquiring Best, Sally Beauty succeeded to all of Best's rights and obligations under the distribution agreement. It further alleges that Nexxus breached the agreement by failing to give Sally Beauty 120 days notice prior to terminating the agreement and by terminating it on other than an anniversary date of

[1] The appellant does not appear to dispute the proposition that Alberto-Culver is Nexxus' direct competitor, see Reply Brief at 8-10; rather it disagrees only with Nexxus' contention that performance by Sally Beauty would necessarily be unacceptable. See infra.

its formation . . . . Nexxus, in its motion for summary judgment, argued that the distribution agreement it entered into with Best was a contract for personal services, based upon a relationship of personal trust and confidence between Reichek and the Redding family. As such, the contract could not be assigned to Sally without Nexxus' consent.

In opposing this motion Sally Beauty argued that the contract was freely assignable because (1) it was between two corporations, not two individuals and (2) the character of the performance would not be altered by the substitution of Sally Beauty for Best. It also argued that "the Distribution Agreement is nothing more than a simple, non-exclusive contract for the distribution of goods, the successful performance of which is in no way dependent upon any particular personality, individual skill or confidential relationship." . . .

In ruling on this motion, the district court framed the issue before it as "whether the contract at issue here between Best and Nexxus was of a personal nature such that it was not assignable without Nexxus' consent." It ruled:

> The court is convinced, based upon the nature of the contract and the circumstances surrounding its formation, that the contract at issue here was of such a nature that it was not assignable without Nexxus's consent. First, the very nature of the contract itself suggests its personal character. A distribution agreement is a contract whereby a manufacturer gives another party the right to distribute its products. It is clearly a contract for the performance of a service. In the court's view, the mere selection by a manufacturer of a party to distribute its goods presupposes a reliance and confidence by the manufacturer on the integrity and abilities of the other party.... In addition, in this case the circumstances surrounding the contract's formation support the conclusion that the agreement was not simply an ordinary commercial contract but was one which was based upon a relationship of personal trust and confidence between the parties. Specifically, Stephen Redding, Nexxus's vice-president, travelled to Texas and met with Best's president personally for several days before making the decision to award the Texas distributorship to Best. Best itself had been in the hair care business for 40 years and its president Mark Reichek had extensive experience in the industry. It is reasonable to conclude that Stephen Redding and Nexxus would want its distributor to be experienced and knowledgeable in the hair care field and that the selection of Best was based upon personal factors such as these. [citations omitted]

The district court also rejected the contention that the character of performance would not be altered by a substitution of Sally Beauty for Best: "Unlike Best, Sally Beauty is a subsidiary of one of Nexxus' direct competitors. This is a significant distinction and in the court's view, it raises serious questions regarding Sally Beauty's ability to perform the distribution agreement in the same manner as Best." . . .

We cannot affirm this summary judgment on the grounds relied on by the district court. . . . Nexxus did not meet its burden on the question of the parties' reasons for entering into this agreement. Although it might be "reasonable to conclude" that Best and Nexxus had based their agreement on "a relationship of personal trust and confidence," and that

Reichek's participation was considered essential to Best's performance, this is a finding of fact. . . . Since the parties submitted conflicting affidavits on this question,[3] the district court erred in relying on Nexxus' view as representing undisputed fact in ruling on this summary judgment motion. . . .[4]

We may affirm this summary judgment, however, on a different ground if it finds support in the record. . . . Sally Beauty contends that the distribution agreement is freely assignable because it is governed by the provisions of the Uniform Commercial Code (the "UCC" or the "Code"), as adopted in Texas. . . . We agree with Sally that the provisions of the UCC govern this contract and for that reason hold that the assignment of the contract by Best to Sally Beauty was barred by the UCC rules on delegation of performance, UCC § 2-210(1) . . . .

III.

The UCC codifies the law of contracts applicable to "transactions in goods." UCC § 2-102, Tex.Bus. & Com.Code Ann. § 2-102 (Vernon 1968). Texas applies the "dominant factor" test to determine whether the UCC applies to a given contract or transaction: was the essence of or dominant factor in the formation of the contract the provision of goods or services? . . . No Texas case addresses whether a distribution agreement is a contract for the sale of goods, but the rule in the majority of jurisdictions is that distributorships (both exclusive and non-exclusive) are to be treated as sale of goods contracts under the UCC. . . .

Several of these courts note that "a distributorship agreement is more involved than a typical sales contract," Quality Performance Lines, 609 P.2d at 1342, but apply the UCC nonetheless because the sales aspect in such a contract is predominant. . . . This is true of the contract at issue here (as embodied in the July 24, 1979 letter from Reichek to Redding). Most of the agreed-to terms deal with Nexxus' sale of its hair care products to Best. We are confident that a Texas court would find the sales aspect of this contract dominant and apply the majority rule that such a distributorship is a contract for "goods" under the UCC.

---

[3] Reichek stated the following in an affidavit submitted in support of Sally Beauty's Memorandum in Opposition to Nexxus' Motion for Summary Judgment:

> At no time prior to the execution of the Distribution Agreement did Steve Redding tell me that he was relying upon my personal peculiar tastes and ability in making his decision to award a Nexxus distributorship to Best. Moreover, I never understood that Steve Redding was relying upon my skill and ability in particular in choosing Best as a distributor. I never considered the Distribution Agreement to be a personal service contract between me and Nexxus or Stephen Redding. I always considered the Distribution Agreement to be between Best and Nexxus as expressly provided in the Distribution Agreement which was written by my brother and me. At all times I conducted business with Nexxus on behalf of Best and not on my own behalf. In that connection, when I sent correspondence to Nexxus, I invariably signed it as president of Best. Neither Stephen Redding nor any other Nexxus employee ever told me that Nexxus was relying on my personal financial integrity in executing the Distribution Agreement or in shipping Nexxus products to Best....

Affidavit of Mark Reichek, ¶¶ 19-21, Appellant's Appendix at 189-190.

[4] It is also possible to read the district court's decision as ruling that all distribution agreements are as a matter of law personal services contracts and therefore nonassignable. For the reasons explained infra, we do not believe that this is an accurate statement of the law.

IV.

The fact that this contract is considered a contract for the sale of goods and not for the provision of a service does not, as Sally Beauty suggests, mean that it is freely assignable in all circumstances. The delegation of performance under a sales contract (whether in conjunction with an assignment of rights, as here, or not) is governed by UCC section 2-210(1), Tex.Bus. & Com.Code § 2-210(a) (Vernon 1968). The UCC recognizes that in many cases an obligor will find it convenient or even necessary to relieve himself of the duty of performance under a contract, see Official Comment 1, UCC § 2-210 ("[T]his section recognizes both delegation of performance and assignability as normal and permissible incidents of a contract for the sale of goods."). The Code therefore sanctions delegation except where the delegated performance would be unsatisfactory to the obligee: "A party may perform his duty through a delegate unless otherwise agreed to or unless the other party has a substantial interest in having his original promisor perform or control the acts required by the contract." UCC § 2-210(1), Tex.Bus. & Com.Code Ann. § 2-210(a) (Vernon 1968). Consideration is given to balancing the policies of free alienability of commercial contracts and protecting the obligee from having to accept a bargain he did not contract for.

We are concerned here with the delegation of Best's duty of performance under the distribution agreement, as Nexxus terminated the agreement because it did not wish to accept Sally Beauty's substituted performance.[6] Only one Texas case has construed section 2-210 in the context of a party's delegation of performance under an executory contract. In McKinnie v. Milford, 597 S.W.2d 953 (Tex.Civ.App.1980, writ ref'd, n.r.e.), the court held that nothing in the Texas Business and Commercial Code prevented the seller of a horse from delegating to the buyer a pre-existing contractual duty to make the horse available to a third party for breeding. "[I]t is clear that Milford [the third party] had no particular interest in not allowing Stewart [the seller] to delegate the duties required by the contract. Milford was only interested in getting his two breedings per year, and such performance could only be obtained from McKinnie [the buyer] after he bought the horse from Stewart." Id. at 957. In McKinnie, the Texas court recognized and applied the UCC rule that bars delegation of duties if there is some reason why the non-assigning party would find performance by a delegate a substantially different thing than what he had bargained for.

In the exclusive distribution agreement before us, Nexxus had contracted for Best's "best efforts" in promoting the sale of Nexxus products in Texas. UCC § 2-306(2), Tex.Bus. & Com.Code Ann. § 2-306(b) (Vernon 1968), states that "[a] lawful agreement by either buyer or seller for exclusive dealing in the kind of goods concerned imposes unless otherwise agreed an obligation by the seller to use best efforts to supply the goods and by the buyer to use best efforts to promote their sale." This implied promise on Best's part was the consideration for Nexxus' promise to refrain from supplying any other distributors within

[6] If this contract is assignable, Sally Beauty would also, of course, succeed to Best's rights under the distribution agreement. But the fact situation before us must be distinguished from the assignment of contract rights that are no longer executory (e.g., the right to damages for breach or the right to payment of an account), which is considered in UCC section 2-210(2), Tex.Bus. & Com.Code Ann. § 2-210(b) (Vernon 1968), and in several of the authorities relied on by appellants. The policies underlying these two situations are different and, generally, the UCC favors assignment more strongly in the latter. See UCC § 2-210(2) (non-executory rights assignable even if agreement states otherwise).

Best's exclusive area. See Official Comment 5, UCC § 2-306. It was this contractual undertaking which Nexxus refused to see performed by Sally.

In ruling on Nexxus' motion for summary judgment, the district court noted: "Unlike Best, Sally Beauty is a subsidiary of one of Nexxus' direct competitors. This is a significant distinction and in the court's view, it raises serious questions regarding Sally Beauty's ability to perform the distribution agreement in the same manner as Best." Memorandum Opinion and Order at 7. In Berliner Foods Corp. v. Pillsbury Co., 633 F.Supp. 557 (D.Md.1986), the court stated the same reservation more strongly on similar facts. Berliner was an exclusive distributor of Haagen-Dazs ice cream when it was sold to Breyer's, manufacturer of a competing ice cream line. Pillsbury Co., manufacturer of Haagen-Dazs, terminated the distributorship and Berliner sued. The court noted, while weighing the factors for and against a preliminary injunction, that "it defies common sense to require a manufacturer to leave the distribution of its products to a distributor under the control of a competitor or potential competitor." Id. at 559-60. We agree with these assessments and hold that Sally Beauty's position as a wholly-owned subsidiary of Alberto-Culver is sufficient to bar the delegation of Best's duties under the agreement.

We do not believe that our holding will work the mischief with our national economy that the appellants predict. We hold merely that the duty of performance under an exclusive distributorship may not be delegated to a competitor in the market place-or the wholly-owned subsidiary of a competitor-without the obligee's consent. We believe that such a rule is consonant with the policies behind section 2-210, which is concerned with preserving the bargain the obligee has struck. Nexxus should not be required to accept the "best efforts" of Sally Beauty when those efforts are subject to the control of Alberto-Culver. It is entirely reasonable that Nexxus should conclude that this performance would be a different thing than what it had bargained for. At oral argument, Sally Beauty argued that the case should go to trial to allow it to demonstrate that it could and would perform the contract as impartially as Best. It stressed that Sally Beauty is a "multi-line" distributor, which means that it distributes many brands and is not just a conduit for Alberto-Culver products. But we do not think that this creates a material question of fact in this case. When performance of personal services is delegated, the trier merely determines that it is a personal services contract. If so, the duty is per se nondelegable. There is no inquiry into whether the delegate is as skilled or worthy of trust and confidence as the original obligor: the delegate was not bargained for and the obligee need not consent to the substitution. And so here: it is undisputed that Sally Beauty is wholly owned by Alberto-Culver, which means that Sally Beauty's "impartial" sales policy is at least acquiesced in by Alberto-Culver-but could change whenever Alberto-Culver's needs changed. Sally Beauty may be totally sincere in its belief that it can operate "impartially" as a distributor, but who can guarantee the outcome when there is a clear choice between the demands of the parent-manufacturer, Alberto-Culver, and the competing needs of Nexxus? The risk of an unfavorable outcome is not one which the law can force Nexxus to take. Nexxus has a substantial interest in not seeing this contract performed by Sally Beauty, which is sufficient to bar the delegation under section 2-210, Tex. Bus. Com. Code Ann. § 2-210 (Vernon 1968). Because Nexxus should not be forced to accept performance of the distributorship agreement by Sally, we hold that the contract was not assignable without Nexxus' consent.

The judgment of the district court is AFFIRMED.

POSNER, Circuit Judge, dissenting.

My brethren have decided, with no better foundation than judicial intuition about what businessmen consider reasonable, that the Uniform Commercial Code gives a supplier an absolute right to cancel an exclusive-dealing contract if the dealer is acquired, directly or indirectly, by a competitor of the supplier. I interpret the Code differently.

Nexxus makes products for the hair and sells them through distributors to hair salons and barbershops. It gave a contract to Best, cancellable on any anniversary of the contract with 120 days' notice, to be its exclusive distributor in Texas. Two years later Best was acquired by and merged into Sally Beauty, a distributor of beauty supplies and wholly owned subsidiary of Alberto-Culver. Alberto-Culver makes "hair care" products, too, though they mostly are cheaper than Nexxus's, and are sold to the public primarily through grocery stores and drugstores. My brethren conclude that because there is at least a loose competitive relationship between Nexxus and Alberto-Culver, Sally Beauty cannot-as a matter of law, cannot, for there has been no trial on the issue-provide its "best efforts" in the distribution of Nexxus products. . . .

My brethren's conclusion that these provisions of the Uniform Commercial Code entitled Nexxus to cancel the contract does not leap out from the language of the provisions or of the contract; so one would expect, but does not find, a canvass of the relevant case law. . . .

. . . So far as appears, the same people who distributed Nexxus's products for Best (except for Best's president) continued to do so for Sally Beauty. Best was acquired, and continues, as a going concern; the corporation was dissolved, but the business wasn't. Whether there was a delegation of performance in any sense may be doubted. . . . The general rule is that a change of corporate form-including a merger-does not in and of itself affect contractual rights and obligations. . . .

The fact that Best's president has quit cannot be decisive on the issue whether the merger resulted in a delegation of performance. The contract between Nexxus and Best was not a personal-services contract conditioned on a particular individual's remaining with Best. . . . If Best had not been acquired, but its president had left anyway, as of course he might have done, Nexxus could not have repudiated the contract.

No case adopts the per se rule that my brethren announce. The cases ask whether, as a matter of fact, a change in business form is likely to impair performance of the contract. . . .

. . . Suppose there had been no merger, but the only child of Best's president had gone to work for Alberto-Culver as a chemist. Could Nexxus have canceled the contract, fearing that Best (perhaps unconsciously) would favor Alberto-Culver products over Nexxus products? That would be an absurd ground for cancellation, and so is Nexxus's actual ground. At most, so far as the record shows, Nexxus may have had grounds for "insecurity" regarding the performance by Sally Beauty of its obligation to use its best efforts to promote Nexxus products, but if so its remedy was not to cancel the contract but to demand assurances of due performance. See UCC § 2-609; Official Comment 5 to § 2-306. No such demand was made. An anticipatory repudiation by conduct requires conduct that makes the repudiating party unable to perform. . . . The merger did not do this. At least there is no evidence it did. The judgment should be reversed and the case remanded for a trial on whether the merger so altered the conditions of performance that Nexxus is entitled to declare the contract broken.

KUNZMAN V. THORSEN
Supreme Court of Oregon
740 P.2d 754 (1987).

CAMPBELL, Justice.

Plaintiffs, vendors on a land sale contract, brought this action for specific performance of the contract against the vendee's assignees. The trial court granted plaintiffs' motion for summary judgment and the Court of Appeals affirmed. . . . We accepted review of this case to consider the circumstances under which the assignees of a vendee's interest in a land sale contract will be held to have assumed the vendee's contract obligations.

The Court of Appeals' summary of the facts reads:

> "In 1977, plaintiffs sold property to David McNabb. Later in the same year, McNabb assigned 'all of [his] right, title and interest' in the property to defendants, with the approval of plaintiffs. After that date, all dealings on the contract were between plaintiffs and defendants; McNabb was no longer involved."
>
> "After the assignment, defendants took possession of the property and exercised exclusive control over it. They alone made payments to plaintiffs under the land sale contract. They mortgaged the land to finance a barn that they had built on it. They rented out pasture, ran cattle on the property, allowed others to run cattle on it and listed it for sale. Pursuant to the terms of the contract, they paid for and received lot releases for certain parcels, which they then sold. In 1979, defendants' attorney threatened plaintiffs with legal action if they did not release deeds to certain parcels in accordance with the contract's lot release provisions."
>
> "In 1984, defendants defaulted, paying neither the annual installment nor the property taxes, and plaintiffs accelerated the contract balance and commenced this action. Defendants contend that the trial court improperly granted summary judgment, because, as assignees of McNabb's rights under the contract, they are not, as a matter of law, obligated on the contract because they did not assume the contract."

The Court of Appeals, relying upon this court's opinion in *Hodges v. Servine,* 211 Or. 428, 316 P.2d 312 (1957), concluded that defendants had impliedly assumed the vendee's contractual duties by "claiming the benefits" of the contract. Defendants argue that their actions did not constitute a claim of contract benefits within the meaning of *Hodges.*

For the reasons set out below, we affirm.

It is well-settled in Oregon that "[e]ither party to a contract for the sale of land generally may have specific performance of the contract." [citation omitted.] A vendor's rights against the assignee of a land sale contract derive from the vendor's status as third party beneficiary to the contract of assignment between the vendee and the vendee's assignee. No independent obligation arises between the vendor and the assignee as a result of the acceptance of contract benefits. The scope of the assignment defines the scope of relief available to the vendor. In essence, the vendor's action is one for specific performance of the assignee's agreement to assume the vendee's duties. *See* 4 Corbin, Contracts 627, § 906 (1964 & Supp 1984).

The dispute in this case is over construction of the instrument of assignment. That instrument conveys to the assignees "all of the vendee's right, title and interest in and to" the land sale contract "and to the real estate described therein." The issue is whether this broad and inclusive language was intended by the parties to impose upon the assignees duties of performance under the original contract. As one treatise has stated:

> "If the words of the assignment transaction clearly purport to do nothing but transfer to the assignee the assignor's right against the third party, interpretation is simple. The same is true if the assignee's words are clearly promissory. The difficulty exists in those cases in which the parties make no clear analysis and do not differentiate in terms between rights and duties; and the assignor purports to assign the "contract" or all of his "right and title to the contract." If the contract is still bilateral in character, so that the assignor has a duty to perform as well as a right to a performance by the third party, interpretation must depend chiefly upon the context and the surrounding circumstances." *Id.* at 628-29, § 906.

In contracts for the sale of goods that ambiguity has been resolved in favor of a presumption that the assignee has assumed the contract duties. ORS 72.2100(4) reads:

> "An assignment of 'the contract' or of 'all my rights under the contract' or an assignment in similar general terms is an assignment of rights and unless the language or the circumstances (as in an assignment for security) indicate the contrary, it is a delegation of performance of the duties of the assignor and its acceptance by the assignee constitutes a promise by the assignee to perform those duties. This promise is enforceable by either the assignor or the other party to the original contract."

The Restatement (Second) of Contracts (and its predecessor, the 1932 Restatement) adopted the same presumption as a general rule of contract construction. Restatement (Second) Contracts § 328 (1981); Restatement Contracts § 164 (1932).[2] The justification

---

[2] Restatement Contracts § 164 (1932) reads:

"(1) Where a party to a bilateral contract which is at the time wholly or partially executory on both sides, purports to assign the whole contract, his action is interpreted, in the absence of circumstances showing a contrary intention, as an assignment of assignor's rights under the contract and a delegation of the assignor's duties."

"(2) Acceptance by the assignee of such an assignment is interpreted, in the absence of circumstances showing a

advanced for this rule is that it most probably conforms to the parties' intent and to their understanding of the meaning of such broad language of assignment. 3 Williston, Contracts 109, § 418A (3d ed 1960); *Langel v. Betz,* 250 N.Y. 159, 162-63, 164 N.E. 890 (1928). However, the Restatement (Second) includes a caveat in which the American Law Institute reserves its opinion as to whether that presumption "applies to an assignment by a purchaser of his rights under a contract for the sale of land." Restatement (Second) Contracts § 328 (1981). The Institute explains this reticence in a comment:

> "When the purchaser under a land contract assigns his rights, the assignment has commonly been treated like a sale of land 'subject to' a mortgage. In this view acceptance of the assignment does not amount to an assumption of the assignor's duties unless the contract of assignment so provides either expressly or by implication. . . . Decisions refusing to infer an assumption of duties by the assignee have been influenced by doctrinal difficulties in the recognition of rights of assignees and beneficiaries. Those difficulties have now been overcome, and it is doubtful whether adherence to such decisions carries out the probable intent of the parties in the usual case. But since the shift in doctrine has not yet produced any definite changes in the body of decisions, the Institute expresses no opinion on the application of Subsection (2) to an assignment by a purchaser under a land contract." Restatement (Second) of Contracts § 328, *comment c* at 46 (1981).

In *Hodges v. Servine, supra,* this court stated the rule of interpretation for use in such cases. The vendee under a land sale contract had assigned the contract to defendants, who took possession of the property and began making payments to plaintiffs. Defendants eventually fell behind in their payments, and the vendors brought an action for strict foreclosure. Defendants answered that plaintiffs had waived strict performance of the payment terms of the contract, breached the contract and repudiated and rescinded the contract. Defendants claimed a lien for the amount of payments received by plaintiffs under the contract and for the value of permanent improvements defendants made on the property. This court affirmed the trial court's judgment for plaintiffs. Among the issues this court addressed was whether defendants were bound by a provision in the contract authorizing attorney fees in the event of a foreclosure. This court concluded:

> "By its decree the court allowed the plaintiffs an attorney's fee in the sum of $500. A provision of the contract authorized such an allowance, but defendants say that this provision is not binding on them because they did

contrary intention, as both an assent to become an assignee of the assignor's rights and as a promise to the assignor to assume the performance of the assignor's duties."

Restatement (Second) Contracts § 328 (1981) reads:
"(1) Unless the language or the circumstances indicate the contrary, as in an assignment for security, an assignment of 'the contract' or of 'all my rights under the contract' or an assignment in similar general terms is an assignment of the assignor's rights and a delegation of his unperformed duties under the contract.
"(2) Unless the language or the circumstances indicate the contrary, the acceptance by an assignee of such an assignment operates as a promise to the assignor to perform the assignor's unperformed duties, and the obligor of the assigned rights is an intended beneficiary of the promise."
"*Caveat:* The Institute expresses no opinion as to whether the rule stated in Subsection (2) applies to an assignment by a purchaser of his rights under a contract for the sale of land."

> not assume the obligations of the contract but merely accepted a bare assignment. The general rule is that the assignee of a contract for the purchase of land or other property assumes no liability to the vendor by reason of the assignment alone. *Urban v. Phy,* [24 F.2d 494 (9th Cir.1928)]; *Coos Bay Wagon Co. v. Crocker,* [4 F. 577, 587 (C.C.Or.1880)]. But 'Where the assignee claims the benefits of the contract he becomes subject to its burdens as fully and to the same extent as though he were the original party to the contract.' 92 CJS 199, Vendor and Purchaser § 311. Without expressing our approval, we take note of the fact that the Restatement of the Law of Contracts, § 164, provides that acceptance by the assignee of an assignment of a bilateral contract which is wholly or partially executory on both sides, 'is interpreted, in the absence of circumstances showing a contrary intention, as both an assent to become an assignee of the assignor's rights and as a promise to the assignor to assume the performance of the assignor's duties.' See the comment on this section in *Langel v. Betz,* 250 N.Y. 159, 164 N.E. 890 [(1928)]. In the present case it is obvious that the assignees are claiming rights under the contract and are therefore charged with the obligations of their assignor, among which is the obligation to pay a reasonable attorney's fee in the event that it should become necessary to bring suit to enforce the provisions of the contract." *Hodges v. Servine, supra,* 211 Or. at 437-38, 316 P.2d 312.

In the instant case the Court of Appeals concluded from this passage that "an assignee may become liable under a contract by engaging in conduct that indicates that he has assumed it." 83 Or.App. at 394, 732 P.2d 49. The court scrutinized defendants' conduct and concluded:

> "The assignees' conduct . . . indicates that they had assumed the contract obligations as well as the rights rising from it. It is undisputed that defendants, in addition to possessing and paying for the property, also demanded and received lot releases pursuant to the contract provisions. Their attorney also threatened to use the courts to enforce the 'Kunzman to Thorsen' contract. We hold that the undisputed facts, as a matter of law, establish that defendants became assuming assignees and are obligated on the contract." 83 Or.App. at 395, 732 P.2d 49.

Defendants argue that their actions did not constitute a claim of the contract's benefits within the meaning of *Hodges,* an argument made possible by the fact that the *Hodges* court did not specify which of the assignees' acts constituted a claim of benefits. Defendants contend that an assignee should be held to have claimed the benefits (and so to have assumed the duties) of a contract only when the assignee has resorted to the courts for relief under the contract. The Court of Appeals disagreed, stating that "[a]lthough bringing an action to enforce a contract is one way to claim its benefits, that is not the exclusive means by which an assignee may become liable." *Id.* Defendants point to the *Hodges* assignees' claim for rescission and to the citation in *Hodges* of the New York case of *Langel v. Betz, supra,* as support for their contention. Our reading of *Langel,* our consideration of the purposes to which it was put by the *Hodges* court and our examination of the other cases in which this court has considered the assumption of contract duties by an assignee on the ground that the assignee accepted the benefits of the contract lead us to agree with the Court of Appeals.

In *Langel v. Betz, supra,* the assignee of a land sale contract requested of the vendors an extension of the date for performance of the contract in order to allow the title company to complete its search and report on the title to the property. The vendors granted this request. However, upon the arrival of the new date for performance, the assignee did not appear. The vendors sought specific performance of the contract against the assignee, arguing that the assignee's request for an extension was an act sufficient to constitute an assumption of the contractual duties. The court recognized that "[t]he assignee may . . . expressly or impliedly, bind himself to perform the assignor's duties," and noted that under its previous decisions "where the assignee of the vendee invokes the aid of a court of equity in an action for specific performance, he impliedly binds himself to perform on his part," but that the converse of this rule, "that the assignee of the vendee would be bound when the vendor began the action," did not follow from those decisions. 250 N.Y. at 162, 164 N.E. 890.

The *Langel* court next discussed and rejected the rule of the first Restatement presuming assumption by the assignee, and it is for this discussion that *Hodges* cites the case. The *Langel* court stated:

> "The proposed change is a complete reversal of our present rule of interpretation as to the probable intention of the parties. It is, perhaps, more in harmony with modern ideas of contractual relations than is 'the archaic view of a contract as creating a strictly personal obligation between the creditor and debtor' (Pollock on Contracts [9th ed.], 232), which prohibited the assignee from suing at law in his own name and which denied a remedy to third party beneficiaries. 'The fountains out of which these resolutions issue' have been broken up if not destroyed (*Seaver v. Ransom,* 224 N.Y. 233, 237 [120 N.E. 639]), but the law remains that no promise of the assignee to assume the assignor's duties is to be inferred from the acceptance of an assignment of a bilateral contract, in the absence of circumstances surrounding the assignment itself which indicate a contrary intention."
> 250 N.Y. at 163-64, 164 N.E. 890.

The court last concluded that because the assignee's request for an extension was not clearly "an assertion of a right" to the extension, the court would reserve consideration of the question of whether a "demand for performance by the vendee's assignee creates a right in the complaining vendor to enforce the contract against him." 250 N.Y. at 165, 164 N.E. 890.

Hodges cites *Betz* not for its tangential reference to the rule of implied assumption where the assignee has sued on the contract, but for its criticism of the Restatement.[3] This court joined the New York court in rejecting the Restatement rule and requiring some objective manifestation of intent to be bound where the words of assignment are

---

3 We note, too, that the claims asserted by the assignees in *Hodges* for recovery of monies paid and improvements made were not dependent upon the existence of the contract and so were not claims of the "benefits of the contract". *See Kneberg v. H.L. Green Co.,* 89 F.2d 100, 104 (7th Cir. 1937).

ambiguous. However, while the New York court declined to consider whether an assertion of a right under the contract might constitute such manifestation, this court held in *Hodges* that a claim of the contract benefits creates a presumption that the assignee assumed the contract obligations.

As we read the opinion in *Hodges,* the court was impressed less with the fact that the assignees sought restitution for their expenditures than with the fact that the assignees took possession of the land and made payments directly to the vendors, behaving generally as if they were party to the original contract. This interpretation of *Hodges* is supported by the only other cases in which this court has determined that acceptance of contract benefits imposed liability upon a contract assignee.

In *Oregon & Western Colonization Co. v. Strang,* 123 Or. 377, 260 P. 1002 (1927), this court considered the issue of whether the assignee of a land sale contract was bound by a provision requiring the vendee to "pay all taxes that may be hereafter levied" on the property. The court stated:

> "Plaintiff claims that defendant Davison, having accepted the assignment of the contract between it and defendant Strang and that contract having provided that vendee Strang should pay the taxes, is bound thereby; *he cannot accept the benefits of said contract without also becoming liable for the obligations.* Plaintiff also claims that the covenant to pay the taxes is a covenant which runs with the land; that defendant Davison having accepted the assignment of contract to purchase said land steps in the place and stead of defendant Strang and is liable to plaintiff to the same extent as his assignor Strang was and is. We think that plaintiff's positions are correct. While the authorities are not uniform we believe that both in reason and by weight of the authorities *defendant Davison became personally liable for the payment of the taxes when he accepted an assignment of the contract, signed the notes given by his assignor Strang to plaintiff and entered into the possession of the land: Corvallis & Alsea R.R. Co. v. Portland E. & E. Ry. Co.,* [84 Or. 524, 534, 163 P. 1173 (1917)]; *Windle v. Hughes,* [40 Or. 1, 5, 65 P. 1058 (1901)]."...
>
> "It is our opinion that the covenant to pay the taxes, which is a part of the contract under which defendant Davison was in possession of the land and enjoyed the benefits thereof, runs with the land: 15 C.J. 1253, § 71." 123 Or. at 382-83, 260 P. 1002 (emphasis added).

In *Miller v. Fernley,* 280 Or. 333, 337, 570 P.2d 1178 (1977), this court cited *Hodges* in holding that an assignee who sold his assigned interest under a separate land sale contract, received payments from his vendee and later defaulted on the payments under the original contract had "assumed the burden of [an attorney fees] provision [in the original contract] since he accepted the benefits of the contract." Because no mention is made of the assertion by the assignee of any claim or counterclaim, it is clear that the court considered the assignee's sale of his interest and his receipt of payments an acceptance of benefits, just as it is clear that the *Strang* court considered the possession of and right to sell the land the "benefits" of the contract.

From this mash of precedent we distill the following principle: An assignee "claims the benefits" of a land sale contract when he or she exercises the rights in the contract's subject matter conferred upon the vendee by the contract. Where a party accepts a broadly worded assignment of a land sale contract, "steps into the shoes" of the assignor and asserts the interests the contract conveys, the presumption arises that the assignee intended also to assume the duties the contract imposes.

Defendants aver that "every assignee, even assignees for security purposes, 'claim the benefits' of contracts assigned to them," and they express concern that the Court of Appeals' decision consequently renders every contract assignee liable for performance of the contract assigned. This concern is unfounded.

Accepting the benefits of a contract does not *impose* liability on an assignee. The *Hodges* rule is a rule of construction only. It considers the probable intent of the parties at the time the assignment was made for the purpose of determining whether expansive words of the assignment imply an assumption of duties by the assignee. Where the parties clearly intend otherwise (as evinced either by the terms of the assignment or by the surrounding circumstances, *e.g.*, an assignment for security), the implication that the assignee assumed the vendor's contractual duties is dispelled.

Defendants further contend that vendees under land sale contracts will be unable to assign their interests in land as freely as mortgagors or grantors of trust deeds, pointing out that holders of those interests can assign their interests in the land "subject to" the mortgage or trust deed. Of course, nothing prevents the parties to an assignment of a vendee's interest in a land sale contract from including such a provision or otherwise limiting the assignee's exposure in the instrument of assignment.

The rule developed in *Hodges, Fernley* and *Strang* is closer to that of the Restatement and the UCC than it is to the probable majority rule on this issue. However, we are not persuaded that a more rigorous test than that adopted in this court's previous decisions is needed to safeguard the interests of the parties to a land sale contract or to its subsequent assignment.

Defendants argue that this case was not appropriately decided by summary judgment because defendants introduced to the trial court "evidence of language and circumstances fairly suggesting an intention not to assume" the contract. Our scrutiny of the affidavit and exhibits introduced by defendants in opposition to plaintiffs' motion reveals no such evidence. Defendants deny having expressly assumed or agreed to assume the contract duties, argue that their situation in this matter was such that they would not have wanted to assume the duties, and maintain that the relative bargaining positions of the parties were such that plaintiffs could have required an express assumption of duties but that the assignor could not. There is no indication that defendants sought affirmatively to disclaim the contract duties or that the understanding of the parties was anything other than that the assignment would affect a delegation and assumption of duties. We agree with the trial judge that this "evidence" was insufficient as a matter of law to dispel the presumption arising from the language of the assignment and the actions of the parties. Even viewed in the light most favorable to the nonmoving party, defendants' submissions to the trial court created no "genuine issue as to any material fact." ORCP 47 C. *See Seeborg v. General*

Motors Corporation, 284 Or. 695, 588 P.2d 1100 (1978).

In this case the trial court and the Court of Appeals properly construed defendants' acts as a claim of the benefits of the land sale contract. The trial court properly concluded that defendants had assumed the duties created by the contract and that summary judgment in favor of plaintiffs was appropriate. We affirm.

NOTES AND QUESTIONS:

1. Generally, the prevailing view regarding assignments and delegations is in line with the U.C.C.'s treatment of such matters. *See* Restatement (Second) of Contracts § 317 and § 318 (1981), reflecting the same view.

2. While adopting the view set forth in the U.C.C. § 2-210(5) and Restatement (Second) of Contracts § 328 regarding the presumption that an assignee's acceptance of rights under a contract obligates him or her to perform the corresponding duties, the *Kunzman* court noted that other jurisdictions diverge from this view. *See e.g.* Langel v. Betz, 164 N.E. 890 (1928).

---

2. MODE OF ASSIGNMENT

HERZOG V. IRACE
Supreme Judicial Court of Maine
594 A.2d 1106 (1991).

BRODY, Justice.

Anthony Irace and Donald Lowry appeal from an order entered by the Superior Court (Cumberland County, Cole, J.) affirming a District Court (Portland, Goranites, J.) judgment in favor of Dr. John P. Herzog in an action for breach of an assignment to Dr. Herzog of personal injury settlement proceeds[1] collected by Irace and Lowry, both attorneys, on behalf of their client, Gary G. Jones. On appeal, Irace and Lowry contend that the District Court erred in finding that the assignment was valid and enforceable against them. They also argue that enforcement of the assignment interferes with their ethical obligations toward their client. Finding no error, we affirm.

The facts of this case are not disputed. Gary Jones was injured in a motorcycle accident and retained Irace and Lowry to represent him in a personal injury action. Soon thereafter, Jones dislocated his shoulder, twice, in incidents unrelated to the motorcycle accident. Dr. Herzog examined Jones's shoulder and concluded that he needed surgery. At the time, however, Jones was unable to pay for the surgery and in consideration for the performance of the surgery by the doctor, he signed a letter dated June 14, 1988, written on Dr. Herzog's letterhead stating:

---

[1] This case involves the assignment of proceeds from a personal injury action, not an assignment of the cause of action itself.

I, Gary Jones, request that payment be made directly from settlement of a claim currently pending for an unrelated incident, to John Herzog, D.O., for treatment of a shoulder injury which occurred at a different time.

Dr. Herzog notified Irace and Lowry that Jones had signed an "assignment of benefits" from the motorcycle personal injury action to cover the cost of surgery on his shoulder and was informed by an employee of Irace and Lowry that the assignment was sufficient to allow the firm to pay Dr. Herzog's bills at the conclusion of the case. Dr. Herzog performed the surgery and continued to treat Jones for approximately one year.

In May, 1989, Jones received a $20,000 settlement in the motorcycle personal injury action. He instructed Irace and Lowry not to disburse any funds to Dr. Herzog indicating that he would make the payments himself. Irace and Lowry informed Dr. Herzog that Jones had revoked his permission to have the bill paid by them directly and indicated that they would follow Jones's directions. Irace and Lowry issued a check to Jones for $10,027 and disbursed the remaining funds to Jones's other creditors. Jones did send a check to Dr. Herzog but the check was returned by the bank for insufficient funds and Dr. Herzog was never paid.

Dr. Herzog filed a complaint in District Court against Irace and Lowry seeking to enforce the June 14, 1988 "assignment of benefits." The matter was tried before the court on the basis of a joint stipulation of facts. The court entered a judgment in favor of Dr. Herzog finding that the June 14, 1988 letter constituted a valid assignment of the settlement proceeds enforceable against Irace and Lowry. Following an unsuccessful appeal to the Superior Court, Irace and Lowry appealed to this court. Because the Superior Court acted as an intermediate appellate court, we review the District Court's decision directly. See Brown v. Corriveau, 576 A.2d 200, 201 (Me.1990). . . .

Validity of Assignment

An assignment is an act or manifestation by the owner of a right (the assignor) indicating his intent to transfer that right to another person (the assignee). See Shiro v. Drew, 174 F.Supp. 495, 497 (D.Me.1959). For an assignment to be valid and enforceable against the assignor's creditor (the obligor), the assignor must make clear his intent to relinquish the right to the assignee and must not retain any control over the right assigned or any power of revocation. Id. The assignment takes effect through the actions of the assignor and assignee and the obligor need not accept the assignment to render it valid. Palmer v. Palmer, 112 Me. 149, 153, 91 A. 281, 282 (1914). Once the obligor has notice of the assignment, the fund is "from that time forward impressed with a trust; it is ... impounded in the [obligor's] hands, and must be held by him not for the original creditor, the assignor, but for the substituted creditor, the assignee." Id. at 152, 91 A. 281. After receiving notice of the assignment, the obligor cannot lawfully pay the amount assigned either to the assignor or to his other creditors and if the obligor does make such a payment, he does so at his peril because the assignee may enforce his rights against the obligor directly. Id. at 153, 91 A. 281.

Ordinary rights, including future rights, are freely assignable unless the assignment would materially change the duty of the obligor, materially increase the burden or risk imposed upon the obligor by his contract, impair the obligor's chance of obtaining return performance, or materially reduce the value of the return performance to the obligor, and unless the law restricts the assignability of the specific right involved. See Restatement (Second) Contracts § 317(2)(a) (1982). In Maine, the transfer of a future right to proceeds from pending litigation has been recognized as a valid and enforceable equitable assignment. McLellan v. Walker, 26 Me. 114, 117-18 (1846). An equitable assignment need not transfer the entire future right but rather may be a partial assignment of that right. Palmer, 112 Me. at 152, 91 A. 281. We reaffirm these well established principles.

Relying primarily upon the Federal District Court's decision in Shiro, 174 F.Supp. 495, a bankruptcy case involving the trustee's power to avoid a preferential transfer by assignment, Irace and Lowry contend that Jones's June 14, 1988 letter is invalid and unenforceable as an assignment because it fails to manifest Jones's intent to permanently relinquish all control over the assigned funds and does nothing more than request payment from a specific fund. We disagree. The June 14, 1988 letter gives no indication that Jones attempted to retain any control over the funds he assigned to Dr. Herzog. Taken in context, the use of the word "request" did not give the court reason to question Jones's intent to complete the assignment and, although no specific amount was stated, the parties do not dispute that the services provided by Dr. Herzog and the amounts that he charged for those services were reasonable and necessary to the treatment of the shoulder injury referred to in the June 14 letter. Irace and Lowry had adequate funds to satisfy all of Jones's creditors, including Dr. Herzog, with funds left over for disbursement to Jones himself. Thus, this case simply does not present a situation analogous to Shiro because Dr. Herzog was given preference over Jones's other creditors by operation of the assignment. Given that Irace and Lowry do not dispute that they had ample notice of the assignment, the court's finding on the validity of the assignment is fully supported by the evidence and will not be disturbed on appeal.

Ethical Obligations

Next, Irace and Lowry contend that the assignment, if enforceable against them, would interfere with their ethical obligation to honor their client's instruction in disbursing funds. Again, we disagree.

Under the Maine Bar Rules, an attorney generally may not place a lien on a client's file for a third party. M.Bar R. 3.7(c). The Bar Rules further require that an attorney "promptly pay or deliver to the client, as requested by the client, the funds, securities, or other properties in the possession of the lawyer which the client is entitled to receive." M.Bar R. 3.6(f)(2)(iv). The rules say nothing, however, about a client's power to assign his right to proceeds from a pending lawsuit to third parties. Because the client has the power to assign his right to funds held by his attorney, McLellan v. Walker, 26 Me. at 117-18, it follows that a valid assignment must be honored by the attorney in disbursing the funds on the client's behalf. The assignment does not create a conflict under Rule 3.6(f)(2)(iv) because the client is not entitled to receive funds once he has assigned them to a third party. Nor does the assignment violate Rule 3.7(c), because the client, not the attorney, is responsible for placing the incumbrance upon the funds. Irace and Lowry were under no ethical obligation, and the record gives no indication that they were under a contractual obligation, to honor their client's instruction to disregard a valid assignment. The District Court correctly concluded that the assignment is valid and enforceable against Irace and Lowry.

The entry is:

Judgment affirmed.

All concurring.

NOTES AND QUESTIONS:

1. As discussed in *Herzog*, a validly created assignment establishes a legal relationship between the obligor and assignee that cannot be satisfied by the obligor's performance of his original duties under the contract to the assignor. What is required for a valid and enforceable assignment? *See also* Restatement (Second) of Contracts § 324 (1981).

2. As between the assignor and the assignee, whether an assignment is enforceable depends on whether it stems from a contractual relationship or has any other basis for enforcement. Just like any other promise, a gratuitous assignment is generally freely revocable by the assignor with some exceptions. Accordingly, unless there is some exchange of value or consideration (or a consideration substitute) to support the assignment, the assignor may revoke the assignment prior to performance by the obligor, and neither will have any liability to the assignee. *See* Restatement (Second) of Contracts § 332 (1981), generally reflecting the treatment of gratuitous assignments.

---

3. NON-ASSIGNMENT CLAUSES AND OTHER LIMITATIONS

BEL-RAY COMPANY V. CHEMRITE LTD.
United States Court of Appeals, Third Circuit
181 F.3d 435 (1999).

STAPLETON, Circuit Judge:

Lubritene Ltd. ("Lubritene") and four of its directors and officers appeal the District Court's order compelling them to arbitrate claims brought against them by Bel-Ray Company, Inc. ("Bel-Ray"). Lubritene claims the District Court erroneously concluded that it was bound under its predecessor's arbitration agreement. The directors and officers contend that the District Court erred because it lacked personal jurisdiction over them, and because they are not bound by their corporate principal's agreement to arbitrate. We agree that Lubritene is bound to arbitrate this dispute and that the District Court had personal jurisdiction over the directors and officers. . . .

I.

Bel-Ray is a New Jersey corporation engaged in the business of manufacturing specialty lubricants for the international mining, industrial and consumer markets. Bel-Ray has developed special formulas and blending technology for its products and maintains them in the highest confidentiality. Between 1983 and 1996, Bel-Ray entered into a series of agreements with Chemrite (Pty.) Ltd., a South African corporation, for the blending and distribution of Bel-Ray products in South Africa. Ivor H. Kahn, Cesare Carbonare, Ian

Robertson, and Pierre Van Der Riet (the "Individual Appellants") were officers or directors, as well as shareholders, of Chemrite.

In January of 1996, the parties entered into the most recent set of these agreements (the "Trade Agreements") by executing a(i) Distributor Sales Agreement, (ii) Blending Manufacturing License Agreement, and (iii) License Agreement to Trade Name. The Trade Agreements allowed Chemrite to market and sell Bel-Ray products, and to produce and market products under Bel-Ray's trade name in South Africa. Each agreement contains two clauses relevant to this appeal. First, each agreement required arbitration of "any and all disputes relating to th[e] agreement or its breach" in Wall Township, New Jersey . . . . Arbitration was to proceed under the American Arbitration Association rules and New Jersey substantive law. Second, the agreements specifically require Bel-Ray's written consent to any assignment of Chemrite's interests under the Trade Agreements.

On August 20, 1996, Chemrite sent Bel-Ray a fax indicating that it had changed its name to "Lubritene (Pty) Ltd." The change became more than nominal on October 10, 1996, when Chemrite sold its lubricant business, expressly including its rights under the Trade Agreements to Lubritene, a newly formed business entity, and Chemrite entered liquidation. Lubritene continued Chemrite's lubricant business at the same location with the same employees and management, and the Individual Appellants became Lubritene shareholders, directors and officers. Lubritene and Bel-Ray continued to conduct business in the same manner under the Trade Agreements. In November of 1996, Lubritene sent Bel-Ray a package of documents that included the October 10th sale of assets documents and thereby informed Bel-Ray that Lubritene was a new and separate company.

In the Spring of 1997, the parties engaged in a series of negotiations. These negotiations were initially motivated by Bel-Ray's interest in acquiring a stake in Lubritene. When it became clear that such an acquisition was not in the cards, the negotiations turned to focus upon modifying the Trade Agreements to add additional industrial products and to extend their terms to six years. During negotiating sessions in South Africa, Lubritene representatives queried Bel-Ray representative Linda Keifer as to whether Bel-Ray believed there was a legally binding agreement between Lubritene and Bel-Ray. According to Keifer:

> [she] explained to them that, not being an attorney, [she] could not comment on the legal enforceability of the [Trade Agreements], but told them that Bel-Ray's attorneys had advised [her] that technically and legally we do have an agreement. Moreover, [she] pointed out that both Bel-Ray and Lubritene had continued to conduct business in the same manner without interruption, since the agreements were signed ... [and] that [she] understood from Bel-Ray's attorneys that as long as we both continued to do business according to the terms of the existing agreements while we discussed a possible new relationship, Bel-Ray had an implied agreement with Lubritene on the same terms as the existing agreements with Chemrite.

Six Lubritene affiants, however, contend that Keifer stated that "technically and legally there is no agreement between Lubritene and Bel-Ray" because any assignment of the Chemrite agreement required Bel-Ray's written consent, which had not yet been granted.

Soon after these negotiations, a former Lubritene director brought internal corporate documents to Bel-Ray's attention. Among these documents were the minutes of a Lubritene board meeting held in anticipation of the Spring 1997 negotiations "to resolve the legal stance Lubritene (Pty) Ltd must take in respect of the Bel-Ray Company Inc[.] agreement." (A127) Lubritene's counsel advised the board at the meeting that:

> while admittedly the [Trade Agreements were] entered into between Chemrite Southern Africa (Pty) Ltd[.,] and Bel-Ray Company Inc.[,] after the deregistration/liquidation of Chemrite Southern Africa (Pty) Ltd [.], Bel-Ray still continued to deal commercially with Lubritene (Pty) Ltd and therefore, Bel-Ray's conduct has basically assumed that the assigned agreements were in fact assigned to Lubritene (Pty) Ltd.[.] However, the agreements state that the transfer of the agreements must be approved in writing by BelRay. Id.

The board then resolved to (i) liquidate Chemrite; (ii) "continue to trade with Bel-Ray Company Inc as is and not [to] suggest any changes to the current agreement when Linda Keifer and Bernie Meeks visit South Africa in April"; (iii) create another new company and transfer all of Lubritene's business other than Bel-Ray to that company so that Lubritene "will have no assets" and "[i]f Bel-Ray decides to take legal action against Lubritene (Pty) Ltd, there will be nothing left in the company and hence Bel-Ray will not recover any damages"; and (iv) when Bel-Ray seeks to renew the Trade Agreements to inform them that the Trade Agreements were with Chemrite, "which does not exist anymore and that the agreements are no longer valid." Id. The minutes end by instructing that "[i]t is vital that we do not alert Bel-Ray to our plans and hence we must be very cautious and circumspect when we ALL meet with them in April." Id.

Bel-Ray alleges that these minutes and the other documents brought to them by the former Lubritene director reveal that Lubritene, and the Individual Appellants as its officers and directors, conspired to misappropriate Bel-Ray's technology and other proprietary information and intentionally defrauded Bel-Ray by leading it to believe that Lubritene would abide by the Trade Agreements. Additionally, they allege that Lubritene marketed Bel-Ray products falsely under Lubritene's trade name, and conversely marketed inferior Lubritene products under Bel-Ray's trade name thereby damaging Bel-Ray's business reputation.

Bel-Ray filed this action in the United States District Court for the District of New Jersey to compel Lubritene and the Individual Appellants to arbitrate their claims under the Trade Agreements' arbitration clauses. Bel-Ray alleges that Lubritene's actions amount to the business torts of (i) unfair competition, (ii) fraud, and (iii) misappropriation. Bel-Ray also claims that these same actions constitute breaches of the Trade Agreements.

Lubritene and the Individual Appellants, jointly represented, filed an answer asserting inter alia lack of personal jurisdiction and counterclaims. The counterclaims alleged that Bel-Ray had commenced related proceedings in South Africa to enjoin Lubritene from continuing to use its intellectual property and trade name, and requested the District Court to either (i) stay the proceedings, or (ii) enjoin Bel-Ray from seeking to compel arbitration because it had waived its right to arbitrate by initiating the South African litigation. Two months later, the Individual Appellants filed a motion on their counterclaims requesting a stay, or alternatively, summary judgment enjoining Bel-Ray from seeking to compel arbitration.

The District Court denied the appellants' motion. Months later, the Court granted Bel-Ray summary judgment and entered an order compelling arbitration on August 10, 1998. Lubritene and the Individual Appellants appeal this order. . . .

III.

We begin with the propriety of the District Court's order to the extent it compelled Lubritene to arbitrate Bel-Ray's claims. Under the Federal Arbitration Act ("FAA"), a court may only compel a party to arbitrate where that party has entered into a written agreement to arbitrate that covers the dispute. See 9 U.S.C. §§ 2 & 206. The arbitration clauses in the Trade Agreements are the only written agreements to arbitrate offered in this case. It is undisputed that these agreements were entered into by Chemrite and Bel-Ray, and that Chemrite subsequently assigned the agreements to Lubritene. If these assignments are effective, then the District Court's order should be affirmed. Lubritene, however, contends that the assignments are ineffective because Bel-Ray did not consent to the assignments in writing as the Trade Agreements require. They therefore argue that there is no written agreement to arbitrate and we must reverse the District Court's order. . . .

Lubritene claims that it cannot be bound by Chemrite's agreement to arbitrate because, as a matter of contract law, the written consent provision prevents it from becoming Chemrite's assignee. . . .

. . . Thus, we now turn to consider that state's contract law. The New Jersey Supreme Court has not yet addressed the effect of contractual provisions limiting or prohibiting assignments. Nevertheless, we are not without guidance because the Superior Court's Appellate Division recently addressed this issue in Garden State Buildings L.P. v. First Fidelity Bank, N.A., 305 N.J.Super. 510, 702 A.2d 1315 (1997). There, a partnership had entered a loan agreement with Midatlantic Bank for the construction of a new hotel. The parties subsequently entered into a modification agreement to extend the loan's maturity date, which provided that: "No party hereto shall assign this Letter Agreement (or assign any right or delegate any obligation contained herein) without the prior written consent of the other party hereto and any such assignment shall be void." Id. at 1318. Midatlantic subsequently assigned the loan to Starwood without obtaining the partnership's prior written consent. The partnership acknowledged Starwood's rights under the loan agreement by making payments to, and eventually entering a settlement agreement with, Starwood. Nonetheless, the partnership filed suit against Midatlantic for damages arising from its breach of the modification agreement's assignment clause. It argued that it was not required to void the assignment, but could recognize its validity while still preserving its right to sue Midatlantic for breach of its covenant not to assign without the partnership's written consent.

To resolve this claim the Appellate Division looked to § 322 of the Restatement (Second) of Contracts, which provides in relevant part:

(2) A contract term prohibiting assignment of rights under the contract, unless a different intention is manifested....

(b) gives the obligor a right to damages for breach of the terms forbidding assignment *but does not render the assignment ineffective* ... Restatement (Second) of Contracts § 322 (1981) (emphasis added).

The Court distinguished between an assignment provision's effect upon a party's "power" to assign, as opposed to its "right" to assign. A party's "power" to assign is only limited where the parties clearly manifest a different intention. According to the Court:

[t]o reveal the intent necessary to preclude the power to assign, or cause an assignment violative of contractual provisions to be wholly void, such clause must contain express provisions that any assignment shall be void or invalid if not made in a certain specified way.

Otherwise, the assignment is effective, and the obligor has the right to damages. Garden State, 702 A.2d at 1321 (quoting University Mews Assoc's v. Jeanmarie, 122 Misc.2d 434, 471 N.Y.S.2d 457, 461 (1984)).

The Court concluded that the parties had sufficiently manifested their intent to limit Midatlantic's power to assign the loan because the anti-assignment clause clearly provided that assignments without the other party's written consent "shall be void." Id. at 1322.

In adopting § 322, New Jersey joins numerous other jurisdictions that follow the general rule that contractual provisions limiting or prohibiting assignments operate only to limit a parties' right to assign the contract, but not their power to do so, unless the parties' manifest an intent to the contrary with specificity. See Cedar Point Apartments, Ltd. v. Cedar Point Inv. Corp., 693 F.2d 748, 754 & n. 4 (8th Cir.1982); Pro Cardiaco Pronto Socorro Cardiologica, S.A. v. Trussell, 863 F.Supp. 135, 137 (S.D.N.Y.1994); Lomas Mortgage U.S.A., Inc. v. W.E. O'Neil Constr. Co., 812 F.Supp. 841, 843-44 (N.D.Ill.1993); Allhusen v. Caristo Const. Corp., 303 N.Y. 446, 103 N.E.2d 891, 893 (1952); Macklowe v. 42nd St. Dev. Corp., 170 A.D.2d 388, 566 N.Y.S.2d 606, 606-07 (1991); Sullivan v. International Fidelity Ins. Co., 96 A.D.2d 555, 465 N.Y.S.2d 235, 237 (1983); University Mews Assoc's v. Jeanmarie, 122 Misc.2d 434, 471 N.Y.S.2d 457, 461 (1984). To meet this standard the assignment provision must generally state that nonconforming assignments (i) shall be "void" or "invalid," or (ii) that the assignee shall acquire no rights or the nonassigning party shall not recognize any such assignment. See Garden State, 702 A.2d at 1321 ("clause must contain express provisions that any assignment shall be void or invalid if not made in a certain specified way"); Cedar Point, 693 F.2d at 754 n. 4 (same); Allhusen, 103 N.E.2d at 893; Sullivan, 465 N.Y.S.2d at 238; University Mews, 471 N.Y.S.2d at 461. In the absence of such language, the provision limiting or prohibiting assignments will be interpreted merely as a covenant not to assign, or to follow specific procedures-typically obtaining the non-assigning party's prior written consent-before assigning. Breach of such a covenant may render the assigning party liable in damages to the non-assigning party. The assignment, however, remains valid and enforceable against both the assignor and the assignee. See Garden State, 702 A.2d at 1321; Cedar Point, 693 F.2d at 754 n. 4; Pro

Cardiaco, 863 F.Supp. at 137; Lomas, 812 F.Supp. at 844; Allhusen, 103 N.E.2d at 892; Sullivan, 465 N.Y.S.2d at 237.

The Trade Agreements in this case contain the following assignment provisions: (i) the Distributor Sales Agreement § 7.06 provides that the "Agreement and the obligations and rights under this Agreement will not be assignable by [Chemrite] without express prior written consent of Bel-Ray, which may be withheld at the sole discretion of Bel-Ray"; (ii) the Blending and Manufacturing License Agreement § 7.05 provides that the "Agreement and the obligations and rights hereunder will not be assignable by [Chemrite] without the express prior written consent of BEL-RAY"; and (iii) the License Agreement to Trade Name § 6.06 provides that the "Agreement, and the obligations and rights under this agreement will not be assignable without the express written consent of all Parties to this Agreement." (A39, A61, A83). None contain terms specifically stating that an assignment without Bel-Ray's written consent would be void or invalid. Several courts have considered virtually identical clauses and concluded that they did not contain the necessary express language to limit the assigning party's power to assign. See Lomas, 812 F.Supp. at 844; Macklowe, 566 N.Y.S.2d at 606-07; Sullivan, 465 N.Y.S.2d at 236-38.

The Trade Agreements' assignment clauses do not contain the requisite clear language to limit Chemrite's "power" to assign the Trade Agreements. Chemrite's assignment to Lubritene is therefore enforceable, and Lubritene is bound to arbitrate claims "relating to" the Trade Agreements pursuant to their arbitration clauses. We therefore agree with the District Court that Bel-Ray was entitled to an order compelling Lubritene to arbitrate. . . .

NOTES AND QUESTIONS:

1. In *Bel-Ray*, the court distinguished between a party's right to assignment and his power to assign where a non-assignment clause is present. Compare this court's ruling with the provisions of U.C.C. § 2-210(2) and § 9-406(d), rendering ineffective any attempt or agreement purporting to prohibit the assignment of one's right to the payment of money. How do these code sections differ from the treatment of such anti-assignment provisions under *Bel-Ray*?

2. *See also* Restatement (Second) of Contracts § 323 (Obligor's Assent to Assignment or Delegation) for treatment of an obligor's consent to future assignments obtained at the time of contracting.

B. RIGHTS AND DEFENSES

1. DEFENSES OF OBLIGOR

MAYO V. CITY NATIONAL BANK & TRUST
Supreme Court of New Jersey
265 A.2d 382 (1970).

HANEMAN, J.

This matter involves the question of the order of precedence of various creditors of an owner-builder to payment out of an installment of a construction mortgage.

On May 10, 1966, The City National Bank and Trust Company of Hackensack (City National Bank) signed a "Mortgage Commitment and Closing Instruction Sheet" agreeing to advance $750,000 to Fairleigh Arms, Inc. (Fairleigh) in unspecified installments, the repayment of which was to be secured by a "Construction Mortgage." Said Commitment reads in part: "Subject to the conditions as stated in a Permanent Commitment by Manhattan Savings Bank, dated December 14, 1965." The Permanent Commitment of the Manhattan Savings Bank above referred to reads in part:

> The loan shall be . . . secured by a first mortgage on the above premises . . . which mortgage shall constitute a valid first lien on a good and marketable title in unencumbered fee simple to the premises and building and improvements now or hereafter erected thereon and all fixtures, equipment and articles of personal property now or hereafter affixed to or used in connection with the operation of the premises.
>
> The mortgage shall be superior to any mechanic's lien which may be filed for construction of the building and proof satisfactory to our counsel that the cost of construction of the building has been paid in full shall be submitted at or prior to the closing.

On May 11, 1966, Fairleigh executed and delivered a mortgage in the face amount of $750,000 to City National Bank. Although the mortgage recites that $750,000 had been "in hand well and truly paid by the Mortgagee at or before the sealing and delivery of these presences," a legend appearing on the top of page one, indicates that it is a "Construction Mortgage" printed by "Irwin Karkus, Law Blank Publisher, Newark, N.J." No place in the body of the instrument is there any finite specification of the time for and amount of future installments. This fact is adverted to, not because it affects the merits of the matter but because it is explanatory of why this Court as well as the trial court, encountered some difficulty in ascertaining the facts. In order that there be no misunderstanding, no such written statements are required to make a valid Construction Mortgage. However, as a matter of propriety and safety this should be done. Bell v. Fleming's Executors, 12 N.J.Eq. 13 (Ch.1858), aff'd 12 N.J.Eq. 490 (E. & A. 1859); Reed v. Rochford, 62 N.J.Eq. 186, 50 A. 70 (Ch.1901). Such statements are helpful in resolving the parties' respective rights and duties. All parties agree that the loan was upon a Construction Mortgage and that advances were to be made by the mortgagee under some oral arrangement subject to the conditions contained in the above mentioned instruments.

On August 22, 1966, Fairleigh executed an assignment to plaintiff of which defendant had notice and which reads:

> For and in consideration of the sum of ONE ($1.00) DOLLAR, and other good and valuable consideration, receipt which is hereby acknowledged, the undersigned hereby assigns to
>
> JOHN MAYO
>
> 205 West Madison Avenue
>
> Dumont, New Jersey
>
> the sum of FIVE THOUSAND ($5,000.00) DOLLARS out of the fifth mortgage payment advance to be made by City National Bank & Trust Company on Mortgage made by Fairleigh Arms, Inc., to City National Bank & Trust Company, on property situate on Anderson Street, Hackensack, New Jersey.
>
> Said City National Bank & Trust Company is hereby authorized and directed to pay the aforesaid sum of $5,000.00 to JOHN MAYO, out of the said fifth mortgage payment.

On September 7, 1966, Fairleigh executed and delivered to Cooper-Horowitz, Inc. (Cooper-Horowitz) a mortgage in the amount of $50,000 which was duly recorded on September 8, 1966. Said mortgage contained the following provision:

> Subject to a certain mortgage from Fairleigh Arms, Inc. to The City National Bank & Trust Company of Hackensack dated May 11, 1966 recorded May 13, 1966 in Book 4413 of mortgages at page 249 in the amount of $750,000.00 of which $607,500.00 has been advanced.
>
> It is a condition of this mortgage that the mortgagor, its successors and assigns pay to the mortgagee, its successors and assigns, the future advances made by The City National Bank and Trust Company of Hackensack pursuant to the aforementioned mortgage unless the debt secured by this mortgage and interest thereon is fully paid.

On September 16, 1966, P. Germinario and Sons, Inc., duly recorded a Mechanic's Notice of Intention. N.J.S.A. 2A:44-71.

On November 14, 1966, City National Bank made a fifth advance in the total amount of $78,500 none of which was paid to Fairleigh or plaintiff. Payments were made to said bank in payment of two interim notes and interest and to its attorney for legal services. In addition $45,000 was paid to Germinario and $5,575 was paid to Cooper-Horowitz.

Plaintiff does not contest the validity of the payments to the bank and its attorney but asserts that he had a right to the payment of $5,000 by virtue of the above referred to assignment which he alleges was prior to the rights to payment of either Germinario or Cooper-Horowitz.

The Chancery Division entered judgment approving the payments as made, 103 N.J.Super. 227, 247 A.2d 33 which judgment was affirmed by the Appellate Division, 107 N.J.Super. 43, 256 A.2d 801. This Court granted certification, 55 N.J. 77, 259 A.2d 228 (1969).

Several additional facts should be noted before a discussion of the primary issue. Fairleigh, the owner of the realty, was its own contractor for the erection of the building here involved and sub-contracted the various phases of construction. There was no independent prime contractor and, of course, no filed building contract. On November 14, 1966, there was due Germinario for plastering work, $100,000. At the same time there were also a number of other contractors who had filed notices of intention and performed work on the construction for which money was owing. The draw of November 14, 1966 took two days of conferences to accomplish. Although the record unsatisfactorily furnishes no detail of the conferences and final agreement between the mortgagees and those who had filed notices of intention, it is implicit in the record and the exhibits, including the "Closing Statement," that it was agreed that Germinario and Cooper-Horowitz should receive the sums paid to them in exchange for a release, postponement or subordination of the balance of their respective liens and that the other mechanic's lien notice of intention creditors also agreed to release, postpone or subordinate their respective lien claims to the lien of the City National Bank Mortgage.

It must be recognized at the outset that the assignment to plaintiff, whether outright or as collateral security, can rise no higher than Fairleigh's entitlement to payment out of the fifth installment. It follows that if Fairleigh, itself, was not entitled to any such payment, plaintiff in turn was not entitled to receive any funds from the fifth draw. . . . Accordingly, we must determine Fairleigh's right to personally receive funds out of the fifth draw.

City National Bank was obliged to advance future funds only if it would receive a "first lien on a good and marketable title in unencumbered fee simple to the premises and building and improvements" to the extent of the funds so advanced. Also, even though probably unnecessary, it was further specifically provided that the lien of the City National Bank mortgage would be superior for each advance to any mechanic's lien. It was, therefore, Fairleigh's duty to furnish City National Bank with a first lien and plaintiff's assignment was subject to the performance of that duty.

On November 14, 1966, City National Bank had a first lien to the extent of $607,500, the money actually advanced to that date and not for the face amount of the mortgage. . . . Where it is optional with the mortgagee whether to make future advances, he does not have a prior lien for those advances made after notice of an existing encumbrance. . . . Here, City National Bank had knowledge of the Germinario notice of intention, the Cooper-Horowitz second mortgage and the other filed notices of intention prior to making the advance on November 14, 1966. At that posture City National Bank could not have obtained a first lien for any additional funds to be advanced on that day unless the liens of the filed notice of intention creditors and the second mortgagee were satisfied, subordinated or postponed to the bank's lien for such an additional advance.

In addition, for City National Bank to become entitled to a priority over the mechanic's liens, the bank was required to comply with N.J.S.A. 2A: 44-89 which reads as far as here pertinent:

> The priority given by section 2A:44-87 (for mortgages) of this title shall also exist when the mortgage secured or the funds secured thereby have been applied:
>
>> e. To the payment to every person, or his legal representative, assignee, receiver or trustee, who shall have furnished labor or material for the building for money due therefor at the time of any advance and who shall have filed, or in whose behalf there shall have been filed a 'mechanic's notice of intention,' as required by this article. All such claimants shall be entitled to participate in each advance made under the mortgage, except when made for payments under paragraphs 'a' to 'd,' inclusive, of this section, unless such person shall have:
>>
>> 1. Subordinated, released, partially released or postponed his right of payment or lien to the lien of the mortgage, but no postponement shall be effective for the purposes of this article, except for the first payment made in reliance thereon and any preceding payments which may have been made;
>>
>> The mortgagee may, if the amount being advanced is not sufficient to pay in full all claimants having a right to participate therein, pay to each such claimant such proportionate amount of his claim as the total amount being advanced bears to the total of the claims of all entitled to participate. All liens or rights of liens conferred by this article shall be subordinate to the mortgage to the extent of the payments so made; . . . .

The terms of this statute are as much a part of the City National Bank-Fairleigh agreement as if recited therein in full. . . . So Fairleigh had by implication agreed to permit the City National Bank to distribute in accordance therewith. Plaintiff as assigned of Fairleigh is similarly bound.

Although, as above noted, the testimony is sparse, it can reasonably be concluded that Cooper-Horowitz and the mechanic's lien claimants, including Germinario, agreed to postpone the priority of their respective liens which exceeded the amount of the advance, waive any further claim, statutory or otherwise, to participation in the advance, and authorize the payment above stated to Germinario and Cooper-Horowitz.

The payment to precedent lien holders in order to provide City National Bank with a first lien for its fifth advance, exhausted the funds available for distribution. It follows that Fairleigh did not qualify for any payment. As Fairleigh, the assignor, was not entitled to participation in the fifth advance, plaintiff, its assignee, was also not entitled to any such participation.

Affirmed.

For affirmance: Chief Justice WEINTRAUB and Justices JACOBS, FRANCIS, PROCTOR, HALL, SCHETTINO and HANEMAN-7.
For reversal: None.

NOTES AND QUESTIONS:

1. As with third party beneficiaries, the rights of assignees stem from the contract. Accordingly, with some exceptions, the rights of assignees are subject to the claims and defenses of the obligor, including all infirmities of the underlying transaction. *See* U.C.C. § 9-404 (Rights Acquired by Assignee; Claims and Defenses Against Assignee).

2. An assignee qualifying as a holder in due course generally has greater rights to enforce an obligation represented by a negotiable instrument than the assignor would have against the obligor. Such an HDC is said to acquire the negotiable instrument subject to all real defenses but free from personal defenses. However, for obligations arising out of a consumer transaction, the consumer-obligor is able to assert all defenses, real and personal, against any assignee, without regard to HDC status. *See* U.C.C. § 3-104 (Negotiable Instrument); § 3-302 (Holder in Due Course); and § 3-305 (Defenses and Claims In Recoupment).

3. Another exception to the general rule that the assignee is subject to all claims and defenses of the obligor is where the obligor agreed at the time of contracting not to assert any defenses against a future assignee seeking to enforce payment of the money obligation. Generally, such a waiver of defense clause contained in the contract will be enforced against the obligor, thereby requiring the obligor to pay the assignee and then pursue the assignor for any claims or damages resulting from the underlying transaction. However, the obligor is still allowed to assert against an assignee any defense that a holder in due course would be allowed to assert (real defenses). Moreover, as with holders in due course, the waiver of defense clause does not apply to a consumer-obligor, thereby allowing him to assert against the assignee all defenses stemming from the contract that he could assert against the assignor. *See* U.C.C. § 9-403 (Agreement Not To Assert Defenses Against Assignee).

SEATTLE-FIRST NATIONAL BANK V. OREGON PACIFIC INDUSTRIES, INC.
Supreme Court of Oregon
500 P.2d 1033 (1972).

DENECKE, Justice.

The plaintiff bank obtained a judgment against the defendant for the amount of an invoice assigned to the bank by Centralia Plywood. The trial court denied defendant's right to a setoff and defendant appeals.

The issue is the interpretation of the assignment section of the secured transactions chapter of the Uniform Commercial Code (ORS 79.3180).

On December 12, 1968, the defendant purchased plywood from Centralia. Centralia assigned the invoice evidencing the purchase to the bank on December 13, and the bank notified the defendant of the assignment. The defendant refused payment and the bank brought this action.

The defendant argues that it has a setoff against the bank's claim. Prior to the bank's assignment the defendant had placed two plywood orders, not included in the assigned invoice, with Centralia. Delivery was never made by Centralia and defendant contends it can set off the damages it suffered thereby against the bank's claim.

Centralia Plywood was insolvent when it assigned the invoice to the bank on December 12 and the bank knew of the insolvency at that time. Both Centralia and the bank are nonresidents. The defendant contends that because of these circumstances it is entitled to the setoff and cites our opinion in Pearson v. Richards, 106 Or. 78, 92, 211 P. 167 (1922), in support.

Assuming defendant's contention is correct in cases not involving the Code, we hold the principle contended for by defendant is not applicable when the Code applies. ORS 79.3180(1) provides:

> . . . (T)he rights of an assignee are subject to:
>
> (a) All the terms of the contract between the account debtor and assignor and any defense or claim arising therefrom; and
>
> (b) Any other defense or claim of the account debtor against the assignor which accrues before the account debtor receives notification of the assignment.

The Code does not expressly provide that a claim can be set off if the assignor was insolvent at the time of the assignment and the assignee had knowledge of this fact or because the assignor and assignee are nonresidents.

One of the prime purposes of the Code was to create a statutory scheme incorporating within its provisions the complete regulation of certain types of commercial dealings. This purpose would be blunted if the rules created by some precode decisions and not expressly provided for in the statutory scheme were nevertheless grafted onto the Code by implication. In Evans Products v. Jorgensen, 245 Or. 362, 372, 421 P.2d 978 (1966), we held generally that we would not engage in this practice.

We recently observed in Investment Service Co. v. North Pacific Lbr. Co., Or., 492 P.2d 470-471 (1972), that the comment to this section of the Code states that this section "makes no substantial change in prior law."[1] Upon further examination, we must

[1] Investment Service Co. v. North Pacific Lbr. Co., Or., 492 P.2d 470-471 (1972), involved ORS 79.3180(1)(a), a setoff arising out of the contract between the account debtor and the assignor.

acknowledge that while the Code retains the essence of the previous law of assignments, the Code has, by specific language, changed some of the details of the previous law of assignments.

The Code distinguishes "between what might be called the contract-related and the unrelated defenses and claims. Defenses and claims 'arising' from the contract can be asserted against the assignee whether they 'arise' before or after notification. . . . Under the Code, 'any other defense or claim' is available against the assignee only if it 'accrues before . . . notification." 2 Gilmore, Security Interests in Personal Property, 1090-1091, s 41.4 (1965).

The setoff or claim the defendant seeks to assert is an unrelated setoff because it arises out of a breach of a contract not connected with the invoice assigned to the bank. For this reason the defendant can assert the setoff only if it accrued before the defendant was notified of Centralia's assignment to the bank.

The controversy thus narrows down to the issue of whether the setoff "accrued" to the defendant before it received notice of the assignment. We could be aided in defining "accrued" if we could determine why the accrual of the setoff was selected as the cutoff event. Accruing of the setoff, however, apparently, was selected arbitrarily. The choice of the event of the accrual was based upon previous decisions, some of which used the phrase "matured" rather than "accrued" claim. 4 Corbin, Contracts, 599, s 897 (1951). 1 Restatement 211, Contracts § 167(1), provided that the obligor could assert its setoff if the setoff was "based on facts arising . . . prior to knowledge of the assignment by the obligor."

It was necessary to permit at least some setoffs to be asserted in order to protect the obligor from being unduly prejudiced by the assignment; but this right of setoff had to be limited in order to give some value and stability to the assignment so that it could be used as an effective security device. If an obligor could not assert any of the defenses or setoffs against an assignee which he could have asserted against his creditor, the assignor, the obligor would be extremely prejudiced by an assignment. On the other hand, if the obligation assigned could be obliterated or diminished by events happening after the assignment and notice of assignment to the obligor, the assignment would be precarious collateral.

The comments to the Oregon Code are of no assistance in interpreting "accrue." The comments to the Washington Code state: "The term 'accrues' appears to mean that the 'claim' shall exist as such, i.e., as a cause of action, before such knowledge." RCWA 62A.9-318, p. 439.

"Accrue," aside from its fiscal use, generally is used in the law to describe when a cause of action comes into being. Its chief use is to determine when the statute of limitations commences. We believe it is advisable to use "accrue" in the Code in its usual sense; that is, a claim or setoff accrues when a cause of action exists.

The parties stipulated that the "breaches of contract (the failure to deliver by Centralia) occurred on or about January 3, 1969." Therefore, the claim "accrued" at that time. Since the claim accrued after defendant had notification of the assignment, the setoff cannot be asserted successfully.

Defendant on appeal contends that by stipulating that the breaches of contract occurred on January 3 it did not intend to stipulate that the cause of action accrued at that time. The normal inference is that the cause of action accrues at the time the breach of contract occurs. In addition, the record indicates that the trial court and the parties so understood the import of the stipulation.

Affirmed.

---

2. MODIFICATION

TEXAS UNIFORM COMMERCIAL CODE
§ 9.405. MODIFICATION OF ASSIGNED CONTRACTS
TEX. BUS. & COM. CODE § 9.405 (2011).

(a) A modification of or substitution for an assigned contract is effective against an assignee if made in good faith. The assignee acquires corresponding rights under the modified or substituted contract. The assignment may provide that the modification or substitution is a breach of contract by the assignor. This subsection is subject to Subsections (b)--(d).

(b) Subsection (a) applies to the extent that:

(1) the right to payment or a part thereof under an assigned contract has not been fully earned by performance; or

(2) the right to payment or a part thereof has been fully earned by performance and the account debtor has not received notification of the assignment under Section 9.406(a).

(c) This section is subject to law other than this chapter that establishes a different rule for an account debtor who is an individual and who incurred the obligation primarily for personal, family, or household purposes.

(d) This section does not apply to an assignment of a health-care-insurance receivable.

---

3. ASSIGNMENT WARRANTIES

LONSDALE V. CHESTERFIELD
Supreme Court of Washington
662 P.2d 385 (1983).

WILLIAM H. WILLIAMS, Chief Justice.

Petitioners, Robert Lonsdale, et al., are assignees of the vendors' interests in certain real estate contracts. They appeal the unpublished decision of the Court of Appeals, Division One, which upheld the dismissal of their class action for rescission and damages. . . . We reverse and remand to the trial court.

In 1968, Chesterfield Land, Inc. (Chesterfield) platted a portion of a development known as Sansaria on land along the Oregon coast near Coos Bay, Oregon. It then sold 81 lots to various purchasers by real estate contracts. In each sales contract Chesterfield agreed to install a water system for the use of the plat. In turn, each purchaser agreed to pay a portion of the cost of installation and to use the water system.

Chesterfield subsequently sold its vendor's interest in some of these real estate contracts to members of the petitioner class who purchased them for investment purposes. The class members paid Chesterfield money and received in return an assignment of the vendor's interest together with a deed to the land corresponding to that particular real estate contract. The deed was intended to secure payment of the outstanding balance on each real estate contract.

In 1969, Jack Chesterfield, the sole owner of Chesterfield, died. Susan Chesterfield, his widow, then sold the remaining undeveloped portion of the development to Sansaria, Inc. (Sansaria), one of the respondents in this case. As part of the consideration for the sale Sansaria assumed Chesterfield's obligation to install a water system for the entire development, including that portion already sold via the real estate contracts. Chesterfield was later dissolved and its assets distributed to Susan Chesterfield. Despite the terms of this contract, neither party installed the system. In a declaratory judgment action brought by Chesterfield against Sansaria, the Superior Court found Sansaria in default on this obligation.

In that action, the trial court found that as a result of failure of both Sansaria and Chesterfield to install the system, many of the original contract purchasers defaulted. Others defaulted for financial reasons and others continued to make the scheduled payments. Some of these purchasers brought suit in Oregon and obtained judgment against both Chesterfield and the individual investors. Thus, the vendors' interests in those contracts became worthless.

In August 1973, petitioners brought suit against Chesterfield to recover for the failure to install the water system. They also sued Sansaria claiming to be third party beneficiaries of the contract between Chesterfield and Sansaria. At the close of petitioners' case, the trial court granted respondents' motion to dismiss, holding Chesterfield's obligation to supply water did not run to petitioners and petitioners were not third party beneficiaries.

Following some procedural confusion, the nature of which is no longer material, petitioners moved to vacate and reenter judgment to allow appeal. This motion was denied on jurisdictional grounds. On appeal, the Court of Appeals reversed on the issue of vacation of judgment but proceeded to decide the case on the merits of petitioners' claim. In so doing the court held: (1) Chesterfield's obligation did run to petitioners and (2) the petitioners were third party beneficiaries of the contract between Chesterfield and Sansaria. Lonsdale v. Chesterfield, 19 Wash.App. 27, 573 P.2d 822 (1978).

On review, this court agreed with the Court of Appeals decision on the jurisdiction issue but reversed and remanded the issues on the merits, since respondents had not been given an opportunity to present evidence at trial. . . . On remand, the trial court reaffirmed its earlier decision. On appeal, a different panel of Division One reversed the prior holding and affirmed. We granted review to decide the following issues: (1) As a contract assignor is Chesterfield liable to the assignees/petitioners for its failure to install the water system? (2) Are petitioners third party beneficiaries of Sansaria's promise to Chesterfield to install the system? We answer both in the affirmative.

I.

ASSIGNOR'S LIABILITY TO ASSIGNEES

It is well established that in every contract, "[t]here is an implied covenant of good faith and fair dealing, ... a covenant or implied obligation by each party to cooperate with the other so that [each] may obtain the full benefit of performance." . . . Petitioners contend that this covenant of fair dealings applies with equal force to assignment contracts. Specifically, they contend that Chesterfield breached an implied warranty of noninterference arising from the assignment. Support for this contention is found in the Restatement of Contracts, which provides in pertinent part:

> § 333. Warranties of An Assignor
>
> (1) Unless a contrary intention is manifested, *one who assigns* or purports to assign a right by assignment under seal or *for value warrants to the assignee*
>
> (a) *that he will do nothing to defeat or impair the value of the assignment and has no knowledge of any fact which would do so;*
>
> (b) that the right, as assigned, actually exists and is subject to no limitations or defenses good against the assignor other than those stated or apparent at the time of the assignment;
>
> (c) that any writing evidencing the right which is delivered to the assignee or exhibited to him to induce him to accept the assignment is genuine and what it purports to be.
>
> (2) An assignment does not of itself operate as a warranty that the obligor is solvent or that he will perform his obligation. (Italics ours.) Restatement (Second) of Contracts § 333 (1981).

The comment to that section of the Restatement explains:

> Unlike an indorser of commercial paper or a collecting bank or its customer, an assignor is not liable for defaults of the obligor and does not warrant his solvency.... *An assignor does warrant his lack of knowledge of facts and his future abstention from conduct which would impair the value of the assigned right.* (Citations omitted. Italics ours.) Restatement (Second) of Contracts § 333,comment a (1981). See also J. Calamari & J. Perillo, Contracts § 18-23 at 661-62 (2d ed. 1977); 3 S. Williston, Contracts § 445 at 316-21 (3d ed. 1960); 4 A. Corbin, Contracts § 904 at 622-25 (1951).

We interpret this section to mean that by the mere fact of the assignment the assignor impliedly guarantees that he will not thereafter interfere with the thing assigned or do anything to defeat or impair the value of the assignment; if he does so interfere, he renders himself liable to the assignee for any damages resulting from the interference. . . .

No cases have been found that consider whether the warranty is also breached by the assignor's failure to perform an obligation to a third party that impairs the value of the assignment. However, we see no good reason to distinguish between an affirmative act and a failure to act when as a practical matter the assignor can impair or defeat the assigned right by doing either. Our conclusion is directly in accord with the established principle of cooperation between contracting parties as expressed in Miller. In this case Chesterfield's failure to perform its obligation to the lot purchasers constituted a breach of this implied covenant of good faith.

In its unpublished opinion, the Court of Appeals found Chesterfield did not act so as to defeat or impair the value of the assignments:

> To the contrary, Chesterfield acted to maintain the value of the assignments by requiring Sansaria, Inc. to assume the obligation to install a water system.

Lonsdale v. Chesterfield, at 5. We reject this reasoning. When a party contracts to perform a specified obligation, he cannot escape liability for nonperformance by delegating his duty to perform; he remains secondarily liable (as a surety) for performance of the duty promised.

In the present case, Chesterfield's failure to perform its obligation to install the water system was a breach of its contracts with the original purchasers of the lots. Even if an assignee is not affirmatively liable for nonperformance of an assignor's duties, an assignee takes subject to defenses assertible against the assignor. . . . Thus, Chesterfield's failure to fulfill its obligation made the assigned rights under the contract virtually worthless, since the purchasers could assert Chesterfield's failure to perform as a defense to an action by petitioners for payment.

The Court of Appeals further determined that petitioners assumed the risk of Chesterfield not performing its obligation because "[i]t was ... quite apparent at the time of the assignments that should the water system not be installed, the purchasers of the land would have a defense that might be raised against the vendor." Lonsdale v. Chesterfield, at 5. We also reject this reasoning.

Were this reasoning accurate, no party to an executory contract would ever be allowed to recover for a breach. In this case, we think it incorrect to assume that petitioners entered into the contracts with no expectation of recovering in the event of a breach. We think it more just to recognize that once Chesterfield received value for the assignments from petitioners, it no longer had the incentive to perform its part of the contract. Were we to hold that Chesterfield is not liable for its failure to perform, the petitioners would be denied the benefit of the bargain, a right long recognized in Washington, and Chesterfield would be unjustly enriched.

Since Chesterfield no longer exists, any recovery must be had against Susan Chesterfield as distributee of the remaining assets of that corporation. It is well-settled that a creditor of a corporation can satisfy his claim against the corporation out of the assets distributed to shareholders upon dissolution. . . . Although the trial court made an alternative finding on damages should its opinion be reversed on appeal, this decision is possibly erroneous in that we find no distinction being made between defaults arising from Chesterfield's breach and defaults in payment caused by other circumstances. The damages issue is remanded to the trial court for resolution.

II.

THIRD PARTY BENEFICIARIES

Whether Sansaria is liable to petitioners depends upon whether petitioners were third party beneficiaries of the contract between Sansaria and Chesterfield. This in turn depends upon whether the parties to the contract intended that Sansaria assume a direct obligation to petitioners. Burke & Thomas, Inc. v. International Organization of Masters, 92 Wash.2d 762, 767, 600 P.2d 1282 (1979); American Pipe and Constr. Co. v. Harbor Constr. Co., 51 Wash.2d 258, 266, 317 P.2d 521 (1957). In Burke & Thomas, Inc., this court observed:

> The creation of a third-party beneficiary contract requires that the parties intend that the promisor assume a direct obligation to the intended beneficiary at the time they enter into the contract. Burke & Thomas, Inc., 92 Wash.2d at 767, 600 P.2d 1282.

In the case of Vikingstad v. Baggott, 46 Wash.2d 494, 496-97, 282 P.2d 824 (1955), this court defined the intent required to create a third party beneficiary contract:

> If the terms of the contract *necessarily require the promisor to confer a benefit upon a third person,* then the contract, and hence the parties thereto, *contemplate a benefit to the third person* .... The 'intent' which is a prerequisite of the beneficiary's right to sue is 'not a desire or purpose to confer a particular benefit upon him,' nor a desire to advance his interests, but an *intent that the promisor shall assume a direct obligation to him.* (Some italics ours.)

In paragraph 3 of their contract, Sansaria assumed Chesterfield's obligation to construct a water system for the entire development. As noted previously, this part of the agreement was later the subject of a declaratory judgment action brought by Chesterfield wherein Sansaria was found to be in default of its obligation to install the water system. The Court of Appeals found no third party beneficiary contract:

> In his oral opinion, the trial judge succinctly stated: "[N]othing was further from the minds of the two contracting parties than intending ... [a] benefit [to] the plaintiffs...." This is fatal to plaintiffs' claim against Sansaria, Inc. Lonsdale v. Chesterfield, at 7.

This interpretation constitutes a misreading of *Vikingstad.* In defining intent this court further stated:

> So long as the contract necessarily and directly benefits the third person, it is immaterial that this protection was afforded ..., not as an end in itself, but for the sole purpose of securing to the promisee some consequent benefit or immunity. *In short, the motive, purpose, or desire of the parties is a quite different thing from their intention.* (Italics ours.) Vikingstad, at 497, 282 P.2d 824.

We, unlike the trial court, may not examine the minds of the parties, searching for evidence of their motives or desires. Rather, we must look to the terms of the contract to determine whether performance under the contract would necessarily and directly benefit the petitioners. The fact that representatives of neither Sansaria nor Chesterfield subjectively intended to benefit the petitioners is not determinative of this issue.

Our interpretation of the meaning of intent in no way departs from the reasoning in our earlier case of Burke & Thomas, Inc. There, members of the public claimed standing to sue a union for breach of a collective bargaining agreement. They claimed to be third party beneficiaries of the employment agreement between the union and the public employer. We then noted: "Petitioners point to no language in the contract which indicates such an intent. Nor do they put forward any other evidence tending to show that the parties here intended any consequence other than the normal agreement to the terms and conditions of employment." Burke & Thomas, Inc., 92 Wash.2d at 767-68, 600 P.2d 1282. We therefore concluded that under the facts presented, the petitioners could not be third party beneficiaries of the contract.

The petitioners in this case present quite different facts. It is not doubted that the contracting parties were motivated by something other than altruism towards the petitioners. Sansaria possibly viewed its promise to install the system merely as additional consideration for gaining ownership of the development. On the other hand, we can assume that Chesterfield only sought release from this obligation. Notwithstanding these motives, paragraph three of the contract necessarily required Sansaria, as the promisor, to confer a benefit upon petitioners. Under the terms of the contract, Sansaria could not fully perform its promise to install the water system without directly benefitting the petitioners as deeded owners of the lots. Petitioners were thus intended third party beneficiaries of the performance due under the contract.

We therefore reverse the Court of Appeals and remand to the trial court for resolution consistent with this holding.

BRACHTENBACH, STAFFORD, UTTER, PEARSON, DOLLIVER, DOE and DEMMICK, JJ., and CUNNINGHAM, J. Pro Tem., concur.

NOTES AND QUESTIONS:

1. Read Restatement (Second) of Contracts § 333 (Warranties of an Assignor) (1981).
